1981 CATHOLIC ALMANAC

The Most Complete One-Volume Encyclopedia Of Catholic Facts And Information On The Church

FELICIAN A. FOY, O.F.M.
EDITOR

OUR SUNDAY VISITOR, INC.
PUBLISHER
HUNTINGTON, INDIANA

Acknowledgments: NC News Service for coverage of news and documentary texts; *The Documents of Vatican II,* Walter M. Abbott, S.J., general editor, Herder and Herder, America Press, New York, 1966, for quotations; *Annuario Pontificio,* 1980; *The Official Catholic Directory,* 1980, P. J. Kenedy & Sons, New York; The United States Catholic Mission Council, 1302 Eighteenth St. N.W., Washington, D.C. 20036, for U.S. foreign mission compilations and statistics; *Catholic Press Directory,* 1980; *CCCB 1980 Directory,* copyright© Concacan, Inc., 1980, with permission of the Canadian Conference of Catholic Bishops, 90 Parent Ave., Ottawa, Ont. K1N 7B1, for Canadian Catholic statistics. Other sources are credited in various entries.

Rose M. Avato, Associate Editor

1981 CATHOLIC ALMANAC

Library of Congress Catalog Card Number: 73-641001

International Standard Serial Number (ISSN) 0069-1208

ISBN 0-87973-251-2 Paperbound Edition
ISBN 0-87973-261-X Clothbound Edition

Published with Ecclesiastical Permission

Published in U.S.A. by
Our Sunday Visitor, Inc.
200 Noll Plaza
Huntington, Indiana 46750

TABLE OF CONTENTS

INDEX

4

Boyer, Charles, Rev. (Death), 647
Boys Town Award, 115
Braga Rite, 239
Brandao Vilela, Avelar, Card., 183
Brazil, 108, 116, 121, 127, 375, 412
  Papal Visit, Addresses, 55-62, 122
Brebeuf, John de, St., 427
Breitenbeck, Joseph M., Bp., 485
Brendan, St., 282
Brennan, Francis (U.S. Cardinals), 197
Brennan, Peter J. (Catholics in Presidents' Cabinets), 449
Brennan, William (Catholics in Supreme Court), 449
Brent Award, 640
Breviary, 238
Bridget (Birgitta), St. (of Sweden), 282, 291
Bridget (Brigid), St. (of Ireland), 282, 291
Bridgettine Sisters, 525
Brief, Apostolic, 335
Brigid, Congregation of St., 525
British Honduras, see Belize
Brizgys, Vincas, Bp., 485
Broadcasters, Religious, and Radio Deregulation, 131
Broadcasters Association, Catholic, see UNDA-USA
Broderick, Edwin B., Bp., 485
Brodeur, Rosario L., Bp., 419
Brothers, 511
  Concept, 94
Brothers, U.S., 466-69, 520-21
  National Assembly, 522
Brothers, Statistics, U.S., 466-69
  World, 409
"Brothers and Sisters to Us," Pastoral Letters, 77-8
Brown, Charles A., M.M., Bp., 485
Brunei, 376
Brunini, Joseph B., Bp., 485
Bruno, St., 283
Brust, Leo J., Bp., 485
Brzana, Stanislaus, Bp., 485
Bucher, Lloyd M., 115
Buddhists, 329
Bueno y Monreal, Jose Maria, Card., 183
  Warning about Alleged Apparition, 104
Bulgaria, 376, 412
Bulgarian Catholics (Byzantine Rite), 300
Bull, Bulla, Bullarium, 335
Bull of Demarcation (1493), 142
Bullock, William H., Bp., 485
Burhoe, Ralph Wendell (Templeton Prize), 116
Burial, Ecclesiastical, 335
  See also Funeral Rites
Burke, Augustin-Emile, Bp., 419
Burke, James C., O.P., Bp., 485
Burma, 376, 412
Burse, 244
Burundi, 376
Bus Transportation, Private Schools, see Church-State Decisions
Buswell, Charles A., Bp., 486
Butler, Pierce (Catholics in Supreme Court), 449
By-Line Award (Marquette Univ.), 103
Byelorussians, 300, 303
Byrne, James J., Abp., 486
Byzantine Rite (Catholic), 300-301, 303-05
  Calendar, 270
  Catholics, 300-301, 303
  Liturgy, Features, Vestments, 303-05
  Ukrainian Bishops' Synod, 65

C

C. Albert Koob Merit Award, 110
Cabana, Georges, Abp., 419
Cabrini, Mother (St. Frances Xavier Cabrini), 284
Cabrini Sisters, see Sacred Heart Missionary Sisters
Caesar, Raymond R., Bp., 486
Caggiano, Antonio, Card. (Death), 647
Caillouet, L. Abel, Bp., 486
Cajetan, St., 283
Calendar, Church, 268-277
  Byzantine, 270
  Gregorian (1582), 143
Califano, Joseph A. (Catholics in Presidents' Cabinets), 449
California, 435, 469, 471, 473, 476, 483, 558, 566, 574, 582, 583, 585, 591, 631
  Missions, 430
  Parochial School Discipline Practices, Indio, 123
  Worldwide Church of God, 118

Calix Society, 603
Callahan, William M. (Death), 647
Callistus I, St., 283
Calumny, 335
Calvary, 335
Calvin, John, 309
Camaldolese Congregation, 514
Camaldolese Hermits, 514
Cambodia (Kampuchea), 390
  Relief Aid, Need, 90, 95, 98, 108
Camerlengo, see Chamberlain
Cameroon, 376
Camillians, 514
Camillus de Lellis, St., 283
Camp Fire, Inc., 601
Campaign for Human Development, 114, 630
Campaign for Surplus Rosaries, 603
Campbell, James (Catholics in Presidents' Cabinets), 448
Campinas, University of (Brazil), 569
Campion Award, 640
Campus Ministry, 565-66
Cana Conferences, 265
Canada, 377, 416-27
  Basilicas, 476-77
  Bishops, Ottawa, Letter to Youth, 100
  Bishops' Biographies, 418-23
  Bishops' Conference, 92, 99, 423
  Catholic Publications, 426-27
  Eastern (Byzantine) Rite Catholics, 425
  Liturgical Abuses, Toronto Archdiocese, 116
  Pontifical Universities, Faculty of, 569, 570
  Quebec Referendum, 116
  Shrines, 426
  Statistics, 424-25, 426
  Threat to Catholic Schools, British Columbia, 131
  YWCA Abortion Policy, 92
Canadian Conference of Catholic Bishops, 92, 99, 423
Canary Islands, 377
Cancer de Barbastro, Louis, 427
Cancer Homes and Hospitals, 589
Cancer Saint (St. Peregrine), 287
Candle, Paschal, 360
Candlemas Day (Presentation), 281
Candles, 245
Canon, 335
  of Bible, 215
  of Mass, 241, 246
Canon Law, 335
  Commissions, 178
  Society of America, 603
Canon Law and Priests in Public Office, 75
Canonization, 335-36
Canonizations, from Leo XIII to Present, 162-63
Canons Regular of Holy Cross (Crosier Fathers), 515
Canons Regular of Premontre (Premonstratensians), 518-19
Canterbury Statement, 346
Canticle, 336
Canticum Laudis (Liturgy of the Hours), 238
Cap-de-la-Madeleine, Shrine, 426
Cape Verde Islands, 377
Capital Punishment, 336
  Abolition Urged, Europe, 124
  Execution by Injection and Physicians, AMA, 123
Capital Sins, 336
Cappa Magna, 243
Cappel, Louis, 225
Caprinica College, Papal Address, 97
Caprio, Giuseppe, Card., 183
Capucci, Hilarion, Abp., 116, 134
Capuchins, 516
Carberry, John, Card., 183
Cardinal, 181
  Bishops, 181, 195
  Deacons, 181, 196
  in Pectore, 182
  Priests, 181, 195
Cardinal Gibbons Medal, 640
Cardinal Mindszenty Foundation, 603
Cardinal Spellman Award, 640
Cardinal Virtues, 336
Cardinal Wright Award, 646
Cardinale, Igino, Abp., 124
Cardinals, 181-97
  American, 196-97
  Biographies, 182-95
  Categories, 195-96

H

Tennessee
Constitutional Convention Vote, 103
Teresa, Mother, 91, 96, 111, 120, 126, 128
Teresa (Theresa) of Avila, St., 230
Teresa of Jesus, Society of St., 541
Teresian Institute, 545
Terrorist Bombing (Bologna), 125
Tertullian (206), 137
Tessier, Maxime, Bp., 423
Test-Tube Baby, see *In Vitro* Fertilization
Testament, Old and New, see Bible
Texas, 446-47, 468, 471, 473, 476, 483, 557, 568, 581, 585,
588, 595-96, 634
School Rights Law, 122-23
Sterilization Proposal, 107
Textbook Loans, see Schools, Catholic, Aid
Thaddeus, Jude, St., 223, 226
Thailand, 404
See also Refugees
Thanksgiving, 370
Theatines, 520
Theatre, Catholic, 627-28
Theism, 370
Theodosian Code (438), 138
Theologians and the Magisterium, 71-2
Theological Commission, International, 180
Deaconess Statement, 342
Theological Virtues, 370
Theology, 370
John Paul II on, 93, 101
Trends (U.S.), 214
Theophany, see Epiphany
Theresa (Teresa) of Avila, St., 230
Therese Couderc, St., 287
Therese of Lisieux, St., 287
Theresians of America, 609
Thessalonians, 223
Thiandoum, Hyacinthe, Card., 194
Thiep, Barnabas, Rev., 103
Third Order Regular of St. Francis, 515
Third Orders (Secular Orders), 546
Thirty-Nine Articles (1563), 143
Thirty Years' War (1648), 143
Thomas, St. (Apostle), 227
See also India
Thomas Aquinas, St., 129, 230
Philosophy of, 89
Pontifical University (Angelicum), 571
Thomas Becket, St., 287
Thomas Christians, see Syro-Malabar Catholics
Thomas More, St., 288
Thomas of Villanova, St., Congregation of Srs., 54
Thomistic Congress, International, 129
Thrones (Angels), 332
Thurible, see Censer
Tibet, 404
Timlin, James C., Bp., 507
Timor, Eastern, 404
Timothy, St., 288
Epistle, 223
Tiso, Joseph, Msgr. (Czechoslovakia), 380
Tito, Marshal, Funeral, 115
Tithing, 371
Titular Archbishop, Bishop, 169
Titular Sees, 371
Titus, St., 288
Epistle, 223
Tobago, 404
Tobin, Maurice J. (Catholics in Presidents' Cabinets), 448
Tobit, 218
Todadilla, Anthony de, 429
Togo, 404
Tokelau Islands, 404
Toleration Act, England (1689), 143
Tomasek, Frantisek, Card., 194
Tonga, 404
Tongues, Gift, see Charismatic Renewal
Tonsure, see Holy Orders
Topel, Bernard J., Bp., 507
Toulouse, Catholic Institute, 569
Tourism, Commission, 114, 178
Tourism, John Paul II, 90
Tracy, Robert, Bp. (Death), 648
Tradition, 211-12
Transfiguration, 281
Transfinalization, 371

Transignification, 371
Transkei, 91, 404
Translations, Bible, 216
Transplants, Organ, 359
Transubstantiation, 371
See also Miracles
Trappists, 514
Treasury of the Church, 371
Treinen, Sylvester, Bp., 507
Trent, Council of, 150
and Canon of Bible, 215
and Celibacy, 337
Doctrine on Mass, 240
Tribunals of Roman Curia, 177
Trident Submarine, USS Michigan, 102
Tridentine Latin Rite Church, 110
Tridentine Mass, see Lefebvre, Marcel, Archbishop
Triduum, 371
Trination, 247
Trinidad, 404
Trinitarians, 520
Trinity, Blessed, Missionary Servants of Most, 541
Trinity, Holy, 281
Missionary Servants of Most, 520
Order of Most, 520
Sisters of Most, 541
Third Order Secular of Most, 546
Trinh van-Can, Joseph-Marie, Card., 194
Triodion, 270
Triumph of the Cross, 281
Truce of God (1027), 140
Truman, Pres. Harry S., 202
Tschoepe, Thomas, Bp., 507
Tunisia, 404
Turibius de Mogrovejo, St., 429
Turin, Papal Visit, 109
Turin, Shroud of, 367
Turkey, 404
Papal Trip, 42-4, 90
Turks and Caicos Islands, 405
Tuvalu (Ellice Islands), 405
Twelve Apostles of Mexico, 429
"Type" (649), 139
Typical Sense (Bible), 224

U

Uganda, 405
Uganda Martyrs (Sts. Charles Lwanga, Companions), 105,
283
Ukraine, Underground Church, 119
Ukrainian Byzantine Rite Catholics, 301
Bishops' Meeting, Rome, 65
in the United States, 303
Patriarchate, 65
Una Voce Canada, 95
Unam Sanctam (1302), 142
Unbaptized, 209
UNDA-USA, 628
Unemployment, Canada, 99
Union of Soviet Socialist Republics, 98, 119, 405
Religious Repression, 112
Union of Superiors General, 90, 543
Unions, Teacher, Catholic Schools, 560
Unitarianism, 310
Unitatis Redintegratio, 150
See also Ecumenism Decree
United Arab Emirates, 405
United Brethren Church (John Hus), 309
United Church of Christ, 314
United Methodist Church, 311
Dialogues, 321-22
United Nations, 100, 127-28
Decade for Women, 415
Educational, Scientific and Cultural Org. (UNESCO),
54-5, 134
Food and Agricultural Org. (UNFAO), 89, 109
United Societies of U.S.A., 609-10
United States
Apostolic Delegates, 200
Bishops, see Bishops, U.S.
Catholic Historical Society, 609
Catholic Population, 115, 466-69
Church in (Abp. Jadot), 127
Eastern Rite Catholics, 303, 469, 473, 555
History, Catholic, 431-48
Jurisdictions, Hierarchy, 455-64, 485-508

EQUAL RIGHTS AMENDMENT

The Equal Rights Amendment was passed by Congress and submitted to the states Mar. 22, 1972, for ratification by Mar. 22, 1979. The amendment, first proposed in 1923, states: "Equality of rights under the law shall not be denied by the United States or by any state on account of sex."

Indiana was the 35th and last state to ratify the amendment, Jan. 18, 1977. With ratification by three more states necessary for enactment, Congress voted in October, 1978, to extend the ratification period to June 30, 1982, and to turn down a proposal that would have permitted states to rescind ratification already given. Four states — Idaho, Nebraska, South Dakota and Tennessee — have voted for rescission.

The U.S. Supreme Court ruled in October, 1980, that boycott activities by the National Organization of Women in support of the amendment were "privileged on the basis of the First Amendment." Since February, 1977, NOW had been urging organizations planning conventions and other meetings not to hold them in any of the 15 states which had not ratified the Equal Rights Amendment.

SYNOD OF BISHOPS: 1980 ASSEMBLY

The fifth ordinary assembly of the Synod of Bishops met Sept. 26 to Oct. 25 at the Vatican for deliberations on the theme, "The Role of the Christian Family in the Modern World."

In attendance were more than 200 voting delegates, including bishops elected by their respective episcopal conferences, 13 Eastern-Rite prelates, 24 papal appointees and 10 superiors general of men religious. Also there were 10 experts and 43 auditors, five of whom were from the United States.

Delegates elected by the National Conference of Catholic Bishops were Archbishops John R. Quinn, president of the conference, Joseph L. Bernardin of Cincinnati, Robert F. Sanchez of Santa Fe, and Auxiliary Bishop James F. Stafford of Baltimore. Cardinal Terence Cooke was a papal appointee.

Archbishop Jozef Tomko was general secretary of the assembly.

PAPAL REFLECTIONS

(By Nancy Frazier)

With a firm "yes" to the indissolubility of marriage and to present church teaching on artificial birth control, Pope John Paul closed the 1980 world Synod of Bishops Oct. 25.

Speaking in Latin to Synod participants in the Sistine Chapel, he said that the only divorced and remarried Catholics who may receive the Eucharist are those who refrain from sexual relations with their second spouse.

He had strong praise for the Synod's affirmation of "the validity and clear truth of the prophetic message — filled with profound meaning and pertaining to today's conditions — contained in the encyclical *"Humanae Vitae."*

Church teaching on contraception and remarriage after divorce were major topics of discussion during the synod, which opened Sept. 26 on "The Role of the Christian Family in the World of Today."

Nearly 300 people involved in the month-long meeting attended the closing ceremony, which began in the Sistine Chapel and concluded at the tomb of St. Peter in St. Peter's Basilica.

Dressed in red vestments, the Pope sat before the huge fresco of Michelangelo's "Last Judgment" as Argentine Cardinal Raul Primatesta of Cordoba, one of three president-delegates for the Synod, read a message of thanks.

Archbishop Jozef Tomko, secretary general of the Synod, read the Synod's "Message to Christian Families in the Modern World." The message confirmed the Church's opposi-

tion to the use of artificial means of contraception and to divorce, but expressed compassion for couples who, "although they sincerely want to observe the moral norms taught by the Church, find themselves unequal to the task."

Pope John Paul gave his own reflections on the message and the 43 propositions which had been presented to him by the Synod but not made public.

Divorced and Remarried

"The Synod, commenting on the pastoral ministry to those who have entered a new marriage after divorce, deservedly praised those spouses who, although faced with great difficulties, nevertheless witness in their own lives to the indissolubility of marriage," he said.

He said divorced and remarried Catholics should "not be considered separate from the Church" but cannot be admitted to the Eucharist unless they "take on themselves the duty to live in complete continence, that is, by abstinence from acts in which only married couples can engage."

On birth control, the Pope said the Synod participants "are not removed in mind and heart from the grave difficulties which many spouses feel in their consciences about moral laws which pertain to transmitting and fostering human life."

In addition to its confirmation of *Humanae Vitae*, the Synod urged theologians to join their talents with the work of the hierarchical magisterium so that the biblical foundation and the so-called 'personalistic' reasons for this doctrine might be continually illustrated," he said.

Synod Hinges

The Pope said all of the discussions at the Synod turned on "two hinges ... namely, fidelity toward the plan of God for the family and a pastoral way of acting."

In discussing the status of women, he quoted from a section of the Synod propositions which urged that "women not be forced to engage in external work ... so that the family might be able to live rightly, that the mother might devote herself fully to the family."

Those in mixed marriages cannot simply "accommodate themselves in a passive and easy manner to existing conditions but must try so that, with patience and good will, they might find a common willingness to be faithful to the duties of Christian marriage," the Pope said.

He also praised the Synod's efforts to achieve "a deeper awareness and consciousness either of the riches which are found in various forms in people's cultures or of the benefits which every culture brings with it."

FAMILY CHARTER

(By Jerry Filteau)

The 1980 world Synod of Bishops asked the Holy See to publish a "Charter of Family Rights" and to propose it to the United Nations for international adoption.

The 16-point charter declared that the family has priority over any other social entity. It demanded respect for the family's freedom.

It called for the protection of marriage and basic family values, and for provision of the necessary means for families to achieve or maintain its rights.

The idea for such a charter originated in the Synod with Ukrainian-Rite Archbishop Maxim Hermaniuk of Winnipeg, Manitoba, who proposed it on Sept. 29.

The proposed charter consisted of two fundamental principles followed by a list of 14 rights.

The first principle in the proposed charter stated: "The family is the basic cell of society, a subject of rights and duties, with priority over the state and any other community."

The second principle was: "The state by its laws and institutions must recognize and protect the family with respect to its liberty and assist it, not replacing it."

Rights

The draft charter stated that the family has rights:

• to exist and progress as a family; every person, especially of the poor, has the right to form a family and sustain it with appropriate assistance;

• to exercise its role in transmitting life right from its conception and to educate children;

• to intimacy of both conjugal and family life;

• to stability of the bond and institution of marriage;

• to believe and profess one's own faith and propagate it;

• to educate one's children according to one's own traditions and religious and cultural values, with the necessary instruments, means and institutions;

• to obtain physical, social, political and economic security, especially for the poor and weak;

• to habitation fit for leading a family life properly;

• to expression and representation before public authorities, economic, social and cultural, and those subject to them, either by oneself or through associates;

• to create associations with other families

and institutions so that one may fulfill one's role fittingly and effectively;

• to protection for minors, with the help of adequate institutions and laws, against harmful drugs, pornography and alcoholism;

• to fruitful leisure which may foster family values;

• to dignified life and dignified death;

• to emigrate as a family to seek a better life.

It was believed that, if the Vatican acted on the Synod suggestion, it would seek refinement of the language and a more comprehensive study of the issues with the help of theologians and such Vatican agencies as the Pontifical Justice and Peace Commission and the Secretariat of State.

The Vatican might also seek cooperation with other international bodies before presenting a proposed charter to the United Nations.

MESSAGE TO FAMILIES

Following are excerpts from the official English version of "A Message to Christian Families in the Modern World" issued by the 1980 assembly of the Synod of Bishops at the close of the Synod Oct. 25.

In our discussions of family life today we have found joys and consolations, sorrows and difficulties. We must look first for the good things and seek to build on them and make them perfect, confident always that God is present everywhere in his creatures and that we can discern his will in the signs of our times. We are encouraged by the many good and positive things that we see. We rejoice that so many families, even in the face of great pressure to do otherwise, gladly fulfill the God-given mission entrusted to them. Their goodness and fidelity in responding to God's grace and shaping their lives by his teaching gave us a great hope.

The number of families who consciously want to live the life of the Gospel, giving witness to the fruits of the Spirit, continues to grow in all our lands.

Underlying many of the problems confronting families, and indeed the world at large, is the fact that many people seem to reject their fundamental vocation to participate in God's life and love. They are obsessed with the desire to possess, the will for power, the quest for pleasure. Instead of looking upon their fellow human beings as brothers and sisters, members of the human family, they regard them as obstacles and adversaries. Where people lose their sense of God, the heavenly Father, they also lose their sense of the human family. How can human beings see one another as brothers and sisters if they have lost their consciousness of having a common Father? The fatherhood of God is the only basis for the unity of the human family.

God's Plan

God's eternal plan ... is that all men and women should participate and share in the divine life and being. ... The Father summons people to realize this plan in union with their fellow human beings, thus forming the people of God.

In a special way the family is called to carry out this divine plan. It is, as it were, the first cell of the Church, helping its members to become agents of the history of salvation and living signs of God's loving plan for the world.

God's plan for marriage and the family can only be fully understood, accepted and lived by persons who have experienced conversion of heart, that radical turning of the self to God by which one puts off the "old" self and puts on the "new." All are called to conversion and sanctity. We must all come to the knowledge and love of the Lord and experience him in our lives, rejoicing in his love and mercy, his patience, compassion and forgiveness, and loving one another as he loves us. Husbands and wives, parents and children, are instruments and ministers of Christ's fidelity and love in their mutual relationships. It is this which makes Christian marriage and family life authentic signs of God's love for us and of Christ's love for the Church.

Family Response

Just as we are doing, you also are seeking to learn what your duties are in today's world. In looking at the world, we see facing you certain important tasks of education. You have the tasks of forming free persons with a keen moral sense and a discerning conscience, together with a perception of their duty to work for the betterment of the human condition and the sanctification of the world. Another task for the family is to form persons in love and also to practice love in all its relationships, so that it does not live closed in on itself but remains open to the community, moved by a sense of justice and concern for others as well as by a consciousness of its responsibility toward the whole of society. It is your duty to form persons in the faith — that is, in knowledge and love of God and eagerness to do his will in all things. It is also your task to hand on sound human and Christian values and to form persons in such a way that they can integrate new values into their lives. The more Christian the family becomes, the more human it becomes.

In fulfilling these tasks, the family will be, as it were, a "domestic church," a community of faith living in hope and love, serving God and the entire human family. Shared prayer and the liturgy are sources of grace for families. In fulfilling its tasks, the family must nourish itself on God's word and participate in the life of the sacraments, especially reconciliation and the Eucharist. Traditional and contemporary devotions, particularly those associated with the Blessed Virgin, are rich sources of growth in piety and grace.

Evangelization and catechesis begin in the family. Formation in faith, chastity and the other Christian virtues, as well as education in human sexuality, must start in the home.

Out of a sense of fidelity to the Gospel, the family should be prepared to welcome new life, to share its goods and resources with the poor, to be open and hospitable to others. Today the family is sometimes obliged to choose a way of life that goes contrary to modern culture in such matters as sexuality, individual autonomy and material wealth. In the face of sin and failure, it gives witness to an authentically Christian spirit, sensitive in its life and in the lives of others there to the values of penance and forgiveness, reconciliation and hope. It gives evidence of the fruits of the Holy Spirit and the Beatitudes. It practices a simple style of life and pursues a truly evangelical apostolate toward others.

Church and Family

Family ministry is of very special interest to the Church. By this we mean efforts made by the whole people of God through local communities, especially through the help of pastors and lay people devoted to pastoral work for families. They work with individuals, couples and families to help them live out their conjugal vocation as fully as possible. This ministry includes preparation for marriage; help given to married couples at all stages of married life; catechetical and liturgical programs directed to the family; help given to childless couples, single-parent families, the widowed, the separated and divorced; and, in particular, to families and couples laboring under burdens like poverty, emotional and psychological tensions, physical and mental handicaps, alcohol and drug abuse, and the problems associated with migration and other circumstances which strain family stability.

As we reach the end of our message, we wish to say to you, brothers and sisters, that we are fully aware of the frailty of our common human condition. In no way do we ignore the very difficult and trying situation of the many Christian couples who, although they sincerely want to observe the moral norms taught by the Church, find themselves unequal to the task because of weakness in the face of difficulties. All of us need to grow in appreciation of the importance of Christ's teachings and his grace and to live by them. Accompanied and assisted by the whole Church, those couples continue along the difficult way toward a more complete fidelity to the commands of the Lord.

Everything we have said about marriage and the family can be summed up in two words: love and life.

POPE JOHN PAUL II IN TURKEY

Pope John Paul made what he called the "first ecumenical voyage" of his pontificate Nov. 28 to 30, 1979, with a visit to Turkey and meetings with Ecumenical Orthodox Patriach Dimitrios I. The key event of the trip was their joint announcement of the establishment of a Catholic-Orthodox commission for the beginning of official dialogue in quest of unity of the churches.

Purpose of the Trip

The Pope stated the purpose of the trip before boarding an Alitalia jetliner for the flight from Rome's Leonardo da Vinci Airport to Ankara. He said:

"I go to this nation to continue with renewed commitment the effort toward the unity of all Christians, based on one of the pre-eminent aims of the Second Vatican Council; to demonstrate, moreover, the importance that the Catholic Church places on relations with the venerable Orthodox Church on the eve of the beginning of a theological dialogue; and, finally, to express my sincere affection and deep love toward all those churches and their patriarchs, particularly toward the Ecumenical Patriarch."

At Ankara and Istanbul

The Pontiff began his 54-hour trip in the morning of Nov. 28 and arrived early in the afternoon at Esenbaga Airport, Ankara, where he was welcomed as a head of state by Prime Minister Suleyman Demirel and other government officials. Later in the day, he met with President Fahri Koruturk, members of the diplomatic corps and other dignitaries.

At a morning prayer service Nov. 29, the Holy Father urged members of the small Catholic community in the Turkish capital to respect the religious and moral values of their Moslem countrymen and to collaborate with them for the good of the nation. He then flew to Istanbul, arriving there early in the afternoon. On hand to receive him at the airport were local government officials and leading churchmen who included Armenian Catholic Patriarch Jean Tcholakiyan, Patriarch Dimitrios and Armenian Orthodox Patriarch Chnork Kalustyan.

A Meeting of Churches

The Patriarch addressed the Pope Nov. 29 during a *Te Deum* service of praise and thanksgiving to God in the Orthodox Patriarchal Cathedral of St. George. He called their coming together "a meeting of the Churches of the West and of the East," and added:

"Our meeting takes place today, and yet it is linked with the long yesterday, the yesterday of our common Apostles, our common fathers, our common martyrs and confessors,

our ecumenical synods; with the concelebration on the same altar and the Communion in the same chalice. But it is also linked with the recent yesterday, the yesterday of our two great predecessors, Pope Paul VI and Athenagoras I. And, thus, the meeting of today is destined for the tomorrow of God, the day of unity again, of common confession again, of full communion again, in the holy Eucharist."

Liturgies and Announcement

Also on Nov. 29, the Patriarch attended a Mass celebrated by the Pope in the Latin-Rite Cathedral of the Holy Spirit.

The following day, the Pope attended the Divine Liturgy celebrated by the Patriarch in the patriarchal cathedral. At the conclusion of the Liturgy, both prelates issued the announcement of the establishment of the unity-seeking, joint theological commission.

The Holy Father ended his Turkish trip with a visit to Meryam Ana, the Marian shrine at the site of the ancient Aegean seacoast city of Ephesus, where the third ecumenical council in 431 defined the title *Theotokos* ("Bearer of God") for Mary, the Mother of the Son of God made Man.

The visit to Turkey was low-keyed, with none of the popular acclaim and mass-attended public appearances that highlighted trips the Pope made earlier in 1979 to Mexico, Poland, Ireland and the United States.

It was the Pontiff's first trip to a predominantly non-Christian country in which about 26,000 Catholics and less than 100,000 Orthodox were outnumbered by Moslems comprising 98 per cent of the total population of 42 million.

NEW PHASE OF RELATIONS

Following are excerpts from the address delivered Nov. 30, 1979, by Ecumenical Patriarch Dimitrios I in the Orthodox Patriarchal Cathedral of St. George, Istanbul.

These excerpts are from the translation circulated by the NC Documentary Service, Origins, Dec. 13, 1979 (Vol. 9, No. 26). Subheads have been added.

We are entering a new phase of our cofraternization, a serious and important phase whose outcome will influence our whole journey toward the goal at which we are aiming, that is, unity.

We are happy today, as the Orthodox Church, to announce that we have both of us designated two theological commissions which, under the form of one mixed theological commission and on the basis of an agenda prepared and approved by the two churches for a first phase, will soon undertake the dialogue.

The Ultimate Goal

Our ultimate and principal goal is not only the unity of the two churches, but the unity of all Christians in one same Lord and in participation in one same chalice.

To those non-Christians who might wonder what significance Christian unity would have for them .. we could answer that the Christian unity sought is not a turning against anyone, but that it constitutes, rather, a positive service for all, independently of their sex, independently of their race, independently of their religion, independently of their social class.

Obstacles To Be Overcome

Various obstacles stand before us. First of all, we have the serious theological problems which concern the essential chapters of the Christian faith, for whose solution we are engaging in theological dialogue. But, at the same time, there are obstacles coming from mistrust, irresponsibility, fear — like that of the disciples in the Garden of Gethsemani: non-theological factors concerning Christian differences, intolerance, and fanaticism which opposes Christians to one another and religions to one another; in a word, all the obstacles which come from the weapons of Lucifer.

We live and we work for the accomplishment of the will of God and for the evangelization of love, of unity and of peace at a critical hour of the history of the human race.

IMPORTANCE OF DIALOGUE

Following are excerpts from the address delivered Nov. 30, 1979, by Pope John Paul II in the Orthodox Patriarchal Cathedral of St. George, Istanbul.

These excerpts are from the translation circulated by the NC Documentary Service, Origins, Dec. 13, 1979 (Vol. 9, No. 26). Subheads have been added.

(Pope John Paul said his visit with the Patriarch showed) the importance that the Catholic Church attaches to the theological dialogue which is going to begin with the Orthodox Church. With realism and wisdom, in conformity with the desire of the Apostolic See of Rome and also with the desire of the Pan-Orthodox Conferences, it was decided (years earlier) to resume between the Catholic Church and the Orthodox Churches relations and contacts which would permit getting to know one another and creating the atmosphere necessary to a fruitful theological dialogue. ... This period has been rightly called the dialogue of charity. This dialogue has permitted regaining consciousness of the profound communion which already unites us and lets us regard one another and treat one another as Sister Churches. Much has already been realized, but this effort must be continued.

Consequences of Dialogue

The consequences of this mutual theological rediscovery must be drawn, wherever Catholics and Orthodox live together. Habits of isolation must be overcome in order to collaborate in all the areas of pastoral activity where such collaboration is made possible by the almost total communion which already exists between us. We must not be afraid to reconsider on both sides, and in consultation with one another, canonical rules established when awareness of our communion — now close, even if it is still incomplete — was still obscured, rules which perhaps no longer correspond to the results of the dialogue of charity and to the possibilities that they have opened up. That is important so that the faithful on both sides might take into account the progress made, and it would be desirable that those who are going to be entrusted with the dialogue be concerned about drawing the consequences, for the life of the faithful, from future progress.

This theological dialogue which is going to begin now will have for its task overcoming the misunderstandings and disagreements which still exist between us, if not at the level of faith, at least at the level of theological formulation. It should go on not only in the atmosphere of the dialogue of charity, which must be developed and intensified, but also in an atmosphere of adoration and availability.

It is only in adoration, with a keen sense of the transcendence of the inexpressible mystery 'which surpasses all understanding' (Eph. 3:19), that we will be able to situate our differences and 'not lay on any burden beyond that which is strictly necessary' (Acts 15:28) in order to reestablish communion (cf. *Decree on Ecumenism*, No. 18; Second Vatican Council).

The Key Question

It seems to me, in fact, that the question we must ask ourselves is not so much whether we can reestablish full communion but, rather, whether we still have the right to remain separate. We must ask ourselves this question in the very name of our fidelity to the will of Christ for his Church. Incessant prayer must make us on both sides ever more disposed toward this fidelity in the course of the theological dialogue.

COMMISSION ESTABLISHED

Following is the text of the joint announcement made Nov. 30, 1979, by Pope John Paul II and Ecumenical Orthodox Patriarch Dimitrios I concerning the establishment of a Catholic-Orthodox theological commission for the beginning of official dialogue in quest of unity of their churches.

This translation was circulated by the NC

Documentary Service, Origins, Dec. 13, 1979 (Vol. 9, No. 26).

We, Pope John Paul II and Ecumenical Patriarch Dimitrios I, thank God who has granted that we meet to celebrate together the feast of the Apostle Andrew, the first called and the brother of the Apostle Peter. "Praised be the God and Father of Our Lord Jesus Christ, who has bestowed on us in Christ every spiritual blessing in the heavens." (Eph. 1:3).

It is in seeking the sole glory of God through the accomplishment of his will that we affirm anew our firm will to do all that is possible to hasten the day when full communion between the Catholic Church and the Orthodox Church will be reestablished and when we will finally be able to concelebrate the Divine Eucharist.

We are grateful to our predecessors, Pope Paul VI and Patriarch Athenagoras I, for all they have done to reconcile our churches and to make them progress in unity.

The progress made in the preparatory stage permits us to announce that the theological dialogue is going to begin and to make public the list of members of the mixed Catholic-Orthodox commission which will be entrusted with it.

This theological dialogue has as its goal not only to progress toward the reestablishment of full communion between the Catholic and Orthodox Sister Churches, but further to contribute to the many dialogues which are going on in the Christian world in quest of its unity.

The dialogue of charity (cf. Jn. 13:34; Eph. 4:1-7), rooted in a complete fidelity to the one Lord Jesus Christ and to his will for his Church (cf. Jn. 17:21), has opened the way to a better understanding of mutual theological positions and, from there, to new approaches to theological work and to a new attitude toward the common past of our Churches. This purification of the collective memory of our Churches is an important fruit of the dialogue of charity and an indispensable condition of future progress. This dialogue of charity must continue and be intensified in the complex situation which we have inherited from the past and which constitutes the reality in which our effort must go on today.

We desire that progress in unity may open new possibilities for dialogue and collaboration with believers of other religions and with all men of good will, so that love and brotherhood may win over hatred and opposition between men. We hope thus to contribute to the coming of a true peace in the world. We implore this gift from him who was, who is and who is to come, Christ our only Lord and our true peace.

Membership

Pope John Paul II and Ecumenical Orthodox Patriarch Dimitrios I, in their joint announcement of Nov. 30, 1979, made the Catholic-Orthodox Mixed Commission for theological dialogue the highest ranking and largest commission of its kind, with an initial membership of 23 Orthodox and 31 Catholic representatives.

Orthodox representatives included prelates and theologians of eight patriarchates (Constantinople, Alexandria, Antioch, Jerusalem, Moscow, Serbia, Rumania and Bulgaria) and the Orthodox Churches of Cyprus, Greece, Georgia (U.S.S.R.) and Finland.

Catholic members were headed by Cardinals Johannes Willebrands, president of the Vatican Secretariat for Promoting Christian Unity, George Basil Hume of Westminster, Joseph Ratzinger of Munich and Freising, Roger Etchegaray of Marseilles and William Baum of Washington, D.C.

One of the priests named to the commission was Father Frederick McManus, a liturgist and canon lawyer on the faculty of the Catholic University of America.

Background of Relations

Events leading to the establishment of the Catholic-Orthodox Mixed Commission for theological dialogue include the following:

• Fraternal meeting of Pope Paul VI and Ecumenical Orthodox Patriarch Athenagoras Jan. 5, 1964, in Jerusalem.

• Mutual nullification Dec. 7, 1965, of excommunications decreed by the Catholic and Orthodox Churches against each other in 1054.

• Meetings of Pope Paul and Patriarch Athenagoras in 1967, in Turkey in July and at the Vatican in October.

• Formation of preparatory commissions for dialogue, announced Dec. 7, 1975.

• Reciprocal meetings and ceremonial visits of Catholic and Orthodox representatives on patronal feasts (Sts. Peter and Paul, June 29, St. Andrew, Nov. 30) and other occasions.

• Meeting at the Vatican Mar. 29 to Apr. 1, 1978, for discussion of the purpose, method and themes of official dialogue.

• Publication of several documents on matters of mutual concern to Catholics and Orthodox (see Eastern Ecumenism).

In the United States, 19 ecumenical dialogue sessions took place between the start of preliminary discussions Sept. 9, 1965, and Mar. 15-16, 1979, under the auspices of the U.S. Bishops' Committee for Ecumenical and Interreligious Affairs and the Standing Conference of Canonical Orthodox Bishops of America (see Ecumenical Dialogues).

The special relationship that exists between the Catholic and Orthodox Churches is sacramental in nature and directly related, despite their differences, to the apostolic succession of their bishops and the validity of orders conferred on their priests.

PAPAL VISIT TO AFRICA

Following is an account of the principal events of Pope John Paul's visit May 2 to 12, 1980, to Zaire, the People's Republic of the Congo, Kenya, Ghana, Upper Volta and Ivory Coast. His visits to Zaire and Ghana coincided with celebrations of the 100th anniversary of the establishment of the Church in those countries.

The Holy Father traveled more than 11,000 miles during what one source called his "spiritual safari." He delivered well over 50 addresses of one kind or another before massive audiences of Catholics as well as people of other beliefs. For most of them, his presence alone was as compelling and inspiring as his messages of pastoral concern.

MAY 2

Pope John Paul departed from Rome's international airport at 9:10 a.m. aboard an Alitalia DC-10 jetliner and arrived at Kinshasa, Zaire, at 3:10 p.m. He was greeted there by Cardinal Joseph Malula, President Mobutu Sese Seko and the first of hundreds of thousands — into the millions — of people who cheered his presence in Africa.

Purpose and Intent

In response to the greetings of officials, he said:

"I come here here as a spiritual leader . . . as a man of religion . . . as a messenger of peace . . . I come here as a man of hope."

He said he rejoiced with independent African nations because "they have taken their destiny into their own hands." He noted that each of them still had "a long road to travel" in developing its own unity, personality and culture, a task which would require peace, independence and the unselfish aid of other nations.

As a religious leader, the Pope said he appreciated "the religious sense so rooted in the African soul," and added that this sense should not be banished but "purified, elevated and strengthened."

His first stop in Kinshasa was at the cathedral where he was formally welcomed by Cardinal Malula. The cardinal asked him to consider carefully and respond positively to developments related to the Africanization of the Church, especially with respect to liturgy, lay leadership and the directions of theological reflection in the country.

The Pope did not respond to the cardinal immediately, but did so implicitly in a homily the following day and in other addresses during the trip.

MAY 3

The Holy Father celebrated Mass for married couples in the morning at St. Peter's Church. Some, but not all, of the features of the experimental Zairean liturgy were used, out of deference to his wishes.

Marriage

In his homily, he said that the wise use of many African traditions could contribute to building Christian homes in Africa and were worthy of imitation by "more advanced populations."

He praised the seriousness with which Africans regard the commitment and preparation for marriage, the priority given the transmission of life, the "law of solidarity" among families, a "sort of coresponsibility" in the raising and educating of children, as well as their reverence for their ancestors.

But, in contrast to polygamous customs native to many African cultures, he presented monogamous marriage as "the design of God." Monogamy is a Semitic concept, he said, which expresses that interpersonal relation in which each of the partners is recognized by the other as equal in value. "This monogamous and personalistic concept of the human person is an absolutely original revelation, which bears the mark of God and deserves to be ever deepened."

The Church and African Culture

The mutual adaptation and accommodation of the Church and African culture was the subject of the Pope's address May 3 to the bishops of Zaire at the Kinshasa Interdiocesan Center.

"The Gospel, certainly, is not identified with cultures and transcends them all. But the kingdom which the Gospel announces is lived by men profoundly linked to a culture; the building of the kingdom cannot be dispensed from borrowing elements of human cultures. . . . The Holy Spirit asks us to believe in fact that the leaven of the Gospel, in its authenticity, has the strength to raise up Christians in the various cultures with all the riches of their patrimony purified and transfigured."

In outlining several principles governing Africanization of the Church, the Pope observed that this church-culture adaptation or accommodation needs to be the "fruit of a progressive maturity in the faith." It calls for theological clarity, spiritual discernment, wisdom, prudence and time. It "is a matter of becoming authentically Christian and authentically African."

Vocation of Religious

The universal character of the vocation of women religious was the subject of a talk by the Pope May 3 at the convent of contemplative nuns in Kinshasa.

"You come to the religious life from very different social environments, countries and even continents. You live in community to confirm — in opposition to nationalism, prejudices, sometimes hate —the possibility and reality of that universal brotherhood to which all peoples aspire."

The Pope said the traditional African values of physical fertility and deep sense of family "can be experienced by the African religious woman in the bosom of a wider and incessantly renewed community, and to the benefit of an absolutely astonishing spiritual fertility."

He stressed the importance of catechetical work. "Women religious who — for reasons of personal affirmation — put aside too easily this precedent-taking ecclesial duty, are they always sure of being faithful to their consecration?" he asked.

Religious women serve the mission of the Church by their life of prayer, their ability to animate the Christian community and the pastoral activities their bishops assign them.

He urged them to work with youth and African women "in a manner analogous to the service performed by the 'mothers of the village.' "

After meeting with the nuns, the Pope made a brief visit to the La Rive leper colony.

Meeting in the evening with leaders of other Christian churches, he told them that interfaith cooperation was a "sign of witness" to Christ.

Influences on Africa

For diplomats invited to the nunciature in Kinshasa, the Pope had another message.

He alluded to the evil of racism and spoke in support of the rights of man, the right of people to rule themselves, and the need nations have for assistance in their "progress toward sovereignty."

He also said: "It is with astonishment . . . that one observes that this continent is marked by influences, directed from either inside or outside, often under the cover of economic aid, which in reality are in the perspective of an interest which is not so truly humanitarian as its label. How one would hope that the various nations which compose Africa could live and grow in peace, outside the ideological or political conflicts which are foreign to its mentality. Let them not be led, for example, to spend on armaments a disproportionate part of their often meager means . . . and may the aid they receive not be dependent on any form of allegiance.

"Such factors can only lead in the long run to violence. . . . That is not worthy of man, and it is particularly unworthy of African man. . . . Fighting and violence have never really solved any problem."

MAY 4

The Pope ordained eight bishops during a morning Mass celebrated before a throng of 750,000 people in the park in front of the Kinshasa People's Palace. Four of the bishops were Zairean, two were from Burundi, one was from Sudan, and one was a French-Canadian missionary. The Holy Father called on all of them to be true to their roles as pastors and spiritual leaders, teachers of faith, leaders in action for social justice and the welfare of the poor.

He met in the afternoon with 5,000 university students and professors.

Life and Ministry of Priests

The Pope spoke about essentials of their way of life and ministry to priests of Zaire May 4 in Kinshasa.

"Leave political responsibilities to those who are charged with them. You have another part, a magnificent part. You are 'leaders' by another right and in another manner, participating in the priesthood of Christ as his ministers. Your sphere of interventions, and it is vast, is that of faith and morals, where it is expected that you preach at the same time by a courageous word and by the example of your life."

Recalling the "essential physiognomy of the priest" — prayer, obedience and celibacy — the Pope urged priests to model themselves on Christ by being mediators between God and man. This has a permanent value. "It is not a question of ignoring the new problems posed by the contemporary world, and also by the African context, for it is important to prepare priests who may be at the same time fully African and authentically Christian. The questions posed by the culture into which the priestly ministry is inserted demand mature reflection."

Priests exercise their ministry of reconciliation by preaching the Gospel and making the sacraments available. They have a responsibility to help the laity fulfill their role. He praised their "concern to raise up collaborators," adding: "It is necessary finally to really know how to collaborate, without monopolizing all the tasks, all the initiatives or all the decisions . . . in the area of (lay persons') competence and their responsibility. It is thus that living communities are formed."

Other meetings of the day were with President Mobutu Sese Seko, 5,000 university students and professors, and Consolata Missionary Sisters to whom he gave an icon of Our Lady of Czestochowa.

An evening cultural program was cancelled because of an early morning accident in which nine persons were trampled to death and more than 70 were injured in the crush of people trying to find place in the park before Mass.

MAY 5

At about 8:00 a.m., the Pope was ferried across the Congo River to Brazzaville, capital of the socialist-oriented People's Republic of the Congo. He was welcomed at dockside by President Denis Sasson Nguesso, three bishops and a host of cheering people.

He addressed an assembly of priests, seminarians and nuns at the cathedral, where he also paid his respects at the tomb of Cardinal Emile Biayenda who was murdered Mar. 23, 1977, in a period of political turmoil.

Church-State Relations

At a second meeting with the president, the Pope called for a "serene and constructive atmosphere" between Church and state. Recognition that the Church and state have different natures and thus different missions, he said, would help to avoid confusion and conflict in their relations. "The state can count on the loyal collaboration of the Church so long as it is a matter of serving man and contributing to his integral progress. And the Church, in the name of its spiritual mission, asks ... the freedom to address consciences as well as the possibility for believers to publicly profess, nourish and proclaim their faith." The Pope said the common goal of service to man should be the subject of more dialogue between Church and state.

Evangelization

During an outdoor Mass concelebrated before a highly enthusiastic throng of 200,000 persons, the Pope preached a homily on the need to continue the work of evangelization.

Conversion does not end with baptism, the Pope said, but must continue throughout life.

"The idols which must be renounced are always being reborn, even if they sometimes have new names, in the old churches of the West as in the young churches of Africa." Materialism can turn people away from the faith by portraying the Gospel message as useless or illusory. Sometimes personal or family habits and social customs dismiss the Gospel ideal as too difficult.

"There is never an end to becoming Christian.

"The Church knows that the sons of this country are capable of an authentic Christian life. They have already proved it to a great extent."

Evangelization also means concern for human development and social progress, he added, urging the people to be "artisans of peace and even the 'salt' and the 'leaven' of which Jesus speaks."

He called on the people to remain close to the universal Church: "The Church makes the new people who have come to it live with its life. No new community grafted onto the tree of the Church can live its life in an independent manner. It lives only in sharing in the great vital current which makes the whole tree live."

The Pope's seven-hour visit to the Congo ended after Mass with his departure by plane for another stop in northern Zaire, Kisangani (formerly Stanleyville), where 38 priests and nuns were killed in the Katangese rebellion in 1964.

His arrival and first hours in Kisangani followed the pattern of other arrivals, with welcoming ceremonies, a motorcade from the airport to the cathedral and a variety of meetings.

MAY 6

The day started with a Mass celebrated in front of the Cathedral of Our Lady of the Rosary.

Agricultural Development

The Pope keyed his homily during Mass to the rural and underdeveloped Upper Congo region of northern Zaire.

He urged the people to transform the conditions of rural life which prevent them from living in dignity, hope and peace. "If you are aware of the dignity of your life and of your work ... you will seek to make them more worthy for yourselves and for others. You will not accept that country folk should be considered second-class men and women. You will not resign yourselves to letting some be crushed by poverty or be victims of injustice."

Agricultural development is a priority in Africa, the Pope said. "Your country must satisfy its food needs. Agricultural products are more necessary than certain luxuries."

It is not the Church's task to propose and develop specific technical programs, but to see that such programs have a human dimension. Christians will "consider themselves managers of God's creation, which cannot be wasted or ravaged at will, for it is entrusted to men for the good of all."

After Mass, the Pope went to the St. Gabriel Mission about three miles outside Kisangani where he addressed a mixed gathering of priests, religious and lay persons.

He left Kisangani shortly after noon on a flight to Kenya, the only East African nation on the tour and one of the most prosperous countries on the continent.

A lengthy, two-hour welcoming ceremony at the Nairobi airport, during which he met President Daniel Arap Moi and other officials, delayed his arrival at Holy Family Cathedral in the city until about 6:00 p.m. He exhorted priests, religious and lay persons gathered there to walk worthily in their respective vocations.

Policy Statement

The Pope delivered what was called a major policy statement on Africa during an evening meeting with diplomats at the nunciature in Nairobi. It covered the following points, among others:

• measures to cope with the needs of four million refugees on the continent;

• respect for the human dignity and moral values essential to the self-identity of Africans;

• African self-determination, with "eco-

nomic independence and freedom from ideological domination";
  • criticism of corruption and abuse of power in official circles;
  • support for religious freedom and the rejection of "atheistic ideology";
  • an end to racial discrimination;
  • an appeal to African nations to work together "to further their development";
  • "the priority of the spiritual" in all efforts toward progress, in place of materialism and selfishness which are "lacking in humanity."

MAY 7

The Pope concelebrated a morning Mass in Nairobi's Uhuru Park with 40 cardinals and bishops before a gathering of 500,000 people.

Political Responsibility

The Pope preached a homily about the Christian duties of citizenship. He told the congregation that it is their "right and duty to share in political life." Christians, "and especially you who are laity, are called by God to be involved in the world in order to transform it according to the Gospel."

"The Christian faith does not provide you with ready-made solutions to the complex problems affecting contemporary society. But it does give you deep insights into the nature of man and his needs, calling you to speak the truth in love, to take up your responsibilities as good citizens and to work with your neighbors to build a society where true human values are nourished and deepened by a shared Christian vision of life."

The duties of the Christian citizen "involve more than shunning corruption, more than not exploiting others." It is the duty of Christians to contribute positively to "the establishment of just laws and structures that foster human values."

After Mass, the Pope had a round of meetings with contemplative nuns; Christian, Moslem and Hindu leaders; bishops of Kenya and other countries whom he exhorted to stimulate Christian life among all their people without any dilution of doctrine.

MAY 8

The Pope departed from Nairobi in the morning on a flight to Ghana.

On arrival at the Accra airport, he was greeted by President Hilla Limann, several bishops and a large crowd, and was then driven to the Cathedral of the Holy Spirit.

In an address to a mixed congregation there on the occasion of the centenary of the Church in the country, he spoke in praise of pioneer Fathers Auguste Moreau and Eugene Murat who established the Church in the land in 1880.

After a mid-afternoon meeting with the president at his residence, the Holy Father concelebrated Mass with the bishops of Ghana and baptized 10 persons in Accra's Independence Square.

He said in a homily that the role of lay people in the church extends in two directions: they help to build up the communion of the faithful and, as responsible citizens, they permeate society with the leaven of the Gospel.

"Your Christian vocation does not take you away from any of your other brothers and sisters. It does not inhibit your involvement in civic affairs nor exempt you from your responsibilities as a citizen. . . . No human activity is foreign to the Gospel. God wishes all of creation to be ordered to his kingdom, and it is especially to the laity that the Lord has entrusted this task."

MAY 9

The Holy Father and Archbishop Robert Runcie of Canterbury, head of the Anglican Communion, met for the first time, for 45 minutes, in the morning.

The Pope flew to the capital of the Ashanti kingdom in the interior of Ghana where he celebrated Mass in the Kumasi Stadium for the particular purpose of honoring catechists. Six of them, each a representative from one of the countries on the Pope's itinerary, were given John XXIII Peace Prizes in recognition of their service to the Church

Catechists and Their Work

The Holy Father said in his homily. "I express the gratitude of the whole Catholic Church to these catechists, . . . to their predecessors in the faith, and to their fellow catechists throughout the continent of Africa — gratitude for helping to make disciples for Christ, for helping people to believe that Jesus is the Son of God, for helping to instruct their brothers and sisters in his life, and thus to build up his body, the Church."

"The dedication of countless catechists and their deep attachment to the Person of Jesus Christ remains a chapter of glory in the history of this land and this continent."

"The Church sees catechists as witnesses of faith, servants of Jesus Christ and his Church, effective collaborators in the mission of establishing, developing and fostering the life of the Christian community."

The Pope noted in particular: "Catechesis is a work of faith that is far beyond any technique. It is a commitment of Christ's Church. Its primary and essential object is the mystery of Christ. Its definitive aim is to put people in communion with Jesus Christ."

MAY 10

The Pope left Ghana in the morning on a flight to Ouagadougou, Upper Volta, the poorest of the Sahelian countries and one of the least Christian nations on the continent.

In a busy five-hour period, he met with government officials and diplomats, bishops and seminarians, and celebrated an outdoor Mass before 200,000 people. His homily was an appeal for aid for the poverty-stricken, drought-ridden, country.

"From here, from Ouagadougou, from the center of one of these countries which can be called the countries of thirst, may I . . . address to everyone, in Africa and beyond this continent, a solemn appeal not to shut their eyes before what has happened and what is happening in the Sahelian region."

The Pope issued "a solemn appeal to the whole world" on behalf of those who are part of and who suffer because of the drama of the Sahel: "Let us not wait till frightening and devastating drought returns! Let us not wait for the sand to bring death again! Let us not permit the future of these peoples to remain forever threatened!"

The Pontiff left Upper Volta after 2:00 p.m. on a flight to Abidjan, Ivory Coast. He was greeted by the usual enthusiastic crowd on arrival, met and spoke with President Felix Houphouet-Boigny about the dangers of materialism, and celebrated an evening Mass with the bishops of Ivory Coast and 13 newly ordained priests. The rich-poor gap and ways to close it were the subjects of his homily.

MAY 11

Meetings and a tour of an Abidjan slum preceded an afternoon flight to Yamoussoukro, the Pope's last stop in Africa.

Challenge to the Young

During the celebration of Mass there, the Pope confirmed 10 youths and, in his homily, challenged the thousands of young people in the congregation to commit themselves to Christ and the service of their people, and to safeguard their African culture.

"Hold fast to your African roots. Safeguard the values of your culture."

He said they should use these values to build "an original and typically African model" incorporating the best of modern civilization but rejecting the worst.

Nor should they abandon their faith, he continued: "Cease, therefore, thinking silently or saying aloud that the Christian faith is good only for children and simple folk. If it still seems to be so, it is because adolescents and adults have seriously neglected to make their faith grow at the pace of their human development." He urged them to make a synthesis between African culture and the modern world, between their role as citizens and their Christian vocation.

MAY 12

The Holy Father's final visit in Africa was to a leper colony 35 miles from Abidjan.

Afterwards, he returned to Abidjan by helicopter and left for Rome on an Air Afrique DC-10.

PAPAL VISIT TO FRANCE

Following is an account of Pope John Paul's pastoral visit to France May 30 to June 2, 1980. The visit was made at the invitation of Mr. Amadou Mahtar M'Bow, general director of the United Nations Educational, Scientific and Cultural Organization.

Paris was the site of all activities of the Pope, except for the final trip to Lisieux.

During his stay, the Holy Father delivered 25 or more addresses and was received much more warmly and by larger crowds than expected by some skeptics. Events during the visit were televised in France and 10 other countries.

Excerpts from several of the Pope's addresses follow the chronology of the visit.

MAY 30

Pope John Paul began the sixth foreign trip of his pontificate early in the afternoon aboard an Alitalia flight from Rome to Orly Airport outside Paris. On arrival there at 4:46 p.m., he was greeted by Cardinal Francois Marty, Archbishop Roger Etchegaray of Marseilles, president of the French Bishops' Conference, Archbishop Angelo Felici, apostolic nuncio, Prime Minister Raymond Barre and other dignitaries. Shortly afterwards, he was welcomed by President Valery Giscard D'Estaing at the Champs Elysees.

The first major event of the trip was the celebration of Mass outside the Basilica of Notre Dame, following a Te Deum of praise and thanksgiving.

The Holy Father keyed his homily to the question, "Do you love?" He said that "human life in general has a value and meaning to the extent to which it is the answer to this question. . . . It is only due to this that life is worth living. . . . The answer given to this question . . . has a universal significance, an abiding value. It constructs in the history of mankind the world of good. Only love constructs this world."

After Mass, the Pope addressed a gathering of priests in the basilica.

He spent this and the next two nights at the nunciature in Paris.

MAY 31

The Pope started the day with an unscheduled meeting with intellectuals.

At a gathering of leaders of other Christian churches, he spoke of the need for mutual forgiveness of faults by all Christians. He also declared that their primary service was to "bear witness to the truth" and to seek its fullness in unity.

He attended a reception at the presidential palace and lunched with Cardinal Marty before visiting the Daughters of Charity of St. Vincent de Paul at their motherhouse on rue du Bac, where the Blessed Virgin Mary appeared to St. Catherine Laboure in 1830. He spoke to the nuns about the nature, gift and significance of the religious life.

The principal events of the day were the papal Mass and homily at the Basilica of St. Denis in the heart of a working-class, communist-voting suburb of Paris. The vocation to love and justice expressed in work was the main subject of the talk, in which the Pope spoke also about the nature of work, the rights of workers, family concerns, and peaceful efforts for the attainment of social justice. The early-evening homily was delivered outside the basilica in clear view of about 50,000 people.

The day ended with two smaller-scale meetings, with priests of the Paris Regional Committee for the Workers' Mission and with leaders of national lay movements. To the latter, the Pope stressed the need of adequate response by them and their organizations to the needs of people and opportunities for evangelization.

JUNE 1

At a morning meeting with 5,000 professors and students at the Catholic Institute in Paris, the Pope called attention to "the more and more obvious failure of all forms of what can be called 'atheistic humanism.' " He noted that the truth about God and man are inseparable, and that "religious knowledge and spiritual progress go hand in hand." He urged his listeners: "Do not let yourselves be suffocated by the weight of secularization. Reject the ferment of doubt, the suspicion of the human sciences, the encroachment of practical materialism."

He concelebrated a mid-morning Mass with a number of bishops at Le Bourget field before a congregation of about 350,000 people. In his homily he asked if France, "the eldest daughter of the Church," was faithful to the promises of her baptism.

The Pope spent much of the afternoon at a plenary meeting of the French bishops held at the Issy-Les Moulineaux Seminary. In an address to the conference, he underscored the need to put directives of the Second Vatican Council into effect, strongly criticized polarized conservatives and liberals in the Church, and pointed to systematic atheism as a serious threat.

He met with students at the seminary and urged them to do all in their power to make themselves available as priests for the service of the Church and all people.

In the evening at the Parc des Princes Stadium, he addressed some 50,000 young people, in response to 21 questions previously submitted to him. Afterwards, he visited the Sacred Heart Basilica in Montmarte, the site of the apparition of Jesus to St. Margaret Mary Alacoque, where prayer for the Church and the intentions of the reigning pope have been offered continuously since 1914.

JUNE 2

The Pope met in the morning with representatives of international Catholic organizations and the staff of the International Catholic Center for the United Nations Educational, Scientific and Cultural Organization.

The highlight of the day — and the reason for the Pope's visit to France — was his address to UNESCO delegates. The link of Christ's message with man and culture, the nature of culture, and the threat to man posed by the destructive potential of some scientific developments were topics of the Pontiff's talk.

The last leg of the visit to France was a flight to Lisieux where the Holy Father celebrated Mass late in the afternoon outside the Basilica of St. Therese and preached about the legacy of the Little Flower of Jesus. Afterwards, he visited and spoke to nuns at the Carmelite convent where Therese spent nine years before her death in 1897 at the age of 24.

The Pope returned to Rome at 10:12 p.m. on a special Air France flight from Deauville Airport.

PURPOSE OF THE VISIT

The Holy Father stated the purpose of his visit to France and sketched the role of the Church in the state May 30 in response to a welcoming address by President Valery Giscard D'Estaing.

The Pope called his visit "a pastoral journey, above all, to . . . encourage Catholics in France; a journey which also intends to express my esteem and friendship for the whole population."

"I have come to encourage you in the way of the Gospel. . . . This way does not pass through resignation, renunciation or abandonment. It does not resign itself to the dulling of the moral sense, and it would like the civil law itself to elevate man. It does not try to bury itself, to remain unnoticed; but, on the contrary, it requires the joyful boldness of the Apostles. So it banishes faintheartedness while being perfectly respectful with regard to those who do not share the same ideal. If the Church claims religious freedom for herself, in fact, and, if she has multiple reasons for expressing satisfaction at enjoying it in France, it is natural that she should also respect the convictions of others. She asks, on her part, that she should be permitted to live, to bear witness publicly, and to appeal to consciences."

He urged Catholics to be proud of their Christian dignity, and added:

"My visit to your country is intended, not

only as a testimony of solidarity with regard to your pastors, but also as an appeal for a new outburst of enthusiasm in face of the numerous tasks that are offered to you."

PRIESTS

The identity and mission of priests, as well as the need for them in the Church and the world, were the themes of an address by the Pope May 30 to a gathering of priests in the Basilica of Notre Dame, Paris.

"It is not the world that establishes our role, . . . our identity. . . . It is Christ Jesus who has chosen us as his friends so that we might bear fruit, who has made us his ministers. . . . It is the Church, the Body of Christ, which for 2,000 years has expressed the indispensable place that bishops, priests and deacons have in it."

"Never will the Church be able to decide to do without priests, holy priests. The more the people of God attains its maturity, the more Christian families and lay Christians assume their role in their multiple apostolic commitments, the more they need priests who are fully priests, precisely in the vitality of their Christian life. And, in another sense, the more the world is de-Christianized or lacks maturity in its faith, the more need there is for priests who are totally devoted to bearing witness to the fullness of the mystery of Christ. That is the assurance which must sustain our own priestly zeal; that is the perspective which must stimulate us to encourage with all our strength — by prayer and witness, by call and formation — vocations of priests and deacons."

Apostolic Concern

"Preserve the apostolic, missionary concern which is so much alive in most French priests. Many — it is particularly striking in the last 35 years — have been obsessed with announcing the Gospel in the heart of the world, in the heart of the life of our contemporaries, in all milieus. . . . And they have done that through new approaches of every kind . . . even going so far as to share the work and living conditions of workers in the perspective of mission."

"Many . . . are striving to confront the spiritual needs of a de-Christianized, secularized world, often agitated by new cultural challenges. This pastoral concern, thought out and carried out in union with your bishops, is to your honor. Let it be ceaselessly pursued and purified."

"Let your ministry always be that of the apostle of Jesus Christ. . . . Never lose sight of the purpose of your ordination: to make men advance in divine life. The Second Vatican Council asks you at the same time not to remain strangers to the life of men and to be 'witnesses and dispensers of a life other than earthly life.' "

WORLD OF WORK AND JUSTICE

The vocation to love and justice expressed in work and the struggle for justice without violence were subjects of the papal homily delivered in the evening of May 31 outside the Basilica of St. Denis in a working-class suburb of Paris before a throng of 50,000 people.

"I am anxious, above all, to encourage the Christian apostolate which is carried out in a real concern for evangelization by priests, sisters, young and adult lay people — all who are devoted to this working-class world."

The Pope said it is easy to lose the place of man in the economic order.

"It is lost when work is envisaged, above all, as one of the elements of production, as 'merchandise' or an 'instrument.' The name of the systems on which this position is based is not important; if man is subordinated to production, if he becomes merely its instrument, then work, human work, is deprived of its dignity and its specific meaning."

"The love that man puts into his work finds its full measure only if he connects it up, if he unites it, with men themselves, and, above all, with those who are his own flesh and blood."

World of Moral Strength

"The world of human work must be, above all, a world constructed on moral strength; it must be the world of love and not the world of hatred. It is the world of construction and not that of destruction. The rights of man, of the family, of the nation, of mankind are deeply inscribed in human work. The future of the world depends on respect for them.

"Does that mean that today the fundamental problem of the world of work is not justice and the struggle for social justice? On the contrary, it means that there is no way of detaching the reality of human work from this justice and this noble struggle."

"These words (of the *Magnificat*, Lk. 1:51-53) tell us that the world willed by God is a world of justice. That the order that must govern relations between men is based on justice. That this order must be continually realized in the world, and even that it must always be realized anew, as situations and social systems grow and develop, in proportion to new conditions and economic possibilities, new possibilities of technology and production, and at the same time new possibilities and necessities of distributing goods."

Freedom To Enjoy Rights

"Man is hungry not only for bread; he is hungry, perhaps even more, for truth. He is hungry for freedom, when some of his fundamental rights are violated, such as the right to freedom of conscience and to religious freedom, the right to the education of his children in conformity with the faith and convictions of parents and families, the right to instruction according to capacities and not, for example, according to a political situation or a conception of the world imposed by force."

"The world of human work . . . must . . . remain sensitive to all . . . dimensions of injustice which have developed in the modern world. Workers must be capable of struggling nobly for every form of justice, for the real good of man, for all the rights of the person, of the family, of the nation, of mankind. This justice is the condition of peace."

"This thirst for righteousness (cf. Mt. 5:6), this eagerness to struggle for truth and moral order in the world, are not and cannot be hate or a source of hate in the world. They cannot be turned into a program of struggle against man, solely because he is, if one may express it so, 'on the other side.' This struggle cannot become a program of destruction of the adversary. It cannot create social and political mechanisms in which there are manifested ever greater forms of collective egoism, powerful and destructive egoism, egoism which sometimes destroys its own society and its own nation, which also destroys others unscrupulously — nations and societies that are weakest from the point of view of human and economic potential and civilization — by depriving them of their independence and their real sovereignty, and by exploiting their resources."

CULTURE AND ETERNAL WISDOM

Man's covenant or alliance with eternal wisdom, in and through Christ, "is the foundation of all culture and of man's real progress." Contemporary humanism, which is not based on this covenant, is deficient and carries within itself the seeds of its own destruction. So stated the Pope in a homily delivered June 1 during a Mass at Le Bourget Airport.

"Mankind has a meaning in the world only insofar as it is the image and resemblance of God. Otherwise, man has no meaning and we could say, as some have said, that he is nothing more than a 'useless passion.' "

"We think that the inner alliance with (eternal) wisdom (in and through Christ) is the foundation of any culture and the true progress of people."

"In this alliance, man must grow and develop himself as a man. He must grow and develop from the very divine basic aspect of his humanity; that is to say, looking like and being the image of God himself. He must grow and develop himself as the son of divine adoption.

"As a son of divine adoption, man must grow and develop himself through all that contributes to the development and the progress of the world he lives in, through all that he makes with his hands and his genius, through the successes of contemporary science and the application of modern techniques, through all that he knows."

Threat of Destruction

"How does it happen that man has discovered for some time that . . . gigantic progress is a source of threat for himself? How has the point been reached where, at the very heart of modern science and techniques, the possibility of a gigantic self-destruction has appeared; that everyday life proves so often that, what should have been for man and should have been of use to him, has been used against him?

"How did we get to this point? Has not man, looking for progress, chosen only one way, the easiest? Has he not neglected the alliance with eternal wisdom?"

The Pope concluded the homily with two questions.

"France, eldest daughter of the Church, are you faithful to the promises of your baptism?

"France, daughter of the Church and teacher of people, are you faithful, for man's sake, to the alliance with the eternal wisdom?"

MISSION OF THE CHURCH

The mission of the Church in de-Christianized society was the central theme of the address delivered by the Pope June 1 at a plenary assembly of the bishops of France.

The task of bishops, the Pontiff said, "remains the acceptance and the realization of Vatican II, according to its genuine content."

"There is nothing surprising about the fact that in this 'postconciliar' stage there have . . . developed, quite intensely, certain interpretations of Vatican II which do not correspond to its authentic magisterium (teaching authority). It is a question here of two well-known trends, 'progressivism' and 'integralism.' "

Progressives vs. Integrists

"The first are always eager to adapt even the content of faith, Christian ethics, the liturgy, ecclesial organization, to changes of mentalities, and to the demands of the 'world' without sufficiently taking into account not only the general feeling of the faithful, who are bewildered, but also the essentials of the faith, already defined, the roots of the Church, her centuries-old experience, the norms necessary for her faithfulness, her unity, her universality. They are obsessed about 'advancing.' But, toward what kind of 'progress,' when all is said and done?

"The others — pointing out these abuses which we are, of course, the first to condemn and correct — adopt an intransigent attitude, shutting themselves up in a given period of the Church at a given stage of theological formulation of liturgical expression which they make an absolute, without sufficiently penetrating its underlying meaning, without considering the totality of history and its legitimate development, fearing new questions, without admitting, in a word, that the Spirit of God is at work in the Church today, with her pastors united with the Successor of Peter.

"These facts are not surprising if we think of similar phenomena in the history of the Church. But it is all the more necessary to concentrate all forces on the correct, that is, authentic, interpretation of the conciliar magisterium as the indispensable foundation of the further self-realization of the Church, for which this magisterium is the source of correct inspiration and orientation."

Polarization

"The two extreme trends which I have pointed out foster not only an opposition, but a regrettable and harmful division, as if they stirred up each other to the extent of creating uneasiness for everyone, even scandal, and of expending in this mutual suspicion and criticism so many energies which would be so useful for a real renewal. It is to be hoped that both parties, which do not lack generosity or faith, will learn humbly, with their pastors, to overcome this opposition between brothers, to accept the authentic interpretation of the council — for that is the fundamental question — and to face up together to the mission of the Church, in the diversity of their pastoral sensitivity."

"Certainly, the vast majority of Christians in your country are ready to manifest their faithfulness and their readiness to follow the Church; they do not share these extreme and unauthorized positions. But a certain number hesitate between the two or are troubled by them; and the problem is that they run the risk of becoming indifferent and of straying from the faith. The time makes it necessary for you to be more than ever the architects of unity, watching over the fundamental questions which are at stake and at the same time the psychological difficulties which prevent ecclesial life in truth and in charity."

"Certainly, the council requires from the Church in our age a faith open to dialogue in the different circles of interlocutors of whom Paul VI spoke; it also requires that her faith should be capable of recognizing all the seeds of truth wherever they may be. But, for this very reason, it requires from the Church a very mature faith, a faith highly conscious of its own truth, and at the same time very deeply animated by love."

Threat of Atheism

"We find ourselves up against the threat of 'systematic' atheization, 'enforced' in a way in the name of man's progress. But on the other hand there is another threat within the Church: it consists of wishing, in many ways, 'to conform to the world' in its present 'advanced' aspect.

"We know how much this desire is radically distinguished from what Christ taught. It is enough to recall the Gospel comparison of the leaven and that of the salt of the earth, to warn the Apostles against conformity with the world.

"Nevertheless there is no lack of pioneers or 'prophets' of this direction of 'progress' in the Church."

Renewal vs. Secularization

"This shows the vastness of the task of pastors as regards 'discernment,' between what is real 'renewal' and what is a cover for the trends of modern 'secularization' and 'laicization,' or else the tendency towards 'compromise' with a system without knowing, perhaps, all its premises.

"It also shows how great is the task of pastors to 'preserve the deposit' (of faith), to remain faithful to the mystery of Christ inscribed in the whole of man's history, and also to remain faithful to this marvelous 'supernatural sense of faith' of the whole people of God, which is generally not the object of publicity in the mass media but which is expressed in the depth of hearts and consciences with the authentic language of the Spirit. Our doctrinal and pastoral ministry must remain particularly in the service of this *sensus fidelium*."

"At a time when people talk so much of 'prophetic charism' — not always using this concept in accordance with its exact meaning — it is necessary to renew deeply and reconstruct the awareness of prophetic charism linked with the episcopal ministry of the teachers of faith and 'guides of the flock,' who incarnate in life, according to an adequate analogy, Christ's words about the 'Good Shepherd.' "

Vigilance and Credibility

"The Good Shepherd is concerned about pasturage, about feeding his sheep. Here, I am thinking particularly of theological publications which spread very quickly and far and wide, and in many environments, and of which the essential parts are popularized in reviews. It is they which, according to their qualities, their depth, their sense of the Church, educate and deepen faith, or on the contrary shake it or dissolve it through the partiality or their methods. French publications have often had, and still have, an international readership, even among the young churches. Your prophetic charism makes it a duty for you to watch particularly over their doctrinal faithfulness and their ecclesial quality."

"The fundamental question that we must ask ourselves, we bishops on whom there weighs a special responsibility as regards the truth of the Gospel and the mission of the Church, is that of the credibility of this mission and of our service.

"Efforts to reach those who are far away, especially in the de-Christianized working-class and rural environments, must preserve fully an evangelical, apostolic and pastoral character. It is not possible to succumb to 'the challenges of politics.' Nor can we accept many resolutions which claim to be only 'just.' We cannot let ourselves be shut up in overall views which are in reality one-sided. It is true that social mechanisms, and also their political and economic characteristics, seem to confirm these overall views and certain painful facts: 'mission country,' 'loss of the working-class.' It seems, however, that we must be ready not only for 'self-criticism' but also for 'criticism' of the mechanisms themselves."

THE CHURCH AND CULTURE

Pope John Paul addressed the United Nations Educational, Scientific and Cultural Organization June 2 at the organizaton's headquarters in Paris. Subjects of the address included the link between the message of Christ and man in his very humanity, the fundamental need of respect for human rights, the nature of culture, and the accomplishments as well as the threat of science.

"Respect for human rights is basic and belongs undeniably to the human person. . . . Any threat whatsoever against the rights of man, whether against his spiritual good or his material well-being, violates this fundamental dimension."

Fundamental Link

"I think . . . of the fundamental link between the Gospel, i.e., the message of Christ and of the Church, and man in his very humanity itself. In order to create culture, it is necessary to consider man in light of his final destiny and in light of his transcendence, his particular and autonomous value. It is necessary to affirm man because of his being a man and not because of any other reason; only because of himself. Even more, it is necessary to love man because he is a human being. It is necessary to claim love for man because of his specific dignity. The whole of affirmations concerning men belongs to the substance of the message of Christ and to the mission of the Church, despite whatever is being said by some critics about this matter and despite what has been done by those of contrary-minded trends, in reference to religion in general and Christianity in particular.

"Throughout history, we have witnessed and continue to witness a development, a manifestation of great importance. Wherever religious institutions have been abolished, wherever ideas and works inspired by religion, and particularly the Christian religion, have not been accepted, men rediscover the same elements outside the institutional context, because of the confrontation between truth and the interior effort, between what constitutes their humanity and what the Christian message conveys."

Destructive "Imperatives"

"Contemporary civilization tries to force upon man a series of apparent imperatives which its spokesmen justify by resorting to the principle of development and progress. Thus, for instance, they replace respect for life with the 'imperative' of eliminating life and destroying it; love, the responsible communion of persons, is replaced by the 'imperative' of maximum sexual pleasure regardless of any sense of responsibility; instead of giving preference to truth in actions, they 'prefer' the fashionable behavior of subjectivity and immediate success.

"All this expresses a great systematic renunciation of the wholesome ambition of being man. Let us not be deceived that 'the system' based on these false imperatives, these fundamental renunciations, determines the future of man and the future of culture."

Sovereignty of Culture

"By all the means at your disposal, watch over (the) fundamental sovereignty which every nation possesses by virtue of its own culture. Protect it as you would your very eyes for the future of the great human family. Protect it. Never permit it to become the prey of political or economic interest. Never permit it to become the victim of totalitarianisms, imperialisms or hegemonies, by which man is regarded only as an object of domination and not as the subject of his own, proper human existence. For these too, the nation . . . is regarded as an object of domination and a lure of diverse interests, and not as a subject — the subject of a sovereignty coming from the authentic culture which is specifically its own. Are there not on the maps of Europe and the world nations which have a marvelous historic sovereignty coming from their culture, and which are nevertheless at the very same time deprived of their full sovereignty? Is this not an important point for the future of human culture, especially important in this age when the elimination of all remains of colonialism is so urgent?"

"We are well aware . . . that the future of man and mankind is threatened, radically threatened, despite very noble intentions, by men of science. And it is menaced because the tremendous results of their research and their discoveries, especially regarding natural science, have been and continue to be exploited — to the prejudice of ethical imperatives — for ends which have nothing to do with the prerequisites of science but with the ends of destruction and death to a degree never before attained, causing unimaginable ravages. Although science is called on to be a service to men's lives, only too often do we see that it is enslaved by these destructive goals, destructive of the true dignity of man and human life. Such is the case when scientific research is itself directed toward these goals or when its results are applied to ends contradictory to those of humanity. This can be verified as well in the realm of genetic manipulations and biological experiments as well as in those of chemical, bacteriological or nuclear armaments."

Nuclear Menace

"Two considerations lead me particularly to submit to your thoughts the nuclear menace which weighs on the world today and which could, if not removed, lead to the destruction of the fruits of all culture, products of a civilization elaborated through successive generations of men who have believed in the primacy of the spirit and who have spared neither their efforts nor fatigue.

The first consideration is the following. The world has been led into an unstable situation due to geopolitical causes, to wounded national pride, to the materialism of our age, to the decadence of moral values. It has been led to a fragile equilibrium which risks being destroyed from one moment to the next because of errors of judgment, information or interpretation.

"Another consideration can be added to this troubling perspective. In our times, can we still be certain that the breakdown of this equilibrium will not lead to war, to a war which would not hesitate to use nuclear weapons? Until now we have been told that nuclear arms have constituted a deterrent force which has prevented the outbreak of 'major' war, and so it is, no doubt. But we can also, at the same time, wonder if it will always be thus. Nuclear weapons, whatever their order of importance or whatever their type, are each year perfected and added to the arsenals of ever more countries. How can we be sure that the use of nuclear arms, even for national defense or limited conflicts, will not lead to an inevitable escalation, ending in a destruction which humanity can never envisage, let alone accept?"

Science Allied with Conscience

"The world will not be able to pursue this route for very long. For the man who has become aware of the situation at stake and who also is inspired by even an elementary sense of the responsibilities incumbent on everyone, the conviction, which is also a moral imperative, is inescapable. Consciences must be mobilized. The efforts of human consciousness must increase as the tension between good and evil, to which man is submitted at the close of the 20th century, grows. We must be convinced of the priority of the ethical over the technical, of the primacy of the human being over things, of the superiority of the spirit over matter. The cause of mankind will be served if science and conscience become allies. The man of science will really help humanity if he preserves the transcendental aspect of man over the world and of God over man."

PAPAL VISIT TO BRAZIL

Following is an account of the principal events of Pope John Paul's pastoral tour of Brazil June 30 to July 11, 1980.

The Holy Father traveled approximately 19,000 miles on this longest of his six trips abroad. He visited 13 cities and delivered 43 addresses at gatherings for Mass and other occasions. He was seen by a total of at least 20 million people. It was estimated that an average of more than 500,000 persons attended each of the Masses the Pope concelebrated with other bishops and priests during the tour.

JUNE 30

Pope John Paul left Rome's Leonardo da Vinci Airport at 6:11 a.m. aboard an Alitalia DC-10 jet bound for Brazil on the first leg of the sixth foreign trip of his pontificate. He arrived shortly before noon, Brazil time, to an exuberant welcome tendered by thousands of people and officials headed by President Joao Baptista Figueriedo.

After kissing the ground of the 13th nation visited by him since he became Pope, the Holy Father addressed the president concerning the purpose and intent of his visit.

"I am here on a purely pastoral and religious mission . . . to strengthen my brother bishops in their mission and, like them, to strengthen the children of the Catholic Church in intrepid and radiant faith. . . . This is the purpose of the visits that I am making to various countries and continents. Because of it, these visits may be called pastoral visits or missionary pilgrimages."

He continued: "My visit is intended as an act of homage to this Church (in Brazil) and to encourage it to be evermore the sacrament of salvation, performing its mission within the framework of the universal Church. . . .

"In the second place, I come because this country with its immense majority of Catholics evidently bears within it a special calling in the contemporary world. . . . Brazil will be able to show itself a country that will have much to offer tomorrow to the grand community of the nations."

Hope for Exemplary Society

The Pope expressed the hope that Brazil might be spurred "to build up an exemplary form of social coexistence by overcoming imbalances and inequalities, in justice and concord, with light and courage, without shocks and ruptures."

The Pontiff was driven in a motorcade to the Esplanade of the Ministries in Brasilia where he celebrated Mass before a congregation of 500,000 people. In a homily backgrounded with references to the meaning of the cross, he said that, "notwithstanding the obstacles and challenges it encounters, the Catholic faith, not just in its abstract formulation but in its practical realization, in the norms that inspire it and the activities that sustain it, is at the roots of the formation of Brazil, especially of its culture."

Talks to President, Diplomats

In the evening, the Pope met again with the president and with members of the diplomatic corps.

Addressing the president, he called for "political, economic, social and cultural programs" that promote "a true civilization which can only be called a civilization of love. . . . The Church does not cease to insist upon indispensable reforms for the protection and promotion of those values without which no society worthy of its name can prosper; that is, reforms which have in mind a society more just and more in accord with the dignity of every human person."

Such reforms, he added, are a way of avoiding reform efforts of another kind on the basis of ideologies that "have recourse to violence and to the direct or indirect suppression of the basic rights and liberties inseparable from the dignity of man."

In a country where a suspicious doctrine of national security impedes effective criticism and action for sound reforms, he told diplomats: "Each country has the duty to preserve its peace and internal security. But it must in some way 'deserve' this peace by assuring the common good and respect for rights."

JULY 1

The Pope started his first full day in Brazil with an 8:00 a.m. visit to the Papuda Prison in the capital city. He told the inmates: "You know from your reading of the Gospel that he, Christ, being without sin, hated sin but loved sinners and visited them in order to bring them his forgiveness. May this prison and all other prisons in Brazil and the world say in its mute language, 'No to lack of love, to violence, to evil. Yes to love.' Because love alone saves and constructs."

From Brasilia the Pope flew to the mining city of Belo Horizonte where he celebrated an outdoor Mass at noon in the Plaza Israel Pinheiro before another throng of 500,000 persons. He told young people for whom the liturgy was particularly intended:

Young Christians

"A young Christian ceases to be young and certainly, is not a Christian when he lets himself be seduced by doctrines or ideologies that preach violence or hate."

"It is indispensable to know how to con-

quer the temptation of the so-called consumer society, of the ambition to have always more, instead of trying to be more, of the ambition to have more while others have less."

"Only true love builds. Only love brings together what is different and produces a union in diversity."

When the Holy Father said toward the end of the homily, "Young people of Belo Horizonte and Brazil, the Pope wishes the best for you," the congregation broke into 20 minutes of wild cheering.

Five hours after touchdown in Belo Horizonte, the Pope was in the air again bound for Rio de Janeiro. He celebrated Mass in the early evening at a monument dedicated to Brazilian soldiers killed in World War II. Family life was the focus of his homily.

Family Life

After calling the "Eucharist a family reunion, a gathering of the big family of Christians," he asked: "How shall we look upon the grave situations in which numerous families are concretely involved among you? How shall we look upon the serious threats that weigh on the family in general?

"Some of these threats are of a social kind. They arise from subhuman conditions, in dwellings, hygiene, health, education. Millions of families are in these conditions, in the interior of the country and on the outskirts of the big cities, by force of unemployment or insufficient wages.

"Other threats belong to the moral order. They are connected with generalized disintegration of the family through ignorance, depreciation or disrespect of human and Christian norms regarding the family in various levels of the population. Others again belong to the civic order. They are linked with legislation referring to the family. Such legislation is becoming more and more permissive throughout the world. It is thus less encouraging for those who try to follow the principles of a more elevated ethic in the matter of the family. Please God that it shall never be so in your country. May it please him that, in accordance with the Christian principles that inspire your culture, those who have responsibility to make and proclaim laws shall do so in respect for the irreplaceable values of a Christian ethic. Outstanding among these is the value of human life, the undeniable right of parents to transmit life. Other threats finally are in the religious order. They derive from scarce knowledge of the sacramental dimensions of matrimony in God's plan."

The Pope called for the development and implementation of well-rounded pastoral programs to assist families to cope with the aforementioned problems and to deepen the Christian dimensions of family life.

The last public event of the day was a meeting with 110 representatives of the intellectual community of Brazil. The Pope spoke about culture.

"In the covenant established between God and humanity, people should imitate God in his infinite love through human culture. Cultural work is a work of love."

Besides expressing the love of God, cultural activity should foster greater love in society. And, in accord with this social love, people should not impose their own culture "on populations that are economically and politically weaker."

Cultural activity should promote freedom and foster the development of a moral order. "There is not the slightest doubt that the primary and fundamental dimension of culture is a wise morality, a moral culture."

JULY 2

The day began with a visit to Vidigal, a hillside slum of Rio de Janeiro, the *favela* of 20,000 squatters. The Pope addressed some of them from the doorway of a makeshift chapel they had erected.

With the expectation of negative answers, he asked: "Do Christ's words about the poor in spirit make one forget about injustices? Do they allow us to leave without solution the difficult problems raised by the whole of the so-called social problem?"

Church of the Poor

He said: "The Church in Brazil wants to be the Church of the poor." And: "The Church of the poor speaks like this: You, particularly the ones who have authority in decision-making, . . . do everything you can so that the life of each man in your country may become 'more human,' more worthy of man."

After reminding people with more to have care for those with less, he called on political and other leaders "to plan a better future for your whole country." He observed ominously that "a society that socially is not just and that does not try to become so has its future in danger."

Before leaving the slum, the Pope removed the gold ring from his finger and handed it to Father Italo Coelho, the priest in charge of ministry among the slum dwellers. The Pontiff said: "I give you my ring for this parish."

At a mid-morning meeting with 164 bishops and additional officials of the Latin American Bishops' Council, the Pope delivered a wide-ranging address covering key developments in the 25-year history of the council as well as a significant number of pastoral and doctrinal concerns.

Social Activism

With regard to social activism, he said that "the Church denounces everything which opposes the plan of God and impedes the development of people. . . . When, in exercising its proper mission, the Church feels the obliga-

tion to denounce, it conforms its exigencies to the Gospel and to the human being without serving the interests of economic or political systems or ideologies of conflict."

"Politics," he added, "must be left to lay persons because of the proper role they have and the tasks which correspond to them, above all in the militancy and leadership of political parties or in the exercise of public office."

The 25th anniversary meeting of CELAM was held in Rio's Sao Sebastiao Cathedral.

From the height of Sugarloaf Mountain, just below the statue of Christ the Redeemer overlooking Rio de Janeiro and the bay, the Holy Father imparted his blessing to the city and all of Brazil early in the afternoon.

Later, at Maracana Stadium, he concelebrated Mass and ordained 70 men to the priesthood.

Essentials of Priesthood

In his homily the Pope gave one of the clearest expositions to date of his concept of the priesthood.

"Let it be very clear that priestly service, if it is to be true to itself, is a service that is essentially and par excellence spiritual. His (the priest's) service is not that of a doctor, of a social worker, of a politician or a union leader. . . . When circumstances demand it, he will not excuse himself from giving material assistance through works of charity and justice. But . . . these are definitely secondary services."

The Pontiff was highly critical of calls for relaxation of discipline concerning celibacy and other aspects of priestly life. "Do not be fooled that the prospect of a priesthood less austere in its demands of sacrifice and renunciation — as, for instance, in the discipline of ecclesiastical celibacy — can increase the number of those who would follow Christ. On the contrary, . . . it is a mentality of vigorous and conscientious faith that is lacking, and we have to create that in our communities."

He attributed the so-called "identity crisis" of some priests to a simple loss of God-oriented priorities, and warned those being ordained not to absorb "the mentality of the world" or to abandon "the external way of presenting oneself distinctively as a priest."

He also said that a priest is a man-for-others only "in virtue of his particular way of being a 'man-for-God.' "

JULY 3

In the morning, the Pope flew from Rio de Janeiro to Sao Paulo where he concelebrated Mass in honor of Blessed Jose de Anchieta, the "Father of the Church in Brazil," who was beatified the previous June 22.

He said in his homily that Blessed Jose went to Brazil in 1554 "with the sole goal of leading men and women to Christ." He added: "Well, I too come to you impelled by the same motive, moved by the same love. I come to you as a humble messenger of Christ."

In a major address delivered later in the day to a crowd of 150,000 workers in Morumbi Stadium, the Pope referred to the commitment to the poor made by the Latin American bishops in 1979 at Puebla, Mexico. He went on from there to say:

Justice for Workers

"When the Church proclaims the Gospel, it also tries, without abandoning its specific role of evangelization, to bring it about that all aspects of social life . . . may undergo a transformation toward justice. The common good of society demands as a fundamental requirement that society be just. Persistent injustice, and lack of justice, threaten the existence of society."

"The common good of society will ever be the new name of justice. It cannot be obtained through violence, because violence destroys what it seeks to create. It does this both when it is used to maintain the privileges of some and when it is used in an attempt to impose necessary transformations. The changes demanded for there to be a just social order ought to be achieved through constant action along the path of peaceful reforms. Such action should always be effective, although often gradual and progressive."

The Pope spoke of the dignity of work and the rights of workers, as well as such problems as unemployment, just wages, humane working conditions and the possibility of worker participation in management decisions.

He said in conclusion that it would not be realistic "to expect that the solution to the problems of pay, social insurance and work conditions will flow naturally from a kind of automatic extension of a certain economic order. The economy will be viable only if it is human, for man and through man.

Other meetings of the day were with children, men and women religious, Orthodox and Jewish leaders.

JULY 4

From Sao Paulo the Holy Father flew to Aparecida where, during a Mass begun before 10:00 a.m., he consecrated the Basilica of Our Lady of Aparecida (Senhora de Aparecida), the national shrine and spiritual capital of Brazil. He did so in testimony to the faith and Marian devotion of the Brazilian people.

Devotion to Mary

This "love and devotion to Mary are fundamental elements in Latin American culture," he said. "Such is one of the characteristic traits of the religiousness of the Brazilian people. I am certain that the pastors of the Church will know how to respect this particular mark, cultivate it and go to meet it so as to put the saying, 'to Jesus through Mary,' into practice.

"What is essential therein is permanent and unalterable. It remains an intrinsic element in Christian devotion if rightly understood and practiced. . . . External forms (however) are by nature subject to the wear of time. . . . They need constant renewal and updating, which are effected in any case with total respect for tradition."

The Pontiff urged people not to let Marian devotion grow cool: "Do not let it be an abstract, but an incarnate, love. Be true to those practices of Marian devotion which are traditional in the Church: the Angelus prayer, the month of Mary (May) and, in a quite special manner, the Rosary."

The Pope visited and addressed students at the Bom Jesus Seminary before leaving Aparecida for Porto Alegre, where he met with representatives of other religious communities and praised the status of interfaith relations.

He also spoke of the need for deepening faith, in the Piazza Deodoro. He said:

"I know that faith is deeply rooted in your land and is lived with intensity in your hearts. I know also that the secret of the great vitality of this faith is in the Christian make-up of the families and in the missionaries, those priests of great merit who evangelized this region extensively more than a century ago.

"In order for us to be convincing witnesses of Jesus Christ, it is important to seek an ever greater authenticity. It is important to be firm in our faith. . . . In our times there is no possibility for survival and for spreading the faith without a deepening of the faith itself, that is to say, without a teaching fitting the circumstances but always conforming with the thinking of the Church."

JULY 5

At a morning Mass in Porto Alegre, the Pope asked in a homily: "Will the Christians of Brazil be ready to face the shock caused by . . . transition from old to new economic and social structures? Will their faith be in a condition to remain unshakeable?"

Need for Catechesis

He said that "the spread of culture, the critical spirit, the publicity given to all questions, and debates require fuller and deeper knowledge of the faith (than before). Popular religion itself ought to be nourished with ever more extensive explanations of revealed truth, and it ought to be freed from elements that make it seem inauthentic. It has need for that solid food of which St. Paul speaks. In other words, a serious and systematic effort at catechesis is imperatively necessary. This is the problem before you today, with all its gravity and urgency."

"The effectiveness of catechesis," he indicated, "will depend largely on . . . capacity to give a Christian meaning to everything that makes up man's life in this time."

The Pope stressed the importance of catechesis in families, parishes and schools, and through the agency of the mass media. To make it credible, he said, the testimony of Christian performance has to match authentic Christian profession.

Seminary Training

After Mass, the Pope addressed a gathering of 10,000 seminarians. He criticized weaknesses in the small-community approach to priestly formation, noting that it reduced the standard seminary curriculum to a minimum "with evident damage to the specific intellectual and spiritual formation that is fitting for a new minister of God."

It was reported that about 30 seminaries in the country had closed and been replaced in the previous 10 years with programs in which eight to 10 students pursued studies and engaged in spiritual and apostolic activities under a director of formation. The numbers of students declined dramatically during that time, leading some bishops to reopen seminaries.

The Pope insisted that all programs of formation are required to comply with norms set by the Second Vatican Council and in related enactments.

The next stop on the itinerary was Curitiba, where the Pope landed late in the afternoon. He was driven for 12 miles past an estimated 500,000 people to the Couto Pereiro Stadium and a Polish festival.

JULY 6

At Mass in the morning, the Pope hailed the Brazilian tradition of open-door hospitality to immigrants and noted how their acceptance without reserve or prejudice had contributed greatly to the welfare of the country.

He left Curitiba at about 11:00 a.m. en route to Salvador da Bahia. On arrival, he was driven through cheering crowds to the cathedral where he extended his greetings to all and recalled that Salvador was the site of the first diocese established in Brazil and also of the first capital when independence was achieved.

In the evening, the Holy Father attended a meeting dedicated to "Builders of a Pluralistic Society Today" and told them, among other things:

Justice One Way or Another

"The Church does not propose a concrete political or economic model in its social doctrine, but it shows the way, presents prin- ciples. And it does so by reason of its evangelizing mission, by reason of the evangelical message which has man as its objective — in his eschatological dimension and also in the concrete context of his historical situation today. It does so because it believes in man's dignity, as being created in God's image, in the dignity that is intrinsic to every man, woman and child, whatever be the place they occupy in society."

"Every society ought to establish a just social order unless it wishes to be destroyed from within. This appeal is not a justification of the class struggle — for the class struggle is destined to sterility and destruction — but it is an appeal to a noble struggle for the sake of social justice throughout society."

"Anyone who reflects on the reality of Latin America as it presents itself at this moment, is led to agree with the statement that the realization of justice on this continent faces a clear dilemma: either it will come through profound and courageous reforms, according to principles that express the supremacy of the dignity of man; or it will come — but without lasting result and without benefit for man, of this I am convinced — through the forces of violence."

JULY 7

The day started with visits to lepers, whom the Pope asked to offer their sufferings for the good of others, and to slum dwellers living in shacks built on sticks in the harbor of Salvador.

During a Mass concelebrated before another massive congregation at the city's administrative center, he spoke about popular religiosity and superstition. The subjects were of major importance because of the prevalence of an admixture of Christian and animist beliefs and rites in the religious experience and practice of many Brazilians. He said:

Popular Religiosity

"Deep within popular religiosity, one always finds a real hunger for the sacred and the divine. It is necessary, therefore, not to discredit it or ridicule it.

"It is necessary to cultivate and use popular religiosity for the better evangelization of the people. Popular religious demonstrations, purified of their negative aspects, of all superstition and magic, are without doubt a providential means for the masses to continue in their adherence to the faith of their ancestors and the Church of Christ. Like the Church as a whole, the religion of the people must be constantly evangelized over and over again."

At Recife, where the Pope arrived a bit after midafternoon, he was welcomed by Archbishop Helder Camara, an internationally known critic of the government since it passed into military hands in 1964. The two prelates greeted each other warmly and, with other bishops and priests, concelebrated Mass before a congregation of 400,000 people.

Land a Gift of God

In his homily, the Pope defended the right of farm workers to land and asked that legal initiatives be taken to improve the lives of workers facing "particularly painful situations," including "unhealthy living conditions, malnutrition, illiteracy and insecurity."

"Land," he said, "is a gift of God," and it is not licit "to use this gift in such a way that its benefits are to the advantage of only a few while others, the immense majority, remain excluded." The development of society must take into account "the men and women who live in the rural areas, those who are ready to make the land productive through the work of their hands. They need land to feed their families."

JULY 8

The Pope left Recife shortly after 8:00 a.m. on a flight to Teresina in the impoverished and drought-stricken northeastern state of Piaui. The stop at the airport there lasted only an hour but was long enough for him to greet a crowd of some 400,000 persons and to plead with those in power to "take up — fully, unreservedly and irrevocably — the cause of your brothers who are trapped in poverty."

Belem, named after Bethlehem and located near the mouth of the Amazon River was the next stop.

The Pope arrived there before noon, and several hours later paid a visit to the Marituba Leprosarium. He reminded the 600 people there of the passion and death of Christ, and of his acceptance of suffering for the sake of mankind. "It is no different in our lives," he added. "Sickness is truly a cross . . . a trial that God permits in the life of a person in the unfathomable mystery of a design that escapes our capacity to understand." He urged them, as he had urged other lepers in Salvador, to offer their sufferings as prayers for the good of others, in imitation of Christ and with the hope of resurrection.

At an open-air Mass where he preached on devotion to Mary, the Pontiff praised popular religiosity but warned against superstition, for the second time in two days. The reference was to widespread quasi-Christian cults that had captured a large number of Catholics in the northeastern and Amazonian regions of Brazil.

JULY 9

In the morning, the Pope flew from Belem to Fortaleza where he began his visit by attending a folk festival in the Castelao Stadium.

The main event of the day was the opening Mass of the five-day, 10th National Eucharistic Congress, concelebrated in the afternoon at an altar erected on the field in front of the soccer stadium. In his homily, the Holy Father related the theme of the congress, "Where Are You Going?" to the Eucharist and migration problems in Brazil.

Eucharistic Encounter

Of the Eucharist, he said:

"Faith assures us that God comes to meet men in the Person of Christ, in whom 'all the fullness of the divinity dwells' (Col. 2:9). So therefore, if man desires to find satisfaction for the thirst for happiness burning in his heart, it is toward Christ that he ought to direct his steps. Christ is not far from him. Our life here on earth is really a continual succession of encounters with Christ: with Christ present in Holy Scripture as the Word of God; with Christ present in his ministers as master, priest and pastor; with Christ present in our neighbor, especially in the poor, in the sick, in those on the fringes of society, who constitute his suffering members; with Christ present in the sacraments, which are the channels of his salvation; with Christ, the silent guest of our hearts, where he dwells and communicates his divine life."

"But the most intimate and transforming is the encounter at the table of the Eucharistic Mystery, at the table of the Bread of the Lord."

"Thus, eucharistic communion constitutes the sign of union of all the faithful. It is a truly suggestive sign, because at the sacred table all differences of race or social class disappear; all that remains is sharing by all in the same sacred food. This participation is identical in all; it signifies and achieves removal of all that divides men and effects a meeting of all on a higher level where every contrast is eliminated. The Eucharist thus becomes the great instrument for men to become close to each other. Whenever the faithful partake of it with a sincere heart, they cannot fail to receive a fresh impulse toward having better relations among each other, with a reciprocal acknowledgment of rights and of corresponding duties as well. Accomplishment of the demands of justice is facilitated in this way, and is due precisely to the particular atmosphere of interpersonal relationships that fraternal charity goes on creating within the community itself."

Migration

In reference to migration, the Pope said:

"Human mobility in this country is broad and complex. . . . In this situation, how can one not think of the cultural and sometimes linguistic uprooting, the temporary or definitive separation from one's family, the difficulties of insertion and integration in a new environment, the many other consequences, especially of an inner, spiritual nature?"

He called for the Church to engage in "concrete pastoral action" relevant to the needs of people on the move and in alien settings, and declared:

"The Church has not and will not ever cease to proclaim the fundamental rights of man: to settle freely in one's own country; to emigrate within and outside the country for legitimate reasons; to be able to have a full family life; to count on the goods necessary for life; to preserve and develop one's own ethnic, cultural and linguistic patrimony; to profess publicly one's own religion; to be recognized and treated in accord with the dignity of one's person in any circumstance."

The Pope prayed during the Mass for three women who were killed in an early morning rush for seats at the folk festival attended later by him.

JULY 10

The main event of the day was a four-hour, morning-to-early-afternoon meeting with well over 200 bishops of Brazil. They heard not only an address by the Pope but also interventions by six of their own.

The Holy Father praised "the image that you Brazilian bishops project through the entire Church and the whole world. It is an image of poverty and simplicity, of full dedication, of closeness to your people and full presence in their lives and problems.... This is an image of bishops who are profoundly evangelical and profoundly in conformity with the model proposed in its documents by the Second Vatican Council."

Support for Bishops

This characterization of the bishops was interpreted as symbolic of the Pope's favorable attitude toward their activism for social and economic reforms. Archbishop Camara commented: "He could not have given more concrete support to the activities of the Church of Christ in Brazil."

The Pope also told the prelates: "Your vocation to be bishops prohibits you with total clarity . . . from everything that has to do with political partisanship and subjection to this or that ideological system. But it does not prohibit you — rather does it call you — to be near and at the service of all men and women, especially the weakest and most needy."

The wide-ranging talk by the Pope covered a variety of other subjects, including evangelization, liturgy, catechetics, vocations to the priesthood and religious life, popular religiosity and small Christian communities (*comunidades de base*).

The Holy Father departed from Fortaleza at about 4:00 p.m. on a two and one-half hour flight to Manaus, the last stop of his tour. On arrival he was driven to the cathedral in the city where he was given a tumultuous welcome.

He met in the evening with 58 leaders of 19 Indian nations who presented him with a record of injustices committed against them by government, industry and wealthy landholders. In describing the extent of these injustices, spokesmen told the Pope that 90 nations had disappeared in this century alone and that the Indian population had declined from six million 480 years ago to the present figure of 210,000.

JULY 11

The Pope concelebrated Mass in the morning before the last of the huge congregations he encountered daily during his pastoral tour. Help for Indians, praise and encouragement for missionaries were the subjects of his homily.

Of the Indians, he said:

"I confide to public authorities and other responsible people the wish I make, with all my heart and in the name of the Lord, for the Indians, whose ancestors were the first inhabitants of this land, that their right to inhabit it in peace and serenity be recognized.

Indians have a fear, a true nightmare, of being expelled, to benefit others who are more powerful, from the vital land needed as a base not only for survival but also for the preservation of their identity as a people."

Main Action of Missionaries

He told missionaries that their sacramental activity "is complemented by much that you should also do to aid the needy to promote themselves by passing from situations of penury and abandonment unworthy of children of God to more humane living conditions. This is what legions of missionaries did before you here in Latin America, here in Brazil itself.

"What matters is that the price paid for your action for the sake of the material promotion of people may never, not even distantly, mean diminution of your strictly religious activity. This would be a dangerous countertestimony, and it would be all the graver if you gave the impression of acting under the urging of some ideological imperative.

"Experience shows, at any rate, that the Church's testimony, declarations and action at any of her levels are credible and truly effective in the social field only if based on testimony, declarations and action that are even more intense in the main field, that of education in the faith and sacramental life. If she truly does this, it is her best way of preparing Christians who will act along the line of deep Christian inspiration without danger of deviations."

"I have another word to say to you. It will be brief, but it is a word charged with feeling. It is a message from a priest to his brother priests.

"The invitation that I would leave with you in remembrance of my visit is a call to be a missionary to such depth that it will never be just a title to you, a beautiful and glorious title, of course, but that it will be the deepest content of your priestly lives. In other words, that being a missionary will be the reason of your whole life, the profound inspiration of your action, the secret of your spirituality."

The last public event of the trip was the Pope's participation as the honored spectator in the traditional St. Peter's Day blessing and parade of boats down the Rio Negro to its juncture with the Amazon and back upriver to Manaus. About 300 boats of various types and sizes accompanied the patrol boat on which the Pope rode.

The Holy Father left Brazil in the early evening with a final blessing for the country and its people.

His Varig flight touched down at the Rome airport July 12 at 9:35 a.m.

THE PARTICULAR SYNOD OF DUTCH BISHOPS

"The pastoral work of the Church in The Netherlands to be exercised in the present situation," was the theme of the Particular Synod of Dutch Bishops convoked by Pope John Paul and held Jan. 14 to 31, 1980, at the Vatican.

Its purposes, as stated by Cardinal Johannes Willebrands in an opening address, were:

"To revive our communion with the universal Church, and especially with the Bishop of Rome. . . .

"To share our information regarding the situation and problems of the Church in The Netherlands.

"To reach agreement in our conceptions and pastoral action."

The Present Situation

The "present situation" noted in the theme of the synod was the product of more than 15 years of ferment in quest of renewal of the Church in Holland — in line with, beyond, or against directives that emanated from the Second Vatican Council. Developments during this period had the following results, among others.

• Strained relations with the Holy See.
• Significant differences among some bishops, and between bishops and priests, religious and lay persons.
• Objectionable views and trends in doctrine, evident especially in: the contents of a new catechism for adults published in 1966 and a high-school religion course published later; writings and teaching concerning the Eucharist, a variety of other subjects, and the encyclical *Humanae Vitae.*
• Extremes in liturgical practice.
• Vigorous advocacy for optional clerical celibacy and for pastoral ministry by priests who had left the priesthood and married.
• Significant departures from the priesthood (e.g., 196 in 1968, 244 in 1969, 243 in 1970) and a lack of candidates, coupled with a dismantling of traditional seminaries in all but one diocese.
• Excessive experimentation affecting the forms of life and work of religious, together with heavy departures from religious life and a serious lack of new candidates.
• Confusion in pastoral ministry regarding the distinctive and respective roles of priests,

deacons and approximately 275 lay pastoral workers.
• Pastoral effects of actions of six sessions of a national pastoral council between January, 1968, and April, 1970, and of a national pastoral consultation in January, 1973.
• Polarization of the faithful, religious and priests into groups of their own ideological and liturgical preferences.

Pope John Paul called the synod, the first of its kind with participation by a Pope and an entire national hierarchy, after consultation with the bishops during their most recent *ad limina* visits to the Vatican. With them, he signed the document (see below) in which they pledged that they would work together to improve the condition of the Church in The Netherlands.

Participants

The principal participants in the synod were the bishops of Holland: Cardinal Johannes Willebrands of Utrecht, the Pope's president-delegate; Hubert C. Ernst of Breda, Johannes B. Moller of Groningen, Theodore H. Zwartkruis of Haarlem, Johannes W.M. Bluyssen of 's-Hertogenbosch, Adrian Simonis of Rotterdam and Johannes Gijsen of Roermond. Archbishop Godfried Danneels of Malines-Brussels, Belgium, served with Cardinal Willebrands as a president-delegate.

Vatican officials at the synod were Cardinals: Franjo Seper, prefect of the Congregation for the Doctrine of the Faith; Sebastiano Baggio, prefect of the Congregation for Bishops; James R. Knox, prefect of the Congregation for the Sacraments and Divine Worship; Silvio Oddi, prefect of the Congregation for the Clergy; Eduardo Pironio, prefect of the Congregation for Religious and Secular Institutes; Gabriel-Marie Garrone, prefect of the Congregation for Catholic Education.

SYNOD DOCUMENT

Following are excerpts and general coverage of the document approved, signed and issued by the Dutch bishops and Pope John Paul II at the conclusion of the Particular Synod of Dutch Bishops Jan. 31, 1980.

The excerpts, with some headings and lead lines added, are from the translation circulated by the NC Documentary Service, Origins, Feb. 14, 1980 (Vol. 9, No. 35).

"Our deliberations dealt with what is desirable for the pastoral work in The Netherlands in the present circumstances. ... The grave problems that confront us as pastors demand a unity, a profound sense of what must be an affective and effective communion."

"Fidelity to the teaching of the Apostles being a condition of communion, the doctrine and discipline of the Church ... remain today the norm of fidelity to fraternal communion."

Bishops, Teachers of Faith

"The bishops ... express their unanimous will to deepen cordial and fraternal relations among themselves."

"The bishops profess their agreement on the content of the Catholic faith according to the teaching of the Roman Catholic Church. They express their full and entire communion with the Pope ... as well as their faith in the hierarchical constitution of the Church; neither bishops nor priests are delegates of the faithful, but are ministers of Jesus Christ at the service of the ecclesial community."

"The point of departure and the objective source of the faith are in divine revelation."

"The bishops intend to announce in its fullness the content of revelation, interpreted by the magisterium, and (to do) that while taking into account the requests of the men of our times."

Sense of the Faith: "There is, among the believing faithful of all times, a *sensus fidei* ("sense of the faith") to which theologians should always pay attention, and of which it is necessary to make use as an element of interpretation of tradition. ... Nevertheless, this *sensus fidei* is not constitutive of revelation and does not have the same force as the normative interpretation given to it by the magisterium of the Church, in submission to this revelation itself."

Religious Experience: "Religious experiences common to all men ... can constitute a point of departure for education to the faith and for catechesis. They must, nevertheless, be evaluated in the light of necessary growth toward the full understanding of the faith. It is necessary, therefore, to move away from certain methods of catechesis which remain at the level of religious experience alone."

"The bishops will watch to see that ... diversity (in expressions of the faith and of doctrine) does not engender confusion among believers."

Episcopal Government

Under the heading of episcopal government and their role as pastors, the bishops committed themselves to efforts to improve relations and collaboration among themselves — individually as well as in and through the operations of their conference — and with the congregations and other agencies of the Roman Curia. They mentioned the "reconciliation (necessary) between the exercise of their proper function within the diocese and their adherence to the directives of the conference or the majority of its members." They pledged that they would "abstain from declarations which could harm a confrere in the episcopate."

They noted their concern about the need for "establishing constant personal contact with priests, men and women religious, committed lay persons" and the faithful in general.

Priests

The bishops were unanimous in professing "the essential distinction between the ministerial or sacramental priesthood and the common priesthood of the baptized," in affirming "the permanent character of the ministerial priesthood," in declaring that "celibacy in view of the kingdom of heaven constitutes a great good for the Church," and in expressing "their will to follow faithfully the decisions of the popes to maintain the rule of celibacy."

They "decided to promote a pastoral activity of priestly and religious vocations, even while continuing research on the various forms that the apostolate of the laity can take."

Priests' Councils Are Not Unions: They cited the nature of associations of priests and priests' councils, in accordance with directives of the Second Vatican Council, and noted: "Possible associations of priests cannot ... be such that they obscure the hierarchical communion of their members with the bishop, the unique nature of the priesthood, and the respective functions of the bishop and of the priests' council. If these associations take on the character of a labor union, they are incompatible with the structures and spirit of the Church."

Training of Priests: The formation of candidates for the priesthood "can be assured only by true seminaries or else seminaries integrally assuring formation ... or else community houses of formation having all the attributes of a seminary" conducted according to conditions stated in official documents of the Church. Verification of such conditions was to be the responsibility of a special commission of bishops.

Religious

The bishops noted their appreciation of the contributions made by men and women religious to the Church in Holland, and also expressed satisfaction "with the relations which exist between the (episcopal) conference and the four assemblies of major superiors."

They added a word of caution "with regard to what is sometimes called emotional integration." They said "the expression is the object of ambiguous interpretations. They recognize the importance of a healthy emotional life, understood in the sense of cordiality and fraternity in relations among persons. They refer to St. Paul and St. John to stress that, rightly understood, love for God and for Christ, in the Spirit, can contribute greatly to integrate the need for affection in fraternal love. With regard to a sort of 'third way,' lived as an ambiguous state between celibacy and marriage, the members of the synod are unanimous in rejecting it."

Critics

"With regard to critical groups, the members of the synod — being aware that these groups include priests and religious — observe that these groups sometimes exercise too great a pressure on the life of the Church. The same is true of several periodicals and other forms of publicity. This criticism emanates from groups opposed among themselves — on the one hand, 'progressive' groups; on the other hand, 'conservative' groups.

"The bishops recognize that the criticisms made are valid to some extent and are sometimes accompanied by reasonable desires and useful stimuli for pastoral activity.

"The influence of these criticisms is negative when there is generalization, fanaticism, aggressiveness, pressure, refusal of dialogue, and unjust attacks against persons and institutions of the Church. They then cause polarization and harm the exercise of the episcopal function and communion among the faithful; they undermine the atmosphere of fraternal love and joy which ought to characterize the Christian life.

"The bishops want to maintain contact with these groups in the hope of being able to play a moderating role and to remain informed in a direct way. But they also propose to denounce their divergences with regard to the faith and discipline of the Church, so that true communion may be manifested."

Pastoral Workers

The bishops proposed the establishment of a commission to study "the various concrete forms that the activity of the laity in the pastoral work of the Church can take," with due regard for "the distinction between the respective pastoral tasks of the priest, the deacon and the lay person." They said there was "no room for envisioning a new 'office' or ministry, or a permanent function of global scope" that might create "a parallel 'clergy' which would be presented as an alternative to the priesthood and the diaconate."

Former Priests: Regarding the status and church-related involvement of priests who had been dispensed from the obligation of celibacy, the bishops quoted a guiding principle noted by the 1971 assembly of the Synod

of Bishops; " 'The priest who has left the exercise of his ministry must be treated justly and fraternally; even if he can contribute to the service of the Church, he must nevertheless not be admitted to exercise priestly functions.' "

Some Areas of Church Life

Liturgy: "To be able to live with Christ, the Church asks the faithful to take part in the Eucharistic celebration — the perfect sacrifice of praise — at least each Sunday and on feasts of obligation."

"The regulation of the liturgy depends uniquely on the authority of the Church. . . . It is through fidelity to Christ and to the Church that the liturgy must be celebrated in full conformity with the official books, renewed in line with Vatican II . . ., using the broad possibilities for adaptation provided for in these books themselves."

Sacrament of Reconciliation: "Reconciliation with the Father and with the Church presupposes the confession of our personal faults and a sincere will of conversion. Despite the present disaffection toward individual confession, the bishops ask priests to seek, in preaching and catechesis, to restore the esteem of the faithful for the sacrament of reconciliation. They beg them, especially, to be willing to remain available to all for confession. . . . Individual confession . . . is the only ordinary means of reconciling them with God and with their brothers and sisters in the faith. Collective absolution is an extraordinary means which the bishops may permit only according to the conditions prescribed by the new rite of the sacrament of reconciliation."

Catechesis: "The lived faith of the universal Church must be expressed. With regard to the pedagogical method, it must be suited to the character, the attitudes, the age and conditions of life of the hearers. In this, a certain research and prudent experimentation are legitimate."

Ecumenism: "The bishops eagerly encourage ecumenical activity as a grave duty flowing from Vatican II. . . . Its objective is to arrive not at a least common denominator but, on the contrary, at the fullness of the faith. That is why ecumenical activity will be supported by the bishops, who will watch out to see that it takes into account the demands of the faith, which reminds us especially that intercommunion among separated brothers is not the response to the call of Christ to perfect unity."

Additional Dispositions: The bishops established a synodal council to oversee the execution of its directives, consisting of Cardinal Gabriel-Marie Garrone (appointed by the Pope), and Cardinal Johannes Willebrands and Bishop Johannes Bluyssen (elected by the bishops).

For the reconciliation of differences between Bishop Johannes Gijsen of Roermond and the other six bishops, the synod directed: "The bishop of Roermond will resume his collaboration with the other bishops in the areas of the Pontifical Mission Works, the Lenten Activity and the Dutch Missionary Week." The other bishops said they were "ready to seek a solution" to the difficulties they had with Bishop Gijsen.

SYNOD OF UKRAINIAN BISHOPS

Pope John Paul convoked an extraordinary synod of Ukrainian bishops of the Byzantine Rite Mar. 24 to 27, 1980, at the Vatican for purposes stated Feb. 5 in a letter to Major Archbishop-Cardinal Josyf Slipyi. The Holy Father said in the letter:

"I have reached the decision to appoint a coadjutor with right of succession to Your Eminence, after a synod of all the Ukrainian bishops of the diaspora (all areas outside of the Ukraine) has been convoked; and, in addition, to grant extraordinary faculties for other synodal meetings of the same bishops for the future, 'at the will of the Supreme Pontiff' . . . to handle business or to propose candidates for the episcopate."

The 15 bishops attending the synod voted by secret ballot for three nominees for the office of coadjutor major archbishop. The Pope's choice, announced Mar. 27, was Archbishop Myroslav Lubachivsky of Philadelphia. His selection assured continuity in the future leadership of Ukrainian Catholics.

No Patriarchate

The synod was intended to emphasize the identity of Ukrainians in the Byzantine Rite, to reaffirm their liturgical and canonical traditions, and, especially, to counteract patriarchal pretensions and advocacy by Cardinal Slipyi and others sharing the views of the Society for the Promotion of a Patriarchal System in the Ukrainian Catholic Church.

The Pope told the cardinal in his letter that he has "no intention to extend the jurisdiction of the major archbishop (of Lvov) beyond the confines of his territory, or to erect a Ukrainian patriarchate."

Pope Paul VI rejected the patriarchate proposal several times during his pontificate, particularly in letters addressed to the cardinal on July 7, 1971, and May 24, 1975.

The reasons against establishment of a patriarchate were:

• Canonical: A patriarch could not exercise his office, as required by church law, in Soviet-controlled Ukraine where the Catholic Church was suppressed in 1946.

• Historical: There never was a Ukrainian patriarchate.

• Practical: There was fear that establishment of a patriarchate would exacerbate rather than improve the condition of underground Catholics in the Soviet Union.

Cardinal Slipyi

Cardinal Slipyi, the key figure in patriarchal controversy, became archbishop of Lvov in 1944. Arrested in 1945 and charged with unspecified crimes by Soviet authorities, he survived the suppression of the Church in the Ukraine and spent 18 years in prison. Released from detention in 1963, he established residence in Rome as an exile and was given the title of major archbishop; two years later he became a cardinal. As the ranking Ukrainian prelate but without canonical sanction, he has used the title of patriarch and has summoned Ukrainian bishops on several occasions to attend meetings he called synods.

EUCHARISTIC MYSTERY AND WORSHIP

The "Mystery and Worship of the Holy Eucharist" was the subject of a letter addressed by Pope John Paul to bishops throughout the world in connection with the celebration of Holy Thursday, Apr. 3, 1980. The Latin title is *Dominicae Coenae.* The letter, dated Feb. 24, was released Mar. 18.

The Holy Father said in the letter: "We shall continue in the future to take special care to promote and follow the renewal of the Church according to the teaching of the Second Vatican Council, in the spirit of an ever living tradition." It is "necessary to continue to actuate a new and intense education, in order to discover all the richness contained in the new liturgy."

The following were among subjects covered in the Holy Father's pastoral reflections.

• the central significance and role of the Eucharist, as sacrifice and sacrament, in the Church;

• the relationship of the Eucharist to the sacrament of penance;

• frequent reception of the Eucharist;

• the place and legitimacy of the use of Latin in the liturgy, under conditions laid down by the Second Vatican Council, for people "educated on the basis of the old (pre-Vatican II) liturgy in Latin";

• the importance of scriptural readings at Mass.

• practical directives in line with liturgical enactments of and since the Second Vatican Council. (See below.)

NORMS FOR WORSHIP

Following are excerpts from an "Instruction on Certain Norms concerning Worship of the Eucharistic Mystery," approved by Pope John Paul Apr. 17 and issued by the Congregation for the Sacraments and Divine Worship May

23, 1980. The Latin title is Inaestimabile Donum ("The Priceless Gift"). Its stated purpose is to reaffirm and to clarify teaching on liturgical renewal contained in enactments of the Second Vatican Council and in several related implementing documents.

These excerpts are from the translation circulated June 5, 1980, by the NC Documentary Service, Origins (Vol. 10, No. 3).

Positive Results: "This sacred congregation notes with great joy the many positive results of the liturgical reform (since the Second Vatican Council):

• "a more active and conscious participation by the faithful in the liturgical mysteries;

• "doctrinal and catechetical enrichment through the use of the vernacular and the wealth of readings from the Bible;

• "a growth in the community sense of liturgical life;

• "successful efforts to close the gap between life and worship, between liturgical piety and personal piety, and between liturgy and popular piety."

Some Abuses: "But these encouraging and positive aspects cannot suppress concern at the varied and frequent abuses being reported from different parts of the Catholic world:

• "the confusion of roles, especially regarding the priestly ministry and the role of the laity (indiscriminate shared recitation of the Eucharistic Prayer, homilies given by lay people, lay people distributing Communion while the priests refrain from doing so);

• "an increasing loss of the sense of the sacred (abandonment of liturgical vestments, the Eucharist celebrated outside church without real need, lack of reverence and respect for the Blessed Sacrament, etc.);

• "misunderstanding of the ecclesial character of the liturgy (the use of private texts, the proliferation of unapproved Eucharistic Prayers, the manipulation of the liturgical texts for social and political ends)."

"In these cases we are face to face with real falsification of the Catholic liturgy."

Right to True Liturgy: "The faithful have a right to a true liturgy, which means the liturgy desired and laid down by the Church.... Undue experimentation, changes and creativity bewilder the faithful. The use of unauthorized texts means a loss of the necessary connection between the law of praying and the law of believing.... 'No person, even if he be a priest, may add, remove or change anything in the liturgy on his own authority.' " (*Constitution on the Sacred Liturgy*, No. 22 (3); Second Vatican Council), and: " 'Anyone who takes advantage of the reform to indulge in arbitrary experiments is wasting energy and offending the ecclesial sense' " (Address of Paul VI, Aug. 22, 1973; *L'Osservatore Romano*, Aug. 23, 1973).

The Mass

Scripture: "The Liturgy of the Word and the Eucharistic Liturgy are so closely connected that they form but one single act of worship. ... Sacred Scripture is ... of the highest importance in the celebration of Mass. ... It would be a serious abuse to replace the word of God with the word of man, no matter who the author may be."

"The reading of the Gospel passage is reserved to the ordained minister, namely, the deacon or the priest. When possible, the other readings should be entrusted to a reader who has been instituted as such or to other spiritually and technically trained lay people."

Homily: "The purpose of the homily is to explain to the faithful the word of God ... and to apply its message to the present. Accordingly, the homily is to be given by the priest or the deacon."

Eucharistic Prayer: "It is reserved to the priest, by virtue of his ordination, to proclaim the Eucharistic Prayer.... It is, therefore, an abuse to have some parts of the Eucharistic Prayer said by the deacon, by a lower minister, or by the faithful.... The assembly ... unites itself to the priest in faith and silence and shows its concurrence by the various interventions provided for in the course of the Eucharistic Prayer.... The *Per Ipsum* (beginning the final acclamation) itself is reserved to the priest."

"Only the Eucharistic Prayers included in the Roman Missal or those that the Apostolic See has by law admitted, in the manner and within the limits laid down by the Holy See, are to be used. To modify the Eucharistic Prayers approved by the Church or to adopt others privately composed is a most serious abuse."

"The Eucharistic Prayer must not be overlaid with other prayers or songs."

Concelebration: "Concelebrants ... are to be present from the beginning of the celebration, they are to wear the prescribed vestments, they are to occupy the place appropriate to their ministry as concelebrants, and they are to observe faithfully the other norms for the seemly performance of the rite."

Matter of the Eucharist: "The bread of the celebration of the Eucharist ... must be made solely of wheat and, in accordance with the tradition proper to the Latin Church, it must be unleavened. (It) 'should appear as actual food.' This is to be understood as linked to the consistency of the bread and not to its form, which remains the traditional one. No other ingredients are to be added to the wheaten flour and water.... The wine for the Eucharistic celebration must be of 'the fruit of the vine,' and be natural and genuine, that is to say, not mixed with other substances."

Holy Communion: "Communion is ... given to the faithful through the minister appointed for this purpose. It is not permitted that the faithful should themselves pick up the consecrated bread and the sacred chalice; still less that they should hand them from one to another."

Eucharistic Ministers: "The faithful . . . authorized as extraordinary ministers of the Eucharist can distribute Communion when there is no priest, deacon or acolyte, when the priest is impeded by illness or advanced age, or when the number of the faithful going to Communion is so large as to make the celebration of Mass excessively long. . . . A reprehensible attitude is shown by those priests who, though present at the celebration, refrain from distributing Communion and leave this task to the laity."

Manner of Reception: "The faithful can receive it (the Eucharist) either kneeling or standing," and under one or both species (bread and wine) in accord with appropriate norms.

Disposition of Fragments: Sacred particles remaining after the distribution of Communion "are to be consumed or taken by the competent minister to the place where the Eucharist is reserved."

"The consecrated wine is to be consumed immediately after Communion and may not be kept. Care must be taken to consecrate only the amount of wine needed for Communion."

Sacred Vessels: The instruction contained directives regarding the form and materials of sacred vessels, and noted: "Use is not to be made of simple baskets or other receptacles meant for ordinary use outside the sacred celebrations, nor are the sacred vessels to be of poor quality or lacking any artistic style."

Ministries of Women: "There are . . . various roles that women can perform in the liturgical assembly. . . . Women are not, however, permitted to act as altar servers."

Other Eucharistic Worship

"Public and private devotion to the Holy Eucharist outside Mass is highly recommended; for the presence of Christ, who is adored by the faithful in the sacrament, derives from the sacrifice and is directed toward sacramental and spiritual Communion."

The instruction listed some details connected with these devotions. It also called attention to the need for priests to acquire deep and authentic understanding and experience of the Mass, for liturgical formation in seminaries, and for development of the work of liturgical commissions on various levels for backgrounding and carrying out liturgical reform and renewal.

EUTHANASIA

Following are excerpts from the "Declaration on Euthanasia" issued June 26, 1980, by the Congregation for the Doctrine of the Faith. The declaration, approved by Pope John Paul, was dated May 5, 1980.

These excerpts are from the official English text circulated by the NC Documentary Service, Origins, Aug. 14, 1980 (Vol. 10, No. 10).

I. Value of Human Life

"Human life is the basis of all goods, and is the necessary source and condition of every human activity and of all society. Most people regard life as something sacred and hold that no one may dispose of it at will, but believers see in life something greater, namely, a gift of God's love which they are called upon to preserve and make fruitful. And it is this latter consideration that gives rise to the following consequences.

• "1. No one can make an attempt on the life of an innocent person without opposing God's love for that person, without violating a fundamental right, and therefore without commiting a crime of the utmost gravity.

• "2. Everyone has the duty to lead his or her life in accordance with God's plan. That life is entrusted to the individual as a good that must bear fruit already here on earth, but that finds its full perfection only in eternal life.

• "3. Intentionally causing one's own death, or suicide, is therefore equally as wrong as murder; such an action on the part of a person is to be considered as a rejection of God's sovereignty and loving plan. Furthermore, suicide is also often a refusal of love for self, the denial of the natural instinct to live, a flight from the duties of justice and charity owed to one's neighbor, to various communities or to the whole of society — although, as is generally recognized, at times there are psychological factors present that can diminish responsibility or even completely remove it.

"However, one must clearly distinguish suicide from that sacrifice of one's life whereby for a higher cause — such as God's glory, the salvation of souls or the service of one's brethren — a person offers his or her own life or puts it in danger (cf. Jn. 15:14)."

II. Euthanasia

"By euthanasia is understood an action or an omission which of itself or by intention causes death, in order that all suffering may in this way be eliminated. Euthanasia's terms of reference . . . are to be found in the intention of the will and in the methods used.

"It is necessary to state firmly once more that nothing and no one can in any way permit the killing of an innocent human being, whether a fetus or an embryo, an infant or an adult, an old person, or one suffering from an incurable disease, or a person who is dying. Furthermore, no one is permitted to ask for this act of killing, either for himself or herself or for another person entrusted to his or her care, nor can he or she consent to it, either explicitly or implicitly. Nor can any authority legitimately recommend or permit such an action. For it is a question of the violation of the divine law, an offense against the dignity of the human person, a crime against life, and an attack on humanity.

"It may happen that, by reason of prolonged and barely tolerable pain, for deeply personal or other reasons, people may be led to believe that they can legitimately ask for death or obtain it for others. Although in these cases the guilt of the individual may be reduced or completely absent, nevertheless the error of judgment into which the conscience falls, perhaps in good faith, does not change the nature of this act of killing, which will always be in itself something to be rejected."

III. Suffering and Painkillers

"Physical suffering is certainly an unavoidable element of the human condition. On the biological level, it constitutes a warning of which no one denies the usefulness. But, since it affects the human psychological makeup, it often exceeds its own biological usefulness and so can become so severe as to cause the desire to remove it at any cost.

"According to Christian teaching, however, suffering, especially suffering during the last moments of life, has a special place in God's saving plan; it is in fact a sharing in Christ's Passion and a unon with the redeeming sacrifice which he offered in obedience to the Father's will."

"Human and Christian prudence suggest for the majority of sick people the use of medicine capable of alleviating or suppressing pain, even though these may cause as a secondary effect semi-consciousness and reduced lucidity. As for those who are not in a state to express themselves, one can reasonably presume that they wish to take these painkillers and have them administered according to doctor's advice."

"It is fitting to recall a declaration by Pius XII, which retains its full force, in answer to a group of doctors who had put the question: 'Is the suppression of pain and consciousness by the use of narcotics permitted by religion and morality to the doctor and the patient (even at the approach of death and if one foresees that the use of narcotics will shorten life)?'

"The Pope said: 'If no other means exist, and if, in the given circumstances, this does not prevent the carrying out of other religious and moral duties: Yes' (Address of Feb. 24, 1957). In this case, of course, death is in no way intended or sought, even if the risk of it is reasonably taken; the intention is simply to relieve pain effectively, using for this purpose painkillers available to medicine.

"However, painkillers that cause unconsciousness need special consideration. For a person not only has to be able to satisfy his or her moral duties and family obligations; he or she also has to prepare himself or herself with full consciousness for meeting Christ. Thus Pius XII warns: 'It is not right to deprive the dying person of consciousness without a serious reason' (Address of Sept. 9, 1958)."

IV. Proportion in Use of Remedies

"A 'right to die' " means "the right to die peacefully with human and Christian dignity. From this point of view, the use of therapeutic means can sometimes pose problems.

"In numerous cases, the complexity of the situation can be such as to cause doubts about the way ethical principles should be applied. In the final analysis, it pertains to the conscience either of the sick person, or of those qualified to speak in the sick person's name, or of the doctors, to decide, in the light of moral obligations and of the various aspects of the case.

"Everyone has the duty to care for his or her own health or to seek such care from others. Those whose task it is to care for the sick must do so conscientiously and administer the remedies that seem necessary or useful.

"However, is it necessary in all circumstances to have recourse to all possible remedies?

"In the past, moralists replied that one is never obliged to use 'extraordinary' means. This reply, which as a principle still holds good, is perhaps less clear today, by reason of the imprecision of the term and the rapid progress made in the treatment of sickness. Thus, some people prefer to speak of 'proportionate' and 'disproportionate' means.

Factors To Be Considered

"In any case, it will be possible to make a correct judgment as to the means by studying the type of treatment to be used, its degree of complexity or risk, its cost and the possibilities of using it, and comparing these elements with the result that can be expected, taking into account the state of the sick person and his or her physical and moral resources.

"In order to facilitate the application of these general principles, the following clarifications can be added:

• "If there are no other sufficient remedies, it is permitted, with the patient's consent, to have recourse to the means provided by the most advanced medical techniques, even if these means are still at the experimental stage and are not without a certain risk. By accepting them, the patient can even show generosity in the service of humanity.

• "It is also permitted, with the patient's

consent, to interrupt these means, where the results fall short of expectations. But for such a decision to be made, account will have to be taken of the reasonable wishes of the patient's family, as also of the advice of the doctors who are specially competent in the matter. The latter may in particular judge that the investment in instruments and personnel is disproportionate to the results foreseen; they may also judge that the techniques applied impose on the patient strain or suffering out of proportion with the benefits which he or she may gain from such techniques.

• "It is also permissible to make do with the normal means that medicine can offer. Therefore, one cannot impose on anyone the obligation to have recourse to a technique which is already in use but which carries a risk or is burdensome. Such a refusal is not the equivalent of suicide; on the contrary, it should be considered as an acceptance of the human condition, or a wish to avoid the application of a medical procedure disproportionate to the results that can be expected, or a desire not to impose excessive expense on the family or the community.

• "When inevitable death is imminent in spite of the means used, it is permitted in conscience to take the decision to refuse forms of treatment that would only secure a precarious and burdensome prolongation of life, so long as the normal care due to the sick person in similar cases is not interrupted. In such circumstances the doctor has no reason to reproach himself with failing to help the person in danger."

KATERI TEKAKWITHA AND OTHERS BEATIFIED

The five Servants of God listed below were declared "Blessed" during beatification ceremonies presided over by Pope John Paul June 22, 1980. All of them figured in the early history of the Church in the Western Hemisphere. Also significant was the fact that their beatifications were decreed more on the basis of their reputations for holiness and veneration than on the specific verification of miracles attributable to their intercession.

Blessed Kateri Tekakwitha

Kateri Tekakwitha, "Lily of the Mohawks," was born in 1656 at Ossernenon (Auriesville), N.Y., the daughter of a Mohawk chief and a Christian Algonquin mother. From the age of four she was raised with the family of an uncle, following the loss of her parents and brother in a smallpox epidemic which left her with a disfigured face and poor eyesight.

Nine years after her first encounter with Jesuit missionaries, she was baptized by one of them, Father Jacques de Lamberville, at Easter, 1676. She left Ossernenon the following year to escape from the animosity and hostility of persons opposed to her conversion and way of life, and went to live at a Christian village about 200 miles away, Sault St. Louis, near Montreal. Besides devoting herself to prayer, penitential practices and the care of the sick and aged, she professed a vow of perpetual virginity Mar. 25, 1679. She died Apr. 17, 1680, and was buried at Caughnawaga, Ontario.

Kateri, who was designated as "Venerable" in 1943, is the first of her people to be declared "Blessed." Basic documentary evidence of her holiness was compiled by three Jesuits within 35 years or so of her death. The National Shrine of Kateri Tekakwitha is located at Fonda, N.Y.

Blessed Bishop Laval

Francois De Montmorency-Laval was born Apr. 30, 1623, at Montigny-sur-Avre, France. Educated at Jesuit institutions, he was ordained to the priesthood in 1647 and served in various assignments in France before being named vicar apostolic of Canada and ordained a bishop in 1658.

He arrived in Canada the following year and set in motion the pioneer organization of pastoral ministry, missionary endeavor, priestly training and educational work that won for him the title of "Founder of the Church in Canada." As bishop of Quebec, following establishment of the diocese in 1674, he exercised jurisdiction over all French-claimed territory in the New World.

Bishop Laval retired from the diocese in 1688 and spent the rest of his life at the Seminary of Quebec which he had established in 1663. He died May 6, 1708, and was interred at the seminary. He was declared "Venerable" in 1960.

Blessed Marie of the Incarnation

Marie Guyard was born Oct. 28, 1599, at Tours, France. She was married in 1617 and bore a son, but suffered the loss of her husband in less than three years. In 1632, after entrusting her son to the care of her sister, she joined the Ursuline nuns and adopted Marie of the Incarnation as her name. Seven years later she and two other nuns who left France with her became the first women missionaries to the New World.

Because of her 33-year-long pioneer role as a religious and educator, Pope John Paul called Marie the "Mother of the Church in Canada." Her mystical experiences and accounts of them merited for her the title of "Teresa of the New World."

Mother Marie died in Quebec Apr. 30, 1672. She was declared "Venerable" in 1911.

Blessed Jose de Anchieta

Jose de Anchieta was born Mar. 19, 1534, at San Cristobal de la Laguna, Tenerife, Canary Islands. He joined the Jesuits in 1551 in Portugal. Two years later he went to Brazil where he spent the rest of his life as an active missionary. He was ordained to the priesthood in 1566, served as a religious superior for a number of years, established the first classical school in the New World, and was the author of catechetical and other religious writings. He is called the "Apostle of Brazil."

Jose died June 9, 1597, at Reritiba. He was declared "Venerable" in 1736.

Blessed Pedro de San Jose Betancur

Pedro de San Jose Betancur was born in March, 1626, at Chasna, Tenerife, Canary Islands. The son of poor parents, he worked as a shepherd there before setting out for Guatemala in 1650.

He arrived at Guatemala City a year later and in 1653 began studies for the priesthood which he did not complete. He joined the Third Order Secular of St. Francis two years later and devoted the rest of his life to the service of the sick and the poor. He founded a hospital, a school, homes for the poor, and a community of like-minded men to carry on the work that gave meaning to his life. He is known as the "St. Francis of the Americas."

Pedro died Apr. 25, 1667. He was declared "Venerable" in 1771.

THE AUGSBURG CONFESSION: 450TH ANNIVERSARY

Joint Catholic-Lutheran celebrations made observance of the 450th anniversary of the Augsburg Confession an outstanding ecumenical event of 1980. The significance of the commemoration lay in the paradoxical hope it generated that the Confession, long a symbol of differences between Catholics and Lutherans, might help to bring them closer to unity of faith.

The Augsburg Confession (*Confessio Augustana*) is the primary statement of Lutheran belief. Written principally by Philipp Melancthon 13 years after Martin Luther triggered the Reformation, it was presented at the invitation of Holy Roman Emperor Charles V to the Imperial Diet at Augsburg June 25, 1530, for the purpose of stating Reformist views, of seeking reconciliation of them with doctrines and practices of the Catholic Church, and of achieving peace and toleration in the troubled German states.

28 Articles

The Confession consists of 21 articles of faith and doctrine, and seven articles concerning matters in dispute and subject to reform.

The doctrinal articles are on God, original sin, Christ, justification by faith, ministry, the new obedience, the Church, baptism, the Lord's Supper, confession, repentance, use of the sacraments, order in the Church, usages of the Church, civil government, divine judgment, freedom of will, the causes of sin, faith and good works, and the cult of saints.

Seven additional articles deal in polemical fashion with reception of the Eucharist under the forms of bread and wine, the authority of bishops, and opposition to clerical celibacy, private Masses, required confession of sins, traditions instituted by the Church, and monastic vows.

A panel of Catholic theologians at the Diet responded to the Confession with a Papalist Confutation which indicated approval of nine articles without reservations, approval of six articles with qualifications, and condemnation of 13 articles. Doctrinal and disciplinary statements of the Confession at variance with the teaching and practice of the Catholic Church were condemned later by the Council of Trent.

New Consensus

The Confession has been a touchstone of contention and division between the Catholic and Lutheran communions for more than four centuries. Now, however, according to Father John Jay Hughes, writing in the Jan. 12, 1980, edition of *America,* there has emerged "a consensus of scholarly opinion that the Confession was an honest and sincere attempt, not motivated by merely tactical or diplomatic considerations, to formulate a statement of reformed, evangelical Catholicism. Its essentially Catholic intent is still insufficiently appreciated, however, outside the small world of professional ecumenists and scholars."

In the same vein, the officially appointed Catholic-Lutheran Commission of ecumenists noted in a statement approved Feb. 23, 1980, at Augsburg: "Research into doctrinal history .. has produced insights favorable to a more objective view of earlier controversies, to a defusing of mutual condemnations. . . ."

The statement also said: "In content and structure this Confession, which is the basis and point of reference for the other Lutheran confessional documents, reflects as no other confession does the ecumenical purpose and Catholic intention of the Reformation. . . .

"The express purpose of the Augsburg Confession is to bear witness to the faith of the one, holy, catholic and apostolic Church. Its concern is not with peculiar doctrines nor indeed with the establishment of a new church . . ., but with the preservation and renewal of the Christian faith in its purity — in harmony with the ancient church, and 'the Church of Rome,' and in agreement with the witness of Holy Scripture. . . .

"Joint studies by Catholic and Lutheran theologians have shown that the contents of the statements of the Augsburg Confession in large measure fulfill this intention and to this extent can be regarded as an expression of the common faith."

But Still Differences

The expression is not complete, however, despite: common faith in the Trinity "and the saving work of God through Jesus Christ in the Holy Spirit"; a broad consensus on the doctrine of justification; a basic but still incomplete accord in understanding of the church. There are persistent differences regarding a variety of subjects including the sacraments, the papal office, the order of bishops, and the teaching authority of the church — not to mention dogmas defined since the Reformation (infallibility, the Immaculate Conception and Assumption of Mary).

The statement, which represents the views of those who produced and signed it, notes that changes in the life and judgment of the churches have removed the grounds for the sharp criticism of abuses made in the last seven articles of the Confession.

Papal Hope

Pope John Paul marked the 450th anniversary of the Confession at the conclusion of a general audience on June 25, 1980. He said, in part:

"As a 'confessional text' it remains today a fundamental document for the confession of faith and the ecclesial life of Lutheran Christians and others. . . .

"The intense and long-standing dialogue with the Lutheran Church, called for and made possible by the Second Vatican Council, has enabled us to discover how great and solid are the common foundations of our Christian faith. . . .

"I want to urge all the faithful, and particularly theologians, and to beg them unceasingly that . . . we may seek all there is in the apostolic heritage that unites us with our brothers and sisters, in order that we may discover anew the treasure of one common creed."

The Holy Father expressed hope that, "from the Gospel of creation by God, of Redemption in Jesus Christ, and of the call to one People of God, there may develop a new force for a confession of faith full of hope, today and tomorrow. The will of Christ and the signs of the times are leading us to a common witness in a growing fullness of truth and love."

DECLARATION ON VIEWS OF FATHER HANS KUNG

The Sacred Congregation for the Doctrine of the Faith, in a declaration dated Dec. 15 and published Dec. 18, 1979, stated that Father Hans Kung, "in his writings, has departed from the integral truth of Catholic faith, and therefore he can no longer be considered a Catholic theologian nor function as such in a teaching role."

This translation of the text of the declaration, issued by the Vatican, was circulated by the NC Documentary Service, Origins, Jan. 3, 1980 (Vol. 9, No. 29).

The Church of Christ has received from God the mandate to keep and to safeguard the deposit of faith so that all the faithful, under the guidance of the sacred magisterium through which Christ himself exercises his role as teacher in the Church, may cling without fail to the faith once delivered to the saints, may penetrate it more deeply by accurate insights, and may apply it more thoroughly to life.[1]

Theologians and Magisterium

In order to fulfill the important task entrusted to itself alone,[2] the magisterium of the Church avails itself of the work of theologians, especially those who in the Church have received from the authorities the task of teaching and who, therefore, have been designated in a certain way as teachers of the truth. In their research the theologians, like scholars in other fields, enjoy a legitimate scientific liberty, though within the limits of the method of sacred theology. Thus, while working in their own way they seek to attain the same specific end as the magisterium itself, namely, "to preserve, to penetrate ever more deeply, to explain, to teach, to defend the sacred deposit of revelation; and in this way to illumine the life of the Church and of the human race with the light of divine truth."[3]

Fidelity to Magisterium

It is necessary, therefore, that theological research and teaching should always be illumined with fidelity to the magisterium, since no one may rightly act as a theologian except in close union with the mission of teaching truth which is incumbent on the Church itself.[4]

When such fidelity is absent, harm is done to all the faithful who, since they are bound to profess the faith which they have received from God through the Church, have a sacred right to receive the word of God uncontaminated, and so they expect that vigilant care should be exercised to keep the threat of error far from them.[5]

If it should happen, therefore, that a teacher of sacred doctrine chooses and disseminates as the norm of truth his own judgment and not the thought of the Church, and if he continues in his conviction, despite the use of all charitable means in his regard, then honesty itself demands that the Church should publicly call attention to his conduct and should state that he can no longer teach with the authority of the mission which he received from her.[6]

This canonical mission is, in fact, a testimony to a reciprocal trust: first, trust on the part of the competent authority that the theologian will conduct himself as a Catholic theologian in the work of his research and teaching; second, trust on the part of the theologian himself in the Church and in her integral teaching, since it is by her mandate that he carries out his task.

Warning

Since some of the writings — spread throughout many countries — and the teaching of Professor Hans Kung, a priest, are a cause of disturbance in the minds of the faithful, the bishops of Germany and this Congregation for the Doctrine of the Faith, acting in common accord, have several times counseled and warned him in order to persuade him to carry on his theological work in full communion with the authentic magisterium of the Church.

In this spirit the Sacred Congregation for the Doctrine of the Faith, in order to fulfill its role of promoting and safeguarding the doctrine of faith and morals in the universal Church,[7] issued a public document on Feb. 15, 1975, declaring that some opinions of Professor Hans Kung were opposed in different degrees to the doctrine of the Church which must be held by all the faithful. Among these opinions it noted especially, as of greater importance, those which pertain to the dogma of faith about infallibility in the Church, to the task of authentically interpreting the unique sacred deposit of the word of God which has been entrusted only to the living magisterium of the Church, and finally to the valid consecration of the Eucharist.

At the same time, this sacred congregation warned Professor Kung that he should not continue to teach such opinions, expecting in the meantime that he would bring his opinions into harmony with the doctrine of the authentic magisterium.[8]

However, up to the present time he has in no way changed his opinion in the matters called to his attention.

This fact is particularly evident in the matter of the opinion which at least puts in doubt the dogma of infallibility in the Church or reduces it to a certain fundamental indefectibility of the Church in truth, with the possibility of error in doctrinal statements which the magisterium of the Church teaches must be held definitively. On this point Hans Kung has in no way sought to conform to the doctrine of the magisterium. Instead, he has recently proposed his view again more explicitly (namely, in his writings, *Kirche-Gehalten in der Wahrheit?* — Benziger Verlag, 1979, and *Zum Geleit,* an introduction to the work of A. B. Hasler titled *Wie der Papst Unfehlbar*

Wurde — Piper Verlag, 1979), even though this sacred congregation had affirmed that such an opinion contradicts the doctrine defined by Vatican Council I and confirmed by Vatican Council II.

Moreover, the consequences of this opinion, especially a contempt for the magisterium of the Church, may be found in other works published by him, undoubtedly with serious harm to some essential points of Catholic faith (e.g., those teachings which pertain to the consubstantiality of Christ with his Father, and to the Blessed Virgin Mary), since the meaning ascribed to these doctrines is different from that which the Church has understood and now understands.

Decision

The Sacred Congregation for the Doctrine of the Faith in the aforesaid document of 1975 refrained at the time from further action regarding the above-mentioned opinions of Professor Kung, presuming that he himself would abandon them. But, since this presumption no longer exists, this sacred congregation by reason of its duty is constrained to declare that Professor Hans Kung, in his writings, has departed from the integral truth of Catholic faith, and therefore he can no longer be considered a Catholic theologian nor function as such in a teaching role.

At an audience granted to the undersigned cardinal prefect, the Supreme Pontiff Pope John Paul II approved this declaration, decided upon at an ordinary meeting of this sacred congregation, and ordered its publication.

In Rome, at the Sacred Congregation for the Doctrine of the Faith, on Dec. 15, 1979.

Franjo Cardinal Seper, Prefect.

Jerome Hamer, O.P., Titular Archbishop of Lorium, Secretary.

Footnotes

(1) Cf. Vatican Council I, *Const. Dogm. Dei Filius,* cap. iv, *"De fide et ratione":* DS 301 8; Vatican Council II, *Const. Dogm. Lumen Gentium,* n. 12.

(2) Vatican Council II, *Const. Dogm. Dei Verbum,* n. 10.

(3) Paul VI, *Allocut. ad Congress. Internat. de Theologia Conc. Vatic. II,* Oct. 1, 1966, *Acta Apostolicae Sedis* 58 (1966), p. 891.

(4) Cf. John Paul II, *Const. Apost. Sapientia Christiana,* Art. 70; *Encyclical Redemptor Hominis,* n. 19, *AAS* 71 (1979), pp. 493, 308.

(5) Cf. Vatican Council II, *Const. Dogm. Lumen Gentium,* nos. 11 and 25; Paul VI, *Exhort. Apost. Quinque iam anni: AAS* 63 (1971), pp. 99 ff.

(6) Cf. *Sapientia Christiana,* Tit. III, art. 27, par. 1: *AAS* 71 (1979), p. 483.

(7) Cf. *Motu proprio Integrae Servandae,* nos. 1, 3 and 4: *AAS* 57 (1965), p. 954.

(8) Cf. *AAS* 67 (1975), pp. 203-204.

CARDINAL'S STATEMENT

Following are excerpts from a declaration on Father Hans Kung issued Dec. 18, 1979, by Cardinal Joseph Hoffner, president of the German Bishops' Conference.

The excerpts are from a translation of the declaration circulated by the NC Documentary Service, Origins, Jan. 3, 1980 (Vol. 9, No. 29).

Professor Hans Kung in his book, *Unfehlbar? Eine Anfrage* ("Infallibility? An Inquiry"), Zurich, 1970, and in other writings reduced this doctrine to the meaning of maintaining a fundamental continuity of the Church in the truth, which, however, could be reconciled with errors of fact in decisions of faith made by the Church in an irrevocable manner. The Church thus would remain in the truth "notwithstanding all the errors ever possible." The Congregation for the Doctrine of the Faith sees in this opinion an attenuation of the gift of the infallibility of the Church and a violation or radical obfuscation of the dogma of 1870. Professor Kung recently spoke of a redress, a "revision of the decisions of Vatican I."

Infallibility

The dogma of infallibility in the Church can seem at first sight to be marginal in the totality of the faith. In reality, in it are concentrated fundamental problems, such as, for example, the knowledge of truth and interpretation of revelation, its verbal form and its tradition, the certainty of the faith and the grounds of the power of authority in the Church. In this area that serves true knowledge of divine revelation, the appearance of errors brings damage to the faith itself.

Christology

The theological method practiced by Professor Kung, with the dangerous limits too often in evidence (in his works), brings as a result a break with the theological tradition of faith and doctrine on principal points. That shows itself above all in Kung's affirmations concerning the person of Jesus Christ. On the central Christological question, whether Jesus Christ is *really* Son of God, in other words, if ᴉe is of the degree and level of being of God, without diminution, Kung, notwithstanding all his attempts at clarification, avoids a confession that is decisive and formulated in binding words.

From ancient times the Christians professed: "We believe . . . in one Lord, Jesus Christ, only-begotten Son of God, born of the Father before all ages: God from God, Light from Light, *true God from true God,* begotten, not made, *one in being with the Father*" (as in the great profession of faith of Nicea, 325). This implies consequences for our salvation; if in Jesus Christ, *God himself* has not given himself for men, then the central point of Christian revelation falls. All the pronounce-

Christian revelation falls. All the pronouncements, even those on the "human" being, that is on the humanity of Jesus, are really important for the Christian faith only if they are intrinsically connected with Jesus Christ as truly being God.

Effects on Other Doctrines

Professor Kung in general asserts that he wants to preserve and strengthen the content of the Christological dogmas, but in fact he obscures and reduces their univocal enunciations. When there is little clarity on fundamental points concerning the mystery of the person of Jesus Christ, the heart not only of the Catholic faith but of Christian faith in general is threatened. Therefore it is no accident that Professor Kung presents the doctrine on the divine Trinity, the Church, the sacraments and Mary in an insufficient way as well.

The Congregation for the Doctrine of the Faith warned Professor Kung about his concepts of the Church back in 1967, after the publication of his book *Die Kirche* ("The Church"), Freiburg im Breisgau, 1967. On April 30, 1968, the congregation communicated to Professor Kung that it had made an examination of his book *Die Kirche.* At the same time the congregation invited Professor Kung for a conversation. Even though he declared himself open to this in principle, the conversation did not take place despite repeated invitations. After the publication of the book *Unfehlbar? Eine Anfrage* ("Infallibility? An Inquiry"), 1970, the congregation began a doctrinal procedure over certain opinions in that book and asked Professor Kung to answer questions sent to him by the congregation. The voluminous exchange of letters did not bring a response satisfactory to the congregation.

As a result, the Congregation for the Doctrine of the Faith, by reason of its duty to safeguard and promote the faith throughout the Church, on July 6, 1973, published the declaration, *Mysterium Ecclesiae* ("The Mystery of the Church"), in which the teachings of the professor of Tubingen were refuted. In reference to the declaration *Mysterium Ecclesiae,* the congregation, through a member, communicated to Professor Kung that the possibility remained open for a conversation concerning the two doctrinal procedures. If Professor Kung should recognize the doctrine contained in the declaration *Mysterium Ecclesiae,* the current procedure concerning the two books would be closed.

No Clarification

Despite the mediation of Cardinal Dopfner, the conversation proposed by Rome to clarify events did not come about. After Professor Kung, in a letter of Sept. 4,

1974, assured the Congregation for the Doctrine of the Faith that he wanted to make use of the "time for reflection" granted him, not excluding as a result "conformity" of his teaching with that of the magisterium, the congregation in a declaration of Feb. 15, 1975, applied to him "*for now*, by mandate of Paul VI, the warning not to maintain such doctrines any longer." The doctrinal procedure of the Congregation for the Doctrine of the Faith was "declared closed *for now* in regard to this theme."

Bishops Ignored

The German Bishops' Conference, in a related declaration of Feb. 17, 1975, reminded Professor Kung of the principles for the basic understanding of Catholic theology, which were not taken sufficiently into account in some of his works. That applied above all to the teaching on the person of Jesus Christ contained in Kung's book *Christ Sein* ("On Being Christian"), Munich, 1974. Since many attempts to assure that Professor Kung had integrated his thought (cf. the conversation of Stuttgart that lasted several hours Jan. 22, 1977) ended in failure, the German Bishops' Conference on Nov. 17, 1977, published a declaration on the book *Christ Sein*. At the same time the related correspondence was also published. The promise made by Kung as a result, to clarify the challenged themes in his most recent work *Existiert Gott?* ("Does God Exist?"), Munich, 1978, again was not borne out. Professor Kung, despite the warning of the Congregation for the Doctrine of the Faith of Feb. 15, 1975, in the spring of 1979 not only repeated his opinions on infallibility in the Church, but represented them in a still sharper manner [cf. *Kirche — Gehalten in der Wahrheit?, Theologische Meditationen* 51, Zurich, 1979 ("The Church — Maintained in Truth?" in "Theological Meditation," No. 51); *Der Neue Stand der Unfehlbarkeitsdebatte*, ("The New State (Standing) of the Infallibility Debate"), preface to the book by A. B. Hasler, *Wie der Papst Unfehlbar Wurde. Macht und Ohnmacht Eines Dogmas*, Munich, 1979, xiii-xxxviii) ("How the Pope Became Infallible. The Force and Non-Force of a Dogma," pp. 13-18).] The Congregation for the Doctrine of the Faith in its decision of Dec. 15, 1979, reflects on this flagrant violation of the conditions imposed for the temporary suspension of the doctrinal procedure in February, 1975.

Inevitable Decision

The decision taken can be understood only in the light of this decade-long period of discussion and controversy. The representatives of the Roman Congregation for the Doctrine of the Faith, the presidents of the German Bishops' Conference, especially Cardinals Julius Dopfner and Hermann Volk, as well as the competent bishop of Rottenburg, Bishop Georg Moser, in many letters of different kinds, in personal conversations and in many initiatives have sought to reach a clarification of the situation that was created. In this they always recognized an important role for theological discussion.

Professor Kung neither accepted the invitations to a colloquy expressed for years by the Congregation for the Doctrine of the Faith nor answered the questions asked of him by the German Bishops' Conference. The temporary suspension of the doctrinal procedure and the "warning" of 1975, which were not foreseen from juridical and procedural points of view, constituted a way to make an encounter most possible and an attempt to overcome the conflicts in a new way.

Professor Kung did not take advantage of this possibility — which is true despite contrary declarations on his part of being available for dialogue; he did not allow himself to determine, either from the vast theological discussion or from the initiatives by the magisterium, to integrate, modify or correct his teachings. His attacks, in part excessive, on the discipline and order of the Church must also be placed in this context.

For these reasons the decision taken on the part of the Congregation for the Doctrine of the Faith was made inevitable.

The German Bishops' Conference asks the faithful of the Catholic Church, other Christians and all men interested in the life of the Church, to see and judge the decision of the Congregation for the Doctrine of the Faith with this background in mind. The events have been known publicly for years and, as such, are verifiable. The authority of the Church will not let itself be dissuaded by this disappointing event from searching, also in the future, whenever it is a matter of reaching a clarification on controverted theological opinions, a solution on the basis of sincere dialogue.

Professor Kung is not, because of this, excluded from the Church. He remains a priest. Regarding the revocation of the *nihil obstat*, however, he loses his mandate to teach Catholic theology in the name of the Church and as a teacher recognized by the Church.

RELATED DEVELOPMENTS

Father Hans Kung, in a statement issued Dec. 18, 1979, said he was "deeply ashamed" of his Church because of what he called the "secret inquisitorial proceedings" against him by the Congregation for the Doctrine of the Faith. Despite the declaration by the congregation that he could not be considered a Catholic theologian, he said he planned "to continue as a Catholic theologian, in the Catholic Church."

Support for Kung's protest was expressed by numerous theologians in several countries

— but without significant advertence to overtures made to him by the Doctrinal Congregation and the German bishops for clarification of his views, and also without substantial comment on the nature of his opinions.

The declaration by the congregation did not accuse Kung of heresy or otherwise affect his status as a priest.

Because of it, however, Bishop Georg Moser of Rottenburg-Stuttgart revoked the commission under which he had taught for 19 years at the University of Tubingen, an institution of the West German State of Baden-Wurttemberg. Such revocation, under terms of an existing concordat or church-state treaty, required Kung's dismissal from his position as professor of dogmatic and ecumenical theology and director of the Institute of Ecumenical Research. Kung said he would contest dismissal in court. A majority of fellow faculty members, who at first rallied to Kung's support, urged him to resign from the university without litigation.

PRIESTS IN POLITICS

Jesuit Father Robert F. Drinan, a Democratic Representative of Massachusetts, announced May 5, 1980, that he would not run for a sixth consecutive term in Congress. He withdrew his expected candidacy in deference to a directive issued by the superior general of the Jesuits, Father Pedro Arrupe, at "the express wish" of Pope John Paul. He accepted the denial of permission to run in the spirit of his vow of obedience, but "with regret and pain."

Father Drinan's provincial superior, Father Edward M. O'Flaherty, declared May 5 in a statement that "the principal reason for the order was the Pope's conviction about the proper role of the priest. . . . There was no intention of singling out Father Drinan for criticism. . . . It is obvious that in the Pope's view the reasons that commended the idea of Father Drinan's candidacy up to now no longer apply."

Existing Discipline

Commentators viewed the order not as a new decision by the Pope but as a reaffirmation of existing church discipline.

Canon 139 of the Code of Canon Law states that clerics shall not seek or accept the office of senator or representative (meaning, generally, elective public office) without the permission of their own bishop as well as that of the bishop of the place where the election takes place. In line with this canon is the requirement that a cleric member of a religious institute also needs the permission of his major superior to run for office. Permission in any case is contingent on special circumstances related to political and social conditions, the qualifications of the candidate and the lack of suitable lay persons to run for office.

In the United States, where participation by Catholic clerics in electoral politics is not and has not been customary, the Third Plenary Council of Baltimore enacted in 1837 a measure forbidding priests to meddle in political affairs unless the defense of morality and sound discipline was at stake.

Synodal and Papal Views

In the same vein, the 1971 assembly of the Synod of Bishops voted 143 to 1 in favor of this statement: "Since political options are by nature contingent and never in an entirely adequate and perennial way interpret the Gospel, the priest, who is the witness of things to come, must keep a certain distance from any political office or involvement."

Pope John Paul addressed the priests-and-politics issue while speaking in January, 1979, in Mexico before a gathering of priests belonging to religious institutes. He said: "Temporal leadership can easily become a source of division, while the priest should be a sign and factor of unity, of brotherhood. . . . You are priests and members of religious orders. You are not social directors, political leaders or functionaries of temporal power."

Secular functions, the Holy Father added, are the proper field of action of the laity, who ought to perfect temporal matters with a Christian spirit. And the Second Vatican Council, in its *Decree on the Apostolate of the Laity,* declared that renewal of the temporal order is the laity's business, with the moral and spiritual support of the clergy.

Withdrawal of Father Cornell

The day after Father Drinan announced he would not run for office in 1980, Norbertine Father Robert J. Cornell said the same thing. In earlier races for the office of Representative of Wisconsin's Eight Congressional District, he was defeated in 1970 and 1972, he won in 1976 and lost again in 1978. He was on the verge of running again but gave up the attempt after being denied permission by Bishop Aloysius J. Wycislo of Green Bay.

Priest-officeholders at the time of the Drinan and Cornell withdrawals were Father John Beno of Pueblo, in the middle of a four-year term in the Colorado Senate, and Father Joseph Simon, S.V.D. a city council member and pro tem mayor of Epworth, Iowa. It seemed likely that they would be permitted to continue in office until the end of their terms.

Past Refusals

Permission to run for public office has been denied to priests in the past. Among them were: Jesuit Father John S. McLaughlin in 1970, an unsuccessful candidate for the Senate from Rhode Island; Charles W. Cobb in 1971, seeking the office of mayor of Meriden, Conn.; Eugene J. Boyle in 1974, running for the California Legislature.

The Drinan order had no effect on priests serving in a variety of ways on community and similar boards, nor on Sister Carolyn Farrell, a member of the Dubuque city council who was elected mayor in January, 1980.

Officeholders in Nicaragua

Priest-officeholders in post-Somoza Nicaragua were reported to be seeking to remain in office even after the bishops' conference said in a statement May 13, 1980: "We feel that, once the exceptional circumstances (of the post-civil-war period) have been surmounted, Catholic laymen can discharge with no less efficacy the public duties now being held by several priests."

The priests were Fathers: Miguel D'Escoto, M.M., foreign minister; Fernando Cardenal, director of the National Literacy Crusade, and his assistants, Ignacio Anezola, S.J., and Ernesto Vallecillo; Edgard Parrales, assistant director of the Social Security Institute; Xavier Gorostiaga, S.J., an economic adviser; Ricardo Falla, S.J., in the Institute on Land Reform; Ernesto Cardenal, minister of culture; Alvaro Arguello, a representative of the Nicaraguan Clergy Association on the Council of State.

WHITE HOUSE CONFERENCE ON FAMILIES

The impact of public policies on families was the central concern of the 1980 White House Conference on Families.

President Jimmy Carter addressed himself to this subject at the first of three national meetings of the conference. Speaking June 5 in Baltimore, he said he was "deeply concerned that official America had lost touch with family America." He urged delegates to "look for creative, compassionate solutions to the problems of families and then consider who or what might best carry them out." He also declared: "Where government involvement is helpful, let it be strengthened. Where it is harmful, let it be changed."

Series of Meetings

The Baltimore assembly was preceded by a series of regional and state meetings that got under way in September, 1979, about two months after overall conference plans were completed and approved by a 40-member National Advisory Committee. Recommendations regarding family-related policies and programs developed at these meetings were filtered upwards through the advisory body to major meetings held June 5 to 7 in Baltimore, June 19 to 21 in Minneapolis, and July 10 to 12 in Los Angeles.

An estimated 100,000 persons took some kind of part in proceedings of the conference. About 2,000 of them were delegates to the national meetings which produced a total of 163 recommendations. These were reviewed Aug. 19 to 22 by a National Task Force which had the responsibility of submitting a report on the conference to the President and Congress. Initial implementation of some conference proposals was due to start in September.

The conference, with a federal budget of $3 million, was held under the general chairmanship of Jim Guy Tucker, a former Congressman from Arkansas. John Carr, former director of education for the U.S. Bishops' Campaign for Human Development, was the executive director.

Agreement and Disagreement

Delegates to the national meetings were in general agreement with respect to many issues, including:

• school-parent partnership in the development of educational policies at national, state and local levels;

• aid to families with disabled and handicapped members;

• health care;

• child care programs for working mothers;

• tax reforms favoring married couples;

• tax aid for home care of the elderly;

• analysis of the impact of public policy on families.

There were sharp differences, however, on such subjects as:

• abortion and a constitutional amendment to protect the right of the unborn to life;

• the Equal Rights Amendment;

• homosexual rights;

• access by minors to contraception, abortion and sterilization.

Chairman Jim Guy Tucker told a press conference at the end of the Los Angeles meeting that 80 per cent of the delegates had agreed on 80 per cent of the overall agenda and that the other 20 per cent of issues were in conflict throughout the country.

Advocacy of divisive issues split constituencies of the conference into a strongly conservative Pro-Family Coalition and a broader based Coalition for the White House Conference on Families.

Some of the pro-family delegates charged that delegate selection — by a combination of peer election and variously arranged appointment — had been rigged against them and that an under-the-table agenda was subversive of traditional family values.

Catholic Participation

The Catholic Coordinating Committee to the White House Conference on Families found itself in disagreement with both coalitions. The conservative group did not share its concern over social issues and the broader based coalition favored unacceptable positions on abortion and several other subjects noted above.

Participants in the Catholic committee included representatives of the National Conference of Catholic Bishops, the U.S. Catholic Conference, the National Conference of Catholic Charities, the National Catholic Educational Association and the National Council of Catholic Women.

Auxiliary Bishop J. Francis Stafford of Baltimore was a member of the National Advisory Committee.

Msgr. Francis J. Lally, chairman of the Catholic committee, felt "positive" about the outcome of the conference. "A great many resolutions," he said, "are thoroughly supportive of our own Catholic social teachings. We were disappointed in some obvious areas that were offensive to our traditional ideas of family — such as gay family life-style, abortion and the payment for abortions, sterilization and contraception."

In a statement addressed to the National Task Force before its meeting in August, the committee noted that the most significant result of the conference "was to put American families firmly on the national agenda." It recommended that "respect for human life itself be a basic underlying principle" of the White House Conference on Families, and urged that its recommendations be developed "within the context of families as traditionally understood, and (that) due consideration be given to family impact analysis."

The committee did not endorse by name any specific recommendations that emanated from the national meetings, but did urge that "recognition be given to the fact that the pro-abortion recommendations were extremely low in ranking, 53rd out of 60 in Baltimore, 56th out of 57 in Los Angeles. The recommendation favoring abortion did not pass in Minneapolis."

The committee said it intended to cooperate in "making effective use" of conference results and would encourage others to do so.

RACISM: PASTORAL LETTER

Following are excerpts from a pastoral letter, entitled "Brothers and Sisters to Us," approved and released during the annual meeting Nov. 12 to 15, 1979, of the National Conference of Catholic Bishops and the U.S. Catholic Conference. Earlier conference statements on the subject were issued in 1958 and 1968, and additional statements of this kind have been published by numerous bishops.

These excerpts are from the text circulated Nov. 29, 1979, by the NC Documentary Service, Origins (Vol. 9, No. 24).

The Evil of Racism: "Racism is an evil which endures in our society and in our Church. Despite apparent advances and even significant changes in the last two decades, the reality of racism remains."

"We do not deny that the ugly external features of racism which marred our society have in part been eliminated. But neither can it be denied that too often what has happened has been only a covering over, not a fundamental change. Today the sense of urgency has yielded to an apparent acceptance of the status quo. The climate of crisis engendered by demonstrations, protests and confrontation has given way to a mood of indifference, and other issues occupy our attention."

A Persistent Presence: "We wish to call attention to the persistent presence of racism and in particular to the relationship between racial and economic justice. Racism and economic oppression are distinct but interrelated forces which dehumanize our society. Movement toward authentic justice demands a simultaneous attack on both evils."

"Economic pressures exacerbate racism, particularly where poor white people are competing with minorities for limited job opportunities."

The Church Must Speak Out: "Mindful of its duty to be the advocate for those who hunger and thirst for justice's sake, the Church cannot remain silent about the racial injustices in society and in its own structures. Our concern over racism follows, as well, from our strong commitment to evangelization. . . . We would betray our commitment to evangelize ourselves and our society were we not to strongly voice our condemnation of attitudes and practices so contrary to the Gospel."

"Racism is a sin: a sin that divides the human family, blots out the image of God among specific members of that family and violates the fundamental human dignity of those called to be children of the same Father. Racism is the sin that says some human beings are inherently superior and others essentially inferior because of race. It is the sin that makes racial characteristics the determining factor for the exercise of human rights. It mocks the words of Jesus: 'Treat others the way you would have them treat you' (Mt. 7:12). Indeed, racism is more than a disregard for the words of Jesus; it is a denial of the truth of the dignity of each human being revealed by the mystery of the Incarnation."

Covert Racism: "Crude and blatant expressions of racist sentiment, though they occasionally exist, are today considered bad form, but racism persists in a covert way. Under the guise of other motives, it is manifest in the tendency to stereotype and marginalize whole segments of the population whose presence is perceived as a threat. . . . Today's racism flourishes in the triumph of private concern over public responsibility, individual success over social commitment and personal fulfillment over authentic compassion."

"Christian ideals of justice must be brought to bear in both the private and the public sectors in order that covert racism be eliminated wherever it exists."

Racism Weakens Witness: "How great . . . is that sin of racism which weakens the Church's witness as the universal sign of unity among all peoples! How great the scandal given by racist Catholics who would make the body of Christ, the Church, a sign of racial oppression! Yet all too often the Church in our country has been for many a 'white church,' a racist institution."

"Each of us as Catholics must acknowledge a share in the mistakes and sins of the past. We have been prisoners of fear and prejudice. Many of us have preached the Gospel while closing our eyes to the racism it condemned. We have allowed conformity to social pressures to replace compliance with social justice."

"But past mistakes must not hinder the Church's response to the challenges of the present."

"The prophetic voice of the Church . . . must not be muted — especially not by the counterwitness of some of its own people. Let the Church speak out, not only in the assemblies of the bishops, but in every diocese and parish in the land, in every chapel and re-

ligious house, in every school, in every social service agency and in every institution that bears the name Catholic."

Proclamation of the Church: "Let the Church proclaim for all to hear that the sin of racism defiles the image of God and degrades the sacred dignity of humankind, which has been revealed by the mystery of the Incarnation. Let all know that it is a terrible sin that mocks the cross of Christ and ridicules the Incarnation. For the brother and sister of our Brother, Jesus Christ, are brother and sister to us."

"Racism is not merely one sin among many, it is a radical evil dividing the human family and denying the new creation of a redeemed world. To struggle against it demands an equally radical transformation in our own minds and hearts as well as in the structure of our society."

Action against Racism: Suggested ways and means of combatting racism included the following: change in personal attitudes and the exertion of personal influence on other people and movements; affirmative action programs in all dioceses; efforts to make the policies and practices of Catholic institutions conform to church teaching on justice; the continuation and expansion of Catholic schools in inner cities and other disadvantaged areas; coping with the needs of undocumented aliens and workers; the promotion of vocations to the priesthood and religious life among minority groups of the faithful.

ENERGY AND ENVIRONMENT

The most important thing religious institutions can do about the energy crisis is to communicate some of its human reality and motivate a human response to it. So stated Bishop William Cosgrove, a member of the Committee for Social Development and World Peace, U.S. Catholic Conference, in an address Jan. 10, 1980, during an Interfaith Consultation on Energy in Washington, D.C.

Education and Advocacy

The bishop said, in part: "We are not talking about abstractions and statistics. . . . We are talking about war and famine and suffering. We are talking about the struggle against cold, against dark, against isolation. We are also talking about brotherhood and sisterhood — or we should be. From all our churches and synagogues, a warning must sound. The energy crisis threatens new dangers, creates new victims. As believers in a just God, we must stand ready to confront these dangers and aid these victims."

Proper motivation will depend to a great extent on proper education. People cannot develop a sound perspective on energy unless they understand the issues in the light of principles drawn from our Judeo-Christian tradi-

tion. For example, that tradition views humanity not in isolation, but as the most important element in a wider creation. It therefore counsels respect for the natural world, emphasizing that we have responsibilities as well as rights in its use. As religious leaders, we must teach our people the urgency of responsible stewardship, which relates to conservation, to air and water pollution, to the prudent use of our remaining supplies of oil and gas, and to many other energy issues."

"The same is true of other general principles such as promotion of the common good; concern about justice for all, whether they be consumers, suppliers or producers; a special care for the needs of the poor, and more. Principles like these are the particular intellectual contribution the religious community can make to the national debate over energy, and it is important to keep them before the public eye."

"The religious community . . . faces a major challenge in interpreting and explaining the energy crisis on the grassroots level. This challenge must be met if moral considerations are to have much weight in helping shape national energy policy."

"Education . . . leads to advocacy. Our

overall approach to energy as religious leaders, I believe, must emphasize generating not only public understanding but also public demand for responsible policies. The voice of the religious community, in its breadth and depth, must be audible in the White House, in the Senate and House chambers, in state legislatures, in the hearing rooms of public-service commissions. We must work for the day when there is a real, informed, grassroots constituency for just energy decisions and legislation.

Environmental Responsibility

Environmental concerns were the subjects of a message of Pope Paul VI to the United Nations Conference on the Human Environment held June 5 to 16, 1972, in Stockholm.

The Pope said, in part: "Today . . . there is an emerging awareness that man and his environment are more than ever inseparable; the environment shapes the life and the development of man, and man improves and elevates his environment by his presence, his work and his contemplation. But man's capacity for creation cannot bear true and lasting fruit except insofar as man respects the laws that govern nature's dynamism and capacity for regeneration. Man and his environment form a totality and share a common future. And so mankind is warned that it must replace the too often blind and brutal drive of unguided material progress with a global and respectful vision of the world, for there is only one earth."

"The moral conscience recoils in horror at man's application of the discoveries of science to the production of means of destruction such as atomic, chemical and bacteriological weapons. And how can we ignore the upheavals in the biosphere provided by the undisciplined exploitation of the planet's physical resources, even when the aim is useful products? Both animal and plant life have been attacked by pollution of the soil, water and air; and non-renewable natural resources have been wasted. These things deplete and break down man's environment to the point of threatening his survival. We must meet the challenge presented to our generation forcefully by going beyond partial and immediate objectives to build for tomorrow's mankind an earth that will be a home for them."

"Solutions will not be found in easy answers. Just as the population problem is not solved by limiting access to life, so the problem of the environment cannot be coped with simply in terms of technology."

"Technical measures will be ineffective unless they are accompanied by a radical change of mentality."

"For man to rule over creation means not to destroy but to build up, not to make the world an uninhabitable chaos but a neat and attractive place to be lived in. No one, then, has a right to take over the environment in an absolute and egoistic way. The world man lives in is not a *res nullius*, the property of no one; it is a *res omnium*, the patrimony of mankind. Those responsible for the environment, both private and public agencies, must regulate the environment for the well-being of all men, for man himself is the first and the greatest wealth of the earth."

LIBERATION THEOLOGY

Liberation theology deals with the relevance of Christian faith and salvation — and, therefore, of the mission of the Church — to efforts for the promotion of human rights, social justice and human development.

It originated in the religious, social, political and economic environment of Latin America, with its contemporary need for a theory and corresponding action by the Church, in the pattern of its overall mission, for human rights and integral human development.

Development of the subject has produced a considerable body of literature by such Latin American authors as Gustavo Gutierrez, Enrique Dussel, Juan Luis Segundo, Jose Porfirio Miranda and others.

Related treatment of the main features of liberation theology have also been expressed in numerous documents authored by episcopal conferences and other sources, and in the writings and conferences of theorists in other countries.

Pope John Paul described integral and authentic liberation theology and pastoral practice in the keynote address he delivered Jan. 28, 1979, during the plenary assembly of Latin American bishops at Puebla, Mexico.

"There are many signs that help to distinguish when the liberation in question is Christian and when, on the other hand, it is based rather on ideologies that rob it of consistency with an evangelical view of man, of things and events. They are signs drawn from the content of what the evangelizers proclaim or from the concrete attitudes that they adopt.

"At the level of content, one must see what is their fidelity to the word of God, to the Church's living tradition and to her magisterium.

"As for attitudes, one must consider what sense of communion they have with the bishops, in the first place, and with the other sectors of the people of God; what contribution they make to the real building up of the community; in what form they lovingly care for the poor, the sick, the dispossessed, the neglected and the oppressed; and in what way they find in them the image of the poor and suffering Jesus, and strive to relieve their need and serve Christ in them."

"Placing responsible confidence in this social doctrine (of the Church) is the guarantee, in a member of the Church, of his commitment in the delicate and demanding social tasks and of his efforts in favor of the liberation or advancement of his brothers and sisters."

COMUNIDADES DE BASE

The concept and operational model of *comunidades de base* envision relatively small, basic communities of the faithful integrated for secular and religious life, with maximum potential for pastoral ministry, apostolic activity, and human, spiritual and social development.

Pope John Paul conveyed a message to leaders of thousands of such communities July 10, 1980, during his pastoral visit to Brazil.

He said that "basic Christian communities can be a valuable instrument of Christian formation and of penetration of the Gospel in society."

Ecclesial Identity

Speaking of essentials, he continued: "Among the dimensions of basic Christian communities, I believe it appropriate to call to your attention that which more profoundly defines them and without which their identity would disappear: ecclesiality. I stress this ecclesiality because it already explains the designation that, above all in Latin America, these communities have received. Being ecclesial is their original character and their mode of existing and operating. They are formed in organic communities to better serve the Church. And the base to which they refer is of a clearly ecclesial character and not merely sociological or otherwise.

"I also stress this ecclesiality because the danger of weakening this dimension, if not of letting it disappear for the benefit of others is neither unreal nor remote, but above all always real. It is particularly prone to interference by the politician. This interference can happen in the beginning and formation of communities which are brought together not on the basis of a vision of the Church, but with criteria and objectives of political ideology. Such interference can also come about in the form of political instrumentalization of communities which originated with an ecclesial perspective.

Instruments of Service

"A delicate attention and a serious and courageous effort to maintain the ecclesial dimension of these communities in all its purity are an eminent service that is good for the communities themselves on the one hand and for the Church on the other. To them, because preserving them in their ecclesial identity guarantees their freedom, effectiveness and survival. To the Church, because communities which live authentically their ecclesial inspiration without dependencies of another order will serve its essential mission of evangelization."

"The base community will be a community above all to the degree that it shows itself as an instrument of service, mutual service within its own community and service to other brothers, above all the neediest."

BIOETHICS

Bioethics "can be defined as the systematic study, in the light of moral values and principles, of human conduct in the area of the life sciences and health care," according to Warren T. Reich, editor of the *Encyclopedia of Bioethics* published by Macmillan and Free Press (New York, 1980).

Subjects of study include: reproductive technologies, prenatal diagnosis, abortion, human experimentation, genetic intervention, behavior control, psychosurgery, definition of death, prolongation of life, euthanasia, right to privacy, allocation of scarce health resources, dilemmas in the maintenance of environmental health. (Several of these subjects are treated in other Almanac entries; see Index.)

The Pope John XXIII Medical-Moral Research and Education Center is devoted specifically to examining the full range of emerging bioethical issues in the light of Catholic theology. Founded in 1973 by the Catholic Hospital Association and located in St. Louis, the center is supported by memberships, contributions and grants.

Similar research is the focus of the Institute for Theological Encounter with Science and Technology, located at St. Louis University and under the direction of Father Robert A. Brungs, S.J.

Papal View

Pope John Paul was critical of genetic experimentation, "irresponsible" medical research and indiscriminate use of drugs, in an address Oct. 27, 1980, to a group of Italian physicians.

"Even in the attempt to cure, the physician can, involuntarily, harm the right of individuals to their proper life," he said in reference to birth deformities caused by thalidomide before it was banned.

The Holy Father called attention to ethical dangers connected with artificial insemination, birth and fertility controls, organ transplants and new drugs. He voiced alarm over the effects of "medicine that cares more for itself than for man whom it must serve."

Need for Ethical Rules

"Science is not the highest value to which all others must be subordinated," he declared. Higher . . . is the right of individuals to their physical and spiritual life and to their psychic and functional integrity. . . . Scientific progress . . . cannot pretend to place itself in a sort of neutral ground. . . . Ethical rules, founded in the respect of the person's dignity, must illuminate and discipline medicine in the research phase as well as in the application of the results achieved."

The Pope said doctors are obliged to consider "the implicit danger to man's right to life of discoveries in the field of artificial insemination, birth and fertility control and hibernation, of retarded death, of genetic engineering, of othe psychic drugs, of organ transplants."

While acknowledging that science has its "proper laws to follow," he said "it must recognize above all an insurmountable limit in the respect of person and in the protection of his right to live in a worthy way as a human being."

"The truth is that the technological development . . . suffers from a deep ambivalence. While it allows man to take control of his own destiny, it exposes him to the temptation of going beyond the limits of a reasonable control of nature, risking the survival and integrity of the human person."

DNA RESEARCH

The U.S. Bishops' Committee for Human Values, in a statement released in May, 1977, expressed concern over the balance of risk and benefit involved in gene-splicing made possible by the identification and experimental use of DNA (deoxyribonucleic acid), the chemical basis and agent of heredity.

The transplanting of genetic material from one species of cells to another produces new cells (forms of life) of an order which can be beneficial or dangerous, depending on the nature of the recombinants and the manner in which they are handled. Such gene-splicing has yielded a remarkable fund of information about the chemistry and mechanisms of heredity.

Pertinent questions are being asked about how far to go with experimentation and whether and how to expand it from generally pharmaceutical confines to industrial use in chemistry, agriculture and food production, without harmful results.

The bishops' committee cautioned against doing whatever science can do with DNA just because it can be done. The statement said: "We ought not now to follow slavishly the technological imperative that 'all that can be done, must be done.' . . . Our actions . . . must reflect the range of human goods in the process" of determining how to proceed toward enlightened public policy, with communication and collaboration between the scientific community and the public.

Guidelines Relaxed

Relaxed guidelines for gene-splitting research were published Jan. 29, 1980, in the *Federal Register* by the National Institutes of Health. The guidelines, which are mandatory for government-sponsored research and voluntary for private industry, eased safety standards for most of the recombinant DNA work being done in this country.

An Associated Press report quoted Dr. Bernard Talbot, special assistant to the director of the National Institutes of Health, as saying: "Experience, new data and a reanalysis of old data lead to the conclusion that some of the previous fears (underlying earlier stringent directives) probably were overblown. This research can proceed safely under the (new) guidelines."

Most DNA work in progress was focused on bacteria and viruses.

Patent Decision

The U.S. Supreme Court ruled June 16, 1980, that new life forms discovered, for example, through genetic engineering could, under existing U.S. law, be patented by the discoverers.

The decision prompted a statement of concern by the general secretaries of three national religious organizations — Bishop Thomas C. Kelly, U.S. Catholic Conference; Claire Randall, National Council of Churches; and Rabbi Bernard Mandelbaum, Synagogue Council of America.

They said that new life forms may have dramatic potential for improving human life, but may also have unforeseen ramifications. A new life form that proves in time to be a threat may not be able to be recalled. The secretaries said that "control of such life forms by any individual or group poses a potential threat to all of humanity."

They called for a review of patent legislation and action by the government to exercise adequate oversight and to address the fundamental ethical questions involved in genetic engineering. They noted that the issue required international collaboration as well.

IN VITRO FERTILIZATION

The first authenticated birth of a child fertilized outside a mother's womb occurred July 25, 1978, in Lancashire, England. The girl, Louise, was the daughter of Gilbert John and Lesley Brown.

(Three other births resulting from *in vitro* fertilization were reported later, one each in England, India and Australia.)

Steps in the conception and birth of the child were surgical removal of an egg from the mother, fertilization by sperm of the father in a laboratory vessel, and subsequent implantation and development of the fetus in the mother's womb.

The doctors who conducted the procedure were Patrick C. Steptoe and Robert G. Edwards.

Praise for the scientific advance represented by the *in vitro* fertilization was matched with scientific and moral cautions. Pope Pius XII and traditional Catholic moral norms were quoted against the procedure because, among other things, of the divorce between normal marital intercourse and procreation.

Moral Considerations

"In vitro fertilization involves externalizing both sperm and ovum," stated Andre E. Hellegers and Father Richard A. McCormick, S.J., in an article published in the Aug. 19, 1978, edition of *America*. They continued: "It is, from the technological point of view, a step beyond artificial insemination that externalizes only the sperm. . . . Thus, at least some of the basic ethical considerations that surround *in vitro* fertilization are already present in the discussion of artificial insemination."

Moral norms relevant to both of these processes were stated by Pope Pius XII on two particular occasions.

Pius XII Statements

In an address to the Fourth International Convention of Catholic Doctors Sept. 29, 1949, he said:

"The practice of artificial insemination, when it is applied to man, cannot be considered exclusively, nor even principally, from the biological and medical viewpoint, while leaving aside the viewpoint of morality and law."

"Artificial insemination outside of marriage is to be condemned purely and simply as immoral."

"Artificial insemination in marriage with the use of an active element from a third person is equally immoral and as such is to be rejected summarily."

"With regard to the lawfulness of artificial insemination in marriage . . . the simple fact that the desired result is obtained by this means does not justify the employment of the method itself; nor does the desire of the marriage partners — most legitimate in itself — to have a child, suffice to prove the lawfulness or a recourse to artificial insemination for the fulfillment of that desire."

Speaking again, before the Second World Congress on Fertility and Sterility May 19, 1956, the Pope said:

"With regard to artificial fecundation, not only is there reason to be extremely reserved, but it must be absolutely rejected. In speaking thus, one is not necessarily forbidding the use of certain artificial means destined solely to facilitate the natural act or to achieve the attainment of the natural act normally performed."

"On the subject of the experiments in artificial fecundation '*in vitro*,' let it suffice for Us to observe that they must be rejected as immoral and absolutely illicit."

Caution

Pressure has been mounting in the U.S. for an end to a five-year moratorium on federal funding for *in vitro* experimentation. The Ethics Advisory Board of the Department of Health, Education and Welfare, in a report issued in March, 1979, concluded that such research is acceptable despite substantial ethical arguments against it. No federal funding, however, was forthcoming in 1980.

The Eastern Virginia Medical School opened a private *in vitro* fertilization clinic in March, 1980, in Norfolk. No induced pregnancies were reported during the first three months of operation.

Issues related to the clinic were the subjects of a pastoral letter written by Bishop Walter F. Sullivan of Richmond in November, 1978, when the medical school was awaiting decision on its request to establish a clinic. The bishop said the school's proposal raised "serious moral and ethical implications" that had not been addressed by society. He also denounced the "cultural schizophrenia" existing in Virginia, "where we announce research into making test-tube babies and at the same time, through legal abortion, deny life to 50,000 healthy babies each year."

CONCERNS OF WOMEN IN CHURCH AND SOCIETY

Concerns of women were on the agenda of the annual general assembly of the National Council of Catholic Women held in September, 1980, in San Francisco.

Two hundred and 84 delegates adopted a statement on justice in which the council declared its intent to "support all efforts that seek to erase any remaining unjust, oppressive or exploitative discrimination based on sex alone."

Views of NCCW

The statement opposed the Equal Rights Amendment, however: "There is a distinction between justice for women and the Equal Rights Amendment. We feel that the proposed amendment is not a viable solution to the problems of injustice to women."

The statement added that laws beneficial to women are necessary, and urged delegates to work at state levels in support of legislation guaranteeing rights to property, credit, insurance, and protection against rape and sexual abuse.

In a paper on women in the Church, the council accepted the official position against the ordination of women, described by the Vatican in 1976 in a "Declaration on the Question of the Admission of Women to the Ministerial Priesthood." But it supported continuing study of the subject and stated its desire to work toward opening other ministries to women and to overcome differences with other women whose views do not always coincide.

"We know that women are impeded from ministries by prejudices that contradict justice and by lags in recognizing the changes in society that make women more equipped and available for modern ministries," the paper said. "NCCW wishes to work together with other women of the Church in seeking to open wider ministries for women," it added. "We affirm those who are requesting an evaluation of the Code of Canon Law in relation to women, in areas where the Code was based on disciplines which served the Church in another age."

Survey Findings

Concerns in favor of change in the Church were expressed by 56 per cent of 950 women engaged in ministry who were questioned in a survey conducted by the Leadership Conference of Women Religious. Twenty per cent favored tradition and 24 per cent said they were "in the middle." A progress report on the survey was published in March, 1980.

The majority favored change in the Mass, in the Church's position on contraception, in the Church's attitude toward divorced Catholics and in the role of women in the Church. Sizable proportions favored changes in structures of the Church, clerical celibacy and the position of the Church with respect to divorce.

Ninety-three per cent agreed with the position of the Church against abortion.

Florence Rosenberg, director of the study, said that only 52 of the women surveyed were nuns. Eighty per cent of the others polled

were married and living with their husbands; most of them had children.

The concerns stated by the women were probably generated by their experiences in several categories of ministry, including: liturgical, general pastoral, spiritual, educational, health care, social service, recreational, social activist and administrative support service.

Strong concerns have been voiced in recent years by individuals and groups of women, especially some women religious, about male domination in the Church as well as general society, sexist language in the Bible and liturgical usage, lack of what is regarded as a feminine theology, male authority over women religious, restrictions on areas of apostolic ministry, alleged second-class status of women because they cannot be ordained to holy orders.

Vatican View

The employment, health and educational needs and concerns of women were stressed by the Vatican delegation to the United Nations Conference on Women, held July 14 to 30, 1980, in Copenhagen.

Bishop Paul Cordes, head of the delegation, told the conference in an address: "Work must be seen not only as a means of earning one's living, but also as a means whereby persons may develop their own creative capacities and skills." The work of women should be given its full value, he added, whether in the work place or in the home, and women should be provided appropriate education and training as well as "enough free time to take up other interests and to develop them."

He urged the conference to support maternal and child health programs and to denounce practices, such as abortion, which "violate physical, moral or social health."

The bishop called for the abandonment of "the prejudices, the ingrained habits and the economic conditions which even today deprive or limit women in their educational aspirations."

More attention must be given, he added, to finding ways to combine work and family duties, developing simpler life-styles and educating people for peace.

(See U.N. Decade for Women.)

ABORTION DEVELOPMENTS

The U.S. Supreme Court, with a 5-to-4 decision June 30, 1980, upheld Hyde Amendment restrictions on Medicaid abortion funding. The conclusion of the majority opinion delivered by Justice Potter Stewart declared:

"We hold that a state that participates in the Medicaid program is not obligated under Title XIX to continue to fund those medically necessary abortions for which federal reimbursement is unavailable under the Hyde Amendment. We further hold that the fund-

ing restrictions of the Hyde Amendment violate neither the Fifth Amendment nor the Establishment Clause of the First Amendment. It is also our view that the appellees lack standing to raise a challenge to the Hyde Amendment under the Free-Exercise clause of the First Amendment."

Hyde Amendment Constitutional

The Hyde Amendment provided: "None of the funds provided for in this paragraph shall be used to perform abortions except where the life of the mother would be endangered if the fetus were carried to term; or except for such medical procedures necessary for the victims of rape or incest, where such rape or incest has been reported promptly to a law enforcement agency or public health service."

Joining Justice Stewart in the majority opinion were Chief Justice Warren Burger and Justices Byron White, Lewis Powell and William Rhenquist. Dissenting were Justices William Brennan, Thurgood Marshall, Harry Blackmun and John Paul Stevens.

The decision in Harris v. McRae overturned a ruling against the constitutionality of the Hyde Amendment handed down Jan. 15, 1980, by U.S. District Judge John F. Dooling, Jr.

Decisions

Backgrounding the pro-Hyde ruling of the Court were a number of earlier decisions and developments.

• In Roe v. Wade, the Court ruled, 7 to 2, Jan. 22, 1973: (1) During the first three months of pregnancy, a woman's right to privacy is paramount. Accordingly, she has an unrestricted right to abortion with the consent and cooperation of a physician. (2) In the second trimester, the principle controlling legislation on abortion is the health or welfare of the mother, understood in the widest possible sense. (3) In the "state subsequent to viability," the controlling principles are the State's "interest in the potentiality of human life" and "the preservation of the life or health of the mother." These rulings canonized the absolutely private right of a woman to have an abortion and denied to the unborn the right to life.

• In Dole v. Bolton, also decided Jan. 22, 1973, the Court ruled, 7 to 2, against restrictions on facilities that could be used in performing abortions.

• In Danforth v. Planned Parenthood, the Court ruled, 6 to 3, July 1, 1976, against the constitutionality of state laws requiring spousal (in the case of a married woman) or parental (in the case of a minor) consent for an abortion.

• The first of three versions of the Hyde Amendment was adopted by Congress Sept. 30, 1976, in an appropriations measure for the Department of Labor and the Department of Health, Education and Welfare.

• An injunction against the amendment was issued Oct. 22, 1976, by U.S. District Court Judge John F. Dooling, Jr., in a suit originally filed by Cora McRae.

• In Maher v. Roe, the Court ruled, 6 to 3, June 20, 1977, that the Constitution does not require states to pay for non-therapeutic (elective) abortions and does not require public hospitals to provide them.

• The Court set aside June 29, 1977, Judge Dooling's injunction against the Hyde Amendment and ordered him to restudy his ruling of the previous October in the light of its decision in Maher v. Roe.

• Funding restrictions of the Hyde Amendment went into effect Aug. 4, 1977, and the McRae case went back to the Dooling courtroom.

• The Court ruled, 6 to 3, Jan. 9, 1979, in Colautti v. Franklin against the constitutionality of a 1974 Pennsylvania law because of its vagueness about the timing of fetal viability. The decision had the effect of meaning that a woman exercising a legal right to have an abortion had the right to a dead fetus and that the doctor performing the abortion could not be charged civilly or criminally for the death of the fetus.

• In Bellotti v. Baird, the Court ruled, 8 to 1, July 2, 1979, against the constitutionality of a Massachusetts law requiring a minor to consult with her parents before having an abortion. In the absence of parental consent (which the Court ruled in 1976 was not required) or parental consultation (not required either), a court could clear the way for the abortion of a minor judged to be mature enough to have one.

• Judge Dooling ruled Jan. 15, 1980, against the constitutionality of the Hyde Amendment but stayed enforcement of his decision to permit an appeal to the Supreme Court.

• The Court responded Feb. 19, 1980, to Judge Dooling's action with a one-sentence order requiring federal and state governments to provide Medicaid funding for abortions deemed "medically necessary." The Court also agreed to rule on the constitutionality of the Hyde Amendment, in connection with another case (Williams v. Zbaraz) that originated in Illinois.

• Finally, in Harris v. McRae, the Court ruled affirmatively on the constitutionality of the Hyde Amendment.

Medicaid payment for "medically necessary" abortions continued for about two and one-half months after the decision of June 30, pending a ruling by the Supreme Court on petitions for reconsideration. The decision not to reconsider was announced Sept. 17 and payment was discontinued thereafter.

Additional Developments

At the time of the June 30 decision, about nine states and the District of Columbia were providing payment for "medically necessary" abortions, and 13 other states had been under court order to do the same.

More than 25 states had "informed consent" bills under consideration, generally requiring: a 24-hour waiting period before an abortion; notification of a parent or husband 24 hours before an abortion; warnings of possible medical dangers; counseling on alternatives to abortion; telling the women that an unborn child "is a human life from the moment of conception."

It was reported in May, 1980, that 19 states had passed resolutions calling for a constitutional convention to act on an amendment to safeguard the right of the unborn to life.

The National Right to Life Committee, meeting in June, 1980, in Anaheim, Calif., reported it had 10 million followers and 1,800 chapters and affiliates across the country.

The annual rate of legal abortions performed in the U.S. since Jan. 22, 1973, was estimated to be a million or more.

Charges Against the Church

The Catholic Church is the largest and strongest institutional opponent of abortion, because of its firm teaching and practice on the subject, and also because of the number of its members who are against it.

Because this is so in a cultural climate favoring abortion and moral liberalism, the Church has been accused and charged with:

• dominating the pro-life movement;

• trying to force its views on others who do not share its faith;

• violating a peculiar interpretation of the principle of separation of Church and state.

These accusations have been implicit and explicit in reporting of the abortion controversy ever since it began.

The Church insists, however, on its right to speak and act on moral issues on an equal basis with others who claim rights of conscience and freedom to influence others in a society which is subject not only to the laws of man but, above all, to universal moral law.

REFUGEES AND ALIENS

U.S. concern for refugees and displaced persons shifted considerably in 1980 from the "boat people" of Southeast Asia to people of the "Freedom Flotilla" who began streaming into the country in the latter part of April. Between that time and the end of summer, approximately 130,000 persons entered the country. Most of them were Cubans, permitted to leave by the Castro regime which apparently regarded them as malcontents. A smaller number were in flight from conditions of tyranny and poverty in Haiti.

Within six months after the arrival of the first wave of Cubans, approximately 105,000 of them were reported resettled in Florida (80 per cent), New Jersey (7 per cent), New York (5 per cent), California (4 per cent), Illinois (1 per cent), and in all but nine of the other states.

The rate of Haitian resettlement during this time was very low.

Migration and Relief Services, U.S. Catholic Conference, was one of the key voluntary agencies which made the government's resettlement program possible and so successful. Working through diocesan and other agencies, to which it provided $200 per person served, MRS was directly involved in the relocation of at least half of the immigrants under conditions of sponsorship for housing, employment and other needs.

Legal Status

These Cubans and Haitians have the legal status of entrants or undocumented aliens seeking asylum in the U.S. As such, they have interim residence rights and, it appears, will be given the opportunity of applying for permanent residence and/or citizenship. Their eligibility for benefits — limited to some federal medical aid and clearance for the purchase of food stamps — is less than that of refugees.

Haitians were not given the same kind of treatment as that accorded to the Cubans until U.S. District Court Judge James L. King ordered the Immigration and Naturalization Service in July to cease automatically deporting Haitians and to consider each request for political asylum on its own merits. He said the service, apparently motivated by racial bias, had engaged in wholesale violations of their rights.

Cubans and Haitians who came to the U.S. in 1980 were admitted under emergency provisions of immigration law which overcame numerical limitations of the quota system with respect to refugees. There seems to be no doubt, however, that they are refugees, in fact, in the meaning of the Refugee Act of 1980 signed into law by President Carter Mar. 17. They clearly are persons outside their own countries who cannot or will not return because of well founded fear or persecution on grounds of race, religion, nationality, membership in a particular social group or political opinion.

Under existing immigration law, 270,000 persons may be admitted to the U.S. annually, on a preferential basis leading with family reunions. An additional 50,000 refugees a year — and more in emergencies — are permitted entry.

Immigration and naturalization law was under review by a presidential commission in 1980. It was expected that recommendations for revisions would be forthcoming in 1981.

The U.N. High Commissioner for Refugees estimated early in 1980 that there were nearly nine million refugees or displaced persons in the world. They included: Palestinians (1.8 million), Ethiopians (1.6 million), Afghans (700,000), Vietnamese "boat people" (300,000), Cambodians (290,000), Haitians (100,000), Chadians (84,000).

Illegal Aliens

A 1980 estimate by the U.S. Bureau of the

Census placed at less than five million the number of illegal or undocumented aliens in this country. The estimate, which was far lower than others of six to 12 million, was supported by the findings of 12 separate studies.

Auxiliary Bishop Anthony J. Bevilacqua, founding director of the Brooklyn Migration and Refugee Office, regarded amnesty coupled with remedial legislation as the most practical solution to the complex problem of undocumented aliens.

Deportation, he said in April, 1980, would not keep aliens from coming to this country, where they fill a gap in society that is not publicly acknowledged.

While noting that the Catholic Church has been in the forefront of efforts to assist undocumented people because most of them were at least nominally Catholic, he declared:

"Amnesty supporters aren't in favor of illegality, aren't in favor of letting people come in illegally. The United States should have a limitation on numbers of immigrants coming in, and has a right to have legislation to limit them in numbers and quality."

He said that existing laws largely denied legal entry to poor and unskilled people. Also, he stated his belief that the U.S. could absorb up to one million new people a year without experiencing any severe problems.

EUCHARISTIC CONGRESS CENTENARY

The 42nd International Eucharistic Congress scheduled for July, 1981, at the Marian Sanctuaries at Lourdes, France, marks the 100th anniversary of the first such congress held late in June, 1881, on the campus of the Catholic University of Lille.

The start of international congresses is credited to Marie Marthe Tamisier (1834 to 1910) of Touraine, a woman of great devotion to the Blessed Sacrament.

The first attempt to hold a congress, at her urging and with the leadership of Msgr. Louis Gaston de Segur, was unsuccessful. The second attempt succeeded, thanks to the intervention of Philibert Vrau of Lille (1829 to 1905), an industrialist active in Catholic social action and education.

Vrau raised money to finance the congress, got the approval of Pope Leo XIII to hold it, and secured the use of space and facilities at the Catholic University of Lille for its proceedings. Its events were attended by 800 persons from France and five neighboring countries. The success of the congress prompted the formation, at its close, of a permanent committee to plan and oversee the conduct of similar assemblies in the future.

Preparations for the 42nd congress were under way in 1980, on the scene at Lourdes under French direction and with overall supervision by the Permanent Committee for International Eucharistic Congresses headed by Cardinal James R. Knox, prefect of the Congregation for the Discipline of the Sacraments and Divine Worship. Sister Regina Casey of New York, superior of the Missionaries of the Sacred Heart of Jesus and president of the International Union of Superiors General, was one of 20 appointees named to the committee in November, 1979.

(See separate entry for additional background and listing of Congresses.)

1980 ELECTION ISSUES

Following are excerpts from statements of position on several election issues presented by Bishop Thomas C. Kelly before the Democratic and Republican platform committees in the summer of 1980. The positions represented views of the U.S. Catholic Conference.

Abortion: "The right to life is a basic human right which should have the protection of law. Abortion is the deliberate destruction of an unborn human being and therefore violates this right."

"We reject the 1973 Supreme Court decisions on abortion. . . . In order to restore basic legal protection for the right to life for the unborn, we urge the adoption of an amendment to the Constitution."

Criminal Justice and Civil Rights: "We support strong and effective action to control handguns, leading to (their) eventual elimination from our society. . . . We oppose capital punishment. A return to the use of the death penalty can only lead to further erosion of respect for life."

"Renewed and effective action is required on the part of government, the private sector and individual citizens to eradicate unjust discrimination in all its forms so that all Americans can exercise their basic human rights."

Defense and the Draft: "We support arms limitation as a necessary step to general disarmament. This objective is part and parcel of the search for international peace. The arms race must be brought under control and nuclear systems reduced through negotiations. The SALT II treaty should be taken up again and ratified. In SALT III negotiations, the U.S. should aggressively pursue real reductions in nuclear weapons on both sides and in Europe."

"In the event that it becomes necessary to conscript persons into military service, and the case for this is clearly made, the same protection under the law should be given to the selective conscientious objector as to the general conscientious objector, providing his objection is well-founded and constitutes a sincerely held moral conviction and he agrees to alternative service."

Education: "We believe that the rising costs of education diminish the right of parents to educate their children in the schools of their choice. Freedom of choice in education is basic to the American tradition and must be maintained if we are to achieve true social justice in our society. We strongly urge support of tuition tax credit legislation and other proposals such as educational opportunity grants which help to insure the right of parents to choose the education which best meets the needs of their children."

"We also urge the support of federal education legislation which provides for the equitable participation of students and teachers attending the nation's non-public schools."

"We advocate policies to improve the educational opportunities available to economically disadvantaged persons and minorities, including bicultural and bilingual education, as well as compliance with legal requirements for racially integrated schools."

Food and Farm Programs: "We support nutrition programs which help to meet the needs of hungry and malnourished Americans. . . . In this context, we feel it is essential that the food stamp program be funded at adequate levels."

"The U.S. government . . . should support an agricultural system based on small and moderate-sized family farms."

"We urge that U.S. policy for overseas food aid: (1) make a clear separation of food aid from strategic and political considerations; (2) give priority to the poorest nations; (3) establish an international system of grain reserves, and (4) promote agricultural development at the level of the small farmer and the rural poor."

Health Care: "We support a national health policy rooted in the fundamental belief that every person has the right to life, to bodily integrity and to the means which are neces-

sary and suitable for the development of life. In spite of the enormous national commitment to health, the present health care system has serious inadequacies. Consequently, we strongly support comprehensive national health insurance. We also strongly oppose the use of national health insurance to pay for abortions."

Human Rights: "The protection of human rights must be given greater weight in U.S. foreign policy. . . . A more sensitive effort should be made: (1) to support those governments, particularly in Central and South America and in Africa, which respect the freedom, rights and legitimate aspirations of their people; (2) to distance U.S. involvement with those governments which commonly violate or repress these rights."

"Recent and current practice has too often offended both of these principles to the detriment of many suffering people and the weakening of U.S. moral influence in the world. We have only to recall our government's determination to send continued military aid to El Salvador in the face of opposition from popular sectors of that country, and indeed from the recently assassinated Archbishop of San Salvador, Oscar Romero."

Immigration and Undocumented Aliens: "A truly just and comprehensive immigration policy should first strive to clarify our immigration goals, laws, policies and structures so that they reflect the best American interests and values."

"Additionally, such a policy should provide a generous amnesty going back several years. . . . The speedy reunification of families should be a goal and integral part of this policy."

"While effective enforcement of immigration laws is needed, it is important to avoid employer sanctions whose practical effect would very likely be to discourage the employment of minority group U.S. citizens and aliens, especially Hispanics, who are in this country legally."

ELECTRONIC EVANGELIZATION

The Electronic Church — defined as primarily "evangelical-Christian in orientation, personality-centered and self-supported by contributions from listeners and viewers" — has a weekly congregation of 115 million television viewers and between 14 and 15 million radio listeners, according to estimates reported by National Religious Broadcasters, Inc. Its preachers are thousands of Protestant ministers and other speakers versed in biblical fundamentalism and born-again Christianity.

The number of authentic evangelicals in this vast congregation is open to question and interpretation. The best estimate probably lies between 30 and 40 million, although other calculations are much higher.

Christianity Today reported a 1980 estimate of 31 million evangelicals in the United States with shared faith, and some differences about its nuances, in: the literalness and absolute authority of the Bible as the rule of faith; the divinity of Christ and his imminent second coming; salvation to be achieved through personal faith in Christ and/or in a conversion experience of spiritual rebirth through Christ in the power of the Spirit. Evangelicals reject the rationale, methods and results of critical biblical scholarship, practice regular Bible reading and attendance at denominational church services, and are generally strong in support of traditional and so-called conservative family and social values.

The pulpits of the evangelical Electronic Church are 1,400 radio and 35 television stations of their own along with the facilities of other stations on leased time paid for by contributions from listeners and viewers. National Religious Broadcasters, Inc., has a membership of 900 organizations; its director, Benjamin Armstrong, coined the term "Electric Church."

Of all the evangelists and services beamed electronically to urban as well as rural areas, the best known include not only Billy Graham, Oral Roberts and Rex Humbard, but also:

• Rev. Jerry Falwell and the Old Time Gospel Hour, carried by 320 TV stations in the U.S. and by 69 stations abroad;

• Dr. Pat Robertson, host of the daily 700 Club carried by 130 TV stations;

• Rev. Robert Schuller and the Hour of Power carried by 148 TV stations;

• Rev. James Robison, promoter of the "Christian vote" effort of some evangelical broadcasters.

• Rev. Jim Bakker of the PTL ("Praise the Lord") Club.

Critique

The so-called Electronic Church, despite its religious dimensions, cannot be called a true church at all when looked at from a theological perspective. Father Richard McBrien, chairman of the theology department of Notre Dame University, noted: "There is no discernible sacramental dimension to their worship, nor is there any meaningful sense of being a particular community of Christ. By itself the Electronic Church cannot substitute for participation in the life of a particular church community."

Rev. Don Oberdorfer, director of video services for the American Lutheran Church, expressed "concern that these preachers have no substantive understanding of the nature of the church. Their concept of church is limited to their own organizations, which are not the kind of church we understand. . . . They don't deal with what a community is. Their approach is simplistic . . . wrapped up in the phrase, 'Jesus is Lord,' and that's it."

A Gallup-American Research Corporation survey reported in the summer of 1980 indicated that viewing and listening to programs of the Electronic Church had no effect on the church connection of two-thirds of the people questioned, had a positive effect on 12.5 per cent and a negative effect on 10 per cent.

The effects of such viewing and listening on the part of Catholics is open to speculation. It is worthy of note that some observers have called attention to a kind of correlation between evangelicals and Catholics (maybe four to six million) in charismatic renewal.

The possible effects of some evangelical political activism on the 1980 elections was viewed with alarm by some observers. The major activist groups were Moral Majority, which registered three million voters between June, 1979, and August, 1980, the Religious Round Table and the Christian Voice. The expressed fear was that their political and religious extremism posed a serious threat to American pluralism.

DISSIDENT ARCHBISHOP MARCEL LEFEBVRE

The symbol of Archbishop Marcel Lefebvre's refusal to acknowledge papal authority and enactments of the Second Vatican Council is the Mass. He celebrates it in the manner prescribed by the Council of Trent (the Tridentine Mass) rather than in the revised form authorized and ordered by Pope Paul VI in 1969, in line with the decision of the Second Vatican Council.

The essence of his dissent is the "Credo" he issued in November, 1974. In it, he declared that the reforms of the council "spring from heresy and end in heresy," and urged his followers to "categorically reject" the council.

Among principal actions of his dissent have been the following.

• The reopening and continuing operation of his seminary and the Priestly Society of St. Pius X after approval of both was withdrawn in May, 1975. The headquarters of both the seminary and society, originally at Econe, was moved later to Rickenbach, Switzerland.

• The unauthorized ordination of 13 men to the priesthood June 29, 1976, for which he was — and remained to the time of writing — suspended from the licit exercise of holy orders.

• Subsequent ordinations of men to the priesthood (probably between 200 and 300), the diaconate and other orders, some of which were abolished by the Second Vatican Council.

• The choice of June 29 — the feast of Sts. Peter and Paul, symbolic of the role of the Pope in the Church — as the date of priestly ordination from 1976 to 1979 appeared to be an option for defiance of the Holy See.

• The establishment in various places of parishes and other institutions, including seminaries in Italy, Germany, Argentina and the United States.

• Visits and public appearances for the celebration of Mass and the administration of sacraments at gatherings of his followers in various countries. As the end of 1977, 10,000 followers were claimed in the U.S., and 50,000 in Europe and elsewhere.

At the end of 1980, there were no signs of reconciliation between the 75-year-old archbishop and the Holy See.

NOVEMBER 1979

VATICAN

Prayers for the Persecuted — Pope John Paul II, addressing 80,000 persons in St. Peter's Square, appealed Nov. 3 for prayers for "those who, in whatever country and on whatever continent, suffer persecution because of Christ . . . those who find themselves in prison and those who suffer torment because of their faith and their fidelity to their convictions."

Can't Cheat on Marriage Doctrine — The Pope strongly reaffirmed church teaching on marriage and birth control in an address Nov. 3 to family planning experts of the Liaison Center for Research Groups and of the Federation of Organizations for Research and Promotion of Natural Family Planning Methods. Declaring that "one cannot cheat on the doctrine of the Church," he said that "the ideal of conjugal relations" presented by Pope Paul VI in the encyclical *Humanae Vitae* does not allow for "a concession more or less broad, more or less admitted, to the principles and the practice of contraceptive customs."

Cardinals' Meeting — The first plenary session of the College of Cardinals in more than 400 years was convened by Pope John Paul Nov. 5 to 9 for deliberations concerning Vatican finances, the structures and operations of the Roman Curia, and the relationship of the Church to modern culture.

Men and Women Have the Same Nature — The account of the creation of woman in the Book of Genesis shows that "male and female are of the same nature," declared the Pope Nov. 7 before a general audience of 20,000 persons. He said: "The second chapter of the Book of Genesis tells of God causing a deep sleep to fall upon the man and, while he slept, taking one of his ribs and making it into a woman." The Bible's "profound truths" and its "imaginative picture of the woman being formed from the man's rib expresses the fact that male and female are of the same nature. . . . This is true not only of their bodies; it is true of the depth of their nature as human beings. They stand together at the summit of God's visible creation."

Appeal for Hostages Rejected — A papal appeal for the release of about 60 American hostages held by Iranian students since Nov. 4 at the U.S. embassy in Teheran was summarily and brusquely rejected Nov. 9 by Ayatollah Ruhollah Khomeini.

Einstein and Galileo — Pope John Paul, addressing a meeting of the Pontifical Academy of Sciences Nov. 10, paid tribute to the work of Albert Einstein on the 100th anniversary of the scientist's birth. He also said he would support an effort to reverse the condemnation issued by a Roman congregation in 1633 against Galileo Galilei for teaching that the earth revolves around the sun.

Hunger — The Holy Father called it the "gravest and most acute" problem in the world, in an address Nov. 12 to 1,500 delegates attending the general convention of the United Nations Food and Agriculture Organization in Rome.

Witness of Women Religious — Pope John Paul mentioned three key components of the witness of women religious to their vocation during an address Nov. 14 to 630 participants in the annual assembly of the International Union of Superiors General.

• "Fidelity to Christ can never be separated from fidelity to the Church."

• Community life is essential "because spiritual ties cannot be created, developed and perpetuated except through daily and prolonged contact."

• Distinctive religious garb provides "a particular witness" and serves as "a sign . . . indicative of the choice you have made to consecrate yourselves totally to the ideals of the kingdom of heaven."

Philosophy of St. Thomas Aquinas — "The philosophy of St. Thomas merits studious attention and acceptance . . . because of its spirit of openness and universalism, characteristics which are difficult to find in many currents of contemporary thought." So stated the Pope Nov. 17 at the closing session of a conference marking the 100th anniversary of the encyclical *Aeterni Patris,* written by Pope Leo XIII to encourage the teaching of scholastic philosophy in general and that of St. Thomas in particular.

Ecumenism — Ecumenism is "an essentially pastoral task," declared the Pope Nov. 23 in an address to delegates of 59 national ecumenical commissions. Underlining its urgency, he said: "Disunity is a scandal, a hindrance, to the spread of the Gospel. . . . Let no one delude himself that work for perfect unity in faith is somehow secondary, optional, peripheral, something that can be indefinitely postponed."

Oppressive Power Systems — Power systems and ideologies that rule by oppression and violence were berated by the Pope Nov. 25. "There are forms of power," he said, "that seek to condition man even in his most interior dimensions, that subordinate him to ideological systems without taking into account whether or not they correspond to his convictions, that make his civic and social life depend more on the acceptance of those systems than on the real merits of the person."

Men Religious — "The charism of each of the institutes you represent is an eloquent sign of the multiform richness of Christ," the Pope stated Nov. 26 during a meeting with 11 members of the Council of the Union of Superiors General. The Church, he said, "welcomes and nurtures orders and institutes" of different types "because all of them together contribute to revealing the varied nature and the multivalent dynamism of the Word of God incarnate and of those who believe in him."

The Pope Also:

• Criticized luxurious tourism as "an insult and provocation" to people in miserable economic conditions, during a meeting Nov. 10 with delegates to the Second World Conference on the Ministry of Tourism.

• Called on laymen from 229 parishes in Rome to discharge their responsibilities to their communities, Nov. 25.

• Appointed 20 persons — including American Sister Regina Casey — to the new Permanent Committee for International Eucharistic Congresses headed by Cardinal James R. Knox.

First Ecumenical Voyage

Pope John Paul's fourth trip abroad during the year, to Turkey Nov. 28 to 30, was, in his words, his "first ecumenical voyage." Its highlights were the first-ever presences of an Orthodox Patriarch at a Mass celebrated by a Pope (Nov. 29 in the Holy Spirit Cathedral, Istanbul) and of a Pope at a Liturgy celebrated by an Orthodox Patriarch (Nov. 30 in the Church of St. George), and the joint announcement by the Pope and Patriarch Dimitrios I of the formation of a Catholic-Orthodox theological commission for ecumenical dialogue. (See Pope John Paul in Turkey.)

NATIONAL

Refugee Aid — At the beginning of the month, Catholic Relief Services dispatched its 25th mercy convoy of trucks carrying food, clothing, medicine and shelter material to refugees along the Cambodia-Thailand border. In Cambodia, the distribution of emergency food supplies by CRS and other relief agencies was seriously hampered by rival political factions, and the 1970 population of almost eight million was down to less than five million; there were few, if any, children between the ages of one and four.

Social Teaching Has To Be Lived — Auxiliary Bishop Thomas J. Gumbleton of Detroit, speaking Nov. 4 in Lafayette, La., said that "we cannot teach the social teachings of the Church unless we also live them. We must be dedicated to some kind of change in our own life-style." He asked: "How is it that, after 80 years of modern social teaching, the Church has been unable to make an imprint

on the consciences of her people? Most of the faithful do not see structural social injustice as sinful, and feel no responsibility for it or any obligation to do something about it."

Identity and Commitment of a Catholic University — These were the subjects of a statement, "The Catholicity of Catholic Universities and Colleges," issued by the Fellowship of Catholic Scholars. While a Catholic university "wishes to communicate every kind of truth," the statement said, "it has a primary concern with communicating the truth it has received from Jesus Christ and to reflect on all other truth in the light of that revelation."

Youth Convention — "Today We Experience, Tomorrow We Reach Out," with emphasis on the development of youth ministry, was the theme of the 15th biennial convention of the National Catholic Youth Federation held Nov. 15 to 18 in Kansas City, Mo. The meeting, at which James Mayo of Lake Charles, La., was elected federation president, was attended by about 3,200 teen-agers and youth ministers.

Treaties on Human Rights — The failure of the Senate to ratify four treaties on human rights dating back to 1966 was called a cause of embarrassment for the U.S. in the international community, by Msgr. Francis J. Lally, secretary of social development and world peace, U.S. Catholic Conference. He said that conference support for the treaties was in line with Catholic social teaching. "That teaching," he noted, "perceives the mission of the Church to teach the Gospel. . . . Increasingly, the Church has seen as essential to that mission its ministry for justice and, specifically with that, the defense and promotion of human rights."

Covenant of Justice — Leaders of major religious bodies joined in an ecumenical prayer service on the Boston Common Nov. 19 to proclaim a "covenant of justice and equity and harmony." The service marked the start of a massive effort for support of the covenant in the racially troubled city. Cardinal Humberto Medeiros told 4,000 persons attending the service that the achievement of racial peace "is not the sole responsibility or competence of religious leaders. . . . It is the responsibility of all the citizens, all the leadership of the city."

Papal Poll — Seventy per cent of 1,500 adults interviewed by telephone in an ABC News-Louis Harris survey conducted three weeks after Pope John Paul's visit to the U.S. agreed that he is "one of the outstanding world leaders of this century." Eighty-four per cent of the 400 Catholics polled registered this opinion. More than half of them, however, opposed his statements of church teaching and discipline on several subjects, including: contraception (63 to 34 per cent), abortion (61 to 34 per cent), divorce (65 to 34 per cent), celibacy for priests (53 per cent). On "matters concerning the doctrine of the Church affecting members of the Church," they said they agreed with the Pope by 56 to 32 per cent.

Mexican-Americans Being Proselytized — Archbishop Patrick Flores of San Antonio said early in the month that "many other religious denominations have been making every possible attempt at proselytizing and converting the Mexican-American from Catholicism to their own denominations." He estimated that 10 to 15 per cent of Mexican-Americans no longer professed the Catholic faith.

National Briefs:

• Retired Archbishop Edward D. Howard of Portland, Ore., the oldest living Catholic bishop, celebrated his 102nd birthday Nov. 5.

• The American Bible Society announced publication of a new Spanish translation of the Bible (*Dios Habla Hoy*, "God Speaks Today") endorsed by the Catholic Bishops of Latin America.

• Honored: Robert MacNeil, co-host of public television's "MacNeil-Lehrer Report," and Bernard Meltzer, host of WOR's "What's Your Problem?," with Morality in Media awards Nov. 12, for enriching the quality of media; Msgr. George G. Higgins of the U.S. Catholic Conference, with the first Interreligious Award of Religion in American Life, Nov. 13.

• Seventeen-year-old Ku Klux Klan member Aaron Morrison was denied a diploma by Holy Spirit High School, Absecon, N.J., because of his involvement with the racist organization.

• "Sharing the Word of God in the Home" was the theme for Catholic observance of the 39th annual National Bible Week, Nov. 18 to 25.

Bishops' Meeting

More than 250 bishops attended the meeting of the National Conference of Catholic Bishops and the U.S. Catholic Conference Nov. 12 to 15 in Washington, D.C. Among other actions, the bishops:

• Issued a pastoral letter on racism, which they said is "a sin that divides the human family, blots out the image of God among specific members of that family, and violates the fundamental human dignity of those called to be children of the same Father."

• Expressed concern in shorter statements for the welfare of American hostages held by Iranian students in Teheran, and for thousands of persons suffering from hunger and oppression in Cambodia.

• Turned down proposals for changes in the words of Eucharistic Prayers and other prayers of the celebrant at Mass regarded in some quarters as male-oriented.

• Approved a conference budget of $14.5 million for 1980.

INTERNATIONAL

Organizations Banned — Bishop Desmond Tutu, general secretary of the South African Council of Churches, reported that several Christian groups were among 34 organizations banned by the Transkei government Nov. 1. He said: "The council is deeply concerned about the effects this action will have on the countless individuals who have been assisted and served" by the banned organizations in programs of community development and relief. Two of the affected groups were the Students' Christian Movement and the Young Christian Workers.

Coup and Violence in Bolivia — Church officials were among mediators of a provisional solution to political turmoil which reached another of many climaxes Nov. 1 with the overthrow of the civilian government of President Walter Guevara Arze by a junta headed by Col. Alberto Natusch Busch. The solution consisted of the ouster of the military regime and the installation of Lydia Gueiler Tejeda as interim president, to serve until elections scheduled for May, 1980. Victims of three weeks of violence were 201 dead, 207 wounded and 211 missing, according to figures reported by the Bolivian Human Rights Commission.

Hard-Hearted Policies — More than 1,000 priests and nuns, in a letter read in many churches of the country Nov. 4, charged that the Peruvian military government's economic policies were producing death and starvation. "The situation of hunger and death," the letter said, was "constantly worsening because of the rising cost of basic necessities." It called the regime's economic policies (currency devaluation, unrealistic wage and price adjustments) "more hard-hearted with each passing day."

Anti-Conversion Legislation in India — A report issued by a committee of the Indian Bishops' Conference said that bills designed to prevent conversions were causing insecurity in the nation's Catholic community. The report was especially critical of a law in effect in the territory of Arunachal Pradesh and of a bill introduced in Parliament which would extend anti-conversion measures throughout the predominantly Hindu country. Leaders of Christian and Moslem minorities said the legislation was aimed against them. The bishops' report said that, although no action had been taken on the bill before Parliament, it would be "naive on our part to be lulled into a false sense of complacency. We must not forget that the plight of our Christian brethren in Arunachal Pradesh continues to be extremely difficult."

Abortion Is Murder — Mother Teresa of Calcutta, in an address to a United Nations conference Nov. 9 in New Delhi, said that "abortion is nothing but murder in the mother's womb. . . . If a mother can destroy her child, then how can you stop people from killing one another?"

Call for Peace in Ireland — "May the paramilitary leaders, the politicians, the governments, those responsible for law and order, the people of the Catholic community, the people of the Protestant community — may they seize this opportunity which the Pope's visit (Sept. 29 to Oct. 1, 1979) has given us to work for peace with consent, with honor, and with justice." This appeal was made in a pastoral letter issued by the Irish Bishops' Conference Nov. 11.

Diplomatic Status — The British Foreign Office confirmed that the government had agreed to regard Archbishop Bruno Heim, apostolic delegate, as a diplomatic agent but that this status, given on a personal basis, did not mean the establishment of full diplomatic relations with Vatican City.

Reconstruction in Equatorial Guinea — "Ten years of ferocious oppression and persecution (under the rule of President Francisco Macias Nguema, who was overthrown Aug. 1, 1979) had not compromised the work done by more than 300 Claretian missionaries during 96 years of evangelization," reported *Fides*, the news service of the Congregation for the Evangelization of Peoples.

Support for Nicaraguan Government — Four months after the overthrow of the regime of Anastasio Somoza Debayle, the bishops of Nicaragua issued a pastoral letter Nov. 16 in which they expressed guarded support for the new revolutionary government and trust that it would work toward realization of the patriotic and Christian expectations of the people. The bishops said: "We trust that the revolution will be creative, original and deeply nationalist, not an imitation of other revolutions. We and the majority of Nicaraguans seek a revolution that firmly leads toward a representative society, not a capitalist, nor a dependent, nor a totalitarian society. . . . We consider as just a social project that guarantees the common destiny of the country's goods and resources to meet the basic needs of all Nicaraguans so that the quality of human life improves for everyone." They rejected any kind of socialism that "pretends to submit the people to the manipulations of those holding power arbitrarily" or that restricts human rights.

CCCB Meeting — Family ministry was the principal subject under discussion at the plenary meeting of the Canadian Conference of Catholic Bishops held late in the month in Ottawa. Archbishops Joseph MacNeil of Edmonton and Henri Legare of Grouard-McLennan were elected president and vice president, respectively.

Expulsions — Expelled during the month for alleged violations of law during their work as missionaries were: American Father James F. Carney, S.J., Nov. 17, from Honduras; West German Father Pauly, Nov. 28, from South Africa.

YWCA Position on Abortion — Catholic members of the YWCA in Canada were asked to request their local boards to disassociate themselves from the national YWCA policy favoring abortion on demand. The policy statement declares: "The YWCA of Canada believes that sections dealing with abortion should be removed from the criminal code of Canada and that, in support of a woman's right to self-determination, abortion should be a private matter of individual conscience decided by a woman and a physician." Archbishop Gilles Ouellet, on behalf of all the bishops, said in a statement: "Because the Catholic Church believes that abortion is the taking of human life, the YWCA's stance is clearly one which faithful Catholics cannot, in conscience, support or to which they may offer adherence."

International Briefs:

• At ceremonies marking Israel's return to Egypt of control over Mount Sinai, Egyptian president Anwar el-Sadat pledged Nov. 19 that the venerable site would be open to access by all peoples and proposed that an interfaith shrine be built there for Moslems, Christians and Jews. Mount Sinai was the place where Moses received the Ten Commandments.

• Polish dissidents were appealing to international opinion for help in bringing about an end to new government crackdowns, according to a report in the Nov. 29 edition of the Italian Catholic newspaper, *Avvenire*. The appeal came in the wake of arrests of several students and faculty members of the "Flying University" of Warsaw,

Letter to Jesuit Superiors

Father Pedro Arrupe, in a letter dated Oct. 19, called on major superiors of the Society of Jesus to take appropriate action for the correction of "questionable" situations affecting Jesuits and the faithful. The letter, which became available late in November, was prompted by remarks made by Pope John Paul II during an audience Sept. 21 with superiors of the society.

Among questions to be addressed were:

• "Is there a sufficient level, in their community, of that austerity and practice of interior and exterior discipline which sustains and develops a faithful prayer life and the apostolic zeal that it inspires?

• "Are there signs of secularizing tendencies in the community or any of its members, for example, a lack of community life, independence of superiors, questionable relationships with others, failures in the observance of the vows; or is there evidence of apostolic work incompatible with the priestly character which ought to mark our activity, however varied and difficult it may be?"

DECEMBER 1979

VATICAN

New Stage in Dialogue — Pope John Paul told a general audience Dec. 5 that his trip to Turkey Nov. 28 to 30 marked the beginning of "a new stage in the ecumenical dialogue between churches of the East and the West." (See John Paul II in Turkey.)

Model Law, Rights of Women — "The law ought to be not just a reflection of what happens but a model and prod for what ought to be done," declared the Pope Dec. 7 at an audience with members of the Italian Women's Center. In an obvious reference to abortion legislation, he said: "The Church is profoundly convinced that the wisdom of legislation is shown most fully at the point where the most energetic defense is taken up of the weakest and most defenseless members (of society), beginning with the first instant of life."

Addressing also the rights of women, he spoke of "making just laws prevail so that every woman can honestly insert herself into society, both humanly and professionally, beyond every fear of discrimination. But it is necessary to guard against allowing claims and proposals, most of them just from the start, to degenerate into embittered polemic or arbitrary and unnatural proclamations."

Immaculate Conception Observance — The Holy Father observed the solemnity of the Immaculate Conception Dec. 8 with the traditional presentation of flowers at the statue of Mary in Rome's *Piazza di Spagna*. Later in the afternoon, he celebrated Mass in the Basilica of St. Mary Major.

Church Law — "Church law," the Pope stated during an audience Dec. 13 with priest-jurists, "is not only a sign of human justice but an expression of the higher communion of life in Christ, so that all canonical justice should shine with charity."

Priests Should Be Priests — This was the substance of the Pope's remarks at an audience Dec. 13 with ecclesiastical assistants to international Catholic organizations. He urged them to be priests "without reservations. . . . The Church wants you to be priests and the laity with whom you are in touch want you to be priests. . . . A confusion of charisms impoverishes the Church."

More Than Technical Approach Needed — The Pope told Catholics working for social justice and economic development in the Third World that they must be faithful to the Christian analysis of social evils and must provide remedies in line with Catholic social teaching. Addressing the executive committee of International Cooperation for Socio-Economic Development Dec. 15, he said that Catholic associations must work "in fidelity to the Church and to a sole, unique spirit," over and above purely technical or political considerations which often determine the assessment of human need and the means of coping with it.

Theology Not an Isolated Discipline — "Theology has never been conceived as an isolated discipline" at the Pontifical Gregorian University, declared the Holy Father Dec. 15 during his first visit as Pope to the famous institution. He said that theology "is never a private affair of a specialist isolated in a sort of ivory tower. It is at the service of the Church and, therefore, must consider itself dynamically inserted in the mission of the Church, particularly in its prophetic mission."

Year-End Address to Cardinals — World problems were the principal subjects of an address by the Pope Dec. 22 to members of the College of Cardinals in Rome. Topics included: violations of human and religious rights, war and the arms race, abortion, pleas for refugees and more efforts to relieve hunger, an attack on avarice apparently aimed at the oil cartel, hope for religious freedom in China, and a plea for a positive social environment for the growth of young people. In an apparent reference to the detention of U.S. hostages in Iran, he scored "violations of firm principles of international law, causing heavy suffering to the persons involved and their families." The Holy Father covered the wide range of his own activities during the first 14 months of his pontificate, and said that his daily concern was "to meet man, to let man meet with Christ."

Christmas Blessing and Message — Pope John Paul extended greetings in 34 languages and imparted his blessing "to the City and the World" at noon on Christmas Day before a gathering of 100,000 persons in St. Peter's Square and a worldwide television audience of millions. In his message, he called Christmas "the feast of all children in the world — all of them, without distinction of race, nationality, language or origin. Christ is born at Bethlehem for them all. And he represents them all. . . . The child is always a new revelation of the life that is given to man by the Creator. . . . The child is also a great and continuous test of our fidelity to ourselves, of our fidelity to humanity. It is a test of our respect for the mystery of life upon which, from the very first moment of conception, the Creator places the imprint of his image and likeness. The dignity of the child demands, on the part of parents and society, a very great sensitivity of conscience. For the child is that delicate spot around which the morality of families, and hence the morality of whole nations and of society, is either formed or broken."

Human Dignity — "In a world context where the person seems to obtain less and less attention because he finds himself subordinated to ideological and economic systems which enslave and exploit him, it is even more necessary to reaffirm with strength that this dignity must stay intact." So declared the Pope in a letter, made public Dec. 28, to members of the European Court for Human Rights and the European Commission for Human Rights.

The Pope Also:

• Expressed his sympathy for Colombians in the aftermath of earthquakes that left 100 persons dead, 200 missing and nearly 200,000 homeless.

• Called on seminarians of the English College in Rome "to be witnesses in this generation to the vitality of the Church's youth."

• Made another impassioned plea for help for the victims of fighting and famine in Cambodia, Dec. 26.

• Appealed on the feast of the Holy Family to "all families of the world" to work together for peace.

Vatican Briefs:

• Church and government officials exchanged documents of ratification completing the process of updating the concordat between the Vatican and Spain, Dec. 4.

• Cardinal Agnelo Rossi, prefect of the Congregation for the Evangelization of Peoples, represented the Pope at two events during the month: the meeting of the International Missionary Congress Dec. 2 to 6 in Manila, and the observance Dec. 8 of the 50th anniversary of the founding of the Catholic Fujen University in Taipei, Taiwan.

• Minimum salaries of Vatican employees were raised from about $500 to $650 a month; maximum salaries went from $720 to $1,000.

• Dutch theologian Father Edward Schillebeeckx, O.P., was questioned Dec. 13 and 14 by members of the Congregation for the Doctrine of the Faith concerning the contents of his book, *Jesus: An Experiment in Christology.*

Hans Kung Not a Catholic Theologian

The Congregation for the Doctrine of the Faith issued a declaration Dec. 18 in which it said that "Professor Hans Kung, in his writings, has departed from the integral truth of Catholic faith, and therefore he can no longer be considered a Catholic theologian nor function as such in a teaching role." (See separate entry under Hans Kung.)

NATIONAL

Promote Pastoral Letter on Racism — The board of directors of the National Catholic Conference for Interracial Justice resolved Dec. 1 to concentrate during the next three years on efforts to combat racism along the lines suggested in the pastoral letter on the subject approved at the November, 1979, meeting of the National Conference of Catholic Bishops and the U.S. Catholic Conference. The title of the letter was "Brothers and Sisters to Us." (See separate entry.)

Brother Concept — A study group of 12 brother-religious, meeting Dec. 2 to 6 in Washington, D.C., issued a statement in which they described the "brother" concept as follows: "To brother is to participate deeply in the sacramental life of the Church . . . to brother is to minister . . . to brother is to understand and appreciate the working of the Spirit in the world and in the lives of men and women . . . to brother is to encourage, enable and support our brothers and sisters in offering, through commitment, their own particular gifts and charisms in ministry to others."

Haitian Refugees — The failure of the U.S. Attorney's Office to use its discretionary powers to admit Haitian refugees could only "spawn the well-founded suspicion that the treatment received by the Haitians is a result of institutional racism," declared Archbishop Edward A. McCarthy of Miami Dec. 4 in testimony before the U.S. Select Commission on Immigration and Refugee Policy. He said there was "a most serious discrepancy" between the refusal of admission and provisions of the U.S. Immigration and Naturalization Act.

Aid for Nicaragua — Thomas E. Quigley, a staff member of the U.S. Catholic Conference, told the Senate Foreign Relations Committee Dec. 6 that the conference fully supported the request of the Carter Administration for $75 million to assist in reconstruction of the Nicaraguan economy, "struggling to rebuild after a destructive conflict and weakened further by the depradations of the outgoing (Somoza) regime."

Too Little for the Hungry — The Presidential Commission on World Hunger said Dec. 10 in an interim report that, "despite ringing rhetoric, legislative mandates and good intentions among development advocates, too small a percentage of U.S. resources . . . actually serves to increase food consumption among the poor."

Death of Archbishop Sheen — Three thousand people attended the Mass of Christian Burial for Archbishop Fulton J. Sheen in St. Patrick's Cathedral Dec. 13, four days after his death in New York City at the age of 84. They were only a minute fraction of the millions who knew him as a priest since 1919, a "Catholic Hour" radio preacher, a teacher at the Catholic University of America from 1926 to 1950, the host of ABC-TV's "Life Is Worth Living" series in the 50s, a bishop since 1951, head of the Society for the Propagation of the Faith from 1950 to 1966, bishop of Rochester from 1966 to 1969, and a widely read columnist and author. In one of many tributes, Archbishop Edward T. O'Meara said of Archbishop Sheen: "A voice is silent in the midst of the Church and in our land, a voice the like of which will not be heard again in our day."

Nativity Scene in Denver — Federal District

Court Judge Richard Matsch issued an order Dec. 17 for the removal of a nativity scene from the premises of the city hall in Denver, on the ground that such display violated the principle of separation of church and state. The 10th U.S. Circuit Court of Appeals stayed the ruling the following day, for 12 days, and subsequently refused to reconsider the stay. The decision of the district court was appealed Dec. 30 to the U.S. Supreme Court by the American Civil Liberties Union, acting on behalf of an atheistic group.

National Briefs:

• The U.S. bishops' Ad Hoc Committee on Women in the Church and Society met with representatives of the Women's Ordination Conference Dec. 5 and 6 in Washington, D.C., in the first session of an official dialogue between the two groups.

• Lillian Block, retiring editor of Religious News Service, was honored at a luncheon hosted Dec. 7 in New York by the Catholic Press Association.

• Georgetown University, the first Catholic university with a full-time Jewish chaplain, was awarded $30,000 by a New York City foundation for its Jewish chaplaincy program.

• A 14-member medical team from Georgetown University left Washington, D.C., Dec. 13 for Thailand to provide aid to refugees from Cambodia.

• A chapel and multi-purpose center for seamen, provided by the Apostleship of the Sea Commission, U.S. Catholic Conference, was opened Dec. 17 in Miami.

• Gannon College in Erie was granted university status by the Commonwealth of Pennsylvania Dec. 19.

• Archbishop James V. Casey announced during Christmas midnight Mass that Denver's Cathedral of the Immaculate Conception had been given the rank of minor basilica.

• The American Bible Society announced publication of the *Good News Bible for Children,* a redesigned version of the *Good News Bible.*

Leading News Stories of 1979

Forty-one editors responding to an NC News Service survey rated the following as the 10 most important news stories of 1979.

1. Pope John Paul's trips to Mexico, Poland, Ireland, the United States and Turkey.
2. Boat people fleeing from Vietnam.
3. Award of the Nobel Peace Prize to Mother Teresa.
4. Food aid to Cambodians by church groups.
5. Focus on Islam, with the ouster of the Shah and actions of the Khomeini regime in Iran.
6. Vatican financial problems, disclosed at a meeting of the College of Cardinals.

7. Ordination of women, in connection with remarks of Sister Theresa Kane before Pope John Paul.
8. Publication of the encyclical letter *Redemptor Hominis.*
9. Conflict between the Church and federal government regarding: an Internal Revenue Service ruling on the tax status of schools; legislation requiring employers to pay for abortions; unemployment compensation taxes for lay employees of church institutions.
10. Pastoral letter of the U.S. bishops on racism.

Pope John Paul and Mother Teresa of Calcutta were rated the two top newsmakers of the year.

INTERNATIONAL

Relief Aid — *Caritas Internationalis,* the international confederation of Catholic organizations for charitable and social action, reported that Catholic charities relief aid to people in Thailand and Cambodia averaged $1 million a week during November.

Lefebvre Headquarters Moved — *Il Tempo,* the Rome daily newspaper, reported Dec. 6 that dissident Archbishop Marcel Lefebvre had moved the headquarters of his Priestly Confraternity of St. Pius X from Econe to Rickenbach, Switzerland.

Latin in the Liturgy — *Una Voce Canada* made another appeal to the Canadian Conference of Catholic Bishops for a pastoral letter on the use of Latin in the liturgy. The organization asked that Latin-language liturgies be permitted along with those in vernacular languages, noting that the "lawfulness and efficacy" of rituals in Latin are affirmed in the General Introduction to the Roman Sacramentary.

Nuclear Arms and Energy — The Holy See's delegate to the general assembly in New Delhi of the International Atomic Energy Agency condemned Dec. 10 the escalation of nuclear arsenals and advised caution in the use of nuclear energy for peaceful purposes. In a strongly worded address, Msgr. Mario Peressin denounced "the terrible scandal of the rapid proliferation of nuclear armaments" and told conferees that their governments could not "remain indifferent to the phenomenon of the nuclear arsenal, with its frightful power of destroying life on this planet."

Rights for Religious — In a public statement released Dec. 12, the heads of 650 institutes of women religious declared that "thousands of religious are daily denied their fundamental human rights in many countries behind the Iron Curtain." Copies of the statement were sent to the embassies in Italy of Czechoslovakia, East Germany, Rumania and the Soviet Union, the countries "where injustices toward religious are most flagrant."

Missing Persons in Argentina — In a "call to reconciliation" issued Dec. 15, the steering committee of the Argentinian Bishops' Conference repeated to the government an appeal of Pope John Paul for clarification of the fate of prisoners and missing persons in the country. Church and human rights groups claimed that from 6,000 to 10,000 persons seized by security agents or paramilitary squads since the mid-1970s were still missing.

Harassment in Lithuania — Keston College, the London-based center for the study of religion and Communism, reported that two priests belonging to the Catholic Committee for the Defense of Believers' Rights had been threatened by Lithuanian officials with stern penalties if they did not stop their pastoral activities. Fathers A. Svarinskas and S. Tamkevicius were accused of spreading falsehoods about Soviet authorities. Letters from more than 2,000 persons who had attended services conducted by the priests protested against the accusations, saying they were made by "malicious people who hate the faith."

Disorder in El Salvador — Appeals for conciliation and cooperation voiced by Archbishop Oscar Romero of San Salvador, other church leaders and moderate spokesmen were having little or no effect on continuing political, economic and social strife in the country. The government, in power since October, was under attack from both the right and left, and violence was rampant. The archbishop was urging the wealthy to come to terms with the revolution and to stop conspiring for a counter-coup in which violence would "take away everything." At the same time, he criticized "the fanatics in the people's organizations" — like the February 28 Popular League, the People's Revolutionary Bloc and the Popular Liberation Forces — "for resorting to violence."

Church in Jeopardy in Cyprus — "The very continuation and existence of the Catholic Church in Cyprus is threatened," declared Father Jean Foradaris, vicar general of the Maronite-Rite Catholic Diocese of Cyprus. In a report to his superior, Archbishop Elias Farah, he said: "The confusion of recent years continues to cause painful upheaval for the Maronites. It has scattered our people, is dampening our spirit, and is weakening our sense of community. . . . as a result of the July, 1974, Turkish invasion, our community (of approximately 5,500) is in danger of losing its identity, its character."

Meeting with Hostages — Auxiliary Bishop Thomas J. Gumbleton of Detroit was one of three U.S. clergymen invited by the Iranian government to visit Christmas Eve with the American hostages held in the U.S. embassy in Teheran.

The other two visitors were the Rev. William Sloane Coffin of New York and the Rev. William Howard of Princeton, N.J.

International Briefs:

• Vatican Radio reported Dec. 6 that the Australian Bishops' Conference and the United Church of Australia had published a "Declaration of Common Understanding" on the sacrament of baptism.

• Cardinal Raul Silva of Santiago was among participants in a telethon that collected nearly $5 million for the funding of new training centers for handicapped children in three cities in Chile.

• *Caritas Buenos Aires* collected more than $30,000 from Catholics in the metropolitan area in an initial effort to provide housing for slum dwellers.

• Participants in a national consultation between the Catholic Health Association of Canada and natural family planning groups recommended a stronger commitment by the Church to the fertility awareness method of natural family planning. The consultation was held in Ottawa.

• In a pastoral letter read Dec. 30 in churches throughout the country, the bishops of Poland called atheism an "alien ideology" to which young people were "forcibly subjected" in government-controlled educational programs. The bishops said that "only in Christian families do the most precious moral values and traditions of the national culture survive."

Mother Teresa, Nobel Medalist

Mother Teresa of Calcutta, foundress of the Missionaries of Charity, was awarded the 1979 Nobel Peace Prize Dec. 10 in Oslo, Norway. She deserved it, declared Nobel Committee Chairman John Sanness, "because she promotes peace in the most fundamental manner — by her confirmation of human dignity." Mother Teresa accepted the prize "in the name of the hungry, of the naked, of the homeless, of the blind, of the lepers, of all those who feel unwanted, unloved, uncared for throughout society."

The 69-year-old nun, Agnes Gonxha Bojaxhiu, was born of Albanian parents in Yugoslavia. She joined the Loreto Sisters in Ireland at the age of 18, taught school in India until 1948, and in 1950 founded the Missionaries of Charity devoted to the care of thousands of the destitute and dying poor and lepers. The community had about 1,200 members, thousands of auxiliaries and other supporters, and 158 establishments in 31 countries.

Mother Teresa indicated that the prize of $192,000, along with a gift of $70,000 from the Norwegian people and $6,000 saved at her request by cancellation of an awards dinner, would be spent to support the work of the Missionaries of Charity for the poorest of the poor.

JANUARY 1980

VATICAN

Peace Message — "The truth will release unsuspected light and energy, and will give a new opportunity for peace in the world." This was the theme of Pope John Paul's address Jan. 1 in connection with the 13th annual observance of the World Day of Peace. Addressing a throng of 50,000 persons in St. Peter's Square, he emphasized that the pursuit of truth is essential to the pursuit of peace. Nontruth, on the other hand, serves the cause of war and is based on a mistaken ideal of man and of the driving forces behind him. "The first lie, the basic falsehood," he said, "is to refuse to believe in man. Encouraged by differing and often contradictory ideologies, the idea is spreading that the individual and all humanity achieve progress principally through violent struggle." He added: "We cannot sincerely condemn recourse to violence unless we engage in a corresponding effort to replace it by courageous political initiatives which aim at eliminating threats to peace by attacking the roots of injustice."

Concern for Migrants and Refugees — In a message marking the observance of Migration Day throughout the world, the Pope called on Catholics to make "the most ample and full response" to the needs of Southeast Asian refugees. The appeal was contained in a letter addressed to Cardinal Sebastiano Baggio, president of the Pontifical Commission for the Ministry of Migration and Tourism. In the U.S., Migration Day was observed Jan. 12.

Harmony with the Hierarchy — The Pope praised members of Italian Catholic Action Jan. 12 while reminding their national councillors to "do nothing without your bishop." He said: "To be faithful to your identity means to work apostolically and always in perfect, happy, faithful, living harmony with the hierarchy."

Afghanistan Threat — Addressing diplomats accredited to Vatican City Jan. 14, the Pope called the Soviet invasion of Afghanistan a serious threat to world peace. He said: "In the face of the dramatic events taking place in Afghanistan, ... one cannot but question the motives that give rise to events so serious and so threatening to international detente."

Self-Giving in Marriage — The ability to give of oneself forms the foundation of marriage, declared Pope John Paul during a general audience Jan. 16. The Book of Genesis, he said, shows that "the human body, as masculine and feminine, is not only a source of procreation but is also what gives man and woman the capacity to express their love, the capacity to give of themselves to one another." They also possess "the corresponding capacity and profound inclination to affirm the other person in his or her own uniqueness as created in the image of God. ... It is this capacity to give of oneself, together with the capacity to affirm the inherent value of the other person, which provides the foundation of a communion of persons which comes about in marriage."

Closed and Open Minds — Knowledge and intelligence are not keys to salvation if they are teamed with a closed mind and heart, the Pope told seminarians at Rome's Capranica College Jan. 21. "Only one who accepts his intellectual and moral limits and recognizes his need for salvation can open himself to faith and in faith to meet, in Christ, his Redeemer," the Holy Father said.

Christian Unity — The Pope called it "an integral part of God's plan of salvation for all mankind," during a general audience Jan. 23, two days before the end of the annual observance of the Week of Prayer for Christian Unity. "This specific week of prayer," he said, "becomes like an annual occasion to examine our conscience before the Lord, to ask forgiveness for the sad divisions which still divide us, and to recommit ourselves to the duty of becoming completely one in Christ."

Military Chaplains — The Pope praised the work of military chaplains Jan. 24 during an audience with 300 Italian priests serving in the armed forces. He said: "Called by Providence to fulfill a qualified priestly service, your life is well spent even if you do not always have the consolation of seeing the effectiveness and results of your ministry. ... You undoubtedly have a great responsibility, because the Church, individual families, superiors and youth themselves have faith in you and expect from you light, guidance, spiritual strength and a solid point of reference."

Moral Values and the International Community — Without spiritual and moral values, efforts to improve the international community "will look like the Tower of Babel," stated the Pope Jan. 26 during a meeting with Grand Duke Jean and Grand Duchess Josephine Charlotte of Luxembourg. He said: "Solidarity with poor and deprived individuals and peoples, respect for human life and the rights of man, and other spiritual and moral values as well, must be guaranteed and promoted at the same time as material progress, or else what we build up will look like the Tower of Babel, with its inhuman character and spiritual emptiness."

The Pope Also:

• Visited about 60 juveniles awaiting trial at a correctional institution in the northern suburbs of Rome, Jan. 6.

• Reminded 200 members of the Italian Association of Catholic Health Workers Jan. 26 that Christians must oppose laws which are "in direct contrast with the good of persons." He made special reference to Italian legislation on abortion.

• On Jan. 26, the "day for the victims of leprosy," appealed for prayers and aid for lepers.

Vatican Briefs:
• Vatican Radio reported Jan. 3 that 15 million hunger-related child deaths occurred in 1979, the International Year of the Child.

• Carlos Chagas, president of the Pontifical Academy of Sciences, expressed "solidarity and sympathy" for Soviet scientist and Nobel laureate Andrei Sakharov who was arrested by Soviet authorities Jan. 22 and removed from Moscow to the off-limits city of Gorki. Chagas conveyed the sentiments of the Pontifical Academy in a telegram to the Soviet Academy of Sciences.

Synod of Dutch Bishops

The unprecedented Particular Synod of Dutch Bishops concluded more than two weeks of deliberations at the Vatican Jan. 31 with a Mass concelebrated with Pope John Paul and the signing of a 22-page, 46-point document detailing ways and means of improving the condition of the Church in The Netherlands. (See separate entry.)

NATIONAL

Boston Covenant — A report disclosed early in the month that approximately 225,000 people in the Boston area had signed a covenant of justice, equity and harmony since Nov. 19, 1979, in an effort to eradicate racism in the troubled city.

Nun Mayor — Sister Carolyn Farrell, a member of the Sisters of Charity of the Blessed Virgin Mary, was elected mayor of Dubuque by the city council Jan. 7. It was believed that she was the first nun ever elected to such an office in Iowa.

In Vitro Clinic — State Health Commissioner James B. Kenley approved Jan. 8 a "certificate of need" permitting the Eastern Virginia Medical School to open the nation's first clinic, at Norfolk General Hospital, for human fertilization outside the body of a mother.

Twenty-two years before the birth of Louise Brown, Pope Pius XII declared on May 19, 1956: "On the subject of the experiments in artificial fecundation *'in vitro,'* let it suffice for Us to observe that they must be rejected as immoral and absolutely illicit."

(See separate entry.)

Stop and Shop for Refugee Aid — Between Jan. 9 and 19, cannisters for donations in support of relief work in Cambodia were placed beside cash registers in 231 Stop and Shop supermarkets and Bradlees department stores. Funds received were earmarked for use by the Interfaith Hunger Appeal, a cooperative effort launched in 1978 by Catholic Relief Ser-

vices, the American-Jewish Joint Distribution Committee, and Church World Service of the National Council of Churches.

Cardinal Baum Named to Roman Curia — Pope John Paul announced Jan. 15 the appointment of Cardinal William W. Baum of Washington as prefect of the Congregation for Catholic Education, to succeed retiring Cardinal Gabriel-Marie Garrone. At the age of 53, the cardinal became the youngest and only American prefect in the Roman Curia.

Bishops' Suit Dismissed — A suit filed in June, 1979, by the National Conference of Catholic Bishops, challenging provisions of the Pregnancy Discrimination Act, was dismissed by U.S. District Court Judge John H. Pratt. The reason for dismissal, he ruled, was that there was no proof that the provisions at issue — requiring employers to pay for abortion and to provide time off for employees seeking abortion — had actually violated an employer's right to freedom of religion. The judge, at a prior hearing Nov. 30, 1979, had said he did not have "an actual case" on which to rule. Bishop Thomas C. Kelly, general secretary of the NCCB, called the dismissal "lamentable" because the judge did not recognize "that the 'chilling effect' of the Pregnancy Discrimination Act could unconstitutionally burden important First Amendment rights."

Draft Registration — *Pax Christi* was one of a number of groups that responded promptly in the negative to the call for draft registration made by President Jimmy Carter Jan. 23 in his State of the Union Address.

March for Life — At least 45,000 persons advocating a constitutional amendment to guarantee the right of the unborn to life took part in the annual March for Life in Washington, D.C., on Jan. 22, the seventh anniversary of the U.S. Supreme Court's 1973 decisions which outlawed anti-abortion legislation. Similar but smaller-scale demonstrations were held in a number of other cities across the country. (See additional coverage under Abortion.)

Right to Die Cases — Eighty-two-year-old Marianist Brother Joseph Fox, comatose since Oct. 2, 1979, died Jan. 24 before the New York Appellate Division issued a ruling for or against the decision of a lower court that would have permitted his removal from a life-supporting respirator. Removal had been sought by Father Philip Eichner, his religious superior, who petitioned the New York Supreme Court to name him as a committee of one to take over the brother's legal right to privacy and to disconnect the respirator if he were found brain-dead.

In Holyoke, dialysis treatments for 78-year-old Earle Spring were resumed Jan. 24 after Massachusetts Supreme Judicial Court Judge Francis J. Quirico overturned a lower court order which had allowed Spring's family to discontinue such treatments. The family had been permitted to do so because of Spring's alleged mental incompetence and presumed desire that he would not want the life-sustaining treatments to continue. In his ruling, Quirico expressed concern that Spring had not been given a complete physical and psychological examination in more than a year.

COCU Agreement — Representatives of 10 Protestant denominations belonging to the Consultation on Church Union approved a statement on ministry Jan. 24 at a meeting in Cincinnati. The document was scheduled for study and response by the member churches in 1981. If approved by the churches, which were already practicing intercommunion, it could enable them to share and exchange ministers (bishops, presbyters or pastors, and deacons).

KKK a Cancer — The Social Action Commission and the Black Secretariat of the Cincinnati archdiocese called the Ku Klux Klan a "developing cancer spreading to and affecting many communities within our nation." In a joint statement issued Jan. 28, the two offices urged people, "individually and collectively, to probe, to question and ultimately to help us create alternatives which will diffuse, alleviate and eventually eradicate both the causes and effects of Klan activity and the white racism it promotes." The statement was prompted by Klan activities in several communities in Ohio.

Medical-Moral Problems — New technologies of birth and death and related moral questions were the principal subjects of discussion at a meeting of 150 U.S. and Canadian bishops Jan. 29 to Feb. 1 in Dallas. The meeting was sponsored by the Pope John XXIII Medical-Moral Research and Education Center with the support of the Knights of Columbus.

National Briefs:

• Archbishop Patrick Flores designated three chapels in the San Antonio archdiocese as places of daily prayer and adoration, beginning Jan. 2.

• The St. Vincent de Paul Medical-Dental Clinic in Phoenix, Ariz., the only agency of its kind conducted in conjunction with a charity dining room, reported it had provided services for 50 persons a week during its first year of operation.

• Sister Theresa Kane was named "American Woman of the Year" for 1979 by the U.S. Section of St. Joan's International Alliance.

• In response to protests by the diocese of Honolulu, the State of Hawaii relinquished claims to the Church of St. Philomena, the site of leper Father Damien's ministry on Molokai.

• Sister Ann Patrick Ware, declaring in a Jan. 10 letter to officials of the National Council of Churches that she found it difficult to serve as an "enthusiastic exponent" of official Catholic positions, announced that she would retire from the council staff in August.

Dooling Decision on Abortion

Federal District Court Judge John F. Dooling, Jr., ruled Jan. 15 in Brooklyn that Congress has no right to limit federal funding of abortions. The ruling, in Harris v. McRae, nullified restrictions imposed on such funding by the Hyde Amendment of 1976 and guidelines subsequently issued by the Department of Health, Education and Welfare.

Judge Dooling stayed enforcement of his decision for 30 days to permit an appeal to the U.S. Supreme Court by HEW. The Court responded Feb. 19 with a one-sentence order requiring federal and state governments to provide Medicaid funding for all abortions deemed "medically necessary." The Court also agreed to rule on the constitutionality of the Hyde Amendment.

(See Abortion for additional coverage.)

INTERNATIONAL

Unemployment in Canada — "Unemployment is not simply a political or economic or social prolem, (but) is a profoundly moral and spiritual problem in our times." So stated the bishops of Canada in a social message issued Jan. 14. In "Unemployment — the Human Costs," they said: "The persistence of poverty, unemployment (of nearly 800,000 persons), regional disparities and a variety of related social problems demonstrates that there is something wrong with our social and economic order. . . . Effective measures (are necessary) to increase the self-sufficiency of Canada's industries, strengthen the manufacturing sector and other job-producing industries, redistribute capital for industrial development in underdeveloped regions, and enhance community ownership and control of local industry."

Socialism with Freedom — As controversy continued about the orientation of the government in control since the overthrow of President Anastasio Somoza Debayle in July, 1979, Archbishop Miguel Obando Bravo of Managua said that socialism with freedom was the way to bridge the gap between the haves and the have-nots and to avoid class hatred in Nicaragua. "As the bishops said in a joint letter," he stated, "we understand to be true socialism the brand that respects human dignity and freedom, the kind that tries to fill the gap between those who have everything and those who have nothing, that looks after the good of the majority, that seeks to enlighten the people about their dignity and rights, as our faith proclaims."

Bolivian Schools — Proposals to nationaize schools in Bolivia were opposed by private school organizations and the bishops. One organization, *Fe y Alegria,* declared in a statement: "Attempts to set up an educational monopoly in the hands of one given group and ideology, or the state, are clear violations of the rights of parents" to guide the education of their children.

Truth and Political Expediency — Truth and objectivity are often sacrificed on the altar of political expediency, complained a Third World diplomat speaking at a World Day of Peace observance for the U.N. Community Jan. 22 at Holy Family Church, New York City. Berenado Vunibobo, Fiji ambassador to the U.N., said: "If one were to examine in some depth the underlying causes which lead to (regional) conflicts, it would be true to say that so many of them were started when truth was either manipulated or strangled, leading to misunderstanding, vilification, and eventually to open conflict." He also said that "the democracies are not immune from the formulation of public policies which are manifestly and intrinsically wrong but which are legitimized because, in many instances, they represent the will of the majority. The minority is only too frequently swamped if not swept aside, irrespective of the substance of their case."

No Peace from Abuse or Violence — The Basque bishops blamed waves of violence and hundreds of its victims on abuse of power by government authorities and on underground groups acting against the will of the people.

Justice and Honesty — These were among the overriding concerns addressed by the bishops of Ontario in a 2,000-word "Letter to Our Youth." They criticized the trend to "look after Number One," saying that it contributes to injustice. "Instead of trying to 'have more,' why can't we 'be more?' " they asked. "Sins of injustice of whatever kind," they said, "are serious failures in our response to Christ." Stressing the need for honesty, the bishops criticized the "don't get caught" and "see if you can get away with it" mentality, noting: "Christ calls each one of us to integrity, to honesty, to real fidelity to him, to ourselves and to others, to all that is truly human. . . . Why not get caught being honest, get caught being a man or woman of integrity, get caught being a disciple of Christ?"

Polish Shrine and the Highway — Vatican Radio reported Jan. 23 that Pope John Paul had "persuaded" the Polish government to abandon plans for the construction of a four-lane highway that would have blocked or hindered access by pilgrims to the national Shrine of Our Lady of Czestochowa. The project had been vigorously opposed by the bishops.

Appeal of Archbishop Romero — As political polarization and fears of full-scale civil war intensified, Archbishop Oscar Arnulfo Romero of San Salvador appealed to right and left wing extremists to "cease violence and terrorism" in El Salvador. "Violence is a sign of ideological weakness," he said in a Sunday homily Jan. 20. The archbishop was a leading advocate of a peaceful and reasonable resolution to the massive political, social and economic crisis crippling the country.

Vandalism in Jerusalem — Vandalism, resulting in some damage to two Christian churches and a bookstore, was reported in Jerusalem. One official of the city called the attacks the work of "baby Khomeinis, fighting a holy war without reason."

Jesuits Threatened — Fifty-two Jesuits in Guatemala were threatened with death by rightists and with expulsion by the military government after publishing Jan. 16 a denunciation of large export profits they said resulted from exploitation of the poor. The threats came from the Secret Anti-Communist Army and the President's Office for Public Relations. The government office called the Jesuits "political clergy" who were subject to trial for misuse of their freedom and for making "irresponsible accusations." The Jesuits quoted in their letter a report of a government agency that death squads had killed 3,252 people in the first 10 months of 1979.

International Briefs:
- "The demand for Scriptures is overwhelming" in East Germany, reported the Rev. Keith Bricknell after a visit to that country.
- Approximately 450,000 people visited the Sanctuaries of Lourdes in 1979.
- Naoko Suganumu, Japan's ambassador to Vatican City, was baptized a Catholic.
- Five hundred and 89 priests, 20 more than reported in 1978, were ordained in 1979 in Poland.

Asian Mission Congress

Bishops along with native and foreign priests attending the International Mission Congress Dec. 2 to 7, 1979, in Manilla focused attention "on the sharing of reflections and experiences leading to a living expression of Christ's message to Asia and the whole world." So stated Filipino Bishop Gaudencio Rosales, according to a delayed report issued by the *Fides* News Agency. One of their principal concerns was the development of small Christian communities for the deepening of spiritual life and its effective expression in local churches and society.

Other subjects under discussion included
- rights of the poor and liberation from oppression;
- dialogue with representatives of other religious traditions;
- enculturation, the adaptation of forms of worship, teaching and practice to specific cultures;
- education, especially of the informal kind, through family life, adult education, the liturgy and ministry.

FEBRUARY 1980

VATICAN

Commitment of Religious — "Your consecration to God — total, definitive and exclusive — is like a continued growth and a splendid blossoming of that initial consecration that took place in the sacrament of baptism," Pope John Paul told more than 10,000 men and women religious of Rome during a Mass Feb. 2 in St. Peter's Basilica. He said the offering of their lives "finds its constant model . . . in the offering that the Son of God makes of himself," and urged them to make their lives a "real testimony to the eternal life" and a "light to illuminate the world and temporal reality."

African Visit — The Pope told a gathering of Rome residents from 31 African countries Feb. 2 that he intended to visit their continent later in the year. (See separate entry.)

Marriage Bond — The Pope rejected Feb. 4 views that "dead" marriages should be recognized as such by the Church and be dissolved or declared null and void. He said: "Matrimony, one and indissoluble, as a human reality is not something mechanical or static. . . . Its success depends on the free cooperation of the spouses with the grace of God, on their response to his own design of love. . . . If, because cooperation in this divine grace is lacking, the union should be bereft of its fruits, the spouses can and must make the grace of God, assured to them by the sacrament, come back. . . . They can and must revive their commitment to live a love which is made up not only of affection and emotions, but also and especially of reciprocal, free, voluntary, total and irrevocable dedication." The Holy Father's reaffirmation of traditional teaching on the indissolubility of valid marriages came in an address to members of the Sacred Roman Rota, the tribunal which has appellate competence in marriage and other cases in church law.

Vatican Radio — The Pope marked the 50th anniversary of Vatican Radio Feb. 5 with a visit to its facilities and an address to its 250 employees. The station, built by Guglielmo Marconi, went on the air for the first time on Feb. 12, 1931.

Kung Declaration Not Anti-Ecumenical — The declaration made public Dec. 18, 1979, by the Congregation for the Doctrine of the Faith — that Father Hans Kung could not be considered a Catholic theologian — was not an anti-ecumenical move. So stated the Pope Feb. 8 at a meeting with members of the Vatican Secretariat for Promoting Christian Unity. He said: "This spirit of fraternal (ecumenical) dialogue that must exist — and I would say it must exist, first of all, among the theologians who, in the Catholic Church, are engaged in the effort of theological renewal — . . . clearly implies that this dialogue should be carried out in truth and fidelity. . . . If authority is obliged to intervene (in doctrinal matters), it is not acting against the ecumenical movement but is bringing to this movement its contribution in warning that certain paths or certain shortcuts do not lead to the goal (of unity) being sought."

Human Development — Its factors are "fundamental demands" involving "the good of persons and of society," the Pope told members of the Pontifical Justice and Peace Commission Feb. 9. He said: "Collective, organic and continuous development is the indispensable presupposition for assuring the concrete exercise of human rights, both those with an economic content and those that directly concern spiritual values. . . . The measure of all real development is the integrity and respect of the human person." The theme of the Feb. 5 to 9 plenary meeting of the commission was "The Church and the Development of Peoples."

Theology — Theology at a Catholic university must uphold "the rigor of the scientific process" and "absolute respect for divine revelation," declared the Pope during a visit Feb. 16 to the Pontifical Lateran University. Without scientific rigor, he said, "the university would descend to the level of a second-class school"; without adherence to revelation, it would lose its "ministry of teaching."

Lay Vocation and Church Unity — The lay vocation "carries with it all the various possibilities" of service to the Church, the Pope said in an address Feb. 17 to more than 30,000 persons in St. Peter's Square. "The laity," he declared, "can participate in diverse ways in the mission of the Church and its apostolate."

The Holy Father also called attention to the first anniversary of the closing of the general assembly of Latin American bishops at Puebla, Mexico. He said: "In the individual churches of Latin America, there has been for the past year work in progress which tends to put into practice the conclusions of that conference. . . . The conclusions and, subsequently, their realization must serve that unity of the Church which is manifested in its entire mission."

Lenten Observance — Pope John Paul marked the start of Lent Feb. 20 by celebrating Ash Wednesday Mass in the Basilica of St. Sabina. Earlier in the day, he told an audience of 2,000 children that penitential ashes are "the symbol of the relative value of everything that is earthly."

Problems of Rome — The Pope urged secular and religious priests of Rome Feb. 21 to "study together, reflect together, examine together, work together" in an effort to solve "the enormous mass of human and social problems" besetting the diocese. He also spoke of his concern over the shortage of priests and candidates for the priesthood.

The Pope Also:

• Condemned the arms race and praised "all worthy initiatives" for world peace, in an address Feb. 7 to students and faculty members of the NATO Defense College.

• Concelebrated a Mass for the sick and handicapped Feb. 11, the feast of Our Lady of Lourdes.

• Praised members of the Roman Association for Transporting Traveling Missionaries for their works of assistance to missionaries, during a private audience Feb. 15.

• Celebrated Mass Feb. 23 for Vittorio Bachelet, former Italian Catholic Action president, who was killed by terrorists Feb. 12.

Vatican Briefs:

• Father Agnellus Andrew, O.F.M., president of the International Catholic Association for Radio and Television, was named Feb. 15 titular bishop of Numana and vice president of the Pontifical Commission for Social Communications.

• Press officer Father Romeo Panciroli declared Feb. 20 that "conversations" of Peter Dragadze with Pope John Paul reported in the March issue of *Ladies' Home Journal* never took place.

Spiritual Formation in Seminaries

A Jan. 6 "Circular Letter on Some of the More Urgent Aspects of Spiritual Formation in Seminaries" was sent during the month to bishops throughout the world by the Congregation for Catholic Education. "Four of the most urgent guidelines" noted in the letter concerned:

• "a sense of interior silence," for openness to the formative influence of the word of God;

• "communion in the mystery of Christ," in Eucharist-centered spirituality;

• "a sense of penance," including the sacrament, a spirit of obedience and recognition of the need for self-denial;

• "filial love toward her who is the Mother of Jesus and whom Christ on the cross gave us as our Mother."

NATIONAL

United Way Decision — Msgr. Charles B. Mynaugh, director of communications for the Philadelphia archdiocese, said early in the month that the archdiocese had not been consulted concerning the decision of United Way of Southeastern Pennsylvania to exclude a coalition of feminist agencies from its fundraising and fund-allocation programs. Controversy erupted in January when United Way denied participation to Women's Way, two of whose six member organizations provided abortion and contraceptive counseling services. A United Way letter to the coalition said that its acceptance would "contravene

United Way's agreement with the archdiocese," reached in 1975.

Corporate Responsibility — Efforts of religious groups to challenge corporation policies with stockholder resolutions were expanding in number and scope, according to a compilation by Ursuline Sister Valerie Heinonen, research manager for the Interfaith Center on Corporate Responsibility. Her report indicated that more than 100 resolutions were filed with 80 corporations in 1980; comparative figures for 1979 were 80 and 60, respectively. Subjects of resolutions included occupational safety and health, nuclear energy, equal employment opportunities and banking practices.

Submarine Insignia — Bishop Francis F. Reh endorsed a directive of the education office of the Saginaw diocese against participation by Catholic school children in a contest to design an insignia for the new Trident submarine, USS Michigan, which he called a "horrifying instrument of unbelievable destructive power." He cited the specter of children being indoctrinated into a world of weaponry as the reason for his opposition to the contest.

Religious Services for Olympians — The local parish of St. Agnes and priests of Lake Placid, N.Y., took part in the efforts of an interdenominational religious affairs committee to provide services for athletes competing in the 1980 Winter Olympics.

Draft Registration — In a statement issued Feb. 15, the Administrative Board of the U.S. Catholic Conference declared:

• "No objection in principle" to registration of men "both in peacetime and in times of national emergency," given "convincing reasons."

• Opposition "to any reinstitution of military conscription except in the case of a national defense emergency."

• Support for "the right of selective conscientious objection."

• Opposition to "a universal or national service corps."

• Opposition to the registration and conscription of women.

Operation Rice Bowl — The fifth annual Operation Rice Bowl got underway with the start of Lent Feb. 20, for the purpose of raising funds to aid the poor in U.S. dioceses and to support overseas development and rehabilitation programs of Catholic Relief Services. Funds collected since 1976, realized from meal-time sacrifices, amounted to approximately $12 million.

U.S. Supreme Court Decisions — A 1974 New York law providing direct cash payment to non-public schools for the costs of certain state-mandated testing was upheld Feb. 20 in a 5-to-4 decision. In a majority opinion written by Justice Byron White, the Court ruled that reimbursement neither advanced the purposes of religion nor excessively entangled the state in the affairs of religion.

Efforts to regulate fund-raising by religious groups and other charitable organizations were dealt a setback the same day when the Court struck down a Schaumburg, Ill., ordinance permitting the solicitation of funds only by groups that spend a specific percentage of their money for charitable purposes. At least 20 states and dozens of cities had laws similar to the ordinance that was struck down.

No in Vitro Insurance Payment — Blue Cross-Blue Shield of Virginia in Richmond voted not to reconsider its policy of prohibiting medical insurance payments for preconception "experimental" services. Applicants for the program of *in vitro* fertilization at Norfolk General Hospital were told it was unlikely that they would receive any help, including Medicaid, in paying the $4,000 medical fee.

Domestic Violence — "The responsibility of the church community to respond to violence in the family is rooted in the concern for human dignity, human life and family life, and is consistent with Judaic-Christian principles of social justice." So stated Catherine Zandler, director of the Phoenix Diocesan Human Development Council, in testimony before the U.S. Civil Rights Commission in Phoenix. "Traditionally, there is a close relationship between the church and the family," she said; "and, historically, the role of the church as sanctuary supports involvement with those in crises who need shelter and safe abode." She added that the focus of concern should not simply be on "binding the wounds" of the abused but on creating an atmosphere which reduces the incidence of violence.

Bigotry — "Bigotry, with all of its ignorance and hatred, is very much alive . . . in our State of South Carolina," declared Father Thomas R. Duffy in an editorial published in the Jan. 17 edition of *The Catholic Banner,* newspaper of the Charleston diocese. The editorial was written in response to an article in which the Rev. Bob Jones wrote: "Where God is not enthroned in men's hearts and Christ is not worshipped, men turn to their idols and worship their false gods. Nowhere has this been so apparent as in the reception accorded the Antichrist figure known as Pope John Paul II." Father Duffy's editorial was answered in a February edition of the Bob Jones University publication. The retort said, in part: "The only 'Good News' of Romanism is Satanic deceit and a false gospel."

National Briefs:

• Lay leadership in the Church was the principal subject of the first Shared Ministry Conference held Feb. 1 to 3 in Washington, D.C.

• Father Barnabas Thiep was appointed to head the 175-member Vietnamese Congregation of the Mother Co-Redemptrix Community headquartered in Carthage, Mo. Priests and brothers of the community were engaged in service to Vietnamese refugees in the U.S.

• Sister Irene Kraus, the first woman and nun to hold the office, was installed Feb. 3 as chairlady of the board of trustees of the American Hospital Association.

• "The Catholic School: One of the Family," was the theme of Catholic Schools Week, Feb. 3 to 9.

• The Tennessee legislature became the 16th state body of its kind of approve a call for a constitutional convention to consider a human life amendment. The bill was sent to the governor for his signature.

• Bishop Thomas C. Kelly and Msgr. George G. Higgins of the U.S. Catholic Conference applauded the Feb. 13 announcement by President Carter that the U.S. would rejoin the International Labor Organization, from which it had withdrawn in 1977 because of the organization's high "level of politicalization."

• Margo Huston, a Pulitzer Prize winner with *The Milwaukee Journal,* was awarded Feb. 29 the 1980 By-Line Award of Marquette University's College of Journalism.

Abortion Payment Ordered

The U.S. Supreme Court, with a 6-to-3, one-sentence order, accepted for review the Jan. 15 decision of Federal District Court Judge John F. Dooling, Jr., against restrictions on abortion funding, and directed the resumption of such funding pending decision on its constitutionality.

INTERNATIONAL

Troubled Relations in Chile — More than six years after the overthrow of the Allende government in September, 1973, Church-state relations were still troubled over such issues as arbitrary arrests, the unknown fate of missing prisoners, labor policies, a land squeeze on small farmers and state control of Catholic universities. The most recent incident of such trouble was the dismissal of 17 professors from the Catholic University in Santiago on orders from the government-appointed rector, retired Admiral Jorge Swett. Opponents of the action called the dismissals a political purge.

Leaving Rhodesia — Bishop Donal Lamont of Umtali announced at a press conference Feb. 6 in Salisbury that he would leave Rhodesia because British authorities were asking him to reapply for the citizenship of which he was stripped when he was expelled from the country in 1977. He said: "It is quite extraordinary that I should be asked to reapply for citizenship," in view of the fact that British officials "absolved from guilt" the whites who rebelled by unilaterally declaring independence in 1965. "I, who was one of the few who publicly defied the rebel regime (of Ian Smith) .;. . am still a prohibited immigrant."

Superstitious Pilgrimages — Cardinal Jose Maria Bueno y Monreal of Seville issued another warning against pilgrimages promoted by a group claiming that some of its members had seen apparitions of the Blessed Virgin Mary at El Palmar de Troya. He said: "Upon learning that the (Carmelite) Order (of the Holy Face) is conducting a promotional campaign in 1980, we want to remind everyone that the condemnation and warning of 1970 are still valid. (Additional warnings were issued in 1972 and 1976.) The perpetrators of these deplorable events have violated the discipline of the Church and continue under excommunication for their schismatic defiance of the Pope and the bishops, having given no signs of repentance." The 1970 condemnation called the alleged apparitions and related events "superstitious" and "damaging."

Hostage Visit — The American hostages held in the U.S. embassy in Teheran since Nov. 4 were visited Feb. 8 by Msgr. John Nolan, president of the Pontifical Mission for Palestine and national secretary of the Catholic Near East Welfare Association, and Melkite-Rite Archbishop Hilarion Capucci. The visit was made with the approval of the Iranian government.

Hope and Terror in Lebanon — Maronite-Rite Patriarch Antoine Pierre Khoraiche of Antioch and other church and state officials inaugurated Feb. 11 a "Year of Hope" for Lebanese throughout the world. The patriarch noted that the proclamation might seem risky in war-torn Lebanon, but said it was designed to emphasize the power of love to overcome what he later called a "climate of terror." He said in a message for Lent that civil war in the country was "a Calvary of five years."

New Trial for Katz — Italy's Court of Cassation ruled Feb. 15 that American author Robert Katz, whose conviction on the same charges was overturned in 1978, must stand trial again for defaming Pope Pius XII in his book, *Death in Rome*. The decision said the book alleges that the Pope — "in a total lack of the spirit of charity and every humanitarian sentiment and in oblivion of his own pastoral mission" — approved the reprisal killing of 335 Italian men by German soldiers on Mar. 24, 1944.

Three Missionaries Killed — Vatican Radio reported the killing of three missionaries Feb. 18 and 19 in Africa: Father Wilfrid Lepine of Canada, during a robbery in Kampala, Uganda; Brother Arnold Knevels of Belgium, by bandits in the Ngozi diocese, Burundi; and Father Killian Huesser of Switzerland, by invaders of his mission at Brejena, Rhodesia.

Reaction to Dutch Synod — The Dutch bishops said that Catholics in The Netherlands were reacting favorably for the most part to conclusions reached at the special synod held Jan. 14 to 31 at the Vatican. The Vatican Radio report of Feb. 20 also indicated that some 'reservations were being expressed "here and there."

Transform Weapons — Cardinal Stefan Wyszynski, primate of Poland, called on all nations to change weapons into bread. During a liturgical ceremony at the Marian Shrine of Jasna Gora near Czestochowa, he said: "Make the missiles become bread. . . . May the world not send missiles and projectiles to the hungry. But may these arms, through human genius, be transformed into bread."

Hostages in Colombia — Archbishop Angelo Acerbi, papal nuncio to Colombia, and U.S. Ambassador Diego C. Asencio were among more than 50 diplomats and Colombian officials taken hostage by leftist guerrillas at the embassy of the Dominican Republic in Bogota Feb. 27.

International Briefs:

• Dominican Father John Orme Mills assumed office Feb. 1 as president of Rome-based Media International, an agency established in 1970 to promote the use of mass media in Christian apostolates.

• Cardinal Tomas O'Fiaich of Armagh named Father Gerard Clifford to serve as an ecumenical advisor, "to aid in healing the wounds of the past" between Catholics and Protestants in Northern Ireland.

• Vatican Radio reported Feb. 18 that there were 62,743 cloistered nuns in 2,651 convents throughout the world. One-third of the nuns were in Spain.

• Aid contributed by Australian Catholics to agencies working on behalf of Cambodian refugees amounted to $1.5 million.

Repression in Czechoslovakia

A report released by Jesuit headquarters in Rome confirmed that the Czechoslovakian government was continuing to violate religious rights and had "intensified its action" against Catholics in the past three years.

The report said that, although the government had signed the Helsinki accords on human rights in 1975:

• "All means possible continue to be used to hinder, to repress, to reduce even more the fundamental liberties of Catholics in the country."

• Priests cannot celebrate Mass outside their own parishes without government permission, cannot visit parishioners freely and cannot lead theological discussion groups. Violations of government regulations result in revocation of a priest's "state license to exercise his ministry."

MARCH 1980

VATICAN

Love and Life — "Only love, the soul of the Gospel, allows us to be always young," Pope John Paul told an audience of more than 8,000 elementary and secondary school students Mar. 2. He said: "Life, in fact, springs up only from love — and thus from another life — or else from a death faced lovingly, as that of Jesus." He urged his young listeners to "cultivate the most genuine love toward all, to be always disposed to help those in need, to pardon those who offend you, and to correct, or at least to pity, those who commit injustice."

Vocations to the Priesthood — The Holy Father called Mar. 2 for more vocations to the priesthood, in his first public appearance following a week-long retreat. He said: "Let us all pray that the ecclesiastical seminaries and novitiates be filled up again so that the individual churches and the (religious) communities as well . . . can look with trust to the future, assured that they will not lack the workers that the Lord sends 'into his harvest.' "

Nicaraguan Reconstruction — During a meeting Mar. 3 with two members of the Nicaraguan government — Violeta Chamorro and Daniel Ortega — the Pope said he encouraged reconstruction efforts underway to improve the conditions of people in their country. "The Church," he declared, "favors all efforts directed at the economic, social, cultural and political development of the human person." He had special praise for the regime's literacy program designed to teach more than 750,000 persons how to read and write.

Religious Life — "Without religious orders, without the consecrated life, the Church would not be fully itself," declared the Pope in a message delivered Mar. 7 to participants in a plenary meeting of the Congregation for Religious and Secular Institutes. He cited the relevance of the theme of the meeting, "The Role of Contemplation in Religious Life," to the "constant danger for apostolic workers . . . to get so involved in their own activity for the Lord as to forget the Lord of every activity."

Infallibility — The infallibility of the Church is a "gift of Christ," declared the Pope Mar. 9. He said: "To believe in the infallibility of the Church does not mean — in any way — to believe in the infallibility of man, but to believe in the gift of Christ; in that gift which allows fallible men to proclaim infallibly and to confess infallibly the truth revealed for our salvation. . . . The Church in our times . . . must have a particular certitude of the gift of Christ, of the gift of power, of the gift of holiness, of the gift of infallibility. The more it is aware of the weakness, sin-

fulness and fallibility of man, the more it must guard the certitude of those gifts which come from its Redeemer and Bridegroom."

Love vs. Violence — "The spiral of violence cynically continues to provoke and to sow hate and death" in Italy, the Holy Father stated Mar. 16 in an address to 10,000 members of the *Communione e Liberazione* youth group. He urged the young people: "Be, now and always, the spokesmen and transmitters of Christian joy. . . . To blind violence and inhuman hate respond with the transcendent force of love." Backgrounding the Pontiff's appeal was a scenario of violence in which 18 people were killed by political terrorists since the beginning of the year.

St. Joseph — The Pope called him "a man of action" during a general audience on his feast day, Mar. 19. While observing that the Gospels contain no words of St. Joseph but report only his actions, the Holy Father said: "His actions were ordinary, everyday actions, but they were full of deep spirituality and significance for the fulfillment of God's promise to mankind."

Church Will Aid Uganda — "I assure you that the Holy See is following closely the developments which are taking place in your country, and is sincerely interested in the welfare of all Ugandan people." So stated the Pope at a meeting with that nation's new ambassador to the Vatican, John Bernard Moli, Mar. 21, nearly a year after the overthrow of Ugandan dictator Idi Amin.

Benedictine Anniversary — The Pope made a flying visit Mar. 23 to Norcia, Italy, to take part in the start of a year-long celebration marking the 1,500th anniversary of the birth of St. Benedict, founder of the Benedictine Order and patron saint of Europe. He came, the Holy Father said, to pray "for peace in Europe and throughout the world . . . for human freedom . . . for social justice . . . for genuine love . . . for an end to the fearsome menace to mankind brought by modern means of destruction, and for an end to the menace hidden in the hearts of people who are ready to kill and destroy."

Sacrilegious Assassination — The Holy Father, in a message to Bishop Jose Eduardo Alvarez Ramirez of San Miguel, El Salvador, said his "soul was pierced with pain and affliction upon learning the fatal news of the sacrilegious assassination" Mar. 24 of Archbishop Oscar Arnulfo Romero y Galdamez of San Salvador. The Pontiff said his "priestly service to the Church remains sealed by the immolation of his life while offering the Eucharist." The archbishop was shot by an unknown assailant while preaching during a Mass in the chapel of the hospital where he lived in San Salvador.

The True Christian — "The Christian, to

authentically call himself such, must be practicing; he must live in the grace of God, observing all the commandments, and must realize concretely and continuously the command of charity." So stated the Pope Mar. 27 during a Mass for employees of firms working at the Vatican.

Appeal to the Lebanese — In a message addressed Mar. 30 to Maronite-Rite Patriarch Antoine Pierre Khoraiche of Antioch, Pope John Paul encouraged "all the people of Lebanon to open their hearts to hope and, confident of the help of God, to make their own contributions to the reconciliation and reconstruction of their country, in collaboration with state authorities, in order to prepare a happy future for the Lebanese nation." The country was beginning its sixth year of strife among Moslems, Christians, Palestinians and Israelis.

The Pope Also:
• Visited Mar. 4 the central offices of his Diocese of Rome, which is administered by a vicar and his staff.
• Expressed "deep-felt sorrow" over the Polish Airlines crash Mar. 14 near Warsaw in which 87 persons, including 22 members of the U.S. amateur boxing team, were killed.
• Was given the millionth copy of Italy's first interconfessional New Testament Mar. 20.

Vatican Briefs:
• Jesuit Father Roberto Tucci, director of the station, reported Mar. 21 that Vatican Radio was receiving an average of 30 to 40 letters a month from China.
• *L'Osservatore Romano* reported that Vatican delegates or observers attended a record number of 199 international meetings in 1979.

Augsburg Confession

Members of the Joint Roman Catholic-Lutheran Commission, sponsored by the Vatican Secretariat for Promoting Christian Unity and the Lutheran World Federation, published a statement on the Augsburg Confession Mar. 26 in which they said:
• Catholics and Lutherans confess a common faith "in the Triune God and the saving work of God through Jesus Christ in the Holy Spirit."
• "A broad consensus emerges on the doctrine of justification, which was decisively important for the Reformation."
• There is "a basic, if still incomplete, accord" on the understanding of the church.
(See separate entry.)

NATIONAL

Court Decisions — The U.S. Supreme Court, refusing Mar. 3 to review a lower court ruling, blocked efforts by a group of Catholics to obtain an injunction against merging of their Sacred Heart Parish with neighboring parishes in Chicago. The lower court ruling maintained that the suit against Cardinal John Cody was a religious matter in which civil courts had no jurisdiction.

The Massachusetts Supreme Judicial Court ruled Mar. 13 that a school prayer law, in effect for a little more than a month, was unconstitutional.

Music Suit Settlement — An $8.6 million copyright infringement suit by FEL Publications, Inc., against the National Conference of Catholic Bishops and the U.S. Catholic Conference was settled without any admission of liability. The settlement involved circulation by the bishops of a letter calling on persons engaged in parish music programs "to curb and discourage any abuse of authors' and composers' rights through the illegal use of copyrighted materials."

Superbaby Project — The project of California industrialist Robert Graham to produce "superbabies" by inseminating women with sperm from Nobel Prize winners was called an effort to "subvert nature and bend it according to arbitrary and egotistical concepts," by Father Domenico Capone, president of the Institute of Moral Theology of the Pontifical Lateran University. Sir Martin Pyle, a 1974 physics laureate, called the plan "absolutely and basically wrong." Sir Geoffrey Wilkinson, a chemistry laureate, said the whole idea was "biological nonsense." Associated Press reports from Denmark and Switzerland compared Graham's plan to the Nazi program for breeding a "master race."

J. P. Stevens Boycott — Six bishops in Georgia, Virginia, North and South Carolina issued a statement Mar. 12 in which they endorsed a union-organized boycott of J. P. Stevens products. They did so "with the hope that their action will serve to promote the workers' right to bargain collectively" with the company. The textile firm, despite having the worst record of NLRB violations in the country, took issue with the bishops' reasons for supporting the boycott.

Racism among Nuns — On the basis of a two-year-long study, four Sisters of St. Joseph of Cleveland recommended that their community make efforts to combat racism among its members and to revise its recruitment materials and methods in order to make them more appealing to blacks and Hispanics.

Health Care — The right to life "clearly implied the right to health care," readily accessible and at reasonable cost, declared Msgr. Bryan O. Walsh, executive director of the Catholic Service Bureau of Miami, in testimony before a Congressional subcommmittee. With respect to national health insurance, he said: "It is our position . . . that coverage should be universal, including all U.S. citizens, resident aliens and aliens admitted for employment. We also believe that benefits should include preventive services, physician services and all in-patient, out-patient and medical services."

Withdrawals from Citibank — Leaders of several religious organizations, at a press conference held late in the month in New York, announced withdrawal of payroll and other accounts from Citibank, claiming that it was "a full-fledged financial partner of South African apartheid." Withdrawals were announced by the National Council of Churches, the World Council of Churches, and the Board of Global Ministries of the United Methodist Church. Pledges to refrain from buying Citibank bonds, notes or certificates of deposit were made by four communities of sisters and one community of priests and brothers.

SEARCH a Partial Success — A study conducted in the San Francisco Bay area indicated that the SEARCH movement was successful in creating a climate for openness and discussion among teen-agers, but that it had little or no effect on participation by teen-agers in church-related activities.

Life-Support Removal — A state appeals court in New York, ruling in the case of terminally ill, comatose Brother Joseph Fox who died in January, upheld the right of his guardian to order the removal of life-sustaining medical equpment. The court continued consideration of the case after the death of the 82-year-old patient in order to "set guidelines for the future in cases of similar circumstances."

Sterilization Opposed — The bishops of Texas issued a statement late in the month in which they criticized a suggestion by Hilmar Moore, chairman of the state's Department of Human Resources, that women on welfare be sterilized if they have a second child. The bishops, without mentioning Moore by name, attacked the suggestion as "callous and abhorrent."

In a related development, Bishop Walter F. Sullivan of Richmond, in a pastoral letter published Feb. 28, called for the repeal of a law under which more than 8,300 patients in Virginia mental institutions were sterilized between 1924 and 1972. The sterilization program ended in 1972, but the law permitting it was still in effect.

National Briefs:

• Idaho's legislature became the 17th state body to approve a petition for a constitutional convention to adopt a right-to-life amendment.

• Wilfred R. Caron, former associate general counsel of the Securities Investor Protection Corporation of Washington, D.C., succeeded George E. Reed as general counsel of the National Conference of Catholic Bishops and the U.S. Catholic Conference.

• The Archdiocese of Newark announced it had received permission from the Vatican to introduce limited tenure for pastors, for an initial period of six years with possible renewal for another six years.

• Funds in the amount of $10,000 were contributed by U.S. Catholics through the National Conference of Catholic Bishops to the literacy program launched by the Nicaraguan government.

• Meetings during the month included those of: representatives of the U.S. bishops and the Women's Ordination Conference, Mar. 6 and 7 in Lemont, Ill.; 400 participants in the 17th National Workshop on Christian Unity, in Seattle; 91 members of the National Conference of Vicars for Religious, who elected Father Angelo Caligiuri of Buffalo their new president.

Anti-Christian Fiction

This was the description given by author Jim Bishop to the three-hour CBS-TV presentation, "The Day Christ Died," scheduled for broadcast early in April.

Bishop, after viewing the film Mar. 26, said it had no relation whatsoever to his book of the same title. He said he was amazed to learn that scriptwriter Edward Anhalt admitted he had not read the book, and that the bishops' Office for Film and Broadcasting had not condemned the film. He called the film a perversion of bible history.

INTERNATIONAL

No Church-State Separation — Voters in a referendum Mar. 1 and 2 overwhelmingly rejected a proposal for the complete separation of church and state in Switzerland. The vote was against the removal of special privileges to the country's two major religious bodies, the Catholic Church and the Evangelican Reformed Church. The Catholic Church received about $232 million a year from ecclesiastical taxes.

Long Kesh Prison Visit — Cardinal Tomas O'Fiaich of Armagh and Bishop Edward Daly of Derry spent most of Mar. 3 visiting the H Block of Maze Prison at Long Kesh, Northern Ireland. The purpose of their visit was to talk with prisoners convicted of terrorist offenses who were being detained under what the cardinal had earlier called "inhuman conditions" of filth and deprivation. The two prelates said in a statement that they believed "no effort should be spared in attempting to avert the development of a second H Block situation, with all the tragedy and anxiety which this entails for prisoners, prison staff, and the families of both."

Congenial Ecumenical Climate — The "new climate" in ecumenical relations provides greater opportunity than before for common witness among Christian churches, according to a report approved at the Feb. 18 to 23 meeting in Marseilles of the Catholic Church-World Council of Churches joint working group.

Plea for Cambodian Aid — Citing a "humanitarian duty above and beyond politics," Edouard Saouma, director general of the U.N. Food and Agriculture Organization, called for a $262 million food-aid program by the end of the year "to ease and end the tragic sufferings of the people of Kampuchea." He said: "The international community has the means and should have the will for this humanitarian duty. This opportunity for international solidarity should not elude us, because inertia and neglect will haunt us all."

Bad Land Policies in Brazil — Brazil's land policies help agribusiness and foreign investors but result in poverty for small farmers and exploitation of Indians, declared the nation's bishops in a statement entitled "The Church and the Land Problem." Citing official figures and statements, the bishops said, among other things:

• Fifty-two per cent of the nation's farms had fewer than 25 acres each.

• Despite legislation designed to protect Indian rights, no tribe had been spared from violence resulting from poor demarcation of land, land invasion by non-Indians, government mismanagement, and encroachment on native cultures and values.

Two Jesuits Removed — Police forcibly evicted two Jesuit priests Mar. 8 from an Indian mission in Guyana in what Bishop Benedict Singh of Georgetown called part of a campaign against church work among Indians. The priests were accused of anti-state activities.

Cardinals Visit China — Cardinal Roger Etchegaray of Marseilles visited China between Feb. 27 and Mar. 14 at the invitation of the Association of Chinese People for Friendship with Foreign Countries. He met and talked with Chinese officials of various grades but had no significant contact with people or officials of the National Association of Patriotic Catholics. He was denied permission to visit Bishop Ignatius Kung of Shanghai, imprisoned by government authorities for 26 years.

Cardinal Franz Koenig, president of the Vatican Secretariat for Non-Believers, ended a 10-day visit on Mar. 20. During his stay, according to the New China News Agency, he met with four bishops of the National Association of Patriotic Catholics. He was vaguely optimistic about change for the better in the government's attitude toward religion. Back in Vienna on Mar. 21, however, he said that "institutionally, no possibility exists of reconciliation between the (schismatic) Chinese Patriotic Catholics and the Vatican."

Threats to Human Values — Cardinal George Basil Hume of Westminster, addressing a seminar on world development Mar. 19 in London, listed six serious threats to human values in the contemporary world: disparity of wealth among nations, environmental dis-

orders, failure to control and distribute energy resources in an equitable manner, the possibility of nuclear war, hunger and lack of respect for life.

Second Revolution in Nicaragua — Catholics of all ages were among thousands of Nicaraguans who took an oath of commitment Mar. 24 as "crusaders" for a second revolution designed to teach reading and writing to more than 750,000 illiterate people and to develop their awareness of political and social issues affecting them.

Churches in Lithuania — *Novosti,* the Soviet press agency, reported that there were 630 Catholic churches in Lithuania and 72 students for the priesthood enrolled in the seminary at Kaunas. The report, circulated in the U.S. by the Soviet embassy in Washington, also said that Catholic churches were functioning in 10 of the 15 constituent republics of the Soviet Union. The reliability of the report was open to question.

International Briefs:

• Catholic and Anglican bishops in Scotland issued a statement in which they expressed agreement that marriage "is a lifelong commitment, with the purpose of providing a relationship within which two people both assist each other's growth and provide a stable environment for the upbringing of children." Differences remained, however, especially regarding mixed marriages and divorce.

• Bishop Franz Hengsbach of Essen, West Germany, was elected president of the Commission of Catholic Bishops' Conferences of the European Community. The commission was established Mar. 3.

• Cardinals George Basil Hume of Westminster and Johannes Willebrands, president of the Vatican Secretariat for Promoting Christian Unity, were among church dignitaries at the installation Mar. 25 of Robert Runcie as the 102nd Archbishop of Canterbury, head of the Church of England and titular head of the worldwide Anglican Communion.

Archbishop Romero Murdered

Archbishop Oscar Arnulfo Romero y Galdamez was shot to death by an unknown sniper Mar. 24 while preaching at a memorial Mass he was celebrating in the chapel of Divine Providence Hospital in San Salvador.

During his three years as head of the archdiocese, Archbishop Romero was a strong opponent of political violence and repression and a courageous advocate for justice and the rights of the poor. He stood in the middle between extremists of the right and the left. He was critical of a government that was unable or unwilling to take effective action to bring some semblance of order out of chaotic political, social and economic conditions. He finally became a victim of the hatred of parties to everything he was against.

APRIL 1980

VATICAN

Orientation of Studies — Scientific and cultural studies must be oriented to the achievement of "man's ultimate aim, which is the glory of God," Pope John Paul told nearly 6,000 university students Apr. 1. He added: "Only with the grace of Christ, with his light and strength, can man place himself on the supernatural level. . . . Moreover, only with this grace does it become possible for him also to realize all the proportionate good of his own human nature."

Praise for Archbishop Romero — The Pope praised slain Archbishop Oscar Romero for his commitment to the poor and alienated, and lamented the deaths of more than 40 persons Mar. 30 in the violence which disrupted his funeral in San Salvador. He expressed hope Apr. 2 that "the death of Archbishop Romero (might) bring a sign of peace and of reconciliation, a type of spiritual catharsis which might dissipate hate, violence and tensions among fellow citizens" of El Salvador.

Confessor — The Pope, unannounced, heard the confessions of about 30 persons on Good Friday, Apr. 4, in St. Peter's Basilica.

Patron of Ecologists — A papal bull declaring St. Francis of Assisi to be "the heavenly patron saint of ecologists" was delivered Apr. 7 to the Franciscan Friars at their convent in Assisi. The bull, signed by Pope John Paul, was dated Nov. 29, 1979. It said that the saint had "a high sentiment of all the Creator's works and, as if divinely inspired, he composed the beautiful 'Canticle of the Creatures.' Through those creatures, especially Brother Sun and Sister Moon and the stars, he gave the almighty and good Lord due praise, glory, honor and every blessing."

Liturgical Service — The Pope spoke in four languages before a congregation of mostly young liturgical ministers attending a Mass Apr. 9 in St. Peter's Basilica. He told the 9,000 servers, lectors, commentators and choir members that they had the "honor and good fortune of intimately approaching Christ" in their ministries.

Visit to Turin — More than a million people saw the Holy Father Apr. 13 during a 12-hour visit to Turin, the great industrial city known also as the city of fear where 13 people were killed by terrorists in the previous two years and 125 incidents of terrorist-related violence were reported in the previous 12 months. In a major address "to the city and world of work," the Pope condemned "social inequalities and other factors" which gave rise to terrorism and violence.

Morality — "A living morality is not made up merely of rules. It is built up when the rules are interiorized and made part of our inward convictions." So stated the Pope Apr.
16 in an address to more than 30,000 persons in St. Peter's Square.

Prayer and Action — The Pope told representatives of international lay organizations Apr. 18 that the relationship between prayer and action "is at the base of the great enterprise of evangelization and of construction of the world according to God's plan." Noting that lay persons are called to sanctify themselves and the world, he said they had multiple opportunities to give Christian witness in "all sectors of human existence — familial, professional, social, cultural, political."

Prayer for Vocations — The Holy Father asked all members of the Church to "evangelize, reflect and pray" for vocations to the priesthood and religious life in a message marking the 17th annual observance of a World Day of Prayer for Vocations, Apr. 27.

St. Catherine of Siena — St. Catherine of Siena was a "marvelous woman" whose Christian zeal is needed today "perhaps more than ever before," declared the Pope Apr. 29 at a Mass marking the sixth centenary of her death. He called her a living model of the saying, "Grace does not suppress but presupposes and perfects nature." He said her natural talents, enhanced by grace and her profound love for God and the Church, were the source of her strong influence on rulers of cities and kingdoms, princes and prelates of the Church, monks and theologians, many of whom frankly venerated her as 'teacher' and 'mother,' " She was proclaimed the second woman Doctor of the Church Oct. 4, 1970.

Social Justice — "The Church, while having the primary mission of directing man toward the supernatural and other-worldly goals which constitute the essential content of its message, can never forget the concrete, earthly situation of civil brotherhood." So stated the Pope Apr. 29 in an address to general council members of the Italian Center for Youth Initiative.

Meeting with Relatives of Hostages — Pope John Paul met Apr. 29 with four relatives of the 53 American hostages held in Iran since Nov. 4, 1979.

In related developments, the Pope sent personal appeals for peace to the world leaders most directly involved in the hostage situation: President Jimmy Carter, U.N. General Secretary Kurt Waldheim, Iranian President Abolhassan Bani-Sadr and the Ayatollah Khomeini.

The Pope Also:
• Received Apr. 5 the first copy of the new monthly Polish edition of *L'Osservatore Romano.*
• Encouraged the development of international economic cooperation at a meeting

Apr. 24 with European political and economic specialists.

• Held the first general papal audience on a Saturday and, for the first time in his pontificate, consecrated a church (dedicated to the honor of the 22 Ugandan Martyrs), Apr. 26.

Vatican Briefs:

• The recently published *Teachings of John Paul II* during the first 257 days of his pontificate contained the texts of 472 addresses and public documents. The *Teachings of Pope John Paul I* contained the speeches and writings of his 34-day pontificate.

• "We think that many are listening, but we don't know how many," said a Vatican spokesman of an Easter Mass beamed to China by Vatican Radio.

The Pope's Holy Week

The Holy Father had the leading part in eight major religious services during the most solemn week of the year.

While commemorating the triumphal entry of Christ into Jerusalem on Passion (Palm) Sunday, he hailed modern-day martyrs of the "Church of Silence." He concelebrated the Mass of Chrism with 1,000 priests in the morning of Holy Thursday; in the evening, he washed the feet of 12 elderly men during the Mass of the Lord's Supper. He led the Way of the Cross at the Colosseum Good Friday evening, and baptized 24 persons from 11 countries during ceremonies of the Easter Vigil. On Easter Sunday he celebrated Mass in St. Peter's Square before a throng of about 300,000 persons.

As he imparted his Easter blessing "to the City and the World," the Pope declared: "Christ rose again so that man could find the true meaning of existence; so that man could live his own life fully; so that man, who comes from God, could live in God." He urged everyone not to refuse a positive response to Christ, "for each one is responsible for his or her destiny and is the builder or destroyer of his or her own existence."

NATIONAL

Clergy Visits to Hostages — Father Darrell Rupiper of Omaha was one of three American clergymen who conducted Easter services for U.S. hostages held at the U.S. embassy in Teheran since Nov. 4, 1979.

Funding for Communication — The U.S. Catholic Conference announced funding in the amount of $667,654 for the first 18 projects under its new Catholic Communication Campaign. Campaign funds came from the proceeds of a national collection taken up in 1979, in which a total of more than $4 million was contributed.

Death Settles Case — Earle Spring, the center of a death-with-dignity controversy, died Apr. 6 at a Holyoke, Mass., nursing home at the age of 78. Death came a day before a panel of three doctors was scheduled to testify at a final court hearing to determine whether or not restored dialysis treatments should be continued.

Schismatic Sect — Bishop Lawrence Welsh of Spokane, in a statement published in the Apr. 10 edition of the *Inland Register*, declared that the Tridentine Latin Rite Church "cannot be identified as a legitimate expression of the Roman Catholic faith." The church, founded by schismatic Bishop Francis K. Schuckardt in 1968 in Couer d'Alene, Ida., used an unauthorized version of the Mass, refused to recognize as true popes the successors of Paul VI, and claimed that reforms of the Second Vatican Council were in "complete contradiction to past papal decrees and doctrines of the Church."

Catholic Press Statistics — Five hundred and nine Catholic newspapers and magazines in the United States and Canada had a total circulation of 27,097,851 in 1979, according to the 1980 edition of the *Catholic Press Directory*, published by the Catholic Press Association.

NCEA Convention — More than 9,500 delegates attended the 77th convention of the National Catholic Educational Association Apr. 7 to 10 in New Orleans. The primary focus was on "Catholic Educators: Partners with the Family," but speakers and related events drew attention to additional aspects of Catholic education, including inner-city schools, non-Catholic students, systematic teaching of religion, seminary training and teacher unions. The prestigious C. Albert Koob Merit Award was presented to Msgr. Wilfrid H. Paradis, project director for the National Catechetical Directory, *Sharing the Light of Faith.*

Ethics Courses — Sissella Bok, co-director of a study conducted under the auspices of the Hastings (N.Y.) Center, reported that "there are by now some 12,000 ethics courses across the country in institutions of higher learning. Most did not exist 12 years ago. Now there is a groundswell of concern about ethical issues."

Ten Commandments — The Kentucky Supreme Court upheld Apr. 22 the constitutionality of a 1978 state law requiring that a copy of the Ten Commandments be posted in public school classrooms. Justice James Stephenson, who voted to uphold the law, said it was his view "that the constitutional wall separating church and state is in no danger" because of the law. He also said: "Tax money is not involved. Neither the school, child nor the faculty member is required to do anything, and the Ten Commandments does have historical as well as religious significance."

Cuban Refugees — As the first of thousands of people fleeing from Cuba began arriving in Florida late in the month, John McCarthy, executive director of Migration and

Relief Services, U.S. Catholic Conference, gave the U.S. government "blanket assurance that there will be jobs and homes for these refugees."

Washington for Jesus — Three priests active in the charismatic movement — Fathers Michael Scanlon, John Bertolucci and John Randall — were national sponsors and speakers at the Washington for Jesus rally Apr. 28 and 29. Father Randall, who addressed a throng of approximately 200,000 people Apr. 29, said, "The significance of the Washington for Jesus rally is that it is a movement of the little people of God" giving witness to their Christian faith.

New Secretary of State — Senator Edmund S. Muskie, the first Catholic named to the office, was chosen by President Carter to succeed Cyrus Vance as Secretary of State.

Vance resigned because of objections, made known to the President in advance, to the ill-fated attempt Apr. 25 to rescue the American hostages held in Teheran.

National Briefs:

• Father Richard McBrien, professor of theology at Boston College, was appointed chairman of the Department of Theology at the University of Notre Dame.

• Ceremonies for the dedication of the Shrine of *La Virgen de San Juan del Valle* were held Apr. 19 and 20 in San Juan, Texas. Devotion to Mary under that title originated early in the 17th century in Mexico.

• Father Paul Marx, O.S.B., was appointed president of the Human Life Center at St. John's University, Collegeville, Minn.

No Evidence of Women Priests

A committee of the Fellowship of Catholic Scholars contested a statement by a task force of the Catholic Biblical Association that evidence "points toward the admission of women to the priestly ministry." A report issued Apr. 28 with a statement by James Hitchcock, president of the fellowship, said that the task force:

• went beyond New Testament evidence and "mistakenly confused women's participation in several ministries of the early Church as a title to priestly ordination which, on the evidence of the New Testament, is a ministry of a different character";

• erred in using St. Paul's assertion of the basic human equality of both sexes before God as an argument favoring a basic sameness in role-playing in the Church;

• distorted "the obvious role of the Twelve and the manner in which the early Church made decisions concerning the priesthood and the Church's leadership."

The fellowship committee concluded: "Since the biblical evidence is often inconclusive, the evidence by itself is not a decisive factor in settling the question whether women are eligible for ordination to the priesthood. On the other hand, we assert that any claim that the New Testament evidence 'points toward the admission of women to the priestly ministry' is incorrect and not in accord with the understanding of the early Church itself."

INTERNATIONAL

No More Honor Ceremonies — Mother Teresa of Calcutta, winner of the 1979 Nobel Peace Prize, said Apr. 1 that she would no longer participate in ceremonies honoring her. "The public gaze that has fallen on me after I received the Nobel Prize is hindering normal work of service to the poor, and I have decided not to participate in any more receptions," she announced.

Ceremonies Cancelled — A spokesman for the Archdiocese of San Salvador announced Apr. 2 that all outdoor religious ceremonies of Holy Week and Easter would be cancelled in order to lessen the likelihood of more violence following the murder Mar. 24 of Archbishop Oscar Romero. Burial services for the archbishop were disrupted Apr. 30 by gunfire, bombing and panic which took a toll of at least 40 lives, and it was feared that additional disturbances might exacerbate tensions in El Salvador.

Archbishop Lefebvre in Venice — Dissident Archbishop Marcel Lefebvre concelebrated the unauthorized Tridentine version of the Mass with eight priests Apr. 7 before a congregation of nearly 700 people in Venice. The event was another demonstration of the archbishop's defiance of the directives of the Second Vatican Council.

New Status for Hans Kung — Father Hans Kung announced that he would continue as a professor of ecumenical theology and director of the Institute for Ecumenical Research at the University of Tubingen but would no longer be connected with the department of Catholic theology there. The Vatican Congregation for the Doctrine of the Faith declared in December, 1979, that he could not be considered a Catholic theologian.

Tension in Mozambique — Tension between Christian churches and the socialist government in Mozambique intensified during the past year, according to Freedom of Faith, an interfaith human right group. The Marxist-influenced Mozambique Liberation Front in control of the government since the achievement of independence from Portugal in 1975 was highly suspicious of the Catholic Church. The Church "has been stung by the confiscation of much of its property and facilities, notably schools and hospitals," Freedom of Faith said, and added that there were recent "reports of detention of a number of clergy and indications that the government would take over and administer all church property."

Ordination and Protest — Vatican Radio reported that more than 5,000 persons crowded in and around the cathedral at Ljubljana, Yugoslavia, for the ordination Apr. 13 of Archbishop Alojzij Sustar. In attendance, "for the first time at a religious rite of this kind," were four unnamed political leaders.

Archbishop Franjo Kuharic of Zagreb, in an Easter message published in the Catholic press, protested against systematic atheistic propaganda in the mass media and in schools. He said: "A systematic atheization is . . . present in our country in all spheres of instruction and education, from kindergarten to the university. This is a fact. . . . We should repeatedly state that this is a violation of the fundamental rights of believing parents when their children are educated in a materialistic ideology which leads to atheism.

Church Representation in Nicaragua — The Catholic Church was among organizations assigned representation Apr. 17 in the 47-member Council of State, the legislative advisory body formed by the country's ruling junta. There was disagreement within the Church, however, over procedures for selecting representatives and their need for appropriate ecclesiastical permission.

Three priests, reportedly with temporary approval of local bishops, were already serving in the government, Fathers: Miguel D'Escoto, foreign minister, Ernesto Cardenal, minister of culture, and Fernando Cardenal, director of the National Literacy Crusade. A fourth priest, Father Xavier Gorostiaga, an economic adviser to the planning ministry, was not a member of the government.

Zimbabwe — Rhodesia became the new nation of Zimbabwe as Prime Minister Robert Mugabe took office Apr. 18, after seven years of civil war in which an estimated 25,000 persons lost their lives. Hope began to rise for a return to normalcy in the work of the Church.

Abortion — Findings of a study issued by the World Health Organization indicated that abortion, whether legal or illegal, was "the most widely used method of fertility regulation." The study also said that "teen-age pregnancy has reached a disturbing level in many countries," and that about half of all pregnancies did not proceed to full term.

Christian Witness of Charismatics — Spiritual experience and social commitment are equally essential in providing true Christ witness, Cardinal Leo J. Suenens told 10,000 participants in the third annual convention of Italian charismatics Apr. 26 in Rimini. He said they should be "in front of God and at the same time open to service to man, apostles of Christ and present in the heart of the city."

Religious Repression in the U.S.S.R. — Amnesty International, in a report released Apr. 29 in the U.S., said that in 1979 at least 25 Ukrainian Catholics and about 10 Jehovah's Witnesses were believed imprisoned because of their religious activities.

Caribbean Boat People — The first hundreds of what eventually became a flood of more than 100,000 persons fleeing from Cuba arrived in Florida by the end of the month. Their entry, together with that of a large number of Haitians, as undocumented aliens posed serious problems to the Immigration and Naturalization Service and began straining the relief and resettlement capabilities of Migration and Refugee Services, U.S. Catholic Conference, and other voluntary agencies.

International Briefs:

• Divine Word Father Edicio de la Torre was freed from jail in the Philippines after being under detention for five years without trial on allegations of conspiracy to commit rebellion and possession of subversive materials.

• Archbishop Angelo Acerbi, papal nuncio to Colombia, and U.S. Ambassador Diego C. Asencio were among 16 diplomats freed in Havana Apr. 27 after spending 61 days as hostages in Bogota, Colombia.

Religion in China

Cardinal Franz Koenig, in an interview published Apr. 25 after his visit to China in March, said that Catholics there were divided into two camps, consisting of members of the National Association of Patriotic Catholics, which rejected ties with the Pope, and of "a great number of priests, sisters and lay persons in work camps and other situations who remain faithful to the Pope."

Describing a meeting with the chairman of the government's Religious Affairs Committee, he said: "He told me that the government supports with all its means the Patriotic Church because it follows a policy of complete independence from every foreign power and from every colonialism. . . . I tried to explain to him that Rome, the Holy See, is only the center of the great world Catholic community, which is not linked to any power. He said he knew this, but they could not allow any church to have foreign ties."

The Standing Committee of the Christian Movement for Self-Government, Self-Support and Self-Propagation invited Catholics to participate in the formaton of a National Association of Christian Churches in China. The stated purposes of the association were "to strengthen relations with Christian communities everywhere, . . . help Christians in their endeavors to glorify God, and bring benefit to men and women." The invitation was issued from a meeting in March of the Three-Self Movement, a government-approved organization like the National Association of Patriotic Catholics. The movement, founded in 1951, was reported to be active again, after being dissolved by the government in the mid-1960s.

MAY 1980

VATICAN

Religious Instruction in Hungary — Pope John Paul, in a letter published in the May 8 edition of *L'Osservatore Romano,* urged Hungarian Catholics to press the government for religious instruction in state schools. He said: "I express the deep hope that Catholic parents, taking advantage of the possibilities offered by legal provisions, will request for their children that religious instruction be given in state schools in order that they can progress in their spiritual formation."

Papal and Patriarchal Blessings — The Pope met Syrian Orthodox Patriarch Mar Ignatius Yacoub III May 14 and, with him, blessed the people at a general audience that day. It was the first time a non-Catholic prelate had joined the Pope on the stage of the audience hall to impart such a blessing.

Missionary Commitment and Support — "A generous missionary commitment is the surest sign of a Church that is not standing still," declared the Holy Father at a meeting May 17 with national directors of pontifical mission aid societies. The Pontifical Missionary Works Council reported that in 1979 the Pontifical Work for the Propagation of the Faith distributed more than $71 million for the support of missionary work, and the Society of St. Peter the Apostle for Native Clergy disbursed more than $22 million for the training of candidates for the priesthood. The Pontifical Society of the Holy Childhood approved subsidies of about $7 million for child care programs in Third World countries.

Communications Day — The relationship between the family and mass media was the theme of the Pope's message for the 1980 observance of the World Day of Social Communications May 18. He said: "It is the duty of parents to educate themselves and their children to appreciate the value of communication, to make an intelligent choice among programs available to them, and then, having made that choice, to make a reasonable and conscious judgment as to whether the message coming from the program merits to be accepted or rejected."

Birthday Greeting, Message and Parish Visit — Sixty-year-old Pope John Paul was the recipient of birthday greetings May 18 from more than 50,000 young people attending a two-day convention of GENFEST, a festival of the new generation. He told them in response how necessary it was for them to build a world united "against those ideologies which have a common materialistic base and which . . . can only result in a fear of mutual destruction." GENFEST, with a membership of about 120,000 in 137 countries, was the youth branch of the Focolari Movement of lay spiritual renewal.

Also on his birthday, the Holy Father visited a 60-year-old parish in Rome where he met with more than 10 groups of parishioners and was given a 231-pound birthday cake bearing his seal and motto.

Dialogue with Non-Christians — Prayer is an essential element of Catholic life and an important aspect of dialogue with non-Christians, the Pope told a group of 19 Japanese bishops May 20. "In this contemplative aspect of the Church's life in Japan," he said, "is there not an excellent element of dialogue with your non-Christian brethren who in their own ancient traditions have given a place of prominence to contemplation?"

Response to Demands of the Gospel — The Pope, at a meeting May 23 with priests of the Order of Our Lady of Mercy, urged them to be totally available to meet the demands of the Gospel. He praised the Mercedarians for their commitment to work among "the most afflicted and oppressed members of the Mystical Body of Christ."

Liturgical Instruction — An "Instruction on Certain Norms concerning Worship of the Eucharistic Mystery" — entitled *Inaestimabile Donum* ("The Priceless Gift") and approved by Pope John Paul Apr. 17 — was released by the Congregaton for the Sacraments and Divine Worship May 23. The congregation called for the correction of reported abuses. (See separate entry.)

Crisis in the French Church — In a videotaped message scheduled for broadcast in France May 27, Pope John Paul said the Church there was "in a special condition" marked by a "crisis of growth." He did not spell out what he meant, but it appeared he was referring to criticisms that there had been disarray in the French Church since the Second Vatican Council, evidenced by a steep decline in vocations to the priesthood and religious life, a slump in church attendance, weak leadership by bishops, strong factionalism on the left and right, and general decline in religious belief and practice.

Autonomy of Bishops' Conference — The Pope told members of the Italian Bishops' Conference May 29 that they should take up their "own responsibilities" and "revive fully the collegial tradition in force in the Church ever since the most ancient times." Addressing "the problem of a correct and well understood autonomy of the bishops' conference for defining and carrying out its own pastoral duties," he said: "This problem is peculiar to Italy since it can seem that the special links through which it has been and is related to the papacy and the Holy See at times have placed and are placing the bishops' conference itself in a shadow. . . . To dissipate this ambiguity," the conference should "know how to revive the collegial tradition in force in the Church ever since the most ancient times. . . . You . . . are the ones in charge of the Church in Italy, and you must be so in an ever more aware and incisive manner."

The Pope Also:

• Recognized the Committee for the Defense of the Rights of Vatican Employees as a legitimately constituted representative body.

• Confirmed 600 young people in St. Peter's Basilica on the solemnity of Pentecost, May 25.

Vatican Briefs:

• Thirty-three recruits were sworn in as Swiss Guards on May 6, the 453rd anniversary of the sack on Rome during which 147 members of the corps lost their lives while defending Pope Clement VII. The addition of the recruits brought total membership of the corps to 98.

• The Pontifical Commission for the Ministry of Migration and Tourism met in plenary assembly May 27 to 29 for the purpose of considering instructions for priests engaged in ministry to people on the move.

Pastoral Visit to Africa

Pope John Paul, on the 5th trip of his pontificate, made a pastoral visit May 2 to 12 to six countries in Black Africa — Zaire, the Congo, Kenya, Ghana, Upper Volta and the Ivory Coast. His main purpose, he said, was to "help the growth of Christian faith in those fields that are already ripe for harvest." (See separate entry.)

NATIONAL

First Nun in Statuary Hall — The statue of Mother Joseph Pariseau of the Sisters of Providence was dedicated May 1 in National Statuary Hall in the U.S. Capitol. Mother Joseph, thus honored by the State of Washington, established 29 institutions — schools, orphanages and hospitals — during the 46 years she spent in the Northwest. She died in 1902.

Statement on Land — Bishops of 44 midwestern dioceses, at the meeting of the National Conference of Catholic Bishops which ended May 1, unanimously approved a statement based on the concept that land is a gift from God to be used for the benefit of all people. The statement, entitled "Strangers and Guests: Toward Community in the Heartland," analyzed land issues in the light of Judeo-Christian principles of stewardship and proposed specific measures designed to bring about "justice in the distribution and use of the earth's resources." The document was the product of a two-year process that involved 12,000 people at 400 open hearings held in a 12-state area.

NFPC Convention — One hundred and 50 delegates from about 100 priests' councils and senates attended the 13th annual convention of the National Federation of Priests' Councils which ended May 1 in Tucson. The theme of the meeting was "Family Ministry and Church Structures." Pastoral and social issues were the subjects of numerous resolutions. Father Neil McCaulley of Pittsburgh was elected the fifth president of the federation.

Payment by Pauline Fathers — The First Bank Minneapolis was holding $2.9 million in principal and interest for transfer to the holders of bonds issued by the financially troubled Pauline Fathers of Doylestown, Pa. The bank was serving as trustee for the funds on behalf of about 1,500 bondholders. Repayment by the Paulines was scheduled to take place under the terms of a basic settlement worked out in 1979.

CPA Convention — Social justice was one of the principal themes of the Catholic Press Association convention held May 12 to 16 near Nashville in conjunction with the Religious Communications Congress. The communicators — journalists, broadcasters, editors, producers — were urged by Pope John Paul in a videotaped message to work for "the service of humanity." The CPA honored Father Thurston H. Davis, S.J., former editor of *America,* with its St. Francis de Sales Award.

Holy Day Proposal — The U.S. Bishops' Committee on the Liturgy began surveying May 13 the opinions of bishops throughout the country concerning a proposal for the observance of only two, instead of six, holy days of obligation a year, the solemnities of Christmas and the Immaculate Conception. If approved, the proposal would require ratification by the Holy See.

Ku Klux Klan — As Justice Department figures indicated a 450 per cent increase in Ku Klux Klan activity, Bishop Raymond J. Gallagher and the Priests' Senate of the Diocese of Lafayette-in-Indiana warned Catholics against membership in the organization. They said in a statement: "We are aware of explicit efforts to recruit Catholics to join the forces of overt racism. . . . Catholics should avoid all association with such groups as the Ku Klux Klan and any other explicitly racist organizations. It is ironic that an organization which in times past persecuted and oppressed Catholics is now recruiting them."

Campaign for Human Development — Father Marvin Mottet, executive director, reported that 1979 contributions to the Campaign for Human Development were expected to reach more than $8.7 million. He said results of the appeal demonstrated "a continuing commitment on the part of the Catholic community to social justice issues and to addressing the causes of poverty." He also reported that about 650 funding requests for self-help projects had been received for 1980.

Christian Brothers' Celebration — Members of the religious community of the Brothers of the Christian Schools marked the 300th anniversary of their founding with a special day of prayer and thanksgiving May 24 at Manhattan College, New York City.

Catholic Population — The 1980 edition of *The Official Catholic Directory,* published by P. J. Kenedy and Sons, reported a U.S. Catholic population of 49,812,178, as of Jan. 1.

Reconciliation Sought in Miami — In the wake of a disastrous weekend of rioting, Archbishop Edward A. McCarthy and other religious leaders in the Miami area called for the observance of a weekend of reconciliation May 25 and 26. They appealed for "a special time of prayer, of reconciliation, of renewed commitment to interracial justice and harmony." Rioting broke out May 17 after four white ex-policemen were acquitted by an all-white jury of all charges in connection with the beating to death in December, 1979, of Arthur McDuffie, a black insurance salesman. The violence in the Liberty City section of Miami resulted in 18 deaths, injuries to more than 300 persons, and property-related damage amounting to about $100 million.

National Briefs:

• The National Conference of Catholic Bishops concluded the last of its semiannual meetings in Chicago May 1.

• More than 200 people participated in the fifth National Workshop on Christian-Jewish Relations which ended May 1 in Dallas.

• The annual spring period of prayer for good crops and harvests, sponsored by the National Catholic Rural Life Conference, ended May 4.

• The Massachusetts Supreme Judicial Court ruled May 13 that Earle Spring, a 78-year-old kidney patient, should have been allowed to die, according to his family's wishes, without kidney dialysis treatments. Spring died of heart failure Apr. 6 while still receiving dialysis treatments.

• The bishops of Indiana, in a statement released May 21, endorsed efforts of field workers, many of them migrants, to organize unions and bargain collectively.

• Honored: Sister Theresa Kane by the *U.S. Catholic,* for furthering the cause of women in the Church; Frederick O'Neal, president of the Catholic Interracial Council of New York, with the George M. Cohan Award of the Catholic Actors' Guild; Lloyd M. Bucher, former commander of the U.S.S. Pueblo, with the Distinguished Alumnus Award of Boys Town.

Priests Won't Run Again

Father Robert F. Drinan, S.J., a five-term member of the House of Representatives, announced May 5 that, in deference to an order from Father Pedro Arrupe, superior general of the Jesuits, he would not run for office again in the fall of 1980. Father Arrupe said his directive reflected "the express wish" of Pope John Paul. The refusal of permission for Father Drinan to seek office again was in line with the Pope's convictions about the proper role of the priest. Father Drinan said he accepted the decision "with regret and pain."

Another priest, Norbertine Father Robert J. Cornell of De Pere, Wis., made an announcement similar to Father Drinan's on May 6. He had served in the Congress for four years in the mid-70s and had been hoping to regain the seat he lost in 1978.

(See Priests in Politics.)

INTERNATIONAL

Religious Activity in Lithuania — The 40th issue of the underground *Chronicle of the Catholic Church in Lithuania* reported that the Soviet government was troubled by the religious activities of young people. While giving an account of a Mass and procession at the National Shrine of Our Lady of Siluva, the publication noted: "Even though Soviet law forbids youngsters to serve Mass, take part in processions, sing in the choir or participate in group religious instruction, these laws are blatantly ignored throughout Lithuania."

Priest Arrested Again — Seventy-eight-year-old Father Stanislaus Shen, one of several priests released from detention in recent years, was arrested again May 5 in Shanghai and returned to the labor camp where he had spent more than 20 years. He was accused of hampering production and modernization, according to sources in Shanghai.

Papal Representative at Tito Funeral — Archbishop Achille Silvestrini, secretary of the Council for the Public Affairs of the Church, represented Pope John Paul II at the state funeral of Marshal Tito May 8 in Belgrade. Despite a background of persecution of the Church during the 35-year regime of Tito, Vatican City and Yugoslavia maintained diplomatic relations.

Killings in Guatemala — "Priests are being killed in Guatemala because they are involved with the poor," declared Miguel Angel Albizures, head of the National Labor Center. "They are not the only ones," he added, in comment about the death and disappearance of missionaries. "Lay helpers as well as student, labor and peasant leaders are being killed as soon as they succeed in any kind of organizing effort for the people." The most recent casualties were Father Walter Voordeckers, who was machine-gunned to death at his parish May 12, and Father Conrado de la Cruz and a catechist who were kidnapped May 1. It was thought that they were victims of the terrorist activities of the Secret Anti-Communist Army.

Torture in Colombia — Two bishops and Priests for Latin America went on record in support of an Amnesty International report denouncing torture and killings in Colombia. The clerical group said: "In 1979, Justice Minister Hugo Escobar boasted of holding 68,000 political prisoners, causing the distress of so many families who had their homes searched and their loved one disappear under arrest, torture and assassination." According to the report:

• There were 33 prison and detention centers in the country.

• Security laws facilitated political arrest, detention without trial, torture and summary trials before military courts.

• Approximately 48 Indians in Cauca Province were murdered under security laws.

Liturgical Abuses — Cardinal G. Emmett Carter warned Toronto archdiocesan clergy against "certain abuses which appear to be creeping into our liturgical celebration and which I would ask you to correct immediately." Observing that some of the abuses stemmed from the notion that the ordained priesthood is not different from the priesthood of the faithful, he said: "This is specifically rejected by the documents of the (Second Vatican) Council and should be corrected not only in its general thrust but also in its liturgical application." Some of the abuses singled out by the cardinal were criticized by the Congregation for the Sacraments and Divine Worship (see Norms for Eucharistic Worship.)

Cooperation in Zimbabwe — In a message marking the independence Apr. 18 of Zimbabwe, formerly Rhodesia, the bishops pledged their cooperation with the government of Prime Minister Robert Mugabe "in the service of the people." They called such cooperation "the purpose, task and goal of Zimbabwe as a state." During the seven years of civil war that preceded independence, the bishops' Justice and Peace Commission was active in efforts to reconcile differences between the black majority and the dominant white minority.

Strike Support — A long strike by about 150,000 auto and metal workers in the industrial belt surrounding San Paulo had the support of Brazilian Cardinal Paulo Evaristo Arns. He, along with Auxiliary Bishop Claudio Humes, said in a joint statement that "strikes are among the just means for making demands, and the Constitution acknowledges that right. ... The Church would not be Christian if it did not provide its support for workers trying to preserve their dignity and defend their rights without being humiliated." Rights to job security, worker participation in management decisions, freedom to organize, true labor representation and pay scales were among the issues involved in the strike. Archdiocesan authorities not only offered churches and other sites to the strikers for meetings, but also sponsored a strike fund through collections in 364 parishes.

Quebec Referendum — Although the bishops of Quebec Province issued two statements on the subject, they took no position regarding the question of acceptance or rejection of a recommendation by the provincial government to negotiate sovereignty-association with the rest of Canada. The predominantly French-speaking electorate voted 59.5 to 40.5 per cent against the recommendation, which could have led to independence of Quebec with economic ties to the Canadian Confederation.

Ecumenical Commission for Religious — Twelve Catholic and Anglican superiors general of religious communities, at an ecumenical consultation May 25 to 27 in Rome, agreed to form a permanent commision to promote ecumenism among religious. The consultation, the third of its kind, was sponsored by the Catholic unions of superiors general of male and female institutes, and by the religious advisory boards of the Anglican Church.

International Briefs:

• Melkite-Rite Archbishop Hilarion Capucci was a key figure in the transfer of the bodies of eight American servicemen from Iran to the United States, May 6. The men were casualties of the aborted attempt to rescue 53 Americans held hostage since Nov. 4, 1979, at the U.S. embassy in Teheran.

• Hundreds of thousands of people took part May 12 and 13 in ceremonies commemorating the 63rd anniversary of the apparitions of Mary to three shepherd children at Fatima, Portugal.

• Ralph Wendell Burhoe of Chicago, noted for his writings on relations between science and religion, was given the 1980 Templeton Prize (of $198,000) for Progress in Religion.

• At least four priests and five Protestant ministers were among the thousand or more people arrested in South Korea in the wake of the military coup which overthrew the government May 17.

British Pastoral Congress

About 2,000 delegates variously representative of the more than four million Catholics of England and Wales took part in the National Pastoral Congress held May 2 to 6 in Liverpool.

A number of recommendations emanating from discussion groups were handed over, without vote, to the bishops for their consideration. Among the recommendations were those calling for: re-examination of church teaching on contraception; admitting non-Catholic partners in mixed marriages to Communion on special occasions; consideration of the ordination of women and married men to the priesthood; more explicit commitment of the Church to social activism; possible membership in the British Council of Churches.

JUNE 1980

VATICAN

End of Visit to France — The Holy Father returned to the Vatican June 2 after a four-day visit to France. (See separate article.)

Appeal to Germans — Pope John Paul urged some 70,000 persons taking part in the 86th *Katholikentag* June 4 in West Berlin to "say 'yes,' in the name of the love of Christ, to all people, especially those who by themselves cannot defend their human dignity, their right to life and liberty." He made the appeal in a special message to the "Catholic Day" lay apostolate meeting focused on the theme, "The Love of Christ Is Stronger."

Meeting with Georgian Orthodox Patriarch — Pope John Paul and Georgian Orthodox Catholicos-Patriarch Iliya met "as brothers in Christ" June 6 at the Vatican. It was the first such meeting in history. The Pope spoke of Christian unity as "our duty to Christ . . . our duty to our fellowmen . . . our duty to each other." The Patriarch called Catholic-Orthodox division a "misfortune," and added: "Despite this sad phenomenon, between our two churches there have always been good mutual relations which found their expression in cultural, spiritual and scientific collaboration."

Address to Indonesian Bishops — The following key points were emphasized by the Pope in an English-language address June 7 to a group of bishops from Indonesia.

• "Primacy must be given to the word of God as the basis for truly effective solutions" to pastoral problems. "The authentic interpretation of the word of God and its applications to life have been made by the Church over the centuries, and this interpretation and these applications form part of the patrimony of Catholic life today."

• "In our ministry at the service of life, we are called to testify to the fullness of the truth we hold so that all may know the stand of the Catholic Church on the utter inviolability of human life from the moment of conception."

Corpus Christi Celebration — The Holy Father celebrated Mass and took part in a procession of the Blessed Sacrament in St. Peter's Square to mark the solemnity of Corpus Christi June 8. He said in a brief homily: "This is the day on which we not only receive the Host of eternal life but also walk with our gaze fixed on the Eucharistic Host, all of us together in procession. This is a symbol of our pilgrimage with Christ in our earthly life."

St. Catherine of Siena — Pope John Paul called St. Catherine of Siena an exemplary model for all members of the Church, in an apostolic letter commemorating the sixth centenary of her death. "In her," the letter said, "the Holy Spirit made shine marvelous riches of grace and humanity through the gifts of knowledge, intellect and science, with which the human mind becomes extremely sensitive to divine inspiration." St. Catherine, a Doctor of the Church, was the author of 381 letters and other writings, was influential in bringing about an end to the Avignon papacy, and is venerated along with St. Francis of Assisi as a patron saint of Italy.

Vietnamese Seminary — The reopening of the Hanoi seminary, closed since the 1950s, was noted by the Pope June 17 in an address to a group of Vietnamese bishops.

Pope and President — Pope John Paul and President Jimmy Carter discussed human rights, peace and problems of the Middle East during a presidential visit to the Vatican June 21. The Holy Father, speaking in public after private conversation with the President, said: "The Holy See is aware of the worldwide aspect of the responsibility that falls to the United States. It is likewise conscious of the risks involved in facing this responsibility. But, despite all inconveniences and problems, despite human limitations, governments of good will must continue to work for peace and for international understanding in the control and reduction of armaments, in the promotion of the North-South dialogue, and in furthering the advancement of developing nations."

Full Understanding of Christ — "The full understanding of Christ cannot be achieved outside the Church, since to it — and not to others — was entrusted the duty to announce the mystery, under the guidance of the Spirit, 'to all nations . . . until the end of the world.' " So stated the Pope in an address June 21 to 30,000 members of Italian Catholic Action.

Catholic-Lutheran Relations — Dialogue between Catholics and Lutherans "has made us discover how great and solid are the common foundations of our Christian faith," declared the Pope June 25 on the 450th anniversary of the Augsburg Confession. Addressing a general audience of 20,000 people in St. Peter's Square, he said that "the will of Christ and the signs of the times lead us to a common witness in the increasing fullness of truth and love." He urged Christians to pray that, faithful to Christ and to the Gospel, . . . we may discover again the good of common belief." (See Augsburg Confession.)

Church Music — The development of "adequate forms of musical expression" was called for by the Pope in a letter addressed to participants in the Seventh International Congress of Sacred Music held June 20 to 26 in Cologne. He said: "It is necessary to develop and increase the musical patrimony of the Church not only in new churches but also in those which for centuries knew the Gregorian and polyphonic chant in the Latin language and now feel the need, after the introduction of national languages in the liturgy, to find adequate forms of musical expression."

State of the Church — The Pope delivered a 90-minute state-of-the-Church address June 28 before an audience of 35 cardinals, 38 archbishops and bishops, and more than 3,000 officials and employees of the Roman Curia. He said the Church was firmly rooted in its "precious heritage" while noting dangers threatening family life (permissiveness, free love, divorce, contraception, abortion). He spoke also about: the responsibility of theologians to reflect the authentic teaching of the Church; the right and duty of the Church's teaching authority to decide what conforms to authentic doctrine and morals and what does not; fidelity to directives on the liturgy; Christian unity, with emphasis on efforts toward Catholic-Orthodox union; collegiality, evidenced by synods of Dutch and Ukrainian bishops during the year.

The Pope Also:

• Asked people to pray "that the aspiration . . . for peace may be realized in a world that is ever more human and Christian." Also on June 8, he said he wanted Cambodian and other refugees to know "that they are very near to my heart and that I remember them constantly to the Lord."

• Named Cardinal Paul Zoungrana of Ouagadougou, Upper Volta, as his special delegate to the second National Eucharistic Congress, June 22 to 28, and the closing of the Church's centenary year in Kinshasa, Zaire.

• At a memorial Mass June 26, praised the wisdom and charity of Cardinal Sergio Pignedoli, president of the Secretariat for Non-Christians, who died June 15.

Vatican Briefs:

• The Vatican Press Office announced publication of the 10th volume of *Acts and Documents of the Holy See Relative to World War II,* covering the period from January, 1944, to July, 1945.

• Recent publication was reported of *Karol Wojtyla in Writings,* a bibliography of 1,490 items by or about Pope John Paul from 1949 to the time of his election to the papacy, Oct. 16, 1978.

Beatifications

Pope John Paul presided June 22 at ceremonies for the beatification of Kateri Tekakwitha, "Lily of the Mohawks" (1656-1680); Mother Marie (Guyard) of the Incarnation, "Teresa of the New World" (1599-1672); Bishop Francois De Montmorency-Laval, "Founder of the Church in Canada" (1623-1708); Jose de Anchieta, "Apostle of Brazil" (1534-1597);

and Pedro de San Jose Betancur, "St. Francis of the Americas" (1626-1667).
(See separate entries.)

NATIONAL

CRS Telethon — The first fund-raising telethon June 1 ever held by Catholic Relief Services raised about $150,000 in pledges and contributions for the support of its activities.

Probe of Worldwide Church of God — The U.S. Supreme Court refused June 2 to stop the State of California from probing into the financial affairs of the Worldwide Church of God, a 100,000-member denomination headed by Herbert W. Armstrong. The court declined to hear an appeal by the church against an investigation being conducted by the state's attorney general in response to charges that church funds were being converted to personal use by officials of the church. The attorney general claimed that the state could conduct the investigation because contributions to a church create a charitable trust which is subject to oversight by the state. The National Council of Churches and the Catholic League for Religious and Civil Rights were among groups contending that the state's action was unconstitutional because of its implications for the involvement of the state in internal church matters.

Abortion Party Rule — John T. Noonan, Jr., professor of law at the University of California, told the Catholic Health Assembly June 3 in Detroit that an "abortion party" had been "the ruler of America for the last decade." He called the party "a coalition of federal judiciary who are almost totally in favor of abortion, together with lawyers who have worked in tandem with them to provide the cadre to give the judges the necessary legal arguments to bring about the pro-abortion decisions." Institutions such as the American Civil Liberties Union and Planned Parenthood, "that have worked so long and hard to create an atmosphere acceptable to abortion in this country," belong to the party, Noonan said. He added: "Doctors, particularly those at leading university hospitals, and the media, which are wholeheartedly in the abortion camp, make up the remaining segments of the abortion party."

Patents for New Life Forms — The U.S. Supreme Court, declaring that there is nothing in patent law which limits patentability to inanimate inventions, ruled June 16 that new life forms created in the laboratory can be patented like any other new invention. The decision prompted a joint statement on genetic engineering by Bishop Thomas C. Kelly, general secretary of the U.S. Catholic Conference; Dr. Claire Randall, general secretary of the National Council of Churches, and Rabbi Bernard Mandelbaum, general secretary of the Synagogue Council of America.

Augsburg Confession — Joint Catholic-Lutheran prayer services and other celebrations marking the 450th anniversary of the key statement of Lutheran doctrine were indicative of the positive results of 15 years of Catholic-Lutheran dialogue. About 5,000 persons attended the largest observance in the U.S., June 22 at St. Patrick's Cathedral in New York.

No Tuition Grants — The Senate, with a vote of 71 to 24, defeated June 24 an amendment proposed by Sen. Daniel P. Moynihan of New York that would have provided federal grants of up to $750 a year for tuition to non-public elementary and high school students of families with incomes of less than $15,000 a year.

Praise for Archbishop Jadot — Bishop Thomas C. Kelly, general secretary of the National Conference of Catholic Bishops, was one of many speaking in praise of Apostolic Delegate Jean Jadot whose appointment as pro-president of the Secretariat for Non-Christians was announced by the Vatican June 27. Bishop Kelly said: "He has traveled widely in this country (since 1973), dialogued freely and given readily of himself to others. Always he has given encouragement and support, frequently calling attention to emerging issues and pointing the way to new pastoral initiatives in response to them."

Cuban and Haitian Exiles — Approximately 130,000 exiles from Cuba and Haiti were awaiting action by the federal government to further define their legal status and eligibility for aid programs. Migration and Refugee Services, U.S. Catholic Conference, reported near the end of the month that it had spent $1 million in resettlement work since April and had nearly 250 persons working with the aliens at several federal installations and in other parts of the country.

Meetings — Meetings during the month included those of the following organizations and movements:

• National conference on the Charismatic Renewal in the Catholic Church, May 30 to June 1 at the University of Notre Dame, attended by 11,000.

• Ninth annual Catholic Health Assembly, June 1 to 5 in Detroit, attended by more than 1,200.

• The 35th annual convention of the Catholic Theological Society of America, in San Francisco, attended by about 200 members; Father Thomas F. O'Meara, O.P., of Washington, D.C., was elected president.

• Ninth annual meeting of the National Assembly of Religious Brothers, June 19 to 22 in Detroit, attended by 70 delegates.

• The National Right to Life Committee, June 26 to 29 in Anaheim, Calif., attended by 1,800; Dr. J. C. Willke of Cincinnati was elected president.

• Sixth international Symposium on Natural Family Planning, in Philadelphia, attend-

ed by 200; sponsored by the Human Life Center, St. John's University (Collegeville, Minn.), and the Philadelphia Archdiocesan Family Life Bureau.

National Briefs:

• Knights of Columbus contributed more than $26 million to charitable causes and over eight million hours in service to their communities in 1979.

• In a letter addressed to two bishops of South Korea, Archbishop John R. Quinn wrote June 13 that the seizure of power by military personnel there was an "unfortunate development" that might hinder justice for the people of their country.

Hyde Amendment Constitutional

The U.S. Supreme Court ruled 5 to 4 June 30 in support of the constitutionality of federal legislation restricting the funding of abortion under the Medicaid program. At issue in the case of Harris v. McRae was the Hyde Amendment which limited federal funding of abortion to cases of danger of maternal death arising from pregnancy, and to cases of rape and incest promptly reported to appropriate authorities.

The Court's decision reversed a Jan. 15, 1980, ruling in which U.S. District Judge John F. Dooling, Jr., held that Congress has no right to place limits on the use of federal funds for welfare abortions.

(See separate entry.)

INTERNATIONAL

Catholic-Orthodox Dialogue — Sixty Catholic and Eastern Orthodox bishops and theologians participated in the inaugural meeting of the mixed commission for official dialogue between representatives of the respective churches. The purpose of the meeting, held May 29 to June 4 on the Greek islands of Patmos and Rhodes, was "to define the procedure and to organize the details of work for the first phase of dialogue." Establishment of the commission was announced jointly by Pope John Paul and Ecumenical Patriarch Dimitrios I in November, 1979.

Underground Church in Ukraine — The Catholic Church was flourishing in the Ukraine despite repression by the Soviet government, according to information reported at a three-day conference held early in the month in Toronto to celebrate the 50th anniversary of the founding of the theological seminary in Lvov. Documentation from the Ukraine said that the Church there, which was forced underground in 1939 when the Soviet Union took over the region, was "very strong and growing." The Toronto conference was attended by about 50 former students of the Lvov seminary, which was established in 1929 and functioned for 10 years.

Israeli Campaign against Schools — Representatives of six educational institutions with predominantly Palestinian student bodies in the West Bank — including Bethlehem University, administered by the Christian Brothers — issued a joint statement in May saying that Israeli authorities were conducting a "reign of terror" against their institutions.

Patriotic Catholics against Loyal Catholics — A crackdown on Chinese Catholics loyal to the Pope was indicated at a synod held in May by the National Association of Patriotic Catholics, according to a delayed report. Bishop Zong Huaide of Jinan, newly elected chairman of the association, said its purposes were to "mobilize all the bishops, priests and laity, unite them closely around the Communist Party and the government, . . . fight hegemonism, safeguard world peace and implement the principle of independent administration of the church."

Missionaries Threatened in Mexico — Bishop Jose A. Llaguno of the Vicariate of Tarahumara in northern Mexico reported that missionaries in his see had been threatened by political bosses and merchants for defending the Indians. "This is not new," he said in a published letter. "When we denounced injustice before, calumny was the answer in efforts to get rid of the priests. But now threats are being added."

More Victims in El Salvador — Franciscan Father Cosme Spessoto, who was shot to death while celebrating Mass June 14, was the ninth priest killed in El Salvador since 1977.

Six hundred men, women and children were massacred by Salvadorean troops and mercenaries a month earlier near the border of Honduras. News of the slaughter was not reported in the media until June 24.

Violence in South Africa — Unrest in South Africa that erupted in violent riots June 16 could be expected to continue until the government takes steps to "remedy the outstanding injustices" to non-white citizens, declared Father Donald de Beer, editor of *The Southern Cross*, in a telephone interview from Cape Town. The latest violence occurred on the fourth anniversary of rioting in the black community of Soweto where 600 persons were killed in 1976. The death toll in 1980 was just under 50. Cardinal Owen McCann of Cape Town deplored the outbreaks of violence and called for "a day of fasting and prayer" June 25 "in reparation and for reconciliation."

Two Abortions per Five Births — *The State of World Population 1980,* issued by the U.N. Fund for Population Activities, reported June 16 a worldwide daily average of 300,000 live births and 120,000 abortions. Also reported was a decrease in the worldwide fertility rate and a prediction that almost two billion more people would be added by the end of this century to the current population of 4.5 billion.

Nuns Back in Equatorial Guinea — *Fides,*

the news service of the Congregation for the Evangelization of Peoples, reported that 11 nuns had resumed work in Equatorial Guinea 11 years after the expulsion of missionaries by the government of President Francisco Macias Nguema.

Test-Tube Baby Clinic — Mrs. Margaret Tighe, president of Right to Life Australia, said in an interview that her organization had opposed the operations of an *in vitro* fertilization clinic in Melbourne out of concern "that the procedure involves a lack of respect for human life," because of the destruction of human embryos.

It was also reported that a baby, Candice Elizabeth Reed, conceived after *in vitro* fertilization at the clinic, was born there June 23. The clinic and its medical personnel were connected with a hospital where 1,400 abortions were performed a year.

Lefebvre Ordinations — Dissident Archbishop Marcel Lefebvre ordained 11 men to the priesthood June 27 at Econe, Switzerland, in another act of defiance of church discipline since he was suspended from the exercise of holy orders in the summer of 1976 for doing the same thing without proper authorization.

International Briefs:

• The tombs of three Jesuit missionaries in Beijing were renovated on orders from the government of the People's Republic of China, according to the New China News Agency. Reasons for the renovations were not disclosed. One of the tombs was that of Father Matteo Ricci, one of the most famous missionaries to China.

• Mother Teresa of Calcutta opened a center for service to the poorest of the poor in the Madrid suburb of Leganes.

Terror in Guatemala

The Guatemalan Bishops' Conference, citing the recent assassination of three priests and other atrocities, denounced "a state of persecution of the Church" in their country. "Church persecution," they said, "relies on a wave of defamation against bishops, priests and nuns, which aims at fostering mistrust among the people toward their pastors and leaders. . . . Even priests who fell as martyrs while preaching the Gospel are the target of insidious calumny intended to mar their Christian witness."

The bishops deplored "indiscriminate assassination, kidnapping, torture. . . . Other forms of violence abound: defamation, false accusations, lies, and the manipulation of minds by the communications media." They attributed the wave of violence "to the loss of spiritual values in our society, which allows the basest instincts and sin to prevail." They said domestic peace must be based "on the justice, truth and brotherly love which are being respected by the silent majority of Guatemalans."

JULY 1980

VATICAN

Brazilian Eucharistic Congress — Through the Eucharist Christ becomes "not only a witness to history, peoples and nations, but like a close friend," the Holy Father declared at the close of Brazil's National Eucharistic Congress in Fortaleza. His message was issued at the Vatican July 13, four days after he had personally opened the congress and one day after his return to the Vatican from Brazil. Describing the congress as the final objective of his trip, June 30 to July 12, he praised the theme of the assembly — "Where Are You Going?" — and noted that he had asked the question often during his visit. "I am convinced that to this question, the most important question for modern generations of your country, for the masses of Brazilians, and in a particular way for those who find themselves in the most difficult conditions of life, the Church in Brazil has come to find the reply precisely rooted in the Eucharist," the Pope said.

Reforms in Brazil — Pope John said that "indispensable and systematic reforms" were necessary for the achievement of social justice in Brazil and for the avoidance of "painful trials and experiences that in recent times have stricken several societies of that region of the world: subversion, revolutions, bloodshed, threats to human rights." He also appealed July 16 for respect for the rights of Indians there, saying: "Justice demands that those who have not gone in the direction of the new civilization, injected by foreigners, be able to maintain fully their traditional identity."

Time for God — The Pope, addressing a gathering of young people July 20 at Castelgandolfo, urged them to use their vacation not only for relaxation but also as a time for thinking about God. "I know," he said, "that among youths there are those for whom summer vacation is also a time for a special encounter with the Lord in fraternal community with others of their same age. How precious, how very precious such vacations are."

Lust — It robs people of their dignity, depersonalizes them and deprives them of the capacity to give of themselves, the Pope told a general audience of 15,000 people in St. Peter's Square July 23. Concupiscence makes the human body "merely an object of desire" and turns "the relationship of self-giving" into a "relationship of appropriation," he said. "The human heart has become a battleground between love and concupiscence, sometimes masquerading under the name of love. There is thus a fundamental difference between concupiscence or lust for another and authentic love or interpersonal communion."

Faith of the Young — "The world needs your faith, your purity, your joy, your help, your smiles," Pope John Paul told 700 youths from 12 countries during a Mass at Castelgandolfo July 24. The young people were members of Oasis, a Catholic group founded by Jesuit Father Virginio Rotondi in 1950. The Pontiff said their movement was called Oasis because, "in the desert of this world, so arid and so parched, it was your desire and your resolute wish that the life of God be born, grow and multiply." After 30 years, he added, "the litte seed (of the Oasis movement) has grown into a great tree," with members in 35 countries. The Pope also told the youths: "Without the light of Christ, all becomes enigmatic, obscure, contradictory and even absurd, as unfortunately so many currents of modern agnosticism confirm."

Equality in Marriage — Men and women must treat each other as equals in marriage, declared the Pope during a general audience July 30. He said that some passages about man and woman in the Old Testament indicated that women suffered "social marginalization" and that these passages were dictated by circumstances of those times. Nevertheless, he stated, the texts convey an underlying truth about the personal, loving union of man and woman desired by God, which is independent of the conditions of time. The Pope's comments were part of a continuing series of talks on the theology of marriage and the body which he began late in 1979.

The Pope Also:

• On June 7, named Cardinal Paolo Bertoli, chamberlain of the Holy Roman Church, as his special envoy to the National Marian Congress to be held Oct. 8 to 12 in Mendoza, Argentina.

• Met July 29 with a group of his former students from the University of Lublin and with members of *Communione e Liberazione,* a youth movement dedicated to efforts to penetrate all areas of society with Catholic moral and social principles.

• Commuted during this (and the following) month from the summer papal residence at Castelgandolfo to the Vatican for a number of general audiences there.

Vatican Briefs:

The Congregation for the Clergy released July 22 a document entitled "Norms for the Cooperation of the Local Churches among Themselves and Especially for a Better Distribution of the Clergy in the World." The document was dated Mar. 25.

• Documents ratifying a new accord between the Vatican and Peru were formally exchanged July 26 in Lima. Subjects of the accord were "several matters of common interest," thought to be Church-state relations in Catholic education, chaplaincies in the armed forces and the legal status of Catholic associations.

Visit to Brazil

Pope John Paul's trip to Brazil June 30 to July 12 was the seventh and longest of his pastoral pilgrimages up to that time of his pontificate. During the trip, he visited 13 cities, celebrated Mass before large and enthusiastic crowds, delivered nearly 50 addresses and was seen by millions of the people of the country with the largest Catholic population in the world. (See separate article.)

NATIONAL

Discrimination against Haitians — U.S. District Judge James L. King ruled July 3 in Miami that the Immigration and Naturalization Service was discriminatory toward Haitians seeking asylum in this country. He said the service ignored the fact that they were "fleeing the most oppressive regime in the Americas. . . . What they found," however, he noted, "was an immigration service which sought to send them back to Haiti without any hearing by an immigration judge on their asylum claims and a systematic program designed to deport them irrespective of the merits of their asylum." Officials of the U.S. Catholic Conference and the Miami archdiocese were among those who urged the government to treat Haitians in the same manner as the most recent "freedom flotilla" arrivals from Cuba.

No Contraceptive Sterilization — In a "Statement on Tubal Ligation" issued July 9, the National Conference of Catholic Bishops reaffirmed that sterilization for contraceptive purposes is objectively immoral "even if done for medical reasons." The statement reiterated other treatments of the subject by Pope Pius XII in 1953, the Vatican again in 1975, and the Administrative Board of the U.S. Catholic Conference in 1977.

Veto of Anti-Cult Law — The New York State Catholic Conference was among groups that recommended veto of a bill intended to help parents reclaim their children from religious cults. J. Alan Davitt, executive director, said the conference considered the legislation "inherently defective" and felt that it could be used as a basis for action against any religious denomination.

End Military Aid to El Salvador — In a renewed attempt to convince the Carter Administration to halt military aid to El Salvador, the U.S. Catholic Conference urged Secretary of State Edmund Muskie to support a proposed international embargo on arms shipments to that country. Bishop Thomas C. Kelly said in a letter to Muskie: "In the three

months since the tragic assassination and funeral of Archbishop Oscar Romero in San Salvador, events in that country have only strengthened the conviction of many that present United States policy toward El Salvador is badly flawed." He also said that U.S. support for "an increasingly unpopular and repressive" government there "is widely perceived as contributing to the killing" and violence of an "undeclared civil war."

White House Conference on Families — The last of three national meetings of the White House Conference on Families was held July 10 to 12 in Los Angeles. The earlier assemblies were held in Baltimore, June 5 to 7, and Minneapolis, June 19 to 21. Together, they produced 163 recommendations for government action on behalf of families. (See separate entry.)

Communication Projects — The U.S. Catholic Conference announced July 14 grants for eight more national-level projects funded by the Catholic Communication Campaign, bringing the total of such awards to 26 since the start of the campaign in 1979. The grants were funded from parish-level collections across the country.

Protesters Arrested — Secret Service personnel arrested 18 Catholics who staged a protest demonstration July 18 too close to the Soviet embassy in Washington. The demonstration was against religious and political repression in the Baltic States, the holding of the Olympics in Moscow and the Soviet invasion of Afghanistan in December, 1979. Father Casimir Pugevicius, director of the Lithuanian Catholic Relgious Aid organization, was among those arrested and freed on bond. "If we forget what happened in Lithuania 40 years ago," he said July 21, "it's a way of condoning what happened in Afghanistan and whatever goes on."

Homosexual Rights — The City Council of Baltimore defeated July 21 by a 12-to-6 vote a measure that would have barred discrimination based on "sexual orientation." Archbishop William D. Borders, who opposed the bill, said in a newsletter to priests of the archdiocese that "the heart of the matter is the meaning of the term, 'sexual orientation,' in civil law. In legal language, the term necessarily indicates not only psychosexual attraction but also acts which flow from it." The Church "has constantly held that homosexual orientation in and by itself and with no relation to homosexual behavior is neither moral nor immoral." The Church has also constantly taught that "homosexual activity is immoral and socially destructive." Passage of the measure, he said in substance, could be interpreted as approval of such activity.

Anti-Alien Law Struck Down — U.S. District Judge Woodrow Seals ruled July 21 in Houston against the constitutionality of a 1975 Texas law that denied free public education to the children of undocumented aliens. He said the denial, affecting scores of thousands of Hispanic children, was a violation of due process and equal protection of the laws. "The Constitution," he declared, "does not permit the states to deny access to education to a discrete group of children within its borders when it has undertaken to provide public education." The ruling was called a human-rights landmark by Pablo Sedillo, director of the Secretariat for Hispanic Affairs, U.S. Catholic Conference. He said: "Education is far too important a matter to be denied to any child anywhere in the world."

Policy for Confirmation — Archbishop Edward T. O'Meara of Indianapolis announced a new plan for administration of the sacrament and ordered its full implementation by the fall of 1982. Accordingly, the sacrament would be administered to persons between the ages of 13 and 18, and the formation process would include 20 hours of catechetical instruction, a minimum of 30 hours in service, a retreat experience and participation in a communal celebration of the sacrament of reconciliation. Sponsors would receive four hours of instruction.

Public School Prayer — A House Judiciary subcommittee held hearings July 29 and 30 on a proposal by Rep. Jesse Helms of North Carolina to prohibit all federal courts, including the U.S. Supreme Court, from ruling on cases involving voluntary prayer in public schools. The Helms Amendment was controversial, with evangelicals in heavy support. The U.S. Catholic Conference took no position on it. There was considerable agreement that the amendment, even if passed in conjunction with a bill already enacted in the Senate, would be declared unconstitutional.

National Briefs:

• A review board set up by the Diocese of San Bernardino reprimanded teachers at a parochial school in Indio, Calif., for using "questionable forms of (physical) discipline."

• The American Medical Association decided July 22 at its annual meeting in Chicago "that a physician should not be a participant in executions by drug injection." Execution by injection was authorized by legislation in four states.

• After two joint meetings, migration commissions of the U.S. and Mexican bishops' conferences announced plans to establish offices and share personnel along the border in order to assist migrants coming into the U.S. from Latin American countries.

Draft Registration

Thousands of young men 20 and 19 years of age, respectively, registered for a military draft during the last two weeks of the month. The registration took place under legislation proposed by President Carter in January and enacted into law by the House of Representatives in April and by the Senate in June. It was estimated that more than 80 per cent of those covered by the law registered as required.

A number of dioceses, as well as other organizations, announced plans to set up and operate informational, counseling and referral services for men required to register. The dioceses included Baltimore, Boston, Detroit, Milwaukee, Newark, St. Paul and Minneapolis, and San Francisco.

INTERNATIONAL

Convictions in South Africa — The conviction and sentencing of 35 religious leaders July 1 in South Africa was called unjust by 16 U.S. churchmen. "We cannot believe that our church colleagues were charged and found guilty simply because they allegedly demonstrated without a permit and obstructed traffic," they said in a letter to Donald Sole, South African ambassador to the U.S. "It is clear that their sentences (to a $70 fine or 50 days in jail) are part of a broad sweep of government actions meant to intimidate and silence opponents of the unjust and racist systems of apartheid."

Defamation and Harassment in Chile — The bishops of Chile, according to a delayed report, said in a mid-June statement that a campaign of defamation and harassment of church personnel would not keep them from defending human rights. The statement denounced the arrest and torture of civilians and a systematic media campaign "against the Church and its institutions."

Christian Atrocities — Maronite-Rite Patriarch Antoine Pierre Khoraiche of Antioch strongly condemned "atrocities" and "abominations" committed by members of Christian factions in Lebanon, in a statement published in the July 15 edition of *L'Osservatore Romano.* He said there were reports of mistreatment of prisoners, disrespect for corpses, the murder of innocent citizens and the destruction of their homes. It was estimated that fighting between Phalangists and National Liberal Party members claimed more than 300 lives in the previous few weeks.

Opposition to Covenanting — Debate during the General Synod of the Church of England surfaced significant opposition to proposals that the church join with four other churches in covenanting together as the first step toward organic unity. The other churches were the Methodist Church, the United Reformed Church, the Moravian Church and the Churches of Christ. Covenant opponents objected to the implications of mutual recognition of ministries, especially to a proposal that would permit some moderators of the United Reformed Church to continue exercising quasi-episcopal office after covenanting without being ordained bishops. Opponents also contended that the recognition of women ministers of other churches might be a step toward introducing women priests into the Church of England by the back door.

School Closed, Priests Arrested — The Iranian Ministry of National Education shut down the Salesian-run Andicheh School in Teheran July 16 and placed under house arrest 11 priests accused of spying for Israel. Superiors of the order in Rome said that the only Israeli connection was with Salesian provincial headquarters located in Bethlehem since 1886. The school was the second Catholic institution closed in several weeks.

Coup in Bolivia — Less than a month after Archbishop Jorge Manrique of La Paz warned that a coup would be "the greatest treason to our country," military officers overthrew July 17 the government headed by provisional President Lydia Gueiler and installed Gen. Luis Garcia Meza in her place. Priests, religious and lay persons were among human rights advocates arrested for what the junta considered communistic and subversive activity. The coup was the 189th in 154 years of Bolivian independence.

Reconstruction in Nicaragua — As Nicaraguans marked the first anniversary July 19 of the overthrow of the Somoza regime, Archbishop Obando Bravo of Managua cautioned people not to "idolize" their revolution, "even if at first there is fervor and mass enthusiasm. . . . We are now in the second phase of facing realities. Many people are happy while others are dissatisfied and frustrated. . . . Now, as a churchman of hope, I want the revolution in Nicaragua to take the path of peace with the common good of all in mind, and particularly with freedom for all."

Martial Law Toll — During eight years of martial law in the Philippines: at least 50,000 persons were jailed; more than 300 were summarily killed; 200 or more disappeared; democratic rights were abrogated; strikes were banned; the poor were evicted from miserable quarters; press freedom was curtailed; the legislature was turned into a rubber stamp. So stated Franciscan Sister Mariani Dimaranan, once a political prisoner, at a press conference in Washington.

Missionaries Hindered in India — Government efforts to tighten restrictions on the activities of Catholic missionaries in West Bengal were viewed "with concern" by Cardinal Lawrence Picachy of Calcutta and six other bishops. They said in a statement: "While the government has a right to regulate the entry, residence and movements of foreigners, including foreign missionaries, we request the government not to place more restrictions on foreign missionaries than are necessary, so that their noble work, especially among the poor, may not be unduly hampered." Alexander Warjri, a member of Parliament, said that missionaries were being made scapegoats for the ineffectiveness of the central and state governments in dealing with separatist tendencies among minority ethnic and tribal groups.

Work toward End of Capital Punishment — Archbishop Igino Cardinale, papal nuncio to Belgium, Luxembourg and the European Community, urged government leaders in Europe July 30 to work for the abolition of the death penalty.

International Briefs:
• Bishop Raphael Nze Abuy, who was exiled from Equatorial Guinea in 1972, was restored to his Diocese of Bata by Pope John Paul.
• Italian priest worker Father Luis Pichler of Bolzano was suspended from exercise of the priesthood July 22 after refusing to follow an order from his bishop to resign from his seat on the city council.

Jerusalem, Capital of Israel

The Israeli Knesset, with a vote of 69 to 15, enacted into law July 30 a bill proclaiming a "complete and united" Jerusalem as the "eternal capital" of Israel. Proponents of the law said it formalized the actual state of affairs existing in the city since Eastern Jerusalem was occupied by Israel during the Six-Day War in 1967. Critics claimed that the law was in direct conflict with U.N. resolutions declaring that territories occupied during the 1967 war should be returned to Arab control.

A month before passage of the law, an unsigned article in *L'Osservatore Romano* said "the Jerusalem question cannot be reduced to 'free access for all to the Holy Places.' " Other necessary considerations were:
• "that the overall character of Jerusalem as a sacred heritage shared by all three monotheistic religions (Judaism, Christianity, Islam) be guaranteed by appropriate measures;
• "that religious freedom in all its aspects be safeguarded for them;
• "that the complex of rights acquired by the various communities over the shrines and centers for spirituality, study and welfare be protected;
• "that the continuance and development of religious, educational and social activity by each community be ensured;
• "that this be actuated with equality of treatment for all three religions;
• "that this be achieved through an 'appropriate juridical safeguard' that does not derive from the will of only one of the parties interested."

Rabbis Martin A. Cohen and David H. Panitz, speaking for the Anti-Defamation League of B'nai B'rith, called the article one-sided and ill-timed, and said it was being used as a "focal point for an assault on Israel and the Jewish people."

AUGUST 1980

VATICAN

Church Must Defend the Poor — "The Church would not be faithful to the Gospel if it were not close to the poor and if it did not defend their rights," declared Pope John Paul in an interview published in the Aug. 2 edition of *L'Osservatore Romano.* "This is the pure and simple mission of the Gospel," he said.

Lament for Terrorist Victims — The Holy Father told a general audience of 15,000 persons Aug. 6 that there were "no words to express adequately the pain, abhorrence and horror" he and the nation felt at "such vile, absurd crimes" as the bombing Aug. 2 of the Bologna railroad station in which 77 people were killed and more than twice that number injured. He prayed for all those "suffering in body or in spirit" because of the tragedy.

Trip to Germany — A spokesman for the Vatican Press Office announced Aug. 6 that the Pope would visit seven West German cities between Nov. 15 and 19 at the invitation of church and civil authorities, "on the occasion of the seventh centenary of the death of St. Albert the Great." Cities to be visited during the Pope's eighth trip outside Italy were Cologne, Bonn, Osnabruck, Mainz, Fulda, Altotting and Munich.

Opposition to Liberal Drug Laws — "The painful experience of some nations has shown that more permissive legislation (regarding the possession and use of drugs) serves neither to prevent nor to redeem." So stated the Pope Aug. 9 during a Mass celebrated for former drug addicts and their families at Castel Gandolfo.

Crisis in Poland — In one of several expressions of concern over the political and labor crisis gripping Poland since strikes began Aug. 14 in the heavily industrialized Baltic region, the Pope declared: "I share in this trial that my homeland and fellow countrymen are once again going through." He made the statement in a letter addressed Aug. 20 to Cardinal Stefan Wyszynski of Warsaw.

Letter on St. Benedict — In a letter marking the 15th centenary of the birth of St. Benedict, Pope John Paul focused attention on three aspects of Benedictine life — prayer, work and the exercise of paternal authority — as antidotes to a new wave of paganism sweeping across the Western world. "Paganism," he said, "which once was converted to the Gospel by numerous bands of missionary monks, today is being propagated more and more in the Western world. This is both the cause and the effect of the loss of that Christian sense of work and its dignity." The Pope had special praise for St. Benedict for attaching a Christian meaning and dignity to all work: "Benedict indeed considered work as an essential part of life, for whatever reason it happened to be done, and he bound each of his monks to it, putting it at the level of a duty of conscience." The title of the apostolic letter was *Sanctorum Altrix* ("Nourisher of Saints); it was dated July 11 but publication was delayed for several weeks.

Instruments of Justice and Peace — The Pope called on 1,000 young people from Ireland Aug. 28 to "fulfill your destiny" by becoming "instruments of justice and builders of peace." Noting that nearly half of the Catholics in the Archdiocese of Dublin were under the age of 21, he asked: "Can you have any doubt that the future of Dublin and the rest of Ireland really does depend on your generosity, your commitment to Christ, and your service to your brothers and sisters?"

Mission of Secular Institutes — This was the theme of an address delivered by the Pope Aug. 28 during a meeting with 350 participants in the World Conference of Secular Institutes. He said: "Your choice of life, characterized and unified by consecration, ministry and secular life, is certainly developed . . . in authentic communion with the pastors of the Church and in participation in the evangelical mission of all the people of God." He pointed to three conditions for the effectiveness of their mission: "You must be true disciples of Christ . . . truly competent in your specific field in order to be able to exercise (your) ministry of witness and commitment," and capable of changing the world from within.

Meeting with Syro-Malabar Bishops — The Pope, meeting with Syro-Malabar-Rite bishops Aug. 29 at Castel Gandolfo, heard their requests for significant changes in the government and structure of their rite. Two points under discussion were:

• some kind of expansion or major reorganization of the rite in India;

• the establishment of formal ecclesiastical jurisdictions outside India for members of the rite under the supervision of Latin-Rite bishops.

The Pope Also:

• Met Aug. 31 with Archbishop William Barden and several Italian Salesians expelled from Iran after spying and related charges against them were dropped.

Vatican Briefs:

• Archbishop Jean Jadot, in his first public message since becoming head of the Secretariat for Non-Christians, expressed "sentiments of brotherhood" to the Moslem world during the Islamic holy month of Ramadan which ended Aug. 11.

• Iranian students arrested by Italian police Aug. 8 after a demonstration in front of St. Peter's Basilica were released from jail Aug. 19. The students said in a letter addressed to the Pope that their demonstration "was not designed to challenge the religious sentiments of men of the Christian faith" but rather to urge Vatican authorities to take "more decisive and concrete positions in favor of the oppressed people of Palestine and for the liberation of Jerusalem and its restitution to its legitimate owners who are the Arabs of Palestine."

Centenary of St. Bernardine

Pope John Paul commemorated the sixth centenary of the birth of St. Bernardine of Siena Aug. 30 with a trip to Aquila where his remains are enshrined in a basilica bearing his name.

He told a gathering of priests and religious there that the Franciscan Doctor of the Church offered them "an example of attachment to truth, of adhesion to the revealed word." He called for "confident obedience" to the teaching authority of the Church, declaring: "There cannot be an authentic exercise of the ministry of the word in the bosom of the Church without obedience of the heart to him who, even if covered with weakness and fragility, has received the mandate to assure the pureness of doctrine."

Before arriving at Aquila, about 100 miles northwest of Rome, the Pope stopped at the construction site of an eight-mile tunnel under 10,000-foot Gran Sasso Mountain and visited the Sanctuary of St. Mary of the Cross in Poggio di Roio.

NATIONAL

Don't Blame Just Refugees — A nun and a priest involved with Cuban refugees at the Fort Indiantown Gap, Pa., processing center attributed riots there Aug. 5 to refugee tension over delays in processing and to a "bad press" which scared away prospective sponsors. Sister Helen McCormac said: "It was not all the fault of the Cubans, nor the fault of the federal police, nor the fault of the military police."

Mother Teresa Missions — Mother Teresa of Calcutta joined members of her Missionaries of Charity for the opening Aug. 6 of a soup kitchen in the South Bronx, New York City. Later in the month, it was announced that four members of the community would open a mission in September in Miami for "shopping-bag ladies" and other women in need.

Formation Program for Ministry — Bishop John C. Reiss of Trenton announced Aug. 7 a program of formation and training for lay persons and religious already serving in what he called the "unordained pastoral ministry." He informed priests of the diocese by letter that he had authorized the Office of Religious Education "to develop and implement a program of formation and training for those persons who wish to serve the Church in a pastoral ministerial role in cooperation with their pastors."

Anniversary of Black Catholic Office — More than 2,500 black Catholics from across the country attended the first convention of the National Office for Black Catholics Aug. 6 to 9 in Chicago. They marked the 10th anniversary of the office while committing themselves to address concerns involving parishes, families, labor issues, politics, youth activities, vocations, education and lay leadership. The convention was held after the annual meeting of the Knights and Ladies of Peter Claver and in conjunction with the convention of the National Black Catholic Clergy Caucus.

Optimistic View of Missions — Despite rising living costs and trends toward isolationism in this country, U.S. Catholics were giving increased support to the missions. So stated Archbishop D. Simon Lourdusamy, secretary of the Congregation for the Evangelization of Peoples, in an interview in New York. Features of his generally optimistic report about missionary activity were:

• More dioceses, as well as mission-sending societies, were assigning personnel to work in developing countries.

• Affluent countries were maintaining a steady flow of material aid and personnel to poverty-ridden countries.

• Ecumenism in mission areas was alive and well.

• Catholics in mission areas were working alongside missionaries from other places.

Evangelization — Approximately 1,700 persons took part in the Second Annual National Catholic Lay Celebration of Evangelization Aug. 21 to 23 in Washington, D.C. A common theme of 32 workshops held during the celebration was that evangelization works best when the evangelizers respect the particular cultural, ethnic, community and individual conditions and needs of the people they are trying to reach.

Suit against Bishops Dismissed — U.S. District Judge June L. Green dismissed Aug. 22 a suit by the Costello Publishing Co. of Northport, N.Y., against the National Conference of Catholic Bishops for breach of anti-trust laws. The company claimed in a suit filed in 1976 that the conference violated anti-trust laws by taking steps to discourage sale of a book entitled *Morning and Evening Prayers* whose text was not submitted, as required by church law, to the conference for approval. The judge noted that the conference was responsible for the approval of liturgical texts for use by Catholics and added: "Concomitantly, the NCCB has the duty to discourage the dissemination and use of unapproved liturgical texts in the dioceses of the United States."

Student Aid in Iowa — The State Department of Public Instruction reported that during the 1979-80 school year Iowa provided almost $5 million in aid to students attending nonpublic schools. About $3.7 million of that amount went to the benefit of students in Catholic schools.

Opinions of Apostolic Delegate — In an address Aug. 24 during the national assembly in San Antonio of the Conference of Major Superiors of Men, Archbishop Jean Jadot urged the religious leaders to help the Church serve the poor more effectively. The former apostolic delegate called attention to "the temptation in the United States to naivete" and the tendency of many priests and nuns to oversimplify complex problems. He also noted "a danger of watering down doctrinal quality" in educational programs, and said that religious leadership in the U.S. was perhaps more managerial than spiritual.

Meetings — The following organizations were among those that held meetings during the month.

• Tekakwitha Conference, Aug. 4 to 7 in Denver, attended by 600 persons; one of the key concerns was the need for Indian priests and their training in programs suiting the cultural needs of their people.

• National Diaconate Institute on Continuing Education, Aug. 6 to 9 at Notre Dame University; the development of regional organizations was given top priority for the coming year.

• Worldwide Marriage Encounter, Aug. 8 to 10 in Los Angeles, attended by 24,000 persons from 49 countries.

• National Assembly of Women Religious, Aug. 7 to 10 in Milwaukee, and the Leadership Conference of Women Religious, Aug. 24 to 29 in Philadelphia; feminist issues in the Church and general society were among topics under consideration.

• The Second Detroit Conference on Theology in the Americas, July 31 to Aug. 6, attended by 500 Christians, with emphasis on social justice and liberation themes.

National Briefs:

• "Day of Rescue" was the slogan of participants in anti-abortion demonstrations Aug. 9 in a number of cities.

• Winifred Coleman, former dean of students at Trinity College, Washington, D.C., succeeded Mary Helen Madden as executive director of the National Council of Catholic Women, Aug. 13.

• The American Bible Society established a special Helen Keller Centennial Fund to provide Scriptures for the blind and visually handicapped.

• Honored: Mrs. Florence Conley, with the second Paulist Fathers' National Award for Catholic Lay Evangelization, Aug. 23; Msgr. Luigi Ligutti, 85, former executive secretary of the National Catholic Rural Life Conference, with the Iowa Award of the Iowa Centennial Memorial Foundation for his work on behalf of people in rural areas.

Plan for Anglicans

Archbishop John R. Quinn, president of the National Conference of Catholic Bishops, announced Aug. 20 that the Vatican had given permission for the conference to develop ways and means of receiving into the Catholic Church:

• members of the Anglican Communion who, "while wishing to retain some elements of Anglican tradition, fully accept Roman Catholic doctrine and the authority of the Pope and bishops."

• married Anglican clergymen, on the same terms and with the way open for them to become Roman Catholic priests on validation of holy orders and to continue in marriage after such validation.

INTERNATIONAL

Jesuit Superior General To Stay On — The Rome headquarters of the Jesuits announced Aug. 1 that Father Pedro Arrupe had cancelled plans to retire as superior general because the Pope had asked him to remain in office "in view of the good of the Church and of the Society of Jesus." If he had resigned, he would have been the first superior general of the society to do so.

Indians Killed in Mexico — Six bishops in southern Mexico joined a protest by Jesuit missionaries over the killing of 13 Tzeital Indians by police and federal troops and the eviction of 723 families during a land dispute in Chiapas. The priests and bishops placed principal blame for the incident on owners of large farms and local authorities who blocked implementation of land reform laws benefitting the landless.

Threat to Missionaries — A Brazilian law that went into effect Aug. 6 could be used to expel or refuse to admit foreigners, including missionaries, according to the Brazilian Bishops' Conference, opposition political leaders and the Brazilian Lawyers' Association. A conference agency said, "The xenophobic nature of this project is unacceptable." The government claimed that the law was aimed at protecting national security and defending the Brazilian work force against an influx of cheap foreign labor.

Famine — The emergency caused by drought and famine in the countries of the Horn of Africa was called "the most serious we've had" by Kenneth Hackett, regional director for Africa of Catholic Relief Services. He said the emergency "covers a larger geographical area than the 1972 famine in Ethiopia, affects more people than the Biafra war crisis, and is compounded by political factors we didn't encounter during the Sahel drought." The affected countries were Kenya, Ethiopia, Sudan, Djibouti and Somaliland.

Balance of Terror — The existing nuclear "balance of terror" is fragile, and the world remains "at the mercy of errors in judgment, in formation and interpretation" regarding nuclear policies, warned Audrys Backis, Vatican representative at the U.N. conference on the Nuclear Non-Proliferation Treaty which began Aug. 11.

Jerusalem Decision Criticized — The Central Committee of the World Council of Churches said in a statement that it "opposes the Israeli unilateral action of annexing East Jerusalem and uniting the city as its eternal capital under its exclusive sovereignty. . . . This decision is contrary to all pertinent U.N. resolutions. It most dangerously undermines all efforts toward the just solution of the Middle East problem and jeopardizes regional and world peace."

The Israeli decision seemed to move Jerusalem away from the status proposed by the Vatican (See related entry.)

Pastoral Congress Praised, but . . . — The bishops of England and Wales praised the National Pastoral Congress held in May, but their endorsement did not extend to recommendations offered on such subjects as general absolution, divorce, contraception and sexual morality, intercommunion and the ordination to orders of women and married men. Many of 2,305 polled readers of *The Universe,* the British Catholic weekly with the largest circulation, agreed with the bishops.

Attitude toward Development — The General Assembly of the United Nations received a message from Pope John Paul Aug. 25, urging the body "to go beyond any static positions that belong to a particular ideology" in tackling problems in international development. The message was read by Cardinal Bernardin Gantin, president of the Pontifical Commission for Justice and Peace.

Missionaries Leave Guatemala — Spanish nuns and priests were forced to leave their posts in the Guatemalan Diocese of Santa Cruz del Quiche. "There is open and total persecution of the Church in Quiche," the priests said in a statement issued in mid-August. "We left the area in solidarity with the bishop and in protest against five years of massacres by the army, which have escalated since . . . January." Three priests and several lay helpers were killed in the previous three and one-half months.

Grants to African Militants — The World Council of Churches announced a record total of $775,000 in grants from its Special Program to Combat Racism, including $350,000 to militant black organizations in southern Africa. In reply to controversy over the grants, the council emphasized that the organizations receiving them had agreed to use the money for humanitarian purposes.

New Welfare Programs Banned — Mother Teresa's Missionaries of Charity was one of 12 foreign-aided organizations prohibited from starting new welfare programs in tribal areas of India's West Bengal State. It was alleged that the groups had links with separatist movements there. The ban came amid growing concern among legislators that freedom of religion was being challenged in several states.

Priests Expelled from Iran — By the end of the month a number of Salesian priests, against whom charges of collusion with Israel had been brought and then dropped, were expelled from Iran along with Latin-Rite Archbishop William Barden. Four Salesians were permitted to remain in Iran for pastoral work only among the few Catholics there.

Strikes in Poland — By the end of the month, approximately 350,000 shipyard, industrial, transport and mining workers were on strike for the establishment of independent labor unions, an end to censorship, access of the Church to the mass media, and government policies to end food shortages. The bishops were in general sympathy with the strikers since the first of them walked out of Gdansk shipyards on Aug. 14. Cardinal Stefan Wyszynski called for peace and calm Aug. 26; he stood for the rights of workers but implicitly counseled against demands he thought might jeopardize the workers' cause and lead to intervention by the Soviet Union.

International Briefs:

• Reuters reported that Catholic churches in Hanoi appeared to be historical monuments rather than places of worship.

• West German Catholics contributed about $56 million to the Misereor aid agency in 1979 for the support of 2,921 projects in 87 Third World countries.

• Father Edgard Parrales became the third priest to hold a cabinet post in the Nicaraguan government, as head of the Ministry of Social Welfare.

Bolivian Archbishop Defended

For second time since the takeover of the government by a military junta on July 17, the Bolivian Bishops' Conference reacted strongly to attacks by the regime and right-wing groups on Archbishop Jorge Manrique of La Paz for his defense of human rights. "We protest and vigorously reject the absurd campaign against this devoted churchman, which employs grievous, untrue assertions and threats," they said in a statement issued late in the month.

About 20 priests and religious seized after the coup were released during the month. Church sources estimated that 2,000 persons were arrested for alleged subversion. The Archdiocese of La Paz opened a legal aid office to help political prisoners and their families. Two bishops of Bolivia interviewed in this country said that the coup which rocked the nation made the outlook grim for the people and Church, especially for the next few months.

SEPTEMBER 1980

VATICAN

World War II Victims Mourned — Pope John Paul mourned the loss of life and the material and moral damage caused by World War II as he marked Sept. 3 the 41st anniversary of the beginning of the conflict.

Urban Planning — Problems of urbanization and population should be considered "from the viewpoint of total human wellbeing," the Pope told 60 big-city mayors Sept. 4. "The good of man — man seen in the totality of his nature and the full dignity of his person — is indeed a determining factor for all human interventions in this field," he said in an address to the International Conference on Population and the Urban Future.

Creative Activities for the Elderly — The Pope urged participants in the International Forum on Active Aging to promote "creative activities for and with the elderly." Such activities, he said Sept. 5, "will bring forth fruitful results for a more humanized society and a renewed civilization that will sustain a greater fellowship of love and communion of hope and peace."

Contraception — While visiting the Roman suburb of Velletri Sept. 7, the Pope criticized artificial means of contraception and praised the townspeople's "three loves — the family, work and the Madonna." In a homily delivered during Mass outside St. Clement's Cathedral, he said the prevalence of contraception "is not worthy of civilization. . . . Instead of increasing the amount of bread on the table of a hungry race as modern means of production are able to do today, there are thoughts of diminishing the number of those at the table through methods that are contrary to honesty." He called for "a responsible and tireless commitment of all honest men and women at every level of civil society" against contraception.

Lust — "Carnal lust stifles in man's heart the deep voice of his conscience and his sense of responsibility before God," declared the Pope Sept. 10 before a general audience of 15,000 people in St. Peter's Square. He said that "Christ is teaching that a look is the threshold of inner truth, and that already in a look we can find the true meaning of lust."

Speaking about the vice again Sept. 17, the Holy Father said: "By lustful desire, the person ceases to be the subject of an eternal attraction and begins to be only the object of the concupiscence of the flesh. At this point there is a profound internal separation from the meaning of the body as it relates to marriage."

Human Rights Message — The Pope sent messages urging respect for human rights and religious freedom to heads of the countries participating in the European security review conference which began sessions Sept. 10 in Madrid. The plenary assembly of the conference was scheduled to open Nov. 11, for review of accords on cooperation, security and human rights signed in 1975 in Helsinki.

Catechists Praised — The Holy Father celebrated Mass for a group of catechists Sept. 12 at Castel Gandolfo. He praised them for their work and offered them "fatherly encouragement for a zealous and intelligent pursuit of your most precious activity."

St. Thomas Aquinas a Pioneer — He was "an authentic pioneer of modern scientific realism" and should also be called "the doctor of humanity," said the Pope in an address Sept. 13 to participants in the eighth International Thomistic Congress sponsored by the Pontifical Roman Academy of St. Thomas Aquinas. The just completed six-day congress marked the centenary of the academy (commonly called the Angelicum) and of the encyclical letter *Aeterni Patris,* in which Pope Leo XIII called for the restoration of scholastic philosophy, particularly that of St. Thomas, as a means of reviving Catholic intellectualism and countering divergent philosophical trends.

Call for Peace and Job Security — The Pope made an urgent plea for peace and called for greater job security for workers during a visit Sept. 20 to Montecassino. He met there with 500 Benedictine abbots from around the world, at the cradle of their order where they were marking the 15th centenary of the birth of St. Benedict.

Abortion Law — Pope John Paul defended his pronouncement against Italy's abortion law amid denunciations, protests and scattered episodes of violence. His main defense was the fact that "this issue is first and foremost an issue of moral responsibility," he told 40,000 people in St. Peter's Square Sept. 21. Pro-abortion forces denouncing the Pope regarded his anti-abortion statements as interference in affairs of state at a time when it appeared likely that there might be a referendum on abortion legislation in coming elections.

Iran vs. Iraq — "The news of the clashes which have broken out between the armies of Iraq and Iran . . . causes deep concern and sadness," stated the Pope Sept. 24 in his first public comment on fighting between the two oil-producing countries. He prayed that the conflict would not lead to "even larger and more devastating dimensions and consequences."

Predecessors Remembered — Pope John Paul II solemnly commemorated the deaths of John Paul I and Paul VI Sept. 28 with a Mass he concelebrated with most of the 216 participants in the 1980 assembly of the Synod of Bishops.

Responsibilities of Christians — The Pope praised a declaration on the responsibilities of European Christians issued Sept. 28 by the Council of European Bishops. Subjects included in the declaration were: insecurity of the unemployed, immigrant workers and refugees; widespread disregard for human life and human rights; the energy crisis and economic recession; social and ideological conflict; violence, the arms race and the fear of war.

The Pope Also:

• Urged members of the Anglican-Roman Catholic International Commission to continue their efforts toward unity of the two churches.

• Declared St. Januarius patron of the Campania, the region around Naples, according to a papal brief announced Sept. 11.

• Ended a two-month stay at Castel Gandolfo and returned to the Vatican Sept. 20.

• Concelebrated Mass Sept. 24 in the Vatican Gardens with nearly 100 Polish priests who had been prisoners in the Nazi concentration camp at Dachau.

Vatican Briefs:

• The Sept. 5 edition of *L'Osservatore Romano* carried an article reporting the end of SODEPAX (Society, Development and Peace) as of Dec. 31, 1980. The organization, for cooperation on social issues, was established in 1968 under the mutual sponsorship of the Pontifical Commission on Justice and Peace and the Unity, Justice and Service Program of the World Council of Churches. It was announced that termination of the organization's mandate would not diminish the commitment of the Vatican or the council to ecumenical cooperation in pursuit of peace and justice.

• The Second International Conference on Ministry to Nomads was held Sept. 11 to 15 under the sponsorship of the Pontifical Commission for the Ministry of Migration and Tourism.

• Msgr. Mario Peressin, head of the Vatican delegation, delivered an intervention for peaceful and beneficial use of nuclear energy Sept. 24 at the 24th conference of the International Atomic Energy Agency.

• The themes of two 1981 observances were announced during the month: "To Serve Peace, Respect Freedom," for the 14th World Day of Peace, Jan. 1, and "Social Communications and Responsible Human Freedom," for World Communications Day, May 31.

Synod of Bishops

"The Role of the Christian Family in the Modern World" was the theme of the sixth assembly of the Synod of Bishops which went into session following a Mass concelebrated Sept. 26 by Pope John Paul and more than 210 delegates.

The Holy Father said in his inaugural homily: "The family is the fundamental object of the Church's evangelization and catechesis, and is also the necessary subject for which nothing else can be substituted." The task of the Synod, he added, was "to show all families their particular role in the mission of the Church."

(See separate entry.)

NATIONAL

CHD Grants — Bishop Thomas C. Kelly, general secretary of the National Conference of Catholic Bishops, announced Sept. 2 that in 1980 the Campaign for Human Development awarded $5,714,000 in 140 grants and $283,866 in loans to self-help projects around the country. These allocations brought to more than $55 million the 10-year total of grants and loans to more than 1,500 projects.

Msgr. Higgins Retires — Msgr. George G. Higgins paid a formal farewell to the organized labor movement Sept. 3 in Washington with an impassioned plea on behalf of the poor and disadvantaged. "I cannot think of anything worse that could happen to our society in a time of economic crisis than the permanent decline of the labor movement," he told 750 guests at a dinner held in his honor by the AFL-CIO. Two days before the dinner, Msgr. Higgins retired from the U.S. Catholic Conference which he had served as a staff member for 36 years.

CRS in 1979 — The activities of Catholic Relief Services in 1979 had a total program value of more than $340 million, according to the agency's annual report. With funding from a variety of sources, the agency's disbursements (in millions) were for: emergency aid and disaster relief ($39.8); refugee aid ($26.2); help for orphans, lepers, aged, handicapped, the seriously ill ($26.8); developmental assistance ($241.2); administration and fund-raising.

Natural Family Planning — A study of 559 couples for a cumulative total of 4,957 months concluded that the ovulation method of natural family planning is just as effective as oral contraceptives. The method effectiveness rate was 99.6 per cent, and the use effectiveness rate was 94.6 per cent. The study was conducted by researchers at Creighton University in Omaha and St. John's Mercy Hospital in St. Louis.

Aid for Nicaragua — President Carter gave final approval Sept. 12 to a controversial aid package for Nicaragua long sought by church officials in the U.S. and Nicaragua itself. Congress approved the $75 million package earlier in the year but stipulated that before most of the aid could be given the President had to certify that the Nicaraguan government was not harboring terrorists or serving as a base for Marxist revolution elsewhere in the region. The White House announced that evidence from the intelligence community and U.S. embassies in Central America convinced the President at last that the Nicaraguan government was not aiding terrorism.

Radio Deregulation — In September rounds of the radio deregulation battle, a representative of the U.S. Catholic Conference termed the plan of the Federal Communications Commission "almost an obituary" for the concept of public service in broadcasting. Father Donald Matthews made this comment nine days before Charles D. Ferris, chairman of the FCC, told the International Radio and Television Society Sept. 24 that he would continue to push for deregulation and to spur competition in the communications industry. The FCC plan would remove the requirement that broadcasters ascertain and address community needs at license renewal time, eliminate current limits on time devoted to commercials, drop minimum requirements for news and public affairs programming, and end the requirement that stations keep programming logs. Father Matthews said: "We see the present proceeding as another attempt to promote the dominance of purely commercial interests in broadcasting to the detriment of the public interest."

Pastoral Letter on Health Care — The administrative board of the U.S. Catholic Conference decided at a meeting Sept. 16 to 18 to send the draft of a letter on health care to the general meeting of the bishops in November for further discussion but not for a vote. The reason for delay in voting on "Health and the Ministry of Healing" was controversy over such topics as national health insurance and union organizing in hospitals. The board also decided that "the conference should actively pursue a dialogue with the Catholic Health Association" concerning the contents of the letter.

Ruling on Abortion Funding Sustained — The U.S. Supreme Court announced Sept. 17 that it had rejected without comment an appeal for rehearing on its decision earlier in the year upholding federal limits on abortion funding. The action opened the way for a complete cut-off of federal abortion funding except in cases of rape or incest or endangerment to the life of a mother. Even though the Court decided the case June 30, federal funding for most abortions continued because of a rule that Supreme Court orders do not take effect until the Court announces its decision on a petition for rehearing.

Legal Aid Office Honored — *Socorro Juridico,* the legal aid office of the Archdiocese of San Salvador, was awarded the Letelier-Moffit Human Rights Award for 1980 by the Washington-based Institute for Policy Studies. The office was established by Archbishop Oscar Romero, who was shot to death in March, to help victims of repression and their families. The award was instituted in 1977 to honor co-workers who, it was believed, were assassinated by Chilean agents in Washington Sept. 21, 1976 — Orlando Letelier, a Chilean diplomat and economist, and American analyst Ronni Moffit.

Legion of Mary Activity — Visits by 120 members of the Legion of Mary to more than 7,200 homes in Holy Family Parish, Philadelphia, during the summer found 225 non-Catholics interested in taking instructions in the Catholic faith. Also found were 265 non-Catholics who were receptive to additional home visits by parish representatives, and almost 100 inactive Catholics who expressed interest in resuming practice of their faith.

National Briefs:

• The Diocese of Cleveland reaffirmed its ban on the admission to Catholic schools of students seeking to avoid desegregation in public schools.

• "The Parish Community: Servant of the Word" was the theme for observance of the 1980 Catechetical Sunday, Sept. 21.

Medeiros Letter on Abortion

On Sept. 12, four days before primary elections in Massachusetts, *The Pilot* published a pastoral letter in which Cardinal Humberto Medeiros of Boston said:

"Those who make abortions possible by law — such as legislators and those who promote, defend and elect these same lawmakers — cannot separate themselves totally from the guilt which accompanies this horrendous crime and deadly sin. If you are for true human freedom — and for life — you will follow your conscience when you vote. You will vote to save 'our children, born and unborn.' Your answer to this call must not be taken lightly since it could be a matter of life or death for millions yet to come."

The letter did not name any names. Its contents were in line with church teaching and its consequences in practice. Two candidates for the House of Representatives who favored public funding for abortion were successful in their primary contests.

INTERNATIONAL

Threat to Catholic Schools — A decision handed down by the Supreme Court of British Columbia in August, that a Catholic teacher in a Catholic school who married a divorced man should be allowed to continue teaching there, "threatens the very existence of Catholic schools in the province." So stated Archbishop James Carney of Vancouver in an article published in the *B.C. Catholic,* the archdiocesan newspaper. He said the decision meant that, "in hiring teachers for our Catholic schools, we are not permitted to choose practicing Catholics over Catholics who, even by a public act, have repudiated the most important Catholic values."

Gospel Liberation — Attendants at a meeting focused on pastoral work among Blacks in Latin America stressed the need to bring them "the true Gospel-inspired liberation from sin, fatalistic beliefs, magic and extreme poverty." The meeting, held in Cartagena, Colombia, was sponsored by the Latin American Bishops' Council. It was estimated that approximately 30 million blacks were in Latin America.

Rights Violated in Bolivia — "Human dignity and freedom to preach the Gospel face a tough test "under the military regime that took control of the country July 17, declared the Bolivian Bishops' Conference in a statement issued Sept. 10. The bishops said they had documentary evidence of murders, physical and psychological torture, persecutions and threats against innocent people, firings of workers, expulsions and unwarranted detentions.

Pax Romana Criticized — In a letter addressed to bishops' conferences around the world, Cardinal Opilio Rossi, president of the Pontifical Council for the Laity, charged that the international Catholic organization for intellectuals was "strongly 'politicized,' " had a "misconceived idea" of the role of lay persons in the Church, had "doctrinal and theological positions that were inadequate," and held "a detached and critical approach to the structure of the Church and a defensive and suspicious attitude to ecclesiastical authorities." Father Bonaventure Pelegri, contacted at Pax Romana headquarters in Geneva, said the letter was based on "misinformation and misunderstandings."

Somoza Assassinated — Anastasio Somoza Debayle, the former dictator of Nicaragua, was shot to death Sept. 17 in Asuncion, Paraguay, where he had been living since he was deposed in July, 1979. His death occurred five days after President Carter released $75 million in aid to the revolutionary regime of the country his family had ruled for nearly 50 years.

Mass on Radio in Poland — In a historic breakthrough under communist rule, Polish State Radio carried the first weekly Mass in a nationwide broadcast Sept. 21. Auxiliary Bishop Jerzy Modzelewski celebrated the Mass in Warsaw's Holy Cross Church and preached on the theme, "You shall know the truth and the truth will make you free." The transmission of Sunday Mass every week was one of the concessions striking shipyard workers in Gdansk won from the government earlier in the month.

Social Service Despite Attacks — The standing committee of the Indian Bishops' Conference reported a decision to increase social service activities despite attacks on the Church, especially by the government of West Bengal State. In a memorandum presented to Prime Minister Indira Ghandi, the bishops said: "There are flagrant attacks on the natural rights of men and grave violations of the fundamental rights assured to every citizen of India by our Constitution. We request you . . . to direct that the fundamental rights as laid down in the Constitution be restored and all legislation be withdrawn which seeks to restrict such rights."

Nicaraguan Developments — The bishops declared in a statement that the challenge of integration, liberation and personal growth in revolutionary Nicaragua called for renewed formation of priests, as they announced reopening of the national seminary which had been closed for several years.

In another development, it was reported that close to 500,000 Nicaraguans, mostly in rural areas, had been taught the basics of reading and writing during the six-month National Literacy Crusade in which Catholic teachers and students were heavily involved.

Criticism of El Salvador Junta — As peasants, leftists and priests occupied several church buildings, including the nunciature, to protest political violence, Bishop Arturo Rivera Damas criticized guerrillas and the government. He said the course being followed by the regime was retrogressive in relation to the populist reforms promised by the military officers who assumed power in October, 1979.

International Briefs:

• Christian family life was the main topic on the agenda of the annual plenary meeting of the Canadian Conference of Catholic Bishops Sept. 22 to 26.

• Various church officials and members of human rights groups expressed dismay at the death sentence imposed on Kim Dae Jung, a South Korean political leader, by a military court in Seoul. He was found guilty of violating a national security law.

The Cardinal and Strike Leader

Cardinal Stefan Wyszynski, primate of Poland, met with strike leader Lech Walesa Sept. 7 in what was regarded as an important show of unity between the Church and the worker movement headed by Walesa.

Strikes led by Walesa in the Gdansk area caused the government to grant workers major concessions, including legal recognition of the right to strike and the establishment of independent trade unions.

The meeting helped smooth over criticism of the cardinal previously aired by some workers. During the strike, he preached a homily in which he supported the demands of the workers while also asking them to exercise responsibility and to remember their duty to produce for the good of the nation. An abridged version of the homily in the state-controlled media seemed to many workers to be a call to end the strike without accomplishing its purposes.

OCTOBER 1980

VATICAN

Rumanian Bishop Mourned — Pope John Paul publicly mourned Oct. 1 the death of Bishop Aaron Marton who for years had been the only Catholic bishop allowed to exercise his office in Rumania. The 84-year-old prelate had been head of the Diocese of Alba Julia for more than 40 years. He was jailed or under house arrest from 1948 to 1971 when he was allowed limited freedom.

Plea for United Lebanon — The Pope called for a united Lebanon Oct. 2 during a meeting with representatives of the Lebanese Parliament. "The unity of Lebanon, with respect for the rights of every citizen and for those of its various religious and socio-cultural components, is very much in the heart of the Holy See," he said.

Synagogue Bombing Deplored — In a telegram addressed to Cardinal Francois Marty, the Pope deplored the terrorist bombing of a Paris synagogue Oct. 3 in which at least three persons were killed and 12 injured. He expressed hope that "similar acts of violence may be definitively banished as unworthy of man."

Christian Realism "The Christian must be realistic and recognize without fear the characteristics of the society in which he is called to live," declared the Pope Oct. 4 during an audience with pilgrims from two Italian dioceses. He encouraged them to continue their efforts "to understand our time, its problems and solutions, its questions, its conquests and its defeats."

A Society of Love — Ancient idolatries of wealth and power, still present in our times, must be counteracted by the construction of a new "society of love," said the Pope in a recent message to an international meeting in Rio de Janeiro. The letter strongly condemned "scandalous opulence insensitive to the appeals of many parts of the world."

New Risks of War — During a 10-hour visit to Otranto, the easternmost city of Italy, Pope John Paul appealed again for an easing of tensions in the Middle East to prevent the outbreak of new hostilities. "The Middle East region," he said, "is pervaded by tensions and disputes, with ever impending risks of the explosion of new wars." The purpose of the visit to the city 350 miles from Rome was to honor the memory of 800 Christians martyred there by Turks because they refused to renounce their faith. During a homily preached during Mass outside the cathedral, the Holy Father also said: "I must turn my gaze beyond the sea to the not distant heroic Church in Albania, disturbed by hard and prolonged persecution but enriched by the witness of its martyrs."

Lust Is against Human Dignity — Lustful desires harm the dignity of men and women, declared the Pope in concluding a six-month series of talks on adultery in the hart. Addressing 10,000 persons in St. Peter's Square Oct. 8, he said that adultery committed in the heart "diminishes the richness of the perennial attraction of persons for interpersonal communion. Through such a reduction, the other person becomes the mere object for satisfying a sexual need." He also said: "Adultery in the heart is committed not only because man looks in such a way at a woman who is not his wife, but precisely because he looks at a woman that way. Even if he looks at a woman who is his wife in this way, he would commit the same adultery in the heart."

NATIONAL

Abortion Funding — The House of Representatives and Senate reached a compromise agreement Oct. 1 on abortion provisions of an emergency funding measure for the federal government. The agreement authorized federal abortion funding only in cases where the life of a mother would be endangered and in cases of rape (reported within 72 hours) and incest.

In a related development, the Illinois Department of Public Aid notified about 380,000 welfare recipients and providers that the state, as of Oct. 22, would no longer pay for abortions except to save the life of a mother.

Carter Appointments — Father Franklyn M. McAfee, writing in the *Arlington Catholic Herald,* charged that President Carter had ignored Catholic values by appointing a number of pro-abortionists to executive positions. Named were: Jack Hood Vaughn, former president of the Planned Parenthood Federation of America, to be chief administrator of U.S. foreign aid programs in Latin America; Sarah Weddington, who argued before the U.S. Supreme Court in favor of overturning abortion laws of the states, a presidential assistant: Koryne Hobal, chairlady of Voters for Choice, a U.S. representative to the U.N. commission on the status of women; Irvin Cushner, former chairman of the Alan Guttmacher Institute of Planned Parenthood, deputy assistant secretary for population affairs in the Department of Health and Human Services.

The New Right — Four religious leaders stated Oct. 6 that the so-called New Right posed a serious threat to American pluralism. They said right-wing political activists did not have the right to claim that theirs was the only Christian position and that those who disagreed with them were un-Christian. Msgr. George G. Higgins said: "I find their highly partisan approach to such issues to be strangely selective and extremely simplistic."

Carter Political Ad — A political advertisement showing President Carter standing with Pope John Paul was called an insult to Catholic voters by the Catholic League for Religious and Civil Rights. "We can only regard this use of the Pope as a visual campaign slogan as demeaning to the Holy Father and insulting to Catholic voters," said Father Virgil Blum, S.J., in a message to officials of the Democratic Party.

Supreme Court Actions — On Oct. 6 the U.S. Supreme Court: refused to hear an appeal of a lower court ruling upholding a New York law permitting the use of federal funds to pay for remedial teaching in non-public schools; refused to consider a lower court ruling that parents have no rights to be notified when their under-age children are provided with contraceptives; heard oral arguments on a challenge to a Utah law requiring that parents be notified when a minor daughter requests an abortion.

Strike Threats — New York archdiocesan schools limped through the first few weeks of the academic year under job action and strike threats by teacher associations seeking favorable working and salary conditions from the archdiocese.

J. P. Stevens Contract — Union workers at seven J. P. Stevens and Co. plants in Roanoke Rapids, N.C., voted Oct. 19 to approve a contract with the nation's second largest textile firm, ending a 17-year battle over unionization. During that time, the company was found guilty of violating federal labor laws 22 times and was the object of a nationwide boycott launched in 1975. The contract affected about 3,000 production and maintenance workers. Stevens had a total of 160 plants and more than 44,000 workers. Catholic bishops and various church groups were involved in the Steven's boycott and efforts to settle disputes between the corporation and its employees over unionization.

INTERNATIONAL

Natural Family Planning — Scientists and natural family planning experts from 40 countries took part in the meeting of the International Federation of Family Life Promotion which ended Oct. 1 in Dublin.

Missionaries Released in Bolivia — Two U.S. missionaries of the Society of St. James were allowed by the Bolivian government Oct. 1 to leave the apostolic nunciature in La Paz and return to their parish in Oruro. Fathers Ronald Rusk and Gerard Leclerc had been arrested Aug. 22. Like others, they were arrested and detained during the period of political crisis following the government coup of July 17.

Some Schools Continue in Iran — Archbishop Hilarion Capucci, acting apparently as an unofficial Vatican mediator, reported early in the month that Iranian authorities had agreed to allow 40 Christian schools to continue functioning. Seven of the schools were Catholic institutions. Seven other Catholic educational institutions, however, were to remain closed. The archbishop, just returned from Iran, carried a letter to the Pope from President Abolhassan Bani-Sadr. He said the letter mentioned neither the situation of the U.S. hostages in Iran nor the war in progress between Iraq and Iran.

Marxist-Inspired Education — Archbishop Miguel Obando Bravo of Managua, after a study of government documents on education, said they were "inspired by Marxist-Leninist theories, since they clearly quote from Russian and Cuban teachers and Fidel Castro."

Sacrifice Necessary — Efforts to achieve a new world economic order require "substantial sacrifices" by the rich in favor of the poor, stated Archbishop Ernesto Gallina, head of a six-member Vatican delegation to the 21st general conference of UNESCO in Belgrade.

No More Nuclear Plants — A joint working group set up by Catholic and Protestant churches in Ireland was "strongly sympathetic" to the view that no more nuclear power stations should be built until a way is found to dispose of nuclear waste in a safe manner.

Guadalupe Celebration — Mexican Catholics were preparing to launch a Marian Year in preparation for the celebration in December, 1981, of the 450th anniversary of the apparitions of Our Lady of Guadalupe to Juan Diego, an Indian laborer. A bishops' committee said in a statement that the celebration would be "a way to purify popular devotion to the Mother of God and achieve the integration of the Mexican community . . . within the goals of justice and brotherhood. . . . Communion and sharing in the Church must show in the implementation of justice and sharing of goods as a result of Christian charity and the Holy Spirit in our life. Such a commitment with justice in building a new society must lead to the radical change of unjust structures and to the creation of new programs for social responsibility."

Stop Bloodshed — Citing a "vertigo of madness that threatens to engulf us all in a sea of fratricidal bloodshed," the bishops of El Salvador pleaded with the nation's warring political factions to end their campaigns of violence. "No more death! No more hatred! No more revenge! In the name of God, stop the bloodshed!" they said in a pastoral letter issued at the end of September. The bishops spoke of the undeclared civil war that had caused about 6,000 deaths since January and called it "the darkest, most tragic moment in our history." The major political violence was caused by leftist guerrillas, government security forces and rightist groups supporting the security forces.

POPE JOHN PAUL II

(See related entries under John Paul II in Index.)

Cardinal-Archbishop Karol Wojtyla of Cracow was elected Bishop of Rome Oct. 16, 1978, on the seventh or eighth ballot cast on the second day of voting at a conclave of 111 cardinals. He chose the name John Paul II and was invested with the pallium, the symbol of his papal office, Oct. 22 in ceremonies attended by more than 250,000 persons in St. Peter's Square.

The 263rd successor of St. Peter as Bishop of Rome and Supreme Pastor of the Universal Church, he is the first non-Italian Pope since Adrian VI (1522-23), the first Polish Pope in the history of the Church, and the youngest at the time of his election since Pius IX (1846-78).

Early Career

Karol Wojtyla was born May 18, 1920, in Wadowice, Poland.

He began higher studies at the age of 18, with major interests in poetry and theater arts. Forced to suspend university courses because of the outbreak of World War II, he went to work in a stone quarry and a chemical plant, thereby earning the later designation of himself as the "Worker Cardinal."

He started studies for the priesthood in 1942 in the underground seminary of Cracow, whose operations had been banned after the Nazi invasion of Poland.

Ordained to the priesthood Nov. 1, 1946, he was immediately sent to Rome for studies at the Angelicum University, where he earned a doctorate in ethics.

Back home in Poland, he worked as an assistant pastor in a village parish and as a chaplain to university students while continuing studies at the Catholic University of Lublin. He was awarded another doctorate there, in moral theology.

He began writing about this time, and eventually produced more than 100 articles and several books on ethical and other themes. Phenomenology was one of his fields of expertise.

University teaching came next, in 1953, with appointment in 1954 to the position of lecturer and later to the chair of ethics at the Catholic University of Lublin, the most prestigious institute of higher learning in Poland.

Bishop and Cardinal

He was ordained Auxiliary Bishop of Cracow Sept. 28, 1958, became vicar capitular in 1962 after the death of Apostolic Administrator Eugeniusz Baziak, and was appointed Archbishop Jan. 13, 1964. He was the first residential head of the see since the death of Cardinal Adam Sapieha in 1951. Between then and 1964 the archdiocese was run by administrators because the Communist government refused to permit the appointment and ministry of a residential bishop.

Archbishop Wojtyla attended all sessions of the Second Vatican Council from 1962 to 1965, and was one of the writers of the *Pastoral Constitution on the Church in the Modern World.* He also contributed input to the *Declaration on Religious Freedom* and the *Decree on the Instruments of Social Communication.*

His efforts to put into effect the directives of the council induced him to write a book, *Foundations of Renewal,* in 1972 and to start that same year an archdiocesan synod he saw concluded as Pope during his visit to Poland in 1979.

He was inducted into the College of Cardinals June 26, 1967, as one of the younger members, and subsequently served actively in the Congregation for the Sacraments and Divine Worship, the Congregation for the Clergy, and the Congregation for Catholic Education.

He also served as a theological consultant to Pope Paul VI.

He attended assemblies of the Synod of Bishops as a representative of the Polish Bishops' Conference and was a member of the synod's permanent council.

From the beginning of his priestly career, and especially during his episcopate, the Cardinal was vigorous in the defense of human and religious rights, the rights of workers, and rights to religious education.

Close to Cardinal Wyszynski and in company with his fellow bishops, he negotiated the tightrope of Catholic survival in a country under Communist control. With them, and as their spokesman at times, he was stalwart in resisting efforts of the regime to impose atheism, materialism and secularism on the people and culture of Poland.

The First Year

Since the beginning of his pontificate, John Paul has been active as Bishop of Rome, with frequent visits to parishes and institutions of the diocese for the celebration of Mass and participation in other events. During these visits, as well as others to places of pilgrimage and historic significance in Italy, he has had perhaps more personal contact with the faithful than any other Pope. The number of attendants at weekly general audiences at the Vatican and Castel Gandolfo has been unprecedented.

Unprecedented also was the attention focused on him during his first three pilgrimages of faith in 1979 — to the Dominican

Republic and Mexico, Poland, Ireland and the United States — when he celebrated Mass, spoke and moved about among millions of people.

The messages he delivered during these trips were the equivalent of doctrinal, pastoral and social encyclical letters on a wide variety of subjects, all related to the key document of the first year of his pontificate. This was the formal encyclical *Redemptor Hominis*, a treatise on Christian anthropology dealing with the divine and human aspects of redemption and the mission of the Church to carry on a dialogue of salvation with all peoples.

Other significant documents issued in 1979 included *Sapientia Christiana*, concerning pontifical institutions of higher learning, a decree in which he promulgated a New Vulgate version of the Bible, and a letter to priests detailing the dignity, fidelity and responsibilities of their calling. Additional statements and addresses, too numerous to mention, covered a wide variety of topics related to Christian life and actual conditions of those to whom they were addressed.

In his relations with the hierarchy in 1979, the Pope met with groups of bishops making required *ad limina* visits to the Vatican, for first-hand reports and admonitions regarding dioceses all over the world. In June, he inducted 14 new cardinals into the Sacred College, raising its membership at that time to 135.

Second Year

The following events, many of which are covered at greater length in other Almanac entries, were among those of significance during the second year of Pope John Paul's pontificate.

Several weeks after the start of the second year, Pope John Paul convoked the first plenary assembly of the College of Cardinals in more than 400 years.

Ecumenical Voyage: This is what the Pope called his trip to Turkey at the end of November, 1979. He met with Orthodox Ecumenical Patriarch Dimitrios I and, with him, announced the establishment of a joint commission of theologians to begin formal dialogue in quest of the union of Roman Catholic and Orthodox Churches.

Doctrinal Concern: In December, the Pope directly confronted the controversial writings of Father Hans Kung by giving his approval to a declaration by the Congregation for the Doctrine of the Faith that he could not be regarded as a Catholic theologian.

Synods: The Holy Father convoked three of them in 1980.

• With the Dutch bishops at the Vatican for a particular synod in January, he called for measures to cope with differences among the prelates, polarization among the people and action to remedy doctrinal and disciplinary problems.

• Meeting with Ukrainian bishops in March, he turned down demands made by some of their people for a patriarchate, and named a successor to Cardinal Josyf Slipyi.

• With more than 200 delegates from episcopal conferences around the world, he held the fifth ordinary assembly of the Synod of Bishops for deliberations on the "Role of the Christian Family in the World."

Pastoral Pilgrimages: The Holy Father made three of them between May and July. A fourth one was scheduled for West Germany Nov. 15 to 19.

• He visited six African nations in May. He spoke about Africanization of the Church, the cultural values of African peoples and the independence they should have from alien influences of other countries.

• In France for an address before the United Nations Educational, Scientific and Cultural Organization in May, he delineated with great clarity the stance of the Church on a wide variety of subjects, with special emphasis on its role in a secularized state, society, and culture.

• During a 13-city tour of Brazil in July, the Pope declared that the Church is on the side of the poor, appealed for across-the-board respect for human rights by governments and people of influence, called for measures of economic and social reform, and indicated his approval of non-violent social activism for the good of all peoples. He attended a plenary assembly of the bishops of the country and took part in opening ceremonies of a national Eucharistic congress.

Audiences and Addresses: The Pope delivered hundreds of addresses during the year at general and private audiences and on special occasions. All of them were thoroughly grounded in doctrinal essentials coupled with relevance to the people being addressed or the events being commemorated.

Reactions to the Pope: "After two years of Pope John Paul's pontificate, three phases can be distinguished," wrote Desmond O'Grady in *Our Sunday Visitor,* Oct. 19, 1980.

"The first was that of curiosity in the Pope who came in from the cold. . . . The second, which began with his trip to the United States and continued with the sanction against Hans Kung, was that of some people still liking the singer but not the song. The third began with his Brazilian trip in which he showed flexibility as well as tact and forcefulness as he unequivocally backed church commitment for social justice."

The two-year record of Pope John Paul's pontificate is testimony to O'Grady's observation that he is a man of decisive leadership for doctrinal orthodoxy and church discipline.

First Century

Early 30's: First Christian Pentecost: gathering together of the Christian community, outpouring of the Holy Spirit, preaching of St. Peter to Jews in Jerusalem, baptism and aggregation of some 3,000 persons to the Christian community.

St. Stephen, deacon, was stoned to death at Jerusalem; he is venerated as the first Christian martyr.

34-64/67: St. Paul, formerly Saul the persecutor of Christians, was converted, baptized and joined to the college of Apostles. After three major missionary journeys, he was martyred in 64 or 67 at Rome.

39: The Gentile Cornelius and his family were baptized by St. Peter.

42: Persecution of Christians in Palestine broke out during the rule of Herod Agrippa; St. James the Greater, the first Apostle to die, was beheaded in 44; St. Peter was imprisoned for a short time; many Christians fled to Antioch and elsewhere.

At Antioch, the followers of Christ were first called Christians.

49: Christians at Rome, who were considered members of a Jewish sect, were adversely affected by a decree of Claudius which forbade Jewish worship there.

51: The Council of Jerusalem, in which all the Apostles participated under the presidency of St. Peter, decreed that circumcision, dietary regulations, and various other prescriptions of Mosaic Law were not obligatory for Gentile converts to the Christian community. The decree was issued in opposition to Judaizers who contended that observance of the Mosaic Law in its entirety was necessary for salvation.

64: Persecution under Nero: The emperor, accusing Christians of starting a fire which destroyed half of Rome, inaugurated the era of major Roman persecutions.

64/65: Martyrdom of St. Peter at Rome during the Neronian persecution. He established his see and spent his last years there after preaching in and around Jerusalem, establishing a see at Antioch, and presiding at the Council of Jerusalem.

70: Destruction of Jerusalem by Titus.

88-97: Pontificate of St. Clement I, third successor of St. Peter as bishop of Rome, one of the Apostolic Fathers. The *First Epistle of Clement to the Corinthians*, with which he has been identified, was addressed by the Church of Rome to the Church at Corinth, the scene of irregularities and divisions in the Christian community.

95: Domitian persecuted Christians, principally at Rome.

c. 100: Death of St. John, Apostle and Evangelist, marking the end of the Age of the Apostles and the first generation of the Church.

Second Century

c. 107: St. Ignatius of Antioch was martyred at Rome. He was the first writer to use the expression, "the Catholic Church."

112: Rescript to Pliny. Emperor Trajan instructed Pliny, governor of Bithynia, not to search out Christians but to punish them if they were publicly denounced and refused to do homage to the Roman gods. The rescript set a pattern of discretionary leniency for Roman magistrates in dealing with Christians.

117-138: Persecution under Hadrian. Many *Acts of Martyrs* date from this period.

c. 125: Spread of Gnosticism.

c. 155: St. Polycarp, bishop of Smyrna and disciple of St. John the Evangelist, was martyred.

c. 156: Beginning of Montanism.

161-180: Reign of Marcus Aurelius. His persecution, launched in the wake of natural disasters, was more violent than those of his predecessors.

165: St. Justin, an important early Christian writer, was martyred at Rome.

c. 180: St. Irenaeus, bishop of Lyons and one of the great early theologians, wrote *Adversus Haereses*. He stated that the teaching and tradition of the Roman See was the standard for belief.

196: Easter Controversy.

The *Didache,* written in the second century, was an important record of Christian belief, practice and government in the first century.

Latin was introduced in the West as a liturgical language.

The Catechetical School of Alexandria, founded about the middle of the century, increased in importance.

Third Century

202: Persecution under Septimius Severus, who wanted to establish one common religion in the Empire.

206: Tertullian, a convert since 197 and the first great ecclesiastical writer in Latin, joined the heretical Montanists. He died in 230.

215: Death of Clement of Alexandria, teacher of Origen and a founding father of the School of Alexandria.

217-235: St. Hippolytus, the first antipope. He was reconciled to the Church while in prison during persecution in 235.

232-254: Origen established the School of Caesarea after being deposed in 231 as head of the School of Alexandria; he died in 254. A scholar and voluminous writer, he was one of the founders of systematic theology and exerted wide influence for many years.

c. 242: Manichaeism originated in Persia.

249-251: Persecution under Decius. Many of those who denied the faith *(lapsi)* sought readmission to the Church at the end of the persecution in 251. Pope St. Cornelius had correspondence with St. Cyprian on the subject and ordered that *lapsi* were to be readmitted after suitable penance.

250-300: Neo-Platonism of Plotinus and Porphyry gained followers.

251: Novatian, an antipope, was condemned at Rome.

256: Pope St. Stephen I upheld the validity of baptism administered by heretics, in the Rebaptism Controversy.

257: Persecution under Valerian, who attempted to destroy the Church as a social structure.

258: St. Cyprian, bishop of Carthage, was martyred.

c. 260: St. Lucian founded the exegetical School of Antioch.

Pope St. Dionysius condemned teachings of Sabellius and the Marcionites.

261: Gallienus issued an edict of toleration which ended general persecution for nearly 40 years.

c. 266: Sabellianism was condemned and Paul of Samosata deposed.

292: Diocletian divided the Roman Empire into East and West. The division emphasized political, cultural and other differences between the two parts of the Empire and influenced the Church in the East and West. The prestige of Rome began to decline.

Fourth Century

303: Persecution broke out under Diocletian. It ended in the West in 306 but continued for 10 years in the East; it was particularly violent in 304.

305: St. Anthony of Heracles established a foundation for hermits near the Red Sea in Egypt.

c. 306: The first local legislation on clerical celibacy was enacted by a council held at Elvira, Spain; bishops, priests, deacons and other ministers were forbidden to have wives.

310: St. Hilarion established a foundation for hermits in Palestine.

311: An edict of toleration issued by Galerius at the urging of Constantine and Licinius officially ended persecution in the West; some persecution continued in the East.

313: The *Edict of Milan* issued by Constantine and Licinius recognized Christianity as a lawful religion and the legal freedom of all religions in the Roman Empire.

314: The Council of Arles condemned Donatism in Africa and declared that baptism by heretics was valid.

318: St. Pachomius established the first foundation of the cenobitic (common) life, as compared with the solitary life of hermits in Upper Egypt.

325: The Ecumenical Council of Nicaea (I),

first of its kind in the history of the Church, condemned Arianism; see separate entry.

326: Discovery of the True Cross on which Christ was crucified.

337: Baptism and death of Constantine.

c. 342: Beginning of a 40-year persecution in Persia.

343-344: A local Council of Sardica reaffirmed doctrine formulated by Nicaea I and declared that bishops had the right of appeal to the pope as the highest authority in the Church.

361-363: Julian the Apostate waged an unsuccessful campaign against the Church in an attempt to restore paganism as the religion of the Empire.

c. 365: Persecution under Valens in the East.

c. 376: Beginning of the barbarian invasion in the West.

379: Death of St. Basil, the Father of Monasticism in the East. His writings contributed greatly to the development of rules for the religious life.

381: The Ecumenical Council of Constantinople (I); see separate entry.

382: The *Decree of Pope St. Damasus* listed the Canon of Sacred Scripture.

382-c. 406: St. Jerome translated the Old and New Testaments into Latin. His work is called the Vulgate Version of the Bible.

396: St. Augustine became bishop of Hippo.

397: A local Council of Carthage published the Canon of Sacred Scripture.

Fifth Century

410: Visigoths sacked Rome.

411: Donatism was condemned by a council at Carthage.

430: St. Augustine, bishop of Hippo for 35 years, died. He was a strong defender of orthodox doctrine against Manichaeism, Donatism and Pelagianism. The depth and range of his writings made him a dominant influence in Christian thought for many centuries.

431: The Ecumenical Council of Ephesus; see separate entry.

432: St. Patrick arrived in Ireland. By the time of his death in 461 most of the country had been converted, monasteries founded and the hierarchy established.

438: The *Theodosian Code,* a compilation of decrees for the Empire, was issued by Theodosius II. It had great influence on subsequent civil and ecclesiastical law.

449: The Robber Council of Ephesus, which did not have ecclesiastical sanction, declared itself in favor of the opinions of Eutyches who contended that Christ had only one nature.

451: The Ecumenical Council of Chalcedon; see separate entry.

452: Pope St. Leo the Great persuaded Attila the Hun to spare Rome.

455: Vandals sacked Rome. The decline of

imperial Rome dates approximately from this time.

484: Patriarch Acacius of Constantinople was excommunicated for signing the *Henoticon*, a unity law published by Emperor Zeno in 482 to end the turmoil associated with the Monophysite heresy. The document capitulated to the heresy. The excommunication triggered a 35-year-long schism.

494: Pope St. Gelasius I declared in a letter to Emperor Anastasius that the pope had power and authority over the emperor in spiritual matters.

496: Clovis, King of the Franks, was converted and became the defender of Christianity in the West. The Franks became a Catholic people.

Sixth Century

520 and later: Irish monasteries flourished as centers for spiritual life, missionary training and scholarly activity.

529: The Second Council of Orange condemned Semi-Pelagianism.

c. 529: St. Benedict founded the Monte Cassino Abbey. Some years before his death in 543 he wrote a monastic rule which exercised tremendous influence on the form and style of religious life. He is called the Father of Monasticism in the West.

533: John II became the first pope to change his name. The practice did not become general until the time of Sergius IV (1009).

533-534: Emperor Justinian promulgated the *Corpus Juris Civilis* for the Roman world. Like the *Theodosian Code*, it influenced subsequent civil and ecclesiastical law.

c. 545: Death of Dionysius Exiguus who was the first to date history from the birth of Christ, a practice which resulted in use of the B.C. and A.D. abbreviations. His calculations were at least four years late.

553: The Ecumenical Council of Constantinople (II); see separate entry.

585: St. Columban founded an influential monastic school at Luxeuil. He died in 615.

589: The most important of several councils of Toledo was held. The Visigoths renounced Arianism, and St. Leander began the organization of the Church in Spain.

590-604: Pontificate of Pope St. Gregory I the Great. He set the form and style of the papacy which prevailed throughout the Middle Ages; exerted great influence on doctrine and liturgy; was strong in support of monastic discipline and clerical celibacy; authored writings on many subjects. Gregorian Chant is named in his honor.

596: Pope St. Gregory I the Great sent St. Augustine of Canterbury and 40 monks to do missionary work in England.

597: St. Columba died. He founded an important monastery at Iona, established schools and did notable missionary work in Scotland.

By the end of the century, monasteries of nuns were common; Western monasticism was flourishing; monasticism in the East, under the influence of Monophysitism and other factors, was losing its vigor.

Seventh Century

613: St. Columban established the influential Monastery of Bobbio in northern Italy.

622: The Hegira (flight) of Mohammed from Mecca to Medina signalled the beginning of Islam, which, by the end of the century, claimed almost all of the southern Mediterranean area.

629: Emperor Heraclius recovered the True Cross from the Persians.

649: A Lateran Council condemned two erroneous formulas *(Ecthesis* and *Type)* issued by emperors Heraclius and Constans II as means of reconciling Monophysites with the Church.

664: Actions of the Synod of Whitby advanced the adoption of Roman usages in England, especially regarding the date for the observance of Easter. (See Easter Controversy.)

680-681: The Ecumenical Council of Constantinople (III); see separate entry.

692: Trullan Synod. Eastern-Church discipline on clerical celibacy was settled, permitting marriage before ordination to the diaconate and continuation in marriage afterwards, but prohibiting marriage following the death of the wife thereafter. Anti-Roman canons contributed to East-West alienation.

During the century, the monastic influence of Ireland and England increased in Western Europe; schools and learning declined; regulations regarding clerical celibacy became more strict in the East.

Eighth Century

711: Moslems began the conquest of Spain.

726: Emperor Leo III, the Isaurian, launched a campaign against the veneration of sacred images and relics; called Iconoclasm (image-breaking), it caused turmoil in the East until about 843.

731: Pope Gregory II and a synod at Rome condemned Iconoclasm, with a declaration that the veneration of sacred images was in accord with Catholic tradition.

Venerable Bede issued his *Ecclesiastical History of the English People*.

732: Charles Martel defeated the Moslems at Poitiers, halting farther advance by them in the West.

744: The Monastery of Fulda was established by St. Sturm, a disciple of St. Boniface.

754: A council of more than 300 Byzantine bishops endorsed Iconoclast errors. This council and its actions were condemned by the Lateran Synod of 769.

Stephen II (III) crowned Pepin ruler of the Franks. Pepin twice invaded Italy, in 754 and 756, to defend the pope against the Lombards. His land grants to the papacy, called the Donation of Pepin, were later extended by Charlemagne (773) and formed part of the States of the Church.

c. 755: St. Boniface (Winfrid) was martyred. He was called the Apostle of Germany for his missionary work and organization of the hierarchy there.

781: Alcuin was chosen by Charlemagne to organize a Palace School, which became a center of intellectual leadership.

787: The Ecumenical Council of Nicaea (II); see separate entry.

792: A council at Ratisbon condemned Adoptionism.

The famous *Book of Kells* ("The Great Gospel of Columcille") dates from the early eighth or late seventh century.

Ninth Century

800: Charlemagne was crowned Emperor by Pope Leo III on Christmas Day.

Egbert became king of West Saxons. He unified England and strengthened the See of Canterbury.

813: Emperor Leo V, the Armenian, revived Iconoclasm, which persisted until about 843.

814: Charlemagne died.

843: The Treaty of Verdun split the Frankish kingdom among Charlemagne's three grandsons.

844: A Eucharistic controversy involving the writings of Paschasius Radbertus, Ratramnus and Rabanus Maurus occasioned the development of terminology regarding the doctrine of the Real Presence.

846: The Moslems invaded Italy and attacked Rome.

847-852: Period of composition of the *False Decretals*, a collection of forged documents attributed to popes from St. Clement (88-97) to Gregory II (715-731). The *Decretals*, which strongly supported the autonomy and rights of bishops, were suspect for a long time before being repudiated entirely about 1628.

848: The Council of Mainz condemned Gottschalk for heretical teaching regarding predestination. He was also condemned by the Council of Quierzy in 853.

857: Photius displaced Ignatius as patriarch of Constantinople. This marked the beginning of the Photian Schism, a confused state of East-West relations which has not yet been cleared up by historical research. Photius, a man of exceptional ability, died in 891.

865: St. Ansgar, Apostle of Scandinavia, died.

868: Sts. Cyril (d. 869) and Methodius (d. 885) were consecrated bishops. The Apostles of the Slavs devised an alphabet and translated the Gospels and liturgy into the Slavonic language.

869: The Ecumenical Council of Constantinople (IV); see separate entry.

871-c. 900: Reign of Alfred the Great, the only English king ever anointed by a pope at Rome.

Tenth Century

910: William, Duke of Aquitaine, founded the Benedictine Abbey of Cluny, which became a center of monastic and ecclesiastical reform.

915: Pope John X played a leading role in the expulsion of Saracens from central and southern Italy.

955: St. Olga, of the Russian royal family, was baptized.

962: Otto I, the Great, crowned by Pope John XII, revived Charlemagne's kingdom, which became the Holy Roman Empire.

966: Mieszko, first of a royal line in Poland, was baptized; he brought Latin Christianity to Poland.

989: Vladimir, ruler of Russia, was baptized. Russia was subsequently Christianized by Greek missionaries.

993: John XV was the first pope to decree the official canonization of a saint (Ulrich) for the universal Church.

997: St. Stephen became ruler of Hungary. He assisted in organizing the hierarchy and establishing Latin Christianity in that country.

999-1003: Pontificate of Sylvester II (Gerbert of Aquitaine), a Benedictine monk and the first French pope.

Eleventh Century

1009: Beginning of lasting East-West schism in the Church, marked by dropping of the name of Pope Sergius IV from the Byzantine diptychs (the listing of persons prayed for during the liturgy). The deletion was made by Patriarch Sergius II of Constantinople.

1012: St. Romuald founded the Camaldolese Hermits.

1025: The Council of Arras, and other councils later, condemned the Cathari (Neo-Manichaeans, Albigenses).

1027: The Council of Elne proclaimed the Truce of God as a means of stemming violence. The truce involved armistice periods of varying length, which were later extended.

1038: St. John Gualbert founded the Vallombrosians.

1043-1059: Constantinople patriarchate of Michael Cerularius, the key figure in a controversy concerning the primacy of the papacy. His and the Byzantine synod's refusal to acknowledge this primacy in 1054 widened and hardened the East-West schism in the Church.

1047: Pope Clement II died. He was the only pope ever buried in Germany.

1049-54: Pontificate of St. Leo IX, who inaugurated a movement of papal, diocesan, monastic and clerical reform.

1055: Condemnation of the Eucharistic doctrine of Berengarius.

1059: A Lateran Council issued new legislation regarding papal elections. Voting power was entrusted to the Roman cardinals.

1066: Death of St. Edward the Confessor, King of England from 1042 and restorer of Westminster Abbey.

Defeat, at Hastings, of Harold by William I, who subsequently exerted strong influence on the life style of the Church in England.

1073-1085: Pontificate of St. Gregory VII (Hildebrand). A strong pope, he carried forward programs of clerical and general ecclesiastical reform and struggled against Henry IV and other rulers to end the evils of lay investiture. He introduced the Latin liturgy in Spain and set definite dates for the observance of ember days.

1077: Henry IV, excommunicated and suspended from the exercise of imperial powers by Gregory VII, sought absolution from the Pope at Canossa. Henry later repudiated this action and in 1084 forced Gregory to leave Rome.

1079: The Council of Rome condemned Eucharistic errors of Berengarius, who retracted.

1084: St. Bruno founded the Carthusians.

1097-1099: The first of several Crusades undertaken between this time and 1265. Recovery of the Holy Places and gaining free access to them for Christians were the original purposes, but these were diverted to less worthy objectives in various ways. Results included: a Latin Kingdom of Jerusalem, 1099-1187; a military and political misadventure in the form of a Latin Empire of Constantinople, 1204-1261; acquisition, by treaties, of visiting rights for Christians in the Holy Land. East-West economic and cultural relationships increased during the period. In the religious sphere, actions of the Crusaders had the effect of increasing the alienation of the East from the West.

1098: St. Robert founded the Cistercians.

Twelfth Century

1108: Beginnings of the influential Abbey and School of St. Victor.

1115: St. Bernard established the Abbey of Clairvaux and inaugurated the Cistercian Reform.

1118: Christian forces captured Saragossa, Spain; the beginning of the Moslem decline in that country.

1121: St. Norbert established the original monastery of the Praemonstratensians near Laon, France.

1122: The Concordat of Worms (Pactum Callixtinum) was formulated and approved by Pope Callistus II and Emperor Henry V to settle controversy concerning the investiture of prelates. The concordat provided that the emperor could invest prelates with symbols of temporal authority but had no right to invest them with spiritual authority, which came from the Church alone, and that the emperor was not to interfere in papal elections. This was the first concordat in history.

1123: The Ecumenical Council of the Lateran (I), the first of its kind in the West; see separate entry.

1139: The Ecumenical Council of the Lateran (II); see separate entry.

1140: St. Bernard met Abelard in debate at the Council of Sens. Abelard, whose rationalism in theology was condemned for the first time in 1121, died in 1142 at Cluny.

1148: The Synod of Rheims enacted strict disciplinary decrees for communities of women religious.

1152: The Synod of Kells reorganized the Church in Ireland.

1160: Gratian, whose *Decretum* became a basic text of Canon Law, died.

Peter Lombard, compiler of the *Four Books of Sentences,* a standard theology text for nearly 200 years, died.

1170: St. Thomas Becket, archbishop of Canterbury, who clashed with Henry II over Church-state relations, was murdered in his cathedral.

1171: Pope Alexander III reserved the process of canonization of saints to the Holy See.

1179: The Ecumenical Council of the Lateran (III); see separate entry.

1184: Waldenses and other heretics were excommunicated by Pope Lucius III.

Thirteenth Century

1198-1216: Pontificate of Innocent III, during which the papacy reached its medieval peak of authority, influence and prestige in the Church and in relations with civil rulers.

1208: Innocent III called for a crusade, the first in Christendom itself, against the Albigensians.

1209: Verbal approval was given by Innocent III to a rule of life for the Order of Friars Minor, started by St. Francis of Assisi.

1212: The Second Order of Franciscans, the Poor Clares, was founded.

1215: The Ecumenical Council of the Lateran (IV); see separate entry.

1216: Formal papal approval was given to a rule of life for the Order of Preachers, started by St. Dominic.

The Portiuncula Indulgence was granted by the Holy See at the request of St. Francis of Assisi.

1221: The Third Order of St. Francis for lay persons was founded.

1226: Death of St. Francis of Assisi.

1245: The Ecumenical Council of Lyons (I); see separate entry.

1247: Preliminary approval was given by the Holy See to a Carmelite rule of life.

1270: St. Louis IX, king of France, died.

Beginning of papal decline.

1274: The Ecumenical Council of Lyons (II); see separate entry.

Death of St. Thomas Aquinas, Doctor of the Church, of lasting influence; see separate entry.

1280: Pope Nicholas III, who made the *Breviary* the official prayer book for clergy of the Roman Church, died.

1281: The excommunication of Michael Palaeologus by Pope Martin IV ruptured the union effected with the Eastern Church in 1274.

Fourteenth Century

1302: Pope Boniface VIII issued the bull *Unam Sanctam*, concerning the unity of the Church and the temporal power of princes, against the background of a struggle with Philip IV of France; it was the most famous medieval document on the subject.

1308-1378: For a period of approximately 70 years, seven popes resided at Avignon because of unsettled conditions in Rome and other reasons; see separate entry.

1311-1312: The Ecumenical Council of Vienne; see separate entry.

1321: Dante Alighieri died a year after completing the *Divine Comedy.*

1324: Marsilius of Padua completed *Defensor Pacis*, a work condemned by Pope John XXII as heretical because of its denial of papal primacy and the hierarchical structure of the Church, and for other reasons. It was a charter for conciliarism.

1337-1453: Period of the Hundred Years' War, a dynastic struggle between France and England.

1338: Four years after the death of Pope John XXII, who had opposed Louis IV of Bavaria in a years-long controversy, electoral princes declared at the Diet of Rhense that the emperor did not need papal confirmation of his title and right to rule. Charles IV later (1356) said the same thing in a *Golden Bull*, eliminating papal rights in the election of emperors.

1347-1350: The Black Death swept across Europe, killing perhaps one-fourth to one-third of the total population; an estimated 40 per cent of the clergy succumbed.

1374: Petrarch, poet and humanist, died.

1378: Return of the papacy from Avignon to Rome.

Beginning of the Western Schism; see separate entry.

Fifteenth Century

1409: The Council of Pisa, without canonical authority, tried to end the Western Schism but succeeded only in complicating it by electing a third claimant to the papacy; see Western Schism.

1414-1418: The Ecumenical Council of Constance ended the Western Schism; see separate entry.

1431: St. Joan of Arc was burned at the stake.

1431-1449: The Council of Basle, which began with convocation by Pope Martin V in 1431, turned into an anti-papal forum of conciliarists seeking to subject the primacy and authority of the pope to the overriding authority of an assembly of bishops. It was not an ecumenical council.

1438: The Pragmatic Sanction of Bourges was enacted by Charles VIII and the French parliament to curtail papal authority over the Church in France, in the spirit of conciliarism. It found expression in Gallicanism and had effects lasting at least until the French Revolution.

1438-1443: The Ecumenical Council of Florence affirmed the primacy of the pope in opposition to conciliarism and effected a measure of union with separated Eastern Christians; see separate entry.

1453: The fall of Constantinople to the Turks.

c. 1456: Gutenberg issued the first edition of the Bible printed from movable type, at Mainz, Germany.

1476: Pope Sixtus IV ordered observance of the feast of the Immaculate Conception on Dec. 8 throughout the Church.

1492: Columbus discovered the Americas.

1493: Pope Alexander VI issued a *Bull of Demarcation* which determined spheres of influence for the Spanish and Portuguese in the Americas.

The Renaissance, a humanistic movement which originated in Italy in the 14th century, spread to France, Germany, the Low Countries and England. A transitional period between the medieval world and the modern secular world, it introduced profound changes which affected literature and the other arts, general culture, politics and religion.

Sixteenth Century

1512-1517: The Ecumenical Council of the Lateran (V); see separate entry.

1517: Martin Luther signalled the beginning of the Reformation by posting 95 theses at Wittenberg. Subsequently, he broke completely from doctrinal orthodoxy in discourses and three published works (1519 and 1520); was excommunicated on more than 40 charges of heresy (1521); remained the dominant figure in the Reformation in Germany until his death in 1546.

1519: Zwingli triggered the Reformation in Zurich and became its leading proponent there until his death in combat in 1531.

1524: Luther's encouragement of German princes in putting down the two-year Peasants' Revolt gained political support for his cause.

1528: The Order of Friars Minor Capuchin was approved as an autonomous division of the Franciscan Order; like the Jesuits, the Capuchins became leaders in the Counter-Reformation.

1530: The *Augsburg Confession* of Lutheran faith was issued; it was later supplemented by the *Smalcald Articles* approved in 1537.

1533: Henry VIII divorced Catherine of Aragon, married Anne Boleyn, was excommunicated. In 1534 he decreed the Act of Supremacy, making the sovereign the head of the Church in England, under which Sts. John Fisher and Thomas More were executed in 1535. Despite his rejection of papal primacy and actions against monastic life in England, he generally maintained doctrinal orthodoxy until his death in 1547.

1536: John Calvin, leader of the Reformation in Switzerland until his death in 1564, issued the first edition of *Institutes of the Christian Religion*, which became the classical text of Reformed (non-Lutheran) theology.

1540: The constitutions of the Society of Jesus (Jesuits), founded by St. Ignatius of Loyola, were approved.

1541: Start of the 11-year career of St. Francis Xavier as a missionary to the East Indies and Japan.

1545-1563: The Ecumenical Council of Trent formulated statements of Catholic doctrine under attack by the Reformers and mobilized the Counter-Reformation; see separate entry.

1549: The first *Book of Common Prayer* was issued by Edward VI. Revised editions were published in 1552, 1559 and 1662.

1553: Start of the five-year reign of Mary Tudor who tried to counteract actions of Henry VIII against the Roman Church.

1555: Enactment of the Peace of Augsburg, an arrangement of religious territorialism rather than toleration, which recognized the existence of Catholicism and Lutheranism in the German Empire and provided that citizens should adopt the religion of their respective rulers.

1558: Beginning of the reign of Elizabeth I, during which the Church of England took on its definitive form.

1559: Establishment of the hierarchy of the Church of England, with the consecration of Matthew Parker as archbishop of Canterbury.

1563: The first text of the *39 Articles* of the Church of England was issued. Also enacted were a new Act of Supremacy and Oath of Succession to the English throne.

1570: Elizabeth I was excommunicated. Penal measures against Catholics subsequently became more severe.

1571: Defeat of the Turkish armada at Lepanto staved off the invasion of Eastern Europe.

1577: The *Formula of Concord*, the classical statement of Lutheran faith, was issued; it was, generally, a Lutheran counterpart of the canons of the Council of Trent. In 1580, along with other formulas of doctrine, it was included in the *Book of Concord.*

1582: The Gregorian Calendar, named for Pope Gregory XIII, was put into effect and was eventually adopted in most countries: England delayed adoption until 1752.

Seventeenth Century

1605: The Gunpowder Plot, an attempt by Catholic fanatics to blow up James I of England and the houses of Parliament, resulted in an anti-Catholic Oath of Allegiance; the Oath was condemned by Pope Paul V in 1606.

1610: Death of Matteo Ricci, outstanding Jesuit missionary to China, pioneer in cultural relations between China and Europe.

Founding of the first community of Visitation Nuns by Sts. Francis de Sales and Jane de Chantal.

1611: Founding of the Oratorians.

1613: Catholics were banned from Scandinavia.

1625: Founding of the Congregation of the Mission (Vincentians) by St. Vincent de Paul. He founded the Sisters of Charity in 1633.

1642: Death of Galileo, scientist, who was censured by the Congregation of the Holy Office for supporting the Copernican theory of the sun-centered planetary system.

Founding of the Sulpicians by Jacques Olier.

1643: Start of publication of the Bollandist *Acta Sanctorum,* a critical work on lives of the saints.

1648: Provisions in the Peace of Westphalia, ending the Thirty Years' War, extended terms of the Peace of Augsburg (1555) to Calvinists and gave equality to Catholics and Protestants in the 300 states of the Holy Roman Empire.

1649: Oliver Cromwell invaded Ireland and began a severe persecution of the Church there.

1653: Pope Innocent X condemned five propositions of Jansenism, a complex theory which distorted doctrine concerning the relations between divine grace and human freedom. Jansenism was also a rigoristic movement which seriously disturbed the Church in France, the Low Countries and Italy in this and the 18th century.

1673: The Test Act in England barred from public office Catholics who would not deny the doctrine of transubstantiation and receive Communion in the Church of England.

1678: Many English Catholics suffered death as a consequence of the Popish Plot, a false allegation by Titus Oates that Catholics planned to assassinate Charles I, land a French army in the country, burn London, and turn over the government to the Jesuits.

1682: The four articles of the *Gallican Declaration,* drawn up by Bossuet, asserted political and ecclesiastical immunities of France from papal control. The articles, which rejected the primacy of the pope, were condemned in 1690.

1689: The Toleration Act granted a measure of freedom of worship to other English dissenters but not to Catholics.

This century is called the age of Enlightenment or Reason because of the predominating rational and scientific approach of its leading philosophers, scientists and writers with respect to religion, ethics and natural law. This approach downgraded the fact and significance of revealed religion. Also characteristic of the Enlightenment were subjectivism, secularism and optimism regarding human perfectibility.

Eighteenth Century

1704: Chinese Rites — involving the Christian adaptation of elements of Confucianism, veneration of ancestors and Chinese terminology in religion — were condemned by Clement XI. An earlier ban was issued in 1645; a later one, in 1742.

1720: The Passionists were founded by St. Paul of the Cross.

1732: The Redemptorists were founded by St. Alphonsus Liguori.

1738: Freemasonry was condemned by Clement XII and Catholics were forbidden to join, under penalty of excommunication; the prohibition was repeated by Benedict XIV in 1751 and by later popes.

1760's: Josephinism, a theory and system of state control of the Church, was initiated in Austria; it remained in force until about 1850.

1764: Febronianism, an unorthodox theory and practice regarding the constitution of the Church and relations between Church and state, was condemned for the first of several times. Proposed by an auxiliary bishop of Trier using the pseudonym Justinus Febronius, it had the effects of minimizing the office of the pope and supporting national churches under state control.

1773: Clement XIV issued a brief of suppression against the Jesuits, following their expulsion from Portugal in 1759, from France in 1764 and from Spain in 1767. Political intrigue and unsubstantiated accusations were principal factors in these developments. The ban, which crippled the Society, contained no condemnation of the Jesuit constitutions, particular Jesuits or Jesuit teaching. The Society was restored in 1814.

1778: Catholics in England were relieved of some civil disabilities dating back to the time of Henry VIII, by an act which permitted them to acquire, own and inherit property. Additional liberties were restored by the Roman Catholic Relief Act of 1791 and subsequent enactments of Parliament.

1789: Religious freedom in the United States was guaranteed under the First Amendment to the Constitution.

Beginning of the French Revolution which resulted in: the secularization of church property and the Civil Constitution of the Clergy in 1790; the persecution of priests, religious and lay persons loyal to papal authority; invasion of the Papal States by Napoleon in 1796; renewal of persecution from 1797-1799; attempts to dechristianize France and establish a new religion; the occupation of Rome by French troops and the forced removal of Pius VI to France in 1798.

Nineteenth Century

1809: Pius VII was made a captive by Napoleon and deported to France where he remained in exile until 1814. During this time he refused to cooperate with Napoleon who sought to bring the Church in France under his own control.

The turbulence in church-state relations in France at the beginning of the century recurred in connection with the Bourbon Restoration, the July Revolution, the second and third Republics, the Second Empire and the Dreyfus case.

1814: The Society of Jesus, suppressed since 1773, was restored.

1817: Reestablishment of the Congregation for the Propagation of the Faith (Propaganda) by Pius VII was an important factor in increasing missionary activity during the century.

1820: Years-long persecution, during which thousands died for the faith, ended in China. Thereafter, communication with the West remained cut off until about 1834. Vigorous missionary work got underway in 1842.

1822: The Pontifical Society for the Propagation of the Faith, inaugurated in France by Pauline Jaricot for the support of missionary activity, was established.

1829: The Catholic Emancipation Act relieved Catholics in England and Ireland of most of the civil disabilities to which they had been subject from the time of Henry VIII.

1832: Gregory XVI, in the encyclical *Mirari Vos,* condemned indifferentism, one of the many ideologies at odds with Christian doctrine which were proposed during the century.

1833: Start of the Oxford Movement which affected the Church of England and resulted in some notable conversions, including that of John Henry Newman in 1845, to the Catholic Church.

Frederick Ozanam founded the Society of St.. Vincent de Paul in France. The society, whose objective was works of charity, became worldwide.

1848: The *Communist Manifesto,* a revolutionary document symptomatic of socio-economic crisis, was issued.

1850: The hierarchy was reestablished in England and Nicholas Wiseman made the first archbishop of Westminster. He was succeeded in 1865 by Henry Manning, an Oxford convert and proponent of the rights of labor.

1853: The Catholic hierarchy was reestablished in Holland.

1854: Pius IX proclaimed the dogma of the Immaculate Conception in the bull *Ineffabilis Deus.*

1858: The Blessed Virgin Mary appeared to

St. Bernadette at Lourdes, France; see separate entry.

1864: Pius IX issued the encyclical *Quanta Cura* and the *Syllabus of Errors* in condemnation of some 80 propositions derived from the scientific mentality and rationalism of the century. The subjects in question had deep ramifications in many areas of thought and human endeavor; in religion, they explicitly and or implicitly rejected divine revelation and the supernatural order.

1867: The first volume of *Das Kapital* was published. Together with the Communist First International, formed in the same year, it had great influence on the subsequent development of Communism and Socialism.

1869: The Anglican Church was disestablished in Ireland.

1869-1870: The First Vatican Council; see separate entry.

1870-1871: Victor Emmanuel II of Sardinia, crowned king of Italy after defeating Austrian and papal forces, marched into Rome in 1870 and expropriated the Papal States after a plebiscite in which Catholics, at the order of Pius IX, did not vote. In 1871, Pius IX refused to accept a Law of Guarantees. Confiscation of church property and hindrance of ecclesiastical administration by the regime followed.

1871: The German Empire, a confederation of 26 states, was formed. Government policy launched a Kulturkampf whose May Laws of 1873 were designed to annul papal jurisdiction in Prussia and other states and to place the Church under imperial control. Resistance to the enactments and the persecution they legalized forced the government to modify its anti-Church policy by 1887.

1878: Beginning of the pontificate of Leo XIII, who was pope until his death in 1903. Leo is best known for the encyclical *Rerum Novarum,* which greatly influenced the course of Christian social thought and the labor movement. His other accomplishments included promotion of a revival of Scholastic philosophy and the impetus he gave to scriptural studies.

1881: The first International Eucharistic Congress was held in Lille, France.

Alexander II of Russia died. His policies of Russification — as well as those of his two predecessors and a successor during the century — caused great suffering to Catholics, Jews and Protestants in Poland, Lithuania, the Ukraine and Bessarabia.

1882: Charles Darwin died. His theory of evolution by natural selection, one of several scientific highlights of the century, had extensive repercussions in the faith-and-science controversy.

1889: The Catholic University of America was founded in Washington, D.C.

1893: The US apostolic delegation was set up in Washington, D.C.

Twentieth Century

1901: Restrictive measures in France forced the Jesuits, Benedictines, Carmelites and other religious orders to leave the country. Subsequently, 14,000 schools were suppressed; religious orders and congregations were expelled; the concordat was renounced in 1905; church property was confiscated in 1906. For some years the Holy See, refusing to comply with government demands for the control of bishops' appointments, left some ecclesiastical offices vacant.

1903: Start of the 11-year pontificate of St. Pius X. He initiated the codification of canon law, 1904; removed the ban against participation by Catholics in Italian national elections, 1905; issued decrees calling upon the faithful to receive Holy Communion frequently and daily, and stating that children should begin receiving the Eucharist at the age of seven, 1905 and 1910, respectively; ordered the establishment of the Confraternity of Christian Doctrine in all parishes throughout the world, 1905; condemned Modernism in the decree *Lamentabili* and the encyclical *Pascendi,* 1907.

1908: The United States and England, long under the jurisdiction of the Congregation for the Propagation of the Faith as mission territories, were removed from its control and placed under the common law of the Church.

1910: Laws of separation were enacted in Portugal, marking a point of departure in church-state relations.

1911: The Catholic Foreign Mission Society of America — Maryknoll, the first US-founded society of its type — was established.

1914: Start of World War I, which lasted until 1918.

Start of the eight-year pontificate of Benedict XV. Much of his pontificate was devoted to seeking ways and means of minimizing the material and spiritual havoc of World War I. In 1917 he offered his services as a mediator to the belligerent nations, but his pleas for settlement of the conflict went unheeded.

1917: The Blessed Virgin Mary appeared to three children at Fatima, Portugal.

A new constitution, embodying repressive laws against the Church, was enacted in Mexico. Its implementation resulted in persecution in the 1920's and 1930's.

Bolsheviks seized power in Russia and set up a Communist dictatorship. The event marked the rise of Communism in Russian and world affairs. One of its immediate, and lasting, results was persecution of the Church, Jews and other segments of the population.

1918: The *Code of Canon Law,* in preparation for more than 10 years, went into effect in the Western Church.

1919: Benedict XV stimulated missionary work through the decree *Maximum Illud,* in which he urged the recruiting and training of native clergy in places where the Church was not firmly established.

1922: Beginning of the 17-year pontificate of Pius XI. He subscribed to the Lateran Treaty, 1929, which settled the Roman Question created by the confiscation of the Papal States in 1871; issued the encyclical *Casti Connubii*, 1930, an authoritative statement on Christian marriage; resisted the efforts of Benito Mussolini to control Catholic Action and the Church, in the encyclical *Non Abbiamo Bisogno*, 1931; opposed various Fascist policies; issued the encyclicals *Quadragesimo Anno*, 1931, developing the social doctrine of Leo XIII's *Rerum Novarum*, and *Divini Redemptoris*, 1937, calling for social justice and condemning atheistic Communism; condemned anti-Semitism, 1937.

Ireland was partitioned. All but two of the predominantly Catholic counties were included in the southern part of the country, which eventually attained the status of an independent republic in 1949.

1926: The Catholic Relief Act repealed virtually all legal disabilities of Catholics in England.

1931: Leftists proclaimed Spain a republic and proceeded to disestablish the Church, confiscate church property, deny salaries to the clergy, expel the Jesuits and ban teaching of the Catholic faith. These actions were preludes to the civil war of 1936-1939.

1933: Emergence of Adolf Hitler to power in Germany. By 1935 two of his aims were clear, the elimination of the Jews and control of a single national church. Persecution decimated the Jews over a period of years. The Church was subject to repressive measures, which Pius XI protested futilely in the encyclical *Mit Brennender Sorge* in 1937.

1936: A three-year civil war broke out in Spain between the leftist Loyalists and forces led by Francisco Franco. The Loyalists were defeated and one-man, one-party rule was established. A number of priests, religious and lay persons fell victims to Loyalist persecution.

1939: Start of World War II, which lasted until 1945.

Start of the 19-year pontificate of Pius XII; see separate entry.

1940: Start of a decade of Communist conquest in more than 13 countries, resulting in conditions of persecution for a minimum of 60 million Catholics as well as members of other faiths; see various countries.

Persecution diminished in Mexico through non-enforcement of anti-religious laws still on record.

1950: Pius XII proclaimed the dogma of the Assumption of the Blessed Virgin Mary.

1954: St. Pius X was canonized.

1957: The Communist regime of China attempted to start a national schismatic church.

1958: Beginning of the five-year pontificate of John XXIII; see separate entry.

1962: The Second Vatican Council began the first of four sessions; see separate entry.

1963: Beginning of 15-year pontificate of Paul VI; see separate entry.

1978: Thirty-four-day pontificate of John Paul I; see separate entry.

Beginning of pontificate of John Paul II; see separate entry.

HERESIES

Heresy is the formal and obstinate denial or doubt by a baptized person, who remains a nominal Christian, of any truth which must be believed as a matter of divine and Catholic faith. Formal heresy involves deliberate resistance to the authority of God who communicates revelation through Scripture and tradition and the teaching authority of the Church. Obstinate refusal to accept the infallible teaching of the Church constitutes the canonical crime of heresy.

Formal heretics automatically incur the penalty of excommunication (Canon 1325 of the Code of Canon Law). Material heretics are those who, in good faith and without formal obstinacy, do not accept articles or matters of divine and Catholic faith.

Heresies have been significant not only as disruptions of unity of faith but also as occasions for the clarification and development of doctrine.

Heresies from the beginning of the Church to the 13th century are listed below.

Judaizers: Early converts who claimed that members of the Church had to observe all the requirements of Mosaic Law as well as the obligations of Christian faith. This view was condemned by the Council of Jerusalem held in 51 under the presidency of St. Peter (Acts 15:28).

Gnosticism: A combination of elements of Platonic philosophy and Eastern mystery religions which claimed that its secret knowledge-principle gave its adherents a deeper insight into Christian doctrine than divine revelation and faith. One Gnostic thesis denied the divinity of Christ; others denied the reality of his humanity, calling it mere appearance (**Docetism, Phantasiasm**).

Modalism: A general term covering propositions (**Monarchianism, Patripassianism, Sabellianism**) that the Father, Son and Holy Spirit are not really distinct divine Persons but are only three different modes of being and self-manifestation of the one God. Various forms of Modalism, which appeared in the East in the second century and spread westward, were all condemned.

Marcionism: A Gnostic creation named for its author, who claimed there was total opposition and no connection at all between the Old Testament and the New Testament, between the God of the Jews and the God of the Christians; and that the canon of Scripture consisted only of portions of Luke's Gospel and 10 Epistles of Paul. Marcion was excommunicated in 144 at Rome, and his tenets were condemned again by a Roman council about 260. The heresy was checked at Rome by 200 but persisted for several centuries in the East and had some adherents as late as the Middle Ages.

Montanism: A form of extremism preached about 170 by Montanus of Phrygia, Asia Minor. Its principal tenets were: an imminent second coming of Christ, denial of the divine nature of the Church and its power to forgive sin, excessively rigorous morality. Condemned by Pope St. Zephyrinus (199-217). Tertullian was one of its victims.

Novatianism: A heresy of excessive rigorism named for its author, a priest of Rome and antipope. Its principal tenet was that persons who fell away from the Church under persecution and/or those guilty of serious sin after baptism could not be absolved and readmitted to communion with the Church. The heresy, condemned by a Roman synod in 251, slowly subsided in the West and died in the East by the end of the seventh century.

Subordinationism, Adoptionism: Christological errors and logical antecedents of Arianism. The key tenet was that Christ, while the most excellent of creatures, was subordinate to God whose Son he was by adoption rather than by nature. First proposed at Rome late in the second century, it was condemned by Pope St. Victor in 190 and again in the following century, in 785 by Pope Adrian I, in 794 by a Council of Frankfurt, and in 1177 by Pope Alexander III.

Arianism: Denial of the divinity of Christ, the most devastating of the early heresies, authored by Arius of Alexandria and condemned by the Council of Nicaea I in 325. Arians and several kinds of **Semi-Arians** propagandized their tenets widely, raised havoc in the Church for several centuries, and established their own hierarchies and churches.

Macedonianism: Denial of the divinity of the Holy Spirit, who was said to be a creature of the Son. Condemned by the Council of Constantinople I in 381. Macedonians were also called **Pneumatomachists,** enemies of the Spirit; and **Marathonians,** after the name of one of their leaders, a bishop of Nicomedia.

Nestorianism: Denial of the real unity of divine and human natures in the single divine Person of Christ, proposed by Nestorius, patriarch of Constantinople. He also held that Mary could not be called the Mother of God *(Theotokos);* that is, of the Second Person of the Trinity made Man. Condemned by the councils of Ephesus in 431 and Chalcedon in 451.

Monophysitism: Denial of Christ's human nature; also called **Eutychianism,** after the name of one of its leading advocates. Condemned by the Council of Chalcedon in 451.

Monothelitism: Denial of the human will of Christ. Severus of Antioch and Sergius, patriarch of Constantinople, were leading advocates of the heresy, which was condemned by the Council of Constantinople III in 681.

Priscillianism: A fourth century amalgamation of elements from various sources — Sabellianism, Arianism, Docetism, Pantheism, belief in the diabolical nature of marriage, corruption of Scripture. Condemned by a Council of Braga in 563 on 17 different counts.

Donatism: A development of the error at the heart of the third century **Rebaptism Controversy** (baptism conferred by heretics is invalid because persons deprived of grace are incapable of being ministers of grace to others). Followers of Donatus the Great asserted throughout the fourth century that sacraments administered by sinners were invalid. Condemnation of the heresy is traced to Pope St. Stephen I (254-257) and the principle that sacraments have their efficacy from Christ, not from their human ministers.

Pelagianism: Denial of the supernatural order of things, proposed by Pelagius (360-420), a Breton monk. Proceeding from the assumption that Adam had a natural right to supernatural life, the theory held that man could attain salvation through the efforts of his own free will and natural powers. The theory involved errors concerning the nature of original sin, the meaning of grace and other matters. St. Augustine opposed the heresy, which was condemned by the Council of Ephesus in 431. **Semi-Pelagianism** was condemned by a Council of Orange in 529.

Iconoclasm: An image-breaking campaign which resulted from an edict issued by Eastern Emperor Leo the Isaurian in 726, that the veneration of images, pictures and relics was idolatrous. The theoretical basis of the heresy was the Monophysite error which denied the humanity of Christ. It was denounced several times before its condemnation by the Council of Nicaea II in 787.

Berengarian Heresy: Denial of the Real Presence of Christ under the appearances of bread and wine, the first clear-cut Eucharistic heresy; proposed by Berengarius of Tours (c. 1000-1088). Condemned by various synods and finally by a council held at Rome in 1079.

Waldensianism: Claimed by Peter Waldo, a merchant of Lyons, to be a return to pure Christianity, the heresy rejected the hierarchical structure of the Church, the sacramental system and other doctrines. Its adherents were excommunicated in 1184 and their tenets were condemned several times thereafter.

Albigensianism, Catharism: Related errors based on the old **Manichaean** assumption that two supreme principles of good and evil were operative in creation and life, and that the supreme objective of human endeavor was liberation from evil (matter). The heresy denied the humanity of Christ, the sacramental system and the authority of the Church (and state), and endorsed a moral code which threatened seriously the fabric of social life in southern France and northern Italy in the 12th and 13th centuries. Condemned by councils of the Lateran III and Lateran IV in 1179 and 1215.

ECUMENICAL COUNCILS

An ecumenical council is an assembly of the college of bishops, with and under the presidency of the pope, which has supreme authority over the Church in matters pertaining to faith, morals, worship and discipline.

The Second Vatican Council stated: "The supreme authority with which this college (of bishops) is empowered over the whole Church is exercised in a solemn way through an ecumenical council. A council is never ecumenical unless it is confirmed or at least accepted as such by the successor of Peter. It is the prerogative of the Roman Pontiff to convoke these councils, to preside over them, and to confirm them" *(Dogmatic Constitution on the Church*, No. 22).

Pope Presides

The pope is the head of an ecumenical council; he presides over it either personally or through legates. Conciliar decrees and other actions have binding force only when confirmed and promulgated by him. If a pope dies during a council, it is suspended until reconvened by another pope. An ecumenical council is not superior to a pope; hence, there is no appeal from a pope to a council.

Collectively, the bishops with the pope represent the whole Church. They do this not as democratic representatives of their faithful in a kind of church parliament, but as the successors of the Apostles with divinely given authority, care and responsibility over the whole Church.

Council participants with a deliberative vote are: cardinals; residential patriarchs, primates, archbishops and bishops, even if they are not yet consecrated; abbots and certain other prelates, an abbot primate, abbot superiors of monastic congregations and heads of exempt clerical religious; titular bishops, on invitation. Experts in theology and canon law may be given a consultative vote. Others, including lay persons, may address a council or observe its actions, but may not vote.

Basic legislation concerning ecumenical councils is contained in Canons 222-229 of the Code of Canon Law. Basic doctrinal considerations were stated by the Second Vatican Council in the *Dogmatic Constitution on the Church.*

Background

Ecumenical councils had their prototype in the Council of Jerusalem in 51, at which the Apostles under the leadership of St. Peter decided that converts to the Christian faith were not obliged to observe all the prescriptions of Old Testament law (Acts 15). As early as the second century, bishops got together in regional meetings, synods or councils to take common action for the doctrinal and pastoral good of their communities of faithful. The expansion of such limited assemblies to ecumenical councils was a logical and historical evolution, given the nature and needs of the Church.

Emperors were active in summoning or convoking the first eight councils, especially the first five and the eighth. Among reasons for intervention of this kind were the facts that the emperors regarded themselves as guardians of the faith; that the settlement of religious controversies, which had repercussions in political and social turmoil, served the cause of peace in the state; and that the emperors had at their disposal ways and means of facilitating gatherings of bishops. Imperial actions, however, did not account for the formally ecumenical nature of the councils.

Some councils were attended by relatively few bishops, and the ecumenical character of several was open to question for a time. However, confirmation and de facto recognition of their actions by popes and subsequent councils established them as ecumenical.

Role in History

The councils have played a highly significant role in the history of the Church by witnessing to and defining truths of revelation, by shaping forms of worship and discipline, and by promoting measures for the ever-necessary reform and renewal of Catholic life. In general, they have represented attempts of the Church to mobilize itself in times of crisis for self-preservation, self-purification and growth.

The first eight ecumenical councils were held in the East; the other 13, in the West. The majority of separated Eastern Churches — e.g., the Orthodox — recognize the ecumenical character of the first seven councils, which formulated a great deal of basic doctrine. Nestorians, however, acknowledge only the first two councils; the Monophysite Armenians, Syrians, and Copts acknowledge the first three.

The 21 Councils

The 21 ecumenical councils in the history of the Church are listed below, with indication of their names or titles (taken from the names of the places where they were held); the dates; the reigning and/or approving popes; the emperors who were instrumental in convoking the eight councils in the East; the number of bishops who attended, when available; the number of sessions; the most significant actions.

1. **Nicaea I**, 325: St. Sylvester I (Emperor Constantine I); attended by approximately 300 bishops; sessions held between May 20 or June 19 to near the end of August. Con-

demned Arianism, which denied the divinity of Christ; contributed to formulation of the Nicene Creed; fixed the date of Easter; passed regulations concerning clerical discipline; adopted the civil division of the Empire as the model for the organization of the Church.

2. Constantinople I, 381: St. Damasus I (Emperor Theodosius I); attended by approximately 150 bishops; sessions held from May to July. Condemned various brands of Arianism, and Macedonianism which denied the divinity of the Holy Spirit; contributed to formulation of the Nicene Creed; approved a canon which made the bishop of Constantinople the ranking prelate in the East, with primacy next to that of the pope. Doubt about the ecumenical character of this council was resolved by the ratification of its acts by popes and the Council of Chalcedon.

3. Ephesus, 431: St. Celestine I (Emperor Theodosius II); attended by 150 to 200 bishops; five sessions held between June 22 and July 17. Condemned Nestorianism, which denied the real unity of the divine and human natures in the Person of Christ; defined *Theotokos* ("Bearer of God") as the title of Mary, Mother of the Son of God made Man; condemned Pelagianism, which reduced the supernatural to the natural order of things.

4. Chalcedon, 451: St. Leo I (Emperor Marcian); attended by approximately 600 bishops; 17 sessions held between Oct. 8 and Nov. 1. Condemned: Monophysitism, also called Eutychianism, which denied the humanity of Christ by holding that he had only one, the divine, nature; and the Monophysite Robber Synod of Ephesus, of 449.

5. Constantinople II, 553: Vigilius (Emperor Justinian I); attended by 165 bishops; eight sessions held between May 5 and June 2. Condemned the *Three Chapters,* Nestorian-tainted writings of Theodore of Mopsuestia, Theodoret of Cyprus and Ibas of Edessa.

6. Constantinople III, 680-681; St. Agatho, St. Leo II (Emperor Constantine IV); attended by approximately 170 bishops; 16 sessions held between Nov. 7, 680, and Sept. 16, 681. Condemned Monothelitism, which held that there was only one will, the divine, in Christ; censured Pope Honorius I for a letter to Sergius, bishop of Constantinople, in which he made an ambiguous but not infallible statement about the unity of will and/or operation in Christ. Constantinople III is also called the Trullan Council because its sessions were held in the domed hall, Trullos, of the imperial palace.

7. Nicaea II, 787: Adrian I (Empress Irene); attended by approximately 300 bishops: eight sessions held between Sept. 24 and Oct. 23. Condemned: Iconoclasm, which held that the use of images was idolatry; and Adoptionism, which claimed that Christ was not the Son of God by nature but only by adoption. This was the last council regarded as ecumenical by Orthodox Churches.

8. Constantinople IV, 869-870: Adrian II (Emperor Basil I); attended by 102 bishops; six sessions held between Oct. 5, 869, and Feb. 28, 870. Condemned Iconoclasm; condemned and deposed Photius as patriarch of Constantinople; restored Ignatius to the patriarchate. This was the last ecumenical council held in the East. It was first called ecumenical by canonists toward the end of the 11th century.

9. Lateran I, 1123: Callistus II; attended by approximately 300 bishops; sessions held between Mar. 18 and Apr. 6. Endorsed provisions of the Concordat of Worms concerning the investiture of prelates: approved reform measures in 25 canons.

10. Lateran II, 1139: Innocent II; attended by 900 to 1,000 bishops and abbots; three sessions held in April. Adopted measures against a schism organized by antipope Anacletus; approved 30 disciplinary measures and canons, one of which stated that holy orders is an invalidating impediment to marriage.

11. Lateran III, 1179: Alexander III; attended by at least 300 bishops; three sessions held between Mar. 5 and 19. Enacted measures against the Waldenses and Albigensians; approved reform decrees in 27 canons; provided that popes be elected by two-thirds vote of the cardinals.

12. Lateran IV, 1215: Innocent III; sessions held between Nov. 11 and 30. Ordered annual confession and Communion; defined and made first official use of the term "transubstantiation"; adopted measures to counteract the Cathari and Albigensians; approved 70 canons.

13. Lyons I, 1245: Innocent IV; attended by approximately 150 bishops; three sessions held between June 28 and July 17. Confirmed the deposition of Emperor Frederick II; approved 22 canons.

14. Lyons II, 1274: Gregory X; attended by approximately 500 bishops; six sessions held between May 7 and July 17. Accomplished a temporary reunion of separated Eastern Churches with the Roman Church; issued regulations concerning conclaves for papal elections; approved 31 canons.

15. Vienne, 1311-1312: Clement V; attended by 132 bishops; three sessions held between Oct. 16, 1311, and May 6, 1312. Suppressed the Knights Templar; enacted a number of reform decrees.

16. Constance, 1414-1418: Gregory XII, Martin V; attended by nearly 200 bishops, plus other prelates and many experts; 45 sessions held between Nov. 5, 1414, and Apr. 22, 1418. Took successful action to end the Western Schism; rejected the teachings of Wycliff; condemned Hus as a heretic. One decree, passed in the earlier stages of the council, asserted the superiority of an ecumenical council over the pope; this was later rejected.

17. Florence (also called Basel-Ferrara-Florence), 1438-1445: Eugene IV; attended by many Latin-Rite and Eastern-Rite bishops; preliminary sessions were held at Basel and Ferrara before definitive work was accomplished at Florence. Reaffirmed the primacy of the pope against the claims of Conciliarists that an ecumenical council is superior to the pope; formulated and approved decrees of union — with the Greeks, July 6, 1439; with the Armenians, Nov. 22, 1439; with the Jacobites, Feb. 4, 1442. These decrees failed to gain general or lasting acceptance in the East.

18. Lateran V, 1512-1517: Julius II, Leo X; 12 sessions held between May 3, 1512, and Mar. 16, 1517. Stated the relation and position of the pope with respect to an ecumenical council; acted to counteract the Pragmatic Sanction of Bourges and exaggerated claims of liberty by the French Church; condemned erroneous teachings concerning the nature of the human soul; stated doctrine concerning indulgences. The council reflected concern for abuses in the Church and the need for reforms but failed to take decisive action in the years immediately preceding the Reformation.

19. Trent, 1545-1563: Paul III, Julius III, Pius IV; 25 sessions held between Dec. 13, 1545, and Dec. 4, 1563. Issued a great number of decrees concerning doctrinal matters opposed by the Reformers, and mobilized the Counter-Reformation. Definitions covered the rule of faith, the nature of justification, grace, faith, original sin and its effects, the seven sacraments, the sacrificial nature of the Mass, the veneration of saints, use of sacred images, belief in purgatory, the doctrine of indulgences, the jurisdiction of the pope over the whole Church. Initiated many reforms for renewal in the liturgy and general discipline in the Church, the promotion of religious instruction, the education of the clergy through the foundation of seminaries, etc. Trent ranks with Vatican II as the greatest ecumenical council held in the West.

20. Vatican I, 1869-1870: Pius IX; attended by approximately 800 bishops and other prelates; four public sessions and 89 general meetings held between Dec. 8, 1869, and July 7, 1870. Defined papal primacy and infallibility in a dogmatic constitution on the Church; covered natural religion, revelation, faith, and the relations between faith and reason in a dogmatic constitution on the Catholic faith. The council suspended sessions Sept. 1 and was adjourned Oct. 20, 1870.

Vatican II

The Second Vatican Council, which was forecast by Pope John XXIII Jan. 25, 1959, was held in four sessions in St. Peter's Basilica.

Pope John convoked it and opened the first session, which ran from Oct. 11 to Dec. 8, 1962. Following John's death June 3, 1963, Pope Paul VI reconvened the council for the other three sessions which ran from Sept. 29 to Dec. 4, 1963; Sept. 14 to Nov. 21, 1964; Sept. 14 to Dec. 8, 1965.

A total of 2,860 Fathers participated in council proceedings, and attendance at meetings varied between 2,000 and 2,500. For various reasons, including the denial of exit from Communist-dominated countries, 274 Fathers could not attend.

The council formulated and promulgated 16 documents — two dogmatic and two pastoral constitutions, nine decrees and three declarations — all of which reflect its basic pastoral orientation toward renewal and reform in the Church. Given below are the Latin and English titles of the documents and their dates of promulgation.

• *Lumen Gentium* (Dogmatic Constitution on the Church), Nov. 21, 1964.

• *Dei Verbum* (Dogmatic Constitution on Divine Revelation), Nov. 18, 1965.

• *Sacrosanctum Concilium* (Constitution on the Sacred Liturgy), Dec. 4, 1963.

• *Gaudium et Spes* (Pastoral Constitution on the Church in the Modern World), Dec. 7, 1965.

• *Christus Dominus* (Decree on the Bishops' Pastoral Office in the Church), Oct. 28, 1965.

• *Ad Gentes* (Decree on the Church's Missionary Activity), Dec. 7, 1965.

• *Unitatis Redintegratio* (Decree on Ecumenism), Nov. 21, 1964.

• *Orientalium Ecclesiarum* (Decree on Eastern Catholic Churches), Nov. 21, 1964.

• *Presbyterorum Ordinis* (Decree on the Ministry and Life of Priests), Dec. 7, 1965.

• *Optatam Totius* (Decree on Priestly Formation), Oct. 28, 1965.

• *Perfectae Caritatis* (Decree on the Appropriate Renewal of the Religious Life), Oct. 28, 1965.

• *Apostolicam Actuositatem* (Decree on the Apostolate of the Laity), Nov. 18, 1965.

• *Inter Mirifica* (Decree on the Instruments of Social Communication), Dec. 4, 1963.

• *Dignitatis Humanae* (Declaration on Religious Freedom), Dec. 7, 1965.

• *Nostra Aetate* (Declaration on the Relationship of the Church to Non-Christian Religions), Oct. 28, 1965.

• *Gravissimum Educationis* (Declaration on Christian Education), Oct. 28, 1965.

The key documents were the four constitutions, which set the ideological basis for all the others. To date, the documents with the most visible effects are those on the liturgy, the Church, the Church in the world, ecumenism, the renewal of religious life, the life and ministry of priests, the lay apostolate.

The main business of the council was to explore and make explicit dimensions of doctrine and Christian life requiring emphasis for the full development of the Church and the better accomplishment of its mission in the contemporary world.

LIST OF POPES

(Source: *Annuario Pontificio*.)

Information includes the name of the pope, in many cases his name before becoming pope, his birthplace or country of origin, the date of accession to the papacy, and the date of the end of reign which, in all but a few cases, was the date of death. Double dates indicate times of election and coronation.

St. Peter (Simon Bar-Jona): Bethsaida in Galilee; d. c. 64 or 67.

St. Linus: Tuscany; 67-76.

St. Anacletus (Cletus): Rome; 76-88.

St. Clement: Rome; 88-97.

St. Evaristus: Greece; 97-105.

St. Alexander I: Rome; 105-115.

St. Sixtus I: Rome; 115-125.

St. Telesphorus: Greece; 125-136.

St. Hyginus: Greece; 136-140.

St. Pius I: Aquileia; 140-155.

St. Anicetus: Syria; 155-166.

St. Soter: Campania; 166-175.

St. Eleutherius: Nicopolis in Epirus; 175-189.

Up to the time of St. Eleutherius, the years indicated for the beginning and end of pontificates are not absolutely certain. Also, up to the middle of the 11th century, there are some doubts about the exact days and months given in chronological tables.

St. Victor I: Africa; 189-199.

St. Zephyrinus: Rome; 199-217.

St. Callistus I: Rome; 217-222.

St. Urban I: Rome; 222-230.

St. Pontian: Rome; July 21, 230, to Sept. 28, 235.

St. Anterus: Greece; Nov. 21, 235, to Jan. 3, 236.

St. Fabian: Rome; Jan. 10, 236, to Jan. 20, 250.

St. Cornelius: Rome; Mar., 251, to June, 253.

St. Lucius I: Rome; June 25, 253, to Mar. 5, 254.

St. Stephen I: Rome; May 12, 254, to Aug. 2, 257.

St. Sixtus II: Greece; Aug. 30, 257, to Aug. 6, 258.

St. Dionysius: July 22, 259, to Dec. 26, 268.

St. Felix I: Rome; Jan. 5, 269, to Dec. 30, 274.

St. Eutychian: Luni; Jan. 4, 275, to Dec. 7, 283.

St. Caius: Dalmatia; Dec. 17, 283, to Apr. 22, 296.

St. Marcellinus: Rome; June 30, 296, to Oct. 25, 304.

St. Marcellus I: Rome; May 27, 308, or June 26, 308, to Jan. 16, 309.

St. Eusebius: Greece; Apr. 18, 309 or 310, to Aug. 17, 309 or 310.

St. Melchiades (Miltiades): Africa; July 2, 311, to Jan. 11, 314.

St. Sylvester I: Rome; Jan. 31, 314, to Dec. 31, 335. (Most of the popes before St. Sylvester I were martyrs.)

St. Marcus: Rome; Jan. 18, 336, to Oct. 7, 336.

St. Julius I: Rome; Feb. 6, 337, to Apr. 12, 352.

Liberius: Rome; May 17, 352, to Sept. 24, 366.

St. Damasus I: Spain; Oct. 1, 366, to Dec. 11, 384.

St. Siricius: Rome; Dec. 15, or 22 or 29, 384, to Nov. 26, 399.

St. Anastasius I: Rome; Nov. 27, 399, to Dec. 19, 401.

St. Innocent I: Albano; Dec. 22, 401, to Mar. 12, 417.

St. Zozimus: Greece; Mar. 18, 417, to Dec. 26, 418.

St. Boniface I: Rome; Dec. 28 or 29, 418, to Sept. 4, 422.

St. Celestine I: Campania; Sept. 10, 422, to July 27, 432.

St. Sixtus III: Rome; July 31, 432, to Aug. 19, 440.

St. Leo I (the Great): Tuscany; Sept. 29, 440, to Nov. 10, 461.

St. Hilary: Sardinia; Nov. 19, 461, to Feb. 29, 468.

St. Simplicius: Tivoli; Mar. 3, 468, to Mar. 10, 483.

St. Felix III (II): Rome; Mar. 13, 483, to Mar. 1, 492.

He should be called Felix II, and his successors of the same name should be numbered accordingly. The discrepancy in the numerical designation of popes named Felix was caused by the erroneous insertion in some lists of the name of St. Felix of Rome, a martyr.

St. Gelasius I: Africa; Mar. 1, 492, to Nov. 21, 496.

Anastasius II: Rome; Nov. 24, 496, to Nov. 19, 498.

St. Symmachus: Sardinia; Nov. 22, 498, to July 19, 514.

St. Hormisdas: Frosinone; July 20, 514, to Aug. 6, 523.

St. John I, Martyr: Tuscany; Aug. 13, 523, to May 18, 526.

St. Felix IV (III): Samnium; July 12, 526, to Sept. 22, 530.

Boniface II: Rome; Sept. 22, 530, to Oct. 17, 532.

John II: Rome; Jan. 2, 533, to May 8, 535.

John II was the first pope to change his name. His given name was Mercury.

St. Agapitus I: Rome; May 13, 535, to Apr. 22, 536.

St. Silverius, Martyr: Campania; June 1 or 8, 536, to Nov. 11, 537 (d. Dec. 2, 537).

St. Silverius was violently deposed in March, 537, and abdicated Nov. 11, 537. His successor, Vigilius, was not recognized as pope by all the Roman clergy until his abdication.

Vigilius: Rome; Mar. 29, 537, to June 7, 555.

Pelagius I: Rome; Apr. 16, 556, to Mar. 4, 561.

John III: Rome; July 17, 561, to July 13, 574.

Benedict I: Rome; June 2, 575, to July 30, 579.

Pelagius II: Rome; Nov. 26, 579, to Feb. 7, 590.

St. Gregory I (the Great): Rome; Sept. 3, 590, to Mar. 12, 604.

Sabinian: Blera in Tuscany; Sept. 13, 604, to Feb. 22, 606.

Boniface III: Rome; Feb. 19, 607, to Nov. 12, 607.

St. Boniface IV: Abruzzi; Aug. 25, 608, to May 8, 615.

St. Deusdedit (Adeodatus I): Rome; Oct. 19, 615, to Nov. 8, 618.

Boniface V: Naples; Dec. 23, 619, to Oct. 25, 625.

Honorius I: Campania; Oct. 27, 625, to Oct. 12, 638.

Severinus: Rome; May 28, 640, to Aug. 2, 640.

John IV: Dalmatia; Dec. 24, 640, to Oct. 12, 642.

Theodore I: Greece; Nov. 24, 642, to May 14, 649.

St. Martin I, Martyr: Todi; July, 649, to Sept. 16, 655 (in exile from June 17, 653).

St. Eugene I: Rome; Aug. 10, 654, to June 2, 657.

St. Eugene I was elected during the exile of St. Martin I, who is believed to have endorsed him as pope.

St. Vitalian: Segni; July 30, 657, to Jan. 27, 672.

Adeodatus II: Rome; Apr. 11, 672, to June 17, 676.

Donus: Rome; Nov. 2, 676, to Apr. 11, 678.

St. Agatho: Sicily; June 27, 678, to Jan. 10, 681.

St. Leo II: Sicily; Aug. 17, 682, to July 3, 683.

St. Benedict II: Rome; June 26, 684, to May 8, 685.

John V: Syria; July 23, 685, to Aug. 2, 686.

Conon: birthplace unknown; Oct. 21, 686, to Sept. 21, 687.

St. Sergius I: Syria; Dec. 15, 687, to Sept. 8, 701.

John VI: Greece; Oct. 30, 701, to Jan. 11, 705.

John VII: Greece; Mar. 1, 705, to Oct. 18, 707.

Sisinnius: Syria; Jan. 15, 708, to Feb. 4, 708.

Constantine: Syria; Mar. 25, 708, to Apr. 9, 715.

St. Gregory II: Rome; May 19, 715, to Feb. 11, 731.

St. Gregory III: Syria; Mar. 18, 731, to Nov., 741.

St. Zachary: Greece; Dec. 10, 741, to Mar. 22, 752.

Stephen II (III): Rome; Mar. 26, 752, to Apr. 26, 757.

After the death of St. Zachary, a Roman priest named Stephen was elected but died (four days later) before his consecration as bishop of Rome, which would have marked the beginning of his pontificate. Another Stephen was elected to succeed Zachary as Stephen II. (The first pope with this name was St. Stephen I, 254-57.) The ordinal III appears in parentheses after the name of Stephen II because the name of the earlier elected but deceased priest was included in some lists. Other Stephens have double numbers.

St. Paul I: Rome; Apr. (May 29), 757, to June 28, 767.

Stephen III (IV): Sicily; Aug. 1 (7), 768, to Jan. 24, 772.

Adrian I: Rome; Feb. 1 (9), 772, to Dec. 25, 795.

St. Leo III: Rome; Dec. 26 (27), 795, to June 12, 816.

Stephen IV (V): Rome; June 22, 816, to Jan. 24, 817.

St. Paschal I: Rome; Jan. 25, 817, to Feb. 11, 824.

Eugene II: Rome; Feb. (May), 824, to Aug., 827.

Valentine: Rome; Aug. 827, to Sept., 827.

Gregory IV: Rome; 827, to Jan., 844.

Sergius II: Rome; Jan., 844 to Jan. 27, 847.

St. Leo IV: Rome; Jan. (Apr. 10), 847, to July 17, 855.

Benedict III: Rome; July (Sept. 29), 855, to Apr. 17, 858.

St. Nicholas I (the Great): Rome; Apr. 24, 858, to Nov. 13, 867.

Adrian II: Rome; Dec. 14, 867, to Dec. 14, 872.

John VIII: Rome; Dec. 14, 872, to Dec. 16, 882.

Marinus I: Gallese; Dec. 16, 882, to May 15, 884.

St. Adrian III: Rome; May 17, 884, to Sept., 885. Cult confirmed June 2, 1891.

Stephen V (VI): Rome; Sept., 885, to Sept. 14, 891.

Formosus: Portus; Oct. 6, 891, to Apr. 4, 896.

Boniface VI: Rome; Apr., 896, to Apr., 896.

Stephen VI (VII): Rome; May, 896, to Aug., 897.

Romanus: Gallese; Aug., 897, to Nov., 897.

Theodore II: Rome; Dec., 897, to Dec., 897.

John IX: Tivoli; Jan., 898, to Jan., 900.

Benedict IV: Rome; Jan. (Feb.), 900, to July, 903.

Leo V: Ardea; July, 903, to Sept., 903.

Sergius III: Rome; Jan. 29, 904, to Apr. 14, 911.

Anastasius III: Rome; Apr., 911, to June, 913.

Landus: Sabina; July, 913, to Feb., 914.

John X: Tossignano (Imola); Mar., 914, to May, 928.

Leo VI: Rome; May, 928, to Dec., 928.

Stephen VII (VIII): Rome; Dec., 928, to Feb., 931.

John XI: Rome; Feb. (Mar.), 931, to Dec., 935.

Leo VII: Rome; Jan. 3, 936, to July 13, 939.

Stephen VIII (IX): Rome; July 14, 939, to Oct., 942.

Marinus II: Rome; Oct. 30, 942, to May, 946.

Agapitus II: Rome; May 10, 946, to Dec., 955.

John XII (Octavius): Tusculum; Dec. 16, 955, to May 14, 964 (date of his death).

Leo VIII: Rome; Dec. 4 (6), 963, to Mar. 1, 965.

Benedict V: Rome; May 22, 964, to July 4, 966.

Confusion exists concerning the legitimacy of claims to the pontificate by Leo VIII and Benedict V. John XII was deposed Dec. 4, 963, by a Roman council. If this deposition was invalid, Leo was an antipope. If the deposition of John was valid, Leo was the legitimate pope and Benedict was an antipope.

John XIII: Rome; Oct. 1, 965, to Sept. 6, 972.

Benedict VI: Rome; Jan. 19, 973, to June, 974.

Benedict VII: Rome; Oct. 974, to July 10, 983.

John XIV (Peter Campenora): Pavia; Dec., 983, to Aug. 20, 984.

John XV: Rome; Aug., 985, to Mar., 996.

Gregory V (Bruno of Carinthia): Saxony; May 3, 996, to Feb. 18, 999.

Sylvester II (Gerbert): Auvergne; Apr. 2, 999, to May 12, 1003.

John XVII (Siccone): Rome; June, 1003, to Dec., 1003.

John XVIII (Phasianus): Rome; Jan., 1004, to July, 1009.

Sergius IV (Peter): Rome; July 31, 1009, to May 12, 1012.

The custom of changing one's name on election to the papacy is generally considered to date from the time of Sergius IV. Before his time, several popes had changed their names. After his time, this became a regular practice, with few exceptions; e.g., Adrian VI and Marcellus II.

Benedict VIII (Theophylactus): Tusculum; May 18, 1012, to Apr. 9, 1024.

John XIX (Romanus): Tusculum; Apr. (May), 1024, to 1032.

Benedict IX (Theophylactus): Tusculum; 1032, to 1044.

Sylvester III (John): Rome; Jan. 20, 1045, to Feb. 10, 1045.

Sylvester III was an antipope if the forcible removal of Benedict IX in 1044 was not legitimate.

Benedict IX (second time): Apr. 10, 1045, to May 1, 1045.

Gregory VI (John Gratian): Rome; May 5, 1045, to Dec. 20, 1046.

Clement II (Suitger, Lord of Morsleben and Hornburg): Saxony; Dec. 24 (25), 1046, to Oct. 9, 1047.

If the resignation of Benedict IX in 1045 and his removal at the December, 1046, synod were not legitimate, Gregory VI and Clement II were antipopes.

Benedict IX (third time): Nov. 8, 1047, to July 17, 1048 (d. c. 1055).

Damasus II (Poppo): Bavaria; July 17, 1048, to Aug. 9, 1048.

St. Leo IX (Bruno): Alsace; Feb. 12, 1049, to Apr. 19, 1054.

Victor II (Gebhard): Swabia; Apr. 16, 1055, to July 28, 1057.

Stephen IX (X) (Frederick): Lorraine; Aug. 3, 1057, to Mar. 29, 1058.

Nicholas II (Gerard): Burgundy; Jan. 24, 1059, to July 27, 1061.

Alexander II (Anselmo da Baggio): Milan; Oct. 1, 1061, to Apr. 21, 1073.

St. Gregory VII (Hildebrand): Tuscany; Apr. 22 (June 30), 1073, to May 25, 1085.

Bl. Victor III (Dauferius; Desiderius): Benevento; May 24, 1086, to Sept. 16, 1087. Cult confirmed July 23, 1887.

Bl. Urban II (Otto di Lagery): France; Mar. 12, 1088, to July 29, 1099. Cult confirmed July 14, 1881.

Paschal II (Raniero): Ravenna; Aug. 13 (14), 1099, to Jan. 21, 1118.

Gelasius II (Giovanni Caetani): Gaeta; Jan. 24 (Mar. 10), 1118, to Jan. 28, 1119.

Callistus II (Guido of Burgundy): Burgundy; Feb. 2 (9), 1119, to Dec. 13, 1124.

Honorius II (Lamberto): Fiagnano (Imola); Dec. 15 (21), 1124, to Feb. 13, 1130.

Innocent II (Gregorio Papareschi): Rome; Feb. 14 (23), 1130, to Sept. 24, 1143.

Celestine II (Guido): Citta di Castello; Sept. 26 (Oct. 3), 1143, to Mar. 8, 1144.

Lucius II (Gerardo Caccjanemici): Bologna: Mar. 12, 1144, to Feb. 15, 1145.

Bl. Eugene III (Bernardo Paganelli di Montemagno): Pisa; Feb. 15 (18), 1145, to July 8, 1153. Cult confirmed Oct. 3, 1872.

Anastasius IV (Corrado): Rome; July 12, 1153, to Dec, 3, 1154.

Adrian IV (Nicholas Breakspear): England; Dec. 4 (5), 1154, to Sept. 1, 1159.

Alexander III (Rolando Bandinelli): Siena; Sept. 7 (20), 1159, to Aug. 30, 1181.

Lucius III (Ubaldo Allucingoli): Lucca; Sept. 1 (6), 1181, to Sept. 25, 1185.

Urban III (Uberto Crivelli): Milan; Nov. 25 (Dec. 1), 1185, to Oct. 20, 1187.

Gregory VIII (Alberto de Morra): Benevento; Oct. 21 (25), 1187, to Dec. 17, 1187.

Clement III (Paolo Scolari): Rome; Dec. 19 (20), 1187, to Mar., 1191.

Celestine III (Giacinto Bobone): Rome; Mar. 30 (Apr. 14), 1191, to Jan. 8, 1198.

Innocent III (Lotario dei Conti di Segni): Anagni; Jan. 8 (Feb. 22), 1198, to July 16, 1216.

Honorius III (Cencio Savelli): Rome; July 18 (24), 1216, to Mar. 18, 1227.

Gregory IX (Ugolino, Count of Segni): Anagni; Mar. 19 (21), 1227, to Aug. 22, 1241.

Celestine IV (Goffredo Castiglioni): Milan; Oct. 25 (28), 1241, to Nov. 10, 1241.

Innocent IV (Sinibaldo Fieschi): Genoa; June 25 (28), 1243, to Dec. 7, 1254.

Alexander IV (Rinaldo, Count of Segni): Anagni; Dec. 12 (20), 1254, to May 25, 1261.

Urban IV (Jacques Pantaléon): Troyes; Aug. 29 (Sept. 4), 1261, to Oct. 2, 1264.

Clement IV (Guy Foulques or Guido le Gros): France; Feb. 5 (15), 1265, to Nov. 29, 1268.

Bl. Gregory X (Teobaldo Visconti): Piacenza; Sept. 1, 1271 (Mar. 27, 1272), to Jan. 10, 1276. Cult confirmed Sept. 12, 1713.

Bl. Innocent V (Peter of Tarentaise): Savoy; Jan. 21 (Feb. 22), 1276, to June 22, 1276. Cult confirmed Mar. 13, 1898.

Adrian V (Ottobono Fieschi): Genoa: July 11, 1276, to Aug. 18, 1276.

John XXI (Petrus Juliani or Petrus Hispanus): Portugal; Sept. 8 (20), 1276, to May 20, 1277.

Elimination was made of the name of John XX in an effort to rectify the numerical designation of popes named John. The error dates back to the time of John XV.

Nicholas III (Giovanni Gaetano Orsini): Rome; Nov. 25 (Dec. 26), 1277, to Aug. 22, 1280.

Martin IV (Simon de Brie): France; Feb. 22 (Mar. 23), 1281, to Mar. 28, 1285.

The names of Marinus I (882-84) and Marinus II (942-46) were construed as Martin. In view of these two pontificates and the earlier reign of St. Martin I (649-55), this pope was called Martin IV.

Honorius IV (Giacomo Savelli): Rome; Apr. 2 (May 20), 1285, to Apr. 3, 1287.

Nicholas IV (Girolamo Masci): Ascoli; Feb. 22, 1288, to Apr. 4, 1292.

St. Celestine V (Pietro del Murrone): Isernia; July 5 (Aug. 29), 1294, to Dec. 13, 1294; d. 1296. Canonized May 5, 1313.

Boniface VIII (Benedetto Caetani): Anagni; Dec. 24, 1294 (Jan. 23, 1295), to Oct. 11, 1303.

Bl. Benedict XI (Niccolo Boccasini): Treviso; Oct. 22 (27), 1303, to July 7, 1304. Cult confirmed Apr. 24, 1736.

Clement V (Bertrand de Got): France; June 5 (Nov. 14), 1305, to Apr. 20, 1314. (First of Avignon popes.)

John XXII (Jacques d'Euse): Cahors; Aug. 7 (Sept. 5), 1316, to Dec. 4, 1334.

Benedict XII (Jacques Fournier): France; Dec. 20, 1334 (Jan. 8, 1335), to Apr. 25, 1342.

Clement VI (Pierre Roger): France; May 7 (19), 1342, to Dec. 6, 1352.

Innocent VI (Etienne Aubert): France; Dec. 18 (30), 1352, to Sept. 12, 1362.

Bl. Urban V (Guillaume de Grimoard): France; Sept. 28 (Nov. 6), 1362, to Dec. 19, 1370. Cult confirmed Mar. 10, 1870.

Gregory XI (Pierre Roger de Beaufort): France; Dec. 30, 1370 (Jan. 5, 1371), to Mar. 26, 1378. (Last of Avignon popes.)

Urban VI (Bartolomeo Prignano): Naples; Apr. 8 (18), 1378, to Oct. 15, 1389.

Boniface IX (Pietro Tomacelli): Naples; Nov. 2 (9), 1389, to Oct. 1, 1404.

Innocent VII (Cosma Migliorati): Sulmona; Oct. 17 (Nov. 11), 1404, to Nov. 6, 1406.

Gregory XII (Angelo Correr): Venice; Nov. 30 (Dec. 19), 1406, to July 4, 1415, when he voluntarily resigned from the papacy to permit the election of his successor. He died Oct. 18, 1417. (See The Western Schism.)

Martin V (Oddone Colonna): Rome; Nov. 11 (21), 1417, to Feb. 20, 1431.

Eugene IV (Gabriele Condulmer): Venice; Mar. 3 (11), 1431, to Feb. 23, 1447.

Nicholas V (Tommaso Parentucelli): Sarzana; Mar. 6 (19), 1447, to Mar. 24, 1455.

Callistus III (Alfonso Borgia): Jativa (Valencia); Apr. 8 (20), 1455, to Aug. 6, 1458.

Pius II (Enea Silvio Piccolomini): Siena; Aug. 19 (Sept. 3), 1458, to Aug. 15, 1464.

Paul II (Pietro Barbo): Venice; Aug. 30 (Sept. 16), 1464, to July 26, 1471.

Sixtus IV (Francesco della Rovere): Savona; Aug. 9 (25), 1471, to Aug. 12, 1484.

Innocent VIII (Giovanni Battista Cibo): Genoa; Aug. 29 (Sept. 12), 1484, to July 25, 1492.

Alexander VI (Rodrigo Borgia): Jativa (Valencia); Aug. 11 (26), 1492, to Aug. 18, 1503.

Pius III (Francesco Todeschini-Piccolomini): Siena; Sept. 22 (Oct. 1, 8), 1503, to Oct. 18, 1503.

Julius II (Giuliano della Rovere): Savona; Oct. 31 (Nov. 26), 1503, to Feb. 21, 1513.

Leo X (Giovanni de' Medici): Florence; Mar. 9 (19), 1513, to Dec. 1, 1521.

Adrian VI (Adrian Florensz): Utrecht; Jan. 9 (Aug. 31), 1522, to Sept. 14, 1523.

Clement VII (Giulio de' Medici): Florence; Nov. 19 (26), 1523, to Sept. 25, 1534.

Paul III (Alessandro Farnese): Rome; Oct. 13 (Nov. 3), 1534, to Nov. 10, 1549.

Julius III (Giovanni Maria Ciocchi del Monte): Rome; Feb. 7 (22), 1550, to Mar. 23, 1555.

Marcellus II (Marcello Cervini): Montepulciano; Apr. 9 (10), 1555, to May 1, 1555.

Paul IV (Gian Pietro Carafa): Naples; May 23 (26), 1555, to Aug. 18, 1559.

Pius IV (Giovan Angelo de' Medici): Milan; Dec. 25, 1559 (Jan. 6, 1560), to Dec. 9, 1565.

St. Pius V (Antonio-Michele Ghislieri): Bosco (Alexandria); Jan. 7 (17), 1566, to May 1, 1572. Canonized May 22, 1712.

Gregory XIII (Ugo Buoncompagni): Bologna; May 13 (25), 1572, to Apr. 10, 1585.

Sixtus V (Felice Peretti): Grottammare (Ripatransone); Apr. 24 (May 1), 1585, to Aug. 27, 1590.

Urban VII (Giovanni Battista Castagna): Rome; Sept. 15, 1590, to Sept. 27, 1590.

Gregory XIV (Niccolo Sfondrati): Cremona; Dec. 5 (8), 1590, to Oct. 16, 1591.

Innocent IX (Giovanni Antonio Facchinetti): Bologna; Oct. 29 (Nov. 3), 1591, to Dec. 30, 1591.

Clement VIII (Ippolito Aldobrandini): Florence; Jan. 30 (Feb. 9), 1592, to Mar. 3, 1605.

Leo XI (Alessandro de' Medici): Florence; Apr. 1 (10), 1605, to Apr. 27, 1605.

Paul V (Camillo Borghese): Rome; May 16 (29), 1605, to Jan. 28, 1621.

Gregory XV (Alessandro Ludovisi): Bologna; Feb. 9 (14), 1621, to July 8, 1623.

Urban VIII (Maffeo Barberini): Florence; Aug. 6 (Sept. 29), 1623, to July 29, 1644.

Innocent X (Giovanni Battista Pamfili): Rome; Sept. 15 (Oct. 4), 1644, to Jan. 7, 1655.

Alexander VII (Fabio Chigi): Siena; Apr. 7 (18), 1655, to May 22, 1667.

Clement IX (Giulio Rospigliosi): Pistoia; June 20 (26), 1667, to Dec. 9, 1669.

Clement X (Emilio Altieri): Rome; Apr. 29 (May 11), 1670, to July 22, 1676.

Bl. Innocent XI (Benedetto Odescalchi): Como; Sept. 21 (Oct. 4), 1676, to Aug. 12, 1689.

Alexander VIII (Pietro Ottoboni): Venice; Oct. 6 (16), 1689, to Feb. 1, 1691.

Innocent XII (Antonio Pignatelli): Spinazzola; July 12 (15), 1691, to Sept. 27, 1700.

Clement XI (Giovanni Francesco Albani): Urbino; Nov. 23, 30 (Dec. 8), 1700, to Mar. 19, 1721.

Innocent XIII (Michelangelo dei Conti): Rome; May 8 (18), 1721, to Mar. 7, 1724.

Benedict XIII (Pietro Francesco — Vincenzo Maria — Orsini): Gravina (Bari); May 29 (June 4), 1724, to Feb. 21, 1730.

Clement XII (Lorenzo Corsini): Florence; July 12 (16), 1730, to Feb. 6, 1740.

Benedict XIV (Prospero Lambertini): Bologna; Aug. 17 (22), 1740, to May 3, 1758.

Clement XIII (Carlo Rezzonico): Venice; July 6 (16), 1758, to Feb. 2, 1769.

Clement XIV (Giovanni Vincenzo Antonio — Lorenzo — Ganganelli): Rimini; May 19, 28 (June 4), 1769, to Sept. 22, 1774.

Pius VI (Giovanni Angelo Braschi): Cesena; Feb. 15 (22), 1775, to Aug. 29, 1799.

Pius VII (Barnaba — Gregorio — Chiaramonti): Cesena; Mar. 14 (21), 1800, to Aug. 20, 1823.

Leo XII (Annibale della Genga): Genga (Fabriano); Sept. 28 (Oct. 5), 1823, to Feb. 10, 1829.

Pius VIII (Francesco Saverio Castiglioni): Cingoli; Mar. 31 (Apr. 5), 1829, to Nov. 30, 1830.

Gregory XVI (Bartolomeo Alberto — Mauro — Cappellari): Belluno; Feb. 2 (6), 1831, to June 1, 1846.

Pius IX (Giovanni M. Mastai Ferretti): Senigallia; June 16 (21), 1846, to Feb. 7, 1878.

Leo XIII (Gioacchino Pecci): Carpineto (Anagni); Feb. 20 (Mar. 3), 1878, to July 20, 1903.

St. Pius X (Giuseppe Sarto): Riese (Treviso); Aug. 4 (9), 1903, to Aug. 20, 1914. Canonized May 29, 1954.

Benedict XV (Giacomo della Chiesa): Genoa; Sept. 3 (6), 1914, to Jan. 22, 1922.

Pius XI (Achille Ratti): Desio (Milan); Feb. 6 (12), 1922, to Feb. 10, 1939.

Pius XII (Eugenio Pacelli): Rome; Mar. 2 (12), 1939, to Oct. 9, 1958.

John XXIII (Angelo Giuseppe Roncalli): Sotto il Monte (Bergamo); Oct. 28 (Nov. 4). 1958 to June 3, 1963.

Paul VI (Giovanni Battista Montini): Concessio (Brescia); June 21 (June 30), 1963 to Aug. 6, 1978. (See separate entry.)

John Paul I (Albino Luciani): Forno di Canale (Belluno); Aug. 26 (Sept. 3) to Sept. 28, 1978. (See separate entry.)

John Paul II (Karol Wojtyla): Wadowice, Poland; Oct. 16 (22), 1978. to

ANTIPOPES

(Source: *Annuario Pontificio.*)

This list of men who claimed or exercised the papal office in an uncanonical manner includes names, birthplaces and dates of alleged reigns.

St. Hippolytus: Rome; 217-235; was reconciled before his death.

Novatian: Rome; 251.

Felix II: Rome; 355 to Nov. 22, 365.

Ursinus: 366-367.

Eulalius: Dec. 27 or 29, 418, to 419.

Lawrence: 498; 501-505.

Dioscorus: Alexandria; Sept. 22, 530, to Oct. 14, 530.

Theodore: ended alleged reign, 687.

Paschal: ended alleged reign, 687.

Constantine: Nepi; June 28 (July 5), 767, to 769.

Philip: July 31, 768; retired to his monastery on the same day.

John: ended alleged reign, Jan., 844.

Anastasius: Aug., 855, to Sept., 855; d. 880.

Christopher: Rome; July or Sept., 903, to Jan., 904.

Boniface VII: Rome; June, 974, to July, 974; Aug., 984, to July, 985.

John XVI: Rossano; Apr., 997, to Feb., 998.

Gregory: ended alleged reign, 1012.

Benedict X: Rome; Apr. 5, 1058, to Jan. 24, 1059.

Honorius II: Verona; Oct. 28, 1061, to 1072.

Clement III: Parma; June 25, 1080 (Mar. 24, 1084), to Sept. 8, 1100.

Theodoric: ended alleged reign, 1100; d. 1102.

Albert: ended alleged reign, 1102.

Sylvester IV: Rome; Nov. 18, 1105, to 1111.

Gregory VIII: France; Mar. 8, 1118, to 1121.

Celestine II: Rome; ended alleged reign, Dec., 1124

Anacletus II: Rome; Feb. 14 (23), 1130, to Jan. 25, 1138.

Victor IV: Mar., 1138, to May 29, 1138; submitted to Pope Innocent II.

Victor IV: Montecelio; Sept. 7 (Oct. 4), 1159, to Apr. 20, 1164; he did not recognize his predecessor (Victor IV, above).

Paschal III: Apr. 22 (26), 1164, to Sept. 20, 1168.

Callistus III: Arezzo; Sept., 1168, to Aug. 29, 1178; submitted to Pope Alexander III.

Innocent III: Sezze; Sept. 29, 1179, to 1180.

Nicholas V: Corvaro (Rieti); May 12 (22), 1328, to Aug. 25, 1330; d. Oct. 16, 1333.

Four antipopes of the Western Schism:

Clement VII: Sept. 20 (Oct. 31), 1378, to Sept. 16, 1394.

Benedict XIII: Aragon; Sept. 28 (Oct. 11), 1394, to May 23, 1423.

Alexander V: Crete; June 26 (July 7), 1409, to May 3, 1410.
John XXIII: Naples; May 17 (25), 1410, to May 29, 1415.
Felix V: Savoy; Nov. 5, 1439 (July 24, 1440), to April 7, 1449; d. 1451.

Avignon Papacy

Avignon was the residence of a series of French popes from Clement V to Gregory XI (1309-77). Prominent in the period were power struggles over the mixed interests of Church and state with the rulers of France (Philip IV, John II), Bavaria (Lewis IV), England (Edward III); factionalism of French and Italian churchmen; political as well as ecclesiastical turmoil in Italy, a factor of significance in prolonging the stay of popes in Avignon. Despite some positive achievements, the Avignon papacy was a prologue to the Western Schism which began in 1378.

Western Schism

The Western Schism was a confused state of affairs which divided Christendom into two and then three papal obediences from 1378 to 1417.

It occurred some 50 years after Marsilius theorized that a general (not ecumenical) council of bishops and other persons was superior to a pope and nearly 30 years before the Council of Florence stated definitively that no kind of council had such authority.

It was a period of disaster preceding the even more disastrous period of the Reformation.

Urban VI, following transfer to Rome of the 70-year papal residence at Avignon, was elected pope Apr. 8, 1378, and reigned until his death in 1389. He was succeeded by Boniface IX (1389-1404), Innocent VII (1404-1406) and Gregory XII (1406-1415). These four are considered the legitimate popes of the period.

Some of the cardinals who chose Urban pope, dissatisfied with his conduct of the office, declared that his election was invalid. They proceeded to elect Clement VII, who claimed the papacy from 1378 to 1394. He was succeeded by Benedict XIII.

Prelates seeking to end the state of divided papal loyalties convoked the Council of Pisa which, without authority, found Gregory XII and Benedict XIII, in absentia, guilty on 30-odd charges of schism and heresy, deposed them, and elected a third claimant to the papacy, Alexander V (1409-1410). He was succeeded by John XXIII (1410-1415).

The schism was ended by the Council of Constance (1414-1418). This council, although originally called into session in an irregular manner, acquired authority after being convoked by Gregory XII in 1415. In its early irregular phase, it deposed John XXIII whose election to the papacy was uncanonical anyway. After being formally convoked, it accepted the abdication of Gregory in 1415 and dismissed the claims of Benedict XIII two years later, thus clearing the way for the election of Martin V on Nov. 11, 1417. The Council of Constance also rejected the theories of John Wycliff and condemned John Hus as a heretic.

20th CENTURY POPES

Leo XIII

Leo XIII (Gioacchino Vincenzo Pecci) was born May 2, 1810, in Carpineto, Italy. Although all but three years of his life and pontificate were of the 19th century, his influence extended well into the 20th century.

He was educated at the Jesuit college in Viterbo, the Roman College, the Academy of Noble Ecclesiastics, and the University of the Sapienza. He was ordained to the priesthood in 1837.

He served as an apostolic delegate to two States of the Church, Benevento from 1838 to 1841 and Perugia in 1841 and 1842. Ordained titular archbishop of Damietta, he was papal nuncio to Belgium from January, 1843, until May, 1846; in the post, he had controversial relations with the government over education issues and acquired his first significant experience of industrialized society.

He was archbishop of Perugia from 1846 to 1878. He became a cardinal in 1853 and chamberlain of the Roman Curia in 1877. He was elected to the papacy Feb. 20, 1878. He died July 20, 1903.

Canonizations: He canonized 18 saints and beatified a group of English martyrs.

Church Administration: He established 300 new dioceses and vicariates; restored the hierarchy in Scotland, set up an English, as contrasted with the Portuguese, hierarchy in India; approved the action of the Congregation for the Propagation of the Faith in reorganizing missions in China.

Encyclicals: He issued 50 encyclicals, on subjects ranging from devotional to social. In the former category were *Annum Sacrum,* on the Sacred Heart, in 1899, and nine letters on Mary and the Rosary.

Interfaith Relations: He was unsuccessful in unity overtures made to Orthodox and Slavic Churches. He declared Anglican orders invalid in the apostolic bull *Apostolicae Curae* Sept. 13, 1896.

International Relations: Leo was frustrated in seeking solutions to the Roman Question arising from the seizure of church lands by the Kingdom of Italy in 1870. He also faced anticlerical situations in Belgium and France and in the Kulturkampf policies of Bismarck in Germany.

Social Questions: Much of Leo's influence stemmed from social doctrine stated in numerous encyclicals, concerning liberalism, liberty, the divine origin of authority; socialism, in *Quod Apostolici Muneris*, 1878; the Christian concept of the family, in *Arcanum*, 1880; socialism and economic liberalism, relations between capital and labor, in *Rerum Novarum*, 1891. Two of his social encyclicals were against the African slave trade.

Studies: In the encyclical *Aeterni Patris* of Aug. 4, 1879, he ordered a renewal of philosophical and theological studies in seminaries along scholastic, and especially Thomistic, lines, to counteract influential trends of liberalism and Modernism. He issued guidelines for biblical exegesis in *Providentissimus Deus* Nov. 18, 1893, and established the Pontifical Biblical Commission in 1902.

In other actions affecting scholarship and study, he opened the Vatican Archives to scholars in 1883 and established the Vatican Observatory.

United States: He authorized establishment of the apostolic delegation in Washington, D.C. Jan. 24, 1893. He refused to issue a condemnation of the Knights of Labor. With a document entitled *Testem Benevolentiae*, he eased resolution of questions concerning what was called an American heresy in 1899.

St. Pius X

St. Pius X (Giuseppe Melchiorre Sarto) was born in 1835 in Riese, Italy.

Educated at the college of Castelfranco and the seminary at Padua, he was ordained to the priesthood Sept. 18, 1858. He served as a curate in Trombolo for nine years before beginning an eight-year pastorate at Salzano. He was chancellor of the Treviso diocese from November, 1875, and bishop of Mantua from 1884 until 1893. He was cardinal-patriarch of Venice from that year until his election to the papacy by the conclave held from July 31 to Aug. 4, 1903.

Aims: Pius' principal objectives as pope were "to restore all things in Christ, in order that Christ may be all and in all," and "to teach (and defend) Christian truth and law."

Canonizations, Encyclicals: He canonized four saints and issued 16 encyclicals. One of the encyclicals was issued in commemoration of the 50th anniversary of the proclamation of the dogma of the Immaculate Conception of Mary.

Catechetics: He introduced a whole new era of religious instruction and formation with the encyclical *Acerbo Nimis* of Apr. 15, 1905, in which he called for vigor in establishing and conducting parochial programs of the Confraternity of Christian Doctrine.

Catholic Action: He outlined the role of official Catholic Action in two encyclicals in 1905 and 1906. Favoring organized action by Catholics themselves, he had serious reservations about interconfessional collaboration.

He stoutly maintained claims to papal rights in the anticlerical climate of Italy. He authorized bishops to relax prohibitions against participation by Catholics in some Italian elections.

Church Administration: With the motu proprio *Arduum Sane* of Mar. 19, 1904, he inaugurated the work which resulted in the Code of Canon Law; the code was completed in 1917 and went into effect in the following year. He reorganized and strengthened the Roman Curia with the apostolic constitution *Sapienti Consilio* of June 29, 1908. While promoting the expansion of missionary work, he removed from the jurisdiction of the Congregation for the Propagation of the Faith the Church in the United States, Canada, Newfoundland, England, Ireland, Holland and Luxembourg.

International Relations: He ended traditional prerogatives of Catholic governments with respect to papal elections, in 1904. He opposed anti-Church and anticlerical actions in several countries: Bolivia in 1905, because of anti-religious legislation; France in 1906, for its 1901 action in annulling its concordat with the Holy See, and for the 1905 Law of Separation by which it decreed separation of Church and state, ordered the confiscation of church property, and blocked religious education and the activities of religious orders; Portugal in 1911, for the separation of Church and state and repressive measures which resulted in persecution later.

In 1912 he called on the bishops of Brazil to work for the improvement of conditions among Indians.

Liturgy: "The Pope of the Eucharist," he strongly recommended the frequent reception of Holy Communion in a decree dated Dec. 20, 1905; in another decree, *Quam Singulari*, of Aug. 8, 1910, he called for the early reception of the sacrament by children. He initiated measures for liturgical reform with new norms for sacred music and the start of work on revision of the *Breviary* for recitation of the Divine Office.

Modernism: Pius was a vigorous opponent of "the synthesis of all heresies," which threatened the integrity of doctrine through its influence in philosophy, theology and biblical exegesis. In opposition, he condemned 65 of its propositions as erroneous in the decree *Lamentabili* July 3, 1907; issued the encyclical *Pascendi* in the same vein Sept. 8, 1907; backed both of these with censures; and published the Oath against Modernism in September, 1910, to be taken by all the clergy. Ecclesiastical studies suffered to some extent from these actions, necessary as they were at the time.

Pius followed the lead of Leo XIII in promoting the study of scholastic philosophy. He established the Pontifical Biblical Institute May 7, 1909.

His death, Aug. 20, 1914, was hastened by the outbreak of World War I. He was beatified in 1951 and canonized May 29, 1954. His feast is observed Aug. 21.

Benedict XV

Benedict XV (Giacomo della Chiesa) was born Nov. 21, 1854, in Pegli, Italy.

He was educated at the Royal University of Genoa and Gregorian University in Rome. He was ordained to the priesthood Dec. 21, 1878.

He served in the papal diplomatic corps from 1882 to 1907; as secretary to the nuncio to Spain from 1882 to 1887, as secretary to the papal secretary of state from 1887, and as undersecretary from 1901.

He was ordained archbishop of Bologna Dec. 22, 1907, and spent four years completing a pastoral visitation there. He was made a cardinal just three months before being elected to the papacy Sept. 3, 1914, He died Jan. 22, 1922. Two key efforts of his pontificate were for peace and the relief of human suffering caused by World War I.

Canonizations: Benedict canonized three saints; one of them was Joan of Arc.

Canon Law: He published the Code of Canon Law, developed by the commission set up by St. Pius X, June 28, 1917; it went into effect the following year.

Curia: He made great changes in the personnel of the Curia. He established the Congregation for the Oriental Churches May 1, 1917, and founded the Pontifical Oriental Institute in Rome later in the year.

Encyclicals: He issued 12 encyclicals. Peace was the theme of three of them. In another, published two years after the cessation of hostilities, he wrote about child victims of the war. He followed the lead of Leo XIII in *Spiritus Paraclitus,* Sept. 15, 1920, on biblical studies.

International Relations: He was largely frustrated on the international level because of the events and attitudes of the war period, but the number of diplomats accredited to the Vatican nearly doubled, from 14 to 26, between the time of his accession to the papacy and his death.

Peace Efforts: Benedict's stance in the war was one of absolute impartiality but not of disinterested neutrality. Because he would not take sides, he was suspected by both sides and the seven-point peace plan he offered to all belligerents Aug. 1, 1917, was turned down. The points of the plan were: recognition of the moral force of right; disarmament; acceptance of arbitration in cases of dispute; guarantee of freedom of the seas; renunciation of war indemnities; evacuation and restoration of occupied territories; examination of territorial claims in dispute.

Relief Efforts: Benedict assumed personal charge of Vatican relief efforts during the war. He set up an international missing persons bureau for contacts between prisoners and their families, but was forced to close it because of the suspicion of warring nations that it was a front for espionage operations.

He persuaded the Swiss government to admit into the country military victims of tuberculosis.

Roman Question: Benedict arranged a meeting of Benito Mussolini and the papal secretary of state, which marked the first step toward final settlement of the question in 1929.

Pius XI

Pius XI (Ambrogio Damiano Achille Ratti) was born May 31, 1857, in Desio, Italy.

Educated at seminaries in Seviso and Milan, and at the Lombard College, Gregorian University and Academy of St. Thomas in Rome, he was ordained to the priesthood in 1879.

He taught at the major seminary of Milan from 1882 to 1888. Appointed to the staff of the Ambrosian Library in 1888, he remained there until 1911, acquiring a reputation for publishing works on palaeography and serving as director from 1907 to 1911. He then moved to the Vatican Library, of which he was prefect from 1914 to 1918. In 1919, he was named apostolic visitor to Poland in April, nuncio in June, and was made titular archbishop of Lepanto Oct. 28. He was made archbishop of Milan and cardinal June 13, 1921, before being elected to the papacy Feb. 6, 1922. He died Feb. 10, 1939.

Aim: The objective of his pontificate, as stated in the encyclical *Ubi Arcano,* Dec. 23, 1922, was to establish the reign and peace of Christ in society.

Canonizations: He canonized 34 saints, including the Jesuit Martyrs of North America, and conferred the title of Doctor of the Church on Sts. Peter Canisius, John of the Cross, Robert Bellarmine and Albertus Magnus.

Eastern Churches: He called for better understanding of the Eastern Churches in the encyclical *Rerum Orientalium* of Sept. 8, 1928, and developed facilities for the training of Eastern-Rite priests. He inaugurated steps for the codification of Eastern-Church law in 1929. In 1935 he made Syrian Patriarch Tappouni a cardinal.

Encyclicals: His first encyclical, *Ubi Arcano,* in addition to stating the aims of his pontificate, blueprinted Catholic Action and called for its development throughout the Church. In *Quas Primas,* Dec. 11, 1925, he established the feast of Christ the King for universal observance. Subjects of some of his other encyclicals were: Christian education, in *Divini Illius Magistri,* Dec. 31, 1929; Christian marriage, in *Casti Connubii,* Dec. 30, 1930; social conditions and pressure for social change in line with the teaching in *Rerum Novarum,* in *Quadragesimo Anno,* May 15, 1931; atheistic Communism, in *Divini Redemptoris,* Mar. 19, 1937; the priesthood, in *Ad Catholici Sacerdotii,* Dec. 20, 1935.

Missions: Following the lead of Benedict XV, Pius called for the training of native clergy in the pattern of their own respective cultures, and promoted missionary developments in various ways. He ordained six native bishops for China in 1926, one for Japan in 1927, and others for regions of Asia, China and India in 1933. He placed the first 40 mission dioceses under native bishops, saw the number of native priests increase from about 2,600 to more than 7,000 and the number of Catholics in missionary areas more than double from nine million.

In the apostolic constitution *Deus Scientiarum Dominus* of May 24, 1931, he ordered the introduction of missiology into theology courses.

Interfaith Relations: Pius was negative to the ecumenical movement among Protestants but approved the Malines Conversations, 1921 to 1926, between Anglicans and Catholics.

International Relations: Relations with the Mussolini government deteriorated from 1931 on, as indicated in the encyclical *Non Abbiamo Bisogno,* when the regime took steps to curb liberties and activities of the Church; they turned critical in 1938 with the emergence of racist policies. Relations deteriorated also in Germany from 1933 on, resulting finally in condemnation of the Nazis in the encyclical *Mit Brennender Sorge,* March, 1937. Pius sparked a revival of the Church in France by encouraging Catholics to work within the democratic framework of the Republic rather than foment trouble over restoration of a monarchy. Pius was powerless before the civil war which erupted in Spain in July, 1936; sporadic persecution and repression by the Calles regime in Mexico; and systematic persecution of the Church in the Soviet Union. Many of the 10 concordats and two agreements reached with European countries after World War I became casualties of World War II.

Roman Question: Pius negotiated for two and one-half years with the Italian government to settle the Roman Question by means of the Lateran Agreement of 1929. The agreement provided independent status for the State of Vatican City; made Catholicism the official religion of Italy, with pastoral and educational freedom and state recognition of Catholic marriages, religious orders and societies; and provided a financial payment to the Vatican for expropriation of the former States of the Church.

Pius XII

Pius XII (Eugenio Maria Giovanni Pacelli) was born Mar. 2, 1876, in Rome.

Educated at the Gregorian University and the Lateran University, in Rome, he was ordained to the priesthood Apr. 2, 1899.

He entered the Vatican diplomatic service in 1901, worked on the codification of canon law, and was appointed secretary of the Congregation for Ecclesiastical Affairs in 1914. Three years later he was ordained titular archbishop of Sardis and made apostolic nuncio to Bavaria. He was nuncio to Germany from 1920 to 1929, when he was made a cardinal, and took office as papal secretary of state in the following year. His diplomatic negotiations resulted in concordats between the Vatican and Bavaria (1924), Prussia (1929), Baden (1932), Austria and the German Republic (1933). He took part in negotiations which led to settlement of the Roman Question in 1929.

He was elected to the papacy Mar. 2, 1939. He died Oct. 9, 1958, at Castel Gandolfo after the 12th longest pontificate in history.

Canonizations: He canonized 33 saints, including Mother Frances X. Cabrini, the first US citizen-Saint.

Cardinals: He raised 56 prelates to the rank of cardinal in two consistories held in 1946 and 1953. There were 57 cardinals at the time of his death.

Church Organization and Missions: He increased the number of dioceses from 1,696 to 2,048. He established native hierarchies in China (1946), Burma (1955), and parts of Africa, and extended the native structure of the Church in India. He ordained the first black bishop for Africa.

Communism: In addition to opposing and condemning Communism on numerous occasions, he decreed in 1949 the penalty of excommunication for all Catholics holding formal and willing allegiance to the Communist Party and its policies. During his reign the Church was persecuted in some 15 countries which fell under Communist domination.

Doctrine and Liturgy: He proclaimed the dogma of the Assumption of the Blessed Virgin Mary Nov. 1, 1950 (apostolic constitution, *Munificentissimus Deus*).

In various encyclicals and other enactments, he provided background for the *aggiornamento* introduced by his successor, John XXIII: by his formulations of doctrine and practice regarding the Mystical Body of Christ, the liturgy, sacred music and biblical studies; by the revision of the Rites of Holy Week; by initiation of the work which led to the calendar-missal-breviary reform ordered into effect Jan. 1, 1961; by the first of several modifications of the Eucharistic fast; by extending the time of Mass to the evening. He instituted the feasts of Mary, Queen, and of St. Joseph the Worker, and clarified teaching concerning devotion to the Sacred Heart.

His 41 encyclicals and nearly 1,000 public addresses made Pius one of the greatest teaching popes. His concern in all his communications was to deal with specific points at issue and/or to bring Christian principles to bear on contemporary world problems.

Peace Efforts: Before the start of World War II, he tried unsuccessfully to get the contending nations — Germany and Poland,

France and Italy — to settle their differences peaceably. During the war, he offered his services to mediate the widened conflict, spoke out against the horrors of war and the suffering it caused, mobilized relief work for its victims, proposed a five-point program for peace in Christmas messages from 1939 to 1942, and secured a generally open status for the city of Rome. After the war, he endorsed the principles and intent of the United Nations and continued efforts for peace.

United States: Pius appointed more than 200 of the 265 American bishops resident in the US and abroad in 1958, erected 27 dioceses in this country, and raised seven dioceses to archiepiscopal rank.

John XXIII

John XXIII (Angelo Roncalli) was born Nov. 25, 1881, at Sotte il Monte, Italy.

He was educated at the seminary of the Bergamo diocese and the Pontifical Seminary in Rome, where he was ordained to the priesthood Aug. 10, 1904.

He spent the first nine or 10 years of his priesthood as secretary to the bishop of Bergamo and as an instructor in the seminary there. He served as a medic and chaplain in the Italian army during World War I. Afterwards, he resumed duties in his own diocese until he was called to Rome in 1921 for work with the Society for the Propagation of the Faith.

He began diplomatic service in 1925 as titular archbishop of Areopolis and apostolic visitor to Bulgaria. A succession of offices followed: apostolic delegate to Bulgaria (1931-1935); titular archbishop of Mesembria, apostolic delegate to Turkey and Greece, administrator of the Latin vicariate apostolic of Istanbul (1935-1944); apostolic nuncio to France (1944-1953). On these missions, he was engaged in delicate negotiations involving Roman, Eastern-Rite and Orthodox relations; the needs of people suffering from the consequences of World War II; and unsettling suspicions arising from wartime conditions.

He was made a cardinal Jan. 12, 1953, and three days later was appointed patriarch of Venice, the position he held until his election to the papacy Oct. 28, 1958. He died of stomach cancer June 3, 1963.

John was a strong and vigorous pope whose influence far outmeasured both his age and the shortness of his time in the papacy.

Second Vatican Council: John announced Jan. 25, 1959, his intention of convoking the 21st ecumenical council in history to renew life in the Church, to reform its structures and institutions, and to explore ways and means of promoting unity among Christians. Through the council, which completed its work two and one-half years after his death, he ushered in a new era in the history of the Church.

Canon Law: He established a commission Mar. 28, 1963, for revision of the Code of Canon Law. The work of this commission, still underway, will greatly influence the future course of Catholic life and the conduct of ecclesiastical affairs.

Canonizations: He canonized 10 saints. He also beatified Mother Elizabeth Ann Seton, the first native of the US ever so honored. He named St. Lawrence of Brindisi a Doctor of the Church.

Cardinals: He created 52 cardinals in five consistories, raising membership of the College of Cardinals above the traditional number of 70; at one time in 1962, the membership was 87. He made the college more international in representation than it had ever been, appointing the first cardinals from the Philippines, Japan and Africa. He ordered episcopal ordination for all cardinals. He relieved the suburban bishops of Rome of ordinary jurisdiction over their dioceses so they might devote all their time to business of the Roman Curia.

Eastern Rites: He made all Eastern-Rite patriarchs members of the Congregation for the Oriental Churches.

Ecumenism: He assigned to the Second Vatican Council the task of finding ways and means of promoting unity among Christians. He established the Vatican Secretariat for Promoting Christian Unity June 5, 1960. He showed his desire for more cordial relations with the Orthodox by sending personal representatives to visit Patriarch Athenagoras I June 27, 1961; approved a mission of five delegates to the General Assembly of the World Council of Churches which met in New Delhi, India, in November, 1961; removed a number of pejorative references to Jews in the Roman-Rite liturgy for Good Friday.

Encyclicals: Of the eight encyclicals he issued, the two outstanding ones were *Mater et Magistra* ("Christianity and Social Progress"), in which he recapitulated, updated and extended the social doctrine stated earlier by Leo XIII and Pius XI; and *Pacem in Terris* ("Peace on Earth"), the first encyclical ever addressed to all men of good will as well as to Catholics, on the natural-law principles of peace.

Liturgy: In forwarding liturgical reforms already begun by Pius XII, he ordered a calendar-missal-breviary reform into effect Jan. 1, 1961. He authorized the use of vernacular languages in the administration of the sacraments and approved giving Holy Communion to the sick in afternoon hours. He selected the liturgy as the first topic of major discussion by the Second Vatican Council.

Missions: He issued an encyclical on the missionary activity of the Church; established native hierarchies in Indonesia, Vietnam and Korea; and called on North American superiors of religious institutes to have one-tenth of their members assigned to work in Latin America by 1971.

Peace: John spoke and used his moral influence for peace in 1961 when tension developed over Berlin, in 1962 during the Algerian revolt from France, and later the same year in the Cuban missile crisis. His efforts were singled out for honor by the Balzan Peace Foundation. In 1963, he was posthumously awarded the U.S. Presidential Medal of Freedom.

Paul VI

Paul VI (Giovanni Battista Montini) was born Sept. 26, 1897, at Concesio in northern Italy.

Educated at Brescia, he was ordained to the priesthood May 29, 1920. He pursued additional studies at the Pontifical Academy for Noble Ecclesiastics and the Pontifical Gregorian University. In 1924 he began 30 years of service in the Secretariat of State; as undersecretary from 1937 until 1954, he was closely associated with Pius XII and was heavily engaged in organizing informational and relief services during and after World War II.

He was ordained archbishop of Milan Dec. 12, 1954, and was inducted into the College of Cardinals Dec. 15, 1958. He was elected to the papacy June 21, 1963, two days after the conclave began. He died of a heart attack Aug. 6, 1978.

Second Vatican Council: He reconvened the Second Vatican Council after the death of John XXIII, presided over its second, third and fourth sessions, formally promulgated the 16 documents it produced, and devoted the whole of his pontificate to the task of putting them into effect throughout the Church. The main thrust of his pontificate — in a milieu of cultural and other changes in the Church and the world — was toward institutionalization and control of the authentic trends articulated and set in motion by the council.

Canonizations: He canonized more saints, 84, than any other pope. They included groups of 22 Ugandan martyrs and 40 martyrs of England and Wales, as well as two Americans — Elizabeth Ann Bayley Seton and John Nepomucene Neumann.

Cardinals: He created more cardinals, 137, than any other pope and gave the Sacred College a more international complexion than it ever had before. He limited participation in papal elections to 120 cardinals under the age of 80.

Collegiality: He established the Synod of Bishops in 1965 and called it into session five times. He stimulated the formation and operation of regional conferences of bishops, and of consultative bodies on other levels.

Creed and Holy Year: On June 30, 1968, he issued a Creed of the People of God in conjunction with the celebration of a Year of

Faith. He proclaimed and led the observance of a Holy Year from Christmas Eve of 1974 to Christmas Eve of 1975.

Diplomacy: He met with many world leaders, including Soviet President Nikolai Podgorny in 1967, Marshal Tito of Yugoslavia in 1971 and President Nicolas Ceausescu of Rumania in 1973. He worked constantly to reduce tension between the Church and the intransigent regimes of Eastern European countries by means of a detente type of policy called Ostpolitik. He agreed to significant revisions of the Vatican's concordat with Spain and initiated efforts to revise the concordat with Italy. More then 40 countries established diplomatic relations with the Vatican during his pontificate.

Encyclicals: He issued seven encyclicals, three of which are the best known. In *Populorum Progressio* ("Development of Peoples") he appealed to wealthy countries to take "concrete action" to promote human development and to remedy imbalances between richer and poorer nations; this encyclical, coupled with other documents and related actions, launched the Church into a new depth of involvement as a public advocate for human rights and for humanizing social, political and economic policies. In *Sacerdotalis Caelibatus* ("Priestly Celibacy") he reaffirmed the strict observance of priestly celibacy throughout the Western Church. In *Humanae Vitae* ("Of Human Life") he condemned abortion, sterilization and artificial birth control, in line with traditional teaching and in "defense of life, the gift of God, the glory of the family, the strength of the people."

Interfaith Relations: He initiated formal consultation and informal dialogue on international and national levels between Catholics and non-Catholics — Orthodox, Anglicans, Protestants, Jews, Moslems, Buddhists, Hindus, and unbelievers. He and Greek Orthodox Patriarch Athenagoras I of Constantinople nullified in 1965 the mutual excommunications imposed by their respective churches in 1054.

Liturgy: He carried out the most extensive liturgical reform in history, involving a new Order of the Mass effective in 1969, a revised church calendar in 1970, revisions and translations into vernacular languages of all sacramental rites and other liturgical texts.

Ministries: He authorized the restoration of the permanent diaconate in the Roman Rite and the establishment of new ministries of lay persons.

Peace: He instituted the annual observance of a World Day of Peace on New Year's Day as a means of addressing a message of peace to all the world's political leaders and the peoples of all nations. The most dramatic of his many appeals for peace and efforts to ease international tensions was his plea for "No more war!" before the United Nations Oct. 4, 1965.

Pilgrimages: A "Pilgrim Pope," he made pastoral visits to the Holy Land and India in 1964, the United Nations and New York City in 1965, Portugal and Turkey in 1967, Colombia in 1968, Switzerland and Uganda in 1969, and Asia, Pacific islands and Australia in 1970. While in Manila in 1970, he was stabbed by a Bolivian artist who made an attempt on his life.

Roman Curia: He reorganized the central administrative organs of the Church in line with provisions of the apostolic constitution, *Regimini Ecclesiae Universae,* streamlining procedures for more effective service and giving the agencies a more international perspective by drawing officials and consultors from all over the world. He also instituted a number of new commissions and other bodies. Coupled with curial reorganization was a simplification of papal ceremonies.

John Paul I

John Paul I (Albino Luciani) was born Oct. 17, 1912, in Forno di Canale (now Canale d'Agordo) in northern Italy.

Educated at the minor seminary in Feltre and the major seminary of the Diocese of Belluno, he was ordained to the priesthood July 7, 1935. He pursued further studies at the Pontifical Gregorian University in Rome and was awarded a doctorate in theology. From 1937 to 1947 he was vice rector of the Belluno seminary, where he taught dogmatic and moral theology, canon law and sacred art. He was appointed vicar general of his diocese in 1947 and served as director of catechetics.

Ordained bishop of Vittorio Veneto Dec. 27, 1958, he attended all sessions of the second Vatican Council, participated in three assemblies of the Synod of Bishops (1971, 1974 and 1977), and was vice president of the Italian Bishops' Conference from 1972 to 1975.

He was appointed archbishop and patriarch of Venice Dec. 15, 1969, and was inducted into the College of Cardinals Mar. 5, 1973.

He was elected to the papacy Aug. 26, 1978, on the fourth ballot cast by the 111 cardinals participating in the largest and one of the shortest conclaves in history. The quickness of his election was matched by the brevity of his pontificate of 33 days, during which he delivered 19 addresses. He died of a heart attack Sept. 28, 1978.

CANONIZATIONS BY LEO XIII AND HIS SUCCESSORS

Canonization is an infallible declaration by the pope that a person who suffered martyrdom and/or practiced Christian virtue to a heroic degree is in glory with God in heaven and is worthy of public honor by the universal Church and of imitation by the faithful.

Leo XIII
(1878-1903)

1881: Clare of Montefalco, virgin (d. 1308); John Baptist de Rossi, priest (1698-1764); Lawrence of Brindisi, doctor (d. 1619).

1883: Benedict J. Labre (1748-1783).

1888: Seven Holy Founders of the Servite Order; Peter Claver, priest (1581-1654); John Berchmans (1599-1621); Alphonsus Rodriguez, lay brother (1531-1617).

1897: Anthony M. Zaccaria, founder of Barnabites (1502-1539); Peter Fourier, co-founder of Augustinian Canonesses of Our Lady (1565-1640).

1900: John Baptist de La Salle, founder of Christian Brothers (1651-1719); Rita of Cascia (1381-1457).

St. Pius X
(1903-1914)

1904: Alexander Sauli, bishop (1534-1593); Gerard Majella, lay brother (1725-1755).

1909: Joseph Oriol, priest (1650-1702); Clement M. Hofbauer, priest (1751-1820).

Benedict XV
(1914-1922)

1920: Gabriel of the Sorrowful Mother

(1838-1862); Margaret Mary Alacoque, virgin (1647-1690); Joan of Arc, virgin (1412-1431).

Pius XI
(1922-1939)

1925: Therese of Lisieux, virgin (1873-1897); Peter Canisius, doctor (1521-1597); Mary Magdalen Postel, foundress of Sisterhood of Christian Schools (1756-1846); Mary Magdalen Sophie Barat, foundress of Society of the Sacred Heart (1779-1865); John Eudes, founder of Eudist Fathers (1601-1680); John Baptist Vianney (Curé of Ars), priest (1786-1859).

1930: Lucy Filippini, virgin (1672-1732); Catherine Thomas, virgin (1533-1574); Jesuit North American Martyrs (see Index); Robert Bellarmine, bishop-doctor (1542-1621); Theophilus of Corte, priest (1676-1740).

1931: Albert the Great, bishop-doctor (1206-1280) (equivalent canonization).

1933: Andrew Fournet, priest (1752-1834); Bernadette Soubirous, virgin (1844-1879).

1934: Joan Antida Thouret, foundress of Sisters of Charity of St. Joan Antida (1765-1826); Mary Michaeli, foundress of Institute of Handmaids of the Blessed Sacrament (1809-1865); Louise de Marillac, foundress of Sisters of Charity (1591-1660); Joseph Benedict Cottolengo, priest (1786-1842); Pompilius M. Pirotti, priest (1710-1756); Teresa Margaret Redi, virgin (1747-1770); John Bosco, founder of Salesians (1815-1888); Conrad of Parzham, lay brother (1818-1894).

1935: John Fisher, bishop-martyr (1469-1535); Thomas More, martyr (1478-1535).

1938: Andrew Bobola, martyr (1592-1657); John Leonardi, founder of Clerics Regular of the Mother of God (c. 1550-1609); Salvatore of Horta, lay brother (1520-1567).

Pius XII
(1939-1958)

1940: Gemma Galgani, virgin (1878-1903); Mary Euphrasia Pelletier, foundress of Good Shepherd Sisters (1796-1868).

1943: Margaret of Hungary, virgin (d. 1270) (equivalent canonization).

1946: Frances Xavier Cabrini, foundress of Missionary Sisters of the Sacred Heart (1850-1917).

1947: Nicholas of Flue, hermit (1417-1487); John of Britto, martyr (1647-1693); Bernard Realini, priest (1530-1616); Joseph Cafasso, priest (1811-1860); Michael Garicoits, founder of Auxiliary Priests of the Sacred Heart (1797-1863); Jeanne Elizabeth des Ages, cofoundress of Daughters of the Cross (1773-1838); Louis Marie Grignon de Montfort, founder of Montfort Fathers (1673-1716); Catherine Laboure, virgin (1806-1876).

1949: Jeanne de Lestonnac, foundress of Religious of Notre Dame of Bordeaux (1556-1640); Maria Josepha Rossello, foundress of Daughters of Our Lady of Pity (1811-1880).

1950: Emily de Rodat, foundress of Congregation of the Holy Family of Villefranche (1787-1852); Anthony Mary Claret, bishop, founder of Claretians (1807-1870); Bartolomea Capitanio (1807-1833) and Vincenza Gerosa (1784-1847), foundresses of Sisters of Charity of Lovere; Jeanne de Valois, foundress of Annonciades of Bourges (1461-1504); Vincenzo M. Strambi, bishop (1745-1824); Maria Goretti, virgin-martyr (1890-1902); Mariana Paredes of Jesus, virgin (1618-1645).

1951: Maria Domenica Mazzarello, cofoundress of Daughters of Our Lady Help of Christians (1837-1881); Emilie de Vialar, foundress of Sisters of St. Joseph "of the Apparition" (1797-1856); Anthony M. Gianelli, bishop (1789-1846); Ignatius of Laconi, lay brother (1701-1781); Francis Xavier Bianchi, priest (1743-1815).

1954: Pius X, pope (1835-1914); Dominic Savio (1842-1857); Maria Crocifissa di Rosa, foundress of Handmaids of Charity of Brescia (1813-1855); Peter Chanel, priest-martyr (1803-1841); Gaspar del Bufalo, founder of Missioners of the Most Precious Blood (1786-1837); Joseph M. Pignatelli, priest (1737-1811).

1958: Herman Joseph, O. Praem., priest (1150-1241) (equivalent canonization).

John XXIII
(1958-1963)

1959: Joaquina de Vedruna de Mas, foundress of Carmelite Sisters of Charity (1783-1854); Charles of Sezze, lay brother (1613-1670).

1960: Gregory Barbarigo, bishop (1625-1697) (equivalent canonization); John de Ribera, bishop (1532-1611).

1961: Bertilla Boscardin, virgin (1888-1922).

1962: Martin de Porres, lay brother (1579-1639); Peter Julian Eymard, founder of Blessed Sacrament Fathers (1811-1868); Anthony Pucci, priest (1819-1892); Francis Mary of Camporosso, lay brother (1804-1866).

1963: Vincent Pallotti, founder of Pallottine Fathers (1795-1850).

Paul VI
(1963-1978)

1964: Charles Lwanga and Twenty-One Companions, Martyrs of Uganda.

1967: Benilde, lay brother (1805-1862).

1969: Julia Billiart, foundress of Sisters of Notre Dame de Namur (1751-1816).

1970: Maria Della Dolorato Torres Acosta, foundress of Servants Sisters of Mary (1826-1887); Leonard Murialdo, priest, founder of Congregation of St. Joseph (1828-1900); Therese Couderc, foundress of Congregation of Our Lady of the Cenacle (1805-1885); John of Avila, preacher and spiritual director (1499-1569); Sts. Nicholas Tavelic, Deodatus of Aquitaine, Peter of Narbonne and Stephen of Cuneo, martyrs (d. 1391); Forty English and Welsh Martyrs (d. 16th cent.).

1974: Teresa of Jesus Jornet Ibars, foundress of Little Sisters of Abandoned Aged (1843-1897).

1975: Vicenta Maria Lopez y Vicuna, foundress of Institute of Daughters of Mary Immaculate (1847-1890); Elizabeth Bayley Seton, foundress of Sisters of Charity in the U.S. (1774-1821); John Masias, Dominican brother-missionary (1585-1645): Oliver Plunket, archbishop-martyr (1629-1681); Justin de Jacobis, missionary bishop (1800-1860); John Baptist of the Conception, priest, reformer of the Order of the Most Holy Trinity (1561-1613).

1976: Beatrice da Silva, foundress of Congregation of the Immaculate Conception of the BVM (1424 or 1426-1490); John Ogilvie, Scottish Jesuit martyr (1579-1615).

1977: Rafaela Maria Porras y Ayllon, foundress of Handmaids of the Sacred Heart (1850-1925); John Nepomucene Neumann, bishop (1811-1860); Sharbel Makhlouf, Maronite rite monk (1828-1898).

Pope John Paul beatified three Servants of God Oct. 26, 1980: Bartolo Longo, founder of a community of nuns; Father Luigi Orione, founder of the Little Society of Divine Providence; Marcelline Sister Maria Anna Sala.

ENCYCLICALS ISSUED BY LEO XIII AND HIS SUCCESSORS

An encyclical letter is a pastoral letter addressed by a pope to the whole Church. In general, it concerns matters of doctrine, morals or discipline. Its formal title consists of the first few words of the official text. A few encyclicals, notably *Pacem in Terris* by John XXIII and *Ecclesiam Suam* by Paul VI, have been addressed to "all men of good will" as well as to bishops and the faithful in communion with the Church.

An encyclical epistle, which is like an encyclical letter in many respects, is addressed to part of the Church, that is, to the bishops and faithful of a particular country or area. Its contents may concern other than doctrinal, moral or disciplinary matters of universal significance; for example, the commemoration of historical events, conditions in a certain country.

The authority of encyclicals was stated by Pius XII in the encyclical *Humani Generis* Aug. 12, 1950.

"Nor must it be thought that what is contained in encyclical letters does not of itself demand assent, on the pretext that the popes do not exercise in them the supreme power of their teaching authority. Rather, such teachings belong to the ordinary magisterium, of which it is true to say: 'He who hears you, hears me' (Lk. 10:16); for the most part, too, what is expounded and inculcated in encyclical letters already appertains to Catholic doctrine for other reasons. But if the supreme pontiffs in their official documents purposely pass judgment on a matter debated until then, it is obvious to all that the matter, according to the mind and will of the same pontiffs, cannot be considered any longer a question open for discussion among theologians."

The following list contains the titles and indicates the subject matter of encyclical letters and epistles. The latter are generally distinguishable by the limited scope of their titles or contents.

Leo XIII
(1878-1903)

1878: Inscrutabili Dei Consilio (Evils of Society), Apr. 21.

Quod Apostolici Muneris (Socialism, Communism, Nihilism), Dec. 28.

1879: Aeterni Patris (Scholastic Philosophy, Especially of Thomas Aquinas), Aug. 4.

1880: Arcanum (Christian Marriage), Feb. 10.

Grande Munus (Sts. Cyril and Methodius), Sept. 30.

Sancta Dei Civitas (Three French Societies), Dec. 3.

1881: Diuturnum (Origin of Civil Power), June 29.

1882: Etsi Nos (Conditions in Italy), Feb. 15.

Auspicato Concessum (Third Order of St. Francis), Sept. 17.

Cum Multa (Conditions in Spain), Dec. 8.

1883: Supremi Apostolatus Officio (The Rosary), Sept. 1.

1884: Nobilissima Gallorum Gens (Religious Question in France), Feb. 8.

Humanum Genus (Freemasonry), Apr. 20.

Superiore Anno (Recitation of the Rosary), Aug. 30.

1885: Immortale Dei (The Christian Constitution of States), Nov. 1.

Quod Auctoritate (Proclamation of Extraordinary Jubilee Year), Dec. 22.

1886: Quod Multum (Liberty of the Church in Hungary), Aug. 22.

Pergrata Nobis (Needs of the Church in Portugal), Sept. 14.

1888: Libertas (Human Liberty), June 20.

Paterna Caritas (Recalling the Dissenting Armenians), July 25.

Quam Aerumnosa (Italian Immigrants in America), Dec. 10.

1889: Quamquam Pluries (Patronage of St. Joseph and the Blessed Virgin Mary), Aug. 15.

1890: Sapientiae Christianae (Chief Duties of Christian Citizens), Jan. 10.

Ab Apostoli (To the Clergy and People of Italy), Oct. 15.

1891: Rerum Novarum (Condition of the Working Classes), May 15.

Octobri Mense (The Rosary), Sept. 22.

1892: Au Milieu des Sollicitudes (Church and State in France), Feb. 16.

Magnae Dei Matris (The Rosary), Sept. 8.

1893: Ad Extremas (Seminaries in the East Indies), June 24.

Constanti Hungarorum (Conditions of the Church in Hungary), Sept. 2.

Laetitiae Sanctae (The Rosary), Sept. 8.

Providentissimus Deus (Study of Holy Scripture), Nov. 18.

1894: Caritatis (Conditions in Poland), Mar. 19.

Iucunda Semper Expectatione (The Rosary), Sept. 8.

Christi Nomen (Society for the Propagation of the Faith), Dec. 24.

1895: Adiutricem (The Rosary), Sept. 5.

1896: Satis Cognitum (Church Unity), June 29.

Fidentum Piumque Animum (The Rosary), Sept. 20.

1897: Divinum Illud Munus (The Holy Spirit, doctrine and devotion), May 9.

Militantis Ecclesiae (Third Centenary of the Death of St. Peter Canisius), Aug. 1.

Augustissimae Virginis (Rosary), Sept. 12.

Affari Vos (The Manitoba School Question), Dec. 8.

1898: Caritatis Studium (The Magisterium of the Church in Scotland), July 25.

Spesse Volte (Catholic Action in Italy) Aug. 5.

1899: Annum Sacrum (Consecration of Mankind to the Sacred Heart), May 25.

Depuis le Jour (Ecclesiastical Education in France), Sept. 8.

1900: Tametsi Futura Prospicientibus (Jesus Christ, Our Redeemer), Nov. 1.

1901: Graves de Communi Re (Christian Democracy), Jan. 18.

1902: Mirae Caritatis (The Most Holy Eucharist), May 28.

Fin dal Principio (Education of the Clergy in Italy), Dec. 8.

Saint Pius X
(1903-1914)

1903: E Supremi (Restoration of All Things in Christ), Oct. 4.

1904: Ad Diem Illum Laetissimum (Jubilee of the Immaculate Conception), Feb. 2.

Iucunda Sane (Thirteenth Centenary of the Death of St. Gregory the Great), Mar. 12.

1905: Acerbo Nimis (Teaching of Christian Doctrine), Apr. 15.

Il Fermo Proposito (Catholic Action in Italy), June 11.

1906: Vehementer Nos (French Separation Law), Feb. 11.

Tribus Circiter (Condemnation of the Mariavites), Apr. 5.

Pieni l'Animo (Clergy in Italy), July 28.

Gravissimo Officio Munere (Forbidding Associations Cultuelles), Aug. 10.

1907: Une Fois Encore (Separation of Church and State in France), Jan. 6.

Pascendi Dominici Gregis (Modernism), Sept. 8.

1909: Communium Rerum (Eighth Centenary of the Death of St. Anselm), Apr. 21.

1910: Editae Saepe (Third Centenary of the Death of St. Charles Borromeo), May 26.

1911: Iamdudum (Separation Law in Portugal), May 24.

1912: Lacrimabili Statu (Indians of South America), June 7.

Singulari Quadam (Labor Organizations in Germany), Sept. 24.

Benedict XV
(1914-1922)

1914: Ad Beatissimi Apostolorum (Appeal for Peace), Nov. 1.

1917: Humani Generis Redemptionem (Preaching), June 15.

1918: Quod Iam Diu (Peace Congress, Paris), Dec. 1.

1919: In Hac Tanta (Twelfth Centenary of St. Boniface), May 14.

Paterno Iam Diu (Christian Charity of the Children of Central Europe), Nov. 24.

1920: Pacem, Dei Munus Pulcherrimum (Peace and Christian Reconciliation), May 23.

Spiritus Paraclitus (Holy Scripture), Sept. 15.

Principi Apostolorum Petro (St. Ephrem the Syrian, declared Doctor), Oct. 5.

Annus Iam Plenus (Child War Victims), Dec. 1.

1921: Sacra Propediem (Seventh Centenary of the Third Order of St. Francis), Jan. 6.

In Praeclara Summorum (Sixth Centenary of Dante's Death), Apr. 30.

Fausto Appetente Die (Seventh Centenary of the Death of St. Dominic), June 29.

Pius XI
(1922-1939)

1922: Ubi Arcano Dei Consilio (Peace of Christ in the Kingdom of Christ), Dec. 23.

1923: Rerum Omnium Perturbationem (Third Centenary of the Death of St. Francis de Sales), Jan. 26.

Studiorum Ducem (Sixth Centenary of the Canonization of St. Thomas Aquinas), June 29.

Ecclesiam Dei (Third Centenary of the Death of St. Josaphat, Archbishop of Polotsk), Nov. 12.

1924: Maximam Gravissimamque (French Diocesan Associations), Jan. 18.

1925: Quas Primas (Feast of Christ the King), Dec. 11.

1926: Rerum Ecclesiae (Catholic Missions), Feb. 28.

Rite Expiatis (Seventh Centenary of the Death of St. Francis of Assisi), Apr. 30.

Iniquis Afflictisque (Persecution of the Church in Mexico), Nov. 18.

1928: Mortalium Animos (Promotion of True Religious Unity), Jan. 6.

Miserentissimus Redemptor (Reparation Due the Sacred Heart), May 8.

Rerum Orientalium (Reunion with the Eastern Churches), Sept. 8.

1929: Mens Nostra (Promotion of Spiritual Exercises), Dec. 20.

Quinquagesimo Ante (Sacerdotal Jubilee), Dec. 23.

Divini Illius Magistri (Rappresentanti in Terra) (Christian Education of Youth), Dec. 31.

1930: Ad Salutem (Fifteenth Centenary of the Death of St. Augustine), Apr. 20.

Casti Connubii (Christian Marriage), Dec. 31.

1931: Quadragesimo Anno (Social Reconstruction), May 15.

Non Abbiamo Bisogno (Catholic Action), June 29.

Nova Impendet (Economic Crisis, Unemployment, Armaments), Oct. 2.

Lux Veritatis (Fifteenth Centenary of the Council of Ephesus), Dec. 25.

1932: Caritate Christi Compulsi (Sacred Heart and World Distress), May 3.

Acerba Animi (Persecution of the Church in Mexico), Sept. 29.

1933: Dilectissima Nobis (Conditions in Spain), June 3.

1935: Ad Catholici Sacerdotii (Catholic Priesthood), Dec. 20.

1936: Vigilanti Cura (Clean Motion Pictures), June 29.

1937: Mit Brennender Sorge (Church in Germany), Mar. 14.

Divini Redemptoris (Atheistic Communism), Mar. 19.

Firmissimam Constantiam (Nos Es Muy Conocida) (Conditions in Mexico), Mar. 28.

Ingravescentibus Malis (The Rosary) Sept. 29.

Pius XII
(1939-1958)

1939: Summi Pontificatus (Function of the State in Modern World), Oct. 20.

Sertum Laetitiae (To the Church in the United States), Nov. 1.

1940: Saeculo Exeunte Octavo (Missions), June 13.

1943: Mystici Corporis Christi (Mystical Body), June 29.

Divino Afflante Spiritu (Biblical Studies), Sept. 30.

1944: Orientalis Ecclesiae Decus (Fifteenth Centenary of the Death of St. Cyril of Alexandria), Apr. 9.

1945: Communium Interpretes Dolorum (Appeal for Prayers), Apr. 15.

Orientales Omnes Ecclesias (Anniversary of the Ruthenian Reunion), Dec. 23.

1946: Quemadmodum (Call for Intensified Aid to Youth), Jan. 6.

Deiparae Virginis Mariae (Proposing to the Bishops the Question of the Definition of the Dogma of the Assumption), May 1.

1947: Fulgens Radiatur (Fourteenth Centenary of the Death of St. Benedict), Mar. 21.

Mediator Dei (Sacred Liturgy), Nov. 20.

Optatissima Pax (Peace and Social Disorders), Dec. 18.

1948: Auspicia Quaedam (Prayer to Blessed Virgin Mary for Peace), May 1.

In Multiplicibus Curis (Crisis in Palestine), Oct. 24.

1949: Redemptoris Nostri (Internationalization of Jerusalem), Apr. 15.

1950: Anni Sacri (Holy Year Call for Public Prayer), Mar. 12.

Summi Maeroris (Renewed Holy Year Call for Public Prayer), July 19.

Humani Generis (Warnings against Attempts to Distort Catholic Truths), Aug. 12.

Mirabile Illud (Call for Renewed Crusade of Prayers for Peace), Dec. 6.

1951: Evangelii Praecones (Call for Greater Missionary Effort), June 2.

Sempiternus Rex (Fifteenth Centenary of the Council of Chalcedon), Sept. 8.

Ingruentium Malorum (Recitation of the Rosary), Sept. 15.

1952: Orientales Ecclesias (Communist Persecution of the Church; Call for Prayers for the Persecuted), Dec. 15.

1953: Doctor Mellifluus (Eighth Centenary of Death of St. Bernard), May 24.

Fulgens Corona (Call for Catholics to Observe Marian Year), Sept. 8.

1954: Sacra Virginitas (Preeminence of Evangelical Chastity), Mar. 25.

Ecclesiae Fastos (Commemoration of St. Boniface), June 5.

Ad Sinarum Gentem (The Church in China), Oct. 7.

Ad Caeli Reginam (Feast of Queenship of Mary), Oct. 11.

1955: Musicae Sacrae (Sacred Music), Dec. 25.

1956: Haurietis Aquas (The Sacred Heart), May 15.

Luctuosissimi Eventus (Prayers for Hungary), Oct. 28.

Laetamur Admodum (Middle East Crisis), Nov. 1.

Datis Nuperrime (Prayers for Peace), Nov. 5.

1957: Fidei Donum (Missionary Effort, especially in Africa), Apr. 21.

Invicti Athletae Christi (Third Centenary of Death of St. Andrew Bobola), May 16.

Le Pelerinage de Lourdes (Centenary of Lourdes Apparitions), July 2.

Miranda Prorsus (Radio, TV and Motion Pictures), Sept. 8.

1958: Ad Apostolorum Principis (Critical Situation of the Church in China), June 29.

Meminisse Juvat (Prayers for Peace and the Persecuted Church), July 14.

John XXIII
(1958-1963)

1959: Ad Petri Cathedram (Appeal to Separated Christians to Reunite with Church), June 29.

Sacerdotii Nostri Primordia (Centenary of the Cure of Ars), Aug. 1.

Grata Recordatio (Rosary), Sept. 26.

Princeps Pastorum (Missions), Nov. 28.

1961: Mater et Magistra (Christianity and Social Progress), May 15.

Aeterna Dei Sapientia (Fifteenth Centenary of the Death of St. Leo the Great), Nov. 11.

1962: Paenitentiam Agere (Appeal for Works of Penance for Success of the Second Vatican Council), July 1.

1963: Pacem in Terris (Peace on Earth), Apr. 11.

Paul VI
(1963-1978)

1964: Ecclesiam Suam (Second Vatican Council Themes), Aug. 6.

1965: Mense Maio (Prayer for Success of Vatican II, Peace), Apr. 29.

Mysterium Fidei (The Eucharist), Sept. 3.

1966: Christi Matri Rosarii (The Rosary), Sept. 15.

1967: Populorum Progressio (Development of Peoples), Mar. 26.

Sacerdotalis Caelibatus (Priestly Celibacy), June 24.

1968: Humanae Vitae (Birth Control), July 25.

John Paul II
(1978-   )

1979: Redemptor Hominis (Redeemer of Man), Mar. 4.

BIBLICAL COMMISSION

The Pontifical Biblical Commission, which has been instrumental in directing the course of Catholic biblical scholarship, was established by Leo XIII Oct. 30, 1902, with the apostolic letter *Vigilantiae Studiique,* at a time when biblical studies were open to great promise as well as to the serious threat of Modernism.

The commission was ordered to promote biblical studies; to safeguard the correct interpretation of Scripture, in the pattern of the rule of faith and against the background of sound scholarship; to state positions which had to be held by Catholics on biblical questions; to indicate questions requiring further study and/or those which were open to the judgment of competent scholars. The commission was also authorized — by St. Pius X in 1904, Pius XI in 1924 and 1931, and Pius XII in 1942 — to set up standards for biblical studies and to grant degrees in Sacred Scripture.

The commission issued 23 decrees or decisions between 1905 and 1953; letters on the scientific study of the Bible (1941) and the Pentateuch (1948); instructions on teaching Scripture in seminaries (1950), biblical associations (1955), and the historical truth of the Gospels (1964).

Pope St. Pius X stated the authority of decisions of the commission in the letter *Illibatae,* which he issued June 29, 1910, on his own initiative:

"All are bound in conscience to submit to the decisions of the Pontifical Biblical Commission pertaining to doctrine, whether already issued or to be issued in the future, in the same way as to the decrees of the Sacred Congregations (of the Roman Curia) approved by the Pontiff; nor can they avoid the stigma both of disobedience and temerity or be free from grave sin who by any spoken or written words impugn these decisions."

Decisions of the commission regarding points of doctrine are not infallible of themselves. They require religious assent, however, so long as there is no positive evidence that they are wrong. They do not close the door to continuing investigation and study.

The commission was reorganized June 27, 1971, in line with directives issued by Paul VI on his own initiative under the title *Sedula Cura.*

Fifteen new norms changed its structure from a virtually independent office of cardinals aided by lifetime consultors into a group of 20 biblical scholars with five-year terms (renewable) linked with the Congregation for the Doctrine of the Faith. Functionally, however, it remains the same.

The commission:

• receives questions and study topics referred to it by a variety of sources, from the pope to Catholic universities and biblical associations;

• is required to meet in plenary session at least once a year and to submit conclusions reached in such meetings to the pope and the Congregation for the Doctrine of the Faith;

• is under directive to promote relationships with non-Catholic as well as Catholic institutes of biblical studies;

• is to be consulted before any new norms on biblical matters are issued;

• retains its authorization to confer academic degrees in biblical studies.

Membership

Cardinal Franjo Seper, prefect of the Congregation for the Doctrine of the Faith, is president of the commission; Albert Descamps, titular bishop of Tunes, is the secretary. The other members, as reported in the 1980 edition of *Annuario Pontificio,* are as follows.

Jose Alonso-Diaz, S.J.; Jean-Dominique Barthelemy, O.P.; Pierre Benoit, O.P.; Henri Cazelles, S.S.; Guy Couturier, C.S.C.; Alfons Deissler; Ignace de la Potterie, S.J.; Jacques Dupont, O.S.B.; Joachim Gnilka; Pierre Grelot; Augustine Jankowski, O.S.B.; Abp. Carlo M. Martini, S.J.; Laurent Nare; Angelo Penna, C.R.L.; Jerome D. Quinn (U.S.); Matthew Vellanickal; Benjamin Wambacq, O.Praem.

Recent Meetings

The commission met in plenary session Apr. 14 to 18, 1980, at the Vatican with attention focused on the hermeneutic problem in Christology, i.e., the interpretation of what Scripture says about the nature and mission of Jesus.

At its 1979 meeting, the commission initiated a study of acculturation in the Old and New Testaments. The purpose of the study, as stated by Pope John Paul, was "to establish the distinction" between what is culturally conditioned (language, manner of expression, historical circumstances) "and what must always retain its value" (truth relating to salvation) in the words and events used to communicate divine revelation in the Bible.

ORGANIZATION AND GOVERNMENT

As a structured society, the Catholic Church is organized and governed along lines corresponding mainly to the jurisdictions of the pope and bishops.

The pope is the supreme head of the Church. He has primacy of jurisdiction as well as honor over the entire Church.

Bishops, in union with and in subordination to the pope, are the successors of the Apostles for care of the Church and for the continuation of Christ's mission in the world. They serve the people of their own dioceses, or local churches, with ordinary authority and jurisdiction. They also share, with the pope and each other, in common concern and effort for the general welfare of the whole Church.

Bishops of exceptional status are Eastern Rite patriarchs who, subject only to the pope, are heads of the faithful belonging to their rites throughout the world.

Subject to the Holy Father and directly responsible to him for the exercise of their ministry of service to people in various jurisdictions or divisions of the Church throughout the world are: resident archbishops and metropolitans (heads of archdioceses), resident bishops (heads of dioceses), vicars and prefects apostolic (heads of vicariates apostolic and prefectures apostolic), certain abbots and prelates, apostolic administrators. Each of these, within his respective territory and according to the provisions of canon law, has ordinary jurisdiction over pastors (who are responsible for the administration of parishes), priests, religious and lay persons.

Also subject to the Holy Father are titular archbishops and bishops (who have delegated jurisdiction), religious orders and congregations of pontifical right, pontifical institutes and faculties, papal nuncios and apostolic delegates.

Assisting the pope and acting in his name in the central government and administration of the Church are cardinals and other officials of the Roman Curia.

THE HIERARCHY

The ministerial hierarchy is the orderly arrangement of the ranks and orders of the clergy to provide for the spiritual care of the faithful, the government of the Church, and the accomplishment of the Church's total mission in the world. Persons belong to this hierarchy by virtue of ordination and canonical mission.

The term hierarchy is also used to designate an entire body or group of bishops; for example, the hierarchy of the Church, the hierarchy of the United States.

Hierarchy of Order: Consists of the pope, bishops, priests and deacons, by divine law. Their purpose, for which they are ordained to holy orders, is to carry out the sacramental and pastoral ministry of the Church.

Hierarchy of Jurisdiction: Consists of the pope and bishops by divine law, and other church officials by ecclesiastical institution and mandate, who have authority to govern and direct the faithful for spiritual ends.

Prelates: Clerics with the authority of public office in the Church — i. e., the authority of jurisdiction in the external forum. They are: the pope, patriarchs, residential archbishops and bishops, certain abbots and prelates, vicars and prefects apostolic, vicars general, certain superiors in clerical exempt religious communities. Titular archbishops and bishops without ordinary jurisdiction are not prelates in the strict sense of the term; neither are pastors, who have very limited jurisdiction in the external forum.

The Pope

His Holiness the Pope is the Bishop of Rome, the Vicar of Jesus Christ, the successor of St. Peter, Prince of the Apostles, the Supreme Pontiff who has the primacy of jurisdiction and not merely of honor over the universal Church, the Patriarch of the West, the Primate of Italy, the Archbishop and Metropolitan of the Roman Province, the Sovereign of the State of Vatican City, Servant of the Servants of God.

Cardinals
(See Index)

Patriarchs

Patriarch, a term which had its origin in the Eastern Church, is the title of a bishop who, second only to the pope, has the highest rank in the hierarchy of jurisdiction. He is the incumbent of one of the sees listed below. Subject only to the pope, an Eastern-Rite patriarch is the head of the faithful belonging to his rite throughout the world. The patriarchal sees are so called because of their special status and dignity in the history of the Church.

The Council of Nicaea (325) recognized three patriarchs — the bishops of Alexandria and Antioch in the East, and of Rome in the West. The First Council of Constantinople (381) added the bishop of Constantinople to the list of patriarchs and gave him rank second only to that of the pope, the bishop of Rome and patriarch of the West; this action was seconded by the Council of Chalcedon (451) and was given full recognition by the

Fourth Lateran Council (1215). The Council of Chalcedon also acknowledged patriarchal rights of the bishop of Jerusalem.

Eastern Rite patriarchs are as follows: one of Alexandria, for the Copts; three of Antioch, one each for the Syrians, Maronites and Greek Melkites (the latter also has the personal title of Greek Melkite patriarch of Alexandria and of Jerusalem). The patriarch of Babylonia, for the Chaldeans, and the patriarch of Sis, or Cilicia, for the Armenians, should be called, more properly, *Katholikos* — that is, a prelate delegated for a universality of causes. These patriarchs are elected by bishops of their rites: they receive approval and the pallium, symbolic of their office, from the pope.

Latin Rite patriarchates were established for Antioch, Jerusalem, Alexandria and Constantinople during the Crusades; afterwards, they became patriarchates in name only. Jerusalem, however, was reconstituted as a patriarchate by Pius IX, in virtue of the bull *Nulla Celebrior* of July 23, 1847. In 1964, the Latin titular patriarchates of Constantinople, Alexandria and Antioch, long a bone of contention in relations with Eastern Rites, were abolished.

As of Oct. 1, 1980, the patriarchs in the Church were:

The Pope, Bishop of Rome, Patriarch of the West; Cardinal Stephanos I Sidarouss, C.M., of Alexandria, for the Copts; Ignace Antoine II Hayek, of Antioch, for the Syrians; Maximos V Hakim, of Antioch, for the Greek Melkites (he also has the titles of Alexandria and Jerusalem for the Greek Melkites); Antoine Khoraiche, of Antioch, for the Maronites; Giacomo Beltritti, of Jerusalem, for the Latin Rite; Paul II Cheikho, of Babylon, for the Chaldeans; Hemaiagh Pierre XVII Ghedighian, of Cilicia, for the Armenians.

The titular patriarchs (in name only) of the Latin Rite were: Cardinal Antonio Ribeiro, of Lisbon; Cardinal Marco Cé of Venice and Archbishop Raul Nicolau Goncalves of the East Indies (Archbishop of Goa and Daman, India). The patriarchate of the West Indies has been vacant since 1963.

Archbishops, Metropolitans

Archbishop: A bishop with the title of an archdiocese.

Metropolitan Archbishop: Head of the principal see, an archdiocese, in an ecclesiastical province consisting of several dioceses. He has the full powers of bishop in his own archdiocese and limited supervisory jurisdiction and influence over the other (suffragan) dioceses in the province.

Titular Archbishop: Has the title of an archdiocese which formerly existed in fact but now exists in title only. He does not have ordinary jurisdiction over an archdiocese.

Archbishop ad personam: A title of personal honor and distinction granted to some bishops. They do not have ordinary jurisdiction over an archdiocese.

Primate: A title given to the ranking prelate of some countries or regions.

Bishops

Residential Bishop: A bishop in charge of a diocese.

Titular Bishops: Have the titles of dioceses which formerly existed in fact but now exist in title only. They have delegated authority of jurisdiction, by grant in line with their assignments, rather than the ordinary jurisdiction of office which belongs to a residential bishop. An auxiliary bishop (titular) is an assistant to a residential bishop. A coadjutor bishop (titular) is an assistant bishop of higher status; some coadjutors have the right of succession to residential sees.

Episcopal Vicar: An assistant, who may or may not be a bishop, appointed by a residential bishop as his deputy for a certain part of a diocese, a determined type of apostolic work, or the faithful of a certain rite.

Eparch, Exarch: Titles of bishops of Eastern-Rite churches.

Nomination of Bishops: Nominees for episcopal ordination are selected in several ways. Final appointment in all cases is subject to decision by the pope.

In the U.S., bishops periodically submit the names of candidates to the archbishop of their province. The names are then considered at a meeting of the bishops of the province, and those receiving a favorable vote are forwarded to the apostolic delegate for transmission to the Holy See. Bishops are free to seek the counsel of priests, religious and lay persons with respect to nominees.

Eastern-Rite churches have their own procedures and synodal regulations for nominating and making final selection of candidates for episcopal ordination.

In some countries where concordat or other special arrangements are in effect, civil governments have specified privileges to express approval or disapproval of candidates for the episcopacy.

Ad Limina Visit: Residential bishops and military vicars are obliged to make a periodic *ad limina* visit ("to the threshold" of the Apostles) to the tombs of Sts. Peter and Paul, have audience with the Holy Father, consult with appropriate Vatican officials and present a written report on conditions in their jurisdictions. The most recent regulations concerning the formalities and scheduling of visits by bishops from various countries, generally every five years, were issued by the Congregation for Bishops in a decree dated Nov. 27, 1975.

Other Prelates

Some prelates and abbots, formerly called

nullius, have jurisdiction over territories (abbacies, prefectures, prelatures) not under the authority of diocesan bishops.

Vicar Apostolic: Usually a titular bishop who has ordinary jurisdiction over a mission territory. A vicar apostolic could also serve as the administrator of a vacant diocese or a diocese whose bishop is impeded from the exercise of his office.

Prefect Apostolic: A prelate with ordinary jurisdiction over a mission territory.

Apostolic Administrator: Usually a bishop appointed to administer an ecclesiastical jurisdiction temporarily. Administrators of lesser rank are also appointed for special and more restricted supervisory duties.

Vicar General: A bishop's deputy for the administration of a diocese. Such a vicar does not have to be a bishop.

Honorary Prelates

Honorary prelates belonging to the Pontifical Household are: Apostolic Prothonotaries, Honorary Prelates of His Holiness, and Chaplains of His Holiness. Their title is Reverend Monsignor.

SYNOD OF BISHOPS

The Synod of Bishops was chartered by Pope Paul VI Sept. 15, 1965, in a document he issued on his own initiative under the title, *Apostolica Sollicitudo.* According to the document:

• The purposes of the Synod are: "to encourage close union and valued assistance between the Sovereign Pontiff and the bishops of the entire world; to insure that direct and real information is provided on questions and situations touching upon the internal action of the Church and its necessary activity in the world of today; to facilitate agreement on essential points of doctrine and on methods of procedure in the life of the Church."

• The Synod is a central ecclesiastical institution, permanent by nature.

• The Synod is directly and immediately subject to the Pope, who has authority to assign its agenda, to call it into session, and to give its members deliberative as well as advisory authority.

• In addition to a limited number of ex officio members and a few heads of male religious institutes, the majority of the members are elective by and representative of national or regional episcopal conferences. The Pope reserved the right to appoint the general secretary, special secretaries and no more than 15 per cent of the total membership.

The Pope is president of the Synod.

The secretary general is Archbishop Jozef Tomko of Czechoslovakia.

First Meeting, 1967

The Synod met for the first time from Sept. 29 to Oct. 29, 1967, in Vatican City. Its objectives, as stated by Pope Paul, were "the preservation and strengthening of the Catholic faith, its integrity, its force, its development, its doctrinal and historical coherence."

One result of synodal deliberations was a recommendation to the Pope to establish an international commission of theologians to assist the Congregation for the Doctrine of the Faith and to broaden approaches to theological research. The commission was subsequently set up by Pope Paul in 1969.

In other actions, the Synod called for the formulation of a Code of Canon Law more pastoral than the one in force since 1918 and more in touch with the mentality, aspirations and needs of people in contemporary circumstances; favored the view that episcopal conferences should have major control over seminaries in their respective areas; suggested some changes in pastoral procedures with respect to mixed marriages, which were authorized in 1970; gave general approval to the New Order of the Mass which was promulgated and put into effect in 1969.

The first meeting of the Synod had 197 participants.

Extraordinary Session

The second Synod of Bishops, meeting in extraordinary session Oct. 11 to 28, 1969, opened the door to wider participation by the bishops with the Pope and each other in the government of the Church.

The business assigned to the meeting by Pope Paul was to seek and examine ways and means of putting into practice the principle of collegiality which figured largely in declarations of the Second Vatican Council on the Church and the pastoral office of bishops.

Accordingly, proceedings were oriented to three main points: (1) the nature and implications of collegiality; (2) the relationships of bishops and their conferences to the Pope; (3) the relationships of bishops and their conferences to each other. The end results were three proposals approved by the bishops and the Pope, and five times that number approved and placed under advisement by the Pope. All proposals pointed in the direction of more cooperative action by all the bishops with the Pope in the conduct of church affairs.

The three proposals which were approved and moved for action provided for regular meetings of the Synod at two-year intervals (later extended to three years), staff organization and operations of the general secretariat in the interim between meetings, and openness of the synodal agenda to suggestions by bishops.

The second meeting had 146 participants.

Between the second and third meetings of the Synod, an advisory council of 15 members (12 elected, three appointed by the Pope) was formed to provide the secretariat with adequate staff for carrying on liaison with episcopal conferences and for drawing up the agenda of synodal meetings. The council, at its first meeting May 12 to 15, 1970, followed the lead of the second assembly by opening the agenda of the 1971 meeting to the suggestions of bishops from all over the world.

Synod '71

The ministerial priesthood and justice in the world were the principal topics of discussion at the third and longest meeting, the Second General Assembly of the Synod, Sept. 30 to Nov. 6, 1971.

Advisory reports on these subjects, compiled from views expressed by the bishops before and during the synodal sessions, were presented to Pope Paul at the end of the meeting. He authorized publication of the reports and said, in a letter made public Dec. 9, that he accepted conclusions reached by the bishops which "conform to the current norms" of church teaching.

The Priesthood

In its report on the priesthood, the Synod described difficulties experienced by priests, stated traditional doctrinal principles on the priesthood, and drew from these principles a set of guidelines for priestly life and ministry in the mission of Christ and the Church, and in the communion of the Church.

The report emphasized the primary and permanent dedication of priests in the Church to the ministry of word, sacrament and pastoral service as a full-time occupation.

The synodal Fathers — with 168 votes in favor without reservations, 21 votes in favor with reservations, and 10 votes against — supported the existing discipline of clerical celibacy. They favored leaving to the discretion of the Pope decisions regarding the ordination of already married men in special circumstances. They did not consider the question of permitting already ordained priests to marry. The majority voted against permitting priests who had left the ministry to resume priestly duties, although they said such priests could serve the Church in other ways and should be treated in a just and fraternal manner.

Justice in the World

In connection with "The Mission of the People of God To Further Justice in the World," a synodal report reviewed a wide range of existing injustices; cited the social-justice imperatives of the Gospel; called for the practice of justice throughout the Church and for greater efforts in education and ecumenical collaboration for justice; and outlined an eight-point program for international action.

Behind the Synod's recommendations were the convictions:

• "The Church . . . has a proper and specific responsibility which is identified with her mission of giving witness before the world of the need for love and justice contained in the Gospel message, a witness to be carried out in church institutions themselves and in the lives of Christians."

• "Action on behalf of justice and participation in the transformation of the world fully appear to us as a constitutive dimension of the preaching of the Gospel; or, in other words, of the Church's mission for the redemption of the human race and its liberation from every oppressive situation."

• "The present situation of the world, seen in the light of faith, calls us back to the very essence of the Christian message, creating in us a deep awareness of its true meaning and of its urgent demands. The mission of preaching the Gospel dictates at the present time that we should dedicate ourselves to the liberation of man even in his present existence in this world. For, unless the Christian message of love and justice shows its effectiveness through action in the cause of justice in the world, it will only with difficulty gain credibility with the men of our times."

The assembly had 210 participants.

Fourth Assembly

"Evangelization of the Modern World" was the theme of the fourth assembly of the Synod, Sept. 27 to Oct. 26, 1974. Its major product was a general statement on the subject, covering the need for it and its relationship to efforts for total human liberation from personal and social evil.

The statement reconfirmed "that the mandate to evangelize all men constitutes the essential mission of the Church," that "the duty to proclaim the Gospel belongs to the whole people of God," and that "this work demands incessant interior conversion on the part of individual Christians and continual renewal of our communities and institutions."

The bishops noted that evangelization is impeded by atheism, secularism, and the repression of religious liberty in a number of countries.

Communication of the Gospel was called "a dynamic process" which "takes place through word, work and life," and which needs "translation," expression and indigenization in terms of the religious and cultural patterns of people in different places.

The statement cited the need and intention for ecumenical collaboration with other Christians for the purpose of rendering "to the world a much broader common witness to Christ, while at the same time working to obtain full union in the Lord."

Liberation

Regarding the relationship between evangelization and human liberation, the bishops said:

"Faithful to her evangelizing mission, the Church, as a truly poor, praying and fraternal community, can do much to bring about the integral salvation or the full liberation of men. She can draw from the Gospel the most profound reasons and ever new incentives to promote generous dedication to the service of all men — the poor especially, the weak and the oppressed — and to eliminate the social consequences of sin which are translated into unjust social and political structures.

"The Church does not remain within merely political, social and economic limits (elements which she must certainly take into account) but leads towards freedom under all its forms — liberation from sin, from individual or collective selfishness — and to full communion with God and with men who are like brothers. In this way the Church, in her evangelical way, promotes the true and complete liberation of all men, groups and peoples."

The assembly had 209 participants.

Synod '77

"Catechetics in Our Time, with Special Reference to Children and Young People," was the theme of the fifth assembly, Sept. 30 to Oct. 29, 1977. Its major products were a "Message to the People of God," the first synodal statement issued since inception of the body, and two documents presented to Pope Paul — a set of 34 propositions and some 900 suggestions regarding the substance of the propositions and the message on catechetics.

The propositions covered six general subjects in considerable detail: the importance of catechetical renewal, the theme of authentic catechesis, the mode of authentic catechizing, the necessity of catechesis for all Christians, the community as the context and milieu of catechesis, attitudes and other factors affecting catechesis.

The "Message to the People of God" consisted of three parts, dealing with: the world, young people and catechesis; the manifestation of salvation in Christ; catechesis as the task of all people in the Church.

The fifth assembly had 204 delegates.

Sixth Assembly

"The Role of the Christian Family in the Modern World" was the theme of the sixth assembly, which began deliberations Sept. 26, 1980.

U.S. delegates elected by the National Conference of Catholic Bishops were: Archbishops John R. Quinn of San Francisco, Joseph L. Bernardin of Cincinnati, Robert F. Sanchez of Santa Fe, and Auxiliary Bishop J. Francis Stafford of Baltimore. The alternates were Bishops Walter W. Curtis of Bridgeport and Lawrence Welsh of Spokane.

Byzantine-Rite Archbishop Stephen J. Kocisko of Pittsburgh was an ex officio delegate. Cardinal Terence J. Cooke was a papal appointee. Rev. Paul Boyle, C.P., and Rev. Stephen Tutas, S.M., were among 10 representatives of religious institutes to the Synod. Dr. and Mrs. Richard McBride of Long Beach, Calif., were auditors.

(See separate entry.)

ROMAN CURIA

The Roman Curia consists of the Secretariat of State, the Sacred Council for the Public Affairs of the Church, nine congregations, three tribunals, three secretariats, and a complex of commissions, councils and offices which administer church affairs at the highest level.

Background

The Curia evolved gradually from advisory assemblies or synods of the Roman clergy with whose assistance the popes directed church affairs during the first 11 centuries. Its original office was the Apostolic Chancery, dating from the fourth century. The antecedents of its permanently functioning agencies and offices were special commissions of cardinals and prelates. Its establishment in a form resembling what it is now dates from the second half of the 16th century.

Pope Paul VI gave the following short account of the background of the Curia in the apostolic constitution *Regimini Ecclesiae Universae* ("For the Government of the Universal Church"), dated Aug. 15, 1967.

"The Roman Pontiffs, successors to Blessed Peter, have striven to provide for the government of the Universal Church by making use of experts to advise and assist them.

"In this connection, we should remember both the Presbyterium of the City of Rome and the College of Cardinals of the Holy Roman Church which in the course of centuries evolved from it. Then, little by little, as we know, out of that office (Apostolic Chancery) which was set up in the fourth century to transmit papal documents, many offices developed; to these was added the Auditorium, which was a well-developed tribunal in the 13th century and which was more thoroughly organized by John XXII (1316-1334).

"With an increase in the volume of things to be dealt with, bodies or commissions of cardinals selected to treat of specific questions began to be more efficiently organized in the 16th century, from which eventually arose the congregations of the Roman Curia. It is to the credit of our predecessor Sixtus V that, in the constitution *Immensa Aeterni Dei* of Jan. 22, 1588, he arranged the sacred councils in an orderly manner and wisely described the structure of the Roman Curia.

"With the progress of time, however, it happened that some of them became obsolete, others had to be added, and others had to be restructured. This is the work our predecessor St. Pius X set out to do with the constitution *Sapienti Consilio* of June 29, 1908. Its provisions, a lasting testimony to that wise and ingenious pastor of the Church, were with a few changes incorporated into the Code of Canon Law" (Canons 242-264).

Reorganization

Pope Paul initiated a four-year reorganization study in 1963 which resulted in the constitution *Regimini Ecclesiae Universae.* The document was published Aug. 18, 1967, and went into full effect in March, 1968.

While the study was underway, the Pope took preliminary steps toward curial reorganization by reorienting and changing the title of the Sacred Congregation of the Holy Office (to the Sacred Congregation for the Doctrine of the Faith) and by appointing a number of non-Italians to key curial positions.

The stated purposes of the reorganization were to increase the efficiency of the Curia and to make it more responsive to the needs and concerns of the Universal Church. The pursuit of these objectives involved various modifications.

Curial Departments

• The Office of the Pope, including the Papal Secretariat or Secretariat of State and the Council for the Public Affairs of the Church.

• Nine congregations, instead of twelve as formerly. The functions of the Sacred Congregation of Ceremonies were transferred to the Prefecture of the Pontifical Household; the duties of the Sacred Congregation for Extraordinary Ecclesiastical Affairs were taken over by the Sacred Council for the Public Affairs of the Church; the Sacred Congregation of the Basilica of St. Peter was reduced in rank. In 1969, the Sacred Congregation of Rites was phased out of existence and its functions were assigned to the Sacred Congregation for the Causes of Saints and the Sacred Congregation for Divine Worship.

In 1975 the Congregation for the Sacraments and Divine Worship was established to replace the Congregation for the Discipline of the Sacraments and the Congregation for Divine Worship.

• Three secretariats, the Council of the Laity and the Pontifical Commission on Justice and Peace.

• Three tribunals.

• Six offices, including the former Apostolic Chancery (abolished in 1973) and Apostolic Chamber, and the newly constituted Prefecture of Economic Affairs, Prefecture of the Pontifical Household, Administration of the Patrimony of the Apostolic See, and Central Statistics Office. Functions of the former Apostolic Datary and the Secretariats of State, of Briefs to Princes, and of Latin Letters were transferred to the Secretariat of State.

Operational Procedures

• The papal secretary or secretary of state has authority to take initiative in coordinating and expediting business through meetings and other cooperative procedures.

• Officials of departments have five-year terms of office, which may be renewed. Resignation is automatic on the death of a pope. The five-year terms of consultors are renewable.

• Diocesan bishops as well as full-time curial personnel have membership in curial departments, in accordance with provisions of the decree *Pro Comperto Sane* of Aug. 6, 1967. Seven diocesan bishops hold five-year membership in each congregation, with full rights to participation in the more important plenary assemblies scheduled once a year. They are also entitled to take part in routine meetings whenever they are in Rome. Three general superiors of male religious institutes hold similar membership in the Sacred Congregation for Religious and Secular Institutes.

• Lay persons are eligible to serve as consultors to curial departments.

• Close liaison with episcopal conferences is required. They should be given prior notice of forthcoming curial decrees affecting them in any special way.

• In line with customary procedure, matters in which the competence of two or more departments is involved are handled on a cooperative basis, with mutual consultation and decision.

• Although Latin remains the official language of the Curia, communication in any of the widely known modern languages is acceptable.

• Informational and financial services are centralized in the Central Statistics Office and the Prefecture of Economic Affairs, respectively.

• Heads of curial departments are required to notify the pope before conducting any serious or extraordinary business.

• Authority to act and decide on many matters belongs to departmental officials in virtue of delegation from the pope.

Internationalization

As of Sept. 10, 1980, principal officials of the Roman Curia (cardinals unless indicated otherwise) were from the following countries: Italy (Baggio, Caprio, Casaroli, Felici, Oddi, Palazzini, Paupini, Opilio Rossi, Vagnozzi); Poland (Rubin, Abp. Deskur, Bp. Majdanski); Germany (Msgr. Ewers, Bp. Cordes); United States (Baum, Bp. Marcinkus); Argentina (Pironio); Australia (Knox); Belgium (Abp. Jadot); Benin (Gantin); Brazil (Agnelo Rossi); Canada (Bp. Gagnon); France (Abp. Poupard); India (Lourdusamy); Netherlands (Willebrands); Scotland (Bp. Andrew); Yugoslavia (Seper).

The international complexion of personnel in the Roman Curia changed considerably during the decade from 1961 to 1970. The number of non-Italians increased from 570 to more than 1,400, a rise of 145 per cent, while the number of Italians increased from 750 to 850, a rise of only 14 per cent. In 1970, 62 per cent were from other countries, as compared with 44 per cent in 1961.

DEPARTMENTS

Secretariat of State: Provides the pope with the closest possible assistance in the care of the Universal Church and in dealings with all departments of the Curia.

The cardinal secretary is the key coordinator of curial operations. He has authority to call meetings of the prefects of all departments for expediting the conduct of business, for consultation and intercommunication. He handles: any and all matters entrusted to him by the pope, and ordinary matters which are not within the competence of other departments; some relations with bishops; relations with representatives of the Holy See, civil governments and their representatives, without prejudice to the competence of the Council for the Public Affairs of the Church.

The cardinal secretary has been likened to a prime minister or head of government because of the significant role he plays in coordinating curial operations at the highest level.

The secretariat has two offices for preparing and writing letters for the pope (functions formerly performed by the Secretariat of Briefs to Princes and the Secretariat of Latin Letters), and a Central Statistics Office.

It also handles work formerly done by the Apostolic Datary (the dating and countersigning of papal documents, and the management of church benefices), and the Apostolic Chancery, abolished in 1973 (care of the pope's leaden seal and the Fisherman's Ring).

It has supervisory duties over the Commission for the Instruments of Social Communication, two Vatican publications, *Acta Apostolicae Sedis* and *Annuario Pontificio*, and the Vatican Personnel Office.

The Prefecture of Vatican City is answerable to the secretary of state.

OFFICIALS: Cardinal Agostino Casaroli, secretary of state, Most Rev. Eduardo Martinez Somalo, undersecretary and secretary of the Cifra.

Council for the Public Affairs of the Church: Handles diplomatic and other relations with civil governments. With the Secretariat of State, it supervises matters concerning nunciatures and apostolic delegations. It also has supervision of the Pontifical Commission for Russia.

OFFICIALS: Cardinal Agostino Casaroli, prefect, secretary of state; Most Rev. Achille Silvestrini, secretary.

BACKGROUND: Originated by Pius VI in 1793 as the Congregation for Extraordinary Affairs from the Kingdom of the Gauls; given wider scope by Pius VII, July 19, 1814; formerly called the Sacred Congregation for Extraordinary Ecclesiastical Affairs.

CONGREGATIONS

Sacred Congregation for the Doctrine of the Faith: Has responsibility to safeguard the doctrine of faith and morals.

Accordingly, it examines doctrinal questions; promotes studies thereon; evaluates theological opinions and, when necessary and after prior consultation with concerned bishops, reproves those regarded as opposed to principles of the faith; examines books on doctrinal matters and can reprove such works, if the contents so warrant, after giving authors the opportunity to defend themselves.

It examines matters pertaining to the Privilege of Faith (Petrine Privilege) in marriage cases, and safeguards the dignity of the sacrament of penance.

It has working relations with the Pontifical Biblical Commission (see separate entry).

In 1969, Pope Paul set up a Theological Commission (see separate entry) as an adjunct to the congregation, to provide it with the advisory services of additional experts in theology and allied disciplines.

OFFICIALS: Cardinal Franjo Seper, prefect; Most Rev. Jerome Hamer, O.P., secretary.

BACKGROUND: At the beginning of the 13th century, legates of Innocent III were commissioned as the Holy Office of the Inquisition to combat heresy; the same task was entrusted to the Dominican Order by Gregory IX in 1231 and to the Friars Minor by Innocent IV from 1243 to 1254. On July 21, 1542 (apostolic constitution *Licet*), Paul III instituted a permanent congregation of cardinals with supreme and universal competence over matters concerning heretics and those suspected of heresy. Pius IV, St. Pius V and Sixtus V further defined the work of the congregation. St. Pius X changed its name to the Congregation of the Holy Office.

Paul VI, in virtue of the motu proprio *Integrae Servandae* of Dec. 7, 1965, began reorganization of the Curia with this body, to which he gave the new title, Sacred Congregation for the Doctrine of the Faith. Its orientation is not merely negative, in the condemnation of error, but positive, in the promotion of orthodox doctrine. The right of appeal, judicial representation, and the consultation of their proper regional conference of bishops, are assured to persons accused of unorthodox doctrine. The office for the censorship of books and the Roman Index of Prohibited Books were abolished.

Sacred Congregation for the Oriental Churches: Has competence in matters concerning the persons and discipline of Eastern Rite Churches. It has jurisdiction over territories in which the majority of Christians belong to Oriental Rites (i.e., Egypt, the Sinai Peninsula, Eritrea, Northern Ethiopia, Southern Albania, Bulgaria, Cyprus, Greece, Iran, Iraq, Lebanon, Palestine, Syria, Jordan, Turkey, Afghanistan, the part of Thrace subject to Turkey); also, over minority communities of Orientals no matter where they live.

To assure adequate and equal representation, it has as many offices as there are rites of Oriental Churches in communion with the Holy See.

It is under mandate to consult with the Secretariat for Promoting Christian Unity on questions concerning separated Oriental Churches, and with the Secretariat for Non-Christians, especially in relations with Moslems.

It has a special commission on the liturgy and an Oriental Church Information Service.

OFFICIALS: Cardinal Wladyslaw Rubin, prefect; Most Rev. Mario Brini, secretary.

Members include all Eastern Rite patriarchs and the president of the Secretariat for Promoting Christian Unity.

BACKGROUND: Special congregations for the affairs of the Greek and other Oriental Churches were founded long before this body was created by Pius IX Jan. 6, 1862 (apostolic constitution *Romani Pontifices*), and united with the Sacred Congregation for the Propagation of the Faith. The congregation was made autonomous by Benedict XV May 1, 1917 (motu proprio *Dei Providentis*), and given wider authority by Pius XI Mar. 25, 1938 (motu proprio *Sancta Dei Ecclesia*). John XXIII appointed six patriarchs, five of Eastern Rites and one of the Roman Rite, to the congregation and gave them the same rights as cardinals belonging to the body, in March, 1963. Paul VI named representatives of all Eastern-Rite bodies to serve as consultors of the congregation, in November, 1963.

Sacred Congregation for Bishops, formerly called the Sacred Consistorial Congregation: Has functions related in one way or another to bishops and the jurisdictions in which they serve.

Its concerns are: the establishment and changing of dioceses, provinces, military vicariates and other jurisdictions; providing for the naming of bishops and other prelates; studying things concerning the persons, work and pastoral activity of bishops; providing for the care of bishops when they leave office; receiving and studying reports on the conditions of dioceses; general supervision of the holding and recognition of particular councils and conferences of bishops; publishing and circulating pastoral norms and guidelines through conferences of bishops.

It supervises the Pontifical Commission for Latin America and the Pontifical Commission for Migration and Tourism.

OFFICIALS: Cardinal Sebastiano Baggio, prefect; Most Rev. Moreira Neves Lucas, O.P., secretary.

Ex officio members are the prefects of the Council for the Public Affairs of the Church, and of the Congregations for the Doctrine of the Faith, for the Clergy, and for Catholic Education. The substitute secretaries and undersecretaries of these curial departments are ex officio consultors.

BACKGROUND: Established by Sixtus V Jan. 22, 1588 (apostolic constitution *Immensa*); given an extension of powers by St. Pius X June 20, 1908, and Pius XII Aug. 1, 1952 (apostolic constitution *Exsul Familia*).

Sacred Congregation for the Sacraments and Divine Worship: Established in 1975 to replace the Congregation for the Discipline of the Sacraments and the Congregation for Divine Worship.

The congregation consists of two sections — for the sacraments and for divine worship. The former supervises the discipline of the sacraments without prejudice to the competencies of the Sacred Congregation for the Doctrine of the Faith and other curial departments. The latter has general competence over the ritual and pastoral aspects of divine worship in the Roman and other Latin Rites.

OFFICIALS: Cardinal James R. Knox, prefect; Most Rev. Antonio Innocenti, secretary.

BACKGROUND: The congregation was established by Paul VI Aug. 1, 1975 (apostolic constitution, *Constans novis studium,* dated July 11, 1975). Formerly its duties were carried out by the Congregation for the Discipline of the Sacraments (instituted by St. Pius X June 29, 1908) and the Congregation for Divine Worship (established by Paul VI, May 8, 1969, to replace the Congregation of Rites instituted by Sixtus V in 1588).

Sacred Congregation for the Causes of Saints: Handles all matters connected with beatification and canonization procedures, and the preservation of relics. These affairs were formerly under the supervision of the Congregation of Rites.

The congregation carries on its work through three sections or offices.

One section is a juridical office with supervisory responsibility over procedures and examinations conducted to determine the holiness of prospective saints. It includes a medical commission for the study of miracles attributed to the intercession of candidates for sainthood.

A second section, headed by the promoter general of the faith, who is popularly called the "Devil's Advocate," serves the purpose of establishing beyond reasonable doubt the evidence of holiness advanced in support of beatification and canonization causes.

Research and evaluation of documentary

evidence figuring in canonization causes are the functions of the historic-hagiographical section.

OFFICIALS: *Cardinal Pietro Palazzini, prefect; Most Rev. Giuseppe Casoria, secretary.*

BACKGROUND: The functions and title of this congregation were determined by Paul VI May 8, 1969 (apostolic constitution *Sacra Rituum Congregatio*). Formerly, its duties were carried out by the Congregation of Rites, which was established by Sixtus V in 1588 and affected by legislation of Pius XI in 1930.

Sacred Congregation for the Clergy, formerly called the Sacred Congregation of the Council: Handles matters concerning the persons, work and pastoral ministry of clerics who exercise their apostolate in a diocese. Such clerics are diocesan deacons and priests, and religious who are engaged in ordinary parochial ministry in a diocese.

It carries on its work through three offices.

One office promotes the spiritual growth and formation as well as the professional competence of priests by encouraging the establishment and operation of pastoral institutes and other study opportunities; oversees the general discipline of the clergy, the establishment and conduct of pastoral councils and senates of priests, and resolves controversies among clerics; has a mandate to draw up a set of general principles to direct a better distribution of priests for pastoral service.

A second office, in view of its primary concern for preaching of the word of God, encourages effective apostolic programs and methods, with special emphasis on catechetical and other forms of religious training and formation for the faithful.

A third office has supervisory responsibility over church property and the temporalities of priestly life; among its functions are efforts to provide for the support of the clergy through suitable salary scales, pensions, security and health insurance programs, and other measures.

OFFICIALS: *Cardinal Silvio Oddi, prefect; Most Rev. Maximino Romero de Lema, secretary.*

BACKGROUND: Established by Pius IV Aug. 2, 1564 (apostolic constitution *Alias Nos*), under the title, Sacred Congregation of the Cardinals Interpreters of the Council of Trent; affected by legislation of Gregory XIII and Sixtus V.

Sacred Congregation for Religious and Secular Institutes, formerly known as the Sacred Congregation of Religious or for the Affairs of Religious: Has dual competence over institutes of religious, together with societies of the common life without vows, and secular institutes.

One section deals with the affairs of all religious institutes and societies of the common life, and their members. It has authority in matters related to the establishment, general direction and suppression of institutes; general discipline in line with their rules and constitutions; the movement toward renewal and adaptation of institutes in contemporary circumstances; the setting up and encouragement of councils and conferences of major religious superiors for intercommunication and other purposes.

A second section has the same competence over the affairs and members of secular institutes as the first has over religious.

OFFICIALS: *Cardinal Eduardo Pironio, prefect; Most. Rev. Augustin Mayer, O.S.B., secretary.*

BACKGROUND: Founded by Sixtus V May 27, 1586, with the title, Sacred Congregation for Consultations of Regulars (apostolic constitution *Romanus Pontifex*); confirmed by the apostolic constitution *Immensa* Jan. 22, 1588; made part of the Congregation for Consultations of Bishops and other Prelates in 1601; made autonomous by St. Pius X in 1908.

Sacred Congregation for Catholic Education, formerly known as the Sacred Congregation of Seminaries and Universities: Has supervisory competence over institutions and works of Catholic education.

It carries on its work through three offices.

One office handles matters connected with the direction, discipline and temporal administration of seminaries, and with the education of diocesan clergy, religious and members of secular institutes.

A second office oversees Catholic universities, faculties of study and other institutions of higher learning inasmuch as they depend on the authority of the Church; encourages cooperation and mutual assistance among Catholic institutions, and the establishment of Catholic hospices and centers on campuses of non-Catholic institutions.

A third office is concerned in various ways with all Catholic schools below the college-university level, with general questions concerning education and studies, and with the cooperation of conferences of bishops and civil authorities in educational matters.

The congregation supervises Pontifical Works for Priestly Vocations.

OFFICIALS: *Cardinal William Wakefield Baum, prefect; Most Rev. Antonio M. Javierre Ortas, secretary.*

BACKGROUND: The title and functions of the congregation were defined by Benedict XV Nov. 4, 1915; Pius XI, in 1931 and 1932, and Pius XII, in 1941 and 1949, extended its functions. Its work had previously been carried on by two other congregations erected by Sixtus V in 1588 and Leo XII in 1824.

Sacred Congregation for the Evangelization of Peoples (for the Propagation of the Faith):

Directs and coordinates missionary work throughout the world.

Accordingly, it has competence over those matters which concern all the missions established for the spread of Christ's kingdom. These include: fostering missionary vocations; providing for the training of missionaries in seminaries; assigning missionaries to fields of work; establishing ecclesiastical jurisdictions and proposing candidates to serve them as bishops and in other capacities; encouraging the recruitment and development of indigenous clergy; mobilizing spiritual and financial support for missionary activity.

In general, the varied competence of the congregation extends to most persons and affairs of the Church in areas classified as mission territories.

To promote missionary cooperation, the congregation has a Supreme Council for the Direction of Pontifical Missionary Works. Subject to this council are the general councils of the Missionary Union of the Clergy, the Society for the Propagation of the Faith, the Society of St. Peter the Apostle for Native Clergy, the Society of the Holy Childhood, and the *Fides* news agency.

OFFICIALS: Cardinal Agnelo Rossi, prefect; Most Rev. D. Simon Lourdusamy, secretary.

The heads of the Secretariats for Promoting Christian Unity, for Non-Christians, and for Non-Believers are ex officio members of the congregation.

BACKGROUND: Originated as a commission of cardinals by Gregory XIII and modified by Clement VIII to promote the reconciliation of separated Eastern Christians; erected as a stable congregation by Gregory XV June 22, 1622 (apostolic constitution *Inscrutabili*).

TRIBUNALS

Sacred Apostolic Penitentiary: Has jurisdiction for the internal forum only (sacramental and non-sacramental). It issues decisions on questions of conscience; grants absolutions, dispensations, commutations, sanations and condonations; has charge of non-doctrinal matters pertaining to indulgences.

OFFICIALS: Cardinal Giuseppe Paupini, major penitentiary; Msgr. Luigi de Magistris, regent.

BACKGROUND: Origin dates back to the 12th century; affected by the legislation of many popes; radically reorganized by St. Pius V in 1569; jurisdiction limited to the internal forum by St. Pius X; Benedict XV annexed the Office of Indulgences to it Mar. 25, 1917.

Apostolic Signatura: The principal concerns of this supreme court of the Church are to resolve questions concerning juridical procedure and to supervise the observance of laws and rights at the highest level. It decides the jurisdictional competence of lower courts and has jurisdiction in cases involving personnel and decisions of the Rota. It is the supreme court of the State of Vatican City.

OFFICIALS: Cardinal Pericle Felici, prefect; Most Rev. Aurelio Sabattani, secretary.

BACKGROUND: A permanent office of the Signatura has existed since the time of Eugene IV in the 15th century; affected by the legislation of many popes; reorganized by St. Pius X in 1908 and made the supreme tribunal of the Church.

Sacred Roman Rota: The ordinary court of appeal for cases appealed to the Holy See. It is best known for its competence and decisions in cases concerning the validity of marriage.

OFFICIAL: Msgr. Heinrich Ewers, dean.

BACKGROUND: Originated in the Apostolic Chancery; affected by the legislation of many popes; reorganized by St. Pius X in 1908 and further revised by Pius XI in 1934.

SECRETARIATS

Secretariat for Promoting Christian Unity: Handles relations with members of other Christian ecclesial communities; deals with the correct interpretation and execution of the principles of ecumenism; initiates or promotes Catholic ecumenical groups and coordinates on national and international levels the efforts of those promoting Christian unity; undertakes dialogue regarding ecumenical questions and activities with churches and ecclesial communities separated from the Apostolic See; sends Catholic observer-representatives to Christian gatherings, and invites to Catholic gatherings observers of other churches; orders into execution conciliar decrees dealing with ecumenical affairs.

The Commission for Catholic-Jewish Relations is attached to the secretariat.

It has two offices, for the West and for the East. Each office is under the immediate direction of a delegate.

The prefects of the Congregation for the Oriental Churches and of the Congregation for the Evangelization of Peoples are ex officio members of the secretariat. Consultors include the secretaries of these two departments.

OFFICIALS: Cardinal Johannes Willebrands, president; Rev. Msgr. Charles Moeller, secretary.

BACKGROUND: Established by John XXIII June 5, 1960, as a preparatory secretariat of the Second Vatican Council; raised to commission status during the first session of the council in the fall of 1962; this status confirmed Jan. 3, 1966.

Secretariat for Non-Christians: Is concerned with persons who are not Christians but profess some kind of religious faith. Its function is to promote studies and dialogue for the purpose of increasing mutual understanding and respect between Christians and non-Christians.

The Commission for Catholic-Moslem Relations is attached to the secretariat.

The prefect of the Congregation for the Evangelization of Peoples is an ex officio member of the secretariat.

OFFICIALS: *Most Rev. Jean Jadot, pro-president; Msgr. Pietro Rossano, secretary.*

BACKGROUND: Established by Paul VI May 19, 1964.

Secretariat for Non-Believers: Studies the background and philosophy of atheism, and initiates and carries on dialogue with non-believers.

OFFICIALS: *Most Rev. Paul Poupard, pro-president; Rev. Vincenzo Miano, S.D.B., secretary.*

BACKGROUND: Established by Paul VI Apr. 9, 1965.

COUNCILS, COMMISSIONS

Laity, Pontifical Council for: Instituted on an experimental basis by Paul VI Jan. 6, 1967; given permanent status Dec. 10, 1976 (motu proprio *Apostolatus Peragendi*); its competence covers the apostolate of the laity in the Church and the discipline of the laity as such. Members are mostly lay people from different parts of the world and involved in different apostolates. The council is headed by a cardinal. The Committee for the Family is attached to the Council while retaining its own identity. Cardinal Opilio Rossi, president.

Justice and Peace, Pontifical Commission: Instituted by Paul VI Jan. 6, 1967, on an experimental basis; reconstituted and made a permanent body Dec. 10, 1976 (motu proprio *Iustitiam et Pacem*). Holy See's organization for examining and studying (from the point of view of doctrine, pastoral practice and the apostolate) problems connected with justice and peace and awakening the sensitivity of the people of God to their responsibility in these areas. Cardinal Bernardin Gantin, president.

Revision of the Code of Canon Law: Instituted by John XXIII Mar. 28, 1963, to replace a former commission dating from 1917; Cardinal Pericle Felici, president.

Revision of the Code of Oriental Canon Law: Reconstituted by Paul VI in 1972 to replace a former commission dating from July 17, 1935, "to prepare . . . the reform of the Code of Oriental Canon Law, both in the sections already published by . . . four motu proprios" (1,950 canons concerning marriage; processes; religious, church property and terminology; Eastern Rites and persons), "and in the remaining sections which have been completed but not published" (the balance of a total of 2,666 canons); Cardinal Joseph Parecattil, president.

Interpretation of the Decrees of the Second Vatican Council: Cardinal Pericle Felici, president.

Social Communication: Instituted on an experimental basis by Pius XII in 1948; reorganized three times in the 1950's; made permanent commission by John XXIII Feb. 22, 1959; name changed to present title Apr. 11, 1964; authorized to implement the *Decree on the Instruments of Social Communication* promulgated by the Second Vatican Council; under supervision of the Secretariat of State and the Council for the Public Affairs of the Church; Most Rev. Andrzej-Marie Deskur, president; Most Rev. Martin J. O'Connor, president emeritus.

Latin America: Instituted by Pius XII Apr. 19, 1958; placed under supervision of the Congregation for Bishops July, 1969; Cardinal Sebastiano Baggio, president.

Migration and Tourism: Instituted by Paul VI Mar. 19, 1970, for pastoral assistance to migrants, nomads, tourists, sea and air travelers; placed under the general supervision and direction of the Congregation for Bishops; Cardinal Sebastiano Baggio, president.

Cor Unum: Instituted by Paul VI July 15, 1971, to provide informational and coordinating services for Catholic aid and human development organizations and projects on a worldwide scale; Cardinal Bernardin Gantin, president.

Theological Commission: Instituted by Paul VI Apr. 11, 1969, as an advisory adjunct of no more than 30 theologians to the Congregation for the Doctrine of the Faith; Cardinal Franjo Seper, president. (See separate entry.)

Biblical Commission: Instituted by Leo XIII Oct. 30, 1902; completely restructured by Paul VI June 27, 1971; Cardinal Franjo Seper, president. (See separate entry.)

Abbey of St. Jerome for the Revision and Emendation of the Vulgate: Instituted by Pius XI June 15, 1933, to replace an earlier commission established by St. Pius X; Rev. Vincent Truijen, superior.

Revision of the New Vulgate: Instituted by Paul VI in 1965 to augment the work of the Abbey of St. Jerome; Most Rev. Edward Schick, president.

Sacred Archeology: Instituted by Pius IX Jan, 6, 1852; Most Rev. Gennaro Verolino, president.

Historical Sciences: Instituted by Pius XII Apr. 7, 1954, as a continuation of a commission dating from 1883; Msgr. Michele Maccarrone, president.

Ecclesiastical Archives of Italy: Instituted by Pius XII Apr. 5, 1955; Msgr. Martino Giusti, president.

Sacred Art in Italy: Instituted by Pius XI Sept. 1, 1924; Most Rev. Giovanni Fallani, president.

Sanctuaries of Pompei and Loreto: Originated by Leo XIII; under supervision of the

Congregation for the Clergy; Cardinal Umberto Mozzoni, president.

Russia: Instituted by Pius XI Apr. 6, 1930, to handle all ecclesiastical affairs of the country; placed under supervision of the Congregation for Extraordinary Ecclesiastical Affairs (now the Council for the Public Affairs of the Church) in 1934, with jurisdiction limited to clergy and faithful of the Roman Rite; under supervision of the Council for the Public Affairs of the Church; Most Rev. Achille Silvestrini, president.

State of Vatican City: Cardinal Agostino Casaroli, president.

Protection of the Historical and Artistic Monuments of the Holy See: Instituted by Pius XI in 1923, reorganized by Paul VI in 1963; Most Rev. Giovanni Fallani, president.

Preservation of the Faith, Erection of New Churches in Rome: Instituted by Pius XI Aug. 5, 1930, to replace a commission dating from 1902; Cardinal Ugo Poletti, president.

Works of Religion: Instituted by Pius XII June 27, 1942, to bank and administer funds for works of religion; replaced an earlier administration established by Leo XIII in 1887; Most Rev. Paul C. Marcinkus, president.

Family, Committee for: Instituted by Paul VI Jan. 11, 1973, for pastoral research and supportive effort with respect to the spiritual, moral and social needs of the family; it is attached to the Pontifical Council for the Laity. Cardinal Opilio Rossi, president; Most Rev. Edouard Gagnon, vice-president.

Catholic-Jewish Relations: Instituted by Paul VI, Oct. 22, 1974, to promote and foster relations of a religious nature between Jews and Christians; attached to the Secretariat for Christian Unity; Cardinal Johannes Willebrands, president.

Catholic-Moslem Relations: Instituted by Paul VI, Oct. 22, 1974, to promote, regulate and interpret relations between Catholics and Moslems; attached to the Secretariat for Non-Christians.

OFFICES

Prefecture of the Economic Affairs of the Holy See: A financial office which coordinates and supervises administration of the temporalities of the Holy See.

OFFICIALS: Cardinal Egidio Vagnozzi, president; Msgr. Giovanni Angelo Abbo, secretary.

BACKGROUND: Established by Paul VI Aug. 15, 1967.

Apostolic Chamber: Administers the temporal goods and rights of the Holy See between the death of one pope and the election of another, in accordance with special laws.

OFFICIALS: Cardinal Paolo Bertoli, chamberlain of the Holy Roman Church; Most Rev. Ettore Cunial, vice-chamberlain.

BACKGROUND: Originated in the 11th century; reorganized by Pius XI in 1934.

Administration of the Patrimony of the Apostolic See: Handles the estate of the Apostolic See under the direction of papal delegates

OFFICIALS: Cardinal Giuseppe Caprio, president; Most Rev. Lorenzo Antonetti, secretary.

BACKGROUND: Some of its functions date back to 1878; established by Paul VI Aug. 15, 1967.

Prefecture of the Pontifical Household: Oversees the papal chapel — which is at the service of the pope in his capacity as spiritual head of the Church — and the pontifical family — which is at the service of the pope as a sovereign. It arranges papal audiences, has charge of preparing non-liturgical elements of papal ceremonies, makes all necessary arrangements for papal visits and trips outside the Vatican, and settles questions of protocol connected with papal audiences and other formalities.

OFFICIALS: Most Rev. Jacques Martin, prefect; Msgr. Dino Monduzzi, regent.

BACKGROUND: Established by Paul VI Aug. 15, 1967, under the title, Prefecture of the Apostolic Palace; it supplanted the Sacred Congregation for Ceremonies founded by Sixtus V Jan. 22, 1588. The office was updated and reorganized under the present title by Paul VI, Mar. 28, 1968.

Central Statistics Office: Compiles. systematizes and analyzes information on the status and condition of the Church and the needs of its pastoral ministry, from parish to top levels.

The office is one of the organs of the Secretariat of State.

BACKGROUND: Established by Paul VI Aug. 15, 1967.

Aid Office: Distributes alms and aid to the aged, sick, handicapped and other persons in need.

OFFICIAL: Most Rev. Antonio M. Travia, director.

BACKGROUND: The office originated as a charitable office in the time of Bl. Gregory X (1271-1276).

Vatican II Archives: Preserves the acts and other documents of the Second Vatican Council.

OFFICIAL: Cardinal Pericle Felici.

Personnel: Set up by Paul VI May 9, 1971, to handle personnel relations in the offices and other agencies of the Vatican.

OFFICIAL: Msgr. Michele Buro.

FIDES

The International Fides Service is the news agency of the Congregation for the Evangelization of Peoples, headquartered at Via di Propaganda, 1C, 00187, Rome, Italy.

It issues a periodic service of news, comment and background information on missionary activity, in several languages.

THEOLOGICAL COMMISSION

Establishment of a Theological Commission as an adjunct to the Congregation for the Doctrine of the Faith was announced by Pope Paul VI Apr. 28, 1969. The move had been recommended by the Second Vatican Council and was proposed by the Synod of Bishops in 1967.

The purpose of the commission is to provide the Doctrinal Congregation with the consultative and advisory services of theologians and scriptural and liturgical experts representative of various schools of thought. The international membership is restricted to 30, and the ordinary term of membership is five years.

Membership

The commission is headed by Cardinal Franjo Seper, prefect of the Doctrinal Congregation. Msgr. Philippe Delhaye of Belgium is secretary. Members listed in the 1980 *Annuario Pontificio* were as follows:

Barnabas Ahern, C.P. (U.S.); Juan Alfaro, S.J. (Spain); Catalino Arevalo, S.J. (Philippines); Hans Urs von Balthasar (Switzerland); Walter Burghardt, S.J. (U.S.); Carlo Caffaro (Italy); Raniero Cantalamessa (Italy); Ives Congar, O.P. (France); Wilhelm Ernst (East Germany); Olegario Gonzalez de Cardedal (Spain); Edouard Hamel, S.J. (Canada); Boguslaw Inlender (Poland); Bonaventure Kloppenburg, O.F.M. (Brazil); Marie-Joseph Le Guillou, O.P. (France); Karl Lehmann (Germany); J. F. Lescrauwaet, M.S.C. (Holland); John Mahoney, S.J. (Great Britain); Gustave Martelet, S.J. (France); Jorge Medina Estevez (Chile); Vincent Mulago (Zaire);

Cardinal Joseph Ratzinger (Germany); Most Rev. Georges Abi-Saber, Maronite Monk (Lebanon); Heinz Schurmann (East Germany); Anton Strle (Yugoslavia); Jean-Marie Tillard, O.P. (Canada); Cipriano Vagaggini, O.S.B. (Italy); Jan Walgrave, O.P. (Belgium).

Meetings

The commission met for the first time Oct. 6 to 8, 1969, for organizational purposes and the assignment of subcommissions to studies on the priesthood, the theology of hope, unity of faith and pluralism in theology, the criteria of moral knowledge, and collegiality.

Week-long general assemblies, for discussion and decision on subjects of individual and group research have been held annually, except in 1978, since 1969.

Twenty-six members attending the second meeting, Oct. 5 to 10, 1970, discussed reports on the priestly ministry and collegiality. Views were exchanged about the question of ordaining married men, but marriage was ruled out for already ordained priests wanting to continue in the ministry. With respect to collegiality, no doubt was raised about the pope's authority to act independently in the Church; the consensus, however, was that he would be prudent to engage in wide consultation before acting.

By early 1971, the commission prepared the basis of a feasible working paper on the priesthood for the Synod of Bishops, which met for the third time in the fall. The ordination of women was one of the subjects covered, but it did not figure significantly in discussion by the commission because the issue was not considered urgent. Agreement was reported on two points: tradition militated against ordination but permitted a form of diaconal ordination with a rite and purpose distinctive and proper to women.

Pluralism in theology — concerning different ways of treating, presenting and expressing in practice the unity of faith — was the main subject under consideration at the fourth general assembly Oct. 5 to 11, 1972.

The October, 1973, meeting, attended by 21 members, completed work on a statement concerning apostolic succession and ordination to holy orders. The necessary sacramental sign of both, the statement said, is the imposition of hands by successors of the Apostles acting in accord with the intention of the Church.

The results of research on Christian morality were discussed at the 1974 meeting, and several articles on the subject were published in 1975.

The majority of members attending the Sept. 25 to Oct. 1, 1975, meeting approved a number of conclusions concerning the relationship between "the mandate given to the ecclesiastical magisterium (the teaching authority of the Church) to protect divine revelation and the task given to theologians to investigate and explain the doctrine of the faith." These conclusions were published by the U.S. Catholic Conference in April, 1977.

Christian salvation and human progress, centering on the nature of and relationship between evangelization and human liberation, was the subject of the meeting held Oct. 4 to 9, 1976. The subject was connected with earlier consideration of the matter by the Synod of Bishops, and also with the contents and tenor of the *Pastoral Constitution on the Church in the Modern World* issued by the Second Vatican Council.

The meeting of Dec. 1 to 6, 1977, focused attention on pastoral aspects of Christian marriage and agreed on a summary of conclusions which: (1) reaffirmed the indissolubility of marriage and the stance of the Church against divorce; (2) declared that the Church should not witness the marriage of Catholics who have rejected the faith and the sacramental nature of marriage.

Various aspects of Christology were under consideration during 1979 and 1980.

COLLEGE OF CARDINALS

Cardinals are chosen by the pope to serve as his principal assistants and advisers in the central administration of church affairs. Collectively, they form the Sacred College of Cardinals.

The college evolved gradually from synods of Roman clergy with whose assistance popes directed church affairs in the first 11 centuries. The first cardinals, in about the sixth century, were priests of the leading churches of Rome who were assigned liturgical, advisory and administrative duties with the Holy See, and the regional deacons of Rome.

For all cardinals except Eastern patriarchs, membership in the college involves aggregation to the clergy of Rome. This aggregation is signified by the assignment to each cardinal, except the patriarchs, of a special or titular church in Rome.

History of the College

The Sacred College of Cardinals was constituted in its present form and categories of membership in the 12th century. Before that time the pope had a body of advisers selected from among the bishops of dioceses neighboring Rome, priests and deacons of Rome. The college was given definite form in 1150, and in 1179 the selection of cardinals was reserved exclusively to the pope. Sixtus V fixed the number at 70, in 1586. John XXIII set aside this rule when he increased membership at the 1959 and subsequent consistories. The number of cardinals reached an all-time high of 145 under Paul VI in 1973. The number of cardinals entitled to participate in papal elections was limited to 120.

In 1567 the title of cardinal was reserved to members of the college; previously it had been used by priests attached to parish churches of Rome and by the leading clergy of other notable churches. The Code of Canon Law promulgated in 1918 decreed that all cardinals must be priests. Previously there had been lay cardinals (e.g., Cardinal Giacomo Antonelli, d. 1876, Secretary of State to Pius IX). John XXIII provided in the motu proprio *Cum Gravissima* Apr. 15, 1962, that all cardinals would henceforth be bishops.

Pope Paul VI placed age limits on the functions of cardinals in the apostolic letter *Ingravescentem Aetatem,* dated Nov. 21, 1970, and effective as of Jan. 1, 1971. At 80, they cease to be members of curial departments and offices, and become ineligible to take part in papal elections. They retain membership in the College of Cardinals, however, with relevant rights and privileges.

Three Categories

The three categories of members of the college are cardinal bishops, cardinal priests and cardinal deacons.

Cardinal bishops include the six titular bishops of the suburban sees of Rome and Eastern patriarchs.

First in rank are the titular bishops of the suburban sees, neighboring Rome: Ostia, Palestrina, Porto and Santa Rufina, Albano, Velletri, Frascati, Sabina and Poggio Mirteto. The dean of the college holds the title of the See of Ostia as well as his other suburban see. These cardinal bishops are engaged in full-time service in the central administration of church affairs in departments of the Roman Curia.

Four Eastern patriarchs, three of whom have since died, were made cardinal bishops by Paul VI in virtue of the motu proprio *Ad Purpuratorum Patrum* Feb. 11, 1965. Full recognition was given to their position as the heads of ancient liturgies and of sees of apostolic origin. Because of their patriarchal dignity and titles, which antedated the dignity and titles of cardinals, they were not aggregated to the Roman clergy and were not, like other cardinals, given title to Roman churches. The patriarchs were assigned rank among the cardinals in order of seniority, following the suburban titleholders. Patriarchs, at their request, were not included among cardinals inducted into the college in later consistories.

Cardinal priests, who were formerly in charge of leading churches in Rome, are bishops whose dioceses are outside Rome.

Cardinal deacons, who were formerly chosen according to regional divisions of Rome, are titular bishops assigned to full-time service in the Roman Curia.

The officers of the college are the dean and sub-dean, a chamberlain and a secretary. Pope Paul decreed Feb. 26, 1965, that the dean and sub-dean were to be elected by the cardinal bishops. He set this ruling aside in December, 1977, however, when he appointed Cardinals Carlo Confalonieri and Paolo Marella, respectively, as dean and sub-dean.

Selection and Duties

Cardinals are selected by the pope and are inducted into the college in a three-step process. Their nomination is announced and approved at a meeting (secret consistory) attended only by the pope and cardinals who are already members of the college; word of their election and confirmation is then communicated to the cardinals designate by means of a document called a *biglietto.* In successive and more public ceremonies, they receive the cardinalatial red biretta and ring, and concelebrate Mass with the pope and their fellow cardinals.

Cardinals under the age of 80: elect the pope when the Holy See becomes vacant (see Papal Election); are major administrators of church affairs, serving in one or more departments of the Roman Curia. All cardinals enjoy a number of special rights and privileges. Their title, while symbolic of high honor, does not signify any extension of the powers of holy orders. They are called princes of the Church.

A **cardinal in pectore** is one whose selection has been made by the pope but whose name has not been disclosed; he has no title, rights or duties until such disclosure is made, at which time he takes precedence from the time of the secret selection.

BIOGRAPHIES OF CARDINALS

Biographies of the cardinals, as of Aug. 15, 1980, are given below in alphabetical order. For historical notes, order of seniority and geographical distribution of cardinals, see separate entries.

An asterisk indicates cardinals ineligible to take part in papal elections.

Alfrink,* Bernard Jan: b. July 5, 1900, Nijkerk, Netherlands; ord. priest Aug. 15, 1924; professor of Sacred Scripture at Utrecht major seminary, 1933; consultor to Pontifical Biblical Commission, Rome, 1944; professor at Catholic University of Nijmegen, 1945; ord. titular archbishop of Tiana and coadjutor archbishop of Utrecht, July 17, 1951; archbishop of Utrecht, 1955-75; cardinal Mar. 28, 1960; titular church, St. Joachim. Former archbishop of Utrecht, member of:
Commission: Revision of Code of Canon Law.

Antonelli,* Ferdinando Giuseppe, O.F.M.: b. July 14, 1896, Subbiano, Italy; solemnly professed in Order of Friars Minor, Apr. 7, 1914; ord. priest July 25, 1922; taught church history, 1928-32, and Christian archeology, 1932-65, at Antonianum; rector magnificus of Antonianum, 1937-43, 1953-59; definitor general of Friars Minor, 1939-45; held various offices in Roman Curia; secretary of Congregation of Rites, 1965-69, and Congregation for Causes of Saints, 1969-73; ord. titular archbishop of Idicra, Mar. 19, 1966; cardinal Mar. 5, 1973; deacon, San Sebastian (on the Palatine).

Aponte Martinez, Luis: b. Aug. 4, 1922, Lajas, Puerto Rico; ord. priest Apr. 10, 1950; parish priest at Ponce; ord. titular bishop of Lares and auxiliary of Ponce, Oct. 12, 1960; bishop of Ponce, 1963-64; archbishop of San Juan, Nov. 4, 1964; cardinal Mar. 5, 1973; titular church, St. Mary Mother of Providence (in Monteverde). Archbishop of San Juan, president of Puerto Rican Episcopal Conference, member of:
Congregation: Causes of Saints.

Aramburu, Juan Carlos: b. Feb. 11, 1912, Reduccion, Argentina; ord. priest in Rome, Oct. 28, 1934; ord. titular bishop of Plataea and auxiliary of Tucuman, Dec. 15, 1946; bishop, 1953, and first archbishop, 1957, of Tucuman; titular archbishop of Torri di

Bizacena and coadjutor archbishop of Buenos Aires, June 14, 1967; archbishop of Buenos Aires, Apr. 22, 1975; cardinal May 24, 1976; titular church, St. John Baptist of the Florentines. Archbishop of Buenos Aires, ordinary for Eastern Rite Catholics in Brazil without ordinaries of their own rites, member of:
Congregations: Oriental Churches, Catholic Education.

Arns, Paulo Evaristo, O.F.M.: b. Sept. 14, 1921, Forquilhinha, Brazil; ord. priest Nov. 30, 1945; held various teaching posts; director of *Sponsa Christi,* monthly review for religious, and of the Franciscan publication center in Brazil; ord. titular bishop of Respetta and auxiliary of Sao Paulo, July 3, 1966; archbishop of Sao Paulo, Oct. 22, 1970; cardinal Mar. 5, 1973; titular church, St. Anthony of Padua (in Via Tuscolana). Archbishop of Sao Paulo, member of:
Congregation: Sacraments and Divine Worship;
Secretariat: Non-Believers.

Bafile, Corrado: b. July 4, 1903, L'Aquila, Italy; practiced law in Rome for six years before beginning studies for priesthood; ord. priest Apr. 11, 1936; served in Vatican secretariat of state, 1939-59; ord. titular archbishop of Antiochia in Pisidia, Mar. 19, 1960; apostolic nuncio to Germany, 1960-75; pro-prefect of Sacred Congregation for Causes of Saints, July 18, 1975; cardinal May 24, 1976; deacon, S. Maria (in Portico); prefect of Sacred Congregation for Causes of Saints, 1976-80. Member of:
Congregation: Clergy;
Tribunal: Apostolic Signatura;
Commission: Revision of Code of Canon Law.

Baggio, Sebastiano: b. May 16, 1913, Rosa, Italy; ord. priest Dec. 21, 1935; ord. titular archbishop of Ephesus, July 26, 1953; served in Vatican diplomatic corps, 1953-69; nuncio to Chile, apostolic delegate to Canada, nuncio to Brazil; cardinal Apr. 28, 1969; archbishop of Cagliari, 1969-73; entered order of cardinal bishops as titular bishop of Velletri, Dec. 12, 1974. Prefect of Sacred Congregation for Bishops, 1973, member of:
Council for Public Affairs of Church;
Congregations: Doctrine of the Faith, Religious and Secular Institutes, Catholic Education, Evangelization of Peoples;
Commissions: Revision of Code of Canon Law, Latin America (President), Migration and Tourism (President), Sanctuaries of Pompei and Loreto, Interpretation of Decrees of Vatican II;
Office: Patrimony of Holy See.

Ballestrero, Anastasio Alberto, O.C.D.: b. Oct. 3, 1913, Genoa, Italy; professed in Order of Discalced Carmelites, 1929; ord. priest June 6, 1936; provincial, 1942-48, and superior general, 1955-67, of Carmelites; author of many books on Christian life; ord. archbishop of Bari, Feb. 2, 1974; archbishop of Turin, Aug. 1, 1977; cardinal June 30, 1979; titular church, S. Maria (sopra Minerva). Archbishop of Turin, president of the Italian Episcopal Conference, 1979, member of:

Congregation: Religious and Secular Institutes;

Commission: Revision of Code of Canon Law.

Baum, William Wakefield: b. Nov. 21, 1926, Dallas, Tex.; moved to Kansas City, Mo., at an early age; ord. priest May 12, 1951; executive director of U.S. bishops commission for ecumenical and interreligious affairs, 1964-69; attended Second Vatican Council as *peritus* (expert adviser); ord. bishop of Springfield-Cape Girardeau, Mo., Apr. 6, 1970; archbishop of Washington, D.C., 1973-80; cardinal May 24, 1976; titular church, Holy Cross (on the Via Flaminia). Prefect of Congregation for Catholic Education, 1980, and member of:

Congregations: Doctrine of the Faith, Bishops;

Secretariat: Non-Christians.

Benelli, Giovanni: b. May 12, 1921, Poggiole, Italy; ord. priest Oct. 31, 1943; entered diplomatic service of Holy See August, 1947, as attaché of secretariat of state; served in apostolic nunciatures in Ireland (1950-53), France (1953-60), Brazil (1960-62), Spain (1962-65); observer of Holy See at UNESCO, 1965-66; ord. titular archbishop of Tusurus, Sept. 11, 1966; pro-nuncio in Senegal and apostolic delegate to Western Africa, 1966-67; under-secretary of state 1967-77; app. archbishop of Florence, June 3, 1977; cardinal June 26, 1977; titular church, St. Prisca. Archbishop of Florence, member of:

Congregations: Bishops, Catholic Education.

Beras Rojas, Octavio: b. Nov. 16, 1906, Seibo, Dominican Republic; ord. priest Aug. 13, 1933; founded national Catholic youth movement; ord. titular archbishop of Euchaitae and coadjutor archbishop of Santo Domingo, Aug. 12, 1945; archbishop of Santo Domingo, Dec. 10, 1961; cardinal May 24, 1976; titular church, San Sisto. Archbishop of Santo Domingo, military vicar of Dominican Republic, member of:

Congregation: Bishops.

Bertoli, Paolo: b. Feb. 1, 1908, Poggio Garfagnana, Italy; ord. priest Aug. 15, 1930; entered diplomatic service of the Holy See, serving in nunciatures in Yugoslavia, France, Haiti and Switzerland; ord. titular archbishop of Nicomedia, May 11, 1952; apostolic delegate to Turkey (1952-53), nuncio to Colombia (1953-59), Lebanon (1959-60), France (1960-69); cardinal Apr. 28, 1969; prefect of Congregation for Causes of Saints, 1969-73; entered order of cardinal bishops as titular bishop of Frascati, 1979. Chamberlain (Cam-

erlengo) of Holy Roman Church, 1979, member of:

Council for Public Affairs of Church:

Congregations: Bishops, Oriental Churches, Evangelization of Peoples;

Tribunal; Apostolic Signatura;

Commissions: Revision of Code of Canon Law, Latin America, State of Vatican City.

Brandao Vilela, Avelar: b. June 13, 1912, Vicosa, Brazil; ord. priest Oct. 27, 1935; professor and spiritual director at diocesan seminary at Aracaju; ord. bishop of Petrolina, Oct. 27, 1946; archbishop of Teresina, Nov. 5, 1955; established 20 social centers and a radio station; introduced agrarian reform of church properties; erected the Institute of Catechetics: archbishop of Sao Salvador da Bahia, Mar. 25, 1971; president of CELAM, 1967-72; co-president of Medellin Conference, 1968; cardinal Mar. 5, 1973; titular church, Sts. Boniface and Alexius. Archbishop of Sao Salvador da Bahia, member of:

Congregations: Clergy, Causes of Saints, Catholic Education:

Commission: Latin America.

Bueno y Monreal, Jose Maria: b. Sept. 11, 1904, Zaragoza, Spain; ord. priest Mar. 19, 1927; ord. bishop of Jaca, Mar. 19, 1946; bishop of Vitoria, May 13, 1950; titular archbishop of Antioch in Pisidia and coadjutor archbishop of Seville, Oct. 27, 1954; archbishop of Seville, Apr. 8, 1957; cardinal Dec. 15, 1958; titular church, Sts. Vitus, Modesuts and Crescentia. Archbishop of Seville.

Caprio, Giuseppe: b. Nov. 15, 1914, Lapio, Italy; ord. priest Dec. 17, 1938; served in diplomatic missions in China (1947-51, when Vatican diplomats were expelled by communists), Belgium (1951-54), and South Vietnam (1954-56); internuncio in China with residence at Taiwan, 1959-67; ord. titular archbishop of Apollonia, Dec. 17, 1961; pro-nuncio in India, 1967-69; secretary of Administration of Patrimony of Holy See, 1969-77; substitute secretary of state, 1977-79; cardinal June 30, 1979; deacon, St. Mary in Via Tuscolana. President of Administration of Patrimony of Holy See, 1979, member of:

Congregation: Evangelization of Peoples:

Commission: Revision of Code of Canon Law.

Carberry, John J.: b. July 31, 1904, Brooklyn, N.Y.; ord. priest July 28, 1929; ord. titular bishop of Elis and coadjutor bishop of Lafayette, Ind., July 25, 1956; bishop of Lafayette, Nov. 20, 1957; bishop of Columbus, Jan. 16, 1965; archbishop of St. Louis, 1968-79; cardinal Apr. 28, 1969; titular church, St. John the Baptist (de Rossi). Former archbishop of St. Louis, member of:

Congregation: Evangelization of Peoples.

Carpino, Francesco: b. May 18, 1905, Palazzolo Acreide, Italy; ord. priest Aug. 14, 1927; ord. titular archbishop of Nicomedia and coadjutor archbishop of Monreale, Apr.

8, 1951; archbishop of Monreale, 1951-61; titular archbishop of Sardica, Jan. 19, 1961; assessor of Sacred Consistorial Congregation, 1961; pro-prefect of Sacred Congregation of the Council, Apr. 7, 1967; cardinal June 26, 1967; archbishop of Palermo, 1967-70; entered order of cardinal bishops as titular bishop of Albano, Jan. 27, 1978. Former archbishop of Palermo, referendary of the Congregation of Bishops, 1970, and member of:
Council for Public Affairs of the Church;
Congregations: Causes of Saints;
Tribunal: Apostolic Signatura.

Carter, Gerald Emmett: b. Mar. 1, 1912, Montreal, Canada; ord. priest May 22, 1937; engaged in pastoral and teaching ministry in Montreal; founder and president of St. Joseph Teachers' College and co-founder and director of Thomas More Institute for adult education; ord. titular bishop of Altiburo and auxiliary bishop of London, Ont., Feb. 2, 1962; bishop of London, 1964-78; vice president, 1971-73, and president, 1975-77, of Canadian Conference of Catholic Bishops; archbishop of Toronto, Apr. 27, 1978; cardinal June 30, 1979; titular church, St. Mary (in Traspontina). Archbishop of Toronto, member of:
Secretariats: Christian Unity, Non-Christians.

Casariego, Mario, C.R.S.: b. Feb. 13, 1909, Figueras de Castropol, Spain; ord. priest July 19, 1936; ord. titular bishop of Pudenziana and auxiliary bishop of Guatemala, Dec. 27, 1958; titular archbishop of Perge and coadjutor archbishop of Guatemala, Nov. 12, 1963; archbishop of Guatemala, Dec. 12, 1964; cardinal Apr. 28, 1969; titular church, St. Mary in Aquiro. Archbishop of Guatemala, member of:
Congregation: Causes of Saints.

Casaroli, Agostino: b. Nov. 24, 1914, Castel San Giovanni, Italy; ord. priest May 27, 1937; entered service of Vatican secretariat of state, 1940; undersecretary, 1961-67, of the Sacred Congregation for Extraordinary Ecclesiastical Affairs, and secretary, 1967-79, of its successor the Council for Public Affairs of the Church; chief negotiator for the Vatican with East European communist governments; missions included visits to Hungary, Yugoslavia, Poland, Czechoslovakia, Bulgaria; headed Vatican delegations to several UN conferences and the Helsinki Conference (1975); ord. titular archbishop of Cartagina, July 16, 1967; cardinal June 30, 1979; titular church, the Twelve Apostles. Secretary of State, 1979, prefect of Council for Public Affairs of the Church, 1979, president of pontifical commission for Vatican City and member of:
Congregations: Doctrine of the Faith, Bishops;
Commissions: Institute for Works of Religion; Revision of Code of Canon Law.

Cé, Marco: b. July 8, 1925, Izano, Italy;

ord. priest Mar. 27, 1948; taught sacred scripture and dogmatic theology at seminary in his home diocese of Crema; rector of seminary, 1957; presided over diocesan liturgical commission, preached youth retreats; ord. titular bishop of Vulturia, May 17, 1970; auxiliary bishop of Bologna, 1970-76; general ecclesiastical assistant of Italian Catholic Action, 1976-78; patriarch of Venice, Dec. 7, 1978; cardinal June 30, 1979; titular church, St. Mark. Patriarch of Venice, member of:
Congregations: Clergy, Catholic Education.

Ciappi, Mario Luigi, O.P.: b. Oct. 6, 1909, Florence, Italy; ord. priest Mar. 26, 1932; papal theologian from 1955, serving Pius XII, John XXIII and Paul VI; ord. titular bishop of Misenum June 18, 1977; cardinal June 27, 1977; deacon, Our Lady of the Sacred Heart (in Piazza Navona). Pro-theologian of pontifical household, member of:
Congregation: Causes of Saints.

Civardi, Ernesto: b. Oct. 21, 1906, Fossarmato, Italy; ord. priest June 29, 1930; assistant rector of Pontifical Lombard Seminary in Rome; held various curial offices; undersecretary, 1953-67, and secretary, 1967-79, of the Congregation for Bishops (known as the Consistorial Congregation until 1967); ord. titular archbishop of Sardica, July 16, 1967; secretary of College of Cardinals, 1967-79; filled office of secretary at 1978 conclaves which elected Popes John Paul I and John Paul II; cardinal June 30, 1979; deacon, St. Theodore. Member of:
Congregation: Causes of Saints;
Tribunal: Apostolic Signatura.

Cody, John P.: b. Dec. 24, 1907, St. Louis, Mo.; ord. priest Dec. 8, 1931, Rome, Italy; served in Rome, 1932-38; ord. titular bishop of Apollonia and auxiliary bishop of St. Louis, July 2, 1947; coadjutor bishop of St. Joseph, Mo., Jan. 27, 1954; apostolic administrator of St. Joseph, May 9, 1955; coadjutor bishop of Kansas City-St. Joseph, Aug. 29, 1956; bishop of Kansas City-St. Joseph, 1956-61; titular archbishop of Bostra and coadjutor archbishop of New Orleans, Aug. 10, 1961; apostolic administrator of New Orleans, June 1, 1962; archbishop of New Orleans, Nov. 8, 1964; archbishop of Chicago, June 14, 1965; cardinal June 26, 1967; titular church, St. Cecilia. Archbishop of Chicago, member of:
Congregation: Clergy.

Colombo, Giovanni: b. Dec. 6, 1902, Caronno, Italy; ord. priest May 29, 1926; rector of Milan Seminary, 1953; ord. titular bishop of Filippopoli and auxiliary bishop of Milan, Dec. 7, 1960; archbishop of Milan, 1963-80; cardinal Feb. 22, 1965; titular church, Sts. Sylvester and Martin (in Montibus). Former archbishop of Milan, member of:
Congregations: Sacraments and Divine

Worship, Evangelization of Peoples, Catholic Education;

Commission: Revision of Code of Canon Law.

Confalonieri,* Carlo: b. July 25, 1893, Seveso, Italy; ord. priest Mar. 18, 1916; private secretary to Pius XI for 17 years, to Pius XII for two years; ord. archbishop of L'Aquila, May 4, 1941; transferred to titular archbishopric of Nicopoli al Nesto, Feb. 22, 1950; cardinal Dec. 15, 1958; titular bishop of suburban see of Palestrina, Mar. 14, 1972, when he entered order of cardinal bishops, and Ostia, Dec. 12, 1977, when he was named dean of College of Cardinals; prefect of Sacred Congregation for Bishops, 1967-73; subdean of college of cardinals, 1974-77. Archpriest of Patriarchal Liberian Basilica, dean of College of Cardinals, Dec. 12, 1977.

Cooke, Terence J.: b. Mar. 1, 1921, New York, N.Y.; ord. priest Dec. 1, 1945; ord. titular bishop of Summa and auxiliary bishop of New York, Dec. 13, 1965; archbishop of New York, Mar. 2, 1968; military vicar for the U.S.; cardinal Apr. 28, 1969; titular church, Sts. John and Paul. Archbishop of New York, military vicar of U.S., member of:

Congregations: Bishops, Oriental Churches, Evangelization of Peoples;

Commission: Migration and Tourism.

Cooray, Thomas B., O.M.I.: b. Dec. 28, 1901, Periyamulla Negombo, Ceylon (now Sri Lanka); ord. priest June 23, 1929; ord. titular archbishop of Preslavo, Mar. 7, 1946; coadjutor archbishop of Colombo, Sri Lanka, 1946-47; succeeded as archbishop of Colombo, July 26, 1947 (retired 1976); cardinal Feb. 22, 1965; titular church, Sts. Nereus and Achilleus. Former archbishop of Colombo, Sri Lanka, member of:

Commission: Revision of Code of Canon Law.

Cordeiro, Joseph: b. Jan. 19, 1918, Bombay, India; ord. priest Aug. 24, 1946; served in educational and other diocesan posts at Karachi, Pakistan; ord. archbishop of Karachi, Aug. 24, 1958, the first native-born prelate in that see; cardinal Mar. 5, 1973; titular church, St. Andrew Apostle ("de Hortis"). Archbishop of Karachi, member of:

Congregation: Religious and Secular Institutes;

Secretariat: Non-Christians;

Commission: Pontifical Council *Cor Unum.*

Corripio Ahumada, Ernesto: b. June 29, 1919, Tampico, Mexico; ord. priest Oct. 25, 1942, in Rome, where he remained until almost the end of World War II; taught and held various positions in local seminary of Tampico, 1945-50; ord. titular bishop of Zapara and auxiliary bishop of Tampico, Mar. 19, 1953; bishop of Tampico, 1956-67; archbishop of Antequera, 1967-76; archbishop of Pueblo de los Angeles, 1976-77; arch-

bishop of Mexico City and primate of Mexico, July 19, 1977; cardinal June 30, 1979; titular church, Mary Immaculate al Tiburtino. Archbishop of Mexico City, member of:

Congregation: Sacraments and Divine Worship;

Commission: Latin America.

Darmojuwono, Justin: b. Nov. 2, 1914, Godean, Indonesia; ord. priest May 25, 1947; ord. archbishop of Semarang, Apr. 6, 1964; cardinal June 26, 1967; titular church, Most Holy Names of Jesus and Mary. Archbishop of Semarang, military vicar of Indonesia, member of:

Congregation: Sacraments and Divine Worship;

Secretariat: Non-Christians.

De Araujo Sales, Eugenio: b. Nov. 8, 1920, Acari, Brazil; ord. priest Nov. 21, 1943; ord. titular bishop of Tibica and auxiliary bishop of Natal, Aug. 15, 1954; archbishop of Sao Salvador, 1968-71; cardinal Apr. 28, 1969; titular church, St. Gregory VII. Archbishop of Rio de Janeiro (1971), ordinary for Eastern Rite Catholics in Brazil without ordinaries of their own rites, member of:

Congregations: Bishops, Clergy, Evangelization of Peoples;

Commission: Social Communications.

Dearden, John F.: b. Oct. 15, 1907, Valley Falls, R. I.; ord. priest Dec. 8, 1932; ord. titular bishop of Sarepta and coadjutor bishop of Pittsburgh, May 18, 1948; bishop of Pittsburgh, Dec. 22, 1950; archbishop of Detroit, 1950-80; first president of the National Conference of Catholic Bishops and the United States Catholic Conference, 1966-71; cardinal Apr. 28, 1969; titular church, St. Pius X (alla Balduina). Former archbishop of Detroit, member of:

Congregation: Sacraments and Divine Worship.

De Furstenberg, Maximilien: b. Oct. 23, 1904, Heerlen, Netherlands; ord. priest Aug. 9, 1931; ord. titular archbishop of Palto and apostolic delegate to Japan, Apr. 25, 1949; internuncio, 1952, when Japan established diplomatic relations with the Vatican; apostolic delegate to Australia, New Zealand and Oceania, Feb. 11, 1960; nuncio to Portugal, 1962-67; cardinal June 26, 1967; titular church, Most Sacred Heart of Jesus (a Castro Pretorio); prefect of the Congregation for the Oriental Churches, 1969-73. Grand Master of Equestrian Order of Holy Sepulchre of Jerusalem, member of:

Council for Public Affairs of Church;

Congregations: Bishops, Religious and Secular Institutes, Evangelization of Peoples;

Tribunal: Apostolic Signatura;

Commissions: Revision of Code of Canon Law, Interpretation of Decrees of Vatican II, State of Vatican City, Institute for Works of Religion.

Duval, Leon-Etienne: b. Nov. 9, 1903, Chenex, France; ord. priest Dec. 18, 1926; ord. bishop of Constantine, Algeria, Feb. 11, 1947; archbishop of Algiers, Feb. 3, 1954; cardinal Feb. 22, 1965; titular church, St. Balbina. Archbishop of Algiers, member of:

Congregation: Evangelization of Peoples;

Commission: Revision of Code of Canon Law.

Ekandem, Dominic: b. 1917, Ibiono, Nigeria; ord. priest Dec. 7, 1947; ord. titular bishop of Gerapoli di Isauri and auxiliary bishop of Calabar, Feb. 7, 1954, the first Nigerian to become a bishop; first bishop of Ikot Ekpene, Mar. 1, 1963; cardinal May 24, 1976; titular church, San Marcello. Bishop of Ikot Ekpene, member of:

Secretariat: Non-Christians.

Enrique y Tarancon, Vicente: b. May 14, 1907, Burriana, Spain; ord. priest Nov. 1, 1929; ord. bishop of Solsona, Mar. 24, 1946; bishop of Oviedo, Apr. 12, 1964; archbishop of Toledo, 1969-71; cardinal Apr. 28, 1969; titular church, St. John Chrysostom. Archbishop of Madrid, 1971, member of:

Congregation: Bishops;

Commission: Revision of Code of Canon Law.

Etchegaray, Roger: b. Sept. 25, 1922, Espelette, France; ord. priest July 13, 1947; deputy director, 1961-66, and secretary general, 1966-70, of French Episcopal Conference; ord. titular bishop of Gemelle di Numidia and auxiliary bishop of Paris, May 27, 1969; archbishop of Marseilles, Dec. 22, 1970; prelate of Mission de France, Nov. 26, 1975; president of French Episcopal Conference; cardinal June 30, 1979; titular church, St. Leo I. Archbishop of Marseilles, prelate of Mission de France, member of:

Congregation: Catholic Education;

Secretariat: Christian Unity;

Commission: Social Communications.

Felici, Pericle: b. Aug. 1, 1911, Segni, Italy; ord. priest Oct. 28, 1933; rector of Pontifical Roman Seminary for Legal Studies, 1938-48; judge of Roman Rota, 1947; served on antepreparatory commissions of the Second Vatican Council; ord. titular archbishop of Samosata, Oct. 28, 1960; secretary-general of the Second Vatican Council; accompanied Pope Paul VI on his trip to the UN, Oct. 4, 1965; cardinal June 26, 1967; titular church, St. Apollinare. Prefect of Apostolic Signatura, 1977, member of:

Council for Public Affairs of Church;

Congregations: Doctrine of Faith, Bishops, Sacraments and Divine Worship, Causes of Saints;

Commissions: Revision of Code of Canon Law (President), Revision of Oriental Code of Canon Law, Interpretation of Decrees of Vatican II (President);

Offices: Administration of Patrimony of Holy See, Vatican II Archives.

Flahiff, George B., C.S.B.: b. Oct. 26, 1905, Paris, Ont., Canada; ord. priest Aug. 17, 1930; professor of medieval history at the University of Toronto and Pontifical Institute of Medieval Studies in Toronto, 1934-54; superior general of Basilian Fathers, 1954; ord. archbishop of Winnipeg, May 31, 1961; president of Canadian Conference of Bishops, 1963-65; cardinal Apr. 28, 1969; titular church, St. Mary della Salute (Primavalle). Archbishop of Winnipeg, member of:

Congregation: Religious and Secular Institutes.

Florit, Ermenegildo: b. July 5, 1901, Fagagna, Italy; ord. priest Apr. 11, 1925; taught Sacred Scripture at Lateran University from 1929; pro-rector of Lateran University and Institute of Civil and Canon Law, 1951-54; ord. titular archbishop of Hieropolis and coadjutor archbishop of Florence, Sept. 12, 1954; archbishop of Florence, 1962-77; cardinal Feb. 22, 1965; titular church, Queen of the Apostles. Former archbishop of Florence, member of:

Congregation: Causes of Saints;

Commission: Revision of Code of Canon Law.

Freeman, James D.: b. Nov. 19, 1907, Sydney, Australia; ord. priest July 13, 1930; ord. titular bishop of Ermopoli minore and auxiliary of Sydney, Jan. 24, 1957; bishop of Armidale, 1968-71; archbishop of Sydney, July 9, 1971; cardinal Mar. 5, 1973; titular church, St. Mary Queen of Peace. Archbishop of Sydney, member of:

Congregation: Catholic Education.

Gantin, Bernardin: b. May 8, 1922, Toffo, Dahomey (now Benin): ord. priest Jan. 14, 1951; ord. titular bishop of Tipasa di Mauritania and auxiliary bishop of Cotonou, Feb. 3, 1957; archbishop of Cotonou, 1960-71; associate secretary (1971-73) and secretary (1973-75) of Sacred Congregation for Evangelization of Peoples; vice-president (1975) and president (1976) of Pontifical Commission for Justice and Peace; cardinal June 27, 1977; deacon, Sacred Heart of Christ the King. Former archbishop of Cotonou, president of Pontifical Commission for Justice and Peace and the Pontifical Council *Cor Unum*, member of:

Congregations: Causes of Saints, Evangelization of Peoples, Oriental Churches, Religious and Secular Institutes, Catholic Education;

Secretariat: Non-Believers;

Tribunal: Apostolic Signatura;

Commission: Institute for Works of Religion.

Garrone, Gabriel-Marie: b. Oct. 12, 1901, Aix-les-Bains, France; ord. priest Apr. 11, 1925; captain during World War II, cited for bravery, taken prisoner; rector of major seminary of Chambery, 1947; ord. titular archbishop of Lemno and coadjutor of Toulouse,

June 24, 1947; archbishop of Toulouse, 1956-66; titular archbishop of Torri di Numidia and pro-prefect of Congregation of Seminaries and Universities, Mar. 24, 1966; cardinal June 26, 1967; titular church, St. Sabina; prefect of Congregation for Catholic Education, 1968-80. Grand chancellor of the Pontifical Gregorian University, member of:

Council for Public Affairs of Church;

Congregations: Doctrine of Faith, Bishops, Evangelization of Peoples, Causes of Saints, Religious and Secular Institutes;

Commission: Revision of Code of Canon Law.

Gonzalez Martin, Marcelo: b. Jan. 16, 1918, Villanubla, Spain; ord. priest June 29, 1941; taught theology and sociology at Valladolid diocesan seminary; founded organization for construction of houses for poor; ord. bishop of Astorga, Mar. 5, 1961; titular archbishop of Case Mediane and coadjutor of Barcelona, Feb. 21, 1966; archbishop of Barcelona, 1967-71; archbishop of Toledo, Dec. 3, 1971; cardinal Mar. 5, 1973; titular church, St. Augustine. Archbishop of Toledo, member of:

Congregation: Evangelization of Peoples.

Gouyon, Paul: b. Oct. 24, 1910, Bordeaux, France; ord. priest Mar. 13, 1937; ord. bishop of Bayonne, Oct. 7, 1957; titular archbishop of Pessinonte and coadjutor archbishop of Rennes, Sept. 6, 1963; archbishop of Rennes, Sept. 4, 1964; cardinal Apr. 28, 1969; titular church, the Nativity (Via Gallia). Archbishop of Rennes, member of:

Secretariat: Non-Believers.

Gray, Gordon J.: b. Aug. 10, 1910, Edinburgh, Scotland; ord. priest June 15, 1935; ord. archbishop of Saint Andrews and Edinburgh, Sept. 21, 1951; chairman of International Committee for English in the Liturgy; cardinal Apr. 28, 1969; titular church, St. Clare. Archbishop of Saint Andrews and Edinburgh, member of:

Congregations: Evangelization of Peoples, Sacraments and Divine Worship;

Commission: Social Communications.

Guerri, Sergio: b. Dec. 25, 1905, Tarquinia, Italy; ord. priest Mar. 30, 1929; ord. titular archbishop of Trevi, Apr. 27, 1969; cardinal Apr. 28, 1969; titular church, Most Holy Name of Mary. Pro-president of Pontifical Commission for State of Vatican City, member of:

Congregations: Oriental Churches, Evangelization of Peoples.

Guyot, Jean: b. July 7, 1905, Bordeaux, France; ord. priest June 29, 1932; held various offices in Bordeaux diocese; ord. titular bishop of Helenopolis and coadjutor of Constance, May 4, 1949; bishop of Constance, 1950-66; archbishop of Toulouse, 1966-78; invested with Legion of Honor by French government; cardinal Mar. 5, 1973; titular church, Saint Agnes Outside the Walls. Former archbishop of Toulouse, member of:

Congregation: Catholic Education.

Hoeffner, Joseph: b. Dec. 24, 1906, Horhausen, Germany; ord. priest Oct. 30, 1932; ord. bishop of Munster, Sept. 14, 1962; titular archbishop of Aquileia and coadjutor archbishop of Cologne, Jan. 6, 1969; archbishop of Cologne, Feb. 23, 1969; cardinal Apr. 28, 1969; titular church, St. Andrew of the Valley. Archbishop of Cologne, member of:

Congregations: Oriental Churches, Religious and Secular Institutes, Evangelization of Peoples, Catholic Education;

Secretariat: Non-Believers;

Office: Prefecture of Economic Affairs.

Hume, George Basil, O.S.B.: b. Mar. 2, 1923, Newcastle-upon-Tyne, England; began monastic studies at Benedictine Abbey of St. Laurence at Ampleforth, 1941; made solemn perpetual vows as Benedictine, 1945; ord. priest July 23, 1950; abbot of Ampleforth, 1963-76; ord archbishop of Westminster, Mar. 25, 1976; cardinal May 24, 1976; titular church, S. Silvestro (in Capite). Archbishop of Westminster, member of:

Congregation: Religious and Secular Institutes;

Secretariat: Christian Unity.

Jubany Arnau, Narciso: b. Aug. 12, 1913, Santa Coloma de Farnes, Spain; ord. priest July 30, 1939; professor of law at Barcelona seminary; served on ecclesiastical tribunal; ord. titular bishop of Ortosia and auxiliary of Barcelona, Jan. 22, 1956; bishop of Gerona, 1964-71; archbishop of Barcelona, Dec. 3, 1971; cardinal Mar. 5, 1973; titular church, San Lorenzo (in Damaso). Archbishop of Barcelona, member of:

Congregations: Sacraments and Divine Worship, Religious and Secular Institutes;

Secretariat: Non-Christians;

Commission: Revision of Code of Canon Law.

Kim, Stephan Sou Hwan: b. May 8, 1922, Tae Gu, Korea; ord. priest Sept. 15, 1951; ord. bishop of Masan, May 31, 1966; archbishop of Seoul, Apr. 9, 1968; cardinal Apr. 28, 1969; titular church, St. Felix of Cantalice (Centocelle). Archbishop of Seoul, apostolic administrator of Pyeong Yang, member of:

Congregation: Evangelization of Peoples;

Secretariat: Non-Christians.

Knox, James R.: b. Mar. 2, 1914, Bayswater, Australia; ord. priest Dec. 22, 1941, at Rome; forced to remain in Rome because of World War II; chaplain and later vice rector of Pontifical Urban University; secretary of apostolic delegation in Japan; ord. titular archbishop of Melitene, Nov. 8, 1953; apostolic delegate to British Africa, 1953-57; internuncio to India and apostolic delegate to Burma and Ceylon (Sri Lanka), 1957-67; archbishop of Melbourne, Australia, 1967-74; cardinal Mar. 5, 1973; titular church, Santa Maria (in Vallicella). Prefect of

Sacred Congregation for the Sacraments and Divine Worship, 1974, member of:

Council for Public Affairs of Church;

Congregations: Bishops, Oriental Churches, Evangelization of Peoples, Catholic Education;

Commissions: Revision of Code of Canon Law, Interpretation of Decrees of Vatican II, Revision of Oriental Code of Canon Law;

Office: Administration of Patrimony of Holy See.

Koenig, Franz: b. Aug. 3, 1905, Rabenstein, Lower Austria; ord. priest Oct. 28, 1933; ord. titular bishop of Livias and coadjutor bishop of Sankt Poelten, Aug. 31, 1952; archbishop of Vienna, May 10, 1956; cardinal Dec. 15, 1958; titular church, St. Eusebius; president of Secretariat for Non-Believers, 1965-80. Archbishop of Vienna, ordinary for faithful of Byzantine Rite living in Austria, member of:

Congregation: Bishops;

Commission: Revision of Code of Canon Law.

Krol, John J.: b. Oct. 26, 1910, Cleveland, Ohio; ord. priest Feb. 20, 1937; ord. titular bishop of Cadi and auxiliary bishop of Cleveland, Sept. 2, 1953; archbishop of Philadelphia, Feb. 11, 1961, installed Mar. 22, 1961; cardinal June 26, 1967; titular church, St. Mary (della Merced) and St. Adrian Martyr; vice-president, 1966-72, and president, 1972-74, of NCCB/USCC. Archbishop of Philadelphia, member of:

Congregation: Oriental Churches;

Commission: Revision of Code of Canon Law.

Landazuri Ricketts, Juan, O.F.M: b. Dec. 19, 1913, Arequipa, Peru; entered Franciscans, 1933; ord. priest Apr. 16, 1939; ord. titular archbishop of Roina and coadjutor archbishop of Lima, Aug. 24, 1952; archbishop of Lima, May 2, 1955; cardinal Mar. 19, 1962; titular church, St. Mary (in Aracoeli). Archbishop of Lima, member of:

Congregations: Clergy, Religious and Secular Institutes, Catholic Education;

Commission: Revision of Code of Canon Law.

Leger, Paul Emile, S.S.: b. Apr. 26, 1904, Valleyfield, Quebec, Canada; ord. priest May 25, 1929; rector Canadian College, Rome, 1947; ord. archbishop of Montreal, Apr. 26, 1950; cardinal Jan. 12, 1953; titular church, St. Mary (of the Angels); resigned as archbishop of Montreal (Apr. 20, 1968) to become missionary to lepers, retired 1979. Former archbishop of Montreal, member of:

Congregation: Evangelization of Peoples;

Commission: Revision of Code of Canon Law.

Lekai, Laszlo: b. Mar. 12, 1910, Zalalovo, Hungary; ord. priest Oct. 28, 1934; professor of philosophy and dogmatic theology at major seminary at Veszprem; arrested and imprisoned by Nazis during World War II; engaged in pastoral work and held diocesan offices after the war; ord. titular bishop of Girus Tirasii and apostolic administrator of Esztergom, Mar. 16, 1972; archbishop of Esztergom and primate of Hungary, Feb. 12, 1976; cardinal May 24, 1976; titular church, S. Teresa (on the Corso d'Italia). Archbishop of Esztergom, member of:

Congregation: Catholic Education.

Lorscheider, Aloisio, O.F.M.: b. Oct. 8, 1924, Linha Geraldo, Brazil; received in Franciscan Order, Feb. 1, 1942; ord. priest Aug. 22, 1948; professor of theology at the Antonianum, Rome, and director of Franciscan international house of studies; ord. bishop of Santo Angelo, Brazil, May 20, 1962; archbishop of Fortaleza, Mar. 26, 1973; president of CELAM, 1975-79; cardinal May 24, 1976; titular church, S. Pietro (in Montorio). Archbishop of Fortaleza, member of:

Congregations: Religious and Secular Institutes, Clergy;

Secretariat: Non-Christians.

McCann, Owen: b. June 29, 1907, Woodstock, South Africa; ord. priest Dec. 21, 1935; ord. titular bishop of Stettorio and vicar apostolic of Cape Town, May 18, 1950; first archbishop of Cape Town, Jan. 11, 1951; opponent of apartheid policy; cardinal Feb. 22, 1965; titular church, St. Praxedes. Archbishop of Cape Town, member of:

Congregation: Evangelization of Peoples.

Macharski, Franciszek: b. May 20, 1927, Cracow, Poland; ord. priest Apr. 2, 1950; engaged in pastoral work, 1950-56; continued theological studies in Fribourg, Switzerland, 1956-60; taught pastoral theology at the Faculty of Theology in Cracow; app. rector of archdiocesan seminary at Cracow, 1970; ord. archbishop of Cracow, Jan. 6, 1979, by Pope John Paul II; cardinal June 30, 1979; titular church, St. John at the Latin Gate. Archbishop of Cracow, member of:

Congregations: Clergy, Catholic Education.

Malula, Joseph: b. Dec. 12, 1917, Kinshasa, Zaire; ord. priest June 9, 1946; ord. titular bishop of Attanaso and auxiliary bishop of Kinshasa, Sept. 20, 1959; archbishop of Kinshasa. July 7, 1964; cardinal Apr. 28, 1969; titular church, Ss. Protomartyrs (Via Aurelia Antica). Archbishop of Kinshasa, member of:

Congregation: Evangelization of Peoples.

Manning, Timothy: b. Nov. 15, 1909, Ballingeary, Ireland; completed studies for the priesthood at St. Patrick's Seminary, Menlo Park, Calif.; ord. priest June 16, 1934; became American citizen, Jan. 14, 1944; ord. titular bishop of Lesvi and auxiliary of Los Angeles, Oct. 15, 1946; first bishop of Fresno, 1967-69; titular archbishop of Capri and coadjutor of Los Angeles, May 26, 1969; archbishop of Los Angeles, Jan. 21, 1970; cardinal Mar. 5,

1973; titular church, Santa Lucia. Archbishop of Los Angeles, member of:

Congregations: Evangelization of Peoples, Religious and Secular Institutes.

Marella,* Paolo: b. Jan. 25, 1895, Rome, Italy; ord. priest Feb. 23, 1918; aide in Congregation for Propagation of the Faith; on staff of apostolic delegation, Washington, D.C., 1923-33; ord. titular archbishop of Doclea, Oct. 29, 1933; apostolic delegate to Japan, 1933-48, to Australia, New Zealand and Oceania, 1948-53; nuncio to France, 1953-59; cardinal Dec. 14, 1959; entered order of cardinal bishops as titular bishop of Porto and Santa Rufina, Mar. 14, 1972; president of Secretariat for Non-Christians, 1967-73. Archpriest of St. Peter's Basilica, sub-dean of College of Cardinals, 1977, member of:

Commission: Sacred Art in Italy (Honorary President).

Marty, Francois: b. May 18, 1904, Pachins, France; ord. priest June 28, 1930; ord. bishop of Saint-Flour, May 1, 1952; titular archbishop of Emesa and coadjutor archbishop of Rheims, Dec. 14, 1959; archbishop of Rheims, May 9, 1960; archbishop of Paris, Mar. 26, 1968; cardinal Apr. 28, 1969; titular church, St. Louis of France. Archbishop of Paris, ordinary for Eastern Rite Catholics in France without ordinaries of their own rites, member of:

Congregations: Oriental Churches, Clergy, Sacraments and Divine Worship;

Commission: Revision of Code of Canon Law.

Maurer,* Jose Clemente, C.SS.R.: b. Mar. 13, 1900, Puttlingen, Germany; ord. priest Sept. 19, 1925; assigned to Bolivian missions, 1926; became a Bolivian citizen; ord. titular bishop of Cea and auxiliary bishop of La Paz, Apr. 16, 1950; archbishop of Sucre, Oct. 27, 1951; cardinal June 26, 1967; titular church, Most Holy Redeemer and St. Alphonsus. Archbishop of Sucre.

Medeiros, Humberto: b. Oct. 6, 1915, Arrifes, S. Miguel, Azores; came to U.S. at age of 15; became American citizen, 1940; ord. priest June 15, 1946; ord. bishop of Brownsville, Tex., June 9, 1966; archbishop of Boston, Sept. 8, 1970; cardinal Mar. 5, 1973; titular church, Santa Susanna. Archbishop of Boston, member of:

Congregations: Bishops, Catholic Education.

Miranda y Gomez,* Miguel Dario: b. Dec. 19, 1895, Leon, Mexico; ord. priest Oct. 28, 1918; ord. bishop of Tulancingo, Dec. 8, 1937; titular archbishop of Selimbra and coadjutor archbishop of Mexico City, Dec. 20, 1955; archbishop of Mexico City, May 28, 1956; served as president of the Latin American Bishops' Council (CELAM); cardinal Apr. 28, 1969; titular church, St. Mary of Guadalupe (Montemario). Former archbishop of Mexico City (resigned 1977).

Motta,* Carlos Carmelo de Vasconcellos: b. July 16, 1890, Bom Jesus do Amparo, Brazil; ord. priest June 29, 1918; ord. titular bishop of Algiza and auxiliary bishop of Diamantina, Oct. 30, 1932; archbishop of Sao Luis do Maranhao, Dec. 19, 1935; archbishop of Sao Paulo del Brasile, 1944-64; cardinal Feb. 18, 1946; titular church, St. Pancratius. Archbishop of Aparecida (1964).

Mozzoni, Umberto: b. June 29, 1904, Buenos Aires, Argentina; holds Italian citizenship; ord. priest Aug. 14, 1927; professor of theology and canon law at Macerata seminary, Italy; served on Vatican diplomatic staff in Canada, England and Portugal; ord. titular archbishop of Side, Dec. 5, 1954; nuncio to Bolivia, 1954-58, Argentina, 1958-69, Brazil, 1969-73; cardinal Mar. 5, 1973; deacon, St. Eugene. Member of:

Congregations: Oriental Churches, Clergy, Religious and Secular Institutes, Evangelization of Peoples, Causes of Saints;

Tribunal: Apostolic Signatura;

Commissions: Sanctuaries of Pompei and Loreto (President), Institute for Works of Religion.

Munoz Duque, Anibal: b. Oct. 3, 1908, Santa Rosa de Osos, Colombia; ord. priest Nov. 19, 1933; ord. bishop of Soccoro y San Gil, May 27, 1951; bishop of Bucaramango, 1952-59; archbishop of Nueva Pamplona, 1959-68; titular archbishop of Cariana and coadjutor archbishop of Bogota, 1968; archbishop of Bogota, July 29, 1972; cardinal Mar. 5, 1973; titular church, St. Bartholomew. Archbishop of Bogota, military vicar, member of:

Congregation: Sacraments and Divine Worship.

Munoz Vega, Pablo, S. J.: b. May 23, 1903, Mira, Ecuador; ord. priest July 25, 1933; ord. titular bishop of Ceramo and auxiliary bishop of Quito, Mar. 19, 1964; archbishop of Quito, June 23, 1967; cardinal Apr. 28, 1969; titular church, St. Robert Bellarmine. Archbishop of Quito, member of:

Congregation: Religious and Secular Institutes.

Nasalli Rocca di Corneliano, Mario: b. Aug. 12, 1903, Piacenza, Italy; ord. priest Apr. 9, 1927; ord. titular archbishop of Anzio, Apr. 20, 1969; cardinal Apr. 28, 1969; titular church, St. John the Baptist. Member of:

Congregations: Sacraments and Divine Worship, Causes of Saints;

Secretariat: Non-Believers.

Nsubuga, Emmanuel: b. Nov. 5, 1914, Kisule, Uganda; ord. priest Dec. 15, 1946; ord. bishop of Kampala, Oct. 30, 1966; cardinal May 24, 1976; titular church, S. Maria Nuova. Archbishop of Kampala, member of:

Congregation: Evangelization of Peoples.

O'Boyle,* Patrick A.: b. July 18, 1896,

Scranton, Pa.; ord. priest May 21, 1921; executive director of War Relief Services, NCWC, 1943; ord. archbishop of Washington, Jan. 14, 1948 (retired, 1973); cardinal June 26, 1967; titular church, St. Nicholas (in Carcere). Former archbishop of Washington.

Oddi, Silvio: b. Nov. 14, 1910, Morfasso, Italy; ord. priest May 21, 1933; ord. titular archbishop of Mesembria, Sept. 27, 1953; served in Vatican diplomatic corps, 1953-69; apostolic delegate to Jerusalem, Palestine, Jordan and Cyprus, internuncio to the United Arab Republic, and nuncio to Belgium and Luxembourg; cardinal Apr. 28, 1969; titular church, St. Agatha of the Goths. Pontifical legate for Patriarchal Basilica of St. Francis of Assisi, prefect of Sacred Congregation for the Clergy, 1979, member of:
Council for Public Affairs of Church;
Congregations: Bishops, Oriental Churches, Causes of Saints, Evangelization of Peoples;
Tribunal: Apostolic Signatura;
Commissions: State of Vatican City, Sanctuaries of Pompei and Loreto.

O'Fiaich, Tomas: b. Nov. 3, 1923; Crossmaglen, Ireland; ord. priest July 6, 1948; lecturer, 1953, and professor, 1959, of modern history at Maynooth College; vice president, 1970, and president, 1974, of Maynooth; prolific author of scholarly works; recognized authority on early Irish Christianity; ord. archbishop of Armagh and primate of All Ireland, Oct. 2, 1977; pledged to work for the cause of peace in Northern Ireland; outspoken in his condemnation of violence; president of Irish Episcopal Conference; cardinal June 30, 1979; titular church, St. Patrick. Archbishop of Armagh, primate of All Ireland, member of:
Congregations: Clergy, Catholic Education;
Secretariat: Christian Unity.

Otunga, Maurice: b. January, 1923, Chebukwa, Kenya; son of pagan tribal chief; baptized 1935, at age of 12; ord. priest Oct. 3, 1950, at Rome; taught at Kisumu major seminary for three years; attaché in apostolic delegation at Mombasa, 1953-56; ord. titular bishop of Tacape and auxiliary of Kisumu, Feb. 25, 1957; bishop of Kisii, 1960-69; titular archbishop of Bomarzo and coadjutor of Nairobi, Nov. 15, 1969; archbishop of Nairobi, Oct. 24, 1971; cardinal Mar. 5, 1973; titular church, St. Gregory Barbarigo. Archbishop of Nairobi, member of:
Congregations: Sacraments and Divine Worship, Religious and Secular Institutes.

Palazzini, Pietro: b. May 19, 1912, Piobbico, Pesaro, Italy; ord. priest Dec. 6, 1934; assistant vice-rector of Pontifical Major Roman Seminary and vice-rector and bursar of Pontifical Roman Seminary for Juridical Studies; professor of moral theology at Lateran University; held various offices in Roman Curia; secretary of Congregation of Council (now Clergy), 1958-73; ord. titular archbishop of Caesarea in Cappadocia, Sept. 21, 1962; author of numerous works on moral theology and law; cardinal Mar. 5, 1973; deacon, St. Jerome. Prefect of Congregation for Causes of Saints, 1980, member of:
Congregations: Oriental Churches, Clergy, Causes of Saints;
Tribunal: Apostolic Signatura;
Commissions: Revision of Code of Canon Law, Interpretation of Decrees of Vatican II.

Pappalardo, Salvatore: b. Sept. 23, 1918, Villafranca Sicula, Sicily; ord. priest Apr. 12, 1941; entered diplomatic service of secretariat of state, 1947; ord. titular archbishop of Miletus, Jan. 16, 1966; pro-nuncio in Indonesia, 1966-69; president of Pontifical Ecclesiastical Academy, 1969-70; archbishop of Palermo, Oct. 17, 1970; cardinal Mar. 5, 1973; titular church, St. Mary Odigitria of the Sicilians. Archbishop of Palermo, member of:
Congregations: Oriental Churches, Clergy.

Parecattil, Joseph: b. Apr. 1, 1912, Kidangoor, India; ord. priest Aug. 24, 1939; ord. titular bishop of Aretusa for Syrians and auxiliary bishop of Ernakulam, Nov. 30, 1953; archbishop of Ernakulam (Chaldean-Malabar Rite), July 20, 1956; vice-president of the Indian Bishops' Conference, 1966; appointed one of seven members of Pope Paul VI's advisory council for Eastern Rite churches, 1968; cardinal Apr. 28, 1969; titular church, Our Lady Queen of Peace. Archbishop of Ernakulam of the Chaldean-Malabar Rite, member of:
Congregation: Oriental Churches;
Secretariat: Non-Christians;
Commissions: Revision of Code of Canon Law, Revision of Oriental Code of Canon Law (President).

Parente,* Pietro: b. Feb. 16, 1891, Casalnuovo, Monterotaro, Italy; ord. priest Mar. 18, 1916; director of Archiepiscopal Seminary at Naples, 1916-26; rector of Pontifical Urban College of Propagation of the Faith, 1934-38; Consultor of the Congregations of the Holy Office, Council, Propagation of the Faith, and Seminaries and Universities; ord. archbishop of Perugia, Oct. 23, 1955; titular archbishop of Tolemaide di Tebaide, Oct. 23, 1959; assessor (1959-65) and secretary (1965-67) of Congregation of Holy Office (now Doctrinal Congregation); cardinal June 26, 1967; titular church, St. Lawrence (in Lucina).

Paupini, Giuseppe: b. Feb. 25, 1907, Mondavio, Italy; ord. priest Mar. 19, 1930; ord. titular archbishop of Sebastopolis in Abasgia, Feb. 26, 1956; served in Vatican diplomatic corps, 1956-69; internuncio to Iran, 1956-57; nuncio to Guatemala and El Salvador, 1957-58, nuncio to Colombia, 1959-69; cardinal Apr. 28, 1969; titular church, All Saints Church. Major penitentiary 1973, member of:
Congregation: Causes of Saints;
Commission: State of Vatican City.

Pellegrino, Michele: b. Apr. 25, 1903, Centallo, Italy; ord. priest Sept. 19, 1925; ord.

archbishop of Turin, Oct. 17, 1965 (resigned 1977); cardinal June 26, 1967; titular church, Most Holy Name of Jesus. Former archbishop of Turin, member of:

Congregation: Catholic Education.

Philippe, Pierre Paul, O.P.: b. Apr. 16, 1905, Paris, France; entered Dominican Order, 1926; ord. priest July 6, 1932; professor at Angelicum, Rome, from 1935; founded Institute of Spirituality for masters of novices at Angelicum, 1950, and school for mistresses of novices, 1953; apostolic visitor of various religious institutes, 1951-56; commissary of the Holy Office, 1955; consultor of various pontifical commissions and congregations from 1958; secretary of Congregation for Religious, 1959; ord. titular archbishop of Heracleopolis Magna, Sept. 21, 1962; secretary of Congregation for Doctrine of Faith, 1967-73; cardinal Mar. 5, 1973; deacon, St. Pius V; prefect of Congregation for Oriental Churches, 1973-80. Member of:

Congregations: Religious and Secular Institutes, Evangelization of Peoples;

Secretariat: Christian Unity;

Commissions: Revision of Code of Canon Law, Revision of Oriental Code of Canon Law.

Picachy, Lawrence Trevor, S.J.: b. Aug. 7, 1916, Lebong, India; ord. priest Nov. 21, 1947; dean, 1950-54, and then rector, 1954-60, of St. Francis Xavier University College, Calcutta; ord. bishop of Jamshedpur, Sept. 9, 1962; archbishop of Calcutta, May 29, 1969; cardinal May 24, 1976; titular church, Sacred Heart of Mary. Archbishop of Calcutta, president of Indian Episcopal Conference, 1975, member of:

Congregation: Evangelization of Peoples.

Pironio, Eduardo: b. Dec. 3, 1920, Nueve de Julio, Argentina; ord. priest Dec. 5, 1943; taught theology at Pius XII Seminary of Mercedes diocese, 1944-59; vicar general of diocese 1958-60; attended Second Vatican Council as *peritus*; ord. titular bishop of Ceciri, May 31, 1964; apostolic administrator of diocese of Avellaneda, 1967-72; secretary general 1967-72, and president, 1973-75, of CELAM; bishop of Mar del Plata, 1972-75; titular archbishop of Thiges and pro-prefect of Sacred Congregation for Religious and Secular Institutes, Sept. 20, 1975; cardinal May 24, 1976; deacon, Sts. Cosmas and Damian. Prefect of the Sacred Congregation for Religious and Secular Institutes, 1976, member of:

Council for Public Affairs of the Church.

Congregations: Bishops, Sacraments and Divine Worship, Catholic Education, Oriental Churches;

Commissions: Council for the Laity, Revision of Code of Canon Law, Latin America, Interpretation of Decrees of Vatican II.

Poletti, Ugo: b. Apr. 19, 1914, Omegna, Italy; ord. priest June 29, 1938; served in various diocesan offices at Novara; ord. titular bishop of Medeli and auxiliary of Novaro, Sept. 14, 1958; president of Pontifical Mission Aid Society for Italy, 1964-67; archbishop of Spoleto, 1967-69; titular archbishop of Cittanova, 1969; served as second viceregent of Rome, 1969-72; pro-vicar general of Rome, 1972, following the sudden death of Cardinal Dell'Acqua; cardinal Mar. 5, 1973; titular church, Sts. Ambrose and Charles. Vicar general of Rome, 1973, archpriest of Patriarchal Lateran Archbasilica, 1973, grand chancellor of Lateran University, member of:

Congregations: Clergy, Sacraments and Divine Worship, Oriental Churches, Religious and Secular Institutes;

Commission: Council for the Laity.

Poma, Antonio: b. June 12, 1910, Villanterio, Italy; ord. priest Apr. 15, 1933; ord. titular bishop of Tagaste and auxiliary bishop of Mantova, Dec. 9, 1951; bishop of Mantova, Sept. 8, 1954; titular archbishop of Gerpiniano and coadjutor archbishop of Bologna, July 16, 1967; archbishop of Bologna, Feb. 12, 1968; cardinal Apr. 28, 1969; titular church, St. Luke (al Prenestino). Archbishop of Bologna, member of:

Congregations: Clergy, Catholic Education.

Primatesta, Raul Francisco: b. Apr. 14, 1919, Capilla del Senor, Argentina; ord. priest Oct. 25, 1942, at Rome; taught at minor and major seminaries of La Plata; contributed to several theology reviews; ord. titular bishop of Tanais and auxiliary of La Plata, Aug. 15, 1957; bishop of San Rafael, 1961-65; archbishop of Cordoba, Feb. 16, 1965; cardinal Mar. 5, 1973; titular church, St. Mary Sorrowful Virgin. Archbishop of Cordoba, Argentina, member of:

Congregations: Bishops, Religious and Secular Institutes, Sacraments and Divine Worship.

Quintero, Jose Humberto: b. Sept. 22, 1902, Mucuchies, Venezuela; ord. priest Aug. 22, 1926; ord. titular archbishop of Acrida and coadjutor archbishop of Merida, Dec. 6, 1953; archbishop of Caracas 1960-80; cardinal Jan. 16, 1961; titular church, Sts. Andrew and Gregory (al Monte Celio). Former archbishop of Caracas.

Ratzinger, Joseph: b. Apr. 16, 1927, Marktl am Inn, Germany; ord. priest June 29, 1951; professor of dogmatic theology at University of Regensburg, 1969-77; member of International Theological Commission; ord. archbishop of Munich-Freising, May 28, 1977; cardinal June 27, 1977; titular church, St. Mary of Consolation (in Tiburtina). Archbishop of Munich-Freising, member of:

Secretariat: Christian Unity;

Commission: International Theological.

Razafimahatratra, Victor, S.J.: b. Sept. 8, 1921, Ambanitsilena-Ranomasina, Madagascar; entered Society of Jesus, 1945; ord. priest July 28, 1956; rector of Fianarantsoa Minor Seminary, 1960-63; superior of Jesuit residence at Ambositra, 1963-69; rector of Tananarive Major Seminary, 1969-71; ord. bishop of

Farafangana, Apr. 18, 1971; archbishop of Tananarive, Apr. 10, 1976; cardinal May 24, 1976; titular church, Holy Cross in Jerusalem. Archbishop of Tananarive, president of Madagascar Episcopal Conference, member of:

Congregation: Evangelization of Peoples.

Renard, Alexandre C.: b. June 7, 1906, Avelin, France; ord. priest July 12, 1931; ord. bishop of Versailles, Oct. 19, 1953; archbishop of Lyons, May 28, 1967; cardinal June 26, 1967; titular church, Most Holy Trinity (at Monte Pincio). Archbishop of Lyons, member of:

Congregations: Religious and Secular Institutes, Evangelization of Peoples.

Ribeiro, Antonio: b. May 21, 1928, Gandarela di Basto, Portugal; ord. priest July 5, 1953; professor of fundamental theology at major seminary at Braga; ord. titular bishop of Tigillava and auxiliary of Braga, Sept. 17, 1967; patriarch of Lisbon, May 10, 1971; cardinal Mar. 5, 1973; titular church, St. Anthony of Padua (in Rome). Patriarch of Lisbon, military vicar, member of:

Congregation: Catholic Education;
Commission: Social Communications.

Righi-Lambertini, Egano: b. Feb. 22, 1906, Casalecchio di Reno, Italy; ord. priest May 25, 1929; entered service of secretariat of state, 1939; served in diplomatic missions in France (1949-54), Costa Rica (1955), England (1955-57); first apostolic delegate to Korea, 1957-60; ord. titular archbishop of Doclea, Oct. 28, 1960; apostolic nuncio in Lebanon, 1960-63, Chile, 1963-67, Italy, 1967-69; France, 1969-79; while nuncio in France he also served as special envoy at the Council of Europe, 1974-79; cardinal June 30, 1979; deacon, St. John Bosco in Via Tuscolana. Member of:

Council for Public Affairs of the Church;
Congregation: Bishops;
Secretariat: Non-Christians.

Rosales, Julio: b. Sept. 18, 1906, Calbayog, Philippines; ord. priest June 2, 1929; ord. bishop of Tagbilaran, Sept. 21, 1946; archbishop of Cebu, Dec. 17, 1949; cardinal Apr. 28, 1969; titular church, Sacred Heart of Jesus (a Vitinia). Archbishop of Cebu, member of:

Congregation: Clergy;
Commission: Revision of Code of Canon Law.

Rossi, Agnelo: b. May 4, 1913, Joaquim Egidio, Brazil; ord. priest Mar. 27, 1937; ord. bishop of Barra do Pirai, Apr. 15, 1956; archbishop of Ribeirao Preto, 1962-64; archbishop of Sao Paulo, 1964-70; cardinal Feb. 22, 1965; titular church, Mother of God. Prefect of Congregation for Evangelization of Peoples, 1970, grand chancellor of Pontifical Urban University, member of:

Council for Public Affairs of Church;
Congregations: Clergy, Doctrine of Faith, Bishops, Oriental Churches, Causes of Saints,

Religious and Secular Institutes, Catholic Education;

Secretariats: Christian Unity, Non-Christians;

Commissions: Revision of Code of Canon Law, Revision of Oriental Code of Canon Law, Institute for Works of Religion.

Rossi, Opilio: b. May 14, 1910, New York, N.Y.; holds Italian citizenship; ord. priest for diocese of Piacenza, Italy, Mar. 11, 1933; served in nunciatures in Belgium, The Netherlands and Germany, 1938-53; ord. titular archbishop of Ancyra, Dec. 27, 1953; nuncio in Ecuador, 1953-59, Chile, 1959-61, Austria, 1961-76; cardinal May 24, 1976; deacon, S. Maria Liberatrice (on the Monte Testaccio). Member of:

Council for Public Affairs of the Church;
Congregations: Bishops, Oriental Churches, Sacraments and Divine Worship, Religious and Secular Institutes, Evangelization of Peoples;

Commissions: Council for Laity (President), Committee for Family (President).

Roy, Maurice: b. Jan. 25, 1905, Quebec, Canada; ord. priest June 12, 1927; chief of chaplains of Canadian Armed Forces during World War II; ord. bishop of Trois Rivieres, May 1, 1946; military vicar, June 8, 1946; archbishop of Quebec, June 2, 1947; primate of Canada, Jan. 25, 1956; cardinal Feb. 22, 1965; titular church, Our Lady of the Most Holy Sacrament and the Holy Canadian Martyrs. Archbishop of Quebec, primate of Canada, military vicar of Canada, member of:

Congregations: Clergy, Catholic Education;

Commission: Revision of Code of Canon Law.

Rubin, Wladyslaw: b. Sept. 20, 1917, Toki, Poland; seminary studies interrupted during World War II when he was arrested and deported to labor camp; completed studies at St. Joseph's University in Beirut; ord. priest in Beirut June 30, 1946 and served Polish community there; sent to Rome for further studies, 1949; chaplain for Polish refugees in Italy, 1953-58; rector of Polish College in Rome, 1959-64; ord. titular bishop of Serta, primate of Poland's delegate for emigration and auxiliary of Gniezno, Nov. 29, 1964; established contact with Polish emigrants throughout the world; secretary general of Synod of Bishops, 1967-79; cardinal June 30, 1979; deacon, St. Mary in Via Lata. Prefect of Congregation for Oriental Churches, 1980, member of:

Congregations: Doctrine of the Faith, Causes of Saints;

Tribunal: Apostolic Signatura;

Commission: Interpretation of Decrees of Vatican II.

Rugambwa, Laurean: b. July 12, 1912, Bukongo, Tanzania; ord. priest Dec. 12,

1943; ord. titular bishop of Febiano and vicar apostolic of Lower Kagera, Feb. 10, 1952; bishop of Rutabo, Mar. 25, 1953; cardinal Mar. 28, 1960; titular church, St. Francis of Assisi (a Ripa); bishop of Bukoba, 1960-68. Archbishop of Dar-es-Salaam, 1968, member of:
Congregation: Causes of Saints;
Commission: Revision of Code of Canon Law.

Salazar Lopez, Jose: b. Jan. 12, 1910, Ameca, Mexico; ord. priest May 26, 1934, in Rome; instrumental in building of new seminary at Guadalajara, the largest in Mexico; vice-rector and later rector of seminary; ord. titular bishop of Prusiade and coadjutor bishop of Zamora, Aug. 20, 1961; bishop of Zamora, 1967-70; archbishop of Guadalajara, Feb. 21, 1970; cardinal Mar. 5, 1973; titular church, Santa Emerentia. Archbishop of Guadalajara, member of:
Congregations: Sacraments and Divine Worship, Clergy.

Samore, Antonio: b. Dec. 4, 1905, Bardi, Italy; ord. priest June 10, 1928; served in apostolic nunciatures at Lithuania and Switzerland; worked in Vatican secretariat of state during World War II; assigned to apostolic delegation in Washington, D.C., 1947; nuncio to Colombia, 1950; ord. titular archbishop of Tirnovo, Apr. 16, 1950; secretary of Congregation of Extraordinary Ecclesiastical Affairs, 1953-67; cardinal June 26, 1967; entered order of cardinal bishops as titular bishop of Sabina and Poggia Mirteto, Dec. 12, 1974; prefect of Congregation for Discipline of Sacraments, 1968-74. Librarian and archivist of Holy Roman Church, 1974, member of:
Council for Public Affairs of Church;
Congregations: Oriental Churches, Bishops, Evangelization of Peoples;
Commission: Revision of Code of Canon Law.

Satowaki, Joseph Asajiro: b. Feb. 1, 1904, Shittsu, Japan; ord. priest Dec. 17, 1932; served in various pastoral capacities in Nagasaki archdiocese after his ordination; apostolic administrator of Taiwan (then a Japanese possession), 1941-45; director of Nagasaki minor seminary, 1945-57; vicar general of Nagasaki, 1945; ord. first bishop of Kagoshima, May 3, 1955; archbishop of Nagasaki, Dec. 19, 1968; president of Japanese Episcopal Conference, 1979-   ; cardinal June 30, 1979; titular church, St. Mary of Peace. Archbishop of Nagasaki, member of:
Congregation: Evangelization of Peoples;
Secretariat: Non-Christians.

Scherer, Alfred Vicente: b. Feb. 5, 1903, Bom Principio, Brazil; ord. priest Apr. 3, 1926; ord. archbishop of Porto Alegre, Feb. 23, 1947; cardinal Apr. 28, 1969; titular church, Our Lady of La Salette. Archbishop of Porto Alegre, Brazil.

Schroeffer, Joseph: b. Feb. 20, 1903, Ingolstadt, Germany; ord. priest Oct. 28, 1928; studied at the Gregorian University, Rome, 1922-31; returned to Germany 1931; professor at Higher Institute for Philosophical and Theological Studies at Eichstatt; vicar general of diocese of Eichstatt, 1941-48; ord. bishop of Eichstatt, Sept. 21, 1948; app. titular archbishop of Volturnum and secretary of Sacred Congregation for Catholic Education, 1968; cardinal May 24, 1976; deacon, San Saba. Member of:
Council for Public Affairs of the Church;
Congregations: Doctrine of the Faith, Bishops;
Tribunal: Apostolic Signatura;
Commissions: Council for Laity, Revision of Code of Canon Law;
Office: Administration of Patrimony of Holy See.

Sensi, Giuseppe Maria: b. May 27, 1907, Cosenza, Italy; ord. priest Dec. 21, 1929; entered Vatican diplomatic service; served in nunciatures in Hungary, Switzerland, Belgium and Czechoslovakia, 1934-49; ord. titular archbishop of Sardes, July 24, 1955; apostolic nuncio to Costa Rica, 1955; apostolic delegate to Jerusalem, 1956-62; nuncio to Ireland, 1962-67, and Portugal, 1967-76; cardinal May 24, 1976; deacon, SS. Biagio e Carlo (ai Catinari). Member of:
Congregations: Oriental Churches, Evangelization of Peoples;
Office: Prefecture of Economic Affairs.

Seper, Franjo: b. Oct. 2, 1905, Osijek, Yugoslavia; ord. priest Oct. 26, 1930; secretary of Cardinal Stepinac, 1934-41; rector of Zagreb's major seminary, 1941-51; ord. titular archbishop of Filippopoli and coadjutor archbishop of Zagreb, Sept. 21, 1954; archbishop of Zagreb, 1960-69; cardinal Feb. 22, 1965; titular church, Sts. Peter and Paul (in Via Ostia). Prefect of Congregation for Doctrine of the Faith, 1968, member of:
Council for Public Affairs of Church;
Congregations: Bishops, Sacraments and Divine Worship, Catholic Education;
Commissions: Biblical (President), Theological (President), Revision of Code.

Shehan,* Lawrence J.: b. Mar. 18, 1898, Baltimore, Md.; ord. priest Dec. 23, 1922; ord. titular bishop of Lidda and auxiliary bishop of Baltimore and Washington, Dec. 12, 1945; bishop of Bridgeport, 1953-61; titular archbishop of Nicopolis ad Nestum and coadjutor archbishop of Baltimore, July 10, 1961; archbishop of Baltimore, 1961-74; cardinal Feb. 22, 1965; titular church, St. Clement. Former archbishop of Baltimore.

Sidarouss, Stephanos I, C.M.: b. Feb. 22, 1904, Cairo, Egypt; ord. priest July 2, 1939; ord. titular bishop of Sais, Jan. 25, 1948; auxiliary to the patriarch of Alexandria for the Copts, 1948-58; patriarch of Alexandria, May 10, 1958; cardinal Feb. 22, 1965. Patriarch of

Alexandria for the Copts, member of:
　Congregation: Oriental Churches;
　Secretariat: Christian Unity;
　Commissions: Revision of Code of Canon Law, Revision of Code of Oriental Canon Law.

Silva Henriquez, Raul, S.D.B.: b. Sept. 27, 1907, Talca, Chile; ord. priest July 3, 1938; ord. bishop of Valparaiso, Nov. 29, 1959; archbishop of Santiago de Chile, Mar. 14, 1961; cardinal Mar. 19, 1962; titular church, St. Bernard (alle Terme). Archbishop of Santiago de Chile, member of:
　Commission: Revision of Code of Canon Law.

Sin, Jaime L.: b. Aug. 31, 1928, New Washington, Philippines; ord. priest Apr. 3, 1954; diocesan missionary in Capiz, 1954-57; app. first rector of the St. Pius X Seminary, Roxas City, 1957; ord. titular bishop of Obba and auxiliary bishop of Jaro, Mar. 18, 1967; apostolic administrator of archdiocese of Jaro, June 20, 1970; titular archbishop of Massa Lubrense and coadjutor archbishop of Jaro, Jan. 15, 1972; archbishop of Jaro, Oct. 8, 1972; archbishop of Manila, Jan. 21, 1974; cardinal May 24, 1976; titular church, S. Maria (ai Monti). Archbishop of Manila, member of:
　Congregations: Evangelization of Peoples, Catholic Education;
　Secretariat: Non-Christians;
　Commission: Social Communications.

Siri, Giuseppe: b. May 20, 1906, Genoa, Italy; ord. priest Sept. 22, 1928; ord. titular bishop of Liviade and auxiliary bishop of Genoa, May 7, 1944; archbishop of Genoa, May 14, 1946; cardinal Jan. 12, 1953; titular church, St. Mary (della Vittoria). Archbishop of Genoa, member of:
　Congregations: Clergy, Catholic Education;
　Commission: Revision of Code of Canon Law.

Slipyi or Slipyj,* Josyf (Kobernyckyj-Dyckowskyj): b. Feb. 17, 1892, Zazdrist in the Ukraine; ord. priest Sept. 30, 1917; ord. titular archbishop of Serre, Dec. 22, 1939; coadjutor archbishop of Lwow for the Ukrainians, 1939-44; archbishop of Lwow, Nov. 1, 1944; imprisoned 1945-63 for unspecified crimes; released by Soviets and allowed to go to Rome in February, 1963; named major archbishop by Paul VI, 1963; cardinal Feb. 22, 1965; titular church, St. Athanasius. Archbishop of Lwow (not permitted to exercise his office; he resides in Vatican City), major archbishop of the Ukraine.

Suenens, Leo Josef: b. July 16, 1904, Brussels, Belgium; ord. priest Sept. 4, 1927; ord. titular bishop of Isinda, Dec. 16, 1945; auxiliary bishop of Mechelen, 1945-61; archbishop of Mechelen-Brussels, 1961-79; cardinal Mar. 19, 1962; titular church, St. Peter in Chains. Former archbishop of Mechelen-

Brussels, member of:
　Congregations: Evangelization of Peoples, Causes of Saints;
　Commission: Revision of Canon Law.

Taofinu'u, Pio, S.M.: b. Dec. 9, 1923, Falealupo, W. Samoa; ord. priest Dec. 8, 1954; joined Society of Mary, 1955; ord. bishop of Apia (now Samoa and Tokelau), May 29, 1968, the first Polynesian bishop; cardinal Mar. 5, 1973; titular church, Sant' Onofrio (on the Janiculum). Bishop of Samoa and Tokelau, member of:
　Congregation: Causes of Saints.

Thiandoum, Hyacinthe: b. Feb. 2, 1921, Poponguine, Senegal; ord. priest Apr. 18, 1949; studied at Gregorian University, Rome, 1951-53; returned to Senegal, 1953; ord. archbishop of Dakar, May 20, 1962; cardinal May 24, 1976; titular church, S. Maria (del Popolo). Archbishop of Dakar, president of Senegal-Mauretania Episcopal Conference, member of:
　Congregation: Religious and Secular Institutes;
　Commission: Social Communications.

Tomasek,* Frantisek: b. June 30, 1899, Studenka, Moravia, Czechoslovakia; ord. priest July 5, 1922; professor of pedagogy and catechetics at the theology faculty of Olomouc, 1934-39; resumed academic activity after liberation in 1945; author, *Catechism of the Catholic Religion;* ord. titular bishop of Butus and auxiliary of Olomouc, Oct. 13, 1949; only Czech bishop to attend Second Vatican Council; apostolic administrator of Prague, Feb. 18, 1965; cardinal May 24, 1976 *(in pectore);* solemnly proclaimed at June 27, 1977, consistory; titular church, Sts. Vitalis, Valeria, Gervase and Protase. Archbishop of Prague, 1977, member of:
　Congregation: Clergy.

Trinh van-Can, Joseph-Marie: b. Mar. 19, 1921, Trac But, Vietnam; ord. priest Dec. 8, 1949; held various offices in Hanoi archdiocese; ord. titular bishop of Ela (with personal title of archbishop) and coadjutor archbishop of Hanoi, June 2, 1963; archbishop of Hanoi, Nov. 27, 1978; cardinal June 30, 1979; titular church, St. Mary in Via. Archbishop of Hanoi, member of:
　Congregation: Evangelization of Peoples.

Ursi, Corrado: b. July 26, 1908, Andria, Italy; ord. priest July 25, 1931; vice-rector and later rector of the Pontifical Regional Seminary of Molfetta, 1931-51; ord. bishop of Nardo, Sept. 30, 1951; archbishop of Acerenza, Nov. 30, 1961; archbishop of Naples, May 23, 1966; cardinal June 26, 1967; titular church, St. Callistus. Archbishop of Naples, member of:
　Congregation: Catholic Education.

Vagnozzi, Egidio: b. Feb. 2, 1906, Rome, Italy; ord. priest Dec. 22, 1928; served in U.S. apostolic delegation; ord. titular archbishop of Mira, May 22, 1949; apostolic delegate to the Philippines, 1949; first nuncio to Philippines, 1951; apostolic delegate to the U.S., 1958-67; cardinal June 26, 1967; titular church, St. Joseph. Chamberlain of the College of Cardinals, president of Prefecture of Economic Affairs of Holy See, member of:

Congregations: Oriental Churches; Evangelization of Peoples;

Tribunal: Apostolic Signatura.

Volk, Hermann: b. Dec. 27, 1903, Steinheim, Germany; ord. priest Apr. 2, 1927; professor of dogmatic theology at University of Muenster; ord. bishop of Mainz, June 5, 1962; cardinal Mar. 5, 1973; titular church, Saints Fabian and Venanzio (at Villa Fiorelli). Bishop of Mainz, member of:

Secretariat: Christian Unity.

Willebrands, Johannes: b. Sept. 4, 1909, Bovenkarspel, Netherlands; ord. priest May 26, 1934; ord. titular bishop of Mauriana, June 28, 1964; secretary of Secretariat for Christian Unity, 1960-69; cardinal Apr. 28, 1969; titular church, St. Sebastian (alle Catacombe). President of Secretariat for Christian Unity, 1969, Archbishop of Utrecht, 1975, military vicar of Netherlands, member of:

Congregations: Doctrine of Faith, Sacraments and Divine Worship, Oriental Churches, Catholic Education, Evangelization of Peoples;

Commissions: Revision of Code of Canon Law, Revision of Oriental Code of Canon Law..

Wyszynski, Stefan: b. Aug. 3, 1901, Zuzela, Poland; ord. priest Aug. 3, 1924; ord. bishop of Lublin, May 12, 1946; archbishop of Gniezno and Warsaw, Nov. 12, 1948; cardinal Jan. 12, 1953; titular church, St. Mary (in Trastavere). He was "deposed" by Polish government in fall of 1953, recognized, 1956. Archbishop of Gniezno and Warsaw, primate of Poland, member of:

Commission: Revision of Canon Law.

Zoungrana, Paul: b. Sept. 3, 1917, Ouagadougou, Upper Volta; ord. priest May 2, 1942, in the Missionaries of Africa; ord. archbishop of Ouagadougou at St. Peter's Basilica by John XXIII, May 8, 1960; cardinal Feb. 22, 1965; titular church, St. Camillus de Lellis. Archbishop of Ouagadougou, member of:

Congregation: Evangelization of Peoples.

CATEGORIES OF CARDINALS
(As of Sept. 10, 1980.)

Information below includes categories of cardinals and dates of consistories at which they were created. Seniority or precedence usually depends on order of elevation, except in the case of cardinal bishops whose seniority depends on date of appointment to suburban see.

Four of these cardinals were named by Pius XII (consistories of Feb. 18, 1946, and Jan. 12, 1953); 10 by John XXIII (consistories of Dec. 15, 1958, Dec. 14, 1959, Mar. 28, 1960, Jan. 16, 1961, and Mar. 19, 1962); 99 by Paul VI (consistories of Feb. 22, 1965, June 26, 1967, Apr. 28, 1969, Mar. 5, 1973, May 24, 1976, and June 27, 1977); 14 by John Paul II (consistory of June 30, 1979).

Order of Bishops

Titular Bishops of Suburban Sees: Carlo Confalonieri, Dean (Dec. 15, 1958); Paolo Marella (Dec. 14, 1959); Antonio Samore (June 26, 1967); Sebastiano Baggio (Apr. 28, 1969); Francesco Carpino (June 26, 1967); Paolo Bertoli (Apr. 28, 1969).

Eastern Rite Patriarch: Stephanos I Sidarouss, C.M. (Feb. 22, 1965).

Order of Priests

1946 (Feb. 18): Carlos Carmelo de Vasconcellos Motta.

1953 (Jan. 12): Giuseppe Siri, Stefan Wyszynski, Paul Emile Leger, S.S.

1958 (Dec. 15): Jose M. Bueno y Monreal, Franz Koenig.

1960 (Mar. 28): Bernard Jan Alfrink, Laurean Rugambwa.

1961 (Jan. 16): Jose Humberto Quintero.

1962 (Mar. 19): Juan Landazuri Ricketts, O.F.M., Raul Silva Henriquez, S.D.B., Leo Josef Suenens.

1965 (Feb. 22): Josyf Slipyi, Thomas B. Cooray, Maurice Roy, Owen McCann, Leon-Etienne Duval, Ermenegildo Florit, Franjo Seper, Paul Zoungrana, Lawrence J. Shehan, Agnelo Rossi, Giovanni Colombo.

1967 (June 26): Gabriel Garrone, Patrick O'Boyle, Egidio Vagnozzi, Maximilien de Furstenberg, Jose Clemente Maurer, C.SS.R., Pietro Parente, Pericle Felici, John J. Krol, John P. Cody, Corrado Ursi, Justin Darmojuwono, Michele Pellegrino, Alexandre Renard.

1969 (Apr. 28): Alfredo Vicente Scherer, Julio Rosales, Gordon J. Gray, Silvio Oddi, Miguel Dario Miranda y Gomez, Giuseppe Paupini, Joseph Parecattil, John F. Dearden, Francois Marty;

George Flahiff, Paul Gouyon, Mario Casariego, Vicente Enrique y Tarancon, Joseph Malula, Pablo Muñoz Vega, S.J., Antonio Poma;

John J. Carberry, Terence J. Cooke, Stephan Sou Hwan Kim, Eugenio de Araujo Sales, Joseph Hoeffner, Johannes Willebrands, Mario Nasalli Rocca di Corneliano, Sergio Guerri.

1973 (Mar. 5): Antonio Ribeiro, James Robert Knox, Avelar Brandao Vilela, Joseph Cordeiro, Anibal Muñoz Duque, Luis Aponte Martinez, Raul Francisco Primatesta, Salvatore Pappalardo, Marcelo Gonzalez Martin, Louis Jean Guyot, Ugo Poletti, Timothy Manning, Maurice Otunga, Jose Salazar Lopez, Humberto S. Medeiros, Paulo

Evaristo Arns, James Darcy Freeman, Narciso Jubany Arnau, Hermann Volk, Pio Taofinu'u.

1976 (May 24): Octavio Beras Rojas, Juan Carlos Aramburu, Hyacinthe Thiandoum, Emmanuel Nsubuga, Lawrence Trevor Picachy, Jaime L. Sin, William W. Baum, Aloisio Lorscheider, Laszlo Lekai, George Basil Hume, O.S.B., Victor Razafimahatratra, Frantisek Tomasek, Dominic Ekandem.

1977 (June 27): Giovanni Benelli, Joseph Ratzinger.

1979 (June 30): Agostino Casaroli, Marco Ce, Joseph-Marie Trinh van-Can, Ernesto Corripio Ahumada, Joseph Asajiro Satowaki, Roger Etchegaray, Anastasio Alberto Ballestrero, O.C.D., Tomas O'Fiaich, Gerald Emmett Carter, Franciszek Macharski.

Order of Deacons

1973 (Mar. 5): Umberto Mozzoni, Pierre Paul Philippe, Pietro Palazzini, Ferdinando Giuseppe Antonelli.

1976 (May 24): Opilio Rossi, Giuseppe Maria Sensi, Corrado Bafile, Joseph Schroeffer, Eduardo Pironio.

1977 (June 27): Bernardin Gantin, Luigi Ciappi.

1979 (June 30): Giuseppe Caprio, Egano Righi-Lambertini, Ernesto Civardi, Wladyslaw Rubin.

Ineligible To Vote

As of Sept. 10, 1980, twelve of the 127 cardinals were ineligible to take part in a papal election in line with the apostolic letter *Ingravescentem Aetatem* effective Jan. 1, 1971, which limited the functions of cardinals after completion of their 80th year.

Cardinals affected were: Alfrink, Antonelli, Confalonieri, Marella, Maurer, Miranda y Gomez, Motta, O'Boyle, Parente, Shehan, Slipyi, Tomasek.

In 1981, four more cardinals will become ineligible to vote: Ermengildo Florit, after July 5; Stefan Wyszynski, after Aug. 3; Gabriel-Marie Garrone, after Oct. 12; and Thomas B. Cooray, O.M.I., after Dec. 28.

DISTRIBUTION OF CARDINALS

As of Sept. 10, 1980, there were 127 cardinals from more than 50 countries or areas. Listed below are areas, countries, number and last names.

Europe — 66

Italy (35): Antonelli, Bafile, Baggio, Ballestrero, Benelli, Bertoli, Caprio, Carpino, Casaroli, Ce, Ciappi, Civardi, Colombo, Confalonieri, Felici, Florit, Guerri, Marella, Mozzoni, Nasalli Rocca di Corneliano, Oddi, Palazzini, Pappalardo, Parente, Paupini, Pellegrino, Poletti, Poma, Righi-Lambertini, Rossi, Samore, Sensi, Siri, Ursi, Vagnozzi.

France (7): Etchegaray, Garrone, Gouyon, Guyot, Marty, Philippe, Renard.

Germany (4): Hoeffner, Ratzinger, Schroeffer, Volk.

Spain (4): Bueno y Monreal, Enrique y Tarancon, Gonzalez Martin, Jubany Arnau.

Netherlands (3): Alfrink, De Furstenberg, Willebrands.

Poland (3): Macharski, Rubin, Wyszynski.

One from each of the following countries: Austria, Koenig; Belgium, Suenens; Czechoslovakia, Tomasek; England, Hume; Hungary, Lekai; Ireland, O'Fiaich; Portugal, Ribeiro; Scotland, Gray; Ukraine (now in USSR), Slipyi; Yugoslavia, Seper.

Asia — 10

India (2): Parecattil, Picachy.

Philippines (2): Rosales, Sin.

One from each of the following countries: Indonesia, Darmojuwono; Japan, Satowaki; Korea, Kim; Pakistan, Cordeiro; Sri Lanka, Cooray; Vietnam, Trinh van-Can.

Oceania — 3

Australia (2): Freeman, Knox; Pacific Islands (Samoa), Taofinu'u.

Africa — 12

One from each of the following countries: Algeria, Duval; Benin, Gantin; Egypt, Sidarouss; Kenya, Otunga; Madagascar, Razafimahatratra; Nigeria, Ekandem; Senegal, Thiandoum; South Africa, McCann; Tanzania, Rugambwa; Uganda, Nsubuga; Upper Volta, Zoungrana; Zaire, Malula.

North America — 18

United States (10): Baum, Carberry, Cody, Cooke, Dearden, Krol, Manning, Medeiros, O'Boyle, Shehan.

Canada (4): Carter, Flahiff, Leger, Roy.

Mexico (3): Corripio Ahumada, Miranda y Gomez, Salazar Lopez.

Puerto Rico (1): Aponte Martinez.

Central and South America — 18

Brazil (7): Arns, Brandao Vilela, De Araujo Sales, Lorscheider, Motta, Rossi, Scherer.

Argentina (3): Aramburu, Pironio, Primatesta.

One from each of the following countries: Bolivia, Maurer; Chile, Silva Henriquez; Colombia, Munoz Duque; Dominican Republic, Beras Rojas; Ecuador, Munoz Vega, S.J.; Guatemala, Casariego (b. Spain); Peru, Landazuri Ricketts; Venezuela, Quintero.

Cardinals of U.S.

As of Sept. 10, 1980, U.S. cardinals, years of elevation and sees.

Lawrence J. Shehan, 1965, Baltimore (retired 1974); Patrick A. O'Boyle, 1967, Washington (retired 1973); John J. Krol, 1967, Philadelphia; John P. Cody, 1967, Chicago; John F. Dearden, 1969, Detroit (retired 1980); John J. Carberry, 1969, St. Louis (retired 1979); Terence J. Cooke, 1969, New

York; Timothy Manning, 1973, Los Angeles; Humberto S. Medeiros, 1973, Boston; William W. Baum, 1976, Washington, D.C. (1973-80); prefect of Congregation for Catholic Education, 1980.

Deceased cardinals of the United States,. Data: years of elevation, sees, years of birth and death.

John McCloskey, 1875, New York, 1810-1885; James Gibbons, 1886, Baltimore, 1834-1921; John Farley, 1911, New York, 1842-1918; William O'Connell, 1911, Boston, 1859-1944; Dennis Dougherty, 1921, Philadelphia, 1865-1951; Patrick Hayes, 1924, New York, 1867-1938; George Mundelein, 1924,

Chicago, 1872-1939; John Glennon, 1946, St. Louis, 1862-1946; Edward Mooney, 1946, Detroit, 1882-1958;

Francis Spellman, 1946, New York, 1889-1967; Samuel Stritch, 1946, Chicago, 1887-1958; John O'Hara, C.S.C., 1958, Philadelphia, 1888-1960; Richard Cushing, 1958, Boston, 1895-1970; Albert Meyer, 1959, Chicago, 1903-1965; Aloysius Muench, 1959, Fargo (and papal nuncio), 1889-1962; Joseph Ritter, 1961, St. Louis, 1892-1967; Francis Brennan, 1967, official of Roman Curia, 1894-1968; James F. McIntyre, 1953, Los Angeles, 1886-1979; John J. Wright, 1969, prefect of Congregation for Clergy, 1909-1979.

REPRESENTATIVES OF THE HOLY SEE

Papal representatives and their functions were the subject of a document entitled *Sollicitudo Omnium Ecclesiarum* which Pope Paul issued on his own initiative under the date of June 24, 1969.

Delegates and Nuncios

Papal representatives "receive from the Roman Pontiff the charge of representing him in a fixed way in the various nations or regions of the world.

"When their legation is only to local churches, they are known as apostolic delegates. When to this legation, of a religious and ecclesial nature, there is added diplomatic legation to states and governments, they receive the title of nuncio, pro-nuncio, and internuncio."

[An apostolic nuncio has the diplomatic rank of ambassador extraordinary and plenipotentiary. Traditionally, because the Vatican diplomatic service has the longest uninterrupted history in the world, a nuncio has precedence among diplomats in the country to which he is accredited and serves as dean of the diplomatic corps on state occasions. Since 1965 pro-nuncios, also of ambassadorial rank, have been assigned to countries in which this prerogative is not recognized.]

(Other representatives, who are covered in the Almanac article, Vatican Representatives to International Organizations, are clerics and lay persons "who form . . . part of a pontifical mission attached to international organizations or take part in conferences and congresses." They are variously called delegates or observers.)

"The primary and specific purpose of the mission of a papal representative is to render ever closer and more operative the ties that bind the Apostolic See and the local churches.

"The ordinary function of a pontifical representative is to keep the Holy See regularly and objectively informed about the conditions of the ecclesial community to which he has been sent, and about what may affect the life of the Church and the good of souls.

"On the one hand, he makes known to the Holy See the thinking of the bishops, clergy,

religious and faithful of the territory where he carries out his mandate, and forwards to Rome their proposals and their requests; on the other hand, he makes himself the interpreter, with those concerned, of the acts, documents, information and instructions emanating from the Holy See."

Service and Liaison

Representatives, while carrying out their general and special duties, are bound to respect the autonomy of local churches and bishops. Their service and liaison responsibilities include the following:

• **Nomination of Bishops:** To play a key role in compiling, with the advice of ecclesiastics and lay persons, and submitting lists of names of likely candidates to the Holy See with their own recommendations.

• **Bishops:** To aid and counsel local bishops without interfering in the affairs of their jurisdictions.

• **Episcopal Conferences:** To maintain close relations with them and to assist them in every possible way. (Papal representatives do not belong to these conferences.)

• **Religious Communities of Pontifical Rank:** To advise and assist major superiors for the purpose of promoting and consolidating conferences of men and women religious and to coordinate their apostolic activities.

• **Church-State Relations:** The thrust in this area is toward the development of sound relations with civil governments and collaboration in work for peace and the total good of the whole human family.

The mission of a papal representative begins with appointment and assignment by the pope and continues until termination of his mandate. He acts "under the guidance and according to the instructions of the cardinal secretary of state and prefect of the Council for the Public Affairs of the Church, to whom he is directly responsible for the execution of the mandate entrusted to him by the Supreme Pontiff." Normally, representatives are required to retire at the age of 75.

NUNCIOS AND DELEGATES

(Sources: *Annuario Pontificio, L'Osservatore Romano,* NC News Service.)

Data, as of Aug. 6, 1980, country, rank of legation (corresponding to rank of legate unless otherwise noted), name of legate (archbishop unless otherwise noted) as available.

Delegate for Papal Representatives: Archbishop Giovanni Coppa. The post was established in 1973 to coordinate papal diplomatic efforts throughout the world. The office entails responsibility for "following more closely through timely visits the activities of papal representatives ... and encouraging their rapport with the central offices" of the Secretariat of State and the Council for the Public Affairs of the Church.

Africa, Southern (Botswana, South Africa, Namibia, Swaziland): Pretoria, South Africa, Apostolic Delegation; Edward Cassidy (also Pro-Nuncio to Lesotho).

Algeria: Algiers, Nunciature; Gabriel Montalvo, Pro-Nuncio (He is also Pro-Nuncio to Morocco and Tunisia and Apostolic Delegate to Libya.)

Angola: Luanda, Apostolic Delegation; Giovanni De Andrea.

Antilles: Apostolic Delegation; Paul Tabat (resides in Port of Spain, Trinidad).

Argentina: Buenos Aires, Nunciature; Pio Laghi.

Australia: Canberra, Nunciature; Luigi Barbarito, Pro-Nuncio.

Austria: Vienna, Nunciature; Mario Cagna.

Bahamas: Nunciature; Paul Tabat, Pro-Nuncio (resides in Port of Spain, Trinidad).

Bangladesh: Dacca, Nunciature; Luigi Accogli, Pro-Nuncio (also serves as Apostolic Delegate to Burma.)

Barbados: Nunciature; Paul Tabat, Pro-Nuncio (resides in Port of Spain, Trinidad).

Belgium: Brussels, Nunciature; Igino Cardinale (also Nuncio to Luxembourg).

Benin (formerly Dahomey): Nunciature; Giuseppe Ferraioli, Pro-Nuncio (resides in Accra, Ghana).

Bolivia: La Paz, Nunciature; Alfio Rapisarda.

Botswana: See Africa, Southern.

Brazil: Brasilia, Nunciature; Carmine Rocco.

Burma: See Bangladesh.

Burundi: Bujumbura, Nunciature; Donato Squicciarini.

Cameroon: Yaounde, Nunciature; Giuseppe Uhac, Pro-Nuncio (also Pro-Nuncio to Gabon Republic and Apostolic Delegate to Equatorial Guinea).

Canada: Ottawa, Nunciature; Angelo Palmas, Pro-Nuncio.

Cape Verde Islands: Nunciature; Luigi Dossena, Pro-Nuncio (resides in Dakar, Senegal).

Central African Republic: Bangui, Nunciature; Oriano Quilici, Pro-Nuncio (also Pro-Nuncio to Congo and Apostolic Delegate to Chad).

Chad: Apostolic Delegation; Oriano Quilici (resides in Bangui, Central African Republic).

Chile: Santiago, Nunciature; Angelo Sodano.

China: Taipei (Taiwan), Nunciature.

Colombia: Bogota, Nunciature; Angelo Acerbi.

Congo Republic: Brazzaville, Nunciature; Oriano Quilici, Pro-Nuncio (resides in Bangui, Central African Republic).

Costa Rica: San Jose, Nunciature; Lajos Kada.

Cuba: Havana, Nunciature; Giuglio Einaudi, Pro-Nuncio.

Cyprus: Nicosia, Nunciature; William A. Carew, Pro-Nuncio (also Apostolic Delegate to Jerusalem).

Denmark: See Scandinavia.

Djibouti: See Red Sea Region.

Dominican Republic: Santo Domingo, Nunciature; Giovanni Gravelli (also Apostolic Delegate to Puerto Rico).

Ecuador: Quito, Nunciature; Vincenzo Farano.

Egypt: Cairo, Nunciature; Achille Glorieux, Pro-Nuncio.

El Salvador: San Salvador, Nunciature; Emanuele Gerada (also Nuncio to Guatemala).

Equatorial Guinea: Santa Isabel, Apostolic Delegation; Giuseppe Uhac (resides in Yaounde, Cameroon).

Ethiopia: Addis Ababa, Nunciature; Raymond Etteldorf, Pro-Nuncio.

Fiji: Nunciature; Antonio Magnoni, Pro-Nuncio (resides in New Zealand).

Finland: Helsinki, Nunciature; Josip Zabkar, Pro-Nuncio (resides in Copenhagen).

France: Paris, Nunciature; Angelo Felici.

Gabon Republic: Libreville, Nunciature; Giuseppe Uhac, Pro-Nuncio (resides in Yaounde, Cameroon).

Gambia: Nunciature; Johannes Dyba, Pro-Nuncio (resides in Monrovia, Liberia).

Germany: Bonn, Nunciature; Guido Del Mestri.

Ghana: Accra, Nunciature; Giuseppe Ferraioli, Pro-Nuncio (also Pro-Nuncio to Benin and Apostolic Delegate to Togo).

Great Britain: London, Apostolic Delegation; Bruno Heim (also Apostolic Delegate to Gibraltar).

Greece: Athens, Nunciature; Giovanni Mariani, Pro-Nuncio.

Grenada: Nunciature.

Guatemala: Guatemala City, Nunciature; Emanuele Gerada (also Nuncio to El Salvador).

Guinea: Conakry, Apostolic Delegation;

Johannes Dyba (resides in Monrovia, Liberia).

Guinea-Bissau: Apostolic Delegation; Luigi Dossena (Delegate resides at Dakar, Senegal).

Haiti: Port-au-Prince, Nunciature; Luigi Conti.

Honduras: Tegucigalpa, Nunciature.

Iceland: Nunciature; Josip Zabkar, Pro-Nuncio (resides in Copenhagen, Denmark).

India: New Delhi, Nunciature; Luciano Storero, Pro-Nuncio.

Indonesia: Jakarta, Nunciature; Pablo Puente, Pro-Nuncio.

Iran: Teheran, Nunciature; Annibale Bugnini, C.M., Pro-Nuncio.

Iraq: Baghdad, Nunciature; Antonio Del Giudice, Pro-Nuncio (also Pro-Nuncio to Kuwait).

Ireland: Dublin, Nunciature; Gaetano Alibrandi.

Italy: Rome, Nunciature; Romolo Carboni.

Ivory Coast: Abidjan, Nunciature; Justo Mullor Garcia, Nuncio (also Pro-Nuncio to Niger and Upper Volta).

Jamaica: Nunciature; Paul Tabat, Pro-Nuncio (resides in Port of Spain, Trinidad).

Japan: Tokyo, Nunciature; Mario Pio Gaspari, Pro-Nuncio.

Jerusalem, Palestine, Jordan, Israel: Jerusalem, Apostolic Delegation; William A. Carew (also Pro-Nuncio to Cyprus).

Kenya: Nairobi, Nunciature; Agostino Cacciavillan, Pro-Nuncio (also Apostolic Delegate to Seychelles Is.).

Korea: Seoul, Nunciature; Luciano Angeloni, Pro-Nuncio.

Kuwait: Al Kuwait, Nunciature; Antonio Del Giudice, Pro-Nuncio (resides in Baghdad, Iraq).

Laos, Malaysia and Singapore: Apostolic Delegation; Silvio Luoni (resides in Bangkok, Thailand).

Lebanon: Beirut, Nunciature; Carlo Furno.

Lesotho: Maseru, Nunciature; Edward Cassidy, Pro-Nuncio (resides in Pretoria, S. Africa).

Liberia: Monrovia, Nunciature; Johannes Dyba, Pro-Nuncio (also Pro-Nuncio to Gambia and Apostolic Delegate to Guinea and Sierra Leone).

Libya: Apostolic Delegation; Gabriel Montalvo (resides in Algiers, Algeria).

Luxembourg: Nunciature; Igino Cardinale (resides in Brussels, Belgium).

Madagascar: Tananarive, Nunciature; Sergio Sebastiani, Pro-Nuncio (also Pro-Nuncio to Mauritius and Apostolic Delegate to Reunion).

Malawi: Lilongwe, Nunciature; Georg Zur, Pro-Nuncio (resides in Zambia).

Mali: Nunciature; Luigi Dossena, Pro-Nuncio (resides in Dakar, Senegal).

Malta: La Valletta, Nunciature.

Mauritania: Nouakchott, Apostolic Delegation; Luigi Dossena (resides in Dakar, Senegal).

Mauritius: Port Louis, Nunciature; Sergio Sebastiani, Pro-Nuncio (resides in Tananarive, Madagascar).

Mexico: Mexico City, Apostolic Delegation; Girolamo Prigione.

Morocco: Rabat, Nunciature; Gabriel Montalvo, Pro-Nuncio (resides in Algiers, Algeria).

Mozambique: Maputo, Apostolic Delegation; Francesco Colasuonna.

Namibia: See Africa, Southern.

Netherlands: The Hague, Nunciature; Bruno Wustenberg, Pro-Nuncio.

New Zealand: Wellington, Nunciature; Antonio Magnoni. (He is also Pro-Nuncio to Fiji and Apostolic Delegate to Pacific Islands).

Nicaragua: Managua, Nunciature.

Niger: Niamey, Nunciature; Justo Mullor Garcia, Pro-Nuncio (resides in Abidjan, Ivory Coast).

Nigeria: Lagos, Apostolic Delegation; Carlo Curis, Pro-Nuncio.

Norway: See Scandinavia.

Pacific Islands: See New Zealand.

Pakistan: Islamabad, Nunciature.

Panama: Panama, Nunciature; Blasco Francisco Collaco.

Papua New Guinea: Port Moresby; Nunciature; Andrea Cordero Lanza di Montezemolo, Pro-Nuncio. (He is also Apostolic Delegate to western and southern Solomon Islands.)

Paraguay: Asuncion, Nunciature; Joseph Mees.

Peru: Lima, Nunciature; Mario Tagliaferri.

Philippines: Manila, Nunciature; Bruno Torpigliani.

Portugal: Lisbon, Nunciature; Sante Portalupi, Nuncio.

Puerto Rico: See Dominican Republic.

Red Sea Region (Somalia, Djibouti, part of Arabian Peninsula): Apostolic Delegation; Giovanni Moretti (resides in Khartoum, Sudan).

Reunion: See Madagascar.

Rhodesia: See Zimbabwe.

Rwanda: Kigali, Nunciature; Thomas White.

Scandinavia (Denmark, Sweden, Norway): Copenhagen, Denmark, Apostolic Delegation; Josip Zabkar (also Pro-Nuncio to Finland and Iceland).

Senegal: Dakar, Nunciature; Luigi Dossena, Pro-Nuncio (also Pro-Nuncio to Cape Verde Islands and Mali; Apostolic Delegate to Guinea-Bissau, and Mauritania.)

Seychelles Islands: See Kenya.

Sierra Leone: Apostolic Delegation; Johannes Dyba (resides in Monrovia, Liberia).

Solomon Islands: Apostolic Delegation;

Andrea Cordero Lanza di Montezemolo (resides in Port Moresby, Papua New Guinea).

Somalia: See Red Sea Region.

South Africa: See Africa, Southern.

Spain: Madrid, Nunciature; Luigi Dadaglio.

Sri Lanka: Colombo, Nunciature; Nicola Rotunno, Pro-Nuncio.

Sudan: Khartoum, Nunciature; Giovanni Moretti, Pro-Nuncio (also Apostolic Delegate to Red Sea Region).

Swaziland: See Africa, Southern.

Sweden: See Scandinavia.

Switzerland: Bern, Nunciature; Ambrogio Marchioni.

Syria (Syrian Arab Republic): Damascus, Nunciature; Angelo Pedroni, Pro-Nuncio.

Tanzania: Dar-es-Salaam, Nunciature; Franco Brambilla, Pro-Nuncio.

Thailand: Bangkok, Nunciature; Silvio Luoni, Pro-Nuncio (also Apostolic Delegate to Laos, Malaysia and Singapore).

Togo: Lome, Apostolic Delegation, Giuseppe Ferraioli (resides in Accra, Ghana).

Trinidad and Tobago: Port of Spain, Trinidad, Nunciature; Paul Tabat, Pro-Nuncio (also Pro-Nuncio to Bahamas, Barbados, Jamaica and Apostolic Delegate to Antilles).

Tunisia: Tunis, Nunciature; Gabriel Montalvo, Pro-Nuncio (resides in Algiers, Algeria).

Turkey: Ankara, Nunciature; Salvatore Asta, Pro-Nuncio.

Uganda: Kampala, Nunciature; Henri Lemaitre, Pro-Nuncio.

United States of America: Washington, D.C., Apostolic Delegation.

Upper Volta: Ouagadougou, Nunciature; Justo Mullor Garcia, Pro-Nuncio (resides in Abidjan, Ivory Coast).

Uruguay: Montevideo, Nunciature; Luigi Bellotti.

Venezuela: Caracas, Nunciature; Ubaldo Calabresi.

Vietnam and Cambodia: Apostolic Delegation.

Yugoslavia: Belgrade, Nunciature; Michele Cecchini, Pro-Nuncio.

Zaire: Kinshasa, Nunciature; Edoardo Rovida, Pro-Nuncio.

Zambia: Lusaka, Nunciature; Georg Zur, Pro-Nuncio (also Pro-Nuncio to Malawi).

Zimbabwe: Nunciature.

Apostolic Delegate to U.S.

As of Aug. 20, 1980, the post of apostolic delegate to the United States was vacant.

Archbishop Jean Jadot held the post from 1973 until June, 1980, when he was appointed Pro-President of the Secretariat for Non-Christians.

The U.S. Apostolic Delegation was established Jan. 21, 1893. It is located at 3339 Massachusetts Ave. N.W., Washington, D.C. 20008.

Archbishop Jadot's predecessors were Archbishops: Francesco Satolli (1893-1896), Sebastiano Martinelli, O.S.A. (1896-1902), Diomede Falconio, O.F.M. (1902-1911), Giovanni Bonzano (1911-1922), Pietro Fumasoni-Biondi (1922-1933), Amleto Cicognani (1933-1958), Egidio Vagnozzi (1958-1967) and Luigi Raimondi (1967-1973).

DIPLOMATS AT VATICAN

(Sources: *Annuario Pontificio, L'Osservatore Romano,* NC News Service. As of Aug. 6, 1980.)

Algeria: Anisse Salel-Bey, Ambassador.

Argentina: Ruben Victor Manuel Blanco, Ambassador.

Australia: Lloyd Thomson, Ambassador.

Austria: Gordian Gudenus, Ambassador.

Bahamas: Ambassador.

Bangladesh: Mohammed Sultan, Ambassador.

Barbados: Ambassador.

Belgium: Felix Standaert, Ambassador.

Benin (formerly Dahomey): Douwa David Gbaguidi, Ambassador.

Bolivia: Juan Vidaurre Pinto, Ambassador.

Brazil: Espedito de Freitas Resende, Ambassador.

Burundi: Lazare Nzorubara, Ambassador.

Cameroon: Ambassador.

Canada: Yvon Beaulne, Ambassador.

Cape Verde Islands: Ambassador.

Central African Republic: Albert Sato, Ambassador.

Chile: Hector Riesle Contreras, Ambassador.

China (Taiwan): Chow Shu-Kai, Ambassador.

Colombia: Raimundo Emiliani Roman, Ambassador.

Congo Republic: Jean-Pierre Nonault, Ambassador.

Costa Rica: Alvaro Aguilar Peralto, Ambassador.

Cuba: Jose Antonio Portuondo Valdor, Ambassador.

Cyprus: Polys Modinos, Ambassador.

Dominican Republic: Miguel Antonio Olavarrieta Perez, Ambassador.

Ecuador: Teodoro Bustamante Munoz, Ambassador.

Egypt: Shaffei Abdel Hamid, Ambassador.

El Salvador: Prudencio Llach Schonenberg, Ambassador.

Ethiopia: Haile Giorgis Tasew, Ambassador.

Fiji: Ambassador.

Finland: Seppo Taito Pietinen, Ambassador.

France: Louis Dauge, Ambassador.

Gabon: Gaston Felicien Olouna, Ambassador.

Gambia: Bocar Ousman Semega-Janneh, Ambassador.

Germany: Walter Gehlhoff, Ambassador.

Ghana: Ambassador.
Great Britain: Mark Evelyn Heath, Minister.
Greece: Stephanos Stathatos, Ambassador.
Grenada: Ambassador.
Guatemala: Luis Valladares y Aycinena, Ambassador.
Haiti: Jean-Claude Andre, Ambassador.
Honduras: Manuel Luna Mejia, Ambassador.
Iceland: Niels P. Sigurdsson, Ambassador.
India: Gurbachan Singh, Ambassador.
Indonesia: Raymond Toto Prawira Supradja, Ambassador.
Iran: Ambassador.
Iraq: Ambassador.
Ireland: Francis A. Coffey, Ambassador.
Italy: Dr. Bruno Bottai, Ambassador.
Ivory Coast: Joseph Amichia, Ambassador.
Jamaica: Keith Johnson, Ambassador.
Japan: Kiyoshi Suganuma, Ambassador.
Kenya: Bethuel A. Kiplagat, Ambassador.
Korea: Hyun Joon Shin, Ambassador.
Kuwait: Essa Ahmad Al-Hamad, Ambassador.
Lebanon: Antoine Fattal, Ambassador.
Lesotho: Julius Nako Ts'Oanamatsie, Ambassador.
Liberia: Ambassador.
Lithuania: Stasys Lozoraitis, Jr., first secretary.
Luxembourg: Charles Reichling, Ambassador.
Madagascar: Ambassador.
Malawi: Victor Timothy Likaku, Ambassador.
Mali: Ambassador.
Malta: Paolo Farrugia, Ambassador.
Mauritius: Leckraz Teelock, Ambassador.
Monaco: Cesar Charles Solamito, Minister.
Morocco: Youssef Ben Abbes, Ambassador.
Netherlands: Josef Laurentius Hubertus Ceulen, Ambassador.
New Zealand: John Vivian Scott, Ambassador.
Nicaragua: Ricardo Agustin Peters Silva, Ambassador.
Niger: Alzouma Tiecoura, Ambassador.
Nigeria: Ignatius Olisemeka, Ambassador.
Order of Malta: Christophe de Kallay, Minister.
Pakistan: Zulfiqar ali Khan, Ambassador.
Panama: Jose Manuel Watson Diez, Ambassador.
Papua New Guinea: Ambassador.
Paraguay: Juan I. Livieres Argana, Ambassador.
Peru: Jorge Nicholson Sologuren, Ambassador.
Philippines: Antonio C. Delgado, Ambassador.
Portugal: Jose Calvet de Magalhaes, Ambassador.
Rwanda: Callixte Hatungimana, Ambassador.

San Marino: Dr. Giovanni Galassi, Minister.
Senegal: Paul Ndiaye, Ambassador.
Spain: Ambassador.
Sri Lanka: Vernon Lorraine Benjamin Mendis, Ambassador.
Sudan: Bashir Bakri, Ambassador.
Syria (Arab Republic): Dia Allah El-Fattal, Ambassador.
Tanzania: Nicholas J. Merinyo Maro, Ambassador.
Thailand: Varachit Nitibhon, Ambassador.
Trinidad and Tobago: Ambassador.
Tunisia: Taoufik Smida, Ambassador.
Turkey: Veedi Turel, Ambassador.
Uganda: John Bernard Moli, Ambassador.
Upper Volta: Pierre Ilboudo, Ambassador.
Uruguay: Carlos Maria Romero, Ambassador.
Venezuela: Ambassador.
Yugoslavia: Zdenko Svete, Ambassador.
Zaire: Tshimbalanga Shala-Dibwe, Ambassador.
Zambia: Miss Lombe Phyllis Chibesakunda, Ambassador.
Zimbabwe: Ambassador.

U.S. — Vatican Relations

Official relations for trade and diplomatic purposes were maintained by the United States and the Papal States while the latter had the character of and acted like other sovereign powers in the international community.

Consular Relations

Consular relations developed in the wake of an announcement, made by the papal nuncio in Paris to the American mission there Dec. 15, 1784, that the Papal States had agreed to open several Mediterranean ports to U.S. shipping.

U.S. consular representation in the Papal States began with the appointment of John B. Sartori, a native of Rome, in June, 1797. Sartori's successors as consuls were: Felix Cicognani, also a Roman, and Americans George W. Greene, Nicholas Browne, William C. Sanders, Daniel LeRoy, Horatio V. Glentworth, W.J. Stillman, Edwin C. Cushman, David M. Armstrong.

Consular officials of the Papal States who served in the U.S. were: Count Ferdinand Lucchesi, 1826 to 1829, who resided in Washington; John B. Sartori, 1829 to 1841, who resided in Trenton, N.J.; Daniel J. Desmond, 1841 to 1850, who resided in Philadelphia; Louis B. Binsse, 1850 to 1895, who resided in New York.

U.S. recognition of the consul of the Papal States did not cease when the states were absorbed into the Kingdom of Italy in 1871, despite pressure from Baron Blanc, the Italian minister. Binsse held the title until his death Mar. 28, 1895. No one was appointed to succeed him.

Diplomatic Relations

The U.S. Senate approved a recommendation, made by President James K. Polk in December, 1847, for the establishment of a diplomatic post in the Papal States. Jacob L. Martin, the first charge d'affaires, arrived in Rome Aug. 2, 1848, and presented his credentials to Pius IX Aug. 19. Martin, who died within a month, was succeeded by Lewis Cass, Jr. Cass became minister resident in 1854 and served in that capacity until his retirement in 1858.

John P. Stockton, who later became a U.S. Senator from New Jersey, was minister resident from 1858 to 1861. Rufus King was named to succeed him but, instead, accepted a commission as a brigadier general in the Army. Alexander W. Randall of Wisconsin took the appointment. He was succeeded in August, 1862, by Richard M. Blatchford who served until the following year. King was again nominated minister resident and served in that capacity until 1867 when the ministry was ended because of objections from some quarters in the U.S. and failure to appropriate funds for its continuation. J. C. Hooker, a secretary, remained in the Papal States until the end of March, 1868, closing the ministry and performing functions of courtesy.

Personal Envoys

Myron C. Taylor was appointed by President Franklin D. Roosevelt in 1939 to serve as his personal representative to Pope Pius XII and continued serving in that capacity during the presidency of Harry S. Truman until 1951. Henry Cabot Lodge was named to the post by President Richard M. Nixon in 1970, served also during the presidency of Gerald Ford, and represented President Carter at the canonization of St. John Neumann in 1977. Neither Taylor nor Lodge had diplomatic status.

President Harry S. Truman nominated Gen. Mark Clark to be ambassador to the Vatican in 1951, but withdrew the nomination at Clark's request because of controversy over the appointment.

None of Truman's three successors — Dwight D. Eisenhower, John F. Kennedy or Lyndon B. Johnson — had a personal representative to the Pope.

Miami attorney David Walters, a Catholic, served as the personal envoy of President Jimmy Carter to the Pope from July, 1977, until his resignation Aug. 16, 1978. He was succeeded by Robert F. Wagner, former mayor of New York, in October, 1978.

At the time of Walters' designation for the non-diplomatic post, the House of Representatives had under consideration an amendment, already passed by the Senate, that would lift an 1867 prohibition against funding for diplomatic relations with the Vatican.

Any initiative for the establishment of formal diplomatic relations would have to be undertaken by the U.S. government.

VATICAN CITY

The State of Vatican City (Stato della Citta del Vaticano) is the territorial seat of the papacy. The smallest sovereign state in the world, it is situated within the city of Rome, embraces an area of 108.7 acres, and includes within its limits the Vatican Palace, museums, art galleries, gardens, libraries, radio station, post office, bank, astronomical observatory, offices, apartments, service facilities, St. Peter's Basilica, and neighboring buildings between the Basilica and Viale Vaticano.

The extraterritorial rights of Vatican City extend to more than 10 buildings in Rome, including the major basilicas and office buildings of various congregations of the Roman Curia, and to the **Villa of Castel Gandolfo** 15 miles southeast of the City of Rome. Castel Gandolfo is the summer residence of the Holy Father.

The government of Vatican City is in the hands of the reigning pope, who has full executive, legislative and judicial power. The administration of affairs, however, is handled by the Pontifical Commission for the State of Vatican City. The legal system is based on Canon Law; in cases where this code does not obtain, the laws of the City of Rome apply. The City is an absolutely neutral state and enjoys all the rights and privileges of a sovereign power. The Secretariat of State (Papal Secretariat) maintains diplomatic relations with other nations. The citizens of Vatican City, and they alone, owe allegiance to the pope as a temporal head of state.

Cardinals of the Roman Curia residing outside Vatican City enjoy the privileges of extraterritoriality.

The normal population is approximately 1,000. While the greater percentage is made up of priests and religious, there are several hundred lay persons living in Vatican City. They are housed in their own apartments in the City and are engaged in secretarial, domestic, trade and service occupations. About 4,000 persons are employed by the Vatican.

Services of honor and order are performed by the Swiss Guards, who have been charged with responsibility for the personal safety of popes since 1506. Additional police and ceremonial functions are under the supervision of a special office. These functions were formerly handled by the Papal Gendarmes, the Palatine Guard of Honor, and the Guard of Honor of the Pope (Pontifical Noble Guard) which Pope Paul disbanded Sept. 14, 1970.

The **Basilica of St. Peter,** built between 1506 and 1626, is the largest church in Christendom and the site of most papal ceremonies. The pope's own patriarchal basilica, however, is **St. John Lateran,** whose origins date back to 324.

St. Ann's is the parish church of Vatican City.

The vicar general of the pope for Vatican City, which is part of the diocese of Rome, is Most Rev. Peter Canisius Van Lierde, O.S.A., titular bishop of Porfireone.

The **Vatican Library,** one of five in the City, has among its holdings 70,000 manuscripts, 770,000 printed books, and 7,500 incunabula.

The independent temporal power of the pope, which is limited to the confines of Vatican City and small areas outside, was for many centuries more extensive than it is now. As late as the nineteenth century, the pope ruled 16,000 square miles of Papal States across the middle of Italy, with a population of over 3,000,000. In 1870 forces of the Kingdom of Italy occupied these lands which, with the exception of the small areas surrounding the Vatican and Lateran in Rome and the Villa of Castel Gandolfo, became part of the Kingdom by the Italian law of May 13, 1871.

The **Roman Question,** occasioned by this seizure and the voluntary confinement of the pope to the limited papal lands, was finally settled with ratification of the Lateran Agreement on June 7, 1929, by the Italian government and Vatican City and provided a financial indemnity for the former Papal States, which became recognized as part of Italy. The Lateran Agreement became Article 7 of the Italian Constitution on Mar. 26, 1947.

Papal Flag

The papal flag consists of two equal vertical stripes of yellow and white, charged with the insignia of the papacy on the white stripe — a triple crown or tiara over two crossed keys, one of gold and one of silver, tied with a red cord and two tassels. The divisions of the crown represent the teaching, sanctifying and ruling offices of the pope. The keys symbolize his jurisdictional authority.

The papal flag is a national flag inasmuch as it is the standard of the Supreme Pontiff as the sovereign of the state of Vatican City. It is also universally accepted by the faithful as a symbol of the supreme spiritual authority of the Holy Father.

In a Catholic church, the papal flag is displayed on a staff on the left side of the sanctuary (facing the congregation), and the American flag is displayed on the right.

Vatican Radio

The declared purpose of Vatican Radio Station HVJ is "that the voice of the Supreme Pastor may be heard throughout the world by means of the ether waves, for the glory of Christ and the salvation of souls." Designed by Guglielmo Marconi, the inventor of radio, and supervised by him until his death, the sta-

tion was inaugurated by Pope Pius XI in 1931. The original purpose has been extended to a wide variety of programming.

Vatican Radio operates on international wave lengths, transmits programs in 33 languages, and serves as a channel of communication between the Vatican, church officials and listeners in general in many parts of the world. The station broadcasts about 220 hours a week throughout the world.

The staff of 300 broadcasters and technicians includes 32 Jesuits and is directed by Father Robert Tucci, S.J. Headquarters are located in Vatican City. Studios and offices are at Palazzo Pio, Piazza Pia, 3. The transmitters are situated at Santa Maria di Galeria, a 200-acre site 16 miles from Rome.

1980 Vatican Stamps

The Vatican Philatelic Office scheduled the following issues of stamps for 1980. (Issue date is given where available.)

• Series commemorating St. Benedict, patron of Europe. Issued Mar. 21, 1980, in five values (80, 100, 150, 220 and 450 lire) featuring five subjects.

• Series of air mail stamps commemorating John Paul II's journeys outside of Italy in 1979. Issued June 24, 1980, in six values (200, 300, 500, 1,000, 1,500, and 2,000 lire) featuring a single subject. A 3000-lire stamp of the series — featuring the meeting between the Pope and Dimitrios I — was to be released at a later date.

• Series commemorating the third centenary of the death of Gian Lorenzo Bernini.

• Series commemorating the seventh centenary of the death of St. Albert the Great.

• Series in honor of the liturgical solemnity of All Saints.

• A new type of aerogram.

Vatican Coins

The Vatican Numismatics Office issued a series of coins Apr. 21, 1980, for the first year of the pontificate of Pope John Paul II. The set consisted of six coins (10, 20, 50, 100, 200 and 500 lire).

Papal Audiences

General audiences are scheduled weekly, on Wednesday at noon.

In Vatican City, they are held in the Audience Hall on the south side of St. Peter's Basilica. The hall, which was opened in 1971, has a seating capacity of 6,800 and a total capacity of 12,000.

Audiences are also held during the summer at Castel Gandolfo when the pope is there on a working vacation.

General audiences last from about 60 to 90 minutes, during which the pope gives a talk and his blessing. A résumé of the talk, which is usually in Italian, is given in several languages.

Arrangements for papal audiences are handled by an office of the Prefecture of the Apostolic Household.

American visitors can obtain passes for general audiences by applying to the Bishops' Office for United States Visitors to the Vatican, Casa Santa Maria, Via dell'Umilita, 30, 00187 Rome.

Private and group audiences are reserved for dignitaries of various categories and for special occasions.

Publications

Acta Apostolicae Sedis: The only "official commentary" of the Holy See, was established in 1908 for the publication of activities of the Holy See, laws, decrees and acts of congregations and tribunals of the Roman Curia. The first edition was published in January, 1909.

St. Pius X made *AAS* an official organ in 1908. Laws promulgated for the Church ordinarily take effect three months after the date of their publication in this commentary.

The publication, mostly in Latin and Italian, is printed by the Vatican Polyglot Press.

The immediate predecessor of this organ was *Acta Sanctae Sedis*, founded in 1865 and given official status by the Congregation for the Propagation of the Faith in 1904.

Annuario Pontificio: The yearbook of the Holy See. It is edited by the Vatican Secretariat of State and is printed in Italian, with some portions in other languages, by the Vatican Polyglot Press. It covers the worldwide organization of the Church, lists members of the hierarchy, and includes a wide range of statistical information.

The publication of a statistical yearbook of the Holy See dates back to 1716, when a volume called *Notizie* appeared. Publication under the present title began in 1860, was suspended in 1870, and resumed again in 1872 under the title *Catholic Hierarchy*. This volume was printed privately at first, but has been issued by the Vatican Press since 1885. The title *Annuario Pontificio* was restored in 1912, and the yearbook was called an "official publication" until 1924.

L'Osservatore Romano: The daily newspaper of the Holy See. It began publication July 1, 1861, as an independent enterprise under the ownership and direction of four Catholic laymen headed by Marcantonio Pacelli, vice minister of the interior under Pope Pius IX and a grandfather of the late Pius XII. Leo XIII bought the publication in 1890, making it the "pope's" own newspaper.

The only official material in *L'Osservatore Romano* is that which appears under the heading, "Nostre Informazioni." This includes notices of appointments by the Holy See, the texts of papal encyclicals and addresses by the Holy Father and others, various types of documents, accounts of decisions and rulings of administrative bodies, and similar items. Additional material includes news and comment on developments in the Church and the world. Italian is the language most used.

The editorial board is directed by Valerio Volpini. A staff of about 15 reporters covers Rome news sources. A corps of correspondents provides foreign coverage.

A weekly roundup edition in English was inaugurated in 1968. Other weekly editions are printed in French, Spanish, Portuguese and German. Publication of a monthly Polish edition was begun in February, 1980.

Vatican Press Office: The establishment of a single Vatican Press Office was announced Feb. 29, 1968, to replace service agencies formerly operated by *L'Osservatore Romano* and an office created for press coverage of the Second Vatican Council. Rev. Romeo Panciroli is the director.

Vatican Polyglot Press: The official printing plant of the Vatican.

The Vatican press was conceived by Marcellus II and Pius IV but was actually founded by Sixtus V on Apr. 27, 1587, to print the Vulgate and the writings of the Fathers of the Church and other authors. A Polyglot Press was established in 1626 by the Congregation for the Propagation of the Faith to serve the needs of the Oriental Church. St. Pius X merged both presses under this title.

The plant has facilities for the printing of a wide variety of material in about 30 languages.

Activities of the Holy See: An annual documentary volume covering the activities of the pope — his daily work, general and special audiences, discourses and messages on special occasions, visits outside the Vatican, missionary and charitable endeavors, meetings with diplomats, heads of state and others — and activities of the congregations, commissions, tribunals and offices of the Roman Curia.

Statistical Yearbook of the Church: Issued by the Central Statistics Office of the Church, it contains principal data concerning the presence and work of the Church in the world. The first issue was published in 1972 under the title *Collection of Statistical Tables, 1969*. It is printed in corresponding columns of Italian and Latin. Some of the introductory material is printed in other languages.

VATICAN REPRESENTATIVES

(Sources: *Annuario Pontificio;* NC News Service.)

The Vatican has representatives to a number of quasi-governmental and international organizations.

Governmental Organizations: United Nations (Abp. Giovanni Cheli, permanent observer); UN Office in Geneva (Abp. Jean Rupp, permanent observer); International Atomic Energy Agency (Dr. Hermann Abs, delegate); UN Organization for Industrial

Development (Msgr. Mario Peressin, permanent observer); UN Food and Agriculture Organization (Bp. Agostino Ferrari-Toniolo, permanent observer); UN Educational, Scientific and Cultural Organization (Msgr. Renzo Frana, permanent observer);

Council of Europe (Very Rev. Fortunato Baldelli, special envoy with function of permanent observer); Council for Cultural Cooperation of the Council of Europe (Msgr. Fortunato Baldelli, delegate); Organization of American States (permanent observer); International Institute for the Unification of Private Law (Prof. Pio Ciprotti, delegate); International Committee of Medicine and Pharmacy (Msgr. Victor Heylen); World Organization of Tourism (Rev. Giovanni Arrighi, O.P.);

Universal Postal Union; International Telecommunications Union; International Council on Grain; World Organization of Intellectual Property; International Union for the Protection of Literary and Artistic Works; International Union for the Protection of Industrial Property; International Organization of Telecommunication via Satellite (Intelsat); European Conference of Postal and Telecommunication Administration (CEPT).

Non-Governmental Organizations: International Committee of Historical Sciences (Msgr. Michele Maccarrone); International Committee of Paleography (Msgr. Jose Ruysschaert); International Committee of the History of Art (Prof. Carlo Pietrangeli); International Committee of Anthropological and Ethnological Sciences;

International Committee for the Neutrality of Medicine (Rev. Michel Riquet, S.J., permanent observer); International Center of Study for the Preservation and Restoration of Cultural Goods (Prof. Carlo Pietrangeli); International Council of Monuments and Sites (Prof. Carlo Pietrangeli); International Alliance on Tourism; International Astronomical Union; International Institute of Administrative Sciences; International Technical Committee for Prevention and Extinction of Fires; World Medical Association.

Rationale of Diplomatic Relations

Reasons for the existence of diplomatic relations between the Vatican and various countries were among the subjects of an address delivered by Pope John Paul Jan. 14, 1980, to the diplomatic corps accredited to the Holy See.

"What . . . is the principle that inspires the Apostolic See when it addresses politicians or occupies itself with political matters? A sentence of the Second Vatican Council would sum it up well; 'The Church, by reason of her role and competence, is not identified with any political community nor bound by ties to any political system. It is at once the sign and the safeguard of the transcendental dimension of the human person' (*Pastoral Constitution on the Church in the Modern World,* No. 74).''

"It is true that the common good of a society, a nation, must be promoted in many ways. . . . 'The Church cannot remain insensible to whatever serves man's true welfare, any more than she can remain indifferent to what threatens it' (Encyclical *Redeemer of Man,* No. 13)."

"Some of your countries, in fact, have ties of centuries-old traditions with the Catholic Church because the sons and daughters of these nations, in the vast majority, have long professed the Catholic faith. In others, the Catholic Church is present only with a small group of faithful, sometimes a very small one, but those who exercise power there consider it opportune, however, to maintain diplomatic relations with the Holy See. I am particularly glad to greet the countries that have established such relations in the course of the past year."

"I cannot help thinking of other countries whose deeply Catholic populations would aspire to establishing closer relations with the Holy See.

"The composition of the diplomatic corps makes it possible to understand better, in a proper way, the important problem of the presence of the Church in the modern world. This form does not, of course, take away anything from the urgency of the apostolate of members of the Church, thanks to their daily witness and their action in all the temporal fields in which their life and their profession give them a place.

"But diplomatic relations permit, at another level, a direct and at the same time discreet presence of the Catholic Church, as such and in her head, among the most different peoples, their governments or their representatives. The Church respects their political systems and their temporal responsibilities while bringing them the assistance of the spiritual and moral exigencies to which she bears witness and which her sons endeavor to put into practice. In this sense, she intends to contribute to the good of the people of every country. And, in exchange, the activity of each of the diplomatic representatives encourages the accomplishment of the mission that the Church considers it her duty to carry out in the modern world, for this mission concerns the various dimensions of human existence and the various communities, and so also the political dimension and political communities."

The Church of Santa Susanna, the national church for Americans in Rome, was established Feb. 28, 1922, and entrusted to the care of the Paulist Fathers.

Doctrine of the Catholic Church

Following are excerpts from the first two chapters of the *Dogmatic Constitution on the Church* promulgated by the Second Vatican Council. They describe the relation of the Catholic Church to the Kingdom of God, the nature and foundation of the Church, the People of God, the necessity of membership and participation in the Church for salvation.

Additional subjects in the constitution are treated in other Almanac entries.

I. MYSTERY OF THE CHURCH

". . . By her relationship with Christ, the Church is a kind of sacrament or sign of intimate union with God, and of the unity of all mankind . . ." (No. 1).

". . . He (the eternal Father) planned to assemble in the holy Church all those who would believe in Christ. Already from the beginning of the world the foreshadowing of the Church took place. She was prepared for in a remarkable way throughout the history of the people of Israel and by means of the Old Covenant. Established in the present era of time, the Church was made manifest by the outpouring of the Spirit. At the end of time she will achieve her glorious fulfillment. Then . . . all just men from the time of Adam, 'from Abel, the just one, to the last of the elect,' will be gathered together with the Father in the universal Church" (No. 2).

"When the work which the Father had given the Son to do on earth (cf. Jn. 17:4) was accomplished, the Holy Spirit was sent on the day of Pentecost in order that He might forever sanctify the Church, and thus all believers would have access to the Father through Christ in the one Spirit (cf. Eph. 2:18). . . .

"The Spirit dwells in the Church and in the hearts of the faithful as in a temple (cf. 1 Cor. 3:16; 6:19). . . . The Spirit guides the Church into the fullness of truth (cf. Jn. 16:13) and gives her a unity of fellowship and service. He furnishes and directs her with various gifts, both hierarchical and charismatic, and adorns her with the fruits of His grace (cf. Eph. 4:11-12; 1 Cor. 12:4; Gal. 5:22). By the power of the gospel He makes the Church grow, perpetually renews her, and leads her to perfect union with her Spouse. . . ." (No. 4).

Foundation of the Church

"The mystery of the holy Church is manifest in her very foundation, for the Lord Jesus inaugurated her by preaching the good news, that is, the coming of God's Kingdom, which, for centuries, had been promised in the Scriptures. . . . In Christ's word, in His works, and in His presence this kingdom reveals itself to men. . . .

"The miracles of Jesus also confirm that the kingdom has already arrived on earth. . . .

"Before all things, however, the kingdom is clearly visible in the very person of Christ, Son of God and Son of Man. . . .

"When Jesus rose up again after suffering death on the cross for mankind, He manifested that He had been appointed Lord, Messiah, and Priest forever (cf. Acts 2:36; Hb. 5:6; 7:17-21), and He poured out on His disciples the Spirit promised by the Father (cf. Acts 2:33). The Church, consequently, equipped with the gifts of her Founder and faithfully guarding His precepts . . . receives the mission to proclaim and to establish among all peoples the kingdom of Christ and of God. She becomes on earth the initial budding forth of that kingdom. While she slowly grows, the Church strains toward the consummation of the kingdom and, with all her strength, hopes and desires to be united in glory with her King" (No. 5).

Figures of the Church

"In the Old Testament the revelation of the kingdom had often been conveyed by figures of speech. In the same way the inner nature of the Church was now to be made known to us through various images. . . .

". . . The Church is a sheepfold . . . a flock . . . a tract of land to be cultivated, the field of God . . . His choice vineyard . . . the true Vine is Christ . . . the edifice of God . . . the house of God . . . the holy temple (whose members are) . . . living stones . . . this Holy City . . . a bride . . . 'our Mother' . . . the spotless spouse of the spotless Lamb . . . an exile. . ." (No. 6).

"In the human nature which He united to Himself, the Son of God redeemed man and transformed him into a new creation (cf. Gal. 6:15; 2 Cor. 5:17) by overcoming death through His own death and resurrection. By communicating His Spirit to His brothers, called together from all peoples, Christ made them mystically into His own body.

"In that body, the life of Christ is poured into the believers, who, through the sacraments, are united in a hidden and real way to Christ who suffered and was glorified. Through baptism we are formed in the likeness of Christ. . . .

"Truly partaking of the body of the Lord in the breaking of the Eucharistic bread, we are taken up into communion with Him and with one another . . ." (No. 7).

One Body in Christ

"As all the members of the human body, though they are many, form one body, so also are the faithful in Christ (cf. 1 Cor. 12:12). Also, in the building up of Christ's body there is a flourishing variety of members and functions. There is only one Spirit who . . . distributes His different gifts for the welfare of the Church (cf. 1 Cor. 12:1-11). Among these gifts stands out the grace given to the apostles. To their authority, the Spirit Himself subjected even those who were endowed with charisms (cf. 1 Cor. 14). . . .

"The head of this body is Christ . . ." (No. 7).

Mystical Body of Christ

"Christ, the one Mediator, established and ceaselessly sustains here on earth His holy Church, the community of faith, hope, and charity, as a visible structure. Through her He communicates truth and grace to all. But the society furnished with hierarchical agencies and the Mystical Body of Christ are not to be considered as two realities, nor are the visible assembly and the spiritual community, nor the earthly Church and the Church enriched with heavenly things. Rather they form one interlocked reality which is comprised of a divine and a human element. For this reason . . . this reality is compared to the mystery of the incarnate Word. Just as the assumed nature inseparably united to the divine Word serves Him as a living instrument of salvation, so, in a similar way, does the communal structure of the Church serve Christ's Spirit, who vivifies it by way of building up the body (cf. Eph. 4:16).

"This is the unique Church of Christ which in the Creed we avow as one, holy, catholic, and apostolic. After His Resurrection our Savior handed her over to Peter to be shepherded (Jn. 21:17), commissioning him and the other apostles to propagate and govern her (cf. Mt. 28:18, ff.). Her He erected for all ages as 'the pillar and mainstay of the truth' (1 Tm. 3:15). This Church, constituted and organized in the world as a society, subsists in the Catholic Church, which is governed by the successor of Peter and by the bishops in union with that successor, although many elements of sanctification and of truth can be found outside of her visible structure. These elements, however, as gifts properly belonging to the Church of Christ, possess an inner dynamism toward Catholic unity.

". . . the Church, embracing sinners in her bosom, is at the same time holy and always in need of being purified, and incessantly pursues the path of penance and renewal.

"The Church, 'like a pilgrim in a foreign land, presses forward . . .' announcing the cross and death of the Lord until He comes (cf. 1 Cor. 11:26) . . ." (No. 8).

II. THE PEOPLE OF GOD

"At all times and among every people, God has given welcome to whosoever fears Him and does what is right (cf. Acts 10:35). It has pleased God, however, to make men holy and save them not merely as individuals without any mutual bonds, but by making them into a single people, a people which acknowledges Him in truth and serves Him in holiness. He therefore chose the race of Israel as a people unto Himself. With it He set up a covenant. Step by step He taught this people by manifesting in its history both Himself and the decree of His will, and by making it holy unto Himself. All these things, however, were done by way of preparation and as a figure of that new and perfect covenant which was to be ratified in Christ. . . .

". . . Christ instituted this new covenant, that is to say, the new testament, in His blood (cf. 1 Cor. 11:25), by calling together a people made up of Jew and Gentile, making them one, not according to the flesh but in the Spirit.

"This was to be the new People of God . . . reborn . . . through the Word of the living God (cf. 1 Pt. 1:23) . . . from water and the Holy Spirit (cf. Jn. 3:5-6) . . . 'a chosen race, a royal priesthood, a holy nation, a purchased people. . . . You who in times past were not a people, but are now the people of God' (1 Pt. 2:9-10).

"That messianic people has for its head Christ. . . . Its law is the new commandment to love as Christ loved us (cf. Jn. 13:34). Its goal is the kingdom of God, which has been begun by God Himself on earth, and which is to be further extended until it is brought to perfection by Him at the end of time. . . .

". . . This messianic people, although it does not actually include all men, and may more than once look like a small flock, is nonetheless a lasting and sure seed of unity, hope, and salvation for the whole human race. Established by Christ as a fellowship of life, charity, and truth, it is also used by Him as an instrument for the redemption of all, and is sent forth into the whole world as the light of the world and the salt of the earth (cf. Mt. 5:13-16).

"Israel according to the flesh . . . was already called the Church of God (2 Ezr. 13:1; cf. Nm. 20:4; Dt. 23:1, ff.). Likewise the new Israel . . . is also called the Church of Christ (cf. Mt. 16:18). For He has bought it for Himself with His blood (cf. Acts 20:28), has filled it with His Spirit, and provided it with those means which befit it as a visible and social unity. God has gathered together as one all those who in faith look upon Jesus as the author of salvation and the source of unity and peace, and has established them as the Church, that for each and all she may be the visible sacrament of this saving unity . . ." (No. 9)

Priesthood

". . . The baptized, by regeneration and the anointing of the Holy Spirit, are consecrated into . . . a holy priesthood. . . ."

(All members of the Church participate in

the priesthood of Christ, through the common priesthood of the faithful. See Priesthood of the Laity.)

"Though they differ from one another in essence and not only in degree, the common priesthood of the faithful and the ministerial or hierarchical priesthood are nonetheless interrelated. Each of them in its own special way is a participation in the one priesthood of Christ . . ." (No. 10).

"It is through the sacraments and the exercise of the virtues that the sacred nature and organic structure of the priestly community is brought into operation . . ." (No. 11). See Role of the Sacraments.)

Prophetic Office

"The holy People of God shares also in Christ's prophetic office. It spreads abroad a living witness to Him, especially by means of a life of faith and charity and by offering to God a sacrifice of praise. . . . The body of the faithful as a whole, anointed as they are by the Holy One (cf. Jn. 2:20, 27), cannot err in matters of belief. Thanks to a supernatural sense of faith which characterizes the People as a whole, it manifests this unerring quality when, 'from the bishops down to the last member of the laity,' it shows universal agreement in matters of faith and morals.

". . . God's People accepts not the word of men but the very Word of God (cf. 1 Thes. 2:13). It clings without fail to the faith once delivered to the saints (cf. Jude 3), penetrates it more deeply by accurate insights, and applies it more thoroughly to life. All this it does under the lead of a sacred teaching authority to which it loyally defers.

"It is not only through the sacraments and Church ministries that the same Holy Spirit sanctifies and leads the People of God. . . . He distributes special graces among the faithful of every rank. By these gifts He makes them fit and ready to undertake the various tasks or offices advantageous for the renewal and upbuilding of the Church. . . . These charismatic gifts . . . are to be received with thanksgiving and consolation, for they are exceedingly suitable and useful for the needs of the Church.

". . . Judgment as to their genuineness and proper use belongs to those who preside over the Church, and to whose special competence it belongs . . . to test all things and hold fast to that which is good (cf. 1 Thes. 5:12; 19-21)" (No. 12).

All Are Called

"All men are called to belong to the new People of God. Wherefore this People, while remaining one and unique, is to be spread throughout the whole world and must exist in all ages, so that the purpose of God's will may be fulfilled. In the beginning God made human nature one. After His children were scattered, He decreed that they should at length be united again (cf. Jn. 11:52). It was for this reason that God sent His Son . . . that He might be Teacher, King, and Priest of all, the Head of the New and universal people of the sons of God. For this God finally sent His Son's Spirit as Lord and Lifegiver. He it is who, on behalf of the whole Church and each and every one of those who believe, is the principle of their coming together and remaining together in the teaching of the apostles and in fellowship, in the breaking of bread and in prayers (cf. Acts 2:42)" (No. 13).

One People of God

"It follows that among all the nations of earth there is but one People of God, which takes its citizens from every race, making them citizens of a kingdom which is of a heavenly and not an earthly nature. For all the faithful scattered throughout the world are in communion with each other in the Holy Spirit . . .the Church or People of God . . . foster(s) and take(s) to herself, insofar as they are good, the ability, resources and customs of each people. Taking them to herself she purifies, strengthens, and enobles them. . . . This characteristic of universality which adorns the People of God is a gift from the Lord Himself. By reason of it, the Catholic Church strives energetically and constantly to bring all humanity with all its riches back to Christ its Head in the unity of His Spirit.

"In virtue of this catholicity each individual part of the Church contributes through its special gifts to the good of the other parts and of the whole Church. Thus through the common sharing of gifts . . . the whole and each of the parts receive increase. . . .

"All men are called to be part of this catholic unity of the People of God. . . . And there belong to it or are related to it in various ways, the Catholic faithful as well as all who believe in Christ, and indeed the whole of mankind. For all men are called to salvation by the grace of God" (No. 13).

The Catholic Church

"This sacred Synod turns its attention first to the Catholic faithful. Basing itself upon sacred Scripture and tradition, it teaches that the Church . . . is necessary for salvation. For Christ, made present to us in His Body, which is the Church, is the one Mediator and the unique Way of salvation. In explicit terms He Himself affirmed the necessity of faith and baptism (cf. Mk. 16:16; Jn. 3:5) and thereby affirmed also the necessity of the Church, for through baptism as through a door men enter the Church. Whosoever, therefore, knowing that the Catholic Church was made necessary by God through Jesus Christ, would refuse to enter her or to remain in her could not be saved.

"They are fully incorporated into the society of the Church who, possessing the Spirit of Christ, accept her entire system and all the means of salvation given to her, and through union with her visible structure are joined to Christ, who rules her through the Supreme Pontiff and the bishops. This joining is effected by the bonds of professed faith, of the sacraments, of ecclesiastical government, and of communion. He is not saved, however, who, though he is part of the body of the Church, does not persevere in charity. He remains indeed in the bosom of the Church, but . . . only in a 'bodily' manner and not 'in his heart.' . . .

"Catechumens who, moved by the Holy Spirit, seek with explicit intention to be incorporated into the Church are by that very intention joined to her. . . . Mother Church already embraces them as her own" (No. 14).

Other Christians, The Unbaptized

"The Church recognizes that in many ways she is linked with those who, being baptized, are honored with the name of Christian, though they do not profess the faith in its entirety or do not preserve unity of communion with the successor of Peter. . . .

" . . . We can say that in some real way they are joined with us in the Holy Spirit, for to them also He gives His gifts and graces, and is thereby operative among them with His sanctifying power . . ." (No. 15).

"Finally, those who have not yet received the gospel are related in various ways to the People of God. In the first place there is the people to whom the covenants and the promises were given and from whom Christ was born according to the flesh (cf. Rom. 9:4-5). On account of their fathers, this people remains most dear to God, for God does not repent of the gifts He makes nor of the calls He issues (cf. Rom. 11:28-29).

"But the plan of salvation also includes those who acknowledge the Creator. In the first place among these are the Moslems. . . . Nor is God Himself far distant from those who in shadows and images seek the unknown God. . . .

"Those also can attain to everlasting salvation who through no fault of their own do not know the gospel of Christ or His Church, yet sincerely seek God and, moved by grace, strive by their deeds to do His will as it is known to them through the dictates of conscience. Nor does divine Providence deny the help necessary for salvation to those who, without blame on their part, have not yet arrived at an explicit knowledge of God, but who strive to live a good life, thanks to His grace. Whatever goodness or truth is found among them is looked upon by the Church as a preparation for the Gospel. She regards such qualities as given by Him who enlightens all men so that they may finally have life . . ." (No. 16).

THE POPE, TEACHING AUTHORITY, COLLEGIALITY

The Roman Pontiff — the successor of St. Peter as the Vicar of Christ and head of the Church on earth — has full and supreme authority over the universal Church in matters pertaining to faith and morals (teaching authority), discipline and government (jurisdictional authority).

The primacy of the pope is real and supreme power. It is not merely a prerogative of honor — that is, of his being regarded as the first among equals. Neither does primacy imply that the pope is just the presiding officer of the collective body of bishops. The pope is the head of the Church.

Catholic belief in the primacy of the pope was stated in detail in the dogmatic constitution on the Church, *Pastor Aeternus*, approved in 1870 by the fourth session of the First Vatican Council. Some elaboration of the doctrine was made in the *Dogmatic Constitution on the Church* which was approved and promulgated by the Second Vatican Council Nov. 21, 1964. The entire body of teaching on the subject is based on Scripture and tradition and the centuries-long experience of the Church.

Infallibility

The essential points of doctrine concerning infallibility in the Church and the infallibility of the pope were stated by the Second Vatican Council in the *Dogmatic Constitution on the Church,* as follows:

"This infallibility with which the divine Redeemer willed his Church to be endowed in defining a doctrine of faith and morals extends as far as extends the deposit of divine revelation, which must be religiously guarded and faithfully expounded. This is the infallibility which the Roman Pontiff, the head of the college of bishops, enjoys in virtue of his office, when, as the supreme shepherd and teacher of all the faithful, who confirms his brethren in their faith (cf. Lk. 22:32), he proclaims by a definitive act some doctrine of faith or morals. Therefore his definitions, of themselves, and not from the consent of the Church, are justly styled irreformable, for they are pronounced with the assistance of the Holy Spirit, an assistance promised to him in blessed Peter. Therefore they need no approval of others, nor do they allow an appeal to any other judgment. For then the Roman Pontiff is not pronouncing judgment as a private person. Rather, as the supreme teacher of the universal Church, as one in whom the charism of the infallibility of the Church herself is individually present, he is expounding or defending a doctrine of Catholic faith.

"The infallibility promised to the Church resides also in the body of bishops when that body exercises supreme teaching authority with the successor of Peter. To the resultant definitions the assent of the Church can never be wanting, on account of the activity of that same Holy Spirit, whereby the whole flock of Christ is preserved and progresses in unity of faith.

"But when either the Roman Pontiff or the body of bishops together with him defines a judgment, they pronounce it in accord with revelation itself. All are obliged to maintain and be ruled by this revelation, which, as written or preserved by tradition, is transmitted in its entirety through the legitimate succession of bishops and especially through the care of the Roman Pontiff himself.

"Under the guiding light of the Spirit of truth, revelation is thus religiously preserved and faithfully expounded in the Church. The Roman Pontiff and the bishops, in view of their office and of the importance of the matter, strive painstakingly and by appropriate means to inquire properly into that revelation and to give apt expression to its contents. But they do not allow that there could be any new public revelation pertaining to the divine deposit of faith" (No. 25).

Authentic Teaching

The pope rarely speaks *ex cathedra* — that is, "from the chair" of St. Peter, for the purpose of making an infallible pronouncement. More often and in various ways he states authentic teaching in line with Scripture, tradition, the living experience of the Church, and the whole analogy of faith. Of such teaching, the Second Vatican Council said in its *Dogmatic Constitution on the Church* (No. 25):

". . . Religious submission of will and of mind must be shown in a special way to the authentic teaching authority of the Roman Pontiff, even when he is not speaking *ex cathedra*. That is, it must be shown in such a way that his supreme magisterium is acknowledged with reverence, the judgments made by him are sincerely adhered to, according to his manifest mind and will. His mind and will in the matter may be known chiefly either from the character of the documents, from his frequent repetition of the same doctrine, or from his manner of speaking."

With respect to bishops, the constitution said: "They are authentic teachers, that is, teachers endowed with the authority of Christ, who preach to the people committed to them the faith they must believe and put into practice. By the light of the Holy Spirit, they make that faith clear, bringing forth from the treasury of revelation new things and old (cf. Mt. 13:52), making faith bear fruit and vigilantly warding off any errors which threaten their flock (cf. Tm. 4:1-4).

"Bishops, teaching in communion with the Roman Pontiff, are to be respected by all as witnesses to divine and Catholic truth. In matters of faith and morals, the bishops speak in the name of Christ and the faithful are to accept their teaching and adhere to it with a religious assent of soul."

Magisterium—Teaching Authority

Responsibility for teaching doctrine and judging orthodoxy belongs to the official teaching authority of the Church.

This authority is personalized in the pope, the successor of St. Peter as head of the Church, and in the bishops together and in union with the pope, as it was originally committed to Peter and to the whole college of Apostles under his leadership. They are the official teachers of the Church.

Others have auxiliary relationships with the magisterium: theologians, in the study and clarification of doctrine; teachers — priests, religious, lay persons — who cooperate with the pope and bishops in spreading knowledge of religious truth; the faithful, who by their sense of faith and personal witness contribute to the development of doctrine and the establishment of its relevance to life in the Church and the world.

The magisterium, Pope Paul noted in an address at a general audience Jan. 11, 1967, "is a subordinate and faithful echo and secure interpreter of the divine word." It does not reveal new truths, "nor is it superior to Sacred Scripture." Its competence extends to the limits of divine revelation manifested in Scripture and tradition and the living experience of the Church, with respect to matters of faith and morals and related subjects.

Official teaching in these areas is infallible when it is formally defined, for belief and acceptance by all members of the Church, by the pope, acting in the capacity of supreme shepherd of the flock of Christg and when doctrine is proposed and taught with moral unanimity of bishops with the pope in a solemn collegial manner as in an ecumenical council, and/or in the ordinary course of events. Even when not infallibly defined, official teaching in the areas of faith and morals is authoritative and requires religious assent.

The teachings of the magisterium have been documented in creeds, formulas of faith, decrees and enactments of ecumenical and particular councils, various kinds of doctrinal statements, and other teaching instruments. They have also been incorporated into the liturgy, with the result that the law of prayer is said to be a law of belief.

Collegiality

The bishops of the Church, in union with the pope, have supreme teaching and pastoral authority over the whole Church in addition to the authority of office they have for their own dioceses.

This collegial authority is exercised in a solemn manner in an ecumenical council and can be exercised in other ways as well, "provided that the head of the college calls them to collegiate action, or at least so approves or freely accepts the united action of the dispersed bishops, that it is made a true collegiate act."

This doctrine is grounded on the fact that: "Just as, by the Lord's will, St. Peter and the other apostles constituted one apostolic college, so in a similar way the Roman Pontiff as the successor of Peter, and the bishops as the successors of the apostles are joined together."

Doctrine on collegiality was stated by the Second Vatican Council in the *Dogmatic Constitution on the Church* (Nos. 22 and 23).

REVELATION

Following are excerpts from the *Constitution on Revelation* promulgated by the Second Vatican Council. They describe the nature and process of divine revelation, inspiration and interpretation of Scripture, the Old and New Testaments, and the role of Scripture in the life of the Church.

I. Revelation Itself

". . . God chose to reveal Himself and to make known to us the hidden purpose of His will (cf. Eph. 1:9) by which through Christ, the Word made flesh, man has access to the Father in the Holy Spirit and comes to share in the divine nature (cf. Eph. 2:18; 2 Pt. 1:4). Through this revelation, therefore, the invisible God (cf. Col. 1:15; 1 Tm. 1:17) . . . speaks to men as friends (cf. Ex. 33:11; Jn. 15:14-15) and lives among them (cf. Bar. 3:38) so that He may invite and take them into fellowship with Himself. This plan of revelation is realized by deeds and words having an inner unity: the deeds wrought by God in the history of salvation manifest and confirm the teaching and realities signified by the words, while the words proclaim the deeds and clarify the mystery contained in them. By this revelation then, the deepest truth about God and the salvation of man is made clear to us in Christ, who is the Mediator and at the same time the fullness of all revelation" (No. 2).

"God . . . from the start manifested Himself to our first parents. Then after their fall His promise of redemption aroused in them the hope of being saved (cf. Gn. 3:15), and from that time on He ceaselessly kept the human race in His care, in order to give eternal life to those who perseveringly do good in search of salvation (cf. Rom. 2:6-7). . . . He called Abraham in order to make of him a great nation (cf. Gn. 12:2). Through the patriarchs, and after them through Moses and the prophets, He taught this nation to acknowledge Himself as the one living and true God . . . and to wait for the Savior promised by Him. In this manner He prepared the way for the gospel down through the centuries" (No. 3).

Revelation in Christ

"Then, after speaking in many places and varied ways through the prophets, God 'last of all in these days has spoken to us by His Son' (Hb. 1:1-2). . . . Jesus perfected revelation by fulfilling it through His whole work of making Himself present and manifesting Himself: through His words and deeds, His signs and wonders, but especially through His death and glorious resurrection from the dead and final sending of the spirit of truth. Moreover, He confirmed with divine testimony what revelation proclaimed: that God is with us to free us from the darkness of sin and death, and to raise us up to life eternal.

"The Christian dispensation, therefore, as the new and definitive covenant, will never pass away, and we now await no further new public revelation before the glorious manifestation of our Lord Jesus Christ (cf. 1 Tm. 6:14; Ti. 2:13)" (No. 4).

II. Transmission of Revelation

". . . God has seen to it that what He had revealed for the salvation of all nations would abide perpetually in its full integrity and be handed on to all generations. Therefore Christ the Lord, in whom the full revelation of the supreme God is brought to completion (cf. 2 Cor. 1:20; 3:16; 4:6), commissioned the apostles to preach to all men that gospel which is the source of all saving truth and moral teaching, and thus to impart to them divine gifts. This gospel had been promised in former times through the prophets, and Christ Himself fulfilled it and promulgated it with His own lips. This commission was faithfully fulfilled by the apostles who, by their oral preaching, by example, and by ordinances, handed on what they had received from . . . Christ . . . or what they had learned through the prompting of the Holy Spirit. The commission was fulfilled, too, by those apostles and apostolic men who under the inspiration of the same Holy Spirit committed the message of salvation to writing" (No. 7).

Tradition

"But in order to keep the gospel forever whole and alive within the Church, the apostles left bishops as their successors, 'handing over their own teaching role' to them. This sacred tradition, therefore, and sacred Scripture of both the Old and the New Testament are like a mirror in which the pilgrim Church on earth looks at God . . ." (No. 7).

". . . The apostolic preaching, which is expressed in a special way in the inspired books, was to be preserved by a continuous succession of preachers until the end of time. Therefore the apostles, handing on what they themselves had received, warn the faithful to hold fast to the traditions which they have learned. . . . Now what was handed on by the apostles includes everything which contributes to the holiness of life, and the increase in faith of the People of God; and so the Church, in her teaching, life, and worship, perpetuates and hands on to all generations all that she herself is, all that she believes" (No. 8).

Development of Doctrine

"This tradition which comes from the apostles develops in the Church with the help of the Holy Spirit. For there is a growth in the understanding of the realities and the words which have been handed down. This happens through the contemplation and study made by believers . . . through the intimate understanding of spiritual things they experience, and through the preaching of those who have received through episcopal succession the sure gift of truth. For, as the centuries succeed one another, the Church constantly moves forward toward the fullness of divine truth until the words of God reach their complete fulfillment in her.

"The words of the holy Fathers witness to the living presence of this tradition, whose wealth is poured into the practice and life of the believing and praying Church. Through the same tradition the Church's full canon of the sacred books is known, and the sacred writings themselves are more profoundly understood and unceasingly made active in her; . . . and the Holy Spirit, through whom the living voice of the gospel resounds in the Church, and through her, in the world, leads unto all truth those who believe and makes the word of Christ dwell abundantly in them (cf. Col. 3:16)" (No. 8).

Tradition and Scripture

"Hence there exist a close connection and communication between sacred tradition and sacred Scripture. For both of them, flowing from the same divine wellspring, in a certain way merge into a unity and tend toward the same end. For sacred Scripture is the word of God inasmuch as it is consigned to writing under the inspiration of the divine Spirit. To the successors of the apostles, sacred tradition hands on in its full purity God's word, which was entrusted to the apostles by Christ the Lord and the Holy Spirit. Thus, led by the light of the Spirit of truth, these successors can in their preaching preserve this word of God faithfully, explain it, and make it more widely known. Consequently, it is not from sacred Scripture alone that the Church draws her certainty about everything which has been revealed. Therefore both sacred tradition and sacred Scripture are to be accepted and venerated with the same sense of devotion and reverence" (No. 9).

"Sacred tradition and sacred Scripture form one sacred deposit of the word of God, which is committed to the Church" (No. 10).

Teaching Authority of Church

"The task of authentically interpreting the word of God, whether written or handed on, has been entrusted exclusively to the living teaching office of the Church, whose authority is exercised in the name of Jesus Christ. This teaching office is not above the word of God, but serves it, teaching only what has been handed on . . . it draws from this one deposit of faith everything which it presents for belief as divinely revealed.

"It is clear, therefore, that sacred tradition, sacred Scripture, and the teaching authority of the Church . . . are so linked and joined together that one cannot stand without the others, and that all together and each in its own way under the action of the one Holy Spirit contribute effectively to the salvation of souls" (No. 10).

III. Inspiration, Interpretation

"Those . . . revealed realities . . . contained and presented in sacred Scripture have been committed to writing under the inspiration of the Holy Spirit. Holy Mother Church, relying on the belief of the apostles, holds that the books of both the Old and New Testament in their entirety, with all their parts, are sacred and canonical because, having been written under the inspiration of the Holy Spirit (cf. Jn. 20:31; 2 Tm. 3:16; 2 Pt. 1:19-21; 3:15-16) they have God as their author and have been handed on as such to the Church herself. In composing the sacred books, God chose men and while employed by Him they made use of their powers and abilities, so that with Him acting in them and through them, they, as true authors, consigned to writing everything and only those things which He wanted" (No. 11).

Inerrancy

"Therefore, since everything asserted by the inspired authors or sacred writers must be held to be asserted by the Holy Spirit, it follows that the books of Scripture must be acknowledged as teaching firmly, faithfully, and without error that truth which God wanted put into the sacred writings for the sake of our salvation. Therefore 'all Scripture is inspired by God and useful for teaching, for reproving, for correcting, for instruction in justice; that the man of God may be perfect, equipped for every good work' (2 Tm. 3:16-17)" (No. 11).

Literary Forms

"However, since God speaks in sacred Scripture through men in human fashion, the interpreter of sacred Scripture, in order to see clearly what God wanted to communicate to us, should carefully investigate what meaning the sacred writers really intended, and what God wanted to manifest by means of their words.

". . . The interpreter must' investigate what meaning the sacred writer intended to express and actually expressed in particular circumstances as he used contemporary literary forms in accordance with the situation of his own time and culture. For the correct understanding of what the sacred author wanted to assert, due attention must be paid to the customary and characteristic styles of perceiving, speaking, and narrating which prevailed at the time of the sacred writer, and to the customs men normally followed at that period in their everyday dealings with one another" (No. 12).

Analogy of Faith

". . . No less serious attention must be given to the content and unity of the whole of Scripture, if the meaning of the sacred texts is to be correctly brought to light. The living tradition of the whole Church must be taken into account along with the harmony which exists between elements of the faith. . . . all of what has been said about the way of interpreting Scripture is subject finally to the judgment of the Church, which carries out the divine commission and ministry of guarding and interpreting the word of God" (No. 12).

IV. The Old Testament

"In carefully planning and preparing the salvation of the whole human race, the God of supreme love, by a special dispensation, chose for Himself a people to whom He might entrust His promises. First He entered into a covenant with Abraham (cf. Gn. 15:18) and, through Moses, with the people of Israel (cf. Ex. 24:8). To this people which He had acquired for Himself, He so manifested Himself through words and deeds as the one true and living God that Israel came to know by experience the ways of God with men. . . . The plan of salvation, foretold by the sacred authors, recounted and explained by them, is found as the true word of God in the books of the Old Testament: these books, therefore, written under divine inspiration, remain permanently valuable . . ." (No. 14).

Principal Purpose

"The principal purpose to which the plan of the Old Covenant was directed was to prepare for the coming both of Christ, the universal Redeemer, and of the messianic kingdom. . . . Now the books of the Old Testament, in accordance with the state of mankind before the time of salvation established by Christ, reveal to all men the knowledge of God and of man and the ways in which God . . . deals with men. These books . . . show us true divine pedagogy . . ." (No. 15).

". . . The books of the Old Testament with all their parts, caught up into the proclamation of the gospel, acquire and show forth their full meaning in the New Testament (cf. Mt. 5:17; Lk. 24:27; Rom. 16:25-26; 2 Cor. 3:14-16) and in turn shed light on it and explain it" (No. 16).

V. The New Testament

"The word of God . . . is set forth and shows its power in a most excellent way in the writings of the New Testament. For when the fullness of time arrived (cf. Gal. 4:4), the Word was made flesh and dwelt among us in the fullness of grace and truth (cf. Jn. 1:14). Christ established the Kingdom of God on earth, manifested His Father and Himself by deeds and words, and completed His work by His death, resurrection, and glorious ascension and by the sending of the Holy Spirit. Having been lifted up from the earth, He draws all men to Himself (cf. Jn. 12:32). . . . This mystery had not been manifested to other generations as it was now revealed to His holy apostles and prophets in the Holy Spirit (cf. Eph. 3:4-6), so that they might preach the Gospel, stir up faith in Jesus, Christ and Lord, and gather the Church together. To these realities, the writings of the New Testament stand as a perpetual and divine witness" (No. 17).

The Gospels and Other Writings

". . . The Gospels have a special preeminence . . . for they are the principal witness of the life and teaching of the incarnate Word, our Savior.

"The Church has always and everywhere held and continues to hold that the four Gospels are of apostolic origin. For what the apostles preached . . . afterwards they themselves and apostolic men, under the inspiration of the divine Spirit, handed on to us in writing: the foundation of faith, namely, the fourfold Gospel, according to Matthew, Mark, Luke, and John" (No. 18).

". . . The four Gospels, . . . whose historical character the Church unhesitatingly asserts, faithfully hand on what Jesus Christ, while living among men, really did and taught for their eternal salvation until the day He was taken up into heaven (see Acts 1:1-2). Indeed, after the ascension of the Lord the apostles handed on to their hearers what He had said and done. . . . The sacred authors wrote the four Gospels, selecting some things from the many which had been handed on by word of mouth or in writing, reducing some of them to a synthesis, explicating some things in view of the situation of their churches, and preserving the form of proclamation but always in such fashion that they told us the honest truth about Jesus. For their intention in writing was that . . . we might know 'the truth' concerning those matters about which we have been instructed (cf. Lk. 1:2-4)" (No. 19).

"Besides the four Gospels, the canon of the New Testament also contains the Epistles of St. Paul and other apostolic writings, composed under the inspiration of the Holy Spirit. In these writings . . . those matters which concern Christ the Lord are confirmed, His true teaching is more and more fully stated, the saving power of the divine work of Christ is preached, the story is told of the beginnings of the Church and her marvelous growth, and her glorious fulfillment is foretold" (No. 20).

VI. Scripture in Church Life

"The Church has always venerated the divine Scriptures just as she venerates the body of the Lord. . . . She has always regarded the Scriptures together with sacred tradition as the supreme rule of faith, and will ever do so. For, inspired by God and committed once and for all to writing, they impart the word of God Himself without change, and make the voice of the Holy Spirit resound in the words of the prophets and apostles. Therefore, like the Christian religion itself, all the preaching of the Church must be nourished and ruled by sacred Scripture . . ." (No. 21).

"Easy access to sacred Scripture should be provided for all the Christian faithful. That is why the Church from the very beginning accepted as her own that very ancient Greek translation of the Old Testament which is named after seventy men (the Septuagint); and she has always given a place of honor to other translations, Eastern and Latin, especially the one known as the Vulgate. But since the word of God should be available at all times, the Church with maternal concern sees to it that suitable and correct translations are made into different languages, especially from the original texts of the sacred books. And if, given the opportunity and the approval of Church authority, these translations are produced in cooperation with the separated brethren as well, all Christians will be able to use them" (No. 22).

Biblical Studies, Theology

The constitution encouraged the development and progress of biblical studies "under the watchful care of the sacred teaching office of the Church." (Such studies have made great progress in recent years.)

It noted also: "Sacred theology rests on the written word of God, together with sacred tradition, as its primary and perpetual foundation," and that "the study of the sacred page is, as it were, the soul of sacred theology" (Nos. 23, 24).

TRENDS IN AMERICAN THEOLOGY

Following are excerpts from a report on trends in American theology submitted by Cardinal William Baum, then chairman of the Bishops' Committee on Doctrine, to the meeting of the National Conference of Catholic Bishops Nov. 12 to 15, 1979.

"In every field of theological inquiry, certain positions have been adopted, even publicly, which are contrary to what the Church believes about the mystery of the human person. Our Holy Father recognized this serious pastoral problem in his address at The Catholic University of America (Oct. 7, 1979): 'It is the right of the faithful not to be troubled by theories and hypotheses that they are not expert in judging or that are easily simplified or manipulated by public opinion for ends that are alien to the truth.' "

Improper Christology

"In my opinion, most of these diverse and troubling positions stem from a single root problem: an improper Christology. Not only are there deficient understandings of the mystery of Christ, but often insufficient attention is paid to this sublime mystery upon which everything else depends. Hence, even those who adhere to the Church's authentic faith in Christ sometimes fail to see its profound implications for every teaching on faith and morals that the Church proposes for belief and acceptance."

"It is clear that what is often denied or neglected is the divinity of the Lord, and this is many times due to the opinion that his divinity is destructive not only of his humanity but also of ours. At stake, then, is the unsurpassable dignity of human nature itself, capable of being divinized in the eternal Son."

"Nowhere does the impoverishment and even falsification of theology which result from deficient Christology become more apparent than in the area of moral theology.

Other Effects

Deficient Christologies also adversely affect the way in which the ministry of orders is discussed today. For example, the priesthood is sometimes discussed in such a way that its inalienable Christological and therefore sacramental dimensions are lost. It is clear that what is most disputed today is the profound, indeed ontological, configuration of the priest to the Person of Christ, so that within the sacred assembly the priest in his person, in fact, speaks and acts in the Person of Christ, our great High Priest.

"Deficient Christologies threaten not only various teachings of the Church, but challenge the very constitution of the Church. If indeed Christ were merely a chosen prophet, but not divine, if indeed he were unaware or even mistaken about his ministry upon earth, then it would not be surprising were the Church to be confused about her mission and identity."

"As it is, no such confusion has ever marked the Church's mission and self-reflection from apostolic times to this very day."

THE BIBLE

The Catholic canon of the Old Testament consists of:

• The Pentateuch, the first five books: Genesis (Gn.), Exodus (Ex.), Leviticus (Lv.), Numbers (Nm.), Deuteronomy (Dt.).

• Historical Books: Joshua (Jos.), Judges (Jgs.), Ruth (Ru.), 1 and 2 Samuel (Sm.), 1 and 2 Kings (Kgs.), 1 and 2 Chronicles (Chr.), Ezra (Ezr.), Nehemiah (Neh.), Tobit (Tb.), Judith (Jdt.), Esther (Est.), 1 and 2 Maccabees (Mc.).

• Wisdom Books: Job (Jb.), Psalms (Ps.), Proverbs (Prv.), Ecclesiastes (Eccl.), Song of Songs (Song), Wisdom (Wis.), Sirach (Sir.).

• The Prophets: Isaiah (Is.), Jeremiah (Jer.), Lamentations (Lam.), Baruch (Bar.), Ezechiel (Ez.), Daniel (Dn.), Hosea (Hos.), Joel (Jl.), Amos (Am.), Obadiah (Ob.), Jonah (Jon.), Micah (Mi.), Nahum (Na.), Habakkuk (Hb.), Zephaniah (Zep.), Haggai (Hg.), Zechariah (Zec.), Malachi (Mal.).

The Catholic canon of the New Testament consists of:

• The Gospels of Matthew (Mt.), Mark (Mk.), Luke (Lk.), John (Jn.)

• The Acts of the Apostles (Acts).

• The Pauline Letters — Romans (Rom.), 1 and 2 Corinthians (Cor.), Galatians (Gal.), Ephesians (Eph.), Philippians (Phil.), Colossians (Col.), 1 and 2 Thessalonians (Thes.), 1 and 2 Timothy (Tm.), Titus (Ti.), Philemon (Phlm.), Hebrews (Heb.); the Catholic Letters — James (Jas.), 1 and 2 Peter (Pt.), 1, 2 and 3 John (Jn.), Jude (Jude).

• Revelation (Rv.).

Catholic and Other Canons

The Catholic canon of the Old Testament was determined by the tradition of the Church. It was firm by the fifth century, despite some questioning by scholars, and was stated by the African councils of Hippo in 393 and Carthage in 397 and 419, by Innocent I in 405, and by the Council of Florence in 1441. It was defined by the Council of Trent in the dogmatic decree *De Canonicis Scripturis,* Apr. 8, 1546.

The Jews, although they generally accepted 22 or 24 books as sacred in the first century A.D., did not have a definite canon of sacred writings until late in the second or early in the third century. This canon was fixed by the consensus of rabbinical schools.

The canon of the Hebrew Masoretic Text, which is accepted by modern Jews, consists of 24 books, as follows:

• The Law: Genesis, Exodus, Leviticus, Numbers, Deuteronomy.

• The Prophets: earlier prophets — Joshua, Judges, Samuel, Kings; later prophets — Isaiah, Jeremiah, Ezekiel, and 12 others in one book (Hosea, Joel, Amos, Obadiah, Jonah, Micah, Nahum, Habakkuk, Zephaniah, Haggai, Zechariah, Malachi).

• The Writings: Psalms, Job, Proverbs, Ruth, Song of Songs, Ecclesiastes, Lamentations, Esther, Daniel, Ezra-Nehemiah, Chronicles.

This canon does not include a number of books in the Alexandrian collection of sacred writings — viz., 1 and 2 Maccabees, Tobit, Judith, Sirach, Wisdom, Baruch, and portions of Esther and Daniel (chapters 13 and 14). These additional books and passages, contained in the Septuagint version of the Old Testament and called deuterocanonical, are in the Catholic canon.

These books and passages, called deuterocanonical in terminology coined by Sixtus of Siena (1520-1569), were under discussion for some time until questions about their canonicity were settled. Books admitted into the canon with little or no debate were called protocanonical. The canonical status of both categories of books is the same in the Catholic Bible.

The Protestant canon, in an arrangement of 39 books, is the same as the Hebrew canon.

The Old Testament canon has not been definitely settled by the Orthodox. Since the time of the Reformation, however, they have given some preference to the Protestant canon.

The New Testament canon was firm by the end of the fourth century. By the end of the second century all of the New Testament books were generally known and most of them were acknowledged as inspired. The Muratorian Fragment, dating from about 200, listed most of the books recognized in later decrees as canonical. Prior to the end of the fourth century, however, there were controversies over the inspired character of several books — viz., the Letter to the Hebrews, James, Jude, 2 Peter, 2 and 3 John, and Revelation. Controversy over these books ended in the fourth century, and the canon stated by the councils of Hippo and Carthage and reaffirmed by Innocent I in 405 was solemnly defined by the Council of Trent (1545-63).

Although Martin Luther eliminated the aforementioned books from his New Testament canon, they were reinstated by his followers by the year 1700. Anglicans and Calvinists always retained them.

The Greek and Russian Orthodox have the same New Testament canon as the Catholic Church. Some variations exist among other separated Eastern churches.

Languages of the Bible

Hebrew, Aramaic and Greek were the original languages of the Bible. Most of the Old Testament books were written in Hebrew. Portions of Daniel, Ezra, Jeremiah, Esther, and probably the books of Tobit and Judith were written in Aramaic. The Book of Wisdom, 2 Maccabees and all the books of the New Testament were written in Greek.

Manuscripts and Versions

The original writings of the inspired authors have been lost. The Bible has been transmitted through ancient copies called manuscripts and through translations or versions.

Authoritative Greek manuscripts include the Sinaitic and Vatican manuscripts of the fourth century and the Alexandrine and Parisian of the fifth century A. D.

The Septuagint and Vulgate translations are in a class by themselves.

The Septuagint version, a Greek translation of the Old Testament, was begun about 250 and completed about 100 B. C. The work of several Jewish translators at Alexandria, it differed from the Hebrew Bible in the arrangement of books and included several, later called deuterocanonical, which were not acknowledged as sacred by the community at Jerusalem.

The Vulgate was a Latin version of the Old and New Testaments produced from the original languages by St. Jerome from about 383 to 404. It became the most widely used Latin text for centuries and was regarded as basic long before the Council of Trent designated it as authentic and suitable for use in public reading, controversy, preaching and teaching. Because of its authoritative character, it became the basis for many translations into other languages. A critical revision, in work since 1965, was completed by a pontifical commission in 1977.

Hebrew and Aramaic manuscripts of great antiquity and value have figured more significantly than before in recent scriptural work by Catholic scholars, especially since their use was strongly encouraged, if not mandated, in 1943 by Pius XII in the encyclical *Divino Afflante Spiritu.*

The English translation of the Bible in general use among Catholics until recent years was the *Douay-Rheims,* so called because of the places where it was prepared and published, the New Testament at Rheims in 1582 and the Old Testament at Douay in 1609. The translation was made from the Vulgate text. As revised and issued by Bishop Richard Challoner in 1749 and 1750, it became the standard Catholic English version for about 200 years.

A revision of the Challoner New Testament, made on the basis of the Vulgate text by scholars of the Catholic Biblical Association of America, was published in 1941 in the United States under the sponsorship of the Episcopal Committee of the Confraternity of Christian Doctrine.

New American Bible

A new translation of the entire Bible, the first ever made directly into English from the original languages under Catholic auspices, was projected in 1944 and completed in the fall of 1970 with publication of the *New American Bible.* The Episcopal Committee of the Confraternity of Christian Doctrine sponsored the NAB. The translators were members of the Catholic Biblical Association of America and several fellow scholars of other faiths. The typical edition was produced by St. Anthony Guild Press, Paterson, N. J.

Old Testament portions of the NAB were published in separate volumes before undergoing final revision and being bound in one cover. Genesis and Psalms were issued in 1948 and 1950; Genesis to Ruth, in 1952; Job to Sirach, in 1955; the Prophets, in 1961; Samuel to the Maccabees, in 1969. The new translation of the New Testament was issued for the first time in 1970.

Versions of the Bible approved for use in the Catholic liturgy are the *Douay-Rheims,* the *New American Bible, A New Translation from the Latin Vulgate* by Ronald A. Knox, the Catholic edition of the *Revised Standard Version,* and the *Jerusalem Bible.*

The *Jerusalem Bible* is an English translation of a French version based on the original languages. It was published by Doubleday & Co., Inc., which is also working toward completion of the *Anchor Bible.*

The Protestant counterpart of the *Douay-Rheims Bible* was the *King James Bible,* called the *Authorized Version* in England. Originally published in 1611, it was in general use for more than three centuries. Its modern revisions include the *English Revised Version,* published between 1881 and 1885; the *American Revised Version,* 1901, and revisions of the New Testament (1946) and the Old Testament (1952) published in 1957 in the United States as the *Revised Standard Version.*

The latest revision, a translation in the language of the present day made from Greek and Hebrew sources, is the *New English Bible,* published Mar. 16, 1970. Its New Testament portion was originally published in 1961.

Biblical Federation

The World Catholic Federation for the Biblical Apostolate, established in 1969, sponsors a program designed to create greater awareness among Catholics of the Bible and its use in everyday life. Mill Hill Father Arnold Jurgens is the general secretary.

The Bible as the source of spiritual development, especially for priests, students for the priesthood and religious, was the theme of the 1978 meeting of the federation held in April in Malta, with an attendance of persons from 45 nations.

The U. S. Center for the Catholic Biblical Apostolate, under the direction of Father Stephen Hartdegen, O.F.M., is related to the Department of Education, U.S. Catholic Conference. Address: 1312 Massachusetts Ave. N.W., Washington, D.C. 20005.

APOCRYPHA

Apocrypha are books which have some resemblance to the canonical books in subject matter and title but which have not been recognized as canonical by the Church. They are characterized by a false claim to divine authority; extravagant accounts of events and miracles alleged to be supplemental revelation; material favoring heresy (especially in "New Testament" apocrypha); minimal, if any, historical value.

Among examples of this type of literature itemized by J. McKenzie, S.J., in *Dictionary of the Bible* are: *the Books of Adam and Eve, Martyrdom of Isaiah, Testament of the Patriarchs, Assumption of Moses, Sibylline Oracles; Gospel of James, Gospel of Thomas, Arabic Gospel of the Infancy, History of Joseph the Carpenter; Acts of John, Acts of Paul, Acts of Peter, Acts of Andrew,* and numerous epistles.

Books of this type are called pseudepigrapha by Protestants. They regard the deuterocanonical books in the Catholic canon of Scripture as apocrypha.

DEAD SEA SCROLLS

The Qumran Scrolls, popularly called the Dead Sea Scrolls, are a collection of manuscripts, all but one of them in Hebrew, found between 1947 and 1956 in caves in the Desert of Juda west of the Dead Sea.

Among the findings were a complete text of Isaiah dating from the second century, B.C., more or less extensive fragments of other Old Testament texts (including the deuterocanonical Tobit), and a commentary on Habakkuk. Until the discovery of these materials, the oldest known Hebrew manuscripts were from the 10th century, A.D.

Also found were messianic and apocalyptic texts, and other writings describing the beliefs and practices of the Essenes, a rigoristic Jewish sect.

The scrolls, dating from about the first century before and after Christ, are important sources of information about Hebrew literature, Jewish history during the period between the Old and New Testaments, and the history of Old Testament texts. They established the fact that the Hebrew text of the Old Testament was fixed before the beginning of the Christian era and have had definite effects in recent critical studies and translations of the Old Testament. Together with other scrolls found at Masada, they are still the subject of intensive study.

A theory was proposed in 1972 by Father Jose O'Callaghan, a Spanish papyrologist, that a scrap of one of the scrolls might be a fragment of St. Mark's Gospel dating from about the year 50. Father Pierre Benoit, O.P., discounted the hypothesis, stating that it was based on an erroneous analysis of a photocopy of the scrap in question.

BOOKS OF THE BIBLE

Old Testament
(Dates are before Christ.)

Pentateuch

The Pentateuch is the collective title of the first five books of the Bible. Substantially, they identify the Israelites as Yahweh's Chosen People, cover their history from Egypt to the threshold of the Promised Land, contain the Mosaic Law and Covenant, and disclose the promise of salvation to come. Principal themes concern the divine promise of salvation, Yahweh's fidelity, and the Covenant. Work on the composition of the Pentateuch was completed in the sixth century.

Genesis: The book of origins, according to its title in the Septuagint. In two parts, covers: religious prehistory, including accounts of the origin of the world and man, the original state of innocence and the fall, the promise of salvation, patriarchs before and after the Deluge, the Tower of Babel narrative, genealogies (first 11 chapters); the covenant with Abraham and patriarchal history from Abraham to Joseph (balance of the 50 chapters). Significant are the themes of Yahweh's universal sovereignty and mercy.

Exodus: Named with the Greek word for departure, is a religious epic which describes the oppression of the 12 tribes in Egypt and their departure, liberation or passover therefrom under the leadership of Moses; Yahweh's establishment of the Covenant with them, making them his Chosen People, through the mediation of Moses at Mt. Sinai; instructions concerning the tabernacle, the sanctuary and Ark of the Covenant; the institution of the priesthood. The book is significant because of its theology of liberation and redemption. In Christian interpretation, the Exodus is a figure of baptism.

Leviticus: Mainly legislative in theme and purpose, contains laws regarding sacrifices, ceremonies of ordination and the priesthood of Aaron, legal purity, the holiness code, atonement, the redemption of offerings, and other subjects. Summarily, Levitical laws provided directives for all aspects of religious observance and for the manner in which the Israelites were to conduct themselves with respect to Yahweh and each other. Leviticus was the liturgical handbook of the priesthood.

Numbers: Taking its name from censuses recounted at the beginning and near the end, is a continuation of Exodus. It combines narrative of the Israelites' desert pilgrimage from Sinai to the border of Canaan with laws related to and expansive of those in Leviticus.

Deuteronomy: The concluding book of the Pentateuch, recapitulates, in the form of a testament of Moses, the Law and much of the desert history of the Israelites; enjoins fidelity to the Law as the key to good or bad fortune for the people; gives an account of the commissioning of Joshua as the successor of Moses. Notable themes concern the election of Israel by Yahweh, observance of the Law, prohibitions against the worship of foreign gods, worship of and confidence in Yahweh, the power of Yahweh in nature. The Deuteronomic Code or motif, embodying all of these elements, was the norm for interpreting Israelite history.

Joshua, Judges, Ruth

Joshua: Records the fulfillment of Yahweh's promise to the Israelites in their conquest, occupation and division of Canaan under the leadership of Joshua. It also contains an account of the return of Transjordanian Israelites and of a renewal of the Covenant. It was redacted in final form probably in the sixth century or later.

Judges: Records the actions of charismatic leaders, called judges, of the tribes of Israel between the death of Joshua and the time of Samuel, and a crisis of idolatry among the people. The basic themes are sin and punishment, repentance and deliverance; its purpose was in line with the Deuteronomic motif, that the fortunes of the Israelites were related to their observance or non-observance of the Law and the Covenant. It was redacted in final form probably in the sixth century.

Ruth: Named for the Gentile (Moabite) woman who, through marriage with Boaz, became an Israelite and an ancestress of David (her son, Obed, became his grandfather). Themes are filial piety, faith and trust in Yahweh, the universality of messianic salvation. Dates ranging from c. 950 to the seventh century have been assigned to the origin of the book, whose author is unknown.

Historical Books

These books, while they contain a great deal of factual material, are unique in their preoccupation with interpreting it, in the Deuteronomic manner, in primary relation to the Covenant on which the nation of Israel was founded and in accordance with which community and personal life were judged.

The books are: Samuel 1 and 2, from the end of Judges (c. 1020) to the end of David's reign (c. 961); Kings 1 and 2, from the last days of David to the start of the Babylonian Exile and the destruction of the Temple (587); Chronicles 1 and 2, from the reign of Saul (c. 1020-1000) to the return of the people from the Exile (538); Ezra and Nehemiah, covering the reorganization of the Jewish community after the Exile (458-397); Maccabees 1 and 2, recounting the struggle against attempted suppression of Judaism (168-142).

Three of the books listed below — Tobit, Judith and Esther — are categorized as religious novels.

Samuel 1 and 2: A single work in concept and contents, containing episodic history of the last two Judges, Eli and Samuel, the establishment and rule of the monarchy under Saul and David, and the political consequences of David's rule. The royal messianic dynasty of David was the subject of Nathan's Oracle in 2 Sm. 7. They were edited in final form probably late in the seventh century or during the Exile.

Kings 1 and 2: Cover the last days of David and the career of Solomon, including the building of the Temple and the history of the kingdom during his reign; stories of the prophets Elija and Elisha; the history of the divided kingdom to the fall of Israel in the North (721) and the fall of Judah in the South (587), the destruction of Jerusalem and the Temple. They reflect the Deuteronomic motif in attributing the downfall of the people to corruption of belief and practice in public and private life. They were completed probably in the sixth century.

Chronicles 1 and 2: A collection of historical traditions interpreted in such a way as to present an ideal picture of one people governed by divine law and united in one Temple worship of the one true God. Contents include genealogical tables from Adam to David, the careers of David and Solomon, coverage of the kingdom of Judah to the Exile, and the decree of Cyrus permitting the return of the people and rebuilding of Jerusalem. Both are related to and were written about 400 by the same author, the Chronicler, who composed Ezra and Nehemiah.

Ezra and Nehemiah: A running account of the return of the people to their homeland after the Exile and of practical efforts, under the leadership of Ezra and Nehemiah, to restore and reorganize the religious and political community on the basis of Israelite traditions, divine worship and observance of the Law. Events of great significance were the building of the second Temple, the building of a wall around Jerusalem, and the proclamation of the Law by Ezra. This restored community was the start of Judaism. Both are related to and were written about 400 by the same author, the Chronicler, who composed Chronicles 1 and 2.

Tobit: Written in the literary form of a novel and having greater resemblance to wisdom than to historical literature, narrates the personal history of Tobit, a devout and charitable Jew in exile, and persons connected with him, viz., his son Tobiah, his kinsman Raguel, and Raguel's daughter Sarah. Its purpose was to teach people how to be good Jews. One of its principal themes is patience under trial, with trust in divine Providence which is symbolized by the presence and action of the angel Raphael. It was written about 200.

Judith: Recounts, in the literary form of a historical novel or romance, the preservation of the Israelites from conquest and ruin through the action of Judith. The essential themes are trust in God for deliverance from danger and emphasis on observance of the Law. It was written probably during the Maccabean period.

Esther: Relates, in the literary form of a historical novel or romance, the manner in which Jews in Persia were saved from annihilation through the central role played by Esther, the Jewish wife of Ahasuerus; a fact commemorated by the Jewish feast of Purim. Like Judith, it has trust in divine Providence as its theme and indicates that God's saving will is sometimes realized by persons acting in unlikely ways. Its origin and date are uncertain; it may have been written about 200 near the beginning of the period of strong Hellenistic influence on the Jews.

Maccabees 1 and 2: While related to some extent because of common subject matter, are quite different from each other.

The first book recounts the background and events of the 40-year (175-135) struggle for religious and political freedom led by Judas Maccabeus and his brothers against the Hellenist Seleucid kings and some Hellenophiles among the Jews. Victory was symbolized by the rededication of the Temple. Against the background of opposition between Jews and Gentiles, the author equated the survival of belief in the one true God with survival of the Jewish people, thus identifying religion with patriotism. It was written probably by a Palestinian Jew after 104.

The second book supplements the first to some extent, covering and giving a theological interpretation to events from 180 to 162. It explains the feast of the Dedication of the Temple, a key event in the survival of Judaism which is commemorated in the feast of Hanukkah; stresses the primacy of God's action in the struggle for survival; and indicates belief in an afterlife and the resurrection of the body. It was written probably by a Jew of Alexandria after 120.

Wisdom Books

With the exceptions of Psalms and the Song of Songs, the titles listed under this heading are called wisdom books because their purpose was to formulate the fruits of human experience in the context of meditation on sacred Scripture and to present them as an aid toward understanding the problems of life. Hebrew wisdom literature was distinctive from pagan literature of the same type, but it had limitations; these were overcome in the New Testament, which added the dimensions of the New Covenant to those of the Old. Solomon was regarded as the archtype of the wise man.

Job: A dramatic, didactic poem consisting mainly of several dialogues between Job and his friends concerning the mystery involved in the coexistence of the just God, evil, and the suffering of the just. It describes an innocent man's experience of suffering and conveys the truth that faith in and submission to God rather than complete understanding, which is impossible, make the experience bearable; also, that the justice of God cannot be defended by affirming that it is realized in this world. Of uncertain authorship, it was written probably between the fifth and third centuries.

Psalms: A collection of 150 religious songs or lyrics reflecting Israelite belief and piety dating from the time of the monarchy to the post-Exilic period, a span of well over 500 years. The psalms, which are a compendium of Old Testament theology, were used in the temple liturgy and were of several types suitable for the king, hymns, lamentations, expressions of confidence and thanksgiving, prophecy, historical meditation and reflection, and the statement of wisdom. About one-half of them are attributed to David; many, by unknown authors, date from the early post-Exilic period.

Proverbs: The oldest book of the wisdom type in the Bible, consisting of collections of sayings attributed to Solomon and other persons regarding a wide variety of subjects including wisdom and its nature, rules of conduct, duties with respect to one's neighbor, the conduct of daily affairs. It reveals many details of Jewish life. Its nucleus dates from the period before the Exile, but no definite date can be assigned for its final compilation.

Ecclesiastes: A treatise about many subjects whose unifying theme is the vanity of strictly human efforts and accomplishments with respect to the achievement of lasting happiness; the only things which are not vain are fear of the Lord and observance of his commandments. The pessimistic tone of the book is due to the absence of a concept of afterlife. It was written by an unknown author about 250.

Song of Songs: A collection of erotic lyrics reflecting various themes, including the celebration of fidelity and love between man and woman. According to one interpretation, the book is a parable of the love of Yahweh for Israel. It was written by an unknown author after the Exile.

Wisdom: Deals with many subjects including the reward of justice; praise of wisdom, a gift of Yahweh proceeding from belief in him and the practice of his Law; the part played by him in the history of his people, especially in their liberation from Egypt; the folly and shame of idolatry. Its contents are taken from the whole sacred literature of the Jews and represent a distillation of its wisdom based on the law, beliefs and traditions of Israel. Contains the first Old Testament affirmation of an afterlife with God. The last book of the Old Testament to be written, it was probably composed about 50 years before Christ by an unknown author to confirm the faith of the Jewish community in Alexandria.

Sirach: Resembling Proverbs, is a collection of sayings handed on by a grandfather to his grandson. It contains a variety of moral instruction and eulogies of patriarchs and other figures in Israelite history. Its moral maxims apply to individuals, the family and community, relations with God, friendship, education, wealth, the Law, divine worship. Its theme is that true wisdom consists in the Law. (It was formerly called Ecclesiasticus, the Church Book, because of its extensive use by the Church for moral instruction.) It was written in Hebrew between 200 and 175, during a period of strong Hellenistic influence, and was translated into Greek after 132.

The Prophets

These books and the prophecies they contain "express judgments of the people's moral conduct, on the basis of the Mosaic alliance between God and Israel. They teach sublime truths and lofty morals. They contain exhortations, threats, announcements of punishment, promises of deliverance. . . . In the affairs of men, their prime concern is the interests of God, especially in what pertains to the Chosen People through whom the Messiah is to come; hence their denunciations of idolatry and of that externalism in worship which exclude the interior spirit of religion. They are concerned also with the universal nature of the moral law, with personal responsibility, with the person and office of the Messiah, and with the conduct of foreign nations" (*The Holy Bible,* Prophetic Books, CCD Edition, 1961; Preface). There are four major (Isaiah, Jeremiah, Ezekiel, Daniel) and 12 minor prophets (distinguished by the length of books), Lamentations and Baruch. Earlier prophets, mentioned in historical books, include Samuel, Gad, Nathan, Elijah and Elisha.

Before the Exile, prophets were the intermediaries through whom God communicated revelation to the people. Afterwards, prophecy lapsed and the written word of the Law served this purpose.

Isaiah: Named for the greatest of the prophets whose career spanned the reigns of three Hebrew kings from 742 to the beginning of the seventh century, in a period of moral breakdown in Judah and threats of invasion by foreign enemies. It is an anthology of poems and oracles credited to him and a number of followers deeply influenced by him. Of special importance are the prophecies concerning Immanuel (6 to 12), including the prophecy of the virgin birth (7:14). Chapters 40 to 55, called Deutero-Isaiah, are attributed to an anonymous poet toward the end of the Exile; this portion contains the Songs of the Servant. The concluding part of the book (56-66) contains oracles by later disciples. One of many themes in Isaiah concerned the saving mission of the remnant of Israel in the divine plan of salvation. It was edited in its present form by 180.

Jeremiah: Combines history, biography and prophecy in a setting of crisis caused by internal and external factors, viz., idolatry and general infidelity to the Law among the Israelites and external threats from the Assyrians, Egyptians and Babylonians. Jeremiah prophesied the promise of a new covenant as well as the destruction of Jerusalem and the Temple. His career began in 626 and ended some years after the beginning of the Exile. The book, the longest in the Bible, was edited in final form after the Exile.

Lamentations: A collection of five laments or elegies over the fall of Jerusalem and the fate of the people in Exile, written by an unknown eyewitness not long after 587. They convey the message that Yahweh struck the people because of their sins and reflect confidence in his love and power to restore his converted people.

Baruch: Against the background of the already begun Exile, it consists of an introduction and several parts: an exile's prayer of confession and petition for forgiveness and the restoration of Israel; a poem praising wisdom and the Law of Moses; a lament in which Jerusalem, personified, bewails the fate of her people and consoles them with the hope of blessings to come; and a polemic against idolatry. Although ascribed to Baruch, Jeremiah's secretary, it was written by several authors probably in the second century.

Ezekiel: Named for the priest-prophet who prophesied in Babylon from 593 to 571, during the first phase of the Exile. To prepare his fellow early exiles for the impending fall of Jerusalem, he reproached the Israelites for past sins and predicted woes to come upon them. After the destruction of the city, the burden of his message was hope and promise of restoration. Ezekiel had great influence on the religion of Israel after the Exile. The book, which contains the substance of his teaching, had a number of authors and editors.

Daniel: The protagonist is a fictional young Jew, taken early to Babylon where he lived until 537, who figured in a series of edifying stories. The stories, which originated from Israelite tradition, recount the trials and triumphs of Daniel and his three companions, and other episodes including those concerning Susannah, Bel, and the Dragon. The book is more apocalyptic than prophetic: it envisions Israel in glory to come and conveys the message that men of faith can resist temptation and overcome adversity. It states the prophetic themes of right conduct, divine control of men and events, and the final triumph of the kingdom. It was written by an unknown author in the 160's to give moral support to Jews during the persecutions of the Maccabean period.

Hosea: Consists of a prophetic parallel between Hosea's marriage and Yahweh's relations with his people. As the prophet was married to a faithless wife whom he would not give up, Yahweh was bound in Covenant with an idolatrous and unjust Israel whom he would not desert but would chastise for purification. Hosea belonged to the Northern Kingdom of Israel and began his career about the middle of the eighth century. He inaugurated the tradition of describing Yahweh's relation to Israel in terms of marriage.

Joel: Is apocalyptic and eschatological regarding divine judgment, the Day of the Lord, which is symbolized by a ravaging invasion of locusts, the judgment of the nations in the Valley of Josaphat, and the outpouring of the Spirit in the messianic era to come. Its message is that God will vindicate and save Israel, in view of the prayer and repentance of the people, and will punish their enemies. It was composed after the period of Nehemiah.

Amos: Consists of an indictment against foreign enemies of Israel; a strong denunciation of the people of Israel, whose infidelity, idolatry and injustice made them subject to divine judgment and punishment; and a messianic oracle regarding Israel's restoration. Amos prophesied in the Northern Kingdom of Israel, at Bethel, in the first half of the eighth century; chronologically, he was the first of the canonical prophets.

Obadiah: A 21-verse prophecy, the shortest and one of the sternest in the Bible, against the Edomites, invaders of southern Judah and enemies of those returning from the Exile to their homeland. It was redacted in final form no later than the end of the fourth century.

Jonah: A parable of divine mercy with the theme that Yahweh wills the salvation of all, not just a few, men who respond to his call. Its protagonist is a disobedient prophet; forced by circumstances beyond his control to preach penance among Gentiles, he is highly successful in his mission but baffled by the divine concern for those who do not belong to the Chosen People. It was written after the Exile.

Micah: Attacks the injustice and corruption of priests, false prophets, officials and people; announces judgment and punishment to come; foretells the restoration of Israel; refers to the saving remnant of Israel. Micah was a contemporary of Isaiah.

Nahum: Dating from about 613, concerns the destruction of Nineveh in 612 and the overthrow of the Assyrian Empire by the Babylonians.

Habakkuk: Dating from about 605-597, concerns sufferings to be inflicted by oppressors on the people of Judah because of their infidelity to the Lord. It also sounds a note of confidence in the Lord, the Savior, and declares that the just will not perish.

Zephaniah: Exercising his ministry in the second half of the seventh century, during a time of widespread idolatry, superstition and religious degradation, he prophesied impending judgment and punishment for Jerusalem and its people. He prophesied too that a holy remnant of the people (Anawim, mentioned also by Amos) would be spared. Zephaniah was a forerunner of Jeremiah.

Haggai: One of the first prophets after the Exile, Haggai in 520 encouraged the returning exiles to reestablish their community and to complete the second Temple (dedicated in 515), for which he envisioned greater glory, in a messianic sense, than that enjoyed by the original Temple of Solomon.

Zechariah: A contemporary of Haggai, he prophesied in the same vein. A second part of the book, called Deutero-Zechariah and composed by one or more unknown authors, relates a vision of the coming of the Prince of Peace, the Messiah of the Poor.

Malachi: Written by an anonymous author, presents a picture of life in the post-Exilic community between 516 and the initiation of reforms by Ezra and Nehemiah about 432. Blame for the troubles of the community is placed mainly on priests for failure to carry out ritual worship and to instruct the people in the proper manner; other factors were religious indifference and the influence of doubters who were scandalized at the prosperity of the wicked. The vision of a universal sacrifice to be offered to Yahweh (1:11) is interpreted in Christian theology as a prophecy of the sacrifice of the Mass. Malachi was the last of the minor prophets.

OLD TESTAMENT DATES

c. 1800 — c. 1600: Period of the patriarchs (Abraham, Isaac, Jacob).

c. 1600: Israelites in Egypt.

c. 1250: Exodus of Israelites from Egypt.

c. 1210: Entrance of Israelites into Canaan.

c. 1210 — c. 1020: Period of the Judges.

c. 1020 — c. 1000: Reign of Saul, first king.

c. 1000 — c. 961: Reign of David.

c. 961 — 922: Reign of Solomon. Temple built during his reign.

922: Division of the Kingdom into Israel (North) and Judah (South).

721: Conquest of Israel by Assyrians.

587-538: Conquest of Judah by Babylonians. Babylonian Captivity and Exile. Destruction of Jerusalem and the Temple, 587. Captivity ended with the return of exiles, following the decree of Cyrus permitting the rebuilding of Jerusalem.

515: Dedication of the Second Temple.

458-397: Restoration and reform of the Jewish religious and political community; building of the Jerusalem wall, 439. Leaders in the movement were Ezra and Nehemiah.

168-142: Period of the Maccabees; war against Syrians.

142: Independence granted to Jews by Demetrius II of Syria.

135-37: Period of the Hasmonean dynasty.

63: Beginning of Roman rule.

37-4: Period of Herod the Great.

New Testament Books

Gospels

The term Gospel is derived from the Anglo-Saxon *god-spell* and the Greek *euangelion,* meaning good news, good tidings. In Christian use, it means the good news of salvation proclaimed by Christ and the Church, and handed on in written form in the Gospels of Matthew, Mark, Luke and John.

The initial proclamation of the coming of the kingdom of God was made by Jesus in and through his Person, teachings and actions, and especially through his Passion, death and resurrection. This proclamation became the center of Christian faith and the core of the oral Gospel tradition with which the Church spread the good news by apostolic preaching for some 30 years before it was committed to writing by the Evangelists.

According to an Instruction issued by the Pontifical Commission for Biblical Studies Apr. 21, 1964:

• The sacred writers selected from the material at their disposal (the oral Gospel tradition, some written collections of sayings and deeds of Jesus, eyewitness accounts) those things which were particularly suitable to the various conditions (liturgical, catechetical, missionary) of the faithful and the aims they had in mind, and they narrated these things in such a way as to correspond with those circumstances and their aims.

• The life and teaching of Jesus were not simply reported in a biographical manner for the purpose of preserving their memory but were "preached" so as to offer the Church the basis of doctrine concerning faith and morals.

• In their works, the Evangelists presented the true sayings of Jesus and the events of his life in the light of the better understanding they had following their enlightenment by the Holy Spirit. They did not transform Christ into a "mythical" Person, nor did they distort his teaching.

Passion narratives are the core of all the Gospels, covering the suffering, death and resurrection of Jesus as central events in bringing about and establishing the New Covenant. Leading up to them are accounts of the mission of John the Baptizer and the ministry of Jesus, especially in Galilee and finally in Jerusalem before the Passion. The infancy of Jesus is covered by Luke and Matthew with narratives inspired by Old Testament citations appropriate to the birth of the Messiah.

Matthew, Mark and Luke, while different in various respects, have so many similarities that they are called Synoptic; their relationships are the subject of the Synoptic Problem.

Matthew: Written in the 70's or 80's for Jewish Christians, with clear reference to Jewish background and identification of Jesus as the divine Messiah, the fulfillment of the Old Testament. Distinctive are the use of Old Testament citations regarding the Person, activity and teaching of Jesus, and the presentation of doctrine in sermons and discourses. The canonical Matthew was written in Greek, with dependence on Mark.

Mark: The first of the Gospels, dating from about 65. Written for Gentile Christians, it is noted for the realism and wealth of concrete details with which it reveals Jesus as Son of God and Savior more by his actions and miracles than by his discourses. Theologically, it is less refined than the other Gospels.

Luke: Written in the 70's or 80's for Gentile Christians. It is noted for the universality of its address, the insight it provides into the Christian way of life, the place it gives to women, the manner in which it emphasizes Jesus' friendship with sinners and compassion for the suffering.

John: Written sometime in the 90's, is the most sublime and theological of the Gospels, and is different from the Synoptics in plan and treatment. Combining accounts of signs with longer discourses and reflections, it progressively reveals the Person and mission of Jesus — as Word, Way, Truth, Life, Light — in line with the purpose, "to help you believe that Jesus is the Messiah, the Son of God, so that through this faith you may have life in his name" (Jn. 20:31). There are questions about the authorship but no doubt about the Johannine tradition behind the Gospel.

Acts of the Apostles

Acts of the Apostles: Written by Luke in the 70's or 80's as a supplement to his Gospel. It describes the origin and spread of Christian communities through the action of the Holy Spirit from the resurrection of Christ to the time of Paul's first Roman imprisonment in the early 60's.

Letters (Epistles)

These letters, the first documents of the New Testament, were written in response to existential needs of the early Christian communities for doctrinal and moral instruction, disciplinary action, practical advice, and exhortation to true Christian living.

Pauline Letters

These letters, which comprise approximately one-fourth of the New Testament, are primary and monumental sources of the development of Christian theology. Several of them may not have had Paul as their actual author, but evidence of the Pauline tradition behind them is strong. The letters to the Colossians, Philippians, Ephesians and Philemon have been called the "Captivity Letters" because of a tradition that they were written while Paul was under house arrest in Rome from 61 to 63.

Romans: Written in the late 50's from

Corinth on the central significance of Christ and faith in him for salvation, and the relationship of Christianity to Judaism; the condition of mankind without Christ; justification and the Christian life; duties of Christians.

Corinthians 1: Written near the beginning of 57 from Ephesus to counteract factionalism and disorders, it covers community dissensions, moral irregularities, marriage and celibacy, conduct at religious gatherings, the Eucharist, spiritual gifts (charisms) and their function in the Church, charity, the resurrection of the body.

Corinthians 2: Written later in the same year as 1 Cor., concerning Paul's defense of his apostolic life and ministry, and an appeal for a collection to aid poor Christians in Jerusalem.

Galatians: Written probably between 54 and 57 (perhaps earlier, according to some scholars) to counteract Judaizing opinions and efforts to undermine his authority, it asserts the divine origin of Paul's authority and doctrine, states that justification is not through Mosaic Law but through faith in Christ, insists on the practice of evangelical virtues, especially charity.

Ephesians: Written probably between 61 and 63, or perhaps in the 70's, mainly on the Church as the Mystical Body of Christ.

Philippians: Written between 61 and 63 primarily to thank the Philippians for their kindness to him while he was under house arrest in Rome.

Colossians: Written while he was under house arrest in Rome from 61 to 63 to counteract the influence of self-appointed teachers who were watering down doctrine concerning Christ. It includes two highly important Christological passages, a warning against false teachers, and an instruction on the ideal Christian life.

Thessalonians 1 and 2: Written within a short time of each other probably in 51 from Corinth, mainly on doctrine concerning the Parousia, the second coming of Christ.

Timothy 1 and 2, Titus: Written between 65 and 67, or perhaps in the 70's, giving pastoral counsels to Timothy and Titus who were in charge of churches in Ephesus and Crete, respectively. 1 Tm. emphasizes pastoral responsibility for preserving unity of doctrine; 2 Tm. describes Paul's imprisonment in Rome.

Philemon: A private letter written between 61 and 63 to a wealthy Colossian concerning a slave, Onesimus, who had escaped from him; Paul appealed for kind treatment of the man.

Hebrews: Dating from some time between the mid-60's and the 80's, a complex theological treatise on Christology, the priesthood and sacrifice of Christ, the New Covenant, and the pattern for Christian living. Critical opinion is divided as to whether it was addressed to Judaeo or Gentile Christians.

Catholic Letters, Revelation

These seven letters have been called "catholic" because it was thought for some time, not altogether correctly, that they were not addressed to particular communities.

James: Written sometime between the mid-60's and the 80's (although datable before 62 according to some scholars) in the spirit of Hebrew wisdom literature and the moralism of Tobit. An exhortation to practical Christian living, it is also noteworthy for the doctrine it states on good works and its citation regarding anointing of the sick.

Peter 1 and 2: The first letter may have been written in the mid-60's; the second dates from 100 to 125. Addressed to Christians in Asia Minor, both are exhortations to perseverance in the life of faith despite trials and difficulties arising from pagan influences, isolation from other Christians, and false teaching.

John 1: Written sometime in the 90's and addressed to Asian churches, its message is that God is made known to us in the Son and that fellowship with the Father is attained by living in the light, justice and love of the Son.

John 2: Written sometime in the 90's and addressed to a church in Asia, it commends the people for standing firm in the faith and urges them to perseverance.

John 3: Written sometime in the 90's, it appears to represent an effort to settle a jurisdictional dispute in one of the churches.

Jude: Written sometime between the 70's and 90's, it is a brief treatise against erroneous teachings and practices opposed to law, authority and true Christian freedom.

Revelation: Written in the 90's along the lines of Johannine thought, it is a symbolic and apocalyptic treatment of things to come combined with warning but hope and assurance to the Church regarding the coming of the Lord in glory.

BIBLICAL AUTHORSHIP

Some books of the Bible were not written by the authors to whom they have been traditionally attributed; New Testament examples are the Gospels of Matthew and John, Hebrews, 1 and 2 Timothy, Titus, James, Jude.

This fact, which has never been the subject of dogmatic definition by the Church, does not militate against the canonicity of the books, since canonicity concerns the theological matter of inspiration rather than the historical question of human authorship.

Questions concerning authorship are explained in various ways: (1) according to an old custom whereby literary works of importance were sometimes attributed to famous persons so they would get a reading; (2) authorship, by a disciple or school of disciples, of works derived from the doctrine of a master; (3) authorship by persons writing in the spirit and tradition of a master.

INTERPRETATION OF THE BIBLE

According to the *Constitution on Revelation* issued by the Second Vatican Council, "the interpreter of Sacred Scripture, in order to see clearly what God wanted to communicate to us, should carefully investigate what meaning the sacred writers really intended, and what God wanted to manifest by means of their words" (No. 12).

Hermeneutics, Exegesis

This careful investigation proceeds in accordance with the rules of hermeneutics, the normative science of biblical interpretation and explanation. Hermeneutics in practice is called exegesis.

The principles of hermeneutics are derived from various disciplines and many factors which have to be considered in explaining the Bible and its parts. These include: the original languages and languages of translation of the sacred texts, through philology and linguistics; the quality of texts, through textual criticism; literary forms and genres, through literary and form criticism; cultural, historical, geographical and other conditions which influenced the writers, through related studies; facts and truths of salvation history; the truths and analogy of faith.

Distinctive to biblical hermeneutics, which differs in important respects from literary interpretation in general, is the premise that the Bible, though written by human authors, is the work of divine inspiration in which God reveals his plan for the salvation of men through historical events and persons, and especially through the Person and mission of Christ.

Textual, Form Criticism

Textual criticism is the study of biblical texts, which have been transmitted in copies several times removed from the original manuscripts, for the purpose of establishing the real state of the original texts. This purpose is served by comparison of existing copies; by application to the texts of the disciplines of philology and linguistics; by examination of related works of antiquity; by study of biblical citations in works of the Fathers of the Church and other authors; and by other means of literary study.

Since about 1920, the sayings of Christ have been a particular object of New Testament study, the purpose being to analyze the forms of expression used by the Evangelists in order to ascertain the words actually spoken by him.

Literary Criticism

Literary criticism aims to determine the origin and kinds of literary composition, called forms or genres, employed by the inspired authors. Such determinations are necessary for decision regarding the nature and purpose and, consequently, the meaning of biblical passages. Underlying these studies is the principle that the manner of writing was conditioned by the intention of the authors, the meaning they wanted to convey, and the then-contemporary literary style, mode or medium best adapted to carry their message — e.g., true , history, quasi-historical narrative, poems, prayers, hymns, psalms, aphorisms, allegories, discourses. Understanding these media is necessary for the valid interpretation of their message.

Literal Sense

The key to all valid interpretation is the literal sense of biblical passages. Regarding this matter and the relevance to it of the studies and procedures described above, Pius XII wrote the following in the encyclical *Divino Afflante Spiritu.*

"What the literal sense of a passage is, is not always as obvious in the speeches and writings of ancient authors of the East as it is in the works of our own time. For what they wished to express is not to be determined by the rules of grammar and philology alone nor solely by the context; the interpreter must, as it were, go back wholly in spirit to those remote centuries of the East and with the aid of history, archeology, ethnology, and other sciences accurately determine what modes of writing, so to speak, the authors of that ancient period would be likely to use and in fact did use. . . . In explaining the Sacred Scripture and in demonstrating and proving its immunity from all error (the Catholic interpreter) should make a prudent use of this means, determine to what extent the manner of expression or literary mode adopted by the sacred writer may lead to a correct and genuine interpretation; and let him be convinced that this part of his office cannot be neglected without serious detriment to Catholic exegesis."

The literal sense of the Bible is the meaning in the mind of and intended by the inspired writer of a book or passage of the Bible. This is determined by the application to texts of the rules of hermeneutics. It is not to be confused with word-for-word literalism.

Typical Sense

The typical sense is the meaning which a passage has not only in itself but also in reference to something else of which it is a type or foreshadowing. A clear example is the account of the Exodus of the Israelites: in its literal sense, it narrates the liberation of the Israelites from death and oppression in Egypt; in its typical sense, it foreshadowed the liberation of men from sin through the redemptive death and resurrection of Christ. The typical sense of this and other passages emerged in the working out of God's plan of salvation history. It did not have to be in the mind of the author of the original passage.

Accommodated Senses

Accommodated, allegorical and consequent senses are figurative and adaptive meanings given to books and passages of the Bible for moral and other purposes. Such interpretations involve the danger of stretching the literal sense beyond proper proportions. Hermeneutical principles require that interpretations like these respect the integrity of the literal sense of the passages in question.

In the Catholic view, the final word on questions of biblical interpretation belongs to the teaching authority of the Church. In other views, generally derived from basic principles stated by Martin Luther, John Calvin and other Reformers, the primacy belongs to individual judgment acting in response to the inner testimony of the Holy Spirit, the edifying nature of biblical subject matter, the sublimity and simplicity of the message of salvation, the intensity with which Christ is proclaimed.

Biblical Studies

The first center for biblical studies, in some strict sense of the term, was the School of Alexandria, founded in the latter half of the second century. It was noted for allegorical exegesis. Literal interpretation was a hallmark of the School of Antioch.

St. Jerome, who produced the Vulgate, and St. Augustine, author of numerous commentaries, were the most important figures in biblical studies during the patristic period. By the time of the latter's death, the Old and New Testament canons had been stabilized. For some centuries afterwards, there was little or no progress in scriptural studies, although collections were made of scriptural excerpts from the writings of the Fathers of the Church, and the systematic reading of Scripture became established as a feature of monastic life.

Advances were made in the 12th and 13th centuries with the introduction of new principles and methods of scriptural analysis stemming from renewed interest in Hebraic studies and the application of dialectics.

By the time of the Reformation, the Bible had become the first book set in movable type, and more than 100 vernacular editions were in use throughout Europe.

The Council of Trent

In the wake of the Reformation, the Council of Trent formally defined the Canon of the Bible; it also reasserted the authoritative role of tradition and the teaching authority of the Church as well as Scripture with respect to the rule of faith. In the heated atmosphere of the 16th and 17th centuries, the Bible was turned into a polemical weapon; Protestants used it to defend their doctrines, and Catholics countered with citations in support of the dogmas of the Church. One result of this state of affairs was a lack of substantial progress in biblical studies during the period.

Toward the end of the 17th century, Louis Cappel, a Protestant, introduced a methodology for textual criticism, and Richard Simon, a Catholic, inaugurated modern literary and historical criticism. Their work was poorly regarded, however, and went into eclipse until about the beginning of the 19th century. It was then taken over by men whose work threatened to destroy the credibility of not only the Bible but Christianity itself.

Rationalists, and later Modernists, denied the reality of the supernatural and doctrine concerning inspiration of the Bible, which they generally regarded as a strictly human production expressive of the religious sense and experience of mankind. In their hands, the tools of positive critical research became weapons for biblical subversion. The defensive Catholic reaction to their work had the temporary effect of alienating scholars of the Church from solid advances in archeology, philology, history, textual and literary criticism.

Catholic Developments

Major influences in bringing about a change in Catholic attitude toward use of these disciplines in biblical studies were two papal encyclicals and two institutes of special study, the Ecole Biblique, founded in Jerusalem in 1890, and the Pontifical Biblical Institute established in Rome in 1909. The encyclical *Providentissimus Deus,* issued by Leo XIII in 1893, marked an important breakthrough; in addition to defending the concept of divine inspiration and the formal inspiration of the Scriptures, it encouraged the study of allied and ancillary sciences and techniques for a more fruitful understanding of the sacred writings. The encyclical *Divino Afflante Spiritu,* 50 years later, gave encouragement for the use of various forms of criticism as tools of biblical research. The documents encouraged the work of scholars and stimulated wide communication of the fruits of their study.

Great changes in the climate and direction of biblical studies have occurred in recent years. One of them has been an increase in cooperative effort among Catholic, Protestant, Orthodox and Jewish scholars. Their common investigation of the Dead Sea Scrolls is well known. More recently productive was the collaboration in England of Catholics and Protestants in turning out a Catholic edition of the Revised Standard Version of the Bible.

The development and results of biblical studies in this century have directly and significantly affected all phases of the contemporary renewal movement in the Church. Their influence on theology, liturgy, catechetics, and preaching indicate the importance of their function in the life of the Church.

APOSTLES AND EVANGELISTS

The Apostles were the men selected, trained and commissioned by Christ to preach the Gospel, to baptize, to establish, direct and care for his Church as servants of God and stewards of his mysteries. They were the first bishops of the Church.

St. Matthew's Gospel lists the Apostles in this order: Peter, Andrew, James the Greater, John, Philip, Bartholomew, Thomas, Matthew, James the Less, Jude, Simon and Judas Iscariot. Matthias was elected to fill the place of Judas. Paul became an Apostle by a special call from Christ. Barnabas was called an Apostle.

Two of the Evangelists, John and Matthew, were Apostles. The other two, Luke and Mark, were closely associated with the apostolic college.

Andrew: Born in Bethsaida, brother of Peter, disciple of John the Baptist, a fisherman, the first Apostle called; according to legend, preached the Gospel in Northern Greece, Epirus and Scythia, and was martyred at Patras about 70; in art, is represented with an x-shaped cross, called St. Andrew's Cross; feast, Nov. 30; is honored as the patron of Russia and Scotland.

Barnabas: Originally called Joseph but named Barnabas by the Apostles, among whom he is ranked because of his collaboration with Paul; a Jew of the Diaspora, born on Cyprus; a cousin of Mark and member of the Christian community at Jerusalem, influenced the Apostles to accept Paul, with whom he became a pioneer missionary outside Palestine and Syria, to Antioch, Cyprus and southern Asia Minor; legend says he was martyred on Cyprus during the Neronian persecution; feast, June 11.

Bartholomew (Nathaniel): A friend of Philip; according to various traditions, preached the Gospel in Ethiopia, India, Persia, and Armenia where he was martyred by being flayed and beheaded; in art, is depicted holding a knife, an instrument of his death; feast, Aug. 24 in the Roman Rite, Aug. 25 in the Byzantine Rite.

James the Greater: A Galilean, son of Zebedee, brother of John (with whom he was called a "son of thunder"), a fisherman; with Peter and John, witnessed the raising of Jairus' daughter to life, the transfiguration, the agony of Jesus in the Garden of Gethsemani; first of the Apostles to die, by the sword in 44 during the rule of Herod Agrippa; there is doubt about a journey legend says he made to Spain and also about the authenticity of relics said to be his at Santiago de Compostela; in art, is depicted carrying a pilgrim's bell; feast, July 25 in the Roman Rite, Apr. 30 in the Byzantine Rite.

James the Less: Son of Alphaeus, called "Less" because he was younger in age or shorter in stature than James the Greater; one of the "catholic" epistles bears his name; was stoned to death in 62 or thrown from the top of the temple in Jerusalem and clubbed to death in 66; in art, is depicted with a club or heavy staff; feast, May 3 in the Roman Rite, Oct. 9 in the Byzantine Rite.

John: A Galilean, son of Zebedee, brother of James the Greater (with whom he was called a "son of thunder"), a fisherman, probably a disciple of John the Baptist, one of the Evangelists, called the "beloved disciple"; with Peter and James the Greater, witnessed the raising of Jairus' daughter to life, the transfiguration, the agony of Jesus in the Garden of Gethsemani; Mary was commended to his special care by Christ; the fourth Gospel, three "catholic" Epistles and Revelation bear his name; according to various accounts, lived at Ephesus in Asia Minor for some time and died a natural death about 100; in art, is represented by an eagle, symbolic of the sublimity of the contents of his Gospel; feast, Dec. 27 in the Roman Rite, May 8 in the Byzantine Rite.

Jude Thaddeus: One of the "catholic" epistles, the shortest, bears his name; various traditions say he preached the Gospel in Mesopotamia, Persia and elsewhere, and was martyred; in art, is depicted with a halberd, the instrument of his death; feast, Oct. 28 in the Roman Rite, June 19 in the Byzantine Rite.

Luke: A Greek convert to the Christian community, called "our most dear physician" by Paul, of whom he was a missionary companion; author of the third Gospel and Acts of the Apostles; the place — Achaia, Bithynia, Egypt — and circumstances of his death are not certain; in art, is depicted as a man, a writer, or an ox (because his Gospel starts at the scene of Temple sacrifice); feast, Oct. 18.

Mark: A cousin of Barnabas and member of the first Christian community at Jerusalem; a missionary companion of Paul and Barnabas, then of Peter; author of the Gospel which bears his name; according to legend, founded the Church at Alexandria, was bishop there and was martyred in the streets of the city; in art, is depicted with his Gospel and a winged lion, symbolic of the voice of John the Baptist crying in the wilderness, at the beginning of his Gospel; feast, Apr. 25.

Matthew: A Galilean, called Levi by Luke and John and the son of Alphaeus by Mark, a tax collector, one of the Evangelists; according to various accounts, preached the Gospel in Judea, Ethiopia, Persia and Parthia, and was martyred; in art, is depicted with a spear, the instrument of his death, and as a winged man in his role as Evangelist; feast, Sept. 21 in the Roman Rite, Nov. 16 in the Byzantine Rite.

Matthias: A disciple of Jesus whom the faithful 11 Apostles chose to replace Judas before the Resurrection; uncertain traditions report that he preached the Gospel in Palestine, Cappadocia or Ethiopia; in art, is represented with a cross and a halberd, the instruments of his death as a martyr; feast, May 14 in the Roman Rite, Aug. 9 in the Byzantine Rite.

Paul: Born at Tarsus, of the tribe of Benjamin, a Roman citizen; participated in the persecution of Christians until the time of his miraculous conversion on the way to Damascus; called by Christ, who revealed himself to him in a special way; became the Apostle of the Gentiles, among whom he did most of his preaching in the course of three major missionary journeys through areas north of Palestine, Cyprus, Asia Minor and Greece; 14 epistles bear his name; two years of imprisonment at Rome, following initial arrest in Jerusalem and confinement at Caesarea, ended with martyrdom, by beheading, outside the walls of the city in 64 or 67 during the Neronian persecution; in art, is depicted in various ways with St. Peter, with a sword, in the scene of his conversion; feasts, June 29, Jan. 25 (Roman Rite).

Peter: Simon, son of Jona, born in Bethsaida, brother of Andrew, a fisherman; called Cephas or Peter by Christ who made him the chief of the Apostles and head of the Church as his vicar; named first in the listings of Apostles in the Synoptic Gospels and the Acts of the Apostles; with James the Greater and John, witnessed the raising of Jairus' daughter to life, the transfiguration, the agony of Jesus in the Garden of Gethsemani; was the first to preach the Gospel in and around Jerusalem and was the leader of the first Christian community there; established a local Church in Antioch; presided over the Council of Jerusalem in 51; wrote two "catholic" epistles to the Christians in Asia Minor; established his see in Rome where he spent his last years and was martyred by crucifixion in 64 or 65 during the Neronian persecution; in art, is depicted carrying two keys, symbolic of his primacy in the Church; feasts, June 29, Feb. 22 (Roman Rite).

Philip: Born in Bethsaida; according to legend, preached the Gospel in Phrygia where he suffered martyrdom by crucifixion; feast, May 3 in the Roman Rite, Nov. 14 in the Byzantine Rite.

Simon: Called the Cananean or the Zealot; according to legend, preached in various places in the Near East and suffered martyrdom by being sawed in two; in art, is depicted with a saw, the instrument of his death, or a book, symbolic of his zeal for the Law; feast, Oct. 28 in the Roman Rite, May 10 in the Byzantine Rite.

Thomas (Didymus): Notable for his initial incredulity regarding the Resurrection and his subsequent forthright confession of the divinity of Christ risen from the dead; according to legend, preached the Gospel in places from the Caspian Sea to the Persian Gulf and eventually reached India where he was martyred near Madras; Thomas Christians trace their origin to him; in art, is depicted kneeling before the risen Christ, or with a carpenter's rule and square; feast, July 3 in the Roman Rite, Oct. 6 in the Byzantine Rite.

JUDAS

The Gospels record only a few facts about Judas, the Apostle who betrayed Christ.

The only non-Galilean among the Apostles, he was from Carioth, a town in southern Juda. He was keeper of the purse in the apostolic band. He was called a petty thief by John. He voiced dismay at the waste of money, which he said might have been spent for the poor, in connection with the anointing incident at Bethany. He took the initiative in arranging the betrayal of Christ. Afterwards, he confessed that he had betrayed an innocent man and cast into the Temple the money he had received for that action. Of his death, Matthew says that he hanged himself; the Acts of the Apostles states that he swelled up and burst open; both reports deal more with the meaning than the manner of his death — the misery of the death of a sinner.

The consensus of speculation over the reason why Judas acted as he did in betraying Christ focuses on disillusionment and unwillingness to accept a suffering Messiah.

APOSTOLIC FATHERS, FATHERS, DOCTORS OF THE CHURCH

The writers listed below, were outstanding and authoritative witnesses to authentic Christian belief and practice, and played significant roles in giving them expression.

Apostolic Fathers

The Apostolic Fathers were Christian writers of the first and second centuries who are known or believed to have had personal relations with the Apostles, and whose writings echo genuine apostolic teaching.

Chief in importance are: St. Clement (d.c. 97), bishop of Rome and third successor of St. Peter in the papacy; St. Ignatius (50-c.

107), bishop of Antioch and second successor of St. Peter in that see, reputed to be a disciple of St. John; St. Polycarp (69-155), bishop of Smyrna and a disciple of St. John. The authors of the *Didache* and the *Epistle of Barnabas* are also numbered among the Apostolic Fathers.

Other early ecclesiastical writers included: St. Justin, martyr (100-165), of Asia Minor and Rome, a layman and apologist; St. Irenaeus (130-202), bishop of Lyons, who opposed Gnosticism; and St. Cyprian (210-258), bishop of Carthage, who opposed Novatianism.

Fathers and Doctors

The Fathers of the Church were theologians and writers of the first eight centuries who were outstanding for sanctity and learning. They were such authoritative witnesses to the belief and teaching of the Church that their unanimous acceptance of doctrines as divinely revealed has been regarded as evidence that such doctrines were so received by the Church in line with apostolic tradition and Sacred Scripture. Their unanimous rejection of doctrines branded them as heretical. Their writings, however, were not necessarily free of error in all respects.

The greatest of these Fathers were: Sts. Ambrose, Augustine, Jerome and Gregory the Great in the West; Sts. John Chrysostom, Basil the Great, Gregory of Nazianzen and Athanasius in the East.

The Doctors of the Church were ecclesiastical writers of eminent learning and sanctity who have been given this title because of the great advantage the Church has derived from their work. These writings, however, were not necessarily free of error in all respects.

Albert the Great, St. (c. 1200-1280): Born in Swabia, Germany; Dominican; bishop of Regensburg (1260-1262); wrote extensively on logic, natural sciences, ethics, metaphysics, Scripture, systematic theology; contributed to development of Scholasticism; teacher of St. Thomas Aquinas; canonized and proclaimed doctor, 1931; named patron of natural scientists, 1941; called Doctor Universalis, Doctor Expertus; feast, Nov. 15.

Alphonsus Liguori, St. (1696-1787): Born near Naples, Italy; bishop of Agatha of the Goths (1762-1775); founder of the Redemptorists; in addition to his principal work, *Theologiae Moralis,* wrote on prayer, the spiritual life, and doctrinal subjects in response to controversy; canonized, 1839; proclaimed doctor, 1871; named patron of confessors and moralists, 1950; feast, Aug. 1.

Ambrose, St. (c. 340-397): Born in Treves, Germany; bishop of Milan (374-397); one of the strongest opponents of Arianism in the West; his homilies and other writings — on faith, the Holy Spirit, the Incarnation, the sacraments and other subjects — were pastoral and practical; influenced the development of a liturgy at Milan which was named for him; Father and Doctor of the Church; feast, Dec. 7.

Anselm, St. (1033-1109): Born in Aosta, Piedmont, Italy; Benedictine; archbishop of Canterbury (1093-1109); in addition to his principal work, *Cur Deus Homo,* on the atonement and reconciliation of man with God through Christ, wrote about the existence and attributes of God and defended the *Filioque* explanation of the procession of the Holy Spirit from the Father and the Son; canonized, 1494; proclaimed doctor, 1720; called Father of Scholasticism; feast, Apr. 21.

Anthony of Padua, St. (1195-1231): Born in Lisbon, Portugal; first theologian of the Franciscan Order; preacher; canonized, 1232; proclaimed doctor, 1946; called Evangelical Doctor; feast, June 13.

Athanasius, St. (c. 297-373): Born in Alexandria, Egypt; bishop of Alexandria (328-373); participant in the Council of Nicaea I while still a deacon; dominant opponent of Arians whose errors regarding Christ he refuted in *Apology against the Arians, Discourses against the Arians,* and other works; Father and Doctor of the Church; called Father of Orthodoxy; feast, May 2.

Augustine, St. (354-430): Born in Tagaste, North Africa; bishop of Hippo (395-430) after conversion from Manichaeism; works include the autobiographical and mystical *Confessions, City of God,* treatises on the Trinity, grace, passages of the Bible, and doctrines called into question and denied by Manichaeans, Pelagians and Donatists; had strong and lasting influence on Christian theology and philosophy; Father and Doctor of the Church; Doctor of Grace; feast, Aug. 28.

Basil the Great, St. (c. 329-379): Born in Caesarea, Cappadocia, Asia Minor; bishop of Caesarea (370-379); wrote three books *Contra Eunomium* in refutation of Arian errors, a treatise on the Holy Spirit, many homilies, and several rules for monastic life, on which he had lasting influence; Father and Doctor of the Church; called Father of Monasticism in the East; feast, Jan. 2.

Bede the Venerable, St. (c. 673-735): Born in Northumberland, England; Benedictine; in addition to his principal work, *Ecclesiastical History of the English Nation* (covering the period 597-731), wrote scriptural commentaries; regarded as probably the most learned man in Western Europe of his time; called Father of English History; feast, May 25.

Bernard of Clairvaux, St. (c. 1090-1153): Born near Dijon, France; abbot; monastic reformer, called the second founder of the Cistercian Order; mystical theologian with great influence on devotional life; opponent of the rationalism brought forward by Abelard and others; canonized, 1174; proclaimed doctor, 1830; called Mellifluous Doctor because of his eloquence; feast, Aug. 20.

Bonaventure, St. (c. 1217-1274): Born near Viterbo, Italy; Franciscan; bishop of Albano (1273-1274); cardinal; wrote *Itinerarium Mentis in Deum, De Reductione Artium ad Theologiam, Breviloquium,* scriptural commentaries, additional mystical works affecting devotional life, and a life of St. Francis of Assisi; canonized, 1482; proclaimed doctor, 1588; called Seraphic Doctor; feast, July 15.

Catherine of Siena, St. (c. 1347-1380): Born in Siena, Italy; member of the Third Order of St. Dominic; mystic; authored a long series of letters, mainly concerning spiritual instruction and encouragement, to associates, and *Dialogue,* a spiritual testament in four treatises; was active in support of a crusade against the Turks and efforts to end war between papal forces and the Florentine allies; had great influence in inducing Gregory XI to return himself and the Curia to Rome in 1376, to end the Avignon period of the papacy; canonized, 1461; proclaimed the second women doctor, Oct. 4, 1970; feast, Apr. 29.

Cyril of Alexandria, St. (c. 376-444): Born in Egypt; bishop of Alexandria (412-444); wrote treatises on the Trinity, the Incarnation and other subjects, mostly in refutation of Nestorian errors; made key contributions to the development of Christology; presided at the Council of Ephesus, 431; proclaimed doctor, 1882; feast, June 27.

Cyril of Jerusalem, St. (c. 315-387): Bishop of Jerusalem (350-387); vigorous opponent of Arianism; principal work, *Catecheses,* a pre-baptismal explanation of the creed of Jerusalem; proclaimed doctor, 1882; feast, Mar. 18.

Ephraem, St. (c. 306-373): Born in Nisibis, Mesopotamia; counteracted the spread of Gnostic and Arian errors with poems and hymns of his own composition; wrote also on the Eucharist and Mary; proclaimed doctor, 1920; called Deacon of Edessa and Harp of the Holy Spirit; feast, June 9.

Francis de Sales, St. (1567-1622): Born in Savoy; bishop of Geneva (1602-1622); spiritual writer with strong influence on devotional life through treatises such as *Introduction to a Devout Life,* and *The Love of God;* canonized, 1665; proclaimed doctor, 1877; patron of Catholic writers and the Catholic press; feast, Jan. 24.

Gregory Nazianzen, St. (c. 330-c. 390): Born in Arianzus, Cappadocia, Asia Minor; bishop of Constantinople (381-390); vigorous opponent of Arianism; in addition to five theological discourses on the Nicene Creed and the Trinity for which he is best known, wrote letters and poetry; Father and Doctor of the Church; called the Christian Demosthenes because of his eloquence and, in the Eastern Church, The Theologian; feast, Jan. 2.

Gregory I, the Great, St. (c. 540-604): Born in Rome; pope (590-604): wrote many scriptural commentaries, a compendium of theology in the *Book of Morals* based on Job, *Dialogues* concerning the lives of saints, the immortality of the soul, death, purgatory, heaven and hell, and 14 books of letters; enforced papal supremacy and established the position of the pope vis-a-vis the emperor; worked for clerical and monastic reform and the observance of clerical celibacy; Father and Doctor of the Church; feast, Sept. 3.

Hilary of Poitiers, St. (c. 315-368): Born in Poitiers, France; bishop of Poitiers (c. 353-368); wrote *De Synodis,* with the Arian controversy in mind, and *De Trinitate,* the first lengthy study of the doctrine in Latin; introduced Eastern theology to the West; contributed to the development of hymnology; proclaimed doctor, 1851; called the Athanasius of the West because of his vigorous defense of the divinity of Christ against Arians; feast, Jan. 13.

Isidore of Seville, St. (c. 560-636): Born in Cartagena, Spain; bishop of Seville (c. 600-636); in addition to his principal work, *Etymologiae,* an encyclopedia of the knowledge of his day, wrote on theological and historical subjects; regarded as the most learned man of his time; proclaimed doctor, 1722; feast, Apr. 4.

Jerome, St. (c. 343-420): Born in Stridon, Dalmatia; translated the Old Testament from Hebrew into Latin and revised the existing Latin translation of the New Testament to produce the Vulgate version of the Bible; wrote scriptural commentaries and treatises on matters of controversy; regarded as Father and Doctor of the Church from the eighth century; called Father of Biblical Science; feast, Sept. 30.

John Chrysostom, St. (c. 347-407): Born in Antioch, Asia Minor; archbishop of Constantinople (398-407); wrote homilies, scriptural commentaries and letters of wide influence in addition to a classical treatise on the priesthood; proclaimed doctor by the Council of Chalcedon, 451; called the greatest of the Greek Fathers; named patron of preachers, 1909; called golden-mouthed because of his eloquence; feast, Sept. 13.

John Damascene, St. (c. 675-c. 749): Born in Damascus, Syria; monk; wrote *Fountain of Wisdom,* a three-part work including a history of heresies and an exposition of the Christian faith, three *Discourses against the Iconoclasts,* homilies on Mary, biblical commentaries and treatises on moral subjects; proclaimed doctor, 1890; called Golden Speaker because of his eloquence; feast, Dec. 4.

John of the Cross, St. (1542-1591): Born in Old Castile, Spain; Carmelite; founder of Discalced Carmelites; one of the greatest mystical theologians, wrote *The Ascent of Mt. Carmel — The Dark Night, The Spiritual Canticle, The Living Flame of Love;* canonized, 1726; proclaimed doctor, 1926; called Doctor of Mystical Theology; feast, Dec. 14.

Lawrence of Brindisi, St. (1559-1619): Born in Brindisi, Italy; Franciscan (Capuchin); vigorous preacher of strong influence in the post-Reformation period; 15 tomes of collected works include scriptural commentaries, sermons, homilies and doctrinal writings; canonized, 1881; proclaimed doctor, 1959; feast, July 21.

Leo I, the Great, St. (c. 400-461): Born in Tuscany, Italy; pope (440-461); wrote the *Tome of Leo,* to explain doctrine concerning the two natures and one Person of Christ, against the background of the Nestorian and Monophysite heresies; other works included sermons, letters, and writings against the errors of Manichaeism and Pelagianism; was instrumental in dissuading Attila from sacking Rome in 452; proclaimed doctor, 1574; feast, Nov. 10.

Peter Canisius, St. (1521-1597): Born in Nijmegen, Holland; Jesuit; wrote popular expositions of the Catholic faith in several catechisms which were widely circulated in 20 editions in his lifetime alone; was one of the moving figures in the Counter-Reformation period, especially in southern and western Germany; canonized and proclaimed doctor, 1925; feast, Dec. 21.

Peter Chrysologus, St. (c. 400-450): Born in Imola, Italy; served as archbishop of Ravenna (c. 433-450); his sermons and writings, many of which were designed to counteract Monophysitism, were pastoral and practical; proclaimed doctor, 1729; feast, July 30.

Peter Damian, St. (1007-1072): Born in Ravenna, Italy; Benedictine; cardinal; his writings and sermons, many of which concerned ecclesiastical and clerical reform, were pastoral and practical; proclaimed doctor, 1828; feast, Feb. 21.

Robert Bellarmine, St. (1542-1621): Born in Tuscany, Italy; Jesuit; archbishop of Capua (1602-1605); wrote *Controversies,* a three-volume exposition of doctrine under attack during and after the Reformation, two catechisms and the spiritual work, *The Art of Dying Well,* was an authority on ecclesiology and Church-state relations; canonized, 1930; proclaimed doctor, 1931; feast, Sept. 17.

Theresa of Avila, St. (1515-1582): Born in Avila, Spain; entered the Carmelite Order, 1535; in the early 1560's, initiated a primitive Carmelite, discalced-Alcantarine reform which greatly influenced men and women religious, especially in Spain; wrote extensively on spiritual and mystical subjects; principal works included her *Autobiography, Way of Perfection, The Interior Castle, Meditations on the Canticle, The Foundations, Visitation of the Discalced Nuns;* canonized, 1614; proclaimed doctor, Sept. 27, 1970; feast, Oct. 15.

Thomas Aquinas, St. (1225-1274): Born near Naples, Italy; Dominican; teacher and writer on virtually the whole range of philosophy and theology; principal works were *Summa contra Gentiles,* a manual and systematic defense of Christian doctrine, and *Summa Theologiae,* a new (at that time) exposition of theology on philosophical principles; canonized, 1323; proclaimed doctor, 1567; called Doctor Communis, Doctor Angelicus, the Great Synthesizer because of the way in which he related faith and reason, theology and philosophy (especially that of Aristotle), and systematized the presentation of Christian doctrine; named patron of Catholic schools and education, 1880; feast, Jan. 28.

CREEDS

Creeds are formal and official statements of Christian doctrine. As summaries of the principal truths of faith, they are standards of orthodoxy and are useful for instructional purposes, for actual profession of the faith, and for expression of the faith in the liturgy.

The classical creeds are the Apostles' Creed and the Creed of Nicaea-Constantinople. Two others are the Athanasian Creed and the Creed of Pius IV.

Apostles' Creed

Text: I believe in God, the Father almighty, Creator of heaven and earth.

And in Jesus Christ, his only Son, our Lord; who was conceived by the Holy Spirit, born of the Virgin Mary, suffered under Pontius Pilate, was crucified, died, and was buried. He descended into hell; the third day he arose again from the dead; he ascended into heaven, sits at the right hand of God, the Father almighty; from thence he shall come to judge the living and the dead.

I believe in the Holy Spirit, the holy Catholic Church, the communion of saints, the forgiveness of sins, the resurrection of the body, and life everlasting. Amen.

Background: The Apostles' Creed reflects the teaching of the Apostles but is not of apostolic origin. It probably originated in the second century as a rudimentary formula of faith professed by catechumens before the reception of baptism. Baptismal creeds in fourth-century use at Rome and elsewhere in the West closely resembled the present text, which was quoted in a handbook of Christian doctrine written between 710 and 724. This text was in wide use throughout the West by the ninth century. The Apostles' Creed is common to all Christian confessional churches in the West, but is not used in Eastern Churches.

Nicene Creed

The following translation of the Latin text of the creed was prepared by the International Committee on English in the Liturgy.

Text: We believe in one God, the Father, the Almighty, maker of heaven and earth, of all that is seen and unseen.

We believe in one Lord, Jesus Christ, the only Son of God, eternally begotten of the Father, God from God, Light from Light, true God from true God, begotten, not made, one in Being with the Father. Through him all things were made. For us men and for our salvation he came down from heaven: by the power of the Holy Spirit he was born of the Virgin Mary, and became man. For our sake he was crucified under Pontius Pilate; he suffered, died, and was buried. On the third day he rose again in fulfillment of the Scriptures; he ascended into heaven and is seated at the right hand of the Father. He will come again in glory to judge the living and the dead, and his kingdom will have no end.

We believe in the Holy Spirit, the Lord, the giver of life, who proceeds from the Father and the Son. With the Father and the Son he is worshiped and glorified. He has spoken through the prophets.

We believe in one holy catholic and apostolic Church. We acknowledge one baptism for the forgiveness of sins. We look for the resurrection of the dead, and the life of the world to come. Amen.

Background: The Nicene Creed (Creed of Nicaea-Constantinople) consists of elements of doctrine contained in an early baptismal creed of Jerusalem and enactments of the Council of Nicaea (325) and the Council of Constantinople (381). Its strong trinitarian content reflects the doctrinal errors, especially of Arianism, it served to counteract. Theologically, it is much more sophisticated than the Apostles' Creed. Since late in the fifth century, the Nicene Creed has been the only creed in liturgical use in the Eastern Churches. The Western Church adopted it for liturgical use by the end of the eighth century.

The Athanasian Creed

The Athanasian Creed, which has a unique structure, is a two-part summary of doctrine concerning the Trinity and the Incarnation-Redemption bracketed at the beginning and end with the statement that belief in the cited truths is necessary for salvation; it also contains a number of anathemas or condemnatory clauses regarding doctrinal errors. Although attributed to St. Athanasius, it was probably written after his death, between 381 and 428, and may have been authored by St. Ambrose. It is not accepted in the East; in the West, it has place in the liturgy of some other Christian churches as well as in the Roman-Rite Liturgy of the Hours and for the Solemnity of the Holy Trinity.

Creed of Pius IV

The Creed of Pius IV, also called the Profession of Faith of the Council of Trent, was promulgated in the bull *Injunctum Nobis,* Nov. 13, 1564. It is a summary of doctrine defined by the council concerning: Scripture and tradition, original sin and justification, the Mass and sacraments, veneration of the saints, indulgences, the primacy of the See of Rome. It was slightly modified in 1887 to include doctrinal formulations of the First Vatican Council.

REDDITIO OF CREED

The "giving back," by profession, of a baptismal creed by candidates for baptism to a bishop or his representative was one of the immediate preliminaries to reception of the sacrament at the conclusion of the catechumenate in the early Church.

MORAL OBLIGATIONS

The basic norm of Christian morality is life in Christ. This involves, among other things, the observance of the Ten Commandments, their fulfillment in the twofold law of love of God and neighbor, the implications of the Sermon on the Mount and the whole New Testament, and membership in the Church established by Christ.

The Ten Commandments

The Ten Commandments, the Decalogue, were given by God through Moses to his Chosen People for the guidance of their moral conduct in accord with the demands of the Covenant he established with them as a divine gift. Their observance was essential to participation in the Covenant and the order of salvation based on it.

In the traditional Catholic enumeration and according to Dt. 5:6-21, the Commandments are:

1. "I, the Lord, am your God . . . You shall not have other gods besides me. You shall not carve idols. . . ."
2. "You shall not take the name of the Lord, your God, in vain. . . ."
3. "Take care to keep holy the Sabbath day. . . ."
4. "Honor your father and your mother. . . ."
5. "You shall not kill."
6. "You shall not commit adultery."
7. "You shall not steal."
8. "You shall not bear dishonest witness against your neighbor."
9. "You shall not covet your neighbor's wife."
10. "You shall not desire your neighbor's house or field, nor his male or female slave, nor his ox or ass, nor anything that belongs to him" (summarily, his goods).

Another version of the Commandments, substantially the same, is given in Ex. 20:1-17.

The traditional enumeration of the Commandments in Protestant usage differs from the above. Thus: two commandments are made of the first, as above; the third and fourth are equivalent to the second and third, as above, and so on; and the 10th includes the ninth and 10th, as above.

Love of God and Neighbor

The first three of the commandments deal directly with man's relations with God, viz.: acknowledgment of one true God and the rejection of false gods and idols; honor due to God and his name; observance of the Sabbath as the Lord's day.

The rest cover interpersonal relationships, viz.: the obedience due to parents and, logically, to other persons in authority, and the obligations of parents to children and of persons in authority to those under their care; respect for life and physical integrity; fidelity in marriage, and chastity; justice and rights; truth; internal respect for faithfulness in marriage, chastity, and the goods of others.

Perfection in Christian Life

The moral obligations of the Ten Commandments are complemented by others flowing from the twofold law of love, the whole substance and pattern of Christ's teaching, and everything implied in full and active membership and participation in the community of salvation formed by Christ in his Church. Some of these matters are covered in other sections of the Almanac under appropriate headings.

Precepts of the Church

The precepts of the Church of Roman Rite oblige Catholics to:

1. Assist at Mass on Sundays and holy days of obligation. (Also, to desist from unnecessary servile work on these days.)

2. Fast and abstain on the days appointed. (The fasting obligation binds persons from the 21st until the 59th birthday; the days of fast are Ash Wednesday and Good Friday. The abstinence obligation binds from the 14th birthday on these days, and is obligatory for all Fridays in Lent in the U.S.) These regulations, which have been modified in recent years, are penitential in purpose but do not exhaust obligations of penance. Other ways of doing penance are left to personal option.

3. Confess their sins at least once a year.

4. Receive Holy Communion during the Easter time. (In the U.S., the Easter time extends from the First Sunday of Lent to Trinity Sunday.)

5. Contribute to the support of the Church.

6. Observe the laws of the Church concerning marriage.

SOCIAL DOCTRINE

(For additional social doctrine, see entries pertaining to Pope John Paul II.)

Since the end of the last century, Catholic social doctrine has been formulated in a progressive manner in a number of authoritative documents. Outstanding examples are the encyclicals: *Rerum Novarum,* issued by Leo XIII in 1891; *Quadragesimo Anno,* by Pius XI in 1931; *Mater et Magistra* ("Christianity and Social Progress") and *Pacem in Terris* ("Peace on Earth"), by John XXIII in 1961 and 1963, respectively; and *Populorum Progressio* ("Development of Peoples"), by Paul VI in 1967. Pius XII, among other accomplishments of ideological importance in the social field, made a distinctive contribution with his formulation of a plan for world peace and order in Christmas messages from 1939 to 1941, and in other documents.

These documents represent the most serious attempts in modern times to systematize the social implications of the Gospel and the rest of divine revelation as well as the socially relevant writings of the Fathers and Doctors of the Church. Their contents are theological penetrations into social life, with particular reference to human rights, the needs of the poor and those in underdeveloped countries, and humane conditions of life, freedom, justice and peace. In some respects, they read like juridical documents; underneath, however, they are Gospel-oriented and pastoral in intention.

Nature of the Doctrine

Pope John, writing in *Christianity and Social Progress,* made the following statement about the nature and scope of the doctrine stated in the encyclicals in particular and related writings in general.

"What the Catholic Church teaches and declares regarding the social life and relationships of men is beyond question for all time valid.

"The cardinal point of this teaching is that individual men are necessarily the foundation, cause, and end of all social institutions . . . insofar as they are social by nature, and raised to an order of existence that transcends and subdues nature.

"Beginning with this very basic principle whereby the dignity of the human person is affirmed and defended, Holy Church — especially during the last century and with the assistance of learned priests and laymen, specialists in the field — has arrived at clear social teachings whereby the mutual relationships of men are ordered. Taking general norms into account, these principles are in accord with the nature of things and the changed conditions of man's social life, or with the special genius of our day. Moreover, these norms can be approved by all."

The Church in the World

Even more Gospel-oriented and pastoral in a distinctive way is the *Pastoral Constitution on the Church in the Modern World* promulgated by the Second Vatican Council in 1965.

Its purpose was to search out the signs of God's presence and meaning in and through the events of this time in human history. Accordingly, it dealt with the situation of men in present circumstances of profound change, challenge and crisis on all levels of life.

The first part of the constitution developed the theme of the Church and man's calling, and focused attention on the dignity of the human person, the problem of atheism, the community of mankind, man's activity throughout the world, and the serving and saving role of the Church in the world. This portion of the document, it has been said, represents the first presentation by the Church in an official text of an organized Christian view of man and society.

The second part of the document considered several problems of special urgency: fostering the nobility of marriage and the family (see Marriage Doctrine), the proper development of culture, socio-economic life, the life of the political community, the fostering of peace (see Peace and War), and the promotion of a community of nations.

In conclusion, the constitution called for action to implement doctrine regarding the role and work of the Church for the total good of mankind.

Following are a number of key excerpts from the ideological heart of the constitution.

One Human Family and Community: "God, who has fatherly concern for everyone, has willed that all men should constitute one family and treat one another in a spirit of brotherhood....

"For this reason, love for God and neighbor is the first and greatest commandment. Sacred Scripture ... teaches us that the love of God cannot be separated from love of neighbor.... To men growing daily more dependent on one another, and to a world becoming more unified every day, this truth proves to be of paramount importance ..." (No. 24).

Human Person Is Central: "Man's social nature makes it evident that the progress of the human person and the advance of society itself hinge on each other. For the beginning, the subject and the goal of all social institutions is and must be the human person, which for its part and by its very nature stands completely in need of social life. This social life is not something added on to man. Hence, through his dealings with others, through reciprocal duties, and through fraternal dialogue he develops all his gifts and is able to rise to his destiny."

Influence of Social Circumstances: "But if by this social life the human person is greatly aided in responding to his destiny, even in its religious dimensions, it cannot be denied that men are often diverted from doing good and spurred toward evil by the social circumstances in which they live and are immersed from their birth. To be sure the disturbances which so frequently occur in the social order result in part from the natural tensions of economic, political, and social forms. But at a deeper level they flow from man's pride and selfishness, which contaminate even the social sphere. When the structure of affairs is flawed by the consequences of sin, man, already born with a bent toward evil, finds there new inducements to sin, which cannot be overcome without strenuous efforts and the assistance of grace" (No. 25).

"Every social group must take account of the needs and legitimate aspirations of other groups, and even of the general welfare of the entire human family."

Human Necessities: "At the same time however, there is a growing awareness of the exalted dignity proper to the human person, since he stands above all things, and his rights and duties are universal and inviolable. Therefore, there must be made available to all men everything necessary for leading a life truly human, such as food, clothing, and shelter; the right to choose a state of life freely and to found a family, the right to education, to employment, to a good reputation, to respect, to appropriate information, to activity in accord with the upright norm of one's own conscience, to protection of privacy and to rightful freedom in matters religious too.

"Hence, the social order and its development must unceasingly work to the benefit of the human person if the disposition of affairs is to be subordinate to the personal realm and not contrariwise, as the Lord indicated when He said that the Sabbath was made for man, and not man for the Sabbath."

Improvement of Social Order: "This social order requires constant improvement. It must be founded on truth, built on justice, and animated by love; in freedom it should grow every day toward a more humane balance. An improvement in attitudes and widespread changes in society will have to take place if these objectives are to be gained.

"God's Spirit, who with a marvelous providence directs the unfolding of time and renews the face of the earth, is not absent from this development. The ferment of the gospel, too, has aroused and continues to arouse in man's heart the irresistible requirements of his dignity" (No. 26).

Regard for Neighbor as Another Self: "Coming down to practical and particularly urgent consequences, this Council lays stress on reverence for man; everyone must consider his every neighbor without exception as another self, taking into account first of all his life and the means necessary to living it with dignity....

"In our times a special obligation binds us to make ourselves the neighbor of absolutely every person, and of actively helping him when he comes across our path...."

Inhuman Evils: "... Whatever is opposed to life itself, such as any type of murder, genocide, abortion, euthanasia, or willful self-destruction, whatever violates the integrity of the human person, such as mutilation, torments inflicted on body or mind, attempts to coerce the will itself; whatever insults human dignity, such as subhuman living conditions, arbitrary imprisonment, deportation, slavery, prostitution, the selling of women and children; as well as disgraceful working conditions, where men are treated as mere tools for profit, rather than as free and responsible persons; all these things and others of their like are infamies indeed. They poison human society, but they do more harm to those who practice them than those who suffer from the injury. Moreover, they are a supreme dishonor to the Creator" (No. 27).

Respect for Those Who Are Different: "Respect and love ought to be extended also to those who think or act differently than we do in social, political, and religious matters. In fact, the more deeply we come to understand their ways of thinking through such courtesy and love, the more easily will we be able to enter into dialogue with them."

Distinction between Error and Person in Error: "This love and good will,, to be sure, must in no way render us indifferent to truth and goodness. Indeed love itself impels the disciples of Christ to speak the saving truth to all men. But it is necessary to distinguish between error, which always merits repudiation, and the person in error, who never loses the dignity of being a person, even when he is flawed by false or inadequate religious notions. God alone is the judge and searcher of hearts; for that reason He forbids us to make judgments about the internal guilt of anyone.

"The teaching of Christ even requires that we forgive injuries, and extends the law of love to include every enemy . . ." (No. 28).

Men Are Equal but Different: "Since all men possess a rational soul and are created in God's likeness, since they have the same nature and origin, have been redeemed by Christ, and enjoy the same divine calling and destiny, the basic equality of all must receive increasingly greater recognition.

"True, all men are not alike from the point of view of varying physical power and the diversity of intellectual and moral resources. Nevertheless, with respect to the fundamental rights of the person, every type of discrimination, whether social or cultural, whether based on sex, race, color, social condition, language, or religion, is to be overcome and eradicated as contrary to God's intent. . . ."

Humane Conditions for All: ". . . Although rightful differences exist between men, the equal dignity of persons demands that a more humane and just condition of life be brought about. For excessive economic and social differences between the members of the one human family and population groups cause scandal, and militate against social justice, equity, the dignity of the human person, as well as social and international peace.

"Human institutions, both private and public, must labor to minister to the dignity and purpose of man. At the same time let them put up a stubborn fight against any kind of slavery, whether social or political, and safeguard the basic rights of man under every political system. Indeed human institutions themselves must be accommodated by degrees to the highest of all realities, spiritual ones, even though, meanwhile, a long enough time will be required before they arrive at the desired goal" (No. 29).

"Profound and rapid changes make it particularly urgent that no one, ignoring the trend of events or drugged by laziness, content himself with a merely individualistic morality. It grows increasingly true that the obligations of justice and love are fulfilled only if each person, contributing to the common good, according to his own abilities and the needs of others, also promotes and assists the public and private institutions dedicated to bettering the conditions of human life."

Social Necessities Are Prime Duties: "Let everyone consider it his sacred obligation to count social necessities among the primary duties of modern man, and to pay heed to them. For the more unified the world becomes, the more plainly do the offices of men extend beyond particular groups and spread by degrees to the whole world. But this challenge cannot be met unless individual men and their associations cultivate in themselves the moral and social virtues, and promote them in society. Thus, with the needed help of divine grace, men who are truly new and artisans of a new humanity can be forthcoming" (No. 30).

"In order for individual men to discharge with greater exactness the obligations of their conscience toward themselves and the various groups to which they belong, they must be carefully educated to a higher degree of culture through the use of the immense resources available today to the human race. . . ."

Living Conditions and Freedom: ". . . A man can scarcely arrive at the needed sense of responsibility unless his living conditions allow him to become conscious of his dignity, and to rise to his destiny by spending himself for God and for others. But human freedom is often crippled when a man falls into extreme poverty, just as it withers when he indulges in too many of life's comforts and imprisons himself in a kind of splendid isolation. Freedom acquires new strength, by contrast, when a man consents to the unavoidable requirements of social life, takes on the manifold demands of human partnership, and commits himself to the service of the human community.

"Hence, the will to play one's role in common endeavors should be everywhere encouraged . . ." (No. 31).

Communitarian Character of Life: "God did not create man for life in isolation, but, for the formation of social unity. So also 'it has pleased God to make men holy and save them not merely as individuals, without any mutual bonds, but by making them into a single people, a people which acknowledges Him in truth and serves Him in holiness' (*Dogmatic Constitution on the Church,* No. 9). So from the beginning of salvation history He has chosen men not just as individuals but as members of a certain community. Revealing His mind to them, God called these chosen ones 'His people' (Ex. 3:7-12), and, furthermore, made a covenant with them on Sinai.

"This communitarian character is developed and consummated in the work of Jesus Christ. For the very Word made flesh willed to share in the human fellowship. He was present at the wedding of Cana, visited the house of Zacchaeus, ate with publicans and sinners. He revealed the love of the Father and the sublime vocation of man in terms of the most common of social realities and by making use of the speech and the imagery of plain everyday life. Willingly obeying the laws of His country, He sanctified those human ties, especially family ones, from which social relationships arise. He chose to lead the life proper to an artisan of His time and place.

"In His preaching He clearly taught the sons of God to treat one another as brothers. In His prayers He pleaded that all His disciples might be 'one.' Indeed, as the Redeemer of all, He offered Himself for all even to the point of death. . . . He commanded His apostles to preach to all peoples the gospel message so that the human race might become the Family of God, in which the fullness of the Law would be love."

The Community Founded by Christ: "As the first-born of many brethren and through the gift of His Spirit, He founded after His death and resurrection a new brotherly community composed of all those who receive Him in faith and in love. This he did through His Body, which is the Church. There everyone, as members one of the other, would render mutual service according to the different gifts bestowed on each" (No. 32).

PEACE AND WAR

The following excerpts, stating principles and objectives of social doctrine concerning peace and war, are from the *Pastoral Constitution on the Church in the Modern World* (Nos. 77 to 82) promulgated by the Second Vatican Council.

Call to Peace: ". . . This Council fervently desires to summon Christians to cooperate with all men in making secure among themselves a peace based on justice and love, and in setting up agencies of peace. This Christians should do with the help of Christ, the Author of peace" (No. 77).

Conditions for Peace: "Peace is not merely the absence of war. Nor can it be reduced solely to the maintenance of a balance of power between enemies. Nor is it brought about by dictatorship. Instead, it is rightly and appropriately called 'an enterprise of justice' (Is. 32:7). Peace results from that harmony built into human society by its divine Founder, and actualized by men as they thirst after ever greater justice.

"The common good of men is in its basic sense determined by the eternal law. Still the concrete demands of this common good are constantly changing as time goes on. Hence peace is never attained once and for all, but must be built up ceaselessly. Moreover, since the human will is unsteady and wounded by sin, the achievement of peace requires that everyone constantly master his passions and that lawful authority keep vigilant.

"But such is not enough. This peace cannot be obtained on earth unless personal values are safeguarded and men freely and trustingly share with one another the riches of their inner spirits and their talents. A firm determination to respect other men and peoples and their dignity, as well as the studied practice of brotherhood, are absolutely necessary for the establishment of peace. Hence peace is likewise the fruit of love, which goes beyond what justice can provide."

Renunciation of Violence: ". . . We cannot fail to praise those who renounce the use of violence in the vindication of their rights and who resort to methods of defense which are otherwise available to weaker parties too, provided that this can be done without injury to the rights and duties of others or of the community itself . . ." (No. 78).

Mass Extermination: ". . . The Council wishes to recall first of all the permanent binding force of universal natural law and its all-embracing principles. Man's conscience itself gives ever more emphatic voice to these principles. Therefore, actions which deliberately conflict with these same principles, as well as orders commanding such actions, are criminal. Blind obedience cannot excuse those who yield to them. Among such must first be counted those actions designed for the methodical extermination of an entire people, nation, or ethnic minority. These actions must be vehemently condemned as horrendous crimes. The courage of those who openly and fearlessly resist men who issue such commands merits supreme commendation."

International Agreements: "On the subject of war, quite a large number of nations have subscribed to various international agreements aimed at making military activity and its consequences less inhuman. Such are conventions concerning the handling of wounded or captured soldiers, and various similar agreements. Agreements of this sort must be honored. They should be improved upon."

Conscientious Objectors: ". . . It seems right that laws make humane provisions for the case of those who for reasons of conscience refuse to bear arms, provided, however, that they accept some other form of service to the human community."

Legitimate Defense: "Certainly, war has not been rooted out of human affairs. As long as the danger of war remains and there is no competent and sufficiently powerful authority at the international level, governments cannot be denied the right to legitimate defense once every means of peaceful settlement has been exhausted. Therefore, government authorities and others who share public responsibility have the duty to protect the welfare of the people entrusted to their care and to conduct such grave matters soberly.

"But it is one thing to undertake military action for the just defense of the people, and something else again to seek the subjugation of other nations. Nor does the possession of war potential make every military or political use of it lawful. Neither does the mere fact that war has unhappily begun mean that all is fair between the warring parties."

Nature of Military Service: "Those who are pledged to the service of their country as members of its armed forces should regard themselves as agents of security and freedom on behalf of their people. As long as they fulfill this role properly, they are making a genuine contribution to the establishment of peace" (No. 79).

Total War Condemned: ". . . This most holy Synod makes its own the condemnations of total war already pronounced by recent Popes, and issues the following declaration:

"Any act of war aimed indiscriminately at the destruction of entire cities or of extensive areas along with their population is a crime against God and man himself. It merits unequivocal and unhesitating condemnation.

"The unique hazard of modern warfare consists in this: it provides those who possess modern scientific weapons with a kind of occasion for perpetrating just such abominations. Moreover, through a certain inexorable chain of events, it can urge men on to the most atrocious decisions. That such in fact may never happen in the future, the bishops of the whole world, in unity assembled, beg all men, especially government officials and military leaders, to give unremitting thought to the awesome responsibility which is theirs before God and the entire human race" (No. 80).

Retaliation and Deterrence: "Scientific weapons, to be sure, are not amassed solely for use in war. The defensive strength of any nation is considered to be dependent upon its capacity for immediate retaliation against an adversary. Hence this accumulation of arms, which increases each year, also serves, in a way heretofore unknown, as a deterrent to possible enemy attack. Many regard this state of affairs as the most effective way by which peace of a sort can be maintained between nations at the present time."

Arms Race: "Whatever be the case with this method of deterrence, men should be convinced that the arms race in which so many countries are engaged is not a safe way to preserve a steady peace. Nor is the so-called balance resulting from this race a sure and authentic peace. Rather than being eliminated thereby, the causes of war threaten to grow gradually stronger.

"While extravagant sums are being spent for the furnishing of ever new weapons, an adequate remedy cannot be provided for the multiple miseries afflicting the whole modern world. Disagreements between nations are not really and radically healed. On the contrary other parts of the world are infected with them. New approaches initiated by reformed attitudes must be adopted to remove this trap and to restore genuine peace by emancipating the world from its crushing anxiety.

"Therefore, it must be said again: the arms race is an utterly treacherous trap for humanity, and one which injures the poor to an intolerable degree. It is much to be feared that, if this race persists, it will eventually spawn all the lethal ruin whose path it is now making ready . . ." (No. 81).

Outlaw War: "It is our clear duty, then, to strain every muscle as we work for the time when all war can be completely outlawed by international consent. This goal undoubtedly requires the establishment of some universal public authority acknowledged as such by all, and endowed with effective power to safeguard, on the behalf of all, security, regard for justice, and respect for rights."

Multilateral and Controlled Disarmament: "But before this hoped-for authority can be set up, the highest existing international centers must devote themselves vigorously to the pursuit of better means for obtaining common security. Peace must be born of mutual trust between nations rather than imposed on them through fear of one another's weapons. Hence everyone must labor to put an end at last to the arms race, and to make a true beginning of disarmament, not indeed a unilateral disarmament, but one proceeding at an equal pace according to agreement, and backed up by authentic and workable safeguards.

"In the meantime, efforts which have already been made and are still under way to eliminate the danger of war are not to be underrated. On the contrary, support should be given to the good will of the very many leaders who work hard to do away with war, which they abominate. . . ."

Public Opinion: ". . . Men should take heed not to entrust themselves only to the efforts of others, while remaining careless about their own attitudes. For government officials, who must simultaneously guarantee the good of their own people and promote the universal good, depend on public opinion and feeling to the greatest possible extent. It does them no good to work at building peace so long as feelings of hostility, contempt, and distrust, as well as racial hatred and unbending ideologies, continue to divide men and place them in opposing camps.

"Hence arises a surpassing need for renewed education of attitudes and for new inspiration in the area of public opinion. Those who are dedicated to the work of education . . . should regard as their most weighty task the effort to instruct all in fresh sentiments of peace" (No. 82).

The nature and purpose of the liturgy, along with norms for its revision, were the subject matter of the *Constitution on the Sacred Liturgy* promulgated by the Second Vatican Council. The principles and guidelines stated in this document, the first issued by the Council, are summarized here and/or are incorporated in other Almanac entries on liturgical subjects.

Nature and Purpose of Liturgy

"It is through the liturgy, especially the divine Eucharistic Sacrifice, that 'the work of our redemption is exercised.' The liturgy is thus the outstanding means by which the faithful can express in their lives, and manifest to others, the mystery of Christ and the real nature of the true Church . . ." (No. 2).

"The liturgy is considered as an exercise of the priestly office of Jesus Christ. In the liturgy the sanctification of man is manifested by signs perceptible to the senses, and is effected in a way which is proper to each of these signs; in the liturgy full public worship is performed by the Mystical Body of Jesus Christ, that is, by the Head and His members.

"From this it follows that every liturgical celebration, because it is an action of Christ the priest and of His Body the Church, is a sacred action surpassing all others. No other action of the Church can match its claim to efficacy, nor equal the degree of it" (No. 7).

"The liturgy is the summit toward which the activity of the Church is directed; at the same time it is the fountain from which all her power flows. For the goal of apostolic works is that all who are made sons of God by faith and baptism should come together to praise God in the midst of His Church, to take part in her sacrifice, and to eat the Lord's Supper.

". . . From the liturgy, therefore, and especially from the Eucharist, as from a fountain, grace is channeled into us; and the sanctification of men in Christ and the glorification of God, to which all other activities of the Church are directed as toward their goal, are most powerfully achieved" (No. 10).

Full Participation

"Mother Church earnestly desires that all the faithful be led to that full, conscious, and active participation in liturgical celebrations which is demanded by the very nature of the liturgy. Such participation by the Christian people as 'a chosen race, a royal priesthood, a holy nation, a purchased people' (1 Pt. 2:9; cf. 2:4-5), is their right and duty by reason of their baptism.

"In the restoration and promotion of the sacred liturgy, this full and active participation by all the people is the aim to be considered before all else; for it is the primary and indispensable source from which the faithful are to derive the true Christian spirit . . ." (No. 14).

"In order that the Christian people may more securely derive an abundance of graces from the sacred liturgy, holy Mother Church desires to undertake with great care a general restoration of the liturgy itself. For the liturgy is made up of unchangeable elements divinely instituted, and elements subject to change. The latter not only may but ought to be changed with the passing of time if features have by chance crept in which are less harmonious with the intimate nature of the liturgy, or if existing elements have grown less functional.

"In this restoration, both texts and rites should be drawn up so that they express more clearly the holy things which they signify. Christian people, as far as possible, should be able to understand them with ease and to take part in them fully, actively, and as befits a community . . ." (No. 21).

Norms

Norms regarding the reforms concern the greater use of Scripture; emphasis on the importance of the sermon or homily on biblical and liturgical subjects; use of vernacular languages for prayers of the Mass and for administration of the sacraments; provision for adaptation of rites to cultural patterns.

Approval for reforms of various kinds — in liturgical texts, rites, etc. — depends on the Holy See, regional conferences of bishops and individual bishops, according to provisions of law. No priest has authority to initiate reforms on his own. Reforms may not be introduced just for the sake of innovation, and any that are introduced in the light of present-day circumstances should embody sound tradition.

To assure the desired effect of liturgical reforms, training and instruction are necessary for the clergy, religious and the laity. The functions of diocesan and regional commissions for liturgy, music and art are to set standards and provide leadership for instruction and practical programs in their respective fields.

Most of the constitution's provisions regarding liturgical reforms have to do with the Roman Rite. The document clearly respects the equal dignity of all rites, leaving to the Eastern Churches control over their ancient liturgies.

(For coverage of the **Mystery of the Eucharist,** see The Mass; **Other Sacraments,** see separate entries.)

Sacramentals

Sacramentals, instituted by the Church, "are sacred signs which bear a resemblance to the sacraments: they signify effects, particularly of a spiritual kind, which are obtained through the Church's intercession. By them men are disposed to receive the chief effect of the sacraments, and various occasions in life are rendered holy" (No. 60).

"Thus, for well-disposed members of the faithful, the liturgy of the sacraments and sacramentals sanctifies almost every event in their lives; they are given access to the stream of divine grace which flows from the paschal mystery of the passion, death, and resurrection of Christ, the fountain from which all sacraments and sacramentals draw their power. There is hardly any proper use of material things which cannot thus be directed toward the sanctification of men and the praise of God" (No. 61).   Some common sacramentals are priestly blessings, blessed palm, candles, holy water, medals, scapulars, prayers and ceremonies of the Roman Ritual.

Liturgy of the Hours

The Liturgy of the Hours (Divine Office) is the public prayer of the Church for praising God and sanctifying the day. Its daily celebration is required as a sacred obligation by men in holy orders and by men and women religious who have professed solemn vows. Its celebration by others is highly commended and is to be encouraged in the communuty of the faithful.

"By tradition going back to early Christian times, the Divine Office is arranged so that the whole course of the day and night is made holy by the praises of God. Therefore, when this wonderful song of praise is worthily rendered by priests and others who are deputed for this purpose by Church ordinance, or by the faithful praying together with the priest in an approved form, then it is truly the voice of the bride addressing her bridegroom; it is the very prayer which Christ Himself, together with His body, addresses to the Father" (No. 84).

"Hence all who perform this service are not only fulfilling a duty of the Church, but also are sharing in the greatest honor accorded to Christ's spouse, for by offering these praises to God they are standing before God's throne in the name of the Church their Mother" (No. 85).

The Latin text of the Liturgy of the Hours, under revision since 1965, was described by Pope Paul in the apostolic constitution *Canticum Laudis,* dated Nov. 1, 1970. Its four complete volumes in authorized English translation have been published since May, 1975.

One-volume, partial editions of the Liturgy of the Hours have been published in approved English translation. Entitled *Christian Prayer,* they contain the Morning and Evening Prayers and other elements. They are intended for use by religious and lay persons who are not bound by obligation to pray the Liturgy of the Hours.

The revised Liturgy of the Hours consists of:

• Office of Readings, for reflection on the word of God. The pruncipal parts are three psalms, biblical and non-biblical readings.

• Morning and Evening Prayer, called the "hinges" of the Liturgy of the Hours. The principal parts are a hymn, two psalms, an Old or New Testament canticle, a brief biblical reading, Zechariah's canticle (the *Benedictus,* morning) or Mary's canticle (the *Magnificat,* evening), responsories, intercessions and a concluding prayer.

• Daytime Prayer. The principal parts are a hymn, three psalms, a brief biblical reading and one of three concluding prayers corresponding to the time at which the prayer is offered (midmorning, midday, midafternoon).

• Night Prayer: The principal parts are one or two psalms, a brief biblical reading, Simeon's canticle *(Nunc Dimittis),* a concluding prayer and an antiphon in honor of Mary.

In the new Office, the hours are shorter than they had been, with greater textual variety, meditation aids, and provision for intervals of silence and meditation. The psalms are distributed over a four-week period instead of a week; some psalms, entirely or in part, are not included. Additional canticles from the Old and New Testaments are assigned for Morning and Evening Prayer. Additional scriptural texts have been added and variously arranged for greater internal unity, correspondence to readings at Mass, and relevance to events and themes of salvation history. Readings include some of the best material from the Fathers of the Church and other authors and improved selections on the lives of saints.

The book used for recitation of the Office is the **Breviary.**

For coverage of the **Liturgical Year,** see Church Calendar.

Sacred Music

"The musical tradition of the universal Church is a treasure of immeasurable value, greater even than that of any other art. The main reason for this pre-eminence is that, as sacred melody united to words, it forms a necessary or integral part of the solemn liturgy.

". . . Sacred music increases in holiness to the degree that it is intimately linked with liturgical action, winningly expresses prayerfulness, promotes solidarity, and enriches sacred rites with heightened solemnity. The Church indeed approves of all forms of true art, and admits them into divine worship when they show appropriate qualities" (No. 112).

The constitution decreed:

• Vernacular languages for the people's parts of the liturgy, as well as Latin, may be used.

• Participation in sacred song by the whole body of the faithful, and not just by choirs, is to be encouraged and brought about.

• Provisions should be made for proper musical training for clergy, religious and lay persons.

• While Gregorian Chant has a unique dignity and relationship to the Latin liturgy, other kinds of music are acceptable.

• Native musical traditions should be used, especially in mission areas.

• Various instruments compatible with the dignity of worship may be used.

Gregorian Chant: A form and style of chant called Gregorian was the basis and most highly regarded standard of liturgical music for centuries. It originated probably during the formative period of the Roman liturgy and developed in conjunction with Gallican and other forms of chant. Gregory the Great's connection with it is not clear, although it is known that he had great concern for and interest in church music. The earliest extant written versions of Gregorian chant date from the ninth century. A thousand years later, the Benedictines of Solesmes, France, initiated a revival of chant which gave impetus to the modern liturgical movement.

Sacred Art and Furnishings

"Very rightly the fine arts are considered to rank among the noblest expressions of human genius. This judgment applies especially to religious art and to its highest achievement, which is sacred art. By their very nature both of the latter are related to God's boundless beauty, for this is the reality which these human efforts are trying to express in some way. To the extent that these works aim exclusively at turning men's thoughts to God persuasively and devoutly, they are dedicated to God and to the cause of His greater honor and glory" (No. 122).

The objective of sacred art is "that all things set apart for use in divine worship should be truly worthy, becoming, and beautiful, signs and symbols of heavenly realities. . . . The Church has . . . always reserved to herself the right to pass judgment upon the arts, deciding which of the works of artists are in accordance with faith, piety, and cherished traditional laws, and thereby suited to sacred purposes.

". . . Sacred furnishings should worthily and beautifully serve the dignity of worship . . ." (No. 122).

According to the constitution:

• Contemporary art, as well as that of the past, shall "be given free scope in the Church, provided that it adorns the sacred buildings and holy rites with due honor and reverence . . ." (No. 123).

• Noble beauty, not sumptuous display, should be sought in art, sacred vestments and ornaments.

• "Let bishops carefully exclude from the house of god and from other sacred places those works of artists which are repugnant to faith, morals, and Christian piety, and which offend true religious sense either by their distortion of forms or by lack of artistic worth, by mediocrity or by pretense.

• "When churches are to be built, let great care be taken that they be suitable for the celebration of liturgical services and for the active participation of the faithful" (No. 124).

• "The practice of placing sacred images in churches so that they may be venerated by the faithful is to be firmly maintained. Nevertheless, their number should be moderate and their relative location should reflect right order. Otherwise they may create confusion among the Christian people and promote a faulty sense of devotion" (No. 125).

• Artists should be trained and inspired in the spirit and for the purposes of the liturgy.

• The norms of sacred art should be revised. "These laws refer especially to the worthy and well-planned construction of sacred buildings, the shape and construction of altars, the nobility, location, and security of the Eucharistic tabernacle, the suitability and dignity of the baptistery, the proper use of sacred images, embellishments, and vestments . . ." (No. 128).

RITES

A rite is the manner in which liturgical worship is carried out. It includes the forms and ceremonial observances of liturgical worship.

Different rites have evolved in the course of Church history, giving to liturgical worship forms and usages peculiar and proper to the nature of worship itself and to the culture of the faithful in various circumstances of time and place. Thus, there has been development since apostolic times in prayers and ceremonies of the Mass, the administration of the sacraments, requirements for celebration of the Divine Office. Practices within the patriarchates of Antioch, Rome, Alexandria and Constantinople were the principal sources of the rites in present use.

Eastern Rites, described elsewhere in the Almanac, are proper to Eastern Catholic Churches.

The **Roman** or **Latin Rite,** described in this section, prevails in the Western Church. It was derived from Roman practices and the use of Latin as an official language from the third century onward. Other rites in limited use in the Western Church have been the Ambrosian, the Mozarabic, the Lyonnais, the Braga, and rites peculiar to some religious orders like the Dominicans, Carmelites and Carthusians.

MASS, EUCHARISTIC SACRIFICE AND BANQUET

Declarations of Vatican II

The Second Vatican Council made the following declarations, among others, with respect to the Mass.

"At the Last Supper, on the night when He was betrayed, our Savior instituted the Eucharistic Sacrifice of His Body and Blood. He did this in order to perpetuate the sacrifice of the Cross throughout the centuries until He should come again, and so to entrust to His beloved spouse, the Church, a memorial of His death and resurrection: a sacrament of love, a sign of unity, a bond of charity, a paschal banquet in which Christ is consumed, the mind is filled with grace, and a pledge of future glory is given to us" (*Constitution on the Sacred Liturgy,* No. 47).

". . . As often as the sacrifice of the cross in which 'Christ, our passover, has been sacrificed' (1 Cor. 5:7) is celebrated on an altar, the work of our redemption is carried on. At the same time, in the sacrament of the Eucharistic bread the unity of all believers who form one body in Christ (cf. 1 Cor. 10:17) is both expressed and brought about. All men are called to this union with Christ . . ." (*Dogmatic Constitution on the Church.* No. 3).

". . . The ministerial priest, by the sacred power he enjoys, molds and rules the priestly people. Acting in the person of Christ, he brings about the Eucharistic Sacrifice, and offers it to God in the name of all the people. For their part, the faithful join in the offering of the Eucharist by virtue of their royal priesthood . . ." (*Ibid.,* No. 10).

Declarations of Trent

Among its decrees on the Holy Eucharist, the Council of Trent stated the following points of doctrine on the Mass.

1. There is in the Catholic Church a true Sacrifice, the Mass instituted by Jesus Christ. It is the Sacrifice of His Body and Blood, Soul and Divinity, Himself, under the appearances of bread and wine.

2. This Sacrifice is identical with the Sacrifice of the Cross, inasmuch as Christ is the Priest and Victim in both. A difference lies in the manner of offering, which was bloody upon the Cross and is bloodless on the altar.

3. The Mass is a propitiatory Sacrifice, atoning for sins of the living and dead for whom it is offered.

4. The efficacy of the Mass is derived from the Sacrifice of the Cross, whose super-abundant merits it applies to men.

5. Although the Mass is offered to God alone, it may be celebrated in honor and memory of the saints.

6. Christ instituted the Mass at the Last Supper.

7. Christ ordained the Apostles priests, giving them power and the command to consecrate His Body and Blood to perpetuate and renew the Sacrifice.

ORDER OF MASS

The Mass consists of two principal divisions called the **Liturgy of the Word,** which features the proclamation of the Word of God, and the **Eucharistic Liturgy,** which focuses on the central act of sacrifice in the Consecration and on the Eucharistic Banquet in Holy Communion. (Formerly, these divisions were called, respectively, the **Mass of the Catechumens** and the **Mass of the Faithful.**) In addition to these principal divisions, there are ancillary introductory and concluding rites.

The following description covers the Mass as celebrated with participation by the people. This Order of the Mass was approved by Pope Paul VI in the apostolic constitution *Missale Romanum* dated Apr. 3, 1969, and promulgated in a decree issued Apr. 6, 1969, by the Congregation for Divine Worship. The assigned effective date was Nov. 30, 1969.

Introductory Rites

Entrance: The introductory rites begin with the singing or recitation of an entrance song while the priest approaches the altar, kisses it, and goes to the place where he will be seated. The song consists of one or more scriptural verses stating the theme of the mystery, season or feast commemorated in the Mass.

Greeting: The priest and people make the Sign of the Cross together. The priest then greets them in one of several alternative ways and they reply in a corresponding manner.

Introductory Remarks: At this point, the priest or another of the ministers may introduce the theme of the Mass.

Penitential Rite: The priest and people together acknowledge their sins as a preliminary step toward worthy celebration of the sacred mysteries. This rite includes a brief examination of conscience, a general confession of sin and plea for divine mercy in one of several ways, and a prayer of absolution by the priest. The *Kyrie, eleison* ("Lord, have mercy") is then said if it was not included in one of the foregoing pleas for divine mercy.

Glory to God: A doxology, a hymn of praise to God, sung or said on festive occasions.

Opening Prayer: A prayer of petition offered by the priest on behalf of the worshipping community.

I. Liturgy of the Word

Readings: The featured elements of this liturgy are several readings of passages from the Bible. If three readings are in order, the first is usually from the Old Testament, the second from the New Testament (Epistles, Acts, Revelation), and the third from one of the Gospels; the final reading is always a selection from a Gospel. The first reading(s) is concluded with the formula, "This is the Word of the Lord," to which the people respond, "Thanks be to God." The Gospel reading is concluded with the formula, "This is the Gospel of the Lord," to which the people respond, "Praise to you, Lord Jesus Christ." Between the readings, psalm verses and a Gospel acclamation are sung or said.

Homily: Sermon on a scriptural or liturgical subject; ideally, it should be related to the liturgical service in progress.

Creed: The Nicene profession of faith, by priest and people, on certain occasions.

Prayer of the Faithful: Litany-type prayers of petition, with participation by the people. Called general intercessions, they concern needs of the Church, the salvation of the world, public authorities, persons in need, the local community.

II. Eucharistic Liturgy

Offertory Song: Scriptural verses related to the theme of the Mass, or a suitable hymn, sung or said while things are prepared at the altar for the Eucharistic Liturgy and while the offerings of bread and wine are brought to the altar.

Offertory Procession: Presentation to the priest of the gifts of bread and wine, principally, by participating members of the congregation.

Offering of the Gifts: Consists of the prayers and ceremonies with which the priest offers bread and wine as the elements of the sacrifice to take place during the Eucharistic Prayer and of the Lord's Supper to be shared in Holy Communion. If singing takes place during the offering, the priest can say the prayers and carry out the action silently; if there is no singing, he says the prayers aloud and the people, after each offering, respond with the words, "Blessed be God forever."

Washing of Hands: After offering the bread and wine, the priest cleanses his fingers with water in a brief ceremony of purification.

Pray, Brethren: Prayer that the sacrifice to take place will be acceptable to God. The first part of the prayer is said by the priest; the second, by the people.

Prayer over the Gifts: A prayer of petition offered by the priest on behalf of the worshiping community.

Eucharistic Prayer

Preface: A hymn of praise, introducing the Eucharistic Prayer or Canon, sung or said by the priest following responses by the people. The Order of the Mass contains a variety of prefaces, for use on different occasions.

Holy, Holy, Holy; Blessed Is He: Divine praises sung or said by the priest and people.

Canon: The Eucharistic Prayer of the Mass whose central portion is the Consecration, when the essential act of the sacrificial offering takes place with the changing of bread and wine into the Body and Blood of Christ. The prayers of the Canon, which are said by the celebrant only, commemorate principal mysteries of salvation history and include petitions for the Church, the living and dead, and remembrances of saints. There are four Eucharistic Prayers, for use on various occasions and at the option of the priest. (Additional Canons for Masses with children and for reconciliation were approved in 1975.)

Doxology: A formula of divine praise sung or said by the priest while he holds aloft the chalice containing the consecrated wine in one hand and the paten containing the consecrated host in the other.

Communion Rite

Lord's Prayer: Sung or said by the priest and people.

Prayer for Deliverance from evil: Called an **embolism** because it is a development of the final petition of the Lord's Prayer; said by the priest. It concludes with a memorial of the return of the Lord to which the people respond, "For the kingdom, the power, and the glory are yours, now and forever."

Prayer for Peace: Said by the priest, with corresponding responses by the people. The priest can, in accord with local custom, bid the people to exchange a greeting of peace with each other.

Lamb of God: A prayer for divine mercy sung or said while the priest breaks the consecrated host and places a piece of it into the consecrated wine in the chalice.

Communion: The priest, after saying a preparatory prayer, administers Holy Communion to himself and then to the people, thus completing the sacrifice-banquet of the Mass. (This completion is realized even if the celebrant alone receives the Eucharist.) On giving the Eucharist to the people, the priest says, "The Body of Christ," to each recipient; the customary response is "Amen." If the Eucharist is administered under the forms of bread and wine, the priest says, "The Body and Blood of Christ."

Communion Song: Scriptural verses or a suitable hymn sung or said during the distribution of Holy Communion. After Holy Communion is received, some moments may be spent in silent meditation or in the chanting of a psalm or hymn of praise.

Prayer after Communion: A prayer of petition offered by the priest on behalf of the worshipping community.

Concluding Rite

Announcements: Brief announcements to the people are in order at this time.

Dismissal: Consists of a final greeting by the priest, a blessing, and a formula of dismissal. This rite is omitted if another liturgical action immediately follows the Mass; e.g., a procession, the blessing of the body during a funeral rite.

Some parts of the Mass are changeable with the liturgical season or feast, and are called the **proper** of the Mass. Other parts are said to be **common** because they always remain the same.

Additional Mass Notes

Catholics are seriously obliged to attend Mass in a worthy manner on Sundays and holy days of obligation. Failure to do so without a proportionately serious reason is gravely wrong.

It is the custom for priests to celebrate Mass daily whenever possible. To satisfy the needs of the faithful on Sundays and holy days of obligation, they are authorized to say Mass twice (**bination**) or even three times (**trination**). Bination is also permissible on weekdays. On Christmas and All Souls' Day every priest may say three Masses. Mass may be celebrated in the morning, afternoon or evening.

The **fruits of the Mass,** which in itself is of infinite value, are: **general,** for all the faithful; **special (ministerial),** for the intentions or persons specifically intended by the celebrant; **most special (personal),** for the celebrant himself. On Sundays and certain other days pastors are obliged to offer Mass for their parishioners. If a priest accepts a stipend or offering for a Mass, he is obliged in justice to apply the Mass for the designated intention. Mass may be applied for the living and the dead, or for any good intention.

Mass can be celebrated in several ways: e.g., with people present, without their presence (privately), with two or more priests as co-celebrants (concelebration), with greater or less solemnity.

Some of the various types of Masses are: **for the dead** (Funeral Mass or Mass of Christian Burial, Mass for the Dead — formerly called Requiem Mass); **nuptial,** for married couples, with or after the wedding ceremony; **votive,** to honor a Person of the Trinity, a saint, or for some special intention. A **red Mass** is a Votive Mass of the Holy Spirit, celebrated for members of the legal profession that they might exercise prudence and equity in their official capacities. **Gregorian Masses** are a series of 30 Masses celebrated on 30 consecutive days for a deceased person.

The only day of the year on which Mass is not celebrated is Good Friday. In its place, there is a **Solemn Liturgical Action.**

Places, Altars for Mass

The ordinary place for celebrating the Eucharist is a church or other sacred place, at a permanent or movable altar.

Outside of a sacred place, Mass may be celebrated in an appropriate place at a suitable table covered with a linen cloth and corporal.

An **altar stone** containing the relics of saints, which was formerly prescribed, is not required by regulations in effect since the promulgation Apr. 6, 1969, of *Institutio Generalis Missalis Romani.*

A **permanent altar** should have a table of stone, be consecrated, and have enclosed within it relics of some saints.

A **movable altar** may be made of any solid and suitable material. If made of stone and consecrated, it should have enclosed within it relics of some saints; if blessed rather than consecrated, the enclosure of relics is not required.

LITURGICAL VESTMENTS

In the early years of the Church, vestments worn by the ministers at liturgical functions were the same as the garments in ordinary popular use. They became distinctive when their form was not altered to correspond with later variations in popular style. Liturgical vestments are symbolic of the sacred ministry and add appropriate decorum to divine worship.

Mass Vestments

Alb: A body-length tunic of white fabric; a vestment common to all ministers of divine worship.

Amice: A rectangular piece of white cloth worn about the neck, tucked into the collar and falling over the shoulders; worn under the alb.

Chasuble: Originally, a large mantle or cloak covering the body, it is the outer vestment of a priest celebrating Mass or carrying out other sacred actions connected with the Mass.

Cincture: A cord which serves the purpose of a belt, holding the alb close to the body.

Dalmatic: The outer vestment worn by a deacon in place of a chasuble.

Stole: A long, band-like vestment worn about the neck and falling to about the knees. (A stole is used for other functions also.)

The material, form and ornamentation of the aforementioned and other vestments are subject to variation and adaptation, according to norms and decisions of the Holy See and concerned conferences of bishops. The overriding norm is that they should be appropriate for use in divine worship. The customary ornamented vestments are the chasuble, dalmatic and stole.

The minimal vestments required for a priest celebrating Mass are the alb, stole and chasuble.

Chasuble-Alb: A vestment combining the features of the chasuble and alb; for use with a stole by concelebrants and, by way of exception, by celebrants in certain circumstances.

Liturgical Colors

The colors of outer vestments vary with liturgical seasons, feasts and other circumstances. The colors and their use are:

Green: For the season of the year; symbolic of hope and the vitality of the life of faith.

Purple: For Advent and Lent; may also be used in Masses for the dead; symbolic of penance.

Red: For the Sunday of the Passion, the Wednesday of Holy Week, Good Friday, Pentecost; feasts of the Passion of Our Lord, the Apostles and Evangelists, martyrs; symbolic of the supreme sacrifice of life for the love of God.

Rose: May be used in place of purple on the Third Sunday of Advent (Gaudete Sunday) and the Fourth Sunday of Lent (Laetare Sunday); symbolic of anticipatory joy during a time of penance.

White: For Christmastide and Eastertide; feasts and commemorations of Our Lord, except those of the Passion; feasts and commemorations of the Blessed Virgin Mary, angels, saints who are not martyrs, All Saints (Nov. 1), St. John the Baptist (June 24), St. John the Evangelist (Dec. 27), the Chair of St. Peter (Feb. 22), the Conversion of St. Paul (Jan. 25). White, symbolic of purity and integrity of the life of faith, may generally be substituted for other colors, and can be used for funeral and other Masses for the dead.

Options are provided regarding the color of vestments used in offices and Masses for the dead. The newsletter of the U.S. Bishops' Committee on the Liturgy, in line with No. 308 of the "General Instruction of the Roman Missal," announced in July, 1970: "In the dioceses of the United States, **white** vestments may be used, in addition to violet (**purple**) and **black**, in offices and Masses for the dead."

On more solemn occasions, better than ordinary vestments may be used, even though their color (e.g., gold) does not match the requirements of the day.

Considerable freedom is permitted in the choice of colors of vestments worn for votive Masses.

Other Vestments

Cappa Magna: Flowing vestment with a train, worn by bishops and cardinals.

Cassock: A full-length, close-fitting robe worn by priests and other clerics under liturgical vestments and in ordinary use; usually black for priests, purple for bishops and other prelates, red for cardinals, white for the pope. In place of a cassock, priests belonging to religious institutes wear the habit proper to their institute.

Cope: A mantle-like vestment open in front and fastened across the chest; worn by sacred ministers in processions and other ceremonies, as prescribed by appropriate directives.

Gremial: A rectangular veil of silk or linen placed over the knees of a bishop when he is seated during various episcopal ceremonies.

Habit: The ordinary garb of members of religious institutes, analogous to the cassock of diocesan priests; the form of habits varies from institute to institute.

Humeral Veil: A rectangular vestment worn about the shoulders by a deacon. or priest in Eucharistic processions and for other prescribed liturgical ceremonies.

Mitre: A headdress worn at some liturgical functions by bishops, abbots and, in certain cases, other ecclesiastics.

Pallium: A circular band of white wool about two inches wide, with front and back pendants, marked with six crosses, worn about the neck. It is a symbol of the fullness of the episcopal office. Pope Paul VI, in a document issued July 20, 1978, on his own initiative and entitled *Inter Eximia Episcopalis,* restricted its use to the pope and archbishops of metropolitan sees. The pallium is made from the wool of lambs blessed by the pope on the feast of St. Agnes (Jan. 21).

Rochet: A knee-length, white linen-lace garment of prelates worn under outer vestments.

Surplice: A loose, flowing vestment of white fabric with wide sleeves. For some functions, it is interchangeable with an alb.

Zucchetto: A skullcap worn by bishops and other prelates.

SACRED VESSELS, LINENS

Vessels

Chalice and Paten: The principal sacred vessels required for the celebration of Mass are the **chalice** (cup) and **paten** (plate) in which wine and bread, respectively, are offered, consecrated and consumed. Both should be made of solid and noble material which is not easily breakable or corruptible. Gold coating is required of the interior parts of sacred vessels subject to rust. The cup of a chalice should be made of non-absorbent material.

Vessels for containing consecrated hosts (see below) can be made of material other than solid and noble metal — e. g., ivory, more durable woods — provided the substitute material is locally regarded as noble or rather precious and is suitable for sacred use.

Sacred vessels should be blessed or consecrated, according to prescribed requirements.

Vessels, in addition to the paten, for containing consecrated hosts are:

Ciborium: Used to hold hosts for distribution to the faithful and for reservation in the tabernacle.

Luna, Lunula, Lunette: A small receptacle which holds the sacred host in an upright position in the monstrance.

Monstrance, Ostensorium: A portable receptacle so made that the sacred host, when enclosed therein, may be clearly seen, as at

244

Vessels — Church Building

Benediction or during extended exposition of the Blessed Sacrament.

Pyx: A watch-shaped vessel used in carrying the Eucharist to the sick.

Linens

Altar Cloth: A white cloth, usually of linen, covering the table of an altar. One cloth is sufficient. Three were used according to former requirements.

Burse: A square, stiff flat case, open at one end, in which the folded corporal is placed; the outside is covered with material of the same kind and color as the outer vestments of the celebrant.

Corporal: A square piece of white linen spread on the altar cloth, on which rest the vessels holding the Sacred Species — the consecrated host(s) and wine — during the Eucharistic Liturgy. The corporal is similarly used whenever the Blessed Sacrament is removed from the tabernacle; e. g., during Benediction the vessel containing the Blessed Sacrament rests on a corporal.

Finger Towel: A white rectangular napkin used by the priest to dry his fingers after cleansing them following the offering of gifts at Mass.

Pall: A square piece of stiff material, usually covered with linen, used to cover the chalice at Mass.

Purificator: A white rectangular napkin used for cleansing sacred vessels after the reception of Communion at Mass.

Veil: The chalice intended for use at Mass is covered with a veil made of the same material as the outer vestments of the celebrant.

THE CHURCH BUILDING

A church is a building set aside and dedicated for purposes of divine worship, the place of assembly for a worshiping community.

A Catholic church is the ordinary place in which the faithful assemble for participation in the Eucharistic Liturgy and other forms of divine worship.

In the early years of Christianity, the first places of assembly for the Eucharistic Liturgy were private homes (Acts 2:46; Rom. 16:5; 1 Cor. 16:5; Col. 4:15) and, sometimes, catacombs. Church building began in the latter half of the second century during lulls in persecution and became widespread after enactment of the Edict of Milan in 313, when it finally became possible for the Church to emerge completely from the underground. The oldest and basic norms regarding church buildings date from about that time.

The essential principle underlying all norms for church building was reformulated by the Second Vatican Council, as follows: "When churches are to be built, let great care be taken that they be suitable for the celebration of liturgical services and for the active participation of the faithful" *(Constitution on the Sacred Liturgy*, No. 124).

This principle was subsequently elaborated in detail by the Congregation for Divine Worship in a document entitled *Institutio Generalis Missalis Romani*, which was approved by Paul VI Apr. 3 and promulgated by a decree of the congregation dated Apr. 6, 1969. Coverage of the following items reflects the norms stated in Chapter V of this document.

Sanctuary: The part of the church where the altar of sacrifice is located, the place where the ministers of the liturgy lead the people in prayer, proclaim the word of God and celebrate the Eucharist. It is set off from the body of the church by a distinctive structural feature — e. g., elevation above the main floor — or by ornamentation. (The traditional **communion rail,** which has been removed in recent years in many churches, served this purpose of demarcation.) The customary location of the sanctuary is at the front of the church; it may, however, be centrally located.

Altar: The main altar of sacrifice and table of the Lord is the focal feature of the sanctuary and entire church. It stands by itself, so that the ministers can move about it freely, and is so situated that they face the people during the liturgical action. In addition to this main altar, there may also be others; in new churches, these are situated in side chapels or alcoves removed to some degree from the body of the church.

Adornment of the Altar: The altar table is covered with a suitable linen cloth. Required candelabra and a cross are placed upon or near the altar in plain sight of the people and are so arranged that they do not obscure their view of the liturgical action.

Seats of the Ministers: The seat of the celebrant, corresponding with his role as the presiding minister of the assembly, is best located behind the altar and facing the people; it is raised a bit above the level of the altar but must not have the appearance of a throne. The seats of other ministers are also located in the sanctuary.

Ambo, Pulpit: The stand at which scriptural lessons and psalm responses are read, the word of God preached, and the prayer of the faithful offered. It is so placed that the ministers can be easily seen and heard by the people.

Places for the People: Seats and kneeling benches (**pews**) and other accommodations for the people are so arranged that they can participate in the most appropriate way in the liturgical action and have freedom of movement for the reception of Holy Communion. Reserved seats are out of order.

Place for the Choir: Where it is located depends on the most suitable arrangement for maintaining the unity of the choir with the congregation and for providing its members maximum opportunity for carrying out their proper function and participating fully in the Mass.

Tabernacle: The best place for reserving the Blessed Sacrament is in a chapel suitable for the private devotion of the people. If this is not possible, reservation should be at a side altar or other appropriately adorned place. In either case, the Blessed Sacrament should be kept in a tabernacle, i.e., a safe-like, secure receptacle.

Statues: Images of the Lord, the Blessed Virgin Mary and the saints are legitimately proposed for the veneration of the faithful in churches. Their number and arrangement, however, should be ordered in such a way that they do not distract the people from the central celebration of the Eucharistic Liturgy. There should be only one statue of one and the same saint in a church.

General Adornment and Arrangement of Churches: Churches should be so adorned and fitted out that they serve the direct requirements of divine worship and the needs and reasonable convenience of the people.

Other Items

Ambry: A box containing the holy oils, attached to the wall of the sanctuary in some churches.

Baptistery: The place for administering baptism. Some churches have baptisteries adjoining or near the entrance, a position symbolizing the fact that persons are initiated in the Church and incorporated in Christ through this sacrament. Contemporary liturgical practice favors placement of the baptistery near the sanctuary and altar, or the use of a portable font in the same position, to emphasize the relationship of baptism to the Eucharist, the celebration in sacrifice and banquet of the death and resurrection of Christ.

Candles: Used more for symbolical than illuminative purposes, they represent Christ, the light and life of grace, at liturgical functions. They are made of beeswax.

Confessional: A booth-like structure for the hearing of confessions, with separate compartments for the priest and penitents and a grating or screen between them. The use of confessionals became general in the Roman Rite after the Council of Trent.

Crucifix: A cross bearing the figure of the body of Christ, representative of the Sacrifice of the Cross.

Cruets: Vessels containing the wine and water used at Mass. They are placed on a credence table in the sanctuary.

Holy Water Fonts: Receptacles containing holy water, usually at church entrances, for the use of the faithful.

Sanctuary Lamp: A lamp which is kept burning continuously before a tabernacle in which the Blessed Sacrament is reserved, as a sign of the Real Presence of Christ.

LITURGICAL DEVELOPMENTS

The principal developments covered in this article are enactments of the Holy See and actions related to their implementation in the United States.

Modern Movement

Origins of the modern movement for renewal in the liturgy date back to the 19th century. The key contributing factor was a revival of liturgical and scriptural studies. Of special significance was the work of the Benedictine monks of Solesmes, France, who aroused great interest in the liturgy through the restoration of Gregorian Chant. St. Pius X approved their work in a motu proprio of 1903 and gave additional encouragement to liturgical study and development.

St. Pius X did more than any other single pope to promote early first Communion and the practice of frequent Communion, started the research behind a revised breviary, and appointed a group to investigate possible revisions in the Mass.

The movement attracted some attention in the 1920's and 30's but made little progress.

Significant pioneering developments in the US during the 20's, however, were the establishment of the Liturgical Press, the beginning of publication of *Orate Fratres* (now *Worship*), and the inauguration of the League of the Divine Office by the Benedictines at St. John's Abbey, Collegeville, Minn. Later events of influence were the establishment of the Pius X School of Liturgical Music at Manhattanville College of the Sacred Heart and the organization of a summer school of liturgical music at Mary Manse College by the Gregorian Institute of America. The turning point toward real renewal was reached during and after World War II.

Pius XII gave it impetus and direction, principally through the background teaching in his encyclicals on the *Mystical Body* (1943), *Sacred Liturgy* (1947), and the *Discipline of Sacred Music* (1955), and by means of specific measures affecting the liturgy itself. His work was continued during the pontificates of John XXIII and Paul VI. The Second Vatican Council, in virtue of its *Constitution on the Sacred Liturgy,* inaugurated changes of the greatest significance.

Before and After Vatican II

The most significant liturgical changes made in the years immediately preceding the Second Vatican Council were the following:

(1) Revision of the Rites of Holy Week, for universal observance from 1956.

(2) Modification of the Eucharistic fast and permission for afternoon and evening Mass, in effect from 1953 and extended in 1957.

(3) The Dialogue Mass, introduced in 1958.

(4) Use of popular languages in administration of the sacraments.

(5) Calendar-missal-breviary reform, in effect from Jan. 1, 1961.

(6) Seven-step administration of baptism for adults, approved in 1962.

The *Constitution on the Sacred Liturgy* approved (2,174 to 4) and promulgated by the Second Vatican Council Dec. 4, 1963, marked the beginning of a profound renewal in the Church's corporate worship. Implementation of some of its measures was ordered by Paul VI Jan. 25, 1964, in the motu proprio *Sacram Liturgiam.* On Feb. 29, a special commission, the Consilium for Implementing the Constitution on the Sacred Liturgy, was formed to supervise the execution of the entire program of liturgical reform. Implementation of the program on local and regional levels was left to bishops acting through their own liturgical commissions and in concert with their fellow bishops in national conferences.

Liturgical reform in the United States has been carried out under the direction of the Liturgy Committee, National Conference of Catholic Bishops. Its secretariat, established early in 1965, is located at 1312 Massachusetts Ave. N.W., Washington, D.C. 20005.

Stages of Development

Liturgical development after the Second Vatican Council proceeded in several stages. It started with the formulation of guidelines and directives, and with the translation into vernacular languages of virtually unchanged Latin ritual texts. Then came structural changes in the Mass, the sacraments, the calendar, the Divine Office and other phases of the liturgy. These revisions were just about completed with the publication of a new order for the sacrament of penance in February, 1974. A continuing phase of development, in progress from the beginning, involves efforts to deepen the liturgical sense of the faithful, to increase their participation in worship and to relate it to full Christian life.

Texts and Translations

The master texts of all documents on liturgical reform were in Latin. Effective dates of their implementation depended on the completion and approval of appropriate translations into vernacular languages. English translations were made by the International Committee for English in the Liturgy.

The principal features of liturgical changes and the effective dates of their introduction in the United States are covered below under topical headings. (For expanded coverage of various items, especially the sacraments, see additional entries.)

The Mass

A new Order of the Mass, supplanting the one authorized by the Council of Trent in the 16th century, was introduced in the U.S. Mar. 22, 1970. It had been approved by Paul VI in the apostolic constitution *Missale Romanum,* dated Apr. 3, 1969.

Preliminary and related to it were the following developments.

Mass in English: Introduced Nov. 29, 1964. In the same year, Psalm 42 was eliminated from the prayers at the foot of the altar.

Incidental Changes: The last Gospel (prologue of John) and vernacular prayers following Mass were eliminated Mar. 7, 1965. At the same time, provision was made for the celebrant to say aloud some prayers formerly said silently.

Rubrics: An instruction entitled *Tres Abhinc Annos,* dated May 4 and effective June 29, 1967, simplified directives for the celebration of Mass, approved the practice of saying the canon aloud, altered the Communion and dismissal rites, permitted purple instead of black vestments in Masses for the dead, discontinued wearing of the maniple, and approved in principle the use of vernacular languages for the canon, ordination rites, and lessons of the Divine Office when read in choir.

Canons or Eucharistic Prayers: Three additional Eucharistic prayers authorized May 23, 1968, were approved for use in vernacular translation the following Aug. 15. They have the same basic structure as the traditional Roman Canon, whose use in English was introduced Oct. 22, 1967.

The customary Roman Canon, which dates at least from the beginning of the fifth century and has remained substantially unchanged since the seventh century, is the first in the order of listing of the Eucharistic prayers. It can be used at any time, but is the one of choice for most Sundays, some special feasts like Easter and Pentecost, and for feasts of the Apostles and other saints who are commemorated in the canon. Any preface can be used with it.

The second Eucharistic prayer, the shortest and simplest of all, is best suited for use on weekdays and various special circumstances. It has a preface of its own, but others may be used with it. This canon bears a close resemblance to the one framed by St. Hippolytus about 215.

The third Eucharistic prayer is suitable for use on Sundays and feasts as an alternative to the Roman Canon. It can be used with any preface and has a special formula for remembrance of the dead.

The fourth Eucharistic prayer, the most sophisticated of them all, presents a broad synthesis of salvation history. Based on the Eastern tradition of Antioch, it is best suited for use at Masses attended by persons versed in Sacred Scripture. It has an unchangeable preface.

English translations of three new canons for Masses with children and two for Masses of reconciliation were approved by the Congregation for Divine Worship June 5, 1975, for an experimental period to end with 1977, later extended to the end of 1980. The choice of one each of the canons was left to the judgment of the National Conference of Catholic Bishops.

Lectionary: A new compilation of scriptural readings and psalm responsories for Mass was introduced Mar. 22, 1970. The *Lectionary* contains a three-year cycle of readings for Sundays and solemn feasts, a two-year weekday cycle, and a one-year cycle for the feasts of saints, in addition to readings for a great variety of Masses, ritual Masses and Masses for various needs. There are also responsorial psalms to follow the first readings, and gospel or alleluia versicles to follow the second readings.

Sacramentary (Missal): The Vatican Polyglot Press began distribution in June, 1970, of the Latin text of a new *Roman Missal*, the first revision published in 400 years. The English translation was authorized for optional use beginning July 1, 1974; the mandatory date for use was Dec. 1, 1974.

The missal is the celebrant's book of prayers and sacramental formulas and does not include the readings of the Mass, such as the Gospel and the Epistle. It contains the texts of entrance songs, prefaces and other prayers of the Mass. The number of prefaces is four times greater than it had been. There are 10 commons (or sets of Mass prayers) of martyrs, two of doctors of the Church, and a dozen for saints or groups of saints of various kinds, such as religious, educators and mothers of families. There are Masses during which certain sacraments are administered and others for religious profession, the Church, the pope, priests, Christian unity, the evangelization of nations, persecuted Christians, and other intentions.

Mass for Special Groups: Reasons and norms for the celebration of Mass at special gatherings of the faithful were the subject of an instruction issued May 15, 1969. Two years earlier, the U.S. Bishops' Liturgy Committee went on record in support of the celebration of Mass in private homes.

Sunday Mass on Saturday: The Congregation for the Clergy, under date of Jan. 10, 1970, granted the request that the faithful, where bishops consider it pastorally necessary or useful, may satisfy the precept of participating in Mass in the late afternoon or evening hours of Saturdays and the days before holy days of obligation.

This permission was subsequently renewed for five-year periods Dec. 14, 1974, and June 13, 1979.

Trination: The Congregation for the Sacraments, under date of Jan. 20, 1970, granted to all U.S. bishops the authority to permit priests to celebrate Mass three times on Saturdays and days preceding holy days of obligation, on condition that the first and second Masses are celebrated for weddings and/or funerals and the third Mass is celebrated in the evening so that the precept (of participating in Mass) will be satisfied by the faithful.

Mass in Latin: According to notices issued by the Congregation for Divine Worship June 1, 1971, and Oct. 28, 1974: (1) Bishops may permit the celebration of Mass in Latin for mixed-language groups. (2) Bishops may permit the celebration of one or two Masses in Latin on weekdays or Sundays in any church, irrespective of mixed-language groups involved (1971). (3) Priests may celebrate Mass in Latin when people are not present. (4) The approved revised Order of the Mass is to be used in Latin as well as vernacular languages . (5) By way of exception, bishops may permit older and handicapped priests to use the Council of Trent's Order of the Mass in private celebration of the holy Sacrifice.

Inter-Ritual Concelebration: The Apostolic Delegation in Washington, D.C., announced in June, 1971, that it had received authorization to permit priests of Roman and Eastern rites to celebrate Mass together in the rite of the host church. It was understood that the inter-ritual concelebrations would always be "a manifestation of the unity of the Church and of communion among particular churches."

Ordo of the Sung Mass: In a decree dated June 24 and made public Aug. 24, 1972, the Congregation for Divine Worship issued a new *Ordo of the Sung Mass* — containing Gregorian chants in Latin — to replace the *Graduale Romanum*.

Mass for Children: Late in 1973, the Congregation for Divine Worship issued special guidelines for children's Masses, providing accommodations to the mentality and spiritual growth of pre-adolescents while retaining the principal parts and structures of the Mass. The *Directory for Masses with Children* was approved by Paul VI Oct. 22 and was dated Nov. 1, 1973. English versions of three canons for Masses with children were approved by the congregation June 5, 1975, for an experimental period to end with 1977. Cardinal John Knox, prefect of the congregation, announced Dec. 10, 1977, that experimental use of Masses with children and the Mass of Reconciliation had been extended to the end of 1980.

Sacraments

The general use of English in administration of the sacraments was approved for the U.S. Sept. 14, 1964. Structural changes of the rites were subsequently made and introduced in the U.S. as follows.

Anointing of the Sick: Revised rites, covering also administration of the Eucharist to sick persons, were approved Nov. 30,. 1972, and published Jan. 18, 1973. The effective date for use of the provisional English prayer formula was Dec. 1, 1974.

Baptism: New rites for the baptism of infants, approved Mar. 19, 1969, were introduced June 1, 1970.

Christian Initiation of Adults: Revised rites were issued Jan. 6, 1972, for the Christian initiation of adults — affecting preparation for and reception of baptism, the Eucharist and confirmation; also, the reception of already baptized adults into the Church. These rites, which were introduced in the U.S. on the completion of English translation, nullified a seven-step baptismal process approved in 1962.

Confirmation: Revised rites, issued Aug. 15, 1971, became mandatory in the U.S. Jan. 1, 1973.

Eucharist: Several enactments concerning the Eucharist have been issued since 1966 when permission was given for the superiors of convents to administer Holy Communion in the absence of priests. Paul VI issued an instruction on *Worship of the Eucharistic Mystery* May 25, 1967, and another on the manner of administering Holy Communion May 20, 1969. Limited permission for lay persons to serve as extraordinary ministers of the Eucharist was given in 1971 and extended in 1972. Also in 1972, instructions were issued regarding administration of the Eucharist to other Christians, and in particular circumstances.

Holy Orders: Revised ordination rites for deacons, priests and bishops, validated by prior experimental use, were approved in 1970. The sacrament of holy orders underwent further revision in 1972 with the elimination of the Church-instituted orders of porter, reader, exorcist, acolyte and subdeacon, and of the tonsure ceremony symbolic of entrance into the clerical state. The former minor orders of reader and acolyte were changed from orders to ministries.

Matrimony: New rites, issued Mar. 19, 1969, were introduced June 1, 1970. Minor revisions had been made in 1964 in conjunction with a directive for imparting the nuptial blessing at all weddings.

Penance: Ritual revision of the sacraments was completed with the approval by Paul VI Dec. 2, 1973, of new directives for the sacrament of penance or reconciliation. The U.S. Bishops' Committee on the Liturgy set Feb. 27, 1977, as the mandatory date for use of the new rite. The committee also declared that it could be used from Mar. 7, 1976, after adequate preparation of priests and people. Earlier, authorization was given by the Holy See in 1968 for the omission of any reference to excommunication or other censures in the formula of absolution unless there was some indication that a censure had actually been incurred by a penitent.

Additional Developments

Calendar: A revised liturgical calendar, approved by Paul VI Feb. 14 and made public May 9, 1969, went into effect in the U.S. in 1972.

Funeral Rites: Revised rites oriented to the resurrection theme went into effect Nov. 1, 1971.

Holy Week: The English version of revised Holy Week rites went into effect in 1971. They introduced concelebration of Mass, placed new emphasis on commemorating the institution of the priesthood on Holy Thursday, and modified Good Friday prayers for other Christians, Jews and other non-Christians.

Liturgy of the Hours: The background, contents, scope and purposes of the revised Divine Office, called the Liturgy of the Hours, were described by Paul VI in the apostolic constitution *Canticum Laudis,* dated Nov. 1, 1970. A provisional English version, incorporating basic features of the master Latin text, was published in 1971. The four complete volumes of the Hours in English have been published since May, 1975. One-volume, partial editions, intended for use by religious and lay persons not bound to pray the Liturgy of the Hours, have also been published in approved form. Nov. 27, 1977, was set by the Congregation for Divine Worship and the National Conference of Catholic Bishops as the effective date for exclusive use in liturgical worship of the translation of the Latin text of the Office approved by the International Committee on English in the Liturgy.

Music: An *Instruction on Music in the Liturgy,* dated Mar. 5 and effective May 14, 1967, encouraged congregational singing during liturgical celebrations and attempted to clarify the role of choirs and trained singer s. More significantly, the instruction indicated that a major development underway in the liturgy was a gradual erasure of the distinctive lines traditionally drawn between the sung liturgy and the spoken liturgy, between what had been called the high Mass and the low Mass.

In the same year, the U.S. Bishops' Liturgy Committee approved the use of contemporary music, as well as guitars and other suitable instruments, in the liturgy. The Holy See authorized in 1968 the use of musical instruments other than the organ in liturgical services, "provided they are played in a manner suitable to worship."

Oils: The Congregation for Divine Worship issued a directive in 1971 permitting the use of other oils — from plants, seeds or coconuts — instead of the traditional olive oil in administering some of the sacraments. The directive also provided that oils could be blessed at other times than at the usual Mass of Chrism on Holy Thursday, and authorized bishops' conferences to permit priests to bless oils in cases of necessity.

Eucharistic Prayers: A three-year extension, through 1980, was granted by the Congregation for Divine Worship for continuing experimental use of approved Eucharistic Prayers in Masses for children and Masses of reconciliation.

Environment and Art in Catholic Worship: A booklet with this title was issued by the U.S. Bishops' Committee on the Liturgy in March, 1978.

Eucharistic Ministers: Approval by the Congregation for Divine Worship was reported in August, 1978, of a provisional translation of a "Rite of Commissioning Special Ministers of Holy Communion." Note was made of the fact that such ministers should be called "special" instead of "extraordinary."

Doxology: The bishops' committee called attention in August, 1978, to the directive that the Doxology concluding the Eucharistic Prayer is said or sung by the celebrant (concelebrants) alone, to which the people respond, "Amen."

Churches, Altars, Chalices: The *Newsletter* of the U.S. Bishops' Committee on the Liturgy reported in November, 1978, that the Congregation for Divine Worship had given provisional approval of a new English translation for the rite of dedicating churches and altars, and of a new form for the blessing of chalices.

Study of the Mass: The Bishops' Committee on the Liturgy, following approval of the project by the National Conference of Catholic Bishops in May, 1979, began a three-year study of the function and position of some elements of the Mass, including the Gloria, the sign of peace, the penitential rite and the readings; some changes might be made on completion of the study. Completion of the first phase of the study was reported in July, 1980; its product was a 175-page study document scheduled for publication in 1981.

Eucharistic Hosts: Father Thomas Krosnicki, secretary of the Bishops' Committee on the Liturgy, reported in July, 1979, that the committee was preparing new guidelines on the preparation of hosts, in compliance with a request from the Congregation for the Doctrine of the Faith. He said the congregation had "questioned the contents of some of the recipes" used in this country. Cardinal Franjo Seper, prefect of the congregation, stressed the importance of carefully observing traditional theological principles relating to the making of hosts — which should be of wheat, unleavened, with the appearance of food, and capable of being broken and distributed to communicants. In 1980, the congregation ruled definitely against changes in the preparation of hosts, and so informed the bishops' committee. The same prohibition was stated in the "Instruction on Certain Norms concerning Worship of the Eucharistic Mystery" approved by the Pope Apr. 17, 1980.

Eucharistic Worship: This was the subject of two documents issued in 1980. *Dominicae Coenae* was a letter addressed by Pope John Paul to bishops throughout the world in connection with the celebration of Holy Thursday; it was dated Feb. 24 and released Mar. 18. It was more doctrinal in content than the "Instruction on Certain Norms concerning Worship of the Eucharistic Mystery" (*Inaestimabile Donum,* "The Priceless Gift"), which was approved by the Pope Apr. 17 and published by the Congregation for the Sacraments and Divine Worship May 23. Its stated purpose was to reaffirm and clarify teaching on liturgical renewal contained in enactments of the Second Vatican Council and in several related implementing documents. (See Eucharistic Mystery and Worship, Norms for Worship.)

Holy Days Proposal Withdrawn: The Bishops' Committee on the Liturgy announced Oct. 2, 1980, that it was withdrawing from the agenda of the November meeting of the National Conference of Catholic Bishops a proposal that could result in ending the obligation to attend Mass on several holy days celebrated in the U.S. The proposal, which had the support of 130 of 197 bishops who responded to a survey, was opposed by most Catholics who responded to surveys conducted by a number of diocesan newspapers. Committee chairman Archbishop Rembert G. Weakland said that, instead of pursuing the proposal under existing circumstances, the committee would develop an instructional program on the nature and purpose of holy days and would continue to explore solutions to problems connected with holy day observance for future implementation by the bishops.

The original proposal called for the retention of only Christmas and the Solemnity of the Immaculate Conception as holy days of obligation. The observance of Ascension Thursday would have been transferred to the following Sunday. The obligation to attend Mass on the three other holy days — the solemnities of Mary the Mother of God (Jan. 1), of the Assumption (Aug. 15), and of All Saints (Nov. 1) — would have been dropped, although they would have remained major feast days.

The administrative committee of the national conference came up with an alternative proposal: that there be no change in the current number of holy days; that a "major catechesis" be developed on the nature of holy days and the moral obligation to observe them; that the Vatican be asked to give individual bishops authority to dispense people in their dioceses from the sometimes confusing back-to-back obligation of Mass attendance when a holy day falls on a Saturday or a Monday. At the time of writing, before the November meeting of the conference, it was not clear what action would be taken with respect to the alternative proposal.

General regulations permit bishops, with the approval of the Holy See, to decide what holy days are to be celebrated in their respective countries. At least two are observed, Christmas and a feast of Mary.

Sunday Communion

More than two-thirds of the U.S. bishops voted (187 to 82) during the general meeting of their national conference in November, 1978, or afterwards for allowing the reception of Holy Communion under the forms of bread and wine on Sundays and holy days — subject to the options of bishops of dioceses, priests celebrating Mass and persons receiving the Eucharist. (Reception of Communion in this manner on certain occasions was already provided for in directives of the Congregation for Divine Worship, but Sundays and holy days were not mentioned.)

COMMUNION IN HAND

(Source: *Notitiae,* the official bulletin of the Congregation for Divine Worship.)

The Holy See has approved in recent years the practice of in-hand reception of Holy Communion in regions and countries where it had the approval of the appropriate bishops' conferences. Areas with this practice and the dates of approval are as follows.

Europe

Belgium (May, 1969), France and Germany (June, 1969), The Netherlands (September, 1969), Luxembourg, Scandinavia and Monaco (October, 1969), Austria (February, 1970), Yugoslavia (January, 1971), Portugal (July, 1975), Spain (February, 1976), England and Wales (March, 1976), Ireland (September, 1976), Scotland (July, 1977), Gibraltar (August, 1977).

Africa

Chad (September, 1969), North Africa (October, 1969), South Africa (February, 1970), Djibouti (March, 1970), Upper Volta and Niger (February, 1971), Zimbabwe (October, 1971), Madagascar (May, 1972), Mozambique (October, 1972), Angola (September, 1973), Zambia (March, 1974), Mali (July, 1974), Zaire (July, 1979).

Asia and Oceania

Japan (June, 1970), Indonesia (March, 1971), Korea (January, 1974), New Zealand (April, 1974), Australia (September, 1975), Pacific Episcopal Conference area: New Caledonia, New Hebrides (now Vanuatu), Wallis and Futuna, Cook, Fiji, and Gilbert Islands (December, 1975), Papua New Guinea (April, 1976), Pakistan (October, 1976), Malaysia-Singapore (October, 1977), Turkey (September, 1978).

Central and South America

Bolivia and Uruguay (October, 1969), Jamaica (March, 1970), Paraguay (September, 1971), Panama (May, 1973), Chile (June, 1973), Costa Rica (September, 1973), Peru and Brazil (March, 1975), Cuba (March, 1978).

North America

Canada (February, 1970), Mexico (September, 1976), United States (June, 1977).

MASS FOR NON-CATHOLICS

The Congregation for the Doctrine of the Faith released a decree June 11, 1976, authorizing the celebration of public Masses for deceased non-Catholic Christians under certain conditions.

The decree noted requests for the celebration of "Mass for deceased persons baptized in other churches or ecclesial communities, particularly when the departed showed special devotion and honor for the Catholic religion or held public office at the service of the whole civil community."

It declared: "There is, of course, no difficulty about the celebration of private Masses for these deceased persons."

"However, the present discipline lays down that they shall not be celebrated (publicly) for those who have died outside of full communion with the Catholic Church."

"In view of the present change in the religious and social situation that gave rise to the above-mentioned discipline, the Sacred Congregation for the Doctrine of the Faith has received inquiries from various quarters to ask if, in certain cases, even public Masses can be said for these deceased persons."

In reply, the congregation decreed:

"I. The present discipline regarding the celebration of public Masses for other Christians who have died shall continue to be the general rule. One reason for this is the consideration due to the conscience of these deceased persons, who did not profess the Catholic faith to the full."

"II. Exceptions can be allowed to this general rule, until the new code (of canon law) is promulgated, whenever both the following conditions are verified:

• "1. The public celebration of the Masses must be explicitly requested by the relatives, friends or subjects of the deceased person for a genuine religious motive.

• "2. In the Ordinary's judgment, there must be no scandal for the faithful.

"III. In these cases public Mass may be celebrated, provided, however, that the name of the deceased is not mentioned in the Eucharistic Prayer, since that mention presupposes full communion with the Catholic Church."

The decree was approved by Pope Paul.

Sacraments

The sacraments are actions of Christ and his Church which signify grace, cause it in the act of signifying it, and confer it upon persons properly disposed to receive it. They perpetuate the redemptive activity of Christ, making it present and effective. They infallibly communicate the fruit of that activity — namely grace — to responsive persons with faith. Sacramental actions consist of the union of sensible signs (matter of the sacraments) with the words of the minister (form of the sacraments).

Christ himself immediately instituted the seven sacraments of the New Law by determining their essence and the efficacy of their signs to produce the grace they signify.

Christ is the principal priest or minister of every sacrament; human agents — an ordained priest, baptized persons contracting marriage with each other, any person conferring emergency baptism in a proper manner — are secondary ministers. Sacraments have efficacy from Christ, not from the personal dispositions of their human ministers.

Each sacrament confers sanctifying grace for the special purpose of the sacrament; this is, accordingly, called sacramental grace. It involves a right to actual graces corresponding to the purposes of the respective sacraments.

While sacraments infallibly produce the grace they signify, recipients benefit from them in proportion to their personal dispositions. One of these is the intention to receive sacraments as sacred signs of God's saving and grace-giving action. The state of grace is also necessary for fruitful reception of the Holy Eucharist, confirmation, matrimony, holy orders and anointing of the sick. Baptism is the sacrament in which grace is given in the first instance and original sin is remitted. Penance is the secondary sacrament of reconciliation, in which persons guilty of serious sin after baptism are reconciled with God and the Church, and in which persons already in the state of grace are strengthened in that state.

Role of Sacraments

The Second Vatican Council prefaced a description of the role of the sacraments with the following statement concerning participation by all the faithful in the priesthood of Christ and the exercise of that priesthood by receiving the sacraments (*Dogmatic Constitution on the Church,* Nos. 10 and 11).

". . . The baptized by regeneration and the anointing of the Holy Spirit are consecrated into a spiritual house and a holy priesthood. Thus through all those works befitting Christian men they can offer spiritual sacrifice and proclaim the power of Him who has called them out of darkness into His marvelous light (cf. 1 Pt. 2:4-10). . . ."

"Though they differ from one another in essence and not only in degree, the common priesthood of the faithful and the ministerial or hierarchical priesthood (of those ordained to holy orders) are nonetheless interrelated. Each of them in its own special way is a participation in the one priesthood of Christ. The ministerial priest, by the sacred power he enjoys, molds and rules the priestly people. Acting in the person of Christ, he brings about the Eucharistic Sacrifice, and offers it to God in the name of all the people. For their part, the faithful join in the offering of the Eucharist by virtue of their royal priesthood. They likewise exercise that priesthood by receiving the sacraments, by prayer and thanksgiving, by the witness of a holy life, and by self-denial and active charity."

"It is through the sacraments and the exercise of the virtues that the sacred nature and organic structure of the priestly community is brought into operation."

Baptism: "Incorporated into the Church through baptism, the faithful are consecrated by the baptismal character to the exercise of the cult of the Christian religion. Reborn as sons of God, they must confess before men the faith which they have received from God through the Church."

Confirmation: "Bound more intimately to the Church by the sacrament of confirmation, they are endowed by the Holy Spirit with special strength. Hence they are more strictly obliged to spread and defend the faith both by word and by deed as true witnesses of Christ."

Eucharist: "Taking part in the Eucharistic Sacrifice, which is the fount and apex of the whole Christian life, they offer the divine Victim to God, and offer themselves along with It. Thus, both by the act of oblation and through holy Communion, all perform their proper part in this liturgical service, not, indeed, all in the same way but each in that way which is appropriate to himself. Strengthened anew at the holy table by the Body of Christ, they manifest in a practical way that unity of God's People which is suitably signified and wondrously brought about by this most awesome sacrament."

Penance: "Those who approach the sacrament of penance obtain pardon from the mercy of God for offenses committed against Him. They are at the same time reconciled with the Church, which they have wounded by their sins, and which by charity, example, and prayer seeks their conversion."

Anointing of the Sick: "By the sacred anointing of the sick and the prayer of her priests, the whole Church commends those who are ill to the suffering and glorified Lord, asking that He may lighten their suffering and save them (cf. Jas. 5:14-16). She exhorts them, moreover, to contribute to the welfare of the whole People of God by associating themselves freely with the passion and death of Christ (cf. Rom. 8:17; Col. 1:24; 2 Tm. 2:11-12; 1 Pt. 4:13)."

Holy Orders: "Those of the faithful who are consecrated by holy orders are appointed to feed the Church in Christ's name with the Word and the grace of God."

Matrimony: "Christian spouses, in virtue of the sacrament of matrimony, signify and partake of the mystery of that unity and fruitful love which exists between Christ and His Church (cf. Eph. 5:32). The spouses thereby help each other to attain to holiness in their married life and by the rearing and education of their children. And so, in their state and way of life, they have their own special gift among the People of God (cf. 1 Cor. 7:7).

"For from the wedlock of Christians there comes the family, in which new citizens of human society are born. By the grace of the Holy Spirit received in baptism these are made children of God, thus perpetuating the People of God through the centuries. The family is, so to speak, the domestic Church. In it parents should, by their word and example, be the first preachers of the faith to their children. They should encourage them in the vocation which is proper to each of them, fostering with special care any religious vocation.

"Fortified by so many and such powerful means of salvation, all the faithful, whatever their condition or state, are called by the Lord, each in his own way, to that perfect holiness whereby the Father Himself is perfect."

Baptism

Baptism is the sacrament of spiritual regeneration by which a person is incorporated in Christ and made a member of His Mystical Body, given grace, and cleansed of original sin. Actual sins and the punishment due for them are remitted also if the person baptized was guilty of such sins (e.g., in the case of a person baptized after reaching the age of reason). The theological virtues of faith, hope and charity are given with grace. The sacrament confers a character on the soul and can be received only once. Baptism has been called a sacrament of the dead because its purpose is to confer sanctifying grace on persons who do not have it.

The matter is the pouring of water. The form is: "I baptize you in the name of the Father and of the Son and of the Holy Spirit."

The minister of solemn baptism is a priest or deacon, but in case of emergency anyone, including a non-Catholic, can validly baptize. The minister pours water on the forehead of the person being baptized and says the words of the form while the water is flowing. The water used in solemn baptism is blessed during the rite.

The Church recognizes as valid baptism by **immersion, aspersion** (sprinkling of the water), or **infusion** (pouring of the water). In the Western Church, i.e., Roman Rite, the method of infusion is prescribed. The Church recognizes as valid baptisms properly performed by non-Catholic ministers. The baptism of infants has always been considered valid and the general practice of infant baptism was well established by the fifth century. Baptism is conferred conditionally when there is doubt about the validity of a previous baptism or the dispositions of the person.

Baptism is necessary for salvation. If a person cannot receive the baptism of water described above, this can be supplied by baptism of blood (martyrdom suffered for the Catholic faith or some Christian virtue) or by baptism of desire (perfect contrition joined with at least the implicit intention of doing whatever God wills that men should do for salvation).

A sponsor is required for the person being baptized. (See Godparents, below).

A person must be validly baptized before he can receive any of the other sacraments.

Christian Initiation of Infants: Infants should be solemnly baptized as soon after birth as conveniently possible. In danger of death, anyone may baptize an infant. If the child survives, the ceremonies of solemn baptism should be supplied.

The sacrament is ordinarily conferred by a priest or deacon of the parents' parish.

Only Catholics, in their 14th year or older, may be **godparents** or sponsors. Only one is required. Two, one of each sex, are permitted. A non-Catholic Christian cannot be a godparent for a Catholic child, but may serve as a witness to the baptism. A Catholic may not be a godparent for a child baptized in a non-Catholic religion, but may be a witness.

The role of godparents in baptismal ceremonies is secondary to the role of the parents. They serve as representatives of the community of faith and with the parents request baptism for the child and perform other ritual functions. Their function after baptism is to serve as proxies for the parents if the parents should be unable or fail to provide for the religious training of the child.

At baptism every child should be given a name with Christian significance, usually the name of a saint, to symbolize newness of life in Christ.

Christian Initiation of Adults: According to the *Ordo Initiationis Christianae Adultorum* ("Rite of the Christian Initiation of Adults") issued by the Congregation for Divine Worship under date of Jan. 6, 1972, adults are prepared for baptism and reception into the Church in several stages:

• An initial period of inquiry, instruction

and evangelization.

• The catechumenate, a period of formal instruction and progressive formation in and familiarity with Christian life. It starts with a statement of purpose and includes a rite in which the catechumen is signed with the cross, blessings, exorcisms, and introduction into church for celebration of the word of God.

• Immediate preparation, called a period of purification and enlightenment, from the beginning of Lent to reception of the sacraments of initiation — baptism, confirmation, Holy Eucharist — at Easter. The period is marked by scrutinies, formal giving of the creed and the Lord's Prayer, the choice of a Christian name, and a final statement of intention.

• A final phase whose objective is greater familiarity with Christian life in the Church through observances of the Easter season and association with the community of the faithful.

The priest who baptizes a catechumen can also administer the sacrament of confirmation.

A sponsor is required for the person being baptized.

The *Ordo* also provides a simple rite of initiation for adults in danger of death and for cases in which all stages of the initiation process are not necessary, and guidelines for: (1) the preparation of adults for the sacraments of confirmation and Holy Eucharist in cases where they have been baptized but have not received further formation in the Christian life; (2) for the formation and initiation of children of catechetical age.

The Church recognizes the right of anyone over the age of seven to request baptism and to receive the sacrament after completing a course of instruction and giving evidence of good will. Practically, in the case of minors in a non-Catholic family or environment, the Church accepts them when other circumstances favor their ability to practice the faith — e.g., well-disposed family situation, the presence of another or several Catholics in the family. Those who are not in such favorable circumstances are prudently advised to defer reception of the sacrament until they attain the maturity necessary for independent practice of the faith.

Reception of Baptized Christians: Procedure for the reception of already baptized Christians into full communion with the Catholic Church is distinguished from the catechumenate, since they have received some Christian formation. Instruction and formation are provided as necessary, however; and conditional baptism is administered if there is reasonable doubt about the validity of the person's previous baptism.

In the rite of reception, the person is invited to join the community of the Church in professing the Nicene Creed and is asked to state: "I believe and profess all that the holy Catholic Church believes, teaches, and proclaims as revealed by God." The priest places his hand on the head of the person, states the formula of admission to full communion, confirms (in the absence of a bishop), gives a sign of peace, and administers Holy Communion during a Eucharistic Liturgy.

Confirmation

Confirmation is the sacrament by which a baptized person, through anointing with chrism and the imposition of hands, is endowed with the gifts and special strength of the Holy Spirit for mature Christian living. The sacrament, which completes the Christian initiation begun wth baptism, confers a character on the soul and can be received only once.

According to the apostolic constitution *Divinae Consortium Naturae* dated Aug. 15, 1971, in conjunction with the *Ordo Confirmationis* ("Rite of Confirmation"): "The sacrament of confirmation is conferred through the anointing with chrism on the forehead, which is done by the imposition of the hand (matter of the sacrament), and through the words: 'N . . . . , receive the seal of the Holy Spirit, the Gift of the Father' " (form of the sacrament). On May 5, 1975, bishops' conferences in English-speaking countries were informed by the Congregation for Divine Worship that Pope Paul had approved this English version of the form of the sacrament: "Be sealed with the gift of the Holy Spirit."

The ordinary minister of confirmation in the Roman Rite is a bishop. Priests may be delegated for the purpose. A pastor can confirm a parishioner in danger of death, and a priest can confirm in ceremonies of Christian initiation.

Ideally, the sacrament is conferred during the Eucharistic Liturgy. Elements of the rite include renewal of the promises of baptism, which confirmation ratifies and completes, and the laying on of hands — by symbolic elevation over the heads of those being confirmed — by the confirming bishop and priests participating in the ceremony.

"The entire rite," according to the *Ordo;* "has a twofold meaning. The laying of hands upon the candidates, done by the bishop and the concelebrating priests, expresses the biblical gesture by which the gift of the Holy Spirit is invoked. . . . The anointing with chrism and the accompanying words clearly signify the effect of the Holy Spirit. Signed with the perfumed oil by the bishop's hand, the baptized person receives the indelible character, the seal of the Lord, together with the Spirit who is given and who conforms the person more perfectly to Christ and gives him the grace of spreading the Lord's presence among men."

A sponsor is required for the person being confirmed. This can be one of the baptismal sponsors or another person. Parents can serve as sponsors for their own children.

In the Roman Rite, it has been customary for children to receive confirmation within a reasonable time after first Communion and confession. There is a developing trend, however, to defer confirmation until later when its significance for mature Christian living becomes more evident. In the Eastern Rites, confirmation is administered at the same time as baptism.

The Holy Eucharist

The Holy Eucharist is a sacrifice (see The Mass) and the sacrament in which Christ is present and is received under the appearances of bread and wine.

The matter is bread of wheat, unleavened in the Roman Rite and leavened in the Eastern Rites, and wine of grape. The form consists of the words of consecration said by the priest at Mass: "This is my body. . . . This is the cup of my blood" (according to the traditional usage of the Roman Rite).

Only a priest can consecrate bread and wine so they become the body and blood of Christ. After consecration, however, the Eucharist can be administered by deacons and, for various reasons, by religious and lay persons.

Priests celebrating Mass receive the Eucharist under the appearances of bread and wine. In the Roman Rite, others usually receive under the appearances of bread only, i.e., the consecrated host; in some circumstances, however, they may receive under the appearances of both bread and wine. In Eastern-Rite practice, the faithful generally receive a piece of consecrated leavened bread which has been dipped into consecrated wine (i.e., by intinction).

Conditions for receiving the Eucharist, commonly called **Holy Communion,** are the state of grace, the right intention, and observance of the Eucharistic fast.

The faithful of Roman Rite are required by a precept of the Church to receive the Eucharist at least once a year, during the Easter time (in the U.S., from the First Sunday of Lent to Trinity Sunday, inclusive).

(See Eucharistic Fast, Mass, Transubstantiation, Viaticum.)

First Communion and Confession: Children are to be prepared for and given opportunity for receiving both sacraments on reaching the age of discretion, at which time they become subject to general norms concerning confession and Communion. This, together with a stated preference for first confession before first Communion, was the central theme of a document entitled *Sanctus Pontifex* and published May 24, 1973, by the Congregation for the Discipline of the Sacraments and the Congregation for the Clergy, with the approval of Pope Paul VI.

What the document prescribed was the observance of practices ordered by St. Pius X in the decree *Quam Singulari* of Aug. 8, 1910. Its purpose was to counteract pastoral and catechetical experiments virtually denying children the opportunity of receiving both sacraments at the same time. Termination of such experiments was ordered by the end of the 1972-73 school year.

At the time the document was issued, two- or three-year experiments of this kind — routinely deferring reception of the sacrament of penance until after the first reception of Holy Communion — were in effect in more than half of the dioceses of the U.S. They have remained in effect in many places, despite the advisory from the Vatican.

One reason stated in support of such experiments is the view that children are not capable of serious sin at the age of seven or eight, when Communion is generally received for the first time, and therefore prior reception of the sacrament of penance is not necessary. Another reason is the purpose of making the distinctive nature of the two sacraments clearer to children.

The Vatican view reflected convictions that the principle and practice of devotional reception of penance are as valid for children as they are for adults, and that sound catechetical programs can avoid misconceptions about the two sacraments.

A second letter on the same subject and in the same vein was released May 19, 1977, by the aforementioned congregations. It was issued in response to the question:

" 'Whether it is allowed after the declaration of May 24, 1973, to continue to have, as a general rule, the reception of first Communion precede the reception of the sacrament of penance in those parishes in which this practice developed in the past few years.'

"The Sacred Congregations for the Sacraments and Divine Worship and for the Clergy, with the approval of the Supreme Pontiff, reply: Negative, and according to the mind of the declaration.

"The mind of the declaration is that one year after the promulgation of the same declaration, all experiments of receiving first Communion without the sacrament of penance should cease so that the discipline of the Church might be restored, in the spirit of the decree, *Quam Singulari.*"

The two letters from the Vatican congregations have not produced uniformity of practice in this country. Simultaneous preparation for both sacraments is provided in some dioceses where a child has the option of receiving either sacrament first, with the counsel of parents, priests and teachers. Programs in other dioceses are geared first to reception of Communion and later to reception of the sacrament of reconciliation.

Commentators on the letters note that: they are disciplinary rather than doctrinal in content; they are subject to pastoral interpretation by bishops; they cannot be interpreted to mean that a person who is not guilty of serious sin must be required to receive the sacrament of penance before (even first) Communion.

Holy Communion under the Forms of Bread and Wine (by separate taking of the consecrated bread and wine or by intinction, the reception of the host dipped in the wine): Such reception is permitted under conditions stated in instructions issued by the Congregation for Divine Worship (May 25, 1967; June 29, 1970), the *General Instruction on the Roman Missal* (No. 242), and directives of bishops' conferences and individual bishops.

Accordingly, Communion can be administered in this way to: persons being baptized, received into communion with the Church, confirmed, receiving anointing of the sick; couples at their wedding or jubilee; religious at profession or renewal of profession; lay persons receiving an ecclesiastical assignment (e.g., lay missionaries); participants at concelebrated Masses, retreats, pastoral commission meetings, daily Masses and on other occasions.

Holy Communion Twice a Day: The reception of Holy Communion at Mass a second time on the same day is permitted in accord with provisions of the "Instruction on Facilitating Communion in Particular Circumstances" *(Immensae Caritatis)* approved by Pope Paul VI Jan. 20 and published by the Congregation for Divine Worship Mar. 29, 1973.

The occasions are: Sunday Mass on Saturday evening or a holy day Mass the previous evening; a second Mass on Christmas or Easter, following reception at midnight Mass or the Mass of the Easter Vigil; the evening Mass of Holy Thursday, following reception at the earlier Mass of Chrism; Masses in which baptism, confirmation, holy orders, matrimony, anointing of the sick, first Communion, Viaticum are administered; some Masses for the dead (e.g., of Christian burial, first anniversary); special occasions — consecration of a church or altar, religious profession, conferring an ecclesiastical assignment (e.g., to lay missionaries), feast of Corpus Christi, parochial visitation, canonical visitation or special meetings of religious, Eucharistic and other congresses, pilgrimages, preaching missions; other occasions designated by the local bishop.

Holy Communion and Eucharistic Devotion outside of Mass: These were the subjects of an instruction *(De Sacra Communione et de Cultu Mysterii Eucharistici extra Missam)* dated June 21 and made public Oct. 18, 1973,

by the Congregation for Divine Worship.

Holy Communion can be given outside of Mass to persons unable for a reasonable cause to receive it during Mass on a given day. The ceremonial rite is modeled on the structure of the Mass, consisting of a penitential act, a scriptural reading, the Lord's Prayer, a sign or gesture of peace, giving of the Eucharist, prayer and final blessing. Viaticum and Communion to the sick can be given by extraordinary ministers (authorized lay persons) with appropriate rites.

Forms of devotion outside of Mass are exposition of the Blessed Sacrament (by men or women religious, especially, or lay persons in the absence of a priest; but only a priest can give the blessing), processions and congresses with appropriate rites.

Intercommunion: Church policy on intercommunion was stated in an "Instruction on the Admission of Other Christians to the Eucharist," dated June 1 and made public July 8, 1972, against the background of the *Decree on Ecumenism* approved by the Second Vatican Council, and the *Directory on Ecumenism* issued by the Secretariat for Promoting Christian Unity in 1967.

Basic principles related to intercommunion are:

• "There is an indissoluble link between the mystery of the Church and the mystery of the Eucharist, or between ecclesial and Eucharistic communion; the celebration of the Eucharist of itself signifies the fullness of profession of faith and ecclesial communion" (1972 Instruction).

• "Eucharistic communion practiced by those who are not in full ecclesial communion with each other cannot be the expression of that full unity which the Eucharist of its nature signifies and which in this case does not exist; for this reason such communion cannot be regarded as a means to be used to lead to full ecclesial communion" (1972 Instruction).

• The question of reciprocity "arises only with those churches which have preserved the substance of the Eucharist, the sacrament of orders and apostolic succession" (1967 Directory).

• "A Catholic cannot ask for the Eucharist except from a minister who has been validly ordained" (1967 Directory).

The policy distinguishes between separated Eastern Christians and other Christians.

With Separated Eastern Christians (e.g., Orthodox): These may be given the Eucharist (as well as penance and anointing of the sick) at their request. Catholics may receive these same sacraments from priests of separated Eastern churches if they experience genuine spiritual necessity, seek spiritual benefit, and access to a Catholic priest is morally or physically impossible. This policy (of reciprocity) derives from the facts that the separated Eastern churches have apostolic succession through their bishops, valid priests, and sacramental beliefs and practices in accord with those of the Catholic Church.

With Other Christians (e.g., members of Reformation-related churches, others): Admission to the Eucharist in the Catholic Church, according to the *Directory on Ecumenism,* "is confined to particular cases of those Christians who have a faith in the sacrament in conformity with that of the Church, who experience a serious spiritual need for the Eucharistic sustenance, who for a prolonged period are unable to have recourse to a minister of their own community and who ask for the sacrament of their own accord; all this provided that they have proper dispositions and lead lives worthy of a Christian." The spiritual need is defined as "a need for an increase in spiritual life and a need for a deeper involvement in the mystery of the Church and of its unity."

Circumstances under which Communion may be given to other properly disposed Christians are danger of death, imprisonment, persecution, grave spiritual necessity coupled with no chance of recourse to a minister of their own community. Judgment regarding these and other special circumstances rests with the local bishop.

Catholics cannot ask for the Eucharist from ministers of other Christian churches who have not been validly ordained to the priesthood.

Penance

Penance is the sacrament by which sins committed after baptism are forgiven and a person is reconciled with God and the Church.

A revised ritual for the sacrament — *Ordo Paenitentiae,* published by the Congregation of Divine Worship Feb. 7, 1974 — reiterates standard doctrine concerning the sacrament; emphasizes the social (communal and ecclesial) aspects of sin and conversion, with due regard for personal aspects and individual reception of the sacrament; prescribes three forms for celebration of the sacrament; and presents models for community penitential services.

The U.S. Bishops' Committee on the Liturgy recommended that adequate preparation of priests and people should precede introduction in this country of the revised ritual in English. Recommended dates for its use, after due preparation, were the first Sunday of Lent, 1976 (optional), and the first Sunday of Lent, 1977 (mandatory).

The basic elements of the sacrament are sorrow for sin because of a supernatural motive, confession (of previously unconfessed mortal or grave sins, required; of venial sins also, but not of necessity), and reparation (by means of prayer or other act enjoined by the confessor), all of which comprise the matter of the sacrament; and absolution, which is the form of the sacrament.

The traditional words of absolution — "I absolve you from your sins in the name of the Father, and of the Son, and of the Holy Spirit" — remain unchanged at the conclusion of a petition in the new rite that God may grant pardon and peace through the ministry of the Church.

The minister of the sacrament is an authorized priest — i.e., one who, besides having the power of orders to forgive sins, also has faculties of jurisdiction granted by an ecclesiastical superior and/or by canon law.

The sacrament can be celebrated in three ways.

• For individuals: The traditional manner remains acceptable but is enriched with additional elements including: reception of the penitent and making of the Sign of the Cross; an exhortation by the confessor to trust in God; a possible reading from Scripture; confession of sins; manifestation of repentance; petition for God's forgiveness through the ministry of the Church and the absolution of the priest; praise of God's mercy, and dismissal in peace. Some of these elements are optional.

• For several penitents, in the course of a community celebration including a liturgy of the Word of God and prayers, individual confession and absolution, and an act of thanksgiving.

• For several penitents, in the course of a community celebration, with general confession and general absolution. This method is reserved for special circumstances in which it is morally or physically impossible for persons to confess and be absolved individually, and in view of their need for reconciliation and reception of the Eucharist. Penitents are required to confess at their next individual confession any grave sins absolved in such a general celebration of the sacrament. Judgment regarding circumstances that warrant general confession and absolution belongs principally to the bishop of the place.

Communal celebrations of the sacrament are not held in connection with Mass.

The place of individual confession, as determined by episcopal conferences in accordance with given norms, can be the traditional confessional or another appropriate setting.

The sacrament is necessary, by the institution of Christ, for the reconciliation of persons guilty of grave sins committed after baptism.

A precept of the Church obliges the faithful guilty of grave sin to confess at least once a year.

The Church favors more frequent reception of the sacrament not only for the reconciliation of persons guilty of serious sins but also for reasons of devotion. Devotional confession — in which venial sins or previously forgiven sins are confessed — serves the purpose of confirming persons in penance and conversion.

Penitential Celebrations: Communal penitential celebrations are designed to emphasize the social dimensions of Christian life — the community aspects and significance of penance and reconciliation.

Elements of such celebrations are community prayer, hymns and songs, scriptural and other readings, examination of conscience, general confession and expression of sorrow for sin, acts of penance and reconciliation, and a form of non-sacramental absolution resembling the one in the penitential rite of the Mass.

If the sacrament is celebrated during the service, there must be individual confession and absolution of sin.

(See Absolution, Confession, Confessional, Confessor, Contrition, Faculties, Forgiveness of Sin, Power of the Keys, Seal of Confession, Sin.)

Anointing of the Sick

This sacrament, promulgated by St. James the Apostle (Jas. 5:13-15), is administered to persons who are seriously ill. By the anointing with blessed oil and the prayer of a priest, the sacrament confers on the person comforting grace; the remission of venial sins and inculpably unconfessed mortal sins, together with at least some of the temporal punishment due for sins; and, sometimes, results in an improved state of health.

The matter of this sacrament is the anointing with blessed oil (of the sick — olive oil, or vegetable oil if necessary) of the forehead and hands; in cases of necessity, a single anointing of another portion of the body suffices. The form is: "Through this holy anointing and his most loving mercy, may the Lord assist you by the grace of the Holy Spirit so that, when you have been freed from your sins, he may save you and in his goodness raise you up."

Anointing of the sick, formerly called extreme unction, may be received more than once, e.g., in new or continuing stages of serious illness. Ideally, the sacrament should be administered while the recipient is conscious and in conjunction with the sacraments of penance and the Eucharist. It may be administered conditionally even after apparent death.

The sacrament can be administered during a communal celebration in some circumstances, as in a home for the aged.

Holy Orders

Holy orders is the sacrament by which spiritual power and grace are given to enable an ordained minister to consecrate the Eucharist, forgive sins, perform other pastoral and ecclesiastical functions, and form the community of the People of God. Holy orders confers a character on the soul and can be received only once. The minister of the sacrament is a bishop.

Holy orders, like matrimony but in a different way, is a social sacrament. As the Second Vatican Council declared in the *Dogmatic Constitution on the Church:*

"For the nurturing and constant growth of the People of God, Christ the Lord instituted in His Church a variety of ministries, which work for the good of the whole body. For those ministers who are endowed with sacred power are servants of their brethren, so that all who are of the People of God, and therefore enjoy a true Christian dignity, can work toward a common goal freely and in an orderly way, and arrive at salvation" (No. 18).

"With their helpers, the priests and deacons, bishops have . . . taken up the service of the community, presiding in place of God over the flock whose shepherds they are, as teachers of doctrine, priests of sacred worship, and officers of good order" (No. 20).

The fullness of the priesthood belongs to those who have received the order of **bishop.** Bishops, in hierarchical union with the pope and their fellow bishops, are the successors of the apostles as pastors of the Church: they have individual responsibility for the care of the local churches they serve and collegial responsibility for the care of the universal Church (see Collegiality). In the ordination or consecration of bishops, the essential form is the imposition of hands by the consecrator(s) and the assigned prayer in the preface of the rite of ordination.

A **priest** is an ordained minister with the power to celebrate Mass, administer the sacraments, preach and teach the word of God, impart blessings, and perform additional pastoral functions, according to the mandate of his ecclesiastical superior.

Concerning priests, the Second Vatican Council stated in the *Dogmatic Constitution on the Church* (No. 28):

". . . The divinely established ecclesiastical ministry is exercised on different levels by those who from antiquity have been called bishops, priests, and deacons. Although priests do not possess the highest degree of the priesthood, and although they are dependent on the bishops in the exercise of their power, they are nevertheless united with the bishops in sacerdotal dignity. By the power of the sacrament of orders, and in the image of Christ the eternal High Priest (Hb. 5:1-10; 7:24; 9:11-28), they are consecrated to preach the gospel, shepherd the faithful, and celebrate divine worship as true priests of the New Testament. . . .

"Priests, prudent cooperators with the episcopal order as well as its aides and instruments, are called to serve the People of God. They constitute one priesthood with their bishop, although that priesthood is comprised of different functions. . . ."

In the ordination of a priest of Roman Rite, the essential matter is the imposition of hands on the heads of those being ordained by the ordaining bishop. The essential form is the accompanying prayer in the preface of the ordination ceremony. Other elements in the rite are the presentation of the implements of sacrifice — the chalice containing wine and the paten containing a host — with accompanying prayers.

Regarding the order of **deacon**, the *Dogmatic Constitution on the Church* (No. 29) stated:

"At a lower level of the hierarchy are deacons, upon whom hands are imposed 'not unto the priesthood, but unto a ministry of service.' For strengthened by sacramental grace, in communion with the bishop and his group of priests, they serve the People of God in the ministry of the liturgy, of the word, and of charity. It is the duty of the deacon, to the extent that he has been authorized by competent authority, to administer baptism solemnly, to be custodian and dispenser of the Eucharist, to assist at and bless marriages in the name of the Church, to bring Viaticum to the dying, to read the sacred Scripture to the faithful, to instruct and exhort the people, to preside at the worship and prayer of the faithful, to administer sacramentals, and to officiate at funeral and burial services. (Deacons are) dedicated to duties of charity and administration. . . ."

". . . The diaconate can in the future be restored as a proper and permanent rank of the hierarchy. It pertains to the competent territorial bodies of bishops, of one kind or another, to decide, with the approval of the Supreme Pontiff, whether and where it is opportune for such deacons to be appointed for the care of souls. With the consent of the Roman Pontiff, this diaconate will be able to be conferred upon men of more mature age, even upon those living in the married state. It may also be conferred upon suitable young men. For them, however, the law of celibacy must remain intact" (No. 29).

The Apostles ordained the first seven deacons (Acts 6:1-6): Stephen, Philip, Prochorus, Nicanor, Timon, Parmenas, Nicholas.

Other Ministries: The Church later assigned ministerial duties to men in several other orders, as:

Subdeacon, with specific duties in liturgical worship, especially at Mass. The order, whose first extant mention dates from about the middle of the third century, was regarded as minor until the 13th century; afterwards, it was called a major order in the West but not in the East.

Acolyte, to serve in minor capacities in liturgical worship; a function now performed by Mass servers.

Exorcist, to perform services of exorcism for expelling evil spirits; a function which came to be reserved to specially delegated priests.

Lector, to read scriptural and other passages during liturgical worship; a function now generally performed by lay persons

Porter, to guard the entrance to an assembly of Christians and to ward off undesirables who tried to gain admittance; an order of early origin and utility but of present insignificance.

Long after it became evident that these positions and functions had fallen into general disuse or did not require clerical ordination, the Holy See started a revision of the orders in 1971. By an indult of Oct. 5, the bishops of the United States were permitted to omit ordaining porters and exorcists. Another indult, dated three days later, permitted the use of revised rites for ordaining acolytes and lectors, and authorized the use of a service celebrating admission to the clerical state in place of the ceremony of tonsure which had previously served this purpose.

To complete the revision, Pope Paul VI abolished Sept. 14, 1972, the orders of porter, exorcist and subdeacon; decreed that laymen, as well as candidates for the diaconate and priesthood, can be installed (rather than ordained) in the ministries (rather than orders) of acolyte and lector; reconfirmed the suppression of tonsure and its replacement with a service of dedication to God and the Church; and stated that a man enters the clerical state on ordination to the diaconate.

There were no doctrinal obstacles to the Pope's action, because the abolished orders had been instituted by the Church for functional purposes and were not considered to be parts of the sacrament of holy orders.

PERMANENT DIACONATE

Authorization for restoration of the permanent diaconate in the Roman Rite — making it possible for men to become deacons permanently, without going on to the priesthood — was promulgated by Pope Paul VI June 18, 1967, in a document entitled *Sacrum Diaconatus Ordinem* ("Sacred Order of the Diaconate").

The Pope's action implemented the desire expressed by the Second Vatican Council for reestablishment of the diaconate as an independent order in its own right not only to supply ministers for carrying on the work of the Church but also to complete the hierarchical structure of the Church of Roman Rite.

Permanent deacons have been traditional in the Eastern Church. The Western Church, however, since the fourth or fifth century, generally followed the practice of conferring the diaconate only as a sacred order preliminary to the priesthood, and of restricting the ministry of deacons to liturgical functions.

The Pope's document, issued on his own initiative, provided:

• Qualified unmarried men 25 years of age or older may be ordained permanent deacons. They cannot marry after ordination.

• Qualified married men 35 years of age or older may be ordained permanent deacons. The consent of the wife of a prospective deacon is required. A married deacon cannot remarry after the death of his wife.

• Preparation for the diaconate includes a course of study and formation over a period of at least three years.

• Candidates who are not religious must be affiliated with a diocese. Reestablishment of the permanent diaconate among religious is reserved to the Holy See.

• Deacons will practice their ministry under the direction of a bishop and with the priests with whom they will be associated. (For functions, see the description of deacon, under Holy Orders.)

Restoration of the permanent diaconate in the United States was approved by the Holy See in October, 1968. Shortly afterwards the U.S. bishops established a committee of the same name, which is chaired by Auxiliary Bishop Eugene A. Marino, S.S.J., of Washington, D.C. The committee operates through a secretariat, of which Msgr. Ernest J. Fiedler is executive director. Its offices are located at 1312 Massachusetts Ave. N. W., Washington, D.C. 20005.

Present Status

The bishops' secretariat reported in October, 1979, that 4,028 permanent deacons had been ordained in the U.S.; that 130 dioceses either had approved programs of formation or were in the process of preparing formation programs; that a total of 2,621 candidates were in training.

Functions

Deacons have various functions, depending on the nature of their assignments. Liturgically, they can officiate at baptisms, weddings, wake services and funerals, can preach and distribute Holy Communion. Some are engaged in religious education work. All are intended to carry out works of charity and pastoral service of one kind or another.

The majority of permanent deacons, 93 per cent of whom are married, continue in their secular work. Their ministry of service is developing in three dimensions: of liturgy, of the word, and of charity. Depending on the individual deacon's abilities and preference, he is assigned by his bishop to either a parochial ministry or to one particular field of service. The latter is the most challenging ministry to develop. Deacons are now active in a variety of ministries including those to prison inmates and their families, the sick in hospitals, nursing homes and homes for the aged,

alienated youth, the elderly and the poor, and in various areas of legal service to the indigent, of education and campus ministry. A few have been assigned as quasi-pastors of multi-county, rural parishes. The unlimited possibilities for diaconal ministry are under realistic assessment, diocese by diocese.

Training Programs

There were 130 training centers for deacons as of October, 1979. The first four were established in 1969. One center may serve two or more dioceses in the formation of diaconal candidates.

Continuing efforts are made to recruit Spanish-speaking, black and other minority candidates in training programs. Of the permanent deacons ordained up to October, 1979, five per cent were black, and 14 per cent were Hispanic.

Training programs of spiritual, doctrinal and pastoral formation are generally based on *Permanent Deacons in the United States: Guidelines on Their Formation and Ministry,* published by the Bishops' Committee on the Permanent Diaconate in September, 1971.

National Association of Permanent Diaconate Directors: Membership organization of directors, vicars and other staff personnel of permanent diaconate programs. Established in 1977 to promote effective communication and facilitate the exchange of information and resources of members; to develop professional expertise and promote research, training and self evaluation; to foster accountability and seek ways to promote means of implementing solutions to problems. NAPDD is governed by an executive board of elected officers. President: Rev. Neal T. Dolan, 1667 Santa Paula Dr., San Diego, Calif. 92111.

AMERICAN COLLEGE, LOUVAIN

The American College was founded by the bishops of the United States in 1857 as a residence and house of formation for U.S. seminarians and graduate students pursuing courses in theology and related subjects at the Catholic Universities of Leuven and Louvain-la-Neuve (dating from 1425) in Belgium.

The college is administered by an American rector and staff, and operates under the auspices of a special committee of the National Conference of Catholic Bishops. Bishop Edward W. O'Rourke of Peoria is chairman of the committee. The present rector, the 10th, is Msgr. William Greytak of Helena, Mont.

The address is: American College, University of Louvain, Naamsestraat 100, B-3000 Leuven, Belgium.

The current enrollment of the American College includes students from more than 35 dioceses in the U.S., Canada, the Bahamas, the United Kingdom, the Netherlands, Australia and Indonesia.

MARRIAGE DOCTRINE

The following excerpts, stating key points of doctrine on marriage, are from the *Pastoral Constitution on the Church in the Modern World* (Nos. 48 to 51) promulgated by the Second Vatican Council.

Conjugal Covenant

"The intimate partnership of married life and love has been established by the Creator and qualified by His laws. It is rooted in the conjugal covenant of irrevocable personal consent. . . .

". . . God Himself is the author of matrimony, endowed as it is with various benefits and purposes. All of these have a very decisive bearing on the continuation of the human race, on the personal development and eternal destiny of the individual members of a family, and on the dignity, stability, peace, and prosperity of the family itself and of human society as a whole. By their very nature, the institution of matrimony itself and conjugal love are ordained for the procreation and education of children, and find in them their ultimate crown.

"Thus a man and a woman . . . render mutual help and service to each other through an intimate union of their persons and of their actions. Through this union they experience the meaning of their oneness and attain to it with growing perfection day by day. As a mutual gift of two persons, this intimate union, as well as the good of the children, imposes total fidelity on the spouses and argues for an unbreakable oneness between them" (No. 48).

Sacrament of Matrimony

"Christ the Lord abundantly blessed this many-faceted love. . . . The Savior of men and the Spouse of the Church comes into the lives of married Christians through the sacrament of matrimony. He abides with them thereafter so that, just as He loved the Church and handed Himself over on her behalf, the spouses may love each other with perpetual fidelity through mutual self-bestowal.

". . . Graced with the dignity and office of fatherhood and motherhood, parents will energetically acquit themselves of a duty which devolves primarily on them, namely education, and especially religious education.

". . . The Christian family, which springs from marriage as a reflection of the loving covenant uniting Christ with the Church, and as a participation in that covenant, will manifest to all men the Savior's living presence in the world, and the genuine nature of the Church . . ." (No. 48).

Conjugal Love

"The biblical Word of God several times urges the betrothed and the married to nourish and develop their wedlock by pure conjugal love and undivided affection. . . .

"This love is an eminently human one since it is directed from one person to another through an affection of the will. It involves the good of the whole person. Therefore it can enrich the expressions of body and mind with a unique dignity, ennobling these expressions as special ingredients and signs of the friendship distinctive of marriage. This love the Lord has judged worthy of special gifts, healing, perfecting, and exalting gifts of grace and of charity.

"Such love, merging the human with the divine, leads the spouses to a free and mutual gift of themselves, a gift proving itself by gentle affection and by deed. Such love pervades the whole of their lives. Indeed, by its generous activity it grows better and grows greater. Therefore it far excels mere erotic inclination, which, selfishly pursued, soon enough fades wretchedly away.

"This love is uniquely expressed and perfected through the marital act. The actions within marriage by which the couple are united intimately and chastely are noble and worthy ones. Expressed in a manner which is truly human, these actions signify and promote that mutual self-giving by which spouses enrich each other with a joyful and a thankful will.

"Sealed by mutual faithfulness and hallowed above all by Christ's sacrament, this love remains steadfastly true in body and in mind, in bright days or dark. It will never be profaned by adultery or divorce. Firmly established by the Lord, the unity of marriage will radiate from the equal personal dignity of wife and husband, a dignity acknowledged by mutual and total love.

"The steady fulfillment of the duties of this Christian vocation demands notable virtue. For this reason, strengthened by grace for holiness of life, the couple will painstakingly cultivate and pray for constancy of love, largeheartedness, and the spirit of sacrifice . . ." (No. 49).

Fruitfulness of Marriage

"Marriage and conjugal love are by their nature ordained toward the begetting and educating of children. Children are really the supreme gift of marriage and contribute very substantially to the welfare of their parents. . . . God Himself . . . wished to share with man a certain special participation in His own creative work. Thus He blessed male and female, saying: 'Increase and multiply' (Gn. 1:28).

"Hence, while not making the other purposes of matrimony of less account, the true practice of conjugal love, and the whole meaning of the family life which results from it, have this aim: that the couple be ready with stout hearts to cooperate with the love of the

Creator and the Savior, who through them will enlarge and enrich His own family day by day.

"Parents should regard as their proper mission the task of transmitting human life and educating those to whom it has been transmitted. They should realize that they are thereby cooperators with the love of God the Creator, and are, so to speak, the interpreters of that love. Thus they will fulfill their task with human and Christian responsibility . . ." (No. 50).

Norms of Judgment

"They will thoughtfully take into account both their own welfare and that of their children, those already born and those which may be foreseen. For this accounting they will reckon with both the material and the spiritual conditions of the times as well as of their state in life. Finally, they will consult the interests of the family group, of temporal society, and of the Church herself.

"The parents themselves should ultimately make this judgment in the sight of God. But in their manner of acting, spouses should be aware that they cannot proceed arbitrarily. They must always be governed according to a conscience dutifully conformed to the divine law itself, and should be submissive toward the Church's teaching office, which authentically interprets that law in the light of the gospel. That divine law reveals and protects the integral meaning of conjugal love, and impels it toward a truly human fulfillment. . . .

"Marriage to be sure is not instituted solely for procreation. Rather, its very nature as an unbreakable compact between persons, and the welfare of the children, both demand that the mutual love of the spouses, too, be embodied in a rightly ordered manner, that it grow and ripen. Therefore, marriage persists as a whole manner and communion of life, and maintains its value and indissolubility, even when offspring are lacking — despite, rather often, the very intense desire of the couple" (No. 50).

Love and Life

"This Council realizes that certain modern conditions often keep couples from arranging their married lives harmoniously, and that they find themselves in circumstances where at least temporarily the size of their families should not be increased. As a result, the faithful exercise of love and the full intimacy of their lives are hard to maintain. But where the intimacy of married life is broken off, it is not rare for its faithfulness to be imperiled and its quality of fruitfulness ruined. For then the upbringing of the children and the courage to accept new ones are both endangered.

"To these problems there are those who presume to offer dishonorable solutions. Indeed, they do not recoil from the taking of life. But the Church issues the reminder that a true contradiction cannot exist between the divine laws pertaining to the transmission of life and those pertaining to the fostering of authentic conjugal love.

"For God, the Lord of Life, has conferred on men the surpassing ministry of safeguarding life — a ministry which must be fulfilled in a manner which is worthy of men. Therefore from the moment of its conception life must be guarded with the greatest care, while abortion and infanticide are unspeakable crimes. The sexual characteristics of man and the human faculty of reproduction wonderfully exceed the dispositions of lower forms of life. Hence the acts themselves which are proper to conjugal love and which are exercised in accord with genuine human dignity must be honored with great reverence" (No. 51).

Church Teaching

"Therefore when there is question of harmonizing conjugal love with the responsible transmission of life, the moral aspect of any procedure does not depend solely on the sincere intentions or on an evaluation of motives. It must be determined by objective standards. These, based on the nature of the human person and his acts, preserve the full sense of mutual self-giving and human procreation in the context of true love. Such a goal cannot be achieved unless the virtue of conjugal chastity is sincerely practiced. Relying on these principles, sons of the Church may not undertake methods of regulating procreation which are found blameworthy by the teaching authority of the Church in its unfolding of the divine law.

"Everyone should be persuaded that human life and the task of transmitting it are not realities bound up with this world alone. Hence they cannot be measured or perceived only in terms of it, but always have a bearing on the eternal destiny of men" (No. 51).

HUMANAE VITAE

Marriage doctrine and morality were the subjects of the encyclical *Humanae Vitae* ("Of Human Life") issued by Pope Paul July 29, 1968. Following are a number of key excerpts from the document, which was framed in the pattern of traditional teaching and statements by the Second Vatican Council.

". . . each and every marriage act ('quilibet matrimonii usus') must remain open to the transmission of life" (No. 11).

"Indeed, by its intimate structure, the conjugal act, while most closely uniting husband and wife, capacitates them for the generation of new lives, according to laws inscribed in the very being of man and of woman. By safeguarding both these essential aspects, the unitive and the procreative, the conjugal act preserves in its fullness the sense of true mutual love and its ordination toward man's most high calling to parenthood" (No. 12).

"It is, in fact, justly observed that a conjugal act imposed upon one's partner without regard for his or her condition and lawful desires is not a true act of love, and therefore denies an exigency of right moral order in the relationships between husband and wife. Hence, one who reflects well must also recognize that a reciprocal act of love which jeopardizes the responsibility to transmit life — which God the Creator, according to particular laws, inserted therein — is in contradiction with the design constitutive of marriage and with the will of the Author of life. To use this divine gift, destroying, even if only partially, its meaning and its purpose, is to contradict the nature both of man and of woman and of their most intimate relationship, and therefore it is to contradict also the plan of God and His will" (No. 13).

Forbidden Actions: ". . . the direct interruption of the generative process already begun, and, above all, directly willed and procured abortion, even if for therapeutic reasons, are to be absolutely excluded as licit means of regulating birth.

"Equally to be excluded . . . is direct sterilization, whether perpetual or temporary, whether of the man or of the woman. Similarly excluded is every action which, either in anticipation of the conjugal act, or in its accomplishment, or in the development of its natural consequences, proposes, whether as an end or as a means, to render procreation impossible.

Inadmissible Principles: "To justify conjugal acts made intentionally infecund, one cannot invoke as valid reasons the lesser evil, or the fact that such acts would constitute a whole together with the fecund acts already performed or to follow later and hence would share in one and the same moral goodness. In truth, if it is sometimes licit to tolerate a lesser evil in order to avoid a greater evil or to promote a greater good, it is not licit, even for the gravest reasons, to do evil so that good may follow therefrom; that is, to make into the object of a positive act of the will something which is intrinsically disorder, and hence unworthy of the human person, even when the intention is to safeguard or promote individual, family or social well-being.

"Consequently, it is an error to think that a conjugal act which is deliberately made infecund, and so is intrinsically dishonest, could be made honest and right by the ensemble of a fecund conjugal life" (No. 14).

Rhythm: "If, then, there are serious motives to space out births, which derive from the physical or psychological conditions of husband and wife, or from external conditions, the Church teaches that it is then licit to take into account the natural rhythms immanent in the generative functions, for the use of marriage in the infecund periods only, and in this way to regulate birth without offending" earlier stated principles (No. 16).

Authoritative Teaching: Pope Paul called the foregoing teaching authoritative, although not infallible. He left it open for further study. As a practical norm to be followed, however, he said it involved the binding force of religious assent.

With pastoral concern, the Pope said: "We do not at all intend to hide the sometimes serious difficulties inherent in the life of Christian married persons; for them, as for everyone else, 'the gate is narrow and the way is hard that leads to life.' But the hope of that life must illuminate their way, as with courage they strive to live with wisdom, justice and piety in this present time, knowing that the figure of this world passes away.

"Let married couples, then, face up to the efforts needed, supported by the faith and hope which 'do not disappoint . . . because God's love has been poured into our hearts through the Holy Spirit, who has been given to us.' Let them implore divine assistance by persevering prayer; above all, let them draw from the source of grace and charity in the Eucharist. And, if sin should still keep its hold over them, let them not be discouraged but rather have recourse with humble perseverance to the mercy of God, which is poured forth in the sacrament of penance" (No. 25).

Reactions: Exception was taken to the binding force of the encyclical — notably by the bishops of Belgium, Austria and France, and many theologians — for several reasons: rights of conscience; questions concerning the natural-law concept underlying the encyclical; the thesis of totality; the proposition that contraception may in some cases be the lesser of two evils. All agreed, however, that conscientious objection to the encyclical could not be taken without serious reasons and reflection.

MARRIAGE LAWS

The Catholic Church, in line with the belief that it was established and commissioned by Christ to provide and administer the means of salvation to men, claims jurisdiction over its members in matters pertaining to marriage, which is a sacrament. The purpose of its laws in this area, consisting of 132 canons, is to safeguard the validity and lawfulness of marriage.

Catholics are bound by all marriage laws of the Church. Non-Catholics, whether baptized or not, are not considered bound by these ecclesiastical laws except in cases of marriage with a Catholic. Certain natural laws, in the Catholic view, bind all men and women, irrespective of their religious beliefs; accordingly, marriage is prohibited before the time of puberty, without knowledge and free mutual consent, in the case of an already existing valid marriage bond, in the case of antecedent and perpetual impotence.

Formalities

These include, in addition to arrangements for the time and place of the marriage ceremony, doctrinal and moral instruction concerning marriage and the recording of data which verifies in documentary form the eligibility and freedom of the persons to marry. Records of this kind, which are confidential, are preserved in the archives of the church where the marriage takes place.

Premarital instructions are the subject matter of Pre-Cana Conferences.

Mixed Marriages

"Mixed Marriages" (*Matrimonia Mixta*) was the subject of: (1) a letter issued under this title by Pope Paul VI Mar. 31, 1970, and (2) a statement, *Implementation of the Apostolic Letter on Mixed Marriages,* approved by the National Conference of Catholic Bishops Nov. 16, 1970.

One of the key points in the bishops' statement referred to the need for mutual pastoral care by ministers of different faiths for the sacredness of marriage and for appropriate preparation and continuing support of parties to a mixed marriage.

Pastoral experience, which the Catholic Church shares with other religious bodies, confirms the fact that marriages of persons of different beliefs involve special problems related to the continuing religious practice of the concerned persons and to the religious education and formation of their children.

Pastoral measures to minimize these problems include instruction of a non-Catholic party in essentials of the Catholic faith for purposes of understanding. Desirably, some instruction should also be given the Catholic party regarding his or her partner's beliefs.

The Catholic party to a mixed marriage is required to declare his (her) intention of continuing practice of the Catholic faith and to promise to do all in his power to share his faith with children born of the marriage by having them baptized and raised as Catholics. No declarations or promises are required of the non-Catholic party, but he (she) must be informed of the declaration and promise made by the Catholic.

Notice of the Catholic's declaration and promise is an essential part of the application made to a bishop for dispensation from the impediment of mixed religion or disparity of worship (see below).

A mixed marriage can take place with a Nuptial Mass. (The bishops' statement added this caution: "To the extent that Eucharistic sharing is not permitted by the general discipline of the Church, this is to be considered when plans are being made to have the mixed marriage at Mass or not.")

The ordinary minister at a mixed marriage is an authorized priest, and the ordinary place is the parish church of the Catholic party. A non-Catholic minister may not only attend the marriage ceremony but may also address, pray with and bless the couple.

For appropriate pastoral reasons, a bishop can grant a dispensation from the Catholic form of marriage and can permit the marriage to take place in a non-Catholic Church with a non-Catholic minister as the officiating minister. A priest may not only attend such a ceremony but may also address, pray with and bless the couple.

"It is not permitted," however, the bishops statement declared, "to have two religious services or to have a single service in which both the Catholic marriage ritual and a non-Catholic marriage ritual are celebrated jointly or successively."

Banns

The banns are public announcements made in their parish churches, usually on three successive Sundays, of the names of persons who intend to marry. Persons who know of reasons in church law why a proposed marriage should not take place, are obliged to make them known to the pastor.

Marital Consent

The exchange of consent to the marriage contract, which is essential for valid marriage, must be rational, free, true and mutual.

Matrimonial consent can be invalidated by an essential defect, substantial error, the strong influence of force and fear, the presence of a condition or intention against the nature of marriage.

Form of Marriage

A Catholic is required, for validity and lawfulness, to contract marriage — with another Catholic or with a non-Catholic — in the presence of a competent priest or deacon and two witnesses.

There are two exceptions to this law. A Roman Rite Catholic (since Mar. 25, 1967) or an Eastern Rite Catholic (since Nov. 21, 1964) can contract marriage validly in the presence of a priest of a separated Eastern Rite Church, provided other requirements of law are complied with. With permission of the competent Roman-Rite or Eastern-Rite bishop, this form of marriage is lawful, as well as valid. (See Eastern Rite Laws, below.)

With these two exceptions, and aside from cases covered by special permission, the Church does not regard as valid any marriages involving Catholics which take place before non-Catholic ministers of religion or civil officials. (See Mixed Marriage Guidelines.)

An excommunication formerly in force against Catholics who celebrated marriage before a non-Catholic minister was abrogated in a decree issued by the Sacred Congregation for the Doctrine of the Faith on Mar. 18, 1966.

The ordinary place of marriage is the parish of the bride, of the Catholic party in case of a mixed marriage, or of an Eastern Rite groom.

Church law regarding the form of marriage does not affect non-Catholics in marriages among themselves. The Church recognizes as valid the marriages of non-Catholics before ministers of religion and civil officials, unless they are rendered null and void on other grounds.

Impediments

Impediments to marriage are factors which render a marriage unlawful or invalid.

Prohibitory Impediments, which make a marriage unlawful but do not affect validity:

• simple vows of virginity, perpetual chastity, celibacy, to enter a religious order or to receive sacred orders;

• difference of religion, which obtains when one party is a Catholic and the other is a baptized non-Catholic.

The impediment of legal relationship is not in force in the US.

Diriment Impediments, which make a marriage invalid as well as unlawful:

• age, which obtains before completion of the 14th year for a woman and the 16th year for a man;

• impotency, if it is antecedent to the marriage and permanent (this differs from sterility, which is not an impediment);

• the bond of an existing valid marriage;

• disparity of worship, which obtains when one party is a Catholic and the other party is unbaptized;

• sacred orders;

• religious profession of the solemn vow of chastity;

• abduction, which impedes the freedom of the person abducted;

• crime, variously involving elements of adultery, promise or attempt to marry, conspiracy to murder a husband or wife;

• blood relationship in the direct line (father-daughter, mother-son, etc.) and within the third degree of the collateral line (brother-sister, first and second cousins);

• affinity, or relationship resulting from a valid marriage, in any degree of the direct line and within the second degree of the collateral line;

• spiritual relationship arising through baptism — between a godchild and godparent, between the person baptized and the one who performed the baptism;

• public honesty, arising from an invalid marriage or from public or notorious concubinage; it renders either party incapable of marrying relatives of the other in the first and second degrees of the direct line.

Dispensations from Impediments: Persons hindered by impediments either may not or cannot marry unless they are dispensed therefrom in view of reasons recognized in canon law. Local bishops can dispense from the impediments most often encountered (e.g., difference of religion, disparity of worship) as well as others.

Decision regarding some dispensations is reserved to the Holy See.

Separation

A valid and consummated marriage of baptized persons cannot be dissolved by any human authority or any cause other than the death of one of the persons.

In other circumstances:

• 1. A valid but unconsummated marriage of baptized persons, or of a baptized and an unbaptized person, can be dissolved:

a. by the solemn religious profession of one of the persons, made with permission of the pope. In such a case, the bond is dissolved at the time of profession, and the other person is free to marry again;

b. by dispensation from the pope, requested for a grave reason by one or both of the persons. If the dispensation is granted, both persons are free to marry again.

Dispensations in these cases are granted for reasons connected with the spiritual welfare of the concerned persons.

• 2. A legitimate marriage, even consummated, of unbaptized persons can be dissolved in favor of one of them who subsequently receives the sacrament of baptism. This is the Pauline Privilege, so called because it was promulgated by St. Paul (1 Cor. 7:12-15) as a means of protecting the faith of converts. Requisites for granting the privilege are:

a. marriage prior to the baptism of either person;

b. reception of baptism by one person;

c. refusal of the unbaptized person to live in peace with the baptized person and without interfering with his or her freedom to practice the Christian faith. The privilege does not apply if the unbaptized person agrees to these conditions.

• 3. A legitimate and consummated marriage of a baptized and an unbaptized person can be dissolved by the pope in virtue of the Privilege of Faith, also called the Petrine Privilege.

Civil Divorce: Because of the unity and the indissolubility of marriage, the Church denies that civil divorce can break the bond of a valid marriage, whether the marriage involves two Catholics, a Catholic and a non-Catholic, or non-Catholics with each other.

In view of serious circumstances of marital distress, the Church permits an innocent and aggrieved party, whether wife or husband, to seek and obtain a civil divorce for the purpose of acquiring title and right to the civil effects of divorce, such as separate habitation and maintenance, and the custody of children. Permission for this kind of action should be obtained from proper church authority. The divorce, if obtained, does not break the bond of a valid marriage.

Under other circumstances — as would obtain if a marriage was invalid (see Decree of Nullity, below) — civil divorce is permitted for civil effects and as a civil ratification of the fact that the marriage bond really does not exist.

Decree of Nullity, sometimes improperly called an annulment. This is a decision by a competent church authority — e.g., a bishop, a diocesan marriage tribunal, the Sacred Roman Rota — that an apparently valid marriage was actually invalid from the beginning because of the unknown or concealed existence, from the beginning, of a diriment impediment, an essential defect in consent, radical incapability for marriage, or a condition placed by one or both of the parties against the very nature of marriage.

Eastern Rite Laws

Marriage laws of the Eastern Church differ in several respects from the legislation of the Roman Rite. The regulations in effect since May 2, 1949, were contained in the motu proprio *Crebre Allatae* issued by Pius XII the previous February.

According to both the Roman Code of Canon Law and the Oriental Code, marriages between Roman Rite Catholics and Eastern Rite Catholics ordinarily take place in the rite of the groom and have canonical effects in that rite.

Regarding the form for the celebration of marriages between Eastern Catholics and baptized Eastern non-Catholics, the Second Vatican Council declared:

"By way of preventing invalid marriages between Eastern Catholics and baptized Eastern non-Catholics, and in the interests of the permanence and sanctity of marriage and of domestic harmony, this sacred Synod decrees that the canonical 'form' for the celebration of such marriages obliges only for lawfulness. For their validity, the presence of a sacred minister suffices, as long as the other requirements of law are honored" (*Decree on Eastern Catholic Churches,* No. 18).

Marriages taking place in this manner are lawful, as well as valid, with permission of a competent Eastern Rite bishop.

The Rota

The Sacred Roman Rota is the ordinary court of appeal for marriage, and some other cases, which are appealed to the Holy See from lower church courts. Appeals are made to the Rota if decisions by diocesan and archdiocesan courts fail to settle the matter in dispute.

Cana Conferences, named for the marriage-miracle passage in St. John's Gospel, are for married couples, with formats covering the multiple aspects of marriage.

PROCEDURAL RULES

Pope Paul VI promulgated, June 11, 1971, a set of 13 rules designed to speed up the handling of cases in which the validity of marriage is questioned. Norms given in the document, which was issued by the Pope on his own initiative and became effective Oct.31, concern "the constitution of ecclesiastical tribunals and . . . the judicial process which will expedite the matrimonial process itself."

The norms do not affect the reasons for the validity or invalidity of marriages, but only the way in which cases of this kind are handled in church courts.

Pope Paul told judges of the Roman Rota Jan. 30, 1975, that national conferences of bishops seemed "unanimously satisfied" with the procedures authorized in 1971. He also said: "We strongly hope that, with the promulgation of the new code of procedures, unnecessary differences among various ecclesiastical regions will be removed."

U. S. Norms

Twenty-three experimental norms — drawn up by the Canon Law Society of America, approved by the National Conference of Catholic Bishops and the Holy See, and in effect since July, 1970 — were broader in some respects than those decreed by Pope Paul. Among other things, they provided for: one-priest tribunals for specific periods of time instead of just for individual cases; dispensation by the NCCB from the need for review of first decisions regarding the validity or invalidity of a marriage; circumstances affecting the competence of tribunals. Continuing use of the experimental procedural norms was authorized by Paul VI in a letter dated May 22 and announced June 8, 1974 — "until the new order of matrimonial court procedure is promulgated for the Latin Church" in connection with the on-going revision of the Code of Canon Law. Termination of their use had been scheduled for June 30, 1974, following an original authorization for one year and an extension for three more years.

Cases of Non-Consummation

Pope Paul VI promulgated May 31, 1972, norms designed to speed up the handling of cases involving questions about the validity of marriages entered legally but never consummated sexually. The regulations which went into effect July 1, granted local bishops powers previously reserved to the Holy See.

Accordingly local bishops can initiate procedures in cases of this type; testimony and documents are acceptable in any modern language and on tape; physical proof of non-consummation can be omitted if the bishop is satisfied with the statements of the parties and/or witnesses; the number of witnesses is left to the discretion of the bishop.

PASTORAL MINISTRY FOR DIVORCED AND REMARRIED

Ministry to divorced and remarried Catholics is a difficult field of pastoral endeavor, situated as it is in circumstances tantamount to the horns of a dilemma.

At Issue

On the one side is firm church teaching on the permanence of marriage and norms against reception of the Eucharist and full participation in the life of the Church by Catholics in irregular unions.

On the other side are men and women with broken unions followed by second and perhaps happier attempts at marriage which the Church does not recognize as valid and which may not be capable of being validated because of the existence of an earlier marriage bond.

The forces at work in these circumstances are those of the Church, upholding its doctrine and practice regarding the permanence of marriage, and those of many men and women in irregular second marriages who desire full participation in the life of the Church.

Sacramental participation is not possible for those whose first marriage was valid, although there is no bar to their attendance at Mass, to sharing in other activities of the Church, or to their efforts to have children baptized and raised in the Catholic faith.

An exception to this rule is the condition of a divorced and remarried couple living in a brother-sister relationship.

There is no ban against sacramental participation by separated or divorced persons who have not attempted a second marriage.

Unverified estimates of the number of U.S. Catholics who are divorced and remarried vary between three and five million.

Tribunal Action

What can the Church do for them and with them in pastoral ministry, is an old question charged with new urgency because of the rising number of divorced and remarried Catholics.

One way to help is through the agency of marriage tribunals charged with responsibility for investigating and settling questions concerning the validity or invalidity of a prior marriage. There are reasons in canon law justifying the Church in declaring a particular marriage null and void from the beginning, despite the short- or long-term existence of an apparently valid union.

Decrees of nullity are not new in the history of the Church. If such a decree is issued, a man or woman is free to validate a second marriage and live in complete union with the Church.

Canonist L. Mason Knox, writing in the Oct. 16, 1976, edition of *America,* reported that 442 formal decisions, of which 338 were declarations of nullity, were issued by U.S.

tribunals in 1968. Following adoption of the American Procedural Norms (see Procedural Rules) in 1970, the number of formal decisions rose in 1974 to 9,293, of which about 80 to 90 per cent were declarations of nullity. Similar decisions were rendered the same year in other canonical processes on grounds of: defect of form (15,722), papal dispensation for non-consummation (120), Pauline Privilege (691), Privilege of Faith (1,761), summary procedure (1,331).

U.S. tribunals handed down approximately 25,000 decisions in 1978.

The increase in the number of declarations of nullity is a result not just of new procedures but also, and more significantly, of tribunal judgments regarding the radical incapability of persons to contract valid marriage in the first place.

Reasons behind Decrees

Pastoral experience reveals that some married persons, a short or long time after contracting an apparently valid marriage, exhibit signs that point back to the existence, at the time of marriage, of latent and serious personal deficiencies which made them incapable of valid consent and sacramental commitment.

Such deficiencies might include gross immaturity and those affecting in a serious way the capacity to love, to have a true interpersonal and conjugal relationship, to fulfill marital obligations, to accept the faith aspect of marriage.

Psychological and behavioral factors like these have been given greater attention by tribunals in recent years and have provided grounds for numerous decrees of nullity.

Decisions of this type do not indicate any softening of the Church's attitude regarding the permanence of marriage. They affirm, rather, that some persons who have married were really not capable of doing so.

Serious deficiencies in the capacity for real interpersonal relationship in marriage were the reasons behind a landmark decree of nullity issued in 1973 by the Roman Rota, the Vatican high court of appeals in marriage cases.

Decree Not Always Possible

The tribunal way to a decree of nullity regarding a previous marriage is not open to many persons in second marriages — because grounds are either lacking or, if present, cannot be verified in tribunal process.

Many men and women in this second category are aligned with and in sympathy with aims of the North American Conference of Separated and Divorced Catholics, which has several hundred support groups in various parts of the United States and Canada. Formed early in 1972, the conference seeks a special pastoral ministry for divorced Catholics in second irregular unions.

This purpose is shared by the Judeans (founded in 1952) and by official ministries in many U.S. dioceses, by other church agencies and by hosts of priests.

The principal problem involved in such ministry is the degree of sacramental participation open to persons in irregular unions.

Unacceptable Solution

The Congregation for the Doctrine of the Faith advised bishops throughout the world in August, 1973, against one solution of the problem called "good conscience procedure." This involves administration of the sacraments of penance and the Eucharist to divorced and remarried Catholics unable to obtain a decree of nullity for a first marriage who are living in a subsequent marriage "in good faith."

This procedure, despite the fact that it has no standing or recognition in church law, is being advocated and practiced by some priests and remarried Catholics.

MARRIAGE ENCOUNTER

Marriage Encounter originated in Spain through the efforts of Father Gabriel Calvo who worked out its principal features between the early 1950s and 1962 with the collaboration of Diego and Fina Bartoneo and other parties interested in ministry to married couples. Along with Charismatic Renewal, it has been called one of the fastest growing contemporary movements in the Church, with an estimated participation of one and one-half to two million couples in more than 50 countries.

The first encounter was held with 28 couples in 1962 in Barcelona. Five years later the first encounter in the U.S. was conducted in conjunction with a convention of the Christian Family Movement at Notre Dame University. Marriage Encounter caught on from this beginning and went nationwide in 1969. Since then, it has developed in two different forms.

Two Forms

National Marriage Encounter is a component of International Marriage Encounter. It is in direct line with the program and movement initiated by Father Calvo and is conducted in accord with guidelines adopted in 1977 by the general assembly of the International Confederation of Christian Family Movements. Its stated purpose is the enhancement and growth of marriage and family relationships.

The executive team of Paul and Margaret Tepper (3021 Runnymede Dr., Norristown, Pa. 19401) and Msgr. Thoralf T. Thielen (Pontifical College Josephinum, Worthington, O. 43085) services approximately 150 groups in the U.S., Canada, the Bahamas, Bermuda, Ireland, Japan and Venezuela.

The international secretariat team consists of Jerry and Marilyn Sexton and Father Tom Hill, O.F.M. Cap., with an address at 955 Lake Dr., St. Paul, Minn. 55120. Their selection, after being nominated by Father Calvo, was announced in 1980 by Roland and Isabelle Leroux of Ottawa, president couple of the International Confederation of Christian Family Movements.

Worldwide Marriage Encounter was formed in the late 1960s and early 1970s by a group that broke away from National Marriage Encounter, changing both the purpose and content of the program. The executive team consists of Tom and Jayne McGuiness and Rev. Robert A. Uzzilio. Headquarters are located at 3711 Long Beach Blvd., Suite 204, Long Beach, Calif. 90807. An international council services the movement in 46 countries.

Marriage Encounter brings couples together for a 44-hour weekend directed by an already encountered team of several couples and a priest, for the purpose of developing their abilities to communicate with each other in their life together as husband and wife. This purpose is served by direction in techniques given by the team and by private dialogue of each couple. Subjects of the dialogue extend to the whole range of personal and marital concerns. The anticipated result is the enrichment of all personal-marital relationships.

This real communication and sharing by husband and wife, spurred by the encounter and open to development by subsequent daily dialogue between them, is the positive substance of the movement.

The composition of Marriage Encounter groups for the encounter varies; some of them are exclusively Catholic while others have participants of different religious, professional or other special-interest affiliations.

Commentators insist that Marriage Encounter is not for troubled marriages and is not an exercise in group dynamics. Neither is it a retreat, although it has potential for spiritual development.

The identifying logo or emblem of Marriage Encounter consists of wedding bands intertwining a cross and surmounted by a red heart.

Engaged Encounter: A development from Marriage Encounter, designed to facilitate and deepen the communication potential of couples intending to marry. With appropriate modifications, it follows the pattern of the Marriage Encounter weekend and subsequent practice of dialogue. The movement is served by a national executive team consisting of Ron and Donna Adamo of Aptos, Calif., and Rev. Robert Harrington of Westfield, N.J.

The Church Calendar

The calendar of the Roman Church consists of an arrangement throughout the year of a series of liturgical seasons and feasts of saints for purposes of divine worship.

The purposes of this calendar were outlined in the *Constitution on the Sacred Liturgy* (Nos. 102-105) promulgated by the Second Vatican Council.

"Within the cycle of a year ... (the Church) unfolds the whole mystery of Christ, not only from His incarnation and birth until His ascension, but also as reflected in the day of Pentecost, and the expectation of a blessed, hoped-for return of the Lord.

"Recalling thus the mysteries of redemption, the Church opens to the faithful the riches of her Lord's powers and merits, so that these are in some way made present at all times, and the faithful are enabled to lay hold of them and become filled with saving grace" (No. 102).

"In celebrating this annual cycle of Christ's mysteries, holy Church honors with special love the Blessed Mary, Mother of God ..." (No. 103).

"The Church has also included in the annual cycle days devoted to the memory of the martyrs and the other saints. . . . (who) sing God's perfect praise in heaven and offer prayers for us. By celebrating the passage of these saints from earth to heaven the Church proclaims the paschal mystery as achieved in the saints who have suffered and been glorified with Christ; she proposes them to the faithful as examples who draw all to the Father through Christ, and through their merits she pleads for God's favors" (No. 104).

". . . In the various seasons of the year and according to her traditional discipline, the Church completes the formation of the faithful by means of pious practices for soul and body, by instruction, prayer, and works of penance and mercy. . ." (No. 105).

THE NEW CALENDAR

Pope Paul VI announced May 9, 1969, his approval of a reorganization of the liturgical year and calendar for the Roman Rite, in implementation of a directive from the Second Vatican Council in 1964. He made the announcement in a document issued on his own initiative and entitled *Paschalis Mysterii*.

The purpose of the action, the Pope said, was "no other . . . than to permit the faithful to communicate in a more intense way, through faith, hope and love, in 'the whole mystery of Christ which ... unfolds within the cycle of a year.' "

The *motu proprio* was dated Feb. 14, 1969. The new calendar was promulgated a month later by a decree of the Congregation for Divine Worship and went into effect Jan. 1, 1970, with provisional modifications. Full implementation of all its parts was delayed in 1970 and 1971, pending the completion of

work on related liturgical texts. The U.S. bishops ordered the whole new calendar into effect for 1972.

The Seasons

Advent: The liturgical year begins with the First Sunday of Advent, which introduces a season of four weeks or slightly less duration with the theme of expectation of the coming of Christ. During the first two weeks, the final coming of Christ as Lord and Judge at the end of the world is the focus of attention. From Dec. 17 to 24, the emphasis shifts to anticipation of the celebration of his Nativity on the Solemnity of Christmas.

Advent has four Sundays. Since the 10th century, the first Sunday has marked the beginning of the liturgical year in the Western Church. In the Middle Ages, a kind of pre-Christmas fast was in vogue during the season.

Christmastide: Christmastide opens with the Solemnity of the Nativity, Dec. 25, and lasts until the Sunday after Epiphany. The Holy Family is commemorated on the Sunday within the Christmas octave. Jan. 1 — formerly called the Octave Day of the Nativity and, before that, the feast of the Circumcision of Jesus — has the title of Solemnity of Mary the Mother of God. The Epiphany, scheduled for Jan. 6 in the universal calendar, is celebrated in the U.S. on the Sunday between Jan. 2 and 8. The Baptism of the Lord, observed on the Sunday following Epiphany, marks the end of Christmastide.

The period between the end of Christmastide and the beginning of Lent belongs to the Ordinary Time of the year. Of variable length, the pre-Lenten phase of this season includes what were formerly called the Sundays after Epiphany and the suppressed Sundays of Septuagesima, Sexagesima and Quinquagesima.

Lent: The penitential season of Lent begins on Ash Wednesday, which occurs between Feb. 4 and Mar. 11, depending on the date of Easter, and lasts until Easter. It has six Sundays and 40 weekdays. The climactic last week is called Holy Week. The last three days (Holy Thursday, Good Friday and Holy Saturday) are called the Paschal Triduum.

The origin of Lenten observances dates back to the fourth century or earlier.

Eastertide: Eastertide, whose theme is resurrection from sin to the life of grace, lasts for 50 days, from Easter to Pentecost. Easter, the first Sunday following the vernal equinox, occurs between Mar. 22 and Apr. 25. The terminal phase of Eastertide, between the Solemnities of the Ascension of the Lord and Pentecost, stresses anticipation of the coming and action of the Holy Spirit.

Ordinary Time: The season of Ordinary Time of the year includes not only the period between the end of Christmastide and the beginning of Lent, as noted above, but also all Sundays after Pentecost to the last Sunday of the liturgical year, which is celebrated as the feast of Christ the King. The number of Sundays before Lent and after Pentecost varies, depending on the date of the key feast of Easter. The overall purpose of the season is to elaborate the themes of salvation history.

The various liturgical seasons are characterized in part by the scriptural readings and Mass prayers assigned to each of them. During Advent, for example, the readings are messianic; during Eastertide, from the Acts of the Apostles, chronicling the Resurrection and the original proclamation of Christ by the Apostles, and from the Gospel of John; during Lent, baptismal and penitential passages. Mass prayers reflect the meaning and purpose of the various seasons.

Feasts of Saints

The feasts of saints are celebrated concurrently with the liturgical seasons and feasts of our Lord. Their purpose is to illustrate the paschal mysteries as reflected in the lives of saints, to honor them as heroes of holiness, and to appeal for their intercession.

In line with revised regulations, some former feasts have been either abolished or relegated to observance in particular places by local option for one of two reasons: (1) lack of sufficient historical evidence for observance of the feasts; (2) lack of universal significance.

The feast of a saint, as a general rule, is observed on the day of his death (*dies natalis,* day of birth to glory with God in heaven). Exceptions to this rule include the feasts of St. John the Baptist, who is honored on the day of his birth; Sts. Basil the Great and Gregory Nazianzen, and the brother Saints, Cyril and Methodius, who are commemorated in joint feasts.

Application of this general rule in the revised calendar resulted in date changes of some feasts.

Sundays and Feast Days

Sunday is the original Christian feast day because of the unusually significant events of salvation history which took place and are commemorated on the first day of the week — viz., the Resurrection of Christ, the key event of his life and the fundamental fact of Christianity; and the descent of the Holy Spirit upon the Apostles on Pentecost, the birthday of the Church. The transfer of observance of the Lord's Day from the Sabbath to Sunday was made in apostolic times. The Mass and Liturgy of the Hours (Divine Office) of each Sunday reflect the themes and set the tones of the various liturgical seasons.

Categories of feasts according to dignity and manner of observance are: solemnity (highest, corresponding to former first-class feasts); feast (corresponding to former second-class feasts); memorial (corresponding to former third-class feasts); optional memorial (observable by local choice). Feasts of the first three categories are observed universally in the Roman Rite.

Fixed feasts are those which are regularly celebrated on the same calendar day each year.

Movable feasts are those which are not observed on the same calendar day each year. Examples of these are Easter (the first Sunday after the first full moon following the vernal equinox), Ascension (40 days after Easter), Pentecost (50 days after Easter), Trinity Sunday (first after Pentecost), Christ the King (last Sunday of the liturgical year).

Holy Days of Obligation

Holy days of obligation are special feasts on which Catholics who have reached the age of reason are seriously obliged, as on Sundays, to assist at Mass and to avoid unnecessary servile work. Serious reasons excuse from the observance of either or both of these obligations.

By enactment of the Third Plenary Council of Baltimore, and with the approval of the Holy See, the holy days of obligation observed in the United States are: Christmas, the Nativity of Jesus, Dec. 25; Solemnity of Mary the Mother of God, Jan. 1; Ascension of the Lord; Assumption of Blessed Mary the Virgin, Aug. 15; All Saints' Day, Nov. 1; Immaculate Conception of Blessed Mary the Virgin, Dec. 8.

In addition to these, there are four other holy days of obligation prescribed in the general law of the Church which are not so observed in the U.S.: Epiphany; St. Joseph, Mar. 19; Corpus Christi; Sts. Peter and Paul, June 29.

Weekdays, Days of Prayer

Weekdays are those on which no proper feast or vigil is celebrated in the Mass or Liturgy of the Hours (Divine Office). On such days, the Mass may be that of the preceding Sunday, which expresses the liturgical spirit of the season, an optional memorial, a votive Mass, or a Mass for the dead. Weekdays of Advent and Lent are in a special category of their own.

Days of prayer: Dioceses, at times to be designated by local bishops, should observe "days or periods of prayer for the fruits of the earth, prayer for human rights and equality, prayer for world justice and peace, and penitential observance outside of Lent." So states the *Instruction on Particular Calendars* (No. 331) issued by the Congregation for the Sacraments and Divine Worship June 24, 1970.

These days are contemporary equivalents of what were formerly called ember and rogation days.

Ember days originated at Rome about the fifth century, probably as Christian replacements for seasonal festivals of agrarian cults. They were observances of penance, thanksgiving, and petition for divine blessing on the various seasons; they also were occasions of special prayer for clergy to be ordained. These days were observed four times a year.

Rogation days originated in France about the fifth century. They were penitential in character and also occasions of prayer for a bountiful harvest and protection against evil.

Days of Abstinence and Fast

The apostolic constitution *Paenitemini*, in effect since Feb. 23, 1966, authorized the substitution of other works of penance for the customary and common observances of abstinence and fast on various days of the year.

In this country, in line with provisions of the constitution and a 1974 decision of the National Conference of Catholic Bishops, Ash Wednesday and Good Friday are days of fast and abstinence, and all Fridays of Lent are days of abstinence.

The obligation to abstain from meat binds Catholics 14 years of age and older. The obligation to fast, limiting oneself to one full meal and two lighter meals in the course of a day, binds Catholics from the ages of 21 to 59.

BYZANTINE CALENDAR

As in the Roman usage, the dating of feasts follows the Gregorian Calendar. Formerly, until well into this century, the Julian Calendar was used. (The Julian Calendar, which is now about 13 days late, is still used by some Eastern-Rite Churches.)

The year has several cycles, which include proper seasons, the feasts of saints, and series of New Testament readings. All of these elements of worship are contained in liturgical books of the rite.

The ecclesiastical calendar, called the **Menologion**, explains the nature of feasts, other observances and matters pertaining to the liturgy for each day of the year. In some cases, its contents include the lives of saints and the history and meaning of feasts.

The Divine Liturgy (Mass) and Divine Office for the proper of the saints, fixed feasts, and the Christmas season are contained in the **Menaion**. The **Triodion** covers the pre-Lenten season of preparation for Easter; Lent begins two days before the Ash Wednesday observance of the Roman Rite. The **Pentecostarion** contains the liturgical services from Easter to the Sunday of All Saints, the first after Pentecost. The **Evangelion** and **Apostolos** are books in which the Gospels, and Acts of the Apostles and the Epistles, respectively, are arranged according to the order of their reading in the Divine Liturgy and Divine Office throughout the year.

The cyclic progression of liturgical music throughout the year, in successive and repetitive periods of eight weeks, is governed by the **Oktoechos**, the Book of Eight Tones.

Sunday Names

Many Sundays are named after the subject of the Gospel read in the Mass of the day or after the name of a feast falling on the day — e.g., Sunday of the Publican and Pharisee, of the Prodigal Son, of the Samaritan Woman, of St. Thomas the Apostle, of the Fore-Fathers (Old Testament Patriarchs). Other Sundays are named in the same manner as in the Roman calendar — e.g., numbered Sundays of Lent and after Pentecost.

Holy Days, Abstinence, Fast

The calendar lists about 28 holy days. Many of the major holy days coincide with those of the Roman calendar, but the feast of the Immaculate Conception is observed on Dec. 9 instead of Dec. 8, and the feast of All Saints falls on the Sunday after Pentecost rather than on Nov. 1. Instead of a single All Souls' Day, there are five All Souls' Saturdays.

According to regulations in effect in the Byzantine-Rite (Ruthenian) Archeparchy of Pittsburgh and its suffragan sees of Passaic and Parma, holy days are obligatory, solemn and simple, and attendance at the Divine Liturgy is required on five obligatory days — the feasts of the Epiphany, the Ascension, Sts. Peter and Paul, the Assumption of the Blessed Virgin Mary, and Christmas. Although attendance at the liturgy is not obligatory on 15 solemn and seven simple holy days, it is recommended.

In the Byzantine-Rite (Ukrainian) Archeparchy of Philadelphia and its suffragan sees of St. Nicholas (Chicago) and Stamford, the obligatory feasts are the Circumcision, Epiphany, Annunciation, Easter, Ascension, Pentecost, Dormition (Assumption of Mary), Immaculate Conception and Christmas.

Lent

The first day of Lent — the Monday before Ash Wednesday of the Roman Rite — and Good Friday are days of strict abstinence for persons between the ages of 21 and 59. No meat, eggs, or dairy products may be eaten on these days.

All persons over the age of 14 must abstain from meat on Fridays during Lent, Holy Saturday, and the vigils of the feasts of Christmas and Epiphany; abstinence is urged, but is not obligatory, on Wednesdays of Lent. The abstinence obligation is not in force on certain "free" or "privileged" Fridays.

Synaxis

An observance without a counterpart in the Roman calendar is the synaxis. This is a commemoration, on the day following a feast, of persons involved with the occasion for the feast — e.g., Sept. 9, the day following the feast of the Nativity of the Blessed Virgin Mary, is the Synaxis of Joachim and Anna, her parents.

JANUARY 1981

1—Thurs. **Solemnity of Mary, Mother of God. Holy day of obligation.** (Nm. 6:22-27; Gal. 4:4-7; Lk. 2:16-21.)

2—Fri. Sts. Basil the Great and Gregory Nazianzen, bishops-doctors; memorial.

3—Sat. Weekday.

4—**Sun. Epiphany of the Lord (in U.S.); solemnity.** (Is. 60:1-6; Eph. 3:2-3a, 5-6; Mt. 2:1-12.) [St. Elizabeth Seton; memorial in U.S.]

5—Mon. St. John Neumann, bishop; memorial (in U.S.).

6—Tues. Weekday (in U.S.).

7—Wed. St. Raymond of Penyafort, priest; optional memorial.

8—Thurs. Weekday.

9—Fri. Weekday.

10—Sat. Weekday.

11—**Sun. Baptism of the Lord; feast.** (Is. 42:1-4, 6-7; Acts 10:34-38; Mt. 3:13-17.)

12—Mon. Weekday. (First Week of the Year.)

13—Tues. St. Hilary, bishop-doctor; optional memorial.

14—Wed. Weekday.

15—Thurs. Weekday.

16—Fri. Weekday.

17—Sat. St. Anthony, Abbot; memorial.

18—**Second Sunday of the Year.** (Is. 49:3, 5-6; 1 Cor. 1:1-3; Jn. 1:29-34.) Beginning of the annual observance of the Week of Prayer for Christian Unity.

19—Mon. Weekday.

20—Tues. St. Fabian, pope-martyr, or St. Sebastian, martyr; optional memorials.

21—Wed. St. Agnes, virgin-martyr; memorial.

22—Thurs. Weekday. St. Vincent, deacon-martyr; memorial.

23—Fri. Weekday.

24—Sat. St. Francis de Sales, bishop-doctor; memorial.

25—**Third Sunday of the Year.** (Is. 8:23b to 9:3; 1 Cor. 1:10-13, 17; Mt. 4:12-23.) [Conversion of St. Paul, apostle; feast.]

26—Mon. Sts. Timothy and Titus, bishops; memorial.

27—Tues. Weekday. St. Angela Merici, virgin; optional memorial.

28—Wed. St. Thomas Aquinas, priest-doctor; memorial.

29—Thurs. Weekday.

30—Fri. Weekday.

31—Sat. St. John Bosco, priest; memorial.

GENERAL PRAYER INTENTION: That all gifts bestowed on Christians, whether of nature or of grace, may contribute to the common welfare toward the unity of Christ's body.

MISSION PRAYER INTENTION: That the children's pious custom of praying and of offering their daily lives for the missions may be more known and practiced.

FEBRUARY 1981

1—**Fourth Sunday of the Year.** (Zep. 2:3 and 3:12-13; 1 Cor. 1:26-31; Mt. 5:1-12a.)

2—Mon. Presentation of the Lord; feast.

3—Tues. Weekday. St. Blase, bishop-martyr, or St. Ansgar, bishop; optional memorials.

4—Wed. Weekday.

5—Thurs. St. Agatha, virgin-martyr; memorial.

6—Fri. Sts. Paul Miki and Companions, martyrs; memorial.

7—Sat. Weekday.

8—**Fifth Sunday of the Year.** (Is. 58:7-10; 1 Cor. 2:1-5; Mt. 5:13-16.) [St. Jerome Emiliani; optional memorial.]

9—Mon. Weekday.

10—Tues. St. Scholastica, virgin; memorial.

11—Wed. Weekday. Our Lady of Lourdes; optional memorial.

12—Thurs. Weekday.

13—Fri. Weekday.

14—Sat. Sts. Cyril, monk, and Methodius, bishop; memorial.

15—**Sixth Sunday of the Year.** (Sir. 15:15-20; 1 Cor. 2:6-10; Mt. 5:17-37.)

16—Mon. Weekday.

17—Tues. Weekday. Seven Holy Founders of the Servite Order; optional memorial.

18—Wed. Weekday.

19—Thurs. Weekday.

20—Fri. Weekday.

21—Sat. Weekday. St. Peter Damien, bishop-doctor; optional memorial.

22—**Seventh Sunday of the Year.** (Lv. 19:1-2, 17-18; 1 Cor. 3:16-23; Mt. 5:38-48.) [Chair of Peter, apostle; feast.]

23—Mon. St. Polycarp, bishop-martyr; memorial.

24—Tues. Weekday.

25—Wed. Weekday.

26—Thurs. Weekday.

27—Fri. Weekday.

28—Sat. Weekday.

GENERAL PRAYER INTENTION: That the handicapped may grow strong enough to place themselves suitably in civil society.

MISSION PRAYER INTENTION: That young Christians of the older churches may give real help to handicapped children in the younger churches.

(Cardinal George Basil Hume of Westminster, England, speaking in May, 1980, in New York, expressed hope that during the 1981 International Year of the Handicapped "there will be a universal reappraisal of our approach to people with handicaps and universal effort to integrate them in practical ways with the rest of the worshipping community." He called the handicapped "God's special friends called to share more closely in the Passion of our Lord.")

MARCH 1981

1—**Eighth Sunday of the Year.** (Is. 49:14-15; 1 Cor. 4:1-5; Mt. 6:24-34.)
2—Mon. Weekday.
3—Tues. Weekday.
4—Ash Wednesday. Beginning of Lent. *Fast and abstinence.* Ashes are blessed on this day and imposed on the forehead of the faithful to remind them of their obligation to do penance for sin and to seek spiritual renewal by means of prayer, fasting, good works, and by bearing with patience and for God's purposes the trials and difficulties of everyday life. [St. Casimir; optional memorial.]
5—Thurs. Weekday of Lent.
6—Fri. Weekday of Lent. *Abstinence.*
7—Sat. Weekday of Lent. [Sts. Perpetua and Felicity, martyrs; memorial.]
8—**First Sunday of Lent.** (Gn. 2:7-9 and 3:1-7; Rom. 5:12-19; Mt. 4:1-11.) [St. John of God, religious; optional memorial.]
9—Mon. Weekday of Lent. [St. Frances of Rome, religious; optional memorial.]
10—Tues. Weekday of Lent.
11—Wed. Weekday of Lent.
12—Thurs. Weekday of Lent.
13—Fri. Weekday of Lent. *Abstinence.*
14—Sat. Weekday of Lent.
15—**Second Sunday of Lent.** (Gn. 12:1-4a; 2 Tm. 1:8b-10; Mt. 17:1-9.)
16—Mon. Weekday of Lent.
17—Tues. Weekday of Lent. [St. Patrick, bishop; optional memorial.]
18—Wed. Weekday of Lent. [St. Cyril of Jerusalem, bishop-doctor; optional memorial.]
19—Thurs. St. Joseph; solemnity. Weekday of Lent.
20—Fri. Weekday of Lent. *Abstinence.*
21—Sat. Weekday of Lent.
22—**Third Sunday of Lent.** (Ex. 17:3-7; Rom. 5:1-2, 5-8; Jn. 4:5-42.)
23—Mon. Weekday of Lent. [St. Turibius, bishop; optional memorial.]
24—Tues. Weekday of Lent.
25—Wed. Annunciation; solemnity. Weekday of Lent.
26—Thurs. Weekday of Lent.
27—Fri. Weekday of Lent. *Abstinence.*
28—Sat. Weekday of Lent.
29—**Fourth Sunday of Lent.** (1 Sm. 16:1b, 6-7, 10-13a; Eph. 5:8-14; Jn. 9:1-41.)
30—Mon. Weekday of Lent.
31—Tues. Weekday of Lent.

GENERAL PRAYER INTENTION: That Christians may more frequently and fruitfully approach the sacrament of reconciliation.
MISSION PRAYER INTENTION: For the Church in Equatorial Guinea (where the resumption of missionary work got underway in August, 1979).

APRIL 1981

1—Wed. Weekday of Lent.
2—Thurs. Weekday of Lent. [St. Francis of Paola, hermit; optional memorial.]
3—Fri. Weekday of Lent. *Abstinence.*
4—Sat. Weekday of Lent. [St. Isidore of Seville, bishop-doctor; optional memorial.]
5—**Fifth Sunday of Lent.** (Ez. 37:12-14; Rom. 8:8-11; Jn. 11:1-45.) [St. Vincent Ferrer, priest; optional memorial.]
6—Mon. Weekday of Lent.
7—Tues. Weekday of Lent. [St. John Baptist de la Salle, priest; memorial.]
8—Wed. Weekday of Lent.
9—Thurs. Weekday of Lent.
10—Fri. Weekday of Lent. *Abstinence.*
11—Sat. Weekday of Lent. [St. Stanislaus, bishop-martyr; memorial.]
12—**Sunday of the Passion (Palm Sunday).** (Procession — Mt. 21:1-11. Mass. — Is. 50:4-7; Phil. 2:6-11; Matt. 26:14 to 27:66.)
13—Monday of Holy Week. [St. Martin I, pope-martyr; optional memorial.]
14—Tuesday of Holy Week.
15—Wednesday of Holy Week.
16—Thursday of Holy Week. Holy Thursday. The Paschal Triduum begins with the evening Mass of the Supper of the Lord.
17—Friday of the Passion of the Lord. Good Friday. *Fast and abstinence.*
18—Holy Saturday. The Easter Vigil.
19—**Easter Sunday; solemnity.** (Acts 10:34a, 37-43; 2 Col. 3:1-4 or 1 Cor. 5:6b-8; Jn. 20:1-9 or Mt. 28:1-10 or (Evening) Luke 24:13-35.)
20—Monday of Easter Octave.
21—Tuesday of Easter Octave. [St. Anselm, bishop-doctor; optional memorial.]
22—Wednesday of Easter Octave.
23—Thursday of Easter Octave. [St. George, martyr; optional memorial.]
24—Friday of Easter Octave. [St. Fidelis of Sigmaringen, priest-martyr; optional memorial.]
25—Saturday of Easter Octave. [St. Mark, evangelist; feast.]
26—**Second Sunday of Easter.** (Acts 2:42-47; 1 Pt. 1:3-9; Jn. 20:19-31.)
27—Mon. Weekday.
28—Tues. Weekday. St. Peter Chanel, priest-martyr; optional memorial.
29—Wed. St. Catherine of Siena, virgin-doctor; memorial.
30—Thurs. Weekday. St. Pius V, pope; optional memorial.

GENERAL PRAYER INTENTION: That young people may be true witnesses to Christ and respond with love to his call.
MISSION PRAYER INTENTION: That missionary vocations in Latin America may multiply.

MAY 1981

1—Fri. Weekday. St. Joseph the Worker; optional memorial.

2—Sat. St. Athanasius, bishop-doctor; memorial.

3—**Third Sunday of Easter.** (Acts 2:14, 22-28; 1 Pt. 1:17-21; Lk. 24:13-35.) [Sts. Philip and James, apostles; feast.]

4—Mon. Weekday.

5—Tues. Weekday.

6—Wed. Weekday.

7—Thurs. Weekday.

8—Fri. Weekday.

9—Sat. Weekday.

10—**Fourth Sunday of Easter.** (Acts 2:14a, 36-41; 1 Pt. 2:20b-25; Jn. 10:1-10.)

11—Mon. Weekday.

12—Tues. Weekday. Sts. Nereus and Achilleus, martyrs, or St. Pancras, martyr; optional memorials.

13—Wed. Weekday.

14—Thurs. St. Matthias, apostle; feast.

15—Fri. Weekday. St. Isidore the Farmer; optional memorial (in U.S.).

16—Sat. Weekday.

17—**Fifth Sunday of Easter.** (Acts 6:1-7; 1 Pt. 2:4-9; Jn. 14:1-12.)

18—Mon. Weekday. St. John I, pope-martyr; optional memorial.

19—Tues. Weekday.

20—Wed. Weekday. St. Bernardine of Siena, priest; optional memorial.

21—Thurs. Weekday.

22—Fri. Weekday.

23—Sat. Weekday.

24—**Sixth Sunday of Easter.** (Acts 8:5-8, 14-17; 1 Pt. 3:15-18; Jn. 14:15-21.)

25—Mon. Weekday. St. Bede the Venerable, priest-doctor, or St. Gregory VII, pope, or St. Mary Magdalene de Pazzi, virgin; optional memorials.

26—Tues. St. Philip Neri, priest; memorial.

27—Wed. Weekday. St. Augustine of Canterbury, bishop; optional memorial.

28—Thurs. Ascension of the Lord; solemnity. Holy day of obligation. (Acts 1:1-11; Eph. 1:17-23; Mt. 28:16-20.)

29—Fri. Weekday.

30—Sat. Weekday.

31—**Seventh Sunday of Easter.** (Acts 1:12-14; 1 Pt. 4:13-16; Jn. 17:1-11a.) [Visitation of Blessed Mary the Virgin; feast.]

GENERAL PRAYER INTENTION: That we may learn to esteem more highly and to enjoy more earnestly the friendship of Jesus who also loves us with a human heart.

MISSION PRAYER INTENTION: That, through a filial love of the Blessed Virgin Mary, Mother of the Church, the fruitfulness of the new churches may increase. (Traditionally, May as been dedicated to the honor of Mary.)

JUNE 1981

1—Mon. St. Justin, martyr; memorial.

2—Tues. Weekday. Sts. Marcellinus and Peter, martyrs; optional memorial.

3—Wed. Sts. Charles Lwanga and Companions, martyrs; memorial.

4—Thurs. Weekday.

5—Fri. St. Boniface, bishop-martyr; memorial.

6—Sat. Weekday. St. Norbert, bishop; optional memorial.

7—**Sun. Pentecost; solemnity.** (Acts 2:1-11; 1 Cor. 12:3b-7, 12-13; Jn. 20:19-23.)

8—Mon. Weekday. (Tenth Week of the Year.)

9—Tues. Weekday. St. Ephraem, deacon-doctor; optional memorial.

10—Wed. Weekday.

11—Thurs. St. Barnabas, apostle; memorial.

12—Fri. Weekday.

13—Sat. St. Anthony of Padua, priest-doctor; memorial.

14—**Trinity Sunday; solemnity.** (Ex. 34:4b-6, 8-9; 2 Cor. 13:11-13; Jn. 3:16-18.)

15—Mon. Weekday. (Eleventh Week of the Year.)

16—Tues. Weekday.

17—Wed. Weekday.

18—Thurs. Weekday.

19—Fri. Weekday. St. Romuald, abbot; optional memorial.

20—Sat. Weekday.

21—**Sun. Corpus Christi (in U.S.); solemnity.** (Dt. 8:2-3, 14b-16a; 1 Cor. 10:16-17; Jn. 6:51-58.) [St. Aloysius Gonzaga, religious; memorial.]

22—Mon. Weekday. St. Paulinus of Nola, bishop, or Sts. John Fisher, bishop-martyr, and Thomas More, martyr, optional memorials. (Twelfth Week of the Year.)

23—Tues. Weekday.

24—Wed. Birth of St. John the Baptist; solemnity.

25—Thurs. Weekday.

26—Fri. Sacred Heart of Jesus; solemnity.

27—Sat. Weekday. Immaculate Heart of Mary, or St. Cyril of Alexandria, bishop-doctor; optional memorials.

28—**Thirteenth Sunday of the Year.** (2 Kgs. 4:8-11, 14-16a; Rom. 6:3-4, 8-11; Mt. 10:37-42.) [St. Irenaeus, bishop-martyr; memorial.]

29—Mon. Sts. Peter and Paul, apostles; solemnity.

30—Tues. Weekday. First Martyrs of the Roman Church; optional memorial.

GENERAL PRAYER INTENTION: That young people may reject a false, drug-induced liberty.

MISSION PRAYER INTENTION: That all who need fraternal help, whether refugees or not, may actually receive it, especially those in Southeast Asia (where the concentration of refugees is enormous).

JULY 1981

1—Wed. Weekday.
2—Thurs. Weekday.
3—Fri. St. Thomas, apostle; feast.
4—Sat. Weekday. St. Elizabeth of Portugal; optional memorial. Independence Day Votive Mass (in U.S.).
5—**Fourteenth Sunday of the Year.** (Zec. 9:9-10; Rom. 8:9, 11-13; Mt. 11:25-30.) [St. Anthony Mary Zaccaria, priest; optional memorial.]
6—Mon. Weekday. St. Maria Goretti, virgin-martyr; optional memorial.
7—Tues. Weekday.
8—Wed. Weekday.
9—Thurs. Weekday.
10—Fri. Weekday.
11—Sat. St. Benedict, abbot; memorial.
12—**Fifteenth Sunday of the Year.** (Is. 55:10-11; Rom. 8:18-23; Mt. 13:1-23.)
13—Mon. Weekday. St. Henry; optional memorial.
14—Tues. Weekday. St. Camillus de Lellis, priest; optional memorial.
15—Wed. St. Bonaventure, bishop-doctor; memorial.
16—Thurs. Weekday. Our Lady of Mt. Carmel; optional memorial.
17—Fri. Weekday.
18—Sat. Weekday.
19—**Sixteenth Sunday of the Year.** (Wis. 12:13, 16-19; Rom. 8:26-27; Mt. 13:24-43.)
20—Mon. Weekday.
21—Tues. Weekday. St. Lawrence of Brindisi, priest-doctor; optional memorial.
22—Wed. St. Mary Magdalene; memorial.
23—Thurs. Weekday. St. Bridget, religious; optional memorial.
24—Fri. Weekday.
25—Sat. St. James, apostle; feast.
26—**Seventeenth Sunday of the Year.** (1 Kgs. 3:5, 7-12; Rom. 8:28-30; Mt. 13:44-52.) [Sts. Joachim and Anne, parents of Mary; memorial.]
27—Mon. Weekday.
28—Tues. Weekday.
29—Wed. St. Martha; memorial.
30—Thurs. Weekday. St. Peter Chrysologus, bishop-doctor; optional memorial.
31—Fri. St. Ignatius of Loyola, priest; memorial.

GENERAL PRAYER INTENTION: That Jesus Christ in the Eucharist may be considered as "bread broken for a new world." (The Second Vatican Council noted in its *Decree on the Life and Ministry of Priests:* "No Christian community (or world) can be built up unless it has its basis and center in the celebration of the Eucharist.")

MISSION PRAYER INTENTION: That the laity in the Indian Ocean islands may actively participate in the Church.

AUGUST 1981

1—Sat. St. Alphonsus Liguori, bishop-doctor; memorial.
2—**Eighteenth Sunday of the Year.** (Is. 55:1-3; Rom. 8:35, 37-39; Mt. 14:13-21.) [St. Eusebius of Vercelli, bishop; optional memorial.]
3—Mon. Weekday.
4—Tues. St. John Vianney, priest; memorial.
5—Wed. Weekday. Dedication of St. Mary Major Basilica; optional memorial.
6—Thurs. Transfiguration of the Lord; feast.
7—Fri. Weekday. Sts. Sixtus II, pope, and Companions, martyrs; or St. Cajetan, priest; optional memorials.
8—Sat. St. Dominic, priest; memorial.
9—**Nineteenth Sunday of the Year.** (1 Kgs. 19:9a, 11-13a; Rom. 9:1-5; Mt. 14:22-33.)
10—Mon. St. Lawrence, deacon-martyr; feast.
11—Tues. St. Clare, virgin; memorial.
12—Wed. Weekday.
13—Thurs. Weekday. Sts. Pontian, pope, and Hippolytus, priest, martyrs; optional memorial.
14—Fri. Weekday.
15—Sat. Assumption of Blessed Mary the Virgin; solemnity. Holy day of obligation. (Rv. 11:19a and 12:1-6a, 10ab; 1 Cor. 15:20-26; Lk. 1:39-56.)
16—**Twentieth Sunday of the Year.** (Is. 56:1, 6-7; Rom. 11:13-15, 29-32; Mt. 15:21-28.) [St. Stephen of Hungary; optional memorial.]
17—Mon. Weekday.
18—Tues. Weekday.
19—Wed. Weekday. St. John Eudes, priest; optional memorial.
20—Thurs. St. Bernard of Clairvaux, abbot-doctor; memorial.
21—Fri. St. Pius X, pope; memorial.
22—Sat. Queenship of Mary; memorial.
23—**Twenty-First Sunday of the Year.** (Is. 22:19-23; Rom. 11:33-36; Mt. 16:13-20.) [St. Rose of Lima, virgin; optional memorial.]
24—Mon. St. Bartholomew, apostle; feast.
25—Tues. Weekday. St. Louis, or St. Joseph Calasanz, priest; optional memorials.
26—Wed. Weekday.
27—Thurs. St. Monica; memorial.
28—Fri. St. Augustine, bishop-doctor; memorial.
29—Sat. Beheading of St. John the Baptist; memorial.
30—**Twenty-Second Sunday of the Year.** (Jer. 20:7-9; Rom. 12:1-2; Mt. 16:21-27.)
31—Mon. Weekday.

GENERAL AND MISSION INTENTIONS: That believers in God give witness to their faith. For mutual respect among Christians and Moslems.

SEPTEMBER 1981

1—Tues. Weekday.
2—Wed. Weekday.
3—Thurs. St. Gregory the Great, pope-doctor; memorial.
4—Fri. Weekday.
5—Sat. Weekday.
6—**Twenty-Third Sunday of the Year.** (Ez. 33:7-9; Rom. 13:8-10; Mt. 18:15-20.)
7—Mon. Weekday.
8—Tues. Birth of Mary; feast.
9—Wed. St. Peter Claver, priest; memorial (in U.S.). Weekday.
10—Thurs. Weekday.
11—Fri. Weekday.
12—Sat. Weekday.
13—**Twenty-Fourth Sunday of the Year.** (Sir. 27:30 to 28:7; Rom. 14:7-8; Mt. 18:21-35.) [St. John Chrysostom, bishopdoctor; memorial.]
14—Mon. Triumph of the Cross; feast.
15—Tues. Our Lady of Sorrows; memorial.
16—Wed. Sts. Cornelius, pope, and Cyprian, bishop, martyrs; memorial.
17—Thurs. Weekday. St. Robert Bellarmine, bishop-doctor; optional memorial.
18—Fri. Weekday.
19—Sat. Weekday. St. Januarius, bishopmartyr; optional memorial.
20—**Twenty-Fifth Sunday of the Year.** (Is. 55:6-9; Phil. 1:20c-24, 27a; Mt. 20:1-16a.)
21—Mon. St. Matthew, apostle-evangelist; feast.
22—Tues. Weekday.
23—Wed. Weekday.
24—Thurs. Weekday.
25—Fri. Weekday.
26—Sat. Weekday. Sts. Cosmas and Damian, martyrs; optional memorial.
27—**Twenty-Sixth Sunday of the Year.** (Ez. 18:25-28; Phil. 2:1-11; Mt. 21:28-32.) [St. Vincent de Paul, priest; memorial.]
28—Mon. Weekday. St. Wenceslaus, martyr; optional memorial.
29—Tues. Sts. Michael, Gabriel, Raphael, archangels; feast.
30—Wed. St. Jerome, priest-doctor; memorial.

GENERAL PRAYER INTENTION: That the right to religious liberty may be granted in fact to individuals and groups.
MISSION PRAYER INTENTION: That all legal discrimination may end in India, especially with respect to citizens belonging to groups known as "Backward Classes" ("Untouchables"), whether they are Christians or members of any other religion. (According to a report circulated early in September, 1980, 15 members of the Indian Parliament told Prime Minister Indira Ghandi that "in a few states the local governments have enacted laws making the preaching of religion a criminal offense.")

OCTOBER 1981

1—Thurs. St. Therese of the Child Jesus, virgin; memorial.
2—Fri. Guardian Angels; memorial.
3—Sat. Weekday.
4—**Twenty-Seventh Sunday of the Year.** (Is. 5:1-7; Phil. 4:6-9; Mt. 21:33-43.) [St. Francis of Assisi; memorial.]
5—Mon. Weekday.
6—Tues. Weekday. St. Bruno, priest; optional memorial.
7—Wed. Our Lady of the Rosary; memorial.
8—Thurs. Weekday.
9—Fri. Sts. Denis, bishop, and Companions, martyrs, or St. John Leonard, priest; optional memorials.
10—Sat. Weekday.
11—**Twenty-Eighth Sunday of the Year.** (Is. 25:6-10a; Phil. 4:12-14, 19-20; Mt. 22:1-14.)
12—Mon. Weekday.
13—Tues. Weekday.
14—Wed. Weekday. St. Callistus I, popemartyr; optional memorial.
15—Thurs. St. Teresa of Avila, virgin-doctor; memorial.
16—Fri. Weekday. St. Hedwig, religious, or St. Margaret Mary Alacoque, virgin; optional memorials.
17—Sat. St. Ignatius of Antioch, bishop-martyr; memorial.
18—**Twenty-Ninth Sunday of the Year.** (Is. 45:1, 4-6; 1 Thes. 1:1-5b; Mt. 22:15-21.) [St. Luke, evangelist; feast.]
19—Mon. Sts. Isaac Jogues, John de Brebeuf, priests, and Companions, martyrs; memorial (in U.S.). Weekday. St. Paul of the Cross, priest; optional memorial.
20—Tues. Weekday.
21—Wed. Weekday.
22—Thurs. Weekday.
23—Fri. Weekday. St. John of Capistrano, priest; optional memorial.
24—Sat. Weekday. St. Anthony Mary Claret, bishop; optional memorial.
25—**Thirtieth Sunday of the Year.** (Ex. 22:20-26; 1 Thes. 1:5c-10; Mt. 22:34-40.)
26—Mon. Weekday.
27—Tues. Weekday.
28—Wed. Sts. Simon and Jude, apostles; feast.
29—Thurs. Weekday.
30—Fri. Weekday.
31—Sat. Weekday.

GENERAL PRAYER INTENTION: That the bond of unity in believing families may grow stronger and stronger through common prayer. ("The Family That Prays Together Stays Together" is the theme of the Family Rosary Crusade.
MISSION PRAYER INTENTION: That all the regional churches may cooperate in evangelizing all parts of the world.

NOVEMBER 1981

1—**Sun. All Saints Day; solemnity.** (Rv. 7:2-4, 9-14; 1 Jn. 3:1-3; Mt. 5:1-12a.)

2—Mon. Commemoration of All the Faithful Departed (All Souls' Day). Three Masses proper. (Thirty-First Week.)

3—Tues. Weekday. St. Martin de Porres, religious; optional memorial.

4—Wed. St. Charles Borromeo, bishop; memorial.

5—Thurs. Weekday.

6—Fri. Weekday.

7—Sat. Weekday.

8—**Thirty-Second Sunday of the Year.** (Wis. 6:12-16; 1 Thes. 4:13-18; Mt. 25:1-13.)

9—Mon. Dedication of St. John Lateran (Archbasilica of Most Holy Savior); feast.

10—Tues. St. Leo the Great, pope-doctor; memorial.

11—Wed. St. Martin of Tours, bishop; memorial.

12—Thurs. St. Josaphat, bishop-martyr; memorial.

13—Fri. St. Frances Xavier Cabrini, virgin; memorial (in U.S.).

14—Sat. Weekday.

15—**Thirty-Third Sunday of the Year.** (Prv. 31:10-13, 19-20, 30-31; 1 Thes. 5:1-6; Mt. 25:14-30.) [St. Albert the Great, bishop-doctor; optional memorial.]

16—Mon. Weekday. St. Margaret of Scotland, or St. Gertrude, virgin; optional memorials.

17—Tues. St. Elizabeth of Hungary, religious; memorial.

18—Wed. Weekday. Dedication of Basilica of Sts. Peter and Paul, apostles; optional memorial.

19—Thurs. Weekday.

20—Fri. Weekday.

21—Sat. Presentation of Mary; memorial.

22—**Sun. Christ the King; solemnity.** (Ez. 34:11-12, 15-17; 1 Cor. 15:20-26, 28; Mt. 25:31-46.) [St. Cecilia, virgin-martyr; memorial.]

23—Mon. Weekday. St. Clement I, pope-martyr, or St. Columban, abbot; optional memorials. (Thirty-Fourth Week of the Year.)

24—Tues. Weekday.

25—Wed. Weekday.

26—Thurs. Thanksgiving Day Votive Mass (in U.S.). Weekday.

27—Fri. Weekday.

28—Sat. Weekday.

29—**First Sunday of Advent:** (Is. 63:16b-17, 19b, and 64:2b-7; 1 Cor. 1:3-9; Mk. 13:33-37.)

30—Mon. St. Andrew, apostle; feast.

GENERAL AND MISSION INTENTIONS: For the dying and those who help them. For the Church throughout southern Africa.

DECEMBER 1981

1—Tues. Weekday of Advent.

2—Wed. Weekday of Advent.

3—Thurs. St. Francis Xavier, priest; memorial.

4—Fri. Weekday of Advent. St. John Damascene, priest-doctor; optional memorial.

5—Sat. Weekday of Advent.

6—**Second Sunday of Advent.** (Is. 40:1-5, 9-11; 2 Pt. 3:8-14; Mk. 1:1-8.) [St. Nicholas, bishop; optional memorial.]

7—Mon. St. Ambrose, bishop-doctor; memorial.

8—**Tues. Immaculate Conception of Blessed Mary the Virgin; solemnity. Holy day of obligation.** (Gn. 3:9-15, 20; Eph. 1:3-6, 11-12; Lk. 1:26-38.)

9—Wed. Weekday of Advent.

10—Thurs. Weekday of Advent.

11—Fri. Weekday of Advent. St. Damasus I, pope; optional memorial.

12—Sat. Our Lady of Guadalupe; memorial (in U.S.). Weekday of Advent. St. Jane Frances de Chantal; optional memorial.

13—**Third Sunday of Advent.** (Is. 61:1-2a, 10-11; 1 Thes. 5:16-24; Jn. 1:6-8, 19-28.) [St. Lucy, virgin-martyr; memorial.]

14—Mon. St. John of the Cross, priest-doctor; memorial.

15—Tues. Weekday of Advent.

16—Wed. Weekday of Advent.

17—Thurs. Weekday of Advent.

18—Fri. Weekday of Advent.

19—Sat. Weekday of Advent.

20—**Fourth Sunday of Advent.** (2 Sm. 7:1-5, 8b-11, 16; Rom. 16:25-27; Lk. 1:26-38.)

21—Mon. Weekday of Advent. [St. Peter Canisius, priest-doctor; optional memorial.]

22—Tues. Weekday of Advent.

23—Wed. Weekday of Advent. [St. John of Kanty, priest; optional memorial.]

24—Thurs. Weekday of Advent.

25—**Fri. Christmas. Birth of the Lord; solemnity. Holy day of obligation.** (Midnight — Is. 9:1-6; Ti. 2:11-14; Lk. 2:1-14. Dawn — Is. 62:11-12; Ti. 3:4-7; Lk. 2:15-20; During the Day — Is. 52:7-10; Heb. 1:1-6; Jn. 1:1-18.)

26—Sat. St. Stephen, first martyr; feast.

27—**Sun. Holy Family; feast.** (Sir. 3:2-6, 12-14; Col. 3:12-21; Lk. 2:22-40.) [St. John, apostle-evangelist; feast.]

28—Mon. Holy Innocents, martyrs; feast.

29—Tues. Fifth Day of Christmas Octave. St. Thomas Becket, bishop-martyr; optional memorial.

30—Wed. Sixth Day of Christmas Octave.

31—Thurs. Seventh Day of Christmas Octave. St. Sylvester I, pope; optional memorial.

INTENTIONS: For the success of peace initiatives. For openness to the Gospel in China.

TABLE OF MOVABLE FEASTS

Year	Ash Wednesday	Easter	Ascension	Pentecost	Weeks of Ordinary Time				First Sunday of Advent
					Before Lent		After Pent.		
					Week	Ends	Week	Begins	
1981	Mar. 4	Apr. 19	May 28	June 7	8	Mar. 3	10	June 8	Nov. 29
1982	Feb. 24	Apr. 11	May 20	May 30	7	Feb. 23	9	May 31	Nov. 28
1983	Feb. 16	Apr. 3	May 12	May 22	6	Feb. 15	8	May 23	Nov. 27
1984	Mar. 7	Apr. 22	May 31	June 10	9	Mar. 6	10	June 11	Dec. 2
1985	Feb. 20	Apr. 7	May 16	May 26	6	Feb. 19	8	May 27	Dec. 1
1986	Feb. 12	Mar. 30	May 8	May 18	5	Feb. 11	7	May 19	Nov. 30
1987	Mar. 4	Apr. 19	May 28	June 7	9	Mar. 3	10	June 8	Nov. 29
1988	Feb. 17	Apr. 3	May 12	May 22	6	Feb. 16	8	May 23	Nov. 27
1989	Feb. 8	Mar. 26	May 4	May 14	5	Feb. 7	6	May 15	Dec. 3
1990	Feb. 28	Apr. 15	May 24	June 3	8	Feb. 27	9	June 4	Dec. 2
1991	Feb. 13	Mar. 31	May 9	May 19	5	Feb. 12	7	May 20	Dec. 1
1992	Mar. 4	Apr. 19	May 28	June 7	9	Mar. 3	10	June 8	Nov. 29
1993	Feb. 24	Apr. 11	May 20	May 30	7	Feb. 23	9	May 31	Nov. 28
1994	Feb. 16	Apr. 3	May 12	May 22	6	Feb. 15	8	May 23	Nov. 27
1995	Mar. 1	Apr. 16	May 25	June 4	8	Feb. 28	9	June 5	Dec. 3
1996	Feb. 21	Apr. 7	May 16	May 26	7	Feb. 20	8	May 27	Dec. 1
1997	Feb. 12	Mar. 30	May 8	May 18	5	Feb. 11	7	May 19	Nov. 30
1998	Feb. 25	Apr. 12	May 21	May 31	7	Feb. 24	9	June 1	Nov. 29
1999	Feb. 17	Apr. 4	May 13	May 23	6	Feb. 16	8	May 24	Nov. 28
2000	Mar. 8	Apr. 23	June 1	June 11	9	Mar. 7	10	June 12	Dec. 3
2001	Feb. 28	Apr. 15	May 24	June 3	7	Feb. 27	9	June 4	Dec. 2
2002	Feb. 13	Mar. 31	May 9	May 19	5	Feb. 12	7	May 20	Dec. 1
2003	Mar. 5	Apr. 20	May 29	June 8	8	Mar. 4	10	June 9	Nov. 30
2004	Feb. 25	Apr. 11	May 20	May 30	7	Feb. 24	9	May 31	Nov. 28

Season of Ordinary Time

Weeks between the end of Christmastide and the beginning of Lent, and from the day after Pentecost to the last Sunday of the liturgical year, belong to the season of Ordinary Time. The table indicates the number and terminal date of the week ending the first part, and the number and starting date of the week beginning the second part, of this season. In some years, a week of this season is eliminated because of calendar conditions.

Readings at Mass

The texts of scriptural readings for Mass on Sundays, holy days and some other days are indicated under the respective dates. The first (A) cycle of readings in the Lectionary is prescribed for the 1981 liturgical year; the second (B) cycle is prescribed for the 1982 liturgical year which begins with the first Sunday of Advent, Nov. 29, 1981.

Weekday cycles of readings are the first and second, respectively, for liturgical years 1981 and 1982.

Holiday Masses

Liturgical experiments in recent years have led to the development of votive Masses for national holidays, like those introduced in the U.S. for Thanksgiving Day in 1969 and July 4 in 1972. This development is in line with a custom whereby "from the earliest times the Church has crowned many non-Christian feasts with Christian fulfillment by instituting its own liturgical festivals" to coincide with them.

Monthly Prayer Intentions

General and mission intentions chosen and recommended by Pope John Paul II to the prayers of the Apostles of Prayer are given under each month of the 1981 calendar. He has expressed his desire that all Catholics make these intentions their own "in the certainty of being united with the Holy Father and praying according to his intentions and desires." These intentions represent the worldwide needs of the Church and its missions as seen through the eyes of the Pope.

HOLY DAYS, OTHER FEASTS

The following list includes the six holy days of obligation observed in the United States and additional observances of devotional and historical significance. The dignity or rank of observances is indicated by the terms: **solemnity** (highest in rank, the equivalent of former first class feasts): **feast** (equivalent to former second class feasts); **memorial** (equivalent to former third class feasts, for universal observance); **optional memorial** (for celebration by choice).

All Saints, Nov. 1, holy day of obligation, solemnity. Commemorates all the blessed in heaven, and is intended particularly to honor the blessed who have no special feasts. The background of the feast dates to the fourth century when groups of martyrs, and later other saints, were honored on a common day in various places. In 609 or 610, the Pantheon, a pagan temple at Rome, was consecrated as a Christian church for the honor of Our Lady and the martyrs (later all saints). In 835, Gregory IV fixed Nov. 1 as the date of observance.

All Souls, Commemoration of the Faithful Departed, Nov. 2 (transferable to Nov. 3). The dead were prayed for from the earliest days of Christianity. By the sixth century it was customary in Benedictine monasteries to hold a commemoration of deceased members of the order at Pentecost. A common commemoration of all the faithful departed on the day after All Saints was instituted in 998 by St. Odilo, of the Abbey of Cluny, and an observance of this kind was generally adopted throughout the Church. In 1915, Benedict XV granted priests throughout the world permission to celebrate three Masses for this commemoration. He also granted a special indulgence for the occasion.

Annunciation of the Lord (formerly, Annunciation of the Blessed Virgin Mary), Mar. 25, solemnity. A feast of the Incarnation which commemorates the announcement by the Archangel Gabriel to the Virgin Mary that she was to become the Mother of Christ (Lk. 1:26-38), and the miraculous conception of Christ by her. The feast was instituted about 430 in the East. The Roman observance dates from the seventh century, when celebration was said to be universal.

Ascension of the Lord, movable observance held 40 days after Easter, holy day of obligation, solemnity. Commemorates the Ascension of Christ into heaven 40 days after his Resurrection from the dead (Mk. 16:19; Lk. 24:51; Acts 1:2). The feast recalls the completion of Christ's mission on earth for the salvation of men and his entry into heaven with glorified human nature. The Ascension is a pledge of the final glorification of all who achieve salvation. Documentary evidence of the feast dates from early in the fifth century, but it was observed long before that time in connection with Pentecost and Easter.

Ash Wednesday, movable observance, six and one-half weeks before Easter. It was set as the first day of Lent by St. Gregory the Great (590-604) with the extension of an earlier and shorter penitential season to a total period including 40 weekdays of fasting before Easter. Ashes, symbolic of penance, are blessed and distributed among the faithful during the day. They are used to mark the forehead with the Sign of the Cross, with the reminder: "Remember, man, that you are dust, and unto dust you shall return," or: "Repent, and believe the Good News."

Assumption Aug. 15, holy day of obligation, solemnity. Commemorates the taking into heaven of Mary, soul and body, at the end of her life on earth, a truth of faith that was proclaimed a dogma by Pius XII on Nov. 1, 1950. One of the oldest and most solemn feasts of Mary, it has a history dating back to at least the seventh century when its celebration was already established at Jerusalem and Rome.

Baptism of the Lord, movable, celebrated on the Sunday after Epiphany, feast. Recalls the baptism of Christ by John the Baptist (Mk. 1:9-11), an event associated with the liturgy of the Epiphany. This baptism was the occasion for Christ's manifestation of Himself at the beginning of his public life.

Birth of Mary, Sept. 8, feast. This is a very old feast which originated in the East and found place in the Roman liturgy in the seventh century.

Candlemas Day, Feb. 2. See Presentation of the Lord.

Chair of Peter, Feb. 22, feast. Commemorates establishment of the see of Antioch by Peter. The feast, which has been in the Roman calendar since 336, is a liturgical expression of belief in the episcopacy and hierarchy of the Church.

Christmas, Birth of Our Lord Jesus Christ, Dec. 25, holy day of obligation, solemnity. Commemorates the birth of Christ (Lk. 2:1-20). This event was originally commemorated in the East on the feast of Epiphany or Theophany. The Christmas feast itself originated in the West; by 354 it was certainly kept on Dec. 25. This date may have been set for the observance to offset pagan ceremonies held at about the same time to commemorate the birth of the sun at the winter solstice. Priests may celebrate three Masses on Christmas Day. Christmastide begins with this feast and continues until the Sunday after Epiphany.

Christ the King, movable, celebrated on the last Sunday of the liturgical year, solemnity. Commemorates the royal prerogatives of Christ and is equivalent to a declaration of his rights to the homage, service and fidelity of men in all phases of individual and social life. Pius XI instituted the feast Dec. 11, 1925.

Corpus Christi, movable observance held in

the US on the Sunday following Trinity Sunday, solemnity. Commemorates the institution of the Holy Eucharist (Mt. 26:26-28). The feast originated at Liege in 1246 and was extended throughout the Church in the West by Urban IV in 1264. St. Thomas Aquinas composed the Office for the feast.

Dedication of St. John Lateran, Nov. 9, feast. Commemorates the first public consecration of a church, that of the Basilica of the Most Holy Savior by Pope St. Sylvester Nov. 9, 324. The church, as well as the Lateran Palace, was the gift of Emperor Constantine. Since the 12th century it has been known as St. John Lateran, in honor of John the Baptist after whom the adjoining baptistery was named. It was rebuilt by Innocent X (1644-55), reconsecrated by Benedict XIII in 1726, and enlarged by Leo XIII (1878-1903). This basilica is regarded as the church of highest dignity in Rome and throughout the Roman Rite.

Dedication of St. Mary Major, Aug. 5, optional memorial. Commemorates the rebuilding and dedication by Sixtus III (432-40) of a church in honor of Blessed Mary the Virgin. This is the Basilica of St. Mary Major on the Esquiline Hill in Rome. An earlier building was erected during the pontificate of Liberius (352-66); according to legend, it was located on a site covered by a miraculous fall of snow seen by a nobleman favored with a vision of Mary.

Easter, movable celebration held on the first Sunday after the full moon following the vernal equinox (between Mar. 22 and Apr. 25), solemnity with an octave. Commemorates the Resurrection of Christ from the dead (Mk. 16:1-7). The observance of this mystery, kept since the first days of the Church, extends throughout the Easter season which lasts until the feast of Pentecost, a period of 50 days. Every Sunday in the year is regarded as a "little" Easter. The date of Easter determines the dates of movable feasts, such as Ascension and Pentecost, and the number of Sundays after Epiphany and Pentecost.

Easter Vigil (Holy Saturday), day before Easter. Ceremonies are all related to the Resurrection and renewal-in-grace theme of Easter: blessing of the new fire and Paschal Candle, reading of prophecies, blessing of water and the baptismal font, the baptism of converts and renewal of baptismal vows by the faithful, the Litany of the Saints, and the celebration of Mass. The vigil ceremonies are held after sundown, preferably at a time that makes possible the celebration of Mass at midnight.

Epiphany of Our Lord, Jan. 6 or (in the US) a Sunday between Jan. 2 and 8, solemnity. Commemorates the manifestations of the divinity of Christ. It is one of the oldest Christian feasts, with an Eastern origin traceable to the beginning of the third century and antedating the Western feast of Christmas. Originally, it commemorated the manifestations of Christ's divinity — or Theophany — in his birth, the homage of the Magi, and baptism by John the Baptist. Later, the first two of these commemorations were transferred to Christmas when the Eastern Church adopted that feast between 380 and 430. The central feature of the Eastern observance now is the manifestation or declaration of Christ's divinity in his baptism and at the beginning of his public life. The Epiphany was adopted by the Western Church during the same period in which the Eastern Church accepted Christmas. In the Roman Rite, commemoration is made in the Mass of the homage of the wise men from the East (Mt. 2:1-12).

Good Friday, the Friday before Easter, privileged feria of Holy Week. Liturgical elements of the observance are commemoration of the Passion and Death of Christ in the reading of the Passion (according to John), special prayers for the Church and people of all ranks, the veneration of the Cross, and a Communion service. The Solemn Liturgical Action takes place between noon and 9 p.m. This is the only day in the year on which the Eucharistic Liturgy is not celebrated in the Roman Rite.

Guardian Angels, Oct. 2, memorial. Commemorates the angels who protect men from spiritual and physical dangers and assist them in doing good. A feast in their honor celebrated in Spain in the 16th century was extended to the whole Church by Paul V in 1608. In 1670, Clement X set Oct. 2 as the date of observance. Earlier, guardian angels were honored liturgically in conjunction with the feast of St. Michael.

Holy Family, movable observance on the Sunday after Christmas, feast. Commemorates the Holy Family of Jesus, Mary and Joseph as the model of domestic society, holiness and virtue. The devotional background of the feast was very strong in the 17th century. In the 18th century, in prayers composed for a special Mass, a Canadian bishop likened the Christian family to the Holy Family. Leo XIII consecrated families to the Holy Family. In 1921, Benedict XV extended the Divine Office and Mass of the feast to the whole Church.

Holy Innocents, Dec. 28, feast. Commemorates the infants who suffered death at the hands of Herod's soldiers seeking to kill the child Jesus (Mt. 2:13-18). A feast has been observed since the fifth century.

Holy Thursday, the Thursday before Easter, privileged feria of Holy Week. Commemorates the institution of the Holy Eucharist (which is later celebrated on the special feast of Corpus Christi) and other events of the Last Supper. Ceremonies include the celebration of a principal Mass between 4 and 9 p.m., the washing of feet in imitation of the act of Christ who washed the feet of the Apostles at the Last Supper, the stripping of the altar at the conclusion of Mass. There is also a procession of the Blessed Sacrament to a special place of reposition where It is reserved for veneration by the faithful until the Solemn Liturgical Action on Good Friday. At a special Mass of Chrism, bishops bless oils (of catechumens, chrism, of the sick) for use during the year.

Immaculate Conception, Dec. 8, holy day of obligation, solemnity. Commemorates the fact that Mary, in view of her calling to be the Mother of Christ and in virtue of his merits, was preserved from the first moment of her conception from original sin and was filled with grace from the very beginning of her life. She was the only person so preserved from original sin. The present form of the feast dates from Dec. 8, 1854, when Pius IX defined the dogma of the Immaculate Conception. An earlier feast of the Conception, which testified to long-existing belief in this truth, was observed in the East by the eighth century, in Ireland in the ninth, and subsequently in European countries. In 1846, Mary was proclaimed patroness of the US under this title.

Immaculate Heart of Mary, Saturday following the second Sunday after Pentecost, optional memorial. On May 4, 1944, Pius XII ordered this feast observed throughout the Church in order to obtain Mary's intercession for "peace among nations, freedom for the Church, the conversion of sinners, the love of purity and the practice of virtue." Two years earlier, he consecrated the entire human race to Mary under this title. Devotion to Mary under the title of her Most Pure Heart originated during the Middle Ages. It was given great impetus in the 17th century by the preaching of St. John Eudes, who was the first to celebrate a Mass and Divine Office of Mary under this title. A feast, celebrated in various places and on different dates, was authorized in 1799.

Joachim and Ann, July 26, memorial. Commemorates the parents of Mary. A joint feast, celebrated Sept. 9, originated in the East near the end of the sixth century. Devotion to Ann, introduced in the eighth century at Rome, became widespread in Europe in the 14th century; her feast was extended throughout the Latin Church in 1584. A feast of Joachim was introduced in the West in the 15th century.

John the Baptist, Birth, June 24, solemnity. The precursor of Christ, whose cousin he was, was commemorated universally in the liturgy by the fourth century. He is the only saint, except the Blessed Virgin Mary, whose birthday is observed as a feast. Another feast, on Aug. 29, commemorates his passion and death at the order of Herod (Mk. 6:14-29).

Joseph, Mar. 19, solemnity. Joseph is honored as the husband of the Blessed Virgin Mary, the patron and protector of the universal Church and workman. Devotion to him already existed in the eighth century in the East, and in the 11th in the West. Various feasts were celebrated before the 15th century when Mar. 19 was fixed for his commemoration; this feast was extended to the whole Church in 1621 by Gregory XV. In 1955, Pius XII instituted the feast of St. Joseph the Workman for observance May 1; this feast, which may be celebrated by local option, supplanted the Solemnity or Patronage of St. Joseph formerly observed on the third Wednesday after Easter. St. Joseph was proclaimed protector and patron of the universal Church in 1870 by Pius IX.

Michael, Gabriel and Raphael, Archangels, Sept. 29, feast. A feast bearing the title of Dedication of St. Michael the Archangel formerly commemorated on this date the consecration in 530 of a church near Rome in honor of Michael, the first angel given a liturgical feast. For a while, this feast was combined with a commemoration of the Guardian Angels. The separate feasts of Gabriel (Mar. 24) and Raphael (Oct. 24) were suppressed by the calendar reform of 1969 and this joint feast of the three archangels was instituted.

Octave of Christmas, Jan. 1. See Solemnity of Mary, Mother of God.

Our Lady of Sorrows, Sept. 15, memorial. Recalls the sorrows experienced by Mary in her association with Christ: the prophecy of Simeon (Lk. 2:34-35), the flight into Egypt (Mt. 2:13-21), the three-day separation from Jesus (Lk. 2:41-50), and four incidents connected with the Passion: her meeting with Christ on the way to Calvary, the crucifixion, the removal of Christ's body from the cross, and his burial (Mt. 27:31-61; Mk. 15:20-47; Lk. 23:26-56; Jn. 19:17-42). A Mass and Divine Office of the feast were celebrated by the Servites, especially, in the 17th century, and in 1817 Pius VII extended the observance to the whole Church.

Our Lady of the Rosary, Oct. 7, memorial. Commemorates the Virgin Mary through recall of the mysteries of the Rosary which recapitulate events in her life and the life of Christ. The feast was instituted to commemorate a Christian victory over invading Mohammedan forces at Lepanto on Oct. 7, 1571, and was extended throughout the Church by Clement XI in 1716.

Passion (Palm) Sunday, the Sunday before Easter. Recalls the triumphal entry of Christ into Jerusalem at the beginning of the last week of his life (Mt. 21:1-9). A procession and other ceremonies commemorating this event were held in Jerusalem from very early Christian times and were adopted in Rome by the ninth century, when the blessing of palm for the occasion was introduced. Full liturgical observance includes the blessing of palm and a procession before the principal Mass of the day. The Passion, by Matthew, Mark or Luke, is read during the Mass.

Pentecost, also called **Whitsunday,** movable celebration held 50 days after Easter, solemnity. Commemorates the descent of the Holy Spirit upon the Apostles, the preaching of Peter and the other Apostles to Jews in Jerusalem, the baptism and aggregation of some 3,000 persons to the Christian community (Acts 2:1-41). It is regarded as the birthday of the Catholic Church. The original observance of the feast antedated the earliest extant documentary evidence from the third century.

Peter and Paul, June 29, solemnity. Commemorates the dual martyrdom of Peter by crucifixion and Paul by beheading during the Neronian persecution. This joint commemoration of the two greatest Apostles dates at least from 258 at Rome.

Presentation of the Lord (formerly called Purification of the Blessed Virgin Mary, also Candlemas), Feb. 2, feast. Commemorates the presentation of Jesus in the Temple — according to prescriptions of Mosaic Law (Lv. 12:2-8; Ex. 13:2; Lk. 2:22-32) — and the purification of Mary 40 days after his birth. In the East, where the feast antedated fourth century testimony regarding its existence, it was observed primarily as a feast of Our Lord; in the West, where it was adopted later, it was regarded more as a feast of Mary until the calendar reform of 1969. Its date was set for Feb. 2 after the celebration of Christmas was fixed for Dec. 25, late in the fourth century. The blessing of candles, probably in commemoration of Christ who was the Light to enlighten the Gentiles, became common about the 11th century and gave the feast the secondary name of Candlemas.

Queenship of Mary, Aug. 22, memorial. Commemorates the high dignity of Mary as Queen of heaven, angels and men. Universal observance of the memorial was ordered by Pius XII in the encyclical *Ad Caeli Reginam* Oct. 11, 1954, near the close of a Marian Year observed in connection with the centenary of the proclamation of the dogma of the Immaculate Conception and four years after the proclamation of the dogma of the Assumption. The original date of the memorial was May 31.

Resurrection. See Easter.

Sacred Heart of Jesus, movable observance held on the Friday after Corpus Christi, solemnity. The object of the devotion is the divine Person of Christ, whose heart is the symbol of his love for men — for whom he accomplished the work of Redemption. The Mass and Office now used on the feast were prescribed by Pius XI in 1929. Devotion to the Sacred Heart was introduced into the liturgy in the 17th century through the efforts of St. John Eudes who composed an Office and Mass for the feast. It was furthered as the

result of the revelations of St. Margaret Mary Alacoque after 1675 and by the work of Claude de la Colombiere, S.J. In 1765, Clement XIII approved a Mass and Office for the feast, and in 1856 Pius IX extended the observance throughout the Roman Rite.

Solemnity of Mary, Mother of God, Jan. 1, holy day of obligation, solemnity. The calendar reform of 1969, in accord with Eastern tradition, reinstated the Marian character of this commemoration on the octave day of Christmas. The former feast of the Circumcision, dating at least from the first half of the sixth century, marked the initiation of Jesus (Lk. 2:21) in Judaism and by analogy focused attention on the initiation of persons in the Christian religion and their incorporation in Christ through baptism. The feast of the Solemnity supplants the former feast of the Maternity of Mary observed on Oct. 11.

Transfiguration of the Lord, Aug. 6, feast. Commemorates the revelation of his divinity by Christ to Peter, James and John on Mt. Tabor (Mt. 17:1-9). The feast, which is very old, was extended throughout the universal Church in 1457 by Callistus III.

Trinity, Most Holy, movable observance held on the Sunday after Pentecost, solemnity. Commemorates the most sublime mystery of the Christian faith, i.e., that there are Three Divine Persons — Father, Son and Holy Spirit — in one God (Mt. 28:18-20). A votive Mass of the Most Holy Trinity dates from the seventh century; an Office was composed in the 10th century; in 1334, John XXII extended the feast to the universal Church.

Triumph of the Cross, Sept. 14, feast. Commemorates the finding of the cross on which Christ was crucified, in 326 through the efforts of St. Helena, mother of Constantine; the consecration of the Basilica of the Holy Sepulchre nearly 10 years later: and the recovery in 628 or 629 by Emperor Heraclius of a major portion of the cross which had been removed by the Persians from its place of veneration at Jerusalem. The feast originated in Jerusalem and spread through the East before being adopted in the West. General adoption followed the building at Rome of the Basilica of the Holy Cross "in Jerusalem," so called because it was the place of enshrinement of a major portion of the cross of crucifixion.

Visitation, May 31, feast. Commemorates Mary's visit to her cousin Elizabeth after the Annunciation and before the birth of John the Baptist, the precursor of Christ (Lk. 1:39-47). The feast had a medieval origin and was observed in the Franciscan Order before being extended throughout the Church by Urban VI in 1389. It is one of the feasts of the Incarnation and is notable for its recall of the Magnificat, one of the few New Testament canticles, which acknowledges the unique gifts of God to Mary because of her role in the redemptive work of Christ. The canticle is recited at Vespers in the Liturgy of the Hours.

SAINTS

Biographical sketches of additional saints are under other Almanac titles. See Index.

An asterisk with a feast date indicates that a memorial or feast is observed according to the revised Roman-Rite calendar.

Adjutor, St. (d. 1131): Norman knight; fought in First Crusade; monk-recluse after his return; legendary accounts of incidents on journey to Crusade probably account for his patronage of yachtsmen; Apr. 30.

Agatha, St. (d. c. 250): Sicilian virgin-martyr; her intercession credited in Sicily with stopping eruptions of Mt. Etna; patron of nurses; Feb. 5*.

Agnes, St. (d. c. 304): Roman virgin-martyr; martyred at age of 10 or 12; patron of young girls; Jan. 21*.

Aloysius Gonzaga, St. (1568-1591): Italian Jesuit; died while nursing plague-stricken; canonized 1726; patron of youth; June 21*.

Amand, St. (d. c. 676): Apostle of Belgium; b. France; established monasteries throughout Belgium; Feb. 6.

Andre Grasset de Saint Sauveur, Bl. (1758-1792): Canadian priest; martyred in France, Sept. 2, 1792, during the Revolution; one of a group called the Martyrs of Paris who were beatified in 1926.

Andrew Corsini, St. (1302-1373): Italian Carmelite; bishop of Fiesoli; mediator between quarrelsome Italian states; canonized 1629; Feb. 4.

Andrew Fournet, St. (1752-1834): French priest; co-founder with St. Jeanne Elizabeth des Anges of the Congregation of Daughters of the Cross; canonized 1933; May 13.

Angela Merici, St. (1474-1540): Italian nun; foundress of Institute of St. Ursula, 1535, the first teaching order of nuns in the Church; canonized 1807; Jan. 27*.

Anne Mary Javouhey, Bl. (1779-1851): French virgin; foundress of Institute of St. Joseph of Cluny, 1812; beatified 1950; July 15.

Ansgar, St. (801-865): Bishop, Benedictine monk; b. near Amiens; missionary in Denmark, Sweden, Norway and Northern Germany; apostle of Denmark; Feb. 3*.

Anthony Abbot, St. (c. 251-c. 354): Egyptian hermit; patriarch of all monks; established communities for hermits which became models for monastic life, especially in the East; friend and supporter of St. Athanasius in the latter's struggle with the Arians; Jan. 17*.

Anthony Mary Claret, St. (1807-1870): Spanish priest; founder of Missionary Sons of the Immaculate Heart of Mary (Claretians), 1849; archbishop of Santiago, Cuba, 1851-57; canonized 1950; Oct. 24*.

Anthony Mary Zaccaria, St. (1502-1539): Italian priest; founder of Barnabites (Clerks Regular of St. Paul), 1530; canonized 1897; July 5*.

Apollonia, St. (d. 249): Deaconess of Alexandria; martyred during persecution of Decius; her patronage of dentists probably rests on tradition that her teeth were broken by pincers by her persecutors; Feb. 9.

Augustine of Canterbury, St. (d. 604 or 605): Italian missionary; apostle of the English; sent by Pope Gregory I with 40 monks to evangelize England; arrived there 597; first archbishop of Canterbury; May 27*.

Benedict of Nursia, St. (c. 480-547): Abbot; founder of monasticism in Western Europe; established monastery at Monte Cassino; proclaimed patron of Europe by Paul VI in 1964; July 11*.

Benedict the Black (il Moro), St. (1526-1589): Sicilian Franciscan; born a slave; joined Franciscans as lay brother; appointed guardian and novice master; canonized 1807; Apr. 4.

Bernadette Soubirous, St. (1844-1879): French peasant girl favored with series of visions of Blessed Virgin Mary at Lourdes (see Lourdes Apparitions); joined Institute of Sisters of Notre Dame at Nevers, 1866; canonized 1933; Apr. 16.

Bernard of Menthon, St. (d. 1081): Italian priest; founded Alpine hospices near the two passes named for him; patron of mountaineers; May 28.

Bernardine of Feltre, Bl. (1439-1494): Italian Franciscan preacher; a founder of montes pietatis.

Bernardine of Siena, St. (1380-1444): Italian Franciscan; noted preacher and missioner; spread of devotion to Holy Name is attributed to him; represented in art holding to his breast the monogram IHS; canonized 1450; May 20*.

Blase, St. (d. c. 316): Armenian bishop; martyr; the blessing of throats on his feast day derives from tradition that he miraculously saved the life of a boy who had half-swallowed a fish bone; Feb. 3*.

Boniface (Winfrid), St. (d. 754): English Benedictine; bishop, martyr; apostle of Germany; established monastery at Fulda which became center of German missionary work; archbishop of Mainz; martyred near Dukkum in Holland; June 5*.

Brendan, St. (c. 489-583): Irish abbot; founded monasteries; his patronage of sailors probably rests on tradition that he made a seven-year voyage in search of a fabled paradise; called Brendan the Navigator; May 16.

Bridget (Brigid), St. (c. 450-525): Irish nun; founded nunnery at Kildare, the first erected on Irish soil; patron, with Sts. Patrick and Columba, of Ireland; Feb. 1.

Bridget (Birgitta), St. (c. 1303-1373): Swedish mystic; widow; foundress of Order of Our Savior (Brigittines); canonized 1391; wrote *Revelationes,* accounts of her visions; patroness of Sweden; July 23*.

Bruno, St. (1030-1101): German monk; founded Carthusians, 1084, in France; Oct. 6*.

Cabrini, Mother: See Index.

Cajetan of Thiene, St. (1480-1547): Italian lawyer; religious reformer; a founder of Oratory of Divine Love, forerunner of the Theatines; canonized 1671; Aug. 7*.

Callistus I, St. (d. 222): Pope, 217-222; martyr; condemned Sabellianism and other heresies; advocated a policy of mercy toward repentant sinners; Oct. 14*.

Camillus de Lellis, St. (1550-1614): Italian priest; founder of Camillians (Ministers of the Sick); canonized 1746; patron of the sick and of nurses; July 14*.

Casimir, St. (1458-1484): Polish prince; grand duke of Lithuania; noted for his piety; buried at cathedral in Vilna, Lithuania; canonized 1521; patron of Poland and Lithuania; Mar. 4*.

Cassian, St. (d. 298): Roman martyr; an official court stenographer who declared himself a Christian; patron of stenographers; Dec. 3.

Catherine Laboure, St. (1806-1876): French nun; favored with series of visions; first Miraculous Medal (see Index) struck as the result of one of the visions; canonized 1947; Dec. 31.

Catherine of Bologna, St. (1413-1463): Italian Poor Clare; mystic, writer, artist; canonized 1712; patron of artists; Mar. 9.

Cecilia, St. (2nd-3rd century): Roman virgin-martyr; traditional patron of musicians; Nov. 22*.

Charles Borromeo, St. (1538-1584): Italian cardinal; nephew of Pope Pius IV; cardinal bishop of Milan; influential figure in Church reform in Italy; promoted education of clergy; canonized 1610; Nov. 4*.

Charles Lwanga and Companions, Sts. (d. 1886 and 1887): Martyrs of Uganda; pages of King Mwanga of Uganda; Charles Lwanga and 12 companions were martyred near Rubaga, June 3, 1886; the other nine were martyred between May 26, 1886, and Jan. 27, 1887; canonized 1964; first martyrs of black Africa; June 3*.

Christopher, St. (3rd cent.): Early Christian martyr inscribed in Roman calendar about 1550; feast relegated to particular calendars because of legendary nature of accounts of his life; traditional patron of travelers; July 25.

Clare, St. (1194-1253): Foundress of Poor Clares; b. at Assisi; later joined in religious life her sisters Agnes and Beatrice, and her mother Ortolana; canonized 1255; patroness of television; Aug. 11*.

Clement I, St. (d. c. 100): Pope, 88-97; third successor of St. Peter; wrote important letter to Church in Corinth settling disputes there; venerated as a martyr; Nov. 23*.

Columba, St. (521-597): Irish monk; founded monasteries in Ireland; missionary in Scotland; established monastery at Iona which became the center for conversion of Picts, Scots, and Northern English; Scotland's most famous saint; June 9.

Columban, St. (545-615): Irish monk; scholar; founded monasteries in England and Brittany (famous abbey of Luxeuil), forced into exile because of his criticism of Frankish court; spent last years in northern Italy where he founded abbey at Bobbio; Nov. 23*.

Contardo Ferrini, Bl. (1859-1902): Italian secular Franciscan; model of the Catholic professor; beatified 1947; patron of universities; Oct. 17.

Cornelius, St. (d. 253): Pope, 251-253; promoted a policy of mercy with respect to readmission of repentant Christians who had fallen away during the persecution of Decius *(lapsi);* banished from Rome during persecution of Gallus; regarded as a martyr; Sept. 16 (with Cyprian)*.

Cosmas and Damian, Sts. (d. c. 303): Arabian twin brothers; physicians who were martyred during Diocletian persecution; patrons of physicians; Sept. 26*.

Crispin and Crispinian, Sts. (3rd cent.): Early Christian martyrs; said to have met their deaths in Gaul; patrons of shoemakers, a trade they pursued; Oct. 25.

Cyprian, St. (d. 258): Early ecclesiastical writer; b. Africa; bishop of Carthage, 249-258; supported Pope St. Cornelius concerning the readmission of Christians who had apostatized in time of persecution; erred in his teaching that baptism administered by heretics and schismatics was invalid; wrote *De Unitate;* Sept. 16 (with St. Cornelius)*.

Cyril and Methodius, Sts.: Greek missionaries; brothers venerated as apostles of the Slavs; Cyril (d. 869) and Methodius (d. 885) began their missionary work in Moravia in 863; developed a Slavonic alphabet; eventually their use of the vernacular in the liturgy was approved; Feb. 14*.

Damasus I, St. (d. 384): Pope, 366-384; opposed Arians and Apollinarians; commissioned St. Jerome to work on Bible translation; developed Roman liturgy; Dec. 11*.

Damian, St.: See Cosmas and Damian, Sts.

David, St. (5th-6th cent.): Welsh monk; founded monastery at Menevia; patron saint of Wales; Mar. 1.

Denis and Companions, Sts. (d. 3rd cent.): Denis, bishop of Paris, and two companions identified by early writers as Rusticus, a priest, and Eleutherius, a deacon; martyred near Paris; Denis is popularly regarded as apostle of France; Oct. 9*.

Dismas, St. (1st cent.): Name given to repentant thief (Good Thief) to whom Jesus promised salvation; regarded as patron of prisoners; Mar. 25.

Dominic, St. (Dominic de Guzman) (1170-1221): Spanish priest; founder of Dominican Order (Friars Preachers), 1215;

preached against the Albigensian heresy; a contemporary of St. Francis of Assisi; canonized 1234; Aug. 8*.

Dominic Savio, St. (1842-1857): Italian youth; pupil of St. John Bosco; died before his 15th birthday; canonized 1954; patron of choir boys; Mar. 9.

Dunstan, St. (c. 910-988): English monk; archbishop of Canterbury; initiated reforms in religious life; royal counselor to several kings; considered one of greatest Anglo-Saxon saints; patron of armorers, goldsmiths, locksmiths, jewelers; May 17.

Dymphna, St. (dates uncertain): Nothing certain known of her life; presumably she was an Irish maiden whose relics were discovered at Gheel near Antwerp, Belgium, in the 13th century; since that time many cases of mental illness and epilepsy have been cured at her shrine; patron of those suffering from mental illness; May 15.

Edmund Campion, St. (1540-1581): English Jesuit; convert 1573; martyred at Tyburn; canonized 1970, one of the Forty English and Welsh Martyrs; Dec. 1.

Elizabeth Bayley Seton, St. (1774-1821): American foundress; convert, 1805; founded Sisters of Charity in the U.S.; beatified 1963; canonized Sept. 14, 1975; the first American-born saint; Jan. 4 (U.S.)*.

Elizabeth of Hungary, St. (1207-1231): Queen; became secular Franciscan after death of her husband in 1227; devoted life to poor and destitute; a patron of the Secular Franciscan Order; Nov. 17*.

Elizabeth of Portugal, St. (1271-1336): Queen of Portugal; b. Spain; retired to Poor Clare convent as a secular Franciscan after the death of her husband; July 4*.

Erasmus, St. (d. 303): Life surrounded by legend; martyred during Diocletian persecution; patron of sailors; June 2.

Ethelbert, St.(552-676): King of Kent; baptized by St. Augustine 597; issued legal code; furthered spread of Christianity; Feb. 24.

Euphrasia Pelletier, St. (1796-1868): French nun; founded Sisters of the Good Shepherd at Angers, 1829; canonized 1940; Apr. 24.

Eusebius of Vercelli, St. (283-370): Italian bishop; exiled from his see for a time because of his opposition to Arianism; considered a martyr because of sufferings he endured; Aug. 2*.

Fabian, St. (d. 250): Pope, 236-250; martyred under Decius; Jan. 20*.

Ferdinand III, St. (1198-1252): King of Castile and Leon; waged successful crusade against Mohammedans in Spain; founded university at Salamanca; canonized 1671; May 30.

Fiacre, St. (d. c. 670): Irish hermit; patron of gardeners; Aug. 30.

Fidelis of Sigmaringen, St. (Mark Rey) (1577-1622): German Capuchin; lawyer before he joined the Capuchins; missionary to

Swiss Protestants; stabbed to death by peasants who were told he was agent of Austrian emperor; Apr. 24*.

Frances of Rome, St. (1384-1440): Italian model for housewives and widows; happily married for 40 years; after death of her husband in 1436 joined community of Benedictine Oblates she had founded; canonized 1608; patron of motorists; Mar. 9*.

Frances Xavier Cabrini, St. (Mother Cabrini) (1850-1917): American foundress; b. Italy; foundress of Missionary Sisters of the Sacred Heart, 1877; settled in the U.S. 1889; became an American citizen at Seattle 1909; worked among Italian immigrants; canonized 1946, the first American citizen so honored; Nov. 13 (U.S.)*.

Francis Borgia, St. (1510-1572): Spanish Jesuit; joined Jesuits after death of his wife in 1546; became general of the Order, 1565; Oct. 10.

Francis of Assisi, St. (Giovanni di Bernardone) (1182-1226): Founder of the Franciscans, 1209; received stigmata 1224; canonized 1228; one of best known and best loved saints; patron of Italy, Catholic Action and ecologists; Oct. 4*.

Francis of Paola, St. (1416-1507): Italian hermit; founder of Minim Friars; Apr. 2*.

Francis Xavier, St. (1506-1552): Spanish Jesuit; missionary to Far East; canonized 1602; patron of foreign missions; considered one of greatest Christian missionaries; Dec. 3*.

Gabriel of the Sorrowful Mother, St. (Francis Possenti) (1838-1862): Italian Passionist; died while a scholastic; canonized 1920; Feb. 27.

Genesius, St. (d. c. 300): Roman actor; according to legend, was converted while performing a burlesque of Christian baptism and was subsequently martyred; patron of actors.

Genevieve, St. (422-500): French nun; a patroness and protectress of Paris; events of her life not authenticated; Jan. 3.

George, St. (d. c. 300): Martyr, probably during Diocletian persecution in Palestine; all other incidents of his life, including story of the dragon, are legendary; patron of England; Apr. 23*.

Gerard Majella, St. (1725-1755): Italian Redemptorist lay brother; noted for supernatural occurrences in his life including bilocation and reading of consciences; canonized 1904; patron of mothers; Oct. 16.

Gertrude, St. (1256-1302): German mystic; writer; helped spread devotion to the Sacred Heart; Nov. 16*.

Gregory VII (Hildebrand), St. (1020?-1085): Pope, 1075-1085; Benedictine monk; adviser to several popes; as pope, strengthened interior life of Church and fought against lay investiture; driven from Rome by Henry IV; died in exile; May 25*.

Gregory the Illuminator, St. (257-332): Martyr; bishop; apostle and patron saint of

Armenia; helped free Armenia from the Persians; Sept. 30.

Hedwig, St. (1174-1243): Moravian noblewoman; married duke of Silesia, head of Polish royal family; fostered religious life in country; canonized 1266; Oct. 16*.

Helena, St. (250-330): Empress; mother of Constantine the Great; associated with discovery of the True Cross; Aug. 18.

Henry, St. (972-1024): Bavarian emperor; cooperated with Benedictine abbeys in restoration of ecclesiastical and social discipline; canonized 1146; July 13*.

Hippolytus, St. (d. c. 236): Roman priest; opposed Pope St. Callistus I in his teaching about the readmission of Christians who had apostasized during time of persecution; elected antipope; reconciled before his martyrdom; important ecclesiastical writer; Aug. 13*.

Hubert, St. (d. 727): Bishop; his patronage of hunters is based on legend that he was converted while hunting; Nov. 3.

Hugh of Cluny (the Great), St. (1024-1109): Abbot of Benedictine foundation at Cluny; supported popes in efforts to reform ecclesiastical abuses; canonized 1120; Apr. 29.

Ignatius of Antioch, St. (d. c. 107): Early ecclesiastical writer; martyr; bishop of Antioch in Syria for 40 years; Oct. 17*.

Ignatius of Loyola, St. (1491-1556): Spanish soldier; renounced military career after recovering from wounds received at siege of Pampeluna (Pamplona) in 1521; founded Society of Jesus (Jesuits), 1534, at Paris; canonized 1622; author *The Book of Spiritual Exercises;* July 31*.

Irenaeus of Lyons, St. (130-202): Early ecclesiastical writer; opposed Gnosticism; bishop of Lyons; traditionally regarded as a martyr; June 28*.

Isidore the Farmer, St. (d. 1170): Spanish layman; farmer; canonized 1622; patron of farmers; May 15 (US)*.

Jane Frances de Chantal, St. (1572-1641): French widow; foundress, under guidance of St. Francis de Sales, of Order of the Visitation; canonized 1767; Dec. 12*.

Januarius (Gennaro), St. (d. 304): Bishop of Benevento; martyred during Diocletian persecution; fame rests on liquefaction of some of his blood preserved in a phial at Naples, an unexplained phenomenon which has occurred regularly about 18 times each year for over 400 years; Sept. 19*.

Jerome Emiliani, St. (1481-1537): Venetian priest; founded Somascan Fathers, 1532, for care of orphans; canonized 1767; patron of orphans and abandoned children; Feb. 8*.

Joan of Arc, St. (1412-1431): French heroine, called The Maid of Orleans, La Pucelle; led French army against English invaders; captured by Burgundians, turned over to ecclesiastical court on charge of heresy, found guilt and burned at the stake; her innocence was declared in 1456; canonized 1920; patroness of France; May 30.

John I, St. (d. 526): Pope, 523-526; martyr; May 18*.

John Baptist de la Salle, St. (1651-1719): French priest; founder of Brothers of the Christian Schools, 1680; canonized 1900; Apr. 7*.

John Berchmans, St. (1599-1621): Belgian Jesuit scholastic; patron of Mass servers; canonized 1888; Aug. 13.

John Bosco, St. (1815-1888): Italian priest; founded Salesians, 1859, for education of boys and cofounded the Daughters of Mary Help of Christians for education of girls; canonized 1934; Jan. 31*.

John Capistran, St. (1386-1456): Italian Franciscan; preacher; papal diplomat; canonized 1690; Oct. 23*.

John Eudes, St. (1601-1680): French priest; founder of Sisters of Our Lady of Charity of Refuge, 1642, and Congregation of Jesus-Mary (Eudists), 1643; canonized 1925; Aug. 19*.

John Fisher, St. (1469-1535): English prelate; theologian; martyr; bishop of Rochester, cardinal; refused to recognize validity of Henry VIII's marriage to Anne Boleyn; upheld supremacy of the pope; beheaded for refusing to acknowledge Henry as head of the Church; canonized 1935; June 22 (with St. Thomas More)*.

John Kanty (Cantius), St. (1395-1473): Polish theologian; canonized 1767; Dec. 23*.

John Leonardi, St. (1550-1609): Italian priest; worked among prisoners and the sick; founded Clerics Regular of the Mother of God; canonized 1938; Oct. 9*.

John Nepomucene, St. (1345-1393): Bohemian priest; regarded as a martyr; canonized 1729; patron of Czechoslovakia; May 16.

John Nepomucene Neumann, St. (1811-1860): American prelate; b. Bohemia; ordained in New York 1836; missionary among Germans near Niagara Falls before joining Redemptorists, 1840; bishop of Philadelphia, 1852; first bishop in U.S. to prescribe Forty Hours devotion in his diocese; beatified 1963; canonized June 19, 1977; Jan. 5 (U.S.)*.

John of God, St. (1495-1550): Portuguese founder; his work among the sick poor led to foundation of Brothers Hospitallers of St. John of God, 1540, in Spain; canonized 1690; patron of sick, hospitals, nurses; Mar. 8*.

John Vianney (Cure of Ars), St. (1786-1859): French parish priest; noted confessor, spent 16 to 18 hours a day in confessional; canonized 1925; patron of parish priests; Aug. 4*.

Josaphat Kuncevyc, St. (1584-1623): Basilian monk; b. Poland; archbishop of Polotsk, Lithuania; worked for reunion of separated Easterners; martyred by mob of schismatics; canonized 1867; Nov. 12*.

Joseph Benedict Cottolengo, St. (1786-1842): Italian priest; established Little Houses of Divine Providence (Piccolo Casa) for care of orphans and the sick; canonized 1934; Apr. 30.

Joseph Cafasso, St. (1811-1860): Italian priest; renowned confessor; promoted devotion to Blessed Sacrament; canonized 1947; June 22.

Joseph Calasanz, St. (1556-1648): Spanish priest; founder of Piarists (Order of Pious Schools); canonized 1767; Aug. 25*.

Joseph of Cupertino, St. (1603-1663): Italian Franciscan; noted for remarkable incidents of levitation; canonized 1767; Sept. 18.

Justin Martyr, St. (100-165): Early ecclesiastical writer; *Apologies for the Christian Religion, Dialog with the Jew Tryphon;* martyred at Rome; June 1*.

Ladislaus, Saint (1040-1095): King of Hungary; supported Pope Gregory VII against Henry IV; canonized 1192; June 27.

Lawrence, St. (d. 258): Widely venerated martyr who suffered death, according to a long-standing but unverifiable legend, by being roasted alive on a gridiron; Aug. 10*.

Leonard of Port Maurice, St. (1676-1751): Italian Franciscan; ascetical writer; preached missions throughout Italy; canonized 1867; patron of parish missions; Nov. 26.

Louis IX, St. (1215-1270): King of France, 1226-1270; participated in Sixth Crusade; patron of Secular Franciscan Order; canonized 1297; Aug. 25*.

Louis de Montfort, St. (1673-1716): French priest; founder of Sisters of Divine Wisdom, 1703, and Missionaries of Company of Mary, 1715; wrote *True Devotion to the Blessed Virgin;* canonized 1947; Apr. 28.

Louise de Marillac, St. (1591-1660): French foundress, with St. Vincent de Paul, of the Sisters of Charity; canonized 1934; Mar. 15.

Lucy, St. (d. 304): Sicilian maiden; martyred during Diocletian persecution; one of most widely venerated early virgin-martyrs; patron of Syracuse, Sicily; invoked by those suffering from eye diseases (based on legend that she offered her eyes to a suitor who admired them); Dec. 13*.

Marcellinus and Peter, Sts. (d.c. 304): Early Roman martyrs; June 2*.

Margaret Clitherow, St. (1556-1586): English martyr; convert shortly after her marriage; one of Forty Martyrs of England and Wales; canonized 1970.

Margaret Mary Alacoque, St. (1647-1690): French nun; spread devotion to Sacred Heart in accordance with revelations made to her in 1675 (see Sacred Heart); canonized 1920; Oct. 16*.

Margaret of Scotland, St. (1050-1093): Queen of Scotland; noted for solicitude for the poor and promotion of justice; canonized 1251; Nov. 16*.

Maria Goretti, St. (1890-1902): Italian virgin-martyr; a model of purity; canonized 1950; July 6*.

Mariana Paredes of Jesus, St. (1618-1645): South American recluse; Lily of Quito; canonized, 1950; May 26.

Martha, St. (1st cent.): Sister of Lazarus and Mary of Bethany; Gospel accounts record her concern for homely details; patron of cooks; July 29*.

Martin I, St. (d. 655): Pope, 649; banished from Rome by emperor because of his condemnation of Monothelites; considered a martyr; Apr. 13*.

Martin of Tours, St. (316-397): Bishop of Tours; opposed Arianism and Priscillianism; pioneer of Western monasticism, before St. Benedict; Nov. 11*.

Mary Magdalene, St. (1st cent.): Gospels record her as devoted follower of Christ to whom he appeared after the Resurrection; her identification with Mary of Bethany (sister of Martha and Lazarus) and the woman sinner (Lk 7:36-50) has been questioned; July 22*.

Mary Magdalene de Pazzi, St. (1566-1607): Italian Carmelite nun; recipient of mystical experiences; canonized 1669; May 25*.

Maximilian Kolbe, Bl. (1894-1941): Polish Conventual Franciscan; prisoner at Auschwitz who heroically offered his life in place of a fellow prisoner; beatified 1971.

Methodius, St.: See Index.

Monica, St. (332-387): Mother of St. Augustine; model of a patient mother; her feast is observed in the Roman calendar the day before her son's; Aug. 27*.

Nereus and Achilleus, Sts. (d. c. 100): Early Christian martyrs; soldiers who, according to legend, were baptized by St. Peter; May 12*.

Nicholas of Myra, St. (4th cent.): Bishop of Myra in Asia Minor; one of most popular saints in both East and West; most of the incidents of his life are based on legend; patron of Russia; Dec. 6*.

Nicholas of Tolentino, St. (1245-1365): Italian hermit; famed preacher; canonized 1446; Sept. 10.

Norbert, St. (1080-1134): German bishop; founder of Norbertines or Premonstratensians, 1120; promoted reform of the clergy, devotion to Blessed Sacrament; canonized 1582; June 6*.

Odilia, St. (d. c. 720): Benedictine abbess; according to legend she was born blind, abandoned by her family and adopted by a convent where her sight was miraculously restored; patron of blind; Dec. 13.

Oliver Plunket, St. (1629-1681): Irish martyr; theologian; archbishop of Armagh and primate of Ireland; beatified 1920; canonized, 1975.

Pancras, St. (d. c. 304): Roman martyr; May 12*.

Paschal Baylon, St. (1540-1592): Spanish Franciscan lay brother; spent life as doorkeeper in various Franciscan friaries; defended doctrine of Real Presence in Blessed Sacrament; canonized 1690; patron of all Eucharistic confraternities and congresses, 1897; May 17.

Patrick, St. (389-461): Famous missionary of Ireland; began missionary work in Ireland about 432; organized the Church there and established it on a lasting foundation; patron of Ireland, with Sts. Bridget and Columba; Mar. 17*.

Paul Miki and Companions, Sts. (d. 1597): Martyrs of Japan; Paul Miki, Jesuit, and twenty-five other priests and laymen were martyred at Nagasaki; canonized 1862, the first canonized martyrs of the Far East; Feb. 6*.

Paul of the Cross, St. (1694-1775): Italian religious; founder of the Passionists; canonized 1867; Oct. 19*.

Paulinus of Nola, St. (d. 451): Bishop of Nola (Spain); writer; June 22*.

Peregrine, St. (1260-1347): Italian Servite; invoked against cancer (he was miraculously cured of cancer of the foot after a vision); canonized 1726; May 1.

Perpetua and Felicity, Sts. (d. 203): Martyrs; Mar. 7*.

Peter Chanel, St. (1803-1841): French Marist; missionary to Oceania, where he was martyred; canonized 1954; Apr. 28*.

Peter Gonzalez, St. (1190-1246): Spanish Dominican; worked among sailors; court chaplain and confessor of King St. Ferdinand of Castile; patron of sailors; Apr. 14.

Peter of Alcantara, St. (1499-1562): Spanish Franciscan; mystic; initiated Franciscan reform; confessor of St. Teresa of Avila; canonized 1669; Oct. 19.

Philip Neri, St. (1515-1595): Italian religious; founded Congregation of the Oratory; considered a second apostle of Rome because of his mission activities there; canonized 1622; May 26*.

Philip of Jesus, St. (1571-1597): Mexican Franciscan; martyred at Nagasaki, Japan; canonized 1862; patron of Mexico City; Feb. 6*.

Pius V, St. (1504-1572): Pope, 1566-1572; enforced decrees of Council of Trent; organized expedition against Turks resulting in victory at Lepanto; canonized 1712; Apr. 30*.

Polycarp, St. (2nd cent.): Bishop of Smyrna; ecclesiastical writer; martyr; Feb. 23*.

Pontian, St. (d. c. 235): Pope, 230-235; exiled to Sardinia by the emperor; regarded as a martyr; Aug. 13 (with Hippolytus)*.

Raymond Nonnatus, St. (d. 1240): Spanish Mercedarian; cardinal; devoted his life to ransoming captives from the Moors; Aug. 31.

Raymond of Penyafort, St. (1175-1275): Spanish Dominican; confessor of Gregory IX; systematized and codified canon law, in effect until 1917; master general of Dominicans, 1238; canonized 1601; Jan. 7*.

Rita of Cascia, St. (1381-1457): Widow; cloistered Augustinian religious of Umbria;

invoked in impossible and desperate cases; May 22.

Robert Southwell, St. (1561-1595): English Jesuit; poet; martyred at Tyburn; canonized 1970, one of the Forty English and Welsh Martyrs.

Roch, St. (1350-1379): French layman; pilgrim; devoted life to care of plague-stricken; widely venerated; invoked against pestilence; Aug. 17.

Romuald, St. (951-1027): Italian monk; founded Camaldolese Benedictines; June 19*.

Rose of Lima, St. (1586-1617): Peruvian Dominican tertiary; first native-born saint of the New World; canonized 1671; Aug. 23*.

Scholastica, St. (d. c. 559): Sister of St. Benedict; regarded as first nun of the Benedictine Order; Feb. 10*.

Sebastian, St. (3rd cent.): Roman martyr; traditionally pictured as a handsome youth; martyred by being pierced with arrows; patron of athletes; Jan. 20*.

Seven Holy Founders of the Servants of Mary (Buonfiglio Monaldo, Alexis Falconieri, Benedict dell'Antello, Bartholomew Amidei, Ricovero Uguccione, Gerardino Sostegni, John Buonagiunta Monetti): Florentine youths who founded Servites, 1233, in obedience to a vision; canonized 1888; Feb. 17*.

Sixtus II and Companions, Sts. (d. 258): Sixtus, pope 257-258, and four deacons, martyrs; Aug. 7*.

Stanislaus, St. (1030-1079): Polish bishop; martyr; canonized 1253; Apr. 11*.

Stephen, St. (d. c. 33): First Christian martyr; chosen by the Apostles as the first of the seven deacons; stoned to death; Dec. 26*.

Stephen, St. (975-1038): King; apostle of Hungary; welded Magyars into national unity; canonized 1087; Aug. 16*.

Sylvester I, St. (d. 335): Pope 314-335; first ecumenical council held at Nicaea during his pontificate; Dec. 31*.

Tarcisius, St. (d. 3rd cent.): Early martyr; according to tradition, was martyred while carrying the Blessed Sacrament to some Christians in prison; patron of first communicants; Aug. 15.

Therese Couderc, St. (1805-1885): French religious; foundress of the Religious of Our Lady of the Retreat in the Cenacle, 1827; canonized 1970; Sept. 26.

Therese of Lisieux, St. (1873-1897): French Carmelite nun; b. Therese Martin; allowed to enter Carmel at 15, died nine years later of tuberculosis; her "little way" of spiritual perfection became widely known through her spiritual autobiography; despite her obscure life, became one of the most popular saints; canonized 1925; patron of foreign missions; Oct. 1*.

Thomas Becket, St. (1118-1170): English martyr; archbishop of Canterbury; chancellor under Henry II; murdered for upholding rights of the Church; canonized 1173; Dec. 29*.

Thomas More, St. (1478-1535): English martyr; statesman, chancellor under Henry VIII; author of *Utopia;* opposed Henry's divorce, refused to renounce authority of the papacy; beheaded; canonized 1935; June 22 (with St. John Fisher)*.

Timothy, St. (d. c. 97): Bishop of Ephesus; disciple and companion of St. Paul; martyr; Jan. 26*.

Titus, St. (d. c. 96): Bishop; companion of St. Paul; recipient of one of Paul's epistles; Jan. 26*.

Valentine, St. (d. 269): Priest, physician; martyred at Rome; legendary patron of lovers; Feb. 14.

Vincent, St. (d. 304): Spanish deacon; martyr; Jan. 22*.

Vincent de Paul, St. (1581?-1660): French priest; founder of Congregation of the Mission (Vincentians, Lazarists) and co-founder of Sisters of Charity; declared patron of all charitable organizations and works by Leo XIII; canonized 1737; Sept. 27*.

Vincent Ferrer, St. (1350-1418): Spanish Dominican; famed preacher; Apr. 5*.

Wenceslaus, St. (d. 935): Duke of Bohemia; martyr; patron of Bohemia; Sept. 28*.

Zita, St. (1218-1278): Italian maid; noted for charity to poor; patron of domestics.

SAINTS—PATRONS AND INTERCESSORS

A patron is a saint who is venerated as a special intercessor before God. Most patrons have been so designated as the result of popular devotion and long-standing custom. In many cases, the fact of existing patronal devotion is clear despite historical obscurity regarding its origin. The Church has made official designation of relatively few patrons; in such cases, the dates of designation are given in the list below. The theological background of the patronage of saints includes the dogmas of the Mystical Body of Christ and the Communion of Saints.

Accountants: St. Matthew.
Actors: St. Genesius.
Advertisers: St. Bernardine of Siena (May 20, 1960).
Alpinists: St. Bernard of Menthon (Aug. 20, 1923).
Altar boys: St. John Berchmans.
Anesthetists: St. Rene Goupil.
Archers: St. Sebastian.
Architects: St. Thomas, Apostle.
Armorers: St. Dunstan.
Art: St. Catherine of Bologna.
Artists: St. Luke, St. Catherine of Bologna.
Astronomers: St. Dominic.
Athletes: St. Sebastian.
Authors: St. Francis de Sales.
Aviators: Our Lady of Loreto (1920), St. Therese of Lisieux, St. Joseph of Cupertino.
Bakers: St. Elizabeth of Hungary, St. Nicholas.
Bankers: St. Matthew.
Barbers: Sts. Cosmas and Damian, St. Louis.
Barren women: St. Anthony of Padua, St. Felicity.
Basket-makers: St. Anthony, Abbot.
Blacksmiths: St. Dunstan.
Blind: St. Odilia, St. Raphael.
Blood banks: St. Januarius.
Bodily ills: Our Lady of Lourdes.
Bookbinders: St. Peter Celestine.
Bookkeepers: St. Matthew.
Booksellers: St. John of God.
Boy Scouts: St. George.

Brewers: St. Augustine of Hippo, St. Luke, St. Nicholas of Myra.
Bricklayers: St. Stephen.
Brides: St. Nicholas of Myra.
Brush makers: St. Anthony, Abbot.
Builders: St. Vincent Ferrer.
Butchers: St. Anthony, Abbot, St. Luke.
Cab drivers: St. Fiacre.
Cabinetmakers: St. Anne.
Cancer patients: St. Peregrine.
Canonists: St. Raymond of Penyafort.
Carpenters: St. Joseph.
Catechists: St. Viator, St. Charles Borromeo, St. Robert Bellarmine.
Catholic Action: St. Francis of Assisi (1916).
Chandlers: St. Ambrose, St. Bernard of Clairvaux.
Charitable societies: St. Vincent de Paul (May 12, 1885).
Children: St. Nicholas of Myra.
Choir boys: St. Dominic Savio (June 8, 1956).
Church: St. Joseph (Dec. 8, 1870).
Clerics: St. Gabriel of the Sorrowful Mother.
Comedians: St. Vitus.
Communications personnel: St. Bernardine.
Confessors: St. Alphonsus Liguori (Apr. 26, 1950), St. John Nepomucene.
Convulsive children: St. Scholastica.
Cooks: St. Lawrence, St. Martha.
Coopers: St. Nicholas of Myra.
Coppersmiths: St. Maurus.
Dairy workers: St. Brigid.
Deaf: St. Francis de Sales.
Dentists: St. Apollonia.
Desperate situations: St. Gregory of Neocaesarea, St. Jude Thaddeus, St. Rita of Cascia.
Dietitians (in hospitals): St. Martha.
Dyers: Sts. Maurice and Lydia.
Dying: St. Joseph.
Ecologists: St. Francis of Assisi (Nov. 29, 1979).
Editors: St. John Bosco.
Emigrants: St. Frances Xavier Cabrini (Sept. 8, 1950).
Epilepsy: St. Vitus.
Engineers: St. Ferdinand III.

Eucharistic congresses and societies: St. Paschal Baylon (Nov. 28, 1897).

Expectant mothers: St. Raymund Nonnatus, St. Gerard Majella.

Eye diseases: St. Lucy.

Falsely accused: St. Raymund Nonnatus.

Farmers: St. George, St. Isidore.

Farriers: St. John Baptist.

Firemen: St. Florian.

Fire prevention: St. Catherine of Siena.

First communicants: St. Tarcisius.

Fishermen: St. Andrew.

Florists: St. Therese of Lisieux.

Forest workers: St. John Gualbert.

Foundlings: Holy Innocents.

Fullers: St. Anastasius the Fuller, St. James the Less.

Funeral directors: St. Joseph of Arimathea, St. Dismas.

Gardeners: St. Adelard, St.' Tryphon, St. Fiacre, St. Phocas.

Glassworkers: St. Luke.

Goldsmiths: St. Dunstan, St. Anastasius.

Gravediggers: St. Anthony, Abbot.

Greetings: St. Valentine.

Grocers: St. Michael.

Hairdressers: St. Martin de Porres.

Happy meetings: St. Raphael.

Hatters: St. Severus of Ravenna, St. James the Less.

Haymakers: Sts. Gervase and Protase.

Headache sufferers: St. Teresa of Avila.

Heart patients: St. John of God.

Hospital administrators: St. Basil the Great, St. Frances X. Cabrini.

Hospitals: St. Camillus de Lellis and St. John of God (June 22, 1886), St. Jude Thaddeus.

Housewives: St. Anne.

Hunters: St. Hubert, St. Eustachius.

Infantrymen: St. Maurice.

Innkeepers: St. Amand, St. Martha.

Invalids: St. Roch.

Jewelers: St. Eligius, St. Dunstan.

Journalists: St. Francis de Sales (Apr. 26, 1923).

Jurists: St. John Capistran.

Laborers: St. Isidore, St. James, St. John Bosco.

Lawyers: St. Ivo, St. Genesius, St. Thomas More.

Learning: St. Ambrose.

Librarians: St. Jerome.

Lighthouse keepers: St. Venerius.

Locksmiths: St. Dunstan.

Maids: St. Zita.

Marble workers: St. Clement I.

Mariners: St. Michael, St. Nicholas of Tolentino.

Medical record librarians: St. Raymond of Penyafort.

Medical social workers: St. John Regis.

Medical technicians: St. Albert the Great.

Mentally ill: St. Dymphna.

Merchants: St. Francis of Assisi, St. Nicholas of Myra.

Messengers: St. Gabriel.

Metal workers: St. Eligius.

Millers: St. Arnulph, St. Victor.

Missions, Foreign: St. Francis Xavier (Mar. 25, 1904), St. Therese of Lisieux (Dec. 14, 1927).

Missions, Negro: St. Peter Claver (1896, Leo XIII), St. Benedict the Black.

Missions, Parish: St. Leonard of Port Maurice (Mar. 17, 1023).

Mothers: St. Monica.

Motorcyclists: Our Lady of Grace.

Motorists: St. Christopher, St. Frances of Rome.

Mountaineers: St. Bernard of Menthon.

Musicians: St. Gregory the Great, St. Cecilia, St. Dunstan.

Nail makers: St. Cloud.

Notaries: St. Luke, St. Mark.

Nurses: St. Camillus de Lellis and St. John of God (1930, Pius XI), St. Agatha, St. Raphael.

Nursing and nursing service: St. Elizabeth of Hungary, St. Catherine of Siena.

Orators: St. John Chrysostom (July 8, 1908).

Organ builders: St. Cecilia.

Orphans: St. Jerome Emiliani.

Painters: St. Luke.

Paratroopers: St. Michael.

Pawnbrokers: St. Nicholas.

Pharmacists: Sts. Cosmas and Damian, St. James the Greater.

Pharmacists (in hospitals): St. Gemma Galgani.

Philosophers: St. Justin.

Physicians: St. Pantaleon, Sts. Cosmas and Damian, St. Luke, St. Raphael.

Pilgrims: St. James.

Plasterers: St. Bartholomew.

Poets: St. David, St. Cecilia.

Poison sufferers: St. Benedict.

Policemen: St. Michael.

Poor: St. Lawrence, St. Anthony of Padua.

Poor souls: St. Nicholas of Tolentino.

Porters: St. Christopher.

Possessed: St. Bruno, St. Denis.

Postal employees: St. Gabriel.

Priests: St. Jean-Baptiste Vianney (Apr. 23, 1929).

Printers: St. John of God, St. Augustine of Hippo, St. Genesius.

Prisoners: St. Dismas, St. Joseph Cafasso.

Protector of crops: St. Ansovinus.

Public relations: St. Bernardine of Siena (May 20, 1960).

Public relations (of hospitals): St. Paul, Apostle.

Radiologists: St. Michael (Jan. 15, 1941).

Radio workers: St. Gabriel.

Retreats: St. Ignatius Loyola (July 25, 1922).

Rheumatism: St. James the Greater.

Saddlers: Sts. Crispin and Crispinian.

Sailors: St. Cuthbert, St. Brendan, St. Eulalia, St. Christopher, St. Peter Gonzales, St. Erasmus, St. Nicholas.

Scholars: St. Brigid.

Schools, Catholic: St. Thomas Aquinas (Aug. 4, 1880), St. Joseph Calasanz (Aug. 13, 1948).

Scientists: St. Albert (Aug. 13, 1948).

Sculptors: St. Claude.

Seamen: St. Francis of Paola.

Searchers for lost articles: St. Anthony of Padua.

Secretaries: St. Genesius.

Seminarians: St. Charles Borromeo.

Servants: St. Martha, St. Zita.

Shoemakers: Sts. Crispin and Crispinian.

Sick: St. Michael, St. John of God and St. Camillus de Lellis (June 22, 1886).

Silversmiths: St. Andronicus.

Singers: St. Gregory, St. Cecilia.

Skaters: St. Lidwina.

Skiers: St. Bernard.

Social workers: St. Louise de Marillac (Feb. 12, 1960).

Soldiers: St. Hadrian, St. George, St. Ignatius, St. Sebastian, St. Martin of Tours, St. Joan of Arc.

Speleologists: St. Benedict.

Stenographers: St. Genesius, St. Cassian.

Stonecutters: St. Clement.

Stonemasons: St. Stephen.

Students: St. Thomas Aquinas.

Surgeons: Sts. Cosmas and Damian, St. Luke.

Swordsmiths: St. Maurice.

Tailors: St. Homobonus.

Tanners: Sts. Crispin and Crispinian, St. Simon.

Tax collectors: St. Matthew.

Teachers: St. Gregory the Great, St. John Baptist de la Salle (May 15, 1950).

Telecommunications workers: St. Gabriel (Jan. 12, 1951).

Telegraph/telephone workers: St. Gabriel.

Television: St. Clare of Assisi (Feb. 14, 1958).

Television workers: St. Gabriel.

Tertiaries (Franciscan): St. Louis of France, St. Elizabeth of Hungary.

Theologians: St. Augustine, St. Alphonsus Liguori.

Throat sufferers: St. Blase.

Travelers: St. Anthony of Padua, St. Nicholas of Myra, St. Christopher, St. Raphael.

Travel hostesses: St. Bona (Mar. 2, 1962).

Universities: Blessed Contardo Ferrini.

Vocations: St. Alphonsus.

Watchmen: St. Peter of Alcantara.

Weavers: St. Paul the Hermit, St. Anastasius the Fuller, St. Anastasia.

Wine merchants: St. Amand.

Women in labor: St. Anne.

Women's Army Corps: St. Genevieve.

Workingmen: St. Joseph.

Writers: St. Francis de Sales (Apr. 26, 1923), St. Lucy.

Yachtsmen: St. Adjutor.

Young girls: St. Agnes.

Youth: St. Aloysius Gonzaga (1729, Benedict XIII; 1926, Pius XI), St. John Berchmans, St. Gabriel of the Sorrowful Mother.

Patrons of Places

Alsace: St. Odile.

Americas: Our Lady of Guadalupe; St. Rose of Lima.

Argentina: Our Lady of Lujan.

Armenia: St. Gregory Illuminator.

Asia Minor: St. John, Evangelist.

Australia: Our Lady Help of Christians.

Belgium: St. Joseph.

Bohemia: Sts. Wenceslaus, Ludmilla.

Borneo: St. Francis Xavier.

Brazil: Nossa Senhora de Aparecida, Immaculate Conception; St. Peter of Alcantara.

Canada: St. Joseph; St. Anne.

Ceylon (Sri Lanka): St. Lawrence.

Chile: St. James; Our Lady of Mt. Carmel.

China: St. Joseph.

Colombia: St. Peter Claver; St. Louis Bertran.

Corsica: Immaculate Conception.

Czechoslovakia: St. Wenceslaus; St. John Nepomucene; St. Procopius.

Denmark: St. Ansgar; St. Canute.

Dominican Republic: Our Lady of High Grace; St. Dominic.

East Indies: St. Thomas, Apostle.

Ecuador: Sacred Heart.

England: St. George.

Europe: St. Benedict.

Finland: St. Henry.

France: Our Lady of the Assumption; St. Joan of Arc; St. Therese.

Germany: Sts. Boniface, Michael.

Gibraltar: Blessed Virgin Mary under title "Our Lady of Europe" (May 31, 1979).

Greece: St. Nicholas; St. Andrew.

Holland: St. Willibrord.

Hungary: Blessed Virgin, "Great Lady of Hungary"; St. Stephen, King.

India: Our Lady of Assumption.

Ireland: Sts. Patrick, Brigid and Columba.

Italy: St. Francis of Assisi; St. Catherine of Siena.

Japan: St. Peter Baptist.

Lesotho: Immaculate Heart of Mary.

Lithuania: St. Casimir, Bl. Cunegunda.

Malta: St. Paul; Our Lady of the Assumption.

Mexico: Our Lady of Guadalupe.

Monaco: St. Devota.

Moravia: Sts. Cyril and Methodius.

New Zealand: Our Lady Help of Christians.

Norway: St. Olaf.

Papua-New Guinea (including northern Solomon Islands): St. Michael the Archangel (May 31, 1979)

Paraguay: Our Lady of Assumption.

Peru: St. Joseph.

Philippines: Sacred Heart of Mary.

Poland: St. Casimir; Bl. Cunegunda; St. Stanislaus of Cracow; Our Lady of Czestochowa.

Portugal: Immaculate Conception; St. Francis Borgia; St. Anthony of Padua; St. Vincent; St. George.

Republic of South Africa: Our Lady of Assumption.

Russia: St. Andrew; St. Nicholas of Myra; St. Therese of Lisieux.

Scandinavia: St. Ansgar.

Scotland: St. Andrew; St. Columba.

Silesia: St. Hedwig.

Slovakia: Our Lady of Sorrows.

South America: St. Rose of Lima.

Spain: St. James; St. Teresa.

Sweden: St. Bridget; St. Eric.

United States: Immaculate Conception.

Uruguay: Our Lady of Lujan.

Wales: St. David.

West Indies: St. Gertrude.

Apostles of Places, Peoples

Alps: St. Bernard of Menthon.

Andalusia (Spain): St. John of Avila.

Antioch: St. Barnabas.

Armenia: St. Gregory the Illuminator; St. Bartholomew.

Austria: St. Severine.

Bavaria: St. Killian.

Brazil: Jose Anchieta.

California: Junipero Serra.

Carinthia (Yugoslavia): St. Virgil.

Colombia: St. Louis Bertran.

Corsica: St. Alexander Sauli.

Crete: St. Titus.

Cyprus: St. Barnabas.

Denmark: St. Ansgar.

England: St. Augustine of Canterbury; St. Gregory the Great.

Ethiopia: St. Frumentius.

Finland: St. Henry.

Florence: St. Andrew Corsini.

France: St. Remigius; St. Martin of Tours; St. Denis.

Friesland (Germany): St. Suitbert; St. Willibrord.

Gaul: St. Irenaeus.

Gentiles: St. Paul.

Georgia (Russia): St. Nino.

Germany: St. Boniface; St. Peter Canisius.

Gothland (Sweden): St. Sigfrid.

Guelderland (Holland): St. Plechelm.

Highlanders (Scotland): St. Columba.

Hungarians (Magyars): St. Stephen, King; St. Gerard; Bl. Astricus.

India: St. Thomas, Apostle.

Indies: St. Francis Xavier.

Ireland: St. Patrick.

Iroquois: Francois Picquit.

Italy: St. Bernardine of Siena.

Japan: St. Francis Xavier.

Malta: St. Paul.

Mexico: The twelve Apostles of Mexico (Franciscans), headed by Fra. Martin de Valencia.

Negro Slaves: St. Peter Claver.

Netherlands: St. Willibrord.

Northumbria (Britain): St. Aidan.

Norway: St. Olaf.

Ottawas (Indians): Fr. Claude Allouez.

Persia: St. Maruthas.

Poland: St. Hyacinth.

Portugal: St. Christian.

Prussia (Slavs): St. Adalbert; St. Bruno of Querfurt.

Rome: St. Philip Neri.

Rumania: St. Nicetas.

Ruthenia: St. Bruno.

Sardinia: St. Ephesus.

Saxony: St. Willihad.

Scandinavia (North): St. Ansgar.

Scotland: St. Palladius.

Slavs: Sts. Cyril and Methodius, St. Adalbert.

Spain: St. James; Sts. Euphrasius and Felix.

Sweden: St. Ansgar.

Switzerland: St. Andeol.

Tournai (Belgium): St. Eligius, St. Piaton.

Emblems of Saints

St. Agatha: Tongs, veil.

St. Agnes: Lamb.

St. Ambrose: Bees, dove, ox, pen.

St. Andrew: Transverse cross.

St. Anne, Mother of the Blessed Virgin: A door.

St. Anthony, Abbot: Bell, hog.

St. Anthony of Padua: Infant Jesus, bread, book, lily.

St. Augustine of Hippo: Dove, child, shell, pen.

St. Barnabas: Stones, ax, lance.

St. Bartholomew: Knife, flayed and holding his skin.

St. Benedict: Broken cup, raven, bell, crosier, bush.

St. Bernard of Clairvaux: Pen, bees, instruments of Passion.

St. Bernardine of Siena: Tablet or sun inscribed with IHS.

St. Blase: Wax, taper, iron comb.

St. Bonaventure: Communion, ciborium, cardinal's hat.

St. Boniface: Oak, ax, book, fox, scourge, fountain, raven, sword.

St. Bridget of Sweden: Book, pilgrim's staff.

St. Bridget of Kildare: Cross, flame over her head, candle.

St. Catherine of Ricci: Ring, crown, crucifix.

St. Catherine of Siena: Stigmata, cross, ring, lily.

St. Cecilia: Organ.

St. Charles Borromeo: Communion, coat of arms with word *Humilitas*.

St. Christopher: Giant, torrent, tree, Child Jesus on his shoulders.

St. Clare of Assisi: Monstrance.

Sts. Cosmas and Damian: A phial, box of ointment.

St. Cyril of Alexandria: Blessed Virgin holding the Child Jesus, pen.

St. Cyril of Jerusalem: Purse, book.

St. Dominic: Rosary, star.

St. Edmund the Martyr: Arrow, sword.

St. Elizabeth of Hungary: Alms, flowers, bread, the poor, a pitcher.

St. Francis of Assisi: Deer, wolf, birds, fish, skull, the Stigmata.

St. Francis Xavier: Crucifix, bell, vessel, Negro.

St. Genevieve: Bread, keys, herd, candle.

St. George: Dragon.

St. Gertrude: Crown, taper, lily.

Sts. Gervase and Protase: Scourge, club, sword.

St. Gregory I (the Great): Tiara, crosier, dove.

St. Helena: Cross.

St. Hilary: Stick, pen, child.

St. Ignatius Loyola: Communion, chasuble, book, apparition of Our Lord.

St. Isidore: Bees, pen.

St. James the Greater: Pilgrim's staff, shell, key, sword.

St. James the Less: Square rule, halberd, club.

St. Jerome: Lion.

St. John Berchmans: Rule of St. Ignatius, cross, rosary.

St. John Chrysostom: Bees, dove, pen.

St. John of God: Alms, a heart, crown of thorns.

St. John the Baptist: Lamb, head cut off on platter, skin of an animal.

St. John the Evangelist: Eagle, chalice, kettle, armor.

St. Josaphat Kuncevyc: Chalice, crown, winged deacon.

St. Joseph, Spouse of the Blessed Virgin: Infant Jesus, lily, rod, plane, carpenter's square.

St. Jude: Sword, square rule, club.

St. Justin Martyr: Ax, sword.

St. Lawrence: Cross, book of the Gospels, gridiron.

St. Leander of Seville: A pen.

St. Liborius: Pebbles, peacock.

St. Longinus: In arms at foot of the cross.

St. Louis IX of France: Crown of thorns, nails.

St. Lucy: Cord, eyes.

St. Luke: Ox, book, brush, palette.

St. Mark: Lion, book.

St. Martha: Holy water sprinkler, dragon.

St. Mary Magdalene: Alabaster box of ointment.

St. Matilda: Purse, alms.

St. Matthew: Winged man, purse, lance.

St. Matthias: Lance.

St. Maurus: Scales, spade, crutch.

St. Meinrad: Two ravens.

St. Michael: Scales, banner, sword, dragon.

St. Monica: Girdle, tears.

St. Nicholas: Three purses or balls, anchor or boat, child.

St. Patrick: Cross, harp, serpent, baptismal font, demons, shamrock.

St. Paul: Sword, book or scroll.

St. Peter: Keys, boat, cock.

St. Philip, Apostle: Column.

St. Philip Neri: Altar, chasuble, vial.

St. Rita of Cascia: Rose, crucifix, thorn.

St. Roch: Angel, dog, bread.

St. Rose of Lima: Crown of thorns, anchor, city.

St. Sebastian: Arrows, crown.

St. Simon: Saw, cross.

St. Simon Stock: Scapular.

St. Teresa of Avila: Heart, arrow, book.

St. Therese of Lisieux: Roses entwining a crucifix.

St. Thomas, Apostle: Lance, ax.

St. Thomas Aquinas: Chalice, monstrance, dove, ox, person trampled under foot.

St. Vincent: Gridiron, boat.

St. Vincent de Paul: Children.

St. Vincent Ferrer: Pulpit, cardinal's hat, trumpet, captives.

THE MOTHER OF JESUS IN CATHOLIC UNDERSTANDING

This article was written by the Rev. Eamon R. Carroll, O. Carm., professor in the Department of Theology, School of Religious Studies, Catholic University of America; author of "Understanding the Mother of Jesus" (published by M. Glazier, Wilmington, Del.; 1979).

Documents of the Second Vatican Council have provided the charter for current Catholic understanding of the Virgin Mary, Mother of Jesus. This conciliar teaching was expanded and applied in the pastoral letter, "Behold Your Mother: Woman of Faith," issued by the U.S. bishops Nov. 21, 1973. Pope Paul VI added guidelines for devotion, in the revised liturgy and with respect to the Rosary, in the letter *Marialis Cultus* ("To Honor Mary"), dated Feb. 2, 1974.

The first conciliar document, the *Constitution on the Sacred Liturgy*, linked Mary with the life, death and exaltation of Jesus, stating: "In celebrating this annual cycle of Christ's mysteries, holy Church honors with special love blessed Mary, Mother of God, who is joined by an inseparable bond to the saving work of her Son. In her the Church holds up and admires the most excellent fruit of the redemption, and joyfully contemplates, as in a faultless manner, that which she herself wholly desires and hopes to be" (No. 103).

The eighth and final chapter of the *Dogmatic Constitution on the Church* is entitled "The Blessed Virgin Mary, Mother of God, in the Mystery of Christ and the Church." The seventh chapter deals with the communion of saints, the bond between the pilgrim Church on earth and the blessed joined to the risen Christ — what John deSatgé, an English Anglican, describes as the "mutual sharing and caring in Christ for one another." At the Eucharist, above all, "in union with the whole Church we honor Mary, the ever-Virgin Mother of Jesus Christ our Lord and God"

(First Eucharistic Prayer; cf. *Constitution on the Church*, No. 50).

What Catholics believe about the Mother of Jesus is the basis for her place in their prayer life, both in the liturgy and particularly the Eucharist, and in other forms of piety, especially the Rosary. The Church's growth in insight about the Blessed Virgin comes about as Christians ponder the meaning of Mary in prayer as well as in study. The Church has come to know Mary's role by experience and by contemplation of her hidden holiness (*Constitution on the Church*, No. 64). The tradition about Mary has been transmitted by doctrinal teaching and also by life and worship, even as in her own life Mary treasured in her heart God's words and deeds (*Dogmatic Constitution on Divine Revelation*, No. 8).

Mary in the Bible

The possibility of consensus on the Virgin Mary in the Bible was the theme of a book published in 1978, entitled *Mary in the New Testament* (edited by R. E. Brown, J. A. Fitzmyer, J. Reumann and K. P. Donfried). Limiting their study to the New Testament and using critical techniques of interpretation, a team of 12 authors — Catholics, Lutherans, Anglicans and others — agreed on a biblical portrait of Mary the Virgin as the great gospel model of faith commitment.

One valuable insight centers on the "true kinsmen" incident (Mk. 3:31-35; Mt. 12:46-50; Lk. 8:19-21). One day while Jesus was preaching, word was sent to him that his "mother and brethren" wished to see him. In St. Mark, the oldest account, there is a sharp distinction between the circle of the hearers of Jesus, who were "inside" and counted as his "true family," and the relatives "outside," who failed to understand him. St. Mark does not clearly place Mary among the outsiders, but neither does he carefully distinguish her from the other relatives who did not esteem Jesus. St. Luke shifts the focus completely, placing the relatives, especially the Mother of Jesus, among the true followers, as he does also in the Acts of the Apostles by mentioning them in the Upper Room before Pentecost.

St. Luke is fond of speaking of the "word of God." At the Annunciation, Mary consented with the statement, "Be it done to me according to your word" (Lk. 1:26-38), and "the Word was made flesh" (Jn. 1:14). Jesus said in reply to the message about his visitors, "My mother and my brothers are those who hear the word of God and do it" (Lk. 8:21). St. Luke relates this event just after the parables of the sower and the seed and the lamp on the lampstand. Consistent with his high praise of the Virgin Mary in the infancy chapters, he regards Mary as the rich soil — she heard the word and brought forth fruit in abundance, the Holy One who is the Son of God. She is the pure light, rekindled by the coming of the Redeemer; she is the "woman clothed with the sun" (Rv. 12:1), for Jesus is the "sun of justice."

St. Luke alone saved one other mention of Mary during the public ministry of Jesus, in the story of the "enthusiastic woman" (Lk. 11:27-28). One day while Jesus was preaching, a woman cried out, "Blessed is the womb that bore you and the breasts that nursed you." He replied, "Still more blessed are those who hear the word of God and keep it." The obedient Mary, handmaid of the Lord, brought together opposed beatitudes — the anonymous woman's praise of her motherhood and Jesus' tribute to her faith.

In the opening chapter of St. Luke, Elizabeth did the same when, filled with the Holy Spirit, she returned Mary's greeting with the loud cry, "Of all women you are the most blessed, and blessed is the fruit of your womb." Continuing in praise of her young cousin's faith, she added: "Yes, blessed is she who has believed, for the things promised her by the Lord will be fulfilled" (Lk. 1:39-45).

Mary the Virgin

Both St. Luke and St. Matthew, whose infancy narratives differ so much otherwise, agree that Mary conceived Jesus virginally, that her Son had no human father. The Creed affirms that Jesus was "conceived of the Virgin Mary by the power of the Holy Spirit."

St. Luke writes of the virginal conception of Jesus from the standpoint of Mary. To her question, "How can this be since I know not man?" the angel replied by appealing to God's power.

St. Matthew's viewpoint is that of Joseph, who was informed in a dream-vision that Mary's child was of no human father. God accomplishes his saving purposes without dependence on the will of the flesh and the will of man (Jn. 1:13). God shows his favor where he chooses — whether for the barren Sara, wife of Abraham, or aged Elizabeth, the wife of Zechariah, or the Virgin Mary. In the words of the promise to Abraham, repeated by Gabriel to Mary, "Nothing is impossible to God" (Lk. 1:37; Gn. 18:14).

Mary and Joseph accepted as God's will the virginal conception, an unprecedented event, the sign of God sending his Son to be the Savior. Their lives were henceforth totally dedicated to the service of Jesus.

As various forms of Christian witness developed in the Church, the conviction that Mary remains always a virgin came to be held as Catholic doctrine. The Gospels leave undecided the identity of the "brethren" of Jesus. From lived experience, by the fourth century the Church had come to see Mary's life-long virginity as part of her commitment to her Son and his mission. Such "development of doctrine" remains a point of difference between Catholics and Protestants, although the great Reformers — Luther, Calvin and later John Wesley — all held that Mary was ever-Virgin.

St. Luke and St. John on Mary

Along with the role of Mary in the childhood of Jesus, St. Luke sees her as part of the fulfillment of messianic prophecy. The Second Vatican Council spoke of "the exalted daughter of Zion in whom the times are fulfilled after the long waiting for the promise, and the new economy inaugurated when the Son of God takes on human nature from her in order to free men from sin by the mysteries of his flesh." The expectations of Israel for the Messiah reach their peak in Mary of Nazareth: "She stands out among the Lord's lowly and poor who confidently look for salvation from him" (*Constitution on the Church,* No. 55).

The Gospel of St. John introduces Mary at the opening and closing of her Son's ministry, which began with the first of his signs at Cana (Jn. 2:1-11) and ended on Calvary (Jn. 19). Both scenes deal with a "third day," both turn on the "hour," not yet come at Cana but achieved in the decisive event of Calvary. In both, Jesus addresses his Mother with the unaccustomed title, "woman." The request of Mary at Cana is for more than wine to save the wedding feast. She stands for Israel of old, symbolized by the water pots required for religious purifications; Mary stands also for the new Israel, the Church, the bride of Christ, symbolized by the abundant choice wine of the messianic banquet. The marriage feast looks forward to the hour when Christ, the bridegroom, will lay down his life in love for his bride, the Church.

When Jesus spoke from the cross to his Mother and the beloved disciple, "Woman, behold your son," and "Behold your Mother," more was meant than that the disciple should provide for Mary's care (Jn. 19:26-27). In his farewell discourse at the Last Supper, Jesus spoke of the woman in agony because her hour had come. "But when she has borne her child, she no longer remembers her pain for joy that a man has been born into the world" (Jn. 16:21). The longing of Israel for the coming of the Messiah was sometimes compared to labor pains. The "daughter of Zion" had been promised she would become the mother of all races and all nations. The words of Jesus on Calvary announced the fulfillment of that promise; Mary stands for the "woman" who is mother Church, new Israel, new People of God.

In St. John's Gospel, it is only after his words to his Mother and the disciple that Jesus, knowing "that everything was now finished," said, "I am thirsty," and then, "Now it is finished." "Then he bowed his head and delivered over his spirit" (Jn. 19:28-29).

The giving up of the spirit means both the expiring of Jesus and the giving of the Holy Spirit to the Church. The wine Mary requested at Cana was the wine of the Spirit, to be poured out at the messianic banquet. The prayer for the wine of the Spirit is answered through the self-surrender of Jesus on the cross. The triumphant Christ "gives up his spirit," and the Church comes into being. The Acts of the Apostles describe the effects of the outpouring of the Spirit at Pentecost and afterwards. What Mary requested at Cana, what she prayed for in agony at the cross of Jesus, what she sought before Pentecost in union with the Apostles and relatives and the women — all "with one accord devoted to prayer" — is the gift of the Spirit. At Nazareth Mary conceived her Son, and God became man by the power of the Holy Spirit; in the Upper Room she prayed for the Spirit that Jesus be born again in the members of his Church (*Constitution on the Church,* No. 59).

The New Eve

To the titles of Mary already familiar from the Gospels — "the Virgin," "Favored One," "Mother of Jesus," "Mother of my Lord" (Elizabeth's greeting, meaning "Mother of the Messianic King") — the early Church added other descriptions. By the mid-second century Mary was being compared to Eve. Eve was deceived by the word of the evil angel and by disobedience brought death; Mary, the obedient Virgin, heeded the message of the good angel and by her consent brought Life to the world. The title of "New Eve" became common for Mary. By the time of St. Jerome (d. 419), it was proverbial to say, "Death through Eve, life through Mary."

Immaculate Conception

Reflecting on the Blessed Virgin, Christians pondered various aspects of her holiness. The question arose of her freedom from original sin, God's gift of grace that came to be called her Immaculate Conception (not to be confused with the virginal conception of Jesus, for Mary was the child of the father and mother recalled as Joachim and Anne). It took centuries of development before the Immaculate Conception was held to be revealed by God and defined as dogma by Pius IX in 1854. The absence of clear scriptural evidence was one delaying factor, another was lack of clarity about the meaning of original sin, and most cogent was the requirement that Mary be beneficiary of the saving work of Christ. As the English Anglican John deSatgé expresses it, "Mary, who rejoiced in her Savior, was the last person to have need of one." The Franciscan John Duns Scotus (d. 1308) suggested that Mary was kept free of original sin by a "preservative redemption" — in anticipation of the foreseen merits of Jesus

Christ — the explanation eventually recognized as revealed truth.

The Assumption

The final facet of Mary's holiness is the Assumption, her union body and soul with the risen Christ in the glory of heaven, defined as dogma by Pope Pius XII in 1950. By the sixth century the feast of the Assumption was being celebrated in the East, a development from a still earlier August 15 feast that had been known as the Memory of Mary (like the birthdays into heaven of the martyrs), as the Passing of Mary, and as the Dormition or Falling Asleep of the Mother of God. There is no compelling biblical testimony; the appeal is to the concordant faith of the Church, convinced that the promise of the resurrection of the flesh in union with the risen Savior has already been fulfilled for the Mother of the Lord, who gave him human birth in her pure body and was his loyal disciple unto the end.

Model of the Church

All beliefs about the Blessed Virgin lead to Christ. God kept her free from original sin for the sake of Jesus, that she might give herself wholeheartedly to his life and work (*Constitution on the Church,* No. 56), and in consideration of his redemptive mission. Mary's Assumption is her reunion with her Son in the power of his resurrection. The Marian privileges of the Immaculate Conception and the Assumption enrich also the self-understanding of the Church, for she is the "most excellent fruit of the redemption, the spotless model of the Church," the one in whom Christians admire God's plan for his Church. "In the most holy Virgin the Church has already reached that perfection whereby she exists without spot or wrinkle (Eph. 5:27)" (*Constitution on the Church,* No. 65).

Mary Immaculate is a sign of the love of Christ for his bride, the Church; the bridegroom purifies her by his blood to make her all-holy. The preface for the Solemnity of the Immaculate Conception (December 8) addresses the Father: "You allowed no stain of sin to touch the Virgin Mary. Full of grace, she was to be a worthy Mother of your Son, your sign of favor to the Church at its beginning, and the promise of its perfection as the bride of Christ, radiantly beautiful."

Faithful to his promise, Christ has prepared a place for his bride, the Church. In Mary, daughter of the Church, now joined to Christ body and soul in glory, the pilgrim Church sees the successful completion of its own journey. The resurrection of Jesus is the central truth; the Assumption of Mary is the living sign of the Church's call to glory, to loving union with the victorious Redeemer. The preface at Mass for August 15 reads: "Today the Virgin Mother of God was taken up into heaven to be the beginning and the pattern of the Church in its perfection, and a sign of sure hope and comfort for your pilgrim people. You would not allow decay to touch her body, for she had given birth in the glory of the Incarnation to your Son, the Lord of all life." (Cf. also *Constitution on the Church,* No. 68.)

Mother of God

In 325 the first ecumenical council, at Nicaea, proclaimed that Jesus is truly Son of God. Defenders of the faith there were the first to call Mary "Mother of God." At the third ecumenical council, Ephesus, in 431, it was solemnly established that the Virgin Mary is indeed "Mother of God," for the Son to whom she gave birth is the pre-existent Second Person of the Blessed Trinity. "Mother of God" had already been used as a popular title in some parts of the Church, and after Ephesus it was adopted in the prayers of the Mass, as is still the practice in the Catholic Church and all Eastern Churches. For example, the current third Eucharistic Prayer reads: "May he (the Holy Spirit) make us an everlasting gift to you (the Father) and enable us to share in the inheritance of your saints, with Mary, the Virgin Mother of God."

Mother of the Church

When the Church began to celebrate the Assumption of Mary, it did so in the conviction Mary did not leave the members of the Church orphans when her days on earth were ended. She continues her interest for them in union with her Son, the supreme intercessor. By the time of the Council of Ephesus in 431, authors of both the East and West — like St. Ephrem of Syria (d. 373) and St. Ambrose of Italy (d. 397) — proposed Mary as the model of Christian life, and the practice of asking her to pray for her clients on earth began to appear. The feasts of the Nativity of Mary (September 8), the Annunciation (March 25) and the Presentation of Jesus (February 2, also known as the Purification of Mary or Candlemas) have been kept from the sixth and seventh centuries.

When the words of Gabriel and Elizabeth from St. Luke's infancy narrative became part of prayer, the first part of the Hail Mary, their use led to deeper awareness of Mary's holiness as well as to counting on her heavenly help — well expressed in the second part of the Hail Mary — "Holy Mary, Mother of God, pray for us sinners now and at the hour of our death," which reached its fixed form only in the fifteenth century. Mary's place in liturgical prayer and in private prayer reflected and strengthened the sense of her continuing role as loving friend in heaven of the Church on earth. People asked Mary's prayers on their behalf, recalling Mary's own "pilgrimage of faith" and trusting in her abiding maternal care.

Greek homilists like St. John of Damascus (d. ca. 749), St. Andrew of Crete (d. 740) and St. Germanus of Constantinople (d. ca. 733) sang Mary's praises and urged confidence in her loving intercession with Christ. In the West, after the upsurge of the Carolingian times (about 800), remembered for the origin of the Saturday observance in honor of Mary, came the flowering of medieval piety, as evidenced in the writings of St. Anselm (d. 1109), St. Bernard (d. 1153) and his fellow Cistercians, and the great scholastic doctors like St. Thomas Aquinas (d. 1274) and St. Bonaventure (d. 1274). The medieval authors described Mary as Mediatrix of grace, Dispensatrix of grace, spiritual Mother. Blessed Guerric, the Cistercian abbot of Igny (France, d. 1157), emphasized the maternal role of Mary in the formation of Christ in the faithful: "Like the Church of which she is a figure, Mary is Mother of all who are born to life."

Christian Unity and Mary

At the Reformation, in reaction to abuses, the invocation of the saints was rejected as harmful to confidence in Christ the unique Mediator. Since the sixteenth century Western Christians have been sharply divided in their understanding of the communion of saints and the legitimacy of "praying to Mary." Recent events, however, hold out hope for a meeting of minds and hearts even in this sensitive area. The Second Vatican Council offered a biblical portrait of Mary without neglecting later developments in doctrine and devotion. The council described the place of Mary in words designed to meet Protestant difficulties; e.g., the much misunderstood word, Mediatrix, was used once only and was explained as completely dependent on the unique mediatorship of Christ (*Constitution on the Church,* Nos. 67, 69).

The conciliar Decree on Ecumenism, issued Nov. 21, 1964, spoke of the "order" or "hierarchy of truths" among Catholic doctrines, which differ in their relationship to the foundation of the faith (No. 11). The foundation is Jesus Christ, and here all Christians share a common profession of faith. The document mentioned realistically some differences that still divide Catholics and other Christians, in this "order of truths": the meaning of the Incarnation and Redemption, the mystery and ministry of the Church, and the role of Mary in the work of salvation (No. 20). The decree also said in this context: "We rejoice to see our separated brethren looking to Christ as the source and center of ecclesiastical communion. Inspired by longing for union with Christ, they feel compelled to search for unity ever more ardently, and to bear witness to their faith among all the peoples of the earth."

The formation of the Ecumenical Society of the Blessed Virgin Mary in England in 1967, and of the American branch in 1976, is an encouraging sign. The American bishops' pastoral, *"Behold Your Mother,"* appealed to the "basic reverence" of all Christians for Mary, "a veneration deeper than doctrinal differences and theological disputes" (Nos. 101-112). Pope Paul VI's major document, *Marialis Cultus,* contains an appeal to other Christians (Nos. 32 and 33). With Christians of the East, said Pope Paul, Catholics honor the Mother of God as "hope of Christians." Catholics join with Anglicans and Protestants in common praise of God, using the Virgin's own words (Lk. 1:46-55).

It may well be that the growing interest in the bonds between the Blessed Virgin and the Holy Spirit will help bring Christians together. The Spirit of unity inspired Mary's prophecy: "All generations will call me blessed, because he who is mighty has done great things for me" (Lk. 1:48-49).

APPARITIONS OF THE BLESSED VIRGIN MARY

Only eight of the best known apparitions of the Blessed Virgin Mary are described briefly below.

The sites of the following apparitions have become shrines and centers of pilgrimage. Miracles of the moral and physical orders have been reported as occurring at these places and/or in connection with related practices of prayer and penance.

Banneux, near Liege, Belgium: Mary appeared eight times between Jan. 15 and Mar. 2, 1933, to an 11-year-old peasant girl, Mariette Beco, in a garden behind the family cottage in Banneux, near Liege. She called herself the Virgin of the Poor, and has since been venerated as Our Lady of the Poor, the Sick, and the Indifferent. A small chapel was built by a spring near the site of the apparitions and was blessed Aug. 15, 1933. Ap-

proval of devotion to Our Lady of Banneux was given in 1949 by Bishop Louis J. Kerkhofs of Liege, and a statue of that title was solemnly crowned in 1956.

Over 100 sanctuaries throughout the world are dedicated to the honor of Our Lady of Banneux.

The **International Union of Prayer,** for devotion to the Virgin of the Poor, has approximately two million members.

Beauraing, Belgium: Mary appeared 33 times between Nov. 29, 1932, and Jan. 3, 1933, to five children in the garden of a convent school in Beauraing. A chapel, which became a pilgrimage center, was erected on the spot. Reserved approval of devotion to Our Lady of Beauraing was given Feb. 2, 1943, and final approbation July 2, 1949, by Bishop Charue of Namur.

The **Marian Union of Beauraing,** a prayer association for the conversion of sinners, has thousands of members throughout the world (see Pro Maria Committee).

Fatima, Portugal: Mary appeared six times between May 13 and Oct. 13, 1917, to three children in a field called Cova da Iria near Fatima, north of Lisbon. She recommended frequent recitation of the Rosary; urged works of mortification for the conversion of sinners; called for devotion to herself under the title of her Immaculate Heart; asked that the people of Russia be consecrated to her under this title, and that the faithful make a Communion of reparation on the first Saturday of each month.

The apparitions were declared worthy of belief in October, 1930, after a seven-year canonical investigation, and devotion to Our Lady of Fatima was authorized under the title of Our Lady of the Rosary. In October, 1942, Pius XII consecrated the world to Mary under the title of her Immaculate Heart. Ten years later, in the first apostolic letter addressed directly to the peoples of Russia, he consecrated them in a special manner to Mary.

Fatima, with its sanctuary and basilica, ranks with Lourdes as the greatest of modern Marian shrines.

(See First Saturday Devotion.)

Guadalupe, Mexico: Mary appeared four times in 1531 to an Indian, Juan Diego, on Tepeyac hill outside of Mexico City, and instructed him to tell Bishop Zumarraga of her wish that a church be built there. The bishop complied with the request about two years later after being convinced of the genuineness of the apparition by the evidence of a miraculously painted life-size figure of the Virgin on the mantle of the Indian. The mantle bearing the picture has been preserved and is enshrined in the Basilica of Our Lady of Guadalupe, which has a long history as a center of devotion and pilgrimage in Mexico. The shrine church, originally dedicated in 1709 and subsequently enlarged, has the title of basilica.

Benedict XIV, in a decree issued in 1754, authorized a Mass and Office under the title of Our Lady of Guadalupe for celebration on Dec. 12, and named Mary the patroness of New Spain. Our Lady of Guadalupe was designated patroness of Latin America by St. Pius X in 1910 and patroness of the Americas by Pius XII in 1945.

Knock, Ireland: An apparition of Mary, along with the figures of St. Joseph and St. John the Apostle, was witnessed by at least 15 persons in the evening of Aug. 21, 1879, near the parish church of Knock, County Mayo. A commission appointed by the Bishop of Tuam to investigate the matter reported that testimony confirming the apparition was "trustworthy and satisfactory."

La Salette, France: Mary appeared as a sorrowing and weeping figure Sept. 19, 1846, to two peasant children, Melanie Matthieu, 15, and Maximin Giraud, 11, at La Salette in southern France. The message she confided to them, regarding the necessity of penance, was communicated to Pius IX in 1851 and has since been known at the "secret" of La Salette. Bishop de Bruillard of Grenoble declared in 1851 that the apparition was credible, and devotion to Mary under the title of Our Lady of La Salette was authorized. The devotion has been confirmed by popes since the time of Pius IX, and a Mass and Office with this title were authorized in 1942. The shrine church was given the title of minor basilica in 1879.

Lourdes, France: Mary, identifying herself as the Immaculate Conception, appeared 18 times between Feb. 11 and July 16, 1858, to 14-year-old Bernadette Soubirous at the grotto of Massabielle near Lourdes in southern France. Her message concerned the necessity of prayer and penance for the conversion of men. Mary's request that a chapel be built at the grotto and spring was fulfilled in 1862 after four years of rigid examination established the credibility of the apparitions. Devotion under the title of Our Lady of Lourdes was authorized later, and a Feb. 11 feast commemorating the apparitions was instituted by Leo XIII. St. Pius X extended this feast throughout the Church in 1907.

The Church of Notre Dame was made a basilica in 1870, and the Church of the Rosary was built later. The underground Church of St. Pius X, consecrated Mar. 25, 1958, is the second largest church in the world, with a capacity of 20,000 persons.

Our Lady of the Miraculous Medal, France: Mary appeared three times in 1830 to Catherine Laboure in the chapel of the motherhouse of the Daughters of Charity of St. Vincent de Paul, Rue de Bac, Paris. She commissioned Catherine to have made the medal of the Immaculate Conception, now known as the Miraculous Medal, and to spread devotion to her under this title. In 1832, the medal was struck according to the model revealed to Catherine.

Secret of Fatima

Sister Lucy, a Carmelite nun and one of the trio of shepherd children to whom Mary appeared, wrote a three-part account of an apparition which occurred July 13, 1917. The first part concerned a vision of hell. The second dealt with the conversion of the peoples of Russia through devotion to Mary under the title of her Immaculate Heart. The third part was the so-called "secret" which, it was said, was not to be opened until 1960 or the death of Sister Lucy, whichever came first. Presumably, the "secret" was a prophecy of dire events. To date, it has not been disclosed.

The Second Vatican Council, in its *Decree on Eastern Catholic Churches,* stated the following points.

"The Catholic Church holds in high esteem the institutions of the Eastern Churches, their liturgical rites, ecclesiastical traditions, and Christian way of life. For, distinguished as they are by their venerable antiquity, they are bright with that tradition which was handed down from the apostles through the Fathers, and which forms part of the divinely revealed and undivided heritage of the universal Church" (No. 1).

"That Church, Holy and Catholic, which is the Mystical Body of Christ, is made up of the faithful who are organically united in the Holy Spirit through the same faith, the same sacraments, and the same government and who, combining into various groups held together by a hierarchy, form separate Churches or rites. . . . It is the mind of the Catholic Church that each individual Church or rite retain its traditions whole and entire, while adjusting its way of life to the various needs of time and place" (No. 2).

"Such individual Churches, whether of the East or of the West, although they differ somewhat among themselves in what are called rites (that is, in liturgy, ecclesiastical discipline, and spiritual heritage) are, nevertheless, equally entrusted to the pastoral guidance of the Roman Pontiff, the divinely appointed successor of St. Peter in supreme government over the universal Church. They are consequently of equal dignity, so that none of them is superior to the others by reason of rite" (No. 3).

Eastern Heritage: "Each and every Catholic, as also the baptized . . . of every non-Catholic Church or community who enters into the fullness of Catholic communion, should everywhere retain his proper rite, cherish it, and observe it to the best of his ability . . ." (No. 4).

". . . The Churches of the East, as much as those of the West, fully enjoy the right, and are in duty bound, to rule themselves. Each should do so according to its proper and individual procedures . . ." (No. 5).

"All Eastern rite members should know and be convinced that they can and should always preserve their lawful liturgical rites and their established way of life, and that these should not be altered except by way of an appropriate and organic development . . ." (No. 6)

Patriarchs: "The institution of the patriarchate has existed in the Church from the earliest times and was recognized by the first ecumenical Synods.

"By the name Eastern Patriarch is meant the bishop who has jurisdiction over all bishops (including metropolitans), clergy, and people of his own territory or rite, in accordance with the norms of law and without prejudice to the primacy of the Roman Pontiff . . ." (No. 7).

"Though some of the patriarchates of the Eastern Churches are of later origin than others, all are equal in patriarchal dignity. Still the honorary and lawfully established order of precedence among them is to be preserved" (No. 8).

"In keeping with the most ancient tradition of the Church, the Patriarchs of the Eastern Churches are to be accorded exceptional respect, since each presides over his patriarchate as father and head.

"This sacred Synod, therefore, decrees that their rights and privileges should be re-established in accord with the ancient traditions of each Church and the decrees of the ecumenical Synods.

"The rights and privileges in question are those which flourished when East and West were in union, though they should be somewhat adapted to modern conditions.

"The Patriarchs with their synods constitute the superior authority for all affairs of the patriarchate, including the right to establish new eparchies and to nominate bishops of their rite within the territorial bounds of the patriarchate, without prejudice to the inalienable right of the Roman Pontiff to intervene in individual cases" (No. 9).

"What has been said of Patriarchs applies as well, under the norm of law, to major archbishops, who preside over the whole of some individual Church or rite" (No. 10).

Sacraments: "This sacred Ecumenical Synod endorses and lauds the ancient discipline of the sacraments existing in the Eastern Churches, as also the practices connected with their celebration and administration . . ." (No. 12).

"With respect to the minister of holy chrism (confirmation), let that practice be fully restored which existed among Easterners in most ancient times. Priests, therefore, can validly confer this sacrament, provided they use chrism blessed by a Patriarch or bishop" (No. 13).

"In conjunction with baptism or otherwise, all Eastern-Rite priests can confer this sacrament validly on all the faithful of any rite, including the Latin; licitly, however, only if the regulations of both common and particular law are observed. Priests of the Latin rite, to the extent of the faculties they enjoy for administering this sacrament, can confer it also on the faithful of Eastern Churches, without prejudice to rite. They do so licitly if the regulations of both common and particular law are observed" (No. 14).

"The faithful are bound on Sundays and feast days to attend the divine liturgy or, according to the regulations or custom of their own rite, the celebration of the Divine Praises. That the faithful may be able to satisfy their obligation more easily, it is decreed that this obligation can be fulfilled from the Vespers of the vigil to the end of the Sunday or the feast day . . ." (No. 15).

"Because of the everyday intermingling of the communicants of diverse Eastern Churches in the same Eastern region or territory, the faculty for hearing confession, duly and unrestrictedly granted by his proper bishop to a priest of any rite, is applicable to the entire territory of the grantor, also to the places and the faithful belonging to any other rite in the same territory, unless an Ordinary of the place explicitly decides otherwise with respect to the places pertaining to his rite" (No. 16).

". . . This sacred Synod ardently desires that where it has fallen into disuse the office of the permanent diaconate be restored. The legislative authority of each individual church should decide about the subdiaconate and the minor orders . . ." (No. 17).

"By way of preventing invalid marriages between Eastern Catholics and baptized Eastern non-Catholics, and in the interests of the permanence and sanctity of marriage and of domestic harmony, this sacred Synod decrees that the canonical 'form' for the celebration of such marriages obliges only for lawfulness. For their validity, the presence of a sacred minister suffices, as long as the other requirements of law are honored" (No. 18).

Worship: "Henceforth, it will be the exclusive right of an ecumenical Synod or the Apostolic See to establish, transfer, or suppress feast days common to all the Eastern Churches. To establish, transfer, or suppress feast days for any of the individual Churches is within the competence not only of the Apostolic See but also of a patriarchal or archiepiscopal synod, provided due consideration is given to the entire region and to other individual Churches" (No. 19).

"Until such time as all Christians desirably concur on a fixed day for the celebration of Easter, and with a view meantime to promoting unity among the Christians of a given area or nation, it is left to the Patriarchs or supreme authorities of a place to reach a unanimous agreement, after ascertaining the views of all concerned, on a single Sunday for the observance of Easter" (No. 20).

"With respect to rules concerning sacred seasons, individual faithful dwelling outside the area or territory of their own rite may conform completely to the established custom of the place where they live. When members of a family belong to different rites, they are all permitted to observe sacred seasons according to the rules of any one of these rites" (No. 21).

"From ancient times the Divine Praises have been held in high esteem among all Eastern Churches. Eastern clerics and religious should celebrate these Praises as the laws and customs of their own traditions require. To the extent they can, the faithful too should follow the example of their forbears by assisting devoutly at the Divine Praises" (No. 22).

Origin

The Church had its beginnings in Palestine, whence it spread to other regions of the world. As it spread, certain cities or jurisdictions became key centers of Christian life and missionary endeavor — notably, Jerusalem, Alexandria, Antioch and Constantinople in the East, and Rome in the West — with the result that their practices became diffused throughout their spheres of influence. Various rites originated from these practices which, although rooted in the essentials of Christian faith, were different in significant respects because of their relationships to particular cultural patterns.

Patriarchal Jurisdictions

The main lines of Eastern Church organization and liturgy were drawn before the Roman Empire was separated into Eastern and Western divisions in 292. It was originally coextensive with the boundaries of the Eastern Empire. Its jurisdictions were those of the patriarchates of Alexandria and Antioch (recognized as such by the Council of Nicaea in 325), and of Jerusalem and Constantinople (given similar recognition by the Council of Chalcedon in 451). These were the major parent bodies of the Eastern Rite Churches which for centuries were identifiable only with limited numbers of nationality and language groups in Eastern Europe, the Middle East and parts of Asia and Africa. Their members are now scattered throughout the world.

RITES AND FAITHFUL OF EASTERN CHURCHES

(Principal source of statistics: *Annuario Pontificio.* The statistics are for Eastern-Rite jurisdictions only, and do not include Eastern-Rite Catholics under the jurisdiction of Roman-Rite bishops. Some of the figures reported are only approximate. Some of the jurisdictions listed may be inactive because of government suppression.)

The Byzantine, Alexandrian, Antiochene, Armenian and Chaldean are the five principal rites used in their entirety or in modified form by the various Eastern churches. The number of Eastern Catholics throughout the world is more than 12 million.

Alexandrian Rite

Called the Liturgy of St. Mark, the Alexandrian Rite was modified by the Copts and

Melkites, and contains elements of the Byzantine Rite of St. Basil and the liturgies of Sts. Mark, Cyril and Gregory of Nazianzen. The liturgy is substantially that of the Coptic Church, which is divided into two branches — the Coptic or Egyptian, and the Ethiopian or Abyssinian.

The faithful of this rite are:

COPTS: Returned to Catholic unity about 1741; situated in Egypt, the Near East; liturgical languages are Coptic, Arabic. Jurisdictions (located in Egypt): patriarchate of Alexandria, three dioceses; 121,242.

ETHIOPIANS: Returned to Catholic unity in 1846: situated in Ethiopia, Eritrea, Jerusalem, Somalia; liturgical language is Geez. Jurisdictions (located in Ethiopia): one archdiocese, two dioceses; 99,650.

Antiochene Rite

This is the source of more derived rites than any of the other parent rites. Its origin can be traced to the Eighth Book of the *Apostolic Constitutions* and to the Liturgy of St. James of Jerusalem, which ultimately spread throughout the whole patriarchate and displaced older forms based on the *Apostolic Constitutions.*

The faithful of this rite are:

MALANKARESE: Returned to Catholic unity in 1930; situated in India; liturgical languages are Syriac, Malayalam. Jurisdictions (located in India): one archdiocese, two dioceses; 232,600.

MARONITES: United to the Holy See since the time of their founder, St. Maron; have no counterparts among the separated Eastern Christians: situated throughout the world: liturgical languages are Syriac, Arabic. Jurisdictions (located in Lebanon, Cyprus, Egypt, Syria, U.S., Brazil, Australia): patriarchate of Antioch, 16 archdioceses and dioceses, one patriarchal vicariate; 1,766,809. Where no special jurisdictions exist, they are under jurisdiction of local Roman-Rite bishops.

SYRIANS: Returned to Catholic unity in 1781; situated in Asia, Africa, the Americas, Australia; liturgical languages are Syriac, Arabic. Jurisdictions (located in Lebanon, Iraq, Egypt, Syria and Turkey): patriarchate of Antioch, seven archdioceses and dioceses, three patriarchal vicariates; 81,798.

Armenian Rite

Substantially, although using a different language, this is the Greek Liturgy of St. Basil; it is considered an older form of the Byzantine Rite, and incorporates some modifications from the Antiochene Rite.

The faithful of this rite are:

ARMENIANS, exclusively: Returned to Catholic unity during the time of the Crusades; situated in the Near East, Europe, Africa, the Americas, Australasia: liturgical language is Classical Armenian. Jurisdictions (located in Lebanon, Iran, Iraq, Egypt, Syria, Turkey, Poland, France, Greece, Rumania): patriarchate of Cilicia, eight archdioceses and dioceses, two patriarchal vicariates, one exarchate, two ordinariates; 84,500.

Byzantine Rite

Based on the Rite of St. James of Jerusalem and the churches of Antioch, and reformed by Sts. Basil and John Chrysostom, the Byzantine Rite is proper to the Church of Constantinople. (The city was called Byzantium before Constantine changed its name; the modern name is Istanbul.) It is now used by the majority of Eastern Catholics and by the Eastern Orthodox Church (which is not in union with Rome). It is, after the Roman, the most widely used rite.

The faithful of this rite are:

ALBANIANS: Returned to Catholic unity about 1628; situated in Albania; liturgical language is Albanian. Jurisdiction (located in Albania): one apostolic administration.

BULGARIANS: Returned to Catholic unity about 1861; situated in Bulgaria; liturgical language is Old Slavonic. Jurisdiction (located in Bulgaria): one apostolic exarchate.

BYELORUSSIANS, also known as WHITE RUSSIANS: Returned to Catholic unity in the 17th century; situated in Europe, the Americas, Australia; liturgical language is Old Slavonic. They have an apostolic visitor residing at Rome.

GEORGIANS: Returned to Catholic unity in 1861; situated in Georgia (Southern Russia), France; liturgical language is Georgian. They have an apostolic administrator.

GREEKS: Returned to Catholic unity in 1829; situated in Greece, Asia Minor, Europe; liturgical language is Greek. Jurisdictions (located in Greece and Turkey): two exarchates; 2,570.

HUNGARIANS: Descendants of Ruthenians who returned to Catholic unity in 1646; situated in Hungary, the rest of Europe, the Americas; liturgical languages are Greek, Hungarian, English. Jurisdictions (located in Hungary): one diocese and one exarchate: 322,800.

ITALO-ALBANIANS: Have never been separated from Rome; situated in Italy, Sicily, the Americas; liturgical languages are Greek, Italo-Albanian. Jurisdictions (located in Italy): two dioceses, one abbacy; 67,376.

MELKITES (GREEK CATHOLICS-MELKITES): Returned to Catholic unity during the time of the Crusades, but definitive reunion did not take place until early in the 18th century; situated in the Middle East, Asia, Africa, Europe, the Americas, Australia; liturgical languages are Greek, Arabic, English, Portuguese, Spanish. Jurisdictions (located in Syria, Lebanon, Jordan, Israel, U.S., Brazil): patriarchate of Antioch (with patriarchal vicariates in Egypt, Sudan, Jerusalem, Iraq and Kuwait), 16 archdioceses and dioceses; 567,490 (*Annuario Pontificio* figures. Some sources estimate 1,000,000.)

ROMANIANS: Returned to Catholic unity in 1697; situated in Rumania, the rest of Europe, the Americas; liturgical language is Modern Romanian. Jurisdictions (located in Rumania): one archdiocese, four dioceses. There were 1.5 million members in 1948 when they were forcibly incorporated into the Romanian Orthodox Church. They have an apostolic visitor in the U.S. where they number approximately 5,000.

RUSSIANS: Returned to Catholic unity about 1905; situated in Europe, the Americas, Australia, China; liturgical language is Old Slavonic. Jurisdictions (located in Russia and China): two exarchates.

RUTHENIANS, or CARPATHO-RUSSIANS (Rusins): Returned to Catholic unity in the Union of Brest-Litovek, 1596, and the Union of Uzhorod, Apr. 24, 1646; situated in Hungary, Czechoslovakia, elsewhere in Europe, the Americas, Australia; liturgical languages are Old Slavonic, English. Jurisdictions (located in Russia and the U.S.): one archdiocese, three dioceses.

SLOVAKS: Jurisdiction (located in Czechoslovakia): one diocese (also has jurisdiction over Byzantine-rite Catholics in Czechoslovakia); 285,620.

UKRAINIANS, or GALICIAN RUTHENIANS: Returned to Catholic unity about 1595; situated in Europe, the Americas, Australasia; liturgical languages are Old Slavonic and Ukrainian. Jurisdictions (located in Russian Galicia, Poland, the U.S., Canada, England, Australia, Germany, France, Brazil, Argentina): three archdioceses, 10 dioceses, five apostolic exarchates: 4,375,000. This total includes the 1943 figure of 3.5 million Ukrainian Catholics in jurisdictions subsequently forced into the Russian Orthodox Church.

YUGOSLAVS, SERBS and CROATIANS: Returned to Catholic unity in 1611; situated in Yugoslavia, the Americas; liturgical language is Old Slavonic. Jurisdiction (located in Yugoslavia): one diocese (which also has jurisdiction over all Byzantine-Rite faithful in Yugoslavia); 48,557. They are under the jurisdiction of Ruthenian bishops elsewhere.

Chaldean Rite

This rite, listed as separate and distinct by the Sacred Congregation for the Oriental Churches, was derived from the Antiochene Rite.

The faithful of this rite are:

CHALDEANS: Descendants of the Nestorians, returned to Catholic unity in 1692; situated throughout the Middle East, in Europe, Africa, the Americas; liturgical languages are Syriac, Arabic. Jurisdictions (located in Iraq, Iran, Lebanon, Syria, Turkey): patriarchate of Babylonia, 19 archdioceses and dioceses; 343,593. There are patriarchal vicars for Jordan and Egypt.

SYRO-MALABARESE: Descended from the St. Thomas Christians of India; situated mostly in the Malabar region of India; they use a Westernized and Latinized form of the Chaldean Rite in Syriac and Malayalam. Jurisdictions (located in India): two archdioceses, 16 dioceses; 2,308,681.

EASTERN JURISDICTIONS

For centuries Eastern-Rite Catholics were identifiable with a limited number of nationality and language groups in certain countries of the Middle East, Eastern Europe, Asia and Africa. The persecution of religion in the Soviet Union since 1917 and in communist-controlled countries since World War II, however — in addition to decimating and destroying the Church in those places — has resulted in the emigration of many Eastern-Rite Catholics from their homelands. This forced emigration, together with voluntary emigration, has led to the spread of Eastern Rites and their faithful to many other countries.

Europe

(Apostolic visitors for Byzantine Rite faithful in western Europe are: Archbishop Miroslav Marusyn, for Ukrainians who have no bishop of their own; Bishop Ceslao Sipovic for Byelorussians.)

ALBANIA: Byzantine Rite, apostolic administration.

AUSTRIA: Byzantine Rite, ordinariate.

BULGARIA: Byzantine Rite (Bulgarians), apostolic exarchate.

CZECHOSLOVAKIA: Byzantine Rite (Slovakians and other Byzantine-Rite Catholics), eparchy.

FRANCE: Byzantine Rite (Ukrainians), apostolic exarchate.

Armenian Rite, apostolic exarchate.

Ordinariate for all other Eastern-Rite Catholics.

GERMANY: Byzantine Rite (Ukrainians), apostolic exarchate.

GREAT BRITAIN: Byzantine Rite (Ukrainians), apostolic exarchate.

GREECE: Byzantine Rite, apostolic exarchate.

Armenian Rite, ordinariate.

HUNGARY: Byzantine Rite (Hungarians), eparchy, apostolic exarchate.

ITALY: Byzantine Rite (Italo-Albanians), two eparchies, one abbacy.

POLAND: Byzantine Rite (Ukrainian), apostolic exarchate.

Armenian Rite, archeparchy.

RUMANIA: Byzantine Rite (Romanians), metropolitan, four eparchies.

Armenian Rite, ordinariate.

RUSSIA: Byzantine Rite (Russians), apostolic exarchate; (Ruthenians), eparchy; (Ukrainians), major archeparchy, two eparchies.

YUGOSLAVIA: Byzantine Rite (Yugoslav and other Byzantine-Rite Catholics), eparchy.

Asia

CHINA: Byzantine Rite (Russians), apostolic exarchate.

CYPRUS: Antiochene Rite (Maronites), archeparchy.

INDIA: Antiochene Rite (Malankarese), metropolitan see, two eparchies.

Chaldean Rite (Syro-Malabarese), two metropolitan sees, 16 eparchies.

IRAN: Chaldean Rite (Chaldeans), two metropolitan sees, one archeparchy, one eparchy.

Armenian Rite, eparchy.

IRAQ: Antiochene Rite (Syrians), two archeparchies.

Byzantine Rite (Greek-Melkites), patriarchal vicariate.

Chaldean Rite (Chaldeans), patriarchate, two metropolitan sees, eight archeparchies and eparchies.

Armenian Rite, archeparchy.

ISRAEL (includes Jerusalem): Antiochene Rite (Syrians), patriarchal vicariate; (Maronites), patriarchal vicariate.

Byzantine Rite (Greek-Melkites), archeparchy, patriarchal vicariate.

Chaldean Rite (Chaldeans), patriarchal vicariate.

Armenian Rite, patriarchal vicariate.

JORDAN: Byzantine Rite (Greek-Melkites), archeparchy.

KUWAIT: Byzantine Rite (Greek-Melkites), patriarchal vicariate.

LEBANON: Antiochene Rite (Maronites), patriarchate, eight archeparchies and eparchies; (Syrians), patriarchate.

Byzantine Rite (Greek-Melkites), seven metropolitan and archeparchal sees.

Chaldean Rite (Chaldeans), eparchy.

Armenian Rite, patriarchate, eparchy.

SYRIAN ARAB REPUBLIC: Antiochene Rite (Maronites), two archeparchies, one eparchy; (Syrians), four archeparchies.

Byzantine Rite (Greek-Melkites), patriarchate, four metropolitan sees, one archeparchy.

Chaldean Rite (Chaldeans), eparchy.

Armenian Rite, archeparchy, eparchy, patriarchal vicariate.

TURKEY (Europe and Asia): Antiochene Rite (Syrians), patriarchal vicariate.

Byzantine Rite (Greeks), apostolic exarchate.

Chaldean Rite (Chaldeans), one archeparchy, two eparchies.

Armenian Rite, archeparchy.

Oceania

AUSTRALIA: Byzantine Rite (Ukrainians), apostolic exarchate.

Antiochene Rite (Maronites), eparchy.

Africa

EGYPT, ARAB REPUBLIC OF: Alexandrian Rite (Copts), patriarchate, three eparchies.

Antiochene Rite (Maronites), eparchy; (Syrians), eparchy.

Byzantine Rite (Greek-Melkites), patriarchal vicariate.

Chaldean Rite (Chaldeans), patriarchal vicariate.

Armenian Rite, eparchy.

ETHIOPIA: Alexandrian Rite (Ethiopians), metropolitan see, two eparchies.

SUDAN: Byzantine Rite (Greek-Melkites), patriarchal vicariate.

North America

CANADA: Byzantine Rite (Ukrainians), one metropolitan, four eparchies; (Slovaks), apostolic visitor.

UNITED STATES: Antiochene Rite (Maronites), eparchy.

Byzantine Rite (Ukrainians), one metropolitan see, two eparchies; (Ruthenians), one metropolitan see, two eparchies; (Greek-Melkites), eparchy; (Romanians), apostolic visitor.

Other Eastern-Rite Catholics are under the jurisdiction of local Roman-Rite bishops. (See Eastern-Rite Catholics in the United States.)

South America

ARGENTINA: Byzantine Rite (Ukrainians), eparchy.

Ordinariate for all other Eastern-Rite Catholics.

BRAZIL: Antiochene Rite (Maronites), eparchy.

Byzantine Rite (Greek-Melkites), eparchy; (Ukrainians), eparchy.

Ordinariate for all other Eastern-Rite Catholics.

SYNODS, ASSEMBLIES

These assemblies are collegial bodies which have pastoral authority over members of the Eastern Rite Churches.

Patriarchal Synods: Maronites: Antoine Khoraiche, patriarch of Antioch of the Maronites.

Melkites: Maximos V Hakim, patriarch of Antioch of the Greek Catholics-Melkites.

Chaldeans: Paul II Cheikho, patriarch of Babylonia of the Chaldeans.

Copts: Cardinal Stephanos I Sidarouss, C.M., patriarch of Alexandria of the Copts.

Syrians: Ignace Antoine II Hayek, patriarch of Antioch of the Syrians.

Armenians: Hemaiagh Pierre XVII Ghedighian, patriarch of Cilicia of the Armenians.

Assemblies: Assembly of Ordinaries of the Arab Republic of Egypt: Cardinal Stephanos I Sidarouss, C.M., patriarch of Alexandria of the Copts, president.

Assembly of Catholic Patriarchs and Bishops of Lebanon: Antoine Khoraiche, patriarch of Antioch of the Maronites, president.

Assembly of Ordinaries of the Syrian Arab Republic: Maximos V Hakim, patriarch of Antioch of the Greek Catholics-Melkites, president.

Interritual Union of the Bishops of Iraq: Paul II Cheikho, patriarch of Babylonia of the Chaldeans, president.

Conference of the Ukrainian Catholic Hierarchy (Feb. 9, 1962).

Malabarese Episcopal Conference (June 4, 1970): Cardinal Joseph Parecattil, Ernakulam, president.

Iranian Episcopal Conference (Aug. 11, 1977).

Of the collegial bodies listed above, the patriarchal synods have the most authority. In addition to other prerogatives, they have the right to elect bishops and regulate discipline for their respective rites.

EASTERN RITES IN U.S.

(Statistics, from the *Official Catholic Directory*, are membership figures reported by Eastern-Rite jurisdictions. Additional Eastern-Rite Catholics are included in statistics for Roman-Rite dioceses.)

Byzantine Rite

Ukrainians: There are 245,180 in three jurisdictions in the U.S.: the metropolitan see of Philadelphia (1924, metropolitan 1958) and the suffragan sees of Stamford, Conn. (1956), and St. Nicholas of Chicago (1961).

Ruthenians: There are 281,080 in three jurisdictions in the U.S.: the metropolitan see of Pittsburgh (est. 1924 at Pittsburgh; metropolitan and transferred to Munhall, 1969; transferred to Pittsburgh, 1977) and the suffragan sees of Passaic, N.J. (1963), and Parma, Ohio (1969). Hungarian and Croatian Byzantine Catholics in the U.S. are also under the jurisdiction of Ruthenian-Rite bishops.

Melkites (Greek Catholics-Melkites): In 1980, 22,358 (of approximately 55,000) were reported under the jurisdiction of the Melkite eparchy of Newton, Mass. (established as an exarchate, 1965; eparchy, 1976).

Romanians: There are approximately 5,000 in 16 Romanian Catholic Byzantine Rite parishes in the U.S., each under the jurisdiction of the Roman-Rite bishop of the territory in which it is located: Cleveland diocese (3 parishes), Detroit (2), Erie (1), Gary (2), Pittsburgh (1), Rockford (2), Trenton (2), and Youngstown (3). No separate statistics are available. The Association of Romanian Catholics of America (see Index) was established in 1948 to preserve the identity of Romanian Catholics within the general framework of the Catholic Church in America. It has petitioned the Holy See for a bishop of the rite in the U.S. In 1972, the Holy See assigned Msgr. Octavian Barlea as an apostolic visitor to Romanians in the U.S.

Byelorussians: Have one parish in the U.S. — Christ the Redeemer, Chicago, Ill. — and are under the jurisdiction of the local Roman-Rite bishop.

Russians: Have parishes in California (St. Andrew, El Segundo, and Our Lady of Fatima Center, San Francisco); Massachusetts (Our Lady of Kazan, Boston); New York (St. Michael's Chapel, Pope John XXIII Reunion Center). They are under the jurisdiction of local Roman-Rite bishops.

Antiochene Rite

In 1980, 30,887 (of approximately 153,000) Maronites were reported under the jurisdiction of the eparchy of St. Maron, Brooklyn (established at Detroit as an exarchate, 1966; eparchy, 1972; transferred to Brooklyn, 1977).

Armenian Rite

Have parishes in California (Our Lady Queen of Martyrs, Los Angeles); Massachusetts (Holy Cross, Cambridge); Michigan (St. Vartan, Detroit); New Jersey (Sacred Heart, Paterson); New York (Armenian Catholic Community, Forest Hills, Brooklyn). They are under the jurisdiction of local Roman-Rite bishops.

Chaldean Rite

Have parishes in California (St. Thomas the Apostle, Turlock, and St. Peter, Spring Valley); Illinois (St. Ephrem, Chicago); Michigan (Mother of God, Southfield, and Sacred Heart, Detroit) and Virginia (St. Joseph, Falls Church). They are under the jurisdiction of local Roman-Rite bishops.

BYZANTINE DIVINE LITURGY

The Divine Liturgy in all rites is based on the consecration of bread and wine by the narration-reactualization of the actions of Christ at the Last Supper. Aside from this fundamental usage, there are differences between the Roman (Latin) Rite and Eastern Rites, and among the Eastern Rites themselves. Following is a general description of the Byzantine Divine Liturgy which is in widest use in the Eastern-Rite Churches.

In the Byzantine, as in all Eastern Rites, the bread and wine are prepared at the start of the Liturgy. The priest does this in a little niche or at a table in the sanctuary. Taking a round loaf of leavened bread stamped with religious symbols, he cuts out a square host and other particles while reciting verses expressing the symbolism of the action. When the bread and wine are ready, he says a prayer of offering and incenses the oblations, the altar, the icons and the people.

At the altar a litany for all classes of people is sung by the priest. The congregation answers, "Lord, have mercy."

The Little Entrance comes next. In procession, the priest leaves the sanctuary carrying the Book of the Gospels, and then returns. He sings prayers especially selected for the day and the feast. These are followed by the solemn singing of the prayer, "Holy God, Holy Mighty One, Holy Immortal One."

The Epistle follows. The Gospel is sung or read by the priest facing the people at the middle door of the sanctuary.

An interruption after the Liturgy of the Catechumens, formerly an instructional period for those learning the faith, is clearly marked. Catechumens, if present, are dismissed with a prayer. Following this are a prayer and litany for the faithful.

The Great Entrance or solemn Offertory Procession then takes place. The priest first says a long silent prayer for himself, in preparation for the great act to come. Again he incenses the oblations, the altar, the icons and people. He goes to the table on the gospel side for the veil-covered paten and chalice. When he arrives back at the sanctuary door, he announces the intention of the Mass in the prayer: "May the Lord God remember all of you in his kingdom, now and forever."

After another litany, the congregation recites the Nicene Creed.

The most solemn portion of the sacrifice is introduced by the preface, which is very much like the preface of the Roman Rite. At the beginning of the last phrase, the priest raises his voice to introduce the singing of the Sanctus. During the singing he reads the introduction to the words of consecration.

The words of consecration are sung aloud, and the people sing "Amen" to both consecrations. As the priest raises the Sacred Species in solemn offering, he sings: "Thine of Thine Own we offer unto Thee in behalf of all and for all."

A prayer to the Holy Spirit is followed by the commemorations, in which special mention is made of the all-holy, most blessed and glorious Lady, the Mother of God and ever-Virgin Mary. The dead are remembered and then the living.

A final litany for spiritual gifts precedes the Our Father. The Sacred Body and Blood are elevated with the words, "Holy Things for the Holy." The Host is then broken and commingled with the Precious Blood. The priest recites preparatory prayers for Holy Communion, consumes the Sacred Species, and distributes Holy Communion to the people under the forms of both bread and wine. During this time a communion verse is sung by the choir or congregation.

The Liturgy closes quickly after this. The consecrated Species of bread and wine are removed to the side table to be consumed later by the priest. A prayer of thanksgiving is recited, a prayer for all the people is said in front of the icon of Christ, a blessing is invoked upon all, and the people are dismissed.

VESTMENTS, APPURTENANCES

Sticharion: A long white garment of linen or silk with wide sleeves and decorated with embroidery; formerly the vestment for clerics in minor orders, acolytes, lectors, chanters, and subdeacons; symbolic of purity.

Epitrachelion: A stole with ends sewn together, having a loop through which the head is passed; its several crosses symbolize priestly duties.

Zone: A narrow clasped belt made of the same material as the epitrachelion; symbolic of the wisdom of the priest, his strength against enemies of the Church and his willingness to perform holy duties.

Epimanikia: Ornamental cuffs; the right cuff symbolizing strength, the left, patience and good will.

Phelonion: An ample cape, long in the back and sides and cut away in front; symbolic of the higher gifts of the Holy Spirit.

Antimension: A silk or linen cloth laid on the altar for the Liturgy; it may be decorated with a picture of the burial of Christ and the instruments of his passion; the relics of martyrs are sewn into the front border.

Eileton: A linen cloth which corresponds to the Roman-Rite corporal.

Poterion: A chalice or cup which holds the wine and Precious Blood.

Diskos: A shallow plate, which may be elevated on a small stand, corresponding to the Roman-Rite paten.

Asteriskos: Made of two curved bands of gold or silver which cross each other to form a double arch; a star depends from the junction, which forms a cross; it is placed over the diskos holding the consecrated bread and is covered with a veil.

Veils: Three are used, one to cover the poterion, the second to cover the diskos, and the third to cover both.

Spoon: Used in administering Holy Communion by intinction; consecrated leavened bread is dipped into consecrated wine and spooned onto the tongue of the communicant.

Lance: A metal knife used for cutting up the bread to be consecrated during the Liturgy.

BYZANTINE FEATURES

Art: Named for the empire in which it developed, Byzantine art is a unique blend of imperial Roman and classic Hellenic culture with Christian inspiration. The art of the Greek Middle Ages, it reached a peak of development in the 10th or 11th century. Characteristic of its products, particularly in mosaic and painting, are majesty, dignity, refinement and grace. Its sacred paintings, called icons, are reverenced highly in all Eastern Rites.

Church Building: The classical model of Byzantine church architecture is the Church of the Holy Wisdom (Hagia Sophia), built in Constantinople in the first half of the sixth century and still standing. The square structure, extended in some cases in the form of a cross, is topped by a distinctive onion-shaped dome and surmounted by a triple-bar cross. The altar is at the eastern end of building, where the wall bellies out to form an apse. The altar and sanctuary are separated from the body of the church by a fixed or movable screen, the iconostas, to which icons or sacred pictures are attached (see below).

Clergy: The Byzantine Rite has married as well as celibate priests. In places other than the US, where married candidates have not been accepted for ordination since about 1929, men already married can be ordained to the diaconate and priesthood and can continue in marriage after ordination. Celibate deacons and priests cannot marry after ordination; neither can a married priest remarry after the death of his wife. Bishops must be unmarried.

Iconostas: A large screen decorated with sacred pictures or icons which separates the sanctuary from the nave of a church; its equivalent in the Roman Rite, for thus separating the sanctuary from the nave, is an altar rail.

An iconostas has three doors through which the sacred ministers enter the sanctuary during the Divine Liturgy: smaller (north and south) Deacons' Doors and a large central Royal Door.

The Deacons' Doors usually feature the icons of Sts. Gabriel and Michael; the Royal Door, the icons of the Evangelists — Matthew, Mark, Luke and John. To the right and left of the Royal Door are the icons of Christ the Teacher and of the Blessed Virgin Mary with the Infant Jesus. To the extreme right and left are the icons of the patron of the church and St. John the Baptist (or St. Nicholas of Myra).

Immediately above the Royal Door is a picture of the Last Supper. To the right are six icons depicting the major feasts of Christ, and to the left are six icons portraying the major feasts of the Blessed Virgin Mary. Above the picture of the Last Supper is a large icon of Christ the King.

Some icon screens also have pictures of the 12 Apostles and the major Old Testament prophets surmounted by a crucifixion scene.

Liturgical Language: In line with Eastern tradition, Byzantine practice has favored the use of the language of the people in the liturgy. Two great advocates of the practice were Sts. Cyril and Methodius, apostles of the Slavs, who devised the Cyrillic alphabet and pioneered the adoption of Slavonic in the liturgy.

Sacraments: Baptism is administered by immersion, and confirmation is conferred at the same time. The Eucharist is administered by intinction, i.e., by giving the communicant a piece of consecrated leavened bread which has been dipped into the consecrated wine. When giving absolution in the sacrament of penance, the priest holds his stole over the head of the penitent. Distinctive marriage ceremonies include the crowning of the bride and groom. Ceremonies for anointing the sick closely resemble those of the Roman Rite. Holy orders are conferred by a bishop.

Sign of the Cross: Eastern-Rite Catholics have a distinctive way of making it (see entry in the Glossary). The sign of the cross in conjunction with a deep bow, instead of a genuflection, expresses reverence for the presence of Christ in the Blessed Sacrament.

SEPARATED EASTERN CHURCHES

Orthodox

Orthodox Churches, the largest and most widespread of the separated Eastern Churches, have much in common with their Eastern Catholic counterparts, including many matters of faith and morals, general discipline, valid orders and sacraments, and liturgy. One important difference is their acceptance of only the first seven ecumenical councils. Another is their rejection of any single supreme head of the Church. They do not acknowledge and hold communion with the pope.

Like their Catholic counterparts, Orthodox Churches are organized in jurisdictions under patriarchs. The patriarchs are the heads of approximately 15 autocephalic and several other autonomous jurisdictions organized along lines of nationality and/or language.

The Ecumenical Patriarch of Constantinople, Dimitrios I, has the primacy of honor among his equal patriarchs but his actual jurisdiction is limited to his own patriarchate. As the spiritual head of worldwide Orthodoxy, he keeps the book of the Holy Canons of the Autocephalous Churches, in which recognized Orthodox Churches are registered, and has the right to call Pan-Orthodox assemblies.

The definitive Orthodox break with Rome dates from 1054.

Top-level relations between the Churches have improved in recent years through the efforts of former Ecumenical Patriarch Athenagoras I, John XXIII, Paul VI and Patriarch Dimitrios I. Pope Paul met with Athenagoras three times before the latter's death in 1972. The most significant action of both spiritual leaders was their mutual nullification of excommunications imposed by the two Churches on each other in 1054.

The largest Orthodox body in the western

hemisphere is the Greek Orthodox jurisdiction consisting of the Archdiocese of New York, nine dioceses in the U.S., and one diocese each in Canada and South America; it is headed by Archbishop Iakovos and has an estimated membership of 1.5 million. The second largest is the Orthodox Church in America, with approximately 850,000 members; it was given independent status by the Patriarchate of Moscow May 18, 1970, against the will of Athenagoras I who refused to register it in the book of the Holy Canons of Autocephalous Churches. An additional 650,000 or more Orthodox belong to smaller national and language jurisdictions.

Heads of Orthodox jurisdictions in this hemisphere hold membership in the Standing Conference of Canonical Orthodox Bishops in the Americas.

Jurisdictions

The principal jurisdictions of the Greek, Russian and other Orthodox Churches are as follows.

Greek: Patriarchate of Constantinople, with jurisdiction in Turkey, Crete, the Dodecanese, Western Europe, the Americas, Australia; Dimitrios I is Ecumenical Patriarch.

Patriarchate of Alexandria, with jurisdiction in Egypt and the rest of Africa; there is also a native African Orthodox Church in Kenya and Uganda.

Patriarchate of Antioch (Melkites or Syrian Orthodox), with jurisdiction in Syria, Lebanon, Iraq, Australasia, the Americas; Syrian or Arabic, in place of Greek, is the liturgical language.

Patriarchate of Jerusalem, with jurisdiction in Israel and Jordan.

Churches of Greece, Cyprus and Sinai are autocephalic but maintain relations with their fellow Orthodox.

Russian: Patriarchate of Moscow with jurisdiction centered in the Soviet Union.

Other: Patriarchate of Serbia, with jurisdiction in Yugoslavia, Western Europe, the Americas, Australasia.

Patriarchates of Rumania and Bulgaria.

Katholikate of Georgia, the Soviet Union.

Byelorussians and Ukrainian Byzantines.

Churches of Albania, China, Czechoslovakia, Estonia, Finland, Hungary, Japan, Latvia, Lithuania, Poland.

Other minor communities in various places; e.g., Korea, the US, Carpatho-Russia.

The Division of Archives and Statistics of the Eastern Orthodox World Foundation reported a 1970 estimate of more than 200 million Orthodox Church members throughout the world. Other sources estimate the total to be approximately 125 million.

Nestorians, Monophysites

Unlike the majority of Eastern Christian Churches, several bodies do not acknowledge all of the first seven ecumenical councils. Nestorians acknowledge only the first two councils; they do not accept the doctrinal definition of the Council of Ephesus concerning Mary as the Mother of God. Monophysite Armenians, Syrians, Copts, Ethiopians and Jacobites acknowledge only the first three councils; they do not accept the doctrinal definition of the Council of Chalcedon concerning the two natures in Christ.

The Armenian Church has communicants in the Soviet Union, the Middle and Far East, the Americas.

The Coptic Church has communicants in Egypt and elsewhere.

The Ethiopian or Abyssinian Church has communicants in Africa, the Middle East, the Americas, India.

The Jacobite Church (West Syrians) has communicants in the Middle East, the Americas, India.

Nestorians (Assyrians) are scattered throughout the world.

It is estimated that there are approximately 10 million or more members of these other Eastern Churches throughout the world. For various reasons, a more accurate determination is not possible.

Conference of Orthodox Bishops

The Standing Conference of Canonical Orthodox Bishops in the Americas was established in 1960 to achieve cooperation among the various ethnic churches.

Member churches of the conference are the: Albanian Orthodox Diocese of America (Ecumenical Patriarchate), American Carpatho-Russian Greek Catholic Diocese, Antiochian Orthodox Christian Archdiocese of New York and All North America, Bulgarian Eastern Orthodox Church, Greek Orthodox Church of North and South America, Orthodox Church in America, Romanian Orthodox Missionary Episcopate in America, Serbian Orthodox Church in the United States of America and Canada, Ukrainian Orthodox Church of America (Ecumenical Patriarchate), Holy Ukrainian Autocephalic Orthodox Church in Exile.

Patriarchs: High-ranking patriarchs of separated Eastern Churches are Ecumenical Orthodox Patriarch Dimitrios I (Papadopoulos) of Constantinople (Istanbul) and Coptic Orthodox Patriarch Shenouda III (Nazeer Gayed) of Alexandria.

New Orthodox Charter

The Greek Orthodox Archdiocese of North and South America, the largest Orthodox jurisdiction in the western hemisphere, announced a new charter of organization and procedure in June, 1978.

In effect since Sept. 1, the charter provided for one diocese each in Canada and South America, one archdiocese (New York) and seven dioceses in the United States (Boston,

Charlotte, Chicago, Denver, Detroit, Pittsburgh and San Francisco). The jurisdictions are under the overall supervision of Archbishop Iakovos, presiding prelate of the Archdiocese of New York.

EASTERN ECUMENISM

The Second Vatican Council, in the *Decree on Eastern Catholic Churches,* pointed out the special role they have to play "in promoting the unity of all Christians, particularly Easterners." The document also stated in part:

"The Eastern Churches in communion with the Apostolic See of Rome have a special role to play in promoting the unity of all Christians, particularly Easterners, according to the principles of this sacred Synod's *Decree on Ecumenism* first of all by prayer, then by the example of their lives, by religious fidelity to ancient Eastern traditions, by greater mutual knowledge, by collaboration, and by a brotherly regard for objects and attitudes" (No. 24).

"If any separated Eastern Christian should, under the guidance of grace of the Holy Spirit, join himself to Catholic unity, no more should be required of him than what a simple profession of the Catholic faith demands. A valid priesthood is preserved among Eastern clerics. Hence, upon joining themselves to the unity of the Catholic Church, Eastern clerics are permitted to exercise the orders they possess, in accordance with the regulations established by the competent authority" (No. 25).

"Divine Law forbids any common worship (*communicatio in sacris*) which would damage the unity of the Church, or involve formal acceptance of falsehood or the danger of deviation in the faith, of scandal, or of indifferentism. At the same time, pastoral experience clearly shows that with respect to our Eastern brethren there should and can be taken into consideration various circumstances affecting individuals, wherein the unity of the Church is not jeopardized nor are intolerable risks involved, but in which salvation itself and the spiritual profit of souls are urgently at issue.

"Hence, in view of special circumstances of time, place, and personage, the Catholic Church has often adopted and now adopts a milder policy, offering to all the means of salvation and an example of charity among Christians through participation in the sacraments and in other sacred functions and objects. With these considerations in mind, and 'lest because of the harshness of our judgment we prove an obstacle to those seeking salvation,' and in order to promote closer union with the Eastern Churches separated from us, this sacred Synod lays down the following policy:

"In view of the principles recalled above, Eastern Christians who are separated in good faith from the Catholic Church, if they ask of their own accord and have the right dispositions, may be granted the sacraments of penance, the Eucharist, and the anointing of the sick. Furthermore, Catholics may ask for these same sacraments from those non-Catholic ministers whose Churches possess valid sacraments, as often as necessity or a genuine spiritual benefit recommends such a course of action, and when access to a Catholic priest is physically or morally impossible" (Nos. 26, 27).

"Again, in view of these very same principles, Catholics may for a just cause join with their separated Eastern brethren in sacred functions, things, and places" (No. 28).

"This more lenient policy with regard to common worship involving Catholics and their brethren of the separated Eastern Churches is entrusted to the care and execution of the local Ordinaries so that, by taking counsel among themselves and, if circumstances warrant, after consultation also with the Ordinaries of the separated Churches, they may govern relations between Christians by timely and effective rules and regulations" (No. 29).

EASTERN ECUMENICAL BRIEFS

Agreed Statement on the Church: Catholic and Orthodox theologians, meeting for their 10th consultation since 1966, issued an "Agreed Statement on the Church" Dec. 10, 1974. One of the central points in the statement was the difference of views regarding the position and status of the Pope and the Patriarch of Constantinople in the hierarchy of their churches.

The statement said:

"The Catholic Church recognizes that the position of Peter in the college of the Apostles finds visible expression in the Bishop of Rome who exercises those prerogatives defined by Vatican Council I within the whole church of Christ in virtue of this primacy.

"The Orthodox Church finds this teaching at variance with its understanding of primacy within the whole church. It appears to destroy the tension between independence and collegiality (in the universal and particular churches). For independence, a basic condition for collegiality, appears to be removed as a consequence of the jurisdictional teaching role attributed to the Patriarch of the West by Vatican Council I. The Orthodox believe that a necessary primacy in the church depends on the consent of the church and is at present exercised by the Patriarch of Constantinople.

"Our two traditions are not easily harmonized. Yet we believe that the Spirit is ever active to show us the way by which we can live together as one and many. We have the hope that we will be open to his promptings wherever they may lead."

The theological consultation was under the joint sponsorship of the U.S. Bishops' Committee for Ecumenical and Interreligious Affairs and the Standing Conference of Canonical Orthodox Bishops in America.

Orthodox Guidelines: A 66-page document entitled "Guidelines for Orthodox Churches in Ecumenical Relations" was published in February, 1974, by the Standing Conference of Canonical Orthodox Bishops in the Americas. Among the subjects of guidelines were:

• Marriage: Normally marriage in the Orthodox Church "takes place only between members of that Church." There are, however, occasions in which an Orthodox priest may perform a "mixed marriage," under certain conditions. Clergy of other churches may give a blessing or exhort a couple, but do not actually "assist" or "participate" in the marriage service.

• Baptism: Orthodox Churches accept baptism in the name of the Trinity in another church if "proof of the fact of baptism" can be authenticated.

• Eucharist: "Holy Communion will not be sought by Orthodox Christians outside the Church, nor will it be offered to those who do not confess the Orthodox Church as their mother."

• Reciprocity: The "principle of reciprocity" governs preaching in ecumenical situations, meaning that Orthodox priests may preach in non-Orthodox churches and non-Orthodox may speak in Orthodox churches.

Bishops and Presbyters: A document published in July, 1976, by the Orthodox-Roman Catholic Consultation in the U.S. Signatories indicated the following points of common understanding: (1) Ordination in apostolic succession is required for pastoral office in the Church. (2) Presiding at the Eucharistic celebration is a task belonging to those ordained to pastoral service. (3) The offices of bishop and presbyter are different realizations of the sacrament of order. (4) Those ordained are claimed permanently for the service of the Church. The statement noted that questions requiring serious study were the possible ordination of women, clerical celibacy, and the compatibility of certain occupations with pastoral office.

Principle of Economy: A statement issued by the same body at the same time, concerning God's plan and activity in human history for salvation. The concept of "economy" was not completely defined. It appeared that Orthodox understanding precludes recognition of the validity of the sacraments of other Christian churches.

Ministry: Ministry, especially that of bishop, was the principal subject under discussion at a meeting of an international group of Catholic and Orthodox theologians held in December, 1977, in Chambesy, Switzerland. In the context of a joint statement on the relationship between the incarnational and spiritual aspects of church life, they said: "There is no church of Christ without ministries of the Spirit, but there are no ministries without the church; hence, (there are) no ministries apart from or above the community" of the church.

Marriage: A statement entitled "The Sanctity of Marriage," issued in December, 1978, by the Eastern Orthodox-Roman Catholic Consultation in the U.S., acknowledged agreement about the sacramental nature and permanence of marriage while noting Orthodox positions regarding divorce (permitted in some circumstances) and validity (the marriage of Orthodox communicants must be blessed by an Orthodox priest).

Meetings

John Paul and Dimitrios: The Pope and Ecumenical Orthodox Patriarch Dimitrios I met Nov. 29 and 30, 1979, in Istanbul and issued a joint announcement of the establishment of a Catholic-Orthodox Mixed Commission for theological dialogue. The highest ranking and largest commission of its kind, it was set up with an initial membership of 23 Orthodox and 31 Catholic representatives. (See Pope John Paul II in Turkey.) The commission held several meetings between May 30 and June 3 on the islands of Patmos and Rhodes, for mutual acquaintance purposes.

The Pope and Other Patriarchs: The Holy Father met at the Vatican with Syrian Orthodox Patriarch Mar Ignatius Yacoub III of Antioch May 14, shortly before the latter's death, and with Georgian Orthodox Catholicos Patriarch Iliya June 6, shortly after the start of Georgian Orthodox participation in talks with Catholic representatives.

Russian Orthodox Dialogue: Catholic and Orthodox delegates met for the fifth time, Mar. 13 to 17, 1980, in Odessa for discussions related to the theme, "The Local Church and the Universal Church." In a communique issued at the end of the meeting, they said they "found themselves fully in accord on the following points:

• "The local church, in the ambit of the diocese, represents the people of God united around the bishop, legitimately ordained in the uninterrupted apostolic succession. The bishop, with whom the other members of the clergy collaborate and to whom they are subordinate, is the teacher of the faith, the minister of the sacraments — first of all, of the Eucharist — and the one in charge of the Christian life of his flock."

• "The concept of catholicity, understood as organic wholeness of the Church, as the fullness of the possession of the truth revealed by God and of the means of grace given for men's salvation, was deepened. The presence of the episcopate in the local churches guarantees the fullness of their Eucharistic life in grace."

• "Despite their state of separation, the Catholic and Orthodox churches recognize one another as sister churches."

Men, Doctrines, Churches of the Reformation

Some of the leading figures, doctrines and churches of the Reformation are covered below. A companion article covers Major Protestant Churches in the United States.

John Wycliff (c. 1320-1384): English priest and scholar who advanced one of the leading Reformation ideas nearly 200 years before Martin Luther — that the Bible alone is the sufficient rule of faith — but had only an indirect influence on the 16th century Reformers. Supporting belief in an inward and practical religion, he denied the divinely commissioned authority of the pope and bishops of the Church; he also denied the Real Presence of Christ in the Holy Eucharist, and wrote against the sacrament of penance and the doctrine of indulgences. Nearly 20 of his propositions were condemned by Gregory XI in 1377; his writings were proscribed more extensively by the Council of Constance in 1415. His influence was strongest in Bohemia and Central Europe.

John Hus (c. 1369-1415): A Bohemian priest and preacher of reform who authored 30 propositions condemned by the Council of Constance. Excommunicated in 1411 or 1412, he was burned at the stake in 1415. His principal errors concerned the nature of the Church and the origin of papal authority. He spread some of the ideas of Wycliff but did not subscribe to his views regarding faith alone as the condition for justification and salvation, the sole sufficiency of Scripture as the rule of faith, the Real Presence of Christ in the Eucharist, and the sacramental system. In 1457 some of his followers founded the Church of the Brotherhood which later became known as the United Brethren or Moravian Church and is considered the earliest independent Protestant body.

Martin Luther (1483-1546): An Augustinian friar, the key figure in the Reformation. In 1517, as a special indulgence was being preached in Germany, and in view of needed reforms within the Church, he published at Wittenberg 95 theses concerning matters of Catholic belief and practice. Leo X condemned 41 statements from Luther's writings in 1520. Luther, refusing to recant, was excommunicated the following year. His teachings strongly influenced subsequent Lutheran theology; its statements of faith are found in the Book of Concord (1580).

Luther's doctrine included the following:

The sin of Adam, which corrupted human nature radically (but not substantially), has affected every aspect of man's being. Justification, understood as the forgiveness of sins and the state of righteousness, is by grace for Christ's sake through faith. Faith involves not merely intellectual assent but an act of confidence by the will. Good works are indispensably necessary concomitants of faith, but do not merit salvation. Of the sacraments, Luther retained baptism, penance and the Holy Communion as effective vehicles of the grace of the Holy Spirit; he held that in the Holy Communion the consecrated bread and wine are the Body and Blood of Christ. The rule of faith is the divine revelation in the Sacred Scriptures. He rejected purgatory, indulgences and the invocation of the saints, and held that prayers for the dead have no efficacy.

Lutheran tenets not in agreement with Catholic doctrine were condemned by the Council of Trent.

Anabaptism: Originated in Saxony in the first quarter of the 16th century and spread rapidly through southern Germany. Its doctrine included several key Lutheran tenets but was not regarded with favor by Luther, Calvin or Zwingli. Anabaptists believed that baptism is for adults only and that infant baptism is invalid. Their doctrine of the Inner Light, concerning the direct influence of the Holy Spirit on the believer, implied rejection of Catholic doctrine concerning the sacraments and the nature of the Church. Eighteen articles of faith were formulated in 1632 in Holland. Mennonites are Anabaptists.

Ulrich Zwingli (1484-1531): A priest who triggered the Reformation in Switzerland with a series of New Testament lectures in 1519, later disputations and by other actions. He held the Gospel to be the only basis of truth; rejected the Mass (which he suppressed in 1525 at Zurich), penance and other sacraments; denied papal primacy and doctrine concerning purgatory and the invocation of saints; rejected celibacy, monasticism and many traditional practices of piety. His symbolic view of the Eucharist, which was at odds with Catholic doctrine, caused an irreconcilable controversy with Luther and his followers. Zwingli was killed in a battle between the forces of Protestant and Catholic cantons in Switzerland.

John Calvin (1509-1564): French leader of the Reformation in Switzerland, whose key tenet was absolute predestination of some persons to heaven and others to hell. He rejected Catholic doctrine in 1533 after becoming convinced of a personal mission to reform the Church. In 1536 he published the first edition of *Institutes of the Christian Religion,* a systematic exposition of his doctrine which became the classic textbook of Reformed — as distinguished from Lutheran — theology. To Luther's principal theses — regarding

Scripture as the sole rule of faith, the radical corruption of human nature, and justification by faith alone — he added absolute predestination, certitude of salvation for the elect, and the incapability of the elect to lose grace. His Eucharistic theory, which failed to mediate the Zwingli-Luther controversy, was at odds with Catholic doctrine. From 1555 until his death Calvin was the virtual dictator of Geneva, the capital of the non-Lutheran Reformation in Europe.

Arminianism: A modification of the rigid predestinationism of Calvin, set forth by acob Arminius (1560-1609) and formally stated in the *Remonstrance* of 1610. Arminianism influenced some Calvinist bodies.

Unitarianism: A 16th century doctrine which rejected the Trinity and the divinity of Christ in favor of a uni-personal God. It claimed scriptural support for a long time but became generally rationalistic with respect to "revealed" doctrine as well as in ethics and its world-view. One of its principal early proponents was Faustus Socinus (1539-1604), a leader of the Polish Brethren.

A variety of communions developed in England in the Reformation and post-Reformation periods.

Anglican Communion: This communion, which regards itself as the same apostolic Church as that which was established by early Christians in England, derived not from Reformation influences but from the renunciation of papal jurisdiction by Henry VIII (1491-1547). His Act of Supremacy in 1534 called Christ's Church an assembly of local churches subject to the prince, who was vested with fullness of authority and jurisdiction. In spite of Henry's denial of papal authority, this Act did not reject substantially other principal articles of faith. Notable changes, proposed and adopted for the reformation of the church, took place in the subsequent reigns of James VI and Elizabeth, with respect to such matters as Scripture as the rule of faith, the sacraments, the nature of the Mass, and the constitution of the hierarchy.

The Anglican Communion is called Episcopal because its prelates have the title and function of bishops. (See Anglican Orders.)

Puritans: Extremists who sought church reform along Calvinist lines in severe simplicity. (Use of the term was generally discontinued after 1660.)

Presbyterians: Basically Calvinistic, called Presbyterian because church polity centers around assemblies of presbyters or elders. John Knox (c. 1513-1572) established the church in Scotland.

Congregationalists: Evangelical in spirit and seeking a return to forms of the primitive church, they uphold individual freedom in religious matters, do not require the acceptance of a creed as a condition for communion, and regard each congregation as autonomous. Robert Browne influenced the beginnings of Congregationalism.

Quakers: Their key belief is in internal divine illumination, the inner light of the living Christ, as the only source of truth and inspiration. George Fox (1624-1691) was one of their leaders in England. Called the Society of Friends, the Quakers are noted for their pacificism.

Baptists: So called because of their doctrine concerning baptism. They reject infant baptism and consider only baptism by immersion as valid. Leaders in the formation of the church were John Smyth (d. 1612) in England and Roger Williams (d. 1683) in America.

Methodists: A group who broke away from the Anglican Communion under the leadership of John Wesley (1703-1791), although some Anglican beliefs were retained. Doctrines include the witness of the Spirit to the individual and personal assurance of salvation. Wesleyan Methodists do not subscribe to some of the more rigid Calvinistic tenets held by other Methodists.

Universalism: A product of 18th-century liberal Protestanism in England. The doctrine is not Trinitarian.

MAJOR PROTESTANT CHURCHES IN THE UNITED STATES

There are more than 250 Protestant church bodies in the United States.

The majority of U.S. Protestants belong to the following denominations: Baptist, Methodist, Lutheran, Presbyterian, Protestant Episcopal, the United Church of Christ, the Christian Church (Disciples of Christ), Holiness Sects.

See Ecumenical Dialogues, Briefs and related entries for coverage of relations between the Catholic Church and other Christian churches.

Baptist Churches

(Courtesy of the Division of Communication, American Baptist Churches in the U.S.A.)

Baptist churches, comprising the largest of all American Protestant denominations, were first established by John Smyth near the beginning of the 17th century in England. The first Baptist church in America was founded at Providence by Roger Williams in 1639.

Largest of the nearly 30 Baptist bodies in the U.S. are:

The Southern Baptist Convention, 460 James Robertson Parkway, Nashville, Tenn. 37219, with 13.4 million members;

The National Baptist Convention, U.S.A., Inc., 915 Spain St., Baton Rouge, La. 70802, with 6.5 million members;

The National Baptist Convention of America, 954 Kings Rd., Jacksonville, Fla. 32204, with 2.6 million members.

The American Baptist Churches in the U.S.A., Valley Forge, Pa. 19481, with 1.5 million members.

The total number of U.S. Baptists is more than 29 million. The world total is 33 million.

Proper to Baptists is their doctrine on baptism. Called an "ordinance" rather than a sacrament, baptism by immersion is a sign that one has experienced and decided in favor of the salvation offered by Christ. It is administered only to persons who are capable of the experience of faith, which is the sole criterion of salvation and which involves the obligation to a life of virtue. Baptism is not administered to infants.

Baptists do not have a formal creed but generally subscribe to two professions of faith formulated in 1689 and 1832 and are in general agreement with classical Protestant theology regarding Scripture as the sole rule of faith, original sin, justification through faith in Christ, and the nature of the Church. Their local churches are autonomous.

Worship services differ in form from one congregation to another. Usual elements are the reading of Scripture, a sermon, hymns, vocal and silent prayer. The Lord's Supper, called an "ordinance," is celebrated at various intervals.

Methodist Churches

(Courtesy of Joe Hale, General Secretary of the World Methodist Council.)

John Wesley (1703-1791), an Anglican clergyman, was the founder of Methodism. In 1738, following a period of missionary work in America and strongly influenced by the Moravians, he experienced a new conversion to Christ and shortly thereafter became a leader in a religious awakening in England. By the end of the 18th century, Methodism was strongly rooted also in America.

The United Methodist Church, formed in 1968 by a merger of the Methodist Church and the Evangelical United Brethren Church, is the second largest Protestant denomination in the U.S., with 9.8 million members; its principal agencies are located in New York, Evanston, Ill., Nashville, Tenn., Washington, D.C., Dayton, O., and Lake Junaluska, N.C. (World Methodist Council, P.O. Box 518. 28745). The second largest body, with more than two million communicants, is the African Methodist Episcopal Church. The four other major churches are the African Methodist Episcopal Zion, Christian Methodist Episcopal, Free Methodist Church and the Wesleyan Church. The total Methodist membership in the U.S. is about 14 million.

Worldwide, there are more than 60 autonomous Methodist/Wesleyan churches in 90 countries, with a membership of more than 21 million. All of them participate in the World Methodist Council, which gives global unity to the witness of Methodist communicants.

Methodism, although it has a base in Calvinistic theology, rejects absolute predestination and maintains that Christ offers grace freely to all men, not just to a select elite. Wesley's distinctive doctrine was the "witness of the Spirit" to the individual soul and personal assurance of salvation. He also emphasized the central themes of conversion and holiness. Methodists are in general agreement with classical Protestant theology regarding Scripture as the sole rule of faith, original sin, justification through faith in Christ, the nature of the Church, and the sacraments of baptism and the Lord's Supper. Church polity is structured along episcopal lines in America, with ministers being appointed to local churches by a bishop; churches stemming from British Methodism do not have bishops but vest appointive powers within an appropriate conference. Congregations are free to choose various forms of worship services; typical elements are readings from Scripture, sermons, hymns and prayers.

Lutheran Churches

(Courtesy of Tom Dorris, assistant director of the Lutheran News Bureau, 360 Park Ave. South, New York, N.Y. 10010.)

The origin of Lutheranism is generally traced to Oct. 31, 1517, when Martin Luther tacked "95 Theses" to the door of the castle church in Wittenberg, Germany. This call to debate on the subject of indulgences and related concerns has come to symbolize the beginning of the Reformation. Luther and his supporters intended to reform the Church they knew. Though Lutheranism has come to be visible in separate denominations and national churches, at its heart it professes itself to be a confessional movement within the one, holy, catholic and apostolic Church.

The world's 70 million Lutherans form the third largest grouping of Christians, following Roman Catholics and Eastern Orthodox. About 53 million belong to churches which make up the Lutheran World Federation, headquartered in Geneva; its president, Josiah Kibira, is bishop of the Northwest Diocese of the Evangelical Lutheran Church in Tanzania. Eight countries count more than one million Lutherans each: West Germany (22.8 million), United States (8.5 million), Sweden (7.5 million), East Germany (6.5 million), Denmark (4.7 million), Finland (4.6 million), Norway (3.8 million), Indonesia (1.7 million).

Numbering about nine million, Lutherans are the fourth largest grouping of North American Christians, exceeded by Roman Catholics, Baptists and Methodists. About 95 per cent of them belong to one of three denominations: Lutheran Church in America, three million members, 231 Madison Avenue,

New York, N.Y. 10016; Lutheran Church-Missouri Synod, 2.7 million, 500 N. Broadway, St. Louis, Mo. 63102; American Lutheran Church, 2.4 million, 422 S. Fifth St., Minneapolis, Minn. 55415.

In addition, there are about a dozen other smaller Lutheran denominations in North America. The three largest are: Wisconsin Evangelical Lutheran Synod, 400,000 members, 3512 W. North Ave., Milwaukee, Wis. 53208; the Association of Evangelical Lutheran Churches, 110,000, 12015 Manchester Rd., St. Louis, Mo. 63131; Evangelical Lutheran Church of Canada, 82,000, 247 First Ave. North, Saskatoon, Saskatchewan S7K 4H5. (This is the only independent Canadian denomination; most other Canadian Lutherans belong to the Lutheran Church in America or the Missouri Synod.)

The three large bodies and the Association of Evangelical Lutheran Churches form the Lutheran Council in the U.S.A., a cooperative agency for work in theological studies; communication; research and planning; institutional, military and campus ministry; governmental affairs; higher education; immigration and refugee services; youth agency relations; American Indian concerns; domestic disaster relief and other social ministries. The council's main offices are at 360 Park Ave. South, New York, N.Y. 10010. A similar organization, the Lutheran Council in Canada, is headquartered at 500-365 Hargrave St., Winnipeg, Manitoba R3B 2K3.

The Lutheran Church in America, the American Lutheran Church and the Association of Evangelical Lutheran Churches also form Lutheran World Ministries, the U.S. agency of the Lutheran World Federation, headquartered at 360 Park Ave. South, New York, N.Y. 10010. Its Canadian counterpart is the Canadian National Committee of the Lutheran World Federation, headquartered at 500-365 Hargrave St., Winnipeg, Manitoba R3B 2K3.

The statements of faith which have shaped the confessional life of Lutheranism are found in the *Book of Concord*. This 1580 collection includes the three ancient ecumenical creeds (Apostles', Nicene and Athanasian), Luther's *Large and Small Catechisms* (1529), the *Augsburg Confession* (1530) and the *Apology* in defense of it (1531), the *Smalcald Articles* (including the "Treatise on the Power and Primacy of the Pope") (1537), and the *Formula of Concord* (1577).

The central Lutheran doctrinal proposition is that Christians "receive forgiveness of sins and become righteous before God by grace, for Christ's sake."

Baptism and the Lord's Supper (Holy Communion, the eucharist) are universally celebrated among Lutherans as sacramental means of grace in which the Word and promise of God are made visible by being bound to earthly elements — water, bread and wine. In baptism, a person is reborn and by God's gracious action is made a member of the Church catholic. Likewise, the eucharist celebrates and re-presents God's gracious action. With the body and blood of Christ — "in, with, and under" the bread and wine — come the gifts of life, salvation, forgiveness.

Lutherans also treasure the Word proclaimed in the reading of the Scriptures, preaching from the pulpit, and pronouncement of absolution. The Word read and preached is always part of the celebration of the sacrament of the altar. Absolution is usually imparted generally, but it may also be given individually in connection with private confession.

Although it was not the wish of the early Lutherans to deny the bishop's place as the ordinary minister of ordination, the general unwillingness of 16th century bishops to ordain Lutheran pastors led to the usual Lutheran system of presbyteral rather than episcopal ordination. Lutherans are concerned to preserve apostolic succession in life and doctrine, and generally concede the value, though not the necessity, of ordination by bishops.

Marriage and confirmation continue as non-sacramental rites among Lutherans. Confirmation has been generally connected with first communion, though recent years have seen a tendency to separate the two. In the U.S., the tendency is to have first communion around grade-five age, though infant communion is not unknown. Confirmation, sometimes called affirmation of the baptismal covenant, generally occurs during the junior high school years, slightly younger than in European practice.

Lutheran jurisdictions corresponding to dioceses are called districts or synods in North America. There are more than 100 of them on the continent. Because they relate to different national denominations, more than one of these jurisdictions includes the same geographic area. The head of a district or synod, chosen by lay and clergy delegates to a convention, is known as a bishop or a president, depending on the denomination and jurisdiction. The terms "diocese" and "bishop" are more common among European Lutherans and Asian, African and Latin American Lutherans whose roots derive from European missionary efforts.

A visitor to a North American Lutheran parish would generally find adornments, vestments, church calendars and an order of service similar to that of many Episcopal or Roman Catholic congregations. Though the Reformers continued to celebrate the eucharist every Sunday and on other special days, Lutherans strayed from their confessional norm under various historical and philosophic influences. The North American practice has until recent years been monthly celebration.

Weekly celebration is increasingly common and is generally stressed as the desired practice by Lutheran liturgical and sacramental theologians. Lutherans generally like to sing in worship, and successive generations have built up a rich tradition of church music and hymnody. A new North American *Lutheran Book of Worship* was introduced in 1978.

Presbyterian Churches

(Courtesy of Gerald W. Gillette, United Presbyterian Church in the U.S.A.; and Office of the General Assembly, Presbyterian Church in the United States.)

Presbyterians are so called because of their tradition of governing the church through a system of representative bodies composed of elders (presbyters).

Presbyterianism is a part of the Reformed Family of Churches that grew out of the theological work of John Calvin following the Lutheran Reformation, to which it is heavily indebted. Countries in which it acquired early strength and influence were Switzerland, France, Holland, Scotland and England.

Presbyterianism spread widely in this country in the latter part of the 18th century and afterwards. Presently, it has approximately 4.5 million communicants in nine bodies. The largest of these are:

The United Presbyterian Church in the U.S.A., 475 Riverside Drive, New York, N.Y. 10027, with 2.5 million members. This body was formed May 28, 1958, by a merger of the Presbyterian Church in the U.S.A and the United Presbyterian Church of North America.

The Presbyterian Church in the United States, 341 Ponce de Leon Avenue N.E., Atlanta, Ga. 30308, with about 860,000 members.

These churches are closely allied with the Reformed Church in America and the United Church of Christ.

In Presbyterian doctrine, baptism and the Lord's Supper, viewed as seals of the covenant of grace, are regarded as sacraments. Baptism, which is not necessary for salvation, is conferred on infants and adults The Lord's Supper is celebrated as a covenant of the Sacrifice of Christ. In both sacraments, a doctrine of the real presence of Christ is considered the central theological principle.

The Church is twofold, being invisible and also visible; it consists of all of the elect and all those Christians who are united in Christ as their immediate head.

Presbyterians are in general agreement with classical Protestant theology regarding Scripture as the sole rule of faith and practice, salvation by grace, and justification through faith in Christ.

Presbyterian congregations are governed by a session composed of elders (presbyters) elected by the communicant membership. On higher levels there are presbyteries, synods and a general assembly with various degrees of authority over local bodies; all such representative bodies are composed of elected elders and ministers in approximately equal numbers.

Worship services, simple and dignified, include sermons, prayer, reading of the Scriptures and hymns. The Lord's Supper is celebrated at intervals.

Doctrinal developments of the past several years included approval in May, 1967, by the General Assembly of the United Presbyterian Church of a contemporary confession of faith to supplement the historic Westminster Confession. The new confession emphasizes the commitment of the Church and its members to reconciliatory and apostolic works in society.

Protestant Episcopal Church

(Courtesy of the Rev. John A. Schultz, assistant secretary, General Convention.)

The Protestant Episcopal Church in the U.S.A., also officially known as the Episcopal Church, regards itself as the same apostolic church as that which was established by early Christians in England. It was established in this country during the Revolutionary period. Its constitution and Prayer Book were adopted at a general convention held in 1789. It has approximately 3 million members.

Offices of the U.S. executive council are located at 815 Second Ave., New York, N.Y. 10017.

This church, which belongs to the Anglican Communion, subscribes to the branch theory of the Church of Christ, holding that it consists of the Church of Rome, the Eastern Orthodox Church, and the Anglican Communion. It accepts the pope as the "first among equals."

Worldwide, the Anglican Communion has 65 million members in 41 provinces. The chief prelate is the Archbishop of Canterbury.

There is considerable variety in Episcopalian beliefs and practices. Official statements of belief and practice are found in the Apostles' Creed, the Nicene Creed and the Book of Common Prayer, but interpretation is not uniform. Scripture has primary importance with respect to the rule of faith, and some authority is attached to tradition.

All seven sacraments, veneration of the saints, and a great many other Catholic teachings are accepted by Episcopalians but are not used by all.

An episcopal system of church government prevails, but clergymen of lower rank and lay persons also have an active voice in ecclesiastical affairs. The levels of government are the general convention, the executive council, territorial provinces and dioceses, and local parishes. At the parish level, the congregation has the right to select its own rector or pastor, with the advice of the bishop.

Liturgical worship is according to the Book of Common Prayer as adopted in 1979, but ceremonial practices correspond with the doctrinal positions of the various congregations and range from a ceremony similar to the Roman Mass to services of a less elaborate character.

United Church of Christ

(Courtesy of Joseph H. Evans, secretary of the United Church of Christ.)

The 1,745,533-member United Church of Christ was formed in 1957 by a union of the Congregational Christian and the Evangelical and Reformed Churches. The former was originally established by the Pilgrims and the Puritans of the Massachusetts Bay Colony, while the latter was founded in Pennsylvania in the early 1700's by settlers from Central Europe. The denomination has 6,502 congregations throughout the United States.

It considers itself "a united and uniting church" and keeps itself open to all ecumenical options.

Its headquarters are located at 105 Madison Ave., New York, N.Y. 10016.

Its statement of faith recognizes Jesus Christ as "our crucified and risen Lord (who) shared our common lot, conquering sin and death and reconciling the world to himself." It believes in the life after death, and the fact that God "judges men and nations by his righteous will declared through prophets and apostles."

The United Church further believes that Christ calls its members to share in his baptism "and eat at his table, to join him in his passion and victory." Ideally, according to its Lord's Day Service, Communion is to be celebrated weekly. Like other Calvinistic bodies, it believes that Christ is spiritually present in the sacrament.

The United Church is governed along congregational lines, and each local church is autonomous. However, the actions of its biennial General Synod are taken with great seriousness by congregations. Between synods, a 43-member executive council oversees the work of the church.

Christian Church (Disciples of Christ)

(Courtesy of Robert L. Friedly, Executive Director, Office of Communication.)

The Christian Church (Disciples of Christ) originated early in the 1800's from two movements against rigid denominationalism led by Presbyterians Thomas and Alexander Campbell in western Pennsylvania and Barton W. Stone in Kentucky. The two movements developed separately for about 25 years before being merged in 1832.

The church, which identifies itself with the Protestant mainstream, now has approximately 1.2 million members in the U.S. and Canada. The greatest concentration of members in the U.S. is located roughly along the old frontier line, in an arc sweeping from Ohio and Kentucky through the Midwest and down into Oklahoma and Texas.

The general offices of the church are located at 222 South Downey Ave., Box 1986, Indianapolis, Ind. 46206.

The Disciples have no official doctrine or dogma. Their worship practices vary widely from more common informal services to what could almost be described as "high church" services. Membership is granted after a simple statement of belief in Jesus Christ and baptism by immersion; many congregations admit un-immersed transfers from other denominations. The Lord's Supper, generally called Communion, is always open to Christians of all persuasions. Lay men and women routinely preside over the Lord's Supper, which is celebrated each Sunday; they often preach and perform other pastoral functions as well. Distinction between ordained and non-ordained members is blurred somewhat because of the Disciples' emphasis on all members of the church as ministers.

The Christian Church is oriented to congregational government, and has a unique structure in which three levels of polity (general, regional and congregational) operate as equals rather than in a pyramid of authority. At the national or international level, it is governed by a general assembly which has voting representation direct from congregations and regions as well as all ordained clergy.

The Holiness Sects

Perfectionist, Pentecostal and a variety of Evangelical churches and sects have a large membership in the U.S.

These groups do not form a denomination in the strict sense of the term, since they are separate and have their own particular characteristics. Classification under a common heading is possible, however, because they all share the same general spirit and spring from a common origin. John Wesley's teaching on justification is the doctrinal thread common to all of these churches — personal holiness, realized in the life of each individual, is the key to a full Christian life. Hence the name, "Holiness Movement." Its origin is traceable to the revival movement of the 19th century.

The Perfectionist branch of this large group includes such foundations as the Church of the Nazarene, the Church of God (Anderson, Ind.), and the Pilgrim Holiness Church. On the Pentecostal side are the Assemblies of God, the numerous Churches of God, and many bodies with the word Pentecostal in their titles. There are also many other very small cults which are similar in spirit to the larger churches.

The modern ecumenical movement, which started about 1910 among Protestants and led to formation of the World Council of Churches in 1948, developed outside the mainstream of Catholic interest for many years. It has now become for Catholics as well one of the great religious facts of our time.

The 'magna charta of ecumenism for Catholics is a complex of several documents which include, in the first place, the *Decree on Ecumenism* promulgated by the Second Vatican Council Nov. 21, 1964. Other enactments underlying and expanding this decree are the *Dogmatic Constitution on the Church,* the *Decree on Eastern Catholic Churches,* and the *Pastoral Constitution on the Church in the Modern World.*

VATICAN II DECREE

The following excerpts from the *Decree on Ecumenism* cover the broad theological background and principles and indicate the thrust of the Church's commitment to ecumenism.

". . . Men who believe in Christ and have been properly baptized are brought into a certain, though imperfect, communion with the Catholic Church. Undoubtedly, the differences that exist in varying degrees between them and the Catholic Church — whether in doctrine and sometimes in discipline, or concerning the structure of the Church — do indeed create many and sometimes serious obstacles to full ecclesiastical communion. These the ecumenical movement is striving to overcome . . ." (No. 3).

Elements Common to Christians

"Moreover some, even very many, of the most significant elements or endowments which together go to build up and give life to the Church herself can exist outside the visible boundaries of the Catholic Church: the written word of God; the life of grace; faith, hope, and charity, along with other interior gifts of the Holy Spirit and visible elements. All of these, which come from Christ and lead back to Him, belong by right to the one Church of Christ" (No. 3).

[In a later passage, the decree singled out a number of elements which the Catholic Church and other churches have in common but not in complete agreement: confession of Christ as Lord and God and as mediator between God and man; belief in the Trinity; reverence for Scripture as the revealed word of God; baptism and the Lord's Supper; Christian life and worship; faith in action; concern with moral questions.]

"The brethren divided from us also carry out many of the sacred actions of the Christian religion. Undoubtedly, in ways that vary according to the condition of each Church or Community, these actions can truly engender a life of grace, and can be rightly described as capable of providing access to the community of salvation.

"It follows that these separated Churches and Communities, though we believe they suffer from defects already mentioned, have by no means been deprived of significance and importance in the mystery of salvation. For the Spirit of Christ has not refrained from using them as means of salvation which derive their efficacy from the very fullness of grace and truth entrusted to the Catholic Church" (No. 3).

Unity Lacking

"Nevertheless, our separated brethren, whether considered as individuals or as Communities and Churches, are not blessed with that unity which Jesus Christ wished to bestow on all those whom He has regenerated and vivified into one body and newness of life — that unity which the holy Scriptures and the revered tradition of the Church proclaim. For it is through Christ's Catholic Church alone, which is the all-embracing means of salvation, that the fullness of the means of salvation can be obtained. It was to the apostolic college alone, of which Peter is the head, that we believe our Lord entrusted all the blessings of the New Covenant, in order to establish on earth the one Body of Christ into which all those should be fully incorporated who already belong in any way to God's People . . ." (No. 3).

What the Movement Involves

"Today, in many parts of the world, under the inspiring grace of the Holy Spirit, multiple efforts are being expended through prayer, word, and action to attain that fullness of unity which Jesus Christ desires. This sacred Synod, therefore, exhorts all the Catholic faithful to recognize the signs of the times and to participate skillfully in the work of ecumenism.

"The 'ecumenical movement' means those activities and enterprises which, according to various needs of the Church and opportune occasions, are started and organized for the fostering of unity among Christians. These are:

● "First, every effort to eliminate words, judgments, and actions which do not respond to the condition of separated brethren with truth and fairness and so make mutual relations between them more difficult.

● "Then, 'dialogue' between competent experts from different Churches and Communities (scholarly ecumenism).

● "In addition, these Communions cooperate more closely in whatever projects a Christian conscience demands for the common good (social ecumenism).

• "They also come together for common prayer, where this is permitted (spiritual ecumenism).

• "Finally, all are led to examine their own faithfulness to Christ's will for the Church and, wherever necessary, undertake with vigor the task of renewal and reform.

". . . It is evident that the work of preparing and reconciling those individuals who wish for full Catholic communion is of its nature distinct from ecumenical action. But there is no opposition between the two, since both proceed from the wondrous providence of God" (No. 4).

Primary Duty of Catholics

"In ecumenical work, Catholics must assuredly be concerned for their separated brethren, praying for them, keeping them informed about the Church, making the first approaches towards them. But their primary duty is to make an honest and careful appraisal of whatever needs to be renewed and achieved in the Catholic household itself, in order that its life may bear witness more loyally and luminously to the teachings and ordinances which have been handed down from Christ through the apostles.

". . . Every Catholic must . . . aim at Christian perfection (cf. Jas. 1:4; Rom. 12:1-2) and, each according to his station, play his part so that the Church . . . may daily be more purified and renewed, against the day when Christ will present her to Himself in all her glory, without spot or wrinkle (cf. Eph. 5:27).

". . . Catholics must joyfully acknowledge and esteem the truly Christian endowments from our common heritage which are to be found among our separated brethren. . . .

"Nor should we forget that whatever is wrought by the grace of the Holy Spirit in the hearts of our separated brethren can contribute to our own edification. Whatever is truly Christian never conflicts with the genuine interests of the faith; indeed, it can always result in a more ample realization of the very mystery of Christ and the Church . . ." (No. 4).

Participation in Worship

Norms concerning participation by Catholics in the worship of other Christian Churches were sketched in this conciliar decree and elaborated in a number of other documents such as: the *Decree on Eastern Catholic Churches,* promulgated by the Second Vatican Council in 1964; *Interim Guidelines for Prayer in Common,* issued June 18, 1965, by the US Bishops' Committee for Ecumenical and Inter-Religious Affairs; a *Directory on Ecumenism,* published in 1967 by the Vatican Secretariat for Promoting Christian Unity; additional communications from the US Bishops' Committee, and numerous sets of guidelines issued locally by and for dioceses throughout the US.

The norms encourage common prayer services for Christian unity and other intentions. Beyond that, they draw a distinction between separated churches of the Reformation tradition and separated Eastern churches, in view of doctrine and practice the Catholic Church has in common with the latter concerning the apostolic succession of bishops, holy orders, liturgy, and other credal matters.

Full participation by Catholics in official Protestant liturgies is prohibited, because it implies profession of the faith expressed in the liturgy. Intercommunion by Catholics at Protestant liturgies is prohibited. Under certain conditions, Protestants may be given Holy Communion in the Catholic Church (see Intercommunion). A Catholic may stand as a witness, but not as a sponsor, in baptism, and as a witness in the marriage of separated Christians. Similarly, a Protestant may stand as a witness, but not as a sponsor, in a Catholic baptism, and as a witness in the marriage of Catholics.

Separated Eastern Churches

The principal norms regarding liturgical participation with separated Eastern Christians are included under Eastern Ecumenism.

ECUMENICAL AGENCIES

Vatican Secretariat

The top-level agency for Catholic ecumenical efforts is the Vatican Secretariat for Promoting Christian Unity, which originated in 1960 as a preparatory commission for the Second Vatican Council. Its purposes are to provide guidance and, where necessary, coordination for ecumenical endeavor by Catholics, and to establish and maintain relations with representatives of other Christian Churches for ecumenical dialogue and action.

The secretariat, first under the direction of Cardinal Augustin Bea, S. J., and now of Cardinal Johannes Willebrands, has established firm working relations with representative agencies of other churches and the World Council of Churches. It has joined in dialogue with Orthodox Churches, the Anglican Communion, the Lutheran World Federation, the World Alliance of Reformed Churches, the World Methodist Council and other religious bodies. In the past several years, staff members and representatives of the secretariat have been involved in one way or another in nearly every significant ecumenical enterprise and meeting held throughout the world, including the Fifth General Assembly of the World Council of Churches.

While the secretariat and its counterparts in other churches have focused primary attention on theological and other related problems of Christian unity, they have also begun, and in increasing measure, to emphasize the responsibilities of the churches for greater unity of witness and effort in areas of humanitarian need.

Bishops' Committee

The U.S. Bishops' Committee for Ecumenical and Interreligious Affairs was established by the American hierarchy in 1964. Its purposes are to maintain relationships with other Christian churches and other religious communities at the national level, to advise and assist dioceses in developing and applying ecumenical policies, and to maintain liaison with corresponding Vatican offices — the Secretariats for Christian Unity and Non-Christian Religions.

This standing committee of the National Conference of Catholic Bishops is chaired by Ernest L. Unterkoefler of Charleston, S.C. Operationally, the committee is assisted by the Rev. John F. Hotchkin, director; the Rev. Joseph W. Witmer, associate director; Dr. Eugene J. Fisher, executive secretary of the Secretariat for Catholic-Jewish Relations; the Rev. John B. Sheerin, consultant for Catholic-Jewish Relations.

The committee co-sponsors several national consultations with other churches and confessional families. These bring together on a regular basis Catholic representatives and their counterparts from the American Baptist Convention, the Christian Church (Disciples of Christ), the Episcopal Church, the Lutheran World Federation (U.S. Committee), the United Methodist Church, the Orthodox Churches, the Oriental Orthodox Churches, the Alliance of Reformed Churches (North American area), the Interfaith Witness Department of the Home Mission Board of the Southern Baptist Convention. Reports of consultations conducted under committee auspices are published periodically and are available through the Publications Office of the U.S. Catholic Conference. (See Ecumenical Dialogues.)

The committee relates with the National Council of Churches of Christ, through membership in the Faith and Order Commission and through observer relationship with the Commission on Regional and Local Ecumenism, and has sponsored a joint study committee investigating the possibility of Roman Catholic membership in that body.

Advisory and other services are provided by the committee to ecumenical commissions and agencies in dioceses.

Through the Secretariat for Catholic-Jewish Relations, the committee is in contact with several national Jewish agencies and bodies. Issues of mutual interest and shared concern are reviewed for the purpose of furthering deeper understanding between the Catholic and Jewish communities.

Through the Secretariat for Non-Christians, the committee promotes activity in wider areas of dialogue. The Rev. John F. Hotchkin serves as executive secretary for this secretariat.

Offices of the committee are located at 1312 Massachusetts Ave. N.W., Washington, D.C. 20005.

World Council

The World Council of Churches is a fellowship of churches which acknowledge "Jesus Christ as Lord and Savior." It is a permanent organization providing constituent members — nearly 300 churches with some 450 million communicants in 100 countries — with opportunities for meeting, consultation and cooperative action with respect to doctrine, worship, practice, social mission, evangelism and missionary work, and other matters of mutual concern.

The WCC was formally established Aug. 23, 1948, in Amsterdam with ratification of a constitution by 147 communions. This action merged two previously existing movements — Life and Work (social mission), Faith and Order (doctrine) — which had initiated practical steps toward founding a fellowship of Christian churches at meetings held in Oxford, Edinburgh and Utrecht in 1937 and 1938. A third movement for cooperative missionary work, which originated about 1910 and, remotely, led to formation of the WCC, was incorporated into the council in 1971 under the title of the International Missionary Council (World Mission and Evangelism).

Four additional general assemblies of the council have been held since the charter meeting of 1948: in Evanston, Ill. (1954), New Delhi, India (1961), Uppsala, Sweden (1968) and Nairobi, Kenya (1975).

Between assemblies, the council operates through a central committee which meets every 12 or 18 months, and an executive committee which meets every six months.

The council continues the work of the International Missionary Council, the Commission on Faith and Order, and the Commission on Church and Society. The structure of the council has three program units: Faith and Witness, Justice and Service, Education and Communication.

Liaison between the council and the Vatican has been maintained since 1966 through a joint working group. Roman Catholic membership in the WCC is a question officially on the agenda of this body. The Joint Commission on Society, Development and Peace (SODEPAX) was an agency of the council and the Pontifical Commission for Justice and Peace from 1968 to Dec. 31, 1980. Roman Catholics serve individually as full members of the Commission on Faith and Order and in various other capacities.

WCC headquarters are located in Geneva, Switzerland. The United States Conference for the World Council of Churches at 475

Riverside Drive, New York, N.Y. 10015, provides liaison between the U.S. churches and Geneva. The WCC also maintains fraternal relations with regional, national and local councils of churches throughout the world.

The Rev. Philip A. Potter, a Methodist from the Island of Dominica, West Indies, was elected secretary general of the WCC in August, 1972.

WCC presidents are: Ms. Annie Jiagge, Ghana; the Rev. J. Miguez-Bonino, Argentina; General T. B. Simatupang, Indonesia; Archbishop O. Sundby, Sweden; Dr. Cynthia Wedel, U.S.A.; His Holiness Ilia, patriarch of the Gregorian Orthodox Church, S.S.R.

National Council

The National Council of the Churches of Christ in the U.S.A., the largest ecumenical organization in the United States, is a cooperative federation of 32 Protestant, Orthodox and Anglican church bodies having about 40 million members.

The NCCC, established by the churches in 1950, was structured through the merger of 12 separate cooperative agencies. Presently, through three main program divisions and five commissions, the NCCC carries on work in behalf of member churches in home and overseas missions, Christian education, communications, disaster relief and rehabilitation, family life, stewardship, regional and local ecumenism, and other areas.

Policies of the NCCC are determined by a governing board of approximately 250 members appointed by the constituent churches. The governing board meets twice a year.

The NCCC's annual budget approximates $29 million, about 75 per cent of which is devoted to compassionate ministries of aid and relief to victims of disasters and endemic poverty in lands overseas.

The president and general secretary, respectively, are Rev. M. William Howard and Dr. Claire Randall.

NCCC headquarters are located at 475 Riverside Drive, New York, N.Y. 10015.

Consultation

The Consultation on Church Union, officially begun in 1962, is a venture of American churches seeking a united church "truly catholic, truly evangelical, and truly reformed." The churches engaged in this process, representing 25 million Christians, are the African Methodist Episcopal Church, the African Methodist Episcopal Zion Church, the Christian Church (Disciples of Christ), the Christian Methodist Episcopal Church, the Episcopal Church, the Presbyterian Church in the United States, the United Church of Christ, the United Methodist Church, and the United Presbyterian Church in the U.S.A. The National Council of Community Churches joined the COCU in 1976.

From 1970 to 1973 the member churches studied the first draft of a plan of union for the proposed Church of Christ Uniting. The responses to this plan, on the one hand, gave evidence of an historic consensus on faith, worship, and ministry; on the other hand, they revealed the need for mature involvement in order to discover the structures of a united church. The 11th plenary at Memphis, April, 1973, called for a future agenda involving the congregations more intimately, explored divisive factors such as racism, and affirmed the doctrinal and liturgical rapprochement already achieved. An affirmation of mutual recognition of membership was accepted and sent to the churches at the 12th plenary held at Cincinnati Nov. 4 to 8, 1974. At the 1976 plenary meeting, six chapters of "an emerging consensus" as a "theological basis for union" were approved for study by COCU members. The 1980 plenary accepted a seventh chapter on ministry.

Two experimental liturgies, "An Order of Worship for The Proclamation of the Word of God and The Celebration of the Lord's Supper With Commentary" (1968) and "An Order for Holy Baptism" (1973), have been developed. An ecumenical lectionary has also been produced. Another series of eucharistic texts was published in 1978. The 1979 plenary accepted a series of questions to be posed to each church arising out of the mutual recognition of members, and moved ahead on a draft agreement on the ordained ministry.

The general secretary of COCU is the Rev. Gerald F. Moede. The Rev. Rachel Henderlite was elected president in November, 1976.

Offices are located at 228 Alexander St., Princeton, N.J. 08540.

ECUMENICAL DIALOGUES

(Source: Bishops' Committee for Ecumenical and Interreligious Affairs, National Conference of Catholic Bishops.)

Following is a list of principal consultations, from Mar. 16, 1965, involving representatives of the U.S. Catholic Bishops' Committee for Ecumenical and Interreligious Affairs and representatives of other Christian Churches, with names of the churches, places and dates of meetings, and the subject matter of discussions.

Baptist Convention, American (Division of Cooperative Christianity): (1) De Witt, Mich., Apr. 3, 1967 — American Baptist and Roman Catholic dialogue; a Baptist view of areas of theological agreement. (2) Green Lake, Wis., Apr. 29, 1968 — Baptism and confirmation; Christian freedom and ecclesiastical authority. (3) Schiller Park, Ill., Apr. 28, 1969 — Nature and communication of grace; Christian freedom and ecclesiastical authority; baptism and confirmation. (4) Atchison, Kan., Apr. 17, 1970 — Role of the Church, resume of years past and the future; Roman Catholic-American Baptist dialogues; observations concerning bilateral ecumenical conversations and the future course of American Baptist-Roman Catholic conversations.

(5) Detroit, Mich., Apr. 23 to 24, 1971 — Theological perspective on clergy and lay issues and relations; theology of the local church; growth in understanding. (6) Liberty, Mo., Apr. 14 to 15, 1972 — Relationships between Church and State.

Baptists, Southern (Ecumenical Institute, Wake Forest University): (1) Winston-Salem, N.C., May 8, 1969 — Impact of biblical criticism on Roman Catholicism and contemporary Christianity in general; holy use of the world; creeds and the Faith; liturgy and spontaneity in worship; retreat, revival and monasticism; world view of ecumenism.

(2) St. Benedict, La., Feb. 4, 1970 — Liturgy and spontaneity in worship; perspectives on Baptist views on Scripture and tradition; the priesthood of all Christians; authority of the Old Testament; Baptist concepts of the Church; retreat, revival and monasticism. (3) Louisville, Ky., May 13, 1970 — The priesthood of all Christians; the ecumenical tide — a pastoral perspective; the enduring meaning of the Old Testament; retreat, revival and monasticism.

(4) Daytona Beach, Fla., Feb. 1 to 3, 1971 — Issues and answers, prepared by the Interfaith Witness Department of the Home Mission Board, Southern Baptist Convention. (5) Houston, Tex., Oct. 16 to 18, 1972 — Second regional conference planned in conjunction with the Interfaith Witness Department.

(6) Marriottsville, Md., Feb. 4 to 6, 1974 — Third regional conference, planned in conjunction with the Interfaith and Witness Department, concerning different types of reform and their appropriateness at different levels of church life. (7) Menlo Park, Calif., Oct. 27 to 29, 1975 — Fourth regional conference. The theme: "Conversion to Christ and Life-Long Growth in the Spirit."

(8) Winston-Salem, N.C., Nov. 10-12, 1975 — Fraternal dialogue, planned in conjunction with the Ecumenical Institute of Wake Forest University and Belmont Abbey College, on the abortion issue in Christian perspective, with publication of a statement and proceedings.

(9) Winston-Salem, N.C., Nov. 3-5, 1976 — Dialogue, planned as above, on Church-state issues, with publication of a statement and proceedings.

(10) Kansas City, Mo., Nov. 28 to 30, 1977 — Fifth regional conference on the theme, "The Theology and Experience of Worship."
(11) Cincinnati, O., Apr. 28 to 30, 1978 — Inauguration of a scholars' dialogue, with presentation of papers on the Church in the New Testament and the experience of God in the Church.

(12) Cincinnati, O., Nov. 3 to 5, 1978 — Roman Catholicism in the U.S.A., an historical perspective; Southern Baptist experience in America; overviews of each tradition by the other; the local congregation or church. (13) St. Louis, Mo., Apr. 20 to 22, 1979 — Salvation as understood and taught in both traditions.

(14) Cincinnati, O., Nov. 9 to 11, 1979 — The authority of Scripture from Southern Baptist and Roman Catholic viewpoints. (15) Conyers, Ga., Apr. 11 to 13, 1980 — Spirituality as understood in each tradition, including sacraments, saints and social justice; Roman Catholic teaching on ministry from the Scriptures and the Fathers of the Church.

Christian Church, Disciples of Christ (Council on Christian Unity): (1) Indianapolis, Ind., Mar. 16, 1967 — A look at Disciples for Catholics. (2) Kansas City, Mo., Sept. 25, 1967 — Roman Catholic view of the nature of unity being sought; opportunities in the contemporary ecumenical movement. (3) St. Louis, Mo., Apr. 29, 1968 — Eucharistic sharing.

(4) Washington, D.C., Oct. 16, 1968 — Disciple of Christ inquiry regarding the sacramentality of marriage; pastoral reflections on mixed marriage. (5) New York, N.Y., Apr. 25, 1969 — Recognition and reconciliation of ministries; theological presuppositions concerning ministry among the Disciples; role of the priest in the Catholic community.

(6) Columbus, O., Nov. 3 to 5, 1970 — The parish concept in a plan of union (Consultation on Church Union); directions emerging in Catholic parish life. (7) New York, N.Y., June 8 to 10, 1971 — Disciples' theology of baptism; meaning of baptism as liberation, incorporation, empowerment.

(8) Indianapolis, Ind., Mar. 8 to 10, 1972 — Ministry of healing and reconciliation as practiced in the two communities. (9) Madison, Wis., June 26 to 28, 1972 — Review and summary of five years of dialogue; planning for future themes.

(10) Pleasant Hill, Shaker Town, Ky., May 22 to 24, 1973 — The Church in the New Testament.

(11) Indianapolis, Ind., Jan. 5-6, 1977 — Planning session, with the Council on Christian Unity of the Christian Church and the International Disciples Ecumenical Consultative Council, for a five-year consultation on the topic, "Apostolicity and Catholicity in the Visible Unity of the Church."

(12) Indianapolis, Ind., Sept. 22 to 27, 1977 — First session of a new and international consultation on the nature of the Church and elements of unity relating to it from New Testament and historical perspectives.
(13) Rome, Italy, Dec. 9 to 14, 1978 —

Baptism, gift and call in the search for unity; study of various modes of baptism.
(14) Annapolis, Md., Sept. 7 to 12, 1979 — The faith of the individual and the faith of the Church; tradition and the faith of the Church; an agreed account on both subjects.

Episcopal (The Anglican-Roman Catholic Consultation, Joint Commission on Ecumenical Relations): (1) Washington, D.C., June 22, 1965 — Preliminary discussions. (2) Kansas City, Mo., Feb. 2, 1966 — Eucharist as source or expression of community; Eucharist as sign and cause of unity, and the Church as a Eucharistic fellowship.
(3) Providence, R.I., Oct. 10, 1966 — Function of the minister in Eucharistic celebration; minister of the Eucharist. (4) Milwaukee, Wis., May 2, 1967 — Eucharist. (5) Jackson, Miss., Jan. 5, 1968 — Various aspects of the ministerial priesthood and the priesthood of the faithful in Eucharistic celebration; the priest's place and function in the Church's mission of service; the laity in Episcopal Church government.
(6) Liberty, Mo., Dec. 2, 1968 — Directions of the ecumenical movement; episcopal symbol of unity in the Christian community; collegiality; Citizens for Educational Freedom; a layman's view of jurisdictional and cultural factors in division; Church and society in contemporary America.
(7) Boynton Beach, Fla., Dec. 8, 1969 — All in each place; toward the reconciliation of the Roman Catholic Church and Churches of the Anglican Communion; an approach to designing a Roman Catholic-Episcopal parish; preparation of joint statement on the meeting. (8) Green Bay, Wis., June 17, 1970 — Is the (COCU — Consultation on Church Union) plan of union truly Catholic, with special reference to the priest and the episcopacy?; Anglican-Roman Catholic dialogue — achievement and prognostication.
(9) St. Benedict, La., Jan. 26 to 29, 1971 — The primacy of jurisdiction of the Roman Pontiff according to the First Vatican Council; the teaching of the Second Vatican Council concerning the hierarchy of truths; analysis of the ground of "Church Elements: An Ecclesiological Investigation."
(10) Liberty, Mo., June 20 to 23, 1971 — Gift of infallibility; sharing in the teaching authority of the Church; official view of episcopacy in the Episcopal Church in the USA; symposium on Hans Kung's *Infallibility? An Inquiry*; dogma as an ecumenical problem; Revelation and statement in Anglicanism; revised working paper on theological truth, propositions and Christian unity; reflections on the teaching ministry of the Church.
(11) New York, N.Y., Jan 20 to 24, 1972 — Theological truth, propositions and Christian unity; the Protestant Episcopal Church's view of authority, tradition and the Bible; a comment on the Windsor "Statement of Eucharistic Agreement" issued by the International Anglican-Roman Catholic Consultation.
(12) Cincinnati, O., June 12 to 15, 1972 — The notion of *typos* and *typoi* as applied to the forms of the Christian Church; correspondences and differences in the Anglican and Roman Catholic understanding and exercise of teaching authority.
(13) Cincinnati, O., Mar. 18 to 22, 1973 — Formulation of a preliminary draft on the purpose of the Church. (14) Vicksburg, Miss., Jan. 6 to 10, 1974 — Formulation of a response to the "Canterbury Statement" of the International Anglican-Roman Catholic Consultation on ministry and ordination; discussion and amendment of a draft on the purpose of the Church; other subjects in a continuing dialogue on the mission of the Church.
(15) Cincinnati, O., Nov. 10 to 13, 1974 — Discussion on the nature of authority in Anglicanism and Roman Catholicism. Report prepared on the purpose of the Church.
(16) Cincinnati, O., June 22 to 25, 1975 — Special ad hoc consultation on women and orders.
(17) Erlanger, Ky., Oct. 21-24, 1975 — Continuation of discussion on women and orders, with release of joint statement on the ordination of women. (18) Overland Park, Kan., Mar. 10-13, 1976 — Continuation of discussion on authority in the Church.
(19) New Orleans, La., Jan. 19-22, 1977 — Presentation and discussion of a paper entitled "Some Implications of a 'Communio Ecclesiology' for the Authority Question"; formulation of an initial response to the "Venice Statement" (see separate entry); near completion of a 12-year report on the consultation.
(20) Cincinnati, O., Aug. 9 to 12, 1977 — Preparation of a second response to the Venice Statement, "Authority in the Church," and of a 12-year report, "Where We are: A Challenge for the Future" (planned for publication). (21) Savannah, Ga., Mar. 7 to 10, 1978 — Christian anthropology and discussion of issues raised by the topic of the 12-year report in dialogue.
(22) Cincinnati, O., Jan. 3 to 6, 1979 — Christian anthropology in the patristic period and documents of the Second Vatican Council on the subject; New Testament arguments for and against the ordination of women.
(23) Cincinnati, O., Oct. 29 to Nov. 1, 1979 — Christian anthropology from the viewpoints of biotechnology/bodiliness, and Mariology. (24) Cincinnati, O., June 17 to 20, 1980 — Maleness and femaleness in Christian anthropology.

Lutheran, U.S.A. (National Committee of the Lutheran World Federation): (1) Baltimore, Md., Mar. 16, 1965 — Exploratory discussion. (2) Baltimore, Md., July 6, 1965 — Nicene Creed as dogma of the Church. (3) Chicago, Ill., Feb. 10, 1966 — Baptism, in the context of the New Testament; Lutheran understanding; teaching of the Council of Trent.

(4) Washington, D.C., Sept. 22, 1966 — Eucharist as sacrifice, in traditional and contemporary Catholic and Lutheran contexts. (5) New York, N.Y., Apr 7, 1967 — Propitiation and five presentations on various aspects of the Eucharist. (6) St. Louis, Mo.. Sept. 29, 1967 — Eucharist. (7) New York, Mar. 8, 1968 — Intercommunion, with respect to Catholic discipline, Lutheran practice, and theological reflections.

(8) Williamsburg, Va., Sept. 27, 1968 — Ministry; the competent minister of the Eucharist; scriptural foundations of diakonia (ministry of service). (9) San Francisco, Calif., Feb. 21, 1969 — Apostolic succession in the patristic era and in a contemporary view; Lutheran view of the validity of Lutheran orders; Christian priesthood in the light of documents of the Second Vatican Council.

(10) Baltimore, Md., Sept. 26, 1969 — The minister of the Eucharist, according to the Council of Trent; the use of "Church" as applied to Protestant denominations in the documents of Vatican II; Lutheran doctrine of the ministry — Catholic and Reformed; the ordained minister and layman in Lutheranism. (11) St. George, Bermuda, Feb. 19, 1970 — Preparation of joint statement on the ministry.

(12) New York, N.Y., May, 1970. (13) Chicago, Ill., Oct. 30 to Nov. 1, 1970. (14) Miami, Fla., Feb. 19 to 22, 1971 — Peter and the New Testament; the papacy in the late patristic era, Middle Ages, Renaissance; text of the *Dogmatic Constitution on the Church* (Vatican II) with respect to the papacy and infallibility.

(15) Seabury, Conn., Sept. 24 to 27, 1971 — An investigation of the concept of divine right *(jus divinum);* teaching of the First Vatican Council on primacy and infallibility; a Lutheran understanding of what papal primacy in the Church might mean.

(16) New Orleans, La., Feb. 18 to 21, 1972 — Further discussion of the concept of divine right; ecumenical projections concerning the Petrine office; teaching authority in the Lutheran Church. (17) Minneapolis, Minn., Sept. 22 to 25, 1972 — Further investigation of the Petrine function; councils and conciliarism.

(18) San Antonio, Tex., Feb. 16 to 19, 1973 — Discussion of work and papers of the Petrine panel concerning ministry and the Church universal, Catholic and Lutheran interpretive statements; work on papal primacy papers. (19) Allentown, Pa., Sept. 21 to 24, 1973 — Work on a joint statement concerning ministry and the Church universal, the concluding session on this topic; selection of

infallibility as the next topic for consideration. (20) Marriottsville, Md., Feb. 15 to 17, 1974 — Start of discussion on infallibility; commissioning of 16 future research papers.

(21) Princeton, N.J., Sept. 19 to 22, 1974 — Scriptural studies re infallibility, inquiries into the teachings of early Lutheranism. (22) St. Louis, Mo., Jan. 30 to Feb. 2, 1975 — Historical and systematic studies of the teaching of infallibility. (23) Washington, D.C., Apr. 2 to 3, 1975 — Special meeting of several Lutheran presidents and Catholic bishops to review the work of the scholars' consultation and propose future directions. Press report issued.

(24) Washington, D.C. Sept. 17 to 21, 1975 — Further historical and case studies re infallibility: ecumenical councils and marian definitions. (25) Scottsdale, Ariz., Feb. 19 to 22, 1976 — Infallibility discussion continued.

(26) Washington, D.C., Apr. 2-3, 1975 — Meeting of Lutheran presidents and Catholic bishops to evaluate the direction and progress of Lutheran-Catholic dialogue in the U.S., with release of a joint statement. (27) Washington, D.C., Feb. 4-5, 1976 — Continuation of discussion concerning the direction and progress of dialogue.

(28) Gettysburg, Pa., Sept. 15-18, 1976 — Presentation of papers entitled: "Draft I — Authority and Doctrine," "The Roman View of the Petrine Office in the Church 366-461," "The Status of the Nicene Creed as Dogma in the Church," "Ecumenical Methodology — Report of Task Force."

(29) Washington, D.C., Feb. 16-20, 1977 — Discussion of the second draft of a common statement; presentation of a "Note on the Papacy as an Object of Faith."

(30) Columbia, S.C., Sept. 14 to 18, 1977 — Continued discussion of the common statement, "Infallibility and Teaching Authority in the Church." (31) Lantana, Fla., Feb. 15 to 19, 1978 — Discussion on the fourth draft of a comon statement reporting the findings of dialogue on infallibility.

(32) Minneapolis, Minn., Sept. 13 to 17, 1978 — Statement on infallibility produced. (33) Cincinnati, O., Feb. 14 to 18, 1979 — Beginning of study of justification. (34) Princeton, N.J., Sept. 13 to 16, 1979 — Further study of justification.

(35) Atlanta, Ga., Mar. 5 to 9, 1980 — Justification by faith, in the Bible and the teaching of the Council of Trent.

Methodist (United Methodist Church): (1) Chicago, Ill., June 28, 1966 — Methodists and Roman Catholics: comments for Catholic-Methodist conversation. (2) Chicago, Ill., Dec. 18, 1966 — Salvation, faith and good works; Catholic Church and faith. (3) Lake Junaluska, N.C., June 28, 1967 — Roman Catholic position regarding the Spirit in the Church; mission of the Holy Spirit, in the

light of the Second Vatican Council's *Dogmatic Constitution on the Church* and the writings of John Wesley.
(4) New York, N.Y., Dec. 17, 1967 — Three generations of Church-State argumentation. (5) San Antonio, Tex., Sept. 30, 1968 — Shared convictions about education. (6) Delaware, O., Oct. 9, 1969 — Major Methodist ecumenical documents; an appraisal of some documents of Vatican II; racial confrontation in Roman Catholicism, Methodism and the National Council of Churches. (7) Chicago, Ill., Jan. 30, 1970 — Review and planning.
(8) Washington, D.C., Dec. 16, 1970 — Completion of a statement of shared convictions about education. Task force meetings during 1971. (9) Cincinnati, O., Feb. 25 to 26, 1972 — Ministry in the United Methodist Church and the spirituality of the ordained ministry; problems of ministry. (10) Dayton, O., Oct. 13 to 14, 1972 — Dialogue on the holiness of the Church and Christian holiness.
(11) Washington, D.C., Mar. 9 to 10, 1973 — Spirituality of the ministry. (12) Washington, D.C., Nov. 1 to 2, 1973 — Start of preparatory work on a consensus statement on spirituality of the ministry.
(13) Washington, D.C., Jan. 30 to Feb. 2, 1975 — Report prepared on Catholic and United Methodist understandings of holiness and spirituality in the ordained ministry; statement on holiness and spirituality of the ordained ministry released in January, 1976.
(14) Washington, D.C., May 16, 1977 — Planning session for the next round of dialogue.
(15) Washington, D.C., Dec. 4 to 6, 1977 — New phase of dialogue on the Eucharist in both traditions. (16) Marriottsville, Md., Apr. 16 to 18, 1978 — Continuing research on Eucharistic theology as developed in the two churches.
(17) Washington, D.C., Oct. 12 to 14, 1978 — Eucharistic practice in both traditions. (18) Marriottsville, Md., May 17 to 19, 1979 — The Eucharist; contemporary eucharistic devotional practices of both traditions.
(19) Washington, D.C., Nov. 4 to 6, 1979 — The presence of Christ in the word, related to Eucharistic presence; the notion of sacrifice in the Eucharist. (20) Washington, D.C., May 4 to 6, 1980 — Comparison of liturgical texts of Methodists and Catholics; further exploration of the relationship of word and sacrament.

Orthodox (Standing Conference of Canonical Orthodox Bishops of America): Sept. 9, 1965 — Preliminary discussions. (1) New York, N.Y., Sept. 29, 1966 — Consultation led to appointment of task forces to investigate differences in theological methods, questions of sacramental sharing, possible co-operation in theological education and the formation of seminarians. (2) Worcester, Mass., May 5, 1967 — Theological diversity and unity; intercommunion; common witness in theological education. (3) Maryknoll, N.Y., Dec. 7, 1968 — Eucharist and Church; indissolubili ty of marriage; cooperation in theological education.
(4) Worcester, Mass., Dec. 12, 1969 — Orthodox and Catholic views of the Eucharist and membership in the Church; an agreed statement on the Eucharist. (5) New York, N.Y., May 19, 1970 — New Order of the Mass; membership of schismatics and heretics in the ancient Church; current legislation of the Catholic Church and current practices of the Greek Orthodox Church concerning common worship; current legislation of the Catholic Church concerning mixed marriages; Orthodox view of mixed marriages; an agreed statement on mixed marriages.
(6) Brookline, Mass., Dec. 4, 1970 — Ministers, doctrine and practice of matrimony in Eastern and Western traditions. (7) Barlin Acres, Mass., Nov. 3 to 4, 1971 — Ethical issues relating to marriage; revision of an agreed statement on mixed marriages; the primacy of Rome as seen by the Eastern Church.
(8) New York, N.Y., Dec. 6, 1973 — Study of a draft statement on the sanctity of marriage. (9) Washington, D.C., May 23 to 24, 1974 — Dialogical process; witness of the Church on the American scene; approval of an agreed statement on respect for life; Orthodox and Catholic views of contemporary Orthodoxy and Catholicism.
(10) New York, N.Y., Dec. 9 to 10, 1974 — Prepared and issued an agreed statement on the Church. (11) Washington, D.C., May 19 to 20, 1975 — Dialogue on the local church and on the theology of priesthood. (12) New York, N.Y., Jan. 23 to 24, 1976 — Further dialogue on the theology of priesthood, et al.
(13) Washington, D.C., May 18-19, 1976 — Additional discussion of theology of the priesthood, and ecumenical councils; release of joint statements entitled "The Principle of Economy" and "The Pastoral Office."
(14) Brookline, Mass., Jan. 13-14, 1977 — Presentations on "Orthodox/Roman Catholic Marriages Revisited" and of two reports on the first pre-synodal Pan-Orthodox Conference in preparation for the coming Great and Holy Council.
(15) Washington, D.C., Sept. 28 to 29, 1977 — Presentation and discussion of papers concerning the agenda of the forthcoming Great and Holy Council of the Orthodox Church, the theology of marriage and Orthodox-Roman Catholic marriages.
(16) New York, N.Y., Jan. 24 to 25, 1978 — Preparation of a common statement on the sanctity of marriage, authorization for writ-

ing a history of the Orthodox-Roman Catholic Consultation.

(17) Washington, D.C., May 15 to 16, 1978 — Additional work on a common statement on the sanctity of marriage, and initial discussion concerning the religious upbringing of children in Orthodox-Catholic marriages.

(18) New York, N.Y., Dec. 7 to 8, 1978 — Study of the religious formation of children of marriages between Eastern Orthodox and Roman Catholics; release of "An Agreed Statement on the Sanctity of Marriage."

(19) Washington, D.C., Mar. 15 to 16, 1979 — Continued study of a draft entitled "Joint Recommendations on the Spiritual Formation of Children of Marriages between Orthodox and Roman Catholics."

(20) Pittsburgh, Pa., Nov. 2 to 3, 1979 — Additional work on a document, "Spiritual Formation of Children"; study of early Christian commissioning rites.

Orthodox, Oriental (Armenian, Coptic, Ethiopian, Indian Malabar and Syrian Orthodox Churches): (1) New York N.Y., Jan. 27, 1978 — Start of a new consultation, with initial consideration of a historical study of Oriental Orthodoxy.

(2) New York, N.Y., May 26 to 27, 1978 — Purpose and method of dialogue; histories of Oriental Orthodox Churches. (3) Washington, D.C., Dec. 1 to 2, 1978 — Presentation of papers on the Council of Chalcedon, Christology and the Church today, concluding that ancient controversy over Christology does not seem to apply at the present time.

(4) New York, N.Y., May 25 to 26, 1979 — Roman Catholic Christology; Eucharistic Liturgy of the Syrian Orthodox Church.

(5) New York, N.Y., Dec. 27 to 28, 1979 — Paper on Byzantine liturgical commentary; reflection on joint statements of Paul VI with Vasken I, Ignatius Jacoub III and Amba Shenouda III. (6) New York, N.Y., Apr. 18 to 19, 1980 — Paper on Coptic Orthodox Divine Liturgy followed by that Eucharistic Liturgy.

Presbyterian and Reformed (The Roman Catholic-Presbyterian Consultation Group, North American Council of the World Alliance of Reformed Churches): (1) Washington, D.C., July 27, 1965 — Exploratory discussions. (2) Philadelphia, Pa., Nov. 26, 1965 — Role of the Holy Spirit in renewal and reform of the Church. (3) New York, May 12, 1966 — Roman Catholic view of Scripture and tradition; apostolic and ecclesiastical tradition.

(4) Chicago, Ill., Oct. 27, 1966 — Development of doctrine; dialogue, a program of peace, prayer and study for Roman Catholics and Protestants. (5) Collegeville, Minn., Apr. 26, 1967 — Order and ministry in the Reformed tradition; validity of orders; changes

in mixed marriage. (6) Lancaster, Pa., Oct. 26, 1967 — Work was begun on a joint statement on ministry. (7) Bristow, Va., May 9, 1968 — Structures and ministries. (8) Allen Park, Mich., Oct. 24, 1968 — Marriage. (9) Charleston, S.C., May 21, 1969 — Validation of ministries and ministry; theological view of marriage.

(10) Macatawa, Mich., Oct. 30, 1969 — Apostles and apostolic succession in the patristic era; report concerning office; divorce and remarriage as understood in the United Presbyterian Church in the USA; the Church and second marriage; recommendations for changes regarding inter-Christian marriages. (11) Morristown, N.J., May 13, 1970 — Joint statements on ministry in the Church and women in Church and society.

(12) Princeton, N.J., Oct. 29 to 30, 1970 — Episcopal presbyteral polity; episcopacy. (13) Columbus, O., May 13 to 15, 1971 — Ministry in the Church; man-woman relationships; the future of the Church. (14) Richmond, Va., Oct. 28 to 30, 1971 — Reports finalized on women in the Church and ministry in the Church. (15) Oct. 26 to 29, 1972 — The shape of the unity we seek.

(16) Columbus, O., May 30 to June 2, 1973 — Theological and sociological views of the shape of unity we seek. (17) Columbus, O., Oct. 24 to 27, 1973 — Renewed discussion of the previous topic. (18) Columbus, O., May 8 to 11, 1974 — Further discussion of the previous topic in the light of Scripture, tradition, theology and reflection on the total Christian experience; worship and belief; discussion of plans for publication of a book on progress of the dialogue.

(17) Cincinnati, O., Oct. 24 to 26, 1974 — Dialogue on the unity we seek in worship and in structures. (18) Washington, D.C., May 22 to 24, 1975 — Report prepared on the mission and nature of the one Church of Christ, with attention to the unity sought in worship, in structure and in common faith.

(19) Princeton, N.J., Oct. 20-23, 1976 — Presentation of: an overview of the history of the consultation; a paper covering a Roman Catholic summary of the diversity and unity of current Christian responses to moral issues facing the Church; a paper on ethics and ethos in the Reformed/Presbyterian tradition.

(20) Washington, D.C., May 25 to 27, 1977 — Human rights, distributive justice and the abortion issue as faced by the churches. (21) Princeton, N.J., Oct. 6 to 7, 1977 — Discussion of racism in South Africa and continuation of a study on human rights.

(22) Washington, D.C., May 30 to June 1, 1978 — Study of the problem of unwanted pregnancies; preparation of statements on abortion and human rights. (23) Washington, D.C., Mar. 4 to 6, 1979 — Re-drafting of pro-

posed statements on abortion and human rights.

(24) Washington, D.C., Sept. 27 to 29, 1979 — Statements on abortion and human rights approved along with commentaries, and an interpretative report.

ECUMENICAL BRIEFS

Statements: The ecumenical statements listed below, and others like them, reflect the views of participants in the dialogues which produced them. They have not been formally accepted by the respective churches as formulations of doctrine or points of departure for practical changes in discipline.

• The "Windsor Statement" on Eucharistic doctrine, published Dec. 31, 1971, by the Anglican-Roman Catholic International Commission of theologians. (For text, see pages 132-33 of the 1973 *Catholic Almanac*.)

• The "Canterbury Statement" on ministry and ordination, published Dec. 13, 1973, by the same commission (For excerpts, see pages 127-30 of the 1975 *Catholic Almanac*.)

• "Papal Primacy / Converging Viewpoints," published Mar. 4, 1974, by the dialogue group sanctioned by the U.S.A. National Convention of the World Lutheran Federation and the U.S. Bishops' Committee for Ecumenical and Interreligious Affairs. (For excerpts, see pages 130-31 of the 1975 *Catholic Almanac*.)

• An "Agreed Statement on the Purpose of the Church," published Oct. 31, 1975, by the Anglican-Roman Catholic Consultation in the U.S., in which the signatories agreed on the purpose and mission of the Church "insofar as it faithfully preaches the Gospel of salvation and manifests the love of God in service." It noted that "Roman Catholics and Episcopalians believe that there is but one Church of Christ," and endorsed social action for human liberation.

• "Christian Unity and Women's Ordination," published Nov. 7, 1975, by the same consultation, in which it was said that the ordination of women (approved in principle by the Anglican Communion but not by the Catholic Church) would "introduce a new element" in dialogue but would not mean the end of consultation nor the abandonment of its declared goal of full communion and organic unity. (A similar view was expressed in an exchange of letters between Pope Paul and Anglican Archbishop Donald Coggan of Canterbury, between July 8, 1975, and Mar. 23, 1976.)

• "Holiness and Spirituality of the Ordained Ministry," issued early in 1976 by theologians of the Catholic Church and the United Methodist Church; the first statement resulting from dialogue begun in 1966.

• "Mixed Marriages," published in the spring of 1976 by the Anglican-Roman Catholic Consultation in the U.S. It was similar in some respects to the statement, "Implementation of the Apostolic Letter on Mixed Marriages," approved by the National Conference of Catholic Bishops Nov. 16, 1970. It differed in softening the statement of a Catholic party's responsibility to do everything possible to raise children in the Catholic faith and favored greater freedom for having the marriage ceremony according to the rite of another Christian church.

• "Bishops and Presbyters," see under Eastern Ecumenical Briefs.

• "The Principle of Economy," see under Eastern Ecumenical Briefs.

• "Venice Statement" on authority in the Church, published Jan. 20, 1977, by the Anglican-Roman Catholic International Commission of theologians. Its major headings were Christian authority, authority of the ordained ministry and of the community, authority in the community of churches, the primacy of the bishop of Rome, authority in matters of faith, conciliar and primatial authority. Differences were cited in Catholic and Anglican views with respect to scriptural passages related to claims of the Roman See to primacy of authority, the divine right of the successors of St. Peter, papal infallibility and universal jurisdiction over the Church.

• "Response to the Venice Statement," issued Jan. 4, 1978, by the Anglican-Roman Catholic Consultation in the U.S.A., citing additional questions regarding the sharing of authority in the Church, the nature of the primacy of Rome, and the relation of indefectibility to infallibility.

• "The Presence of Christ in Church and World," published early in 1978 by representatives of the Vatican Secretariat for Promoting Christian Unity and the World Alliance of Reformed Churches. The wide-ranging statement noted considerable degrees of mutual understanding and some agreement, along with substantial differences of view on several subjects — especially papal infallibility.

• "An Ecumenical Approach to Marriage," published in January, 1978, in the form of a report on five or more years of dialogue among representatives of the Catholic Church, the Lutheran World Federation and the World Alliance of Reformed Churches. Significant agreement was reported on doctrinal and pastoral aspects of marriage. Objections continued from the Lutheran and Reformed sides, however, with respect to the sacramental nature of marriage, and to Catholic requirements in cases of mixed marriages: (1) that the marriage normally take place with a priest as the officiating minister, and (2) that the Catholic party promise to do everything possible to raise children in the Catholic faith.

• "Teaching Authority and Infallibility in the Church," released in October, 1978, by the Catholic-Lutheran dialogue group in the U.S., noting similarities and differences between Lutheran understanding of the indefectibility of the Church and the Catholic doctrine of papal infallibility.

• "The Eucharist," reported early in 1979, in which the Roman Catholic-Lutheran Commission indicated developing convergence of views concerning the nature and sacrificial aspect of the Mass, and the significance of believing, active participation in the Eucharist.

• "The Holy Spirit," issued Feb. 12, 1979, by the International Catholic-Methodist Commission, citing points of common faith in the Holy Spirit.

• An agreed statement on the Augsburg Confession (*Confessio Augustana*), approved Feb. 23, 1980, by the Catholic-Lutheran commission, on the 450th anniversary of the basic credal statement of Lutherans. The statement said: "In content and structure this Confession, which is the basis and point of reference for the other Lutheran confessional documents, reflects as no other confession does the ecumenical purpose and Catholic intention of the Reformation." (See separate entry.)

Kung Controversy: Questions were raised about the possibly adverse effect on interfaith relations of the declaration issued by the Congregation for the Doctrine of the Faith in December, 1979, that Father Hans Kung could not be regarded as a Catholic theologian. Pope John Paul said the document was issued to clarify points of doctrine and opinion, and should not impede further ecumenical developments and relations.

Work to Continue: Pope John Paul, at a meeting Sept. 4, 1980, with the 20 members of the Anglican-Roman Catholic International Commission, urged them to continue their work toward unity of the two churches. He said: "We have a common treasure whose fullness we must share, not losing certain characteristic qualities and gifts which have been ours in our divided state."

Models of Unity: Ways of approaching Christian unity were under study at a meeting Mar. 15 to 21, 1976, in Liebfrauenberg, France, of the Joint Working Group of theologians co-sponsored by the Lutheran World Federation and the Vatican Secretariat for Promoting Christian Unity. The models were those keyed to the concepts of: organic union (advocated by church union movements), conciliar fellowship (in the manner of the World Council of Churches), concord (as among Lutherans and Reformed Christians), reconciled diversity (as among world confessional families), and sister churches (as in dialogue among Catholics, Orthodox and Anglicans).

Mutual Christian witness by members of different religious bodies, through pastoral and social service, is also considered a way of moving toward the goal of Christian unity.

CATHOLIC-JEWISH RELATIONS

The Second Vatican Council, in addition to the *Decree on Ecumenism* concerning the movement for unity among Christians, stated the mind of the Church on a similar matter in a *Declaration on the Relationship of the Church to Non-Christian Religions*. This document, as the following excerpts indicate, backgrounds the reasons and directions of the Church's regard for the Jews. (Other portions of the document, not cited here, refer to Hindus, Buddhists and Moslems.)

Spiritual Bond

"As this sacred Synod searches into the mystery of the Church, it recalls the spiritual bond linking the people of the New Covenant with Abraham's stock.

"For the Church of Christ acknowledges that, according to the mystery of God's saving design, the beginnings of her faith and her election are already found among the patriarchs, Moses, and the prophets. She professes that all who believe in Christ, Abraham's sons according to faith (cf. Gal. 3:7), are included in the same patriarch's call, and likewise that the salvation of the Church was mystically foreshadowed by the Chosen People's exodus from the land of bondage.

"The Church, therefore, cannot forget that she received the revelation of the Old Testament through the people with whom God in His inexpressible mercy deigned to establish the Ancient Covenant. Nor can she forget that she draws sustenance from the root of that good olive tree onto which have been grafted the wild olive branches of the Gentiles (cf. Rom.11:17-24). Indeed, the Church believes that by His cross Christ, our Peace, reconciled Jew and Gentile, making them both one in Himself (cf. Eph. 2:14-16).

". . . The Jews still remain most dear to God because of their fathers, for He does not repent of the gifts He makes nor of the calls He issues (cf. Rom. 11:28-29). In company with the prophets and the same Apostle (Paul), the Church awaits that day, known to God alone, on which all peoples will address the Lord in a single voice and 'serve him with one accord' (Zeph. 3:9; Cf. Is. 66:23; Ps. 65:4; Rom. 11:11-32).

No Anti-Semitism

"Since the spiritual patrimony common to Christians and Jews is thus so great, this sacred Synod wishes to foster and recommend that mutual understanding and respect which is the fruit above all of biblical and theological studies, and of brotherly dialogues.

"True, authorities of the Jews and those who followed their lead pressed for the death of Christ (cf. Jn. 19:6); still, what happened in His passion cannot be blamed upon all the Jews then living, without distinction, nor upon the Jews of today. Although the Church is the new People of God, the Jews should not be presented as repudiated or cursed by God, as if such views followed from the holy Scriptures. All should take pains, then, lest in catechetical instruction and in the preaching of God's Word they teach anything out of harmony with the truth of the gospel and the spirit of Christ.

"The Church repudiates all persecutions against any man. Moreover, mindful of her common patrimony with the Jews, and motivated by the gospel's spiritual love and by no political considerations, she deplores the hatred, persecutions, and displays of anti-Semitism directed against the Jews at any time and from any source. . . ." (4).

". . . The Church rejects, as foreign to the mind of Christ, any discrimination against men or harassment of them because of their race, color, condition of life, or religion. . . ." (No. 5).

Bishops' Secretariat

The American hierarchy's first move toward implementation of the Vatican II *Declaration on the Relationship of the Church to Non-Christian Religions* was to establish, in 1965, a Subcommission for Catholic-Jewish Relations in the framework of its Commission for Ecumenical and Interreligious Affairs. This subcommission was reconstituted and given the title of secretariat in September, 1967. Its moderator is Bishop Francis J. Mugavero of Brooklyn. The Secretariat for Catholic-Jewish Relations is located at 1312 Massachusetts Ave. N.W., Washington, D.C. 20005. The executive director is Dr. Eugene J. Fisher.

According to the key norm of a set of guidelines issued by the secretariat Mar. 16, 1967: "The general aim of all Catholic-Jewish meetings (and relations) is to increase our understanding both of Judaism and the Catholic faith, to eliminate sources of tension and misunderstanding, to initiate dialogue or conversations on different levels, to multiply intergroup meetings between Catholics and Jews, and to promote cooperative social action."

Vatican Guidelines

In a document issued Jan. 3, 1975, the Vatican Commission for Religious Relations with the Jews offered a number of suggestions and guidelines for implementing the Christian-Jewish portion of the Second Vatican Council's *Declaration on Relations with Non-Christian Religions.*

Among "suggestions from experience" were those concerning dialogue, liturgical links between Christian and Jewish worship, the interpretation of biblical texts, teaching and education for the purpose of increasing mutual understanding, and joint social action.

The document concluded with the statement:

"On Oct. 22, 1974, the Holy Father instituted for the universal Church this Commission for Religious Relations with the Jews, joined to the Secretariat for Promoting Christian Unity. This special commission, created to encourage and foster religious relations between Jews and Catholics — and to do so in collaboration with other Christians — will be, within the limits of its competence, at the service of all interested organizations, providing information for them and helping them to pursue their task in conformity with the instructions of the Holy See.

"The commission wishes to develop this collaboration in order to implement, correctly and effectively, the express intentions of the (Second Vatican) Council."

NCCB Statement

In a statement issued Nov. 20, 1975, in commemoration of the 10th anniversary of the Second Vatican Council's declaration on non-Christian religions, the National Conference of Catholic Bishops welcomed the Vatican guidelines and hailed the "new era in Catholic-Jewish affairs" which "ended a centuries-long silence between Church and Synagogue."

Lamenting the "de-Judaizing process" that set in early in the Church's history — and which "dulled our awareness of our Jewish beginnings," the bishops affirmed that "most essential concepts in the Christian creed grew at first in Judaic soil. Uprooted from that soil, these basic concepts cannot be perfectly understood."

The bishops called on theologians to reconsider the "long-neglected passages" of the Letter to the Romans (Chapters 9 to 11) as a base for "exploring the continuing relationship of the Jewish people with God and their spiritual bonds with the New Covenant" in a positive manner.

Noting also that "an overwhelming majority of Jews see themselves bound in one way or another to the land of Israel," the bishops stated that, "whatever difficulties Christians may experience in sharing this view, they should strive to understand this link between land and people which Jews have expressed in their writings and worship throughout two millenia as a longing for the homeland, holy Zion."

International Liaison Committee

The International Catholic-Jewish Liaison Committee held its seventh and eighth annual meetings in April, 1978, in Madrid, and in October, 1979, in Regensburg, Germany. The proceedings at both meetings provided evidence of the healing of wounds that had taken place between Jews and Catholics since the Second Vatican Council. In Madrid, the group analyzed the progress made in portraying Judaism in Catholic educational materials throughout the world, as well as the portrait of Christianity provided in Jewish textbooks, especially in the United States and Israel. In Regensburg, the committee discussed religious liberty and education for pluralism.

The mission and witness of the Church was the subject of an address delivered at the sixth meeting of the committee in 1977, by Federico Tommaso, a consultor to the Commission for Religious Relations with the Jews.

U.S. Dialogues

National Workshops on Christian-Jewish Relations are a major form of dialogue. The fifth workshop of this kind, held Apr. 28 to May 1, 1980, in Dallas, featured a major address by Msgr. Jorge Mejia, a member of the Vatican Commission for Religious Relations with the Jews. The American dialogue, he said, was marked by an exciting "frankness and openness" of exchange; he predicted it would have great international significance.

A major dialogue on religion and social justice — sponsored by the Synagogue Council of America and the Secretariat for Catholic-Jewish Relations, National Conference of Catholic Bishops — completed its second round in June, 1980, at Notre Dame University.

The Holocaust and related themes of Jewish-Christian concern were standard subjects of discussion at academic discussions on the university level.

JUDAISM

Judaism is the religion of the Old Testament and of contemporary Jews. Divinely revealed and with a patriarchal background (Abraham, Isaac, Jacob), it originated with the Mosaic Covenant, was identified with the Israelites, and achieved distinctive form and character as the religion of The Law from this Covenant and reforms initiated by Ezra and Nehemiah after the Babylonian Exile.

Judaism does not have a formal creed but its principal points of belief are clear. Basic is belief in one transcendent God who reveals himself through The Law, the prophets, the life of his people and events of history. The fatherhood of God involves the brotherhood of men. Religious faith and practice are equated with just living according to The Law. Moral conviction and practice are regarded as more important than precise doctrinal formulation and profession. Formal worship, whose principal act was sacrifice from Canaanite times to 70 A.D., is by prayer, reading and meditating upon the sacred writings, and observance of the Sabbath and festivals.

Judaism has messianic expectations of the complete fulfillment of the Covenant, the coming of God's kingdom, the ingathering of his people, final judgment and retribution for all men. Views differ regarding the manner in which these expectations will be realized — through a person, the community of God's people, an evolution of historical events, an eschatological act of God himself. Individual salvation expectations also differ, depending on views about the nature of immortality, punishment and reward, and related matters.

The sacred books are the 24 books of the Masoretic Hebrew Text of The Law, the Prophets and the Writings (see The Bible). Together, they contain the basic instruction or norms for just living. In some contexts, the term Law or Torah refers only to the Pentateuch (Genesis, Exodus, Leviticus, Numbers, Deuteronomy); in others, it denotes all the sacred books and/or the whole complex of written and oral tradition.

Also of great authority are two Talmuds which were composed in Palestine and Babylon in the fourth and fifth centuries A.D., respectively. They consist of the Mishna, a compilation of oral laws, and the Gemara, a collection of rabbinical commentary on the Mishna. Midrash are collections of scriptural comments and moral counsels.

Priests were the principal official ministers during the period of sacrificial and temple worship. Rabbis were, and continue to be, teachers and leaders of prayer. The synagogue is the place of community worship. The family and home are focal points of many aspects of Jewish worship and practice.

Of the various categories of Jews, Orthodox are the most conservative in adherence to strict religious traditions. Others — Reformed, Conservative, Reconstructionist — are liberal in comparison with the Orthodox. They favor greater or less modification of religious practices in accommodation to contemporary culture and living conditions.

Principal events in Jewish life include the circumcision of males, according to prescriptions of the Covenant; the bar mitzvah which marks the coming-of-age of boys in Judaism at the age of 13; marriage; and observance of the Sabbath and festivals.

Sabbath and Festivals

Observances of the Sabbath and festivals begin at sundown of the previous calendar day and continue until the following sundown.

Sabbath: Saturday, the weekly day of rest prescribed in the Decalogue.

Booths (Tabernacles): A seven-to-nine-day festival in the month of Tishri (Sept.-Oct.), marked by some Jews with Covenant-renewal and reading of The Law. It originated as an agricultural feast at the end of the harvest and got its name from the temporary shelters used by workers in the fields.

Hanukkah (The Festival of Lights, the Feast of Consecration and of the Maccabees): Commemorates the dedication of the new altar in the Temple at Jerusalem by Judas Maccabeus in 165 B.C. The eight-day festival, during which candles in an eight-branch candelabra are lighted in succession, one each day, occurs near the winter solstice, close to Christmas time.

Passover: A seven-day festival commemorating the liberation of the Israelites from Egypt. The narrative of the Exodus, the Haggadah, is read at ceremonial Seder meals on the first and second days of the festival, which begins on the 14th day of Nisan (Mar.-Apr.).

Pentecost (Feast of Weeks): Observed 50 days after Passover. Some Jews regard it as commemorative of the anniversary of the revelation of The Law to Moses.

Purim: A joyous festival observed on the 14th day of Adar (Feb.-Mar.), commemorating the rescue of the Israelites from massacre by the Persians through the intervention of Esther. The festival is preceded by a day of fasting. A gift- and alms-giving custom became associated with it in medieval times.

Rosh Hashana (Feast of the Trumpets, New Year): Observed on the first day of Tishri (Sept.-Oct.), the festival focuses attention on the day of judgment and is marked with meditation on the ways of life and the ways of death. It is second in importance only to the most solemn observance of Yom Kippur, which is celebrated 10 days later.

Yom Kippur (Day of Atonement): The highest holy day, observed with strict fasting. It occurs 10 days after Rosh Hashana.

ISLAM

Islam is the religion of Mohammed and his followers, called Moslems, or Muslims. Islam, meaning submission to God, originated with Mohammed (570-632), an Arabian, who taught that he had received divine revelation and was the last and greatest of the prophets.

Moslems believe in one God. There were six great prophets—Adam, Noah, Abraham, Moses, Jesus and Mohammed—and Mohammed was the greatest. The creed states: "There is no God but Allah and Mohammed is the prophet of Allah."

The principal duties of Moslems are to: profess the faith by daily recitation of the creed; pray five times a day facing in the direction of the holy city of Mecca; give alms; fast daily from dawn to dusk during the month of Ramadan; make a pilgrimage to Mecca once if possible.

Moslems believe in a final judgment, heaven and hell. Polygamy is practiced. Some dietary regulations are in effect. The weekly day of worship is Friday, and the principal service is at noon in a mosque. Moslems do not have an ordained ministry.

The basis of Islamic belief is the Koran, the created word of God revealed to Mohammed by the angel Gabriel over a period of 20 years. The contents of this sacred book are complemented by the Sunna, a collection of sacred traditions, and reinforced by Ijma, the consensus of Moslems which guarantees them against error in matters of belief and practice.

There are several sects of Moslems.

Conciliar Statement

The attitude of the Church toward Islam was stated as follows in the Second Vatican Council's *Declaration on the Relationship of the Church to Non-Christian Religions* (No. 3).

"Upon the Moslems, too, the Church looks with esteem. They adore one God, living and enduring, merciful and all-powerful, Maker of heaven and earth and Speaker to men. They strive to submit wholeheartedly even to His inscrutable decrees, just as did Abraham, with whom the Islamic faith is pleased to associate itself. Though they do not acknowledge Jesus as God, they revere Him as a prophet. They also honor Mary, His virgin mother; at times they call on her, too, with devotion. In addition they await the day of judgment when God will give each man his due after raising him up. Consequently, they prize the moral life, and give worship to God especially through prayer, almsgiving and fasting.

"Although in the course of the centuries many quarrels and hostilities have arisen between Christians and Moslems, this most sacred Synod urges all to forget the past and to strive sincerely for mutual understanding. On behalf of all mankind, let them make common cause of safeguarding and fostering social justice, moral values, peace and freedom."

Dialogue

The purposes of Catholic-Moslem dialogue, which has been rather sketchy, were the subject of joint agreement between the Vatican Secretariat for Non-Christians, and a delegation of the Supreme Council of Islamic Affairs, at a Vatican meeting Dec. 16 to 20, 1970.

Their objectives, as stated in a communique, were to:

• hold regular consultations on Moslem-Christian relations, social, cultural and spiritual questions;

• do everything possible to develop good relations between Christians and Moslems, in order to strengthen the fraternity existing among believers who share respect for all religious values and faith in God;

• continue efforts for justice and peace.

NON-REVEALED RELIGIONS

Hinduism: The traditional religion of India with origins dating to about 5,000 B.C. Its history is complex, including original Vedic Hinduism, with a sacred literature (Veda) of hymns, incantations and other elements, and with numerous nature gods; Brahmanism, with emphasis on ceremonialism and its power over the gods; philosophical speculation, reflected in the Upanishads, with development of ideas concerning Karma, reincarnation, Brahman, and the manner of achieving salvation; the cults of Vishnu, Shiva and other deities; reforms in Hinduism and in relation to Islam and Christianity.

The principal tenets of Hinduism are open to various interpretations. Karma is the law of the deed, of sowing and reaping, of retribution. It determines the progress of a person toward liberation from the cycle of rebirths necessary for salvation. Liberation is accomplished in stages, through successive reincarnations which indicate the previous as well as the existing state of a person. The means of liberation are the practice of ceremonialism and asceticism; faith in, devotion to and worship of the gods Vishnu and Shiva in their several incarnations; and/or knowledge attained through disciplined meditation called Yoga. Salvation, according to philosophical Hinduism, consists in absorption in Brahman, the neuter world-soul. Vishnu, the sun-god, and Shiva, the destroyer or generative force of the universe, are the principal popular deities. Ancient belief in nature gods (pantheism) is reflected in sacred respect for some animals. The concept of reincarnation underlies the caste system in Indian society.

There are many sects in Hinduism, which does not have a definite creed. It lends itself easily to syncretism or amalgamation with other beliefs, as evidenced in the 15th century Sikh movement which adopted the monotheism and militancy of Islam. Hindu rituals are various and elaborate, with respect to foods, festivals, pilgrimages, marriage and other life-events.

Buddhism: Originated in the sixth century B.C. in reaction to formalism, pantheism and other trends in Hinduism. The Buddha, the Enlightened One, was Sidartha Gautama, an Indian prince, who sought to explain human suffering and evil and to find a middle way between the extremes of austerity and sensuality.

The four noble truths of Buddhism are: (1) existence involves suffering or pain; (2) suffering comes from craving; (3) craving can be overcome; (4) the way to overcome craving is to follow the "noble eightfold path" of right views, right intention, right speech, right action, right livelihood, right effort, right mindfulness and right concentration.

Karma, the deed-principle of judgment and retribution, and reincarnation are elements of Buddhism. The ultimate objective of life is Nirvana — the absorption of a person in the absolute — which ends the cycles of rebirth.

Buddhism is essentially atheistic and more of a moral philosophy and ethical system than a religion. It has a cultic element in veneration for Buddha. Monasteries, temples and shrines are places of contemplation and ritualistic observance. There are several categories of Buddhist monks and nuns.

Buddhism has many sects. Mahayana Buddhism, with an elaborate ideology, is strong in China, Korea and Japan. Hinayana Buddhism is common in Southeast Asia. Zen Buddhism is highly contemplative. Lamaism in Tibet is a combination of Buddhism and local demonolatry.

Confucianism: An ethical system based on the teachings of Confucius (c. 551-479 B.C.). It is oriented toward the moral perfection of individuals and society, the attainment of the harmony of individual and social life with the harmony of the universe, through conduct governed by the relationships of humanity, justice, ritual and courtesy, wisdom, and fidelity. Originally and basically humanistic, Confucianism was eventually mingled with elements of Chinese religion. It exerted a strong influence on national life in China from 125 to the beginning of the 20th century,

Taoism: Originated in China several centuries before the Christian era and became a fully developed religious system by the fifth century A.D. As a religion of mystery, it developed extreme polytheism, with the Jade Emperor as the highest deity; sought blessings and long life by means of alchemy; fostered superstition and witchcraft; took on organizational and other aspects of Buddhism, with several categories of priests and nuns; exerted strong ethical influence on the lower classes; split into many sects; adopted features from other religions; became the starting point of many secret societies. One of its key tenets — that the way of nature is the guide to human conduct — resulted in a form of quietism opposed to the social concern of Confucianism.

Shinto: The way of the gods, the sum total of the cultic beliefs and practices of the ancestral religion of Japan which originated from nature and ancestor worship. Shinto is pantheistic and has many objects of devotion, the highest being the Ruler of Heaven; is practiced with detailed rituals in public shrines, which are cultic centers; has strong social influence. Sectarian Shinto has about 13 recognized sects and many offshoots. Shinto, with principal concern for this-worldly blessing, has ben affected by Buddhist and Confucian influences.

Glossary

A

Abbess: The female superior of a monastic community of nuns; e.g., Benedictines, Poor Clares, some others. Elected by members of the community, an abbess has general authority over her community but no sacramental jurisdiction. Earliest evidence of the use of the title, a feminine derivative of the Aramaic *abba* (father), dates from early in the sixth century.

Abbey: See Abbot, Monastery.

Abbot: The male superior of a monastic community of men religious; e.g., Benedictines, Cistercians, some others. Elected by members of the community, an abbot has ordinary jurisdiction and general authority over his community. He has some episcopal privileges. The title derives from the Aramaic *abba* (father); first given to the spiritual fathers and guides of hermits in Egypt in the fourth century, it was appropriated in the Rule of St. Benedict to the heads of abbeys and monasteries. Eastern-Rite equivalents of an abbot are a *hegumen* and an *archimandrite.*

A regular abbot is the head of an abbey or monastery. An abbot general or archabbot is the head of a congregation consisting of several monasteries. An abbot primate is the head of the modern Benedictine Confederation.

A few regular abbots have had jurisdiction, similar in some respects to that of a bishop in his diocese, over the residents and institutions of districts (*abbacies nullius*) not belonging to a diocese. Pope Paul stated in a document issued on his own initiative Dec. 29, 1976, that no more such abbacies would be established, except in cases of extraordinary necessity; also, that such abbacies, with the possible exception of ones of historical significance (like Monte Cassino, the cradle of the Benedictine Order) would be phased out of existence. The only *abbacy nullius* ever in the U.S. was Belmont Abbey, N.C.

Abjuration: Renunciation of apostasy, heresy or schism by a solemn oath.

Ablution: A term derived from Latin, meaning washing or cleansing, and referring to the cleansing of the hands of a priest celebrating Mass, after the offering of gifts; and to the cleansing of the chalice with water and wine after Communion.

Abortion: The expulsion of a nonviable human fetus from the womb of the mother, with moral implications stemming from the humanity of the fetus from the moment of conception and its consequent right to life.

Accidental expulsion, as in cases of miscarriage, is without moral fault.

Direct abortion, in which a fetus is intentionally removed from the womb, constitutes a direct attack on an innocent human being, a violation of the Fifth Commandment. It is punished in church law by the penalty of excommunication, which is automatically incurred by all baptized persons involved; i.e., the consenting mother and necessary physical and/or moral cooperators. Direct abortion is not justifiable for any reason, e.g.: therapeutic, for the physical and/or psychological welfare of the mother; preventive, to avoid the birth of a defective or unwanted child; social, in the interests of family and/or community.

Indirect abortion, which occurs when a fetus is expelled during medical or other treatment of the mother for a reason other than procuring expulsion, is permissible under the principle of double effect for a proportionately serious reason; e.g., when a medical or surgical procedure is necessary to save the life of the mother.

Absolution: The act by which an authorized priest, acting as the agent of Christ and minister of the Church, grants forgiveness of sins in the sacrament of penance. The essential formula of absolution is: "I absolve you from your sins; in the name of the Father, and of the Son, and of the Holy Spirit. Amen.

Priests receive the power to absolve in virtue of their ordination and the right to exercise this power in virtue of faculties of jurisdiction given them by their bishop, their religious superior, or by canon law. The faculties of jurisdiction can be limited or restricted regarding certain sins and penalties or censures.

In cases of necessity, and also in cases of the absence of their own confessors, Eastern and Roman Rite Catholics may ask for and receive sacramental absolution from a priest of a separated Eastern Church. Separated Eastern Christians may similarly ask for and receive sacramental absolution from an Eastern or Roman Rite priest.

Any priest can absolve a person in danger of death; in the absence of a priest with the usual faculties, this includes a laicized priest or a priest under censure.

(See additional entry under Sacraments.)

Absolution, General: (1) Sacramental absolution given without confession of sin, when confession is impossible. Persons so absolved are required to confess, in their next confession, the mortal sins from which they were so absolved.

(2) A blessing of the Church to which a plenary indulgence is attached, given at the hour of death, and at stated times to members of religious institutes and third orders.

Accessory to Another's Sin: One who culpably assists another in the performance of an evil action. This may be done by counsel, command, provocation, consent, praise, flattery, concealment, participation, silence, defense of the evil done.

Adoration: The highest act and purpose of religious worship, which is directed in love and reverence to God alone in acknowledgment of his infinite perfection and goodness, and of his total dominion over creatures. Adoration, which is also called *latria,* consists of internal and external elements, private and social prayer, liturgical acts and ceremonies, and especially sacrifice.

Adultery: (1) Sexual intercourse between a married person and another to whom one is not married; a violation of the obligations of chastity and justice. The Sixth Commandment prohibition against adultery is also regarded as a prohibition against all external sins of a sexual nature.

(2) Any sin of impurity (thought, desire, word, action) involving a married person who is not one's husband or wife has the nature of adultery.

Adventists: Members of several Christian sects whose doctrines are dominated by belief in a more or less imminent second advent or coming of Christ upon earth for a glorious 1,000-year reign of righteousness. This reign, following victory by the forces of good over evil in a final Battle of Armageddon, will begin with the resurrection of the chosen and will end with the resurrection of all other men and the annihilation of the wicked. Thereafter, the just will live forever in a renewed heaven and earth. A sleep of the soul takes place between the time of death and the day of judgment. There is no hell. The Bible, in fundamentalist interpretation, is regarded as the only rule of faith and practice.

About six sects have developed in the course of the Adventist movement which originated with William Miller (1782-1849) in the United States. Miller, on the basis of calculations made from the Book of Daniel, predicted that the second advent of Christ would occur between 1843 and 1844. After the prophecy went unfulfilled, divisions occurred in the movement and the Seventh Day Adventists, whose actual formation dates from 1860, emerged as the largest single body. The observance of Saturday instead of Sunday as the Lord's Day dates from 1844.

Advent Wreath: A wreath of laurel, spruce, or similar foliage with four candles which are lighted successively in the weeks of Advent to symbolize the approaching celebration of the birth of Christ, the Light of the World, at Christmas. The wreath originated among German Protestants.

Agape: A Greek word, meaning love, love feast, designating the meal of fellowship eaten at some gatherings of early Christians. Although held in some places in connection with the Mass, the agape was not part of the Mass, nor was it of universal institution and observance. Legislation against it was passed by the Council of Carthage (397) and other councils because of abuses. It was infrequently observed by the fifth century and disappeared altogether between the sixth and eighth centuries. In recent years, a limited revival has taken place in the course of the liturgical and ecumenical movements.

Age of Reason: (1) The time of life when one begins to distinguish between right and wrong, to understand an obligation and take on moral responsibility; seven years of age is the presumption in church law.

(2) Historically, the 18th century period of Enlightenment in England and France, the age of the Encyclopedists and Deists. According to a basic thesis of the Enlightenment, human experience and reason are the only sources of certain knowledge of truth; consequently, faith and revelation are discounted as valid sources of knowledge, and the reality of supernatural truth is called into doubt and/or denied.

Aggiornamento: An Italian word having the general meaning of bringing up to date, renewal, revitalization, descriptive of the processes of spiritual renewal and institutional reform and change in the Church; fostered by the Second Vatican Council.

Agnosticism: A theory which holds that man cannot have certain knowledge of immaterial reality, especially the existence of God and things pertaining to him. Immanuel Kant, one of the philosophical fathers of agnosticism, stood for the position that God, as well as the human soul, is unknowable on speculative grounds; nevertheless, he found practical imperatives for acknowledging God's existence, a view shared by many agnostics. The First Vatican Council declared that the existence of God and some of his attributes can be known with certainty by human reason, even without divine revelation. The word agnosticism was first used, in the sense given here, by T. H. Huxley in 1869.

Agnus Dei: A Latin phrase, meaning Lamb of God.

(1) A title given to Christ, the Lamb (victim) of the Sacrifice of the New Law (on Calvary and in Mass).

(2) A prayer said at Mass before the reception of Holy Communion.

(3) A sacramental. It is a round paschal-candle fragment blessed by the pope. On one side it bears the impression of a lamb, symbolic of Christ. On the reverse side, there may be any one of a number of impressions; e.g., the figure of a saint, the name and coat of arms of the reigning pope. The *agnus dei* may have originated at Rome in the fifth century. The first definite mention of it dates from about 820.

Alleluia: An exclamation of joy derived from Hebrew, All hail to him who is, praise God. It is used in the liturgy and other prayer on joyful occasions during the church year.

Allocution: A formal type of papal address,

as distinguished from an ordinary sermon or statement of views.

Alms: An act, gift or service of compassion, motivated by love of God and neighbor, for the help of persons in need; an obligation of charity, which is measurable by the ability of one person to give assistance and by the degree of another's need. Almsgiving, along with prayer and fasting, is regarded as a work of penance as well as an exercise of charity. (See Corporal and Spiritual Works of Mercy.)

Alpha and Omega: The first and last letters of the Greek alphabet, used to symbolize the eternity of God (Rv. 1:8) and the divinity and eternity of Christ, the beginning and end of all things (Rv. 21:6; 22:13). Use of the letters as a monogram of Christ originated in the fourth century or earlier.

Amen: A Hebrew word meaning truly, it is true. In the Gospels, Christ used the word to add a note of authority to his statements. In other New Testament writings, as in Hebrew usage, it was the concluding word to doxologies. As the concluding word of prayers, it expresses assent to and acceptance of God's will.

Anathema: A Greek word with the root meaning of cursed or separated and the adapted meaning of excommunication, used in church documents, especially the canons of ecumenical councils, for the condemnation of heretical doctrines and of practices opposed to proper discipline.

Anchorite: A kind of hermit living in complete isolation and devoting himself exclusively to exercises of religion and severe penance according to a rule and way of life of his own devising. In early Christian times, anchorites were the forerunners of the monastic life. The closest contemporary approach to the life of an anchorite is that of Carthusian and Camaldolese hermits.

Angels: Purely spiritual beings with intelligence and free will, whose name indicates their mission as ministers of God and ministering spirits to men. They were created before the creation of the visible universe; the devil and bad angels, who were created good, fell from glory through their own fault. In addition to these essentials of defined doctrine, it is held that angels are personal beings; they can intercede for men; fallen angels were banished from God's glory in heaven to hell; bad angels can tempt men to commit sin. The doctrine of guardian angels, although not explicitly defined as a matter of faith, is rooted in long-standing tradition. No authoritative declaration has ever been issued regarding choirs or various categories of angels: according to theorists, there are nine choirs, consisting of seraphim, cherubim, thrones, dominations, principalities, powers, virtues, archangels and angels. In line with scriptural usage, only three angels can be named—Michael, Raphael and Gabriel.

Angelus: A devotion which commemorates the Incarnation of Christ. It consists of three versicles, three Hail Marys and a special prayer, and recalls the announcement to Mary by the Archangel Gabriel that she was chosen to be the Mother of Christ, her acceptance of the divine will, and the Incarnation (Lk. 1:26-38). The Angelus is recited at 6 a.m., noon and 6 p.m. The practice of reciting the Hail Mary in honor of the Incarnation was introduced by the Franciscans in 1263. The *Regina Caeli,* commemorating the joy of Mary at Christ's Resurrection, replaces the Angelus during the Easter season.

Anger: Passionate displeasure arising from some kind of offense suffered at the hands of another person, frustration or other cause, combined with a tendency to strike back at the cause of the displeasure; a violation of the Fifth Commandment and one of the capital sins if the displeasure is out of proportion to the cause and/or if the retaliation is unjust.

Anglican Orders: Holy orders conferred according to the rite of the Anglican (Episcopal) Church, which Leo XIII declared null and void in the bull *Apostolicae Curae,* Sept. 13, 1896. The orders were declared null because they were conferred according to a rite that was considered substantially defective in form and intent, and because of a break in apostolic succession that occurred when Matthew Parker became head of the Anglican hierarchy in 1559.

In making his declaration, Pope Leo cited earlier arguments against validity made by Julius III in 1553 and 1554 and by Paul IV in 1555. He also noted related directives requiring absolute ordination, according to the Catholic ritual, of convert ministers who had been ordained according to the Anglican Ordinal.

Antichrist: The man of sin, the lawless and wicked antagonist of Christ and the work of God; a mysterious figure of prophecy mentioned in the New Testament. Supported by Satan, submitting to no moral restraints, and armed with tremendous power, Antichrist will set himself up in opposition to God, work false miracles, persecute the People of God, and employ unimaginable means to lead men into error and evil during a period of widespread defection from the Christian faith before the end of time; he will be overcome by Christ. Catholic thinkers have regarded Antichrist as a person, a caricature of Christ, who will lead a final violent struggle against God and His people; they have also applied the title to personal and impersonal forces in history hostile to God and the Church. Official teaching has said little about Antichrist. In 1318, it labeled as partly heretical, senseless, and fanciful the assertions made by the Fraticelli about his coming; in 1415, the Council of Constance condemned the Wycliff thesis that excommunications made by the pope and other prelates were the actions of Antichrist.

Antiphon: (1) A short verse or text, generally from Scripture, recited in the Liturgy of the Hours before and after psalms and canticles.

(2) Any verse sung or recited by one part of a choir or congregation in response to the other part, as in antiphonal or alternate chanting.

Apologetics: The science and art of building and presenting the case for, accounting for, explaining, defending, justifying the reasonableness of the Christian faith, by a wide variety of means including facts of experience, history, science, philosophy. The constant objective of apologetics, as well as of the total process of pre-evangelization, is preparation for response to God in faith; its ways and means, however, are subject to change in accordance with the various needs of people and different sets of circumstances.

Apostasy: (1) The total and obstinate rejection or abandonment of the Christian faith by a baptized person who continues to call himself a Christian. External manifestation of this rejection constitutes the crime of apostasy, and the person, called an *apostate,* automatically incurs a penalty of excommunication.

(2) Apostasy from orders is the unlawful withdrawal from or rejection of the obligations of the clerical state by a man who has received major orders. The canonical penalty for such apostasy is excommunication.

(3) Apostasy from the religious life occurs when a religious with perpetual vows unlawfully leaves the community with the intention of not returning, or actually remains outside the community for 30 days without permission. The canonical penalty for such apostasy is excommunication.

Apostolate: The ministry or work of an apostle. In Catholic usage, the word is an umbrella-like term covering all kinds and areas of work and endeavor for the service of God and the Church and the good of people. Thus, the apostolate of bishops is to carry on the mission of the Apostles as pastors of the People of God: of priests, to carry out the sacramental and pastoral ministry for which they are ordained; of religious, to follow and do the work of Christ in conformity with the evangelical counsels and their rule of life; of lay persons, as individuals and/or in groups, to give witness to Christ and build up the kingdom of God through practice of their faith, professional competence and the performance of good works in the concrete circumstances of daily life. Apostolic works are not limited to those done within the Church or by specifically Catholic groups, although some apostolates are officially assigned to certain persons or groups and are under the direction of church authorities. Apostolate derives from the commitment and obligation of baptism, confirmation, holy orders, matrimony, the duties of one's state in life, etc.

Apostolic Succession: Bishops of the Church, who form a collective body or college, are successors to the Apostles by ordination and divine right; as such they carry on the mission entrusted by Christ to the Apostles as guardians and teachers of the deposit of faith, principal pastors and spiritual authorities of the faithful. The doctrine of apostolic succession is based on New Testament evidence and the constant teaching of the Church, reflected as early as the end of the first century in a letter of Pope St. Clement to the Corinthians. A significant facet of the doctrine is the role of the pope as the successor of St. Peter, the vicar of Christ and head of the college of bishops. The doctrine of apostolic succession means more than continuity of apostolic faith and doctrine; its basic requisite is ordination by the laying on of hands in apostolic succession.

Archangel: An angel who carries out special missions for God in his dealings with men. Three of them are named in the Bible: Michael, leader of the angelic host and protector of the synagogue; Raphael, guide of Tobiah and healer of his father, who is regarded as the patron of travelers; Gabriel, called the angel of the Incarnation because of his announcement to Mary that she was to be the Mother of Christ.

Archdiocese: An ecclesiastical jurisdiction headed by an archbishop. An archdiocese is usually a metropolitan see, i.e., the principal one of a group of dioceses comprising a province; the other dioceses in the province are suffragan sees.

Archives: Documentary records, and the place where they are kept, of the spiritual and temporal government and affairs of the Church, a diocese, church agencies like the departments of the Roman Curia, bodies like religious institutes, and individual parishes. The collection, cataloguing, preserving, and use of these records are governed by norms stated in canon law and particular regulations. The strictest secrecy is always in effect for confidential records concerning matters of conscience, and documents of this kind are destroyed as soon as circumstances permit.

Archpriest: For some time, before and during the Middle Ages, a priest who took the place of a bishop at liturgical worship. In Europe, the term is sometimes used as an honorary title. It is also an honorary title in Eastern-Rite Churches.

Asceticism: The practice of self-discipline. In the spiritual life, asceticism — by personal prayer, meditation, self-denial, works of mortification, and outgoing interpersonal works — is motivated by love of God and contributes to growth in holiness.

Ashes: Religious significance has been associated with their use as symbolic of penance since Old Testament times. Thus, ashes of palm blessed on the previous Sunday of the Passion are placed on the foreheads of the faithful on Ash Wednesday to remind them to do works of penance, especially during the season of Lent, and that they are dust and unto dust will return. Ashes are a sacramental.

Aspergillum: A vessel or device used for sprinkling holy water. The ordinary type is a metallic rod with a bulbous tip which absorbs the water and discharges it at the motion of the user's hand.

Aspersory: A portable metallic vessel, similar to a pail, for carrying holy water.

Aspiration: Short exclamatory prayer; e.g., My Jesus, mercy.

Atheism: Denial of the existence of God, finding expression in a system of thought (speculative atheism) or a manner of acting (practical atheism) as though there were no God.

The Second Vatican Council, in its *Pastoral Constitution on the Church in the Modern World* (Nos. 19 to 21), noted that a profession of atheism may represent an explicit denial of God. the rejection of a wrong notion of God, an affirmation of man rather than of God, an extreme protest against evil. It said that such a profession might result from acceptance of such propositions as: there is no absolute truth; man can assert nothing, absolutely nothing, about God; everything can be explained by scientific reasoning alone; the whole question of God is devoid of meaning.

The constitution also cited two opinions of influence in atheistic thought. One of them regards recognition of dependence on God as incompatible with human freedom and independence. The other views belief in God and religion as a kind of opiate which sedates man on earth, reconciling him to the acceptance of suffering, injustice, shortcomings, etc., because of hope for greater things after death, and thereby hindering him from seeking and working for improvement and change for the better here and now.

All of these views, in one way or another, have been involved in the No-God and Death-of-God schools of thought in recent and remote history.

Atonement: The redemptive activity of Christ, who reconciled man with God through his Incarnation and entire life, and especially by his suffering and Resurrection. The word also applies to prayer and good works by which men join themselves with and take part in Christ's work of reconciliation and reparation for sin.

Attributes of God: Perfections of God. God possesses—and is—all the perfections of being, without limitation. Because he is infinite, all of these perfections are one, perfectly united in him. Man, however, because of the limited power of understanding, views these perfections separately, as distinct characteristics—even though they are not actually distinct in God. God is: almighty, eternal, holy, immortal, immense, immutable, incomprehensible, ineffable, infinite, invisible, just, loving, merciful, most high, most wise, omnipotent, omniscient, omnipresent, patient, perfect, provident, supreme, true.

Avarice (Covetousness): A disorderly and unreasonable attachment to and desire for material things; called a capital sin because it involves preoccupation with material things to the neglect of spiritual goods and obligations of justice and charity.

Ave Maria: See Hail Mary.

B

Baldachino: A canopy over an altar.

Beatification: A preliminary step toward canonization of a saint. It begins with an investigation of the candidate's life, writings and heroic practice of virtue, and the certification of at least two miracles worked by God through his intercession. If the findings of the investigation so indicate, the pope decrees that the Servant of God may be called *Blessed* and may be honored locally or in a limited way in the liturgy. Additional procedures lead to canonization (see separate entry).

Beatific Vision: The intuitive, immediate and direct vision and experience of God enjoyed in the light of glory by all the blessed in heaven. The vision is a supernatural mystery.

Beatitude: A literary form of the Old and New Testaments in which blessings are promised to persons for various reasons. Beatitudes are mentioned 26 times in the Psalms, and in other books of the Old Testament. The best known beatitudes — identifying blessedness with participation in the kingdom of God and his righteousness, and descriptive of the qualities of Christian perfection — are those recounted in Mt. 5:3-11 and Lk. 6:20-22.

In Matthew's account, the beatitudes are:

"How blest are the poor in spirit: the reign of God is theirs.

"Blest too are the sorrowing; they shall be consoled.

"(Blest are the lowly; they shall inherit the land.)

"Blest are they who hunger and thirst for holiness; they shall have their fill.

"Blest are they who show mercy; mercy shall be theirs.

"Blest are the single-hearted for they shall see God.

"Blest too are the peacemakers; they shall be called sons of God.

"Blest are those persecuted for holiness' sake; the reign of God is theirs.

"Blest are you when they insult you and persecute you and utter every kind of slander against you because of me."

In Luke's account, the beatitudes are:

"Blest are you poor; the reign of God is yours.

"Blest are you who hunger; you shall be filled.

"Blest are you who are weeping; you shall laugh.

"Blest shall you be when men hate you, when they ostracize you and insult you and proscribe your name as evil because of the Son of Man."

Benediction of the Blessed Sacrament: A short exposition of the Eucharist for adoration by and blessing of the faithful. Devotional practices include the singing of Eucharistic and other hymns, and recitation of the Divine Praises. Benediction, in its present form, dates from about the 15th century and is a form of liturgical worship.

Benedictus: The canticle or hymn of Zechariah at the circumcision of St. John the Baptist (Lk. 1:68-79). It is an expression of praise and thanks to God for sending John as a precursor of the Messiah. The *Benedictus* is recited in the Liturgy of the Hours as part of the Morning Prayer.

Bible Service: A devotion consisting essentially of common prayer of a biblical or liturgical character, several readings from Scripture, and a homily on the texts.

Biglietto: A papal document of notification of appointment to the cardinalate.

Biretta: A stiff, square hat with three ridges on top worn by clerics in church and on other occasions.

Blasphemy: Any expression of insult or contempt with respect to God, principally, and to holy persons and things, secondarily; a violation of the honor due to God in the context of the First and Second Commandments.

Blasphemy of the Spirit: Deliberate resistance to the Holy Spirit, called the unforgivable sin (Mt. 12:31) because it makes his saving action impossible. Thus, the only unforgivable sin is the one for which a person will not seek pardon from God.

Blessing: Invocation of God's favor, by official ministers of the Church or by private individuals. Blessings are recounted in the Old and New Testaments, and are common in the Christian tradition. The Church, through its ordained ministers (bishops and priests, especially), invokes divine favor in liturgical blessings; e.g., of the people at Mass, of the gifts to be consecrated at Mass, of persons and things on various occasions. Sacramentals — such as crucifixes, crosses, rosaries, scapulars, medals — are blessed by ministers of the Church for the invocation of God's favor on those who use them in the proper manner. Many types of blessings are listed in the *Roman Ritual.* Private blessings, as well as those of an official kind, are efficacious. Blessings are imparted with the Sign of the Cross and appropriate prayer.

Boat: A small vessel used to hold incense which is to be placed in the censer.

Brief, Apostolic: A papal letter, less formal than a bull, signed for the pope by a secretary and impressed with the seal of the Fisherman's Ring. Simple apostolic letters of this kind are issued for beatifications and with respect to other matters.

Bull, Apostolic: The most solemn form of papal document, beginning with the name and title of the pope (e.g., Paul VI, Servant of the Servants of God), dealing with an important subject, and having attached to it either a leaden seal called a *bulla* or a red ink imprint of the device on the seal. Bulls are known as apostolic letters with the seal. The seal, on one side, has representations of the heads of Sts. Peter and Paul; on the other side, the name of the reigning pope. Bulls are issued to confer the titles of bishops and cardinals, to promulgate canonizations, and for other purposes. A collection of bulls is called a *bullarium.*

Burial, Ecclesiastical: Interment with church rites and in consecrated ground. Catechumens as well as baptized Catholics have a right to ecclesiastical burial. A non-Catholic partner in a mixed marriage may be buried in a Catholic cemetery with the Catholic partner.

C

Calumny: Harming the name and good reputation of a person by lies; a violation of obligations of justice and truth. Restitution is due for calumny.

Calvary: A knoll about 15 feet high just outside the western wall of Jerusalem where Christ was crucified, so called from the Latin *calvaria* (skull) which described its shape.

Canon: A Greek word meaning rule, norm, standard, measure.

(1) The word designates the Canon of Sacred Scripture, which is the list of books recognized by the Church as inspired by the Holy Spirit.

(2) In the sense of regulating norms, the word designates the body or corpus of Canon Law enacted and promulgated by ecclesiastical authority for the orderly administration and government of the Church. The Code of Canon Law now in force in the Roman Church has been in effect since 1918. It consists of 2,414 canons which are divided into five books covering general rules, ecclesiastical persons, sacred things, trials, crimes and punishments. The code is now under review for the purpose of revision. Eastern-Rite Churches have their own canon law.

(3) The term also designates the four canons, (Eucharistic prayers, anaphoras) of the Mass, the core of the liturgy.

(4) Certain dignitaries of the Church have the title of Canon, and some religious are known as Canons.

Canonization: An infallible declaration by the pope that a person, who died as a martyr and/or practiced Christian virtue to a heroic degree, is now in heaven and is worthy of honor and imitation by all the faithful. Such a declaration is preceded by the process of beatification and another detailed investigation concerning the person's reputation for holiness, his writings, and (except in the case of martyrs) miracles ascribed to his intercession after his death. Miracles are not required for martyrs. The pope can dispense from some of the formalities ordinarily required in canonization procedures (equivalent canonization), as Pope John XXIII did in the canonization of St. Gregory Barbarigo on May 26, 1960. A saint is worthy of honor in liturgical worship throughout the universal Church.

From its earliest years the Church has venerated saints. Public official honor always required the approval of the bishop of the place. Martyrs were the first to be honored. St. Martin of Tours, who died in 397, was an early non-martyr venerated as a saint. The first official canonization by a pope for the universal Church was that of St. Ulrich by John XV in 993. Alexander III reserved the process of canonization to the Holy See in 1171. In 1588 Sixtus V established the Sacred Congregation of Rites for the principal purpose of handling causes for beatification and canonization: this function is now the work of the Congregation for the Causes of Saints. The present procedure is outlined in canons 1999-2141 of the Code of Canon Law and in a 1969 enactment by Paul VI.

The essential portion of a canonization decree states:

"For the honor of the holy and undivided Trinity; for the exaltation of the Catholic faith and the increase of Christian life; with the authority of our Lord Jesus Christ, of the blessed Apostles Peter and Paul, and with our own authority; after mature deliberation and with the divine assistance, often implored; with the counsel of many of our brothers.

"We decree and define that (name) is a saint and we inscribe him (her) in the Catalogue of Saints, stating that he (she) shall be venerated in the universal Church with pious devotion.

"In the name of the Father and of the Son and of the Holy Spirit. Amen."

The official listing of saints and blessed is contained in the *Roman Martyrology* and related decrees issued after its last publication. Butler's unofficial *Lives of the Saints* (1956) contains 2,565 entries.

The Church regards all persons in heaven as saints, not just those who have been officially canonized.

(See Beatification, Saints, Canonizations by Leo XIII and His Successors.)

Canticle: A scriptural chant or prayer differing from the psalms. Three of the canticles prescribed for use in the Liturgy of the Hours are: The *Magnificat* (Lk. 1:46-55), the *Benedictus* (Lk. 1:68-79), and the *Nunc Dimittis* (Lk. 2:29-32).

Capital Punishment: Punishment for crime by means of the death penalty. The political community, which has authority to provide for the common good, has the right to defend itself and its members against unjust aggression and may in extreme cases punish with the death penalty persons found guilty before the law of serious crimes against individuals and a just social order. Such punishment is essentially vindictive. Its value as a crime deterrent is a matter of perennial debate. The prudential judgment as to whether or not there should be capital punishment belongs to the civic community. The U.S. Supreme Court, in a series of decisions dating from June 29, 1972, ruled against the constitutionality of statutes on capital punishment except in specific cases and with appropriate consideration, with respect to sentence, of mitigating circumstances of the crime.

Capital punishment was the subject of a statement issued Mar. 1, 1978, by the Committee on Social Development and World Peace, U.S. Catholic Conference. The statement said, in part: "The use of the death penalty involves deep moral and religious questions as well as political and legal issues. In 1974, out of a commitment to the value and dignity of human life, the Catholic bishops of the United States declared their opposition to capital punishment. We continue to support this position, in the belief that a return to the use of the death penalty can only lead to the further erosion of respect for life in our society. Violent crime in our society is a serious matter which should not be ignored. We do not challenge society's right to punish the serious and violent offender, nor do we wish to debate the merits of the arguments concerning this right. Past history, however, shows that the death penalty in its present application has been discriminatory with respect to the disadvantaged, the indigent and the socially impoverished. Furthermore, recent data from correction sources definitely question the effectiveness of the death penalty as a deterrent to crime."

Additional statements against capital punishment have been issued by numerous bishops and other sources.

Capital Sins: Moral faults which, if habitual, give rise to many more sins. They are pride, covetousness, lust, anger, gluttony, envy, sloth.

The opposite virtues are: humility, liberality, chastity, meekness, temperance, brotherly love, diligence.

Cardinal Virtues: The four principal moral virtues are prudence, justice, temperance and fortitude.

Catacombs: Underground Christian cemeteries in various cities of the Roman Empire and Italy, especially in the vicinity of Rome; the burial sites of many martyrs and other Christians. Developed from aboveground cemeteries, their passageways, burial niches and assembly rooms were dug out of tuffa, a soft clay which hardened into rock-like consistency on drying. The earliest ones date from the third century; in the fourth, they became the scene of memorial services as the veneration of martyrs increased in popularity; in the seventh and eighth centuries, they were plundered by the Lombards and other invaders. The relics of many martyrs were removed to safer places in the ninth century; afterwards, the catacombs fell into neglect and oblivion until interest in them revived in the 16th century. The catacombs have been excavated extensively, yielding considerable information about early Christian symbolism and art, dating from the third century on, and other aspects of Christian life and practice.

Catafalque: A small structure like a bier, used at services for the dead in the absence of the corpse.

Catechism: A summary of Christian doctrine in question and answer form, used for purposes of instruction.

Catechumen: A person preparing, in a program of instruction and spiritual formation for baptism and reception into the Church.

Cathedra: A Greek word for chair, designating the chair or seat of a bishop in the principal church of his diocese, which is therefore called a cathedral (see separate entry).

Cathedraticum: The tax paid to a bishop by all churches and benefices subject to him for the support of episcopal administration and for works of charity.

Catholic: A Greek word, meaning universal, first used in the title Catholic Church in a letter written by St. Ignatius of Antioch about 107 to the Christians of Smyrna.

Celebret: A Latin word, meaning Let him celebrate, the name of a document issued by a bishop or other superior stating that a priest is in good standing and therefore should be given opportunity to celebrate Mass or perform other priestly functions.

Celibacy: The unmarried state of life, required in the Roman or Latin Church of candidates for holy orders and of men already ordained to holy orders, for the practice of perfect chastity and total dedication to the service of people in the ministry of the Church. Celibacy is enjoined as a condition for ordination by church discipline and law, not by dogmatic necessity.

In the Roman Church, a consensus in favor of celibacy developed in the early centuries while the clergy included both celibates and men who had been married once. The first local legislation on the subject was enacted by a local council held in Elvira, Spain, about 306; it forbade bishops, priests, deacons and other ministers to have wives. Similar enactments were passed by other local councils from that time on, and by the 12th century

particular laws regarded marriage by clerics in major orders to be not only unlawful but also null and void. The latter view was translated by the Second Lateran Council in 1139 into what seems to be the first written universal law making holy orders an invalidating impediment to marriage. In 1563 the Council of Trent ruled definitely on the matter and established the discipline still in force in the Roman Church.

Some exceptions to this discipline have been made in recent years. Several married Protestant ministers who became converts and were subsequently ordained to the priesthood have been permitted to continue in marriage. Married men over the age of 35 can be ordained to the permanent diaconate.

Recent agitation for optional rather than mandatory celibacy for priests has diminished, without change in church law.

Eastern Church discipline on celibacy differs from that of the Roman Church. In line with legislation enacted by the Synod of Trullo in 692 and still in force, candidates for holy orders may marry before becoming deacons and may continue in marriage thereafter, but marriage after ordination is forbidden. Eastern-Rite bishops in the US, however, do not ordain married candidates for the priesthood. Eastern-Rite bishops are unmarried.

Cenacle: The room in Jerusalem where Christ ate the Last Supper with his Apostles.

Censer: A metal vessel with a perforated cover and suspended by chains, in which incense is burned. It is used at some Masses, Benediction of the Blessed Sacrament and other liturgical functions.

Censorship of Books: An exercise of vigilance by the Church for safeguarding authentic religious teaching.

According to a decree issued by the Congregation for the Doctrine of the Faith Apr. 9, 1975, the following regulations are in effect.

(1) Pre-publication clearance is required for: editions of Sacred Scripture, liturgical texts and books of private devotion, catechisms and other writings relating to catechetical instruction. Books dealing with Scripture, theology, canon law, church history and religious or moral disciplines may not be used as basic texts in educational institutions (from elementary to university levels) unless they have been published with the approval of competent church authority.

(2) Pre-publication clearance is recommended for all books on the aforementioned subjects, even though they are not used as basic texts in teaching.

(3) Books or other writings dealing with religion or morals may not be displayed, sold or given out in churches or oratories unless published with the approval of competent ecclesiastical authority.

(4) Except for a just and reasonable cause,

Catholics should not write for newspapers, magazines or periodicals which regularly and openly prove to be inimical to the Catholic religion and good morals. The approval of the local bishop is required before clerics or members of religious institutes (who also need the approval of their superior) may write for such publications.

Permission to publish works of a religious character, together with the apparatus of reviewing them beforehand, falls under the authority of the bishop of the place where the writer lives or where the works are published.

Clearance for publication is usually indicated by the terms *Nihil obstat* (Nothing stands in the way) issued by the censor and *Imprimatur* (Let it be printed) authorized by the bishop. The clearing of works for publication does not necessarily imply approval of an author's viewpoint or his manner of handling a subject.

Censures: Spiritual⁴ penalties inflicted by the Church on baptized persons for committing certain serious sins, which are classified as crimes in canon law, and for being or remaining obstinate therein. Excommunication, suspension and interdict have been the censures in force since the time of Innocent III (1214). Their intended purposes are to deter persons from committing sins which, more seriously and openly than others, threaten the common good of the Church and its members; to punish and correct offenders; and to provide for the making of reparation for harm done to the community of the Church. Censures may be incurred automatically (*ipso facto*) on the commission of certain offenses for which fixed penalties have been laid down in church law (*latae sententiae*); or they may be inflicted by sentence of a judge (*ferendae sententiae*). Obstinacy in crime— also called contumacy, disregard of a penalty, defiance of church authority — is presumed by law in the commission of crimes for which automatic censures are decreed. The presence and degree of contumacy in other cases, for which judicial sentence is required, is subject to determination by a judge. Absolution can be obtained from any censure, provided the person repents and desists from obstinacy. Absolution may be reserved to the pope, the bishop of a place, or the major superior of an exempt clerical religious institute. In danger of death, any priest can absolve from all censures; in other cases, faculties to absolve from reserved censures can be exercised by competent authorities or given to other priests.

Ceremonies, Master of: One who directs the proceedings of a rite or ceremony during the function.

Chamberlain: (1) The Chamberlain of the Holy Roman Church is a cardinal who administers the property and revenues of the Holy See. On the death of the pope he becomes head of the College of Cardinals and summons and directs the conclave until a new pope is elected.

(2) The Chamberlain of the Sacred College of Cardinals has charge of the property and revenues of the College and keeps the record of business transacted in consistories.

(3) The Chamberlain of the Roman Clergy is the president of the secular clergy of Rome.

Chancellor: Notary of a diocese, who draws up written documents in the government of the diocese; takes care of, arranges and indexes diocesan archives, records of dispensations and ecclesiastical trials.

Chancery (1) A branch of church administration that handles written documents used in the government of a diocese.

(2) The administrative office of a diocese, a bishop's office.

Chapel: A building or part of another building used for divine worship; a portion of a church set aside for the celebration of Mass or for some special devotion.

Chaplain: A priest appointed for the pastoral service of any division of the armed forces, religious communities, institutions, various groups of the faithful.

Chaplet: A term, meaning little crown, applied to a rosary or, more commonly, to a small string of beads used for devotional purposes; e.g., the Infant of Prague chaplet.

Chapter: A general meeting of delegates of religious orders for elections and the handling of other important affairs of their communities.

Charisms: Gifts or graces given by God to men for the good of others and the Church. Examples are special gifts for apostolic work, prophecy, healing, discernment of spirits, the life of evangelical poverty, here-and-now witness to faith in various circumstances of life.

The Second Vatican Council made the following statement about charisms in the *Dogmatic Constitution on the Church* (No. 12):

"It is not only through the sacraments and Church ministries that the same Holy Spirit sanctifies and leads the People of God and enriches it with virtues. Allotting His gifts 'to everyone according as he will' (1 Cor. 12:11), He distributes special graces among the faithful of every rank. By these gifts He makes them fit and ready to undertake the various tasks or offices advantageous for the renewal and upbuilding of the Church, according to the words of the Apostle: 'The manifestation of the Spirit is given to everyone for profit' (1 Cor. 12:7). These charismatic gifts, whether they be the most outstanding or the more simple and widely diffused, are to be received with thanksgiving and consolation, for they are exceedingly suitable and useful for the needs of the Church.

"Still, extraordinary gifts are not to be rashly sought after, nor are the fruits of apostolic labor to be presumptuously expected from them. In any case, judgment as to their genuineness and proper use belongs to those who preside over the Church, and to whose special competence it belongs, not indeed to extinguish the Spirit, but to test all things and hold fast to that which is good" (cf. 1 Thes. 5:12; 19-21).

Charity: Love of God above all things for his own sake, and love of one's neighbor as oneself because and as an expression of one's love for God; the greatest of the three theological virtues. The term is sometimes also used to designate sanctifying grace.

Chastity: Properly ordered behavior with respect to sex. In marriage, the exercise of the procreative power is integrated with the norms and purposes of marriage. Outside of marriage, the rule is self-denial of the voluntary exercise and enjoyment of the procreative faculty in thought, word or action.

The vow of chastity, which reinforces the virtue of chastity with the virtue of religion, is an evangelical counsel and one of the three vows professed by religious.

Chirograph or Autograph Letter: A letter written by a pope himself, in his own handwriting.

Christ: The title of Jesus, derived from the Greek translation *Christos* of the Hebrew term *Messiah,* meaning the Anointed of God, the Savior and Deliverer of his people. Christian use of the title is a confession of belief that Jesus is the Savior.

Christianity: The sum total of things related to belief in Christ — the Christian religion, Christian churches, Christians themselves, society based on and expressive of Christian beliefs, culture reflecting Christian values.

Christians: The name first applied about the year 43 to followers of Christ at Antioch, the capital of Syria. It was used by the pagans as a contemptuous term. The word applies to persons who profess belief in the divinity and teachings of Christ and who give witness to him in life.

Christian Science: A religious doctrine consisting of Mary Baker Eddy's interpretation and formulation of the actions and teachings of Christ. Its basic tenets reflect Mrs. Eddy's ideas regarding the reality of spirit and its control and domination of what is not spirit. The basic statement of the doctrine is contained in *Science and Health, with Key to the Scriptures,* which she first published in 1875, nine years after being saved from death and healed on reading the New Testament.

Mary Baker Eddy (1821-1910) established the church in 1879, and in 1892 founded at Boston the First Church of Christ, Scientist, of which all other Christian Science churches are branches. The individual churches are self-governing and self-supporting under the general supervision of a board of directors. Services consist of readings of portions of Scripture and *Science and Health.* One of the church's publications, *The Christian Science Monitor,* has a worldwide reputation as a journal of news and opinion.

Church: (1) See several entries under Church, Catholic. The universal Church is the Church spread throughout the world. The local Church is the Church in a particular locality; e.g., a diocese. Inasmuch as the members of the Church are on earth, in purgatory, or in glory in heaven, the Church is called militant, suffering, or triumphant.

(2) In general, any religious body.

(3) Place of divine worship.

Churching: A rite of thanksgiving in which a blessing is given to women after childbirth. The rite is reminiscent of the Old Testament ceremony of purification (Lv. 12:2-8).

Circumcision: A ceremonial practice symbolic of initiation and participation in the covenant between God and Abraham.

Circumincession: The indwelling of each divine Person of the Holy Trinity in the others.

Clergy: Men ordained to holy orders and assigned to pastoral and other ministries for the service of the people and the Church.

(1) Diocesan or secular clergy are committed to pastoral ministry in parishes and in other capacities in a local church (diocese) under the direction of their bishop, to whom they are bound by a promise of obedience.

(2) Regular clergy belong to religious institutes (orders, congregations, societies) and are so called because they observe the rule (*regula,* in Latin) of their respective institutes. They are committed to the ways of life and apostolates of their institutes. In ordinary pastoral ministry, they are under the direction of local bishops as well as their own superiors.

Clericalism: A term generally used in a derogatory sense to mean action, influence and interference by the Church and the clergy in matters with which they allegedly should not be concerned. Anticlericalism is a reaction of antipathy, hostility, distrust and opposition to the Church and clergy arising from real and/or alleged faults of the clergy, overextension of the role of the laity, or for other reasons.

Cloister: The enclosure of a convent or monastery, which members of the community may not leave or outsiders enter without due permission. Enclosure is of two kinds: papal, in monasteries of religious with solemn vows; episcopal, in the houses of other religious.

Code: A digest of rules or regulations, such as the Code of Canon Law.

Collegiality: The bishops of the Church, in union with and subordinate to the pope — who has full, supreme and universal power over the Church which he can always exercise independently — have supreme teaching and pastoral authority over the whole Church. In addition to their proper authority of office for the good of the faithful in their respective dioceses or other jurisdictions, the bishops have authority to act for the good of the universal Church. This collegial authority is exercised in a solemn manner in an ecumenical council and can also be exercised in other ways sanctioned by the pope. Doctrine on collegiality was set forth by the Second Vatican Council in the *Dogmatic Constitution on the Church*. (See separate entry.)

By extension, the concept of collegiality is applied to other forms of participation and co-responsibility by members of a community.

Commissariat of the Holy Land: A special jurisdiction within the Order of Friars Minor, whose main purposes are the collecting of alms for support of the Holy Places in Palestine and staffing of the Holy Places and missions in the Middle East with priests and brothers. There are 69 such commissariats in 33 countries. One of them has headquarters at Mt. St. Sepulchre, Washington, D.C. Franciscans have had custody of the Holy Places since 1342.

Communion of Faithful, Saints: The communion of all the People of God — on earth, in heavenly glory, in purgatory — with Christ and each other in faith, grace, prayer and good works.

Concelebration: The liturgical act in which several priests, led by one member of the group, offer Mass together, all consecrating the bread and wine. Concelebration has always been common in churches of Eastern Rite. In the Roman Rite, it was long restricted, taking place only at the ordination of bishops and the ordination of priests. The *Constitution on the Sacred Liturgy* issued by the Second Vatican Council set new norms for concelebration.

Concordance, Biblical: An alphabetical verbal index enabling a user knowing one or more words of a scriptural passage to locate the entire text.

Concordat: A Church-state treaty with the force of law concerning matters of mutual concern — e.g., rights of the Church, appointment of bishops, arrangement of ecclesiastical jurisdictions, marriage laws, education. Approximately 150 agreements of this kind have been negotiated since the Concordat of Worms in 1122.

Concupiscence: Any tendency of the sensitive appetite. The term is most frequently used in reference to desires and tendencies for sinful sense pleasure.

Confession: Sacramental confession is the act by which a person tells or confesses his sins to a priest who is authorized to give absolution in the sacrament of penance.

Confessor: (1) A male saint who lived a life of eminent sanctity and heroic virtue, but who did not suffer martyrdom for his faith.

(2) A priest who administers the sacrament of penance.

Confraternity: An association whose members practice a particular form of religious devotion and/or are engaged in some kind of apostolic work. When a confraternity reaches the stage where affiliations similar to itself are formed and adopt its rules, it takes the name of archconfraternity.

Conscience: Practical judgment concerning the moral goodness or sinfulness of an action. In the Catholic view, this judgment is made by reference of the action, its attendant circumstances and the intentions of the person to the requirements of divine law as expressed in the Ten Commandments, the summary law of love for God and neighbor, the life and teaching of Christ, and the authoritative teaching and practice of the Church with respect to the total demands of divine Revelation.

A person is obliged: (1) to obey a certain and correct conscience; (2) to obey a certain conscience even if it is inculpably erroneous; (3) not to obey, but to correct, a conscience known to be erroneous or lax; (4) to rectify a scrupulous conscience by following the advice of a confessor and by other measures; (5) to resolve doubts of conscience before acting.

It is legitimate to act for solid and probable reasons when a question of moral responsibility admits of argument (see Probabilism). It is also legitimate to resolve doubts in difficult cases by having recourse to a reflex principle (e.g., by following the manner of acting of a well-informed and well-intentioned group of persons in similar circumstances).

Conscience, Examination of: Self-examination to determine one's spiritual state before God, especially regarding one's sins and faults. It is recommended as a regular practice and is practically necessary in preparing for the sacrament of penance. The *particular examen* is a regular examination to assist in overcoming specific faults and imperfections.

Consecration of a Church: See Dedication of a Church.

Consistory: An assembly of cardinals presided over by the pope. Consistories are secret (pope and cardinals only), semi-public (plus other prelates), and public (plus other attendants).

Constitution: (1) An apostolic or papal constitution is a document in which a pope enacts and promulgates law.

(2) A formal and solemn document issued by an ecumenical council on a doctrinal or pastoral subject, with binding force in the whole Church; e.g., the four constitutions issued by the Second Vatican Council on the Church, liturgy, Revelation, and the Church in the modern world.

(3) The constitutions of religious orders spell out details of and norms drawn from the various rules for the guidance and direction of the life and work of members of each institute.

Consubstantiation: A theory which holds that the Body and Blood of Christ coexist with the substance of bread and wine in the Holy Eucharist. This theory, also called *impanation,* is incompatible with the doctrine of transubstantiation.

Contraception: Anything done by positive interference to prevent sexual intercourse from resulting in conception. Direct contraception is against the order of nature. Indirect contraception — as a secondary effect of medical treatment or other action having a necessary, good, non-contraceptive purpose — is permissible under the principle of the double effect. The practice of rhythm is not contraception because it does not involve positive interference with the order of nature.

Contrition: Sorrow for sin coupled with a purpose of amendment. Contrition arising from a supernatural motive is necessary for the forgiveness of sin.

(1) Perfect contrition is total sorrow for and renunciation of attachment to sin, arising from the motive of pure love of God. Perfect contrition, which implies the intention of doing all God wants done for the forgiveness of sin, is sufficient for the forgiveness of serious sin and the remission of all temporal punishment due for sin. Confession is required before the reception of another sacrament. (The intention to receive the sacrament of penance is implicit — even if unrealized, as in the case of some persons — in perfect contrition.)

(2) Imperfect contrition or attrition is sorrow arising from a quasi-selfish supernatural motive; e.g., the fear of losing heaven, suffering the pains of hell, etc. Imperfect contrition is sufficient for the forgiveness of serious sin when joined with absolution in confession, and sufficient for the forgiveness of venial sin even outside of confession.

Contumely: Personal insult, reviling a person in his presence by accusation of moral faults, by refusal of recognition or due respect; a violation of obligations of justice and charity.

Corporal Works of Mercy: Feeding the hungry, giving drink to the thirsty, clothing the naked, visiting the imprisoned, sheltering the homeless, visiting the sick, burying the dead.

Councils: Bodies representative of various categories of members of the Church which participate with bishops and other church authorities in making decisions and carrying out action programs for the good of the Church and the accomplishment of its mission to its own members and society in general. Examples are priests' senates or councils, councils of religious and lay persons, parish councils, diocesan pastoral councils.

Councils, Plenary: National councils or councils of the bishops of several ecclesiastical provinces, assembled under the presidency of a papal legate to take action related to the life and mission of the Church in the area under their jurisdiction. The membership of such councils is fixed by canon law; their decrees, when approved by the Holy See, are binding in the territory (see Index, Plenary Councils of Baltimore).

Councils, Provincial: Meetings of the bishops of a province. The metropolitan, or ranking archbishop, of an ecclesiastical province convenes and presides over such councils in a manner prescribed by canon law to take action related to the life and mission of the Church in the province. Acts and decrees must be approved by the Holy See before being promulgated. Provincial councils should be held at least once every 20 years.

Counsels, Evangelical: Gospel counsels of perfection, especially voluntary poverty, perfect chastity and obedience, which were recommended by Christ to those who would devote themselves exclusively and completely to the immediate service of God. Religious bind themselves by public vows to observe these counsels in a life of total consecration to God and service to people through various kinds of apostolic works.

Counter-Reformation: The period of approximately 100 years following the Council of Trent, which witnessed a reform within the Church to stimulate genuine Catholic life and to counteract effects of the Reformation.

Covenant: A bond of relationship between parties pledged to each other. God-initiated covenants in the Old Testament included those with Abraham, Noah, Moses, Levi, David. The Mosaic (Sinai) covenant made Israel God's Chosen People on terms of fidelity to true faith, true worship, and righteous conduct according to the Decalogue. The New Testament covenant, prefigured in the Old Testament, is the bond men have with God through Christ. All men are called to be parties to this perfect and everlasting covenant, which was mediated and ratified by Christ.

Creation: The production by God of something out of nothing. The biblical account of creation is contained in the first two chapters of Genesis.

Creator: God, the supreme, self-existing Being, the absolute and infinite First Cause of all things.

Creature: Everything in the realm of being is a creature, except God.

Cremation: The reduction of a human corpse to ashes by means of fire. Cremation is not in line with Catholic tradition and practice, even though it is not opposed to any article of faith. It can be permitted for serious reasons. The general practice, however, was forbidden in a decree issued May 19, 1886, by the Sacred Congregation of the Holy Office.

This ruling was incorporated in the Code of Canon Law (Canons 1203, 1240), which generally banned the practice of cremation, forbade following orders for cremation, and deprived of the last rites and ecclesiastical burial those who directed that their bodies be cremated and did not retract the directions.

The principal reason behind the prohibition against cremation was the fact that, historically, the practice had represented an attempt to deny the doctrine of the resurrection of the body. It also appeared to be a form of violence against the body which, as the temple of the Holy Spirit during life, should be treated with reverence.

The Congregation for the Doctrine of the Faith, under date of May 8, 1963, circulated among bishops an instruction which upheld the traditional practices of Christian burial but modified anti-cremation legislation. Cremation may be permitted for serious reasons, of a private as well as public nature, provided it does not involve any contempt of the Church or of religion, or any attempt to deny, question, or belittle the doctrine of the resurrection of the body. The person may receive the last rites and be given ecclesiastical burial. A priest may say prayers for the deceased at the crematorium, but full liturgical ceremonies may not take place there.

Crib: A devotional representation of the birth of Jesus. The custom of erecting cribs is generally attributed to St. Francis of Assisi who in 1223 obtained from Pope Honorius III permission to use a crib and figures of the Christ Child, Mary, St. Joseph, and others, to represent the mystery of the Nativity.

Crosier: The bishop's staff, symbolic of his pastoral office, responsibility and authority.

Crypt: An underground or partly underground chamber; e.g., the lower part of a church used for worship and/or burial.

Cura Animarum: A Latin phrase, meaning care of souls, designating the pastoral ministry and responsibility of bishops and priests.

Curia: The personnel and offices through which (1) the pope administers the affairs of the universal Church, the *Roman Curia* (see separate entry), or (2) a bishop the affairs of a diocese, *diocesan curia*. The principal officials of a diocesan curia are the vicar general of the diocese, the chancellor, officials of the diocesan tribunal or court, examiners, consultors, auditors, notaries.

Custos: A religious superior who presides over a number of convents collectively called a custody. In some religious institutes, a custos may be the deputy of a higher superior.

D

Deaconess — A woman officially appointed and charged by the Church to carry out service-like functions. Phoebe apparently was one (Rom. 16:1-2); a second probable reference to the office is in Tm. 3:11.

The office — for assistance at the baptism of women, for pastoral service to women and for works of charity — had considerable development in the third and also in the fourth century when the actual term came into use (in place of such designations as *diacona, vidua, virgo canonica*). Its importance declined subsequently with the substitution of infusion in place of immersion as the common method of baptism in the West, and with the increase of the practice of infant baptism. There is no record of the ministry of deaconess in the West after the beginning of the 11th century.

Several Christian churches have had revivals of the office of deaconess since the 1830s. There is a contemporary movement in support of such a revival among some Catholics.

The Vatican's Theological Commission, in a paper prepared in 1971, noted that there had been in the past a form of diaconal ordination for women. With a rite and purpose distinctive to women, it differed essentially from the ordination of deacons, which had sacramental effects.

Dean: (1) A priest with supervisory responsibility over a section of a diocese known as a deanery. The post-Vatican II counterpart of a dean is an episcopal vicar.

(2) The senior or ranking member of a group.

Dean of the Sacred College: The president of the College of Cardinals (the ranking cardinal bishop). He is elected by the cardinals holding title to the suburban sees of Rome.

Decision: A judgment or pronouncement on a cause or suit, given by a church tribunal or official with judicial authority. A decision has the force of law for concerned parties.

Declaration: (1) An ecclesiastical document which presents an interpretation of an existing law.

(2) A position paper on a specific subject; e.g., the three declarations issued by the Second Vatican Council on religious freedom, non-Christian religions, and Christian education.

Decree: An edict or ordinance issued by a pope and/or by an ecumenical council, with binding force in the whole Church; by a department of the Roman Curia, with binding force for concerned parties; by a territorial body of bishops, with binding force for persons in the area; by individual bishops, with binding force for concerned parties until revocation or the death of the bishop.

The nine decrees issued by the Second Vatican Council were combinations of doctrinal and pastoral statements with executive orders for action and movement toward renewal and reform in the Church.

Dedication of a Church: The ceremony whereby a church is solemnly set apart for the worship of God. The custom of dedicating churches had an antecedent in Old Testament ceremonies for the dedication of the Temple, as in the times of Solomon and the Maccabees. The earliest extant record of the dedication of a Christian church dates from early in the fourth century, when it was done simply by the celebration of Mass. Other ceremonies developed later. A church can be dedicated by a simple blessing or a solemn consecration. The rite of consecration is performed by a bishop.

Definitors: Members of the governing council of a religious order, each one having a decisive vote equal to the vote of the general or provincial superior.

Deism: A system of natural religion which acknowledges the existence of God but regards him as so transcendent and remote from man and the universe that divine revelation and the supernatural order of things are irrelevant and unacceptable. It developed from rationalistic principles in England in the 17th and 18th centuries, and had Voltaire, Rousseau and the Encyclopedists among its advocates in France.

Despair: Abandonment of hope for salvation arising from the conviction that God will not provide the necessary means for attaining it, that following God's way of life for salvation is impossible, or that one's sins are unforgivable; a serious sin against the Holy Spirit and the theological virtues of hope and faith, involving distrust in the mercy and goodness of God and a denial of all the truths that God wills the salvation of all men and provides sufficient grace for it. Real despair is distinguished from unreasonable fear with respect to the difficulties of attaining salvation, from morbid anxiety over the demands of divine justice, and from feelings of despair.

Detachment: Control of affection for creatures by two principles: (1) supreme love and devotion belong to God; (2) love and service of creatures should be an expression of love for God.

Detraction: Revelation of true but hidden faults of a person without sufficient and justifying reason; a violation of requirements of justice and charity, involving the obligation to make restitution when this is possible without doing more harm to the good name of the offended party. In some cases, e.g., to prevent evil, secret faults may and should be disclosed.

Devil: (1) Lucifer, Satan, chief of the fallen angels who sinned and were banished from heaven. Still possessing angelic powers, he can cause such diabolical phenomena as possession and obsession, and can tempt men to sin.

(2) Any fallen angel.

Devil's Advocate: See Promoter of the Faith.

Devotion: (1) Religious fervor, piety; dedication.

(2) The consolation experienced at times during prayer; a reverent manner of praying.

Devotions: Pious practices of members of the Church include not only participation in various acts of the liturgy but also in other acts of worship generally called popular or private devotions. Concerning these, the Second Vatican Council said in the *Constitution on the Sacred Liturgy* (No. 13): "Popular devotions of the Christian people are warmly commended, provided they accord with the laws and norms of the Church. Such is especially the case with devotions called for by the Apostolic See. Devotions proper to the individual churches also have a special dignity. . . . These devotions should be so drawn up that they harmonize with the liturgical seasons, accord with the sacred liturgy, are in some fashion derived from it, and lead the people to it, since the liturgy by its very nature far surpasses any of them."

Devotions of a liturgical type are Benediction of the Blessed Sacrament, recitation of the Little Office of the Blessed Virgin Mary or of Vespers and Compline. Examples of paraliturgical devotion are a Bible Service or Vigil, and the Angelus, Rosary and Stations of the Cross, which have a strong scriptural basis.

Dies Irae: The opening Latin words, Day of Wrath, of a hymn for requiem Masses, written in the 13th century by the Franciscan Thomas of Celano.

Diocese: A fully organized ecclesiastical jurisdiction under the pastoral direction of a bishop as local ordinary.

Discalced: Of Latin derivation and meaning without shoes, the word is applied to religious orders or congregations whose members go barefoot or wear sandals.

Disciple: A term used sometimes in reference to the Apostles but more often to a larger number of followers (70 or 72) of Christ mentioned in Lk. 10:1.

Disciplina Arcani: A Latin phrase, meaning discipline of the secret and referring to a practice of the early Church, especially during the Roman persecutions, to: (1) conceal Christian truths from those who, it was feared, would misinterpret, ridicule and profane the teachings, and persecute Christians for believing them; (2) instruct catechumens in a gradual manner, withholding the teaching of certain doctrines until the catechumens proved themselves of good faith and sufficient understanding.

Dispensation: The relaxation of a law in a particular case. Laws made for the common good sometimes work undue hardship in particular cases. In such cases, where sufficient reasons are present, dispensations may be granted by proper authorities. Bishops, religious superiors and others may dispense from certain laws; the pope can dispense from all ecclesiastical laws. No one has authority to dispense from obligations of the divine law.

Divination: Attempting to foretell future or hidden things by means of things like dreams, necromancy, spiritism, examination of entrails, astrology, augury, omens, palmistry, drawing straws, dice, cards, etc. Practices like these attribute to creatural things a power which belongs to God alone and are violations of the First Commandment.

Divine Praises: Fourteen praises recited or sung at Benediction of the Blessed Sacrament in reparation for sins of sacrilege, blasphemy and profanity. Some of these praises date from the end of the 18th century.

Blessed be God.

Blessed be his holy Name.

Blessed be Jesus Christ, true God and true Man.

Blessed be the Name of Jesus.

Blessed be his most Sacred Heart.

Blessed be his most Precious Blood.

Blessed be Jesus in the most holy Sacrament of the Altar.

Blessed be the Holy Spirit, the Paraclete.

Blessed be the great Mother of God, Mary most holy.

Blessed be her holy and Immaculate Conception.

Blessed be her glorious Assumption.

Blessed be the name of Mary, Virgin and Mother.

Blessed be St. Joseph, her most chaste Spouse.

Blessed be God in his Angels and in his Saints.

Double Effect Principle: Actions sometimes have two effects closely related to each other, one good and the other bad, and a difficult moral question can arise: Is it permissible to place an action from which two such results follow? It is permissible to place the action, if: the action is good in itself and is directly productive of the good effect; the circumstances are good; the intention of the person is good; the reason for placing the action is proportionately serious to the seriousness of the indirect bad effect. For example: Is it morally permissible for a pregnant woman to undergo medical or surgical treatment for a pathological condition if the indirect and secondary effect of the treatment will be the loss of the child? The reply is affirmative, for these reasons: The action, i.e., the treatment, is good in itself, cannot be deferred until a later time without very serious consequences, and is ordered directly to the cure of critically grave pathology. By means of the treatment, the woman intends to save her life, which she has a right to do. The loss of the child is not directly sought as a means for the cure of the mother but results indirectly and in a secondary manner from the placing of the action, i.e., the treatment, which is good in itself.

The double effect principle does not support the principle that the end justifies the means.

Doxology: (1) The lesser doxology, or ascription of glory to the Trinity, is the Glory

be to the Father. The first part dates back to the third or fourth century, and came from the form of baptism. The concluding words, As it was in the beginning, etc., are of later origin.

(2) The greater doxology, Glory to God in the highest, begins with the words of angelic praise at the birth of Christ recounted in the Infancy Narrative (Lk. 2:14). It is often recited at Mass. Of early Eastern origin, it is found in the *Apostolic Constitutions* in a form much like the present.

Dulia: A Greek term meaning the veneration or homage, different in nature and degree from that given to God, paid to the saints. It includes honoring the saints and seeking their intercession with God.

Duty: A moral obligation deriving from the binding force of law, the exigencies of one's state in life, and other sources.

E

Easter Controversy: A three-phase controversy over the time for the celebration of Easter.

Some early Christians in the Near East, called Quartodecimans, favored the observance of Easter on the 14th day of Nisan, the spring month of the Hebrew calendar, whenever it occurred. Against this practice, Pope St. Victor I, about 190, ordered a Sunday observance of the feast.

The Council of Nicaea, in line with usages of the Church at Rome and Alexandria, decreed in 325 that Easter should be observed on the first Sunday following the first full moon of spring.

Uniformity of practice in the West was not achieved until several centuries later, when the British Isles, in delayed compliance with measures enacted by the Synod of Whitby in 664, accepted the Roman date of observance.

Unrelated to the controversy is the fact that some Eastern Christians, in accordance with traditional calendar practices, celebrate Easter at a different time than the Roman and Eastern-Rite churches.

Easter Duty: The serious obligation binding Catholics of Roman Rite, by a precept of the Church, to receive Holy Communion during the Easter time; in the US, from the first Sunday of Lent to Trinity Sunday.

Easter Water: Holy water blessed with special ceremonies and distributed on the Easter Vigil; used during Easter Week for blessing the faithful and homes.

Ecclesiology: Study of the nature, constitution, members, mission, functions, etc., of the Church.

Ecstasy: An extraordinary state of mystical experience in which a person is so absorbed in God that the activity of the exterior senses is suspended.

Ecumenism: The movement of Christians and their churches toward the unity willed by

Christ. The Second Vatican Council called the movement "those activities and enterprises which, according to various needs of the Church and opportune occasions, are started and organized for the fostering of unity among Christians" (*Decree on Ecumenism,* No. 4). Spiritual ecumenism, i.e., mutual prayer for unity, is the heart of the movement. The movement also involves scholarly and pew-level efforts for the development of mutual understanding and better interfaith relations in general, and collaboration by the churches and their members in the social area.

Elevation: The raising of the host after consecration at Mass for adoration by the faithful. The custom was introduced in the Diocese of Paris about the close of the 12th century to offset an erroneous teaching of the time which held that transubstantiation of the bread did not take place until after the consecration of the wine in the chalice. The elevation of the chalice following the consecration of the wine was introduced in the 15th century.

End Justifies the Means: An unacceptable ethical principle which states that evil means may be used to produce good effects.

Envy: Sadness over another's good fortune because it is considered a loss to oneself or a detraction from one's own excellence; one of the seven capital sins, a violation of the obligations of charity.

Epikeia: A Greek word meaning reasonableness and designating a moral theory and practice, a mild interpretation of the mind of a legislator who is prudently considered not to wish positive law to bind in certain circumstances. Use of the principle is justified in practice when the lawgiver himself cannot be appealed to and when it can be prudently assumed that in particular cases, e.g., because of special hardship, he would not wish the law to be applied in a strict manner. Epikeia may not be applied with respect to acts that are intrinsically wrong or those covered by laws which automatically make them invalid.

Episcopate: (1) The office, dignity and sacramental powers bestowed upon a bishop at his ordination.

(2) The body of bishops collectively.

Equivocation: (1) The use of words, phrases, or gestures having more than one meaning in order to conceal information which a questioner has no strict right to know. It is permissible to equivocate (have a broad mental reservation) in some circumstances.

(2) A lie, i.e., a statement of untruth. Lying is intrinsically wrong. A lie told in joking, evident as such, is not wrong.

Eschatology: Doctrine concerning the last things: death, judgment, heaven and hell, and the final state of perfection of the People and Kingdom of God at the end of time.

Eternity: The interminable, perfect possession of life in its totality without beginning or end; an attribute of God, who has no past or future but always is. Man's existence has a beginning but no end and is, accordingly, called immortal.

Ethics: Moral philosophy, the science of the morality of human acts deriving from natural law, the natural end of man, and the powers of human reason. It includes all the spheres of human activity — personal, social, economic, political, etc. Ethics is distinct from but can be related to moral theology, whose primary principles are drawn from divine Revelation.

Eucharistic Congresses: Public demonstrations of faith in the Holy Eucharist. Combining liturgical services, other public ceremonies, subsidiary meetings, different kinds of instructional and inspirational elements, they are unified by central themes and serve to increase understanding of and devotion to Christ in the Eucharist, and to relate this liturgy of worship and witness to life.

The first international congress developed from a proposal by Marie Marthe Tamisier of Touraine, organizing efforts of Msgr. Louis Gaston de Segur, and backing by industrialist Philibert Vrau. It was held with the approval of Pope Leo XIII at the University of Lille, France, and was attended by some 800 persons from France, Belgium, Holland, England, Spain and Switzerland.

International congresses are planned and held under the auspices of a permanent committee for international Eucharistic congresses. Participants include clergy, religious and lay persons from many countries, and representatives of national and international Catholic organizations. Popes have usually been represented by legates, but Paul VI attended two congresses personally, the 38th at Bombay and the 39th at Bogota.

Forty-one international congresses were held from 1881 to 1976:

Lille (1881), Avignon (1882), Liege (1883), Freiburg (1885), Toulouse (1886), Paris (1888), Antwerp (1890), Jerusalem (1893), Rheims (1894), Paray-le-Monial (1897), Brussels (1898), Lourdes (1899), Angers (1901), Namur (1902), Angouleme (1904), Rome (1905), Tournai (1906), Metz (1907), London (1908), Cologne (1909), Montreal (1910), Madrid (1911), Vienna (1912), Malta (1913), Lourdes (1914), Rome (1922), Amsterdam (1924), Chicago (1926), Sydney (1928), Carthage (1930), Dublin (1932), Buenos Aires (1934), Manila (1937), Budapest (1938), Barcelona (1952), Rio de Janeiro (1955), Munich, Germany (1960), Bombay, India (1964), Bogota, Colombia (1968), Melbourne, Australia (1973), Philadelphia (1976).

The Vatican announced in June, 1977, that the 42nd international congress would be held in 1981 at Lourdes.

Eugenics: The science of heredity and environment for the physical and mental improvement of offspring. Extreme eugenics is untenable in practice because it advocates immoral means, such as compulsory breeding of the select, sterilization of persons said to be unfit, abortion, and unacceptable methods of birth regulation.

Euthanasia: Mercy killing, the direct causing of death by painless means for the purpose of ending human suffering. Euthanasia is murder and is totally illicit, for the natural law forbids the direct taking of one's own life or that of an innocent person.

The use of drugs to relieve suffering in serious cases, even when this results in a shortening of life as an indirect and secondary effect, is permissible under conditions of the double effect principle. It is also permissible for a seriously ill person to refuse to follow — or for other responsible persons to refuse to permit — extraordinary medical procedures even though the refusal might entail shortening of life.

Evolution: Scientific theory concerning the development of the physical universe from unorganized matter (inorganic evolution) and, especially, the development of existing forms of vegetable, animal and human life from earlier and more primitive organisms (organic evolution). Various ideas about evolution were advanced for some centuries before scientific evidence in support of the main-line theory of organic evolution, which has several formulations, was discovered and verified in the second half of the 19th century and afterwards. This evidence — from the findings of comparative anatomy and other sciences — confirmed evolution within species and cleared the way to further investigation of questions regarding the processes of its accomplishment. While a number of such questions remain open with respect to human evolution, a point of doctrine not open to question is the immediate creation of the human soul by God.

For some time, theologians regarded the theory with hostility, considering it to be in opposition to the account of creation in the early chapters of Genesis and subversive of belief in such doctrines as creation, the early state of man in grace, and the fall of man from grace. This state of affairs and the tension it generated led to considerable controversy regarding an alleged conflict between religion and science. Gradually, however, the tension was diminished with the development of biblical studies from the latter part of the 19th century onwards, with clarification of the distinctive features of religious truth and scientific truth, and with the refinement of evolutionary concepts.

So far as the Genesis account of creation is concerned, the Catholic view is that the writer(s) did not write as a scientist but as the communicator of religious truth in a manner adapted to the understanding of the people of his time. He used anthropomorphic language, the figure of days and other literary devices to state the salvation truths of creation, the fall of man from grace, and the promise of redemption. It was beyond the competency and purpose of the writer(s) to describe creation and related events in a scientific manner.

Excommunication: A penalty or censure by which a baptized person is excluded from the communion of the faithful, for committing and remaining obstinate in certain sins specified in canon law and technically called crimes. As by baptism a person is made a member of the Church in which there is a communication of spiritual goods, so by excommunication he is deprived of the same spiritual goods until he repents and receives absolution. Even though excommunicated, a person is still responsible for the normal obligations of a Catholic.

Existentialism: A philosophy with radical concern for the problems of individual existence and identity viewed in particular here-and-now patterns of thought which presuppose irrationality and absurdity in human life and the whole universe. It is preoccupied with questions about freedom, moral decision and responsibility against a background of denial of objective truth and universal norms of conduct; is characterized by prevailing anguish, dread, fear, pessimism, despair; is generally atheistic, although its modern originator, Soren Kierkegaard (d. 1855), and Gabriel Marcel attempted to give it a Christian orientation. Pius XII called it "the new erroneous philosophy which, opposing itself to idealism, immanentism and pragmatism, has assumed the name of existentialism, since it concerns itself only with the existence of individual things and neglects all consideration of their immutable essences" (Encyclical *Humani Generis,* Aug. 12, 1950).

Exorcism: (1) Driving out evil spirits; a rite in which evil spirits are charged and commanded on the authority of God and with the prayer of the Church to depart from a person or to cease causing harm to a person suffering from diabolical possession or obsession. The sacramental is officially administered by a priest delegated for the purpose by the bishop of the place. Elements of the rite include the Litany of Saints; recitation of the Our Father, one or more creeds, and other prayers; specific prayers of exorcism; the reading of Gospel passages, and use of the Sign of the Cross. Private exorcism for the liberation of a person from the strong influence of evil spirits, through prayer and the use of sacramentals like holy water, can be done by anyone.

(2) Exorcisms which do not imply the conditions of either diabolical possession or obsession form part of the ceremony of baptism, and are also included in other formulas.

F

Faculties: Grants of jurisdiction, or authority, granted by the law of the Church or superiors (pope, bishop, religious superior) for exercise of the powers of holy orders; e.g., priests are given faculties to hear confessions, officiate at weddings; bishops are given faculties to grant dispensations, etc.

Faith: In religion, faith has several aspects. Catholic doctrine calls faith the assent of the mind to truths revealed by God, the assent being made with the help of grace and by command of the will on account of the authority and trustworthiness of God revealing. The term faith also refers to the truths that are believed (content of faith) and to the way in which a person, in response to Christ, gives witness to and expresses his belief in daily life (living faith).

All of these elements, and more, are included in the following statement:

" 'The obedience of faith' (Rom. 16:26; cf. 1:5; 2 Cor. 10:5-6) must be given to God who reveals, an obedience by which man entrusts his whole self freely to God, offering 'the full submission of intellect and will to God who reveals' (First Vatican Council, *Dogmatic Constitution on the Catholic Faith,* Chap. 3), and freely assenting to the truth revealed by Him. If this faith is to be shown, the grace of God and the interior help of the Holy Spirit must precede and assist, moving the heart and turning it to God, opening the eyes of the mind, and giving 'joy and ease to everyone in assenting to the truth and believing it' " (Second Council of Orange, Canon 7) (Second Vatican Council, *Constitution on Revelation,* No. 5). Faith is necessary for salvation.

Faith, Rule of: The norm or standard of religious belief. The Catholic doctrine is that belief must be professed in the divinely revealed truths in the Bible and tradition as interpreted and proposed by the infallible teaching authority of the Church.

Fast, Eucharistic: Eating and the drinking of any liquids except water are prohibited for one hour before the reception of Holy Communion. Water never breaks the Eucharistic fast, which is prescribed for reasons of reverence and preparation. By way of exception, the period of fasting is 15 minutes for the sick and aged, even though not confined to bed or a home, and those caring for them who wish to receive Communion with them but cannot fast for an hour without inconvenience (Instruction, *Immensae Caritatis,* Congregation for the Discipline of the Sacraments, Jan. 29, 1973).

Those who are ill, even though not confined to bed, may take nonalcoholic beverages and liquid or solid medicine before Holy Communion without any time limit.

Father: A title of priests, who are regarded as spiritual fathers because they are the ordinary ministers of baptism, by which persons are born to supernatural life, and because of their pastoral service to people.

Fear: A mental state caused by the apprehension of present or future danger. Grave fear does not necessarily remove moral responsibility for an act, but may lessen it.

First Friday: A devotion consisting of the reception of Holy Communion on the first Friday of nine consecutive months in honor of the Sacred Heart of Jesus and in reparation for sin. (See Sacred Heart, Promises.)

First Saturday: A devotion tracing its origin to the apparitions of the Blessed Virgin Mary at Fatima in 1917. Those practicing the devotion go to confession and, on the first Saturday of five consecutive months, receive Holy Communion, recite five decades of the Rosary, and meditate on the mysteries for 15 minutes.

Fisherman's Ring: A signet ring engraved with the image of St. Peter fishing from a boat, and encircled with the name of the reigning pope. It is not worn by the pope. It is used to seal briefs, and is destroyed after each pope's death.

Forgiveness of Sin: Catholics believe that sins are forgiven by God through the mediation of Christ in view of the repentance of the sinner and by means of the sacrament of penance. (See Penance.)

Fortitude: Courage to face dangers or hardships for the sake of what is good; one of the four cardinal virtues and one of the seven gifts of the Holy Spirit.

Fortune Telling: Attempting to predict the future or the occult by means of cards, palm reading, etc.; a form of divination, prohibited by the First Commandment.

Forty Hours Devotion: A Eucharistic observance consisting of solemn exposition of the Blessed Sacrament in commemoration of the time Christ's body lay in the tomb, coupled with special Masses and forms of prayer, for the purposes of making reparation for sin and praying for God's blessings of grace and peace. The devotion was instituted in 1534 in Milan. St. John Neumann of Philadelphia was the first bishop in the U.S. to prescribe its observance in his diocese. For many years in this country, the observance was held annually on a rotating basis in all parishes of a diocese. Simplified and abbreviated Eucharistic observances have taken the place of the devotion in some places.

Forum: The sphere in which ecclesiastical authority or jurisdiction is exercised.

(1) External: Authority is exercised in the external forum to deal with matters affecting the public welfare of the Church and its members. Those who have such authority because of their office (e.g., diocesan bishops) are called ordinaries.

(2) Internal: Authority is exercised in the internal forum to deal with matters affecting the private spiritual good of individuals. The

sacramental forum is the sphere in which the sacrament of penance is administered; other exercises of jurisdiction in the internal forum take place in the non-sacramental forum.

Franciscan Crown: A seven-decade rosary used to commemorate the seven Joys of the Blessed Virgin: the Annunciation, the Visitation, the Nativity of Our Lord, the Adoration of the Magi, the Finding of the Child Jesus in the Temple, the Apparition of the Risen Christ to his Mother, the Assumption and Coronation of the Blessed Virgin. Introduced in 1422, the Crown originally consisted only of seven Our Fathers and 70 Hail Marys. Two Hail Marys were added to complete the number 72 (thought to be the number of years of Mary's life), and one Our Father, Hail Mary and Glory be to the Father are said for the intention of the pope.

Freedom, Religious: The Second Vatican Council declared that the right to religious freedom in civil society "means that all men are to be immune from coercion on the part of individuals or of social groups and of any human power, in such wise that in matters religious no one is to be forced to act in a manner contrary to his own beliefs. Nor is anyone to be restrained from acting in accordance with his own beliefs, whether privately or publicly, whether alone or in association with others, within due limits" of requirements for the common good. The foundation of this right in civil society is the "very dignity of the human person" (*Declaration on Religious Freedom,* No. 2).

The conciliar statement did not deal with the subject of freedom within the Church. It noted the responsibility of the faithful "carefully to attend to the sacred and certain doctrine of the Church" (No. 14).

Freemasons: A fraternal order which originated in London in 1717 with the formation of the first Grand Lodge of Freemasons. From England, the order spread to Europe and elsewhere. Its original deistic and non-denominational ideology was transformed in Latin countries into a compound of atheism, anticlericalism and irreligion. Since 1877, Grand Orient Freemasonry has been denied recognition by the Scottish and York Rites because of its failure to require belief in God and the immortality of the soul as a condition of membership. In some places, Freemasonry has been regarded as subversive of the state; in Catholic quarters, it has been considered hostile to the Church and its doctrine. In the United States, Freemasonry is generally known as a fraternal and philanthropic order.

Catholics have been forbidden to join the Freemasons, under penalty of excommunication, for serious pastoral reasons. Eight different popes in 17 different pronouncements, and at least six different local councils, condemned Freemasonry. The first condemnation was made by Clement XII in 1738. Eastern Orthodox and many Protestant bodies have also opposed the order.

The existing prohibition against membership in the Freemasons by Catholics was modified by the contents of a letter written in 1974 by Cardinal Franjo Seper, prefect of the Congregation for the Doctrine of the Faith. The letter said that Catholic laymen may join Masonic lodges which do not plot against the Church. The letter also said: "Clerics, religious and members of secular institutes are still forbidden in every case to join any Masonic association."

Free Will: The faculty or capability of making a reasonable choice among several alternatives. Freedom of will underlies the possibility and fact of moral responsibility.

Friar: Term applied to members of mendicant orders to distinguish them from members of monastic orders. (See Mendicants.)

Fruits of the Holy Spirit: Charity, joy, peace, patience, benignity, goodness, longanimity, mildness, faith, modesty, continence, chastity.

G

Gambling: The backing of an issue with a sum of money or other valuables, which is permissible if the object is honest, if the two parties have the free disposal of their stakes without prejudice to the rights of others, if the terms are thoroughly understood by both parties, and if the outcome is not known beforehand. Gambling often falls into disrepute and may be forbidden by civil law, as well as by divine law, because of cheating, fraud and other accompanying evils.

Gehenna: Greek form of a Jewish name, *Gehinnom,* for a valley near Jerusalem, the site of Moloch worship; used as a synonym for hell.

Genuflection: Bending of the knee, a natural sign of adoration or reverence, as when persons genuflect with the right knee in passing before the tabernacle to acknowledge the Eucharistic presence of Christ.

Gethsemani: A Hebrew word meaning oil press, designating the place on the Mount of Olives where Christ prayed and suffered in agony the night before he died.

Gifts of the Holy Spirit: Supernatural habits disposing a person to respond promptly to the inspiration of grace; promised by Christ and communicated through the Holy Spirit, especially in the sacrament of confirmation. They are: wisdom, understanding, counsel, fortitude, knowledge, piety, fear of the Lord.

Gluttony: An unreasonable appetite for food and drink; one of the seven capital sins.

God: The infinitely perfect Supreme Being, uncaused and absolutely self-sufficient, eternal, the Creator and final end of all things.

The one God subsists in three equal Persons, the Father and the Son and the Holy Spirit. God, although transcendent and distinct from the universe, is present and active in the world in realization of his plan for the salvation of men, principally through Revelation, the operations of the Holy Spirit, the life and ministry of Christ, and the continuation of Christ's ministry in the Church.

The existence of God is an article of faith, clearly communicated in divine Revelation. Even without this Revelation, however, the Church teaches, in a declaration by the First Vatican Council, that men can acquire certain knowledge of the existence of God and some of his attributes. This can be done on the bases of principles of reason and reflection on human experience.

Non-revealed arguments or demonstrations for the existence of God have been developed from the principle of causality; the contingency of man and the universe; the existence of design, change and movement in the universe; human awareness of moral responsibility; widespread human testimony to the existence of God.

Grace: A free gift of God to men (and angels), grace is a created sharing or participation in the life of God. It is given to men through the merits of Christ and is communicated by the Holy Spirit. It is necessary for salvation. The principal means of grace are the sacraments (especially the Eucharist), prayer and good works.

Sanctifying or habitual grace makes men holy and pleasing to God, adopted children of God, members of Christ, temples of the Holy Spirit, heirs of heaven capable of supernaturally meritorious acts. With grace, God gives men the supernatural virtues and gifts of the Holy Spirit. The sacraments of baptism and penance were instituted to give grace to those who do not have it; the other sacraments, to increase it in those already in the state of grace. The means for growth in holiness, or the increase of grace, are prayer, the sacraments, and good works. Sanctifying grace is lost by the commission of serious sin.

Each sacrament confers sanctifying grace for the special purpose of the sacrament; in this context, grace is called sacramental grace.

Actual grace is a supernatural help of God which enlightens and strengthens a person to do good and to avoid evil. It is not a permanent quality, like sanctifying grace. It is necessary for the performance of supernatural acts. It can be resisted and refused. Persons in the state of serious sin are given actual grace to lead them to repentance.

Grace at Meals: Prayers said before meals, asking a blessing of God, and after meals, giving thanks to God. In addition to traditional prayers for these purposes, many variations suitable for different occasions are possible, at personal option.

H

Habit: (1) A disposition to do things easily, given with grace (and therefore supernatural) and/or acquired by repetition of similar acts.

(2) The garb worn by religious.

Hagiography: Writings or documents about saints and other holy persons.

Hail Mary: A prayer addressed to the Blessed Virgin Mary; also called the *Ave Maria* (Latin equivalent of Hail Mary) and the Angelic Salutation. In three parts, it consists of the words addressed to Mary by the Archangel Gabriel on the occasion of the Annunciation, in the Infancy Narrative (Hail full of grace, the Lord is with you, blessed are you among women.); the words addressed to Mary by her cousin Elizabeth on the occasion of the Visitation (Blessed is the fruit of your womb.); a concluding petition (Holy Mary, Mother of God, pray for us sinners now and at the hour of our death. Amen.). The first two salutations were joined in Eastern Rite formulas by the sixth century, and were similarly used at Rome in the seventh century. Insertion of the name of Jesus at the conclusion of the salutations was probably made by Urban IV about 1262. The present form of the petition was incorporated into the breviary in 1514.

Heaven: The state of those who, having achieved salvation, are in glory with God and enjoy the beatific vision.

The phrase, kingdom of heaven, refers to the order or kingdom of God, grace, salvation.

Hell: The state of punishment of the damned — i.e., those who die in mortal sin, in a condition of self-alienation from God and of opposition to the divine plan of salvation. The punishment of hell begins immediately after death and lasts forever.

Hermit: See Anchorite.

Heroic Act of Charity: The completely unselfish offering to God of one's good works and merits for the benefit of the souls in purgatory rather than for oneself. Thus a person may offer to God for the souls in purgatory all the good works he performs during life, all the indulgences he gains, and all the prayers and indulgences that will be offered for him after his death. The act is revocable at will, and is not a vow. Its actual ratification depends on the will of God.

Heterodoxy: False doctrine, teaching or belief; a departure from truth.

Holy See: (1) The diocese of the pope, Rome.

(2) The pope himself and/or the various officials and bodies of the Church's central administration at Vatican City — the Roman Curia — which act in the name and by authority of the pope.

Holy Spirit: God the Holy Spirit, third Person of the Holy Trinity, who proceeds from the Father and the Son and with whom he is equal in every respect; inspirer of the prophets and writers of sacred Scripture; promised by Christ to the Apostles as their advocate and strengthener; appeared in the form of a dove at the baptism of Christ and as tongues of fire at his descent upon the Apostles; soul of the Church and guarantor, by his abiding presence and action, of truth in doctrine; communicator of grace to men, for which reason he is called the sanctifier.

Holy Water: Water blessed by the Church and used as a sacramental, a practice which originated in apostolic times.

Holy Year: A year during which the pope grants the plenary Jubilee Indulgence to the faithful who fulfill certain conditions. For those who make a pilgrimage to Rome during the year, the conditions are reception of the sacraments of penance and the Eucharist, visits and prayer for the intention of the pope in the basilicas of St. Peter, St. John Lateran, St. Paul and St. Mary Major. For those who do not make a pilgrimage to Rome, the conditions are reception of the sacraments and prayer for the pope during a visit or community celebration in a church designated by the bishop of the locality.

Holy Year observances have biblical counterparts in the Years of Jubilee observed at 50-year intervals by the pre-exilic Israelites — when debts were pardoned and slaves freed (Lv. 25:25-54) — and in sabbatical years observed from the end of the Exile to 70 A.D. — in which debts to fellow Jews were remitted.

The practice of Christians from early times to go on pilgrimage to the Holy Land, the shrines of martyrs and the tombs of the Apostles in Rome influenced the institution of Holy Years. There was also a prevailing belief among the people that every 100th year was a year of "Great Pardon." Accordingly, even before Boniface VIII formally proclaimed the first Holy Year Feb. 22, 1300, scores of thousands of pilgrims were already on the way to or in Rome.

Medieval popes embodied in the observance of Holy Years the practice of good works (reception of the sacraments of penance and the Eucharist, pilgrimages and/or visits to the tombs of the Apostles, and related actions) and spiritual benefits (particularly, special indulgences for the souls in purgatory). These and related practices, with suitable changes for celebrations in local churches, remain staple features of Holy Year observances.

The first three Holy Years were observed in 1300, 1350 and 1390. Subsequent ones were celebrated at 25-year intervals except in 1800 and 1850 when, respectively, the French invasion of Italy and political turmoil made observance impossible. Pope Paul II (1464-1471) set the 25-year timetable. In 1500, Pope Alexander VI prescribed the start and finish ceremonies — the opening and closing of the Holy Doors in the major basilicas on successive Christmas Eves. All but a few of the earlier Holy Years were classified as ordinary. Several, like the one held in 1933 to commemorate the 19th centenary of the death and resurrection of Christ, were in the extraordinary category.

Holy Year 1975 coincided with the 10th anniversary of the closing of the Second Vatican Council. Its themes also coincided with the renewal emphasis which dominated the council, and were related to the main topic — the evangelization of the modern world — on the 1974 agenda of the Synod of Bishops.

Homosexuality: The condition of a person whose sexual orientation is toward persons of the same rather than the opposite sex. Some psychologists regard it as an arrested state of emotional development. The condition, usually discovered during adolescence rather than deliberately caused, is not normal but is not sinful in itself. Homosexual acts against nature are objectively wrong; subjective responsibility for such acts, however, may be conditioned and diminished by compulsion and related factors.

Hope: One of the three theological virtues, by which one firmly trusts that God wills his salvation and will give him the means to attain it.

Hosanna: A Hebrew word, meaning O Lord, save, we pray.

Host, The Sacred: The bread under whose appearances Christ is and remains present in a unique manner after the consecration which takes place during Mass. (See Transubstantiation.)

Humility: A virtue which induces a person to evaluate himself at his true worth, to recognize his dependence on God, and to give glory to God for the good he has and can do.

Hyperdulia: The special veneration accorded the Blessed Virgin Mary because of her unique role in the mystery of Redemption, her exceptional gifts of grace from God, and her pre-eminence among the saints. Hyperdulia is not adoration; only God is adored.

Hypnosis: A mental state resembling sleep, induced by suggestion, in which the subject does the bidding of the hypnotist. Hypnotism is permissible under certain conditions: the existence of a serious reason, e.g., for anesthetic or therapeutic purposes, and the competence and integrity of the hypnotist. Hypnotism may not be practiced for the sake of amusement. Experiments indicate that, contrary to popular opinion, hypnotized subjects may be induced to perform immoral acts which, normally, they would not do.

Hypostatic Union: The union of the human and divine natures in the one divine Person of Christ.

I

Icons: Byzantine-style paintings or representations of Christ, the Blessed Virgin and other saints, venerated in the Eastern Churches where they take the place of statues.

Idolatry: Worship of any but the true God; a violation of the First Commandment.

IHS: In Greek, the first three letters of the name of Jesus — Iota, Eta, Sigma.

Immortality: The survival and continuing existence of the human soul after death.

Immunity of the Clergy: Exemption of clerics from military duty and civil service.

Impurity: Unlawful indulgence in sexual pleasure. (See Chastity.)

Incardination: The affiliation of a priest to his diocese. Every secular priest must belong to a certain diocese. Similarly, every priest of a religious community must belong to some jurisdiction of his community; this affiliation, however, is not called incardination.

Incarnation: (1) The coming-into-flesh or taking of human nature by the Second Person of the Trinity. He became human as the Son of Mary, being miraculously conceived by the power of the Holy Spirit, without ceasing to be divine. His divine Person hypostatically unites his divine and human natures.

(2) The supernatural mystery coextensive with Christ from the moment of his human conception and continuing through his life on earth; his sufferings and death; his resurrection from the dead and ascension to glory with the Father; his sending, with the Father, of the Holy Spirit upon the Apostles and the Church; and his unending mediation with the Father for the salvation of men.

Incense: A granulated substance which, when burnt, emits an aromatic smoke. It symbolizes the zeal with which the faithful should be consumed, the good odor of Christian virtue, the ascent of prayer to God.

Incest: Sexual intercourse with relatives by blood or marriage; a sin of impurity and also a grave violation of the natural reverence due to relatives. Other sins of impurity (desire, etc.) concerning relatives have the nature of incest.

Index of Prohibited Books: A list of books which Catholics were formerly forbidden to read, possess or sell, under penalty of excommunication. The books were banned by the Holy See after publication because their treatment of matters of faith and morals and related subjects were judged to be erroneous or serious occasions of doctrinal error. Some books were listed in the Index by name; others were covered under general norms. The Congregation for the Doctrine of the Faith declared June 14, 1966, that the Index and its related penalties of excommunication no longer had the force of law in the Church. Persons are still obliged, however, to take normal precautions against occasions of doctrinal error.

The first *Roman Index of Prohibited Books,* which served the same purposes as earlier lists, was published in 1559 by the Holy Office at the order of Paul IV. The Council of Trent, with the approval of the same pope, authorized another Index in 1564. Seven years later, St. Pius V set up a special Congregation for the Reform of the Index and Correction of Books, and gave it universal jurisdiction. In the course of time, many additions and modifications affecting the Index were made. In 1897, Leo XIII issued complete legislation on the subject, and in 1917 Benedict XV turned over to the Congregation of the Holy Office the function of censoring publications in accordance with the provisions of canon law.

Indifferentism: A theory that any one religion is as true and good — or false — as any other religion, and that it makes no difference, objectively, what religion one professes, if any. The theory is completely subjective, finding its justification entirely in personal choice without reference to or respect for objective validity. It is also self-contradictory, since it regards as equally acceptable — or unacceptable — the beliefs of all religions, which in fact are not only not all the same but are in some cases opposed to each other.

Indulgence: According to *The Doctrine and Practice of Indulgences,* an apostolic constitution issued by Paul VI Jan. 1, 1967, an indulgence is the remission before God of the temporal punishment due for sins already forgiven as far as their guilt is concerned, which a follower of Christ — with the proper dispositions and under certain determined conditions — acquires through the intervention of the Church. The Church grants indulgences in accordance with doctrine concerning the superabundant merits of Christ and the saints, the Power of the Keys, and the sharing of spiritual goods in the Communion of Saints.

An indulgence is partial or plenary, depending on whether it does away with either part or all of the temporal punishment due for sin. Both types of indulgences can always be applied to the dead by way of suffrage; the actual disposition of indulgences applied to the dead rests with God.

(1) Partial indulgence: Properly disposed faithful who perform an action to which a partial indulgence is attached obtain, in addition to the remission of temporal punishment acquired by the action itself, an equal remission of punishment through the intervention of the Church. (This grant was formerly designated in terms of days and years.) The proper dispositions for gaining a partial indulgence are sorrow for sin and freedom from serious sin, performance of the required good work, and the intention (which can be general or immediate) to gain the indulgence.

In addition to customary prayers and other good works to which partial indulgences are attached, the *Enchiridion Indulgentiarum* published in 1968 included general grants of partial indulgences to the faithful who: (a) with some kind of prayer, raise their minds to God with humble confidence while carrying out their duties and bearing the difficulties of everyday life; (b) motivated by the spirit of faith and compassion, give of themselves or their goods for the service of persons in need; (c) in a spirit of penance, spontaneously refrain from the enjoyment of things which are lawful and pleasing to them.

(2) Plenary indulgence: To gain a plenary indulgence, it is necessary for a person to be free of all attachment to sin, to perform the work to which the indulgence is attached, and to fulfill the three conditions of sacramental confession, Eucharistic Communion, and prayer for the intention of the pope. The three conditions may be fulfilled several days before or after the performance of the prescribed work, but it is fitting that Communion be received and prayers for the intentions of the pope be offered on the same day the work is performed. The condition of praying for the pope's intention is fully satisfied by praying one Our Father and one Hail Mary, and sometimes the Creed, but persons are free to choose other prayers.

Four of the several devotional practices for which a plenary indulgence is granted are: (a) adoration of the Blessed Sacrament for at least one-half hour; (b) devout reading of sacred Scripture for at least one-half hour; (c) the Way of the Cross; (d) recitation of the Marian Rosary in a church or public oratory or in a family group, a religious community or pious association. Only one plenary indulgence can be gained in a single day.

Indult: A favor or privilege granted by competent ecclesiastical authority, giving permission to do something not allowed by the common law of the Church.

Infant Jesus of Prague: An 18-inch-high wooden statue of the Child Jesus which has figured in a form of devotion to the Holy Childhood and Kingship of Christ since the 17th century. Of uncertain origin, the statue was presented by Princess Polixena to the Carmelites of Our Lady of Victory Church, Prague, in 1628.

Infused Virtues: The theological virtues of faith, hope, and charity; principles or capabilities of supernatural action, they are given with sanctifying grace by God rather than acquired by repeated acts of a person. They can be increased by practice; they are lost by contrary acts. Natural-acquired moral virtues, like the cardinal virtues of prudence, justice, temperance, and fortitude, can be considered infused in a person whose state of grace gives them supernatural orientation.

Inquisition: A tribunal for dealing with heretics, authorized by Gregory IX in 1231 to search them out, hear and judge them, sentence them to various forms of punishment, and in some cases to hand them over to civil authorities for punishment. The Inquisition was a creature of its time when crimes against faith, which threatened the good of the Christian community, were regarded also as crimes against the state, and when heretical doctrines of such extremists as the Cathari and Albigensians threatened the very fabric of society. The institution, which was responsible for many excesses, was most active in the second half of the 13th century.

Inquisition, Spanish: An institution peculiar to Spain and the colonies in Spanish America. In 1478, at the urging of King Ferdinand, Pope Sixtus IV approved the establishment of the Inquisition for trying charges of heresy brought against Jewish (Marranos) and Moorish (Moriscos) converts. It acquired jurisdiction over other cases as well, however, and fell into disrepute because of irregularities in its functions, cruelty in its sentences, and the manner in which it served the interests of the Spanish crown more than the accused persons and the good of the Church. Protests by the Holy See failed to curb excesses of the Inquisition, which lingered in Spanish history until early in the 19th century.

I N R I: The first letters of words in the Latin inscription atop the cross on which Christ was crucified: (I)esus (N)azaraenus, (R)ex (J)udaeorum — Jesus of Nazareth, King of the Jews.

Insemination, Artificial: The implanting of human semen by some means other than consummation of natural marital intercourse. In view of the principle that procreation should result only from marital intercourse, donor insemination is not permissible. The use of legitimate artificial means to further the fruitfulness of marital intercourse is permissible.

In Sin: The condition of a person called spiritually dead because he does not possess sanctifying grace, the principle of supernatural life, action and merit. Such grace can be regained through repentance.

Instruction: A document containing doctrinal explanations, directive norms, rules, recommendations, admonitions, issued by the pope, a department of the Roman Curia or other competent authority in the Church. To the extent that they so prescribe, instructions have the force of law.

Intercommunion: The common celebration and reception of the Eucharist by members of different Christian churches; a pivotal issue in ecumenical theory and practice. Catholic participation and intercommunion in the Eucharistic liturgy of another church without a valid priesthood and with a variant Eucharistic belief is out of order. Under certain conditions, other Christians may receive the Eucharist in the Catholic Church (see additional Intercommunion entry). Intercommunion is acceptable to some Protestant churches and unacceptable to others.

Interdict: An ecclesiastical penalty imposed on persons and places for certain violations of church law. If the interdict is personal, the interdicted persons may not take part in certain liturgical services, administer or receive certain sacraments. If the interdict is local, persons may not take part in certain liturgical services, administer or receive certain sacraments in the interdicted places.

Interdict is different from excommunication, and does not involve exclusion of a person from the community of the faithful.

Interregnum: The period of time between the death of a pope and the election of his successor. Another term applied to the period is *Sede vacante,* meaning the See (of Rome) being vacant.

The main concerns during an interregnum are matters connected with the death and burial of the pope, the election of his successor, and the maintenance of ordinary routine for the proper functioning of the Roman Curia and the Diocese of Rome.

Interregnum procedures follow norms contained in the apostolic constitution *Romano Pontifici Eligendo* (concerning the vacancy of the Apostolic See and the election of the Roman Pontiff) issued by Paul VI Oct. 1, 1975. This constitution superseded two others previously in force: *Vacantis Apostolicae Sedis,* issued by Pius XII Dec. 8, 1945, and *Summi Pontificis Electione,* issued by John XXIII Sept. 5, 1962.

"During the vacancy of the Apostolic See," the constitution states, "the government of the Church is entrusted to the Sacred College of Cardinals for the sole dispatch of ordinary business and of matters which cannot be postponed, and for the preparation of everything necessary for the election of the new pope."

The general congregation of the whole college, presided over by the dean, sub-dean or senior cardinal, has responsibility for major decisions during an interregnum. Other decisions of a routine nature are left to a particular congregation consisting of the chamberlain of the Holy Roman Church and three assistant cardinals.

The chamberlain of the Holy Roman Church and the dean of the college are the key officials, with directive responsibilities before and during the electoral conclave. The chamberlain is in general charge of ordinary administration. He — or the dean prior to a chamberlain's election by the cardinals — certifies the death of the pope; orders the destruction of the Fisherman's Ring and personal seals of the pope; and sets in motion procedures, carried out in collaboration with the dean, for informing the world about the pope's death, for funeral preparations, and for summoning and supervising the conclave for the election of a new pope.

Cardinals in charge of departments of the Roman Curia relinquish their offices at the death of the pope. Remaining in office, however, are the vicar of Rome, for ordinary jurisdiction over the diocese, and the major penitentiary. The substitute secretary of state or papal secretariat maintains the secretariat in a status quo. Papal representatives, such as nuncios and apostolic delegates, remain in office.

The congregations, offices and tribunals of the Curia retain ordinary jurisdiction for routine affairs but may not initiate new business during an interregnum.

If the pope should die during sessions of an ecumenical council or the Synod of Bishops, they would automatically be suspended.

The deceased pope is buried in St. Peter's Basilica, following prescribed ceremonies and traditional customs during a mourning period of nine days.

The conclave for the election of a new pope begins no sooner than 15 and no later than 20 days after the death of his predecessor. On the election of the new pope, the interregnum comes to an end. (See Papal Election.)

Intinction: A method of administering Holy Communion under the dual appearances of bread and wine, in which the consecrated host is dipped in the consecrated wine before being given to the communicant. The administering of Holy Communion in this manner, which has been traditional in Eastern-Rite liturgies, was authorized in the Roman Rite for various occasions by the *Constitution on the Sacred Liturgy* promulgated by the Second Vatican Council.

Irenicism: Peace-seeking, conciliation, as opposed to polemics; an important element in ecumenism, provided it furthers pursuit of the Christian unity willed by Christ without degenerating into a peace-at-any-price disregard for religious truth.

Irregularity: An impediment to the lawful reception or exercise of holy orders. The Church instituted irregularities — which include apostasy, heresy, homicide, attempted suicide — out of reverence for the dignity of the sacraments.

Itinerarium: Prayers for a spiritually profitable journey.

J

Jansenism: Opinions developed and proposed by Cornelius Jansenius (1585-1638). He held that: human nature was radically and intrinsically corrupted by original sin; some men are predestined to heaven and others to hell; Christ died only for those predestined to heaven; for those who are predestined, the operations of grace are irresistible. Jansenism also advocated an extremely rigorous code of morals and asceticism. The errors were proscribed by Urban VIII in 1642, by Innocent X in 1653, by Clement XI in 1713, and by other popes. Despite these condemnations, the rigoristic spirit of Jansenism lingered for a long time afterwards, particularly in France.

Jehovah's Witnesses: The Witnesses, together with the Watchtower and Bible Tract Society, trace their beginnings to a Bible class organized by Charles Taze Russell in 1872 at Allegheny, Pa. They take their name from a passage in Isaiah (43:12): " 'You are my witnesses,' says Jehovah." They are generally fundamentalist and revivalist with respect to the Bible, and believe that Christ is God's Son but is inferior to God. They place great emphasis on the Battle of Armageddon (as a decisive confrontation of good and evil) that is depicted vividly in Revelation, believing that God will then destroy the existing system of things and that, with the establishment of Jehovah's Kingdom, a small band of 144,000 spiritual sons of God will go to heaven, rule with Christ, and share in some way their happiness with some others.

Each Witness is considered by the society to be an ordained minister charged with the duty of spreading the message of Jehovah, which is accomplished through publications, house-to-house visitations, and other methods. The Witnesses refuse to salute the flag of any nation, regarding this as a form of idolatry, or to sanction blood transfusions even for the saving of life. There are approximately one million Witnesses in more than 22,000 congregations in some 80 countries. The freedom and activities of Witnesses are restricted in some places.

Jesus: The name of Jesus, meaning Savior in Christian usage, derived from the Aramaic and Hebrew *Yeshua* and *Joshua,* meaning *Yahweh* is salvation.

Jesus Prayer: A form of prayer dating back to the fifth century, "Lord Jesus Christ, Son of God, have mercy on me (a sinner)."

Joys of the Blessed Virgin Mary, Seven: (See Franciscan Crown.)

Judgment: (1) Last or final judgment: Final judgment by Christ, at the end of the world and the general resurrection.

(2) Particular judgment: The judgment that takes place immediately after a person's death, followed by entrance into heaven, hell or purgatory.

Jurisdiction: Right, power, authority to rule. Jurisdiction in the Church is of divine institution; has pastoral service for its purpose; includes legislative, judicial and executive authority; can be exercised only by persons with the power of orders.

(1) Ordinary jurisdiction is attached to ecclesiastical offices by law; the officeholders, called ordinaries, have authority over those who are subject to them.

(2) Delegated jurisdiction is that which is granted to persons rather than attached to offices. Its extent depends on the terms of the delegation.

Justice: One of the four cardinal virtues by which a person gives to others what is due to them as a matter of right. (See Cardinal Virtues.)

Justification: The act by which God makes a person just, and the consequent change in the spiritual status of a person, from sin to grace; the remission of sin and the infusion of sanctifying grace through the merits of Christ and the action of the Holy Spirit.

K

Kerygma: Proclaiming the word of God, in the manner of the Apostles, as here and now effective for salvation. This method of preaching or instruction, centered on Christ and geared to the facts and themes of salvation history, is designed to dispose people to faith in Christ and/or to intensify the experience and practice of that faith in those who have it.

Keys, Power of the: Spiritual authority and jurisdiction in the Church, symbolized by the keys of the kingdom of heaven. Christ promised the keys to St. Peter, as head-to-be of the Church (Mt. 16:19), and commissioned him with full pastoral responsibility to feed his lambs and sheep (Jn. 21:15-17). The pope, as the successor of St. Peter, has this power in a primary and supreme manner. The bishops of the Church also have the power, in union with and subordinate to the pope. Priests share in it through holy orders and the delegation of authority.

Examples of the application of the Power of the Keys are the exercise of teaching and pastoral authority by the pope and bishops, the absolving of sins in the sacrament of penance, the granting of indulgences, the imposing of spiritual penalties on persons who commit certain serious sins.

L

Laicization: (1) The process by which a man ordained to holy orders is relieved of the obligations of orders and the ministry and is returned to the status of a lay person. Applications by diocesan clergy are filed with their bishop and forwarded for processing to the congregation of the Roman Curia authorized to grant the indult of laicization.

(2) The process by which a religious is relieved of the obligations of vows and membership in his or her institute. Applications are filed with the proper religious superior and forwarded for processing to the Congregation for Religious which is authorized to grant the appropriate indult.

Languages of the Church: The first language in church use, for divine worship and the conduct of ecclesiastical affairs, was Aramaic, the language of the first Christians in and around Jerusalem. As the Church spread westward, Greek was adopted and prevailed until the third century when it was supplanted by Latin for official use in the West.

According to traditions established very early in churches of the Eastern Rites, many different languages were adopted for use in divine worship and for the conduct of ecclesiastical affairs. The practice was, and still is, to use the vernacular or a language closely related to the common tongue of the people.

In the Western Church, Latin prevailed as the general official language until the promulgation on Dec. 4, 1963, of the *Constitution on the Sacred Liturgy* by the second session of the Second Vatican Council. Since that time, vernacular languages have come into use in the Mass, administration of the sacraments, and the Liturgy of the Hours. The change was introduced in order to make the prayers and ceremonies of divine worship more informative and meaningful to all. Latin, however, remains the official language for administrative and procedural matters.

Law: An ordinance or rule governing the activity of things.

(1) Natural law: Moral norms corresponding to man's nature by which he orders his conduct toward God, neighbor, society and himself. This law, which is rooted in human nature, is of divine origin, can be known by the use of reason, and binds all men having the use of reason. The Ten Commandments are declarations and amplifications of natural law. The primary precepts of natural law, to do good and to avoid evil, are universally recognized, despite differences with respect to understanding and application resulting from different philosophies of good and evil.

(2) Divine positive law: That which has been revealed by God. Among its essentials are the twin precepts of love of God and love of neighbor, and the Ten Commandments.

(3) Ecclesiastical law: That which is established by the Church for the spiritual welfare of the faithful and the orderly conduct of ecclesiastical affairs. (See Canon Law.)

(4) Civil law: That which is established by a socio-political community for the common good.

Lector: A reader of scriptural passages and other selections at Mass and other services of worship.

Legitimation: Removal of the status of illegitimacy; e.g., by marriage of the parents.

Liberalism: A multiphased trend of thought and movement favoring liberty, independence and progress in moral, intellectual, religious, social, economic and political life. Traceable to the Renaissance, it developed through the Enlightenment, the rationalism of the 19th century, and modernist- and existentialist-related theories of the 20th century. Evaluations of various kinds of liberalism depend on the validity of their underlying principles. Extremist positions — regarding subjectivism, libertinarianism, naturalist denials of the supernatural, and the alienation of individuals and society from God and the Church were condemned by Gregory XVI in the 1830's, Pius IX in 1864, Leo XIII in 1899, and St. Pius X in 1907. There is, however, nothing objectionable about forms of libera-

lism patterned according to sound principles of Christian doctrine.

Life in Outer Space: Whether rational life exists on other bodies in the universe besides earth, is a question for scientific investigation to settle. The possibility can be granted, without prejudice to the body of revealed truth.

Limbo: The limbo of the fathers was the state of rest and natural happiness after death enjoyed by the just of pre-Christian times until they were admitted to heaven following the Ascension of Christ. Belief in this matter is stated in the Apostles' Creed. The existence of a limbo for unbaptized persons of infant status — a state of rest and natural happiness — has never been formally defined.

Litany: A prayer in the form of responsive petition; e.g., St. Joseph, pray for us, etc. There are seven litanies approved for liturgical use: Litanies of Loreto (Litany of the Blessed Mother), the Holy Name, All Saints, the Sacred Heart, the Precious Blood, St. Joseph, Litany for the Dying. Others may be used privately.

Little Office of the Blessed Virgin Mary: A shortened version of a Liturgy of the Hours honoring the Blessed Virgin. It dates from about the middle of the eighth century.

Liturgical Languages: (See Languages of the Church.)

Loreto, House of: A Marian shrine in Loreto, Italy, consisting of the home of the Holy Family which, according to an old tradition, was transported in a miraculous manner from Nazareth to Dalmatia and finally to Loreto between 1291 and 1294. Investigations conducted shortly after the appearance of the structure in Loreto revealed that its dimensions matched those of the house of the Holy Family missing from its place of enshrinement in a basilica at Nazareth. Among the many popes who regarded it with high honor was John XXIII, who went there on pilgrimage Oct. 4, 1962. The house of the Holy Family is enshrined in the Basilica of Our Lady.

Lust: A disorderly desire for sexual pleasure; one of the seven capital sins.

M

Magi: In the Infancy Narrative of St. Matthew's Gospel (2:1-12), three wise men from the East whose visit and homage to the Child Jesus at Bethlehem indicated Christ's manifestation of himself to non-Jewish people. The narrative teaches the universality of salvation. The traditional names of the Magi are Caspar, Melchior and Balthasar.

Magnificat: The canticle or hymn of the Virgin Mary on the occasion of her visitation to her cousin Elizabeth (Lk. 1:46-55). It is an expression of praise, thanksgiving and acknowledgment of the great blessings given by God to Mary, the Mother of the Second Person of the Blessed Trinity made Man. The Magnificat is recited in the Liturgy of the

Hours as part of the Evening Prayer.

Martyr: A Greek word, meaning witness, denoting one who voluntarily suffered death for the faith or some Christian virtue.

Martyrology: A catalogue of martyrs and other saints, arranged according to the calendar. The *Roman Martyrology* contains the official list of saints venerated by the Church. Additions to the list are made in beatification and canonization decrees of the Congregation for the Causes of Saints. The Martyrology is being revised to conform with other liturgical books.

Mass for the People: On Sundays and certain feasts throughout the year pastors are required to offer Mass for the faithful committed to their care. If they cannot offer the Mass on these days, they must do so at a later date or provide that another priest offer the Mass.

Master of Novices: The person in charge of the training and formation of candidates for a religious institute during novitiate.

Materialism: Theory which holds that matter is the only reality, and everything in existence is merely a manifestation of matter; there is no such thing as spirit, and the supernatural does not exist. Materialism is incompatible with Christian doctrine.

Meditation: Mental, as distinguished from vocal, prayer, in which thought, affections, and resolutions of the will predominate. There is a meditative element to all forms of prayer, which always involves the raising of the heart and mind to God.

Mendicants: A term derived from Latin and meaning beggars, applied to members of religious orders without property rights; the members, accordingly, worked or begged for their support. The original mendicants were Franciscans and Dominicans in the early 13th century; later, the Carmelites, Augustinians, Servites and others were given the mendicant title and privileges, with respect to exemption from episcopal jurisdiction and wide faculties for preaching and administering the sacrament of penance. The practice of begging is limited at the present time, although it is still allowed with the permission of competent superiors and bishops. Mendicants are supported by free will offerings and income received for spiritual services and other work.

Mercy, Divine: The love and goodness of God, manifested particularly in a time of need.

Merit: In religion, the right to a supernatural reward for good works freely done for a supernatural motive by a person in the state of and with the assistance of grace. The right to such reward is from God, who binds himself to give it. Accordingly, good works, as described above, are meritorious for salvation.

Metempsychosis: Theory of the passage or migration of the human soul after death from one body to another for the purpose of purification from guilt. The theory denies the unity of the soul and human personality, and the doctrine of individual moral responsibility.

Millennium: A thousand-year reign of Christ and the just upon earth before the end of the world. This belief of the Millenarians, Chiliasts, and some sects of modern times is based on an erroneous interpretation of Rv. 20.

Miracles: Observable events or effects in the physical or moral order of things, with reference to salvation, which cannot be explained by the ordinary operation of laws of nature and which, therefore, are attributed to the direct action of God. They make known, in an unusual way, the concern and intervention of God in human affairs for the salvation of men. The most striking examples are the miracles worked by Christ. Numbering about 35, they included his own Resurrection; the raising of three persons to life (Lazarus, the daughter of Jairus, the son of the widow of Naim); the healing of blind, leprous and other persons; nature miracles; and prophecies, or miracles of the intellectual order.

The foregoing notion of miracles, which is based on the concept of a fixed order of nature, was not known by the writers of Sacred Scripture. In the Old Testament, particularly, they called some things miraculous which, according to the definition in contemporary use, may or may not have been miracles. Essentially, however, the occurrences so designated were regarded as exceptional manifestations of God's care and concern for the salvation of his people. The miracles of Christ were miracles in the full sense of the term.

The Church believes it is reasonable to accept miracles as manifestations of divine power for purposes of salvation. God, who created the laws of nature, is their master; hence, without disturbing the ordinary course of things, he can — and has in the course of history before and after Christ — occasionally set aside these laws and has also produced effects beyond their power of operation. The Church does not call miraculous anything which does not admit of easy explanation; on the contrary, miracles are admitted only when the events have a bearing on the order of grace and every possible natural explanation has been tried and found wanting.

(The transubstantiation — i.e., the conversion of the whole substance of bread and wine, their sensible appearances alone remaining, into the Body and Blood of Christ in the act of Consecration at Mass — is not an observable event. Traditionally, however, it has been called a miracle.)

Missal: A liturgical book of Roman Rite also called the *Sacramentary*, containing the celebrant's prayers of the Mass, along with general instructions and ceremonial directives. The Latin text of the new *Roman Missal*, replacing the one authorized by the Council of Trent in the 16th century, was published by the Vatican Polyglot Press in 1970. Its use in English was made mandatory in the U.S. from Dec. 1, 1974. Readings and scriptural responsories formerly in the missal are contained in the *Lectionary*.

Missiology: Study of the missionary nature, constitution and activity of the Church in all aspects: theological reasons for missionary activity, laws and instructions of the Holy See, history of the missions, social and cultural background, methods, norms for carrying on missionary work.

Mission: (1) Strictly, it means being sent to perform a certain work, such as the mission of Christ to redeem mankind, the mission of the Apostles and the Church and its members to perpetuate the prophetic, priestly and royal mission of Christ.

(2) A place where: the Gospel has not been proclaimed; the Church has not been firmly established; the Church, although established, is weak.

(3) An ecclesiastical territory with the simplest kind of canonical organization, under the jurisdiction of the Congregation for the Evangelization of Peoples.

(4) A church or chapel without a resident priest.

(5) A special course of sermons and spiritual exercises conducted in parishes for the purpose of renewing and deepening the spiritual life of the faithful and for the conversion of lapsed Catholics.

Modernism: The "synthesis of all heresies," which appeared near the beginning of the 20th century. It undermines the objective validity of religious beliefs and practices which, it contends, are products of the subconscious developed by mankind under the stimulus of a religious sense. It holds that the existence of a personal God cannot be demonstrated, the Bible is not inspired, Christ is not divine, nor did he establish the Church or institute the sacraments. A special danger lies in modernism, which is still influential, because it uses Catholic terms with perverted meanings. St. Pius X condemned 65 propositions of modernism in 1907 in the decree *Lamentabili* and issued the encyclical *Pascendi* to explain and analyze its errors.

Monastery: The dwelling place, as well as the community thereof, of monks belonging to the Benedictine and Benedictine-related orders like the Cistercians and Carthusians; also, the Augustinians and Canons Regular. Distinctive of monasteries are: their separation from the world; the papal enclosure or strict cloister; the permanence or stability of attachment characteristic of their members; autonomous government in accordance with a monastic rule, like that of St. Benedict in the West or of St. Basil in the East; the special dedication of its members to the community celebration of the liturgy as well as to work that is suitable to the surrounding area and the needs of its people. Monastic superiors of men have such titles as abbot and prior; of women, abbess and prioress. In most essentials, an abbey is the same as a monastery.

Monk: A member of a monastic order — e.g., the Benedictines, the Benedictine-related Cistercians and Carthusians, and the Basilians, who bind themselves by religious profession to stable attachment to a monastery, the contemplative life and the work of their community. In popular use, the title is wrongly applied to many men religious who really are not monks.

Monotheism: Belief in and worship of one God.

Morality: Conformity or difformity of behavior to standards of right conduct. (See Commandments of God, Precepts of the Church, Conscience, Law.)

Mormons: Members of the Church of Jesus Christ of Latter-Day Saints. The church was established by Joseph Smith (1805-1844) at Fayette, N.Y., three years after he said he had received from an angel golden tablets containing the *Book of the Prophet Mormon.* This book, the Bible, *Doctrine and Covenants,* and *The Pearl of Great Price,* are the basic doctrinal texts of the church. Characteristic of the Mormons are strong belief in the revelations of their leaders, among whom was Brigham Young; a strong community of religious-secular concern; a dual secular and spiritual priesthood, and vigorous missionary activity. The headquarters of the church are located at Salt Lake City, Utah, where the Mormons first settled in 1847.

Mortification: Acts of self-discipline, including prayer, hardship, austerities and penances undertaken for the sake of progress in virtue.

Motu Proprio: A Latin phrase designating a document issued by a pope on his own initiative. Documents of this kind often concern administrative matters.

Mysteries of Faith: Supernatural truths whose existence cannot be known without revelation by God and whose intrinsic truth, while not contrary to reason, can never be wholly understood even after revelation. These mysteries are above reason, not against reason. Among them are the divine mysteries of the Trinity, Incarnation and Eucharist.

Some mysteries — e.g., concerning God's attributes — can be known by reason without revelation, although they cannot be fully understood.

N

Necromancy: Supposed communication with the dead; a form of divination.

Non-Expedit: A Latin expression. It is not expedient (fitting, proper), used to state a prohibition or refusal of permission.

Novena: A term designating public or private devotional practices over a period of nine consecutive days; or, by extension, over a period of nine weeks, in which one day a week is set aside for the devotions.

Novice: A person preparing, in a formal period of trial and formation called the *novitiate*, for membership in a religious institute. The novitiate lasts more than a year and ends with the profession of temporary vows or other temporary commitment to the religious life. Current norms require a total 12-month period of seclusion for novices; to this is added other periods of time spent in apostolic work for the sake of experience. A novice, while acquiring experience of the religious life, is not bound by the obligations of professed members of the institute, is free to leave at any time, and may be discharged at the discretion of competent superiors. The immediate superior of a novice is a master or mistress of novices.

Nun (1) Strictly, a member of a religious order of women with solemn vows (moniales).

(2) In general, all women religious, even those in simple vows who are more properly called sisters.

Nunc Dimittis: The canticle or hymn of Simeon at the sight of Jesus at the Temple on the occasion of his presentation (Lk. 2:29-32). It is an expression of joy and thanksgiving for the blessing of having lived to see the Messiah. It is one of the canticles prescribed in the Liturgy of the Hours.

O

Oath: Calling upon God to witness the truth of a statement. Violating an oath, e.g., by perjury in court, or taking an oath without sufficient reason, is a violation of the honor due to God.

Obedience: Submission to one in authority. General obligations of obedience fall under the Fourth Commandment. The vow of obedience professed by religious is one of the evangelical counsels.

Obsession, Diabolical: The extraordinary state of one who is seriously molested by evil spirits in an external manner. Obsession is more than just temptation.

Occultism: Practices involving ceremonies, rituals, chants, incantations, other cult-related activities intended to affect the course of nature, the lives of practitioners and others, through esoteric powers of magic, diabolical or other forces; one of many forms of superstition.

Octave: A period of eight days given over to the celebration of a major feast such as Easter.

Oils, Holy: The oils consecrated by bishops on Holy Thursday or another suitable day, and by priests under certain conditions for use in certain sacraments and consecrations.

(1) The oil of catechumens (olive or vegetable oil), used at baptism and the ordination of priests.

(2) Chrism (olive or vegetable oil mixed with balm), used at baptism, in confirmation, at the ordination of a bishop, in the consecration of churches, altars, altarstones, chalices, patens, and in the blessing of bells.

(3) Oil of the sick (olive or vegetable oil) used in anointing the sick.

Old Catholics — Several sects, including: (1) the Church of Utrecht, which severed relations with Rome in 1724; (2) the National Polish Church in the U.S., which had its origin near the end of the 19th century; (3) German, Austrian and Swiss Old Catholics, who broke away from union with Rome following the First Vatican Council in 1870 because they objected to the dogma of papal infallibility.

The formation of the Old Catholic communion of Germans, Austrians and Swiss began in 1870 at a public meeting held in Nuremberg under the leadership of A. Dollinger. Four years later episcopal succession was established with the ordination of an Old Catholic German bishop by a prelate of the Church of Utrecht. In line with the "Declaration of Utrecht" of 1889, they accept the first seven ecumenical councils and doctrine formulated before 1054, but reject communion with the pope and a number of other Catholic doctrines and practices. They have a valid priesthood and valid sacraments. *The Oxford Dictionary of the Christian Church* notes that they have recognized Anglican ordinations since 1925, that they have had full communion with the Church of England since 1932, and that their bishops, using their own formula, have taken part in the ordination of Anglican bishops.

This communion does not recognize the "Old Catholic" status of several smaller sects calling themselves such. In turn, connection with it is disavowed by the Old Roman Catholic Church headquartered in Chicago, which contends that it has abandoned the traditions of the Church of Utrecht.

The United States is the only English-speaking country with Old Catholic communities.

Oratory: A chapel.

Ordinariate: An ecclesiastical jurisdiction for special purposes and people. Examples are the military ordinariate of the US, for service personnel, and Eastern-Rite ordinariates in places where Eastern-Rite dioceses do not exist.

Ordinary: One who has the jurisdiction of an office: the pope, diocesan bishops, vicars general, prelates of missionary territories, vicars apostolic, prefects apostolic, vicars capitular during the vacancy of a see, superiors general, abbots primate and other major superiors of men religious.

Ordination: The consecration of sacred ministers for divine worship and the service of men in things pertaining to God. The power of ordination comes from Christ and the Church, and must be conferred by a minister capable of communicating it.

Organ Transplants: The transplanting of organs from one person to another is permissible for serious reasons provided it is done with the consent of the concerned parties and does not result in the death or essential mutilation of the donor. Advances in methods and technology have increased the range of transplant possibilities in recent years. Despite such progress, unresolved problems have slowed the pace of some transplant practice, especially with respect to the heart. The first successful heart transplant was performed Dec. 3, 1967, on Louis Washkansky, 56, by a team headed by Dr. Christian Barnard in Cape Town, South Africa.

Original Sin: The sin of Adam (Gn. 2:8—3:24), personal to him and passed on to all men as a state of privation of grace. Despite this privation and the related wounding of human nature and weakening of natural powers, original sin leaves unchanged all that man himself is by nature. The scriptural basis of the doctrine was stated especially by St. Paul in 1 Cor. 15:21, ff., and Romans 5:12-21. Original sin is remitted by baptism and incorporation in Christ, through whom grace is given to persons.

O Salutaris Hostia: The first three Latin words, O Saving Victim, of a Benediction hymn.

Ostpolitik: Policy adopted by Pope Paul VI in an attempt to improve the situation of Eastern European Catholics through diplomatic negotiations with their governments.

Oxford Movement: A movement in the Church of England from 1833 to about 1845 which had for its objective a threefold defense of the church as a divine institution, the apostolic succession of its bishops, and the Book of Common Prayer as the rule of faith. The movement took its name from Oxford University and involved a number of intellectuals who authored a series of influential *Tracts for Our Times.* Some of its leading figures — e.g., F. W. Faber, John Henry Newman and Henry Edward Manning — became converts to the Catholic Church. In the Church of England, the movement affected the liturgy, historical and theological scholarship, the status of the ministry, and other areas of ecclesiastical life.

P

Paganism: A term referring to non-revealed religions, i.e., religions other than Christianity, Judaism and Mohammedanism.

Palms: Blessed palms are a sacramental. They are blessed and distributed on the Sunday of the Passion in commemoration of the triumphant entrance of Christ into Jerusalem. Ashes of the burnt palms are used on Ash Wednesday.

Pange Lingua: First Latin words, Sing, my tongue, of a hymn in honor of the Holy Eucharist, used particularly on Holy Thursday and in Eucharistic processions.

Pantheism: Theory that all things are part of God, divine, in the sense that God realizes himself as the ultimate reality of matter or spirit through being and/or becoming all things that have been, are, and will be. The theory leads to hopeless confusion of the Creator and the created realm of being, identifies evil with good, and involves many inherent contradictions.

Papal Election: The pope is elected by members of the College of Cardinals in a secret conclave or meeting convened ordinarily in secluded quarters of the Vatican Palace between 15 and 20 days after the death of his predecessor. Cardinals under the age of 80, totaling no more than 120, are eligible to participate in a papal election.

Following are some of the principal regulations decreed by Paul VI Oct. 1, 1975, in the apostolic constitution *Romano Pontifici Eligendo* (concerning the vacancy of the Apostolic See and the election of the Roman Pontiff).

The ordinary manner of election is by scrutiny, with two votes each morning and afternoon in the Sistine Chapel until one of the candidates receives a two-thirds plus one vote majority.

Alternative methods, which can be adopted by unanimous agreement of the cardinals in difficult cases, are provided for: (1) by delegation, in which the cardinals designate a limited number (nine to 15) to make the choice; (2) by changing the majority rule from two-thirds plus one vote to an absolute majority plus one; (3) by limiting final choice, if the procedure in force becomes protracted, to one between the two candidates who received the largest numbers of votes, but not a required majority, in the most recent balloting.

An unusual manner of election is by acclamation or inspiration — that is, by spontaneous, unanimous choice without any need for normal voting procedure.

The elected candidate is asked by the dean of the college if he accepts the election. If he does so and is already a bishop, he immediately becomes the bishop of Rome and pope, and signifies the name by which he will be called. The cardinals then pledge their obedience to him before the senior cardinal deacon proclaims his election to the world from the main balcony of the Vatican and the new pope imparts his blessing *Urbi et Orbi.* If the candidate is not a bishop, he is so ordained before receiving the pledge of obedience and being proclaimed pope. The subsequent coronation of the pope is a ceremonial recognition of the fact of his election.

The pope is elected for life. If one should resign, a new pope would be elected in accordance with the foregoing regulations.

Rigid rules govern the conclave — its personnel, freedom from internal and external influence and interference, absolute secrecy (with a ban on recording devices and a prohibition against any disclosures).

Ordinarily, the first indication that a new pope has been elected is a plume of white smoke rising from the Vatican on burning of the last ballots.

(See College of Cardinals, Interregnum.)

Early methods of electing a pope — with various degrees of participation by the clergy and people of Rome and others — were set aside by Pope Nicholas II, who decreed in 1059 that cardinal bishops would be the electors. Further modification of the process was decreed by the Lateran Council in 1179 (that election would take place by a two-thirds majority vote of the cardinals) and by Pope Gregory X in 1274 (regarding a secluded conclave arrangement for elections).

Paraclete: A title of the Holy Spirit meaning, in Greek, Advocate, Consoler.

Parental Duties: All duties related to the obligation of parents to provide for the welfare of their children. These obligations fall under the Fourth Commandment.

Parish: A community of the faithful served by a pastor charged with responsibility for providing them with full pastoral service. Most parishes are territorial, embracing all of the faithful in a certain area of a diocese: some are personal or national, for certain classes of people, without strict regard for their places of residence.

Parousia: The coming, or saving presence, of Christ which will mark the completion of salvation history and the coming to perfection of God's kingdom at the end of the world.

Paschal Candle: A large candle, symbolic of the risen Christ, blessed and lighted on the Easter Vigil and placed at the Gospel side of the altar until Ascension Day. It is ornamented with five large grains of incense, representing the wounds of Christ, inserted in the form of a cross; the Greek letters Alpha and Omega, symbolizing Christ the beginning and end of all things, at the top and bottom of the shaft of the cross; and the figures of the current year of salvation in the quadrants formed by the cross.

Paschal Precept: The church law requiring the faithful to receive Holy Communion during the Easter time.

Passion of Christ: Sufferings of Christ, recorded in the four Gospels.

Pastor: An ordained minister charged with responsibility for the doctrinal, sacramental and related service of people committed to his care; e.g., a bishop for the people in his diocese, a priest for the people of his parish.

Pater Noster: The initial Latin words, Our Father, of the Lord's Prayer.

Peace, Sign of: A gesture of greeting — e.g., a handshake — exchanged by the ministers and participants at Mass.

Pectoral Cross: A cross worn on a chain about the neck and over the breast by bishops and abbots as a mark of their office.

Penance or Penitence: (1) The spiritual change or conversion of mind and heart by which a person turns away from sin, and all that it implies, toward God, through a personal renewal under the influence of the Holy Spirit. In the apostolic constitution *Paenitemini*, Pope Paul VI called it "a religious, personal act which has as its aim love and surrender to God." Penance involves sorrow and contrition for sin, together with other internal and external acts of atonement. It serves the purposes of reestablishing in one's life the order of God's love and commandments, and of making satisfaction to God for sin. A divine precept states the necessity of penance for salvation: "Unless you do penance, you shall all likewise perish" (Lk. 13:3) . . . "Be converted and believe in the Gospel" (Mk. 1:15).

In the penitential discipline of the Church, the various works of penance have been classified under the headings of prayer (interior), fasting and almsgiving (exterior). The Church has established minimum requirements for the common and social observance of the divine precept by Catholics — e.g., by requiring them to fast and/or abstain on certain days of the year. These observances, however, do not exhaust all the demands of the divine precept, whose fulfillment is a matter of personal responsibility; nor do they have any real value unless they proceed from the internal spirit and purpose of penance.

Related to works of penance for sins actually committed are works of mortification. The purpose of the latter is to develop — through prayer, fasting, renunciations and similar actions — self-control and detachment from things which could otherwise become occasions of sin.

(2) Penance is a virtue disposing a person to turn to God in sorrow for sin and to carry out works of amendment and atonement.

(3) The sacrament of penance and sacramental penance.

Perjury: Taking a false oath, lying under oath, a violation of the honor due to God.

Persecution, Religious: A campaign waged against a church or other religious body by persons and governments intent on its destruction. The best known campaigns of this type against the Christian Church were the Roman persecutions which occurred intermittently from about 54 to the promulgation of the Edict of Milan in 313, The most extensive persecutions took place during the reigns of Nero, the first major Roman persecutor, Domitian, Trajan, Marcus Aurelius, and Diocletian. Besides the Roman persecutions, the Catholic Church has been subject to many others, including those of the 20th century in Communist-controlled countries.

Peter's Pence: A collection made each year among Catholics for the maintenance of the pope and his works of charity. It was originally a tax of a penny on each house, and was collected on St. Peter's day, whence the name. It originated in England in the eighth century.

Petition: One of the four purposes of prayer. In prayers of petition, persons ask of God the blessings they and others need.

Pharisees: Influential class among the Jews, referred to in the Gospels, noted for their self-righteousness, legalism, strict interpretation of the Law, acceptance of the traditions of the elders as well as the Law of Moses, and beliefs regarding angels and spirits, the resurrection of the dead and judgment. Most of them were laymen, and they were closely allied with the Scribes; their opposite numbers were the Sadducees. The Pharisaic and rabbinical traditions had a lasting influence on Judaism following the destruction of Jerusalem in 70 A.D.

Pious Fund: Property and money originally accumulated by the Jesuits to finance their missionary work in Lower California. When the Jesuits were expelled from the territory in 1767, the fund was appropriated by the Spanish Crown and used to support Dominican and Franciscan missionary work in Upper and Lower California. In 1842 the Mexican government took over administration of the fund, incorporated most of the revenue into the national treasury, and agreed to pay the Church interest of six per cent a year on the capital so incorporated. From 1848 to 1967 the fund was the subject of lengthy negotiations between the US and Mexican governments because of the latter's failure to make payments as agreed. A lump-sum settlement was made in 1967 with payment by Mexico to the US government of more than $700,000, to be turned over to the Archdiocese of San Francisco.

Polytheism: Belief in and worship of many gods or divinities, especially prevalent in pre-Christian religions.

Poor Box: Alms-box; found in churches from the earliest days of Christianity.

Pope Joan: Alleged name of a woman falsely said to have been pope from 855-858, the years of the reign of Benedict III. The myth was not heard of before the 13th century.

Portiuncula: (1) Meaning little portion (of land), the Portiuncula was the chapel of Our Lady of the Angels near Assisi, Italy, which the Benedictines gave to St. Francis early in the 13th century. He repaired the chapel and made it the first church of the Franciscan Order. It is now enshrined in the Basilica of St. Mary of the Angels in Assisi.

(2) The Portiuncula Indulgence, or Pardon of Assisi, was authorized by Honorius III. Originally, it could be gained for the souls in purgatory only in the chapel of Our Lady of the Angels; by later concessions, it could be gained also in other Franciscan and parish churches. According to legislation now in force, the Portiuncula Indulgence can be gained once on the day of Aug. 2, or on the following Sunday with permission of the bishop of the place. The conditions are, in addition to freedom from attachment to sin: reception of the sacraments of penance and the Eucharist on or near the day; a visit to a parish church on the day, during which the Our Father and Creed are offered for the intentions of the pope.

Possession, Diabolical: The extraordinary state of a person who is tormented from within by evil spirits who exercise strong influence over his powers of mind and body.

Postulant: One of several names used to designate a candidate for membership in a religious institute during the period before novitiate.

Poverty: (1) The quality or state of being poor, in actual destitution and need, or being poor in spirit. In the latter sense, poverty means the state of mind and disposition of persons who regard material things in proper perspective as gifts of God for the support of life and its reasonable enrichment, and for the service of others in need. It means freedom from unreasonable attachment to material things as ends in themselves, even though they may be possessed in small or large measure.

(2) One of the evangelical counsels professed by religious as a vow. It involves the voluntary renunciation of rights of ownership and of independent use and disposal of material goods (solemn vow); or, the right of independent use and disposal, but not of the radical right of ownership (simple vow). Religious institutes provide their members with necessary and useful goods and services from common resources. The manner in which goods are received and/or handled by religious is determined by poverty of spirit and the rule and constitutions of their institute. Practice of the vow of poverty is undergoing some change in the contemporary renewal in religious life.

Pragmatism: Theory that the truth of ideas, concepts and values depends on their utility or capacity to serve a useful purpose rather than on their conformity with objective standards; also called utilitarianism.

Prayer: The raising of the mind and heart to God in adoration, thanksgiving, reparation and petition. Prayer, which is always mental because it involves thought and love of God, may be vocal, meditative, private and personal, social, and official. The official prayer of the Church as a worshipping community is called the liturgy.

Precepts: Commands or orders given to individuals or communities in particular cases; they establish law for concerned parties. Preceptive documents are issued by the pope, departments of the Roman Curia and other competent authority in the Church.

Presence of God: A devotional practice of increasing one's awareness of the presence and action of God in daily life.

Presumption: A violation of the theological virtue of hope, by which a person striving for salvation either relies too much on his own capabilities or expects God to do things which he cannot do, in keeping with his divine attributes, or does not will to do, according to his divine plan. Presumption is the opposite of despair.

Preternatural Gifts: Exceptional gifts, beyond the exigencies and powers of human nature, enjoyed by Adam in the state of original justice: immunity from suffering and death, superior knowledge, integrity or perfect control of the passions. These gifts were lost as the result of original sin; their loss, however, implied no impairment of the integrity of human nature.

Pride: Unreasonable self-esteem; one of the seven capital sins.

Prie-Dieu: A French phrase, meaning pray God, designating a kneeler or bench suitable for kneeling while at prayer.

Priesthood of the Laity: Lay persons share in the priesthood of Christ in virtue of the sacraments of baptism and confirmation. They are not only joined with Christ for a life of union with him but are also deputed by him for participation in his mission, now carried on by the Church, of worship, teaching, witness and apostolic works. St. Peter called Christians "a royal priesthood" (1 Pt. 2:9) in this connection. St. Thomas Aquinas declared: "The sacramental characters (of baptism and confirmation) are nothing else than certain sharings of the priesthood of Christ, derived from Christ himself."

The priesthood of the laity differs from the official ministerial priesthood of ordained priests and bishops — who have the power of holy orders for celebrating the Eucharist, administering the other sacraments, and providing pastoral care. The ministerial priesthood, by divine commission, serves the universal priesthood. (See Role of Sacraments.)

Primary Option: The life-choice of a person for or against God which shapes the basic orientation of moral conduct.

Prior: A superior or an assistant to an abbot in a monastery.

Privilege: A favor, an exemption from the obligation of a law. Privileges of various kinds, with respect to ecclesiastical laws, are granted by the pope, departments of the Roman Curia and other competent authority in the Church.

Probabilism: A moral system for use in cases of conscience which involve the obligation of doubtful laws. There is a general principle that a doubtful law does not bind. Probabilism, therefore, teaches that it is permissible to follow an opinion favoring liberty, provided the opinion is certainly and solidly probable. Probabilism may not be invoked when there is question of: a certain law or the certain obligation of a law; the certain right of another party; the validity of an action; something which is necessary for salvation.

Pro-Cathedral: A church used as a cathedral.

Promoter of the Faith: An official of the Congregation for the Causes of Saints, whose role in beatification and canonization procedures is to establish beyond reasonable doubt the validity of evidence regarding the holiness of prospective saints and miracles attributed to their intercession.

Prophecies of St. Malachy: These so-called prophecies, listing the designations of 102 popes and 10 antipopes, bear the name they have because they have been falsely attributed to St. Malachy, bishop of Armagh, who died in 1148. Actually, they are forgeries by an unknown author and came to light only in the last decade of the 16th century.

The first 75 prophecies cover the 65 popes and 10 antipopes from Celestine II (1143-1144) to Gregory XIV (1590-91), and are exact with respect to names, coats of arms, birthplaces, and other identifying characteristics. This portion of the work, far from being prophetic, is the result of historical knowledge or hindsight. The 37 designations following that of Gregory are vague, fanciful, and subject to wide interpretation. According to the prophecies, John Paul II, from the Labor of the Sun, will have only two successors before the end of the world.

Prophecy: (1) The communication of divine revelation by inspired intermediaries, called prophets, between God and his people. Old Testament prophecy was unique in its origin and because of its ethical and religious content, which included disclosure of the saving will of Yahweh for the people, moral censures of sin and violations of the Law and Covenant, in the form of promises, admonitions, reproaches and threats. Although Moses and other earlier figures are called prophets, the period of prophecy is generally dated from the early years of the monarchy to about 100 years after the Babylonian Exile. From that time on the written Law and its interpreters supplanted the prophets as guides of the people. Old Testament prophets are cited in the New Testament, with awareness that God spoke through them and that some of their oracles were fulfilled in Christ. John the Baptist is the outstanding prophetic figure in the New Testament. Christ never claimed the title of prophet for himself, although some people thought he was one. There were prophets in the early Church, and St. Paul mentioned the charism of prophecy in 1 Cor. 14:1-5. Prophecy disappeared after New Testament times. Revelation is classified as the prophetic book of the New Testament.

(2) In contemporary non-scriptural usage, the term is applied to the witness given by persons to the relevance of their beliefs in everyday life and action.

Province: (1) A territory comprising one archdiocese called the metropolitan see and one or more dioceses called suffragan sees. The head of the archdiocese, an archbishop, has metropolitan rights and responsibilities over the province.

(2) A division of a religious order under the jurisdiction of a provincial superior.

Prudence: Practical wisdom and judgment regarding the choice and use of the best ways and means of doing good; one of the four cardinal virtues.

Punishment Due for Sin: The punishment which is a consequence of sin. It is of two kinds:

(1) Eternal punishment is the punishment of hell, to which one becomes subject by the commission of mortal sin. Such punishment is remitted when mortal sin is forgiven.

(2) Temporal punishment is a consequence of venial sin and/or forgiven mortal sin; it is not everlasting and may be remitted in this life by means of penance. Temporal punishment unremitted during this life is remitted by suffering in purgatory.

Purgatory: The state or condition in which those who have died in the state of grace, but with some attachment to sin, suffer for a time before they are admitted to the glory and happiness of heaven. In this state and period of passive suffering, they are purified of unrepented venial sins, satisfy the demands of divine justice for temporal punishment due for sins, and are thus converted to a state of worthiness of the beatific vision.

R

Racism: A theory which holds that any one or several of the different races of the human family are inherently superior or inferior to any one or several of the others. The teaching denies the essential unity of the human race, the equality and dignity of all men because of their common possession of the same human nature, and the participation of all men in the divine plan of redemption. It is radically opposed to the virtue of justice and the precept of love of neighbor. Differences of superiority and inferiority which do exist are the result of accidental factors operating in a wide variety of circumstances, and are in no way due to essential defects in any one or several of the branches of the one human race. The theory of racism, together with practices related to it, is incompatible with Christian doctrine.

Rash Judgment: Attributing faults to another without sufficient reason; a violation of the obligations of justice and charity.

Rationalism: A theory which makes the mind the measure and arbiter of all things, including religious truth. A product of the Enlightenment, it rejects the supernatural, divine revelation, and authoritative teaching by any church.

Recollection: Meditation, attitude of concentration or awareness of spiritual matters and things pertaining to salvation and the accomplishment of God's will.

Relativism: Theory which holds that all truth, including religious truth, is relative, i.e., not absolute, certain or unchanging; a product of agnosticism, indifferentism, and an unwarranted extension of the notion of truth in positive science. Relativism is based on the tenet that certain knowledge of any and all truth is impossible. Therefore, no religion, philosophy or science can be said to possess the real truth; consequently, all religions, philosophies and sciences may be considered to have as much or as little of truth as any of the others.

Relics: The physical remains and effects of saints, which are considered worthy of veneration inasmuch as they are representative of persons in glory with God. First class relics are parts of the bodies of saints, and instruments of their penance and death; second class relics are objects which had some contact with their persons. Catholic doctrine proscribes the view that relics are not worthy of veneration. In line with norms laid down by the Council of Trent and subsequent enactments, discipline concerning relics is subject to control by the Congregation for the Causes of Saints.

Religion: The adoration and service of God as expressed in divine worship and in daily life. Religion is concerned with all of the relations existing between God and man, and between man and man because of the central significance of God. Objectively considered, religion consists of a body of truth which is believed, a code of morality for the guidance of conduct, and a form of divine worship. Subjectively, it is man's total response, theoretically and practically, to the demands of faith; it is living faith, personal engagement, self-commitment to God. Thus, by creed, code and cult, a person orders and directs his life in reference to God and, through what the love and service of God implies, to his fellow men and all things.

Reliquary: A vessel for the preservation and exposition of a relic; sometimes made like a small monstrance.

Reparation: The making of amends to God for sin committed; one of the four ends of prayer and the purpose of penance.

Rescript: A written reply by an ecclesiastical superior regarding a question or request; its provisions bind concerned parties only. Papal dispensations are issued in the form of rescripts.

Reserved Case: A sin or censure, absolution from which is reserved to religious superiors, bishops, the pope, or confessors having special faculties. Reservations are made because of the serious nature and social effects of certain sins and censures.

Restitution: An act of reparation for an injury done to another. The injury may be caused by taking and/or retaining what belongs to another or by damaging either the property or reputation of another. The intention of making restitution, usually in kind, is required as a condition for the forgiveness of sins of injustice, even though actual restitution is not possible.

Ring: In the Church a ring is worn as part of the insignia of bishops, abbots, et al.; by sisters to denote their consecration to God and the Church. The wedding ring symbolizes the love and union of husband and wife.

Ritual: A book of prayers and ceremonies used in the administration of the sacraments and other ceremonial functions. In the Roman Rite, the standard book of this kind is the Roman Ritual. Revisions have been made — e.g., in the rites of baptism — since the Second Vatican Council.

Rogito: The official notarial act or document testifying to the burial of a pope.

Rosary: A form of mental and vocal prayer centered on mysteries or events in the lives of Jesus and Mary. Its essential elements are meditation on the mysteries and the recitation of a number of decades of Hail Marys, each beginning with the Lord's Prayer. Introductory prayers may include the Apostles' Creed, an initial Our Father, three Hail Marys and a Glory be to the Father; each decade is customarily concluded with a Glory be to the Father; at the end, it is customary to say the Hail, Holy Queen and a prayer from the liturgy for the feast of the Blessed Virgin Mary of the Rosary.

The **Mysteries of the Rosary,** which are the subject of meditation, are: (1) Joyful — the Annunciation to Mary that she was to be the Mother of Christ, her visit to Elizabeth, the birth of Jesus, the presentation of Jesus in the Temple, the finding of Jesus in the Temple. (2) Sorrowful — Christ's agony in the Garden of Gethsemani, scourging at the pillar, crowning with thorns, carrying of the Cross to Calvary, and crucifixion. (3) Glorious — the Resurrection and Ascension of Christ, the descent of the Holy Spirit upon the Apostles, Mary's Assumption into heaven and her crowning as Queen of angels and men.

The complete Rosary, called the Dominican Rosary, consists of 15 decades. In customary practice, only five decades are usually said at one time. Rosary beads are used to aid in counting the prayers without distraction.

The Rosary originated through the coalescence of popular devotions to Jesus and Mary from the 12th century onward. Its present form dates from about the 15th century. Carthusians contributed greatly toward its development; Dominicans have been its greatest promoters.

S

Sabbath: The seventh day of the week, observed by Jews and Sabbatarians as the day for rest and religious observance.

Sacramentary: One of the first liturgical books, containing the celebrant's part of the Mass and rites for administration of the sacraments. The earliest book of this kind, the Leonine Sacramentary, dates from the middle or end of the sixth century.

The sacramentary, incorporating most of the contents of the *Roman Missal,* was reintroduced in the Roman Rite following the promulgation of the *Constitution on the Sacred Liturgy* by the Second Vatican Council.

Sacrarium: A basin with a drain leading directly into the ground; standard equipment of a sacristy.

Sacred Heart, Enthronement: An acknowledgment of the sovereignty of Jesus Christ over the Christian family, expressed by the installation of an image or picture of the Sacred Heart in a place of honor in the home, accompanied by an act of consecration.

Sacred Heart, Promises: Twelve promises to persons having devotion to the Sacred Heart of Jesus, which were communicated by Christ to St. Margaret Mary Alacoque in a private revelation in 1675: (1) I will give them all the graces necessary in their state in life. (2) I will establish peace in their homes. (3) I will comfort them in all their afflictions. (4) I will be their secure refuge during life and, above all, in death. (5) I will bestow abundant blessing upon all their undertakings. (6) Sinners shall find in my Heart the source and the infinite ocean of mercy. (7) By devotion to my Heart tepid souls shall grow fervent. (8) Fervent souls shall quickly mount to high perfection. (9) I will bless every place where a picture of my Heart shall be set up and honored. (10) I will give to priests the gift of touching the most hardened hearts. (11) Those who promote this devotion shall have their names written in my Heart, never to be blotted out. (12) I will grant the grace of final penitence to those who communicate (receive Holy Communion) on the first Friday of nine consecutive months.

Sacrilege: Violation of and irreverence toward a person, place or thing that is sacred because of public dedication to God; a sin against the virtue of religion. Personal sacrilege is violence of some kind against a cleric or religious, or a violation of chastity with a

cleric or religious. Local sacrilege is the dese-
cration of sacred places. Real sacrilege is irreverence with respect to sacred things, such
as the sacraments and sacred vessels.

Sacristy: A utility room where vestments,
church furnishings and sacred vessels are kept
and where the clergy vest for sacred functions.

Sadducees: The predominantly priestly
party among the Jews in the time of Christ,
noted for extreme conservatism, acceptance
only of the Law of Moses, and rejection of the
traditions of the elders. Their opposite
numbers were the Pharisees.

Saints, Cult of: The veneration, called
dulia, of holy persons who have died and are
in glory with God in heaven; it includes honoring them and petitioning them for their intercession with God. Liturgical veneration is
given only to saints officially recognized by
the Church; private veneration may be given
to anyone thought to be in heaven. The veneration of saints is essentially different from the
adoration given to God alone; by its very nature, however, it terminates in the worship of
God.

According to the Second Vatican Council's
Dogmatic Constitution on the Church (No.
50): "It is supremely fitting . . . that we love
those friends and fellow heirs of Jesus Christ,
who are also our brothers and extraordinary
benefactors, that we render due thanks to
God for them and 'suppliantly invoke them
and have recourse to their prayers, their
power and help in obtaining benefits from
God through His Son, Jesus Christ, our Lord,
who is our sole Redeemer and Savior.' For by
its very nature every genuine testimony of
love which we show to those in heaven tends
toward and terminates in Christ, who is the
'crown of all saints.' Through Him it tends
toward and terminates in God, who is wonderful in His saints and is magnified in them."

Salvation: The liberation of men from sin
and its effects, reconciliation with God in and
through Christ, the attainment of union with
God forever in the glory of heaven as the supreme purpose of life and as the God-given
reward for fulfillment of his will on earth. Sal-
vation-in-process begins and continues in this
life through union with Christ in faith professed and in action; its final term is union
with God and the whole community of the
saved in the ultimate perfection of God's
kingdom. The Church teaches that: God wills
the salvation of all men; men are saved in and
through Christ; membership in the Church
established by Christ, known and understood
as the community of salvation, is necessary
for salvation; men with this knowledge and
understanding who deliberately reject this
Church, cannot be saved. In the context of
Catholic belief, the Catholic Church is the
Church founded by Christ. (See below, Salvation outside the Church.)

Salvation History: The facts and the record
of God's relations with men, in the past,
present and future, for the purpose of leading
them to live in accordance with his will for the
eventual attainment after death of salvation,
or everlasting happiness with him in heaven.

The essentials of salvation history are:
God's love for all men and will for their salvation; his intervention and action in the world
to express this love and bring about their salvation; the revelation he made of himself and
the covenant he established with the Israelites
in the Old Testament; the perfecting of this
revelation and the new covenant of grace
through Christ in the New Testament; the
continuing action-for-salvation carried on in
and through the Mystical Body of Christ, the
Church; the communication of saving grace
to men through the merits of Christ and the
operations of the Holy Spirit in the here-and-
now circumstances of daily life and with the
cooperation of men themselves.

Salvation outside the Church: The Second
Vatican Council covered this subject summarily in the following manner: "Those also
can attain to everlasting salvation who
through no fault of their own do not know
the gospel of Christ or His Church, yet sincerely seek God and, moved by grace, strive
by their deeds to do His will as it is known to
them through the dictates of conscience. Nor
does divine Providence deny the help necessary for salvation to those who, without
blame on their part, have not yet arrived at an
explicit knowledge of God, but who strive to
live a good life, thanks to His grace. Whatever good or truth is found among them is
looked upon by the Church as a preparation
for the gospel. She regards such qualities as
given by Him who enlightens all men so that
they may finally have life" *(Dogmatic Constitution on the Church,* No. 16).

Satanism: Worship of the devil, a blasphe-
mous inversion of the order of worship which
is due to God alone.

Scandal: Conduct which is the occasion of
sin to another person.

Scapular: (1) A part of the habit of some
religious orders like the Benedictines and Dominicans; a nearly shoulder-wide strip of
cloth worn over the tunic and reaching almost
to the feet in front and behind. Originally a
kind of apron, it came to symbolize the cross
and yoke of Christ.

(2) Scapulars worn by lay persons as a sign
of association with religious orders and for
devotional purposes are an adaptation of monastic scapulars. Approved by the Church as
sacramentals, they consist of two small
squares of woolen cloth joined by strings and
are worn about the neck. They are given for
wearing in a ceremony of investiture or enrollment. There are nearly 20 scapulars for
devotional use: the five principal ones are
generally understood to include those of Our
Lady of Mt. Carmel (the brown Carmelite
Scapular), the Holy Trinity, Our Lady of the

Seven Dolors, the Passion, the Immaculate Conception.

Scapular Medal: A medallion with a representation of the Sacred Heart on one side and of the Blessed Virgin Mary on the other. Authorized by St. Pius X in 1910, it may be worn or carried in place of a scapular by persons already invested with a scapular.

Scapular Promise: According to a legend of the Carmelite Order, the Blessed Virgin Mary appeared to St. Simon Stock in 1251 at Cambridge and declared that wearers of the brown Carmelite Scapular would be saved from hell and taken to heaven by her on the first Saturday after death. The validity of the legend has never been the subject of official decision by the Church. Essentially, it expresses belief in the intercession of Mary and the efficacy of sacramentals in the context of truly Christian life.

Schism: Derived from a Greek word meaning separation, the term designates formal and obstinate refusal by a baptized person, called a *schismatic,* to be in communion with the pope and the Church. The canonical penalty is excommunication. One of the most disastrous schisms in history resulted in the definitive separation of the Church in the East from union with Rome about 1054.

Scholasticism: The term usually applied to the Catholic theology and philosophy which developed in the Middle Ages.

Scribes: Hebrew intellectuals noted for their knowledge of the Law of Moses, influential from the time of the Exile to about 70 A.D. Many of them were Pharisees. They were the antecedents of rabbis and their traditions, as well as those of the Pharisees, had a lasting influence on Judaism following the destruction of Jerusalem in 70 A.D.

Scruple: A morbid, unreasonable fear and anxiety that one's actions are sinful when they are not, or more seriously sinful than they actually are. Compulsive scrupulosity is quite different from the transient scrupulosity of persons of tender or highly sensitive conscience, or of persons with faulty moral judgment.

Seal of Confession: The obligation of secrecy which must be observed regarding knowledge of things learned in connection with the confession of sin in the sacrament of penance. The seal covers matters whose revelation would make the sacrament burdensome. Confessors are prohibited, under penalty of excommunication, from making any direct revelation of confessional matter; this prohibition holds, outside of confession, even with respect to the person who made the confession unless the person releases the priest from the obligation. Persons other than confessors are obliged to maintain secrecy, but not under penalty of excommunication. General, non-specific discussion of confessional matter does not violate the seal.

Secularism: A school of thought, a spirit and manner of action which ignores and/or repudiates the validity or influence of supernatural religion with respect to individual and social life. In describing secularism in their annual statement in 1947, the bishops of the United States said in part: ". . . There are many men — and their number is daily increasing — who in practice live their lives without recognizing that this is God's world. For the most part they do not deny God. On formal occasions they may even mention his name. Not all of them would subscribe to the statement that all moral values derive from merely human conventions. But they fail to bring an awareness of their responsibility to God into their thought and action as individuals and members of society. This, in essence, is what we mean by secularism."

See: Another name for diocese or archdiocese.

Seminary: A house of study and formation for men, called seminarians, preparing for the priesthood. Traditional seminaries date from the Council of Trent in the middle of the 16th century; before that time, candidates for the priesthood were variously trained in monastic schools, universities under church auspices, and in less formal ways. At the present time, seminaries are undergoing considerable change for the improvement of academic and formation programs and procedures.

Sermon on the Mount: A compilation of sayings of Our Lord in the form of an extended discourse in Matthew's Gospel (5:1 to 7:27) and, in a shorter discourse, in Luke (6:17-49). The passage in Matthew, called the "Constitution of the New Law," summarizes the living spirit of believers in Christ and members of the kingdom of God. Beginning with the Beatitudes and including the Lord's Prayer, it covers the perfect justice of the New Law, the fulfillment of the Old Law in the New Law of Christ, and the integrity of internal attitude and external conduct with respect to love of God and neighbor, justice, chastity, truth, trust and confidence in God.

Servile Work: Work that is mainly physical and done for the sake of material purposes, in distinction from so-called liberal and artistic work which, although involving physical effort, is of a mental and intellectual nature. Commonly classified as servile are such works as farming, manufacturing, commercial operations, mining, etc. Liberal works are those like studying, teaching, designing, writing, typing, etc. The classification of work as servile or otherwise depends in part on custom and cultural interpretation. The reception of pay for work has nothing to do with its classification. Servile work is prohibited on Sundays and holy days of obligation unless there is sound reason for it.

Seven Last Words of Christ: Words of Christ on the Cross. (1) "Father, forgive them; for they do not know what they are doing." (2) To the penitent thief: "I assure you: today you will be with me in Paradise." (3) To Mary and his Apostle John: "Woman, there is your son . . . There is your mother." (4) "My God, my God, why have you forsaken me?" (5) "I am thirsty." (6) "Now it is finished." (7) "Father, into your hands I commend my spirit."

Shrine, Crowned: A shrine approved by the Holy See as a place of pilgrimage. The approval permits public devotion at the shrine and implies that at least one miracle has resulted from devotion at the shrine. Among the best known crowned shrines are those of the Virgin Mary at Lourdes and Fatima.

Shroud of Turin: A strip of brownish linen cloth, 14 feet, three inches in length and three feet, seven inches in width, bearing the front and back imprint of a human body. A tradition dating from the seventh century, which has not been verified beyond doubt, claims that the shroud is the fine linen in which the body of Christ was wrapped for burial. The early history of the shroud is obscure. It was enshrined at Lirey, France, in 1354 and was transferred in 1578 to Turin, Italy, where it has been kept in the cathedral down to the present time. Scientific investigation, which began in 1898, seems to indicate that the markings on the shroud are those of a human body. The shroud, for the first time since 1933, was placed on public view from Aug. 27 to Oct. 8, 1978, and was seen by an estimated 3.3 million people. Scientists conducted intensive studies of it for several days after the end of public viewing.

Sick Calls: When a person is confined at home by illness or other cause and is unable to go to church for reception of the sacraments, a parish priest should be informed and arrangements made for him to visit the person at home. Such visitations are common in pastoral practice, both for special needs and for providing persons with regular opportunities for receiving the sacraments.

Prepared for the visit should be: a conveniently placed table covered with a white cloth; on it should be a crucifix, two lighted candles, a glass with water, a spoon and napkin.

The priest, carrying the Blessed Sacrament, should be escorted to and from the sick person by someone carrying a lighted candle. Members of the household should be present when the sick person receives Holy Communion and/or anointing of the sick.

Sign of the Cross: A sign, ceremonial gesture or movement in the form of a cross by which a person confesses faith in the Holy Trinity and Christ, and intercedes for the blessing of himself, other persons, and things. In Roman-Rite practice, a person making the sign touches the fingers of the right hand to his forehead, below the breast, left shoulder and right shoulder while saying: "In the name of the Father, and of the Son, and of the Holy Spirit." The sign is also made with the thumb on the forehead, the lips, and the breast. For the blessing of persons and objects, a large sign of the cross is made by movement of the right hand. In Eastern-Rite practice, the sign is made with the thumb and first two fingers of the right hand joined together and touching the forehead, below the breast, the right shoulder and the left shoulder; the formula generally used is the doxology, "O Holy God, O Holy Strong One, O Immortal One." The Eastern manner of making the sign was general until the first half of the 13th century; by the 17th century, Western practice involved the whole right hand and the reversal of direction from shoulder to shoulder.

Signs of the Times: Contemporary events, trends and features in culture and society, the needs and aspirations of people, all the factors that form the context in and through which the Church has to carry on its saving mission. The Second Vatican Council spoke on numerous occasions about these signs and the relationship between them and a kind of manifestation of God's will, positive or negative, and about subjecting them to judgment and action corresponding to the demands of divine revelation through Scripture, Christ, and the experience, tradition and teaching authority of the Church.

Simony: The deliberate intention and act of selling and/or buying spiritual goods or material things so connected with the spiritual that they cannot be separated therefrom; a violation of the virtue of religion, and a sacrilege, because it wrongfully puts a material price on spiritual things, which cannot be either sold or bought. In church law, actual sale or purchase is subject to censure in some cases. The term is derived from the name of Simon Magus, who attempted to buy from Sts. Peter and John the power to confirm people in the Holy Spirit (Acts 8:4-24).

Sin: (1) Actual sin is rejection of God manifested by free and deliberate violation of his law by thought, word or action. (a) Mortal sin — involving serious matter, sufficient reflection and full consent — results in total alienation from God, making a person dead to sanctifying grace, incapable of performing meritorious supernatural acts and subject to everlasting punishment. (b) Venial sin — involving less serious matter, reflection and consent — does not have such serious consequences.

(2) Original sin (See separate entry).

Sins against the Holy Spirit: Despair of salvation, presumption of God's mercy, impugning the known truths of faith, envy at another's spiritual good, obstinacy in sin, final impenitence. Those guilty of such sins stubbornly resist the influence of grace and, as long as they do so, cannot be forgiven.

Sins, Occasions of: Circumstances (persons, places, things, etc.) which easily lead to sin. There is an obligation to avoid voluntary proximate occasions of sin, and to take precautions against the dangers of unavoidable occasions.

Sins That Cry to Heaven for Vengeance: Willful murder, sins against nature, oppression of the poor, widows and orphans, defrauding laborers of their wages.

Sister: Any woman religious, in popular speech; strictly, the title applies only to women religious belonging to institutes whose members never professed solemn vows. Most of the institutes whose members are properly called sisters were established during and since the 19th century. Women religious with solemn vows, or belonging to institutes whose members formerly professed solemn vows, are properly called nuns.

Sisterhood: A generic term referring to the whole institution of the life of women religious in the Church, or to a particular institute of women religious.

Situation Ethics: A subjective, individualistic ethical theory which denies the binding force of ethical principles as universal laws and preceptive norms of moral conduct, and proposes that morality is determined only by situational conditions and considerations and the intention of the person. In an instruction issued on the subject in May, 1956, the Congregation for the Holy Office said:

"It ignores the principles of objective ethics. This 'New Morality,' it is claimed, is not only the equal of objective morality, but is superior to it.

"The authors who follow this system state that the ultimate determining norm for activity is not the objective order as determined by the natural law and known with certainty from this law. It is instead some internal judgment and illumination of the mind of every individual by which the mind comes to know what is to be done in a concrete situation.

"This ultimate decision of man is, therefore, not the application of the objective law to a particular case after the particular circumstances of a 'situation' have been considered and weighed according to the rules of prudence, as the more important authors of objective ethics teach; but it is, according to them, immediate, internal illumination and judgment.

"With regard to its objective truth and correctness, this judgment, at least in many things, is not ultimately measured, is not to be measured or is not measurable by any objective norm found outside man and independent of his subjective persuasion, but it is fully sufficient in itself. . . .

"Much that is stated in this system of 'Situation Ethics' is contrary to the truth of reality and to the dictate of sound reason. It gives evidence of relativism and modernism, and deviates far from the Catholic teaching handed down through the ages."

Slander: Attributing to a person faults which he does not have; a violation of the obligations of justice and charity, for which restitution is due.

Sloth: One of the seven capital sins; spiritual laziness, involving distaste and disgust for spiritual things; spiritual boredom, which saps the vigor of spiritual life. Physical laziness is a counterpart of spiritual sloth.

Sorcery: A kind of black magic in which evil is invoked by means of diabolical intervention; a violation of the virtue of religion.

Soteriology: The division of theology which treats of the mission and work of Christ as Redeemer.

Species, Sacred: The appearances of bread and wine (color, taste, smell, etc.) which remain after the substance has been changed at the Consecration of the Mass into the Body and Blood of Christ. (See Transubstantiation.)

Spiritism: Attempts to communicate with spirits and departed souls by means of seances, table tapping, ouija boards, and other methods; a violation of the virtue of religion. Spiritualistic practices are noted for fakery.

Spiritual Works of Mercy: Works of spiritual assistance, motivated by love of God and neighbor, to persons in need: counseling the doubtful, instructing the ignorant, admonishing sinners, comforting the afflicted, forgiving offenses, bearing wrongs patiently, praying for the living and the dead.

Stational Churches, Days: Churches, especially in Rome, where the clergy and lay people were accustomed to gather with their bishop on certain days for the celebration of the liturgy. The 25 early titular or parish churches of Rome, plus other churches, each had their turn as the site of divine worship in practices which may have started in the third century. The observances were rather well developed toward the latter part of the fourth century, and by the fifth they included a Mass concelebrated by the pope and attendant priests. On some occasions, the stational liturgy was preceded by a procession from another church called a collecta. There were 42 Roman stational churches in the eighth century, and 89 stational services were scheduled annually in connection with the liturgical seasons. Stational observances fell into disuse toward the end of the Middle Ages. Some revival was begun by John XXIII in 1959 and continued by Paul VI.

Stations of the Cross: A series of meditations on the sufferings of Christ: his condemnation to death and taking up of the Cross; the first fall on the way to Calvary; meeting his Mother; being assisted by Simon of Cyrene, and by Veronica who wiped his face; the second fall; meeting the women of Jerusalem; the third fall; being stripped and nailed to the Cross; his death; the removal of his body from the Cross and his burial. Depictions of these scenes are mounted in most churches, chapels and in some other places, beneath small crosses.

A person making the Way of the Cross passes before these Stations, or stopping points, pausing at each for meditation. If the Stations are made by a group of people, only the leader has to pass from Station to Station. Prayer for the intentions of the pope is required for gaining the indulgence.

Those unable to make the Stations in the ordinary manner, because they are impeded from visiting a church or other place where the Stations are, can still practice the devotion by meditating on the sufferings of Christ; praying the Our Father, Hail Mary and Glory for each Station and five times in commemoration of the wounds of Christ; and praying for the intentions of the pope. This practice has involved the use of a Stations Crucifix.

A recent development in this devotion is toward greater awareness of the relation of the Passion to the Resurrection-Ascension; this trend, in some circles, has led to the erection of a 15th — unofficial — station. The concept amounts to an extension of the whole customary thrust of the devotion.

The Stations originated, remotely, from the practice of Holy Land pilgrims who visited the actual scenes of incidents in the Passion of Christ. Representations elsewhere of at least some of these scenes were known as early as the fifth century. Later, the Stations evolved in connection with and as a consequence of strong devotion to the Passion in the 12th and 13th centuries. Franciscans, who were given custody of the Holy Places in 1342, promoted the devotion widely; one of them, St. Leonard of Port Maurice, became known as the greatest preacher of the Way of the Cross in the 18th century. The general features of the devotion were fixed by Clement XII in 1731.

Statutes: Virtually the same as decrees (see separate entry), they almost always designate laws of a particular council or synod rather than pontifical laws.

Stigmata: Marks of the wounds suffered by Christ in his crucifixion, in hands and feet by nails, and side by the piercing of a lance. Some persons, called stigmatists, have been reported as recipients or sufferers of marks like these. The Church, however, has never issued any infallible declaration about their possession by anyone, even in the case of St. Francis of Assisi whose stigmata seem to be the best substantiated and may be commemorated in the Roman-Rite liturgy. Ninety percent of some 300 reputed stigmatists have been women. Judgment regarding the presence, significance, and manner of causation of stigmata would depend, among other things, on irrefutable experimental evidence.

Stipend, Mass: An offering given to a priest for applying the fruits of the Mass according to the intention of the donor. The offering is a contribution to the support of the priest. The disposition of the fruits of the sacrifice, in line with doctrine concerning the Mass in particular and prayer in general, is subject to the will of God. In the early Christian centuries, when Mass was not offered for the intentions of particular persons, the participants made offerings of bread and wine for the sacrifice and their own Holy Communion, and of other things useful for the support of the clergy and the poor. Some offerings may have been made as early as the fourth century for the celebration of Mass for particular intentions, and there are indications of the existence of this practice from the sixth century when private Masses began to be offered. The earliest certain proof of stipend practice, however, dates from the eighth century. By the 11th century, along with private Mass, it was established custom.

Stole Fee: An offering given on certain occasions; e.g., at a baptism, wedding, funeral, for the support of the clergy who administer the sacraments and perform other sacred rites.

Stoup: A vessel used to contain holy water.

Suffragan See: Any diocese, except the archdiocese, within a province.

Suicide: The taking of one's own life; a violation of God's dominion over human life. Ecclesiastical burial is denied to persons who deliberately commit suicide while in full possession of their faculties; it is permitted in cases of doubt.

Supererogation: Good and virtuous actions which go beyond the obligations of duty and the requirements enjoined by God's law as necessary for salvation. Examples of these works are the profession and observance of the evangelical counsels of poverty, chastity, and obedience, and efforts to practice charity to the highest degree.

Supernatural: Above the natural; that which exceeds and is not due or owed to the essence, exigencies, requirements, powers and merits of created nature. While man has no claim on supernatural things and does not need them in order to exist and act on a natural level, he does need them in order to exist and act in the higher order or economy of grace established by God for his salvation.

God has freely given to man certain things which are beyond the powers and rights of his human nature. Examples of the supernatural are: grace, a kind of participation by man in the divine life, by which man becomes capable of performing acts meritorious for salvation; divine revelation by which God manifests himself to man and makes known truth that is inaccessible to human reason alone; faith, by which man believes divine truth because of the authority of God who reveals it through Sacred Scripture and tradition and the teaching of his Church.

Superstition: A violation of the virtue of religion, by which God is worshipped in an unworthy manner or creatures are given honor which belongs to God alone. False, vain, or futile worship involves elements which are incompatible with the honor and respect due to God, such as error, deception, and bizarre practices. Examples are: false and exaggerated devotions, chain prayers and allegedly unfailing prayers, the mixing of unbecoming practices in worship. The second kind of superstition attributes to persons and things powers and honor which belong to God alone. Examples are: idolatry, divination, magic, spiritism, necromancy.

Suspension: A penalty by which a cleric is forbidden to exercise some or all of his powers of orders and jurisdiction, or to accept the financial support of his benefices.

Swearing: Taking an oath; calling upon God to witness the truth of a statement; a legitimate thing to do for serious reasons and under proper circumstances, as in a court of law. To swear without sufficient reason is to dishonor God's name; to swear falsely in a court of law is perjury.

Swedenborgianism: A doctrine developed in and from the writings of Emmanuel Swedenborg (1688-1772), who claimed that during a number of visions he had in 1745 Christ taught him the spiritual sense of Sacred Scripture and commissioned him to communicate it to others. He held that, just as Christianity succeeded Judaism, so his teaching supplemented Christianity. He rejected belief in the Trinity, original sin, the Resurrection, and all the sacraments except baptism and the Eucharist. His followers are members of the Church of the New Jerusalem or of the New Church.

Syllabus, The: (1) When not qualified, the term refers to the list of 80 errors accompanying Pope Pius IX's encyclical *Quanta Cura,* issued in 1864.

(2) The *Syllabus* of St. Pius X in the decree *Lamentabili,* issued by the Holy Office July 4, 1907, condemning 65 heretical propositions of modernism. This schedule of errors was followed shortly by that pope's encyclical *Pascendi,* the principal ecclesiastical document against modernism, issued Sept. 8, 1907.

Synod, Diocesan: Meeting of representative persons of a diocese — priests, religious, lay persons — with the bishop, called by him for the purpose of considering and taking action on matters affecting the life and mission of the Church in the diocese. Persons taking part in a synod have consultative status; the bishop alone is the legislator, with power to authorize synodal decrees. According to canon law, every diocese should have a synod every 10 years.

T

Te Deum: The opening Latin words, Thee, God, of a hymn of praise and thanksgiving prescribed for use in the Office of Readings (Matins of the Liturgy of the Hours) on many Sundays, solemnities and feasts.

Temperance: Moderation, one of the four cardinal virtues.

Temptation: Any enticement to sin, from any source: the strivings of one's own faculties, the action of the devil, other persons, circumstances of life, etc. Temptation itself is not sin. Temptation can be avoided and overcome with the use of prudence and the help of grace.

Thanksgiving: An expression of gratitude to God for his goodness and the blessings he grants; one of the four ends of prayer.

Theism: A philosophy which admits the existence of God and the possibility of divine revelation; it is generally monotheistic and acknowledges God as transcendent and also active in the world. Because it is a philosophy rather than a system of theology derived from revelation, it does not include specifically Christian doctrines, like those concerning the Trinity, the Incarnation and Redemption.

Theological Virtues: The virtues which have God for their direct object: faith, or belief in God's infallible teaching; hope, or confidence in divine assistance; charity, or love of God. They are given to a person with grace in the first instance, through baptism and incorporation in Christ.

Theology: Knowledge of God and religion, deriving from and based on the data of divine Revelation, organized and systematized according to some kind of scientific method. It involves systematic study and presentation of the truths of divine Revelation in Sacred Scripture, tradition, and the teaching of the Church.

The Second Vatican Council made the following declaration about theology and its relation to divine Revelation: "Sacred theology rests on the written word of God, together with sacred tradition, as its primary and perpetual foundation. By scrutinizing in the light of faith all truth stored up in the mystery of Christ, theology is most powerfully strengthened and constantly rejuvenated by that word. For the sacred Scriptures contain the word of God and, since they are inspired, really are the word of God; and so the study of the sacred page is, as it were, the soul of sacred theology" *(Constitution on Revelation.* No. 24).

Theology has been divided under various subject headings. Some of the major fields have been: dogma, moral, pastoral, ascetics (the practice of virtue and means of attaining holiness and perfection), mysticism (higher states of religious experience). Other subject headings include ecumenism (Christian unity, interfaith relations), ecclesiology (the nature and constitution of the Church), Mariology (doctrine concerning the Blessed Virgin Mary), the sacraments, etc.

Tithing: Contribution of a portion of one's income, originally one-tenth, for purposes of religion and charity. The practice is mentioned 46 times in the Bible. In early Christian times, tithing was adopted in continuance of Old Testament practices of the Jewish people, and the earliest positive church legislation on the subject was enacted in 567. Catholics are bound in conscience to contribute to the support of their church, but the manner in which they do so is not fixed by law. Tithing, which amounts to a pledged contribution of a portion of one's income, has aroused new attention in recent years in the United States.

Titular Sees: Dioceses where the Church once flourished but which later were overrun by pagans or Moslems and now exist only in name or title. Bishops without a territorial or residential diocese of their own; e.g., auxiliary bishops, are given titular sees.

Transfinalization, Transignification: Terms coined to express the sign value of consecrated bread and wine with respect to the presence and action of Christ in the Eucharistic sacrifice and the spiritually vivifying purpose of the Eucharistic banquet in Holy Communion. The theory behind the terms has strong undertones of existential and "sign" philosophy, and has been criticized for its openness to interpretations at variance with the doctrine of transubstantiation and the abiding presence of Christ under the appearances of bread and wine after the sacrifice of the Mass and Communion have been completed. The terms, if used as substitutes for transubstantiation, are unacceptable; if they presuppose transubstantiation, they are acceptable as clarifications of its meaning.

Transubstantiation; "The way Christ is made present in this sacrament (Holy Eucharist) is none other than by the change of the whole substance of the bread into his Body, and of the whole substance of the wine into his Blood (in the Consecration at Mass) . . . this unique and wonderful change the Catholic Church rightly calls transubstantiation" (encyclical *Mysterium Fidei* of Paul VI, Sept. 3, 1965). The first official use of the term was made by the Fourth Council of the Lateran in 1215. Authoritative teaching on the subject was issued by the Council of Trent.

Treasury of the Church: The superabundant merits of Christ and the saints from which the Church draws to confer spiritual benefits, such as indulgences.

Triduum: A three-day series of public or private devotions.

U-Z

Usury: Excessive interest charged for the loan and use of money; a violation of justice.

Veronica: A word resulting from the combination of a Latin word for true, *vera*, and a Greek word for image, *eikon*, designating a likeness of the face of Christ or the name of a woman said to have given him a cloth on which he caused an imprint of his face to appear. The veneration at Rome of a likeness depicted on cloth dates from about the end of the 10th century; it figured in a popular devotion during the Middle Ages, and in the Holy Face devotion practiced since the 19th century. A faint, undiscernible likeness said to be of this kind is preserved in St. Peter's Basilica. The origin of the likeness is uncertain, and the identity of the woman is unknown. Before the 14th century, there were no known artistic representations of an incident concerning a woman who wiped the face of Christ with a piece of cloth while He was carrying the Cross to Calvary.

Viaticum: Holy Communion given to those in danger of death. The word, derived from Latin, means provision for a journey through death to life hereafter.

Vicar General: A prelate appointed by a bishop to help him, as a deputy, in the administration of his diocese. Because of his office, he has the same jurisdictional authority as the bishop except in cases reserved to the bishop by himself or by church law.

Virginity: Observance of perpetual sexual abstinence. The state of virginity, which is embraced for the love of God by religious with a public vow or by others with a private vow, was singled out for high praise by Christ (Mt. 19:10-12) and has always been so regarded by the Church. In the encyclical *Sacra Virginitas*, Pius XII stated: "Holy virginity and that perfect chastity which is consecrated to the service of God is without doubt among the most perfect treasures which the founder of the Church has left in heritage to the society which he established."

Paul VI approved in 1970 a rite in which women can consecrate their virginity "to Christ and their brethren" without becoming members of a religious institute. The *Ordo Consecrationis Virginum*, a revision of a rite promulgated by Clement VII in 1596, is traceable to the Roman liturgy of about 500.

Virtue: A habit or established capability for performing good actions. Virtues are *natural* (acquired and increased by repeating good acts) and/or *supernatural* (given with grace by God).

Vocation: A call to a way of life. Generally, the term applies to the common call of all men, from God, to holiness and salvation. Specifically, it refers to particular states of life, each called a vocation, in which response is made to this universal call; viz., marriage, the religious life and/or priesthood, the single state freely chosen or accepted for the accomplishment of God's will. The term also applies to the various occupations in which persons make a living. The Church supports the freedom of each individual in choosing a particular vocation, and reserves the right to pass on the acceptability of candidates for the priesthood and religious life. Signs or indicators of particular vocations are many, including a person's talents and interests, circumstances and obligations, invitations of grace and willingness to respond thereto.

Vow: A promise made to God with sufficient knowledge and freedom, which has as its object a moral good that is possible and better than its voluntary omission. A person who professes a vow binds himself by the virtue of religion to fulfill his promise. The best known examples of vows are those of poverty, chastity and obedience professed by religious (see Evangelical Counsels, individual entries).

Public vows are made before a competent person, acting as an agent of the Church, who accepts the profession in the name of the Church, thereby giving public recognition to the person's dedication and consecration to God and divine worship. Vows of this kind are either solemn, rendering all contrary acts invalid as well as unlawful; or simple, rendering contrary acts unlawful. Solemn vows are for life; simple vows are for a definite period of time or for life. Vows professed without public recognition by the Church are called private vows. The Church, which has authority to accept and give public recognition to vows, also has authority to dispense persons from their obligations for serious reasons.

Week of Prayer for Christian Unity: Eight days of prayer, from Jan. 18 to 25, for the union of all men in the Church established by Christ. On the initiative of Father Paul James Francis, S.A., of Graymoor, N.Y., it originated in 1908 as the Chair of Unity Octave. In recent years, its observance on an interfaith basis has increased greatly.

Witness, Christian: Practical testimony or evidence given by Christians of their faith in all circumstances of life — by prayer and general conduct, through good example and good works, etc.; being and acting in accordance with Christian belief; actual practice of the Christian faith.

Zucchetto: A skullcap worn by bishops and other prelates.

OUR LADY OF CZESTOCHOWA

The Black Madonna, the icon of Our Lady of Czestochowa, is enshrined on the "Hill of Light," Jasna Gora, above the city of Czestochowa in south central Poland. Long the center and focus of Marian devotion since it was brought there in 1382, it is the primary symbol of Polish religious faith and freedom.

The icon is a portrayal of Mary holding the Child Jesus. Their faces and hands are dark, as though they had been burned or stained by smoke. Three cuts are on one of Mary's cheeks, put there by robbers who desecrated the icon in 1430.

The origin of the icon is not clear. Elements of the legend say it was painted by St. Luke on a panel made by St. Joseph for the home of the Holy Family in Nazareth; that it was transported from the Holy Land to Constantinople; that it was given in 988 to a Ukrainian princess, Anna, the wife of Vladimir of Kiev; and that it eventually was brought to Czestochowa in 1382. The *Catholic Encyclopedia* notes another possibility, that the icon was of Greek-Italian origin in the ninth century.

The location of the icon on the hill above Czestochowa was related to the establishment of a priory of Paulite monks there, also in 1382. A shrine was built some time after 1386. A church was erected in 1644, and a 344-foot tower was raised in 1702.

Our Lady of Czestochowa was declared the Queen of Poland in 1656, and the icon was solemnly crowned in 1717 during the pontificate of Pope Clement XI.

The shrine has a long history as the greatest pilgrimage and religious center in Central Europe.

The shrine has undergone changes, some of them violent, in the years since 1382. Even in this century it has been a target of search and harassment by officials of the Communist government in control of the country since the end of World War II.

One thing has not changed, however; that is the significance of the icon and Czestochowa in the religious and patriotic life of the Polish people.

There are those who claim that Czestochowa is a more important capital of the nation than Warsaw.

AGRIMISSIO

Agrimissio is a service office established for the purpose of assisting missionaries in rural development work. Founded in 1970 by Msgr. Luigi Ligutti, its honorary president, it is sponsored by the Union of Superiors General (of male religious), the International Union of Superiors General (of female religious), and the National Catholic Rural Life Conference in the U.S. It promotes cooperation among missionaries, the Rome headquarters of religious orders, governmental and nongovernmental organizations, especially the international Food and Agriculture Organization.

Msgr. John F. McDonald is executive secretary. Headquarters are located at the Palazzo S. Calisto, 00120, Vatican City.

O'HARA INSTITUTE

The (Archbishop) Edwin V. O'Hara Institute for Rural Ministry Education was founded May 1, 1978, to provide training and other resource services for priests, seminarians, religious and lay persons beginning or already involved in rural ministry.

Msgr. Charles Fortier is director of the institute. Address: P.O. Box M, Des Moines, Iowa 50311.

(Principal sources for statistics: *Annuario Pontificio, 1980; Statistical Yearbook of the Church, 1977* (the latest available edition). Figures are as of Jan. 1, 1979, or Jan. 1 of the year indicated. See Index under names of countries for additional entries on 1980 events.)

Abbreviation code: archd. — archdiocese; dioc. — diocese; ap. ex. — apostolic exarchate; prel. — prelature; abb. — abbacy; v.a. — vicariate apostolic; p.a. — prefecture apostolic; a.a. — apostolic administration; card. — cardinal; abp. — archbishop; nat. — native; bp. — bishop; priests (dioc. — diocesan or secular priests; rel. — those belonging to religious orders); sem. — seminarians (major diocesan, unless indicated otherwise); p.d. — permanent deacons; bros. — brothers (1978); srs. — sisters; sch. — schools (elementary and secondary); bap. — baptisms; Caths. — Catholic population; tot. pop. — total population.

Afars and Issas: See Djibouti.

Afghanistan: Republic in south-central Asia; capital, Kabul. Christianity antedated Moslem conquest in the seventh century but was overcome by it. All inhabitants are subject to the law of Islam. Christian missionaries are prohibited. Population (est.), 20,000,000.

Albania: Communist people's republic in the Balkans, bordering the Adriatic Sea; capital, Tirana. Christianity was introduced before the middle of the fourth century. The Byzantine-Rite Church broke from unity with Rome following the schism of 1054; it has been suppressed. The Latin (Roman) Church, which prevailed in the north, has been wiped out by persecution since 1945, with the expulsion of Italian missionaries; a number of death and prison sentences and other repressive measures against bishops, priests, religious and lay persons; the closing of Catholic schools and a seminary; the cutting of lines of communication with the Holy See. In 1967, the government proclaimed itself the first atheist state in the world.

Archd., 2; dioc., 3; abb., 1; a.a. 1; bp., 3 (impeded). No statistics are available. The Catholic population was estimated at 10% of the population in 1969. Tot. pop. (1977 est.), 2,620,000.

Algeria: Republic in northwest Africa: capital, Algiers. Christianity, introduced at an early date, succumbed to Vandal devastation in the fifth century and Moslem conquest in 709, but survived for centuries in small communities into the 12th century. Missionary work was unsuccessful except in service to traders, military personnel and captives along the coast. Church organization was established after the French gained control of the territory in the 1830's. A large number of Catholics were among the estimated million Europeans who left the country after it secured independence from France July 5, 1962. Islam is the state religion. Algeria maintains diplomatic relations with Vatican City.

Archd., 1; dioc., 3; card., 1; abp., 1; bp., 3 (1 nat.); parishes, 86; priests, 211 (89 dioc., 122 rel.); sem. 2; p.d., 3; bros., 23; srs., 541; bap., 63; Caths., 57,000 (.3%); tot. pop., 18,510,000.

Andorra: Autonomous principality in the Pyrenees, under the rule of co-princes — the French head of state and the bishop of Urgel, Spain; capital, Andorra la Vella. Christianity was introduced at an early date. Catholicism is the state religion. The principality is under the ecclesiastical jurisdiction of the Spanish diocese of Urgel.

Parishes, 6; priests, 15 (9 dioc., 6 rel.); srs., 25; sch., 3; bap., 489; Caths., 29,000 (95%); tot. pop., 31,000 (1978).

Angola: Independent (Nov. 11, 1975) republic in west Africa; capital, Luanda. Evangelization by Catholic missionaries, dating from about 1570, reached high points in the 17th and 18th centuries. Independence from Portugal in 1975 left the Church with a heavy loss of personnel when about half of the foreign missionaries fled the country. In 1977, two ecclesiastical provinces were established. All but one of the hierarchy are from the native clergy. Angola has an apostolic delegate.

Archd., 3; dioc., 9; abp., 3 (nat.); bp., 8 (7 nat.); parishes, 202; priests, 258 (93 dioc., 165 rel.); sem., 41; bros., 40; srs., 511; bap., 75,769; Caths., 2,996,389 (42.2%); tot. pop., 7,100,000.

Anguilla: Self-governing British island territory in the Caribbean. Under ecclesiastical jurisdiction of St. John's diocese, Antigua. Statistics included in St. Christopher (Kitts)-Nevis.

Antigua: Self-governing British Associated State in the Caribbean; capital, St. John's.

Dioc., 1; bp., 1; parishes, 2; priests, 3 (rel.); sem., 1; bros., 7; srs., 8; sch., 4; bap., 115; Caths., 7,000 (9.1%); tot. pop., 72,000 (1978).

Arabian Peninsula: Christianity, introduced in various parts of the peninsula in early Christian centuries, succumbed to Islam in the seventh century. The native population is entirely Moslem. The only Christians are foreigners. Most of the peninsula is under the ecclesiastical jurisdiction of the Vicariate Apostolic of Arabia located in Abu Dhabi, United Arab Emirates. The area has an apostolic delegate (to the Red Sea Region). See individual countries: Bahrain, Oman, Qatar, Saudi Arabia, United Arab Emirates, Yemen, and Peoples Democratic Republic of Yemen.

Argentina: Republic in southeast South America, bordering on the Atlantic; capital,

Buenos Aires. Priests were with the Magellan exploration party and the first Mass in the country was celebrated Apr. 1, 1519. Missionary work began in the 1530's, diocesan organization in the late 1540's, and effective evangelization about 1570. Independence from Spain was proclaimed in 1816. Since its establishment in the country, the Church has been influenced by Spanish cultural and institutional forces, antagonistic liberalism, government interference and opposition; the latter reached a climax during the last five years of the first presidency of Juan Peron (1946-1955). Political chaos in recent years has resulted in widespread violations of human rights and increased terrorist violence. Catholicism is the state religion. Argentina maintains diplomatic relations with Vatican City.

Archd., 12; dioc., 44; prel., 2; ord., 1; card., 3; abp., 10; bp., 63; parishes, 2,136; priests, 4,877 (2,217 dioc., 2,660 rel.); sem., 771; p.d., 25; bros., 1,043; srs., 11,939; sch., 2,624; bap., 545,846; Caths. 24,331,580 (92.2%); tot. pop., 26,390,000.

Australia: Commonwealth, member of the British Commonwealth, island continent southeast of Asia; capital, Canberra. The first Catholics in the country were Irish under penal sentence, 1795-1804; the first public Mass was celebrated May 15, 1803. Official organization of the Church dates from 1820. The country was officially removed from mission status in March, 1976. Australia established diplomatic relations with Vatican City in 1973.

Archd., 7; dioc., 20; abb., 1; mission "sui juris," 1; ap. ex., 1; card., 2; abp., 6; bp., 36; parishes, 1,403; priests, 3,585 (2,212 dioc., 1,373 rel.); sem., 293; p.d., 4; bros., 2,128; srs., 12,729; sch., 1,829; bap., 72,480; Caths., 3,733,500 (26.2%); tot. pop. 14,250,000.

Austria: Republic in central Europe; capital, Vienna. Christianity was introduced by the end of the third century, strengthened considerably by conversion of the Bavarians from about 600, and firmly established in the second half of the eighth century. Catholicism survived and grew stronger as the principal religion in the country in the post-Reformation period, but suffered from Josephinism in the 18th century. Although liberated from much government harassment in the aftermath of the Revolution of 1848, it came under pressure again some 20 years later in the Kulturkampf. During this time the Church became involved with a developing social movement. The Church faced strong opposition from Socialists after World War I and suffered persecution from 1938 to 1945 during the Nazi regime. Some Church-state matters are regulated by a concordat originally concluded in 1934. Austria maintains diplomatic relations with Vatican City.

Archd., 2; dioc., 7; abb., 1; ord., 1; card., 1;

abp., 2; bp., 14; parishes, 3,046; priests, 5,877 (3,488 dioc., 2,389 rel.); sem., 357; p.d., 92; bros., 695; srs., 11,801; sch., 312; bap., 78,454; Caths., 6,587,192 (86.7%); tot. pop., 7,590,000.

Azores: North Atlantic island group 750 miles west of Portugal, of which it is part. Christianity was introduced in the second quarter of the 15th century.

Bahamas: Independent (July 10, 1973) island group in the British Commonwealth, consisting of some 700 (30 inhabited) small islands southeast of Florida and north of Cuba; capital, Nassau. On Oct. 12, 1492, Columbus landed on one of these islands, where the first Mass was celebrated in the New World. Organization of the Catholic Church in the Bahamas dates from about the middle of the 19th century. Established diplomatic relations with Vatican City in 1979.

Dioc., 1; bp., 1; parishes, 29; priests, 36 (10 dioc., 26 rel.); sem., 4; p.d., 4; bros., 5; srs., 53; sch., 18; bap., 1,657; Caths., 31,000 (13%); tot. pop., 230,000.

Bahrain: Island state in Persian Gulf; capital, Manama. Under ecclesiastical jurisdiction of Arabia vicariate apostolic.

Priests, 2 (rel); srs., 11; sch., 2; bap., 100; Caths., 4,000 (1.5%) tot. pop., 267,000 (1978).

Balearic Islands: Spanish province consisting of an island group in the western Mediterranean. Statistics are included in those for Spain.

Bangladesh: Formerly the eastern portion of Pakistan. Officially constituted as a separate nation Dec. 16, 1971; capital, Dacca. Islam is the principal religion; freedom of religion is granted. There were Jesuit, Dominican and Augustinian missionaries in the area in the 16th century. A vicariate apostolic (of Bengali) was established in 1834; the hierarchy was erected in 1950. Bangladesh established diplomatic relations with Vatican City in 1972.

Archd., 1; dioc., 3; abp., 1 (nat.); bp., 3 (nat.); parishes, 43; priests, 120 (40 dioc., 80 rel.); sem., 53; bros., 48; srs., 456; sch., 316; bap., 5,509; Caths., 152,717 (.18%); tot. pop. 83,421,683.

Barbados: Parliamentary democracy in the British Commonwealth (independent since 1966), easternmost of the Caribbean islands; capital, Bridgetown. About 70 per cent of the people are Anglicans. Established diplomatic relations with Vatican City in 1979.

Dioc., 1; bp., 1; parishes, 6; priests, 8 (3 dioc., 5 rel.); sem., 1; p.d., 2; bros., 5; srs., 50; sch., 5; bap., 223; Caths., 10,000 (3.9%); tot. pop., 254,000 (1978).

Belgium: Constitutional monarchy in northwestern Europe; capital, Brussels. Christianity was introduced about the first quarter of the fourth century and major evangelization was completed about 730. During the rest of the medieval period the Church had firm diocesan and parochial organization, generally vigorous monastic life, and influential monastic and cathedral schools. Lutherans and Calvinists made some gains during the Reformation period but there was a strong Catholic restoration in the first half of the 17th century, when the country was under Spanish rule. Jansenism disturbed the Church from about 1640 into the 18th century. Josephinism, imposed by an Austrian regime, hampered the Church late in the same century. Repressive and persecutory measures were enforced during the Napoleonic conquest. Freedom came with separation of Church and state in the wake of the Revolution of 1830, which ended the reign of William I. Thereafter, the Church encountered serious problems with philosophical liberalism and political socialism. Catholics have long been engaged in strong educational, social and political movements. Except for one five-year period (1880-1884), Belgium has maintained diplomatic relations with Vatican City since 1835.

Archd., 1; dioc., 7; card., 1; abp., 1; bp., 13; parishes, 3,928; priests, 13,024 (8,273 dioc., 4,751 rel.); sem., 305; p.d., 184; bros., 2,261; srs., 27,106; sch., 5,194; bap., 107,605; Caths., 9,009,410 (90.7%); tot. pop., 9,925,314.

Belize (formerly British Honduras): Self-governing colony in Central America; capital, Belmopan. Its history has points in common with Guatemala, where evangelization began in the 16th century.

Dioc., 1; bp., 1; parishes, 12; priests, 36 (9 dioc., 27 rel.); sem., 3; bros., 9; srs., 83; sch., 113; bap., 3,325; Caths., 90,000 (60%); tot. pop., 150,000.

Benin (formerly Dahomey): Republic in west Africa, bordering on the Atlantic; capitals, Cotonou, Porto Novo. Missionary work was very limited from the 16th to the 18th centuries. Effective evangelization dates from 1894. The hierarchy was established in 1955. The majority of Christians are Catholics. Benin maintains diplomatic relations with Vatican City.

Archd., 1; dioc., 5; card., 1 (nat.); abp., 1 (nat.); bp., 5 (4 nat.); parishes, 113; priests, 144 (76 dioc., 68 rel.); sem., 39; bros., 21; srs., 280; bap., 11,517; Caths., 524,618 (15.5%); tot. pop., 3,380,000.

Bermuda: British dependency, consisting of 360 islands (20 of them inhabited) nearly 600 miles east of Cape Hatteras; capital, Hamilton. Catholics were not permitted until about 1800. Occasional pastoral care was provided the few Catholics there by visiting priests during the 19th century. Early in the 1900's priests from Halifax began serving the area. A prefecture apostolic was set up in 1953. The first bishop assumed jurisdiction in 1956. The only Catholic school in Bermuda was the first to admit black students, in 1961.

Dioc., 1; bp., 1; parishes, 7; priests, 9 (1 dioc., 8 rel.); p.d., 1; srs., 9; sch., 2; bap., 90; Caths., 9,000 (15%); tot. pop., 60,000.

Bhutan: Constitutional monarchy in the Himalayas, northeast of India; capital, Thimphu. Most of the population are Buddhists. Ecclesiastical jurisdiction is under the Darjeeling diocese, India.

Priests, 6 (rel.); bros., 7; srs., 8; sch., 7; bap., 5; Caths., 200; tot. pop., 1,232,000 (1978).

Bolivia: Republic in central South America; capital, Sucre; seat of government, La Paz. Catholicism, the official religion, was introduced in the 1530's and the first bishopric was established in 1552. Effective evangelization among the Indians, slow to start, reached high points in the middle of the 18th and the beginning of the 19th centuries and was resumed about 1840. Independence from Spain was proclaimed in 1825, at the end of a campaign that started in 1809. The republic inherited the Spanish right of nominating candidates for bishoprics. Church-state relations are regulated by a 1951 concordat with the Holy See. In recent years, human rights violations in conditions of political, economic and social turmoil have occasioned strong protests by members of the hierarchy and other people of the Church. Bolivia maintains diplomatic relations with Vatican City.

Archd., 4; dioc., 3; prel., 3; v.a., 6; card., 1; abp., 3; bp., 18; parishes, 424; priests, 819 (217 dioc., 602 rel.); sem., 95; p.d., 19; bros., 216; srs., 1,589; sch., 926; bap., 167,645; Caths., 5,643,917 (93%); tot. pop., 6,063,499. (Population figures are from the Annuario Pontificio; other sources report a total population of 5.2 million.)

Botswana: Republic (independent since 1966) in southern Africa, member of the British Commonwealth; capital, Gaborone. Botswana has an apostolic delegate (to Southern Africa).

Dioc., 1; bp., 1; priests, 24 (3 dioc., 21 rel.); sem., 2; bros., 2; srs., 53; sch., 12; bap., 995; Caths., 29,199 (3.7%); tot. pop., 793,000.

Brazil: Republic in northeast South America; capital, Brasilia. One of several priests with the discovery party celebrated the first Mass in the country Apr. 26, 1500. Evangelization began some years later and the first diocese was erected in 1551. During the colonial period, which lasted until 1822, evangelization made some notable progress — especially in the Amazon region between 1680 and 1750 — but was seriously hindered by government policy and the attitude of colonists regarding Amazon Indians the missionaries tried to protect from exploitation and slavery. The Jesuits were suppressed in 1782 and other missionaries expelled as well. Liberal anti-Church influence grew in strength. The government gave minimal support but exercised maximum control over the Church. After the proclamation of independence from Portugal in 1822 and throughout the regency, government control was tightened and the Church suffered greatly from dissident actions of ecclesiastical brotherhoods, Masonic anti-clericalism and general decline in religious life. Church and state were separated by the constitution of 1891, proclaimed two years after the end of the empire. The Church carried into the 20th century a load of inherited liabilities and problems amid increasingly difficult political, economic and social conditions affecting the majority of the population. A number of bishops, priests, religious and lay persons have been active in movements for social and religious reform. Brazil maintains diplomatic relations with Vatican City. (See Index for coverage of the papal visit to Brazil in 1980.)

Archd., 35; dioc., 160; prel., 28; abb., 2; ord., 1; card., 7; abp., 37; bp., 235; parishes, 6,311; priests, 13,246 (5,174 dioc., 8,072 rel.); sem., 3,052; p.d., 242; bros., 2,696; srs., 35,862; sch., 4,512; bap., 2,590,652; Caths., 101,101,000 (90.1%); tot. pop., 112,239,000 (1978, except for jurisdictions, hierarchy).

Brunei: State under British protection, on the northern coast of Borneo; scheduled for independence in 1983; capital, Bandai Seri Begawan (Brunei). Under ecclesiastical jurisdiction of Miri diocese, Malaysia.

Parishes, 3; priests, 6 (3 dioc., 3 rel.); srs., 3; sch., 8; bap., 172; Caths., 4,000; tot. pop., 190,000 (1978).

Bulgaria: People's republic in southeastern Europe on the eastern part of the Balkan peninsula; capital, Sofia. Christianity was introduced before 343 but disappeared with the migration of Slavs into the territory. The baptism of Boris I about 865 ushered in a new period of Christianity which soon became involved in switches of loyalty between Constantinople and Rome. Through it all the Byzantine, and later Orthodox, element remained stronger and survived under the rule of Ottoman Turks into the 19th century. The few modern Latin Catholics in the country are traceable to 17th century converts from heresy. The Byzantines are products of a reunion movement of the 19th century. In 1947 the constitution of the new republic decreed the separation of Church and state. Catholic schools and institutions were abolished and foreign religious banished in 1948. A year later the apostolic delegate was expelled. Ivan Romanoff, vicar general of Plovdiv, died in prison in 1952. Bishop Eugene Bossilkoff, imprisoned in 1948, was sentenced to death in 1952; his fate remained unknown until 1975 when the Bulgarian government informed the Vatican that he had died in prison shortly after being sentenced. Roman and Bulgarian Rite vicars apostolic were permitted to attend the Second Vatican Council from 1962 to 1965. All church activity is under surveillance and/or control by the government, which professes to be atheistic. Pastoral and related activities are strictly limited. Most of the population is Orthodox. There was some improvement in Bulgarian-Vatican relations in 1975, following a visit of Bulgarian President Todor Zhivkov to Pope Paul VI June 19 and talks between Vatican and Bulgarian representatives at the Helsinki Conference in late July. The needs of the church in Bulgaria were outlined by Pope John Paul II in a private audience with the Bulgarian foreign minister in December, 1978. In 1979, the Sofia-Plovdiv vicariate apostolic was raised to a diocese and a bishop was appointed for the vacant see of Nicopoli.

Dioc., 2; ap. ex., 1; bp., 3; Caths. (est.), 65,000 (.7%); tot. pop., 8,810,000.

Burma: Union of Burma, a republic in southeast Asia, on the Bay of Bengal; capital, Rangoon. Christianity was introduced about 1500. Small-scale evangelization had limited results from the middle of the 16th century until the 1850's when effective organization of the Church began. The hierarchy was established in 1955. Buddhism was declared the state religion in 1961, but the state is now officially secular. In 1965, church schools and hospitals were nationalized. In 1966, all foreign missionaries who had entered the country after 1948 for the first time were forced to leave when the government refused to renew their work permits. Despite these setbacks, the Church has shown some progress in recent years. Burma has an apostolic delegate (pro-nuncio to Bangladesh).

Archd., 2; dioc., 6; p.a., 1; abp., 2 (nat.); bp., 6 (nat.); parishes, 126; priests, 212 (174 dioc., 38 rel.); sem., 124; bros., 59; srs., 638; sch., 132; bap., 17,423; Caths., 352,807 (1.1%); tot. pop., 32,210,000.

Burundi: Republic since 1966, near the equator in east-central Africa; capital, Bujumbura. The first permanent Catholic mission station was established late in the 19th century. Large numbers of persons were received into the Church following the ordination of the first Burundi priests in 1925. The first native bishop was appointed in 1959. Most education takes place in schools under Catholic auspices. In 1972-73, the country was torn by tribal warfare between the Tutsis, the ruling minority, and the Hutus. Burundi maintains diplomatic relations with Vatican City.

Archd., 1; dioc., 6; abp., 1 (nat.); bp., 6 (nat.); parishes, 192; priests, 383 (170 dioc., 213 rel.); sem., 71; bros., 138; srs., 701; sch., 367; bap., 73,095; Caths., 2,198,178 (54.9%); tot. pop., 4,000,000.

Cambodia: See Kampuchea.

Cameroon: Republic in west Africa, bordering on the Gulf of Guinea; capital, Yaounde. Effective evangelization began in the 1890's, although Catholics had been in the country long before that time. In the 40-year period from 1920 to 1960, the number of Catholics increased from 60,000 to 700,000. The first native priests were ordained in 1935. Twenty years later the first native bishops were ordained and the hierarchy established. Cameroon maintains diplomatic relations with Vatican City.

Archd., 1; dioc., 12; abp., 1 (nat.); bp., 14 (10 nat.); parishes, 332; priests, 753 (294 dioc., 459 rel.); sem., 195; p.d., 27; bros., 197; srs., 1,168; sch., 948; bap., 62,091; Caths., 2,083,477 (26.5%); tot. pop., 7,851,759.

Canada: Independent federation in the British Commonwealth, comprising the northern half of North America; capital, Ottawa. Canada maintains diplomatic relations with Vatican City. (See The Church in Canada.)

Archd., 18; dioc., 51; abb., 1; card., 4; abp., 24 (17 residential; 7 retired); bp., 100 (73 residential and auxiliary; 27 retired); parishes 5,729; priests, 12,986 (7,632 dioc., 5,354 rel.); p.d., 219; bros., 4,340; srs., 38,858; Caths., 10,123,329 (42.9%); tot. pop., 23,597,600. (Statistics, except for hierarchy, are from 1980 Directory of Canadian Conference of Catholic Bishops.)

Canary Islands: Two Spanish provinces, consisting of seven islands, off the northwest coast of Africa. Evangelization began about 1400. Almost all of the one million inhabitants are Catholics. Statistics are included in those for Spain.

Cape Verde Islands: Independent (July 5, 1975) island group in the Atlantic 300 miles west of Senegal; formerly a Portuguese overseas province; capital, Praia, San Tiago Island. Evangelization began some years before the establishment of the first diocese in 1532. Cape Verde Islands established diplomatic relations with Vatican City in 1976.

Dioc., 1; bp., 1; parishes, 30; priests, 45 (11 dioc., 34 rel.); bros., 4; srs., 29; sch., 7; bap., 4,600; Caths., 292,795 (93.8%); tot. pop., 312,000.

Caroline and Marshall Islands: U.S. trust territory in the southwest Pacific; scheduled for independence in 1981. Effective evangelization began in the late 1880's.

Dioc., 1; bp., 1; parishes, 23; priests, 33 (2 dioc., 31 rel.); sem., 6; p.d., 22; bros., 8; srs., 33; sch., 12; bap., 1,717; Caths., 48,604 (42.3%); tot. pop., 114,841.

Cayman Islands: British colony in Caribbean; capital, George Town on Grand Cayman. Under ecclesiastical jurisdiction of Kingston diocese, Jamaica.

Priest, 1 (rel.); srs., 2; sch., 1 (elementary); bap., 8; Caths., 200; tot. pop., 11,000 (1978).

Central African Republic: Former French colony (independent since 1960) in central Africa; capital, Bangui. Effective evangelization dates from 1894. The region was organized as a mission territory in 1909. The first native priest was ordained in 1938. The hierarchy was organized in 1955. The Central African Republic established diplomatic relations with Vatican City in 1975.

Archd., 1; dioc., 5; abp., 1 (nat.); bp., 3; parishes, 75; priests, 201 (30 dioc., 171 rel.); sem., 65; p.d., 1; bros., 47; srs., 282; sch., 20; bap., 12,501; Caths., 348,264 (15.3%); tot. pop., 2,250,000.

Ceuta: Spanish possession (city) on the northern tip of Africa, south of Gibraltar. Statistics are included in those for Spain.

Ceylon: See Sri Lanka, Republic of.

Chad: Republic (independent since 1960) in north-central Africa; former French possession; capital, N'Djamena (Fort Lamy). Evangelization began in 1929, leading to firm organization in 1947 and establishment of the hierarchy in 1955. Chad has an apostolic delegate (pro-nuncio, Central African Republic).

Archd., 1; dioc., 3; abp., 1 (nat.); bp., 3 (1 nat.); parishes, 12; priests, 169 (21 dioc., 148 rel.); sem., 15; bros., 40; srs., 225; sch., 54; bap., 10,034; Caths., 227,411 (5.2%); tot. pop., 4,310,000.

Chile: Republic on the southwestern coast of South America; capital, Santiago. Priests were with the Spanish conquistadores on their entrance into the territory early in the 16th century. The first parish was established in 1547 and the first bishopric in 1561. Overall organization of the Church took place later in the century. By 1650 most of the peaceful Indians in the central and northern areas were evangelized. Missionary work was more difficult in the southern region. Church activity was hampered during the campaign for independence, 1810 to 1818, and through the first years of the new government, to 1830. Later gains were made, into this century, but hindering factors were shortages of native clergy and religious and attempts by the government to control church administration through the patronage system in force while the country was under Spanish control. Separation of Church and state were decreed in the constitution of 1925. Church-state relations were strained during the regime of Marxist president Salvator Allende Gossens (1970-73). He was overthrown in a bloody coup and was reported to have committed suicide Sept. 11, 1973. Conditions remained unsettled under the military government which assumed control after the coup. Since 1974, the Chilean bishops have issued several statements criticizing government policies violating human rights and urging release of political prisoners. The Church-backed Vicariate of Solidarity was established in 1976 to give legal aid to political prisoners and aid their families. Chile maintains diplomatic relations with Vatican City.

Archd., 5; dioc., 14; prel., 3; v.a., 2; card., 1; abp., 4; bp., 22; parishes, 798; priests, 1,940 (709 dioc., 1,231 rel.); sem., 374; p.d., 193; bros., 369; srs., 4,991; sch., 903; bap., 174,538;

Caths., 9,282,455 (85.4%); tot. pop., 10,860,000.

China (*This article concerns mainland China which has been under Communist control since 1949*): People's Republic in eastern part of Asia; capital, Beijing (Peking). Christianity was introduced by Nestorians who had some influence on part of the area from 635 to 845 and again from the 11th century until 1368. John of Monte Corvino started a Franciscan mission in 1294; he was ordained an archbishop about 1307. Missionary activity involving more priests increased for a while thereafter but the Franciscan mission ended in 1368. The Jesuit Matteo Ricci initiated a remarkable period of activity in the 1580's. By 1700 the number of Catholics was reported to be 300,000. The Chinese Rites controversy, concerning the adaptation of rituals and other matters to Chinese traditions and practices, ran throughout the 17th century, ending in a negative decision by mission authorities in Rome. Bl. Francis de Capillas, the protomartyr of China, was killed in 1648. Persecution, a feature of Chinese history as recurrent as changes in dynasties, occurred several times in the 18th century and resulted in the departure of most missionaries from the country. The Chinese door swung open again in the 1840's and progress in evangelization increased with an extension of legal and social tolerance. At the turn of the 20th century, however, the Boxer Rebellion took one or the other kind of toll among an estimated 30,000 victims. Missionary work in the 1900's reached a new high in every respect before the disaster of persecution initiated by Communists before and especially since they established the republic in 1949. The Reds began a savage persecution as soon as they came into power. Among its results were the expulsion of over 5,000 foreign missionaries, 510 of whom were American priests, brothers and nuns; the arrest, imprisonment and harassment of all members of the native religious, clergy and hierarchy; the forced closing of 3,932 schools, 216 hospitals, 781 dispensaries, 254 orphanages, 29 printing presses and 55 periodicals; denial of the free exercise of religion to all the faithful; the detention of hundreds of priests, religious and lay persons in jail and their employment in slave labor; the proscription of the Legion of Mary and other Catholic Action groups for "counter-revolutionary activities" and "crimes against the new China"; complete outlawing of missionary work and pastoral activity. The government formally established a Patriotic Association of Chinese Catholics in July, 1957. Relatively few priests and lay persons joined the organization, which was condemned by Pius XII in 1958. The government formed the nucleus of what it hoped might become the hierarchy of a schismatic Chinese church by "electing" 26 bishops and having them consecrated validly but illicitly between Apr. 13, 1958, and Nov. 15, 1959, without the permission or approval of the Holy See. By Jan. 21, 1962, a total of 42 bishops were consecrated in this manner. In March, 1960, Bishop James E. Walsh, M.M., the last American missionary in China, was sentenced and placed in custody for a period of 20 years. He was released in the summer of 1970. There seemed to be an opening to the West by China in 1979. What this, along with renewed activity of the Patriotic Association in 1980, might mean for the Church in that country is open to question.

Archd., 20; dioc., 93; p.a., 29. No Catholic statistics are available. In 1949 there were between 3,500,000-4,000,000 Catholics, about .7 per cent of the total population; the 1969 "CSMC World Mission Map" estimated 3,200,000 Catholics, .5 per cent of the population. The latter figure is only an estimate; there is no way of knowing the actual situation. Tot. pop. (1979 est.), 958,230,000.

Colombia: Republic in northwest South America, with Atlantic and Pacific borders; capital, Bogota. Evangelization began in 1508. The first two dioceses were established in 1534. Vigorous development of the Church was reported by the middle of the 17th century despite obstacles posed by the multiplicity of Indian languages, government interference through patronage rights and otherwise, rivalry among religious orders and the small number of native priests among the predominantly Spanish clergy. Some persecution, including the confiscation of property, followed in the wake of the proclamation of independence from Spain in 1819. The Church was affected in many ways by the political and civil unrest of the nation through the 19th century and into the 20th. Various aspects of Church-state relations are regulated by a concordat with the Vatican signed July 12, 1973, and ratified July 2, 1975. The new concordat replaced one which had been in effect with some modifications since 1887. In late 1976, the bishops released a statement reaffirming their concern for social justice but rejecting actions of radical Catholic groups such as Priests for Latin America and Christians for Socialism as Marxist-oriented and destructive of Church unity. Colombia maintains diplomatic relations with Vatican City.

Archd., 11; dioc., 30; prel., 2; v.a., 9; p.a., 7; card., 1; abp., 10; bp., 46; parishes, 2,185; priests, 5,080 (3,047 dioc., 2,033 rel.); sem., 999; p.d., 10; bros., 1,106; srs., 18,170; sch., 2,549; bap., 701,265; Caths., 24,614,400 (96%); tot. pop., 25,640,000.

Comoro Islands: Consists of main islands of Grande Comore, Anjouan, Moheli and Mayotte in Indian Ocean off southeast coast of Africa; capital, Moroni, Grande Comore Island. Former French territory; independent (July 6, 1975) except Mayotte which voted to remain part of France. The majority of the population is Moslem. An apostolic administration for Catholics (formerly under administration of the Ambanja diocese, Madagascar) was established June 20, 1975.

A.a., 1; bp., 1; priests, 3 (rel.); bros., 1; srs., 1; bap., 7; Caths., 1,225 (.38%); tot. pop., 314,400.

Congo Republic: Republic (independent since 1960) in west central Africa; former French possession; capital, Brazzaville. Small-scale missionary work with little effect preceded modern evangelization dating from the 1880's. The work of the Church has been affected by political instability, Communist influence, tribalism and hostility to foreigners. The hierarchy was established in 1955. Congo established diplomatic relations with the Vatican in 1977. (See Index for coverage of the papal visit to the Congo in 1980.)

Archd., 1; dioc., 2; abp., 1 (nat.); bp., 2 (nat); parishes, 91; priests, 126 (52 dioc., 74 rel.); sem., 31; p.d., 2; bros., 17; srs., 89; bap., 11,775; Caths., 637,609 (44%); tot. pop., 1,446,762 (1980 Annuario Pontificio).

Cook Islands: Self-governing territory of New Zealand, an archipelago of small islands in Oceania. Evangelization by Protestant missionaries started in 1821, resulting in a predominantly Protestant population. The first Catholic missionary work began in 1894. The hierarchy was established in 1966.

Dioc., 1; bp., 1; parishes, 13; priests, 13 (2 dioc., 11 rel.); bros., 3; srs., 13; sch., 3; bap., 82; Caths., 2,500 (11.3%); tot. pop., 21,790.

Costa Rica: Republic in Central America; capital, San Jose. Evangelization began about 1520 and proceeded by degrees to real development and organization of the Church in the 17th and 18th centuries. The republic became independent in 1838. Twelve years later church jurisdiction also became independent with the establishment of a bishopric in the present capital. Costa Rica maintains diplomatic relations with Vatican City.

Archd., 1; dioc., 3; v.a., 1; abp., 1; bp., 6; parishes, 157; priests, 399 (253 dioc., 146 rel.); sem., 110; bros., 36; srs., 785; sch., 63; bap., 55,668; Caths., 1,971,230 (93.6%); tot. pop., 2,106,091.

Cuba: Republic under Communist dictatorship, south of Florida; capital, Havana. Effective evangelization began about 1514, leading eventually to the predominance of Catholicism on the island. Native vocations to the priesthood and religious life were unusually numerous in the 18th century but declined in the 19th. The island became independent of Spain in 1902 following the Spanish-American War. Fidel Castro took control of the government Jan. 1, 1959. In 1961, after Cuba was officially declared a socialist state, the University of Villanueva was closed, 350 Catholic schools were nationalized and 136 priests expelled. A greater number of foreign priests and religious had already left the country. Freedom of worship and religious instruction are limited to church premises and no social action is permitted the Church, which survives under surveillance. A new constitution approved in 1976 guaranteed freedom of conscience but restricted its exercise. Cuba maintains diplomatic relations with Vatican City.

Archd., 2; dioc., 5 (new one erected in 1979); abp., 2; bp., 5; parishes, 221; priests, 203 (110 dioc., 93 rel.); sem., 40; bros., 27; srs., 217; bap., 21,760; Caths. (est.), 4,032,000 (42%); tot. pop., 9,600,000.

Cyprus: Republic in the eastern Mediterranean; capital, Nicosia. Christianity was preached on the island in apostolic times and has a continuous history from the fourth century. Latin and Eastern rites were established but the latter prevailed and became Orthodox after the schism of 1054. Roman and Orthodox Christians have suffered under many governments, particularly during the period of Turkish dominion from late in the 16th to late in the 19th centuries, and from differences between the 80 per cent Greek majority and the Turkish minority. About 80 per cent of the population are Orthodox. Cyprus established diplomatic relations with Vatican City in 1973. Maronite Rite Catholics are under the jurisdiction of the archdiocese of Cyprus (of the Maronites), whose archbishop resides in Lebanon. Roman Rite Catholics are under the jurisdiction of the Roman Rite patriarchate of Jerusalem.

Archd., 1 (Maronite); abp., 1 (resides in Lebanon); parishes, 9; priests, 24 (7 dioc., 17 rel.); bros., 3; srs., 96; sch., 18; bap., 95; Caths., 7,000 (1.1%); tot. pop., 640,000 (1978).

Czechoslovakia: Federal socialist republic (since 1969) in Central Europe, consisting of the Czech Socialist Republic, capital Prague; and the Slovak Socialist Republic, capital Bratislava. The republics have local autonomy but are subordinate to the Federal Assembly at Prague made up of representatives from both regions. The Czech and Slovak regions of the country have separate religious and cultural backgrounds. Christianity was introduced in Slovakia in the 8th century by Irish and German missionaries and the area was under the jurisdiction of German bishops. In 863, at the invitation of the Slovak ruler Rastislav who wanted to preserve the cultural and liturgical heritage of the people, Sts. Cyril and Methodius began pastoral and missionary work in the region, ministering to the people in their own language. The saints introduced Old Slovak (Old Church Slavonic) into the liturgy and did so much to evangelize the territory that they are venerated as the apostles of Slovakia. A diocese established at Nitra in 880 had a continuous history except for a century ending in 1024. The Church in Slovakia was severely tested by the Reformation and political upheavals. After World War I, when it became part of the Republic of Czechoslovakia, it was 75 per cent Catholic. In the Czech lands, the martyrdom of Prince Wenceslaus in 929 triggered the spread of Christianity. Prague has had a continuous history as a diocese since 973. A parish system was organized about the 13th century in Bohemia and Moravia, the land of the Czechs. Mendicant orders strengthened relations with the Latin Rite in the 13th century. In the next century the teachings of John Hus in Bohemia brought trouble to the Church in the forms of schism and heresy, and initiated a series of religious wars which continued for decades following his death at the stake in 1415. Church property was confiscated, monastic communities were scattered and even murdered, ecclesiastical organization was shattered, and so many of the faithful joined the Bohemian Brethren that Catholics became a minority. The Reformation, with the way prepared by the Hussites and cleared by other factors, affected the Church seriously. A Counter Reformation got underway in the 1560's and led to a gradual restoration through the thickets of Josephinism, the Enlightenment, liberalism and troubled politics. In 1920, two years after the establishment of the Republic of Czechoslovakia, the schismatic Czechoslovak Church was proclaimed at Prague, resulting in numerous defections from the Catholic Church in the Czech region. In Ruthenia, 112,000 became Russian Orthodox between 1918 and 1930. Vigorous persecution of the church began in Slovakia before the end of World War II when Communists mounted a 1944 offensive against bishops, priests and religious. In 1945, church schools were nationalized, youth organizations were disbanded, the Catholic press was curtailed, the training of students for the priesthood was seriously impeded. Msgr. Josef Tiso, president of the Slovak Republic, was tried for "treason" in December, 1947, and was executed the following April. Between 1945 and 1949 approximately 10 per cent of the Slovak population spent some time in jail or a concentration camp. Persecution began later in the Czech part of the country, following the accession of the Gottwald regime to power early in 1948. Hospitals, schools and property were nationalized and Catholic organizations were liquidated. A puppet organization was formed in 1949 to infiltrate the Church and implement an unsuccessful plan for establishing a schismatic church. In the same year Archbishop Josef Beran of Prague was placed under house arrest. (He left the country in 1965, was made a cardinal, and died in 1969 in Rome.) A number of theatrical trials of bishops and priests were staged in 1950. All houses of religious were taken over between March, 1950, and the end of 1951. An Eastern Rite diocese,

Presov, in Slovakia, was dissolved in 1950 and pressure was applied on the clergy and faithful to join the Orthodox Church. Diplomatic relations with Vatican City were terminated in 1950. About 3,000 priests were deprived of liberty in 1951 and attempts were made to force "peace priests" on the people. In 1958 it was reported that 450 to 500 priests were in jail; an undisclosed number of religious and Byzantine Rite priests had been deported; two bishops released from prison in 1956 were under house arrest; one bishop was imprisoned at Leopoldov and two at the Mirov reformatory. In Bohemia, Moravia and Silesia, five of six dioceses were without ruling bishops; one archbishop and two bishops were active but subject to "supervision"; most of the clergy refused to join the "peace priests." In 1962 only three bishops were permitted to attend the first session of the Second Vatican Council. From January to October, 1968, Church-state relations improved to some extent under the Dubcek regime: a number of bishops were reinstated; some 3,000 priests were engaged in the pastoral ministry, although 1,500 were still barred from priestly work; the "peace priests" organization was disbanded; the Eastern Rite Church, with 147 parishes, was reestablished. In 1969, an end was ordered to rehabilitation trials for priests and religious, but no wholesale restoration of priests and religious to their proper ways of life and work was in prospect. In 1972 the government ordered the removal of nuns from visible but limited apostolates to farms and mental hospitals where they would be out of sight. In 1973, the government allowed the ordination of four bishops — one in the Czech region and three in the Slovak region. Reports from Slovakia late in the same year stated that authorities there had placed severe restrictions on the education of seminarians and the functioning of priests. Government restrictions continued to hamper the work of priests and nuns in recent years.

Archd., 3; *dioc.*, 10; *card.*, 1; *bp.*, 6 (1 impeded); parishes, 4,189; priests, 3,995 (3,454 dioc., 541 rel.); sem., 243; bros., 43; srs., 5,115; bap., 127,782; Caths. (est.), 10,840,240 (71.6%); tot. pop., 15,140,000.

Dahomey: See Benin.

Danzig (Gdansk): Baltic seaport at the mouth of the Vistula River; incorporated into Poland after World War II. The diocese has a Christian history dating from the 10th century. Statistics are included in those for Poland.

Denmark, including the Faroe Islands and Greenland: Constitutional monarchy in northwestern Europe, north of West Germany; capital, Copenhagen. Christianity was introduced in the ninth century and the first diocese for the area was established in 831. Intensive evangelization and full-scale organization of the Church occurred from the second half of the 10th century and ushered in a period of great development and influence in the 12th and 13th centuries. Decline followed, resulting in almost total loss to the Church during the Reformation when Lutheranism became the national religion. Catholics were considered foreigners until religious freedom was legally assured in 1849. Modern development of the Church dates from the second half of the 19th century. About 95 per cent of the population are Evangelical Lutherans. Denmark has an apostolic delegate (to Scandinavia).

Dioc., 1; bp., 1; parishes, 52; priests, 114 (35 dioc., 79 rel.); sem., 3; bros., 7; srs., 480; sch., 36; Caths., 26,215 (.5%); tot. pop., 5,143,678.

Djibouti (formerly French Territory of Afars and Issas): Independent (1977) republic in east Africa, on the Gulf of Aden; capital, Djibouti. Christianity in the area, formerly part of Ethiopia, antedated but was overcome by the Arab invasion of 1200. Modern evangelization, begun in the latter part of the 19th century, had meager results. The hierarchy was established in 1955. The territory has an apostolic delegate (to the Red Sea Region).

Dioc., 1; bp., 2; parishes, 5; priests, 7 (1 dioc., 6 rel.); p.d., 1; bros., 7; srs., 23; sch., 14; bap., 38; Caths., 12,000; tot. pop., 300,000.

Dominica: Independent (Nov. 3, 1978) state in Caribbean; capital, Roseau. Evangelization began in 1642.

Dioc., 1; bp., 1; parishes, 16; priests, 26 (3 dioc., 23 rel.); sem., 1; p.d., 1; bros., 4; srs., 36; sch., 6; bap., 1,355; Caths., 65,000 (86.6%); tot. pop., 75,000.

Dominican Republic: Caribbean republic on the eastern two-thirds of the island of Hispaniola, bordering on Haiti; capital, Santo Domingo. Evangelization began shortly after discovery by Columbus in 1492 and church organization, the first in America, was established by 1510. Catholicism is the state religion. The Dominican Republic maintains diplomatic relations with Vatican City.

Archd., 1; dioc., 7; card., 1; abp., 2; bp., 10; parishes, 200; priests, 481 (116 dioc., 365 rel.); sem., 119; p.d., 27; bros., 63; srs., 1,388; sch., 294; bap., 95,951; Caths., 4,823,304 (93.2%); tot. pop., 5,174,293.

Ecuador: Republic on the west coast of South America; capital, Quito. Evangelization began in the 1530's. The first diocese was established in 1545. A synod, one of the first in the Americas, was held in 1570 or 1594. Multiphased missionary work, spreading from the coastal and mountain regions into the Amazon, made the Church highly influential during the colonial period. The Church was practically enslaved by the constitution enacted in 1824, two years after Ecuador, as part of Colombia, gained independence from Spain. Some change for the better took place later in the century, but from 1891 until the

1930's the Church labored under serious liabilities imposed by liberal governments. The concordat of 1866 was violated; foreign missionaries were barred from the country for some time; the property of religious orders was confiscated; education was taken over by the state; traditional state support was refused; legal standing was denied; attempts to control church offices were made through insistence on rights of patronage. A period of harmony and independence for the Church began after agreement was reached on Church-state relations in 1937. Ecuador maintains diplomatic relations with Vatican City.

Archd., 3; dioc., 10; prel., 1; v.a., 5; p.a., 3; card., 1; abp., 2; bp., 22; parishes, 693; priests, 1,394 (619 dioc., 775 rel.); sem., 78; p.d., 6; bros., 331; srs., 3,781; sch., 971; bap., 216,559; Caths., 7,033,626 (91%); tot. pop., 7,726,851.

Egypt, Arab Republic of: Republic in northeastern Africa, bordering on the Mediterranean; capital, Cairo. Alexandria was the influential hub of a Christian community established by the end of the second century; it became a patriarchate and the center of the Coptic Church, and had great influence on the spread of Christianity in various parts of Africa; Monasticism developed from desert communities of hermits in the third and fourth centuries. Arianism was first preached in Egypt in the 320's. In the fifth century, the Coptic church went Monophysite through failure to accept doctrine formulated by the Council of Chalcedon in 451 with respect to the two natures of Christ. The country was thoroughly Arabized after 640 and was under the rule of Ottoman Turks from 1517 to 1798. English influence was strong during the 19th century. A monarchy established in 1922 lasted about 30 years, ending with the proclamation of a republic in 1953-54. By that time Egypt had become the leader of pan-Arabism against Israel. It waged two unsuccessful wars against Israel in 1948-49 and 1967. Between 1958 and 1961 it was allied with Syria and Yemen, in the United Arab Republic. Islam, the religion of some 90 percent of the population, is the state religion. Egypt maintains diplomatic relations with Vatican City.

Patriarchate, 2 (Alexandria for the Copts and for the Melkites); dioc., 6; v.a., 3; card., 1; bp., 10; parishes, 205; priests, 337 (168 dioc., 169 rel.); sem., 69; p.d., 1; bros., 74; srs., 1,702; sch., 213; bap., 2,344; Caths., 146,517 (.36%); tot. pop., 39,640,000.

El Salvador: Republic in Central America; capital, San Salvador. Evangelization affecting the whole territory followed Spanish occupation in the 1520's. The country was administered by the captaincy general of Guatemala until 1821 when independence from Spain was declared and it was annexed to Mexico. El Salvador joined the Central American Federation in 1825, decreed its own independence in 1841 and became a republic formally in 1856. In recent years, Church efforts to achieve social justice have resulted in persecution of the Church. (See Index for coverage of the assassination of Archbishop Romero and other 1980 events.) El Salvador maintains diplomatic relations with Vatican City.

Archd., 1; dioc., 4; bp., 5; parishes, 229; priests, 378 (176 dioc., 202 rel.); sem., 72; bros., 69; srs., 749; sch., 159; bap., 112,731; Caths., 3,878,476 (91.8%); tot. pop., 4,224,612.

England: Center of the United Kingdom of Great Britain (England, Scotland, Wales) and Northern Ireland, off the northwestern coast of Europe; capital, London. The arrival of St. Augustine of Canterbury and a band of monks in 597 marked the beginning of evangelization. Real organization of the Church took place some years after the Synod of Whitby, held in 663. Heavy losses were sustained in the wake of the Danish invasion in the 780's, but recovery starting from the time of Alfred the Great and dating especially from the middle of the 10th century led to Christianization of the whole country and close Church-state relations. The Norman Conquest of 1066 opened the Church in England to European influence. The 13th century was climactic, but decline had already set in by 1300 when the country had an all-time high of 17,000 religious. In the 14th century, John Wycliff presaged the Protestant Reformation. Henry VIII, failing in 1529 to gain annulment of his marriage to Catherine of Aragon, refused to acknowledge papal authority over the Church in England, had himself proclaimed its head, suppressed all houses of religious, and persecuted persons — Sts. Thomas More and John Fisher, among others — for not subscribing to the Oath of Supremacy and Act of Succession. He held the line on other-than-papal doctrine, however, until his death in 1547. Doctrinal aberrations were introduced during the reign of Edward VI (1547-53), through the Order of Communion, two books of Common Prayer, and the Articles of the Established Church. Mary Tudor's attempted Catholic restoration (1553-58) was a disaster, resulting in the deaths of more than 300 Protestants. Elizabeth (1558-1603) firmed up the Established Church with formation of a hierarchy, legal enactments and multi-phased persecution. One hundred and 11 priests and 62 lay persons were among the casualties of persecution during the underground Catholic revival which followed the return to England of missionary priests from France and The Lowlands. Several periods of comparative toleration ensued after Elizabeth's death. The first of several apostolic vicariates was established in 1685; this form of church government was maintained until the restoration of the hierarchy and diocesan organization in 1850. The revolution of 1688 and subsequent developments to about 1781 subjected Catholics to a wide variety of penal laws and disabilities in religious, civic and social life. The situation began to improve in 1791, and from 1801 Parliament frequently considered proposals for the repeal of penal laws against Catholics. The Act of Emancipation restored citizenship rights to Catholics in 1829. Restrictions remained in force for some time afterwards, however, on public religious worship and activity. The hierarchy was restored in 1850. Since then the Catholic Church, existing side by side with the Established Churches of England and Scotland, has followed a general pattern of growth and development. England has a diplomatic minister to Vatican City; there is an apostolic delegate in England.

Archd., 4; dioc., 15; ap. ex., 1; card., 1; abp., 3; bp., 33; parishes, 2,520; priests, 6,164 (4,134 dioc., 2,030 rel.); sem., 461; p.d., 38; srs., 11,097; sch., 2,572; bap., 68,672; Caths., 4,032,289 (8.7%); tot. pop., 46,369,240.

Equatorial Guinea: Republic on the west coast of Africa, consisting of Rio Muni on the mainland and the islands of Fernando Po and Annobon in the Gulf of Guinea: capital, Malabo (Santa Isabel). Evangelization began in 1841. Repressive measures were enacted against the Church after the country became independent of Spain in 1968. Developments following the August, 1979, overthrow of President Francisco Macias Nguema indicated some measure of improvement in Church-state relations. Equatorial Guinea has an apostolic delegate.

Dioc., 1; bp., 1 (nat., restored to his see of Bata, August, 1980); parishes, 20; priests, 23 (14 dioc., 9 rel.); sem., 9; bros., 5; srs., 33; bap., 6,799; Caths., 240,000 (73%); tot. pop., 330,000.

Estonia: Baltic republic forcibly absorbed by the U.S.S.R. in 1941; capital Tallinn. Catholicism was introduced in the 11th and 12th centuries. Jurisdiction over the area was made directly subject to the Holy See in 1215. Lutheran penetration was general in the Reformation period and Russian Orthodox influence was strong from early in the 18th century until 1917 when independence was attained. The first of several apostolic administrators was appointed in 1924. The small Catholic community was hard hit during and since Russian occupation in 1941. The Russian takeover of Estonia has not been recognized by the Holy See or the United States.

Ethiopia (Abyssinia): Constitutional monarchy in northeast Africa; capital, Addis Ababa. The country was evangelized by missionaries from Egypt in the fourth century and had a bishop by about 340. Following the lead of its parent body, the Egyptian (Coptic) Church, the Church in the area succumbed to the Monophysite heresy in the sixth century.

Catholic influence was negligible for centuries. An ordinariate for the Ethiopian Rite was established in Eritrea in 1930. An apostolic delegation was set up in Addis Ababa in 1937 and several jurisdictions were organized, some under the Congregation for the Oriental Churches and others under the Congregation for the Evangelization of Peoples. Most of the Catholics in the country are in the former Italian colony of Eritrea. Ethiopia maintains diplomatic relations with Vatican City.

Archd., 1; dioc., 2; v.a., 4; p.a., 1; abp., 1; bp., 5; parishes, 163; priests, 465 (155 dioc., 310 rel.); sem. 72; bros., 115; srs., 780; sch., 233; bap., 10,763; Caths., 200,905 (.7%); tot. pop., 29,647,000.

Falkland Islands: British colony off the southern tip of South America.

P.a., 1; parish, 1; priests, 2 (rel.); bap., 5; Caths., 192; tot. pop., 1,900.

Faroe Islands: Island group in North Atlantic; Danish possession. Under ecclesiastical jurisdiction of Copenhagen diocese.

Parish, 1; priest, 1 (rel.); srs., 12; sch., 2; Caths., 100; tot. pop., 41,000 (1978).

Fiji: Independent member of the British Commonwealth, 100 inhabited islands in the southwest Pacific; capital, Suva. Marist missionaries began work in 1844 after Methodism had been firmly established. A prefecture apostolic was organized in 1863. The hierarchy was established in 1966. Established diplomatic relations with Vatican City, 1978.

Archd., 1; abp., 1; parishes, 33; priests, 71 (16 dioc., 55 rel.); sem., 7; bros., 38; srs., 257; sch., 55; bap., 1,807; Caths., 51,894 (8.5%); tot. pop., 611,826.

Finland: Republic in northern Europe; capital, Helsinki. Swedes evangelized the country in the 12th century. The Reformation swept the country, resulting in the prohibition of Catholicism in 1595, general reorganization of ecclesiastical life and affairs, and dominance of the Evangelical Lutheran Church. Catholics were given religious liberty in 1781 but missionaries and conversions were forbidden by law. The first Finnish priest since the Reformation was ordained in 1903 in Paris. A vicariate apostolic for Finland was erected in 1920. A law on religious liberty, enacted in 1923, banned the foundation of monasteries. Finland maintains diplomatic relations with Vatican City.

Dioc., 1; bp., 1; parishes, 5; priests, 18 (2 dioc., 16 rel.); bros., 2; srs., 33; sch., 2; bap., 60; Caths., 3,221 (.06%); tot. pop., 4,758,449.

France: Republic in western Europe; capital, Paris. Christianity was known around Lyons by the middle of the second century. By 250 there were 30 bishoprics. The hierarchy reached a fair degree of organization by the end of the fourth century. Vandals and Franks subsequently invaded the territory and caused barbarian turmoil and doctrinal problems because of their Arianism. The Frankish nation was converted following the baptism of Clovis about 496. Christianization was complete by some time in the seventh century. From then on the Church, its leaders and people, figured in virtually every important development — religious, cultural, political and social — through the periods of the Carolingians, feudalism, the Middle Ages and monarchies to the end of the 18th century. The great University of Paris became one of the intellectual centers of the 13th century. Churchmen and secular rulers were involved with developments surrounding the Avignon residence of the popes and curia from 1309 until near the end of the 14th century and with the disastrous Western Schism that followed. Strong currents of Gallicanism and conciliarism ran through ecclesiastical and secular circles in France; the former was an ideology and movement to restrict papal control of the Church in the country, the latter sought to make the pope subservient to a general council. Calvinism invaded the country about the middle of the 16th century and won a strong body of converts. Jansenism with its rigorous spirit and other aberrations appeared in the next century, to be followed by the highly influential Enlightenment. The Revolution which started in 1789 and was succeeded by the Napoleonic period completely changed the status of the Church, taking a toll of numbers by persecution and defection and disenfranchising the Church in practically every way. Throughout the 19th century the Church was caught up in the whirl of imperial and republican developments and made the victim of official hostility, popular indifference and liberal opposition. In this century, the Church has struggled with problems involving the heritage of the Revolution and its aftermath, the alienation of intellectuals, liberalism, the estrangement of the working classes because of the Church's former identification with the ruling class, and the massive needs of contemporary society. France maintains diplomatic relations with Vatican City. (See Index for coverage of the papal visit to France in 1980.)

Archd., 18; dioc., 75; prel., 1; ap. ex., 2; ord., 1; card., 7; abp., 16; bp., 98; parishes, 38,197; priests, 40,680 (33,442 dioc., 7,238 rel.); sem., 1,320; p.d., 57; bros., 5,003; srs., 87,891; sch., 9,566; bap., 529,827; Caths., 45,102,000 (84.9%); tot. pop., 53,105,000 (1978 figures, except for hierarchy).

Gabon: Republic on the west coast of Equatorial Africa; capital, Libreville. Sporadic missionary effort took place before 1881 when effective evangelization began. The hierarchy was established in 1955. Gabon maintains diplomatic relations with Vatican City.

Archd., 1; dioc., 3; abp., 1 (nat.); bp., 3 (nat.); parishes, 56; priests, 107 (28 dioc., 79 rel.); sem., 14; bros., 39; srs., 151; sch., 264;

bap., 8,276; Caths., 415,461 (57.1%); tot. pop., 727,515 (population figures were compiled from 1980 Annuario Pontificio; other sources report total population of 530-560,000 with an estimated Catholic percentage of 25 to 45%).

Gambia, The: Republic (1970) on the northwestern coast of Africa, smallest state in Africa, member of the British Commonwealth; capital, Banjui. The country was under the jurisdiction of a vicariate apostolic until 1931. The hierarchy was established in 1957. Established diplomatic relations with Vatican City, 1978.

Dioc., 1; bp., 1; parishes, 3; priests, 20 (rel.); sem. 14; bros., 1; srs., 21; sch., 40; bap., 625; Caths., 12,300 (2.1%); tot. pop., 575,938.

Germany: Country in northern Europe partitioned in 1949 into the Communist German Democratic Republic in the East (capital, East Berlin) and the German Federal Republic in the West (capital, Bonn). Christianity was introduced in the third century, if not earlier. Trier, which became a center for missionary activity, had a bishop by 400. Visigoth invaders introduced Arianism in the fifth century but were converted in the seventh century by the East Franks, Celtic and other missionaries. St. Boniface, the apostle of Germany, established real ecclesiastical organization in the eighth century. The Church had great influence during the Carolingian period. Bishops from that time onward began to act in dual roles as pastors and rulers, a state of affairs which led inevitably to confusion and conflict in Church-state relations and perplexing problems of investiture. The Church developed strength and vitality through the Middle Ages but succumbed to abuses which antedated and prepared the ground for the Reformation. Luther's actions from 1517 made Germany a confessional battleground. Religious strife continued until conclusion of the Peace of Westphalia at the end of the Thirty Years' War in 1648. Nearly a century earlier the Peace of Augsburg (1555) had been designed, without success, to assure a degree of tranquillity by recognizing the legitimacy of different religious confessions in different states, depending on the decisions of princes. The implicit principle that princes should control the churches emerged in practice into the absolutism and Josephinism of subsequent years. St. Peter Canisius and his fellow Jesuits spearheaded a Counter Reformation in the second half of the 16th century. Before the end of the century, however, 70 per cent of the population of north and central Germany were Lutheran. Calvinism also had established a strong presence. The Church gained internal strength in a defensive position. Through much of the 19th century, however, its influence was eclipsed by Protestant intellectuals and other influences. It suffered some impoverishment also as a result of shifting boundaries and the

secularization of property shortly after 1800. It came under direct attack in the Kulturkampf of the 1870's but helped to generate the opposition which resulted in a dampening of the campaign of Bismarck against it. Despite action by Catholics on the social front and other developments, discrimination against the Church spilled over into the 20th century and lasted beyond World War I. Catholics in politics struggled with others to pull the country through numerous postwar crises. The dissolution of the Center Party, agreed to by the bishops in 1933 without awareness of the ultimate consequences, contributed negatively to the rise of Hitler to supreme power. Church officials protested the Nazi anti-Church and anti-Semitic actions, but to no avail. After World War II Christian leadership had much to do with the recovery of Western Germany. East Germany, gone Communist under Russian auspices, initiated a program of control and repression of the Church in 1948 and 1949. With no prospect of success for measures designed to split bishops, priests, religious and lay persons, the regime has concentrated most of its attention on mind control, especially of the younger generation, by the elimination of religious schools, curtailment of freedom for religious instruction and formation, severe restriction of the religious press, and the substitution since the mid-50's of youth initiation and Communist ceremonies for the rites of baptism, confirmation, marriage, and funerals. Bishops are generally forbidden to travel outside the Republic. The number of priests is decreasing, partly because of reduced seminary enrollments ordered by the government since 1958. In 1973, the Vatican appointed three apostolic administrators and one auxiliary (all titular bishops) for the areas of three West German dioceses located in East Germany. West Germany maintains diplomatic relations with Vatican City.

West Germany: Archd., 5; dioc., 17 (includes Berlin which covers part of East Germany); ap., ex., 1; card., 4; abp., 3; bp., 60; parishes, 11,763; priests, 23,086 (17,143 dioc., 5,943 rel.); sem., 2,515; p.d., 463; bros., 2,900; srs., 65,538; sch., 1,002; bap., 247,961; Caths., 28,751,000 (46.8%); tot. pop., 61,396,000. (1978, except for hierarchy).

East Germany: Dioc., 1 (Meissen); a.a., 1 (Gorlitz; there are also 3 territories with apostolic administrators); bp., 9; parishes, 920; priests, 1,520 (1,280 dioc., 240 rel.); sem., 174; p.d., 26; bros., 56; srs., 3,244; bap., 9,178; Caths., 1,279,000 (7.6%); tot. pop., 16,765,000. (1978, except for hierarchy).

Ghana: Republic on the western coast of Africa, bordering on the Gulf of Guinea, member of the British Commonwealth; capital, Accra. Priests visited the country in 1482, 11 years after discovery by the Portuguese, but missionary effort — hindered by the slave trade and other factors — was slight until 1880 when systematic evangelization began. A prefecture apostolic was set up in 1879. The hierarchy was established in 1950. Ghana maintains diplomatic relations with Vatican City. (See Index for coverage of the papal visit to Ghana in 1980.)

Archd., 2; dioc., 7; abp., 2 (nat.); bp., 7 (nat.); parishes, 143; priests, 409 (163 dioc., 246 rel.); sem., 206; bros., 103; srs., 407; sch., 1,805; bap., 38,765; Caths., 1,296,532 (12.3%); tot. pop., 10,480,000.

Gibraltar: British colony on the tip of the Spanish Peninsula on the Mediterranean. Evangelization took place after the Moors were driven out near the end of the 15th century. The Church was hindered by the British who acquired the colony in 1713. Most of the Catholics were, and are, Spanish and Italian immigrants and their descendants. A vicariate apostolic was organized in 1817. The diocese was erected in 1910.

Dioc., 1; bp., 1; parishes, 4; priests, 14 (13 dioc., 1 rel.); sem., 2; srs., 23; sch., 2; bap., 325; Caths., 21,197 (71.9%); tot. pop., 30,197.

Gilbert Islands: See Kiribati.

Greece, including Crete: Kingdom in southeastern Europe on the Balkan Peninsula; capital, Athens. St. Paul preached the Gospel at Athens and Corinth on his second missionary journey and visited the country again on his third tour. Other Apostles may have passed through also. Two bishops from Greece attended the First Council of Nicaea. After the division of the Roman Empire, the Church remained Eastern in rite and later broke ties with Rome as a result of the schism of 1054. A Latin-Rite jurisdiction was set up during the period of the Latin Empire of Constantinople, 1204-1261, but crumbled afterwards. Unity efforts of the Council of Florence had poor results. The country now has Greek Catholic and Latin jurisdictions. The Greek Orthodox Church is predominant. Established diplomatic relations with Vatican City in 1980.

Archd., 4; dioc., 4; v.a., 1; ap. ex., 1; ord., 1; abp., 3; bp., 2; parishes, 72; priests, 102 (61 dioc., 41 rel.); sem., 6; bros., 45; srs., 161; sch., 36; bap., 350; Caths., 46,243 (.5%); tot. pop., 9,300,000.

Greenland (Kalaallit Nunaat): Danish island province northeast of North America; granted self rule in 1979; capital, Nuuk (Godthaab). Catholicism was introduced about 1000. The first diocese was established in 1124 and a line of bishops dated from then until 1537. The first known churches in the western hemisphere, dating from about the 11th century, were on Greenland; the remains of 19 have been unearthed. The departure of Scandinavians and spread of the Reformation reduced the Church to nothing. The Moravian Brethren evangelized the Eskimos from the 1720's to 1901. By 1930 the Danish Church —

Evangelical Lutheran — was in full possession. Since 1930 priests have been in Greenland, which is part of the Copenhagen diocese. There are about 60 Catholics in the area.

Grenada: Independent island state in the West Indies; capital, St. George's. Established diplomatic relations with Vatican City in 1979.

Dioc., 1; bp., 1; parishes, 20; priests, 22 (6 dioc., 16 rel.); sem., 3; p.d., 2; bros., 7; srs., 23; sch., 33; bap., 1,360; Caths., 69,031; tot. pop., 110,445.

Guadeloupe: French overseas department in the Leeward Islands of the West Indies; capital, Basse-Terre. Catholicism was introduced in the islands in the 16th century.

Dioc., 1; bp., 1; parishes, 46; priests, 89 (49 dioc., 40 rel.); sem., 6; bros., 6; srs., 203; sch., 22; bap., 4,957; Caths., 300,000; tot. pop., 370,000.

Guam: U.S. territory in the southwest Pacific; capital, Agana. The first Mass was offered in the Mariana Islands in 1521. The islands were evangelized by the Jesuits, from 1668, and other missionaries. The first native Micronesian bishop was ordained in 1970.

Dioc., 1; bp., 1 (nat.); parishes, 35; priests, 57 (21 dioc., 36 rel.); sem., 4; p.d., 10; bros., 8; srs., 138; sch., 14; bap., 2,530; Caths., 120,659; tot. pop., 129,428.

Guatemala: Republic in Central America; capital, Guatemala City. Evangelization dates from the beginning of Spanish occupation in 1524. The first diocese, for all Central American territories administered by the captaincy general of Guatemala, was established in 1534. The country became independent in 1839, following annexation to Mexico in 1821, secession in 1823 and membership in the Central American Federation from 1825. In 1870, a government installed by a liberal revolution repudiated the concordat of 1853 and took active measures against the Church. Separation of Church and state was decreed; religious orders were suppressed and their property seized; priests and religious were exiled; schools were secularized. Full freedom was subsequently granted. Guatemala maintains diplomatic relations with Vatican City.

Archd., 1; dioc., 8; prel., 2; a.a., 2; card., 1; bp., 12; parishes, 336; priests, 679 (217 dioc., 462 rel.); sem., 84; p.d., 3; bros., 118; srs., 1,121; sch., 246; bap., 185,155; Caths. 5,667,000 (88%); tot. pop. 6,436,000. (Catholic and total population figures are from 1977 Statistical Yearbook of the Church; others are from 1980 Annuario Pontificio.)

Guiana, French (Cayenne): French overseas department on the northeast coast of South America; capital, Cayenne. Catholicism was introduced in the 17th century. The Cayenne diocese was established in 1956.

Dioc., 1; bp., 1; parishes, 27; priests, 26 (6

dioc., 20 rel.); bros., 2; srs., 85; sch., 7; bap., 1,102; Caths., 49,000; tot. pop., 62,000.

Guinea: Republic on the west coast of Africa; capital, Conakry. Occasional missionary work followed exploration by the Portuguese about the middle of the 15th century; organized effort dates from 1877. The hierarchy was established in 1955. Following independence from France in 1958, Catholic schools were nationalized, youth organizations banned and missionaries restricted. Foreign missionaries were expelled in 1967. Archbishop Tchidimbo of Conakry, sentenced to life imprisonment in 1971 on a charge of conspiring to overthrow the government, was released in August, 1979; he resigned his see. Guinea has an apostolic delegate.

Archd., 1; dioc., 1; p.a., 1; abp., 1 (nat.); bp., 1 (nat.); parishes, 28; priests, 19 (18 dioc., 1 rel.); sem., 14; bros., 1; srs., 22; bap., 914; Caths., 43,508 (.9%); tot. pop., 4,650,000. (Some statistics date from 1968.)

Guinea-Bissau (formerly Portuguese Guinea): Independent state on the west coast of Africa; capital, Bissau. Catholicism was introduced in the second half of the 15th century but limited missionary work, hampered by the slave trade, had meager results. Missionary work in this century dates from 1933. A prefecture apostolic was established in 1955 (made a diocese in 1977). Guinea-Bissau has an apostolic delegate.

Dioc., 1; bp., 1; parishes, 15; priests, 36 (rel); bros., 11; srs., 16; bap., 759; Caths., 41,000; tot. pop., 650,000 (some figures are from 1975).

Guyana: Republic on the northern coast of South America; capital, Georgetown. In 1899 the Catholic Church and other churches were given equal status with the Church of England and the Church of Scotland, which had sole rights up to that time. Most of the Catholics are Portuguese. The Georgetown diocese was established in 1956, 10 years before Guyana became independent of England. The first native bishop was appointed in 1971. Schools were nationalized in 1976.

Dioc., 1; bp., 1; parishes, 26; priests, 61 (8 dioc., 53 rel.); sem., 3; bros., 6; srs., 53; bap., 2,253; Caths., 94,500 (11.5%); tot. pop., 820,000.

Haiti: Caribbean republic on the western third of Hispaniola adjacent to the Dominican Republic; capital, Port-au-Prince. Evangelization followed discovery by Columbus in 1492. Capuchins and Jesuits did most of the missionary work in the 18th century. From 1804, when independence was declared, until 1860, the country was in schism. Relations were regularized by a concordat concluded in 1860, when an archdiocese and four dioceses were established. Factors hindering the development of the Church have been a shortage of native clergy, inadequate religious instruction and the prevalence of voodoo. Political upheavals in the 1960's had serious effects on the Church. Haiti maintains diplomatic relations with Vatican City.

Archd., 1; dioc., 6; abp., 1; bp., 7; parishes, 186; priests, 387 (184 dioc., 203 rel.); sem., 85; p.d., 2; bros., 207; srs., 860; sch., 709; bap., 104,076; Caths., 4,725,634 (83%); tot. pop. 5,691,412 (1980 Annuario Pontificio figures; other sources give lower population figures with the percentage of Catholics ranging from 80 to 90%).

Honduras: Republic in Central America; capital, Tegucigalpa. Evangelization preceded establishment of the first diocese in the 16th century. Under Spanish rule and after independence from 1823, the Church held a favored position until 1880 when equal legal status was given to all religions. Honduras maintains diplomatic relations with Vatican City.

Archd., 1; dioc., 4; prel., 1; abp., 1; bp., 6; parishes, 109; priests, 229 (73 dioc., 156 rel.); sem., 24; p.d., 1; bros., 20; srs., 278; sch., 52; bap., 118,891; Caths., 3,087,840 (92%); tot. pop., 3,360,000.

Hong Kong: British crown colony at the mouth of the Canton River, adjacent to the southeast Chinese province of Kwangtung. A prefecture apostolic was established in 1841. Members of the Pontifical Institute for Foreign Missions began work there in 1858. The Hong Kong diocese was erected in 1946.

Dioc., 1; bp., 1; parishes, 29; priests, 351 (71 dioc., 280 rel.); sem., 16; bros., 111; srs., 774; sch., 311; bap., 5,637; Caths., 258,817 (5.5%); tot. pop., 4,720,000.

Hungary: People's republic in east central Europe; capital, Budapest. The early origins of Christianity in the country, whose territory was subject to a great deal of change, is not known. Magyars accepted Christianity about the end of the 10th century. St. Stephen I (d. 1038) promoted its spread and helped to organize some of its historical dioceses. Bishops early became influential in politics as well as in the Church. For centuries the country served as a buffer for the Christian West against barbarians from the East, notably the Mongols in the 13th century. Religious orders, whose foundations started from the 1130's, provided the most effective missionaries, pastors and teachers. Outstanding for years were the Franciscans and Dominicans; the Jesuits were noted for their work in the Counter-Reformation from the second half of the 16th century onwards. Hussites and Waldensians prepared the way for the Reformation which struck at almost the same time as the Turks. The Reformation made considerable progress after 1526, resulting in the conversion of large numbers to Lutheranism and Calvinism by the end of the century. Most of them or their descendants returned to the Church later, but many Magyars remained staunch Calvinists. Turks repressed the churches, Protestant as well as Catholic, during a reign of 150 years but they managed to survive. Domination of the Church was one of the objectives of government policy during the reigns of Maria Theresa and Joseph II in the second half of the 18th century; their Josephinism affected Church-state relations until the first World War. More than 100,000 Eastern Rite schismatics were reunited with Rome about the turn of the 18th century. Secularization increased in the second half of the 19th century, which also witnessed the birth of many new Catholic organizations and movements to influence life in the nation and the Church. Catholics were involved in the social chaos and anti-religious atmosphere of the years following World War I, struggling with their compatriots for religious as well as political survival. After World War II Communist strength, which had manifested itself with less intensity earlier in the century, was great long before it forced the legally elected president out of office in 1947 and imposed a Soviet type of constitution on the country in 1949. The campaign against the Church started with the disbanding of Catholic organizations in 1946. In 1948, "Caritas," the Catholic charitable organization, was taken over and all Catholic schools, colleges and institutions were suppressed. Interference in church administration and attempts to split the bishops preceded the arrest of Cardinal Mindszenty on Dec. 26, 1948, and his sentence to life imprisonment in 1949. (He was free for a few days during the unsuccessful uprising of 1956. He then took up residence at the U.S. Embassy in Budapest where he remained until September, 1971, when he was permitted to leave the country. He died in 1975 in Vienna.) In 1950, religious orders and congregations were suppressed and 10,000 religious were interned. At least 30 priests and monks were assassinated, jailed or deported. About 4,000 priests and religious were confined in jail or concentration camps. The government sponsored a national "Progressive Catholic" church and captive organizations for priests and "Catholic Action," which attracted only a small minority. Signs were clear in 1965 and 1966 that a 1964 agreement with the Holy See regarding episcopal appointments had settled nothing. Six bishops were appointed by the Holy See and some other posts were filled, but none of the prelates were free from government surveillance and harassment. Four new bishops were appointed by the Holy See in January and ordained in Budapest in February, 1969; three elderly prelates resigned their sees. Shortly thereafter, peace priests complained that the "too Roman" new bishops would not deal with them. Talks between Vatican and Hungarian representatives during the past several years have resulted in the appointment of bishops to fill all of Hungary's 11 residential sees.

Archd., 3; dioc., 8; abb., 1; ap. ex., 1; card, 1; abp., 2; bp., 16; parishes, 2,185; priests, 3,269 (3,134 dioc., 135 rel.); sem., 270; bros., 26; srs., 55; sch., 11; bap., 85,947; Caths., 6,500,000 (60.8%); tot. pop., 10,690,000.

Iceland: Island republic between Norway and Greenland; capital, Reykjavik. Irish hermits were there in the eighth century. Missionaries subsequently evangelized the island and Christianity was officially accepted about 1000. The first bishop was ordained in 1056. The Black Death had dire effects and spiritual decline set in during the 15th century. Lutheranism was introduced from Denmark between 1537 and 1552 and made the official religion. Some Catholic missionary work was done in the 19th century. Religious freedom was granted to the few Catholics in 1874. A vicariate was erected in 1929 (made a diocese in 1968). Iceland maintains diplomatic relations with Vatican City.

Dioc., 1; bp., 1; parishes, 2; priests, 7 (1 dioc., 6 rel.); sem., 4; srs., 53; sch., 3; bap., 12; Caths., 1,439; tot. pop., 225,000.

India: Republic on the subcontinent of south central Asia, member of the British Commonwealth; capital, New Delhi. Long-standing tradition credits the Apostle Thomas with the introduction of Christianity in the Kerala area. Evangelization followed the establishment of Portuguese posts and the conquest of Goa in 1510. Jesuits, Franciscans, Dominicans, Augustinians and members of other religious orders figured in the early missionary history. An archdiocese for Goa, with two suffragan sees, was set up in 1558. Five provincial councils were held between 1567 and 1606. The number of Catholics in 1572 was estimated to be 280,000. This figure rose to 800,000 in 1700 and declined to 500,000 in 1800. Missionaries had some difficulties with the British East India Co. which exercised virtual government control from 1757 to 1858. They also had trouble because of a conflict that developed between policies of the Portuguese government, which pressed its rights of patronage in episcopal and clerical appointments, and the Congregation for the Propagation of the Faith, which sought greater freedom of action in the same appointments. This struggle eventuated in the schism of Goa between 1838 and 1857. In 1886, when the number of Catholics was estimated to be one million, the hierarchy for India and Ceylon was restored. Jesuits contributed greatly to the development of Catholic education from the second half of the 19th century. A large percentage of the Catholic population is located around Goa and Kerala and farther south. The country is predominantly Hindu. India maintains diplomatic relations with Vatican City. So-called anti-conversion laws in effect in several states have had a restrictive effect on pastoral ministry and social service.

Patriarchate, 1 (titular of East Indies); archd., 19; dioc., 88; p.a., 2; card., 2; abp., 16; bp., 85; parishes, 4,431; priests, 10,642 (6,453 dioc., 4,189 rel.); sem., 4,662; p.d., 16; bros., 2,555; srs., 43,951; sch., 8,545; bap., 274,172; Caths., 9,704,000 (1.6%); tot. pop., 625,818,000 (1978, except for jurisdictions, hierarchy).

Indonesia: Republic southeast of Asia, consisting of some 3,000 islands including Kalimantan (most of Borneo), Sulawesi (Celebes), Java, the Lesser Sundas, Moluccas, Sumatra, Timor and West Irian (Irian Jaya, western part of New Guinea); capital, Jakarta. Evangelization by the Portuguese began about 1511. St. Francis Xavier, greatest of the modern missionaries, spent some 14 months in the area. Christianity was strongly rooted in some parts of the islands by 1600. Islam's rise to dominance began at this time. The Dutch East Indies Co., which gained effective control in the 17th century, banned evangelization by Catholic missionaries for some time but Dutch secular and religious priests managed to resume the work. A vicariate of Batavia for all the Dutch East Indies was set up in 1841. About 90 per cent of the population is Moslem. The hierarchy was established in 1961. Indonesia maintains diplomatic relations with Vatican City.

Archd., 7; dioc., 24; p.a., 2; card., 1; abp., 6; bp., 21; parishes, 361; priests, 1,526 (165 dioc., 1,361 rel.); sem., 358; p.d., 8; bros., 686; srs., 3,853; sch., 4,021; bap., 135,780; Caths., 3,024,000 (2.1%); tot. pop., 143,282,000. (Statistics for former Portuguese Timor which was annexed by Indonesia in 1976 are listed separately; see Timor, Eastern.)

Iran: Constitutional monarchy in southwestern Asia, between the Caspian Sea and the Persian Gulf; capital, Teheran. Some of the earliest Christian communities were established in this area outside the (then) Roman Empire. They suffered persecution in the fourth century and were then cut off from the outside world. Nestorianism was generally professed in the late fifth century. Islam became dominant after 640. Some later missionary work was attempted but without success. Religious liberty was granted in 1834, but Catholics were the victims of a massacre in 1918. Islam is the religion of perhaps 98 per cent of the population. In 1964 the country had 100,000 Monophysites, the largest group of Christians, and some 20,000 Nestorians. Catholics belong to the Latin, Armenian and Chaldean rites. Iran (Persia until 1935) maintains diplomatic relations with Vatican City. In developments connected with the Islamic revolution in the summer of 1980, Archbishop William Barden of Ispahan and several Salesians were expelled, and Catholic schools were closed.

Archd., 4; dioc., 2; abp., 4; bp., 1; parishes, 24; priests, 64 (17 dioc., 47 rel.); sem., 1; p.d.,

1; bros., 3; srs., 71; sch., 17; bap., 491; Caths., 25,900 (.1%); tot. pop., 35,210,000.

Iraq: Republic in southwestern Asia, between Iran and Saudi Arabia; capital, Baghdad. Some of the earliest Christian communities were established in the area, whose history resembles that of Iran. Catholics belong to the Armenian, Chaldean, Latin and Syrian rites; Chaldeans are most numerous. Islam is the religion of some 90 per cent of the population. Iraq maintains diplomatic relations with Vatican City.

Patriarchate, 1; archd., 9; dioc., 5; mission "sui juris," 1; patriarch, 1; abp., 9; bp., 4; parishes, 81; priests, 148 (115 dioc., 33 rel.); sem., 22; bros., 22; srs., 212; bap., 5,032; Caths. (approx.), 300,000; tot. pop., 12,300,000.

Ireland: Republic in the British Isles; capital, Dublin. St. Patrick, who is venerated as the apostle of Ireland, evangelized parts of the island for some years after the middle of the fifth century. Conversion of the island was not accomplished, however, until the seventh century or later. Celtic monks were the principal missionaries. The Church was organized along monastic lines at first, but a movement developed in the 11th century for the establishment of jurisdiction along episcopal lines. By that time many Roman usages had been adopted. The Church gathered strength during the period from the Norman Conquest of England to the reign of Henry VIII despite a wide variety of rivalries, wars, and other disturbances. Henry introduced an age of repression of the faith which continued for many years under several of his successors. The Irish suffered from proscription of the Catholic faith, economic and social disabilities, subjection to absentee landlords and a plantation system designed to keep them from owning property, and actual persecution which took an uncertain toll of lives up until about 1714. Most of those living in the northern part of Ireland became Anglican and Presbyterian in the 1600's but the south remained strong in faith. Some penal laws remained in force until emancipation in 1829. Nearly 100 years later Ireland was divided by two enactments which made Northern Ireland, consisting of six counties, part of the United Kingdom (1920) and gave dominion status to the Irish Free State, made up of the other 26 counties (1922). This state (Eire, in Gaelic) was proclaimed the Republic of Ireland in 1949. The Catholic Church predominates but religious freedom is guaranteed for all. Ireland maintains diplomatic relations with Vatican City.

Archd., 4; dioc., 23; card., 1; abp., 4; bp., 30; parishes, 1,289; priests, 5,892 (3,772 dioc., 2,120 rel.); sem., 628; bros., 1,879; srs., 12,759; sch., 4,244; bap., 79,227 (preceding figures include Northern Ireland); Caths., 2,970,400 (94%); tot. pop., 3,160,000 (1978).

Ireland, Northern: Part of the United Kingdom, it consists of six of the nine counties of Ulster in the northeast corner of Ireland; capital, Belfast. History is given under Ireland, above. For recent developments, see Index.

Caths. (approx.), 505,000 (32%); tot. pop. (1975 est.), 1,537,000 (other statistics are included in Ireland).

Israel: Parliamentary democracy in the Middle East, at the eastern end of the Mediterranean; capitals, Jerusalem and Tel Aviv (diplomatic). Israel was the birthplace of Christianity, the site of the first Christian communities. Some persecution was suffered in the early Christian era and again during the several hundred years of Roman control. Moslems conquered the territory in the seventh century and, except for the period of the Kingdom of Jerusalem established by Crusaders, remained in control most of the time up until World War I. The Church survived in the area, sometimes just barely, but it did not prosper greatly or show any notable increase in numbers. The British took over the protectorate of the area after World War I. Partition into Israel for the Jews and Palestine for the Arabs was approved by the United Nations in 1947. War broke out a year later with the proclamation of the Republic of Israel. The Israelis won the war and 50 percent more territory than they had originally been ceded. War broke out again for six days in June, 1967, and in October, 1973, resulting in a Middle East crisis which persists to the present time. Caught in the middle of the conflict are hundreds of thousands of dispossessed Palestinian refugees. Judaism is the faith professed by about 85 percent of the inhabitants; approximately one-third of them are considered observants. Most of the Arab minority are Moslems. The Acre archdiocese for Melkites is situated in Israel. Maronites are subject to the bishop of Tyr, Lebanon. Latins are under the jurisdiction of the Roman patriarchate of Jerusalem. Israel has an apostolic delegate. The *1977 Statistical Yearbook of the Church* reported a Catholic population of 73,000 in a total population of 3,611,000.

Italy: Republic in southern Europe; capital, Rome. A Christian community was formed early at Rome, probably by the middle of the first century. St. Peter established his see there. He and St. Paul suffered death for the faith there in the 60s. The early Christians were persecuted at various times there, as in other parts of the empire, but the Church developed in numbers and influence, gradually spreading out from towns and cities in the center and south to rural areas and the north. Organization, in the process of formation in the second century, developed greatly between the fifth and eighth centuries. By the latter date the Church had already come to grips with serious problems, including doctrinal and disciplinary disputes that threatened the unity of faith, barbarian invasions, and the need for the pope and bishops to take over civil responsibilities because of imperial default. The Church has been at the center of life on the peninsula throughout the centuries. It emerged from underground in 313, with the Edict of Milan, and rose to a position of prestige and lasting influence. It educated and converted the barbarians, preserved culture through the early Middle Ages and passed it on to later times, suffered periods of decline and gained strength through recurring reforms, engaged in military combat for political reasons and intellectual combat for the preservation and development of doctrine, saw and patronized the development of the arts, experienced all human strengths and weaknesses in its members, knew triumph and the humiliation of failure. For long centuries, from the fourth to the 19th, the Church was a temporal as well as spiritual power. This temporal aspect complicated its history in Italy. Since the 1870's, however, when the Papal States were annexed by the Kingdom of Italy, the history became simpler — but remained complicated — as the Church, shorn of temporal power, began to find new freedom for the fulfillment of its spiritual mission. Italy maintains diplomatic relations with Vatican City.

Patriarchate, 1; archd., 56; dioc., 215; prel., 4; abb., 9; card., 35; abp., 44; bp. (approx.), 200; parishes, 28,384; priests, 61,984 (41,212 dioc., 20,772 rel.); sem., 5,230; p.d., 91; bros., 6,358; srs., 144,107; sch., 3,737; bap., 748,811; Caths., 55,030,000 (97.5%); tot. pop., 56,446,000 (1978, except for hierarchy).

Ivory Coast: Republic in western Africa; capital, Abidjan. The Holy Ghost Fathers began systematic evangelization in 1895. The first native priests from the area were ordained in 1934. The hierarchy was set up in 1955. Ivory Coast maintains diplomatic relations with Vatican City. (See Index for coverage of the papal visit to Ivory Coast in 1980.)

Archd., 1; dioc., 7; abp., 1 (nat.); bp., 8 (nat.); parishes, 151; priests, 395 (122 dioc., 273 rel.); sem., 54; p.d., 1; bros., 92; srs., 503; sch., 336; bap., 15,916; Caths., 675,032 (9.1%); tot. pop., 7,415,000.

Jamaica: Parliamentary democracy in the West Indies, member of the British Commonwealth; capital, Kingston. Franciscans and Dominicans evangelized the island from about 1512 until 1655. Missionary work was interrupted after the English took possession but was resumed by Jesuits about the turn of the 19th century. A vicariate apostolic was organized in 1837. The hierarchy was established in 1967. Established diplomatic relations with Vatican City in 1979.

Archd., 1; dioc., 1; abp., 1; bp., 1; parishes, 29; priests, 107 (23 dioc., 84 rel.); p.d., 2; bros.,

13; srs., 191; bap., 3,222; Caths., 187,220 (8.9%); tot. pop., 2,090,000.

Japan: Constitutional monarchy in the northwest Pacific; capital, Tokyo. Jesuits began evangelization in the middle of the 16th century and about 300,000 converts, most of them in Kyushu, were reported at the end of the century. The Nagasaki Martyrs were victims of persecution in 1597. Another persecution took some 4,000 lives between 1614 and 1651. Missionaries, banned for two centuries, returned about the middle of the 19th century and found Christian communities still surviving in Nagasaki and other places in Kyushu. A vicariate was organized in 1846. Religious freedom was guaranteed in 1889. The hierarchy was established in 1891. Japan maintains diplomatic relations with Vatican City.

Archd., 3; dioc., 13; p.a., 1; card., 1; abp., 2; bp., 14; parishes, 727; priests, 1,932 (488 dioc., 1,444 rel.); sem., 79; p.d., 1; bros., 418; srs., 6,980; sch., 334; bap., 20,601; Caths., 386,262 (.3%); tot. pop., 114,900,000.

Jerusalem: The entire city, site of the first Christian community, has been under Israeli control since the Israeli-Arab war of June, 1967. There are two patriarchates in the city, Melkite and Latin. Jerusalem has an apostolic delegate.

Jordan: Constitutional monarchy in the Middle East; capital, Amman. Christianity there dates from apostolic times. Survival of the faith was threatened many times under the rule of Moslems from 636 and Ottoman Turks from 1517 to 1918, and in the Islamic Emirate of Trans-Jordan from 1918 to 1949. Since the creation of Israel, some 500,000 Palestinian refugees, some of them Christians, have been in Jordan. Islam is the state religion but religious freedom is guaranteed for all. Jordan has an apostolic delegate.

The statistics which follow are for the Greek Melkite-Rite Catholics of the Archdiocese of Petra and Philadelphia in Jordan. Separate statistics are not available for the Latin (Roman)-Rite Catholics under the jurisdiction of the Latin patriarchate of Jerusalem.

Archd., 1; abp., 1; parishes, 32; priests, 21 (17 dioc., 4 rel.); sem. 2; srs., 38; sch., 17; Caths., 18,240; tot. pop., 2,780,000.

Kampuchea (Democratic Kampuchea): Former names — Khmer Republic, Cambodia. Republic (Oct. 9, 1970) in southeast Asia, bordering on the Gulf of Siam, Thailand, Laos and Vietnam; capital Phnom Penh. Evangelization dating from the second half of the 16th century had limited results, more among Vietnamese than Khmers. Thousands of Catholics of Vietnamese origin were forced to flee in 1970 because of Khmer hostility. The status of the Church remained uncertain following the Khmer Rouge take-over in April, 1975. Foreign missionaries were expelled immediately. Local clergy and religious were sent to work the land; whether they

would be able to minister to the faithful was not known. Buddhism is the state religion. The country has an apostolic delegate.

V.a., 1; p.a., 2. No statistics available. Catholics numbered 13,835 (2% of the total population) in 1973. Tot. pop. (1978), 8,606,000.

Kashmir and Jammu: Statistics included in India.

Kenya: Republic in eastern Africa bordering on the Indian Ocean, member of the British Commonwealth; capital, Nairobi. Systematic evangelization by the Holy Ghost Fathers began in 1892, nearly 40 years after the start of work by Protestant missionaries. The hierarchy was established in 1953. Kenya maintains diplomatic relations with Vatican City. (See Index for coverage of the papal visit to Kenya in 1980.)

Archd., 1; dioc., 13; p.a., 1; card., 1 (nat.); bp., 13 (9 nat.); parishes, 247; priests, 796 (181 dioc., 615 rel.); sem., 1,758; p.d., 1; bros., 175; srs., 1,758; sch., 3,352; bap., 170,530; Caths., 2,615,360 (17.6%); tot. pop., 14,860,000.

Kiribati (Gilbert Islands): Former British colony in Oceania; became independent July 12, 1979; capital Bairiki on Tarawa. French Missionaries of the Sacred Heart began work in the islands in 1888. A vicariate for the islands was organized in 1897. The hierarchy was established in 1966.

Dioc., 1; bp., 1; parishes, 22; priests, 20 (2 dioc., 18 rel.); sem., 2; bros., 1; srs., 42; sch., 3; bap., 1,049; Caths., 29,300; tot. pop., 63,600. (Statistics are for the Tarawa, Nauru and Funafuti diocese which includes Kiribati, Republic of Nauru and the Tuvalu Islands.)

Korea: Peninsula in eastern Asia, east of China, divided into the (Communist) Democratic People's Republic in the North, formed May 1, 1948, with Pyongyang as its capital; and the Republic of Korea in the South, with Seoul as the capital. Some Catholics may have been in Korea before it became a "hermit kingdom" toward the end of the 16th century and closed its borders to foreigners. The real introduction to Catholicism came through lay converts in the last quarter of the 18th century. A priest arriving in the country in 1794 found 4,000 Catholics there who had never seen a priest. A vicariate was erected in 1831 but was not manned for several years thereafter. There were 15,000 Catholics by 1857. Four persecutions in the 19th century took a terrible toll; several thousands died in the last one, 1866-69. Freedom of religion was granted in 1883 when Korea opened its borders. Progress was made thereafter. The hierarchy was established in 1962. Since the war of 1950-1953, there have been no signs of Catholic life in the North, which has been blanketed by a news blackout. In July, 1972, both Koreas agreed to seek peaceful means of reunification. The South maintains diplomatic relations with Vatican City. Bishop Tji of Won Ju, South Korea, convicted and sentenced to 15 years' imprisonment in 1974 on a charge of inciting to rebellion, was released in February, 1975.

North Korea: Dioc., 2; abb., 1; bp., 1 (exiled); tot. pop., 16,650,000. No recent Catholic statistics available; there were an estimated 100,000 Catholics reported in 1969.

South Korea: Archd., 3; dioc., 11; card., 1; abp., 2; bp., 13; parishes, 564; priests, 900 (637 dioc., 263 rel.); sem., 491; bros., 143; srs., 2,949; sch., 87; bap., 52,850; Caths. 1,136,556 (3%); tot. pop., 37,115,789.

Kuwait: Constitutional monarchy (sultanate or sheikdom) in southwest Asia bordering on the Persian Gulf. Remote Christian origins probably date to apostolic times. Islam is the predominant and official religion. Kuwait maintains diplomatic relations with Vatican City.

V.a., 1; bp., 1; parishes, 3; priests, 7 (3 dioc., 4 rel.); srs., 30; sch., 6; bap., 488; Caths., 28,000 (2.3%); tot. pop., 1,200,000.

Laos: Constitutional monarchy in southeast Asia, surrounded by China, Vietnam, Kampuchea, Thailand and Burma; capital, Vientiane. Systematic evangelization by French missionaries started about 1881; earlier efforts ended in 1688. A vicariate apostolic was organized in 1899 when there were 8,000 Catholics and 2,000 catechumens in the country. Most of the foreign missionaries were expelled following the communist takeover in 1975. Buddhism is the state religion. Laos has an apostolic delegate.

V.a., 4; bp., 3 (nat.). No statistics available. Catholics numbered 35,000 (1% of the total population) in 1974. Tot. pop. (1978), 3,464,000.

Latvia: Baltic republic forcibly absorbed by the U.S.S.R. in the early 1940s; capital, Riga. Catholicism was introduced late in the 12th century. Lutheranism became the dominant religion after 1530. Catholics were free to practice their faith during the long period of Russian control and during independence from 1918 to 1940. The relatively small Catholic community has been repressed since the start of Soviet occupation. The Russian takeover of Latvia has not been recognized by the Holy See or the United States.

Lebanon: Republic in the Middle East, north of Israel; capital, Beirut. Christianity, introduced in apostolic times, was firmly established by the end of the fourth century and has remained so despite heavy Moslem influence since early in the seventh century. The country is the center of the Maronite Rite. Lebanon maintains diplomatic relations with Vatican City.

There are 18 ecclesiastical jurisdictions in Lebanon serving the following rites: Armenian (1 diocese); Chaldean (1 diocese); Roman (1 vicariate apostolic); Maronite (3 archdioceses and 5 dioceses); Greek Melkite (1 metropolitan see, 6 archdioceses); the Syrians are served by

a patriarchal vicar. The patriarchs of Antioch of the Syrians and Antioch of the Maronites reside in Lebanon. Catholics (est.), 1,000,000; tot. pop., 3,030,000.

Lesotho: Constitutional monarchy, an enclave in the southeastern part of the Republic of South Africa; capital, Maseru. Oblates of Mary Immaculate, the first Catholic missionaries in the area, started evangelization in 1862. A prefecture apostolic was organized in 1894. The hierarchy was established in 1951. Lesotho maintains diplomatic relations with Vatican City.

Archd., 1; dioc., 3; abp., 1 (nat.); bp., 3 (2 nat.); parishes, 72; priests, 120 (19 dioc., 101 rel.); sem., 17; bros., 55; srs., 740; sch., 508; bap., 22,357; Caths., 545,092 (49.3%); tot. pop., 1,102,604.

Liberia: Republic in western Africa, bordering on the Atlantic; capital, Monrovia. Missionary work and influence, dating interruptedly from the 16th century, were slight before the Society of African Missions undertook evangelization in 1906. Liberia maintains diplomatic relations with Vatican City.

V.a., 2; bp., 2 (nat.); parishes, 43; priests, 42 (7 dioc., 35 rel.); sem., 19; p.d., 3; bros., 23; srs., 49; sch., 67; bap., 2,892; Caths., 31,720 (1.7%); tot. pop., 1,800,000.

Libya: Arab republic in northern Africa, on the Mediterranean between Egypt and Tunisia; capitals are Tripoli and Benghasi. Christianity was probably preached in the area at an early date but was overcome by the spread of Islam from the 630's. Islamization was complete by 1067 and there has been no Christian influence since then. The Catholics in the country belong to the foreign colony. Islam is the state religion. Libya has an apostolic delegate.

V.a., 3; p.a., 1; bp., 2; parishes, 3; priests, 9 (rel.); srs., 142; bap., 10; Caths., 27,000 (1.1%); tot. pop., 2,500,000 (Catholic population figure is from 1977 Statistical Yearbook of the Church).

Liechtenstein: Constitutional monarchy in central Europe, in the Alps and on the Rhine between Switzerland and Austria; capital, Vaduz. Christianity in the country dates from the fourth century; the area has been under the jurisdiction of Chur, Switzerland, since about that time. The Reformation had hardly any influence in the country. Catholicism is the state religion but religious freedom for all is guaranteed by law.

Parishes, 10; priests, 27 (dioc.); sch., 1; srs., 120; sch., 1; bap., 500; Caths., 21,000; tot. pop., 23,000 (1978).

Lithuania: Baltic republic forcibly absorbed and under Soviet domination since 1945; captial, Vilna (Vilnius). Catholicism was introduced in 1251 and two dioceses were established by 1260. Effective evangelization took place between 1385 and 1417, when Catholicism became the state religion. Losses to

Lutheranism in the 16th century were overcome. Efforts of czars to "russify" the Church between 1795 and 1918 were strongly resisted. Concordat relations with the Vatican were established in 1927, nine years after independence from Russia and 13 years before the start of another kind of Russian control with the following results, among others: all convents closed since 1940; four seminaries shut down; appointment to one seminary (Kaunas) only with government approval; priests restricted in pastoral ministry and subject to appointment by government officials; no religious services outside churches; no religious press; religious instruction banned; parish installations and activities controlled by directives enacted in 1976; two bishops — Msgr. Vincentas Sladkevicius and Msgr. Julijonas Steponavicius — forbidden to act as bishops and relegated to remote parishes since 1957 and 1961, respectively; arrest, imprisonment or detention in Siberia for four bishops, 185 priests, 275 lay persons between 1945 and 1955. Despite such developments and conditions, there remains a strong and vigorous underground Church in Lithuania, where the Soviet government finds its repressive potential limited by the solidarity of popular resistance. The Soviet takeover of Lithuania is not recognized by the Holy See or the United States.

Luxembourg: Constitutional monarchy in western Europe, between Belgium, Germany and France; capital, Luxembourg. Christianity, introduced in the fifth and sixth centuries, was firmly established by the end of the eighth century. A full-scale parish system was in existence in the ninth century. Monastic influence was strong until the Reformation, which had minimal influence in the country. The Church experienced some adverse influence from the currents of the French Revolution. Luxembourg maintains diplomatic relations with Vatican City.

Dioc., 1; bp., 1; parishes, 274; priests, 475 (373 dioc., 102 rel.); sem., 20; bros., 30; srs., 1,288; sch., 12; bap., 3,295; Caths. 341,184 (95%); tot. pop., 360,000.

Macao: Portuguese province in southeast Asia across the Pearl River estuary from Hong Kong. Christianity was introduced by the Jesuits in 1557. Diocese was established in 1576. Macao served as a base for missionary work in Japan and China.

Dioc., 1; bp., 1; parishes, 8; priests, 73 (38 dioc., 35 rel.); sem., 3; bros., 14; srs., 201; sch., 47; bap., 715; Caths., 39,010; tot. pop., 300,636.

Madagascar (Malagasy Republic): Republic off the eastern coast of Africa; capital, Tananarive. Missionary efforts were generally fruitless from early in the 16th century until the Jesuits were permitted to start open evangelization about 1845. A prefecture apostolic was set up in 1850 and a vicariate apostolic in

the north was placed in charge of the Holy Ghost Fathers in 1898. There were 100,000 Catholics by 1900. The first native bishop was ordained in 1936. The hierarchy was established in 1955. Madagascar maintains diplomatic relations with Vatican City.

Archd., 3; dioc., 14; card., 1 (nat.); abp., 2 (nat.); bp., 15 (12 nat.); parishes, 131; priests, 662 (140 dioc., 522 rel.); sem., 98; bros., 330; srs., 1,674; bap., 75,915; Caths., 1,840,330 (21.5%); tot. pop. 8,530,000.

Madeira Islands: Portuguese province, an archipelago 340 miles west of the northwestern coast of Africa; capital, Funchal. Catholicism has had a continuous history since the first half of the 15th century. Statistics are included in those for Portugal.

Malawi: Republic in the interior of eastern Africa, member of the British Commonwealth; capital, Lilongwe. Missionary work, begun by Jesuits in the late 16th and early 17th centuries, was generally ineffective until the end of the 19th century. The White Fathers arrived in 1889 and later were joined by others. A vicariate was set up in 1897. The hierarchy was established in 1959. Malawi maintains diplomatic relations with Vatican City.

Archd., 1; dioc., 6; abp., 1 (nat.); bp., 6 (4 nat.); parishes, 124; priests, 318 (96 dioc., 222 rel.); sem., 155; bros., 83; srs., 550; sch., 855; bap., 46,028; Caths., 1,312,047 (21.9%); tot. pop., 5,967,964.

Malaysia: Parliamentary democracy in southeastern Asia, member of the British Commonwealth, federation of former states of Malaya, Sabah (former Br. North Borneo), and Sarawak; capital, Kuala Lumpur. Christianity, introduced by Portuguese colonists about 1511, was confined almost exclusively to Malacca until late in the 18th century. The effectiveness of evangelization increased from then on because of the recruitment and training of native clergy. Singapore (see separate entry), founded in 1819, became a center for missionary work. Seventeen thousand Catholics were in the Malacca diocese in 1888. Effective evangelization in Sabah and Sarawak began in the second half of the 19th century. The hierarchy was established in 1973. Malaysia has an apostolic delegate.

Archd., 2; dioc., 4; abp., 2; bp., 4 (nat.); parishes, 137; priests, 262 (172 dioc., 90 rel.); sem., 38; p.d., 1; bros., 106; srs., 561; sch., 375; bap., 14,038; Caths., 392,328 (3.1%); tot. pop., 12,528,800.

Maldives: Republic, an archipelago 400 miles southwest of India and Ceylon; capital, Male. No serious attempt was ever made to evangelize the area, which is completely Moslem.

Tot. pop., 141,000.

Mali: Republic, inland in western Africa; capital, Bamako. Catholicism was introduced late in the second half of the 19th century.

Missionary work made little progress in the midst of the predominantly Moslem population. A vicariate was set up in 1921. The hierarchy was established in 1955. Established diplomatic relations with Vatican City in 1979.

Archd., 1; dioc., 5; abp., 1 (nat.); bp., 5 (3 nat.); parishes, 40; priests, 137 (23 dioc., 114 rel.); sem., 15; bros., 11; srs., 97; sch., 54; bap., 2,125; Caths., 59,711 (1%); tot. pop., 6,100,000.

Malta: Parliamentary democracy, member of the British Commonwealth, 58 miles south of Sicily; capital, Valletta. Early catacombs and inscriptions are evidence of the early introduction of Christianity. St. Paul was shipwrecked on Malta in 60. Saracens controlled the island(s) from 870 to 1090, a period of difficulty for the Church. The line of bishops extends from 1090 to the present. Malta maintains diplomatic relations with Vatican City.

Archd., 1; dioc., 1; abp., 1; bp., 1; parishes, 79; priests, 1,028 (547 dioc., 481 rel.); sem., 79; bros., 112; srs., 1,679; sch., 42; bap., 5,840; Caths., 309,644 (94.9%); tot. pop., 326,134.

Mariana Islands: U.S. Trust territory in Pacific (scheduled to become a U.S. commonwealth). Under ecclesiastical jurisdiction of Agana diocese, Guam. Statistics included in Guam.

Martinique: French overseas department in the West Indies, about 130 miles south of Guadeloupe; capital, Fort-de-France. Catholicism was introduced in the 16th century. The hierarchy was established in 1967.

Archd., 1; abp., 1; parishes, 47; priests, 96 (43 dioc., 53 rel.); sem., 10; bros., 14; srs., 210; sch., 10; bap., 4,510; Caths., 300,000; tot. pop., 369,000.

Mauritania: Islamic republic on the northwest coast of Africa; capital, Nouakchott. With few exceptions, the Catholics in the country are members of the foreign colony. Mauritania has an apostolic delegate.

Dioc., 1; bp., 1; parishes, 6; priests, 9 (2 dioc., 7 rel.); bros., 2; srs., 21; sch., 2; bap., 41; Caths., 5,000 (.3%); tot. pop., 1,500,000.

Mauritius: Self-governing island state, member of the British Commonwealth, 500 miles east of Madagascar; capital, Port Louis. Catholicism was introduced by Vincentians in 1722. Port Louis, made a vicariate in 1819, was a jumping-off point for missionaries to Australia, Madagascar and South Africa. Mauritius maintains diplomatic relations with Vatican City.

Dioc., 1; bp., 1; parishes, 43; priests, 93 (55 dioc., 38 rel.); sem., 5; bros., 31; srs., 308; sch., 67; bap., 6,946; Caths., 325,000 (33.5%); tot. pop., 970,000.

Melilla: Spanish possession in northern Africa. Statistics are included in those for Spain.

Mexico (United States of Mexico): Republic in Middle America. Christianity was introduced early in the 16th century. Mexico City, made a diocese in 1530, became the missionary and cultural center of the whole country. Missionary work, started in 1524 and forwarded principally by Franciscans, Dominicans, Augustinians and Jesuits, resulted in the baptism of all persons in the central plateau by the end of the century. Progress there and in the rest of the country continued in the following century but tapered off and went into decline in the 18th century, for a variety of reasons ranging from diminishing government support to relaxations of Church discipline. The wars of independence, 1810-21, in which some Catholics participated, created serious problems of adjustment for the Church. Social problems, political unrest and government opposition climaxed in the constitution of 1917 which practically outlawed the Church. Persecution took serious tolls of life and kept the Church underground, under Calles, 1924-1928, again in 1931, and under Cardenas in 1934. President Camacho, 1940-1946, ended persecution and instituted a more lenient policy. The Church, however, still labors under legal and practical disabilities. Mexico has an apostolic delegate.

Archd., 11; dioc., 53; prel., 7; v.a., 2; card., 3; abp., 9; bp., 73; parishes, 3,692; priests, 9,615 (7,003 dioc., 2,612 rel.); sem., 2,746; p.d., 12; bros., 932; srs., 24,572; sch., 2,574; bap., 1,910,374; Caths., 61,016,000 (94.5%); tot. pop., 64,594,000 (1978, except for hierarchy).

Monaco: Constitutional monarchy, an enclave on the Mediterranean coast of France near the Italian border; capital, Monaco-Ville. Christianity was introduced before 1000. Catholicism is the official religion but freedom is guaranteed for all. Monaco has a minister at Vatican City.

Dioc., 1; bp., 1; parishes, 5; priests, 32 (12 dioc., 20 rel.); sem., 6; p.d., 1; bros., 39; srs., 67; sch., 8; bap., 239; Caths., 21,790 (87%); tot. pop., 25,030.

Mongolian Peoples' Republic: Republic in north central Asia; capital Ulan Bator. Christianity was introduced by Nestorians. Some Franciscans were in the country in the 13th and 14th centuries, en route to China. Limited evangelization efforts from the 18th century had little success among the Mongols in Outer Mongolia, where Buddhism has predominated for hundreds of years. No Christians were known to be there in 1953. There may be a few Catholics in Inner Mongolia. No foreign missionaries have been in the country since 1953.

Pop., 1,500,000.

Montserrat: British island possession in Caribbean; capital, Plymouth. Under ecclesiastical jurisdiction of St. John's diocese, Antigua.

Parish, 1; priests, 1 (rel.); srs., 3; sch., 1; bap., 37; Caths., 1,000; tot. pop., 13,000.

Morocco: Constitutional monarchy in northwest Africa with Atlantic and Mediterranean coastlines; capital, Rabat. Christianity was known in the area by the end of the third century. Bishops from Morocco attended a council at Carthage in 484. Catholic life survived under Visigoth and, from 700, Arab rule; later it became subject to influence from the Spanish, Portuguese and French. Islam is the state religion. The hierarchy was established in 1955. Morocco maintains diplomatic relations with Vatican City.

Archd., 2; abp., 2; parishes, 65; priests, 110 (29 dioc., 81 rel.); bros., 18; srs., 452; sch., 61; bap., 246; Caths., 69,780 (.36%); tot. pop., 19,021,400.

Mozambique: Independent (June 25, 1975) republic in southeast Africa, bordering on the Indian Ocean; former Portuguese territory; capital, Maputo (formerly Lourenco Marques). Christianity was introduced by Portuguese Jesuits about the middle of the 16th century. Evangelization continued from then until the 18th century when it went into decline largely because of the Portuguese government's expulsion of the Jesuits. Conditions worsened in the 1830's, improved after 1881, but deteriorated again during the anticlerical period from 1910 to 1925. Conditions improved in 1940, the year Portugal concluded a new concordat with the Holy See and the hierarchy was established. Outspoken criticism by missionaries of Portuguese policies in Mozambique resulted in Church-state tensions in the years immediately preceding independence. Tension continues to be a factor, although to a smaller degree, in relations between the Church and the Marxist-oriented government in power since 1975. The first two native bishops were ordained March 9, 1975. Mozambique has an apostolic delegate.

Archd., 1; dioc., 8; abp., 1 (nat.); bp., 8 (6 nat.); parishes, 243; priests, 299 (37 dioc., 262 rel.); sem., 17; p.d., 2; bros., 94; srs., 526; bap., 24,773; Caths., 1,556,971 (15.6%); tot. pop., 9,987,933.

Namibia (South West Africa): Territory in South Africa in dispute between the Republic of South Africa and the United Nations; capital, Windhoek. The area shares the history of the Republic of South Africa. Namibia has an apostolic delegate (to South Africa).

V.a., 2; bp., 2 (1 nat); parishes, 61; priests, 70 (2 dioc., 68 rel.); bros., 49; srs., 287; sch., 93; bap., 6,808; Caths., 148,921 (16.9%); tot. pop., 880,764.

Nauru: Independent republic in western Pacific; capital, Yaren District. Under ecclesiastical jurisdiction of Tarawa, Nauru and Funafuti diocese. Statistics included in Kiribati.

Nepal: Constitutional monarchy, the only Hindu kingdom in the world, in central Asia south of the Himalayas between India and Tibet; capital, Katmandu. Little is known of the country before the 15th century. Some Jesuits passed through from 1628 and some sections were evangelized in the 18th century, with minimal results, before the country was closed to foreigners. Conversions from Hinduism, the state religion, are not recognized in law. Christian missionary work is not allowed. Catholics in the country have been under the jurisdiction of the Patna diocese, India, since 1919.

Parish, 1; priests, 22 (rel.); bros., 1; srs., 14; bap., 18; Caths., 200; tot. pop., 13,136,000.

Netherlands: Kingdom in northwestern Europe; capital, Amsterdam (seat of the government, The Hague). Evangelization, begun about the turn of the sixth century by Irish, Anglo-Saxon and Frankish missionaries, resulted in Christianization of the country by 800 and subsequent strong influence on The Lowlands. Invasion by French Calvinists in 1572 brought serious losses to the Catholic Church and made the Reformed Church dominant. Catholics suffered a practical persecution of official repression and social handicap in the 17th century. The schism of Utrecht occurred in 1724. Only one-third of the population was Catholic in 1726. The Church had only a skeleton organization from 1702 to 1853, when the hierarchy was re-established. Despite this upturn, cultural isolation was the experience of Catholics until about 1914. From then on new vigor came into the life of the Church, and a whole new climate of interfaith relations began to develop. Before and for some years following the Second Vatican Council, the thrust and variety of thought and practice in the Dutch Church moved it to the vanguard position of "progressive" renewal. The Netherlands maintains diplomatic relations with Vatican City. (See Index for coverage of the Synod of Dutch Bishops.)

Archd., 1; dioc., 6; card., 3; bp., 6; parishes, 1,798; priests (1978), 6,280 (2,742 dioc., 3,538 rel.); sem., 258; p.d., 6; bros., 3,508; srs., 22,034; bap., 57,961; Caths., 5,550,390 (39.9%); tot. pop., 13,896,553.

Netherlands Antilles (Curacao): Autonomous part of the Kingdom of The Netherlands. Consists of two groups of islands in the Caribbean: Curacao, Aruba and Bonaire, off the northern coast of Venezuela; and St. Eustatius, Saba and the southern part of St. Martaan, southeast of Puerto Rico; capital, Willemstad on Curacao. Christianity was introduced in the 16th century. Apostolic delegation was established in 1975.

Dioc., 1; bp., 1; parishes, 43; priests, 53 (6 dioc., 47 rel.); sem., 4; bros., 66; srs., 177; sch., 195; bap., 3,454; Caths., 210,000 (84%); tot. pop., 250,000.

New Caledonia: French territory consisting of several islands in Oceania east of Queensland, Australia; capital, Noumea. Catholicism was introduced in 1843, nine years after Protestant missionaries began evangelization. A vicariate was organized in 1847. The hierarchy was established in 1966.

Archd., 1; abp., 1; bp., 1; parishes, 36; priests, 61 (11 dioc., 50 rel.); sem., 3; bros., 66; srs., 192; sch., 71; bap., 1,898; Caths., 90,000 (65.2%); tot. pop., 138,000.

New Guinea: See Papua New Guinea.

New Hebrides: See Vanuatu.

New Zealand: Dominion in the British Commonwealth, a group of islands in Oceania 1,200 miles southeast of Australia: capital, Wellington. Protestant missionaries were the first evangelizers. On North Island, Catholic missionaries started work before the establishment of two dioceses in 1848; their work among the Maoris was not organized until about 1881. On South Island, whose first resident priest arrived in 1840, a diocese was established in 1869. These three jurisdictions were joined in a province in 1896. The Marists were the outstanding Catholic missionaries in the area. New Zealand established diplomatic relations with Vatican City in 1973.

Archd., 1; dioc., 5; abp., 1; bp., 8; parishes, 283; priests, 772 (445 dioc., 327 rel.); sem., 43; bros., 315; srs., 2,144; sch., 316; bap., 8,078; Caths. 486,734 (15.4%); tot. pop., 3,150,000.

Nicaragua: Republic in Central America: capital, Managua. Evangelization began shortly after the Spanish conquest about 1524 and eight years later the first bishop took over jurisdiction of the Church in the country. Jesuits were leaders in missionary work during the colonial period, which lasted until the 1820's. Evangelization endeavor increased after establishment of the republic in 1838. In this century it was extended to the Atlantic coastal area where Protestant missionaries had begun work about the middle of the 1900's. Many church leaders, clerical and lay, supported the aims but not necessarily all the methods of the revolution which forced the resignation and flight July 17, 1979, of Anastasio Somoza Debayle, whose family had controlled the government since the early 1930s. (See News Events for 1980 developments.) Nicaragua maintains diplomatic relations with Vatican City.

Archd., 1; dioc., 4; prel., 1; v.a., 1; abp., 1; bp., 6; parishes, 185; priests, 307 (135 dioc., 172 rel.); sem., 57; p.d., 13; bros., 86; srs., 590; sch., 275; bap., 74,859; Caths., 2,346,315 (92.8%); tot. pop., 2,528,650.

Niger: Republic in west central Africa; capital, Niamey. The first mission was set up in 1831. A prefecture apostolic was organized in 1942 and the first diocese was established in 1961. The country is predominantly Moslem. Niger maintains diplomatic relations with Vatican City.

Dioc., 1; bp., 1; parishes, 10; priests, 24 (4 dioc., 20 rel.); sem., 1; bros., 14; srs., 72; sch., 15; bap., 169; Caths., 12,500 (.2%); tot. pop., 5,100,000.

Nigeria: Republic in western Africa; capital, Lagos. The Portuguese introduced Catholicism in the coastal region in the 15th century. Capuchins did some evangelization in the 17th century but systematic missionary work did not get underway along the coast until about 1840. A vicariate for this area was organized in 1870. A prefecture was set up in 1911 for missions in the northern part of the country where Islam was strongly entrenched. From 1967, when Biafra seceded, until early in 1970 the country was torn by civil war. The hierarchy was established in 1950. Nigeria has an apostolic delegate.

Archd., 3; dioc., 26; card., 1 (nat.); abp., 3 (nat.); bp., 26 (19 nat.); parishes, 326; priests, 999 (514 dioc., 485 rel.); sem., 831; p.d., 4; bros., 120; srs., 980; sch., 1,263; bap., 334,954; Caths., 5,591,287 (7.2%); tot. pop., 76,956,833.

Norway: Constitutional monarchy in northern Europe, the western part of the Scandinavian peninsula; capital, Oslo. Evangelization begun in the ninth century by missionaries from England and Ireland put the Church on a firm footing about the turn of the 11th century. The first diocese was set up in 1153 and development of the Church progressed until the Black Death in 1349 inflicted losses from which it never recovered. Lutheranism, introduced from outside in 1537 and furthered cautiously, gained general acceptance by about 1600 and was made the state religion. Legal and other measures crippled the Church, forcing priests to flee the country and completely disrupting normal activity. Changes for the better came in the 19th century, with the granting of religious liberty in 1845 and the repeal of many legal disabilities in 1897. Norway was administered as a single apostolic vicariate from 1892 to 1932, when it was divided into three jurisdictions under the supervision of the Congregation for the Propagation of the Faith, Norway has an apostolic delegate (to Scandinavia).

Dioc., 1; prel., 2; bp., 3; parishes, 27; priests, 58 (20 dioc., 38 rel.); bros., 3; srs., 367; sch., 5; bap., 227; Caths., 13,260 (.3%); tot. pop., 4,082,000.

Oman: Independent monarchy in eastern corner of Arabian Peninsula; capital, Muscat. Under ecclesiastical jurisdiction of Arabia vicariate apostolic.

Parish, 1; priests, 2 (rel.); bap., 22; Caths., 1,000 (.1%); tot. pop., 817,000 (1978).

Pakistan: Islamic republic in southwestern Asia, member of the British Commonwealth; capital, Islamabad. (Formerly included East Pakistan which became the independent nation of Bangladesh in 1971.) Islam, firmly established in the eighth century, is the state religion. Christian evangelization of the native population began about the middle of the

19th century, years after earlier scattered attempts. The hierarchy was established in 1950. Pakistan maintains diplomatic relations with Vatican City.

Archd., 1; dioc., 5; card., 1 (nat.); bp., 5 (3 nat.); parishes, 50; priests, 232 (84 dioc., 148 rel.); sem., 18; p.d., 2; bros., 51; srs., 627; sch., 211; bap., 17,785; Caths., 413,680 (.6%); tot. pop., 74,500,000.

Panama: Republic in Central America; capital, Panama City. Catholicism was introduced by Franciscan missionaries and evangelization started in 1514. The Panama diocese, oldest in the Americas, was set up at the same time. The Catholic Church has favored status and state aid for missions, charities and parochial schools, but religious freedom is guaranteed to all religions. Panama maintains diplomatic relations with Vatican City.

Archd., 1; dioc., 3; prel., 1; v.a., 1; abp., 1; bp., 6; parishes, 136; priests, 285 (70 dioc., 215 rel.); sem., 32; p.d., 7; bros., 61; srs., 445; sch., 72; bap., 37,203; Caths., 1,634,885 (88.7%); tot. pop., 1,843,106.

Papua New Guinea: Independent (Sept. 16, 1975) republic (formerly under Australian administration) in southwest Pacific; member of British Commonwealth. Consists of the eastern half of the southwestern Pacific island of New Guinea and the Northern Solomon Islands; capital, Port Moresby. (For statistics on the Indonesian portion of New Guinea, see Indonesia.) Marists began evangelization about 1844 but were handicapped by many factors, including "spheres of influence" laid out for Catholic and Protestant missionaries. A prefecture apostolic was set up in 1896 and placed in charge of the Divine Word Missionaries. The territory suffered greatly during World War II. Hierarchy was established for New Guinea and adjacent islands in 1966. Papua New Guinea established diplomatic relations with the Vatican in 1977.

Archd., 3; dioc., 13; abp., 3; bp., 13; parishes, 243; priests, 480 (52 dioc., 428 rel.); sem., 62; p.d., 1; bros., 280; srs., 927; sch., 826; bap., 29,338; Caths., 815,000 (28.1%); tot. pop., 2,905,000 (1978).

Paraguay: Republic in central South America; capital, Asuncion. Catholicism was introduced in 1542, evangelization began almost immediately. A diocese erected in 1547 was occupied for the first time in 1556. On many occasions thereafter dioceses in the country were left unoccupied because of political and other reasons. Jesuits who came into the country after 1609 devised the reductions system for evangelizing the Indians, teaching them agriculture, husbandry, trades and other useful arts, and giving them experience in property use and community life. The reductions were communes of Indians only, under the direction of the missionaries. About 50 of them were established in southern Brazil,

Uruguay and northeastern Argentina as well as in Paraguay. They had an average population of three to four thousand. At their peak, some 30 reductions had a population of 100,000. Political officials regarded the reductions with disfavor because they did not control them and feared that the Indians trained in them might foment revolt and upset the established colonial system under Spanish control. The reductions lasted until about 1768 when their Jesuit founders and directors were expelled from Latin America. Church-state relations following independence from Spain in 1811 were tense as often as not because of government efforts to control the Church through continued exercise of Spanish patronage rights and by other means. The Church as well as the whole country suffered a great deal during the War of the Triple Alliance from 1865-70. After that time, the Church had the same kind of experience in Paraguay as in the rest of Latin America with forces of liberalism, anticlericalism, massive educational needs, poverty, a shortage of priests and other personnel. Most recently church leaders have been challenging the government to initiate long-needed economic and social reforms. Paraguay maintains diplomatic relations with Vatican City.

Archd., 1; dioc., 8; prel., 2; v.a., 2; abp., 1; bp., 12; parishes, 257; priests, 473 (178 dioc., 295 rel.); sem., 77; p.d., 4; bros., 105; srs., 837; sch., 297; bap., 77,971; Caths., 2,774,217 (90.8%); tot. pop., 3,053,825.

Peru: Republic on the western coast of South America; capital, Lima. An effective diocese became operational in 1537, five years after the Spanish conquest. Evangelization, already underway, developed for some time after 1570 but deteriorated before the end of the colonial period in the 1820's. The first native-born saint of the new world was a Peruvian, Rose of Lima, a Dominican tertiary who died in 1617 and was canonized in 1671. In the new republic founded after the wars of independence the Church experienced problems of adjustment and many of the difficulties that cropped up in other South American countries: government efforts to control it through continuation of the patronage rights of the Spanish crown; suppression of houses of religious and expropriation of church property; religious indifference and outright hostility. The Church was given special status but was not made the established religion. Repressive measures by the government against labor protests have been condemned by Church leaders in the past several years. Peru maintains diplomatic relations with Vatican City.

Archd., 7; dioc., 12; prel., 14; v.a., 8; card., 1; abp., 6; bp., 37; parishes, 1,123; priests, 2,140 (867 dioc., 1,273 rel.); sem., 456 (dioc. and rel.); p.d., 25; bros., 399; srs., 4,423; sch.,

674; bap., 455,272; Caths., 15,571,000 (95.2%); tot. pop., 16,358,000 (1978).

Philippine Islands: Republic, an archipelago of 7,000 islands off the southeast coast of Asia; capital, Quezon City. Systematic evangelization was begun in 1564 and resulted in firm establishment of the Church by the 19th century. During the period of Spanish rule, which lasted from the discovery of the islands by Magellan in 1521 to 1898, the Church experienced difficulties with the patronage system under which the Spanish crown tried to control ecclesiastical affairs through episcopal and other appointments. This system ended in 1898 when the United States gained possession of the islands and instituted a policy of separation of Church and state. Anticlericalism flared late in the 19th century. The Aglipayan schism, an attempt to set up a nationalist church, occurred a few years later, in 1902. The martial-law government of Ferdinand Marcos, imposed in 1972, has been under attack by people of the church for the past several years for violations of human rights. The republic maintains diplomatic relations with Vatican City.

Archd., 14; dioc., 33; prel., 13; v.a., 4; card., 2; abp., 13; bp., 64; parishes, 1,895; priests, 4,553 (2,370 dioc., 2,183 rel.); sem., 3,405 dioc. and rel); p.d., 5; bros., 546; srs., 7,454; sch., 1,309; bap., 1,201,390; Caths., 36,610,000 (81.3%); tot. pop., 45,028,000 (1978, except for jurisdictions, hierarchy).

Poland: People's republic in eastern Europe; capital, Warsaw. The first traces of Christianity date from the second half of the ninth century. Its spread was accelerated by the union of the Slavs in the 10th century. The first bishopric was set up in 968. The Gniezno archdiocese, with suffragan sees and a mandate to evangelize the borderlands as well as Poland, was established in 1000. Steady growth continued thereafter, with religious orders and their schools playing a major role. Some tensions with the Orthodox were experienced. The Reformation, supported mainly by city dwellers and the upper classes, peaked from about the middle of the 16th century, resulting in numerous conversions to Lutheranism, the Reformed Church and the Bohemian Brethren. A successful Counter-Reformation, with the Jesuits in a position of leadership, was completed by about 1632. The movement served a nationalist as well as religious purpose; in restoring religious unity to a large degree, it united the country against potential invaders, the Swedes, Russians and Turks. The Counter-Reformation had bad side effects, leading to the repression of Protestants long after it was over and to prejudice against Orthodox who returned to allegiance with Rome in 1596 and later. The Church, in the same manner as the entire country, was adversely affected by the partitions of the 18th and 19th centuries. Russification hurt the Orthodox who had reunited with Rome and the Latins who were in the majority. Germans extended their Kulturkampf to the area they controlled. The Austrians exhibited some degree of tolerance. In the republic established after World War I the Church reorganized itself, continued to serve as a vital force in national life, and enjoyed generally harmonious relations with the state. Progressive growth was strong until 1939 when disaster struck in the form of invasion by German and Russian forces and six years of war. In 1945, seven years before the adoption of a Soviet-type of constitution, the Communist-controlled government initiated a policy that included a constant program of atheistic propaganda; a strong campaign against the hierarchy and clergy; the imprisonment in 1948 of 700 priests and even more religious; rigid limitation of the activities of religious; censorship and curtailment of the Catholic press and Catholic Action; interference with church administration and appointments of the clergy; the "deposition" of Cardinal Wyszynski in 1953 and the imprisonment of other members of the hierarchy; the suppression of "Caritas," the Catholic charitable organization; promotion of "Progressive Catholic" activities and a small minority of "patriotic priests." Establishment of the Gomulka regime, the freeing of Cardinal Wyszynski in October, 1956, and the signing of an agreement two months later by bishops and state officials, led to some improvement of conditions. The underlying fact, however, was that the regime conceded to Catholics only so much as was necessary to secure support of the government as a more tolerable evil than the harsh and real threat of a Russian-imposed puppet government like that in Hungary. This has been the controlling principle in Church-state relations. Auxiliary Bishop Ladislaw Rubin of Gniezno sketched the general state of affairs in March, 1968. He said that there was no sign that the government had any intention of releasing its oppressive grip on the Church. As evidence of the "climate of asphyxiation" in the country he cited: persistent questioning of priests by officials concerning their activities; the prohibition against Catholic schools, hospitals and charitable works; the financial burden of a 60 per cent tax on church income. Cardinal Wyszynski denounced "enforced atheism" in a Lenten pastoral in the same year. In May, 1969, the bishops drafted a list of grievances against the government which, they said, were "only some examples of difficulties which demonstrated the situation of the Church in our homeland." The grievances were: refusal of permits to build new churches and establish new parishes; refusal of permission "for the organization of new religion classes"; pressure on Catholics who attend religious ceremonies; censorship and the lack of an independent Catholic daily newspaper; lack of representation in public life; restriction of "freedom to conduct normal pastoral work" in the western portion of the country. There was a move toward improvement in Church-state relations in 1971-72. In 1973, the Polish bishops issued a pastoral letter urging Catholics to resist the official atheism imposed by the government. In 1974 the Polish bishops expressed approval of renewed Vatican efforts at regularizing Church-state relations but insisted that they (the bishops) be consulted on every step of the negotiations. The bishops have continued their sharp criticism of anti-religious policies and programs of the government. Regular contacts on a working level were established by the Vatican and Poland in 1974.

Archd., 7; dioc., 21; card., 3; abp., 2; bp., 68; parishes, 7,240; priests, 18,845 (14,970 dioc., 3,875 rel.); sem., 3,598; bros., 1,251; srs., 25,494; sch., 14; bap., 612,777; Caths., 32,648,000 (94.1%); tot. pop., 34,698,000 (1978).

Polynesia, French: French possession in the southern Pacific, including Tahiti and the Marquesas Islands; capital, Papeete. The first phase of evangelization in the Marquesas Islands, begun in 1838, resulted in 216 baptisms in 10 years. A vicariate was organized in 1848 but real progress was not made until after the baptism of native rulers in 1853. Persecution caused missionaries to leave the islands several times. By the 1960's, more than 95 per cent of the population was Catholic. Isolated attempts to evangelize Tahiti were made in the 17th and 18th centuries. Two Picpus Fathers began missionary work in 1831. A vicariate was organized in 1848. By 1908, despite the hindrances of Protestant opposition, disease and other factors, the Church had firm roots.

Archd., 1; dioc., 1; abp., 1 (nat.); bp., 1; parishes, 73; priests, 42 (9 dioc., 33 rel.); sem., 3; bros., 28; srs., 67; sch., 21; bap., 1,185; Caths., 48,660; tot. pop., 141,570.

Portugal: Republic in the western part of the Iberian peninsula; capital, Lisbon. Christianity was introduced before the fourth century. From the fifth century to early in the eighth century the Church experienced difficulties from the physical invasion of barbarians and the intellectual invasion of doctrinal errors in the forms of Arianism, Priscillianism and Pelagianism. The Church survived under the rule of Arabs from about 711 and of the Moors until 1249. Ecclesiastical life was fairly vigorous from 1080 to 1185, and monastic influence became strong. A decline set in about 1450. Several decades later Portugal became the jumping-off place for many missionaries to newly discovered colonies. The Reformation had little effect in the country. Beginning about 1750, Pombal, minister of foreign affairs and prime minister, mounted a frontal attack on the Jesuits whom he succeeded in expelling from Portugal and the colonies. His anti-Jesuit campaign successful Pombal also attempted, and succeeded to some extent, in controlling the Church in Portugal until his fall from power about 1777. Liberal revolutionaries with anti-Church policies made the 19th century a difficult one for the Church. Similar policies prevailed in Church-state relations in this century until the accession of Salazar to power in 1928. In 1940 he concluded a concordat with the Holy See which regularized Church-state relations but still left the Church in a subservient condition. The prevailing spirit of church authorities in Portugal has been conservative. In 1971 several priests were tried for subversion for speaking out against colonialism and for taking part in guerrilla activities in Angola. A military coup of Apr. 25, 1974, triggered a succession of chaotic political developments which led to an attempt by Communists, after receiving only 18 per cent of the votes cast in a national election, to take over the government in the summer of 1975. Portugal maintains diplomatic relations with Vatican City.

Patriarchate, 1; archd., 2; dioc., 17; card., 1; abp., 2; bp., 22; parishes, 4,334; priests, 4,959 (3,988 dioc., 971 rel.); sem., 321; p.d., 2; bros., 568; srs., 7,818; sch., 342; bap., 167,881; Caths., 8,774,880 (95.3%); tot. pop., 9,207,550 (1978).

Puerto Rico: A U.S. commonwealth, the smallest of the Greater Antilles, 885 miles southeast of the southern coast of Florida; capital, San Juan. Following its discovery by Columbus in 1493, the island was evangelized by Spanish missionaries and remained under Spanish ecclesiastical as well as political control until 1898 when it became a possession of the United States. The original diocese, San Juan, was erected in 1511. The present hierarchy was established in 1960. Puerto Rico has an apostolic delegate (nuncio to Dominican Republic).

Archd., 1; dioc., 4; card., 1; bp., 8; parishes, 256; priests, 705 (265 dioc., 440 rel.); sem., 101; p.d., 44; bros., 129; srs., 1,430; sch., 190; bap., 52,939; Caths., 2,729,049 (82.9%); tot. pop., 3,289,310.

Qatar: Independent state in the Persian Gulf; capital, Doha. Under ecclesiastical jurisdiction of Arabia vicariate apostolic.

Priest, 1 (rel.); bap., 46; Caths., 2,000; tot. pop., 98,000.

Reunion: French overseas department, 450 miles east of Madagascar; capital, Saint-Denis. Catholicism was introduced in 1667 and some intermittent missionary work was done through the rest of the century. A prefecture apostolic was organized in 1712. Vincentians began work there in 1817 and were joined later by Holy Ghost Fathers. Reunion has an apostolic delegate.

Dioc., 1; bp., 1; parishes, 69; priests, 116 (59

dioc., 57 rel.); sem., 5; bros., 40; srs., 454; sch., 37; bap., 11,300; Caths., 445,000; tot. pop., 495,000.

Rhodes: Greek island in the Aegean Sea, 112 miles from the southwestern coast of Asia Minor. A diocese was established about the end of the third century. A bishop from Rhodes attended the Council of Nicaea in 325. Most of the Christians followed the Eastern Churches into schism in the 11th century and became Orthodox. Turks controlled the island from 1522 to 1912. The small Catholic population, for whom a diocese existed from 1328 to 1546, lived in crossfire between Turks and Orthodox. After 1719 Franciscans provided pastoral care for the Catholics, for whom an archdiocese was erected in 1928. Statistics are included in Greece.

Rhodesia: See Zimbabwe.

Rumania: Socialist republic in southeastern Europe; capital, Bucharest. Latin Christianity, introduced in the third century, all but disappeared during the barbarian invasions. The Byzantine Rite was introduced by the Bulgars about the beginning of the eighth century and established firm roots. It eventually became Orthodox, but a large number of its adherents returned later to union with Rome. Attempts to reintroduce the Latin Rite on any large scale have been unsuccessful. Communists took over the government following World War II, forced the abdication of Michael I in 1947, and enacted a Soviet type of constitution in 1952. By that time a campaign against religion was already in progress. In 1948 the government denounced a concordat concluded in 1929, nationalized all schools and passed a law on religions which resulted in the disorganization of Church administration. The 1.5 million-member Rumanian Byzantine Rite Church, by government decree, was incorporated into the Rumanian Orthodox Church, and the Orthodox bishops then seized the cathedrals of Roman Catholic bishops. Five of the six Latin Rite bishops were immediately disposed of by the government, and the last was sentenced to 18 years' imprisonment in 1951, when a great many arrests of priests and laymen were made. Religious orders were suppressed in 1949. Since 1948 more than 50 priests have been executed and 200 have died in prison. One hundred priests were reported in prison at the end of 1958. Some change for the better in Church-state relations was reported after the middle of the summer of 1964, although restrictions were still in effect. About 1,200 priests were engaged in parish work in August, 1965.

Archd., 2; dioc., 8; ord., 1; bp., 2. No recent statistics are available on the number of Catholics. There were an estimated 1,140,000 Catholics (5.9% of the population) in 1969. Tot. pop., 21,658,000.

Rwanda: Republic in east central Africa; capital, Kigali. Catholicism was introduced about the turn of the 20th century. The hierarchy was established in 1959. Intertribal warfare between the ruling Hutus (90 per cent of the population) and the Tutsis (formerly the ruling aristocracy) has plagued the country for several years. Rwanda maintains diplomatic relations with Vatican City.

Archd., 1; dioc., 5; abp., 1 (nat.); bp., 5 (4 nat.); parishes, 106; priests, 420 (239 dioc., 181 rel.); sem., 136; bros., 179; srs., 685; sch., 736; bap., 86,543; Caths., 2,014,396 (41.4%); tot. pop., 4,859,711.

Ryukyu Islands: Consists of Okinawa and 72 other islands in western Pacific. Statistics included in Japan.

St. Christopher (Kitts)-Nevis: British Associated State in West Indies; capital, Basseterre, on St. Christopher. Under ecclesiastical jurisdiction of St. John's diocese, Antigua.

Parishes, 7; priests, 3 (rel.); srs., 8; sch., 2; bap., 94; Caths., 4,000; tot. pop., 66,000 (1978). Statistics include Anguilla.

St. Lucia: British Associated State in West Indies; capital, Castries.

Archd., 1; parishes, 22; priests, 30 (8 dioc., 22 rel.); sem., 2; p.d., 1; bros., 2; srs., 32; sch., 58; bap., 3,464; Caths., 100,000; tot. pop., 120,000.

St. Pierre and Miquelon: French overseas territory, islands near the southwest coast of Newfoundland. Catholicism was introduced about 1689.

V.a., 1; bp., 1; parishes, 3; priests, 5 (1 dioc., 4 rel.); bros., 1; srs., 15; sch., 6; bap., 112; Caths., 6,180; tot. pop., 6,210.

St. Vincent: Independent State in West Indies; capital, Kingstown. Under ecclesiastical jurisdiction of Bridgetown-Kingstown diocese, Barbados.

Parishes, 5; priests, 5 (rel.); bros., 5; srs., 10; sch., 5; bap., 360; Caths., 13,000; tot. pop., 98,000 (1978).

Samoa, American: Unincorporated U.S. territory in southwestern Pacific, consisting of six small islands; capital, Fagotogo on the Island of Tutuila. Under ecclesiastical jurisdiction of Samoa and Tokelau diocese, Samoa.

Parishes, 5; priests, 5 (1 dioc., 4 rel.); bros., 6; srs., 13; sch., 5; bap., 196; Caths., 4,000; tot. pop., 34,000 (1978).

Samoa, Western: Independent state in the southwestern Pacific; capital, Apia. Catholic missionary work began in 1845. Most of the missions now in operation were established by 1870 when the Catholic population numbered about 5,000. Additional progress was made in missionary work from 1896. The first Samoan priest was ordained in 1892. The hierarchy was established in 1966.

Dioc., 1; card., 1; parishes, 18; priests, 31 (11 dioc., 20 rel.); sem., 24; bros., 24; srs., 104;

sch., 16; bap., 1,411; Caths., 32,000 (20.9%); tot. pop., 153,000 (1978).

San Marino: Republic, a 24-square-mile enclave in northeastern Italy; capital, San Marino. The date of initial evangelization is not known, but a diocese was established by the end of the third century. Ecclesiastically, it forms part of the diocese of San Marino-Montefeltro in Italy. San Marino is represented by a minister at Vatican City.

Parishes, 12; priests, 26 (15 dioc., 11 rel.); srs., 28; bap., 181; Caths., 20,000 (95.2%); tot. pop., 21,000.

Sao Tome and Principe: Independent republic (July 12, 1975), consisting of two islands off the western coast of Africa in the Gulf of Guinea; former Portuguese territory; capital Sao Tome. Evangelization was begun by the Portuguese who discovered the islands in 1471-72. The Sao Tome diocese was established in 1534.

Dioc., 1; parishes, 12; priests, 7 (1 dioc., 6 rel.); bros., 1; srs., 15; bap., 2,673; Caths., 70,000; tot. pop., 83,000.

Saudi Arabia: Monarchy occupying four-fifths of Arabian peninsula; capital, Riyadh (Taif, summer capital). Under ecclesiastical jurisdiction of Arabia vicariate apostolic.

Priests, 6 (rel.); srs., 2; bap., 56; Caths., 10,000; tot. pop., 9,522,000 (1978).

Scotland: Part of the United Kingdom, in the northern British Isles; capital, Edinburgh. Christianity was introduced by the early years of the fifth century. The arrival of St. Columba and his monks in 563 inaugurated a new era of evangelization which reached into remote areas by the end of the sixth century. He was extremely influential in determining the character of the Celtic Church, which was tribal, monastic, and in union with Rome. Considerable disruption of church activity resulted from Scandinavian invasions in the late eighth and ninth centuries. By 1153 the Scottish Church took a turn away from its insularity and was drawn into closer contact with the European community. Anglo-Saxon religious and political relations, complicated by rivalries between princes and ecclesiastical superiors, were not always the happiest. Religious orders expanded greatly in the 12th century. From shortly after the Norman Conquest of England to 1560 the Church suffered adverse effects from the Hundred Years' War, the Black Death, the Western Schism and other developments. In 1560 parliament abrogated papal supremacy over the Church in Scotland and committed the country to Protestantism in 1567. The Catholic Church was proscribed, to remain that way for more than 200 years, and the hierarchy was disbanded. Defections made the Church a minority religion from that time on. Presbyterian church government was ratified in 1690. Priests launched the Scottish Mission in 1653, incorporating themselves as a mission body under a prefect apostolic and working underground to serve the faithful in much the same way their confreres did in England. About 100 heather priests, trained in clandestine places in the heather country, were ordained by the early 19th century. Catholics got some relief from legal disabilities in 1793 and more later. Many left the country about that time. Some of their numbers were filled subsequently by immigrants from Ireland. The hierarchy was restored in 1878. Scotland, though predominantly Protestant, has a better record for tolerance than Northern Ireland.

Archd., 2; dioc., 6; card., 1; abp., 1; bp., 9; parishes, 474; priests, 1,063 (808 dioc., 255 rel.); sem., 125; bros., 163; srs., 1,278; sch., 245; bap., 4,458; Caths., 816,804; tot. pop., 5,200,000.

Senegal: Republic in western Africa; capital, Dakar. The country had its first contact with Catholicism through the Portuguese some time after 1460. Some incidental missionary work was done by Jesuits and Capuchins in the 16th and 17th centuries. A vicariate for the area was placed in charge of the Holy Ghost Fathers in 1779. More effective evangelization efforts were accomplished after the Senegambia vicariate was organized in 1863. The hierarchy was established in 1955. Senegal maintains diplomatic relations with Vatican City.

Archd., 1; dioc., 4; p.a., 1; card., 1 (nat.); bp., 4 (nat.); parishes, 53; priests, 196 (41 dioc., 155 rel.); sem., 58; bros., 112; srs., 524; sch., 148; bap., 7,435; Caths., 212,791 (4%); tot. pop., 5,300,000.

Seychelles Islands: Independent (1976) group of 92 islands in the Indian Ocean 970 miles east of Kenya; capital, Victoria on Mahe. Catholicism was introduced in the 18th century. A vicariate apostolic was organized in 1852. All education in the islands was conducted under Catholic auspices until 1954. The colony has an apostolic delegate (pro-nuncio to Kenya).

Dioc., 1; bp., 1 (nat.); parishes, 17; priests, 21 (6 dioc., 15 rel.); bros., 11; srs., 61; sch., 33; bap., 1,515; Caths., 56,750; tot. pop., 63,250.

Siberia: Republic in the USSR, in northern Asia.

Dioc., 1; v.a. 1.

Sierra Leone: Republic, member of the British Commonwealth, on the western coast of Africa; capital, Freetown. Catholicism was introduced in 1858. Members of the African Missions Society, the first Catholic missionaries in the area, were joined by Holy Ghost Fathers in 1864. Protestant missionaries were active in the area before their Catholic counterparts. Educational work had a major part in Catholic endeavor. The hierarchy was established in 1950. Sierra Leone has an apostolic delegate.

Archd., 1; dioc., 2; abp., 1; bp., 2 (1 nat.);

parishes, 14; priests, 109 (12 dioc., 97 rel.); sem., 26; bros., 12; srs., 85; sch., 488; bap., 3,104; Caths., 56,850 (1.6%); tot. pop., 3,470,000.

Sikkim: Associated state of India in the Himalayas south of Tibet; capital, Gangtok. Some evangelization took place after 1848. Buddhism is the state religion. The territory is under the jurisdiction of the diocese of Darjeeling, India.

Singapore: Independent island republic off the southern tip of the Malay Peninsula; member of the British Commonwealth; capital, Singapore. Christianity was introduced in the area by Portuguese colonists about 1511. Singapore was founded in 1819; the first parish church was built in 1846. Singapore has an apostolic delegate.

Archd., 1; abp., 1 (nat.); parishes, 24; priests, 86 (56 dioc., 30 rel.); sem., 7; bros., 45; srs., 232; sch., 55; bap., 2,691; Caths., 83,103 (3.4%); tot. pop., 2,400,000.

Solomon Islands: Independent (July 7, 1978) island group in Oceania; capital, Honiara, on Guadalcanal. Evangelization of the Southern Solomons, begun earlier but interrupted because of violence against them, was resumed by the Marists in 1898. A vicariate apostolic was organized in 1912. A similar jurisdiction was set up for the Western Solomons in 1959. World War II caused a great deal of damage to mission installations. Catholic statistics for the Northern Solomons, where Catholic missionary work started in 1899 and a vicariate was set up in 1930, are included in those reported for Papua New Guinea. The area has an apostolic delegate.

Archd., 1; dioc., 1; abp., 1; bp., 2; parishes, 24; priests, 37 (7 dioc., 30 rel.); sem., 2; bros., 26; srs., 120; sch., 9; bap., 1,337; Caths., 43,572; tot. pop., 249,323.

Somalia: Republic on the eastern coast of Africa; capital, Mogadishu. The country has been Moslem for centuries. Pastoral activity has been confined to immigrants. Schools and hospitals were nationalized in 1972, resulting in the departure of some foreign missionaries. Somalia has an apostolic delegate (to the Red Sea Region).

Dioc., 1; bp., 1; parishes, 2; priests, 6 (rel.); bros., 2; srs., 65; bap., 6; Caths., 2,100; tot. pop., 3,450,000.

South Africa: Republic in the southern part of Africa; capitals, Cape Town (legislative) and Pretoria (administrative). Christianity was introduced by the Portuguese who discovered the Cape of Good Hope in 1498. Boers, who founded Cape Town in 1652, expelled Catholics from the region. There was no Catholic missionary activity from that time until the 19th century. After a period of British opposition, a bishop established residence in 1837 and evangelization got underway thereafter among the Bantus and white

immigrants. In recent years church authorities have strongly protested the white supremacy policy of apartheid which seriously infringes the human rights of the native blacks and impedes the Church from carrying out its pastoral, educational and social service functions. The hierarchy was established in 1951. South Africa has an apostolic delegate.

Archd., 4; dioc., 18; abb., 1; p.a., 3; card., 1; abp., 3; bp., 19; parishes, 524; priests, 1,084 (269 dioc., 815 rel.); sem., 61; p.d., 32; bros., 410; srs., 4,085; sch., 456; bap., 72,911; Caths., 1,938,265 (7.3%); tot. pop., 26,250,000.

South West Africa: See Namibia.

Spain: Nominal monarchy on the Iberian peninsula in southwestern Europe; capital, Madrid. Christians were on the peninsula by 200; some of them suffered martyrdom during persecutions of the third century. A council held in Elvira about 304/6 enacted the first legislation on clerical celibacy in the West. Vandals invaded the peninsula in the fifth century, bringing with them an Arian brand of Christianity which they retained until their conversion following the baptism of their king Reccared, in 589. One of the significant developments of the seventh century was the establishment of Toledo as the primatial see. The Visigoth kingdom lasted to the time of the Arab invasion, 711-14. The Church survived under Moslem rule but experienced some doctrinal and disciplinary irregularities as well as harassment. Reconquest of most of the peninsula was accomplished by 1248; unification was achieved during the reign of Ferdinand and Isabella. The discoveries of Columbus and other explorers ushered in an era of colonial expansion in which Spain became one of the greatest mission-sending countries in history. In 1492, in repetition of anti-Semitic actions of 694, the expulsion of unbaptized Jews was decreed, leading to mass baptisms but a questionable number of real conversions in 1502. (The Jewish minority numbered about 165,000.) Activity by the Inquisition followed. Spain was not seriously affected by the Reformation. Ecclesiastical decline set in about 1650. Anti-Church actions authorized by a constitution enacted in 1812 resulted in the suppression of religious and other encroachments on the leaders, people and goods of the Church. Political, religious and cultural turmoil recurred during the 19th century and into the 20th. A revolutionary republic was proclaimed in 1931, triggering a series of developments which led to civil war from 1936 to 1939. During the conflict, which pitted leftist Loyalists against the forces of Francisco Franco, 6,632 priests and religious and an unknown number of lay persons perished in addition to thousands of victims of combat. One-man, one-party rule, established after the civil war and with rigid control policies with respect to personal liberties and social and economic issues, continued for more than 35 years before giving way after the death of Franco to democratic reforms. The Catholic Church, long the established religion, was disestablished under a new constitution providing guarantees of freedom for other religions as well. Disestablishment was ratified with modifications of a 1976 revision of the earlier concordat of 1953. Spain maintains diplomatic relations with Vatican City.

Archd., 13; dioc., 50; prel., 1; card., 4; abp., 11; bp., 61; parishes, 21,475; priests, 33,629 (23,137 dioc., 10,492 rel.); sem., 3,050 (dioc. and rel.); p.d., 5; bros., 6,995; srs., 80,524; sch., 5,086; bap., 662,039; Caths., 36,195,000 (98.7%); tot. pop., 36,672,000 (1978).

Spanish North Africa: Includes the cities of Ceuta and Melilla on the northern coast of Africa, which are considered part of metropolitan Spain.

Spanish Sahara: See Western Sahara.

Sri Lanka (formerly Ceylon): Independent socialist republic, island southeast of India; capital, Colombo. Effective evangelization began in 1543 and made great progress by the middle of the 17th century. The Church was seriously hampered during the Dutch period from about 1650 to 1795. Anti-Catholic laws were repealed by the British in 1806. The hierarchy was established in 1886. Leftist governments and other factors have worked against the Church since the country became independent in 1948. The high percentage of indigenous clergy and religious has been of great advantage to the Church. Sri Lanka maintains diplomatic relations with Vatican City.

Archd., 1; dioc., 6; p.a., 1; card., 1 (nat.); abp., 1 (nat.); bp., 7 (nat.); parishes, 286; priests, 540 (327 dioc., 213 rel.); sem., 160; p.d., 1; bros., 291; srs., 2,329; sch., 49; bap., 28,755; Caths., 995,000 (7%); tot. pop., 14,100,000.

Sudan: Republic in northeastern Africa, the largest country on the continent; capital, Khartoum. Christianity was introduced from Egypt and gained acceptance in the sixth century. Under Arab rule, it was eliminated in the northern region. No Christians were in the country in 1600. Evangelization attempts begun in the 19th century in the south yielded hard-won results. By 1931 there were nearly 40,000 Catholics there, and considerable progress was made by missionaries after that time. In 1957, a year after the republic was established, Catholic schools were nationalized. An act restrictive of religious freedom went into effect in 1962, resulting in the harassment and expulsion of foreign missionaries. By 1964 all but a few Sudanese missionaries had been forced out of the southern region. The northern area, where Islam predominates, is impervious to Christian influence. Late in 1971 some missionaries were allowed to return to work in the South. Southern Sudan was granted regional autonomy within a unified country in March, 1972, thus ending often bitter fighting between the North and South dating back to 1955. The hierarchy was established in 1974. Sudan maintains diplomatic relations with Vatican City.

Archd., 2; dioc., 5; abp., 2 (1 nat.); bp., 6 (nat.); parishes, 83; priests, 142 (58 dioc., 84 rel.); sem., 34; bros., 40; srs., 199; sch., 43; bap., 19,347; Caths., 694,000 (4.1%); tot. pop., 16,953,000 (Catholic and total population figures are from 1977 Statistical Yearbook of the Church).

Surinam (formerly Dutch Guiana): Independent (Nov. 25, 1975) state in northern South America; capital, Paramaribo, Catholicism was introduced in 1683. Evangelization began in 1817.

Dioc., 1; bp., 1; parishes, 9; priests, 42 (5 dioc., 37 rel.); sem., 1; p.d., 1; bros., 30; srs., 105; sch., 136; bap., 2,410; Caths., 76,000 (16.8%); tot. pop., 450,000.

Swaziland: Constitutional monarchy in southern Africa; almost totally surrounded by the Republic of South Africa; capital, Mbabane. Missionary work was entrusted to the Servites in 1913. A prefecture apostolic was organized in 1923. The hierarchy was established in 1951. Swaziland has an apostolic delegate (to Southern Africa).

Dioc., 1; bp., 1 (nat.); priests, 36 (3 dioc., 33 rel.); sem., 2; bros., 13; srs., 130; sch., 60; bap., 1,132; Caths., 35,000; tot. pop., 500,000.

Sweden: Kingdom in northwestern Europe; capital, Stockholm. Christianity was introduced by St. Ansgar, a Frankish monk, in 829/30. The Church became well established in the 12th century and was a major influence at the end of the Middle Ages. Political and other factors favored the introduction and spread of the Lutheran Church which became the state religion in 1560. The Augsburg Confession of 1530 was accepted by the government; all relations with Rome, in the country since the 12th century, were severed; monasteries were suppressed; the very presence of Catholics in the country was forbidden in 1617. A decree of tolerance for foreign Catholics was issued about 1781. Two years later a vicariate apostolic was organized for the country. In 1873 Swedes were given the legal right to leave the Lutheran Church and join another Christian church. (Membership in the Lutheran Church is presumed by law unless notice is given of membership in another church.) In 1923 there were only 11 priests and five churches in the country. Since 1952 Catholics have enjoyed almost complete religious freedom. The hierarchy was reestablished in 1953. Hindrances to growth of the Church are the strongly entrenched established church, limited resources, a clergy shortage and the size of the country. Sweden has an apostolic delegate (to Scandinavia).

Dioc., 1; bp., 1; parishes, 29; priests, 94 (29 dioc., 65 rel.); bros., 6; srs., 228; sch., 2; bap., 771; Caths., 87,362; tot. pop., 8,300,000.

Switzerland: Republic in central Europe; capital, Bern. Christianity was introduced in the fourth century or earlier and was established on a firm footing before the barbarian invasions of the sixth century. Constance, established as a diocese in the seventh century, was a stronghold of the faith against the pagan Alamanni, in particular, who were not converted until some time in the ninth century. During this period of struggle with the barbarians, a number of monasteries of great influence were established. The Reformation in Switzerland was triggered by Zwingli in 1519 and furthered by him at Zurich until his death in battle against the Catholic cantons in 1531. Calvin set in motion the forces that made Geneva the international capital of the Reformation and transformed it into a theocracy. Catholics mobilized a Counter-Reformation in 1570, six years after Calvin's death. Struggle between Protestant and Catholic cantons was a fact of Swiss life for several hundred years. The Helvetic Constitution enacted at the turn of the 19th century embodied anti-Catholic measures and consequences, among them the dissolution of 130 monasteries. The Church was reorganized later in the century to meet the threats of liberalism, radicalism and the Kulturkampf. In the process, the Church, even though on the defensive, gained the strength and cohesion that characterizes it to the present time. The six dioceses in the country are immediately subject to the Holy See. In 1973, constitutional articles banning Jesuits from the country and prohibiting the establishment of convents and monasteries were repealed. There is a papal nuncio to Switzerland, but Switzerland does not have a diplomatic officer accredited to Vatican City.

Dioc., 6; abb., 2; bp., 8; parishes, 1,726; priests, 4,349 (2,689 dioc., 1,660 rel.); sem., 191; p.d., 6; bros., 322; srs., 9,941; sch., 120; bap., 37,165; Caths., 3,237,190 (49%); tot. pop., 6,600,000.

Syria: Arab republic in southwest Asia; capital, Damascus. Christian communities were formed in apostolic times. It is believed that St. Peter established a see at Antioch before going to Rome. Damascus became a center of influence. The area was the place of great men and great events in the early history of the Church. Monasticism developed there in the fourth century. So did the Monophysite and Monothelite heresies to which portions of the Church succumbed. Byzantine Syrians who remained in communion with Rome were given the name Melkites. Christians of various persuasions — Jacobites, Orthodox and Melkites — were subject to various degrees of harassment from the Arabs who took over in 638 and from the Ottoman Turks who isolated the country and remained in control from 1516 to the end of World War II. Syria maintains diplomatic relations with Vatican City.

There are 19 ecclesiastical jurisdictions in Syria serving the following rites: Armenian (1 archdiocese, 1 diocese); Chaldean (1 diocese); Roman (1 vicariate apostolic); Maronite (1 patriarchate, whose patriarch resides in Lebanon, 2 archdioceses and 1 diocese); Greek Melkite (1 patriarchate, 5 archdioceses); Syrian (1 patriarchate, whose patriarch resides in Lebanon, 4 archdioceses). Catholics, 210,000 (2.7%); tot. pop., 7,845,000 (1978).

Taiwan (Formosa): Location of the Nationalist Government of the Republic of China, an island 100 miles off the southern coast of mainland China; capital, Taipei. Attempts to introduce Christianity in the 17th century were unsuccessful. Evangelization in the 19th century resulted in some 1,300 converts in 1895. Missionary endeavor was hampered by the Japanese who occupied the island following the Sino-Japanese war of 1894-95. Nine thousand Catholics were reported in 1938. Great progress was made in missionary endeavor among the Chinese who emigrated to the island following the Communist take-over of the mainland in 1949. The hierarchy was established in 1952. Nationalist China maintains diplomatic relations with Vatican City.

Archd., 1; dioc., 6; abp., 1; bp., 5; parishes, 517; priests, 747 (222 dioc., 525 rel.); sem., 58; bros., 89; srs., 1,199; sch., 47; bap., 4,833; Caths., 278,000 (1.7%); tot. pop., 16,410,000 (1978).

Tanzania: Republic (consisting of former Tanganyika on the eastern coast of Africa and former Zanzibar, an island group off the eastern coast); capital, Dar es Salaam (future capital, Dodoma). The first Catholic mission in the former Tanganyikan portion of the republic was manned by Holy Ghost Fathers in 1868. The hierarchy was established there in 1953. Zanzibar was the landing place of Augustinians with the Portuguese in 1499. Some evangelization was attempted between then and 1698 when the Arabs expelled all priests from the territory. There was no Catholic missionary activity from then until the 1860's. The Holy Ghost Fathers arrived in 1863 and were entrusted with the mission in 1872. Zanzibar was important as a point of departure for missionaries to Tanganyika, Kenya and other places in East Africa. A vicariate for Zanzibar was set up in 1906. Tanzania maintains diplomatic relations with Vatican City.

Archd., 2; dioc., 23; card., 1 (nat.); abp., 1 (nat.); bp., 23 (21 nat.); parishes, 597; priests, 1,374 (693 dioc., 681 rel.); sem., 363; p.d., 1; bros., 326; srs., 3,413; sch., 156; bap., 133,788; Caths., 3,186,123 (19.7%); tot. pop., 16,100,000.

Thailand (Siam): Constitutional monarchy in southeastern Asia; capital, Bangkok. The first Christians in the region were Portuguese traders who arrived early in the 16th century. A number of missionaries began arriving in 1554 but pastoral care was confined mostly to the Portuguese until the 1660's. Evangelization of the natives got underway from about that time. A seminary was organized in 1665, a vicariate was set up four years later, and a point of departure was established for missionaries to Tonkin, Cochin China and China. Persecution and death for some of the missionaries ended evangelization efforts in 1688. It was resumed, however, and made progress from 1824 onwards. In 1881 missionaries were sent from Siam to neighboring Laos. The hierarchy was established in 1965. Thailand maintains diplomatic relations with Vatican City.

Archd., 2; dioc., 8; abp., 2 (nat.); bp., 8 (7 nat.); parishes, 160; priests, 316 (137 dioc., 179 rel.); sem., 176; bros., 153; srs., 1,142; sch., 231; bap., 6,478; Caths., 180,000 (.4%); tot. pop., 44,039,000 (1978).

Tibet: Autonomous region of China in eastern Asia, north of the Himalayas; capital, Lhasa. Christian contact and evangelization attempts have been almost fruitless. Some 1,200 Catholics were reported in Tibet about 1950. Syrians visited the area in the seventh century and evangelization attempts were made by Jesuits, 1624-35 and later, Capuchins, 1707-45, and others afterwards. They all met resistance and some met death. Missionaries do not have access to the country.

Tot. pop., 2,000,000.

Timor, Eastern: Former Portuguese overseas province in the Malay archipelago; annexed by Indonesia in 1976.

Dioc., 1; priests, 32 (25 dioc., 7 rel.); bros., 4; srs., 27; Caths., 208,000; tot. pop., 720,000.

Togo: Republic on the western coast of Africa; capital, Lome. The first Catholic missionaries in the area, where slave raiders operated for nearly 200 years, were members of the African Missions Society who arrived in 1563. They were followed by Divine Word Missionaries in 1914, when a prefecture apostolic was organized. At that time the Catholic population numbered about 19,000. The African Missionaries returned after their German predecessors were deported following World War I. The first native priest was ordained in 1922. The hierarchy was established in 1955. Togo has an apostolic delegate.

Archd., 1; dioc., 3; abp., 1 (nat.); bp., 3 (2 nat.); parishes, 65; priests, 153 (59 dioc., 94 rel.); sem., 32; bros., 40; srs., 279; sch., 273; bap., 11,048; Caths., 485,657 (20%); tot. pop., 2,421,829.

Tokelau Islands: Pacific islands administered by New Zealand. Under ecclesiastical jurisdiction of Samoa and Tokelau diocese, Western Samoa.

Parish, 1; priest, 1 (rel.); bap., 33; Caths., 1,000.

Tonga: Polynesian monarchy in the southwestern Pacific, consisting of about 150 islands, member of the British Commonwealth; capital Nuku'alofa. Marists started missionary work in 1842, some years after Protestants had begun evangelization. By 1880 the Catholic population numbered about 1,700. A vicariate was organized in 1937. The hierarchy was established in 1966.

Dioc., 1; bp., 1 (nat); parishes, 13; priests, 25 (9 dioc., 16 rel.); sem., 5; bros., 5; srs., 64; sch., 8; bap., 548; Caths., 15,329 (16.5%); tot. pop., 93,000.

Transkei: Independent (Oct. 26, 1976) state carved out of South Africa; capital, Umtata. Statistics included in South Africa.

Trinidad and Tobago: Independent nation, consisting of two islands in the Caribbean, member of the British Commonwealth; capital, Port-of-Spain. The first Catholic church in Trinidad was built in 1591, years after several missionary ventures had been launched and a number of missionaries killed. Capuchins were there from 1618 until about 1802. Missionary work continued after the British gained control early in the 19th century. Cordial relations have existed between the Church and state, both of which have manifested their desire for the development of native clergy. Established diplomatic relations with Vatican City in 1978.

Archd., 1; abp., 1; parishes, 61; priests, 116 (23 dioc., 93 rel.); sem., 8; p.d., 3; bros., 25; srs., 201; sch., 154; bap., 8,281; Caths., 370,000 (33%); tot. pop., 1,120,000.

Tunisia: Republic on the northern coast of Africa; capital, Tunis. There were few Christians in the territory until the 19th century. A prefecture apostolic was organized in 1843 and the Carthage archdiocese was established in 1884. The Catholic population in 1892 consisted of most of the approximately 50,000 Europeans in the country. When Tunis became a republic in 1956, most of the Europeans left the country. The Holy See and the Tunisian government concluded an agreement in 1964 which changed the Carthage archdiocese into a prelacy and handed over some ecclesiastical property to the republic. A considerable number of Moslem students are in Catholic schools, but the number of Moslem converts to the Church has been small. Tunisia maintains diplomatic relations with Vatican City.

Prel., 1; abp., 1; parishes, 24; priests, 62 (27 dioc., 35 rel.); p.d., 1; bros., 17; srs., 250; sch., 31; bap., 58; Caths., 19,000 (.3%); tot. pop., 6,065,000.

Turkey: Republic in Asia Minor and southeastern Europe, capital, Ankara. Christian communities were established in apostolic times, as attested in the Acts of the Apostles, some of the Epistles of St. Paul, and Revelation. The territory was the scene of heresies and ecumenical councils, the place of residence of Fathers of the Church, the area in which ecclesiastical organization reached the dimensions of more than 450 sees in the middle of the seventh century. The region remained generally Byzantine except for the period of the Latin occupation of Constantinople from 1204 to 1261, but was conquered by the Ottoman Turks in 1453 and remained under their domination until establishment of the republic in 1923. Christians, always a minority, numbered more Orthodox than Latins; they were all under some restriction during the Ottoman period. They suffered persecution in the 19th and 20th centuries, the Armenians being the most numerous victims. Turkey is overwhelmingly Moslem. Catholics are tolerated to a degree. Turkey maintains diplomatic relations with Vatican City. (See Index for coverage of the papal visit to Turkey.)

Patriarchate, 1 (Cilicia for the Armenians, the patriarch resides in Lebanon); archd., 2; dioc., 2; v.a., 2; mission "sui juris," 1; ap. ex., 1; Caths., 26,000; tot. pop., 42,130,000.

Tuvalu (Ellice Islands): Independent island nation in Oceania. Statistics included in Kiribati.

Turks and Caicos Islands: British possession in West Indies; capital, Grand Turk. Under ecclesiastical jurisdiction of Nassau diocese, Bahamas.

Caths., 400; tot. pop., 6,000.

Uganda: Republic in eastern Africa, member of the British Commonwealth; capital, Kampala. The White Fathers were the first Catholic missionaries, starting in 1879. Persecution broke out from 1885 to 1887, taking a toll of 22 Catholic martyrs, who were canonized in 1964, and a number of Anglican victims. (Pope Paul honored all those who died for the faith during a visit to Kampala in 1969.) By 1888, there were more than 8,000 Catholics. Evangelization was resumed in 1894, after being interrupted by war, and proceeded thereafter. The first native African bishop was ordained in 1939. The hierarchy was established in 1953. The Church was suppressed during the erratic regime of Pres. Idi-Amin, who was deposed in the spring of 1979. Uganda maintains diplomatic relations with Vatican City.

Archd., 1; dioc., 11; card., 1 (nat.); bp., 11 (8 nat.); parishes, 298; priests, 704 (359 dioc., 345 rel.); sem., 921; p.d., 1; bros., 316; srs., 1,922; sch., 1,698; bap., 230,456; Caths., 4,433,650 (35.9%); tot. pop., 12,350,000.

Union of Soviet Socialist Republics: Union of 15 Soviet Socialist Republics in northern Eurasia, from the Baltic Sea to the Pacific; Russian capital, Moscow. The Orthodox Church has been predominant in Russian history. It developed from the Byzantine Church before 1064. Some of its members subsequently established communion with Rome as the result of reunion movements but most of them remained Orthodox. The government has always retained some kind of general or particular control of this church. Latins, always a minority, had a little more freedom. From the beginning of the Communist government in 1917, all churches of whatever kind — including Jews and Moslems — became the targets of official campaigns designed to negate their influence on society and/or to eliminate them entirely. An accurate assessment of the situation of the Catholic Church in Russia is difficult to make. Its dimensions, however, can be gauged from the findings of a team of research specialists made public by the Judiciary Committee of the U.S. House of Representatives in 1964. It was reported: "The fate of the Catholic Church in the USSR and countries occupied by the Russians from 1917 to 1959 shows the following: (a) the number killed: 55 bishops; 12,800 priests and monks; 2.5 million Catholic believers; (b) imprisoned or deported: 199 bishops; 32,000 priests and 10 million believers; (c) 15,700 priests were forced to abandon their priesthood and accept other jobs; and (d) a large number of seminaries and religious communities were dissolved; 1,600 monasteries were nationalized, 31,779 churches were closed. 400 newspapers were prohibited, and all Catholic organizations were dissolved." Several Latin Rite churches are open; e.g., in Moscow, Leningrad, Odessa and Tiflis. An American chaplain is stationed in Moscow to serve Catholics at the U.S. embassy there. Recent reports indicate that, despite repression and attempts at Sovietization, the strongholds of Catholicism in the USSR are Lithuania (incorporated in the USSR in 1940, together with Estonia and Latvia) and the Ukraine.

Ecclesiastical jurisdictions, 21 (including 7 in Lithuania, 2 in Latvia, 1 in Estonia); card., 1 (Cardinal Slipyi of the Ukraine, living in Rome since his release in 1963 from 18 years' imprisonment); bp., 9 (apostolic administrators or auxiliaries; four are impeded or exiled; 1 bishop was ordained in 1972, Valerians Zondaks, titular bishop of Tabaicara and auxiliary to the apostolic administrator of Riga and Liepaja, Latvia); tot. pop., 262,400,000. No Catholic statistics are available.

United Arab Emirates: Independent state along Persian Gulf; capital, Abu Dhabi.

V.a., 1; bp., 1; priests, 7 (2 dioc., 5 rel.); srs., 16; sch., 10; bap., 313; Caths., 12,000; tot. pop., 655,000.

United States: See Catholic History in the United States, Statistics of the Church in the United States.

Upper Volta: Republic inland in western Africa; capital, Ouagadougou. White Fathers started the first missions in 1900 and 1901. White Sisters began work in 1911. A minor and a major seminary were established in 1926 and 1942, respectively. The first native bishop in modern times from West Africa was ordained in 1956 and the first cardinal created in 1965. The hierarchy was established in 1955. Upper Volta established diplomatic relations with Vatican City in 1973. (See Index for coverage of the papal visit to Upper Volta in 1980.)

Archd., 1; dioc., 8; card., 1 (nat.); bp., 8 (nat.); parishes, 98; priests, 383 (143 dioc., 240 rel.); sem., 91; bros., 138; srs., 597; sch., 20; bap., 21,247; Caths., 464,722 (7.2%); tot. pop., 6,400,000.

Uruguay: Republic (called the Eastern Republic of Uruguay) on the southeast coast of South America; capital, Montevideo. The Spanish established a settlement in 1624 and evangelization followed. Missionaries followed the reduction pattern to reach the Indians, form them in the faith and train them in agriculture, husbandry, other useful arts, and the experience of managing property and living in community. Montevideo was made a diocese in 1878. The constitution of 1830 made Catholicism the religion of the state and subsidized some of its activities, principally the missions to the Indians. Separation of Church and state was provided for in the constitution of 1917. Uruguay maintains diplomatic relations with Vatican City.

Archd., 1; dioc., 9; abp., 1; bp., 11; parishes, 224; priests, 555 (200 dioc., 355 rel.); sem., 35; p.d., 12; bros., 148; srs., 1,571; sch., 306; bap., 42,562; Caths., 2,223,060 (79%); tot. pop., 2,814,000.

Vanuatu (New Hebrides): Independent (July 29, 1980) island group in the southwest Pacific, about 500 miles west of Fiji; formerly under joint British-French administration; capital, Vila. Effective, though slow, evangelization by Catholic missionaries began about 1887. A vicariate apostolic was set up in 1904. The hierarchy was established in 1966.

Dioc., 1; bp., 1; parishes, 16; priests, 24 (3 dioc., 21 rel.); sem., 4; bros., 12; srs., 66; sch., 32; bap., 691; Caths., 16,971; tot. pop., 102,000.

Vatican City: See separate entry.

Venezuela: Republic in northern South America; capital, Caracas. Evangelization began in 1513-14 and involved members of a number of religious orders who worked in assigned territories, developing missions into pueblos or towns and villages of Indian converts. Nearly 350 towns originated as missions. Fifty-four missionaries met death by violence from the start of missionary work until 1817. Missionary work was seriously hindered during the wars of independence in the second decade of the 19th century and continued in decline through the rest of the century as dictator followed dictator in a period of political turbulence. Restoration of the missions got underway in 1922. The first diocese was established in 1531. Most of the bishops have been native Venezuelans. The first diocesan synod was held in 1574. Church-state relations are regulated by an agreement concluded with the Holy See in 1964. Venezuela maintains diplomatic relations with Vatican City.

Archd., 6; dioc., 18; v.a., 4; card., 1; abp., 5; bp., 31; parishes, 967; priests, 2,025 (850 dioc., 1,175 rel.); sem., 209; p.d., 18; bros., 314; srs., 3,958; sch., 892; bap., 336,315; Caths., 12,169,760 (92.7%); tot. pop., 13,120,000.

Vietnam: Country in southeastern Asia, reunited officially July 2, 1976, as the Socialist Republic of Vietnam; capital, Hanoi. Previously, from 1954, partitioned into the Democratic Peoples' Republic of Vietnam in the North (capital, Hanoi) and the Republic of Vietnam in the South (capital, Saigon). Catholicism was introduced in 1533 but missionary work was intermittent until 1615 when Jesuits arrived to stay. One hundred thousand Catholics were reported in 1639. Two vicariates were organized in 1659. A seminary was set up in 1666 and two native priests were ordained two years later. A congregation of native women religious formed in 1670 is still active. Severe persecution broke out in 1698, three times in the 18th century, and again in the 19th. Between 100,000 and 300,000 persons suffered in some way from persecution during the 50 years before 1883 when the French moved in to secure religious liberty for the Catholics. Most of the 117 beatified Martyrs of Vietnam were killed during this 50-year period. After the French were forced out of Vietnam in 1954, the country was partitioned at the 17th parallel. The North went Communist and the Viet Cong, joined by North Vietnamese regular army troops in 1964, fought to gain control of the South. In 1954 there were approximately 1,114,000 Catholics in the North and 480,000 in the South. More than 650,000 fled to the South to avoid the government repression that silenced the Church in the North. In South Vietnam, the Church continued to develop during the war years. Fragmentary reports about the status of the Church since the end of the war in 1975 have been ominous. Freedom of religious belief and practice was promised by the Revolutionary Government in May, 1975, shortly after its capture of Saigon (Ho Chi Min City). The hierarchy was established in 1960. The apostolic delegation, formerly in Saigon, was transferred to Hanoi in 1976; it is presently vacant.

Archd., 3; dioc., 22; card., 1 (1979); abp., 5; bp., 30. No statistics are available. There were 2,749,475 Catholics (6.4% of the total population) in 1974. Pop., 47,872,000.

Virgin Islands: Organized unincorporated U.S. territory, about 34 miles east of Puerto Rico; capital, Charlotte Amalie on St. Thomas (one of the three principal islands). The islands were discovered by Columbus in 1493 and named for St. Ursula and her virgin companions. Missionaries began evangelization in the 16th century. A church on St. Croix dates from about 1660; another, on St. Thomas, from 1774. The Baltimore archdiocese had jurisdiction over the islands from 1804 to 1820 when it was passed on to the first of several places in the Caribbean area. Some trouble arose over a pastoral appointment in the 19th century, resulting in a small schism. The Redemptorists took over pastoral care in 1858; normal conditions have prevailed since.

Dioc., 1; bp., 1; parishes, 6; priests, 14 (1 dioc., 13 rel.); bros., 1; srs., 21; sch., 5; bap., 818; Caths., 27,000; tot. pop., 110,000.

Wales: Part of the United Kingdom, on the western part of the island of Great Britain. Celtic missionaries completed evangelization by the end of the sixth century, the climax of what has been called the age of saints. Welsh Christianity received its distinctive Celtic character at this time. Some conflict developed when attempts were made — and proved successful later — to place the Welsh Church under the jurisdiction of Canterbury; the Welsh opted for direct contact with Rome. The Church made progress despite the depredations of Norsemen in the eighth and ninth centuries. Norman infiltration occurred near the middle of the 12th century, resulting in a century-long effort to establish territorial dioceses and parishes to replace the Celtic organizational plan of monastic centers and satellite churches. The Western Schism produced split views and allegiances. Actions of Henry VIII in breaking away from Rome had serious repercussions. Proscription and penal laws crippled the Church, resulted in heavy defections and touched off a 150-year period of repression in which more than 91 persons died for the faith. Methodism prevailed by 1750. Modern Catholicism came to Wales with Irish immigrants in the 19th century, when the number of Welsh Catholics was negligible. Catholic emancipation was granted in 1829. The hierarchy was restored in 1850.

Archd., 1; dioc., 1; abp., 1; bp., 2; parishes, 172; priests, 337 (182 dioc., 155 rel.); sem., 26; bros., 19; srs., 708; sch., 126; bap., 2,927; Caths., 146,134 (5.1%); tot. pop., 2,837,221.

Wallis and Futuna Islands: French territory in the southwestern Pacific. Marists, who began evangelizing the islands in 1836-7, were the first Catholic missionaries. The entire populations of the two islands were baptized by the end of 1842 (Wallis) and 1843 (Futuna). The first missionary to the latter island was killed in 1841; he was the first martyr of the Pacific. Most of the priests on the islands are native Polynesians. The hierarchy was established in 1966.

Dioc., 1; bp., 1 (nat.); parishes, 6; priests, 13 (6 dioc., 7 rel.); sem., 2; bros., 6; srs., 49; sch., 8; bap., 260; Caths., 9,896; tot. pop., 9,939.

Western Sahara: Former Spanish overseas province (Spanish Sahara) on the northwestern coast of Africa. Territory is under control of Morocco and Mauritania (1976). Islam is the religion of non-Europeans. A prefecture apostolic was established in 1954 for the European Catholics there.

P.a., 1; parishes, 3; priests, 3 (rel.); Caths., 365.

Yemen: Arab republic in southwestern Arabia; capital, Sana. Christians perished in the first quarter of the sixth century. Moslems have been in control since the seventh century. The state religion is Islam. In 1973, for the first time in 1,400 years, Catholic personnel — priests, religious, lay persons — were invited to work in the country as staff of a government hospital; they were not to engage in proselytizing. Under ecclesiastical jurisdiction of Arabia vicariate apostolic.

Tot. pop., 7,080,000.

Yemen, Peoples Democratic Republic of: Republic in the southern part of the Arabian peninsula; capitals, Aden and Medina as-Shaab. No Christian community has existed there since the Moslem conquest of the seventh century. Under ecclesiastical jurisdiction of Arabia vicariate apostolic.

Tot. pop., 1,801,000.

Yugoslavia: Socialist republic in southeastern Europe; capital, Belgrade. Christianity was introduced from the seventh to ninth centuries in the regions which were combined to form the nation after World War I. Since these regions straddled the original line of demarcation for the Western and Eastern Empires (and churches), and since the Reformation had little lasting effect, the Christians are nearly all either Roman Catholics or Byzantines (some in communion with Rome, the majority Orthodox). Yugoslavia was proclaimed a Socialist republic in 1945. Repression of religion became government policy. Between May, 1945, and December, 1950, persecution took the following toll: almost two-thirds of 22 dioceses lost their bishops; about 348 priests were killed; 200 priests were under arrest and in prison; 12 of 18 seminaries were closed; the Catholic press was confiscated; religious instruction was suppressed in all schools; 300 religious houses and institutions were confiscated, and nuns and other religious driven out; all Church property was expropriated; the ministry of priests was severely restricted and subject to government interference; many thousands of the faithful shared the fate of priests and religious in death, imprisonment and slave labor. Cardinal Stepinac, arrested in 1946 and the symbol of the Church under persecution in Yugoslavia, died Feb. 10, 1960. In an agreement signed June 25, 1966, the government recognized the Holy See's spiritual jurisdiction over the Church in the country and guaranteed to bishops the possibility of maintaining contact with Rome in ecclesiastical and religious matters. The Holy See confirmed the principle that the activity of ecclesiastics, in the exercise of priestly functions, must take place within the religious and ecclesiastical sphere, and that abuse of these functions for political ends would be illegal. Less than two months after the agreement was signed, a group of exiled Croatian priests issued a statement in which they accused the Yugoslav government of failing to abide by it. According to others, an improvement was noticeable. Yugoslavia maintains diplomatic relations with Vatican City.

Archd., 8; dioc., 14; a.a., 1; card., 1; abp., 7; bp., 22; parishes, 2,782; priests, 4,046 (2,647 dioc., 1,399 rel.); sem., 527; p.d., 3; bros., 357; srs., 6,587; sch., 3; bap., 84,923; Caths., 6,942,300 (31.7%); tot. pop., 21,900,000.

Zaire (formerly the Congo): Republic in south central Africa; capital, Kinshasa. Christianity was introduced in 1484 and evangelization began about 1490. The first native bishop in black Africa was ordained in 1518. Subsequent missionary work was hindered by faulty methods of instruction and formation, inroads of the slave trade, wars among the tribes, and Portuguese policy based on the patronage system and having all the trappings of anti-clericalism in the 18th and 19th centuries. Modern evangelization started in the second half of the 19th century. The hierarchy was established in 1959. In the civil disorders which followed independence in 1960, some missions and other church installations were abandoned, thousands of people reverted to tribal religions and many priests and religious were killed. Church-state tensions have developed in recent years because of the Church's criticism of the anti-Christian thrust of Pres. Mobutu's "Africanization" policies. Zaire maintains diplomatic relations with Vatican City. (See Index for coverage of the papal visit to Zaire in 1980.)

Archd., 6; dioc., 41; card., 1 (nat.); abp., 5 (nat.); bp., 45 (39 nat.); parishes, 848; priests, 2,438 (707 dioc., 1,731 rel.); sem., 753; p.d., 42; bros., 876; srs., 4,126; bap., 285,039; Caths., 11,799,000 (44.7%); tot. pop., 26,376,000 (1978).

Zambia: Republic in central Africa; capital, Lusaka. Portuguese priests did some evangelizing in the 16th and 17th centuries but no results of their work remained in the 19th century. Jesuits began work in the south in the 1880's and White Fathers in the north and east in 1895. Evangelization of the western region began for the first time in 1831. The number of Catholics doubled in the 20 years following World War II. Zambia maintains diplomatic relations with Vatican City.

Archd., 2; dioc., 7; abp., 2 (nat.); bp., 7 (5 nat.); parishes, 198; priests, 435 (76 dioc., 359 rel.); sem., 100; p.d., 1; bros., 156; srs., 663; sch., 43; bap., 50,588; Caths., 1,263,570 (23.1%); tot. pop., 5,470,000.

Zimbabwe (formerly Rhodesia): Independent republic (Apr. 18, 1980) in south central Africa; capital, Salisbury. Earlier unsuccessful missionary ventures preceded the introduction of Catholicism in 1879. Missionaries began to make progress after 1893. The hierarchy was established in 1955; the first black bishop was ordained in 1973. In 1969, four years after the government of Ian Smith made a unilateral declaration of independence from England, a new constitution was enacted for the purpose of assuring continued white supremacy over the black majority. Catholic and Protestant prelates in the country protested rigorously against the constitution and related enactments as opposed to human rights of the blacks and restrictive of the Church's freedom to carry out its pastoral, educational and social service functions. The Smith regime was ousted in 1979 after seven years of civil war in which at least 25,000 people were killed. Diplomatic relations with the Vatican were established in 1980. (See Index for 1980 events.)

Archd., 1; dioc., 4; p.a., 1; abp., 1 (nat.); bp., 4 (2 nat.); parishes, 69; priests, 322 (60 dioc., 262 rel.); sem., 86; bros., 124; srs., 926; sch., 130; bap., 20,632; Caths., 625,556 (9.3%); tot. pop., 6,740,000.

COMMUNISM

The substantive principles of modern Communism, a theory and system of economics and social organization, were stated about the middle of the 19th century by Karl Marx, author of *The Communist Manifesto* and, with Friedrich Engels, *Das Kapital.*

The elements of Communist ideology include: radical materialism; dialectical determinism; the inevitability of class struggle, tablishment of a worldwide classless society; common ownership of productive and other goods; the subordination of all persons and institutions to the dictatorship of the collectivity; denial of the rights, dignity and liberty of persons; militant atheism and hostility to religion; utilitarian morality.

Communism in theory and practice has been the subject of many papal documents and statements. Pius IX condemned it in 1846. Leo XIII dealt with it at length in the encyclicals *Quod Apostolici Muneris* in 1878 and *Rerum Novarum* in 1891. Pius XI wrote on the same subject in the encyclicals *Quadragesimo Anno* in 1931 and *Divini Redemptoris* in 1937.

During the pontificate of Paul VI, Vatican diplomats have held talks and conducted negotiations with officials of Communist governments in Eastern Europe in efforts to improve the status of the Church, especially in Hungary, Bulgaria and Poland. Results have been partially to the good, particularly with respect to the appointment of several bishops as heads of long-vacant dioceses. Otherwise, negotiations have not substantially eased government suppression of religion.

CATHOLIC WORLD STATISTICS

(Principal sources: Annuario Pontificio, 1980; Statistical Yearbook of the Church, 1977, the latest available edition.)

Patriarchates: 13 Eastern Rites, 8 (Asia, 6; Africa, 2). Roman Rite, 5 (Asia, 2; Europe, 2; West Indies, 1).

Archdioceses: 494 (Asia, 120; Oceania, 15; Africa, 52; Europe, 145; South America, 85; North and Middle America, 77).

Dioceses: 1,835 (Asia, 346; Oceania, 48; Africa, 293; Europe, 537; South America, 311; North and Middle America, 300).

Prelatures: 92 (Asia, 14; Africa, 1; Europe, 8; South America, 57; North and Middle America, 12).

Abbacies: 20 (Asia, 1; Oceania, 1; Africa, 1; Europe, 14; South America, 2; North and Middle America, 1).

Vicariates Apostolic: 73 (Asia, 15; Africa, 14; Europe, 2; South America, 36; North and Middle America, 6).

Prefectures Apostolic: 59 (Asia, 38; Africa, 10; South America, 11).

Apostolic Administrations: 8 (Asia, 1; Africa, 1; Europe, 4; North and Middle America, 2).

Missions "Sui Juris": 3 (Asia, 2; Oceania, 1).

Apostolic Exarchates, Ordinariates: 18 (Asia, 1; Oceania, 1; Europe, 14; South America, 2).

Cardinals (as of Oct. 6, 1980): **127** (Asia, 10; Oceania, 3; Africa, 12; Europe, 66; South America, 16; North and Middle America, 20).

Archbishops: 411 (Asia, 88; Oceania, 13; Africa, 48; Europe, 103; South America, 79; North and Middle America, 80).

Bishops: 2,434 (Asia, 291; Oceania, 69; Africa, 311; Europe, 729; South America, 499; North and Middle America, 535).

Priests, Total: 403,672 (Asia, 22,946; Oceania, 5,270; Africa, 15,534; Europe, 241,306; South America, 32,680; North and Middle America, 85,936).

Priests, Diocesan: 257,126 (Asia, 11,657; Oceania, 2,809; Africa, 5,129; Europe, 171,596; South America, 14,097; North and Middle America, 51,838).

Priests, Religious: 146,546 (Asia, 11,289; Oceania, 2,461; Africa, 10,405; Europe, 69,710; South America, 18,583; North and Middle America, 34,098).

Brothers: 66,940 (Asia, 5,393; Oceania, 2,954; Africa, 4,799; Europe, 33,229; South America, 6,767; North and Middle America, 13,798).

Seminarians: 61,013 (Asia, 10,956; Oceania, 952; Africa, 5,165; Europe, 22,716; South America, 7,219; North and Middle America, 14,005). Figures, from the *Statistical Yearbook of the Church*, are for diocesan (39,422) and religious order (21,591) major seminarians.

Permanent Deacons: 5,775 (Asia, 36; Oceania 39; Africa, 133; Europe, 575; South America, 555; North and Middle America, 4,437).

Sisters: 938,881 (Asia, 74,088; Oceania, 16,953; Africa, 33,673; Europe, 527,649; South America, 87,373; North and Middle America, 199,145).

Baptisms: 16,932,849 (Asia, 1,796,847; Oceania, 124,640; Africa, 2,000,233; Europe, 3,725,885; South America, 5,314,395; North and Middle America, 3,970,849).

Catholic Population: 739,126,000 (18.1 percent of the total world population of 4,094,206,000). Asia, 56,013,000 (2.3 percent; total population, 2,403,931,000). Oceania, 5,475,000 (25 percent; total population, 21,883,000). Africa, 52,508,000 (12.4 percent; total population, 422,738,000). Europe, 266,034,000 (39.8 percent; total population, 669,350,000). South America, 204,104,000 (91.3 percent; total population, 223,556,000). North and Middle America, 154,992,000 (43.9 percent; total population, 352,748,000). Figures, as of the beginning of 1978, are from the *Statistical Yearbook of the Church*.

EPISCOPAL CONFERENCES

(Principal source: *Annuario Pontificio.*)

Episcopal conferences, organized and operating under general norms and particular statutes approved by the Holy See, are official bodies in and through which the bishops of a given country or territory act together as pastors of the Church.

Listed below according to countries or regions are titles and addresses of conferences and names and sees of presidents (archbishops unless otherwise noted).

Africa, North: Conference Episcopale d'Afrique du Nord, 13 rue Khelifa Boukhalfa, Algiers, Algeria. Card. Leon-Etienne Duval (Algiers).

Africa, South: Southern African Catholic Bishops' Conference (SACBC), P.O. Box 941, Pretoria 0001, S. Africa. Abp.-Bp. Joseph P. Fitzgerald, O.M.I. (Johannesburg).

Angola: Conferencia Episcopal de Angola e Sao Tome (CEAST), C.P. 1230, Luanda, Angola. Eduardo Andre Muaca (Luanda).

Antilles: Antilles Episcopal Conference, 27 Maraval Rd., Port of Spain, Trinidad. Gordon Anthony Pantin (Port of Spain).

Arab Countries: Conference des Eveques Latins dans les Regions Arabes (CELRA), Latin Patriarchate, P.O. Box 14152, Jerusalem (Old City). Patriarch Giacomo Beltritti (Jerusalem).

Argentina: Conferencia Episcopal Argentina (CEA), Calle Paraguay 1867, Buenos Aires. Card. Raul Francisco Primatesta (Cordoba).

Australia: Australian Episcopal Conference, P.O. Box 297, Kingston, A.C.T., 2604. Card. James Darcy Freeman (Sydney).

Austria: Osterreichische Bischofskonferenz, Rotenturmstrasse 2, A1010 Vienna. Card. Franz Koenig (Vienna).

Bangladesh: Catholic Bishops' Conference (CBCB), P.O. Box 3, Ramna, Dacca-2. Michael Rozario (Dacca).

Belgium: Bisschoppenconferentie van Belgie — Conference Episcopale de Belgique, Wollemarkt 15, B-2800 Mechelen.

Benin: Conference Episcopale du Benin, B.P. 491, Cotonou. Christophe Adimou (Cotonou).

Bolivia: Conferencia Episcopal de Bolivia (CEB), Casilla 129, Cochabamba. Jose Armando Guttierrez Granier (Cochabamba).

Brazil: Conferencia Nacional dos Bispos do Brasil (CNBB), C.P. 13-2067, 70000 Brasilia, D.F. Bp. Jose Ivo Lorscheiter (Santa Maria).

Bulgaria: Ulitza Pashovi 10-B, Sofia VI. Bp. Metodio Dimitrow Stratiew (Apostolic Exarch, Sofia).

Burma: Burma Catholic Bishops' Conference (BCBC), 292 Prome Rd., Sanchaung P.O. Alphonse U Than Aung (Mandalay).

Cameroon: Conference Episcopale Nationale du Cameroun, P.O. Box 82, Mankon-Bamenda. Bp. Paul Verdzekov (Bamenda).

Canada: See Index: Canadian Conference of Catholic Bishops.

Central African Republic: Conference Episcopale Centrafricaine (CECA), B.P. 798, Bangui. Joachim N'Dayen (Bangui).

Chad: Conference Episcopale du Tchad, B.P., 456, N'Djamena. Paul Dalmais, S.J. (N'Djamena).

Chile: Conferencia Episcopal de Chile (CECH), Casilla 13191, Correo 21, Santiago de Chile. Bp. Jose Manuel Santos Ascarza (Valdivia).

China (Republic of China, Taiwan): Regional Episcopal Conference of China, Lane 32, Kuangfu Rd., Taipeh 34, Taiwan. Matthew Kia Yen-Wen (Taipeh).

Colombia: Conferencia Episcopal de Colombia, Apartado 7448, Bogota D.E. Mario Revollo Bravo (Nueva Pamplona).

Congo: Conference Episcopale du Congo.

Costa Rica: Conferencia Episcopal de Costa Rica (CECOR), Apartado 497, San Jose. Roman Arrieta Villalobos (San Jose de Costa Rica).

Cuba: Conferencia Episcopal de Cuba (CEC), Apartado 26, Santiago de Cuba. Pedro Meurice Estiu (Santiago de Cuba).

Dominican Republic: Conferencia del Episcopado Dominicano (CED), Ave. Garcia Godoy 32, La Vega. Bp. Juan Dominico Flores Santan (La Vega).

Ecuador: Conferencia Episcopal Ecuatoriana, Apartado 1081, Quito. Card. Pablo Munoz Vega, S.J. (Quito).

El Salvador: Conferencia Episcopal de El Salvador (CEDES). Apartado Postal 43, San Miguel. Bp. Jose Alvarez Ramirez, C.M. (San Miguel).

Ethiopia: Conferenza Episcopale di Etiopia, P.O. Box 21903, Addis Ababa. Paulos Tzadua (Addis Ababa).

France: Conference Episcopale Francaise, 106 rue du Bac, 75341 Paris CEDEX 07. Card. Roger Etchegaray (Marseilles).

Gabon: Conference Episcopale du Gabon, B.P. 2146, Libreville. Andre Fernand Anguile (Libreville).

Gambia, Liberia and Sierra Leone: Inter-Territorial Episcopal Conference, P.O. Box 893, Freetown, Sierra Leone. Bp. Augustus Azzolini, S.X. (Makeni, Sierra Leone).

Germany: Deutsche Bischofskonferenz, Kaiserstrasse 163, D-5300 Bonn. Card. Joseph Hoeffner (Cologne). Berliner Bischofskonferenz, Franzosische Strasse 34, DDR-108 Berlin. Bp. Gerhard Schaffran (Meissen).

Ghana: Ghana Bishops' Conference, P.O. Box 247, Accra. Bp. Dominic Kodwo Andoh (Accra).

Great Britain: Bishops' Conference of England and Wales, Archbishop's House, Westminster, London, S.W. 1. Card. George Basil Hume, O.S.B. (Westminster). Bishops' Conference of Scotland, 42 Greenhill Gardens, Edinburgh 10. Card. Gordon J. Gray (Saint Andrews and Edinburgh).

Greece: Conferenza Episcopale di Grecia, Archeveche Catholique, Corfu. Antonio Varthalitis (Corfu, Zante and Cefalonia.)

Guatemala: Conferencia Episcopal de Guatemala (CEG), 4 Calle 9-45, zona 1, Ciudad de Guatemala. Bp. Angelico Melotto Mazzardo, O.F.M. (Solola).

Guinea: Conference Episcopale de la Guinee, B.P. 1006 Bis, Conakry.

Haiti: Conference Episcopale de Haiti (CEH), Eveche, Hinche. Bp. Jean-Baptiste Decoste (Hinche).

Honduras: Conferencia Episcopal de Honduras (CEH), Arzobispado, Tegucigalpa. Hector Enrique Santos Hernandez (Tegucigalpa).

Hungary: Magyar Puspoki Kar, Berenyi Zsigmond u. 2, Pf. 25, H-2501 Esztergom. Card. Laszlo Lekai (Esztergom).

India: Catholic Bishops' Conference of India (CBCI), 1 Ashok Place, New Delhi-110001. Card. Lawrence Trevor Picachy (Calcutta).

Indonesia: General Conference of the Ordinaries of Indonesia (MAWI), Taman Cut Mutiah 10, Jakarta II/14. Card. Justinus Darmojuwono (Semarang).

Ireland: Episcopal Meetings, "Ara Coeli," Armagh. Card. Tomas O'Fiaich (Armagh).

Italy: Conferenza Episcopale Italiana (CEI), Circonvallazione Aurelia, 50, 00165 Roma. Card. Anastasio Alberto Ballestrero, O.C.D. (Turin).

Ivory Coast: Conference Episcopale de la Cote d'Ivoire, B.P. 1287, Abidjan. Bernard Yago (Abidjan).

Japan: Japan Catholic Bishops' Conference, Catholic Center, 10-34 Uenomachi, Nagasaki-shi. Card. Joseph Asajiro Satowaki (Nagasaki).

Kenya: Kenya Episcopal Conference (KEC), P.O. Box 842, Eldoret. Bp. John Njenga (Eldoret).

Korea: Catholic Conference of Korea, Box 16, Seoul. Victorinus Kong-Hi Youn (Kwang Ju).

Laos and Cambodia: Conference Episcopale du Laos et de la Cambodge, Centre Catholique, Vientiane, Laos. Bp. Thomas Nantha (Succuba, Laos).

Latvia: Pils Jela, 2, Riga. Bp. Giuliano Vaivods (Ap. Admin., Riga and Liepaja).

Lesotho: Lesotho Catholic Bishops' Conference, P.O. Box 267, Maseru. Alfonso Liguori Morapeli (Maseru).

Liberia: See Gambia, Liberia and Sierra Leone.

Lithuania: Vilniaus gatve 4, 233000 Kaunas. Bp. Liudas Povilonis (Ap. Admin., Kaunas and Vilkaviskis).

Madagascar: Conference Episcopale du Madagascar, 102 bis, Av. Marechal Joffre Antanimena, B. P 667, Tananarive. Card. Victor Razafimahatratra (Tananarive).

Malawi: Episcopal Conference of Malawi, P.O. Box 5368, Limbe. James Chiona (Blantyre).

Malaysia-Singapore-Brunei: Catholic Bishops' Conference of Malaysia-Singapore-Brunei, P.O. Box 327, Kuching, Malaysia. Peter Chung Hoan Ting (Kuching, Malaysia).

Mali: Conference Episcopale du Mali, B.P. 298, Bamako. Luc Auguste Sangare (Bamako).

Malta: Conferenza Episcopale Maltese, Archbishop's Curia, Valletta. Joseph Mercieca (Malta).

Mexico: Conferencia del Episcopado Mexicano (CEM), Apartado Postal 1-331, Gaudalajara. Card. Jose Salazar Lopez (Guadalajara).

Mozambique: Conferencia Episcopal de Mocambique (CEM), C.P. 286, Maputo. Bp. Jaime Pedro Goncalves (Beira).

Netherlands: Nederlandse Bisschoppen Konferentie, Postbus 13049, Biltstraat 121, Utrecht. Card. Johannes Willebrands (Utrecht).

New Zealand: New Zealand Episcopal Conference, 227 Rattray St., Dunedin C. 2. Bp. John Kavanagh (Dunedin).

Nicaragua: Conferencia Episcopal de Nicaragua, Arzobispado, Managua. Miguel Obando Bravo, O.S.B. (Managua).

Nigeria: National Episcopal Conference of Nigeria, P.O. Box 951, Lagos. Francis Arinze (Onitsha).

Pacific: Conference des Eveques du Pacifique (CEPAC), P.O. Box 1200, Suva, Fiji. Bp. Patelisio Punou-Ki-Hihifo Finau, S.M. (Tonga).

Pakistan: Pakistan Episcopal Conference,

St. Patrick's Cathedral, Karachi 3. Card. Joseph Cordeiro (Karachi).

Panama: Conferencia Episcopal de Panama (CEP), Apartado 386, Panama 1. Marcos Gregorio McGrath, C.S.C. (Panama).

Papua New Guinea and Solomon Islands: Bishops' Conference of Papua New Guinea and Solomon Islands, P.O. Box 69, Mendi, Papua New Guinea. Bp. Firmin Schmidt, O.F.M. Cap. (Mendi).

Paraguay: Conferencia Episcopal Paraguaya (CEP), Calle Alberdi 782, Casilla Correo 1436, Asuncion. Bp. Felipe Santiago Benitez Avalos (Villarrica).

Peru: Conferencia Episcopal Peruana, Apartado 310, Lima 1. Card. Juan Landazuri Ricketts (Lima).

Philippine Islands: Catholic Bishops' Conference of the Philippines (CBCP), P.O. Box 1160, Manila. Card. Jaime L. Sin (Manila).

Poland: Konferencja Episkopatu Polski, Ul. Miodowa 17, 00-246 Warsaw. Card. Stefan Wyszynski (Gniezno and Warsaw).

Portugal: Conferencia Episcopal Portuguesa, Campo dos martires de Patria, 43-1 Esq., Lisbon 1. Card. Antonio Ribeiro (Patriarch of Lisbon).

Puerto Rico: Conferencia Episcopal Puertorriquena (CEP), Apartado 1967, San Juan de Puerto Rico 00903. Card. Luis Aponte Martinez (San Juan).

Rhodesia: See Zimbabwe.

Rumania: Palatul Episcopiei, Alba Julia. Bp. Aaron Marton (Alba Julia).

Rwanda-Burundi: Conference des Ordinaires du Rwanda et du Burundi (COREB), B.P. 690, Bujumbura, Burundi. Bp. Michel Ntuyahaga (Bujumbura).

Scandinavia: Conferentia Episcopalis Scandiae, Bredgade 69 A, DK 1260 Copenhagen K, Denmark. Bp. John W. Gran, O.C.S.O. (Oslo, Norway).

Senegal-Mauritania: Conference Episcopale du Senegal-Mauritania, B.P. 5082, Dakar, Fann. Senegal. Card. Hyacinthe Thiandoum (Dakar).

Sierra Leone: See Gambia, Liberia and Sierra Leone.

Spain: Conferencia Episcopal Espanola, Alfonso XI, 4, 1º, Madrid 14. Card. Vicente Enrique y Tarancon (Madrid).

Sri Lanka: Catholic Bishops' Conference of Sri Lanka, Archbishop's House, Borella, Colombo 8. Bp. Anthony de Saram (Galle).

Sudan: Sudan Episcopal Conference (SEC), P.O. Box 49, Khartoum. Gabriel Zubeir Wako (Coadjutor, Khartoum).

Switzerland: Conference des Eveques Suisses, Secretariat, av. Moleson 30, CH-1700 Fribourg 1. Bp. Otmar Mader (Sankt Gallen).

Tanzania: Tanzania Episcopal Conference (TEC), P.O. Box 2133, Dar-es-Salaam. Bp. Mario Epifanio Abdallah Mgulunde (Iringa).

Thailand: Conference des Eveques de Thailand, Assumption Cathedral, Bangkok 5. Michael Michai Kitbunchu (Bankok).

Togo: Conference Episcopale du Togo, B.P. 348, Lome. Robert Dosseh Anyron (Lome).

Turkey: Conferenza Episcopale di Turchia, Olcek Sokak 83, Harbiya, Istanbul. Bp. Gauthier Pierre Dubois, O.F.M. Cap. (Atenia).

Uganda: Uganda Episcopal Conference, P.O. Box 2886, Kampala. Bp. Hadrian Ddungu (Masaka).

United States: See National Conference of Catholic Bishops.

Upper Volta and Niger: Conference des Eveques de la Haute-Volta et du Niger, B.P. 90, Ouagadougou, Upper Volta. Bp. Dieudonne Yougbare (Koupela, Upper Volta).

Uruguay: Conferencia Episcopal Uruguaya (CEU), Avenida Uruguay 1319, Montevideo. Bp. Jose Gottardi Cristelli, S.D.B. (Belcastro).

Venezuela: Conferencia Episcopal de Venezuela (CEV), Apartado Postal 954, Caracas 101. Domingo Roa Perez (Maracaibo).

Vietnam: Conference Episcopale du Vietnam, Phan-Dinh-Ohung, Hochiminhville 180. Paul Nguyen van Binh (Hochiminhville).

Yugoslavia: Biskupska Konferencija Jugoslavije, Kaptol 31, P.B. 02-406, Zagreb. Franjo Kuharic (Zagreb).

Zaire: Conference Pleniere des Ordinaires du Zaire, B.P. 3258, Gombe-Kinshasa. Bp. Kaseba (Kalemie-Kirungu).

Zambia: Zambia Episcopal Conference, P.O. Box 1965, Lusaka. Bp. Dennis Harold De Jong (Ndola).

Zimbabwe: Zimbabwe Catholic Bishops' Conference, P.O. Box 8135, Causeway, Salisbury. Patrick Chakaipa (Salisbury).

Territorial Conferences

Territorial as well as national episcopal conferences have been established in some places. Some conferences of this kind are still in the planning stage.

Africa: Association of Member Episcopal Conferences in Eastern Africa (AMECEA): Represents Uganda, Kenya, Tanzania, Zambia and Malawi; Ethiopia was accepted as associate member in 1977. Bishop Medard Joseph Mazombwe, Chipata, Zambia, president. Address: P.O. Box 21191, Nairobi, Kenya.

Symposium of Episcopal Conferences of Africa and Madagascar (Malagasy Republic) (Symposium des Conferences Episcopales d'Afrique et de Madagascar, SCEAM): Cardinal Hyacinthe Thiandoum, Dakar, Senegal, president. Address: Secretariat, P.O. Box 7530, Accra-North, Ghana.

Regional Episcopal Conference of French-Speaking West Africa (Conference Episcopale Regionale de l'Afrique de l'Ouest Francophone, CERAO): Card. Paul Zoungrana, Ouagadougou, president. Address: B.P. 1471, Ouagadougou, Upper Volta.

Association of Episcopal Conferences of Anglo-Speaking West Africa (AECAWA): Card. Dominic Ignatius Ekandem, Ikot Ekpene, Nigeria, president. Address: P.O. Box 951, Lagos, Nigeria.

Association of Episcopal Conferences of Congo, Central African Republic and Chad: Abp. Joachim N'Dayen, Bangui, Central African Republic, president. Address: Secretariat, B.P. 1518, Bangui, Central African Republic.

Asia: Federation of Asian Bishops' Conferences (FABC): Represents 14 Asian episcopal conferences (excluding the Middle East). Headquarters, P.O. Box 2948, Hong Kong. Established in 1970; statutes approved experimentally Dec. 6, 1972. Bishop Mariano Gaviola, Military Vicar, Philippines, secretary general.

Europe: Council of European Bishops' Conferences (Consilium Conferentiarum Episcopalium Europae, CCEE): Card. George Basil Hume, O.S.B., Westminster, England, president. Address of secretariat: Klosterhof 6b, CH-9000 St. Gallen, Switzerland.

Central and South America: Latin American Bishops' Conference (Consejo Episcopal LatinoAmericano, CELAM): Established in 1956; statutes approved Nov. 9, 1974. Represents 22 Latin American national bishops' conferences. Abp. Alfonso Lopez Trujillo, Medellin, Colombia, president. Address of the secretariat: Apartado Aereo 5278, Bogota, D.E., Colombia.

Episcopal Secretariat of Central America and Panama (Secretariado Episcopal de America Central y Panama, SEDAC): Statutes approved experimentally Sept. 26, 1970. Archbishop Miguel Obando Bravo, Managua, Nicaragua, president.

INTERNATIONAL CATHOLIC ORGANIZATIONS

(Principal sources: Conference of International Catholic Organizations; Pontifical Council for the Laity; Almanac survey.)

Guidelines

International organizations wanting to call themselves "Catholic" are required to meet standards set by the Vatican's Council for the Laity and to register with and get the approval of the Papal Secretariat of State, according to guidelines published in *Acta Apostolicae Sedis* under date of Dec. 23, 1971. The guidelines were made public in March, 1972.

Among conditions for the right of organizations to "bear the name Catholic" are:
• leaders "will always be Catholics," and

candidates for office will be approved by the Secretariat of State;

• adherence by the organization to the Catholic Church, its teaching authority and teachings of the Gospel;

• evidence that the organization is really international with a universal outlook and that it fulfills its mission through its own management, meetings and accomplishments.

The guidelines also stated that leaders of the organizations "will take care to maintain necessary reserve as regards taking a stand or engaging in public activity in the field of politics or trade unionism. Abstention in these fields will normally be the best attitude for them to adopt during their term of office."

The guidelines were in line with a provision stated by the Second Vatican Council in the *Decree on the Apostolate of the Laity*: "No project may claim the name 'Catholic' unless it has obtained the consent of the lawful church authority."

They made it clear that all organizations are not obliged to apply for recognition, but that the Church "reserves the right to recognize as linked with her mission and her aims those organizations or movements which see fit to ask for such recognition."

Conference

Conference of International Catholic Organizations: A permanent body for collaboration among various organizations which seek to promote the development of international life along the lines of Christian principles. Eleven international Catholic organizations participated in its foundation and first meeting in 1927 at Fribourg, Switzerland. In 1951, the conference established its general secretariat and adopted governing statutes which were approved by the Vatican Secretariat of State in 1953.

The permanent secretariat is located at 37-39 rue de Vermont, CH-1202 Geneva 20, Switzerland. Other conference addresses are: 1 rue de Varembe, C.P. 43, CH-1211 Geneva 20, Switzerland (Information Center); 9, rue Cler, F-75007 Paris, France (International Catholic Center for UNESCO); ICO Information Center, 323 East 47th St., New York, N.Y. 10017.

International Organizations

International Catholic organizations are listed below. Information includes name, date and place of establishment (when available), address of general secretariat. An asterisk indicates that the organization is a member of the Conference of International Catholic Organizations. Approximately 24 of the organizations have consultative status with other international or regional non-governmental agencies.

Ad Lucem (1932, Lille, France): 12, rue Guy de la Brosse, F-75005, Paris, France. Work for the Third World.

Apostleship of Prayer (1849): Borgo Santo Spirito 5, I-00193 Rome, Italy. National secretariat in most countries. (See Index.)

Apostolatus Maris (Apostleship of the Sea) (1922, Glasgow, Scotland): Pontifical Commission for Migration and Tourism, Piazza San Calisto 16, I-00153 Rome, Italy. (See Index.)

Associationes Juventutis Salesianae (Associations of Salesian Youth) (1847): Via della Pisana, 1111, 00163 Rome, Italy.

Blue Army of Our Lady of Fatima: (See Index.)

Caritas Internationalis* (1951, Rome, Italy): Piazza San Calisto 16, I-00153, Rome, Italy. Coordinates relief aid on an international level.

Catholic International Education Office* (1952): 60, rue des Eburons, B-1040 Brussels, Belgium.

Catholic International Federation for Physical and Sports Education (1911; present name, 1957): 5, rue Cernuschi, F-75017 Paris, France.

Catholic International Union for Social Service* (1925, Milan, Italy): rue de la Poste 111, B-1030 Brussels, Belgium (general secretariat).

Christian Fraternity of the Sick and Handicapped: 9, Avenue de la Gare, CH-1630, Bulle, Switzerland.

"Focolari" (1943, Trent, Italy): Via di Frascati, 302, I-00040 Rocca di Papa (Rome), Italy. (See Index: Focolare Movement.)

International Association of Charities of St. Vincent de Paul* (1617, Chatillon les Dombes, France): 38, rue d'Alsace-Lorraine, B-1050 Brussels, Belgium. (See Index: St. Vincent de Paul Society.)

International Association of Children of Mary (1847): 67 rue de Sèvres, F-75006 Paris, France.

International Catholic Association for Service to Young Women and Girls* (1897): 37-39 rue de Vermont, CH-1202 Geneva, Switzerland. Welfare of Catholic girls living away from home.

International Catholic Auxiliaries (1937, Belgium): 91, rue de la Servette, CH-1202 Geneva, Switzerland.

International Catholic Child Bureau* (1947): 65, rue de Lausanne, CH-1202 Geneva, Switzerland.

International Catholic Conference of Guiding* (1965): Avenida Marechal Camara, 186, 20.000 Rio de Janeiro, Brazil. Founded by member bodies of interdenominational World Association of Guides and Girl Scouts.

International Catholic Conference of Scouting* (1948): Calle Reina Victoria, 16, Barcelona 21, Spain.

International Catholic Film Organization* (1928, The Hague, The Netherlands): 8, rue de l'Orme, B-1040 Brussels, Belgium, (general secretariat). Federation of national Catholic film offices.

International Catholic Migration Commission* (1951): 65, rue de Lausanne, CH-1202 Geneva, Switzerland. Coordinates Catholic activities to help migrants.

International Catholic Rural Association (1962, Rome): Piazza San Calisto 16, I-00153 Rome, Italy. International body for agricultural and rural organizations.

International Catholic Union of the Press*: 37-39 rue de Vermont, Case Postale 197 CH-1211 Geneva 20 CIC, Switzerland. Coordinates and represents at the international level the activities of Catholics and Catholic federations or associations in the field of press and information. Has five specialized branches: International Federation of Catholic Dailies and Periodicals (1928); International Federation of Catholic Journalists (1927); International Federation of Catholic Press Agencies (1950); International Catholic Association of Teachers and Scientific or Technical Research Workers on Information (1968); Federation of Church Press Associations (1974).

International Centre for Studies in Religious Education* (1934-35, Louvain, Belgium, under name Catechetical Documentary Centre; present name, 1956): 184, rue Washington, B-1050 Brussels, Belgium. Also referred to as Lumen Vitae Centre; concerned with all aspects of religious formation.

International Committee of Catholic Nurses* (1933): Piazza San Calisto, 16, 00153 Rome, Italy.

International Cooperation for Socio-Economic Development (1965, Rome, Italy): 104, Avenue Elisabeth, B-1030 Brussels, Belgium.

International Council of Catholic Men* (Unum Omnes) (1948): Piazza San Calisto 16, I-00153 Rome, Italy.

International Crusade for the Blind (1957): 88, Avenue Denfert-Rochereau, F-75014 Paris, France, Coordinates action of Catholic groups and associations for the blind and develops their apostolate.

International Federation of Catholic Medical Associations (1954)): D'Monte Park Rd., 64, Bandra, Bombay, 400.050, India.

International Federation of Catholic Parochial Youth Communities* (1962, Rome, Italy): Kipdorp 30, B-2000 Antwerp, Belgium.

International Federation of Catholic Pharmacists* (1954): 60 avenue des Pages, F-78110 Le Vesinet, France.

International Federation of Catholic Rural Movements* (1964, Lisbon, Portugal): 92, rue Africaine, B-1050 Brussels, Belgium.

International Federation of Catholic Universities* (1949): 77 bis, rue de Grenelle, F-75007 Paris, France.

International Federation of Institutes for Social and Socio-Religious Research (1952): Vlamingenstraat, 116, B-3000 Leuven, Belgium.

International Military Apostolate (1967): Mariahilfestrasse, 20, rue Notre-Dame des Champs, F-75006 Paris, France. Comprised of organizations of military men.

International Movement of Apostolate of Children* (1929, France): 8, rue Duguay-Trouin, F-75006 Paris, France.

International Movement of Apostolate in Middle and Upper Classes* (1963): Piazza San Calisto 16, I-00153 Rome, Italy. Evangelization of adults of the independent milieus (that part of population known as old or recent middle class, aristocracy, bourgeoisie or "white collar").

International Movement of Catholic Agricultural and Rural Youth (1954, Annevoie, Belgium): Diestsevest 68, B-3000 Leuven, Belgium (permanent secretariat).

International Young Catholic Students* (1946, Fribourg, Switzerland; present name, 1954): 171 rue de Rennes, F-75006 Paris, France.

International Young Christian Workers* (1925, Belgium): 26, rue Juste Lipse, B-1040 Brussels, Belgium.

Laity and Christian Community (1966, Algiers, Algeria): 80, rue de Tourbillon, CH-1950 Sion, Switzerland. Universal brotherhood.

Legion of Mary* (1921, Dublin, Ireland): De Montfort House, North Brunswick St., Dublin, Ireland. (See Index.)

Medicus Mundi: Mozartstrasse 9, 5100 Aachen, Germany. Place medicine at service of poor.

Movement for a Better World (1952): Centro Internationale Pio XII, Via dei Laghi Km. 10, I-00040 Rocca di Papa, Italy. (See Index.)

Our Lady's Teams (Equipes Notre-Dame) (1937, France): 49, rue de la Glacière, F-75013 Paris, France. Movement for spiritual formation of couples.

Pax Christi (1950): Kerkstraat, 150, B-2000 Antwerp, Belgium. (See Index.)

Pax Romana* (1921, Fribourg, Switzerland, divided into two movements, 1947):

  International Movement of Catholic Students* (1921): 171, rue de Rennes, F-75006, Paris, France. For undergraduates.

  International Catholic Movement for Intellectual and Cultural Affairs* (1947): 37-39 rue de Vermont, CH-1202 Geneva 20, Switzerland. For university graduates. Has professional secretariats at: Stradhouderskade 86, Amsterdam, The Netherlands (artists); Biesseltsebaan, 40, Nijmegen, The Netherlands (teachers); 18 rue de Varenne, F-75007 Paris, France (engineers); via della Conciliazione 4d, I-00193 Rome, Italy (lawyers).

St. Joan's International Alliance (1911 in England; present title, 1931): 48, chemin des Coudriers, CH-1121 Geneva, Switzerland.

Salesian Cooperators (1876): Via Maria Ausiliatrice 32, 10100 Turin, Italy. Third

Salesian family founded by St. John Bosco; Members commit themselves to an apostolate at the service of the Church, giving particular attention to youth in the Salesian spirit and style.

Secular Franciscan Order (1221, first Rule approved): Via delle Mura Aurelis, 9, I-00165, Rome, Italy. (See Index.)

Serra International (1953, in U.S.): (See Index.)

Society of St. Vincent de Paul* (1933): 5, rue Pré-aux-Clercs, F-75007 Paris, France.

The Grail (1921), Nijmegen, The Netherlands): 5, Sayad Sokkar St. Matareya, Cairo, Egypt. (See Index.).

Third Order of St. Dominic (1285): Convento Santa Sabina, Piazza Pietro d'Illiria, Aventino, I-00153 Rome, Italy. (See Index.)

UNDA: International Catholic Association for Radio and Television* (1928, Cologne, Germany): rue de l'Orme, 12, B-1040 Brussels, Belgium. (See Index.)

Unio Internationalis Laicorum in Servitio Ecclesiae (1965, Aachen, Germany): Postfach 990125, Am Kielshof 2, 5000 Cologne, Germany 91. Consists of national and diocesan associations of persons who give professional services to the Church.

Union of Adorers of the Blessed Sacrament (1937): Largo dei Monti Parioli 3, I-00197, Rome, Italy.

World Catholic Federation for the Biblical Apostolate (1969, Rome): Mittelstrasse, 12, D 7000, Stuttgart 1, Germany.

World Federation of Catholic Youth* (1926; present title, 1968, with amalgamation of World Federation of Catholic Young Women and Girls and the International Catholic Youth Federation): 31 avenue de l'Hôpital-Francais, B-1080 Brussels, Belgium.

World Federation of Christian Life Communities* (1953): 8, Borgo Santo Spirito, C.P. 6139, I-00100 Rome, Italy. First Sodality of Our Lady founded in 1563.

World Movement of Christian Workers* (1961): 90, rue des Palais, B-1030 Brussels, Belgium.

World Organization of Former Students of Catholic Schools (1967, Rome): 19, Boulevard de Picpus, F-75012 Paris, France.

World Union of Catholic Philosophical Societies (1948, Amsterdam, The Netherlands): The Catholic University of America, Washington, D.C. 20064.

World Union of Catholic Teachers* (1951): Piazza San Calisto 16, I-00153, Rome, Italy.

World Union of Catholic Women's Organizations* (1910): 20, rue Notre Dame des Champs, F-75006 Paris, France.

Regional Organizations

European Federation for Catholic Adult Education (1963, Lucerne, Switzerland): Urstadtstraat 2, 5300 Bonn, Germany.

European Forum of National Committees of the Laity (1968): rue du Marechal de Lattre de Tassigny, 17, F-78150 Le Chesnay, France.

Movimiento Familiar Cristiano (1949-50, Montevideo and Buenos Aires): Carrera 17 n. 4671, Bogota, D.E., Colombia. Christian Family Movement of Latin America.

U.N. DECADE FOR WOMEN

The Holy See was represented by a delegation of five women and three men at the World Conference for the United Nations Decade for Women. The conference, which was held in Copenhagen and ended July 30, 1980, reviewed events of the first half of the decade that started in 1975 and produced a Program of Action for the next five years. Bishop Josef Cordes was head of the Vatican delegation.

In a statement issued at the end of the conference, the delegation declared: "The Holy See, by its emphasis on the ethical, spiritual and religious perspectives, strives to foster every initiative which contributes to a fuller realization by all women and by each woman in the socio-economic, political, cultural and religious dimensions of human life, and to the attainment of a greater solidarity between all human persons and all nations in peace, justice, truth and love."

Reservations

The delegation abstained from voting on the Program of Action because of several reservations explained in its statement.

• "It would have been desirable" to have "the objectives of the second half of the decade — which bring out very clearly and richly the 'total development' and 'integral perfection' in the personal and collective life of the human person — translated more effectively in the Program of Action."

• "The general propositions have more often than not tended to reduce the participation of woman to the sole domain — even if very important — of an economic development that does not take sufficiently into consideration the potential or contribution of women in other areas of human and social development."

• "The Program of Action could have had a more global and deeper perspective on the family."

• "The delegation of the Holy See has been obliged to reserve its position with respect to some references concerning family planning. The interpretation and utilization of these recommendations could lead to indiscriminate use of methods which violate human dignity and responsible parenthood."

"It is important to appreciate the essential and unique role of woman, which can best be exercised in partnership with man, whether in the intimacy of a family or in a wider social or political domain."

The Catholic Church in Canada

The first date in the remote background of the Catholic history of Canada was July 7, 1534, when a priest in the exploration company of Jacques Cartier celebrated Mass on the Gaspe Peninsula.

Successful colonization and the significant beginnings of the Catholic history of the country date from the foundation of Quebec in 1608 by Samuel Champlain and French settlers. Montreal was established in 1642.

The earliest missionaries were Franciscan Recollects and Jesuits who arrived in 1615 and 1625, respectively. They provided some pastoral care for the settlers but worked mainly among the 100,000 Indians — Algonquins and Huron-Iroquois — in the interior and in the Lake Ontario region. Five Jesuits of the group of eight North American Martyrs were killed in the 1640s; Isaac Jogues and two lay missionaries were martyred at Ossernenon (Auriesville, N.Y.). Sulpician Fathers, who arrived in Canada late in the 1640's, played a part in the great missionary period which ended about 1700.

Kateri Tekakwitha, "Lily of the Mohawks," who was baptized in 1676 and died in 1680, was declared "Blessed" June 22, 1980.

The communities of women religious with the longest histories in Canada are the Canonesses of St. Augustine, since 1637; the Ursulines, since 1639; and the Hospitallers of St. Joseph, since 1642. Communities of Canadian origin are the Congregation of Notre Dame, founded by Bl. Marguerite Bourgeoys in 1658, and the Grey Nuns, formed by Bl. Marie Marguerite d'Youville in 1738.

Mother Marie (Guyard) of the Incarnation, an Ursuline nun, was one of the first three women missionaries to New France; called "Mother of the Church in Canada," she was declared "Blessed" June 22, 1980.

Start of Church Organization

Ecclesiastical organization began with the appointment in 1658 of Francois De Montmorency-Laval, "Father of the Church in Canada," as vicar apostolic of New France. He was the first bishop of Quebec from 1674 to 1688, with jurisdiction over all French-claimed territory in North America. He was declared "Blessed" June 22, 1980.

In 1713, the French Canadian population numbered 18,000. In the same year, the Treaty of Utrecht ceded Acadia, Newfoundland and the Hudson Bay Territory to England. The Acadians were scattered among the American Colonies in 1755.

The English acquired possession of Canada and its 70,000 French-speaking inhabitants in virtue of the Treaty of Paris in 1763. Anglo-French and Anglican-Catholic differences and tensions developed. The pro-British government at first refused to recognize the titles of church officials, hindered the clergy in their work and tried to install a non-Catholic educational system. Laws were passed which guaranteed religious liberties to Catholics (Quebec Act of 1774, Constitutional Act of 1791, legislation approved by Queen Victoria in 1851), but it took some time before actual respect for these liberties matched the legal enactments. The initial moderation of government antipathy toward the Church was caused partly by the loyalty of Catholics to the Crown during the American Revolution and the War of 1812.

Growth

The 15 years following the passage in 1840 of the Act of Union, which joined Upper and Lower Canada, were significant. New communities of men and women religious joined those already in the country. The Oblates of Mary Immaculate, missionaries par excellence in Canada, advanced the penetration of the West which had been started in 1818 by Abbe Provencher. New jurisdictions were established, and Quebec became a metropolitan see in 1844. The first Council of Quebec was held in 1851. The established Catholic school system enjoyed a period of growth.

Laval University was inaugurated in 1854 and canonically established in 1876.

Archbishop Elzear-Alexandre Taschereau of Quebec was named Canada's first cardinal in 1886.

The apostolic delegation to Canada was set up in 1899. It became a nunciature October 16, 1969, with the establishment of diplomatic relations with the Vatican.

Early in this century, Canada had eight ecclesiastical provinces, 23 dioceses, three vicariates apostolic, 3,500 priests, 2.4 million Catholics, about 30 communities of men religious, and 70 or more communities of women religious. The Church in Canada was phased out of mission status and removed from the jurisdiction of the Congregation for the Propagation of the Faith in 1908.

The greatest concentration of Catholics is in the eastern portion of the country. In the northern and western portions, outside metropolitan centers, there are some of the most difficult parish and mission areas in the world. Bilingual (English-French) differences in the general population are reflected in the Church; for example, in the parallel structures of the Canadian Conference of Catholic Bishops, which was established in 1943. Quebec is the center of French cultural influence. Many language groups are represented among Catholics, who include about 206,265 members of Eastern Rite in a metropolitan see and four eparchies.

ECCLESIASTICAL JURISDICTIONS OF CANADA

Provinces

Names of ecclesiastical provinces and metropolitan sees in bold face: suffragan sees in parentheses. The Winnipeg archdiocese (Latin) is not a metropolitan see.

Edmonton (Calgary, St. Paul).

Grouard-McLennan (Mackenzie-Ft. Smith, Prince George, Whitehorse).

Halifax (Antigonish, Charlottetown, Yarmouth).

Keewatin-LePas (Churchill-Hudson Bay, Labrador-Schefferville, Moosonee).

Kingston (Alexandria-Cornwall, Peterborough, Sault Ste. Marie).

Moncton (Bathurst, Edmundston, St. John).

Montreal (Joliette, St. Jean-de-Quebec, St. Jerome, Valleyfield).

Ottawa (Hearst, Hull, Mont-Laurier, Pembroke, Rouyn-Noranda, Timmins).

Quebec (Amos, Chicoutimi, Ste.-Anne-de-la-Pocatiere, Trois Rivieres).

Regina (Gravelbourg, Prince Albert, Saskatoon, Abbey of St. Peter).

Rimouski (Gaspe, Hauterive).

St. Boniface (no suffragans).

St. John's (Grand Falls, St. George).

Sherbrooke (Nicolet, St. Hyacinthe).

Toronto (Hamilton, London, St. Catharines, Thunder Bay).

Vancouver (Kamloops, Nelson, Victoria).

Winnipeg — Ukrainian (Edmonton, New Westminster, Saskatoon, Toronto).

Archdioceses, Archbishops

Edmonton, Alta. (St. Albert, 1871; archdiocese, transferred Edmonton, 1912): Joseph N. MacNeil, archbishop, 1973.

Grouard-McLennan, Alta. (v.a. Athabaska-Mackenzie, 1862; Grouard, 1927; archdiocese Grouard-McLennan, 1967); Henri Legare, O.M.I., archbishop, 1972.

Halifax, N.S. (1842; archdiocese, 1852): James M. Hayes, archbishop, 1967.

Keewatin-Le Pas, Man. (v.a., 1910; archdiocese, 1967): Paul Dumouchel, O.M.I., archbishop, 1967.

Kingston, Ont. (1826; archdiocese, 1889): Joseph L. Wilhelm, archbishop, 1966.

Moncton, N.B. (1936): Donat Chiasson, archbishop, 1972.

Montreal, Que. (1836; archdiocese, 1886): Paul Gregoire, archbishop, 1968. Lawrence P. Whelan, Valerien Belanger, Andre Cimichella, O.S.M., Leonard Crowley, Jean-Marie Lafontaine, auxiliaries.

Ottawa, Ont. (Bytown, 1847, name changed, 1854; archdiocese, 1886): Joseph Aurele Plourde, archbishop, 1967. John Beahen, Gilles Belisle, auxiliaries.

Quebec, Que. (v.a., 1658; diocese, 1674; archdiocese, 1819; metropolitan, 1844; primatial see, 1956): Cardinal Maurice Roy, archbishop, 1947. Lionel Audet, Louis Vachon, Jean-Paul Labrie, auxiliaries.

Regina, Sask. (1910; archdiocese, 1915): Charles A. Halpin, archbishop, 1973.

Rimouski, Que. (1867; archdiocese, 1946): Gilles Ouellet, P.M.E., archbishop, 1973.

St. Boniface, Man. (1847; archdiocese, 1871): Antoine Hacault, archbishop, 1974.

St. John's, Nfld. (p.a., 1784; v.a., 1796; diocese, 1847; archdiocese, 1904): Alphonsus Penney, archbishop, 1979.

Sherbrooke, Que. (1874; archdiocese, 1951); J.-M. Fortier, archbishop, 1968.

Toronto, Ont. (1841; archdiocese, 1870): Cardinal G. Emmett Carter, archbishop, 1978. Aloysius M. Ambrozic, Michael Pearse Lacey, Robert B. Clune, Leonard J. Wall, auxiliaries.

Vancouver, B. C. (v.a. British Columbia, 1863; diocese New Westminster, 1890; archdiocese Vancouver, 1908): James F. Carney, archbishop, 1969. Lawrence Sabatini, C.S., auxiliary.

Winnipeg, Man. (1915): Cardinal George B. Flahiff, C.S.B., archbishop, 1961.

Winnipeg, Man. (Ukrainian Byzantine Rite) (Ordinariate of Canada, 1912; ap. ex. Central Canada, 1948; ap. ex. Manitoba, 1951; archdiocese Winnipeg, 1956): Maxim Hermaniuk, C.SS.R., archbishop, 1956.

Dioceses, Bishops

Alexandria-Cornwall, Ont. (1890): Eugene Philippe LaRocque, bishop, 1974.

Amos, Que. (1938): Gerard Drainville, bishop, 1978.

Antigonish, N.S. (Arichat, 1844; transferred, 1886): William E. Power, bishop, 1960.

Bathurst, N.B. (Chatham, 1860; transferred, 1938): Edgar Godin, bishop, 1969.

Calgary, Alta. (1912): Paul J. O'Byrne, bishop, 1968.

Charlottetown, P.E.I. (1829): Francis J. Spence, bishop, 1970.

Chicoutimi, Que. (1878): Jean-Guy Couture, bishop, 1979. Roch Pedneault, auxiliary.

Churchill-Hudson Bay, Man. (p.a., 1925; v.a. Hudson Bay, 1931; diocese Churchill, 1967; Churchill-Hudson Bay, 1968): Omer Robidoux, O.M.I., bishop, 1970.

Edmonton, Alta. (Ukrainian Byzantine Rite) (ap. ex., 1948; diocese, 1956): Nile Nicholas Savaryn, O.S.B.M., bishop, 1948. Martin Greschuk, auxiliary.

Edmundston, N.B. (1944): Fernand Lacroix, C.J.M., bishop, 1970.

Gaspe, Que. (1922): Bertrand Blanchet, bishop, 1973.

Grand Falls, Nfld. (Harbour Grace, 1856;

present title, 1964): Joseph Faber Mac-Donald, bishop, 1980.

Gravelbourg, Sask. (1930): Noel Delaquis, bishop, 1974.

Hamilton, Ont. (1856): Paul F. Reding, bishop, 1973. James H. MacDonald, C.S.C., auxiliary.

Hauterive, Que. (p.a., 1882; v.a., 1905; diocese Gulf of St. Lawrence, 1945; name changed, 1960): Roger Ebacher, bishop, 1979.

Hearst, Ont. (p.a., 1918; v.a., 1920; diocese, 1938): Roger Despatie, bishop, 1973.

Hull, Que. (1963): Adolphe Proulx, bishop, 1974.

Joliette, Que. (1904): Rene Audet, bishop, 1968.

Kamloops, B.C. (1945): Adam Exner, O.M.I., bishop, 1974.

Labrador (Nfld.)-Schefferville, Que. (v.a. Labrador, 1945; diocese, 1967): Peter A. Sutton, O.M.I., bishop, 1974.

London, Ont. (1855; transferred Sandwich, 1859; London, 1869): John Sherlock, bishop, 1978. Marcel Gervais, auxiliary.

Mackenzie-Fort Smith, N.W.T. (v.a. Mackenzie, 1901; diocese Mackenzie-Fort Smith, 1967): Paul Piché, O.M.I., bishop, 1967.

Mont-Laurier, Que. (1913): Jean Gratton, bishop, 1978.

Moosonee, Ont. (v.a. James Bay, 1938; diocese Moosonee, 1967): Jules Leguerrier, O.M.I., bishop, 1967.

Nelson, B.C. (1936): Wilfred Emmett Doyle, bishop, 1958.

New Westminster, B.C. (Ukrainian Byzantine Rite) (1974): Jerome Chimy, O.S.B.M., bishop, 1974.

Nicolet, Que. (1885): Albertus Martin, bishop, 1950.

Pembroke, Ont. (v.a. 1882; diocese, 1898): Joseph R. Windle, bishop, 1971.

Peterborough, Ont. (1882): James L. Doyle, bishop, 1976.

Prince Albert, Sask. (v.a., 1890; diocese, 1907): Laurent Morin, bishop, 1959.

Prince George, B.C. (p.a., 1908; v.a. Yukon and Prince Rupert, 1944; diocese Prince George, 1967): J. Fergus O'Grady, O.M.I., bishop, 1967.

Rouyn-Noranda, Que. (1973): Jean-Guy Hamelin, bishop, 1974.

Sainte-Anne-de-la-Pocatiere, Que. (1951): C.-H. Levesque, bishop, 1968.

St. Catharines, Ont. (1958): Thomas B. Fulton, bishop, 1978.

St. George's, Nfld. (p.a., 1870; v.a., 1890; diocese, 1904): Richard T. McGrath, bishop, 1970.

St. Hyacinthe, Que. (1852): Louis-de-Gonzague Langevin, bishop, 1979.

Saint-Jean-de-Quebec (1933): Bernard Hubert, bishop, 1978.

St. Jerome, Que. (1951): Charles Valois,

bishop, 1977. Raymond Saint-Delais, auxiliary.

Saint John, N.B. (1842): Arthur J. Gilbert, bishop, 1974.

St. Paul in Alberta (1948): Raymond Roy, bishop, 1972.

Saskatoon, Sask. (1933): James P. Mahoney, bishop, 1967.

Saskatoon, Sask. (Ukrainian Byzantine Rite) (ap. ex., 1951; diocese, 1956): Andrew J. Roborecki, bishop, 1951.

Sault Ste. Marie, Ont. (1904): Alexander Carter, bishop, 1958. Bernard F. Pappin, Gerard Dionne, auxiliaries.

Thunder Bay, Ont. (Ft. William, 1952; transferred, 1970): John A. O'Mara, bishop, 1976.

Timmins, Ont. (v.a. Temiskaming, 1908; diocese Haileybury, 1915; present title, 1938): Jacques Landriault, bishop, 1971.

Toronto, Ont. (Ukrainian Byzantine Rite) (ap. ex., 1948; diocese, 1956): Isidore Borecky, bishop, 1948, Michael Rusnak, C.SS.R., auxiliary.

Trois-Rivieres, Que. (1852): Laurent Noel, bishop, 1975.

Valleyfield, Que. (1892): Robert Lebel, bishop, 1976.

Victoria, B.C. (diocese Vancouver Is., 1846; archdiocese, 1903; diocese Victoria, 1908): Remi J. De Roo, bishop, 1962.

Whitehorse, Y.T. (v.a., 1944; diocese 1967): Hubert P. O'Connor, O.M.I., bishop, 1971.

Yarmouth, N.S. (1953): Augustin-Emile Burke, bishop, 1968.

Military Vicariate of Canada (1951): Cardinal Maurice Roy, military vicar.

Abbacy of St. Peter, Muenster, Sask. (1921): Jerome Weber, O.S.B. (blessed, 1960).

CANADIAN BISHOPS

(Sources: Almanac survey; *1980 Directory of Canadian Conference of Catholic Bishops; Annuario Pontificio.* Data as of Aug. 1, 1980.)

Ambrozic, Aloysius M.: b. Jan. 27, 1930; ord. priest June 4, 1955; ord. titular bishop of Valabria and auxiliary bishop of Toronto, May 27, 1976.

Audet, Lionel: b. May 22, 1908, Ste. Marie de Beauce, Que.; ord. priest July 8, 1934; ord. titular bishop of Tibari and auxiliary bishop of Quebec, May 1, 1952.

Audet, Rene: b. Jan. 18, 1920, Montreal, Que.; ord. priest May 30, 1948; ord. titular bishop of Chonochora and auxiliary bishop of Ottawa, July 31, 1963; bishop of Joliette, Jan. 3, 1968.

Baudoux, Maurice: b. July 10, 1902, Louviere, Belgium; ord. priest July 17, 1929; ord. bishop of St. Paul in Alberta, Oct. 28, 1948; titular archbishop of Preslavus and coadjutor archbishop of St. Boniface, Mar. 4, 1952; archbishop of St. Boniface, Sept. 14, 1955; retired Sept. 7, 1974.

Beahen, John: b. Feb. 14, 1922, Ottawa, Ont.; ord. priest June 15, 1946; ord. titular bishop of Ploaghe and auxiliary bishop of Ottawa, June 21, 1977.

Belanger, Valerien: b. Apr. 6, 1902, Valleyfield, Que.; ord. priest May 29, 1926; ord titular bishop of Cyrene and auxiliary bishop of Montreal, May 11, 1956.

Belisle, Gilles: b. Oct. 7, 1923, Clarence Creek, Ont.; ord. priest Feb. 2, 1950; ord. titular bishop of Uccula and auxiliary bishop of Ottawa, June 21, 1977.

Blais, Leo: b. Apr. 28, 1904, Dollar Bay, Mich.; ord. priest June 14, 1930; ord. bishop of Prince Albert, Aug. 28, 1952; titular bishop of Geron and auxiliary bishop of Montreal, Feb. 28, 1959; retired 1959.

Blanchet, Bertrand: b. Sept. 19, 1932, Saint Thomas de Montmagny, Que.; ord. priest May 20, 1956; ord. bishop of Gaspe, Dec. 8, 1973.

Borecky, Isidore: b. Oct. 1, 1911, Ostrovec, Ukraine; ord. priest July 17, 1938; ord. titular bishop of Amathus in Cypro and exarch of Toronto, May 27, 1948; bishop of Toronto (Ukrainians), Nov. 3, 1956.

Brodeur, Rosario L.: b. Oct. 30, 1889, Acton Vale, Que.; ord. priest June 17, 1916; ord. titular bishop of Mideo and coadjutor bishop of Alexandria, June 30, 1941; bishop of Alexandria, July 27, 1941; retired Oct. 15, 1966.

Burke, Augustin-Emile: b. Jan. 22, 1922, Sluice Point, N.S.; ord. priest Mar. 25, 1950; ord. bishop of Yarmouth, May 14, 1968.

Cabana, Georges: b. Oct. 23, 1894, Notre Dame de Granby, Que; ord. priest July 28, 1918; ord. titular archbishop of Anchialo and coadjutor archbishop of St. Boniface, June 30, 1941; coadjutor archbishop of Sherbrooke, Jan. 20, 1952; archbishop of Sherbrooke, May 28, 1952; retired Feb. 7, 1968.

Carew, William A.: b. Oct. 23, 1922, St. John's, Nfld., ord. priest June 15, 1947; ord. titular archbishop of Telde, Jan. 4, 1970; nuncio to Rwanda and Burundi, 1970-74; apostolic delegate to Jerusalem and Palestine and pro-nuncio to Cyprus, 1974.

Carney, James F.: b. June 28, 1915, Vancouver, B.C.; ord. priest Mar. 21, 1942; ord. titular bishop of Obori and auxiliary bishop of Vancouver, Feb. 11, 1966; archbishop of Vancouver, Jan. 8, 1969.

Carter, Alexander: b. Apr. 16, 1909, Montreal, Que.; ord. priest June 6, 1936; ord. titular bishop of Sita and coadjutor bishop of Sault Ste. Marie, Feb. 2, 1957; bishop of Sault Ste. Marie, Nov. 22, 1958.

Carter, G. Emmett: (See Cardinals, Biographies.)

Charbonneau, Paul E.: b. May 4, 1922, Ste. Therese de Blainville, Que.; ord. priest May 31, 1947; ord. titular bishop of Thapsus and auxiliary bishop of Ottawa, Jan. 18, 1961; first bishop of Hull, May 21, 1963; retired Apr. 12, 1973, because of ill health.

Chiasson, Donat: b. Jan. 2, 1930, Paquetville, N.B.; ord. priest May 6, 1956; ord. archbishop of Moncton, June 1, 1972.

Chimy, Jerome I., O.S.B.M.: b. Mar. 12, 1919, Radway, Alta.; ord. priest, June 29, 1944; ord. first bishop of New Westminster, B.C., for the Ukrainians, Sept. 5, 1974.

Cimichella, Andre, O.S.M.: b. Feb. 21, 1921, Grotte Santo Stefano, Italy; ord. priest May 26, 1945; ord. titular bishop of Quiza and auxiliary of Montreal, July 16, 1964.

Clune, Robert B.: b. Sept. 18, 1920, Toronto, Ont.; ord. priest May 26, 1945; ord. titular bishop of Lacubaza and auxiliary bishop of Toronto, June 21, 1979.

Coderre, Gerard Marie: b. Dec. 19, 1904, St. Jacques de Montcalm, Que.; ord. priest May 30, 1931; ord. titular bishop of Aegae and coadjutor bishop of St.-Jean-de-Quebec, Sept. 12, 1951; bishop of St.-Jean-de-Quebec, Feb. 3, 1955. Retired May 3, 1978.

Couture, Jean-Guy: b. May 6, 1929, St.-Jean-Baptiste de Quebec, Que.; ord. priest May 30, 1953; ord. bishop of Hauterive, Que., Aug. 15, 1975; bishop of Chicoutimi, Apr. 5, 1979.

Couturier, Gerard: b. Jan. 12, 1913, St. Louis du Ha Ha, Que; ord. priest Mar. 25, 1938; ord. bishop of Hauterive, Feb. 28, 1957; resigned see Sept. 7, 1974.

Crowley, Leonard: b. Dec. 28, 1921, Montreal, Que.; ord. priest May 31, 1947; ord. titular bishop of Mons and auxiliary bishop of Montreal, Mar. 24, 1971.

Decosse, Aime: b. June 21, 1903, Somerset, Man.; ord. priest July 4, 1926; ord. bishop of Gravelbourg, Jan. 20, 1954; retired May 12, 1973.

Delaquis, Noel: b. Dec. 25, 1934, Notre-Dame-de-Lourdes, Man.; ord. priest June 5, 1958; ord. bishop of Gravelbourg, Feb. 19, 1974.

De Roo, Remi J.: b. Feb. 24, 1924, Swan Lake, Man.; ord. priest June 8, 1950; ord. bishop of Victoria, Dec. 14, 1962.

Despatie, Roger: b. Apr. 12, 1927, Sudbury, Ont.; ord. priest Apr. 12, 1952; ord. titular bishop of Usinaza and auxiliary bishop of Sault Ste. Marie, June 28, 1968; bishop of Hearst, Feb. 8, 1973.

Dionne, Gerard: b. June 19, 1919, Saint-Basile, N.B.; ord. priest May 1, 1948; ord. titular bishop of Garba and auxiliary bishop of Sault Ste. Marie, Apr. 8, 1975.

Douville, Arthur: b. July 22, 1894, St. Casimir de Portneuf, Que.; ord. priest May 25, 1919; ord. titular bishop of Vita and auxiliary bishop of St. Hyacinthe, Jan. 29, 1940; coadjutor bishop of St. Hyacinthe, Mar. 21, 1942; bishop of St. Hyacinthe, Nov. 27, 1942; retired June 13, 1967.

Doyle, James L.: b. June 20, 1929, Chatham, Ont.; ord. priest June 12, 1954; ord. bishop of Peterborough June 28, 1976.

Doyle, W. Emmett: b. Feb. 18, 1913, Calgary, Alta.: ord. priest June 5, 1938; ord. bishop of Nelson, Dec. 3, 1958.

Drainville, Gerard: b. May 20, 1930, L'Isle-du-Pas, Que.; ord. priest May 30, 1953; ord. bishop of Amos, June 12, 1978.

Dumouchel, Paul, O.M.I.: b. Sept. 19, 1911, St. Boniface, Man.; ord. priest June 24, 1936; ord. titular bishop of Sufes and vicar apostolic of Keewatin, May 24, 1955; archbishop of Keewatin-Le Pas, July 13, 1967.

Ebacher, Roger: b. Oct. 6, 1936, Amos, Que.; ord. priest May 27, 1961; ord. bishop of Hauterive, July 31, 1979.

Exner, Adam, O.M.I.: b. Dec. 24, 1928, Killaly, Sask.; ord. priest July 7, 1957; ord. bishop of Kamloops, B.C., Mar. 12, 1974.

Flahiff, George F.: (See Cardinals Biographies.)

Fortier, Jean-Marie: b. July 1, 1920, Quebec, Que.; ord. priest June 16, 1944; ord. titular bishop of Pomaria and auxiliary bishop of Ste. Anne-de-la-Pocatiere, Jan. 23, 1961; bishop of Gaspe, Jan. 19, 1965; archbishop of Sherbrooke, Apr. 20, 1968.

Frenette, Emilien: b. May 6, 1905, Montreal, Que.; ord. priest May 30, 1931; ord. bishop of St. Jerome, Sept. 12, 1951; retired June 11, 1971.

Fulton, Thomas B.: b. Jan. 13, 1918, St. Catharines, Ont.; ord. priest June 7, 1941; ord. titular bishop of Cursola and auxiliary bishop of Toronto, Jan. 6, 1969; bishop of St. Catharines, July 7, 1978.

Gagnon, Edouard, P.S.S.: b. Jan. 15, 1918, Port Daniel, Que.; ord. priest Aug. 15, 1940; ord. bishop Mar. 25, 1969; bishop of St. Paul in Alberta 1969-72; rector of Canadian College in Rome, 1972-   ; vice-president and secretary of Vatican Committee for the Family, 1973.

Gervais, Marcel A.: b. 1932, Elie, Man.; ord. priest 1958; app. titular bishop of Rosmarkaeum and auxiliary bishop of London, Ont., Apr. 23, 1980.

Gilbert, Arthur J.: b. Oct. 26, 1915, Oromocto, N.B.; ord. priest June 3, 1943; ord. bishop of St. John, N.B., June 19, 1974.

Godin, Edgar: b. May 31, 1911, Neguac, N.B.; ord. priest June 15, 1941; ord. bishop of Bathurst, July 25, 1969.

Gratton, Jean: b. Dec. 4, 1924, Wendover, Ont.; ord. priest Apr. 27, 1952; ord. bishop of Mont Laurier, June 29, 1978.

Gregoire, Paul: b. Oct. 24, 1911, Verdun, Que.; ord. priest May 22, 1937; ord. titular bishop of Curubis and auxiliary bishop of Montreal, Dec. 27, 1961; archbishop of Montreal, Apr. 20, 1968.

Greschuk, Martin: b. Nov. 7, 1923, Innisfree, Alta.; ord. priest June 11, 1950; ord. titular bishop of Nazianus and auxiliary bishop of Edmonton of the Ukrainians, Oct. 3, 1974.

Hacault, Antoine: b. Jan. 17, 1926, Brux-elles, Man.; ord. priest May 20, 1951; ord. titular bishop of Media and coadjutor of St. Boniface, Sept. 8, 1964; archbishop of St. Boniface, Sept. 7, 1974.

Hains, Gaston: b. Sept. 10, 1921, Drummondville, Que.; ord. priest June 15, 1946; ord. titular bishop of Belesana and auxiliary bishop of St. Hyacinthe, Oct. 10, 1964; coadjutor bishop of Amos, 1967; bishop of Amos, Oct. 31, 1968; retired 1978.

Halpin, Charles A.: b. Aug. 30, 1930, St. Eustache, Man.; ord. priest May 27, 1956; ord. archbishop of Regina, Nov. 26, 1973.

Hamelin, Jean-Guy: b. Oct. 8, 1925, St. Severin-de-Proulxville, Que.; ord. priest June 11, 1949; ord. first bishop of Rouyn-Noranda, Que., Feb. 9, 1974.

Hayes, James M.: b. May 27, 1924, Halifax, N.S.; ord. priest June 15, 1947; ord. titular bishop of Reperi and apostolic administrator of Halifax, Apr. 20, 1965; archbishop of Halifax, June 22, 1967.

Hermaniuk, Maxim, C.SS.R.: b. Oct. 30, 1911, Nove Selo, Ukraine; ord. priest Sept. 4, 1938; ord. titular bishop of Sinna and exarch of Manitoba (Ukrainians), June 29, 1951; archbishop of Winnipeg (Ukrainians), Nov. 3, 1956.

Hubert, Bernard: b. June 1, 1929, Beloeil, Que.; ord. priest May 30, 1953; ord. bishop of St. Jerome, Sept. 12, 1971; coadjutor bishop of Saint-Jean-de-Quebec, 1977; succeeded as bishop of Saint-Jean-de-Quebec, May 3, 1978.

Jennings, Edward Q.: b. Oct. 4, 1896, Saint John, N.B.; ord. priest Dec. 27, 1925; ord. titular bishop of Sala and auxiliary bishop of Vancouver, June 11, 1941; bishop of Kamloops, Feb. 22, 1946; bishop of Fort William (now Thunder Bay), May 14, 1952; resigned Sept. 18, 1969.

Jette, Edouard: b. Aug. 9, 1898, St. Jacques, Que.; ord. priest May 31, 1923; ord. titular bishop of Tabe and auxiliary of Joliette, Apr. 14, 1948; retired 1968.

Jordan, Anthony, O.M.I.: b. Nov. 10, 1901, Broxburn, Scotland; ord. priest June 23, 1929; ord. titular bishop of Vada and vicar apostolic of Prince Rupert, B.C., Sept. 8, 1945; titular archbishop of Silyum and coadjutor of Edmonton, Apr. 17, 1955; archbishop of Edmonton, Aug. 11, 1964; retired July 2, 1973.

Labrie, Jean-Paul: b. Nov. 4, 1922, Laurieville, Que.; ord. priest May 20, 1951; ord. titular bishop of Urci and auxiliary bishop of Quebec, May 14, 1977.

Lacey, Michael Pearse: b. Nov. 27, 1917, Toronto, Ont.; ord. priest May 23, 1943; ord. titular bishop of Diano and auxiliary bishop of Toronto, June 21, 1979.

Lacroix, Fernand, C.J.M.: b. Oct. 16, 1919, Quebec; ord. priest Feb. 10, 1946; ord. bishop of Edmundston, Oct. 20, 1970.

Lafontaine, Jean-Marie: b. Apr. 4, 1923,

Montreal, Que.; ord. priest May 22, 1948; ord. titular bishop of Ursona and auxiliary bishop of Montreal, May 27, 1979.

Landriault, Jacques: b. Sept. 23, 1921, Alfred, Ont.; ord. priest Feb. 9, 1947; ord. titular bishop of Cadi and auxiliary bishop of Alexandria, July 25, 1962; bishop of Hearst, May 27, 1964; app. bishop of Timmins, Mar. 24, 1971.

Langevin, Louis-de-Gonzague, P.B.: b. Oct. 31, 1921, Oka, Que.; ord. priest Feb. 2, 1950; ord. titular bishop of Rosemarkie and auxiliary of St. Hyacinthe Sept. 23, 1974; bishop of St. Hyacinthe, July 18, 1979.

LaRocque, Eugene Philippe: b. Mar. 27, 1927, Windsor, Ont.; ord. priest June 7, 1952; ord. bishop of Alexandria, Ont., Sept. 3, 1974; title of see changed to Alexandria-Cornwall, 1976.

Lebel, Robert: b. Nov. 8, 1924, Trois-Pistoles, Que.; ord. priest June 18, 1950; ord. titular bishop of Alinda and auxiliary of St. Jean de Quebec, May 12, 1974; bishop of Valleyfield, May 12, 1976.

Le Blanc, Camille A.: b. Aug. 25, 1898, Barachois, N.B.; ord. priest Apr. 5, 1924; ord. bishop of Bathurst, Sept. 8, 1942; retired Jan. 8, 1969.

Legare, Henri, O.M.I.: b. Feb. 20, 1918, Willow Bunch, Sask.; ord. priest June 29, 1943; ord. first bishop of Labrador-Schefferville, Sept. 9, 1967; archbishop of Grouard-McLennan, Nov. 21, 1972.

Leger, Paul-Emile: (See Cardinals, Biographies).

Leguerrier, Jules, O.M.I.: b. Feb. 18, 1915, Clarence Creek, Ont.; ord. priest June 19, 1943; ord. titular bishop of Bavagaliana and vicar apostolic of James Bay, June 29, 1964; first bishop of Moosonee, July 13, 1967.

Lemieux, Marie Joseph, O.P.: b. May 10, 1902, Quebec, Que.; ord. priest Apr. 15, 1928; ord. bishop of Sendai, Japan, June 29, 1936; titular bishop of Calydon, 1941; apostolic administrator of Gravelbourg, 1942; bishop of Gravelbourg, 1944; archbishop of Ottawa, 1953; retired 1966.

Levesque, Charles Henri: b. Dec. 29, 1921, St. Andre de Kamouraska, Que.; ord. priest June 13, 1948; ord. titular bishop of Guzabeta and auxiliary bishop of Ste.-Anne-de-la-Pocatiere, Dec. 27, 1965; bishop of Ste.-Anne-de-la-Pocatiere, Aug. 17, 1968.

Levesque, Louis: b. May 27, 1908, Amqui, Que.; ord. priest June 26, 1932; ord. bishop of Hearst, Aug. 15, 1952; titular archbishop of Egnatia and coadjutor of Rimouski, Apr. 13, 1964; archbishop of Rimouski, Feb. 25, 1967; retired May 14, 1973.

Lussier, Philippe, C.SS.R.: b. Oct. 3, 1911, Weedon, Que.; ord. priest Sept. 18, 1937; ord. bishop of St. Paul in Alberta, Aug. 17, 1952; retired Aug. 17, 1968.

McCarthy, Thomas J.: b. Oct. 4, 1905, Goderich, Ont.; ord. priest May 25, 1929;

ord. bishop of Nelson, Aug. 1, 1955; bishop of St. Catharines, Nov. 9, 1958. Retired 1978.

MacDonald, James H.: b. Apr. 28, 1925, Wycogama, N.S.; ord. priest June 28, 1953; ord. titular bishop of Gibba and auxiliary bishop of Hamilton April 17, 1978.

MacDonald, Joseph Faber: b. Jan. 20, 1932, Little Pond, P.E.I.; ord. priest Mar. 28, 1963; ord. bishop of Grand Falls, Mar. 19, 1980.

MacEachern, Malcolm A.: b. Oct. 5, 1901, Broad Cove Chapel, N.S.; ord. priest June 11, 1927; ord. bishop of Charlottetown, Jan. 18, 1955; retired Feb. 24, 1970.

McGrath, Richard T.: b. June 17, 1912, Oderin, Placentia Bay, Nfld.; ord. priest June 24, 1936; ord. bishop of St. George's, Nfld., July 22, 1970.

MacNeil, Joseph N.: b. Apr. 15, 1924, Sydney, N.S.; ord. priest May 23, 1948; ord. bishop of St. John, N.B., June 24, 1969; archbishop of Edmonton, July 6, 1973. President Canadian Conference of Catholic Bishops, 1979.

Mahoney, James P.: b. Dec. 7, 1927, Saskatoon, Sask.; ord. priest June 7, 1952; ord. bishop of Saskatoon, Dec. 13, 1967.

Martin, Albertus: b. Oct. 4, 1913, Southbridge, Mass.; ord. priest May 18, 1939; ord. titular bishop of Bassiana and coadjutor bishop of Nicolet, Oct. 7, 1950; bishop of Nicolet, Nov. 8, 1950.

Melancon, Georges: b. Apr. 7, 1886, Saint-Guillaume d'Upton, Que.; ord. priest Sept. 12, 1909; ord. bishop of Chicoutimi, July 23, 1940; retired Feb. 18, 1961.

Morin, Laurent: b. Feb. 14, 1908, Montreal, Que.; ord. priest May 27, 1934; ord. titular bishop of Arsamosata and auxiliary bishop of Montreal, Oct. 30, 1955; bishop of Prince Albert, Feb. 28, 1959.

Noel, Laurent: b. Mar. 19, 1920, Saint-Just-de-Bretenieres, Que.; ord. priest June 16, 1944; ord. titular bishop of Agathopolis and auxiliary bishop of Quebec, Aug. 29, 1963; bishop of Trois Rivieres, Nov. 5, 1975.

O'Byrne, Paul J.: b. Dec. 21, 1922, Calgary, Alta.; ord. priest Feb. 21, 1948; ord. bishop of Calgary, Aug. 22, 1968.

O'Connor, Hubert P., O.M.I.: b. Feb. 17, 1928, Huntingdon, Que.; ord. priest June 5, 1955; ord. bishop of Whitehorse, Dec. 8, 1971.

O'Grady, John Fergus, O.M.I.: b. July 27, 1908, Macton, Ont.; ord. priest June 29, 1934; ord. titular bishop of Aspendus and vicar apostolic of Prince Rupert, Mar. 7, 1956; first bishop of Prince George, July 13, 1967.

O'Mara, John A.: b. Nov. 17, 1924, Buffalo, N.Y.; ord. priest June 1, 1951; ord. bishop of Thunder Bay, June 29, 1976.

O'Neill, Michael C.: b. Feb. 15, 1898, Kemptville, Ont.; ord. priest Dec. 21, 1927; ord. archbishop of Regina, Apr. 14, 1948; retired Sept. 26, 1973.

Ouellet, Gilles, P.M.E.: b. Aug. 14, 1922,

Bromptonville, Que.; ord. priest June 30, 1946; ord. bishop of Gaspe, Nov. 23, 1968; app. archbishop of Rimouski, Apr. 27, 1973. President Canadian Conference of Catholic Bishops, 1977-79.

Ouellette, Andre: b. Feb. 4, 1913, Salem, Mass.; ord. priest June 11, 1938; ord. titular bishop of Carre and auxiliary bishop of Mont-Laurier, Feb. 25, 1957; bishop of Mont-Laurier, Mar. 27, 1965; retired Feb. 1978.

Pappin, Bernard F.: b. July 10, 1928, Westmeath, Ont.; ord. priest May 27, 1954; ord. titular bishop of Aradi and auxiliary bishop of Sault Ste. Marie, Apr. 11, 1975.

Pare, Marius: b. May 22, 1903, Montmagny, Que.; ord. priest July 3, 1927; ord. titular bishop of Aegae and auxiliary bishop of Chicoutimi, May 1, 1956; bishop of Chicoutimi, Feb. 18, 1961. Retired Apr. 5, 1979.

Parent, Charles Eugene: b. Apr. 22, 1902, Notre Dame-de-Neiges-des-Trois-Pistoles, Que.; ord. priest Mar. 7, 1925; ord. titular bishop of Diana and auxiliary bishop of Rimouski, May 24, 1944; app. archbishop of Rimouski, Mar. 2, 1951; retired Feb. 25, 1967.

Pedneault, Roch: b. Apr. 10, 1927, Saint Joseph d'Alma, Que.; ord. priest Feb. 8, 1953; ord. titular bishop of Aggersel and auxiliary of Chicoutimi, Que., June 29, 1974.

Pelletier, Georges Leon: b. Aug. 19, 1904, Saint-Epiphane, Que.; ord. priest June 24, 1931; ord. titular bishop of Hephaestus and auxiliary bishop of Quebec, Feb. 24, 1943; bishop of Trois Rivieres, July 26, 1947; retired Oct. 31, 1975.

Penney, Alphonsus L.: b. Sept. 17, 1924, St. John's, Nfld.; ord. priest June 29, 1949; ord. bishop of Grand Falls, Jan. 18, 1973; archbishop of St. John's, Nfld., Apr. 5, 1979.

Piche, Paul, O.M.I.: b. Sept. 14, 1909, Gravelbourg, Sask.; ord. priest Dec. 23, 1934; ord. titular bishop of Orcistus and vicar apostolic of Mackenzie, June 11, 1959; first bishop of Mackenzie-Fort Smith, July 13, 1967.

Plourde, Joseph Aurele: b. Jan. 12, 1915, St. Francois de Madawaska, N.B.; ord. priest May 7, 1944; ord. titular bishop of Lapda and auxiliary bishop of Alexandria, Aug. 26, 1964; archbishop of Ottawa, Jan. 2, 1967.

Pocock, Philip: b. July 2, 1906, St. Thomas, Ont.; ord. priest June 14, 1930; ord. bishop of Saskatoon, June 29, 1944; titular archbishop of Aprus and coadjutor archbishop of Winnipeg, Aug. 6, 1951; archbishop of Winnipeg, Jan. 14, 1952; titular archbishop of Isauropolis and coadjutor archbishop of Toronto, Feb. 18, 1961; archbishop of Toronto, Mar. 30, 1971; retired Apr. 29, 1978.

Power, William E.: b. Sept. 27, 1915; Montreal, Que.; ord. priest June 7, 1941; ord. bishop of Antigonish, July 20, 1960; president Canadian Conference of Catholic Bishops, 1971-73.

Proulx, Adolphe J.: b. Dec. 12, 1927, Hanmer, Ont., Canada; ord. priest Apr. 17, 1954; ord. titular bishop of Missua and auxiliary bishop of Sault Ste. Marie, Feb. 24, 1965; bishop of Alexandria, Apr. 28, 1967; bishop of Hull, Feb. 13, 1974.

Reding, Paul F.: b. Feb. 14, 1925, Hamilton, Ont.; ord. priest June 3, 1950; ord. titular bishop of Liberalia and auxiliary bishop of

Hamilton, Sept. 14, 1966; bishop of Hamilton, Sept. 14, 1973.

Robidoux, Omer, O.M.I.: b. Nov. 19, 1913 Saint-Pierre-Jolys, Man.; ord. priest June 29, 1939; ord. bishop of Churchill-Hudson Bay, May 20, 1970.

Roborecki, Andrew: b. Dec. 12, 1910, in western Ukraine; arrived Winnipeg, Man., 1912; ord. priest July 18, 1934; ord. titular bishop of Tanais and auxiliary bishop of Ukrainian Catholic Diocese of Central Canada, May 27, 1948; exarch of Saskatchewan, 1951; bishop of Saskatoon (Ukrainians), Nov. 3, 1956.

Routhier, Henri, O.M.I.: b. Feb. 28, 1900, Pincher Creek, Alta.; ord. priest Sept. 7, 1924; ord. titular bishop of Naissus and coadjutor vicar apostolic of Grouard, Sept. 8, 1945; vicar apostolic of Grouard, 1953; archbishop of Grouard-McLennan, July 13, 1967; retired Nov. 21, 1972.

Roy, Maurice: (Cardinals, Biographies.)

Roy, Raymond: b. May 3, 1919, St. Boniface, Man.; ord. priest May 31, 1947; ord. bishop of St. Paul in Alberta, July 18, 1972.

Rusnak, Michael, C.SS.R.: b. Aug. 21, 1921, Beaverdale, Pa.; ord. priest July 3, 1949; ord. titular bishop of Tzernicus and auxiliary bishop of Toronto eparchy and apostolic visitator to Slovak Catholics of Byzantine rite in Canada, Jan. 2, 1965.

Ryan, Joseph F.: b. Mar. 1, 1897, Dundas, Ont.; ord. priest May 21, 1921; ord. bishop of Hamilton, Oct. 19, 1937; retired Mar. 27, 1973.

Sabatini, Lawrence, C.S.: b. May 15, 1930, Chicago, Ill.; ord. priest Mar. 19, 1957; ord. titular bishop of Nasai and auxiliary bishop of Vancouver, Sept. 21, 1978.

Saint-Delais, Raymond: Superior of the seminary at St. Hyacinthe; appointed titular bishop of Diana and auxiliary bishop of St. Jerome, July 9, 1980.

Sanschagrin, Albert, O.M.I.: b. Aug. 5, 1911, Saint-Tite, Que.; ord. priest May 24, 1936; ord. titular bishop of Bagi and coadjutor bishop of Amos Sept. 14, 1957; bishop of Saint-Hyacinthe, June 13, 1967. Retired July 18, 1979.

Savaryn, Nile Nicholas, O.S.B.M.: b. May 19, 1905, Stary Sambir, Ukraine; ord. priest Aug. 23, 1931; ord. titular bishop of Jos and auxiliary bishop of the Catholic Ukrainian diocese in Canada, July 1, 1943; bishop of apostolic exarchate for western Canada,

1948; bishop of Edmonton (Ukrainians), Nov. 3, 1956.

Sherlock, John M.: b. Jan. 20, 1926, Regina, Sask.; ord. priest June 3, 1950; ord. titular bishop of Macriana and auxiliary of London, Ont., Aug. 28, 1974; bishop of London, July 7, 1978.

Skinner, Patrick J., C.J.M.: b. Mar. 9, 1904, St. John's, Nfld.; ord. priest May 30, 1929; ord. titular bishop of Zenobia and auxiliary bishop of St. John's, Mar. 17, 1950; archbishop of St. John's, Mar. 23, 1951. Retired Apr. 5, 1979.

Smith, William J.: b. Jan. 2, 1897, Greenfield, Ont.; ord. priest June 16, 1927; ord. bishop of Pembroke, July 25, 1945; retired Feb. 8, 1971.

Spence, Francis J.: b. June 3, 1926, Perth, Ont.; ord. priest Apr. 16, 1950; ord. titular bishop of Nova and auxiliary bishop of the military vicariate, June 15, 1967; bishop of Charlottetown, Aug. 15, 1970.

Sutton, Peter A., O.M.I.: b. Oct. 18, 1934, Chandler, Que.; ord. priest Oct. 22, 1960; ord. bishop of Labrador-Schefferville, July 18, 1974.

Tessier, Maxime: b. Oct. 9, 1906, St. Sebastien, Que.; ord. priest June 14, 1930; ord. titular bishop of Christopolis and auxiliary bishop of Ottawa, Aug. 2, 1951; coadjutor bishop of Timmins, 1953; bishop of Timmins, May 8, 1955; retired Mar. 24, 1971.

Vachon, Louis-Albert: b. Feb. 4, 1912, Saint-Frederic, Que.; ord. priest June 11, 1938; ord. titular bishop of Mesarfelta and auxiliary bishop of Quebec, May 14, 1977.

Valois, Charles: b. Apr. 24, 1924, Montreal, Que.; ord. priest June 3, 1950; ord. bishop of St. Jerome, June 29, 1977.

Wall, Leonard J.: b. Sept. 27, 1924, Windsor, Ont.; ord. priest June 11, 1949; ord. titular bishop of Leptiminus and auxiliary bishop of Toronto, June 21, 1979.

Webster, Benjamin I.: b. Mar. 7, 1898, Spofforth, Eng.; ord. priest May 26, 1923; ord. titular bishop of Paphos and auxiliary bishop of Toronto, Nov. 21, 1946; bishop of Peterborough, Apr. 21, 1954; retired Mar. 12, 1968.

Whelan, Lawrence P.: b. Oct. 16, 1899, Montreal, Que.; ord. priest Dec. 19, 1925; ord. titular bishop of Opus and auxiliary bishop of Montreal, Aug. 15, 1941.

Wilhelm, Joseph L.: b. Nov. 16, 1909, Walkerton, Ont.; ord. priest June 9, 1934; ord. titular bishop of Saccaea and auxiliary bishop of Calgary, Aug. 22, 1963; archbishop of Kingston, Dec. 14, 1966.

Windle, Joseph R.: b. Aug. 28, 1917, Ashdad, Ont.; ord. priest May 16, 1943; ord. titular bishop of Uzita and auxiliary bishop of Ottawa, Jan. 18, 1961; coadjutor bishop of Pembroke, 1969; bishop of Pembroke, Feb. 15, 1971.

CANADIAN CONFERENCE OF CATHOLIC BISHOPS

The Canadian Conference of Catholic Bishops was established Oct. 12, 1943, as a permanent voluntary association of the bishops of Canada, was given official approval by the Holy See in 1948, and acquired the status of an episcopal conference after the Second Vatican Council.

The CCCB acts in two ways: (1) as a strictly ecclesiastical body through which the bishops act together with pastoral authority and responsibility for the Church throughout the country; (2) as an operational secretariat through which the bishops act on a wider scale for the good of the Church and society.

At the top of the CCCB organizational table are the president, an executive committee, an administrative board and a plenary assembly. The membership consists of all the bishops of Canada.

Departments and Offices

The CCCB's work is planned and co-ordinated by a Pastoral Team of 14 members — six bishops and six staff members (lay and clergy) and the two general secretaries.

The CCCB has six departments and four offices all of which work in both French and English: (I) Department for Theology and Canon Law; (II) Department for Christian Education and Migration and Tourism; (III) Department for Social Affairs and Laity; (IV)

Department for Missions, Ecumenism and Non-Believers; (V) Department for Clergy and Religious; (VI) Department for Liturgy and Social Communications. Offices for (1) Christian Education (2) Liturgy (3) Missions (4) Social Affairs.

The general secretariat consists of a French and an English general secretary and their assistants and directors of public relations.

Administrative services for purchasing, archives and library, accounting, personnel, publications, printing and distribution are supervised by directors who relate to the general secretaries.

Various advisory councils and committees with mixed memberships of lay persons, religious, priests and bishops also serve the CCCB on a variety of topics.

Operations

Meetings for the transaction of business are held at least once a year by the plenary assembly, eight times a year by the executive committee, and four times a year by the administrative board.

Archbishop Joseph N. MacNeil of Edmonton, Alta., is president of the CCCB; Archbishop Henri Legare of Grouard-McLennan, Alta., is vice-president.

Headquarters are located at 90 Parent Ave., Ottawa, K1N 7B1, Canada.

STATISTICS OF CATHOLIC CHURCH IN CANADA

(Principal source: *1980 Directory of the Canadian Conference of Catholic Bishops.* Permanent deacon statistics are from the *1980 Annuario Pontificio.* Archdioceses are indicated by an asterisk. For dioceses marked +, see Canadian Dioceses with Interprovincial Lines.)

Canada's 10 civil provinces and two territories are divided into 17 ecclesiastical provinces consisting of 17 metropolitan sees (archdioceses) and 52 suffragan sees (51 dioceses and one abbacy); there is also one archdiocese immediately subject to the Holy See. (See listing of Ecclesiastical Provinces elsewhere in this section.)

This table presents a regional breakdown of Catholic statistics. In some cases, the totals are approximate because diocesan boundaries fall within several civil provinces.

Civil Province Diocese	Cath. Pop.	Dioc. Priests	Rel. Priests	Total Priests	Perm. Deacs.	Bros.	Srs.	Parishes
Newfoundland	**204,775**	**120**	**44**	**164**	—	**99**	**530**	**167**
*St. John's	113,792	58	21	79	—	64	328	40
Grand Falls	35,140	31	1	32	—	15	72	45
Labrador- Schefferville+	20,000	1	21	22	—	10	51	24
St. George's	35,843	30	1	31	—	10	79	58
Prince Edward Island								
Charlottetown	**51,215**	**80**	**3**	**83**	**1**	—	**240**	**56**
Nova Scotia	**275,597**	**296**	**50**	**346**	**5**	**10**	**951**	**241**
*Halifax	113,000	76	21	97	5	1	420	73
Antigonish	126,333	195	11	206	—	8	468	127
Yarmouth	36,264	25	18	43	—	1	63	41
New Brunswick	**326,227**	**308**	**119**	**427**	—	**62**	**1,226**	**273**
*Moncton	76,340	80	63	143	—	28	414	64
Bathurst	106,578	90	28	118	—	21	345	70
Edmundston	53,309	59	14	73	—	11	237	38
St. John	90,000	79	14	93	—	2	230	101
Quebec	**5,397,300**	**4,414**	**2,900**	**7,314**	**70**	**3,574**	**27,002**	**1,895**
*Montreal	1,533,777	729	1,190	1,919	—	950	8,568	280
*Quebec	828,469	857	587	1,444	35	806	6,243	275
*Rimouski	161,681	248	63	311	—	47	986	117
*Sherbrooke	235,445	323	137	460	1	138	1,533	131
Amos	106,410	98	24	122	—	23	329	82
Chicoutimi	268,550	298	103	401	2	130	1,015	107
Gaspe	103,077	111	21	132	1	9	318	63
Hauterive	115,000	64	30	94	—	32	297	50
Hull	186,000	90	72	162	1	23	363	65
Joliette	150,508	151	56	207	—	144	662	55
Mont Laurier	68,124	77	48	125	—	58	247	62
Nicolet	164,768	240	38	278	7	163	1,181	85
Rouyn-Noranda	54,942	40	25	65	—	23	202	44
Ste.-Anne-de-la Pocatiere	90,845	197	10	207	—	16	464	54
St. Hyacinthe	290,249	261	109	370	16	342	1,723	112
St. Jean de Quebec	410,000	171	95	266	—	169	840	88
St. Jerome	228,155	112	127	239	2	152	343	66
Trois Rivieres	240,195	218	108	326	5	241	1,282	97
Valleyfield	161,105	129	57	186	—	108	406	62
Ontario	**2,474,306**	**1,427**	**1,295**	**2,722**	**105**	**357**	**5,234**	**1,169**
*Kingston	61,570	83	6	89	—	—	303	78
*Ottawa	285,303	164	242	406	7	117	1,264	110
*Toronto	950,000	298	532	830	78	113	1,025	212
Alexandria-Cornwall	51,212	46	7	53	1	11	123	34
Hamilton	290,093	146	162	308	—	30	460	145
Hearst	34,997	40	8	48	—	3	68	43
London	314,667	256	115	371	—	22	792	177

Civil Province Diocese	Cath. Pop.	Dioc. Priests	Rel. Priests	Total Priests	Perm. Deacs.	Bros.	Srs.	Par- ishes
Ontario								
Moosonee+	3,000	—	11	11	1	12	18	10
Pembroke+	55,418	86	17	103	—	4	285	72
Peterborough	43,276	63	4	67	—	1	168	35
St. Catharines	100,000	55	38	93	—	—	98	47
Sault Ste. Marie	170,000	135	94	229	18	15	454	115
Thunder Bay	55,000	26	41	67	—	6	68	54
Timmins	59,770	29	18	47	—	23	108	37
Manitoba	**207,500**	**151**	**220**	**371**	**18**	**67**	**1,020**	**252**
*Keewatin-LePas+	25,000	—	37	37	1	11	50	52
*St. Boniface	80,000	97	76	173	4	39	616	110
*Winnipeg	97,500	54	86	140	13	12	344	68
Churchill-Hudson Bay+	5,000	—	21	21	—	5	10	22
Saskatchewan	**205,134**	**210**	**160**	**370**	**—**	**34**	**861**	**431**
*Regina	91,500	93	48	141	—	5	271	194
Gravelbourg	14,175	30	8	38	—	4	115	58
Prince Albert	42,959	47	34	81	—	8	209	92
Saskatoon	44,500	40	42	82	—	3	174	63
St. Peter Muenster (Abb.)	12,000	—	28	28	—	14	92	24
Alberta	**350,000**	**239**	**235**	**474**	**1**	**52**	**948**	**431**
*Edmonton	161,000	109	118	227	—	29	616	176
*Grouard-McLennan	30,000	5	40	45	—	6	85	48
Calgary	130,000	97	64	161	1	15	152	127
St. Paul	29,000	28	13	41	—	2	95	80
British Columbia	**310,557**	**174**	**173**	**347**	**—**	**48**	**645**	**335**
*Vancouver	175,000	90	100	190	—	31	357	88
Kamloops	27,000	18	13	31	—	4	52	80
Nelson	37,557	32	17	49	—	—	55	42
Prince George	26,000	5	23	28	—	7	51	74
Victoria	45,000	29	20	49	—	6	130	51
Yukon Territory								
Whitehorse+	7,258	—	17	17	—	2	17	24
Northwest Territories								
MacKenzie-Ft. Smith+	34,000	1	38	39	—	17	36	30
Eastern Rites	**206,265**	**157**	**75**	**232**	**19**	**18**	**142**	**365**
*Winnipeg	55,000	38	18	56	5	3	30	44
Edmonton	41,065	31	15	46	3	9	35	98
New Westminster	7,000	10	4	14	1	—	4	20
Saskatoon	20,000	18	20	38	1	—	40	130
Toronto	83,200	60	18	78	9	6	33	73
Military Vicariate	**73,195**	**55**	**25**	**80**	**—**	**—**	**6**	**60**
TOTALS 1980	**10,123,329**	**7,632**	**5,354**	**12,986**	**219**	**4,340**	**38,858**	**5,729**
Totals 1979	**9,991,243**	**7,734**	**5,316**	**13,050**	**185**	**4,418**	**40,241**	**5,836**

Dioceses with Interprovincial Lines

The following dioceses, indicated by + in the table, have interprovincial lines.

Churchill-Hudson Bay includes part of Northwest Territories.

Keewatin-Le Pas includes part of Manitoba and Saskatchewan provinces.

Labrador-Schefferville includes the Labrador region of Newfoundland and the northern part of Quebec province.

MacKenzie-Fort Smith, Northwest Territories, includes part of Alberta and Saskatchewan provinces.

Moosonee, Ont., includes part of Quebec province.

Pembroke, Ont., includes one county of Quebec province.

Whitehorse, Y.T., includes part of British Columbia.

PERCENTAGE OF CATHOLICS

Catholic population statistics are from the 1980 Directory of the Canadian Conference of Catholic Bishops; total population figures are 1979 estimates.

The table presents a regional breakdown of Catholic percentage in total population. In some cases, the Catholic totals are approximate because diocesan boundaries fall within several civil provinces. See Index: Canadian Dioceses with Interprovincial Lines.

Civil Province Territory	Cath. Pop.	Total Pop.	Cath. Pct.
Alberta	350,000	1,985,200	17.6
British Columbia	310,557	2,555,800	12.1
Manitoba	207,500	1,029,900	20.1
New Brunswick	326,227	699,200	46.6
Newfoundland	204,775	572,900	35.7
Nova Scotia	275,597	845,400	32.6
Ontario	2,474,306	8,479,900	29.1
Prince Edward Is.	51,215	122,300	41.8
Quebec	5,397,300	6,289,600	85.8
Saskatchewan	205,134	952,500	21.5
Northwest Territories	34,000	43,100	78.8
Yukon	7,258	21,800	33.3
Eastern Rites	206,265	—	—
Military Ordinariate	73,195	—	—
TOTALS 1980	10,123,329	23,597,600	42.9
Totals 1979	9,991,243	23,444,200	42.6

CANADIAN SHRINES

Our Lady of the Cape (Cap de la Madeleine), Queen of the Most Holy Rosary: The Three Rivers, Quebec, parish church, built of fieldstone in 1714 and considered the oldest stone church on the North American continent preserved in its original state, was rededicated June 22, 1888, as a shrine of the Queen of the Most Holy Rosary. Thereafter, the site increased in importance as a pilgrimage and devotional center, and in 1904 St. Pius X decreed the crowning of a statue of the Blessed Virgin which had been donated 50 years earlier to commemorate the dogma of the Immaculate Conception. In 1909, the First Plenary Council of Quebec declared the church a shrine of national pilgrimage. In 1964, the church at the shrine was given the status and title of minor basilica.

St. Anne de Beaupre: The devotional history of this shrine in Quebec, which has been called the "Lourdes of the New World," began with the reported cure of a cripple, Louis Grimont, on Mar. 16, 1658, the starting date of construction work on a small chapel of St. Anne. The original building was successively enlarged and replaced by a stone church which was given the rank of minor basilica in 1888. The present structure, a Romanesque-Gothic basilica, houses the shrine proper in its north transept. The centers of attraction are an eight-foot-high oaken statue and the great relic of St. Anne, a portion of her forearm.

St. Joseph's Oratory: The massive oratory basilica standing on the western side of Mount Royal and overlooking the city of Montreal had its origin in a primitive chapel erected there by Brother Andre, C.S.C., in 1904. Eleven years later, a large crypt was built to accommodate an increasing number of pilgrims, and in 1924 construction work was begun on the large church. A belfry, housing a 60-bell carillon and standing on the site of the original chapel, was dedicated May 15, 1955, as the first major event of the jubilee year observed after the oratory was given the rank of minor basilica.

Martyrs' Shrine: A shrine commemorating several of the Jesuit Martyrs of North America who were killed between 1642 and 1649 in the Ontario and northern New York area is located on the former site of old Forte Sainte Marie.

CATHOLIC PUBLICATIONS

(Sources: *Catholic Press Directory*, Canadian Conference of Catholic Bishops.)

Newspapers

British Columbia Catholic, The, w; 150 Robson St., Vancouver, B.C. V6B 2A7.

Catholic New Times (national), biweekly; 80 Sackville St., Toronto, Ont. M5A 3E5.

Catholic Register, The, (national), w; 67 Bond St., Toronto, Ont. M5B 1X6.

Catholic Times, The, 10 times a year; 190 Bolton Ave., St. Lambert, Que. J4R 1W1.

Diocesan News, m; P.O. Box 1689, Charlottetown, P.E.I. CIA 7N4.

Esprit Vivant, w; 1915 est, Blvd. Gouin, Montreal, Que. H2B 1W7.

Monitor, The, m; P.O. Box 986, St. John's, Nfld. A1C 5M3.

New Freeman, The, w; Box 6609, Sta. A, St. John, N.B. E2L 4S1.

Prairie Messenger, w; St. Peter's Press, Muenster, Sask. SOK 2Y0.

Presence, m; 256 King Edward Ave., Ottawa, Ont. K1N 7M1.

Teviskes, Ziburiai (Lithuanian), w; 2185 Stavebank Rd., Mississauga, Ont. L5C 1T3.

Western Catholic Reporter, w; 10562 109th St., Edmonton, Alta. T5H 3B2.

Magazines

Annals of St. Anne de Beaupre, m; Box 1000, St. Anne de Beaupre, Que. GOA 3CO; Basilica of St. Anne.

Apostolat, bm; 460, Primiere Rue, Richelieu, Que. J3L 4B5, Oblates of Mary Immaculate.

Bulletin Le Bulletin (French-English), m; 324 E. Laurier St., Ottawa, Ont. K1N 6P6. Canadian Religious Conference.

Canadian Layman, The, bm; 88 Plymouth

St., Box 5438, Ottawa, Ont. K2C 3J1.

Canadian League, The, 4 times a year; 2375 A Ness Ave., Winnipeg, Man. R3J 1A5.

Chesterton Review, two times a year; 1437 College Dr., Saskatoon, Sask. S7N 0W8.

Centre News, q; 830 Bathurst St., Toronto, Ont. M5R 3G1.

Christian Communications, 4 times a year; 223 Main St., Ottawa, Ont. K1S 1C4.

Companion of St. Francis and St. Anthony, m; P.O. Box 535, Sta. F., Toronto, Ont. M4Y 2L8; Conventual Franciscan Fathers.

Field At Home, q; 10 Montcrest Blvd., Toronto Ont. M4K 1J7.

Indian Record, 6 times a year; 1301 Wellington Crescent, Winnipeg, Man. R3N 0A9.

Kateri (English-French), q; P.O. Box 70, Caughnawaga, Que. JO1 1BO.

Logos (Ukrainian, English and French), q; 165 Catherine St., P.O. Box 220, Yorkton, Sask. S3N 2V7.

Magazine Actualite, m; 2120 Sherbrooke St. E., Montreal, Que. H2K 1C2.

Martyrs' Shrine Message, q; Midland, Ont. L4R 4K3.

Messager de Saint Antoine, 10 times a year; Lac-Bouchette, Que. GOW IVO.

Messenger of the Sacred Heart, m; 833 Broadview Ave., Toronto, Ont. M4K 2P9.

Missions Etrangeres, 6 times a year; 59 Rue Desnoyers, Laval, Que. H7G 14A.

Oblate Missions, q; 17 Graham Ave., Ottawa, Ont. K1S 0B6.

Oratory, 5 times a year; 3800 Ch. Reine-Marie, Montreal Que. H3V 1H6.

Our Family, m; P.O. Box 249, Battleford, Sask.; S0M 0E0; Oblates of Mary Immaculate.

Prete et Pasteur, m; 4450 St. Hubert St., Montreal, Que. H2J 2W9.

Redeemer's Voice, m; 165 Catherine St., P.O. Box 220, Yorkton, Sask. S3N 2V7.

Regard de Foi, 6 times a year; 5875 Est. rue Sherbrooke, Montreal, Que. H1N 1B6.

Relations, m; 8100 Blvd., Saint-Laurent, Montreal Que. H2P 2L9; Jesuit Fathers.

Restoration, m; Madonna House, Combermere, Ont., KOJ ILO.

Sainte Anne de Beaupre, m; Basilica of St. Anne, Que. GOA 3CO.

Scarboro Missions, m; 2685 Kingston Rd., Scarboro, Ont. M1M 1M4.

Spiritan News, 4 times a year; 2475 Queen St., Toronto, Ont. M4E 1H8.

Unity, bm; 308 Young St., Montreal, Que. H3C 2G2.

MISSIONARIES TO THE AMERICAS

Allouez, Claude Jean (1622-1689): French Jesuit; missionary in Canada and midwestern US; preached to 20 different tribes of Indians and baptized over 10,000; vicar general of Northwest.

Altham, John (1589-1640): English Jesuit; missionary among Indians in Maryland.

Anchieta, Jose de, Bl. (1534-1597): Portuguese Jesuit, b. Canary Islands; missionary in Brazil; writer; beatified June 22, 1980.

Andreis, Felix de (1778-1820): Italian Vincentian; missionary and educator in western US.

Aparicio, Bl. Sebastian (1502-1600): Franciscan brother, born Spain; settled in Mexico, c. 1533; worked as road builder and farmer before becoming Franciscan at about the age of 70; beatified, 1787; feast, Feb. 25.

Badin, Stephen T. (1768-1853): French missioner; came to US, 1792, when Sulpician seminary in Paris was closed; ordained, 1793, Baltimore, the first priest ordained in US; missionary in Kentucky, Ohio and Michigan; bought land on which Notre Dame University now stands; buried on its campus.

Baraga, Frederic (1797-1868): Slovenian missionary bishop in US; studied at Ljubljana and Vienna, ordained, 1823; came to US, 1830; missionary to Indians of Upper Michigan; first bishop of Marquette, 1857-1868; wrote Chippewa grammar, dictionary, prayer book and other works.

Bertran, St. Louis (1526-1581): Spanish Dominican; missionary in Colombia and Caribbean, 1562-69; canonized, 1671; feast, Oct. 9.

Bourgeoys, Bl. Marguerite (1620-1700): French foundress, missionary; settled in Canada, 1653; founded Congregation of Notre Dame de Montreal, 1658; beatified, 1950; feast, Jan. 19.

Brebeuf, St. John de (1593-1649): French Jesuit; missionary among Huron Indians in Canada; martyred by Iroquois, Mar. 16, 1649; canonized, 1930; one of Jesuit North American martyrs; feast, Oct. 19.

Cancer de Barbastro, Louis (1500-1549): Spanish Dominican; began missionary work in Middle America, 1533; killed at Tampa Bay, Fla.

Castillo, Bl. John de (1596-1628): Spanish Jesuit; worked in Paraguay Indian mission settlements (reductions); martyred; beatified, 1934; feast, Nov. 17.

Catala, Magin (1761-1830): Spanish Franciscan; worked in California mission of Santa Clara for 36 years.

Chabanel, St. Noel (1613-1649): French Jesuit; missionary among Huron Indians in Canada; murdered by renegade Huron, Dec. 8, 1649; canonized, 1930; one of Jesuit North American martyrs; feast, Oct. 19.

Chaumonot, Pierre Joseph (1611-1693): French Jesuit; missionary among Indians in Canada.

Claver, St. Peter (1581-1654): Spanish Jesuit; missionary among Negroes of South America and West Indies; canonized, 1888;

patron of Catholic missions among Negroes; feast, Sept. 9.

Daniel, St. Anthony (1601-1648): French Jesuit; missionary among Huron Indians in Canada; martyred by Iroquois, July 4, 1648; canonized, 1930; one of Jesuit North American martyrs; feast, Oct. 19.

De Smet, Pierre Jean (1801-1873): Belgian-born Jesuit; missionary among Indians of northwestern US; served as intermediary between Indians and US government; wrote on Indian culture.

Duchesne, Bl. Rose Philippine (1769-1852): French nun; educator and missionary in the US; established first convent of the Society of the Sacred Heart in the US, at St. Charles, Mo. (later Florissant); founded schools for girls; did missionary work among Indians; beatified, 1940; feast, Nov. 17.

Farmer, Ferdinand (family name, Steinmeyer) (1720-1786): German Jesuit; missionary in Philadelphia, where he died; one of the first missionaries in New Jersey.

Flaget, Benedict J. (1763-1850): French Sulpician bishop; came to US, 1792; missionary and educator in US; first bishop of Bardstown, Ky. (now Louisville), 1810-32; 1833-50.

Gallitzin, Demetrius (1770-1840): Russian prince; born The Hague; convert, 1787; ordained priest at Baltimore, 1795; frontier missionary, known as Father Smith; Gallitzin, Pa., named for him.

Garnier, St. Charles (c. 1606-1649): French Jesuit; missionary among Hurons in Canada; martyred by Iroquois, Dec. 7, 1649; canonized, 1930; one of Jesuit North American martyrs; feast, Oct. 19.

Gibault, Pierre (1737-1804): Canadian missionary in Illinois and Indiana; aided in securing states of Ohio, Indiana, Illinois, Michigan and Wisconsin for the Americans during Revolution.

Gonzalez, Bl. Roch (1576-1628): Paraguayan Jesuit; worked in Paraguay Indian mission settlements (reductions); martyred; beatified, 1934; feast, Nov. 17.

Goupil, St. Rene (1607-1642): French Jesuit brother; missionary companion of St. Isaac Jogues among the Hurons; martyred, Sept. 29, 1642; canonized, 1930; one of Jesuit North American martyrs; feast, Oct. 19.

Gravier, Jacques (1651-1708): French Jesuit; missionary among Indians of Canada and midwestern US.

Jesuit North American Martyrs: Isaac Jogues, Anthony Daniel, John de Brebeuf, Gabriel Lalemant, Charles Garnier, Noel Chabanel (Jesuit priests), and Rene Goupil and John Lalande (lay missionaries) who were martyred between Sept. 29, 1642, and Dec. 9, 1649, in the missions of New France; canonized June 29, 1930; feast, Oct. 19. See separate entries.

Jogues, St. Isaac (1607-1646): French

Jesuit; missionary among Indians in Canada; martyred near present site of Auriesville, N.Y., by Mohawks, Oct. 18, 1646; canonized, 1930; one of Jesuit North American martyrs; feast, Oct. 19.

Kino, Eusebio (1645-1711): Italian Jesuit; missionary and explorer in US; arrived Southwest, 1681; established 25 Indian missions, took part in 14 exploring expeditions in northern Mexico, Arizona and southern California; helped develop livestock raising and farming in the area. He was selected in 1965 to represent Arizona in Statuary Hall.

Lalande, St. John (d. 1646): French lay missionary, companion of Isaac Jogues; martyred by Mohawks at Auriesville, N.Y., Oct. 19, 1646; canonized, 1930; one of Jesuit North American martyrs; feast, Oct. 19.

Lalemant, St. Gabriel (1610-1649): French Jesuit; missionary among the Hurons in Canada; martyred by the Iroquois, Mar. 17, 1649; canonized, 1930; one of Jesuit North American martyrs; feast, Oct. 19.

Lamy, Jean Baptiste (1814-1888): French prelate; came to US, 1839; missionary in Ohio and Kentucky; bishop in Southwest from 1850; first bishop (later archbishop) of Santa Fe, 1850-1885. He was nominated in 1951 to represent New Mexico in Statuary Hall.

Las Casas, Bartolome (1474-1566): Spanish Dominican; missionary in Haiti, Jamaica and Venezuela; reformer of abuses against Indians and Negroes; bishop of Chalapas, Mexico, 1544-47; historian.

Manogue, Patrick (1831-1895): Missionary bishop in US, b. Ireland; migrated to US; miner in California; studied for priesthood at St. Mary's of the Lake, Chicago, and St. Sulpice, Paris; ordained, 1861; missionary among Indians of California and Nevada; coadjutor bishop, 1881-84, and bishop, 1884-86, of Grass Valley; first bishop of Sacramento, 1886-1895, when see was transferred there.

Margil, Antonio (1657-1726): Spanish Franciscan; missionary in Middle America; apostle of Guatemala; established missions in Texas.

Marie of the Incarnation, Bl. (Marie Guyard) (1599-1672): French Ursuline nun; arrived in Canada, 1639; first superior of Ursulines in Quebec; missionary to Indians; writer; beatified June 22, 1980.

Marquette, Jacques (1637-1675): French Jesuit; missionary and explorer in America; sent to New France, 1666; began missionary work among Ottawa Indians on Lake Superior, 1668; accompanied Joliet down the Mississippi to mouth of the Arkansas, 1673, and returned to Lake Michigan by way of Illinois River; made a second trip over the same route; his diary and map are of historical significance. He was selected in 1895 to represent Wisconsin in Statuary Hall.

Massias, St. John de (1585-1645); Dominican brother, a native of Spain; entered Dominican Friary at Lima, Peru, 1622; served as doorkeeper until his death; beatified, 1837; canonized 1975; feast, Sept. 18.

Mazzuchelli, Samuel C. (1806-1864): Italian Dominican; missionary in midwestern US; called Builder of the West; writer.

Membre, Zenobius (1645-1687): French Franciscan; missionary among Indians of Illinois; accompanied LaSalle expedition down the Mississippi (1681-1682) and Louisiana colonizing expedition (1684) which landed in Texas; murdered by Indians.

Nerinckx, Charles (1761-1824): Belgian priest; missionary in Kentucky; founded Sisters of Loretto at the Foot of the Cross.

Nobrega, Manoel (1517-1570): Portuguese Jesuit; leader of first Jesuit missionaries to Brazil, 1549.

Padilla, Juan de (d. 1542): Spanish Franciscan; missionary among Indians of Mexico and southwestern US; killed by Indians in Kansas; protomartyr of the U.S.

Palou, Francisco (c. 1722-1789): Spanish Franciscan; accompanied Junipero Serra to Mexico, 1749; founded Mission Dolores in San Francisco; wrote history of the Franciscans in California.

Pariseau, Mother Mary Joseph (1833-1902): Canadian Sister of Charity of Providence; missionary in state of Washington from 1856; founded first hospitals in northwest territory; artisan and architect. Represents Washington in National Statuary Hall.

Peter of Ghent (d. 1572): Belgian Franciscan brother; missionary in Mexico for 49 years.

Porres, St. Martin de (1579-1639): Peruvian Dominican oblate; his father was a Spanish soldier and his mother a Negro freedwoman from Panama; called wonder worker of Peru; beatified, 1837; canonized, 1962; feast, Nov. 3.

Quiroga, Vasco de (1470-1565): Spanish missionary in Mexico; founded hospitals; bishop of Michoacan, 1537.

Ravalli, Antonio (1811-1884): Italian Jesuit; missionary in far-western United States, mostly Montana, for 40 years.

Raymbaut, Charles (1602-1643): French Jesuit; missionary among Indians of Canada and northern US.

Richard, Gabriel (1767-1832): French Sulpician; missionary in Illinois and Michigan; a founder of University of Michigan; elected delegate to Congress from Michigan, 1823; first priest to hold seat in the House of Representatives.

Rodriguez, Bl. Alonso (1598-1628): Spanish Jesuit; missionary in Paraguay; martyred; beatified, 1934; feast, Nov. 17.

Rosati, Joseph (1789-1843): Italian Vincentian; missionary bishop in US (vicar apostolic of Mississippi and Alabama, 1822; coadjutor of Louisiana and the Two Floridas, 1823-26;

administrator of New Orleans, 1826-29; first bishop of St. Louis, 1826-1843).

Sahagun, Bernardino de (c. 1500-1590): Spanish Franciscan; missionary in Mexico for over 60 years; expert on Aztec archaeology.

Seelos, Francis X. (1819-1867): Redemptorist missionary, born Bavaria; ordained, 1844, at Baltimore; missionary in Pittsburgh and New Orleans.

Serra, Junipero (1713-1784): Spanish Franciscan, b. Majorca; missionary in America; arrived Mexico, 1749, where he did missionary work for 20 years; began work in Upper California in 1769 and established nine of the 21 Franciscan missions along the Pacific coast; baptized some 6,000 Indians and confirmed almost 5,000; a cultural pioneer of California. Represents California in Statuary Hall.

Seghers, Charles J. (1839-1886): Belgian missionary bishop in North America; Apostle of Alaska; archbishop of Oregon City (now Portland), 1880-1884; murdered by berserk companion while on missionary journey.

Solanus, St. Francis (1549-1610): Spanish Franciscan; missionary in Paraguay, Argentina and Peru; Wonder Worker of the New World; canonized, 1726.

Sorin, Edward F. (1814-1893): French priest; member of Congregation of Holy Cross; sent to US in 1841; founder and first president of the University of Notre Dame; missionary in Indiana and Michigan.

Todadilla, Anthony de (1704-1746): Spanish Capuchin; missionary to Indians of Venezuela; killed by Motilones.

Turibius de Mogrovejo, St. (1538-1606): Spanish archbishop of Lima, Peru, c. 1580-1606; canonized 1726; feast, Apr. 27.

Twelve Apostles of Mexico (early 16th century): Franciscan priests; arrived in Mexico, 1524: Fathers Martin de Valencia (leader), Francisco de Soto, Martin de la Coruna, Juan Suares, Antonio de Ciudad Rodrigo, Toribio de Benevente, Garcia de Cisneros, Luis de Fuensalida, Juan de Ribas, Francisco Ximenes; Brothers Andres de Coroboda, Juan de Palos.

Valdivia, Luis de (1561-1641): Spanish Jesuit; defender of Indians in Peru and Chile.

Vasques de Espinosa, Antonio (early 17th century): Spanish Carmelite; missionary and explorer in Mexico, Panama and western coast of South America.

Vieira, Antonio (1608-1687): Portuguese Jesuit; preacher; missionary in Peru and Chile; protector of Indians against exploitation by slave owners and traders; considered foremost prose writer of 17th-century Portugal.

White, Andrew (1579-1656): English Jesuit; missionary among Indians in Maryland.

Wimmer, Boniface (1809-1887): German Benedictine; missionary among German immigrants in the US.

Youville, Bl. Marie Marguerite d'
(1701-1771): Canadian widow; foundress of
Sisters of Charity (Grey Nuns), 1738, at
Montreal: beatified, 1959.

Zumarraga, Juan de (1468-1548): Spanish
Franciscan; missionary; first bishop of Mexico; introduced first printing press in New
World, published first book in America, a
catechism for Aztec Indians; extended missions in Mexico and Central America; vigorous opponent of exploitation of Indians; approved of devotions at Guadalupe; leading
figure in early church history in Mexico.

FRANCISCAN MISSIONS

The 21 Franciscan missions of Upper California were established during the 54-year period from 1769 to 1822. Located along the old
El Camino Real, or King's Highway, they extended from San Diego to San Francisco and
were the centers of Indian civilization, Christianity and industry in the early history of the
state.

Fray Junipero Serra was the great pioneer
of the missions of Upper California. He and
his successor as superior of the work, Fray
Fermin Lasuen, each directed the establishment of nine missions. One hundred and 46
priests of the Order of Friars Minor, most of
them Spaniards, labored in the region from
1769 to 1845; 67 of them died at their posts,
two as martyrs. The regular time of mission
service was 10 years.

The missions were secularized by the Mexican government in the 1830's but were subsequently restored to the Church by the US
government. They are now variously used as
the sites of parish churches, a university,
houses of study and museums.

The names of the missions and the order of
their establishment were as follows:

San Diego de Alcala, San Carlos Borromeo
(El Carmelo), San Antonio de Padua, San
Gabriel Arcangel, San Luis Obispo de
Tolosa, San Francisco de Asis (Dolores), San
Juan Capistrano;

Santa Clara de Asis, San Buenaventura,
Santa Barbara, La Purisima Concepcion de
Maria Santisima, Santa Cruz, Nuestra
Senora de la Soledad, San Jose de
Guadalupe;

San Juan Bautista, San Miguel Arcangel,
San Fernando Rey de Espana, San Luis Rey
de Francia, Santa Ines, San Rafael Arcangel,
San Francisco Solano de Sonoma (Sonoma).

APPALACHIA COMMITTEE

The 600-member Catholic Committee of
Appalachia consists of bishops, priests, religious and lay persons engaged in pastoral
and social justice ministry in the 13-state region. Appalachia has been defined by Congress as including all of West Virginia and
parts of Alabama, Georgia, Kentucky, Maryland, Mississippi, New York, North Carolina, Ohio, Pennsylvania, South Carolina, Tennessee and Virginia.

In 1975, "This Land Is Home to Me: A
Pastoral Letter on Powerlessness in Appalachia," was issued by the Catholic bishops
of the region. Implementation of the document — through personal presence and assistance in circumstances of need experienced
by its members and community groups — is
the primary purpose of the committee. Members are involved with community groups in
cooperative efforts on such matters of concern as flood prevention, housing, land ownership, health care, labor rights at J. P.
Stevens, Campbell Foods, United Farm
Workers and the Stearns and Jericol mines,
nuclear disarmament, and the improvement
of schools.

The committee is the Catholic Caucus of
the Commission on Religion in Appalachia,
an interfaith group with members from 17
communions and 13 ecumenical units.

Sister Honor Murphy, O.P., is executive director. Address: 31-A S. Third Ave., Pres-
tonburg, Ky. 41653.

NATIONAL SHRINE

The National Shrine of the Immaculate
Conception is dedicated to the honor of the
Blessed Virgin Mary, who was declared pa-
troness of the United States in 1846. It is the
youngest of all national shrines dedicated to
Mary in the Americas.

The shrine project was launched in 1914;
the site and foundation stone were blessed in
1920; the crypt, an underground church, was
completed in 1926; the main church and su-
perstructure were dedicated Nov. 20, 1959;
more than 56 chapels and additional interior
furnishings have been installed since the dedication. The shrine has a distinctive bell tower
housing a 56-bell carillon.

The shrine is the seventh largest religious
building in the world and the largest Catholic
church in the Western Hemisphere, with normal seating and standing accommodations
for 6,000 persons. It contains some of the
largest mosaics in the world.

As part of its mission to serve as a national
model for worship of Christ and devotion to
Mary, the shrine has developed a spectrum of
liturgical, musical and educational programs
of ministry. It also participates in the Ecumenical Society of the Blessed Virgin Mary,
organized in 1917 to encourage dialogue and
prayer among the Catholic, Orthodox and
Protestant communities.

Approximately one million persons visit
the shrine each year. Open daily, it is located
adjacent to the Catholic University of America, Fourth St. and Michigan Ave. N.E.,
Washington, D.C., 20017.

The shrine director is Msgr. John J.
Murphy.

The Catholic Church in the United States

The starting point of the mainstream of Catholic history in the United States was Baltimore at the end of the Revolutionary War, although before that time Catholic explorers had traversed much of the country and missionaries had done considerable work among the Indians in the Southeast, Northeast and Southwest.

Beginning of Organization

Father John Carroll's appointment as superior of the American missions on June 9, 1784, was the first step toward organization of the Church in this country.

At that time, according to a report he made to Rome in 1785, there were approximately 25,000 Catholics in the general population of four million. Many of them had been in the Colonies for several generations. Among them were such outstanding figures as Charles Carroll, a member of the Continental Congress and signer of the Declaration of Independence; Thomas FitzSimons of Philadelphia and Oliver Pollock, the Virginia agent, who raised funds for the militia; Commander John Barry, father of the American Navy, and numerous high-ranking army officers. For the most part, however, Catholics were an unknown minority laboring under legal and social handicaps.

Father Carroll, the brother of Charles Carroll, was named the first American bishop in 1789 and placed in charge of the Diocese of Baltimore, whose boundaries were coextensive with those of the United States. He was consecrated in England Aug. 15, 1790, and installed in his see the following Dec. 12.

Ten years later, Father Leonard Neale became his coadjutor and the first bishop ordained in the United States. Bishop Carroll became an archbishop in 1808 when Baltimore was designated a metropolitan see and the new dioceses of Boston, New York, Philadelphia and Bardstown were established. These jurisdictions were later subdivided, and by 1840 there were, in addition to Baltimore, 15 dioceses, 500 priests and 663,000 Catholics in the general population of 17 million.

Priests and First Seminaries

The number of the 24 original priests was gradually augmented with the arrival of others from France, after the Civil Constitution on the Clergy went into effect there, and other countries. Among the earliest arrivals were several Sulpicians who established the first seminary in the US, St. Mary's, Baltimore, in 1791. By 1815, 30 alumni of the school had been ordained to the priesthood. By that time, two additional seminaries were in operation: Mt. St. Mary's, established in 1809 at Emmitsburg, Md., and St. Thomas, founded two years later, at Bardstown, Ky.

These and similar institutions founded later played key roles in the development and growth of the American clergy.

Early Schools

Early educational enterprises included the establishment in 1791 of a school at Georgetown which later became the first Catholic university in the US; the opening of a secondary school for girls, conducted by Visitation Nuns, in 1792 at Georgetown; and the start of a similar school in the first decade of the 19th century at Emmitsburg, Md., by Saint Elizabeth Ann Seton and the Sisters of Charity of St. Joseph, the first religious community of American foundation.

By the 1840's, which saw the beginnings of the present public school system, more than 200 Catholic elementary schools, half of them west of the Alleghenies, were in operation. From this start, the Church subsequently built the greatest private system of education in the world.

Trusteeism

The initial lack of organization in ecclesiastical affairs, nationalistic feeling among Catholics and the independent action of some priests were factors involved in several early crises.

In Philadelphia, some German Catholics withdrew from one parish in 1789 and founded one of their own, Holy Trinity, which they maintained until 1802. Controversy over the affair reached the point of schism in 1796. Philadelphia was also the scene of the Hogan Schism, which developed in the 1820's when Father William Hogan, with the aid of lay trustees, seized control of St. Mary's Cathedral. His movement, for churches and parishes controlled by other than canonical procedures and run in extra-legal ways, was nullified by a decision of the Pennsylvania Supreme Court in 1822.

Similar troubles seriously disturbed the peace of the Church in other places, principally New York, Baltimore, Buffalo, Charleston and New Orleans.

Dangers arising from the exploitation of lay control were gradually diminished with the extension and enforcement of canonical procedures and with changes in civil law about the middle of the century.

Bigotry

Bigotry against Catholics waxed and waned during the 19th century and into the 20th. The first major campaign of this kind, which developed in the wake of the panic of 1819 and lasted for about 25 years, was mounted in 1830 when the number of Catholic immigrants began to increase to a noticeable degree. Nativist anti-Catholicism generated a great deal of violence, represented by climaxes in loss of life and property in Charlestown, Mass., in 1834, and in Philadelphia 10 years later. Later bigotry was fomented by the Know-Nothings, in the 1850's; the Ku Klux Klan, from 1866; the American Protective Association, from 1887; and the Guardians of Liberty. Perhaps the last eruption of overt anti-Catholicism occurred during the campaign of Alfred E. Smith for the presidency in 1928. Observers feel the issue was laid to rest in the political area with the election of John F. Kennedy to the presidency in 1960.

Growth and Immigration

Between 1830 and 1900, the combined factors of natural increase, immigration and conversion raised the Catholic population to 12 million. A large percentage of the growth figure represented immigrants: some 2.7 million, largely from Ireland, Germany and France, between 1830 and 1880; and another 1.25 million during the 80's when eastern and southern Europeans came in increasing numbers. By the 1860's the Catholic Church, with most of its members concentrated in urban areas, was one of the largest religious bodies in the country.

The efforts of progressive bishops to hasten the acculturation of Catholic immigrants occasioned a number of controversies, which generally centered around questions concerning national or foreign-language parishes. One of them, called Cahenslyism, arose from complaints that German Catholic immigrants were not being given adequate pastoral care.

Immigration continued after the turn of the century, but its impact was more easily cushioned through the application of lessons learned earlier in dealing with problems of nationality and language.

Councils of Baltimore

The bishops of the growing US dioceses met at Baltimore for seven provincial councils between 1829 and 1849.

In 1846, they proclaimed the Blessed Virgin Mary patroness of the United States under the title of the Immaculate Conception, eight years before the dogma was proclaimed.

After the establishment of the Archdiocese of Oregon City in 1846 and the elevation to metropolitan status of St. Louis, New Orleans, Cincinnati and New York, the first of the three plenary councils of Baltimore was held.

The first plenary assembly was convoked on May 9, 1852, with Archbishop Francis P. Kenrick of Baltimore as papal legate. The bishops drew up regulations concerning parochial life, matters of church ritual and ceremonies, the administration of church funds and the teaching of Christian doctrine.

The second plenary council, meeting from Oct. 7 to 21, 1866, under the presidency of Archbishop Martin J. Spalding, formulated a condemnation of several current doctrinal errors and established norms affecting the organization of dioceses, the education and conduct of the clergy, the management of ecclesiastical property, parochial duties and general education.

Archbishop (later Cardinal) James Gibbons called into session the third plenary council which lasted from Nov. 9 to Dec. 7, 1884. Among highly significant results of actions taken by this assembly were the preparation of the line of Baltimore catechisms which became a basic means of religious instruction in this country; legislation which fixed the pattern of Catholic education by requiring the building of elementary schools in all parishes; the establishment of the Catholic University of America in Washington, D.C., in 1889; and the determination of six holy days of obligation for observance in this country.

The enactments of the three plenary councils have had the force of particular law for the Church in the United States.

The Holy See established the Apostolic Delegation at Washington, D.C., on Jan. 24, 1893.

Slavery and Negroes

In the Civil War period, as before, Catholics reflected attitudes of the general population with respect to the issue of slavery. Some supported it, some opposed it, but none were prominent in the Abolition Movement. Gregory XVI had condemned the slave trade in 1839, but no contemporary pope or American bishop published an official document on slavery itself. The issue did not split Catholics in schism as it did Baptists, Methodists and Presbyterians.

Catholics fought on both sides in the Civil War. Five hundred members of 20 or more sisterhoods served the wounded of both sides.

One hundred thousand of the four million slaves emancipated in 1863 were Catholics; the highest concentrations were in Louisiana, about 60,000, and Maryland, 16,000. Three years later, their pastoral care was one of the subjects covered in nine decrees issued by the Second Plenary Council of Baltimore. The measures had little practical effect with respect to integration of the total Catholic community, predicated as they were on the proposition that individual bishops should handle questions regarding segregation in churches and related matters as best they could in the pattern of local customs.

Long entrenched segregation practices continued in force through the rest of the 19th century and well into the 20th. The first effective efforts to alter them were initiated by Cardinal Joseph Ritter of St. Louis in 1947, Cardinal (then Archbishop) Patrick O'Boyle of Washington in 1948, and Bishop Vincent Waters of Raleigh in 1953.

Friend of Labor

The Church became known during the 19th century as a friend and ally of labor in seeking justice for the working man. Cardinal Gibbons journeyed to Rome in 1887, for example, to defend and prevent a condemnation of the Knights of Labor by Leo XIII. The encyclical *Rerum Novarum* was hailed by many American bishops as a confirmation, if not vindication, of their own theories. Catholics have always formed a large percentage of union membership, and some have served unions in positions of leadership.

The American Heresy

Near the end of the century some controversy developed over what was characterized as Americanism or the phantom heresy. It was alleged that Americans were discounting the importance of contemplative virtues, exalting the practical virtues, and watering down the purity of Catholic doctrine for the sake of facilitating convert work.

The French translation of Father Walter Elliott's *Life of Isaac Hecker,* which fired the controversy, was one of many factors that led to the issuance of Leo XIII's *Testem Benevolentiae* in January, 1899, in an attempt to end the matter. It was the first time the orthodoxy of the Church in the US was called into question.

Schism

In the 1890's, serious friction developed between Poles and Irish in Scranton, Buffalo and Chicago, resulting in schism and the establishment of the Polish National Church. A central figure in the affair was Father Francis Hodur, who was excommunicated by Bishop William O'Hara of Scranton in 1898. Nine years later, his ordination by the Old Catholic Archbishop of Utrecht gave the new church its first bishop.

Another schism of the period led to formation of the American Carpatho-Russian Orthodox Greek Catholic Church.

Coming of Age

In 1900, there were 12 million Catholics in the total US population of 76 million, 82 dioceses in 14 provinces, and 12,000 priests and members of about 40 communities of men religious. Many sisterhoods, most of them of European origin and some of American foundation, were engaged in Catholic educational and hospital work, of which they have always been the main support.

The Church in the United States was removed from mission status with promulgation of the apostolic constitution *Sapienti Consilio* by Pope St. Pius X on June 29, 1908.

Before that time, and even into the early 20's, the Church in this country received financial assistance from mission-aid societies in France, Bavaria and Austria. Already, however, it was making increasing contributions of its own. At the present time, it is the heaviest national contributor to the world-wide Society for the Propagation of the Faith.

American foreign missionary personnel increased from 14 or less in 1906 to 7,148 by 1975 (197 diocesan priests, 3,692 religious priests and brothers, 2,850 sisters, 65 seminarians, 344 lay persons). The first missionary seminary in the US was in operation at Techny, Ill., in 1909, under the auspices of the Society of the Divine Word. Maryknoll, the first American missionary society, was established in 1911 and sent its first priests to China in 1918. Despite these contributions, the Church in the US has not matched the missionary commitment of some other nations.

Bishops' Conference

A highly important apparatus for mobilizing the Church's resources was established in 1917 under the title of the National Catholic War Council. Its name was changed to National Catholic Welfare Conference several years later, but its objectives remained the same: to serve as an advisory and coordinating agency of the American bishops for advancing works of the Church in fields of social significance and impact — education, communications, immigration, social action, legislation, youth and lay organizations.

The forward thrust of the bishops' social thinking was evidenced in a program of social reconstruction they recommended in 1919. By 1945, all but one of their twelve points had been enacted into legislation.

The NCWC was renamed the United States Catholic Conference (USCC) in November, 1966, when the hierarchy also organized itself as a territorial conference with pastoral-juridical authority under the title, National Conference of Catholic Bishops. The USCC is carrying on the functions of the former NCWC.

Pastoral Concerns

The potential for growth of the Church in this country by immigration was sharply reduced but not entirely curtailed after 1921 with the passage of restrictive federal legislation. As a result, the Catholic population became more stabilized and, to a certain extent and for many reasons, began to acquire an identity of its own.

Some increase-from-outside has taken place in the past 50 years, however; from Canada, from central and eastern European countries, and from Puerto Rico and Latin American countries since World War II. This influx, while not as great as that of the 19th century and early 20th, has enriched the Church here with a sizable body of Eastern-Rite Catholics for whom eight ecclesiastical jurisdictions were established between 1924 and 1969. It has also created a challenge for pastoral care of the Spanish-speaking.

The Church continues to grapple with serious pastoral problems in rural areas, where about 600 counties are no-priest land. The National Catholic Rural Life Conference was established in 1922 in an attempt to make the Catholic presence felt on the land, and the Glenmary Society since its foundation in 1939 has devoted itself to this single apostolate. Religious communities and diocesan priests are similarly engaged.

Other challenges lie in the cities and suburbs where 75 percent of the Catholic population lives. Conditions peculiar to each segment of the metropolitan area have developed in recent years as the flight to the suburbs has not only altered some traditional aspects of parish life but has also, in combination with many other factors, left behind a complex of special problems in the inner city.

Phenomena of Change

The Church in the US is presently in a stage of transition from a relatively stable and long established order of life and action to a new order of things. Some of the phenomena of this period are:

• differences in trends and emphasis in theology, and in interpretation and implementation of directives of the Second Vatican Council, resulting in situations of conflict;

• the changing spiritual formation, professional education, style of life and ministry of priests and religious (men and women), which are altering influential patterns of pastoral and specialized service;

• vocations to the priesthood and religious life, which are generally in decline;

• departures from the priesthood and religious life which, while small percentage-wise, are numerous enough to be a matter of serious concern;

• decline of traditional devotional practices;

• exercise of authority along the lines of collegiality and subsidiarity;

• structure and administration, marked by a trend toward greater participation in the life and work of the Church by its members on all levels, from the parish on up;

• alienation from the Church, leading some persons into the catacombs of an underground church, "anonymous Christianity" and religious indifferentism;

• education, undergoing crisis and change in Catholic schools and seeking new ways of reaching out to the young not in Catholic schools and to adults;

• social witness in ministry to the world, which is being shaped by the form of contemporary needs — e.g., race relations, poverty, the peace movement, the Third World;

• ecumenism, involving the Church in interfaith relations on a wider scale than before.

BACKGROUND DATES IN U.S. CATHOLIC CHRONOLOGY

Dates in this section refer mostly to earlier "firsts" and developments in the background of Catholic history in the United States. For other dates, see various sections of the Almanac.

Alabama

1540: Priests crossed the territory with De Soto's expedition.

1560: Five Dominicans in charge of mission at Santa Cruz des Nanipacna.

1682: La Salle claimed territory for France.

1704: Jesuits established first parish church at Fort Louis de la Mobile.

1722: Mobile, formerly under the Quebec diocese, became part of a vicariate apostolic with Florida. Capuchins, Carmelites and Jesuits working there.

1829: Mobile-Birmingham diocese established; made two separate dioceses, 1969.

1830: Spring Hill College, Mobile, established.

1834: Visitation Nuns established an academy at Summerville.

1980: Mobile made metropolitan see.

Alaska

1779: Mass celebrated for first time on shore of Port Santa Cruz on lower Bucareli Bay on May 13 by Franciscan Juan Riobo.

1868: Alaska placed under jurisdiction of Vancouver Island.

1879: Father John Althoff became first resident missionary.

1886: Archbishop Charles J. Seghers, "Apostle of Alaska," murdered by a guide; had surveyed southern and northwest Alaska in 1873 and 1877, respectively.

Sisters of St. Anne first nuns in Alaska.

1894: Alaska made prefecture apostolic.

1901: Jesuits reorganized their missions, established a church at Nome.

1905: Sisters of Providence opened hospital at Nome.

1916: Alaska made vicariate apostolic.

1917: In first ordination in territory, Rev. G. Edgar Gallant raised to priesthood.

1951: Juneau diocese established.

1962: Fairbanks diocese established.

1966: Anchorage archdiocese established.

Arizona

1539: Franciscan Marcos de Niza explored the state.

1540: Franciscans Juan de Padilla, Juan de la Cruz and Marcos de Niza accompanied Coronado expedition through the territory.

1629: Spanish Franciscans began work among Moqui Indians.

1632: Franciscan Martin de Arvide killed by Indians.

1680: Franciscans Jose de Espeleta, Augustin de Santa Maria, Jose de Figueroa and Jose de Trujillo killed in Pueblo Revolt.

1700: Jesuit Eusebio Kino established mission at San Xavier del Bac, near Tucson.

1767: Jesuits expelled; Franciscans took over 10 missions.

1828: Spanish missionaries expelled by Mexican government.

1863: Jesuits returned to San Xavier.

1869: Sisters of Loretto arrived to conduct schools at Bisbee and Douglas.

1897: Tucson diocese established.

1969: Phoenix diocese established.

Arkansas

1541: Priests accompanied De Soto expedition through the territory.

1673: Marquette visited Indians in east.

1686: Henri de Tonti established trading post, first white settlement in territory.

1702: Fr. Nicholas Foucault working among Indians.

1805: Bishop Carroll of Baltimore appointed Administrator Apostolic of Arkansas.

1838: Sisters of Loretto opened first Catholic school.

1843: Little Rock diocese established. There were about 700 Catholics in state, two churches, one priest.

1853: Sisters of Mercy founded St. Mary's Convent at Fort Smith.

California

1542: Cabrillo discovered Upper (Alta) California; name of priest accompanying expedition unknown.

1602: On Nov. 12 Carmelite Andres de la Ascencion offered first recorded Mass in California on shore of San Diego Bay.

1697: Missionary work in Lower and Upper Californias entrusted to Jesuits.

1767: Jesuits expelled from territory. Spanish Crown confiscated their property, including the Pious Fund for Missions. Upper California missions entrusted to Franciscans.

1769: Franciscan Junipero Serra began establishment of Franciscan missions in California, near present San Diego. (See Franciscan Missions of Upper California.)

1775: Franciscan Luis Jayme killed by Indians at San Diego Mission.

1779: Diocese of Sonora, Mexico, which included Upper California, established.

1781: On Sept. 4 an expedition from San Gabriel Mission founded present city of Los Angeles — Pueblo "de Nuestra Senora la Reina de Los Angeles."

Franciscans Francisco Hermenegildo Garces, Juan Antonio Barreneche, Juan Marcello Diaz and Jose Matias Moreno killed by Indians.

1812: Franciscan Andres Quintana killed at Santa Cruz Mission.

1822: Interference and aggression toward missions initiated by Mexican government.

Dedication on Dec. 8 of Old Plaza Church, "Assistant Mission of Our Lady of the Angels," oldest church in Los Angeles.

1833: Missions secularized, finally confiscated.

1840: Pope Gregory XVI established Diocese of Both Californias.

1846: Peter H. Burnett, first governor of California, received into Catholic Church.

1848: Upper California ceded to the United States.

1850: Monterey diocese erected; title changed to Monterey-Los Angeles, 1859; and to Los Angeles, 1922.

1851: University of Santa Clara chartered.

1852: Lower California detached from Monterey diocese.

1853: San Francisco archdiocese established.

1855: US returned confiscated California missions to Church.

1863: Sisters of Notre Dame de Namur opened women's College of Notre Dame at Belmont.

1868: Grass Valley diocese established; transferred to Sacramento in 1886.

1922: Monterey-Fresno diocese established; became separate dioceses, 1967.

1934: Sesquicentennial of Serra's death observed; Serra Year officially declared by Legislature and Aug. 24 observed as Serra Day.

1936: Los Angeles made archdiocese. San Diego diocese established.

1952: Law exempting non-profit, religious-sponsored elementary and secondary schools from taxation upheld in referendum, Nov. 4.

1953: Archbishop James Francis McIntyre of Los Angeles made cardinal by Pius XII.

1962: Oakland, Santa Rosa and Stockton dioceses established.

1973: Archbishop Timothy Manning of Los Angeles made cardinal by Pope Paul VI.

1976: Orange diocese established.

1978: San Bernardino diocese established.

Colorado

1858: First parish in Colorado established.

1864: Sisters of Loretto at the Foot of the Cross, first nuns in the state, established academy at Denver.

1868: Vicariate Apostolic of Colorado and Utah established.

1887: Denver diocese established.

1888: Regis College founded.

1951: Denver made archdiocese. Pueblo diocese established.

Connecticut

1651: Probably first priest to enter state was Jesuit Gabriel Druillettes; ambassador of Governor of Canada, he participated in a New England Colonial Council at New Haven.

1755: Catholic Acadians, expelled from Nova Scotia, settled in the state.

1791: Rev. John Thayer, first missionary to visit state's Catholics on regular basis, offered Mass at home of Noah Webster.

1808: Connecticut became part of Boston diocese.

1818: Religious freedom established by new constitution, although the Congregational Church remained, in practice, the state church.

1828: Father Bernard O'Cavanaugh became first resident priest in state.

1829: First Catholic church in state established at Hartford.

Catholic Press of Hartford established.

1843: Hartford diocese established.

1882: Knights of Columbus founded by Father Michael J. McGivney.

1942: Fairfield University founded.

1953: Norwich and Bridgeport dioceses established. Hartford made archdiocese.

1956: Byzantine Rite Exarchate of Stamford established; made eparchy, 1958.

Delaware

1730: Mount Cuba, New Castle County, the scene of Catholic services.

1750: Jesuit mission at Apoquiniminck administered from Maryland.

1772: First permanent parish established at Coffee Run.

1792: French Catholics from Santo Domingo settled near Wilmington.

1816: St. Peter's Church, later the cathedral of the diocese, erected at Wilmington.

1830: Daughters of Charity opened school and orphanage at Wilmington.

1868: Wilmington diocese established.

1869: Visitation Nuns established residence in Wilmington.

District of Columbia

1641: Jesuit Andrew White evangelized Anacosta Indians.

1774: Father John Carroll ministered to Catholics.

1789: Georgetown, first Catholic college in US, established.

1791: Pierre Charles L'Enfant designed the Federal City of Washington. His plans were not fully implemented until the early 1900's.

1792: James Hoban designed the White House.

1794: Father Anthony Caffrey began St. Patrick's Church, first parish church in the new Federal City.

1801: Poor Clares opened school for girls in Georgetown; first school established by nuns in US.

1802: First mayor of Washington, appointed by President Jefferson, was Judge Robert Brent.

1889: Catholic University of America founded.

1893: Apostolic Delegation established with Archbishop Francesco Satolli as the first delegate.

1919: National Catholic Welfare Conference (now the United States Catholic Conference) organized by American hierarchy to succeed National Catholic War Council.

1920: Cornerstone of National Shrine of Immaculate Conception laid.

1939: Washington made archdiocese of equal rank with Baltimore, under direction of same archbishop.

1947: Washington archdiocese received its own archbishop, was separated from Baltimore; became a metropolitan see in 1965.

1967: Archbishop Patrick A. O'Boyle of Washington made cardinal by Pope Paul VI.

1976: Archbishop William Baum of Washington made a cardinal by Pope Paul VI; transferred to Roman Curia in 1980 as prefect of Sacred Congregation for Catholic Education.

Florida

1513: Ponce de Leon discovered Florida.

1521: Missionaries accompanying Ponce de Leon and other explorers probably said first Masses within present limits of US.

1528: Franciscans landed on western shore.

1539: Twelve missionaries landed with De Soto at Tampa Bay.

1549: Dominican Luis Cancer de Barbastro and two companions slain by Indians near Tampa Bay.

1565: City of St. Augustine, oldest in US, founded by Pedro Menendez de Aviles, who was accompanied by four secular priests.

America's oldest mission, Nombre de Dios, was established.

Father Martin Francisco Lopez de Mendoza Grajales became the first parish priest of St. Augustine, where the first parish in the US was established.

1572: St. Francis Borgia, general of the Society, withdrew Jesuits from Florida.

1606: Bishop Juan de las Cabeyas de Altamirano, O.P., conducted the first episcopal visitation in the US.

1620: The chapel of Nombre de Dios was dedicated to Nuestra Senora de la Leche y Buen Parto (Our Nursing Mother of the Happy Delivery); oldest shrine to the Blessed Mother in the US.

1704: Destruction of Florida's northern missions by English and Indian troops led by Governor James Moore of South Carolina. Franciscans Juan de Parga, Dominic Criodo, Tiburcio de Osorio, Augustine Ponze de Leon, Marcos Delgado and two Indians, Anthony Enixa and Amador Cuipa Feliciano, were slain by the invaders.

1735: Bishop Francis Martinez de Tejadu Diaz de Velasco, auxiliary of Santiago, was the first bishop to take up residence in US, at St. Augustine.

1793: Florida and Louisiana were included in Diocese of New Orleans.

1857: Eastern Florida made a vicariate apostolic.

1870: St. Augustine diocese established.
1917: Convent Inspection Bill passed; repealed 1935.
1958: Miami diocese established.
1968: Miami made metropolitan see; Orlando and St. Petersburg dioceses established.
1976: Pensacola-Tallahassee diocese established.

Georgia

1540: First priests to enter were chaplains with De Soto. They celebrated first Mass within territory of 13 original colonies.
1566: Pedro Martinez, first Jesuit martyr of the New World, was slain by Indians on Cumberland Island.
1569: Jesuit mission was opened at Guale Island by Father Antonio Sedeno.
1572: Jesuits withdrawn from area.
1595: Five Franciscans assigned to Province of Guale.
1597: Five Franciscan missionaries (Fathers Pedro de Corpa, Blas de Rodriguez, Miguel de Anon, Francisco de Berascolo and Brother Antonio de Badajoz) killed in coastal missions.
1606: Bishop Altamirano, O.P., conducted visitation of the Georgia area.
1612: First Franciscan province in US erected under title of Santa Elena; it included Georgia, South Carolina and Florida.
1655: Franciscans had nine flourishing missions among Indians.
1702: Spanish missions ended as result of English conquest.
1796: Augustinian Father Le Mercier was first post-colonial missionary to Georgia.
1798: Catholics granted right of refuge.
1800: First church erected in Savannah on lot given by city council.
1810: First church erected in Augusta on lot given by State Legislature.
1850: Savannah diocese established; became Savannah-Atlanta, 1937; divided into two separate sees, 1956.
1962: Atlanta made metropolitan see.

Hawaii

1825: Pope Leo XII entrusted missionary efforts in Islands to Sacred Hearts Fathers.
1827: The first Catholic missionaries arrived — Fathers Alexis Bachelot, Abraham Armand and Patrick Short, along with three lay brothers. After three years of persecution, the priests were forcibly exiled.
1836: Father Arsenius Walsh, SS. CC., a British subject, was allowed to remain in Islands but was not permitted to proselytize or conduct missions.
1839: Hawaiian government signed treaty with France granting Catholics freedom of worship and same privileges as Protestants.
1844: Vicariate Apostolic of Sandwich Islands (Hawaii) erected.
1873: Father Damien de Veuster of the Sacred Hearts Fathers arrived in Molokai and spent the remainder of his life working among lepers.
1941: Honolulu diocese established, made a suffragan of San Francisco.

Idaho

1840: Jesuit Pierre de Smet preached to the Flathead and Pend d'Oreille Indians; probably offered first Mass in state.
1842: Jesuit Nicholas Point opened a mission among Coeur d'Alene Indians near Maries.
1863: Secular priests sent from Oregon City to administer to incoming miners.
1867: Sisters of Holy Names of Jesus and Mary opened first Catholic school at Idaho City.
1868: Idaho made a vicariate apostolic.
1870: First church in Boise established.
Church lost most of missions among Indians of Northwest Territory when Commission on Indian Affairs appointed Protestant missionaries to take over.
1893: Boise diocese established.

Illinois

1673: Jesuit Jacques Marquette, accompanying Joliet, preached to Indians.
1674: Pere Marquette set up a cabin for saying Mass in what later became City of Chicago.
1675: Pere Marquette established Mission of the Immaculate Conception among Kaskaskia Indians.
1679: La Salle brought with him Franciscans Louis Hennepin, Gabriel de la Ribourde, and Zenobius Membre.
1680: Father Ribourde was killed by Kickapoo Indians.
1689: Jesuit Claude Allouez died after 32 years of missionary activity among Indians of Midwest; he had evangelized 100,000 Indians of 20 different tribes and baptized 10,000. Jesuit Jacques Gravier succeeded Allouez as vicar general of Illinois.
1730: Father Gaston, a diocesan priest, was killed at the Cahokia Mission.
1763: British conquest of the territory resulted in banishment of Jesuits.
1778: Father Pierre Gibault championed Colonial cause in the Revolution and aided greatly in securing states of Ohio, Indiana, Illinois, Michigan and Wisconsin for Americans.
1827: The present St. Patrick's Parish at Ruma, oldest English-speaking Catholic congregation in state, was founded.
1833: Visitation Nuns established residence in Kaskaskia.
1843: Chicago diocese established.
1853: Quincy diocese established; transferred to Alton, 1857; Springfield, 1923.
1860: Quincy College founded.
1877: Peoria diocese established.
1880: Chicago made archdiocese.

1887: Belleville diocese established.
1908: Rockford diocese established.
First American Missionary Congress held in Chicago.
1924: Archbishop Mundelein of Chicago made cardinal by Pope Pius XI.
1926: The 28th International Eucharistic Congress, first held in US, convened in Chicago.
1946: Blessed Frances Xavier Cabrini, former resident of Chicago, was canonized; first US citizen raised to dignity of altar.
Archbishop Samuel A. Stritch of Chicago made cardinal by Pope Pius XII.
1948: Joliet diocese established.
1958: Cardinal Stritch appointed Pro-Prefect of the Sacred Congregation for the Propagation of the Faith — the first US-born prelate to be named to the Roman Curia.
1959: Archbishop Albert G. Meyer of Chicago made cardinal by Pope John XXIII.
1961: Eparchy of St. Nicholas of the Ukrainians established at Chicago.
1967: Archbishop John P. Cody of Chicago made cardinal by Pope Paul VI.

Indiana

1679: Recollects Louis Hennepin and Gabriel de la Ribourde entered state.
1686: Land near present Notre Dame University at South Bend given by French government to Jesuits for mission.
1732: Church of St. Francis Xavier founded at Vincennes.
1778: Father Gibault aided George Rogers Clark in campaign against British in conquest of Northwest Territory.
1793: First school in Indiana built at Vincennes by Father John Francis Rivet.
1834: Vincennes diocese, later Indianapolis, established.
1840: Sisters of Providence founded St. Mary-of-the-Woods College for women.
1842: University of Notre Dame founded by Holy Cross Fathers.
1843: Immigration of German farmers to Indiana swelled Catholic population.
1853: First Benedictine community established in state at St. Meinrad.
1857: Fort Wayne diocese established; changed to Fort Wayne-South Bend, 1960.
1944: Indianapolis made archdiocese. Lafayette and Evansville dioceses established.
1957: Gary diocese established.

Iowa

1673: A Peoria village on Mississippi was visited by Pere Marquette.
1679: Fathers Louis Hennepin and Gabriel de la Ribourde visited Indian villages.
1836: First permanent church, St. Raphael's, founded at Dubuque by Dominican Samuel Mazzuchelli.
1837: Dubuque diocese established.
1838: St. Joseph's Mission founded at Council Bluffs by Jesuit Father De Smet.

1843: Sisters of Charity of the Blessed Virgin Mary were first sisterhood in state.
Sisters of Charity opened Clarke College, Dubuque.
1844: Brothers of St. Joseph opened academy for boys at Dubuque.
1850: First Trappist Monastery in state, Our Lady of New Melleray, was begun.
1881: Davenport diocese established.
1882: St. Ambrose College, Davenport, established.
1893: Dubuque made archdiocese.
1902: Sioux City diocese established.
1911: Des Moines diocese established.

Kansas

1542: Franciscan Juan de Padilla, first martyr of the United States, was killed in central Kansas.
1858: St. Benedict's College founded.
1863: Sisters of Charity opened orphanage at Leavenworth, and St. John's Hospital in following year.
1877: Leavenworth diocese established; transferred to Kansas City in 1947.
1887: Dioceses of Concordia (transferred to Salina in 1944) and Wichita established.
1888: Oblate Sisters of Providence opened an orphanage for Negro boys at Leavenworth, first west of Mississippi.
1951: Dodge City diocese established.
1952: Kansas City made archdiocese.

Kentucky

1775: First settlers in Kentucky were Catholics.
1787: Father Charles Francis Whelan, first resident priest, ministered to settlers of Bardstown.
1793: Father Stephen T. Badin began missionary work in Kentucky.
1806: Dominican Fathers built Priory of St. Rose, later founded St. Thomas Aquinas College.
1808: Bardstown diocese established with Benedict Flaget as its first bishop; transferred to Louisville, 1840.
1811: Rev. Guy L. Chabrat became first priest ordained west of the Allegheny Mountains.
1812: Sisters of Loretto founded by Rev. Charles Nerinckx; first religious community in US without foreign affiliation.
Sisters of Charity of Nazareth founded, the second native community of women founded in the West.
1814: Nazareth College for women established.
1816: Cornerstone of St. Joseph's Cathedral, Bardstown, laid; called "The Cathedral in the Wilderness."
41817: St. Thomas Seminary founded.
1830: Hon. Benjamin J. Webb founded *Catholic Advocate* first Catholic weekly in Kentucky.

1847: Trappist monks took up residence in Gethsemani.

1849: Cornerstone of Cathedral of the Assumption laid at Louisville.

1852: Know-Nothing troubles in state.

1853: Covington diocese established.

1937: Louisville made archdiocese. Owensboro diocese established.

1956: State Court of Appeals upheld right of Catholic Sisters to teach in state's public schools even though they wore religious habits.

Louisiana

1682: La Salle's expedition, accompanied by two priests, completed discoveries of De Soto at mouth of Mississippi. LaSalle named territory Louisiana.

1699: French Catholics founded colony of Louisiana.

First recorded Mass offered Mar. 3, by Franciscan Father Anastase Douay.

1706: Father John Francis Buisson de St. Cosme was killed near Donaldsonville.

1717: Franciscan Anthony Margil established first Indian mission school of San Miguel de Linares.

1718: City of New Orleans founded by Jean Baptiste Le Moyne de Bienville.

1720: First resident priest in New Orleans was the French Recollect Prothais Boyer.

1725: Capuchin Fathers opened school for boys.

1727: Ursuline Nuns founded convent in New Orleans, oldest convent in what is now US; they conducted a school, hospital and orphan asylum.

1793: New Orleans diocese established.

1850: New Orleans made archdiocese.

1853: Natchitoches diocese established; transferred to Alexandria in 1910; became Alexandria-Shreveport in 1976.

1892: Sisters of Holy Family, a Negro congregation, established at New Orleans.

1912: Loyola University of South established.

1918: Lafayette diocese established.

1925: Xavier University established in New Orleans.

1961: Baton Rouge diocese established.

1962: Catholic schools on all levels desegregated in New Orleans archdiocese.

1977: Houma-Thibodaux diocese established.

1980: Lake Charles diocese established.

Maine

1604: First Mass in territory celebrated by Father Nicholas Aubry, accompanying De Monts' expedition which was authorized by King of France to begin colonizing region.

1605: Colony founded on St. Croix Island; two secular priests served as chaplains.

1613: Four Jesuits attempted to establish permanent French settlement near mouth of Kennebec River.

1619: French Franciscans began work among settlers and Indians; driven out by English in 1628.

1630: New England made a prefecture apostolic in charge of French Capuchins.

1633: Capuchin Fathers founded missions on Penobscot River.

1646: Jesuits established Assumption Mission on Kennebec River.

1688: Church of St. Anne, oldest in New England, built at Oldtown.

1704: English soldiers destroyed French missions.

1724: English forces again attacked French settlements, killed Jesuit Sebastian Rale.

1853: Portland diocese established.

1854: Know-Nothing uprising resulted in burning of church in Bath.

1856: Anti-Catholic feeling continued; church at Ellsworth burned.

1864: Sisters of Congregation of Notre Dame from Montreal opened academy at Portland.

1875: James A. Healy, first bishop of Negro blood consecrated in US, became second Bishop of Portland.

Maryland

1634: Maryland established by Lord Calvert. Two Jesuits among first colonists.

First Mass offered on Island of St. Clement in Lower Potomac by Jesuit Father Andrew White.

St. Mary's founded by English and Irish Catholics.

1641: St. Ignatius Parish founded by English Jesuits at Chapel Point, near Port Tobacco.

1649: Religious Toleration Act passed by Maryland Assembly. It was repealed in 1654 by Puritan-controlled government.

1651: Cecil Calvert, second Lord Baltimore, gave Jesuits 10,000 acres for use as Indian mission.

1658: Lord Baltimore restored Toleration Act.

1672: Franciscans came to Maryland under leadership of Father Massius Massey.

1688: Maryland became royal colony as a result of the Revolution in England; Anglican Church became the official religion (1692); Toleration Act repealed; Catholics disenfranchised and persecuted until 1776.

1784: Father John Carroll appointed prefect apostolic for the territory embraced by new Republic.

1789: Baltimore became first diocese established in US, with John Carroll as first bishop.

1790: Carmelite Nuns founded convent at Port Tobacco, the first in the English-speaking Colonies.

1791: First Synod of Baltimore held.

St. Mary's Seminary, first seminary in US, established.

1793: Rev. Stephen T. Badin first priest ordained by Bishop Carroll.

1800: Jesuit Leonard Neale became first bishop consecrated in present limits of US.

1806: Cornerstone of Assumption Cathedral, Baltimore, was laid.

1808: Baltimore made archdiocese.

1809: St. Joseph's College, first women's college in US, founded.

Sisters of Charity of St. Joseph founded by St. Elizabeth Ann Seton; first native American sisterhood.

1821: Assumption Cathedral, Baltimore, formally opened.

1829: Oblate Sisters of Providence, a Negro congregation, established at Baltimore.

First Provincial Council of Baltimore held; six others followed, in 1833, 1837, 1840, 1843, 1846 and 1849.

1836: Roger B. Taney appointed Chief Justice of Supreme Court by President Jackson.

1852: First of the three Plenary Councils of Baltimore convened. Subsequent councils were held in 1866 and 1884.

1855: German Catholic Central Verein founded.

1886: Archbishop Gibbons of Baltimore made cardinal by Pope Leo XIII.

1965: Archbishop Shehan of Baltimore made cardinal by Pope Paul VI.

Massachusetts

1630: New England made a prefecture apostolic in charge of French Capuchins.

1647: Massachusetts Bay Company enacted an anti-priest law.

1732: Although Catholics were not legally admitted to colony, a few Irish families were in Boston; a priest was reported working among them.

1755-56: Acadians landing in Boston were denied services of a Catholic priest.

1775: General Washington discouraged Guy Fawkes Day procession in which pope was carried in effigy, and expressed surprise that there were men in his army "so void of common sense as to insult the religious feelings of the Canadians with whom friendship and an alliance are being sought."

1780: The Massachusetts State Constitution granted religious liberty, but required a religious test to hold public office and provided for tax to support Protestant teachers of piety, religion and morality.

1788: First public Mass said in Boston on Nov. 2 by Abbe de la Poterie, first resident priest.

1803: Church of Holy Cross erected in Boston with financial aid given by Protestants headed by John Adams.

1808: Boston diocese established.

1831: Irish Catholic immigration increased.

1832: St. Vincent's Orphan Asylum, oldest charitable institution in Boston, opened by Sisters of Mercy.

1834: Ursuline Convent in Charlestown burned by a Nationalist mob.

1843: Holy Cross College founded.

1855: Catholic militia companies disbanded; nunneries' inspection bill passed.

1859: St. Mary's, first parochial school in Boston, opened.

1860: Portuguese Catholics from Azores settled in New Bedford.

1870: Springfield diocese established.

1875: Boston made archdiocese.

1904: Fall River diocese established.

1911: Archbishop O'Connell of Boston made cardinal by Pope Pius X.

1950: Worcester diocese established.

1958: Archbishop Richard J. Cushing of Boston made cardinal by Pope John XXIII.

1966: Apostolic Exarchate for Melkites in the US established, with headquarters in Boston; made an eparchy in 1976.

1973: Archbishop Humberto S. Medeiros of Boston made cardinal by Pope Paul VI.

Michigan

1641: Jesuits Isaac Jogues and Charles Raymbaut preached to Chippewas; named Sault-Sainte Marie Rapids.

1660: Jesuit Rene Menard opened first regular mission in Lake Superior region.

1668: Pere Marquette founded Sainte Marie Mission at Sault-Sainte Marie.

1671: Pere Marquette founded St. Ignace Mission at Michilimackinac.

1701: Fort Pontchartrain founded on present site of Detroit and placed in command of Antoine de la Mothe Cadillac. The Chapel of Sainte-Anne-de-Detroit founded.

1706: Franciscan Father Delhalle killed by Indians at Detroit.

1823: Father Gabriel Richard elected delegate to Congress from Michigan territory; he was the first priest chosen for the House of Representatives.

1833: Father Frederic Baraga celebrated first Mass in present Grand Rapids.

Detroit diocese established, embracing whole Northwest Territory.

1843: *Western Catholic Register* founded at Detroit.

1845: St. Vincent's Hospital, Detroit, opened by Sisters of Charity.

1848: Cathedral of Sts. Peter and Paul, Detroit, consecrated.

1853: Vicariate Apostolic of Upper Michigan established.

1857: Sault-Ste. Marie diocese established; later transferred to Marquette.

1877: University of Detroit founded.

1882: Grand Rapids diocese established.

1897: Nazareth College for women founded.

1937: Detroit made archdiocese. Lansing diocese established.

1938: Saginaw diocese established.

1946: Archbishop Edward Mooney of Detroit created cardinal by Pope Pius XII.

1949: Opening of St. John's Theological (major) Seminary at Plymouth; this was first seminary in US serving an entire ecclesiastical province (Detroit).

1966: Apostolic Exarchate for Maronites in US established, with headquarters in Detroit; made an eparchy in 1972; transferred to Brooklyn, 1977.

1969: Archbishop John Dearden of Detroit made cardinal by Pope Paul VI.

1971: Gaylord and Kalamazoo dioceses established.

Minnesota

1680: Falls of St. Anthony discovered by Franciscan Louis Hennepin.

1727: First chapel, St. Michael the Archangel, erected near town of Frontenac and placed in charge of French Jesuits.

1732: Fort Charles built; Jesuits ministered to settlers.

1736: Jesuit Jean Pierre Aulneau killed by Indians.

1839: Swiss Catholics from Canada settled near Fort Snelling; Bishop Loras of Dubuque, accompanied by Father Pellamourgues, visited the Fort and administered sacraments.

1841: Father Lucian Galtier built Church of St. Paul, thus forming nucleus of modern city of same name.

1850: St. Paul diocese established.

1851: Sisters of St. Joseph arrived in state.

1857: University of St. John founded.

1888: St. Paul made archdiocese; name changed to St. Paul-Minneapolis in 1966.

1889: Duluth, St. Cloud and Winona dioceses established.

1909: Crookston diocese established.

1958: New Ulm diocese established.

Mississippi

1540: Chaplains with De Soto expedition entered territory.

1682: Franciscans Zenobius Membre and Anastase Douay preached to Taensa and Natchez Indians. Father Membre offered first recorded Mass in the state on Mar. 29, Easter Sunday.

1698: Priests of Quebec Seminary founded missions near Natchez and Fort Adams.

1702: Father Nicholas Foucault murdered by Indians near Fort Adams.

1721: Missions practically abandoned, with only Father Juif working among Yazoos.

1725: Jesuit Mathurin de Petit carried on mission work in northern Mississippi.

1729: Indians tomahawked Jesuit Paul du Poisson near Fort Rosalie; Father Jean Souel shot by Yazoos.

1736: Jesuit Antoine Senat burned at stake by Chickasaws.

1822: Vicariate Apostolic of Mississippi and Alabama established.

1825: Mississippi made a separate vicariate apostolic.

1837: Natchez diocese established; became Natchez-Jackson in 1956; transferred to Jackson in 1977.

1848: Sisters of Charity opened orphan asylum and school in Natchez.

1977: Biloxi diocese established.

Missouri

1700: Jesuit Gabriel Marest established a mission among Kaskaskia Indians near St. Louis.

1734: French Catholic miners and traders settled Old Mines and Sainte Genevieve.

1750: Jesuits visited French settlers.

1762: Mission established at St. Charles.

1767: Carondelet mission established.

1770: First church founded at St. Louis.

1811: Jesuits established Indian mission school at Florissant.

1818: Bishop Dubourg arrrrived at St. Louis, with Vincentians Joseph Rosati and Felix de Andreis. St. Louis University, the diocesan (Kenrick) seminary and the Vincentian Seminary in Perryville trace their origins to them.

1826: St. Louis diocese established.

1828: Sisters of Charity opened first hospital west of the Mississippi, at St. Louis.

1832: *The Shepherd of the Valley,* first Catholic paper west of the Mississippi.

1845: First conference of Society of St. Vincent de Paul in US founded at St. Louis.

1847: St. Louis made archdiocese.

1865: A Test Oath Law passed by State Legislature (called Drake Convention) to crush Catholicism in Missouri. Law declared unconstitutional by Supreme Court in 1866.

1867: College of St. Teresa for women founded at Kansas City.

1868: St. Joseph diocese established.

1880: Kansas City diocese established.

1946: Archbishop John J. Glennon of St. Louis made cardinal by Pope Pius XII.

1956: Kansas City and St. Joseph dioceses combined into one see. Jefferson City and Springfield-Cape Girardeau dioceses established.

1961: Archbishop Joseph E. Ritter of St. Louis made cardinal by Pope John XXIII.

1969: Archbishop John J. Carberry of St. Louis made cardinal by Pope Paul VI.

Montana

1743: Pierre and Francois Verendrye, accompanied by Jesuit Father Coquart, may have explored territory.

1833: Indian missions handed over to care of Jesuits by Second Provincial Council of Baltimore.

1840: Jesuit Pierre De Smet began missionary work among Flathead and Pend d'Oreille Indians.

1841: St. Mary's Mission established by Father De Smet and two companions on the Bitter Root River in present Stevensville.

1845: Jesuit Antonio Ravalli placed in charge of St. Mary's Mission; Ravalli County named in his honor.

1859: Fathers Point and Hoecken established St. Peter's Mission near the Great Falls.

1869: Sisters of Charity founded a hospital, school and orphanage in Helena.

1877: Vicariate Apostolic of Montana established.

1884: Helena diocese established.

1904: Great Falls diocese established; redesignated Great Falls-Billings in 1980.

1910: Carroll College founded.

1935: Rev. Joseph M. Gilmore became first Montana priest elevated to hierarchy.

Nebraska

1541: Coronado expedition, accompanied by Franciscan Juan de Padilla, reached the Platte River.

1673: Pere Marquette visited Nebraska Indians.

1720: Franciscan Juan Miguel killed by Indians near Columbus.

1855: Father J. F. Tracy administered to Catholic settlement of St. Patrick and to Catholics in Omaha.

1856: Land was donated by Governor Alfred Cumming for a church in Omaha.

1857: Nebraska vicariate apostolic established.

1878: Creighton University established.

1881: Poor Clares, first contemplative group in state, arrived in Omaha.

Duchesne College established.

1885: Omaha diocese established.

1887: Lincoln diocese established.

1912: Kearney diocese established; name changed to Grand Island, 1917.

1917: Father Flanagan founded Boy's Town for homeless boys, an institution which gained national and international recognition in subsequent years.

1945: Omaha made archdiocese.

Nevada

1774: Franciscan missionaries passed through Nevada on way to California missions.

1860: First parish, serving Genoa, Carson City and Virginia City, established.

1862: Rev. Patrick Manogue appointed pastor of Virginia City. He established a school for boys and girls, an orphanage and hospital.

1871: Church erected at Reno.

1931: Reno diocese established; name changed to Reno-Las Vegas, 1977.

New Hampshire

1630: Territory made part of a prefecture apostolic embracing all of New England.

1784: State Constitution included a religious test which barred Catholics from public office; local support was provided for public Protestant teachers of religion.

1818: The Barber family of Claremont was visited by their son Virgil (converted to Catholicism in 1816) accompanied by Father Charles Ffrench, O.P. The visit led to the conversion of the entire Barber family.

1823: Father Virgil Barber, minister who became a Jesuit priest, built first Catholic church and school at Claremont.

1830: Church of St. Aloysius erected at Dover.

1853: New Hampshire made part of the Portland diocese.

1858: Sisters of Mercy began to teach school at St. Anne's, Manchester.

1877: Catholics obtained full civil liberty and rights.

1884: Manchester diocese established.

1893: St. Anselm's College founded; St. Anselm's Abbey canonically erected.

1937: Francis P. Murphy became first Catholic governor of New Hampshire.

New Jersey

1668: William Douglass of Bergen was refused a seat in General Assembly because he was a Catholic.

1672: Fathers Harvey and Gage visited Catholics in Woodbridge and Elizabethtown.

1701: Tolerance granted to all but "papists."

1744: Jesuit Theodore Schneider of Pennsylvania visited German Catholics of New Jersey.

1762: Fathers Ferdinand Farmer and Robert Harding working among Catholics in state.

1776: State Constitution tacitly excluded Catholics from office.

1799: Foundation of first Catholic school in state, St. John's at Trenton.

1803: First parish in northern New Jersey founded at Echo Lake.

1814: First church in Trenton erected.

1844: Catholics obtained full civil liberty and rights.

1853: Newark diocese established.

1856: Seton Hall University established.

1881: Trenton diocese established.

1937: Newark made archdiocese. Paterson and Camden dioceses established.

1947: US Supreme Court ruled on N.J. bus case, permitting children attending non-public schools to ride on buses and be given other health services provided for those in public schools.

1957: Seton Hall College of Medicine and Dentistry established: the first medical school in state; it was run by Seton Hall until 1965.

1963: Byzantine Eparchy of Passaic established.

New Mexico

1539: Territory explored by Franciscan Marcos de Niza.

1544: Franciscans Juan de la Cruz and Louis de Ubedan lay brother, killed by Indians.

1581: Franciscans Augustin Rodriguez, Juan de Santa Maria and Francisco Lopez named the region "New Mexico"; they later died at hands of Indians.

1598: Juan de Onate founded a colony at Chamita, where first chapel in state was built.

1609: Santa Fe founded, future headquarters for missions of New Mexico.

1631: Franciscan Pedro de Miranda was killed by Indians.

1632: Franciscan Francisco Letrado was killed by Indians.

1672: Franciscan Pêdro de Avila y Ayala was killed by Indians.

1675: Franciscan Alonso Gil de Avila was killed by Indians.

1680: Indians massacred 21 missionaries; missions destroyed.

1684: Franciscan Manuel Beltran was killed by Indians.

1692: Missions restored.

1696: Indians rebelled, massacred five more missionaries.

1850: Jean Baptiste Lamy appointed head of newly established Vicariate Apostolic of New Mexico.

1852: Sisters of Loretto arrived in Santa Fe.

1853: Santa Fe diocese established.

1859: Christian Brothers arrived, established first school for boys in New Mexico (later St. Michael's College).

1865: Sisters of Charity started first orphanage and hospital in Santa Fe. It was closed in 1966.

1875: Santa Fe made archdiocese.

1939: Gallup diocese established.

New York

1524: Giovanni de Verrazano was first white man to enter New York Bay.

1627: Franciscan Joseph d'Aillon discovered oil at Seneca Springs, near Cuba, N.Y.

1642: Jesuits Isaac Jogues and Rene Goupil were mutilated by Mohawks; Rene Goupil was killed by them shortly afterwards. Dutch Calvinists rescued Father Jogues.

1646: Jesuit Isaac Jogues and John Lalande were martyred by Iroquois at Ossernenon, now Auriesville.

1654: The Onondagas were visited by Jesuits from Canada.

1655: First permanent mission established near Syracuse.

1656: Church of St. Mary erected near Lake Onondaga.

Kateri Tekakwitha, "Lily of the Mohawks," was born at Ossernenon, now Auriesville (d. in Canada, 1680). She was beatified in 1980.

1658: Indian uprisings destroyed missions among Cayugas, Senecas and Oneidas.

1664: English took New Amsterdam and replaced French priests with their own missionaries.

Duke of York ordered religious freedom in Province of New York.

1667: Missions were restored under protection of Garaconthie, Onondaga chief.

1678: Franciscan Louis Hennepin, first white man to view Niagara Falls, celebrated Mass there.

1682: Thomas Dongan appointed governor by Duke of York.

1683: English Jesuits came to New York, later opened a school.

1700: Although Assembly enacted a bill calling for religious toleration of all Christians in 1683, other penal laws were now enforced against Catholics; all priests were ordered out of the province.

1709: Jesuit missions were abandoned.

1741: Because of an alleged popish plot to burn city of New York, four whites were hanged and 11 Negroes burned at stake.

1777: A rejected amendment of the State Constitution stated that Catholics ought not to hold lands or participate in civil rights unless they swore that no pope or priests may absolve them from allegiance to the state.

1785: Cornerstone was laid for St. Peter's Church, New York City, first permanent structure of Catholic worship in state.

Trusteeism began to cause trouble at New York.

1806: State Test Oath repealed.

1808: New York diocese established.

1828: New York State Legislature enacted a law upholding sanctity of seal of confession.

1834: First native New Yorker to become a secular priest, Rev. John McCloskey, was ordained.

1841: Fordham University and Manhattanville College established.

1847: Albany and Buffalo dioceses established.

1850: New York made archdiocese.

1853: Brooklyn diocese established.

1856: Present St. Bonaventure University and Christ the King Seminary founded at Allegany.

1858: Cornerstone of St. Patrick's Cathedral, New York City, was laid.

1868: Rochester diocese established.

1872: Ogdensburg diocese established.

1875: Archbishop John McCloskey of New York made first American cardinal by Pope Pius IX.

1878: Franciscan Sisters of Allegany were first native American community to send members to foreign missions.

1880: William R. Grace was first Catholic mayor of New York City.

1886: Syracuse diocese established.

1911: Archbishop John M. Farley of New York made cardinal by Pope Pius X.

Catholic Foreign Mission Society of America (Maryknoll) opened a seminary for foreign missions, the first of its kind in US. The Maryknollers were also unique as the first US-established foreign mission society.

1917: Military Ordinariate established with headquarters at New York.

1919: Alfred E. Smith became first elected Catholic governor.

1924: Archbishop Patrick Hayes of New York made cardinal by Pope Pius XI.

1930: Jesuit Martyrs of New York and Canada were canonized on June 29.

1946: Archbishop Francis J. Spellman of New York made cardinal by Pope Pius XII.

1957: Rockville Centre diocese established.

1969: Archbishop Terence Cooke of New York made cardinal by Pope Paul VI.

North Carolina

1526: The Ayllon expedition attempted to establish a settlement on Carolina coast.

1540: De Soto expedition, accompanied by chaplains, entered state.

1776: State Constitution denied office to "those who denied the truths of the Protestant religion."

1805: The few Catholics in state were served by visiting missionaries.

1821: Bishop John England celebrated Mass in the ballroom of the home of William Gaston at New Bern, marking the start of organization of the first parish, St. Paul's, in the state.

1835: William Gaston, State Supreme Court Justice, succeeded in having repealed the article denying religious freedom.

1852: First Catholic church erected in Charlotte.

1868: North Carolina vicariate apostolic established.

Catholics obtained full civil liberty and rights.

1874: Sisters of Mercy arrived, opened an academy, several schools, hospitals and an orphanage.

1878: Belmont Abbey College founded.

1910: Mary Help of Christians Abbey Nullius established at Belmont; suppressed in 1977.

1924: Raleigh diocese established.

1971: Charlotte diocese established.

North Dakota

1742: Pierre and Francois Verendrye, accompanied by Jesuit Father Coquart, explored territory.

1818: Canadian priests ministered to Catholics in area.

1839: Jesuit Father De Smet made first of five trips among Mandan and Gros Ventre Indians.

1848: Father George Belcourt, first American resident priest in territory, reestablished Pembena Mission.

1874: Grey Nuns invited to conduct a school at Fort Totten.

1889: Fargo diocese established.

1893: Benedictines founded St. Gall Monastery at Devil's Lake. (It became an abbey in 1903.)

1909: Bismarck diocese established.

1959: Archbishop Aloysius J. Muench, bishop of Fargo, made cardinal by Pope John XXIII.

Ohio

1749: Jesuits in expedition of Celeron de Bienville preached to Indians.

First religious services were held within present limits of Ohio. Jesuits Joseph de Bonnecamp and Peter Potier celebrated Mass at mouth of Little Miami River and in vicinity of Sandusky Bay, respectively.

1751: First Catholic settlement founded among Huron Indians near Sandusky by Father de la Richardie.

1790: Benedictine Pierre Didier ministered to French immigrants.

1812: Bishop Flaget of Bardstown visited and baptized Catholics of Lancaster and Somerset Counties.

1818: Dominican Father Fenwick built St. Joseph's Church and established first Dominican convent in Ohio.

1821: Cincinnati diocese established.

1831: Xavier University founded.

1843: Seven members of Congregation of Most Precious Blood arrived in Cincinnati from France.

1845: Cornerstone laid for St. Peter's Cathedral, Cincinnati; this was first cathedral west of Alleghenies.

1847: Cleveland diocese established.

1850: Cincinnati made archdiocese.

Marianists opened St. Mary's Institute, now University of Dayton.

1865: Sisters of Charity opened hospital in Cleveland, first institution of its kind in city.

1868: Columbus diocese established.

1871: Ursuline College for women opened at Cleveland.

1910: Toledo diocese established.

1935: Archbishop John T. McNicholas, O.P., founded the Institutum Divi Thomae in Cincinnati for fundamental research in natural sciences.

1943: Youngstown diocese established.

1944: Steubenville diocese established.

1969: Byzantine Rite Eparchy of Parma established.

Oklahoma

1540: De Soto expedition, accompanied by chaplains, explored territory.

1541: Coronado expedition, accompanied by Franciscan Juan de Padilla, explored state.

1630: Spanish Franciscan Juan de Salas labored among Indians.

1700: Scattered Catholic families were visited by priests from Kansas and Arkansas.

1874: First Catholic church built by Father Smyth at Atoka.

1876: Prefecture Apostolic of Indian Territory established with Benedictine Isidore Robot as its head.

1886: First Catholic day school for Choctaw and white children opened by Sisters of Mercy at Kribs.

1891: Vicariate Apostolic of Oklahoma and Indian Territory established.

1905: Oklahoma diocese established; title changed to Oklahoma City and Tulsa, 1930.

1917: Benedictine Heights College for women founded.

Carmelite Sisters of St. Theresa of the Infant Jesus founded at Oklahoma City.

1972: Oklahoma City made archdiocese. Tulsa diocese established.

Oregon

1603: Vizcaino explored northern Oregon coast.

1774: Franciscan missionaries accompanied Juan Perez on his expedition to coast, and Heceta a year later.

1811: Catholic Canadian trappers and traders with John J. Astor expedition founded first American settlement — Astoria.

1834: Indian missions in Northwest entrusted to Jesuits by Holy See.

1838: Abbe Blanchet appointed vicar general to Bishop of Quebec with jurisdiction over area which included Oregon Territory.

1839: First Mass celebrated at present site of St. Paul.

1843: Oregon vicariate apostolic established.

St. Joseph's College for boys opened.

1844: Jesuit Pierre de Smet established Mission of St. Francis Xavier near St. Paul.

Sisters of Notre Dame de Namur, first to enter Oregon, opened an academy for girls.

1846: Vicariate made an ecclesiastical province with Bishop Blanchet as first Archbishop of Oregon City (now Portland).

Walla Walla diocese established; suppressed in 1853.

1847: First priest was ordained in Oregon.

1848: First Provincial Council of Oregon.

1857: Death of Dr. John McLoughlin, "Father of Oregon."

1865: Rev. H. H. Spalding, a Protestant missionary, published the Whitman Myth to hinder work of Catholic missionaries.

1874: Catholic Indian Mission Bureau established.

1875: St. Vincent's Hospital, first in state, opened at Portland.

1903: Baker diocese established.

1922: Anti-private school bill sponsored by Scottish Rite Masons was passed by popular vote, 115,506 to 103,685.

1925: US Supreme Court declared Oregon anti-private school bill unconstitutional.

1953: First Trappist monastery on West Coast established in Willamette Valley north of Lafayette.

Pennsylvania

1673: Priests from Maryland ministered to Catholics in the Colony.

1682: Religious toleration was extended to members of all faiths.

1720: Jesuit Joseph Greaton became first resident missionary of Philadelphia.

1734: St. Joseph's Church, first Catholic church in Philadelphia, was opened.

1741: Jesuit Fathers Schneider and Wappeler ministered to German immigrants.

Conewego Chapel, a combination chapel and dwelling, was built by Father William Wappeler, S.J., a priest sent to minister to the German Catholic immigrants who settled in the area in the 1730's.

1782: St. Mary's Parochial School opened at Philadelphia.

1788: Holy Trinity Church, Philadelphia, was incorporated; first exclusively national church organized in US.

1797: Augustinian Matthew Carr founded St. Augustine parish, Philadelphia.

1799: Prince Demetrius Gallitzin (Father Augustine Smith) built church in western Pennsylvania, at Loretto.

1808: Philadelphia diocese established.

1814: St. Joseph's Orphanage was opened at Philadelphia; first Catholic institution for children in US.

1842: University of Villanova founded by Augustinians.

1843: Pittsburgh diocese established.

1844: Thirteen persons killed, two churches and a school burned in Know-Nothing riots at Philadelphia.

1846: First Benedictine Abbey in New World founded near Latrobe by Father Boniface Wimmer.

1852: Redemptorist John Nepomucene Neumann became fourth bishop of Philadelphia. He was beatified in 1963 and canonized in 1977.

1853: Erie diocese established.

1868: Scranton and Harrisburg dioceses established.

1871: Chestnut Hill College, first for women in state, founded.

1875: Philadelphia made archdiocese.

1901: Altoona-Johnstown diocese established.

1913: Byzantine Rite Apostolic Exarchate of Philadelphia established; became metropolitan see, 1958.

1921: Archbishop Dennis Dougherty made cardinal by Pope Benedict XV.

1924: Byzantine Rite Apostolic Exarchate of Pittsburgh established; made an eparchy in 1963; raised to metropolitan status and transferred to Munhall, 1969; transferred back to Pittsburgh in 1977.

1951: Greensburg diocese established.

1958: Archbishop John O'Hara, C.S.C., of Philadelphia made cardinal by Pope John.

1961: Allentown diocese established.

1967: Archbishop John J. Krol of Philadelphia made cardinal by Pope Paul VI.

1969: Bishop John J. Wright of Pittsburgh made cardinal by Pope Paul VI and transferred to Curia post.

1976: The 41st International Eucharistic Congress, the second held in the U.S. convened in Philadelphia, August 1-8.

Rhode Island

1663: Colonial Charter granted freedom of conscience.

1719: Laws denied Catholics the right to hold public office.

1829: St. Mary's Church, Pawtucket, was first Catholic church in state.

1837: Parochial schools inaugurated in state.

First Catholic church in Providence was built.

1851: Sisters of Mercy began work in Rhode Island.

1872: Providence diocese established.

1900: Trappists took up residence in state.

1917: Providence College founded.

South Carolina

1569: Jesuit Juan Rogel was the first resident priest in the territory.

1573: First Franciscans arrived in southeastern section.

1606: Bishop Altamirano conducted visitation of area.

1655: Franciscans had two missions among Indians; later destroyed by English.

1697: Religious liberty granted to all except "papists."

1790: Catholics given right to vote.

1820: Charleston diocese established.

1822: Bishop England founded *U.S. Catholic Miscellany,* first Catholic paper of a strictly religious nature in US.

1830: Sisters of Our Lady of Mercy, first in state, took up residence at Charleston.

1847: Cornerstone of Cathedral of St. John the Baptist, Charleston, was laid.

1861: Cathedral and many institutions destroyed in Charleston fire.

South Dakota

1842: Father Augustine Ravoux began ministrations to French and Indians at Fort Pierre, Vermilion and Prairie du Chien; printed devotional book in Sioux language the following year.

1867: Parish organized among the French at Jefferson.

1878: Benedictines opened school for Sioux children at Fort Yates.

1889: Sioux Falls diocese established.

1902: Lead diocese established; transferred to Rapid City, 1930.

1950: Mount Marty College for women founded.

1952: Blue Cloud Abbey, first Benedictine foundation in state, was dedicated.

Tennessee

1541: Cross planted on shore of Mississippi by De Soto; accompanying the expedition were Fathers John de Gallegos and Louis De Soto.

1682: Franciscan Fathers Membre and Douay accompanied La Salle to present site of Memphis; may have offered the first Masses in the territory.

1800: Catholics were served by priests from Bardstown, Ky.

1822: Non-Catholics assisted in building church in Nashville.

1837: Nashville diocese established.

1843: Sisters of Charity opened a school for girls in Nashville.

1921: Sisters of St. Dominic opened Siena College for women at Memphis.

1940: Christian Brothers College founded at Memphis.

1970: Memphis diocese established.

Texas

1541: Missionaries with De Soto and Coronado entered territory.

1553: Dominicans Diego de la Cruz, Hernando Mendez, Juan Ferrer, Brother Juan de Mina killed by Indians.

1675: Bosque-Larios missionary expedition entered region; Father Juan Larios offered first recorded Mass.

1689: Four Franciscans founded first mission, San Francisco de los Tejas.

1703: Mission San Francisco de Solano founded on Rio Grande.

1717: Franciscan Antonio Margil founded six missions in northeast.

1721: Franciscan Brother Jose Pita killed by Indians at Carnezeria.

1728: Site of San Antonio settled.

1738: Construction of San Fernando Cathedral at San Antonio.

1744: Mission of San Francisco de Solano rebuilt as the Alamo.

1750: Franciscan Francisco Xavier was killed by Indians; so were Jose Ganzabal in 1752, and Alonzo Ferrares and Jose San Esteban in 1758.

1793: Mexico secularized missions.

1825: Government of Texas secularized all Indian missions.

1830: Irish priests ministered to settlements of Refugio and San Patricio.

1841: Vicariate of Texas established.

1847: Ursuline Sisters established their first academy in territory at Galveston.

Galveston diocese established.

1852: Oblate Fathers and Franciscans arrived in Galveston to care for new influx of German Catholics.

St. Mary's College founded at San Antonio.

1854: Know-Nothing Party began to stir up hatred against Catholics.

1858: Texas Legislature passed law entitling all schools granting free scholarships and meeting state requirements to share in school fund.

1874: San Antonio diocese established.

1881: St. Edward's College founded: became first chartered college in state in 1889.

Sisters of Charity founded Incarnate Word College at San Antonio.

1890: Dallas diocese established; changed to Dallas-Ft. Worth, 1953; made two separate dioceses, 1969.

1912: Corpus Christi diocese established.

1914: El Paso diocese established.

1926: San Antonio made archdiocese. Amarillo diocese established.

1947: Austin diocese established.

1961: San Angelo diocese established.

1965: Brownsville diocese established.

1966: Beaumont diocese established.

Utah

1776: Franciscans Silvestre de Escalante and Atanasio Dominguez reached Utah (Salt) Lake; first white men known to enter the territory.

1858: Jesuit Father De Smet accompanied General Harney as chaplain on expedition sent to settle troubles between Mormons and US Government.

1866: On June 29 Father Edward Kelly offered first Mass in Salt Lake City in Mormon Assembly Hall.

1886: Utah vicariate apostolic established.

1891: Salt Lake City diocese established.

1926: College of St. Mary-of-the-Wasatch for women was founded.

Vermont

1609: Champlain expedition passed through territory.

1666: Captain La Motte built fort and shrine of St. Anne on Isle La Motte; Sulpician Father Dollier de Casson celebrated first Mass.

1668: Bishop Laval of Quebec (beatified in 1980), administered confirmation in region; this was the first area in northeastern US to receive an episcopal visit.

1710: Jesuits ministered to Indians near Lake Champlain.

1793: Discriminatory measures against Catholics were repealed.

1830: Father Jeremiah O'Callaghan became first resident priest in state.

1853: Burlington diocese established.

1854: Sisters of Charity arrived to conduct St. Joseph's Orphanage at Burlington.

1904: St. Michael's College founded.

1951: First Carthusian foundation in America established at Whitingham.

Virginia

1526: Dominican Antonio de Montesinos offered first Mass on Virginia soil.

1561: Dominicans visited the coast.

1571: Father John Baptist de Segura and seven Jesuit companions killed by Indians.

1642: Priests outlawed and Catholics denied right to vote.

1689: Capuchin Christopher Plunket was captured and exiled to a coastal island where he died in 1697.

1776: Religious freedom granted.

1791: Father Jean Dubois arrived at Richmond with letters from Lafayette. The House of Delegates was placed at his disposal for celebration of Mass.

1796: A church was built at Alexandria.

1820: Richmond diocese established.

1822: Trusteeism created serious problems in diocese; Bishop Kelly resigned the see.

1848: Sisters of Charity opened an orphan asylum at Norfolk.

1866: School Sisters of Notre Dame and Sisters of Charity opened academies for girls at Richmond.

1974: Arlington diocese established.

Washington

1775: Spaniards explored the region.

1838: Fathers Blanchet and Demers, "Apostles of the Northwest," were sent to territory by archbishop of Quebec.

1840: Log church for Indians was built on Whidby Island, Puget Sound.

1843: Vicariate Apostolic of Oregon, including Washington, was established.

1844: Mission of St. Paul founded at Colville.

Six Sisters of Notre Dame de Namur began work in area.

1850: Nesqually diocese established; transferred to Seattle, 1907.

1856: Providence Academy, the first permanent Catholic school in the Northwest, was built at Fort Vancouver by Mother Joseph Pariseau of the Sisters of Charity of Providence.

1887: Gonzaga University founded.

1913: Spokane diocese established.

1951: Seattle made archdiocese. Yakima diocese established.

West Virginia

1749: Father Joseph de Bonnecamps, accompanying the Bienville expedition, may have offered first Mass in the territory.

1821: First Catholic church in Wheeling.

1838: Sisters of Charity founded school at Martinsburg.

1848: Visitation Nuns established academy for girls at Mt. de Chantal.

1850: Wheeling diocese established;

name changed to Wheeling-Charleston, 1974.
Wheeling Hospital incorporated, the oldest Catholic charitable institution in territory.
1955: Wheeling College established.

Wisconsin

1661: Jesuit Rene Menard, first known missionary in the territory, was killed or lost in the Black River district.
1665: Jesuit Claude Allouez founded Mission of the Holy Ghost at La Pointe Chegoimegon, now Bayfield; was the first permanent mission in region.
1673: Father Marquette and Louis Joliet traveled from Green Bay down the Wisconsin and Mississippi rivers.
1762: Suppression of Jesuits in French Colonies closed many missions for 30 years.
1843: Milwaukee diocese established.
1853: St. John's Cathedral, Milwaukee, was built.
1864: Marquette University established.
1868: Green Bay and La Crosse dioceses established.
1875: Milwaukee made archdiocese.
1905: Superior diocese established.
1946: Madison diocese established.

Wyoming

1840: Jesuit Pierre de Smet offered first Mass near Green River.
1851: Father De Smet held peace conference with Indians near Fort Laramie.
1867: Father William Kelly, first resident priest, arrived in Cheyenne and built first church a year later.
1873: Father Eugene Cusson became first resident pastor in Laramie.
1875: Sisters of Charity of Leavenworth opened school and orphanage at Laramie.
1884: Jesuits took over pastoral care of Shoshone and Arapaho Indians.
1887: Cheyenne diocese established.
1949: Weston Memorial Hospital opened near Newcastle.

Puerto Rico

1493: Island discovered by Columbus on his second voyage; he named it San Juan de Borinquen (the Indian name for Puerto Rico).
1509: Juan Ponce de Leon, searching for gold, colonized the island and became its first governor; present population descended mainly from early Spanish settlers.
1511: Diocese of Puerto Rico established as suffragan of Seville, Spain; Bishop Alonso, sailing from Spain in 1512, became first bishop to take up residence in New World.
1645: Synod held in Puerto Rico to regulate frequency of Masses according to distances people had to walk.
1898: Puerto Rico ceded to U.S. (became self-governing Commonwealth in 1952); inhabitants granted U.S. citizenship in 1917.

1924: Diocese of Puerto Rico renamed San Juan de Puerto Rico and made immediately subject to the Holy See; Ponce diocese established.
1948: Catholic University of Puerto Rico founded at Ponce through efforts of Bishop James E. McManus, C.SS.R., 1947-63.
1960: San Juan made metropolitan see. Arecibo diocese established.
1964: Caguas diocese established.
1973: Archbishop Luis Aponte Martinez of San Juan made first native Puerto Rican cardinal by Pope Paul VI.
1976: Mayaguez diocese established.
Virgin of Providence officially approved as Patroness of Puerto Rico by Pope Paul VI.

Catholics in Presidents' Cabinets

Roger B. Taney, Attorney General 1831-33, Secretary of Treasury 1833-34; app. by Andrew Jackson.
James Campbell, Postmaster General 1853-57; app. by Franklin Pierce.
John B. Floyd, Secretary of War 1857-61; app. by James Buchanan.
Joseph McKenna, Attorney General 1897-98; app. by William McKinley.
Robert J. Wynne, Postmaster General 1904-05; app. by Theodore Roosevelt.
Charles Bonaparte, Secretary of Navy 1905-06, Attorney General 1906-09; app. by Theodore Roosevelt.
James A. Farley, Postmaster General 1933-40; app. by Franklin D. Roosevelt.
Frank Murphy, Attorney General 1939-40; app. by Franklin D. Roosevelt.
Frank C. Walker, Postmaster General 1940-45; app. by Franklin D. Roosevelt.
Robert E. Hannegan, Postmaster General 1945-47; app. by Harry S. Truman.
J. Howard McGrath, Attorney General 1949-52; app. by Harry S. Truman.
Maurice J. Tobin, Secretary of Labor; 1949-53; app. by Harry S. Truman.
James P. McGranery, Attorney General 1952-53; app. by Harry S. Truman.
Martin P. Durkin, Secretary of Labor 1953; app. by Dwight D. Eisenhower.
James P. Mitchell, Secretary of Labor 1953-61; app. by Dwight D. Eisenhower.
Robert F. Kennedy, Attorney General 1961-65; app. by John F. Kennedy, reapp. by Lyndon B. Johnson.
Anthony Celebrezze, Secretary of Health, Education and Welfare 1962-65; app. by John F. Kennedy, reapp. by Lyndon B. Johnson.
John S. Gronouski, Postmaster General 1963-65; app. by John F. Kennedy, reapp. by Lyndon B. Johnson.
John T. Connor, Secretary of Commerce 1965-67; app. by Lyndon B. Johnson.
Lawrence O'Brien, Postmaster General 1965-68; app. by Lyndon B. Johnson.
Walter J. Hickel, Secretary of Interior 1969-71; app. by Richard M. Nixon.

John A. Volpe, Secretary of Transportation 1969-72; app. by Richard M. Nixon.

Maurice H. Stans, Secretary of Commerce, 1969-72; app. by Richard M. Nixon.

Peter J. Brennan, Secretary of Labor, 1973-75; app. by Richard M. Nixon, reapp. by Gerald R. Ford.

William E. Simon, Secretary of Treasury, 1974-76; app. by Richard M. Nixon, reapp. by Gerald R. Ford.

Joseph A. Califano, Jr., Secretary of Health, Education and Welfare, 1977-79; app. by Jimmy Carter.

Benjamin Civiletti, Attorney General, 1979-; app. by Jimmy Carter.

Moon Landrieu, Secretary of Housing and Urban Development, 1979- ; app. by Jimmy Carter.

Edmund S. Muskie, Secretary of State, 1980- ; app. by Jimmy Carter.

Men who became Catholics after leaving Cabinet posts: Thomas Ewing, Secretary of Treasury under William A. Harrison; and Secretary of Interior under Zachary Taylor; Luke E. Wright, Secretary of War under Theodore Roosevelt; Albert B. Fall, Secretary of Interior under Warren G. Harding.

Catholic Justices
of the Supreme Court

Roger B. Taney, Chief Justice 1836-64; app. by Andrew Jackson.

Edward D. White, Associate Justice 1894-1910, app. by Grover Cleveland; Chief Justice 1910-21, app. by William H. Taft.

Joseph McKenna, Associate Justice 1898-1925; app. by William McKinley.

Pierce Butler, Associate Justice 1923-39; app. by Warren G. Harding.

Frank Murphy, Associate Justice 1940-49; app. by Franklin D. Roosevelt.

William Brennan, Associate Justice 1956-; app. by Dwight D. Eisenhower.

Sherman Minton, Associate Justice from 1949 to 1956, became a Catholic several years before his death in 1965.

Catholics Represented in
National Statuary Hall

Statues of 13 Catholics deemed worthy of national commemoration by the donating states are among 93 enshrined in National Statuary Hall and other places in the US Capitol. The Hall, formerly the chamber of the House of Representatives, was erected by Act of Congress July 2, 1864.

Donating states, names and years of placement are listed. An asterisk indicates placement of a statue in the Hall itself.

Arizona: Rev. Eusebio Kino, S. J., missionary, 1965.

California: Rev. Junipero Serra, O. F. M.* missionary, 1931.

Hawaii: Father Damien, missionary, 1969.

Illinois: Gen. James Shields, statesman, 1893.

Louisiana: Edward D. White, Justice of the US Supreme Court (1894-1921), 1955.

Maryland: Charles Carroll,* statesman, 1901.

Nevada: Patrick A. McCarran,* statesman, 1960.

New Mexico: Dennis Chavez, statesman, 1966. (Archbishop Jean B. Lamy, pioneer prelate of Santa Fe, was nominated for Hall honor in 1951.)

North Dakota: John Burke,* US treasurer, 1963.

Oregon: Dr. John McLoughlin, pioneer, 1953.

Washington: Mother Mary Joseph Pariseau, pioneer missionary and humanitarian.

West Virginia: John E. Kenna, statesman, 1901.

Wisconsin: Rev. Jacques Marquette, S.J., missionary, explorer, 1895.

CHURCH-STATE DECISIONS

(Among sources of this listing of US Supreme Court decisions was *The Supreme Court on Church and State,* Joseph Tussman, editor; Oxford University Press, New York, 1962.)

Terrett v. Taylor, 9 Cranch 43 (1815): The Court declared unconstitutional an act of the Virginia Legislature which denied property rights to Protestant Episcopal churches in the state. Religious corporations, like other corporations, have rights to their property.

Vidal v. Girard's Executors, 2 Howard 205 (1844): The Court upheld the will of Stephen Girard, which barred ministers of any religion from serving as faculty members or visitors in a school he established for orphans.

Watson v. Jones, 13 Wallace 679 (1872): The Court declared that a member of a religious organization may not appeal to secular courts against a decision made by a church tribunal within the area of its competence.

Reynolds v. United States, 98 US 145 (1879): The Court declared, in reference to the Mormon practice of polygamy, that one may not knowingly violate by external practices the law of the land on religious grounds, since such conduct would make the professed doctrines of belief superior to federal or state law. One must keep the external practice of religion within the framework of laws enacted for the common welfare. This was the first decision rendered on the Free Exercise Clause of the First Amendment.

Davis v. Beason, 133 US 333 (1890): The Court upheld the denial of the right of Mormons to vote in Idaho if they refused to sign a registration oath stating that they were not bigamists or polygamists and would not encourage or preach bigamy or polygamy.

Church of Latter-Day Saints v. United States, 136 US 1 (1890): The Court upheld an

Act of Congress which annulled the charter of the Corporation of the Church of Jesus Christ of Latter-Day Saints, and declared "forfeited to the government all its real estate except a small portion used exclusively for public worship" (Tussman, *op. cit.,* p. 33). The Court held that the Corporation used its power to violate laws prohibiting polygamy.

Church of the Holy Trinity v. United States, 143 US 226 (1892): The Court declared it is not "a misdemeanor for a church of this country to contract for the services of a Christian minister residing in another nation" (from the text of the decision).

Bradfield v. Roberts, 175 US 291 (1899): The Court denied that an appropriation of government funds for an institution (Providence Hospital, Washington, D.C.) run by Roman Catholic sisters violated the No Establishment Clause of the First Amendment.

Pierce v. Society of Sisters, 268 US 510 (1925): The Court denied that a state can require children to attend public schools only. The Court held that the liberty of the Constitution forbids standardization by such compulsion, and that the parochial schools involved had claims to protection under the Fourteenth Amendment.

Cochran v. Board of Education, 281 US 370 (1930): The Court upheld a Louisiana statute providing textbooks at public expense for children attending public or parochial schools. The Court held that the children and state were beneficiaries of the appropriations, with incidental secondary benefit going to the schools.

United States v. MacIntosh, 283 US 605 (1931): The Court denied that anyone can place allegiance to the will of God above his allegiance to the government, since such a person could make his own interpretation of God's will the decisive test as to whether he would or would not obey the nation's law. The Court stated that the nation, which has a duty to survive, can require citizens to bear arms in its defense.

Hamilton v. Regents of University of California, 293 US 245 (1934): The Court rejected a "claim to exemption from R.O.T.C. based on conscientious objection to war" (Tussman *op. cit.,* p. 64). If such an exemption were allowed, the liberties of the objector might be extended to the point of refusal to pay taxes in furtherance of a war or any other end condemned by his conscience. This would be an undue exaltation of the right of private judgment.

Cantwell v. Connecticut, 310 US 296 (1940): The Court declared that the right to religious freedom is violated by a statute requiring a person to secure a permit from a government official before soliciting money for alleged religious purposes from someone not of his or her sect. Such a practice would constitute censorship of religion.

Minersville School District v. Gobitis, 310 US 586 (1940): The Court upheld the right of a state to require the salute to the national flag from school children, even from those who refused to do so for sincere religious reasons.

Jones v. City of Opelika, 316 US 584 (1942): The court upheld licensing ordinances in three municipalities against "the claim by Jehovah's Witnesses that they interfere with the free exercise of religion" (Tussman, *op. cit.,* p. 91).

Murdock v. Commonwealth of Pennsylvania, 319 US 105 (1943): In a reversal of the decision handed down in Jones v. City of Opelika, the Court declared the licensing unconstitutional since it violated a freedom guaranteed under the First Amendment. The selling of religious literature by traveling preachers does not make evangelism the equivalent of a commercial enterprise taxable by the State.

Jones v. City of Opelika, 316 US 584 105 (1943): The Court declared that the Constitution denies a city the right to control the expression of men's minds and denies also the right of men to win others to their views through a program of taxes levied against such activity.

Douglas v. City of Jeannette, 319 US 157 (1943): The Court again upheld the proselytizing rights of Jehovah's Witnesses, ruling unconstitutional the action of any public authority in regulating or taxing such activity.

West Virginia State Board of Education v. Barnette, 319 US 624 (1943): In a reversal of the decision handed down in Minersville School District v. Gobitis, the Court declared unconstitutional a state statute requiring of all children a salute to the national flag and a pledge of allegiance which a child may consider contrary to sincere religious beliefs.

Prince v. Commonwealth of Massachusetts, 321 US 158 (1944): The Court upheld a "child-labor regulation against the claim that it prevents a child from performing her religious duty" (Tussman, *op. cit.,* p. 170). The Court asserted a general principle that the state has a wide range of power for limiting parental freedom and authority in things affecting the child's welfare.

United States v. Ballard, 322 US 78 (1944): The Court upheld the general principle that "the truth of religious claims is not for secular authority to determine" (Tussman, *op. cit.,* p. 181).

In Re Summers, 325 US 561 (1945): The Court upheld "the denial, to an otherwise qualified applicant, of admission to the bar on the basis of the applicant's religiously motivated 'conscientious scruples against participation in war' " (Tussman, *op. cit.,* p. 192). The petitioner was barred because he could not in good faith take the prescribed oath to support the Constitution of Illinois which required service in the state militia in times of necessity.

Girouard v. United States, 328 US 61 (1946): In a ruling related to that handed down in United States v. MacIntosh, the Court affirmed the opinion that the refusal of an alien to bear arms does not deny him citizenship.

Everson v. Board of Education, 330 US 1 (1947): The Court upheld the constitutionality of a New Jersey statute authorizing free school bus transportation for parochial as well as public school students. The Court expressed the opinion that the benefits of public welfare legislation, included under such bus transportation, do not run contrary to the concept of separation of Church and State.

McCollum v. Board of Education, 333 US 203 (1948): The Court declared unconstitutional a program for releasing children, with parental consent, from public school classes so they could receive religious instruction on public school premises from representatives of their own faiths.

Zorach v. Clauson, 343 US 306 (1952): The Court upheld the constitutionality of a New York statute permitting, on a voluntary basis, the release during school time of students from public school classes for religious instruction given off public school premises.

Kedroff v. St. Nicholas Cathedral, 344 US 94 (1952): The Court ruled against an action of New York in taking "control of St. Nicholas Cathedral away from the Moscow hierarchy" (Tussman, *op. cit.,* p. 292), on the ground that the controversy involved a matter of church government.

Fowler v. Rhode Island, 345 US 67 (1953): The Court upheld the right of a Jehovah's Witness to preach in a public park against a city ordinance which forbade such preaching. The Court held that the ordinance, as construed and applied, discriminated against the Witness and therefore amounted to preferment by the state of other religious groups.

Torcaso v. Watkins, 367 US 488 (1961): The Court declared unconstitutional a Maryland requirement that one must make a declaration of belief in the existence of God as part of the oath of office for notaries public.

McGowan v. Maryland, 81 Sp Ct 1101; Two Guys from Harrison v. McGinley, 81 Sp Ct 1135; Gallagher v. Crown Kosher Super Market, 81 Sp Ct 1128; Braunfield v. Brown, 81 Sp Ct 1144 (1961): The Court ruled that Sunday closing laws do not violate the No Establishment of Religion Clause of the First Amendment, even though the laws were religious in their inception and still have some religious overtones. The Court held that, "as presently written and administered, most of them, at least, are of a secular rather than of a religious character, and that presently they bear no relationship to establishment of religion as those words are used in the Constitution of the United States."

Engel v. Vitale, 370 US 42 (1962): The Court declared that the voluntary recitation in public schools of a prayer composed by the New York State Board of Regents is unconstitutional on the ground that it violates the No Establishment of Religion Clause.

Abington Township School District v. Schempp and **Murray v. Curlett, 83 Sp Ct 1560 (1963):** The Court ruled that Bible reading and recitation of the Lord's Prayer in public schools, with voluntary participation by students, are unconstitutional on the ground that they violate the No Establishment of Religion Clause of the First Amendment.

Sherbert v. Verner, 83 A Sp Ct 1790 (1963): The Court ruled that individuals of any religious faith may not, because of their faith or lack of it, be deprived of the benefits of public welfare legislation.

Chamberlin v. Dade County, 83 Sp Ct 1864 (1964): The Court reversed a decision of the Florida Supreme Court concerning the constitutionality of prayer and devotional Bible reading in public schools during the school day, as sanctioned by a state statute which specifically related the practices to a sound public purpose.

Board of Education v. Allen, No. 660 (1968): The Court declared constitutional the New York school book loan law which requires local school boards to purchase books with state funds and lend them to parochial and private school students.

Flast v. Cohen, No. 416 (1968): The Court held that individual taxpayers can bring suits to challenge federal expenditures on grounds that they violate the principle of separation of Church and State even though generally taxpayers cannot challenge federal expenditures in court.

Walz v. Tax Commission of New York (1970): The Court upheld the constitutionality of a New York statute exempting church-owned property from taxation.

Earle v. DiCenso, Robinson v. DiCenso, Lemon v. Kurtzman, Tilton v. Richardson (1971): In Earle v. DiCenso and Robinson v. DiCenso, the Court ruled unconstitutional a 1969 Rhode Island statute which provided salary supplements to teachers of secular subjects in parochial schools; in Lemon v. Kurtzman, the Court ruled unconstitutional a 1968 Pennsylvania statute which authorized the state to purchase services for the teaching of secular subjects in nonpublic schools. The principal argument against constitutionality in these cases was that the statutes and programs at issue entailed excessive entanglement of government with religion. In Tilton v. Richardson, the Court held that this argument did not apply to a prohibitive degree with respect to federal grants, under the Higher Education Facilities Act of 1963, for the construction of facilities for nonreligious purposes by four church-related institutions of higher learning, three of which were Catholic, in Connecticut.

Amish Decision (1972): In a case appealed on behalf of Yoder, Miller and Yutzy, the Court ruled that Amish parents were exempt from a Wisconsin statute requiring them to send their children to school until the age of 16. The Court said in its decision that secondary schooling exposed Amish children to attitudes, goals and values contrary to their beliefs, and substantially hindered "the religious development of the Amish child and his integration into the way of life of the Amish faith-community at the crucial adolescent state of development."

Committee for Public Education and Religious Liberty, et al., v. Nyquist, et al., No. 72-694 (1973): The Court ruled that provisions of a 1972 New York statute were unconstitutional on the grounds that they were violative of the No Establishment Clause of the First Amendment and had the "impermissible effect" of advancing the sectarian activities of church-affiliated schools. The programs ruled unconstitutional concerned: (1) maintenance and repair grants, for facilities and equipment, to ensure the health, welfare and safety of students in nonpublic, non-profit elementary and secondary schools serving a high concentration of students from low income families; (2) tuition reimbursement ($50 per grade school child, $100 per high school student) for parents (with income less than $5,000) of children attending nonpublic elementary or secondary schools; tax deduction from adjusted gross income for parents failing to qualify under the above reimbursement plan, for each child attending a nonpublic school.

Sloan, Treasurer of Pennsylvania, et al., v. Lemon, et al., No. 72-459 (1973): The Court ruled unconstitutional a Pennsylvania Parent Reimbursement Act for Nonpublic Education which provided funds to reimburse parents (to a maximum of $150) for a portion of tuition expenses incurred in sending their children to nonpublic schools. The Court held that there was no significant difference between this and the New York tuition reimbursement program (above), and declared that the Equal Protection Clause of the Fourteenth Amendment cannot be relied upon to sustain a program held to be violative of the No Establishment Clause.

Levitt, et al., v. Committee for Public Education and Religious Liberty, et al., No. 72-269 (1973): The Court ruled unconstitutional the Mandated Services Act of 1970 under which New York provided $28 million ($27 per pupil from first to seventh grade, $45 per pupil from seventh to 12th grade) to reimburse nonpublic schools for testing, recording and reporting services required by the state. The Court declared that the act provided "impermissible aid" to religion in contravention of the No Establishment Clause.

In related decisions handed down June 25, 1973, the Court: (1) affirmed a lower court decision against the constitutionality of an Ohio tax credit law benefiting parents with children in nonpublic schools; (2) reinstated an injunction against a parent reimbursement program in New Jersey; (3) affirmed South Carolina's right to grant construction loans to church-affiliated colleges, and dismissed an appeal contesting its right to provide loans to students attending church-affiliated colleges (**Hunt v. McNair, Durham v. McLeod**).

Wheeler v. Barrera (1974): The Court ruled that nonpublic school students in Missouri must share in federal funds for educationally deprived students on a comparable basis with public school students under Title I of the Elementary and Secondary Education Act of 1965.

Norwood v. Harrison (93 S. Ct. 2804): The Court ruled that public assistance which avoids the prohibitions of the "effect" and "entanglement" tests (and which therefore does not substantially promote the religious mission of sectarian schools) may be confined to the secular functions of such schools.

Wiest v. Mt. Lebanon School District (1974): The Court upheld a lower court ruling that invocation and benediction prayers at public high school commencement ceremonies do not violate the principle of separation of Church and state.

Meek v. Pittenger (1975): The Court ruled unconstitutional portions of a Pennsylvania law providing auxiliary services for students of nonpublic schools; at the same time, it ruled in favor of provisions of the law permitting textbook loans to students of such schools. In denying the constitutionality of auxiliary services, the Court held that they had the "primary effect of establishing religion" and involved "excessive entanglement" of Church and state officials with respect to supervision; objection was also made against providing such services only on the premises of non-public schools and only at the request of such schools.

Roemer v. Board of Public Works of Maryland, 96 S. Ct. 2337 (1976): The Court ruled that a Maryland statute which authorized state funds to any private institution meeting certain minimal criteria was constitutional. The Court said the statute met the test previously outlined in Lemon v. Kurtzman because the colleges were not pervasively sectarian and the aid was in fact intended only for secular purposes.

Serbian Eastern Orthodox Diocese v. Milivojevich, 96 S. Ct. 2372 (1976): The Court held unconstitutional the decision of the Illinois Supreme Court that the Serbian Orthodox Church had arbitrarily removed one of its bishops and that its reorganization of the diocese was beyond the power of the church. The Court declared that the First Amendment does not permit civil courts to make ecclesiastical decisions.

TWA, Inc., v. Hardison, 75-1126; International Association of Machinists and Aero Space Workers v. Hardison, 75-1385 (1977): The Court ruled that federal civil rights legislation does not require employers to make more than minimal efforts to accommodate employees who want a particular working day off as their religion's Sabbath Day, and that an employer cannot accommodate such an employee by violating seniority systems determined by a union collective bargaining agreement. The Court noted that its ruling was not a constitutional judgment but an interpretation of existing law.

Wolman v. Walter (1977): The Court ruled constitutional portions of an Ohio statute providing tax-paid textbook loans and some auxiliary services (standardized and diagnostic testing, therapeutic and remedial services, off school premises) for nonpublic school students. It decided that other portions of the law, providing state funds for nonpublic school field trips and instructional materials (audio-visual equipment, maps, tape recorders), were unconstitutional.

THE WALL OF SEPARATION

Thomas Jefferson, in a letter written to the Danbury (Conn.) Baptist Association Jan. 1, 1802, coined the metaphor, "a wall of separation between Church and State," to express a theory concerning interpretation of the religion clauses of the First Amendment: "Congress shall make no law respecting an establishment of religion or prohibiting the free exercise thereof."

The metaphor was cited for the first time in judicial proceedings in 1879, in the opinion by Chief Justice Waite in Reynolds v. United States. It did not, however, figure substantially in the decision.

Accepted as Rule

In 1947 the wall of separation gained acceptance as a constitutional rule, in the decision handed down in Everson v. Board of Education. Associate Justice Black, in describing the principles involved in the No Establishment Clause, wrote:

"Neither a state nor the Federal Government can set up a church. Neither can pass laws which aid one religion, aid all religions, or prefer one religion over another. Neither can force nor influence a person to go to or to remain away from church against his will or force him to profess a belief or disbelief in any religion. No person can be punished for entertaining or professing religious beliefs or disbeliefs, for church attendance or non-attendance. No tax in any amount, large or small, can be levied to support any religious activities or institutions, whatever they may be called, or whatever form they may adopt to teach or practice religion. Neither a state nor the Federal Government can, openly or secretly, participate in the affairs of any religious organizations or groups and vice versa. In the words of Jefferson, the clause against establishment of religion by law was intended to erect 'a wall of separation between Church and State.' "

Mr. Black's associates agreed with his statement of principles, which were framed without reference to the Freedom of Exercise Clause. They disagreed, however, with respect to application of the principles, as the split decision in the case indicated. Five members of the Court held that the benefits of public welfare legislation — in this case, free bus transportation to school for parochial as well as public school students — did not run contrary to the concept of separation of Church and State embodied in the First Amendment.

Different Opinions

Inside and outside the legal profession, opinion is divided concerning the wall of separation and the balance of the religion clauses of the First Amendment.

The view of absolute separationists, carried to the extreme, would make government the adversary of religion. The bishops of the United States, following the McCollum decision in 1948, said that the wall metaphor had become for some persons the "shibboleth of doctrinaire secularism."

Proponents of governmental neutrality toward religion are of the opinion that such neutrality should not be so interpreted as to prohibit incidental aid to religious institutions providing secular services.

In the realm of practice, federal and state legislatures have enacted measures involving incidental benefits to religious bodies. Examples of such measures are the tax exemption of church property; provision of bus rides, book loans and lunch programs to students in church-related as well as public schools; military chaplaincies; loans to church-related hospitals; the financing of studies by military veterans at church-related colleges under GI bills of rights.

CHURCH TAX EXEMPTION

The exemption of church-owned property was ruled constitutional by the US Supreme Court May 4, 1970, in the case of Walz v. The Tax Commission of New York.

Suit in the case was brought by Frederick Walz, who purchased in June, 1967, a 22-by-29-foot plot of ground in Staten Island valued at $100 and taxable at $5.24 a year. Shortly after making the purchase, Walz instituted a suit in New York State, contending that the exemption of church property from taxation authorized by state law increased his own tax rate and forced him indirectly to support churches in violation of his constitutional right to freedom of religion under the First Amendment. Three New York courts dismissed the suit, which had been instituted by mail. The Supreme Court, judging that it had probable jurisdiction, then took the case.

In a 7-1 decision affecting Church-state relations in every state in the nation, the Court upheld the New York law under challenge.

For and Against

Chief Justice Warren E. Burger, who wrote the majority opinion, said that Congress from its earliest days had viewed the religion clauses of the Constitution as authorizing statutory real estate tax exemption to religious bodies. He declared: "Nothing in this national attitude toward religious tolerance and two centuries of uninterrupted freedom from taxation has given the remotest sign of leading to an established church or religion, and on the contrary it has operated affirmatively to help guarantee the free exercise of all forms of religious beliefs."

Justice William O. Douglas wrote in dissent that the involvement of government in religion as typified in tax exemption may seem inconsequential but: "It is, I fear, a long step down the establishment path. . . . Perhaps I have been misinformed. But, as I read the Constitution and the philosophy, I gathered that independence was the price of liberty."

Burger rejected Douglas' "establishment" fears. If tax exemption is the first step toward establishment, he said, "the second step has been long in coming."

The basic issue centered on the following question: Is there a contradiction between federal constitutional provisions against the establishment of religion, or the use of public funds for religious purposes, and state statutes exempting church property from taxation?

In the Walz' decision, the Supreme Court ruled that there is no contradiction.

Legal Background

The U.S. Constitution makes no reference to tax exemption.

There was no discussion of the issue in the Constitutional Convention nor in debates on the Bill of Rights.

In the Colonial and post-Revolutionary years, some churches had established status and were state-supported. This state of affairs changed with enactment of the First Amendment, which laid down no-establishment as the federal norm. This norm was adopted by the states which, however, exempted churches from tax liabilities.

No establishment, no hindrance, was the early American view of Church-state relationships.

This view, reflected in custom law, was not generally formulated in statute law until the second half of the 19th century, although specific tax exemption was provided for churches in Maryland in 1798, in Virginia in 1800, and in North Carolina in 1806.

The first major challenge to church property exemption was initiated by the Liberal League in the 1870's. It reached the point that President Grant included the recommendation in a State of the Union address in 1875, stating that church property should bear its own proportion of taxes. The plea fell on deaf ears in Congress, but there was some support for the idea at state levels. The exemption, however, continued to survive various challenges.

About 36 state constitutions contain either mandatory or permissive provisions for exemption. Statutes provide for exemption in all other states.

There has been considerable litigation challenging this special exemption, but most of it focused on whether a particular property satisfied statutory requirements. Few cases before Walz focused on the strictly constitutional question, whether directly under the First Amendment or indirectly under the Fourteenth Amendment.

Unrelated Income

Taxation of the unrelated business income of churches is a different matter. In a joint statement on this subject issued in May, 1969, the U.S. Catholic Conference and the National Council of Churches said they favored "elimination of the specific exemption of churches from taxation on income from regularly conducted commercial business activities which are unrelated to their exempt functions."

The two groups prefaced the statement with the observation:

"Under existing law many types of organizations are granted exemption from the income tax. Certain exempt organizations, including charitable, educational and some religious organizations, labor unions, business leagues, etc., are nevertheless subjected to tax upon their incomes from any unrelated business; and rents derived from debt-financed property (under leases for periods in excess of five years) are included in unrelated business taxable income.

"The tax upon unrelated business taxable income does not apply to churches, or conventions or associations of churches.

"Such exemption makes available to churches a potential advantage over taxpaying organizations engaged in commercial business activities."

The organizational structure of the Catholic Church in the United States consists of 33 provinces with as many archdioceses (metropolitan sees), 136 suffragan sees (dioceses), two jurisdictions immediately subject to the Holy See — the Eparchy of St. Maron for the Maronites and the Melkite Eparchy of Newton — and the Military Ordinariate. Each of these jurisdictions is under the direction of an archbishop or bishop, called an ordinary, who has apostolic responsibility and authority for the pastoral service of the people in his care.

The structure includes the territorial episcopal conference known as the National Conference of Catholic Bishops. In and through this body, which is strictly ecclesiastical and has defined juridical authority, the bishops exercise their collegiate pastorate over the Church in the entire country (see Index).

Related to the NCCB is the United States Catholic Conference, a civil corporation and operational secretariat through which the bishops, in cooperation with other members of the Church, act on a wider-than-ecclesiastical scale for the good of the Church and society in the United States (see Index).

The representative of the Holy See to the Church in this country is an Apostolic Delegate.

ECCLESIASTICAL PROVINCES

(Sources: *The Official Catholic Directory,* NC News Service.)

The 33 ecclesiastical provinces bear the names of archdioceses, i.e., of metropolitan sees.

Anchorage: Archdiocese of Anchorage and suffragan sees of Fairbanks, Juneau. Geographical area: Alaska.

Atlanta: Archdiocese of Atlanta (Ga.) and suffragan sees of Savannah (Ga.), Charlotte and Raleigh (N.C.), Charleston (S.C.). Geographical area: Georgia, North Carolina, South Carolina.

Baltimore: Archdiocese of Baltimore (Md.) and suffragan sees of Wilmington (Del.), Arlington and Richmond (Va.), Wheeling-Charleston (W. Va.). Geographical area: Maryland (except five counties), Delaware, Virginia, West Virginia.

Boston: Archdiocese of Boston (Mass.) and suffragan sees of Fall River, Springfield and Worcester (Mass.), Portland (Me.), Manchester (N.H.), Burlington (Vt.). Geographical area: Massachusetts, Maine, New Hampshire, Vermont.

Chicago: Archdiocese of Chicago and suffragan sees of Belleville, Joliet, Peoria, Rockford, Springfield. Geographical area: Illinois.

Cincinnati: Archdiocese of Cincinnati and suffragan sees of Cleveland, Columbus, Steubenville, Toledo, Youngstown. Geographical area: Ohio.

Denver: Archdiocese of Denver (Colo.) and suffragan sees of Pueblo (Colo.), Cheyenne (Wyo.). Geographical area: Colorado, Wyoming.

Detroit: Archdiocese of Detroit and suffragan sees of Gaylord, Grand Rapids, Kalamazoo, Lansing, Marquette, Saginaw. Geographical area: Michigan.

Dubuque: Archdiocese of Dubuque and suffragan sees of Davenport, Des Moines, Sioux City. Geographical area: Iowa.

Hartford: Archdiocese of Hartford (Conn.) and suffragan sees of Bridgeport and Norwich (Conn.), Providence (R.I.). Geographical area: Connecticut, Rhode Island.

Indianapolis: Archdiocese of Indianapolis and suffragan sees of Evansville, Fort Wayne-South Bend, Gary, Lafayette. Geographical area: Indiana.

Kansas City (Kans.): Archdiocese of Kansas City and suffragan sees of Dodge City, Salina, Wichita. Geographical area: Kansas.

Los Angeles: Archdiocese of Los Angeles and suffragan sees of Fresno, Monterey, Orange, San Bernardino, San Diego. Geographical area: Southern and Central California.

Louisville: Archdiocese of Louisville (Ky.) and suffragan sees of Covington and Owensboro (Ky.), Memphis and Nashville (Tenn.). Geographical area: Kentucky, Tennessee.

Miami: Archdiocese of Miami and suffragan sees of Orlando, Pensacola-Tallahassee, St. Augustine, St. Petersburg. Geographical area: Florida.

Milwaukee: Archdiocese of Milwaukee and suffragan sees of Green Bay, La Crosse, Madison, Superior. Geographical area: Wisconsin.

Mobile: Archdiocese of Mobile, Ala., and suffragan sees of Birmingham (Ala.) and Biloxi and Jackson (Miss.). Geographical area: Alabama, Mississippi.

Newark: Archdiocese of Newark and suffragan sees of Camden, Paterson, Trenton. Geographical area: New Jersey.

New Orleans: Archdiocese of New Orleans and suffragan sees of Alexandria-Shreveport, Baton Rouge, Houma-Thibodaux, Lafayette and Lake Charles. Geographical area: Louisiana.

New York: Archdiocese of New York and suffragan sees of Albany, Brooklyn, Buffalo, Ogdensburg, Rochester, Rockville Centre, Syracuse. Geographical area: New York.

Oklahoma City: Archdiocese of Oklahoma City (Okla.) and suffragan sees of Tulsa (Okla.) and Little Rock (Ark.). Geographical area: Oklahoma, Arkansas.

Omaha: Archdiocese of Omaha and suffragan sees of Grand Island, Lincoln. Geographical area: Nebraska.

Philadelphia: Archdiocese of Philadelphia and suffragan sees of Allentown, Altoona-Johnstown, Erie, Greensburg, Harrisburg, Pittsburgh, Scranton. Geographical area: Pennsylvania.

Philadelphia (Byzantine Rite): Metropolitan See of Philadelphia (Byzantine Rite) and Eparchies of St. Nicholas of the Ukrainians in Chicago and Stamford, Conn. The jurisdiction extends to all Ukrainian Catholics in the U.S. from the ecclesiastical province of Galicia in the Ukraine.

Pittsburgh (Byzantine Rite): Metropolitan See of Pittsburgh, Pa. and Eparchies of Passaic (N.J.), Parma (Ohio).

Portland: Archdiocese of Portland (Ore.) and suffragan sees of Baker (Ore.), Boise (Ida.), Great Falls-Billings and Helena (Mont.). Geographical area: Oregon, Idaho, Montana.

St. Louis: Archdiocese of St. Louis and suffragan sees of Jefferson City, Kansas City-St. Joseph, Springfield-Cape Girardeau. Geographical area: Missouri.

St. Paul and Minneapolis: Archdiocese of St. Paul and Minneapolis (Minn.) and suffragan sees of Crookston, Duluth, New Ulm, St. Cloud and Winona (Minn.), Bismarck and Fargo (N.D.), Rapid City and Sioux Falls (S.D.). Geographical area: Minnesota, North Dakota, South Dakota.

San Antonio: Archdiocese of San Antonio (Tex.) and suffragan sees of Amarillo, Austin, Beaumont, Brownsville, Corpus Christi, Dallas, Fort Worth, Galveston-Houston and San Angelo (Tex.). Geographical area: Texas (except the Diocese of El Paso).

San Francisco: Archdiocese of San Francisco (Calif.) and suffragan sees of Oakland, Sacramento, Santa Rosa and Stockton (Calif.), Agaña (Guam), Honolulu (Hawaii), Reno-Las Vegas (Nev.), Salt Lake City (Utah). Geographical area: Northern California, Nevada, Utah, Hawaii, Guam, the Marianas Islands and Ryukyus Islands.

Santa Fe: Archdiocese of Santa Fe (N.M.) and suffragan sees of Gallup (N.M.), Phoenix and Tucson (Ariz.), El Paso (Tex.). Geographical area: New Mexico, Arizona, Diocese of El Paso (Tex.).

Seattle: Archdiocese of Seattle and suffragan sees of Spokane, Yakima. Geographical area: Washington.

Washington: Archdiocese of Washington, D.C., and suffragan see of St. Thomas (Virgin Islands). Geographical area: District of Columbia, five counties of Maryland, Virgin Islands.

ARCHDIOCESES, DIOCESES, ARCHBISHOPS, BISHOPS

(Sources: *The Official Catholic Directory;* NC News Service. As of Oct. 1, 1980.)

Archdioceses are indicated by an asterisk.

Albany, N.Y. (1847): Howard J. Hubbard, bishop, 1977.

Former bishops: John McCloskey, 1847-64; John J. Conroy, 1865-77; Francis McNeirny, 1877-94; Thomas M. Burke, 1894-1915; Thomas F. Cusack, 1915-18; Edmund F. Gibbons, 1919-54; William A. Scully, 1954-69; Edwin B. Broderick, 1969-76.

Alexandria-Shreveport, La. (1853): Lawrence P. Graves, bishop, 1973. William B. Friend, auxiliary.

Established at Natchitoches, transferred to Alexandria 1910; present title 1976.

Former bishops: Augustus M. Martin, 1853-75; Francis X. Leray, 1877-79, administrator, 1879-83; Anthony Durier, 1885-1904; Cornelius Van de Ven, 1904-32; D. F. Desmond, 1933-45; Charles P. Greco, 1946-73.

Allentown, Pa. (1961): Joseph M. McShea, bishop, 1961.

Altoona-Johnstown, Pa. (1901): James J. Hogan, bishop, 1966.

Established as Altoona, name changed, 1957.

Former bishops: Eugene A. Garvey, 1901-20; John J. McCort, 1920-36; Richard T. Guilfoyle, 1936-57; Howard J. Carroll, 1958-60; J. Carroll McCormick, 1960-66.

Amarillo, Tex. (1926): Leroy T. Matthiesen, bishop, 1980.

Former bishops; Rudolph A. Gerken,

1927-33; Robert E. Lucey, 1934-41; Laurence J. Fitzsimon, 1941-58; John L. Morkovsky, 1958-63; Lawrence M. De Falco, 1963-79.

Anchorage, * **Alaska** (1966): Francis T. Hurley, archbishop, 1976.

Former archbishop: Joseph T. Ryan, 1966-75.

Arlington, Va. (1974): Thomas J. Welsh, bishop, 1974.

Atlanta, * **Ga.** (1956; archdiocese, 1962): Thomas A. Donnellan, archbishop, 1968.

Former ordinaries: Francis E. Hyland, 1956-61; Paul J. Hallinan, first archbishop, 1962-68.

Austin, Tex. (1947): Vincent M. Harris, bishop, 1971.

Former bishop: Louis J. Reicher, 1947-71.

Baker, Ore. (1903): Thomas J. Connolly, bishop, 1971.

Established as Baker City, name changed, 1952.

Former bishops: Charles J. O'Reilly, 1903-18; Joseph F. McGrath, 1919-50; Francis P. Leipzig, 1950-71.

Baltimore, * **Md.** (1789; archdiocese, 1808): William D. Borders, archbishop, 1974. T. Austin Murphy, P. Francis Murphy, J. Francis Stafford, auxiliaries.

Former ordinaries: John Carroll, 1789-1815, first archbishop; Leonard Neale, 1815-17; Ambrose Marechal, S.S., 1817-28; James Whitfield, 1828-34; Samuel Eccleston, S.S., 1834-51; Francis P. Kenrick, 1851-63; Martin J. Spalding, 1864-72; James R.

Bayley, 1872-77; Cardinal James Gibbons, 1877-1921; Michael J. Curley, 1921-47; Francis P. Keough, 1947-61, Cardinal Lawrence J. Shehan, 1961-74.

Baton Rouge, La. (1961): Joseph V. Sullivan, bishop, 1974.

Former bishop: Robert E. Tracy, 1961-74.

Beaumont, Tex. (1966): Bernard J. Ganter, bishop, 1977.

Former bishops: Vincent M. Harris, 1966-71; Warren L. Boudreaux, 1971-77.

Belleville, Ill. (1887): William M. Cosgrove, bishop, 1976. Stanley G. Schlarman, auxiliary.

Former bishops: John Janssen, 1888-1913; Henry Althoff, 1914-47; Albert R. Zuroweste, 1948-76.

Biloxi, Miss. (1977): (Joseph) Lawson E. Howze, bishop, 1977.

Birmingham, Ala. (1969): Joseph G. Vath, bishop, 1969.

Bismarck, N. Dak. (1909): Hilary B. Hacker, bishop, 1957.

Former bishops: Vincent Wehrle, O.S.B., 1910-39; Vincent J. Ryan, 1940-51; Lambert A. Hoch, 1952-56.

Boise, Ida. (1893): Sylvester Treinen, bishop, 1962.

Former bishops: Alphonse J. Glorieux, 1893-1917; Daniel M. Gorman, 1918-27; Edward J. Kelly, 1928-56; James J. Byrne, 1956-62.

Boston,* Mass. (1808; archdiocese, 1875): Cardinal Humberto S. Medeiros, archbishop, 1970. Lawrence J. Riley, Thomas V. Dailey, John M. D'Arcy, John J. Mulcahy, Daniel A. Hart, auxiliaries.

Former ordinaries: John L. de Cheverus, 1810-23; Benedict J. Fenwick, S.J., 1825-46; John B. Fitzpatrick, 1846-66; John J. Williams, 1866-1907, first archbishop; Cardinal William O'Connell, 1907-44; Cardinal Richard Cushing, 1944-70.

Bridgeport, Conn. (1953): Walter W. Curtis, bishop, 1961.

Former bishop: Lawrence J. Shehan, 1953-61.

Brooklyn, N.Y. (1853): Francis J. Mugavero, bishop, 1968. Charles R. Mulrooney, Joseph P. Denning, auxiliaries.

Former bishops: John Loughlin, 1853-91; Charles E. McDonnell, 1892-1921; Thomas E. Molloy, 1921-56; Bryan J. McEntegart, 1957-68.

Brownsville, Tex. (1965): John J. Fitzpatrick, bishop, 1971.

Former bishops: Adolph Marx, 1965; Humberto S. Medeiros, 1966-70.

Buffalo, N.Y. (1847): Edward D. Head, bishop, 1973. Pius A. Benincasa, Bernard J. McLaughlin, auxiliaries.

Former bishops: John Timon, C.M., 1847-67; Stephen V. Ryan, C.M., 1868-96; James E. Quigley, 1897-1903; Charles H. Colton, 1903-15; Dennis J. Dougherty, 1915-18;

William Turner, 1919-36; John A. Duffy, 1937-44; John F. O'Hara, C.S.C., 1945-51; Joseph A. Burke, 1952-62; James McNulty, 1963-72.

Burlington, Vt. (1853): John A. Marshall, bishop, 1972.

Former bishops: Louis De Goesbriand, 1853-99; John S. Michaud, 1899-1908; Joseph J. Rice, 1910-38; Matthew F. Brady, 1938-44; Edward F. Ryan, 1945-56; Robert F. Joyce, 1957-71.

Camden, N.J. (1937): George H. Guilfoyle, bishop, 1968. James L. Schad, auxiliary.

Former bishops: Bartholomew J. Eustace, 1938-56; Justin J. McCarthy, 1957-59; Celestine J. Damiano, 1960-67.

Charleston, S.C. (1820): Ernest L. Unterkoefler, bishop, 1964.

Former bishops: John England, 1820-42; Ignatius W. Reynolds, 1844-55; Patrick N. Lynch, 1858-82; Henry P. Northrop, 1883-1916; William T. Russell, 1917-27; Emmet M. Walsh, 1927-49; John J. Russell, 1950-58; Paul J. Hallinan, 1958-62; Francis F. Reh, 1962-64.

Charlotte, N.C. (1971): Michael J. Begley, bishop, 1972.

Cheyenne, Wyo. (1887): Joseph Hart, bishop, 1978.

Former bishops: Maurice F. Burke, 1887-93; Thomas M. Lenihan, 1897-1901; James J. Keane, 1902-11; Patrick A. McGovern, 1912-51; Hubert M. Newell, 1951-78.

Chicago,* Ill. (1843; archdiocese, 1880): Cardinal John Cody, archbishop, 1965; Alfred L. Abramowicz, Nevin W. Hayes, O. Carm., auxiliaries.

Former ordinaries: William Quarter, 1844-48; James O. Van de Velde, S.J., 1849-53; Anthony O'Regan, 1854-58; James Duggan, 1859-70; Thomas P. Foley, administrator, 1870-79; Patrick A. Feehan, 1880-1902, first archbishop; James E. Quigley, 1903-15; Cardinal George Mundelein, 1915-39; Cardinal Samuel Stritch, 1939-58; Cardinal Albert Meyer, 1958-65.

Cincinnati,* Ohio (1821; archdiocese, 1850): Joseph L. Bernardin, archbishop, 1972. Nicholas Elko (titular archbishop), Daniel E. Pilarczyk, auxiliaries.

Former ordinaries: Edward D. Fenwick, O.P., 1822-32; John B. Purcell, 1833-83, first archbishop; William H. Elder, 1883-1904; Henry Moeller, 1904-1925; John T. McNicholas, O.P., 1925-50; Karl J. Alter, 1950-69; Paul F. Leibold, 1969-72.

Cleveland, Ohio (1847): Vacant as of Sept. 1, 1980. Anthony M. Pilla, auxiliary, apostolic administrator, 1980. Gilbert I. Sheldon, James P. Lyke, O.F.M., James A. Griffin, auxiliaries.

Former bishops: L. Amadeus Rappe, 1847-70; Richard Gilmour, 1872-91; Ignatius F. Horstmann, 1892-1908; John P. Farrelly, 1909-21; Joseph Schrembs, 1921-45; Edward

F. Hoban, 1945-66; Clarence G. Issenmann, 1966-74; James A. Hickey, 1974-80.

Columbus, Ohio (1868): Edward J. Herrmann, bishop, 1973. George A. Fulcher, auxiliary.

Former bishops: Sylvester H. Rosecrans, 1868-78; John A. Watterson, 1880-99; Henry Moeller, 1900-03; James J. Hartley, 1904-44; Michael J. Ready, 1944-57; Clarence Issenmann, 1957-64; John J. Carberry, 1965-68; Clarence E. Elwell, 1968-73.

Corpus Christi, Tex. (1912): Thomas J. Drury, bishop, 1965.

Former bishops; Paul J. Nussbaum, C.P., 1913-20; Emmanuel B. Ledvina, 1921-49; Mariano S. Garriga, 1949-65.

Covington, Ky. (1853): William A. Hughes, bishop, 1979.

Former bishops: George A. Carrell, S.J., 1853-68; Augustus M. Toebbe, 1870-84; Camillus P. Maes, 1885-1914; Ferdinand Brossart, 1916-23; Francis W. Howard, 1923-44; William T. Mulloy, 1945-59; Richard Ackerman, C.S.Sp., 1960-78.

Crookston, Minn. (1909): Victor Balke, bishop, 1976.

Former bishops: Timothy Corbett, 1910-38; John H. Peschges, 1938-44; Francis J. Schenk, 1945-60; Laurence A. Glenn, 1960-70; Kenneth J. Povish, 1970-75.

Dallas, Tex. (1890): Thomas Tschoepe, bishop, 1969.

Established 1890, as Dallas, title changed to Dallas-Ft. Worth 1953; redesignated Dallas, 1969, when Ft. Worth was made diocese.

Former bishops: Thomas F. Brennan, 1891-92; Edward J. Dunne, 1893-1910; Joseph P. Lynch, 1911-54; Thomas K. Gorman, 1954-69.

Davenport, Ia. (1881): Gerald F. O'Keefe, bishop, 1966.

Former bishops: John McMullen, 1881-83; Henry Cosgrove, 1884-1906; James Davis, 1906-26; Henry P. Rohlman, 1927-44; Ralph L. Hayes, 1944-66.

Denver,* Colo. (1887; archdiocese, 1941): James V. Casey, archbishop, 1967. George R. Evans, Richard C. Hanifen, auxiliaries.

Former ordinaries: Joseph P. Machebeuf, 1887-89; Nicholas C. Matz, 1889-1917; J. Henry Tihen, 1917-31; Urban J. Vehr, 1931-67, first archbishop.

Des Moines, Ia. (1911): Maurice J. Dingman, bishop, 1968.

Former bishops: Austin Dowling, 1912-19; Thomas W. Drumm, 1919-33; Gerald T. Bergan, 1934-48; Edward C. Daly, O.P., 1948-64; George J. Biskup, 1965-67.

Detroit,* Mich. (1833; archdiocese, 1937): Vacant as of Sept. 1, 1980. Thomas J. Gumbleton, Walter J. Schoenherr, Arthur H. Krawczak, auxiliaries.

Former ordinaries: Frederic Rese, 1833-71; Peter P. Lefevere, administrator, 1841-69; Caspar H. Borgess, 1871-88; John S. Foley,

1888-1918; Michael J. Gallagher, 1918-37; Cardinal Edward Mooney, 1937-58, first archbishop; Cardinal John F. Dearden, 1958-80.

Dodge City, Kans. (1951): Eugene J. Gerber, bishop, 1976.

Former bishops: John B. Franz, 1951-59; Marion F. Forst, 1960-76.

Dubuque,* Iowa (1837; archdiocese, 1893): James J. Byrne, archbishop, 1962. Francis J. Dunn, auxiliary.

Former ordinaries: Mathias Loras, 1837-58; Clement Smyth, O.C.S.O., 1858-65; John Hennessy, 1866-1900, first archbishop; John J. Keane, 1900-11; James J. Keane, 1911-29; Francis J. Beckman, 1930-46; Henry P. Rohlman, 1946-54; Leo Binz, 1954-61.

Duluth, Minn. (1889): Paul F. Anderson, bishop, 1969.

Former bishops: James McGolrick, 1889-1918; John T. McNicholas, O.P., 1918-25; Thomas A. Welch, 1926-59; Francis J. Schenk, 1960-69.

El Paso, Tex. (1914): Raymond J. Pena, bishop, 1980.

Former bishops: Anthony J. Schuler, S.J., 1915-42; Sidney M. Metzger, 1942-78. Patrick F. Flores, 1978-79.

Erie, Pa. (1853): Alfred M. Watson, bishop, 1969. Michael J. Murphy, coadjutor.

Former bishops: Michael O'Connor, 1853-54; Josue M. Young, 1854-66; Tobias Mullen, 1868-99; John E. Fitzmaurice, 1899-1920; John M. Gannon, 1920-66; John F. Whealon, 1966-69.

Evansville, Ind. (1944): Francis Raymond Shea, bishop, 1970.

Former bishops: Henry J. Grimmelsman, 1944-65; Paul F. Leibold, 1966-69.

Fairbanks, Alaska (1962): Robert L. Whelan, S.J., bishop, 1968.

Former bishop: Francis D. Gleeson, S.J., 1948-68.

Fall River, Mass. (1904): Daniel A. Cronin, bishop, 1970.

Former bishops: William Stang, 1904-07; Daniel F. Feehan, 1907-34; James E. Cassidy, 1934-51; James L. Connolly, 1951-70.

Fargo, N. Dak. (1889): Justin A. Driscoll, bishop, 1970.

Established at Jamestown, transferred, 1897.

Former bishops: John Shanley, 1889-1909; James O'Reilly, 1910-34; Aloysius J. Muench, 1935-59; Leo F. Dworschak, 1960-70.

Fort Wayne-South Bend, Ind. (1857): William E. McManus, bishop, 1976. Joseph R. Crowley, auxiliary.

Established as Fort Wayne, name changed, 1960.

Former bishops: John H. Luers, 1858-71; Joseph Dwenger, C.Pp. S., 1872-93; Joseph Rademacher, 1893-1900; Herman J. Alerding, 1900-24; John F. Noll, 1925-56; Leo A. Pursley, 1957-76.

Fort Worth, Tex. (1969): John J. Cassata, bishop, 1969 (resigned Sept. 15, 1980).

Fresno, Calif. (1967): Joseph J. Madera, M.Sp.S., bishop, 1980.

Formerly Monterey-Fresno, 1922.

Former bishops (Monterey-Fresno): John J. Cantwell, administrator, 1922-24; John B. MacGinley, first bishop, 1924-32; Philip G. Sher, 1933-53; Aloysius J. Willinger, 1953-67.

Former bishops (Fresno): Timothy Manning, 1967-69; Hugh A. Donohoe, 1969-80.

Gallup, N. Mex. (1939): Jerome J. Hastrich, bishop, 1969.

Former bishop: Bernard T. Espelage, O.F.M., 1940-69.

Galveston-Houston, Tex. (1847): John L. Morkovsky, bishop, 1975. John E. McCarthy, auxiliary.

Established as Galveston, name changed, 1959.

Former bishops: John M. Odin, C.M., 1847-61; Claude M. Dubuis, 1862-92; Nicholas A. Gallagher, 1892-1918; Christopher E. Byrne, 1918-50; Wendelin J. Nold, 1950-75.

Gary, Ind. (1957): Andrew G. Grutka, bishop, 1957.

Gaylord, Mich. (1971): Edmund C. Szoka, bishop, 1971.

Grand Island, Neb. (1912): Lawrence McNamara, bishop, 1978.

Established at Kearney, transferred, 1917.

Former bishops: James A. Duffy, 1913-31; Stanislaus V. Bona, 1932-44; Edward J. Hunkeler, 1945-51; John L. Paschang, 1951-72; John J. Sullivan, 1972-77.

Grand Rapids, Mich. (1882): Joseph M. Breitenbeck, bishop, 1969. Joseph C. McKinney, auxiliary.

Former bishops: Henry J. Richter, 1883-1916; Michael J. Gallagher, 1916-18; Edward D. Kelly, 1919-26; Joseph G. Pinten, 1926-40; Joseph C. Plagens, 1941-43; Francis J. Haas, 1943-53; Allen J. Babcock, 1954-69.

Great Falls-Billings, Mont. (1904): Thomas J. Murphy, bishop, 1978.

Established as Great Falls; name changed, 1980.

Former bishops: Mathias C. Lenihan, 1904-30; Edwin V. O'Hara, 1930-39; William J. Condon, 1939-67; Eldon B. Schuster, 1968-77.

Green Bay, Wis. (1868): Aloysius J. Wycislo, bishop, 1968. Robert F. Morneau, auxiliary.

Former bishops: Joseph Melcher, 1868-73; Francis X. Krautbauer, 1875-85; Frederick X. Katzer, 1886-91; Sebastian G. Messmer, 1892-1903; Joseph J. Fox, 1904-14; Paul P. Rhode, 1915-45; Stanislaus V. Bona, 1945-67.

Greensburg, Pa. (1951): William G. Connare, bishop, 1960. Norbert F. Gaughan, auxiliary.

Former bishop: Hugh L. Lamb, 1951-59.

Harrisburg, Pa. (1868): Joseph T. Daley, bishop, 1971. William H. Keeler, auxiliary.

Former bishops: Jeremiah F. Shanahan, 1868-86; Thomas McGovern, 1888-98; John W. Shanahan,1899-1916; Philip R. McDevitt, 1916-35; George L. Leech, 1935-71.

Hartford,* Conn. (1843; archdiocese, 1953): John F. Whealon, archbishop, 1969. John F. Hackett, Peter A. Rosazza, auxiliaries.

Former ordinaries: William Tyler, 1844-49; Bernard O'Reilly, 1850-56; F. P. MacFarland, 1858-74; Thomas Galberry, O.S.A., 1876-78; Lawrence S. McMahon, 1879-93; Michael Tierney, 1894-1908; John J. Nilan, 1910-34; Maurice F. McAuliffe, 1934-44; Henry J. O'Brien, 1945-68, first archbishop.

Helena, Mont. (1884): Elden F. Curtiss, bishop, 1976.

Former bishops: John B. Brondel, 1884-1903; John P. Carroll, 1904-25; George J. Finnigan, C.S.C., 1927-32; Ralph L. Hayes, 1933-35; Joseph M. Gilmore, 1936-62; Raymond Hunthausen, 1962-75.

Honolulu, Hawaii (1941): John J. Scanlan, bishop, 1968. Joseph A. Ferrario, auxiliary.

Former bishop: James J. Sweeney, 1941-68.

Houma-Thibodaux, La. (1977): Warren L. Boudreaux, bishop, 1977.

Indianapolis,* Ind. (1834; archdiocese, 1944): Edward T. O'Meara, archbishop, 1980. Established at Vincennes, transferred, 1898.

Former ordinaries: Simon G. Bruté, 1834-39; Celestine de la Hailandiere, 1839-47; John S. Bazin, 1847-48; Maurice de St. Palais, 1849-77; Francis S. Chatard, 1878-1918; Joseph Chartrand, 1918-33; Joseph E. Ritter, 1934-46, first archbishop; Paul C. Schulte, 1946-70; George J. Biskup, 1970-79.

Jackson, Miss. (1837): Joseph B. Brunini, bishop, 1968. William R. Houck, auxiliary.

Established at Natchez; title changed to Natchez-Jackson, 1956; transferred to Jackson, 1977 (Natchez made titular see).

Former bishops: John J. Chanche, S.S., 1841-52; James Van de Velde, S.J., 1853-55; William H. Elder, 1857-80; Francis A. Jansens, 1881-88; Thomas Heslin, 1889-1911; John E. Gunn, S.M., 1911-24; Richard O. Gerow, 1924-67.

Jefferson City, Mo. (1956): Michael F. McAuliffe, bishop, 1969.

Former bishop: Joseph Marling, C.Pp.S., 1956-69.

Joliet, Ill. (1948): Joseph I. Imesch, bishop, 1979. Raymond J. Vonesh, auxiliary.

Former bishop: Martin D. McNamara, 1949-66. Romeo Blanchette, 1966-79.

Juneau, Alaska (1951): Michael H. Kenny, bishop, 1979.

Former bishops: Dermot O'Flanagan, 1951-68; Joseph T. Ryan, administrator, 1968-71; Francis T. Hurley, 1971-76, administrator, 1976-79.

Kalamazoo, Mich. (1971): Paul V. Donovan, bishop, 1971.

Kansas City,* Kans. (1877; archdiocese,

1952): Ignatius J. Strecker, archbishop, 1969. Marion F. Forst, auxiliary.

Established as vicariate apostolic, 1850, became Diocese of Leavenworth, 1877, transferred to Kansas City 1947.

Former ordinaries: J. B. Miege, vicar apostolic, 1851-74; Louis M. Fink, O.S.B., vicar apostolic, 1874-77, first bishop, 1877-1904; Thomas F. Lillis, 1904-10; John Ward, 1910-29; Francis Johannes, 1929-37; Paul C. Schulte, 1937-46; George J. Donnelly, 1946-50; Edward Hunkeler, 1951-69, first archbishop.

Kansas City-St. Joseph, Mo. (Kansas City, 1880; St. Joseph, 1868; united 1956): John J. Sullivan, bishop, 1977. George K. Fitzsimons, auxiliary.

Former bishops (Kansas City): John J. Hogan, 1880-1913; Thomas F. Lillis, 1913-38; Edwin V. O'Hara, 1939-56; John P. Cody, 1956-61; Charles H. Helmsing, 1962-77.

Former bishops (St. Joseph): John J. Hogan, 1868-80, administrator, 1880-93; Maurice F. Burke, 1893-1923; Francis Gilfillan, 1923-33; Charles H. Le Blond, 1933-56.

La Crosse, Wis. (1868): Frederick W. Freking, bishop, 1965. John J. Paul, auxiliary.

Former bishops: Michael Heiss, 1868-80; Kilian C. Flasch, 1881-91; James Schwebach, 1892-1921; Alexander J. McGavick, 1921-48; John P. Treacy, 1948-64.

Lafayette, Ind. (1944): Raymond J. Gallagher, bishop, 1965.

Former bishops: John G. Bennett, 1944-57; John J. Carberry, 1957-65.

Lafayette, La. (1918): Gerard L. Frey, bishop, 1973.

Former bishops: Jules B. Jeanmard, 1918-56; Maurice Schexnayder, 1956-72.

Lake Charles, La. (1980): Jude Speyrer, bishop, 1980.

Lansing, Mich. (1937): Kenneth J. Povish, bishop, 1975. James Sullivan, auxiliary.

Former bishops: Joseph H. Albers, 1937-65; Alexander Zaleski, 1965-75.

Lincoln, Neb. (1887): Glennon P. Flavin, bishop, 1967.

Former bishops: Thomas Bonacum, 1887-1911; J. Henry Tihen, 1911-17; Charles J. O'Reilly, 1918-23; Francis J. Beckman, 1924-30; Louis B. Kucera, 1930-57; James V. Casey, 1957-67.

Little Rock, Ark. (1843): Andrew J. McDonald, bishop, 1972.

Former bishops: Andrew Byrne, 1844-62; Edward Fitzgerald, 1867-1907; John Morris, 1907-46; Albert L. Fletcher, 1946-72.

Los Angeles,* Calif. (1840; archdiocese, 1936): Cardinal Timothy Manning, archbishop, 1970. John J. Ward, Juan A. Arzube, Thaddeus A. Shubsda, Manuel D. Moreno, auxiliaries.

Former ordinaries: Francisco Garcia Diego y Moreno, O.F.M., 1840-46; Joseph S. Alemany, O.P., 1850-53; Thaddeus Amat,

C.M., 1854-78; Francis Mora, 1878-96; George T. Montgomery, 1896-1903; Thomas J. Conaty, 1903-15; John J. Cantwell, 1917-47, first archbishop; Cardinal James McIntyre, 1948-70.

Louisville,* Ky. (1808; archdiocese, 1937): Thomas J. McDonough, archbishop, 1967. Charles G. Maloney, auxiliary.

Established at Bardstown, transferred, 1841.

Former ordinaries: Benedict J. Flaget, S.S. 1810-32; John B. David, S.S., 1832-33; Benedict J. Flaget, S.S., 1833-50; Martin J. Spalding, 1850-64; Peter J. Lavialle, 1865-67; William G. McCloskey, 1868-1909; Denis O'Donaghue, 1910-24; John A. Floersh, 1924-67, first archbishop.

Madison, Wis. (1946): Cletus F. O'Donnell, bishop, 1967. George O. Wirz, auxiliary.

Former bishop: William P. O'Connor, 1946-67.

Manchester, N.H. (1884): Odore J. Gendron, bishop, 1974. Robert Mulvee, auxiliary.

Former bishops: Denis M. Bradley, 1884-1903; John B. Delany, 1904-06; George A. Guertin, 1907-32; John B. Peterson, 1932-44; Matthew F. Brady, 1944-59; Ernest J. Primeau, 1960-74.

Marquette, Mich. (1857): Mark F. Schmitt, bishop, 1978.

Former bishops: Frederic Baraga, 1857-68; Ignatius Mrak, 1869-78; John Vertin, 1879-99; Frederick Eis, 1899-1922; Paul J. Nussbaum, C.P., 1922-35; Joseph C. Plagens, 1935-40; Francis Magner, 1941-47; Thomas L. Noa, 1947-68; Charles A. Salatka, 1968-77.

Memphis, Tenn. (1970): Carroll T. Dozier, bishop, 1971.

Miami,* Fla. (1958; archdiocese, 1968): Edward A. McCarthy, archbishop, 1977. John J. Nevins, Agustin A. Roman, auxiliaries.

Former ordinary: Coleman F. Carroll, 1958-77, first archbishop.

Milwaukee,* Wis. (1843; archdiocese, 1875): Rembert G. Weakland, O.S.B., archbishop, 1977. Leo J. Brust, Richard J. Sklba, auxiliaries.

Former ordinaries: John M. Henni, 1844-81, first archbishop; Michael Heiss, 1881-90; Frederick X. Katzer, 1891-1903; Sebastian G. Messmer, 1903-30; Samuel A. Stritch, 1930-39; Moses E. Kiley, 1940-53; Albert G. Meyer, 1953-58; William E. Cousins, 1959-77.

Mobile,* Ala. (1829; archdiocese, 1980): Oscar H. Lipscomb, first archbishop, 1980.

Former bishops: Michael Portier, 1829-59; John Quinlan, 1859-83; Dominic Manucy, 1884; Jeremiah O'Sullivan, 1885-96; Edward P. Allen, 1897-1926; Thomas J. Toolen, 1927-69; John L. May, 1969-80.

Monterey in California (1967): Harry A. Clinch, bishop, 1967.

Formerly Monterey-Fresno, 1922.

Former bishops (Monterey-Fresno): John J. Cantwell, administrator, 1922-24; John B.

MacGinley, first bishop, 1924-32; Philip G. Sher, 1933-53; Aloysius J. Willinger, 1953-67.

Nashville, Tenn. (1837): James D. Niedergeses, bishop, 1975.

Former bishops: Richard P. Miles, O.P., 1838-60; James Whelan, O.P., 1860-64; Patrick A. Feehan, 1865-80; Joseph Rademacher, 1883-93; Thomas S. Byrne, 1894-1923; Alphonse J. Smith, 1924-35; William L. Adrian, 1936-69; Joseph A. Durick, 1969-75.

Newark,* N.J. (1853; archdiocese, 1937): Peter L. Gerety, archbishop, 1974. John J. Dougherty, Jerome Pechillo, T.O.R., Robert F. Garner, Joseph A. Francis, S.V.D., Dominic A. Marconi, auxiliaries.

Former ordinaries: James R. Bayley, 1853-72; Michael A. Corrigan, 1873-80; Winand M. Wigger, 1881-1901; John J. O'Connor, 1901-27; Thomas J. Walsh, 1928-52, first archbishop; Thomas A. Boland, 1953-74.

New Orleans,* La. (1793; archdiocese, 1850): Philip M. Hannan, archbishop, 1965. Harold R. Perry, S. V. D., Stanley J. Ott, auxiliaries.

Former ordinaries: Luis Penalver y Cardenas, 1793-1801; John Carroll, administrator, 1809-15; W. Louis Dubourg, S.S., 1815-25; Joseph Rosati, C.M., administrator, 1826-29; Leo De Neckere, C.M., 1829-33; Anthony Blanc, 1835-60, first archbishop; Jean Marie Odin, C.M., 1861-70; Napoleon J. Perche, 1870-83; Francis X. Leray, 1883-87; Francis A. Janssens, 1888-97; Placide L. Chapelle, 1897-1905; James H. Blenk, S.M., 1906-17; John W. Shaw, 1918-34; Joseph F. Rummel, 1935-64; John P. Cody, 1964-65.

Newton, Mass. (Melkite Rite) (1966; eparchy, 1976): Archbishop Joseph Tawil, exarch, 1969, first eparch, 1976.

Former ordinary: Justin Najmy, 1966-68.

New Ulm, Minn. (1957): Raymond A. Lucker, bishop, 1975.

Former bishop: Alphonse J. Schladweiler, 1958-75.

New York,* N.Y. (1808; archdiocese, 1850): Cardinal Terence J. Cooke, archbishop, 1968. Patrick V. Ahern, James P. Mahoney, Anthony F. Mestice, Theodore E. McCarrick, Austin Vaughan, Francisco Garmendia, auxiliaries.

Former ordinaries: Richard L. Concanen, O.P., 1808-10; John Connolly, O.P., 1814-25; John Dubois, S.S., 1826-42; John J. Hughes, 1842-64, first archbishop; Cardinal John McCloskey, 1864-85; Michael A. Corrigan, 1885-1902; Cardinal John Farley, 1902-18; Cardinal Patrick Hayes, 1919-38; Cardinal Francis Spellman, 1939-67.

Norwich, Conn. (1953): Daniel P. Reilly, bishop, 1975.

Former bishops: Bernard J. Flanagan, 1953-59; Vincent J. Hines, 1960-75.

Oakland, Calif. (1962): John S. Cummins, bishop, 1977.

Former bishop: Floyd L. Begin, 1962-77.

Ogdensburg, N.Y. (1872): Stanislaus J. Brzana, bishop, 1968.

Former bishops: Edgar P. Wadhams, 1872-91; Henry Gabriels, 1892-1921; Joseph H. Conroy, 1921-39; Francis J. Monaghan, 1939-42; Bryan J. McEntegart, 1943-53; Walter P. Kellenberg, 1954-57; James J. Navagh, 1957-63; Leo R. Smith, 1963; Thomas A. Donnellan, 1964-68.

Oklahoma City,* Okla. (1905; archdiocese, 1972): Charles A. Salatka, archbishop, 1977.

Former ordinaries: Theophile Meerschaert, 1905-24; Francis C. Kelley, 1924-48; Eugene J. McGuinness, 1948-57; Victor J. Reed, 1958-71; John R. Quinn, 1971-77, first archbishop.

Omaha,* Nebr. (1885; archdiocese, 1945): Daniel E. Sheehan, archbishop, 1969.

Former ordinaries: James O'Gorman, O.C.S.O., 1859-74, vicar apostolic; James O'Connor, vicar apostolic, 1876-85, first bishop, 1885-90; Richard Scannell, 1891-1916; Jeremiah J. Harty, 1916-27; Francis Beckman, administrator, 1926-28; Joseph F. Rummel, 1928-35; James H. Ryan, 1935-47, first archbishop; Gerald T. Bergan, 1948-69.

Orange, Calif. (1976): William R. Johnson, bishop, 1976.

Orlando, Fla. (1968): Thomas J. Grady, bishop, 1974.

Former bishop: William Borders, 1968-74.

Owensboro, Ky. (1937): Henry J. Soenneker, bishop, 1961.

Former bishop: Francis R. Cotton, 1938-60.

Parma, Ohio (Byzantine Rite) (1969): Emil Mihalik, eparch, 1969.

Passaic, N.J. (Byzantine Rite) (1963): Michael J. Dudick, eparch, 1968. Thomas V. Dolinay, auxiliary.

Former bishop: Stephen Kocisko, 1963-68.

Paterson, N.J. (1937): Frank J. Rodimer, bishop, 1978.

Former bishops: Thomas H. McLaughlin, 1937-47; Thomas A. Boland, 1947-52; James A. McNulty, 1953-63; James J. Navagh, 1963-65; Lawrence B. Casey, 1966-77.

Pensacola-Tallahassee, Fla. (1975): Rene H. Gracida, bishop, 1975.

Peoria, Ill. (1877): Edward W. O'Rourke, bishop, 1971.

Former bishops: John L. Spalding, 1877-1908; Edmund M. Dunne, 1909-29; Joseph H. Schlarman, 1930-51; William E. Cousins, 1952-58; John B. Franz, 1959-71.

Philadelphia,* Pa. (1808; archdiocese, 1875): Cardinal John Krol, archbishop, 1961. John J. Graham, Martin J. Lohmuller, Edward T. Hughes, auxiliaries.

Former ordinaries: Michael Egan, O.F.M., 1810-14; Henry Conwell, 1820-42; Francis P. Kenrick, 1842-51; John N. Neumann, C.SS.R., 1852-60; James F. Wood, 1860-83, first archbishop; Patrick J. Ryan, 1884-1911; Edmond F. Prendergast, 1911-18; Cardinal

Dennis Dougherty, 1918-51; Cardinal John O'Hara, C.S.C., 1951-60.

Philadelphia,* Pa. (Byzantine Rite) (1924; metropolitan, 1958): Myroslav J. Lubachivsky (coadjutor archbishop of Lwow of the Ukrainians), apostolic administrator, 1980.

Former ordinaries: Stephen Ortynsky, O.S.B.M., 1907-16; Constantine Bohachevsky, 1924-61; Ambrose Senyshyn, O.S.B.M., 1961-76; Joseph Schmondiuk, 1977-78; Myroslav J. Lubachivsky, 1979-80.

Phoenix, Ariz. (1969): James S. Rausch, bishop, 1977.

Former bishop: Edward A. McCarthy, 1969-76.

Pittsburgh,* Pa. (Byzantine Rite) (1924; metropolitan, 1969): Stephen J. Kocisko, eparch, 1968, first metropolitan, 1969. John M. Bilock, auxiliary.

Former ordinaries: Basil Takach 1924-48; Daniel Ivancho, 1948-54; Nicholas T. Elko, 1955-67.

Pittsburgh, Pa. (1843): Vincent M. Leonard, bishop, 1969. John B. McDowell, Anthony G. Bosco, auxiliaries.

Former bishops: Michael O'Connor, 1843-53, 1854-60; Michael Domenec, C.M., 1860-76; J. Tuigg, 1876-89; Richard Phelan, 1889-1904; J.F. Regis Canevin, 1904-20; Hugh C. Boyle, 1921-55; John F. Dearden, 1950-58; John J. Wright, 1959-69.

Portland, Me. (1853): Edward C. O'Leary, bishop, 1974. Amedee W. Proulx, auxiliary.

Former bishops: David W. Bacon, 1855-74; James A. Healy, 1875-1900; William H. O'Connell, 1901-06; Louis S. Walsh, 1906-24; John G. Murray, 1925-31; Joseph E. McCarthy, 1932-55; Daniel J. Feeney, 1955-69; Peter L. Gerety, 1969-74.

Portland,* Ore. (1846): Cornelius M. Power, archbishop, 1974. Paul E. Waldschmidt, C.S.C., Kenneth D. Steiner, auxiliaries.

Established as Oregon City, name changed, 1928.

Former ordinaries: Francis N. Blanchet, 1846-80 vicar apostolic, first archbishop; Charles J. Seghers, 1880-84; William H. Gross, C.SS.R., 1885-98; Alexander Christie, 1899-1925; Edward D. Howard, 1926-66; Robert J. Dwyer, 1966-74.

Providence, R.I. (1872): Louis E. Gelineau, bishop, 1972. Kenneth A. Angell, auxiliary.

Former bishops: Thomas F. Hendricken, 1872-86; Matthew Harkins, 1887-1921; William A. Hickey, 1921-33; Francis P. Keough, 1934-47; Russell J. McVinney, 1948-71.

Pueblo, Colo. (1941): Arthur N. Tafoya, bishop, 1980.

Former bishops: Joseph C. Willging, 1942-59; Charles A. Buswell, 1959-79.

Raleigh, N.C. (1924): F. Joseph Gossman, bishop, 1975. George E. Lynch, auxiliary.

Former bishops: William J. Hafey, 1925-37; Eugene J. McGuinness, 1937-44; Vincent S. Waters, 1945-75.

Rapid City, S. Dak. (1902): Harold J. Dimmerling, bishop, 1969.

Established at Lead, transferred, 1920.

Former bishops: John Stariha, 1902-09; Joseph F. Busch, 1910-15; John J. Lawler, 1916-48; William T. McCarty, C.SS.R., 1948-69.

Reno-Las Vegas, Nev. (1931): Norman F. McFarland, bishop, 1976.

Established at Reno; title changed to Reno-Las Vegas, 1976.

Former bishops: Thomas K. Gorman, 1931-52; Robert J. Dwyer, 1952-66; Joseph Green, 1967-74.

Richmond, Va. (1820): Walter F. Sullivan, bishop, 1974.

Former bishops: Patrick Kelly, 1820-22; Richard V. Whelan, 1841-50; John McGill, 1850-72; James Gibbons, 1872-77; John J. Keane, 1878-88; Augustine Van de Vyver, 1889-1911; Denis J. O'Connell, 1912-26; Andrew J. Brennan, 1926-45; Peter L. Ireton, 1945-58; John J. Russell, 1958-73.

Rochester, N.Y. (1868): Matthew H. Clark, bishop, 1979. Dennis W. Hickey, auxiliary.

Former bishops: Bernard J. McQuaid, 1868-1909; Thomas F. Hickey, 1909-28; John F. O'Hern, 1929-33; Edward F. Mooney, 1933-37; James E. Kearney, 1937-66; Fulton J. Sheen, 1966-69; Joseph L. Hogan, 1969-78.

Rockford, Ill. (1908): Arthur J. O'Neill, bishop, 1968.

Former bishops: Peter J. Muldoon, 1908-27; Edward F. Hoban, 1928-42; John J. Boylan, 1943-53; Raymond P. Hillinger, 1953-56; Loras T. Lane, 1956-68.

Rockville Centre, N.Y. (1957): John R. McGann, bishop, 1976. Gerald Ryan, James Daly, auxiliaries.

Former bishop: Walter P. Kellenberg, 1957-76.

Sacramento, Calif. (1886): Francis A. Quinn, bishop, 1979.

Former bishops: Patrick Manogue, 1886-95; Thomas Grace, 1896-1921; Patrick J. Keane, 1922-28; Robert J. Armstrong, 1929-57; Joseph T. McGucken, 1957-62; Alden J. Bell, 1962-79.

Saginaw, Mich. (1938): Vacant as of Sept. 1, 1980.

Former bishops: William F. Murphy, 1938-50; Stephen S. Woznicki, 1950-68; Francis F. Reh, 1969-80.

St. Augustine, Fla. (1870): John J. Snyder, bishop, 1979.

Former bishops: Augustin Verot, S.S., 1870-76; John Moore, 1877-1901; William J. Kenny, 1902-13; Michael J. Curley, 1914-21; Patrick J. Barry, 1922-40; Joseph P. Hurley, 1940-67; Paul F. Tanner, 1968-79.

St. Cloud, Minn. (1889): George H. Speltz, bishop, 1968.

Former bishops: Otto Zardetti, 1889-94; Martin Marty, O.S.B., 1895-96; James Trobec, 1897-1914; Joseph F. Busch, 1915-53; Peter Bartholome, 1953-68.

St. Louis,* Mo. (1826; archdiocese, 1847): John L. May, archbishop, 1980. George J. Gottwald, Charles R. Koester, John Wurm, auxiliaries.

Former ordinaries: Joseph Rosati, C.M., 1827-43; Peter R. Kenrick, 1843-95, first archbishop; John J. Kain, 1895-1903; Cardinal John Glennon, 1903-46; Cardinal Joseph Ritter, 1946-67; Cardinal John J. Carberry, 1968-79.

St. Maron, Brooklyn, N.Y. (Maronite Rite) (1966; diocese, 1972): Francis Zayek, exarch, 1966, first eparch, 1972.

Established at Detroit; transferred to Brooklyn, 1977.

St. Nicholas in Chicago (Byzantine Rite Eparchy of St. Nicholas of the Ukrainians) (1961): Vacant as of Sept. 1, 1980.

Former bishop: Jaroslav Gabro, 1961-80.

St. Paul and Minneapolis,* Minn. (1850; archdiocese, 1888): John R. Roach, archbishop, 1975. John F. Kinney, William H. Bullock, auxiliaries.

Former ordinaries: Joseph Cretin, 1851-57; Thomas L. Grace, O.P., 1859-84; John Ireland, 1884-1918, first archbishop; Austin Dowling, 1919-30; John G. Murray, 1931-56; William O. Brady, 1956-61; Leo Binz, 1962-75.

St. Petersburg, Fla. (1968): W. Thomas Larkin, bishop, 1979.

Former bishop: Charles McLaughlin, 1968-78.

Salina, Kans. (1887): Daniel W. Kucera, O.S.B., bishop, 1980.

Established at Concordia, transferred, 1944.

Former bishops: Richard Scannell, 1887-91; John J. Hennessy, administrator, 1891-98; John F. Cunningham, 1898-1919; Francis J. Tief, 1921-38; Frank A. Thill, 1938-57; Frederick W. Freking, 1957-64; Cyril J. Vogel, 1965-79.

Salt Lake City, Utah (1891): William K. Weigand, bishop, 1980.

Former bishops: Lawrence Scanlan, 1891-1915; Joseph S. Glass, C.M., 1915-26; John J. Mitty, 1926-32; James E. Kearney, 1932-37; Duane G. Hunt, 1937-60; J. Lennox Federal, 1960-80.

San Angelo, Tex. (1961): Joseph A. Fiorenza, bishop, 1979.

Former bishops: Thomas J. Drury, 1962-65; Thomas Tschoepe, 1966-69; Stephen A. Leven, 1969-79.

San Antonio,* Tex. (1874; archdiocese, 1926): Patrick F. Flores, archbishop, 1979. Hugo Gerbermann, M.M., auxiliary.

Former ordinaries: Anthony D. Pellicer, 1874-80; John C. Neraz, 1881-94; John A. Forest, 1895-1911; John W. Shaw, 1911-18; Arthur Jerome Drossaerts, 1918-40, first archbishop; Robert E. Lucey, 1941-69; Francis Furey, 1969-79.

San Bernardino, Calif. (1978): Phillip F. Straling, bishop, 1978.

San Diego, Calif. (1936): Leo T. Maher, bishop, 1969. Gilbert Espinoza Chavez, auxiliary.

Former bishops: Charles F. Buddy, 1936-66; Francis J. Furey, 1966-69.

San Francisco,* Calif. (1853): John R. Quinn, archbishop, 1977. Roland Pierre Du Maine, auxiliary.

Former ordinaries: Joseph S. Alemany, O.P., 1853-84; Patrick W. Riordan, 1884-1914; Edward J. Hanna, 1915-35; John Mitty, 1935-61; Joseph T. McGucken, 1962-77.

Santa Fe,* N. Mex. (1850; archdiocese, 1875): Robert Sanchez, archbishop, 1974.

Former ordinaries: John B. Lamy, 1850-85, first archbishop; John B. Salpointe, 1885-94; Placide L. Chapelle, 1894-97; Peter Bourgade, 1899-1908; John B. Pitaval, 1909-18; Albert T. Daeger, O.F.M., 1919-32; Rudolph A. Gerken, 1933-43; Edwin V. Byrne, 1943-63; James P. Davis, 1964-74.

Santa Rosa, Calif. (1962): Mark J. Hurley, bishop, 1969.

Former bishop: Leo T. Maher, 1962-69.

Savannah, Ga. (1850): Raymond W. Lessard, bishop, 1973.

Former bishops: Francis X. Gartland, 1850-54; John Barry, 1857-59; Augustin Verot, S.S., 1861-70; Ignatius Persico, O.F.M. Cap., 1870-72; William H. Gross, C.SS.R., 1873-85; Thomas A. Becker, 1886-99; Benjamin J. Keiley, 1900-22; Michael Keyes, S.M., 1922-35; Gerald P. O'Hara, 1935-59; Thomas J. McDonough, 1960-67; Gerard L. Frey, 1967-72.

Scranton, Pa. (1868): J. Carroll McCormick, bishop, 1966. James C. Timlin, auxiliary.

Former bishops: William O'Hara, 1868-99; Michael J. Hoban, 1899-1926; Thomas C. O'Reilly, 1928-38; William J. Hafey, 1938-54; Jerome D. Hannan, 1954-65.

Seattle,* Wash. (1850; archdiocese, 1951): Raymond G. Hunthausen, archbishop, 1975. Nicholas E. Walsh, auxiliary.

Established as Nesqually, name changed, 1907.

Former ordinaries; Augustin M. Blanchet, 1850-79; Aegidius Junger, 1879-95; Edward J. O'Dea, 1896-1932; Gerald Shaughnessy, S.M., 1933-50; Thomas A. Connolly, first archbishop, 1950-75.

Sioux City, Ia. (1902): Frank H. Greteman, bishop, 1970.

Former bishops: Philip J. Garrigan, 1902-19; Edmond Heelan, 1919-48; Joseph M. Mueller, 1948-70.

Sioux Falls, S. Dak. (1889): Paul V. Dudley, bishop, 1978.

Former bishops: Martin Marty, O.S.B., 1889-94; Thomas O'Gorman, 1896-1921; Bernard J. Mahoney, 1922-39; William O. Brady, 1939-56; Lambert A. Hoch, 1956-78.

Spokane, Wash. (1913): Lawrence H. Welsh, bishop, 1978.

Former bishops: Augustine F. Schinner, 1914-25; Charles D. White, 1927-55; Bernard J. Topel, 1955-78.

Springfield-Cape Girardeau, Mo. (1956): Bernard F. Law, bishop, 1973.

Former bishops: Charles Helmsing, 1956-62; Ignatius J. Strecker, 1962-69; William Baum, 1970-73.

Springfield, Ill. (1853): Joseph A. McNicholas, bishop, 1975.

Established at Quincy, transferred to Alton 1857; transferred to Springfield 1923.

Former bishops: Henry D. Juncker, 1857-68; Peter J. Baltes, 1870-86; James Ryan, 1888-1923; James A. Griffin, 1924-48; William A. O'Connor, 1949-75.

Springfield, Mass. (1870): Joseph F. Maguire, bishop, 1977. Leo E. O'Neil, auxiliary.

Former bishops: Patrick T. O'Reilly, 1870-92; Thomas D. Beaven, 1892-1920; Thomas M. O'Leary, 1921-49; Christopher J. Weldon, 1950-77.

Stamford, Conn. (Byzantine Rite) (1956): Basil Losten, eparch, 1977.

Former eparchs: Ambrose Senyshyn, O.S.B.M., 1956-61; Joseph Schmondiuk, 1961-77.

Steubenville, Ohio (1944): Albert H. Ottenweller, bishop, 1977.

Former bishop: John K. Mussio, 1945-77.

Stockton, Calif. (1962): Roger M. Mahony, bishop, 1980.

Former bishops: Hugh A. Donohoe, 1962-69; Merlin J. Guilfoyle, 1969-79.

Superior, Wis. (1905): George A. Hammes, bishop, 1960. Raphael M. Fliss, coadjutor.

Former bishops: Augustine F. Schinner, 1905-13; Joseph M. Koudelka, 1913-21; Joseph G. Pinten, 1922-26; Theodore M. Reverman, 1926-41; William P. O'Connor, 1942-46; Albert G. Meyer, 1946-53; Joseph Annabring, 1954-59.

Syracuse, N.Y. (1886): Francis J. Harrison, bishop, 1976. Thomas J. Costello, auxiliary.

Former bishops: Patrick A. Ludden, 1887-1912; John Grimes, 1912-22; Daniel J. Curley, 1923-32; John A. Duffy, 1933-37; Walter A. Foery, 1937-70; David F. Cunningham, 1970-76.

Toledo, Ohio (1910): Vacant as of Sept. 1, 1980. James R. Hoffman, auxiliary.

Former bishops: Joseph Schrembs, 1911-21; Samuel A. Stritch, 1921-30; Karl J. Alter, 1931-50; George J. Rehring, 1950-67; John A. Donovan, 1967-80.

Trenton, N.J. (1881): John C. Reiss, bishop, 1980.

Former bishops: Michael J. O'Farrell, 1881-94; James A. McFaul, 1894-1917; Thomas J. Walsh, 1918-28; John J. McMahon, 1928-32; Moses E. Kiley, 1934-40; William A. Griffin, 1940-50; George W. Ahr,

1950-79.

Tucson, Ariz. (1897): Francis J. Green, bishop, 1960.

Former bishops: Peter Bourgade, 1897-99; Henry Granjon, 1900-22; Daniel J. Gercke, 1923-60.

Tulsa, Okla. (1972): Eusebius J. Beltran, bishop, 1978.

Former bishop: Bernard J. Ganter, 1973-77.

Washington,* D.C. (1939): James A. Hickey, archbishop, 1980. Thomas W. Lyons, Eugene A. Marino, S.S.J., Thomas Kelly, O.P., auxiliaries.

Former ordinaries: Michael J. Curley, 1939-47; Cardinal Patrick O'Boyle, 1948-73; Cardinal William Baum, 1973-80.

Wheeling-Charleston, W. Va. (1850): Joseph H. Hodges, bishop, 1962. James E. Michaels, S.S.C., auxiliary.

Established as Wheeling; name changed, 1974.

Former bishops: Richard V. Whelan, 1850-74; John J. Kain, 1875-93; Patrick J. Donahue, 1894-1922; John J. Swint, 1922-62.

Wichita, Kans. (1887): David M. Maloney, bishop, 1967.

Former bishops: John J. Hennessy, 1888-1920; Augustus J. Schwertner, 1921-39; Christian H. Winkelmann, 1940-46; Mark K. Carroll, 1947-67.

Wilmington, Del. (1868): Thomas J. Mardaga, bishop, 1968.

Former bishops: Thomas A. Becker, 1868-86; Alfred A. Curtis, 1886-96; John J. Monaghan, 1897-1925; Edmond Fitzmaurice, 1925-60; Michael Hyle, 1960-67.

Winona, Minn. (1889): Loras J. Watters, bishop, 1969.

Former bishops: Joseph B. Cotter, 1889-1909; Patrick R. Heffron, 1910-27; Francis M. Kelly, 1928-49; Edward A. Fitzgerald, 1949-69.

Worcester, Mass. (1950): Bernard J. Flanagan, bishop, 1959. Timothy J. Harrington, auxiliary.

Former bishop: John J. Wright, 1950-59.

Yakima, Wash. (1951): William Skylstad, bishop, 1977.

Former bishops: Joseph P. Dougherty, 1951-69; Cornelius M. Power, 1969-74; Nicholas E. Walsh, 1974-76.

Youngstown, Ohio (1943): James W. Malone, bishop, 1968. Benedict C. Franzetta, auxiliary.

Former bishops: James A. McFadden, 1943-52; Emmet M. Walsh, 1952-68.

Military Ordinariate (1917): Cardinal Terence J. Cooke, military vicar, 1968. Joseph T. Ryan, coadjutor archbishop, 1975. William J. Moran, John J. O'Connor, military delegates.

Former military vicars: Cardinal Patrick Hayes, 1917-38; Cardinal Francis Spellman, 1939-67.

Military Ordinariate

The Military Ordinariate or Vicariate, is the diocese which serves members of the armed forces of the United States wherever they are. It has jurisdiction over: military and Veterans Administration hospital chaplains; personnel of the armed forces and members of their families and dependents habitually living with them; members of the Coast Guard, National Guard, Air National Guard and Civil Air Patrol when on active duty; persons living on military installations and/or attached to military offices or VA facilities.

The ordinariate was canonically established on a permanent basis by a decree of the Sacred Consistorial Congregation dated Sept. 8, 1957. Cardinal Terence J. Cooke, Archbishop of New York, is Military Vicar. Offices of the ordinariate are located at 1011 First Ave., New York, N.Y. 10022.

MISSIONARY BISHOPS

Africa

Namibia (South West Africa): Keetmanshoop (vicariate apostolic), Edward F. Schlotterback, O.S.F.S.

Nigeria: Sokoto (diocese), Michael J. Dempsey, O.P.

South Africa: De Aar (diocese), Joseph A. De Palma, S.C.J.

Keimos (diocese), John Minder, O.S.F.S.

Tanzania: Arusha (diocese), Dennis V. Durning, C.S.Sp.

Nachingwea (diocese), Arnold R. Cotey, S.D.S.

Asia

China: Chowtsun (diocese), Henry A. Pinger, O.F.M. Expelled.

Wuchow (diocese), Frederick A. Donaghy, M.M. Expelled.

India: Bhagalpur (diocese), Urban McGarry, T.O.R.

Indonesia: Agats (diocese), Alphonse A. Sowada, O.S.C.

Iraq: Mossul (Chaldean-rite archdiocese), George Garmo.

Korea: Inchon (diocese), William J. McNaughton, M.M.

Pakistan: Multan (diocese), Ernest B. Boland, O.P.

Philippine Islands: Cotabato (archdiocese), Philip M. Smith, O.M.I.

Jolo (vicariate apostolic), Georges Dion, O.M.I.

Marbel (prelacy), Reginald Arliss, C.P.

Taiwan: Taichung (diocese), William F. Kupfer, M.M.

Central America, West Indies

Bahamas: Nassau (diocese), Paul L. Hagarty, O.S.B.

Belize: Belize (diocese), Robert L. Hodapp, S.J.

Dominican Republic: San Juan de la Maguana (diocese), Ronald G. Connors, C.SS.R.,

Honduras: Comayagua (diocese), Gerald Scarpone, O.F.M.

Nicaragua: Bluefields (vicariate apostolic), Salvator Schlaefer, O.F.M.Cap.

Virgin Islands: St. Thomas (diocese), Edward Harper, C.SS.R.

North America

Mexico: Mexico City (archdiocese), Ricardo Watty Urquidi, M.Sp.S., auxiliary.

Oceania

Caroline and Marshall Islands (diocese), Martin J. Neylon, S.J.

Papua New Guinea: Goroko (diocese), Raymond R. Caesar, S.V.D.

Kavieng (diocese), Alfred M. Stemper, M.S.C.

Madang (archdiocese), Leo Arkfeld, S.V.D.

Mendi (diocese), Firmin Schmidt, O.F.M.Cap.

Mount Hagen (diocese), George Bernarding, S.V.D.

Wewak (diocese), Raymond P. Kalisz, S.V.D.

Vanuatu (New Hebrides): Port Vila (diocese), Francis Lambert, S.M.

South America

Bolivia: Coroico (prelacy), Thomas R. Manning, O.F.M.

La Paz (archdiocese), Andrew B. Schierhoff, auxiliary.

Santa Cruz (archdiocese), Charles A. Brown, M.M., auxiliary.

Brazil: Abaete do Tocantins (prelacy), Angelo Frosi, S.X.

Belem do Para (archdiocese), Jude Prost, O.F.M., auxiliary.

Borba (prelacy), Adrian J. M. Veigle, T.O.R.

Cristalandia (prelacy), James A. Schuck, O.F.M.

Jatai (diocese), Benedict D. Coscia, O.F.M. Michael P. Mundo, auxiliary.

Paranagua (diocese), Bernard Nolker, C.SS.R.

Rui Barbosa (diocese), Mathias Schmidt, O.S.B.

Santarem (diocese), James C. Ryan, O.F.M.

Sao Paulo (archdiocese), Alfred Novak, C.SS.R., auxiliary.

Sao Salvador da Bahia (archdiocese), Thomas W. Murphy, C.SS.R., auxiliary.

Peru: Chulucanas (prelacy), John McNabb, O.S.A.

CATHOLIC POPULATION OF THE UNITED STATES

(Source: *The Official Catholic Directory, 1980;* figures as of Jan. 1, 1980. Archdioceses are indicated by an asterisk; for dioceses marked +, see Dioceses with Interstate Lines.)

Section, State Diocese	Catholics	Dioc.	Priests Rel.	Total	Perm. Deacons	Bros.	Sisters	Parishes
NEW ENGLAND	5,681,871	4,146	2,547	6,693	344	716	12,775	1,696
Maine, Portland	275,376	232	128	360	—	33	868	143
New Hampshire, Manchester	285,301	281	97	378	—	46	1,155	126
Vermont, Burlington	156,596	167	69	236	—	29	369	100
Massachusetts	3,036,478	2,166	1,687	3,853	121	318	7,294	785
*Boston	2,017,133	1,306	1,171	2,477	92	212	4,797	408
Fall River	338,322	229	206	435	—	44	747	113
Springfield	352,949	275	145	420	—	25	980	136
Worcester	328,074	356	165	521	29	37	770	128
Rhode Island, Providence	601,063	387	216	603	63	170	1,256	159
Connecticut	1,327,057	913	350	1,263	160	120	1,833	383
*Hartford	790,764	530	153	683	137	61	791	223
Bridgeport	340,441	240	119	359	19	5	694	86
Norwich+	195,852	143	78	221	4	54	348	74
MIDDLE ATLANTIC	13,010,743	9,624	5,618	15,242	794	1,834	35,262	3,908
New York	6,393,532	4,470	3,077	7,547	319	1,121	16,285	1,715
*New York	1,825,090	1,066	1,632	2,698	116	450	5,700	410
Albany	408,648	387	190	577	35	90	1,422	201
Brooklyn	1,338,554	936	400	1,336	54	276	2,414	223
Buffalo	850,000	603	356	959	37	69	2,411	298
Ogdensburg	169,845	194	43	237	—	33	376	122
Rochester	369,840	394	156	550	—	54	1,045	161
Rockville Centre	1,040,517	484	151	635	50	133	2,119	129
Syracuse	391,038	406	149	555	27	16	798	171
New Jersey	2,925,087	1,934	978	2,912	405	337	5,548	695
*Newark	1,390,427	832	443	1,275	200	167	2,521	248
Camden	349,879	378	45	423	45	27	571	127
Paterson	317,515	293	263	556	69	61	1,061	105
Trenton	867,266	431	227	658	91	82	1,395	215
Pennsylvania	3,692,124	3,220	1,563	4,783	70	376	13,429	1,498
*Philadelphia	1,359,987	985	646	1,631	1	225	5,884	307
Allentown	259,418	308	105	413	—	20	961	152
Altoona-Johnstown	151,320	193	99	292	1	28	232	120
Erie	218,768	284	63	347	—	11	731	128
Greensburg	229,105	193	117	310	1	12	465	118
Harrisburg	206,424	182	79	261	42	13	871	112
Pittsburgh	912,959	636	321	957	25	59	3,088	321
Scranton	354,143	439	133	572	—	8	1,197	240
SOUTH ATLANTIC	2,973,898	2,198	2,031	4,229	292	581	6,947	1,253
Delaware, Wilmington+	120,827	123	95	218	1	29	420	55
Maryland, *Baltimore	413,321	363	349	712	89	137	1,972	151
District of Columbia								
*Washington+	397,288	350	676	1,026	92	173	974	128
Virginia	285,161	220	165	385	30	32	707	157
Arlington	174,150	82	99	181	29	23	293	57
Richmond	111,011	138	66	204	1	9	414	100
West Virginia								
Wheeling-Charleston	102,192	134	92	226	10	19	453	114
North Carolina	94,496	123	75	198	2	17	354	120
Charlotte	47,805	57	51	108	—	8	229	62
Raleigh	46,691	66	24	90	2	9	125	58
South Carolina, Charleston	59,027	82	54	136	18	25	272	75
Georgia	149,288	158	123	281	24	49	401	97
*Atlanta	99,742	89	89	178	6	36	191	52
Savannah	49,546	69	34	103	18	13	210	45
Florida	1,352,298	645	402	1,047	26	100	1,394	356
*Miami	830,700	304	204	508	22	49	662	130
Orlando	163,043	126	33	159	—	—	195	61

Section, State Diocese	Catholics	Dioc.	Priests Rel.	Total	Deacons	Bros.	Sisters	Par- ishes
Florida								
Pensacola-Tallahassee	40,823	52	13	65	—	—	65	38
St. Augustine	65,416	53	25	78	1	—	117	44
St. Petersburg	252,316	110	127	237	3	51	355	83
EAST NORTH CENTRAL	**10,237,208**	**7,886**	**4,958**	**12,844**	**1,027**	**1,876**	**31,250**	**4,202**
Ohio	**2,372,393**	**2,055**	**1,019**	**3,074**	**197**	**505**	**7,301**	**977**
*Cincinnati	505,666	467	444	911	57	272	1,890	256
Cleveland	979,300	642	288	930	23	132	2,516	256
Columbus	204,816	235	72	307	17	13	703	108
Steubenville	53,578	166	14	180	1	9	151	74
Toledo	347,594	281	129	410	88	32	1,531	166
Youngstown	281,439	264	72	336	11	47	510	117
Indiana	**717,799**	**743**	**625**	**1,368**	**36**	**245**	**3,692**	**453**
*Indianapolis	202,087	235	192	427	—	87	1,913	142
Evansville	91,701	132	21	153	15	5	448	74
Ft. Wayne-South Bend	147,438	125	270	395	16	116	887	89
Gary	190,033	141	79	220	1	30	325	86
Lafayette	86,540	110	63	173	4	7	119	62
Illinois	**3,575,931**	**2,241**	**1,821**	**4,062**	**525**	**636**	**8,731**	**1,101**
*Chicago	2,406,728	1,264	1,289	2,553	400	309	5,040	444
Belleville	122,147	164	50	214	2	10	434	130
Joliet	411,000	205	181	386	36	262	1,100	111
Peoria	234,844	252	113	365	36	16	699	170
Rockford	217,573	175	82	257	51	7	470	102
Springfield	183,639	181	106	287	—	32	988	144
Michigan	**2,004,288**	**1,326**	**642**	**1,968**	**146**	**182**	**5,155**	**812**
*Detroit	1,190,042	619	432	1,051	93	133	3,050	337
Gaylord	84,425	61	21	82	—	5	153	59
Grand Rapids	148,128	163	40	203	17	9	669	92
Kalamazoo	93,430	58	38	96	12	10	306	46
Lansing	221,338	153	59	212	8	16	560	84
Marquette	98,528	129	24	153	—	2	156	89
Saginaw	168,397	143	28	171	16	7	261	105
Wisconson	**1,566,797**	**1,521**	**851**	**2,372**	**123**	**308**	**6,371**	**859**
*Milwaukee	706,712	646	515	1,161	89	172	3,720	266
Green Bay	337,139	295	219	514	34	87	965	194
La Crosse	218,754	266	43	309	—	22	718	174
Madison	215,255	209	55	264	—	26	727	138
Superior	88,937	105	19	124	—	1	241	87
EAST SOUTH CENTRAL	**686,172**	**953**	**448**	**1,401**	**136**	**331**	**4,045**	**629**
Kentucky	**368,751**	**516**	**171**	**687**	**44**	**149**	**2,823**	**287**
*Louisville	210,154	255	124	379	44	122	1,462	126
Covington	108,500	185	28	213	—	11	1,081	85
Owensboro	50,097	76	19	95	—	16	280	76
Tennessee	**113,169**	**134**	**67**	**201**	**47**	**77**	**341**	**95**
Memphis	47,188	57	26	83	21	57	173	35
Nashville	65,981	77	41	118	26	20	168	60
Alabama	**109,233**	**160**	**137**	**297**	**32**	**37**	**464**	**132**
*Mobile	55,830	93	79	172	15	25	273	77
Birmingham	53,403	67	58	125	17	12	191	55
Mississippi	**95,019**	**143**	**73**	**216**	**13**	**68**	**417**	**115**
Biloxi	52,434	66	30	96	4	57	93	42
Jackson	42,585	77	43	120	9	11	324	73
WEST NORTH CENTRAL	**3,380,367**	**4,060**	**2,209**	**6,269**	**283**	**726**	**15,732**	**2,702**
Minnesota	**1,040,548**	**993**	**476**	**1,469**	**47**	**163**	**4,348**	**697**
*St. Paul and Minneapolis	554,662	396	221	617	41	67	1,642	217
Crookston	41,925	50	23	73	—	3	320	49
Duluth	101,487	101	35	136	1	1	334	78
New Ulm	71,039	114	10	124	1	1	179	94

Section, State Diocese	Catholics	Priests Dioc.	Priests Rel.	Total	Deacons	Bros.	Sisters	Parishes
Minnesota								
St. Cloud	151,682	160	170	330	5	65	1,129	135
Winona	119,753	172	17	189	—	26	744	124
Iowa	**540,929**	**908**	**349**	**1,257**	**45**	**58**	**2,462**	**510**
*Dubuque	242,744	378	101	479	25	40	1,467	190
Davenport	105,000	196	18	214	—	17	457	119
Des Moines	80,427	126	10	136	16	—	205	84
Sioux City	112,758	208	220	428	4	1	333	117
Missouri	**797,768**	**934**	**748**	**1,682**	**107**	**344**	**4,419**	**498**
*St. Louis	531,108	575	527	1,102	29	214	3,395	246
Jefferson City	79,905	127	14	141	33	15	157	94
Kansas City-St. Joseph	137,766	158	166	324	43	52	640	97
Springfield-Cape Girardeau	48,989	74	41	115	2	63	227	61
North Dakota	**185,928**	**220**	**95**	**315**	**11**	**23**	**547**	**189**
Bismarck	76,817	76	66	142	—	18	298	73
Fargo	109,111	144	29	173	11	5	249	116
South Dakota	**140,383**	**182**	**110**	**292**	**9**	**41**	**587**	**178**
Rapid City	40,138	38	41	79	7	14	100	56
Sioux Falls	100,245	144	69	213	2	27	487	122
Nebraska	**335,142**	**422**	**210**	**632**	**63**	**67**	**1,158**	**272**
*Omaha	216,779	223	180	403	63	46	844	136
Grand Island	51,846	82	2	84	—	—	144	50
Lincoln	66,517	117	28	145	—	21	170	86
Kansas	**339,669**	**401**	**221**	**622**	**1**	**30**	**2,211**	**358**
*Kansas City	145,000	125	138	263	—	22	1,225	119
Dodge City	37,174	56	11	67	1	—	190	46
Salina	60,145	79	44	123	—	5	345	98
Wichita	97,350	141	28	169	—	3	451	95
WEST SOUTH CENTRAL	**3,866,075**	**2,040**	**1,719**	**3,759**	**580**	**612**	**7,097**	**1,585**
Arkansas, Little Rock	**56,911**	**108**	**66**	**174**	**2**	**52**	**534**	**85**
Louisiana	**1,316,441**	**692**	**544**	**1,236**	**92**	**278**	**2,109**	**477**
*New Orleans	529,706	229	316	545	40	196	1,275	134
Alexandria-Shreveport	83,432	118	44	162	1	13	226	84
Baton Rouge	173,564	94	67	161	2	10	125	69
Houma-Thibodaux	130,391	57	8	65	15	10	73	35
Lafayette	399,348	194	109	303	34	49	410	155
Lake Charles	No separate statistics available.							
Oklahoma	**117,563**	**170**	**66**	**236**	**24**	**29**	**502**	**126**
*Oklahoma City	67,093	107	39	146	16	20	278	72
Tulsa	50,470	63	27	90	8	9	224	54
Texas	**2,375,160**	**1,070**	**1,043**	**2,113**	**462**	**253**	**3,952**	**897**
*San Antonio	575,245	203	263	466	77	133	1,500	165
Amarillo	89,051	66	24	90	33	1	168	62
Austin	136,935	101	51	152	5	30	190	83
Beaumont	83,973	57	34	91	6	2	121	44
Brownsville	317,656	46	74	120	1	16	170	60
Corpus Christi	177,714	81	90	171	14	19	226	76
Dallas	165,483	103	108	211	101	5	355	61
El Paso+	223,926	92	78	170	39	21	370	82
Fort Worth	91,439	69	40	109	18	16	165	78
Galveston-Houston	437,000	199	257	456	105	10	649	142
San Angelo	76,738	53	24	77	63	—	38	44
MOUNTAIN	**1,668,663**	**1,187**	**815**	**2,002**	**276**	**254**	**3,136**	**795**
Montana	**130,292**	**223**	**62**	**285**	**11**	**13**	**273**	**133**
Great Falls-Billings	65,792	89	38	127	4	5	192	74
Helena	64,500	134	24	158	7	8	81	59
Idaho, Boise	**70,416**	**96**	**27**	**123**	**1**	**8**	**143**	**67**
Wyoming, Cheyenne+	**46,500**	**60**	**7**	**67**	**2**	**2**	**89**	**39**
Colorado	**411,545**	**290**	**274**	**564**	**64**	**49**	**1,152**	**190**
*Denver	309,839	188	223	411	61	35	931	131
Pueblo	101,706	102	51	153	3	14	221	59

Section, State Diocese	Catholics	Dioc.	Priests Rel.	Total	Deacons	Bros.	Sisters	Parishes
New Mexico	372,456	201	151	352	52	113	573	151
*Santa Fe	324,357	152	94	246	45	87	410	95
Gallup+	48,099	49	57	106	7	26	163	56
Arizona	467,710	214	202	416	123	37	665	135
Phoenix	269,710	121	115	236	62	27	317	79
Tucson	198,000	93	87	180	61	10	348	56
Utah, Salt Lake City	59,744	52	45	97	22	17	110	39
Nevada, Reno-Las Vegas	110,000	51	47	98	1	15	131	41
PACIFIC	5,902,676	2,784	2,754	5,538	343	969	9,792	1,527
Washington	488,309	383	382	765	65	40	1,444	227
*Seattle	358,460	222	253	475	49	30	895	130
Spokane	73,649	99	113	212	16	10	488	58
Yakima	56,200	62	16	78	—	—	61	39
Oregon	320,313	237	252	489	1	68	964	152
*Portland	294,952	194	241	435	1	68	869	123
Baker	25,361	43	11	54	—	—	95	29
California	4,844,744	2,075	1,950	4,025	243	781	6,898	1,029
*Los Angeles	2,069,682	583	682	1,265	91	287	2,545	278
*San Francisco	629,366	317	577	894	36	132	1,617	153
Fresno	307,000	118	56	174	—	16	177	85
Monterey	95,000	84	34	118	—	23	203	43
Oakland	390,099	147	238	385	30	176	607	87
Orange	338,023	120	104	224	31	26	475	49
Sacramento	240,570	186	80	266	1	43	327	91
San Bernardino	228,734	146	56	202	18	21	222	87
San Diego	345,000	244	67	311	33	13	505	87
Santa Rosa	88,660	80	24	104	2	38	127	38
Stockton	112,610	50	32	82	1	6	93	31
Alaska	39,310	39	57	96	33	9	103	55
*Anchorage	20,038	20	20	40	—	—	38	18
Fairbanks	14,000	6	36	42	26	9	51	27
Juneau	5,272	13	1	14	7	—	14	10
Hawaii, Honolulu	210,000	50	113	163	1	71	383	64
EASTERN RITES	579,505	540	104	644	18	42	481	497
*Philadelphia	166,344	113	14	127	1	1	212	109
St. Nicholas	30,030	34	12	46	2	—	20	36
Stamford	48,806	59	19	78	—	24	49	52
*Pittsburgh	151,601	82	9	91	—	6	140	84
Parma	32,874	56	4	60	—	—	19	56
Passaic	96,605	88	16	104	2	1	29	86
St. Maron	30,887	74	2	76	3	6	8	48
Newton	22,358	34	28	62	10	4	4	26
MILITARY VICARIATE	1,825,000	—	—	—	—	—	—	—
TOTALS 1980	49,812,178	35,418	23,203	58,621	4,093	7,941	126,517	18,794
Totals 1979	49,602,035	35,472	22,958	58,430	3,296	7,965	128,378	18,695
Totals 1970	47,872,089	37,272	21,920	59,192	—	11,623	160,931	18,224

Dioceses with Interstate Lines

Diocesan lines usually fall within a single state and in some cases include a whole state.

The following dioceses, with their statistics as reported in tables throughout the Almanac, are exceptions.

Norwich, Conn., includes Fisher's Island, N.Y.

Wilmington, Del., includes all of Delaware and nine counties of Maryland.

Baltimore, includes all of Maryland except nine counties under the jurisdiction of Wilmington and five under Washington.

Washington, D.C., includes five counties of Maryland.

El Paso, Tex., includes seven counties of New Mexico.

Gallup, N.M., has jurisdiction over several counties of Arizona.

Cheyenne, Wyo., includes all of Yellowstone National Park.

PERCENTAGE OF CATHOLICS IN U.S. POPULATION

(Source: *The Official Catholic Directory, 1980;* figures are as of Jan. 1, 1980. Total general population figures at the end of the table are U.S. Census Bureau estimates for Jan. 1 of the respective years. Archdioceses are indicated by an asterisk; for dioceses marked +, see Dioceses with Interstate Lines.)

Section, State Diocese	Catholic Pop.	Total Pop.	Cath. Pct.
NEW ENGLAND	**5,681,871**	**14,148,453**	**40.16**
Maine, Portland	275,376	1,028,000	26.79
New Hampshire			
Manchester	285,301	784,000	36.39
Vermont, Burlington	156,596	493,300	31.74
Massachusetts	3,036,478	7,750,873	39.18
*Boston	2,017,133	5,789,478	34.84
Fall River	338,322	530,000	63.83
Springfield	352,949	791,642	44.58
Worcester	328,074	639,753	51.28
Rhode Island, Providence	601,063	929,000	62.03
Connecticut	1,327,057	3,163,280	41.95
*Hartford	790,764	1,748,380	45.23
Bridgeport	340,441	837,000	40.67
Norwich+	195,852	577,900	33.89
MIDDLE ATLANTIC	**13,010,743**	**37,949,195**	**34.28**
New York	6,393,532	18,335,283	34.87
*New York	1,825,090	5,044,800	36.18
Albany	408,648	1,472,684	27.15
Brooklyn	1,338,554	4,218,000	31.73
Buffalo	850,000	1,716,725	49.51
Ogdensburg	169,845	404,806	41.96
Rochester	369,840	1,467,300	25.21
Rockville Centre	1,040,517	2,787,258	37.33
Syracuse	391,038	1,223,710	31.96
New Jersey	2,925,087	8,010,180	36.77
*Newark	1,390,427	2,758,000	50.41
Camden	349,879	1,131,212	30.93
Paterson	317,515	1,518,762	20.91
Trenton	867,266	2,602,206	33.33
Pennsylvania	3,692,124	11,603,732	31.82
*Philadelphia	1,359,987	3,559,530	38.21
Allentown	259,418	1,000,000	25.94
Altoona-Johnstown	151,320	624,800	24.22
Erie	218,768	857,037	25.53
Greensburg	229,105	756,173	30.30
Harrisburg	206,424	1,600,500	12.90
Pittsburgh	912,959	2,241,430	40.73
Scranton	354,143	964,262	36.73
SOUTH ATLANTIC	**2,973,898**	**35,043,492**	**8.49**
Delaware, Wilmington+	120,827	860,500	14.04
Maryland, *Baltimore	413,321	2,449,721	16.87
District of Columbia			
*Washington+	397,288	2,098,200	18.93
Virginia	285,161	5,003,220	5.70
Arlington	174,150	1,317,500	13.22
Richmond	111,011	3,685,720	3.01
West Virginia			
Wheeling-Charleston	102,192	1,744,237	5.86
North Carolina	94,496	5,820,022	1.62
Charlotte	47,805	2,850,000	1.68
Raleigh	46,691	2,970,022	1.57

Section, State Diocese	Catholic Pop.	Total Pop.	Cath. Pct.
South Carolina			
Charleston	59,027	2,876,000	2.05
Georgia	149,288	4,877,422	3.06
*Atlanta	99,742	3,246,250	3.07
Savannah	49,546	1,631,172	3.04
Florida	1,352,298	9,314,170	14.52
*Miami	830,700	3,406,900	24.38
Orlando	163,043	1,785,500	9.13
Pensacola-Tallahassee	40,823	819,811	4.98
St. Augustine	65,416	1,047,000	6.25
St. Petersburg	252,316	2,254,959	11.19
EAST NORTH CENTRAL	**10,237,208**	**40,628,126**	**25.20**
Ohio	2,372,393	10,593,514	22.39
*Cincinnati	505,666	2,668,300	18.95
Cleveland	979,300	2,758,337	35.50
Columbus	204,816	1,901,100	10.77
Steubenville	53,578	545,060	9.83
Toledo	347,594	1,438,800	24.16
Youngstown	281,439	1,281,917	21.95
Indiana	717,799	5,207,615	13.78
*Indianapolis	202,087	2,022,366	9.99
Evansville	91,701	435,177	21.07
Ft. Wayne-S. Bend	147,438	980,952	15.03
Gary	190,033	782,300	24.29
Lafayette	86,540	986,880	8.77
Illinois	3,575,931	11,209,644	31.90
*Chicago	2,406,728	5,750,405	41.85
Belleville	122,147	807,682	15.12
Joliet	411,000	1,191,000	34.51
Peoria	234,844	1,434,428	16.37
Rockford	217,573	934,938	23.27
Springfield	183,639	1,091,191	16.83
Michigan	2,004,288	8,971,250	22.34
*Detroit	1,190,042	4,425,800	26.89
Gaylord	84,425	419,700	20.12
Grand Rapids	148,128	899,238	16.47
Kalamazoo	93,430	796,812	11.73
Lansing	221,338	1,511,910	14.64
Marquette	98,528	304,347	32.37
Saginaw	168,397	613,443	27.45
Wisconsin	1,566,797	4,646,043	33.72
*Milwaukee	706,712	2,039,217	34.66
Green Bay	337,139	736,053	45.80
La Crosse	218,754	667,849	32.76
Madison	215,255	861,020	25.00
Superior	88,937	341,904	26.01
EAST SOUTH CENTRAL		**686,172**	**13,575,679**	**5.05**
Kentucky	368,751	3,479,786	10.60
*Louisville	210,154	1,302,017	16.14
Covington	108,500	1,500,000	7.23
Owensboro	50,097	677,769	7.39

Section, State Diocese	Catholic Pop.	Total Pop.	Cath. Pct.
Tennessee	113,169	4,266,093	2.65
Memphis	47,188	1,500,000	3.15
Nashville	65,981	2,766,093	2.39
Alabama	109,233	3,550,500	3.08
*Mobile	55,830	1,350,500	4.13
Birmingham	53,403	2,200,000	2.43
Mississippi	95,019	2,279,300	4.17
Biloxi	52,434	579,300	9.05
Jackson	42,585	1,700,000	2.50
WEST NORTH CENTRAL	**3,380,367**	**16,407,899**	**20.60**
Minnesota	1,040,548	3,804,046	27.35
*St. Paul and Minneapolis	554,662	2,017,225	27.50
Crookston	41,925	220,132	19.05
Duluth	101,487	421,400	24.08
New Ulm	71,039	279,054	25.46
St. Cloud	151,682	349,853	43.36
Winona	119,753	516,382	23.19
Iowa	540,929	2,780,146	19.46
*Dubuque	242,744	956,078	25.39
Davenport	105,000	687,000	15.28
Des Moines	80,427	624,185	12.89
Sioux City	112,758	512,883	21.99
Missouri	797,768	4,699,595	16.98
*St. Louis	531,108	1,924,220	27.60
Jefferson City	79,905	670,706	11.91
Kansas City-St. Joseph	137,766	1,271,000	10.84
Springfield-Cape Girardeau	48,989	833,669	5.88
North Dakota	185,928	617,737	30.10
Bismarck	76,817	244,777	31.38
Fargo	109,111	372,960	29.26
South Dakota	140,383	662,208	21.20
Rapid City	40,138	178,208	22.52
Sioux Falls	100,245	484,000	20.71
Nebraska	335,142	1,568,537	21.37
*Omaha	216,779	758,125	28.59
Grand Island	51,846	299,012	17.40
Lincoln	66,517	511,400	13.01
Kansas	339,669	2,275,630	14.93
*Kansas City	145,000	882,028	16.44
Dodge City	37,174	218,907	16.98
Salina	60,145	327,903	18.34
Wichita	97,350	846,792	11.50
WEST SOUTH CENTRAL	**3,866,075**	**22,279,405**	**17.35**
Arkansas, Little Rock	56,911	2,186,000	2.60
Louisiana	1,316,441	3,948,139	33.34
*New Orleans	529,706	1,263,200	41.93
Alexandria-Shreveport	83,432	1,083,132	7.70
Baton Rouge	173,564	645,500	26.89
Houma-Thibodaux	130,391	182,000	71.64
Lafayette	399,348	774,307	51.57
Lake Charles	No separate statistics available.		
Oklahoma	117,563	2,784,700	4.22
*Oklahoma City	67,093	1,624,900	4.13
Tulsa	50,470	1,159,800	4.35
Texas	2,375,160	13,360,566	17.78
*San Antonio	575,245	1,376,074	41.80
Amarillo	89,051	800,000	11.13

Section, State Diocese	Catholic Pop.	Total Pop.	Cath. Pct.
Texas			
Austin	136,935	990,864	13.82
Beaumont	83,973	586,598	15.34
Brownsville	317,656	442,518	71.78
Corpus Christi	177,714	545,000	32.61
Dallas	165,483	2,778,656	5.96
El Paso+	223,926	800,000	27.99
Fort Worth	91,439	1,523,895	6.00
Galveston-Houston	437,000	2,960,000	14.76
San Angelo	76,738	556,961	13.78
MOUNTAIN	**1,668,663**	**10,176,275**	**16.40**
Montana	130,292	728,258	17.89
Great Falls-Billings	65,792	351,858	18.70
Helena	64,500	376,400	17.14
Idaho, Boise	70,416	915,960	7.69
Wyoming, Cheyenne+	46,500	425,000	10.94
Colorado	411,545	2,599,929	15.83
*Denver	309,839	2,203,221	14.06
Pueblo	101,706	396,708	25.64
New Mexico	372,456	1,103,028	33.77
*Santa Fe	324,357	780,000	41.58
Gallup+	48,099	323,028	14.89
Arizona	467,710	2,387,100	19.59
Phoenix	269,710	1,524,900	17.69
Tucson	198,000	862,200	22.96
Utah, Salt Lake City	59,744	1,367,000	4.37
Nevada, Reno-Las Vegas	110,000	650,000	16.92
PACIFIC	**5,902,676**	**29,834,394**	**19.78**
Washington	488,309	3,822,450	12.77
*Seattle	358,460	2,825,350	12.69
Spokane	73,649	610,100	12.07
Yakima	56,200	387,000	14.52
Oregon	320,313	2,496,300	12.83
*Portland	294,952	2,195,800	13.43
Baker	25,361	300,500	8.44
California	4,844,744	22,260,344	21.76
*Los Angeles	2,069,682	7,908,300	26.17
*San Francisco	629,366	2,694,200	23.36
Fresno	307,000	1,377,500	22.29
Monterey	95,000	484,363	19.61
Oakland	390,099	1,718,500	22.70
Orange	338,023	1,808,225	18.69
Sacramento	240,570	1,872,000	12.85
San Bernardino	228,734	1,358,844	16.83
San Diego	345,000	1,851,350	18.64
Santa Rosa	88,660	558,102	15.89
Stockton	112,610	628,960	17.90
Alaska	39,310	359,300	10.94
*Anchorage	20,038	195,000	10.28
Fairbanks	14,000	117,000	11.97
Juneau	5,272	47,300	11.15
Hawaii, Honolulu	210,000	896,000	23.44
EASTERN RITES	**579,505**	—	—
MILITARY VICARIATE	**1,825,000**	—	—
TOTALS 1980	**49,812,178**	**221,719,000**	**22.47**
Totals 1979	**49,602,035**	**219,484,000**	**22.60**
Totals 1970	**47,872,089**	**203,184,772**	**23.56**

INFANT BAPTISMS AND CONVERTS IN THE UNITED STATES

(Source: *The Official Catholic Directory, 1980;* figures as of Jan. 1, 1980. Archdioceses are indicated by an asterisk; for dioceses marked +, see Dioceses with Interstate Lines.)

Section, State Diocese	Infant Baptisms	Converts
NEW ENGLAND	**81,135**	**2,837**
Maine, Portland	4,620	458
New Hampshire, Manchester	4,816	250
Vermont, Burlington	2,468	156
Massachusetts	43,337	1,266
*Boston	27,611	761
Fall River	5,591	98
Springfield	5,214	235
Worcester	4,921	172
Rhode Island, Providence	7,174	223
Connecticut	18,720	484
*Hartford	11,166	252
Bridgeport	4,582	124
Norwich+	2,972	108
MIDDLE ATLANTIC	**209,668**	**11,249**
New York	109,688	4,919
*New York	30,731	1,266
Albany	6,961	518
Brooklyn	25,509	546
Buffalo	10,090	601
Ogdensburg	2,841	268
Rochester	6,998	720
Rockville Centre	18,676	275
Syracuse	7,882	725
New Jersey	45,033	1,630
*Newark	17,492	471
Camden	6,495	439
Paterson	6,547	208
Trenton	14,499	512
Pennsylvania	54,947	4,700
*Philadelphia	20,303	1,740
Allentown	3,959	165
Altoona-Johnstown	2,519	290
Erie	4,158	506
Greensburg	3,105	314
Harrisburg	3,955	565
Pittsburgh	11,393	788
Scranton	5,555	332
SOUTH ATLANTIC	**49,861**	**9,479**
Delaware, Wilmington+	2,540	271
Maryland, *Baltimore	7,125	1,159
District of Columbia		
*Washington+	6,354	1,274
Virginia	5,792	1,137
Arlington	3,410	518
Richmond	2,382	619
West Virginia		
Wheeling-Charleston	1,826	582
North Carolina	2,124	564
Charlotte	969	294
Raleigh	1,155	270
South Carolina, Charleston	1,394	408

Section, State Diocese	Infant Baptisms	Converts
Georgia	3,139	1,019
*Atlanta	2,045	551
Savannah	1,094	468
Florida	19,567	3,065
*Miami	10,527	1,204
Orlando	2,994	555
Pensacola-Tallahassee	882	357
St. Augustine	1,360	326
St. Petersburg	3,804	623
EAST NORTH CENTRAL	**172,037**	**20,028**
Ohio	37,913	5,038
*Cincinnati	8,935	1,123
Cleveland	12,786	1,616
Columbus	3,646	531
Steubenville	1,190	217
Toledo	6,645	846
Youngstown	4,711	705
Indiana	14,000	2,831
*Indianapolis	4,209	960
Evansville	1,816	351
Ft. Wayne-South Bend	3,032	660
Gary	3,265	372
Lafayette	1,678	488
Illinois	56,834	5,352
*Chicago	34,144	2,090
Belleville	2,263	716
Joliet	7,594	462
Peoria	4,468	862
Rockford	4,751	532
Springfield	3,614	690
Michigan	35,325	4,640
*Detroit	19,045	2,042
Gaylord	1,545	235
Grand Rapids	2,996	704
Kalamazoo	1,780	374
Lansing	4,766	782
Marquette	1,901	180
Saginaw	3,292	323
Wisconsin	27,965	2,167
*Milwaukee	12,451	867
Green Bay	5,643	334
La Crosse	4,291	427
Madison	3,576	391
Superior	2,004	148
EAST SOUTH CENTRAL	**14,201**	**3,247**
Kentucky	7,935	1,235
*Louisville	4,058	647
Covington	2,676	317
Owensboro	1,201	271
Tennessee	2,351	781
Memphis	907	312
Nashville	1,444	469

Section, State Diocese	Infant Baptisms	Converts	Section, State Diocese	Infant Baptisms	Converts
Alabama	1,971	718	Texas		
*Mobile	1,111	397	Fort Worth	2,718	405
Birmingham	860	321	Galveston-Houston	12,562	1,299
Mississippi	1,944	513	San Angelo	2,674	144
Biloxi	1,109	254			
Jackson	835	259	**MOUNTAIN**	**42,860**	**4,193**
			Montana	3,049	723
WEST NORTH CENTRAL	**70,940**	**9,943**	Great Falls-Billings	1,614	220
Minnesota	22,245	1,795	Helena	1,435	503
*St. Paul and			Idaho, Boise	1,975	500
Minneapolis	11,533	861	Wyoming, Cheyenne+	1,670	206
Crookston	988	142	Colorado	11,490	901
Duluth	1,914	164	*Denver	9,129	734
New Ulm	1,707	186	Pueblo	2,361	167
St. Cloud	3,454	224	New Mexico	8,925	553
Winona	2,649	218	*Santa Fe	7,419	310
Iowa	11,437	1,855	Gallup+	1,506	243
*Dubuque	4,589	636	Arizona	12,555	791
Davenport	2,532	494	Phoenix	6,863	536
Des Moines	1,745	339	Tucson	5,692	255
Sioux City	2,571	386	Utah, Salt Lake City	1,515	239
Missouri	14,867	2,951	Nevada, Reno-Las Vegas	1,681	280
*St. Louis	9,607	1,540			
Jefferson City	1,584	348	**PACIFIC**	**145,155**	**10,899**
Kansas City-St. Joseph	2,774	766	Washington	8,566	1,637
Springfield-Cape Girardeau	902	297	*Seattle	5,547	1,123
North Dakota	3,781	254	Spokane	1,505	380
Bismarck	1,715	182	Yakima	1,514	134
Fargo	2,066	72	Oregon	5,058	1,063
South Dakota	3,476	499	*Portland	4,347	902
Rapid City	1,200	98	Baker	711	161
Sioux Falls	2,276	401	California	125,792	7,647
Nebraska	7,524	1,169	*Los Angeles	57,621	2,445
*Omaha	4,583	654	*San Francisco	13,407	1,173
Grand Island	1,215	225	Fresno	10,583	424
Lincoln	1,726	290	Monterey	3,621	175
Kansas	7,610	1,420	Oakland	6,759	583
*Kansas City	2,913	480	Orange	8,387	511
Dodge City	832	167	Sacramento	6,069	747
Salina	1,460	230	San Bernardino	6,080	415
Wichita	2,405	543	San Diego	8,096	733
			Santa Rosa	1,897	229
WEST SOUTH CENTRAL	**103,630**	**7,876**	Stockton	3,272	212
			Alaska	933	198
Arkansas, Little Rock	1,383	517	*Anchorage	560	151
Louisiana	26,565	1,963	Fairbanks	288	32
*New Orleans	9,591	751	Juneau	85	15
Alexandria-Shreveport	1,991	432	Hawaii, Honolulu	4,806	354
Baton Rouge	3,500	309			
Houma-Thibodaux	2,427	83	**EASTERN RITES**	**3,794**	**261**
Lafayette	9,056	388	*Philadelphia	833	25
Lake Charles	No separate statistics available.		St. Nicholas	341	41
Oklahoma	2,596	842	Stamford	308	2
*Oklahoma City	1,684	616	*Pittsburgh	656	63
Tulsa	912	226	Parma	382	37
Texas	73,086	4,554	Passaic	568	34
*San Antonio	14,938	551	St. Maron	371	28
Amarillo	3,420	195	Newton	335	31
Austin	3,631	368			
Beaumont	1,808	275	**MILITARY VICARIATE**	**17,225**	**1,956**
Brownsville	8,411	125	**TOTALS 1980**	**910,506**	**81,968**
Corpus Christi	7,847	175	Totals 1979	896,151	77,205
Dallas	5,208	830	Totals 1970	1,086,858	92,670
El Paso+	9,869	187			

STATISTICAL SUMMARY OF THE CHURCH IN THE U.S.

(Principal source: *The Official Catholic Directory, 1980*. Comparisons are with figures reported in the previous edition.)

Catholic Population: 49,812,178; increase, 210,143. Percent of total population, 1980 — 22.47; 1979 — 22.60.

Jurisdictions: 33 archdioceses, 138 dioceses (including Guam); the military vicariate.

Cardinals: 10 (5 head archiepiscopal sees, 1 is a Roman Curia official, 4 are retired). As of Sept. 1, 1980.

Archbishops: 56 (32 residential archbishops, including 5 cardinals; 2 titular archbishops; 18 retired, including 4 cardinals; 4 serving outside the U.S.). As of Sept. 1, 1980.

Bishops: 357 (130 residential bishops; 1 coadjutor bishop; 104 auxiliary bishops; 75 retired; 47 serving outside the U.S.) As of Sept. 1, 1980.

Abbots: 85.

Priests: 58,621; increase, 191. Includes diocesan or secular priests, 35,418 (decrease, 54); religious order priests, 23,203 (increase, 245).

Permanent Deacons: 4,093; increase, 797.

Brothers: 7,941; decrease, 24.

Sisters: 126,517; decrease, 1,861.

Seminarians: 13,226; decrease, 734. Includes: diocesan seminarians, 8,552 (decrease, 142); religious order seminarians, 4,674 (decrease, 592).

Infant Baptisms: 910,506; increase, 14,355.

Converts: 81,968; increase, 4,763.

Marriages: 345,521; increase, 5,032.

Deaths: 408,651; increase, 1,549.

Parishes: 18,794; increase, 99.

Seminaries, Diocesan: 92; no change.

Religious Seminaries, Novitiates, Scholasticates: 252; decrease, 6.

Colleges and Universities: 239; decrease, 2. Students, 505,076; increase, 21,316.

High Schools: 1,527; decrease, 15. Students, 846,559; decrease, 7,047.

Elementary Schools: 8,149; decrease, 91. Students, 2,317,200; decrease, 62,616.

Teachers: 167,713; decrease, 1,436. Includes: priests, 5,444 (decrease, 356); scholastics, 200 (increase, 38); brothers, 3,271 (increase, 92); sisters, 41,135 (decrease, 2,578); lay teachers, 117,663 (increase, 1,368).

Public School Students in Religious Instruction Programs: 4,572,597; decrease, 213,432. Includes: high school students, 996,979 (decrease, 89,171); elementary school students, 3,575,618 (decrease, 124,261).

Catholic Hospitals: 720. Patients treated, 34,728,822; increase, 557,257.

Nurses Schools: 121. Student nurses, 19,423; decrease, 713.

Homes for Aged: 497; decrease, 1. Residents, 63,245; increase, 342.

Orphanages: 207; children, 13,628. Children in foster homes, 16,456.

CATHEDRALS IN THE UNITED STATES

A cathedral is the principal church in a diocese, the one in which the bishop has his seat *(cathedra)*. He is the actual rector, although many functions of the church, which usually serves a parish, are the responsibility of a priest serving as the administrator. Because of the dignity of a cathedral, the dates of its dedication and its patronal feast are observed throughout a diocese.

The pope's cathedral, the Basilica of St. John Lateran, is the highest-ranking church in the world.

Albany, N.Y.: Immaculate Conception.

Alexandria-Shreveport, La.: St. Francis Xavier. (Alexandria); St. John Berchmans (Shreveport Co-Cathedral).

Allentown, Pa.: St. Catherine of Siena.

Altoona-Johnstown, Pa.: Blessed Sacrament (Altoona); St. John Gualbert (Johnstown Co-Cathedral).

Amarillo, Tex.: St. Laurence.

Anchorage,* Alaska: Holy Family.

Arlington, Va: St. Thomas More.

Atlanta,* Ga.: Christ the King.

Austin, Tex.: St. Mary (Immaculate Conception).

Baker, Ore.: St. Francis de Sales.

Baltimore,* Md.: Mary Our Queen; Basilica of the Assumption of the Blessed Virgin Mary (Co-Cathedral).

Baton Rouge, La.: St. Joseph.

Beaumont, Tex.: St. Anthony (of Padua).

Belleville, Ill.: St. Peter.

Biloxi, Miss.: Nativity of the Blessed Virgin.

Birmingham, Ala.: St. Paul.

Bismarck, N.D.: Holy Spirit.

Boise, Ida.: St. John the Evangelist.

Boston,* Mass.: Holy Cross.

Bridgeport, Conn.: St. Augustine.

Brooklyn, N.Y.: St. James.

Brownsville, Tex.: Immaculate Conception.

Buffalo, N.Y.: St. Joseph.

Burlington, Vt.: Immaculate Conception.

Camden, N.J.: Immaculate Conception.

Charleston, S.C.: St. John the Baptist.

Charlotte, N.C.: St. Patrick.

Cheyenne, Wyo.: St. Mary.

Chicago,* Ill.: Holy Name (of Jesus).

Cincinnati,* Ohio: St. Peter in Chains.

Cleveland, Ohio: St. John the Evangelist.

Columbus, Ohio: St. Joseph.

Corpus Christi, Tex.: Corpus Christi.

Covington, Ky.: Basilica of the Assumption.

Crookston, Minn.: Immaculate Conception.

Dallas, Tex.: Cathedral-Santuario de Guadalupe.

Davenport, Ia.: Sacred Heart.

Denver,* Colo.: Immaculate Conception (Minor Basilica).

Des Moines, Ia.: St. Ambrose.
Detroit,* Mich.: Blessed Sacrament.
Dodge City, Kans.: Sacred Heart.
Dubuque,* Ia.: St. Raphael.
Duluth, Minn.: Holy Rosary.
El Paso, Tex.: St. Patrick.
Erie, Pa.: St. Peter.
Evansville, Ind.: Most Holy Trinity (Pro-Cathedral).
Fairbanks, Alaska: Sacred Heart.
Fall River, Mass.: St. Mary of the Assumption.
Fargo, N.D.: St. Mary.
Fort Wayne-S. Bend, Ind.: Immaculate Conception (Fort Wayne); St. Matthew (South Bend Co-Cathedral).
Fort Worth, Tex.: St. Patrick.
Fresno, Calif.: St. John the Baptist.
Gallup, N.M.: Sacred Heart.
Galveston-Houston, Tex.: St. Mary (Minor Basilica, Galveston); Sacred Heart (Houston Co-Cathedral).
Gary, Ind.: Holy Angels.
Gaylord, Mich.: St. Mary, Our Lady of Mt. Carmel.
Grand Island, Nebr.: Nativity of Blessed Virgin Mary.
Grand Rapids, Mich.: St. Andrew.
Great Falls-Billings, Mont.: St. Ann (Great Falls); St. Patrick (Billings Co-Cathedral).
Green Bay, Wis.: St. Francis Xavier.
Greensburg, Pa.: Blessed Sacrament.
Harrisburg, Pa.: St. Patrick.
Hartford,* Conn.: St. Joseph.
Helena, Mont.: St. Helena.
Honolulu, Hawaii: Our Lady of Peace.
Houma-Thibodaux, La.: St. Francis de Sales (Houma); St. Joseph (Thibodaux Co-Cathedral).
Indianapolis,* Ind.: Sts. Peter and Paul.
Jackson, Miss.: St. Peter.
Jefferson City, Mo.: St. Joseph.
Joliet, Ill.: St. Raymond Nonnatus.
Juneau, Alaska: Nativity of the Blessed Virgin Mary.
Kalamazoo, Mich.: St. Augustine.
Kansas City,* Kans.: St. Peter the Apostle.
Kansas City-St. Joseph, Mo.: Immaculate Conception (Kansas City); St. Joseph (St. Joseph Co-Cathedral).
La Crosse, Wis.: St. Joseph.
Lafayette, Ind.: St. Mary.
Lafayette, La.: St. John the Evangelist.
Lake Charles, La.: Immaculate Conception.
Lansing, Mich.: St. Mary.
Lincoln, Nebr.: Cathedral of the Risen Christ.
Little Rock, Ark.: St. Andrew.
Los Angeles,* Calif.: St. Vibiana.
Louisville,* Ky.: Assumption.
Madison, Wis.: St. Raphael.
Manchester, N.H.: St. Joseph.
Marquette, Mich.: St. Peter.
Memphis, Tenn.: Immaculate Conception.

Miami,* Fla.: St. Mary (Immaculate Conception).
Milwaukee,* Wis.: St. John.
Mobile,* Ala.: Immaculate Conception (Minor Basilica).
Monterey, Calif.: San Carlos Borromeo.
Nashville, Tenn.: Incarnation.
Newark,* N.J.: Sacred Heart.
New Orleans,* La.: Cathedral (Basilica) of St. Louis.
Newton, Mass. (Melkite Rite): Our Lady of the Annunciation (Roslindale, Boston).
New Ulm, Minn.: Holy Trinity.
New York,* N.Y.: St. Patrick.
Norwich, Conn.: St. Patrick.
Oakland, Calif.: St. Francis de Sales.
Ogdensburg, N.Y.: St. Mary (Immaculate Conception).
Oklahoma City,* Okla.: Our Lady of Perpetual Help.
Omaha,* Nebr.: St. Cecilia.
Orange, Calif.: Holy Family.
Orlando, Fla.: St. James.
Owensboro, Ky.: St. Stephen.
Parma, Ohio (Byzantine Rite): St. John the Baptist.
Passaic, N.J. (Byzantine Rite): St. Michael.
Paterson, N.J.: St. John the Baptist.
Pensacola-Tallahassee, Fla.: Sacred Heart (Pensacola); St. Thomas More (Tallahassee Co-Cathedral).
Peoria, Ill.: St. Mary.
Philadelphia,* Pa.: Sts. Peter and Paul (Minor Basilica).
Philadelphia,* Pa. (Byzantine Rite): Immaculate Conception.
Phoenix, Ariz.: Sts. Simon and Jude.
Pittsburgh,* Pa. (Byzantine Rite): St. John the Baptist, Munhall.
Pittsburgh, Pa.: St. Paul.
Portland, Me.: Immaculate Conception.
Portland,* Ore.: Immaculate Conception.
Providence, R.I.: Sts. Peter and Paul.
Pueblo, Colo.: Sacred Heart.
Raleigh, N.C.: Sacred Heart.
Rapid City, S.D.: Our Lady of Perpetual Help.
Reno-Las Vegas, Nev.: St. Thomas Aquinas (Reno), Guardian Angel (Las Vegas Co-Cathedral).
Richmond, Va.: Sacred Heart.
Rochester, N.Y.: Sacred Heart.
Rockford, Ill.: St. Peter.
Rockville Centre, N.Y.: St. Agnes.
Sacramento, Calif.: Blessed Sacrament.
Saginaw, Mich.: St. Mary.
St. Augustine, Fla.: St. Augustine (Minor Basilica).
St. Cloud, Minn.: St. Mary.
St. Louis,* Mo.: St. Louis.
St. Maron, Brooklyn, N.Y. (Maronite Rite): Our Lady of Lebanon.
St. Nicholas in Chicago (Byzantine Rite): St. Nicholas.
St. Paul and Minneapolis,* Minn.: St. Paul

(St. Paul); Basilica of St. Mary (Minneapolis Co-Cathedral).

St. Petersburg, Fla.: St. Jude the Apostle.
Salina, Kans.: Sacred Heart.
Salt Lake City, Utah: The Madeleine.
San Angelo, Tex.: Sacred Heart.
San Antonio,* Tex.: San Fernando.
San Bernardino, Calif: Our Lady of the Rosary.
San Diego, Calif.: St. Joseph.
San Francisco,* Calif.: St. Mary (Assumption).
Santa Fe,* N.M.: San Francisco de Asis.
Santa Rosa, Calif.: St. Eugene.
Savannah, Ga.: St. John the Baptist.
Scranton, Pa.: St. Peter.
Seattle,* Wash.: St. James.
Sioux City, Ia.: Epiphany.
Sioux Falls, S.D.: St. Joseph.
Spokane, Wash.: Our Lady of Lourdes.
Springfield, Ill.: Immaculate Conception.
Springfield, Mass.: St. Michael.
Springfield-Cape Girardeau, Mo.: St. Agnes (Springfield): St. Mary (Cape Girardeau Co-Cathedral).
Stamford, Conn. (Byzantine Rite): St. Vladimir (Pro-Cathedral).
Steubenville, Ohio: Holy Name.
Stockton, Calif: Annunciation.
Superior, Wis.: Christ the King.
Syracuse, N.Y.: Immaculate Conception.
Toledo, Ohio: Blessed Virgin Mary of the Holy Rosary.
Trenton, N.J.: St. Mary (Assumption).
Tucson, Ariz.: St. Augustine.
Tulsa, Okla.: Holy Family.
Washington,* D.C.: St. Matthew.
Wheeling-Charleston, W. Va.: St. Joseph (Wheeling); Sacred Heart (Charleston Co-Cathedral).
Wichita, Kans.: Immaculate Conception.
Wilmington, Del.: St. Peter.
Winona, Minn.: Sacred Heart.
Worcester, Mass.: St. Paul.
Yakima, Wash.: St. Paul.
Youngstown, Ohio: St. Columba.

BASILICAS IN U.S., CANADA

Basilica is a title assigned to certain churches because of their antiquity, dignity, historical importance or significance as centers of worship. Major basilicas have the papal altar and holy door, which is opened at the beginning of a Jubilee Year; minor basilicas enjoy certain ceremonial privileges.

Among the major basilicas are the patriarchal basilicas of St. John Lateran, St. Peter, St. Paul Outside the Walls and St. Mary Major in Rome; St. Francis and St. Mary of the Angels in Assisi, Italy.

The patriarchal basilica of St. Lawrence, Rome, is a minor basilica.

The dates in the listings below indicate when the churches were designated as basilicas.

Minor Basilicas in U.S., Puerto Rico

Alabama: Mobile, Cathedral of the Immaculate Conception (Mar. 10, 1962).

California: San Francisco, Mission Dolores (Feb. 8, 1952); Carmel, Old Mission of San Carlos (Feb. 5, 1960); Alameda, St. Joseph (Jan. 21, 1972); San Diego, Mission San Diego de Alcala (Nov. 17, 1975).

Colorado: Denver, Cathedral of the Immaculate Conception (Nov. 3, 1979).

Florida: St. Augustine, Cathedral of St. Augustine (Dec. 4, 1976).

Illinois: Chicago, Our Lady of Sorrows (May 4, 1956), Queen of All Saints (Mar. 26, 1962).

Indiana: Vincennes, Old Cathedral (Mar. 14, 1970).

Iowa: Dyersville, St. Francis Xavier (May 11, 1956).

Kentucky: Trappist, Our Lady of Gethsemani (May 3, 1949); Covington, Cathedral of Assumption (Dec. 8, 1953).

Louisiana: New Orleans, St. Louis King of France (Dec. 9, 1964).

Maryland: Baltimore, Assumption of the Blessed Virgin Mary (Sept. 1, 1937).

Massachusetts: Roxbury, Perpetual Help ("Mission Church") (Sept. 8, 1954).

Michigan: Grand Rapids, St. Adalbert (Aug. 22, 1979).

Minnesota: Minneapolis. St. Mary (Feb. 1, 1926).

Missouri: Conception, Basilica of Immaculate Conception (Sept. 14, 1940); St. Louis, St. Louis King of France (Jan. 27, 1961).

New York: Brooklyn, Our Lady of Perpetual Help (Sept. 5, 1969); Buffalo, St. Adalbert's (Aug. 11, 1907); Lackawanna, Our Lady of Victory (1926); Youngstown, Blessed Virgin Mary of the Rosary of Fatima (Oct. 7, 1975).

Ohio: Carey, Shrine of Our Lady of Consolation (Oct. 21, 1971).

Pennsylvania: Latrobe, St. Vincent Basilica, Benedictine Archabbey (Aug. 22, 1955); Conewago, Basilica of the Sacred Heart (June 30, 1962); Philadelphia, Sts. Peter and Paul (Sept. 27, 1976).

Texas: Galveston, St. Mary Cathedral (Aug. 11, 1979).

Wisconsin: Milwaukee, St. Josaphat (Mar. 10, 1929).

Puerto Rico: San Juan, Cathedral of San Juan (Jan. 25, 1978).

Minor Basilicas in Canada

Manitoba: St. Boniface, Cathedral Basilica of St. Boniface (June 10, 1949).

Newfoundland: St. John's, Cathedral Basilica of St. John the Baptist.

Nova Scotia: Halifax, St. Mary's Basilica (June 14, 1950).

Ontario: Ottawa, Basilica of Notre Dame; London, St. Peter's Cathedral (Dec. 13, 1961).

Prince Edward Island: Charlottetown, Basilica of St. Dunstan.

Quebec: Sherbrooke, Cathedral Basilica of St. Michael (July 31, 1959). Montreal, Cathedral Basilica of St. James the Greater; St. Joseph of Mount Royal. Cap-de-la-Madeleine, Basilica of Our Lady of the Cape (Aug. 15, 1964). Quebec, Basilica of Notre Dame; St. Anne de Beaupre, Basilica of St. Anne.

CHANCERY OFFICES OF U.S. ARCHDIOCESES AND DIOCESES

A chancery office, under this or another title, is the central administrative office of an archdiocese or diocese.

(Archdioceses are indicated by asterisk.)

Albany, N.Y.: 465 State St., Box 6297, Quail Station. 12206.

Alexandria-Shreveport, La.: 2315 Texas Ave., P.O. Box 7417, Alexandria. 71306.

Allentown, Pa.: 202 N. 17th St., P.O. Box F. 18105.

Altoona-Johnstown, Pa.: Box 126, Logan Blvd., Hollidaysburg, Pa. 16648.

Amarillo, Tex.: 1800 N. Spring St., P.O. Box 5644. 79107.

Anchorage,* Alaska: P.O. Box 2239. 99510.

Arlington, Va.: 200 N. Glebe Rd. 22203.

Atlanta,* Ga.: Catholic Center, 680 W. Peachtree St. N.W. 30308.

Austin, Tex.: N. Congress and 16th, P.O. Box 13327. Capitol Sta. 78711.

Baker, Ore.: Baker and First Sts., P.O. Box 826, 97814.

Baltimore,* Md.: 320 Cathedral St. 21201.

Baton Rouge, La.: P.O. Box 2028. 70821.

Beaumont, Tex.: 703 Archie St., P.O. Box 3948. 77704.

Belleville, Ill.: 5312 W. Main St., Box 1048. 62223.

Biloxi, Miss.: P.O. Box 1189. 39533.

Birmingham, Ala.: P.O. Box 2086. 35201.

Bismarck, N.D.: 420 Raymond St., Box 1575. 58501.

Boise, Ida.: Box 769. 83701.

Boston,* Mass.: 2121 Commonwealth Ave., Brighton, Mass. 02135.

Bridgeport, Conn.: The Catholic Center, 238 Jewett Ave. 06606.

Brooklyn, N.Y.: 75 Greene Ave., P.O. Box C. 11202.

Brownsville, Tex.: P.O. Box 2279. 78520.

Buffalo, N.Y.: 35 Lincoln Parkway. 14222.

Burlington, Vt.: 351 North Ave. 05401.

Camden, N.J.: 1845 Haddon Ave., P.O. Box 709, 01801.

Charleston, S.C.: 119 Broad St., P.O. Box 818. 29402.

Charlotte, N.C.: P.O. Box 3776. 28203.

Cheyenne, Wyo.: Box 426. 82001.

Chicago,* Ill,: 155 E. Superior. 60611.

Cincinnati,* O.: 100 E. 8th St. 45202.

Cleveland, O.: Chancery Bldg., 1027 Superior Ave. 44114.

Columbus, O.: 198 E. Broad St. 43215.

Corpus Christi, Tex.: 620 Lipan St. 78401.

Covington, Ky.: 1140 Madison Ave., P.O. Box 192. 41012.

Crookston, Minn.: 1200 Memorial Dr., P.O. Box 610. 56716.

Dallas, Tex.: 3915 Lemmon Ave., P.O. Box 19507. 75219.

Davenport, Ia.: St. Vincent Center, 2706 Gaines St. 52804.

Denver,* Colo.: 200 Josephine St. 80206.

Des Moines, Ia.: 2910 Grand Ave., P.O. Box 1816. 50306.

Detroit,* Mich.: 1234 Washington Blvd. 48226.

Dodge City, Kans.: 910 Central Ave., P.O. Box 849. 67801.

Dubuque,* Ia.: 1229 Mt. Loretta Ave. 52001.

Duluth, Minn.: 215 W. 4th St. 55806.

El Paso, Tex.: 1200 N. Mesa St. 79902.

Erie, Pa.: 205 W. 9th St. 16501.

Evansville, Ind.: P.O. Box 4169. 47711.

Fairbanks, Alaska: 1316 Peger Rd. 99701.

Fall River, Mass.: 47 Underwood St., Box 2577. 02722.

Fargo, N.D.: 1310 Broadway, Box 1750. 58107.

Fort Wayne-South Bend, Ind.: P.O. Box 390, Fort Wayne. 46801.

Fort Worth, Tex.: 1206 Throckmorton St. 76102.

Fresno, Calif.: P.O. Box 1668, 1550 N. Fresno St. 93717.

Gallup, N. Mex.: 711 S. Puerco Dr., P.O. Box 1338. 87301.

Galveston-Houston, Tex.: 1700 San Jacinto St., Houston. 77002.

Gary, Ind.: 975 W. Sixth Ave., P.O. Box M-474. 46401.

Gaylord, Mich.: M-32 West, P.O. Box 700. 49735.

Grand Island, Nebr.: 311 W. 17th St., P.O. Box 996. 68801.

Grand Rapids, Mich.: 265 Sheldon Ave. S.E. 49503.

Great Falls-Billings, Mont.: P.O. Box 1399, Great Falls. 59403.

Green Bay, Wis.: Box 66. 54305.

Greensburg, Pa.: 723 E. Pittsburgh St. 15601.

Harrisburg, Pa.: P.O. Box 2153. 17105.

Hartford,* Conn.: 134 Farmington Ave. 06105.

Helena, Mont.: 612 Harrison Ave., P.O. Box 1729. 59601.

Honolulu, Hawaii: 1184 Bishop St. 96813.

Houma-Thibodaux, La.: 1220 Aycock St., P.O. Box 9077, Houma, La. 70361.

Indianapolis,* Ind.: 1350 N. Pennsylvania St. 46202.

Jackson, Miss.: 237 E. Amite St., P.O. Box 2248. 39205.

Jefferson City, Mo.: 605 Clark Ave. P.O. Box 417. 65101.

Joliet, Ill.: 425 Summit St. 60435.

Juneau, Alaska: 416 5th St. 99801.

Kalamazoo, Mich.: 215 N. Westnedge. Ave. 49005.

Kansas City,* Kans.: 2220 Central Ave., P.O. Box 2328. 66110.

Kansas City-St. Joseph, Mo.: P.O. Box 1037, Kansas City. 64141.

La Crosse, Wis.: P.O. Box 69. 54601.

Lafayette in Indiana: 610 Lingle Ave. 47902.

Lafayette, La.: P.O. Drawer 3387. 70502.

Lake Charles, La.: P.O. Box 3223. 70601.

Lansing, Mich.: 300 W. Ottawa. 48933.

Lincoln, Nebr.: 3400 Sheridan Blvd., P.O. Box 80328. 68501.

Little Rock, Ark.: 2415 N. Tyler St. 72217.

Los Angeles,* Calif.: 1531 W. 9th St. 90015.

Louisville,* Ky.: 212 E. College St., P.O. Box 1073. 40201.

Madison, Wis.: 15 E. Wilson St. 53701.

Manchester, N. H.: 153 Ash St. 03105.

Marquette, Mich.: 444 S. Fourth St., P.O. Box 550. 49855.

Memphis, Tenn.: 1325 Jefferson Ave., 38104.

Miami,* Fla.: 6301 Biscayne Blvd. 33138.

Milwaukee,* Wis.: 345 N. 95th St., P.O. Box 2018. 53201.

Mobile,* Ala.: 400 Government St., P.O. Box 1966. 36601.

Monterey, Calif.: 580 Fremont Blvd. 93940.

Nashville, Tenn.: 2400 21st Ave. S. 37219.

Newark,* N.J.: 31 Mulberry St. 07102.

New Orleans,* La.: 7887 Walmsley Ave. 70125.

Newton, Mass. (Melkite Rite): 19 Dartmouth St., W. Newton, Mass. 02165.

New Ulm, Minn.: 1400 Chancery Drive. 56073.

New York,* N.Y.: 1011 First Ave. 10022.

Norwich, Conn.: 201 Broadway, P.O. Box 587. 06360.

Oakland, Calif.: 2900 Lakeshore Ave. 94610.

Ogdensburg, N.Y.: 622 Washington St. 13669.

Oklahoma City,* Okla.: P.O. Box 18838. 73154.

Omaha,* Nebr.: 100 N. 62nd St. 68132.

Orange, Calif.: 440 S. Batavia St. 92668.

Orlando, Fla.: P.O. Box 1800. 32802.

Owensboro, Ky.: 4003 Frederica St. 42301.

Parma, Ohio (Byzantine Rite): 1900 Carlton Rd. 44134.

Passaic, N.J. (Byzantine Rite): 101 Market St. 07055.

Paterson, N.J.: 777 Valley Rd., Clifton. 07013.

Pensacola-Tallahassee, Fla.: 11 N. "B" St., Pensacola. 32501.

Peoria, Ill.: 607 N.E. Madison Ave., P.O. Box 1406. 61655.

Philadelphia,* Pa.: 222 N. 17th St. 19103.

Philadelphia,* Pa. (Byzantine Rite): 815 N. Franklin St. 19123.

Phoenix, Ariz.: 400 E. Monroe St. 85004.

Pittsburgh,* Pa. (Byzantine Rite): 54 Riverview Ave. 15214.

Pittsburgh, Pa.: 111 Blvd. of the Allies. 15222.

Portland, Me.: 510 Ocean Ave., Woodfords P.O. Box H. 04103.

Portland in Oregon*: 2838 E. Burnside St. 97214.

Providence, R.I.: One Cathedral Sq. 02903.

Pueblo, Colo.: 1426 Grand Ave. 81003.

Raleigh, N.C.: 300 Cardinal Gibbons Dr. 27606.

Rapid City, S.D.: 606 Cathedral Dr., P.O. Box 678. 57709.

Reno-Las Vegas, Nev.: 515 Court St., Reno 89509. (Mailing address: P.O. Box 1211, Reno. 89504.)

Richmond, Va.: 811 Cathedral Pl., Suite C. 23220.

Rochester, N.Y.: 1150 Buffalo Rd. 14624.

Rockford, Ill.: 1245 N. Court St. 61101.

Rockville Centre, N.Y.: 50 N. Park Ave. 11570.

Sacramento, Calif.: 1119 K St., P.O. Box 1706. 95808.

Saginaw, Mich.: 5800 Weiss St. 48603.

St. Augustine, Fla.: Suite 1648, Gulf Life Tower, Jacksonville, Fla. 32207.

St. Cloud, Minn.: P.O. Box 1248. 56301.

St. Louis,* Mo.: 4445 Lindell Blvd. 63108.

St. Maron (Maronite Rite), Brooklyn, N.Y.: 205 82nd St., P.O. Box 333, Ft. Hamilton Sta., Brooklyn. 11209.

St. Nicholas in Chicago (Byzantine Rite): 2245 W. Rice St. 60622.

St. Paul and Minneapolis,* Minn.: 226 Summit Ave., St. Paul. 55102.

St. Petersburg, Fla.: 6363 9th Ave. N. 33710. P.O. Box 13109. 33733.

Salina, Kans.: 421 Country Club Rd., P.O. Box 999. 67401.

Salt Lake City, Utah: 333 E. S. Temple. 84111.

San Angelo, Tex.: 116 S. Oakes. Box 1829. 76902.

San Antonio,* Tex.: 9123 Lorene Lane, P.O. Box 32648. 78284.

San Bernardino, Calif.: 1450 North D St. 92405.

San Diego, Calif.: P.O. Box 80428. 92138.

San Francisco,* Calif.: 445 Church St. 94114.

Santa Fe,* N. Mex.: 202 Morningside Dr. S.E., Albuquerque. 87108.

Santa Rosa, Calif.: 547 "B" St., P.O. Box 1297. 95402.

Savannah, Ga.: 225 Abercorn St., P.O. Box 8789. 31412.

Scranton, Pa.: 300 Wyoming Ave. 18503.

Seattle,* Wash.: 907 Terry Ave. 98104.

Sioux City, Ia.: P.O. Box 1530. 51102.

Sioux Falls, S.D.: 423 N. Duluth Ave. 57104.

Spokane, Wash.: 1023 W. Riverside Ave. 99201.

Springfield, Illinois: 524 E. Lawrence Ave. 62705.

Springfield, Mass.: 76 Elliot St. 01105. P.O. Box 1730, 01101.

Springfield-Cape Girardeau, Mo.: 200 McDaniel Bldg., Springfield. 65806.

Stamford, Conn. (Byzantine Rite): 161 Glenbrook Rd. 06902.

Steubenville, Ohio: 422 Washington St., P.O. Box 969. 43952.

Stockton, Calif.: 1105 N. Lincoln St. 95203. P.O. Box 4237. 95204.

Superior, Wis.: 1201 Hughitt Ave. 54880.

Syracuse, N.Y.: 240 E. Onondaga St., 13202.

Toledo, Ohio: 2544 Parkwood Ave. 43610.

Trenton, N.J.: 701 Lawrenceville Rd. 08648.

Tucson, Ariz.: 192 S. Stone Ave., Box 31, 85702.

Tulsa, Okla.: P.O. Box 2009. 74101.

Washington,* D.C.: 1721 Rhode Island Ave. N.W. 20036.

Wheeling-Charleston, W. Va.: 1300 Byron St., Wheeling. 26003.

Wichita, Kans.: 424 N. Broadway. 67202.

Wilmington, Del.: P.O. Box 2030. 19899.

Winona, Minn.: P.O. Box 588. 55987.

Worcester, Mass.: 49 Elm St. 01609.

Yakima, Wash.: 222 Washington Mutual Bldg., P.O. Box 505. 98907.

Youngstown, Ohio: 144 W. Wood St. 44503.

NATIONAL CATHOLIC CONFERENCES

The two conferences described below are related in membership and directive control but distinct in nature, purpose and function.

The National Conference of Catholic Bishops (NCCB) is a strictly ecclesiastical body in and through which the bishops of the United States act together, officially and with authority as pastors of the Church. It is the sponsoring organization of the United States Catholic Conference.

The United States Catholic Conference (USCC) is a civil corporation and operational secretariat in and through which the bishops, together with other members of the Church, act on a wider scale for the good of the Church and society. It is sponsored by the National Conference of Catholic Bishops.

The principal officers of both conferences are: Archbishop John R. Quinn, president; Archbishop John R. Roach, vice president; Archbishop Thomas A. Donnellan, treasurer; Bishop Thomas C. Kelly, O.P., general secretary.

The membership of the Administrative Committee of the NCCB and the Administrative Board of the USCC is identical.

Headquarters of both conferences are located at 1312 Massachusetts Ave. N.W., Washington, D.C. 20005.

NCCB

The National Conference of Catholic Bishops, established by action of the U.S. hierarchy Nov. 14, 1966, is a strictly ecclesiastical body with defined juridical authority over the Church in this country. It was set up with the approval of the Holy See and in line with directives from the Second Vatican Council. Its constitution was formally ratified during the November, 1967, meeting of the U.S. hierarchy.

The NCCB is a development from the Annual Meeting of the Bishops of the United States, whose pastoral character was originally approved by Pope Benedict XV Apr. 10, 1919.

The address of the Conference is 1312 Massachusetts Ave. N.W., Washington, D.C. 20005.

Pastoral Council

The conference, one of many similar territorial conferences envisioned in the conciliar *Decree on the Pastoral Office of Bishops in the Church* (No. 38), is "a council in which the bishops of a given nation or territory (in this case, the United States) jointly exercise their pastoral office to promote the greater good which the Church offers mankind, especially through the forms and methods of the apostolate fittingly adapted to the circumstances of the age."

Its decisions, "provided they have been approved legitimately and by the votes of at least two-thirds of the prelates who have a deliberative vote in the conference, and have been recognized by the Apostolic See, are to have juridically binding force only in those cases prescribed by the common law or determined by a special mandate of the Apostolic See, given either spontaneously or in response to a petition of the conference itself."

All bishops who serve the Church in the U.S., its territories and possessions, have membership and voting rights in the NCCB.

Officers, Committees

The conference operates through a number of bishops' committees with functions in specific areas of work and concern. Their basic assignments are to prepare materials on the basis of which the bishops, assembled as a conference, make decisions, and to put suitable action plans into effect.

The principal officers are: Archbishop John R. Quinn, president; Archbishop John R. Roach, vice president; Archbishop Thomas A. Donnellan, treasurer; Bishop Thomas C. Kelly, O.P., general secretary.

These officers, with several other bishops, hold positions on executive-level committees — Executive Committee, the Committee on Budget and Finance, the Committee on Personnel and Administrative Services, and the Committee on Research, Plans and Programs. They also, with other bishops, serve on the NCCB Administrative Board.

The standing committees and their chairmen (Archbishops and Bishops) are as follows.

American Board of Catholic Missions, John J. Fitzpatrick.

Boundaries of Dioceses and Provinces, John R. Quinn.

Canon Law, Joseph L. Bernardin.

Church in Latin America, Juan Arzube.

Conciliation and Arbitration, George H. Guilfoyle.

Doctrine, James A. Hickey.

Ecumenical and Interreligious Affairs, Ernest L. Unterkoefler.

Human Values, Austin B. Vaughan.

Laity, Albert H. Ottenweller.

Liaison with Priests, Religious and Laity, Joseph A. McNicholas.

Liturgy, Rembert Weakland, O.S.B.

Men Religious, Joseph A. Francis.

Missions, William G. Connare.

Nomination of Bishops, John R. Quinn.

North American College, Louvain, Edward W. O'Rourke

North American College, Rome, Andrew G. Grutka.

Pastoral Research and Practices, Norman F. McFarland.

Permanent Diaconate, Eugene A. Marino.

Priestly Formation, Michael J. Murphy.

Priestly Life and Ministry, Justin A. Driscoll.

Vocations, Kenneth J. Povish.

Welfare Emergency Relief, John R. Quinn.

Women Religious, Frank J. Harrison.

Ad hoc committees and their chairmen are as follows.

Call to Action Plan, John R. Roach.

Catholic Charismatic Renewal, Kenneth J. Povish.

Evangelization, Edward T. O'Meara.

Farm Labor, James S. Rausch.

Hispanic Affairs, Robert Sanchez.

Inter-Rite, William G. Connare.

Liaison with National Office for Black Catholics, Eugene A. Marino.

Marxism-Communism, Joseph A. McNicholas.

Migration and Tourism, Rene H. Gracida.

Parishes, Edward C. O'Leary.

Pro-Life Activities, Cardinal Terence J. Cooke.

Women in Society and Church, Michael F. McAuliffe.

USCC

The United States Catholic Conference, Inc. (USCC), is the operational secretariat and service agency of the National Conference of Catholic Bishops for carrying out the civic-religious work of the Church in this country. It is a civil corporation related to the NCCB in membership and directive control but distinct from it in purpose and function.

The address of the Conference is 1312 Massachusetts Ave. N.W., Washington, D.C. 20005.

Service Secretariat

The USCC, as of Jan. 1, 1967, took over the general organization and operations of the former National Catholic Welfare Conference, Inc., whose origins dated back to the National Catholic War Council of 1917. The council underwent some change after World War I and was established on a permanent basis Sept. 24, 1919, as the National Catholic Welfare Council to serve as a central agency for organizing and coordinating the efforts of U.S. Catholics in carrying out the social mission of the Church in this country. In 1923, its name was changed to National Catholic Welfare Conference, Inc., and clarification was made of its nature as a service agency of the bishops and the Church rather than as a conference of bishops with real juridical authority in ecclesiastical affairs.

The Official Catholic Directory states that the USCC assists "the bishops in their service to the Church in this country by uniting the people of God where voluntary collective action on a broad interdiocesan level is needed. The USCC provides an organizational structure and the resources needed to insure coordination, cooperation, and assistance in the public, educational and social concerns of the Church at the national or interdiocesan level."

Officers, Departments

The principal officers of the USCC are Archbishop John R. Quinn, president; Archbishop John R. Roach, vice president; Archbishop Thomas A. Donnellan, treasurer; Bishop Thomas C. Kelly, O.P., general secretary. These officers, with several other bishops, hold positions on executive-level committees — the Executive Committee; the Committee on Research, Plans and Programs; the Committee on Budget and Finance; the Committee on Personnel and Administrative Services. They also serve on the Administrative Board.

The Executive Committee, organized in 1969, is authorized to handle matters of urgency between meetings of the Administrative Board and the general conference, to coordinate items for the agenda of general meetings, and to speak in the name of the USCC.

The major departments and their chairmen (Archbishops and Bishops) are: Communications, Norbert F. Gaughan; Education, Daniel E. Pilarczyk; Social Development and World Peace, Edward D. Head. Each department is supervised by a committee composed of an equal number of episcopal and non-episcopal members, including lay persons.

A national Advisory Council of bishops, priests, men and women religious, lay men and women advises the Administrative Board on overall plans and operations of the USCC.

The administrative general secretariat, in addition to other duties, supervises staff-service offices of Finance and Administration, General Counsel, Government Liaison, and Research, Plans and Programs.

Most of the organizations and associations affiliated with the USCC are covered in separate Almanac entries.

NCCB-USCC REGIONS

For meeting and other operational purposes, the members of the National Conference of Catholic Bishops and the U.S. Catholic Conference are grouped in the following geographical regions.

I. Maine, Vermont, New Hampshire, Massachusetts, Rhode Island, Connecticut.

II. New York.

III. New Jersey, Pennsylvania.

IV. Delaware, District of Columbia, Florida, Georgia, Maryland, North Carolina, South Carolina, Virgin Islands, Virginia, West Virginia.

V. Alabama, Kentucky, Louisiana, Mississippi, Tennessee.

VI. Michigan, Ohio.

VII. Illinois, Indiana, Wisconsin.

VIII. Minnesota, North Dakota, South Dakota, Wyoming, Colorado.

IX. Iowa, Kansas, Missouri, Nebraska.

X. Arizona, Arkansas, New Mexico, Oklahoma, Texas.

XI. California, Hawaii, Nevada, Utah, Caroline-Marshall Islands, Guam.

XII. Idaho, Montana, Alaska, Washington, Oregon.

MEETINGS OF THE CONFERENCES OF BISHOPS

November 12 to 15, 1979

The meeting, held in Washington, D.C., was attended by more than 250 members of the U.S. hierarchy. The presiding officer was Archbishop John R. Quinn, president of the National Conference of Catholic Bishops and the U.S. Catholic Conference.

Budget: Approved, 119 to 32, a 1980 budget of $14.5 million and an increase, to 10 cents a Catholic, in diocesan assessments for support of the conferences and their operations on the national level. (The 1979 budget was $12.6 million.)

Cambodia: Issued a statement on the critical condition of the population and refugees in Cambodia, declaring that the situation there would "require concerted international action for many months to avert the death of a nation." The statement commended emergency assistance rendered by Catholic Relief Services and its supporters.

Census: Agreed to encourage participation in the federal census of 1980, especially by undocumented aliens, but refused direct involvement in registration procedures.

Communications: Received a report stating that the sum of $1 million had been collected in 1979 for the support (50-50) of national and diocesan media projects. Additional funds were expected from other sources.

Conciliation and Arbitration: Authorized a committee to bring conference-level due-process procedures "into line with procedures already endorsed for use on the diocesan level."

Hostages: Issued a statement on the plight of American hostages detained since Nov. 4 by Iranian students in the U.S. embassy in Teheran. They called the situation "a test of law for the international community and a test of policy for the United States," and noted that the survival and release of the hostages were the subjects of most urgent concern.

Liturgical Language: Turned down, for want of two-thirds majority votes, two proposals of the Committee on the Liturgy for the elimination of some words and the substitution of others explicitly referring to both sexes in: (1) the formula for the consecration of wine in the eucharistic prayers, in which the generic word, "men," is used; (2) other prayers of the Mass, the Liturgy of the Hours and sacramental rituals. The votes in favor of the proposals — 157 to 98 and 142 to 113, respectively — were short of the 189 required for passage. It was noted that changes were not proposed for Christological texts or scriptural translations. (If the proposals had been adopted, they would have required additional approval of the Holy See.)

Papal Visit and Dialogue: Heard addresses by Archbishop John R. Quinn, president of the conferences, and Archbishop Jean Jadot, apostolic delegate to the U.S., in praise of the visit of Pope John Paul to the U.S. Oct. 1 to 7, 1979; and passed a resolution of gratitude to the Holy Father. An amendment to the resolution, signed by 27 bishops and referred to a committee for action, requested an opportunity for dialogue with the Pope for the purpose of representing to him "the experience and needs of the local church."

Plans and Meetings: Approved a three-year planning program for activities of the conferences and a proposal to meet once instead of twice a year, starting in 1981. Also favored was a recommendation to convene occasionally for special purposes, as the bishops of Latin America did at Puebla, Mexico, early in 1979. (For coverage of the Puebla meeting, see Third General Assembly of Latin American Bishops, 1979 *Catholic Almanac,* pp. 85 to 87.)

Racism: Approved, 215 to 30, and issued a pastoral letter on racism, entitled "Brothers and Sisters to Us." (See separate entry.)

Reports: Received reports on a variety of subjects.

• Meeting of the Latin American bishops, Jan. 27 to Feb. 13, 1979, at Puebla, Mexico, by Archbishop Marcos McGrath of Panama.

• Meeting of the College of Cardinals with Pope John Paul, Nov. 5 to 9. (See entry in News Events.)

• Progress of plans and programs for family ministry, starting with the 1980 Family Year.

• Need for military chaplains, whose ratio was one to 2,800 Catholics in the armed services.

• Appeal for support of the 100-year-old Bureau of Catholic Indian Missions.

• Follow-up programs of the 1976 Call to Action Conference, in effect in no more than 30 dioceses.

• Program for the training of students for the priesthood, for further consideration and decision by November, 1980.

April 29 to May 1, 1980

Two hundred and 50 bishops attended the meeting in Chicago. It was the last such spring meeting of this type.

Presidential Address: Archbishop John R. Quinn reviewed a number of developments since the previous meeting which posed "complex and burdensome" challenges to the Church and the world. These included pastoral concerns regarding the family, sexual morality, subjects related to the censure of Father Hans Kung, and the moral implications of a wide variety of national and international issues.

Budget: A cut of $857,000 in the current budget of $14.5 million was approved, involving the probable discharge of 36 of 365 employees and the curtailment of some services. Also approved was a 1981 assessment of 10 cents per Catholic for conference support.

Communications: A committee report recommended steps toward establishment of a national Catholic telecommunications network through the use of satellite technology.

Extraordinary Meeting: Approval was voted for a proposal calling for a special meeting devoted to in-depth consideration of the role of bishops. It was thought the meeting might be held in 1982.

Health Ministry: The general approach of a pastoral letter was approved, with further action deferred until the November, 1980, meeting. The draft indicated support for a national health insurance program despite reservations on the part of the Catholic Health Association and some Catholic professionals in health care. (The administrative board decided in September to submit a draft of the letter at the November, 1980, meeting for discussion and to delay voting until differences of opinion could be ironed out.)

Hispanic Ministry: The bishops received a report citing critical needs in this ministry. One commentator called attention to the necessity of a "fundamental change of attitude" toward this ministry, with full regard for Hispanic identity, culture and tradition.

Iranian Crisis: The bishops approved a resolution in which they urged President Carter to follow a policy of restraint. The resolution said, in part:

"While we recognize the frustrations of the Iranian people, we nonetheless condemn, on religious, moral and legal grounds, the taking and holding of hostages.

"We also understand and share the frustration of the American people over the repeated thwarting of our President's patient negotiations to free the hostages from imprisonment.

"The teaching of the Church on peace, however, affirms that resort to military force is not justifiable when other courses of action are available. We question whether resorting to military force in the present circumstances would meet the moral criteria of prudence and justice."

Liturgy: Archbishop Rembert Weakland reported that the Liturgy Committee had approved a resolution dealing with the problem of holy days of obligation which fall back-to-back with Sundays. The resolution was not released to the press. It was also reported that the question of so-called sexist language in liturgical texts might be raised at a future meeting of the conference.

Priorities: Studies were ordered of the direction, resources and influence of conference structures, programs and activities, for establishing and ordering priorities. Leading priorities were said to be doctrinal concern, pro-life activities, government liaison and services of the general counsel. Continuation was approved of the Secretariat for the Laity and the Ad Hoc Committee for Evangelization, subject to priority decisions and budgetary consideratons.

Refugees from Cuba and Haiti: The bishops approved a resolution urging President Carter to grant asylum and permanent residence to the refugees. Archbishop Edward A. McCarthy of Miami introduced the proposal, saying: "We assure the Administration, as we have in the past, that the Church will do its utmost to provide resettlement opportunities, including employment and housing, for these people."

STATE CONFERENCES

These conferences are agencies of bishops and dioceses in the various states. Their general purposes are to develop and sponsor cooperative programs designed to cope with pastoral and common-welfare needs, and to represent the dioceses before governmental bodies, the public, and in private sectors. Their membership consists of representatives from the dioceses in the states — bishops, clergy and lay persons in various capacities.

The **National Association of State Catholic Conference Directors** maintains liaison with the general secretariat of the United States Catholic Conference. Thomas A. Horkan, Jr., of Florida is president.

Alaska Catholic Conference, 416 5th St., Juneau, Alaska 99801; exec. dir., Frank W. Matulich.

Arizona Catholic Conference, 400 E. Monroe St., Phoenix, Ariz. 85004; exec. dir., Thomas F. Allt.

California Catholic Conference, 926 J St., Suite 1100, Sacramento, Calif. 95814; exec. dir., Msgr. John A. Dickie.

Colorado Catholic Conference, 200 Josephine St., Denver, Colo. 80206; exec. dir., Sr. Loretto Anne Madden, S.L.

Connecticut Catholic Conference, 134 Farmington Ave., Hartford, Conn. 06105; exec. dir., William Wholean.

Florida Catholic Conference, P.O. Box 1571, Tallahassee, Fla. 32302; exec. dir., Thomas A. Horkan, Jr.

Georgia Catholic Conference, P.O. Box 4129, Augusta, Ga. 30907; exec. dir., Cheatham E. Hodges, Jr.

Hawaii Catholic Conference, 1184 Bishop St., Honolulu, H.I. 96813; exec. sex., Mrs. Maggie Bunson.

Illinois Catholic Conference, One East Superior St., Chicago, Ill. 60611; 300 E. Monroe St., Springfield, Ill. 62701; exec. dir., Rev. William J. Lion.

Indiana Catholic Conference, Suite 315, 5435 Emerson Way N., Indianapolis, Ind. 46226; exec. dir., Raymond R. Rufo.

Iowa Catholic Conference, 818 Insurance Exchange Building, Des Moines, Iowa 50309; exec. dir., Timothy McCarthy.

Kansas Catholic Conference, 702 Commercial National Bank Bldg., Kansas City, Kan. 66101; exec. dir., Vincent W. DeCoursey.

Kentucky Catholic Conference, P.O. Box 1073, Louisville, Ky. 40201; chairman, Most Rev. Thomas J. McDonough, Archbishop of Louisville.

Louisiana Catholic Conference, P.O. Box 52948, New Orleans, La. 70152; exec. dir., Emile Comar.

Maryland Catholic Conference, 320 Cathedral St., Baltimore, Md. 21201; exec. dir., Francis X. McIntyre.

Massachusetts Catholic Conference, Parker House, Room 180, Boston, Mass. 02107; exec. dir., Gerald D. D'Avolio, Esq.

Michigan Catholic Conference, P.O. Box 10157, Lansing, Mich. 48901; exec. dir., Msgr. Herman H. Zerfas.

Minnesota Catholic Conference, 145 University Ave., W., St. Paul, Minn. 55103; exec. dir., Msgr. James D. Habiger.

Missouri Catholic Conference, P.O. Box 1022, Jefferson City, Mo. 65102; exec. dir., Miss Peggy J. Keilholz.

Montana Catholic Conference, P.O. Box 1708, Helena, Mont. 59601; exec. dir., John Frankino.

Nebraska Catholic Conference, 521 S. 14th St., Lincoln, Nebr. 68508; exec. dir., James R. Cunningham.

New Jersey Catholic Conference, 211 N. Warren St., Trenton, N.J. 08618; exec. dir., Edward J. Leadem.

New York State Catholic Conference, 11 N. Pearl St., Albany, N.Y. 12207; exec. dir., J. Alan Davitt.

North Dakota Catholic Conference, 107 N. 4th St. — Room 11, Bismarck, N. Dak. 58501; exec. dir., Mrs. Kitty Engelstad.

Ohio, Catholic Conference of, 174 E. Long St., Suite 600, Columbus, Ohio 43215; exec. dir., Theodore N. Staudt.

Oregon Catholic Conference, 2838 E. Burnside, Portland, Ore. 97214; sec., Rev. Joseph Jacobberger.

Pennsylvania Catholic Conference, 509 N. Second St., Harrisburg, Pa. 17105; exec. dir., Howard J. Fetterhoff.

Texas Catholic Conference, 3001 S. Congress Ave., Austin, Tex. 78704; exec. dir., Bro. Richard Daly, C.S.C.

Washington State Catholic Conference, 1319 2nd Ave., Seattle, Wash. 98101; exec. dir. Rev. D. Harvey McIntyre.

Wisconsin Catholic Conference, 30 W. Mifflin St., Suite 910, Madison, Wis. 53703; exec. dir., Charles M. Phillips.

The Internal Revenue Service informed the United Church of Christ in October, 1980, that it could resume publishing voting records of members of Congress because the records were not tied to a political campaign. The decision was made only days after the church instituted suit against the IRS on the grounds that a 1978 ruling, limiting the publication of voting records and other voter education projects by tax-exempt, non-profit organizations, was a violation of freedom of speech.

The decision was announced in a 'private letter ruling,' of a type requested by specific organizations seeking clarification of IRS regulations affecting them. An IRS spokesman said the agency was not free to comment on interpretations of the ruling or its impact on other tax exempt groups — including diocesan newspapers — publishing voter education material.

Biographies of American Bishops

(Sources: Almanac survey, *The Official Catholic Directory,* NC News Service. As of Oct. 1, 1980.)

A

Abramowicz, Alfred L.: b. Jan. 27, 1919, Chicago, Ill.; educ. St. Mary of the Lake Seminary (Mundelein, Ill.), Gregorian Univ. (Rome); ord. priest May 1, 1943; ord. titular bishop of Paestum and auxiliary bishop of Chicago, June 13, 1968.

Ackerman, Richard Henry, C.S.Sp.: b. Aug. 30, 1903, Pittsburgh, Pa.; educ. Duquesne Univ. (Pittsburgh, Pa.), St. Mary's Scholasticate (Norwalk, Conn.), Univ. of Fribourg (Switzerland); ord. priest Aug. 28, 1926; ord. titular bishop of Lares and auxiliary bishop of San Diego, May 22, 1956; app. bishop of Covington, Apr. 4, 1960; resigned Nov. 28, 1978.

Ahern, Patrick V.: b. Mar. 8, 1919, New York, N.Y.; educ. Manhattan College and Cathedral College (New York City), St. Joseph's Seminary (Yonkers, N.Y.), St. Louis Univ. (St. Louis, Mo.), Notre Dame Univ. (Notre Dame, Ind.); ord. priest Jan. 27, 1945; ord. titular bishop of Naiera and auxiliary bishop of New York, Mar. 19, 1970.

Ahr, George William: b. June 23, 1904, Newark, N.J.; educ. St. Vincent College (Latrobe, Pa.), Seton Hall College (S. Orange, N.J.), North American College (Rome); ord. priest July 29, 1928; ord. bishop of Trenton, Mar. 20, 1950; resigned 1979.

Anderson, Paul F.: b. Apr. 20, 1917, Roslindale, Mass.; educ. Boston College (Chestnut Hill, Mass.), St. John's Seminary (Brighton, Mass.); ord. priest Jan. 6, 1943; ord. titular bishop of Polignando and coadjutor bishop of Duluth, Oct. 17, 1968; bishop of Duluth, Apr. 30, 1969.

Angell, Kenneth A.: b. Aug. 3, 1930, Providence, R.I.; educ. St. Mary's Seminary (Baltimore, Md.); ord. priest May 26, 1956; ord. titular bishop of Septimunicia and auxiliary bishop of Providence, R.I., Oct. 7, 1974.

Arkfeld, Leo, S.V.D.: b. Feb. 4, 1912, Butte, Nebr.; educ. Divine Word Seminary (Techny, Ill.), Sacred Heart College (Girard, Pa.); ord. priest Aug. 15, 1943; ord. titular bishop of Bucellus and vicar apostolic of Central New Guinea, Nov. 30, 1948; name of vicariate changed to Wewak, May 15, 1952; first bishop of Wewak, Nov. 15, 1966; app. archbishop of Madang, Papua New Guinea, Dec. 19, 1975.

Arliss, Reginald, C.P.: b. Sept. 8, 1906, East Orange, N.J.; educ. Immaculate Conception Seminary (Jamaica, N.Y.) and other Passionist houses of study; ord. priest Apr. 28, 1934; missionary in China for 16 years, expelled 1951; missionary in Philippines; rector of the Pontifical Philippine College Seminary in Rome, 1961-69; ord. titular bishop of Cerbali and prelate of Marbel, Philippines, Jan. 30, 1970.

Arzube, Juan: b. June 1, 1918, Guayaquil, Ecuador; educ. Rensselaer Polytechnic Institute (Troy, N.Y.), St. John's Seminary (Camarillo, Calif.); ord. priest May 5, 1954; ord. titular bishop of Civitate and auxiliary bishop of Los Angeles, Mar. 25, 1971.

B

Balke, Victor: b. Sept. 29, 1931, Meppen, Ill.; educ. St. Mary of the Lake Seminary (Mundelein, Ill.), St. Louis Univ. (St. Louis, Mo.); ord. priest May 24, 1958; ord. bishop of Crookston, Sept. 2, 1976.

Bartholome, Peter William: b. Apr. 2, 1893, Bellechester, Minn.; educ. Campion College (Prairie du Chien, Wis.), St. Paul Seminary (St. Paul, Minn.), Apollinare (Rome); ord. priest June 12, 1917; ord. titular bishop of Lete and coadjutor bishop of St. Cloud, Mar. 3, 1942; bishop of St. Cloud, May 31, 1953; resigned 1968.

Baum, William W.: (See Cardinals, Biographies.)

Begley, Michael J.: b. Mar. 12, 1909, Mattineague, Mass.; educ. Mt. St. Mary Seminary (Emmitsburg, Md.); ord. priest May 26, 1934; ord. first bishop of Charlotte, N.C., Jan. 12, 1972.

Bell, Alden J.: b. July 11, 1904, Peterborough, Ont., Canada; educ. St. Joseph's College (Mountain View, Calif.), St. Patrick's Seminary (Menlo Park, Calif.), Catholic Univ. (Washington, D.C.); ord. priest May 14, 1932; ord. titular bishop of Rhodopolis and auxiliary bishop of Los Angeles, June 4, 1956; app. bishop of Sacramento, Mar. 30, 1962; resigned 1979.

Beltran, Eusebius J.: b. Aug. 31, 1934, Ashley, Pa.; educ. St. Charles Seminary (Philadelphia, Pa.); ord. priest May 14, 1960; ord. bishop of Tulsa Apr. 20, 1978.

Benincasa, Pius A.: b. July 8, 1913, Niagara Falls, N.Y.: educ. Propaganda Univ. and Lateran Univ. (Rome); ord. priest Mar. 27, 1937; served in Vatican Secretariat of State, 1954-64; ord. titular bishop of Buruni and auxiliary bishop of Buffalo, June 29, 1964.

Bernardin, Joseph L.: b. Apr. 2, 1928, Columbia, S.C.; educ. St. Mary's Seminary (Baltimore, Md.), Catholic Univ. (Washington, D.C.); ord. priest Apr. 26, 1952; ord. titular bishop of Lugura and auxiliary bishop of Atlanta, Apr. 26, 1966; general secretary of the USCC and NCCB, 1968-72; app. archbishop of Cincinnati, Nov. 21, 1972; installed Dec. 19, 1972; president NCCB/USCC, 1974-77.

Bernarding, George, S.V.D.: b. Feb. 15, 1912, Carrick, Pa.; educ. Divine Word Seminary (Girard, Pa.); ord. priest Aug. 13, 1939; ord. titular bishop of Belabitene and first vicar apostolic of Mount Hagen, New Guinea, Apr. 21, 1960; first bishop of Mount Hagen, Nov. 15, 1966.

Bilock, John M.: b. June 20, 1916, McAdoo, Pa.; educ. St. Procopius College and Seminary (Lisle, Ill.); ord. priest Feb. 3, 1946; vicar general of Byzantine archdiocese of Munhall, 1969; ord. titular bishop of Pergamum and auxiliary bishop of Munhall, May 15, 1973; title of see changed to Pittsburgh, 1977.

Blanchette, Romeo: b. Jan. 6, 1913, St. George, Ill.; educ. St. Mary of the Lake Seminary (Mundelein, Ill.), Gregorian Univ. (Rome); ord. priest Apr. 3, 1937; vicar general of Joliet, 1950-66; ord. titular bishop of Maxita and auxiliary of Joliet, Apr. 3, 1965; app. bishop of Joliet, July 19, 1966, installed Aug. 31, 1966; resigned 1979.

Boccella, John H., T.O.R.: b. June 25, 1912, Castelfranci, Italy; came to US at the age of two; educ. St. Francis College and Seminary (Loretto, Pa.), Angelicum Univ. (Rome), Catholic Univ. (Washington, D.C.); ord. priest Mar. 29, 1941; minister general of Third Order Regular, 1947-65; ord. archbishop of Izmir, Turkey, Apr. 17, 1968; transferred to titular see of Ephesus, Dec. 7, 1978.

Bokenfohr, John, O.M.I.: b. Jan. 28, 1903, West Point, Nebr.; ord. priest July 11, 1927; ord. bishop of Kimberley, S. Africa, May 3, 1963; resigned July 17, 1974.

Boland, Ernest B., O.P.: b. July 10, 1925, Providence, R.I.; educ. Providence College (Rhode Island), Dominican Houses of Study (Somerset, Ohio; Washington, D.C.); ord. priest June 9, 1955; ord. bishop of Multan, Pakistan, July 25, 1966.

Borders, William D.: b. Oct. 9, 1913, Washington, Ind.; educ. St. Meinrad Seminary (St. Meinrad, Ind.), Notre Dame Seminary (New Orleans, La.), Notre Dame Univ. (Notre Dame, Ind.); ord. priest May 18, 1940; ord. first bishop of Orlando, June 14, 1968; app. archbishop of Baltimore, Apr. 2, 1974, installed June 26, 1974.

Bosco, Anthony G.: b. Aug. 1, 1927, New Castle, Pa.; educ. St. Vincent Seminary (Latrobe, Pa.), Lateran Univ. (Rome); ord. priest June 7, 1952; ord. titular bishop of Labicum and auxiliary of Pittsburgh, June 30, 1970.

Boudreaux, Warren L.: b. Jan. 25, 1918, Berwick, La.; educ. St. Joseph's Seminary (St. Benedict, La.), St. Sulpice Seminary (Paris, France), Notre Dame Seminary (New Orleans, La.), Catholic Univ. (Washington, D.C.); ord. priest May 30, 1942; ord. titular bishop of Calynda and auxiliary bishop of Lafayette, La., July 25, 1962; app. bishop of Beaumont, June 5, 1971; app. first bishop of Houma-Thibodaux, installed June 5, 1977.

Breitenbeck, Joseph M.: b. Aug. 3, 1914, Detroit, Mich.; educ. University of Detroit, Sacred Heart Seminary (Detroit, Mich.), North American College and Lateran Univ. (Rome), Catholic Univ. (Washington, D.C.); ord. priest May 30, 1942; ord. titular bishop of Tepelta and auxiliary bishop of Detroit, Dec. 20, 1965; app. bishop of Grand Rapids, Oct. 15, 1969, installed Dec. 2, 1969.

Brizgys, Vincas: b. Nov. 10, 1903, Plyniai, Lithuania; ord. priest June 5, 1927; ord. titular bishop of Bosano and auxiliary bishop of Kaunas, Lithuania, May 10, 1940; taken into custody and deported to Germany, 1944; liberated by Americans, 1945; U.S. citizen, 1958.

Broderick, Edwin B.: b. Jan. 16, 1917, New York, N.Y.; educ. Cathedral College (New York City), St. Joseph's Seminary (Yonkers, N.Y.), Fordham Univ. (New York City); ord. priest May 30, 1942; ord. titular bishop of Tizica and auxiliary of New York, Apr. 21, 1967; bishop of Albany, 1969-76; executive director of Catholic Relief Services, 1976.

Brown, Charles, A., M.M.: b. Aug. 20, 1919, New York, N.Y.; educ. Cathedral College (New York City), Maryknoll Seminary (Maryknoll, N.Y.); ord. priest June 9, 1946; ord. titular bishop of Vallis and auxiliary bishop of Santa Cruz, Bolivia, Mar. 27, 1957.

Brunini, Joseph B.: b. July 24, 1909, Vicksburg, Miss.; educ. Georgetown Univ. (Washington, D.C.), North American College (Rome), Catholic Univ. (Washington, D.C.); ord. priest Dec. 5, 1933; ord. titular bishop of Axomis and auxiliary bishop of Natchez-Jackson, Jan. 29, 1957; apostolic administrator of Natchez-Jackson, 1966; app. bishop of Natchez-Jackson, Dec. 2, 1967, installed Jan. 29, 1968; title of see changed to Jackson, 1977.

Brust, Leo J.: b. Jan. 7, 1916, St. Francis, Wis.; educ. St. Francis Seminary (Milwaukee, Wis.), Canisianum (Innsbruck, Austria), Catholic Univ. (Washington, D.C.); ord. priest May 30, 1942; ord. titular bishop of Suelli and auxiliary bishop of Milwaukee. Oct. 16, 1969.

Brzana, Stanislaus J.: b. July 1, 1917, Buffalo, N.Y.; educ. Christ the King Seminary (St. Bonaventure, N.Y.), Gregorian Univ. (Rome); ord. priest June 7, 1941; ord. titular bishop of Cufruta and auxiliary bishop of Buffalo, June 29, 1964; bishop of Ogdensburg, Oct. 22, 1968.

Bullock, William H.: b. 1927, Maple Lake, Minn.; educ. St. Thomas College and St. Paul Seminary (St. Paul, Minn.), Notre Dame Univ. (South Bend, Ind.); ord. priest 1952; ord. titular bishop of Natchez and auxiliary bishop of St. Paul and Minneapolis, Aug. 12, 1980.

Burke, James C., O.P.: b. Nov. 30, 1926, Philadelphia, Pa.; educ. King's College (Wilkes-Barre, Pa.), Providence College (R.I.); ord. priest June 8, 1956; ord. titular bishop of Lamiggiga and prelate of Chimbote, Peru, May 25, 1967, resigned 1978. Vicar for urban affairs, Wilmington, Del., diocese.

Buswell, Charles A.: b. Oct. 15, 1913, Homestead, Okla.; educ. St. Louis Preparatory Seminary (St. Louis, Mo.), Kenrick Seminary (Webster Groves, Mo.), American College, Univ. of Louvain (Belgium); ord. priest July 9, 1939; ord. bishop of Pueblo, Sept. 30, 1959; resigned Sept. 18, 1979.

Byrne, James J.: b. July 28, 1908, St. Paul, Minn.; educ. Nazareth Hall Preparatory Seminary and St. Paul Seminary (St. Paul, Minn.), Univ. of Minnesota (Minneapolis, Minn.); Louvain Univ. (Belgium); ord. priest June 3, 1933; ord. titular bishop of Etenna and auxiliary bishop of St. Paul, July 2, 1947; app. bishop of Boise, June 16, 1956; app. archbishop of Dubuque, Mar. 19, 1962, installed May 8, 1962.

C

Caesar, Raymond R., S.V.D.: b. Feb. 14, 1932, Eunice, La.; educ. Divine Word Seminary (Bay St. Louis, Miss.); Catholic Univ. (Washington, D.C.); ord. priest June 4, 1961; missionary in New Guinea from 1962; ord. coadjutor bishop of Goroka, Papua New Guinea, Oct. 25, 1978; bishop of Goroko, Aug. 30, 1980.

Caillouet, L. Abel.: b. Aug. 2, 1900, Thibodaux, La.; educ. St. Joseph's Preparatory Seminary (St. Benedict, La.), St. Mary's Seminary (Baltimore, Md.), North American College (Rome); ord. priest Mar. 7, 1925; ord. titular bishop of Setea and auxiliary bishop of New Orleans, Oct. 28, 1947; retired July 7, 1976.

Carberry, John J.: (See Cardinals, Biographies.)

Carroll, Mark K.: b. Nov. 19, 1896, St. Louis, Mo.; educ. St. Louis Preparatory Seminary and Kenrick Seminary (St. Louis, Mo.); ord. priest June 10, 1922; ord. bishop of Wichita, Apr. 23, 1947; retired, 1963, but retained title; resigned, 1967.

Casey, James V.: b. Sept. 22, 1914, Osage, Ia.; educ. Loras College (Dubuque, Ia.), North American College (Rome), Catholic Univ. (Washington, D.C.); ord. priest Dec. 8, 1939; ord. titular bishop of Citium and auxiliary bishop of Lincoln, Apr. 24, 1957; bishop of Lincoln, June 14, 1957; app. archbishop of Denver, Feb. 22, 1967, installed May 17, 1967.

Cassata, John J.: b. Nov. 8, 1908, Galveston, Tex.; educ. St. Mary's Seminary (La Porte, Tex.), North American College, Urbana Univ. and Gregorian Univ. (Rome); ord. priest Dec. 8, 1932; ord. titular bishop of Bida and auxiliary bishop of Dallas-Fort Worth, June 5, 1968; app. bishop of Fort Worth, Aug. 27, 1969, installed Oct. 21, 1969; retired September, 1980.

Chavez, Gilbert Espinoza: b. May 9, 1932, Ontario, Calif.; educ. St. Francis Seminary

(El Cajon, Calif.), Immaculate Heart Seminary (San Diego), Univ. of California; ord. priest Mar. 19, 1960; ord. titular bishop of Magarmel and auxiliary of San Diego, June 21, 1974.

Clark, Matthew H.: b. July 15, 1937, Troy, N.Y.; educ. St. Bernard's Seminary (Rochester, N.Y.), Gregorian Univ. (Rome); ord. priest Dec. 19, 1962; ord. bishop of Rochester, May 27, 1979; installed June 26, 1979.

Clinch, Harry A.: b. Oct. 27, 1908, San Anselmo, Calif.; educ. St. Joseph's College (Mountain View, Calif.), St. Patrick's Seminary (Menlo Park, Calif.); ord. priest June 6, 1936; ord. titular bishop of Badiae and auxiliary bishop of Monterey-Fresno, Feb. 27, 1957; app. first bishop of Monterey in California, installed Dec. 14, 1967.

Cody, John P.: (See Cardinals, Biographies.)

Cohill, John Edward, S.V.D.: b. Dec. 13, 1907, Elizabeth, N.J.; educ. Divine Word Seminary (Techny, Ill.); ord. priest Mar. 20, 1936; ord. first bishop of Goroko, Papua New Guinea, Mar. 11, 1967; resigned Aug. 30, 1980.

Comber, John W., M.M.: b. Mar. 12, 1906, Lawrence, Mass.; educ. St. John's Preparatory College (Danvers, Mass.), Boston College (Boston, Mass.), Maryknoll Seminary (Maryknoll, N.Y.); ord. priest Feb. 1, 1931; superior general of Maryknoll, 1956-66; ord. titular bishop of Foratiana, Apr. 9, 1959.

Connare, William G.: b. Dec. 11, 1911, Pittsburgh, Pa.; educ. Duquesne Univ. (Pittsburgh, Pa.), St. Vincent Seminary (Latrobe, Pa.); ord. priest June 14, 1936; ord. bishop of Greensburg, May 4, 1960.

Connolly, James L.: b. Nov. 15, 1894, Fall River, Mass.; educ. St. Charles College (Catonsville, Md.), St. Mary's Seminary (Baltimore, Md.), Catholic Univ. (Washington, D.C.), Louvain Univ. (Belgium); ord. priest Dec. 21, 1923; rector of St. Paul (Minn.) minor seminary 1940-43, major seminary 1943-45; ord. titular bishop of Mylasa and coadjutor of Fall River, May 24, 1945; bishop of Fall River, May 17, 1951; resigned Oct. 30, 1970.

Connolly, Thomas Arthur: b. Oct. 5, 1899, San Francisco, Calif.; educ. St. Patrick's Seminary (Menlo Park, Calif.), Catholic Univ. (Washington, D.C.); ord. priest June 11, 1926; ord. titular bishop of Sila and auxiliary bishop of San Francisco, Aug. 24, 1939; app. coadjutor bishop of Seattle, Feb. 28, 1948; succeeded as bishop of Seattle, May 18, 1950; first archbishop of Seattle, June 23, 1951; retired Feb. 25, 1975.

Connolly, Thomas J.: b. July 18, 1922, Tonopah, Nev.; educ. St. Patrick's Seminary (Menlo Park, Calif.), Catholic Univ. (Washington, D.C.), Lateran Univ. (Rome); ord.

priest Apr. 8, 1947; ord. bishop of Baker, June 30, 1971.

Connors, Ronald G., C.SS.R.: b. Nov. 1, 1915, Brooklyn, N.Y.; ord. priest June 22, 1941; ord. titular bishop of Equizetum and coadjutor bishop of San Juan de la Maguana, Dominican Republic, July 20, 1976; succeeded as bishop of San Juan de la Maguana, July 20, 1977.

Cooke, Terence J.: (See Cardinals, Biographies.)

Coscia, Benedict Dominic, O.F.M.: b. Aug. 10, 1922, Brooklyn, N.Y.; educ. St. Francis College (Brooklyn, N.Y.), Holy Name College (Washington, D.C.); ord. priest June 11, 1949; ord. bishop of Jatai, Brazil, Sept. 21, 1961.

Cosgrove, William M.: b. Nov. 26, 1916, Canton, Ohio; educ. John Carroll Univ. (Cleveland, O.); ord. priest Dec. 18, 1943; ord. titular bishop of Trisipa and auxiliary bishop of Cleveland, Sept. 3, 1968; app. bishop of Belleville, installed Oct. 28, 1976.

Costello, Thomas J.: b. Feb. 23, 1929, Camden, N.Y.; educ. Niagara Univ. (Niagara Falls, N.Y.), St. Bernard's Seminary (Rochester, N.Y.), Catholic Univ. (Washington, D.C.); ord. priest June 5, 1954; ord. titular bishop of Perdices and auxiliary bishop of Syracuse Mar. 13, 1978.

Cotey, Arnold R., S.D.S.: b. June 15, 1921, Milwaukee, Wis.; educ. Divine Savior Seminary (Lanham, Md.), Marquette Univ. (Milwaukee, Wis.); ord. priest June 7, 1949; ord. first bishop of Nachingwea, Tanzania, Oct. 20, 1963.

Cousins, William E.: b. Aug. 20, 1902, Chicago, Ill.; educ. Quigley Seminary (Chicago, Ill.), St. Mary of the Lake Seminary (Mundelein, Ill.); ord. priest Apr. 23, 1927; ord. titular bishop of Forma and auxiliary bishop of Chicago, Mar. 7, 1949; app. bishop of Peoria, May 21, 1952; archbishop of Milwaukee, Jan. 27, 1959; retired 1977.

Cronin, Daniel A.: b. Nov. 14, 1927, Newton, Mass.; educ. St. John's Seminary (Boston, Mass.), North American College and Gregorian Univ. (Rome); ord. priest Dec. 20, 1952; attaché apostolic nunciature (Addis Ababa), 1957-61; served in papal Secretariat of State, 1961-68; ord. titular bishop of Egnatia and auxiliary bishop of Boston, Sept. 12, 1968; bishop of Fall River, Dec. 16, 1970.

Crowley, Joseph R.: b. Jan. 12, 1915, Fort Wayne, Ind.; educ. St. Mary's College (St. Mary, Ky.), St. Meinrad Seminary (St. Meinrad, Ind.); served in US Air Force, 1942-46; ord. priest May 1, 1953; editor of *Our Sunday Visitor* 1958-67; ord. titular bishop of Maraguis and auxiliary bishop of Fort Wayne-South Bend, Aug. 24, 1971.

Cummins, John S.: b. Mar. 3, 1928, Oakland, Calif.; educ. St. Patrick's Seminary (Menlo Park, Calif.), Catholic Univ. (Washington, D.C.), Univ. of California; ord. priest

Jan. 24, 1953; executive director of the California Catholic Conference 1971-76; ord. titular bishop of Lambaesis and auxiliary bishop of Sacramento, May 16, 1974; app. bishop of Oakland, installed June 30, 1977.

Curtis, Walter W.: b. May 3, 1913, Jersey City, N.J.; educ. Fordham Univ. (New York City), Seton Hall Univ. (South Orange, N.J.), Immaculate Conception Seminary (Darlington, N.J.), North American College and Gregorian Univ. (Rome), Catholic Univ. (Washington, D.C.); ord. priest Dec. 8, 1937; ord. titular bishop of Bisica and auxiliary bishop of Newark, Sept. 24, 1957; app. bishop of Bridgeport, 1961, installed Nov. 21, 1961.

Curtiss, Elden F.: b. June 16, 1932, Baker, Ore.; educ. St. Edward Seminary College and St. Thomas Seminary (Kenmore, Wash.); ord. priest May 24, 1958; ord. bishop of Helena, Mont., Apr. 28, 1976.

D

Daily, Thomas V.: b. Sept. 23, 1927, Belmont, Mass.; educ. Boston College, St. John's Seminary (Brighton, Mass.); ord. priest Jan. 10, 1952; missionary in Peru for five years as a member of the Society of St. James the Apostle; ord. titular bishop of Bladia and auxiliary bishop of Boston, Feb. 11, 1975.

Daley, Joseph T.: b. Dec. 21, 1915, Connerton, Pa.; educ. St. Charles Borromeo Seminary (Philadelphia, Pa.); ord. priest June 7, 1941; ord. titular bishop of Barca and auxiliary bishop of Harrisburg, Pa., Jan. 7, 1964; coadjutor bishop of Harrisburg, Aug. 2, 1967; bishop of Harrisburg, Oct. 19, 1971.

Daly, James: b. Aug. 14, 1921, New York, N.Y.; educ. Cathedral College (Brooklyn, N.Y.), Immaculate Conception Seminary (Huntington, L.I.); ord. priest May 22, 1948; ord. titular bishop of Castra Nova and auxiliary bishop of Rockville Centre, May 9, 1977.

Danglmayr, Augustine: b. Dec. 11, 1898, Muenster, Tex.; educ. Subiaco College (Arkansas), St. Mary's Seminary (La Porte, Tex.), Kenrick Seminary (St. Louis, Mo.); ord. priest June 10, 1922; ord. titular bishop of Olba, Oct. 7, 1942; auxiliary bishop of Dallas-Ft. Worth, 1942-69.

D'Antonio, Nicholas, O.F.M.: b. July 10, 1916, Rochester, N.Y.; educ. St. Anthony's Friary (Catskill, N.Y.); ord. priest June 7, 1942; ord. titular bishop of Giufi Salaria and prelate of Olancho, Honduras, July 25, 1966; resigned 1977; app. vicar general of New Orleans archdiocese and episcopal vicar for Spanish Speaking, August, 1977.

D'Arcy, John M.: b. Aug. 18, 1932, Brighton, Mass.; educ. St. John's Seminary (Brighton, Mass.), Angelicum Univ. (Rome); ord. priest Feb. 2, 1957; spiritual director of St. John's Seminary; ord. titular bishop of Mediana and auxiliary bishop of Boston, Feb. 11, 1975.

Dargin, Edward Vincent: b. Apr. 25, 1898,

New York, N.Y.; educ. Fordham Univ. (New York City), St. Joseph Seminary (Dunwoodie, N.Y.), Catholic Univ. (Washington, D.C.); ord. priest Sept. 23, 1922; ord. titular bishop of Amphipolis and auxiliary bishop of New York, Oct. 5, 1953; app. episcopal vicar, 1966. Retired.

Davis, James Peter: b. June 9, 1904, Houghton, Mich.; educ. St. Joseph's College (Mountain View, Calif.), St. Patrick's Seminary (Menlo Park, Calif.); ord. priest May 19, 1929; ord. bishop of San Juan, Puerto Rico, Oct. 6, 1943; app. first archbishop of San Juan, July 30, 1960; app. archbishop of Santa Fe, installed Feb. 25, 1964; resigned June 4, 1974.

Dearden, John Francis: (See Cardinals, Biographies.)

Deksnys, Antanas L.: b. May 9, 1906, Buteniskiai, Lithuania; educ. Metropolitan Seminary and Theological and Philosophical Faculty at Vytautas the Great Univ. (all at Kaunas, Lithuania), Univ. of Fribourg (Switzerland); ord. priest May 30, 1931; served in US parishes at Mt. Carmel, Pa., and East St. Louis, Ill.; ord. titular bishop of Lavellum, June 15, 1969; assigned to pastoral work among Lithuanians in Western Europe.

Dempsey, Michael J., O.P.: b. Feb. 22, 1912, Providence, R.I.; entered Order of Preachers (Dominicans), Chicago province, 1935; ord. priest June 11, 1942; ord. bishop of Sokoto, Nigeria, Aug. 15, 1967.

Denning, Joseph P.: b. Jan. 4, 1907, Flushing, L.I.; educ. Cathedral College (Brooklyn, N.Y.), Immaculate Conception Seminary (Huntington, L.I.), St. Mary's Seminary (Baltimore, Md.); ord. priest May 21, 1932; ord. titular bishop of Mallus and auxiliary bishop of Brooklyn, Apr. 22, 1959.

De Palma, Joseph A., S.C.J.: b. Sept. 4, 1913, Walton, N.Y.; ord. priest May 20, 1944; superior general of Congregation of Priests of the Sacred Heart, 1959-67; ord. first bishop of De Aar, South Africa, July 19, 1967.

Dimmerling, Harold J.: b. Sept. 23, 1914, Braddock, Pa.; educ. St. Fidelis Preparatory Seminary (Herman, Pa.), St. Charles Seminary (Columbus, O.), St. Francis Seminary (Loretto, Pa.); ord. priest May 2, 1940; ord. bishop of Rapid City, Oct. 30, 1969.

Dingman, Maurice J.: b. Jan. 20, 1914, St. Paul, Ia.; educ. St. Ambrose College (Davenport, Ia.), North American College and Gregorian Univ. (Rome), Catholic Univ. (Washington, D.C.); ord. priest Dec. 8, 1939; ord. bishop of Des Moines, June 19, 1968.

Dion, Georges E., O.M.I.: b. Sept. 25, 1911, Central Falls, R.I.; educ. Holy Cross College (Worcester, Mass.), Oblate Juniorate (Colebrook, N.H.), Oblate Scholasticates (Natick, Mass., and Ottawa, Ont.); ord. priest June 24, 1936; ord. titular bishop of Arpaia and vicar apostolic of Jolo, Philippine Islands, Apr. 23, 1980.

Dolinay, Thomas V.: b. July 24, 1923, Uniontown, Pa.; educ. St. Procopius College (Lisle, Ill.); ord. priest May 16, 1948; editor *Eastern Catholic Life,* 1966- ; ord. titular bishop of Tiatira and auxiliary bishop of Byzantine rite diocese of Passaic, Nov. 23, 1976.

Donaghy, Frederick Anthony, M.M.: b. Jan. 13, 1903, New Bedford, Mass.; educ. Holy Cross College (Worcester, Mass.), St. Mary's Seminary (Baltimore, Md.), Maryknoll Seminary (Maryknoll, N.Y.); ord. priest Jan. 29, 1929; ord. titular bishop of Setea and vicar apostolic of Wuchow, China, Sept. 21, 1939; title changed to bishop of Wuchow, Apr. 11, 1946; expelled by Communists.

Donahue, Stephen Joseph: b. Dec. 10, 1893, New York, N. Y.; educ. Cathedral College (New York, N.Y.), St. Joseph's Seminary (Dunwoodie, N.Y.), North American College (Rome); ord. priest May 22, 1918; ord. titular bishop of Medea and auxiliary bishop of New York, May 1, 1934. Retired.

Donnellan, Thomas A.: b. Jan. 24, 1914, New York, N.Y.; educ. Cathedral College and St. Joseph's Seminary (New York, N.Y.), Catholic Univ. (Washington, D.C.); ord. priest June 3, 1939; ord. bishop of Ogdensburg, Apr. 9, 1964; app. archbishop of Atlanta, installed July 16, 1968.

Donohoe, Hugh A.: b. June 28, 1905, San Francisco, Calif.; educ. St. Patrick's Preparatory and Major Seminaries (Menlo Park, Calif.), Catholic Univ. (Washington, D.C.); ord. priest June 14, 1930; ord. titular bishop of Taium and auxiliary bishop of San Francisco, Oct. 7, 1947; app. first bishop of Stockton, Jan. 27, 1962; app. bishop of Fresno, Aug. 27, 1969, installed Oct. 7, 1969; retired July 1, 1980.

Donovan, John A.: b. Aug. 5, 1911, Chatham, Ont., Canada; educ. Sacred Heart Seminary (Detroit, Mich.), North American College and Gregorian Univ. (Rome); ord. priest Dec. 8, 1935; ord. titular bishop of Rhasus and auxiliary bishop of Detroit, Oct. 26, 1954; app. bishop of Toledo, installed Apr. 18, 1967; retired July, 1980.

Donovan, Paul V.: b. Sept. 1, 1924, Bernard, Iowa; educ. St. Gregory's Seminary (Cincinnati, Ohio), Mt. St. Mary's Seminary (Norwood, Ohio), Lateran Univ. (Rome); ord. priest May 20, 1950; ord. first bishop of Kalamazoo, Mich., July 21, 1971.

Dougherty, John J.: b. Sept. 16, 1907, Jersey City, N.J.; educ. Seton Hall Univ. (S. Orange, N.J.), Immaculate Conception Seminary (Darlington, N.J.), North American College, Gregorian Univ., Pontifical Biblical Institute (Rome); ord. priest July 23, 1933; ord. titular bishop of Cotenna and auxiliary bishop of Newark, Jan. 24, 1963.

Dozier, Carroll T.: b. Aug. 18, 1911, Richmond, Va.; educ. Holy Cross College

(Worcester, Mass.), Gregorian Univ. (Rome); ord. priest, Mar. 19, 1937, Rome; ord. first bishop of Memphis, Jan. 6, 1971.

Driscoll, Justin A.: b. Sept. 30, 1920, Bernard, Ia.; educ. Loras College (Dubuque, Ia.), Catholic Univ. (Washington, D.C.); ord. priest July 28, 1945; president of Loras College, 1967-70; ord. bishop of Fargo, Oct. 28, 1970.

Drury, Thomas J.: b. Jan. 4, 1908, Co. Sligo, Ireland; educ. St. Benedict's College (Atchison, Kans.), Kenrick Seminary (St. Louis, Mo.); ord. priest June 2, 1935; ord. first bishop of San Angelo, Tex., Jan. 24, 1962; app. bishop of Corpus Christi, installed Sept. 1, 1965.

Dudick, Michael J.: b. Feb. 24, 1916, St. Clair, Pa.; educ. St. Procopius College and Seminary (Lisle, Ill.); ord. priest Nov. 13, 1945; ord. bishop of Byzantine Rite Eparchy of Passaic, Oct. 24, 1968.

Dudley, Paul: b. Nov. 27, 1926, Northfield, Minn.; educ. Nazareth College and St. Paul Seminary (St. Paul, Minn.); ord. priest June 2, 1951; ord. titular bishop of Ursona and auxiliary bishop of St. Paul and Minneapolis, Jan. 25, 1977; app. bishop of Sioux Falls, installed Dec. 13, 1978.

Duhart, Clarence James, C.SS.R.: b. Mar. 23, 1912, New Orleans, La.; ord. priest June 29, 1937; ord. bishop of Udon Thani, Thailand, Apr. 21, 1966; resigned Oct. 2, 1975.

DuMaine, Roland Pierre: b. Aug. 2, 1931, Paducah, Ky.; educ. St. Joseph's College (Mountain View, Calif.), St. Patrick's College and Seminary (Menlo Park, Calif.), Univ. of California (Berkley), Catholic Univ. (Washington, D.C.); ord. priest June 5, 1957; ord. titular bishop of Sarda and auxiliary bishop of San Francisco, June 29, 1978.

Dunn, Francis J.: b. Mar. 22, 1922, Elkader, Ia.; educ. Loras College (Dubuque, Ia.), Kenrick Seminary (St. Louis, Mo.), Angelicum (Rome, Italy); ord. priest Jan. 11, 1948; chancellor of Dubuque, Aug. 27, 1960; ord. titular bishop of Turris Tamallani and auxiliary bishop of Dubuque, Aug. 27, 1969, app. vicar general, Aug. 28, 1969.

Durick, Joseph Aloysius: b. Oct. 13, 1914, Dayton, Tenn.; educ. St. Bernard Minor Seminary (St. Bernard, Ala.), St. Mary's Seminary (Baltimore, Md.), Urban Univ. (Rome); ord. priest May 23, 1940; ord. titular bishop of Cerbal and auxiliary bishop of Mobile-Birmingham, Mar. 24, 1955; app. coadjutor bishop of Nashville, Tenn., installed Mar. 3, 1964; apostolic administrator, 1966; bishop of Nashville, Sept. 10, 1969; resigned Apr. 4, 1975, to work with inmates of Federal correctional institutions and their families.

Durning, Dennis V., C.S.Sp.: b. May 18, 1923, Germantown, Pa.; educ. St. Mary's Seminary (Ferndale, Conn.); ord. priest June 3, 1949; ord. first bishop of Arusha, Tanzania, May 28, 1963.

E

Elko, Nicholas T.: b. Dec. 14, 1909, Donora, Pa.; educ. Duquesne Univ. (Pittsburgh, Pa.), Seminary of Uzhorod (Czechoslovakia) Louvain Univ. (Belgium); ord. priest Sept. 30, 1934; ord. titular bishop of Apollonias and apostolic administrator of Byzantine-Rite exarchy of Pittsburgh, Mar. 6, 1955; succeeded as exarch of Pittsburgh, Sept. 5, 1955; became eparch when Pittsburgh was raised to eparchy, July, 1963; app. titular archbishop of Dara, 1967, and ordaining prelate for Byzantine Rite in Rome; head of Oriental liturgical commission; app. auxiliary bishop of Cincinnati, Aug. 10, 1971.

Etteldorf, Raymond P.: b. Aug. 12, 1911, Ossian, Ia.; educ. Loras College (Dubuque, Ia.), Gregorian Univ. (Rome); ord. priest Dec. 8, 1937; secretary general of Supreme Council for direction of Pontifical Missionary Works, 1964-68; secretary of Pontifical Commission for Economic Affairs, 1968-69; ord. titular archbishop of Tindari, Jan. 6, 1969; papal representative to New Zealand and the Pacific Islands, 1968-74; pro-nuncio to Ethiopia, 1974.

Evans, George R.: b. Sept. 25, 1922, Denver, Colo.; educ. Notre Dame Univ. (Notre Dame, Ind.), St. Thomas Seminary (Denver, Colo.), Apollinare Univ. (Rome, Italy); ord. priest May 31, 1947; ord. titular bishop of Tubyza and auxiliary bishop of Denver, Apr. 23, 1969.

F

Federal, Joseph Lennox: b. Jan. 13, 1910, Greensboro, N.C.; educ. Belmont Abbey College (Belmont Abbey, N.C.), Niagara Univ. (Niagara Falls, N.Y.), Univ. of Fribourg (Switzerland), North American College and Gregorian Univ. (Rome); ord. priest Dec. 8, 1934; ord. titular bishop of Appiaria and auxiliary bishop of Salt Lake City, Apr. 11, 1951; app. coadjutor with right of succession, May, 1958; bishop of Salt Lake City, Mar. 31, 1960; retired Apr. 22, 1980.

Ferrario, Joseph A.: b. Mar. 3, 1926, Scranton, Pa.; educ. St. Charles College (Catonsville, Md.), St. Mary's Seminary (Baltimore, Md.), Catholic Univ. (Washington, D.C.); Univ. of Scranton; ord. priest May 19, 1951; ord. titular bishop of Cuse and auxiliary bishop of Honolulu Jan. 13, 1978.

Fiorenza, Joseph A.: b. Jan. 25, 1931, Beaumont, Tex.; educ. St. Mary's Seminary (LaPorte, Tex.); ord. priest May 29, 1954; ord. bishop of San Angelo, Oct. 25, 1979.

Fitzpatrick, John J.: b. Oct. 12, 1918, Trenton, Ont., Canada; educ. Urban Univ. (Rome), Our Lady of the Angels Seminary (Niagara Falls, N.Y.); ord. priest Dec. 13, 1942; ord. titular bishop of Cenae and auxiliary bishop of Miami, Aug. 28, 1968; bishop of Brownsville, Tex., May 28, 1971.

Fitzsimons, George K.: b. Sept. 4, 1928,

Kansas City, Mo.; educ. Rockhurst College (Kansas City, Mo.), Immaculate Conception Seminary (Conception, Mo.); ord. priest Mar. 18, 1961; ord. titular bishop of Pertusa and auxiliary bishop of Kansas City-St. Joseph, July 3, 1975.

Flanagan, Bernard Joseph: b. Mar. 31, 1908, Proctor, Vt.; educ. Holy Cross College (Worcester, Mass.), North American College (Rome), Catholic Univ. (Washington, D.C.); ord. priest Dec. 8, 1931; ord. first bishop of Norwich, Nov. 30, 1953; app. bishop of Worcester, installed, Sept. 24, 1959.

Flavin, Glennon P.: b. Mar. 2, 1916, St. Louis, Mo.; educ. Kenrick Seminary (St. Louis, Mo.); ord. priest Dec. 20, 1941; ord. titular bishop of Joannina and auxiliary bishop of St. Louis, May 30, 1957; app. bishop of Lincoln, installed Aug. 17, 1967.

Fliss, Raphael M.: b. Oct. 25, 1930, Milwaukee, Wis.; educ. St. Francis Seminary (Milwaukee, Wis.), Catholic University (Washington, D.C.), Pontifical Lateran Univ. (Rome); ord. priest May 26, 1956; ord. coadjutor bishop of Superior with right of succession, Dec. 20, 1979.

Flores, Felixberto C.: b. Jan. 13, 1921, Agana, Guam; educ. St. John's Seminary (Brighton, Mass.), Fordham Univ. (New York); ord. priest Apr. 30, 1949; ord. titular bishop of Stonj, May 17, 1970, and apostolic administrator of the diocese of Agana, Guam; installed second residential bishop of Agana, July 12, 1972.

Flores, Patrick F.: b. July 26, 1929, Ganado, Tex.; educ. St. Mary's Seminary (Houston, Tex.); ord. priest May 26, 1956; ord. titular bishop of Itolica and auxiliary bishop of San Antonio, May 5, 1970 (first Mexican-American bishop); app. bishop of El Paso, Apr. 4, 1978, installed May 29, 1978; app. archbishop of San Antonio 1979.

Forst, Marion F.: b. Sept. 3, 1910, St. Louis, Mo.; educ. St. Louis Preparatory Seminary (St. Louis, Mo.), Kenrick Seminary (Webster Groves, Mo.); ord. priest June 10, 1934; ord. bishop of Dodge City, Mar. 24, 1960; app. titular bishop of Scala and auxiliary bishop of Kansas City, Kans. Oct. 16, 1976.

Francis Joseph A., S.V.D.: b. Sept. 30, 1923, Lafayette, La.; educ. St. Augustine Seminary (Bay St. Louis, Miss.), St. Mary Seminary (Techny, Ill.), Catholic Univ. (Washington, D.C.); ord. priest Oct. 7, 1950; president Conference of Major Superiors of Men, 1974-76, and the National Black Catholic Clergy Caucus; ord. titular bishop of Valliposita and auxiliary bishop of Newark, June 25, 1976.

Franz, John B.: b. Oct. 29, 1896, Springfield, Ill.; educ. Quincy College (Quincy, Ill.), Kenrick Seminary (Webster Groves, Mo.), Catholic Univ. (Washington, D.C.); ord. priest June 13, 1920; ord. first bishop of Dodge City, Aug. 29, 1951; app. bishop of Peoria, installed Nov. 4, 1959; resigned May 24, 1971.

Franzetta, Benedict C.: b. Aug. 1, 1921, East Liverpool, O.; educ. St. Charles College (Catonsville, Md.), St. Mary Seminary (Cleveland, O.); ord. priest Apr. 29, 1950; ord. titular bishop of Oderzo and auxiliary bishop of Youngstown, Sept. 4, 1980.

Freking, Frederick W.: b. Aug. 11, 1913, Heron Lake, Minn.; educ. St. Mary's College (Winona, Minn.), North American College and Gregorian Univ. (Rome), Catholic Univ. (Washington, D.C.); ord. priest July 31, 1938; ord. bishop of Salina, Nov. 30, 1957; app. bishop of La Crosse, Dec. 30, 1964, installed Feb. 24, 1965.

Frey, Gerard L.: b. May 10, 1914, New Orleans, La.; educ. Notre Dame Seminary (New Orleans, La.); ord. priest Apr. 2, 1938; ord. bishop of Savannah, Aug. 8, 1967; app. bishop of Lafayette, La., Nov. 7, 1972, installed Jan, 7, 1973.

Friend, William B.: b. Oct. 22, 1931, Miami, Fla.; educ. St. Mary's College (St. Mary, Ky.), Mt. St. Mary Seminary (Emmitsburg, Md.), Catholic Univ. (Washington, D.C.), Notre Dame Univ. (Notre Dame, Ind.); ord. priest May 7, 1959; ord. titular bishop of Pomaria and auxiliary bishop of Alexandria-Shreveport, La., Oct. 30, 1979.

Frosi, Angelo, S. X.: b. Jan. 31, 1924, Baffano Cremona, Italy; ord. priest May 6, 1948; U.S. citizen; ord. titular bishop of Magneto, May 1, 1970, and prelate of Abaete do Tocantins, Brazil.

Fulcher, George A.: b. Jan. 30, 1922, Columbus, Ohio; educ. St. Charles Borromeo Seminary (Columbus, O.), Mt. St. Mary of the West Seminary (Norwood, O.), North American College and Angelicum (Rome); ord. priest Feb. 28, 1948; ord. titular bishop of Morosbisdus and auxiliary bishop of Columbus, July 18, 1976.

Furlong, Philip J.: b. Dec. 8, 1892, New York, N.Y.; educ. Cathedral College (New York, N.Y.), St. Joseph's Seminary (Yonkers, N.Y.); ord. priest May 18, 1918; ord. titular bishop of Araxa and auxiliary to military vicar, Jan. 25, 1956. Retired.

G

Gallagher, Raymond J.: b. Nov. 19, 1912, Cleveland, Ohio; educ. John Carroll Univ. and Our Lady of the Lake Seminary (Cleveland, O.); ord. priest Mar. 25, 1939; secretary of the National Conference of Catholic Charities 1961-65; ord. bishop of Lafayette in Indiana, Aug. 11, 1965.

Ganter, Bernard J.: b. July 17,1928, Galveston, Tex.; educ. Texas A & M Univ. (College Sta., Tex.), St. Mary's Seminary (La Porte, Tex.), Catholic Univ. (Washington, D.C.); ord. priest May 22, 1952; chancellor of Galveston-Houston diocese, 1966-73; ord.

first bishop of Tulsa, Feb. 7, 1973; app. bishop of Beaumont, Tex., Oct. 18, 1977, installed Dec. 13, 1977.

Garmendia, Francisco: b. Nov. 6, 1924, Lozcano, Spain; ord. priest June 29, 1947, in Spain; came to New York in 1964; became naturalized citizen; ord. titular bishop of Limisa and auxiliary bishop of New York, June 29, 1977. Vicar for Spanish pastoral development in New York archdiocese.

Garmo, George: b. Dec. 8, 1921, Telkaif, Iraq; educ. St. Peter Chaldean Patriarchal Seminary (Mossul, Iraq), Pontifical Urban Univ. (Rome); ord. priest Dec. 8, 1945; pastor of Chaldean parish in Detroit archdiocese, 1960-64, 1966-80; ord. archbishop of Mossul, Iraq, Sept. 14, 1980.

Garner, Robert F.: b. Apr. 27, 1920, Jersey City, N.J.; educ. Seton Hall Univ. (S. Orange, N.J.), Immaculate Conception Seminary (Darlington, N.J.); ord. priest June 15, 1946; ord. titular bishop of Blera and auxiliary bishop of Newark, June 25, 1976.

Gaughan, Norbert F.: b. May 30, 1921, Pittsburgh, Pa.; educ. St. Vincent College (Latrobe, Pa.), Univ. of Pittsburgh; ord. priest Nov. 4, 1945; ord. titular bishop of Taraqua and auxiliary bishop of Greensburg, June 26, 1975.

Gelineau, Louis E.: b. May 3, 1928, Burlington, Vt.; educ. St. Michael's College (Winooski, Vt.), St. Paul's Univ. Seminary (Ottawa, Ont.), Catholic Univ. (Washington, D.C.); ord. priest June 5, 1954; ord. bishop of Providence, R.I., Jan. 26, 1972.

Gendron, Odore: b. Sept. 13, 1921, Manchester, N.H.; educ. St. Charles Borromeo Seminary (Sherbrooke, Que., Canada), Univ. of Ottawa, St. Paul Univ. Seminary (Ottawa, Ont., Canada); ord. priest May 31, 1947; ord. bishop of Manchester, Feb. 3, 1975.

Gerber, Eugene J.: b. Apr. 30, 1931, Kingman, Kans.; educ. St. Thomas Seminary (Denver, Colo.), Wichita State Univ.; Catholic Univ. (Washington, D.C.), Angelicum (Rome); ord. priest May 19, 1959; ord. bishop of Dodge City, Dec. 14, 1976.

Gerbermann, Hugo, M.M.: b. Sept. 11, 1913, Nada, Tex.; educ. St. John's Minor and Major Seminary (San Antonio, Tex.), Maryknoll Seminary (Maryknoll, N.Y.); ord. priest Feb. 7, 1943; missionary work in Ecuador and Guatemala; ord. titular bishop of Amathus and prelate of Huehuetenango, Guatemala, July 22, 1962; first bishop of Huehuetenango, Dec. 23, 1967; app. titular bishop of Pinkel and auxiliary bishop of San Antonio, July 24, 1975.

Gerety, Peter L.: b. July 19, 1912, Shelton, Conn.; educ. Sulpician Seminary (Paris, France); ord. priest June 29, 1939; ord. titular bishop of Crepedula and coadjutor bishop of Portland, Me., with right of succession, June 1, 1966; app. apostolic administrator of Portland, 1967; bishop of Portland, Me.,

Sept. 15, 1969; app. archbishop of Newark, Apr. 2, 1974; installed June 28, 1974.

Gerrard, James J.: b. June 9, 1897, New Bedford, Mass.; educ. St. Laurent College (Montreal, Que.), St. Bernard's Seminary (Rochester, N.Y.); ord. priest May 26, 1923; ord. titular bishop of Forma and auxiliary bishop of Fall River, Mar. 19, 1959. Retired January, 1976.

Gleeson, Francis D., S.J.: b. Jan. 17, 1895, Carrollton, Mo.: educ. Mount St. Michael's Scholasticate (Spokane, Wash.), St. Francis Xavier College (Ona, Spain); entered the Society of Jesus, 1912; ord. priest July 29, 1926; ord. titular bishop of Cotenna and vicar apostolic of Alaska, Apr. 5, 1948; first bishop of Fairbanks, Aug. 8, 1962; retired Nov. 15, 1968.

Glenn, Laurence A.: b. Aug. 25, 1900, Bellingham, Wash.; educ. St. John's Univ. (Collegeville, Minn.), Catholic Univ. (Washington, D.C.); ord. priest June 11, 1927; ord. titular bishop of Tuscamia and auxiliary bishop of Duluth, Sept. 12, 1956; app. bishop of Crookston, Jan. 27, 1960, installed Apr. 20, 1960; resigned 1970.

Glennie, Ignatius T., S.J.: b. Feb. 5, 1907, Mexico City; educ. Mt. St. Michael's Scholasticate (Spokane, Wash.), Pontifical Seminary (Kandy, Ceylon), St. Mary's College (Kurdeong, India); entered Society of Jesus, 1924; ord. priest Nov. 21, 1938; ord. bishop of Trincomalee, Ceylon, Sept. 21, 1947; title of see changed to Trincomalee-Batticaloa (Sri Lanka), 1967; resigned Feb. 15, 1974.

Gossman, F. Joseph: b. Apr. 1, 1930, Baltimore, Md.: educ. St. Charles College (Catonsville, Md.), St. Mary's Seminary (Baltimore, Md.), North American College (Rome), Catholic Univ. (Washington, D.C.); ord. priest Dec. 17, 1955; ord. titular bishop of Agunto and auxiliary bishop of Baltimore, Sept. 11, 1968; named urban vicar, June 13, 1970; app. bishop of Raleigh April 8, 1975.

Gottwald, George J.: b. May 12, 1914, St. Louis, Mo.; educ. Kenrick Seminary (Webster Groves, Mo.); ord. priest June 9, 1940; ord. titular bishop of Cedamusa and auxiliary bishop of St. Louis, Aug. 8, 1961.

Gracida, Rene H.: b. June 9, 1923, New Orleans, La.; educ. Rice Univ. and Univ. of Houston (Houston, Tex.), Univ. of Fribourg (Switzerland); ord. priest May 23, 1959; ord. titular bishop of Masuccaba and auxiliary bishop of Miami, Jan. 25, 1972; app. first bishop of Pensacola-Tallahassee, Oct. 1, 1975, installed Nov. 6, 1975.

Grady, Thomas J.: b. Oct. 9, 1914, Chicago, Ill.; educ. St. Mary of the Lake Seminary (Mundelein, Ill.), Gregorian Univ. (Rome), Loyola Univ. (Chicago, Ill.); ord. priest Apr. 23, 1938; ord. titular bishop of Vamalla and auxiliary bishop of Chicago, Aug. 24, 1967; app. bishop of Orlando, Fla., Nov. 11, 1974, installed Dec. 16, 1974.

Graham, John J.: b. Sept. 11, 1913, Philadelphia, Pa.; educ. St. Charles Borromeo Seminary (Philadelphia, Pa.), Pontifical Roman Seminary (Rome, Italy); ord. priest Feb. 26, 1938; ord. titular bishop of Sabrata and auxiliary bishop of Philadelphia, Jan. 7, 1964.

Graner, Lawrence L., C.S.C.: b. Apr. 3, 1901, Franklin, Pa.; educ. Holy Cross Seminary (Notre Dame, Ind.), Holy Cross Mission Seminary (Washington, D.C.); entered Congregation of the Holy Cross, 1924; ord. priest June 24, 1928; ord. bishop of Dacca, India, Apr. 23, 1947; title changed to archbishop of Dacca, July 15, 1950; retired Nov. 23, 1967.

Graves, Lawrence P.: b. May 4, 1916, Texarkana, Ark.; educ. St. John's Seminary (Little Rock, Ark.), North American College (Rome), Catholic Univ. (Washington, D.C.); ord. priest June 11, 1942; ord. titular bishop of Vina and auxiliary bishop of Little Rock, Apr. 25, 1969; app. bishop of Alexandria, May 22, 1973, installed Sept. 18, 1973; title of see changed to Alexandria-Shreveport, Jan. 12, 1977.

Graziano, Lawrence, O.F.M.: b. Apr. 5, 1921, Mt. Vernon, N.Y.; educ. Mt. Alvernia Seminary (Wappingers Falls, N.Y.); ord. priest Jan. 26, 1947; ord. titular bishop of Limata and auxiliary bishop of Santa Ana, El Salvador, Sept. 21, 1961; app. coadjutor bishop of San Miguel, El Salvador, with right of succession, 1965; bishop of San Miguel, Jan. 10, 1968; resigned June 27, 1969.

Greco, Charles Paschal: b. Oct. 29, 1894, Rodney, Miss.; educ. St. Joseph's Seminary (St. Benedict, La.), Louvain Univ. (Belgium), Dominican Univ. (Fribourg, Switzerland); ord. priest July 25, 1918; ord. bishop of Alexandria Feb. 25, 1946; retired May 22, 1973.

Green, Francis J.: b. July 7, 1906, Corning, N.Y.; educ. St. Patrick's Seminary (Menlo Park, Calif.); ord. priest May 15, 1932; ord. titular bishop of Serra and auxiliary bishop of Tucson, Sept. 17, 1953; named coadjutor of Tucson with right of succession, May 11, 1960; bishop of Tucson, Oct. 26, 1960.

Green, Joseph: b. Oct. 13, 1917, St. Joseph, Mich.; educ. St. Joseph Seminary (Grand Rapids, Mich.). St. Gregory Seminary (Cincinnati, O.), St. Mary's Seminary (Norwood, O.), Lateran Univ. (Rome); ord. priest July 14, 1946; ord. titular bishop of Trisipa and auxiliary bishop of Lansing, Aug. 28, 1962; app. bishop of Reno, installed May 25, 1967; resigned Dec. 6, 1974.

Grellinger, John B.: b. Nov. 5, 1899, Milwaukee, Wis.; educ. Marquette Univ. and St. Francis Seminary (Milwaukee, Wis.), Urban Univ. and Gregorian Univ. (Rome); ord. priest July 14, 1929; ord. titular bishop of Syene and auxiliary bishop of Green Bay, July 14, 1949; retired Sept. 22, 1974.

Greteman, Frank H.: b. Dec. 25, 1907, Willey, Ia.; educ. Loras Academy and Loras College (Dubuque, Ia.), North American College (Rome), Catholic Univ. (Washington, D.C.); ord. priest Dec. 8, 1932; ord. titular bishop of Vissalsa and auxiliary bishop of Sioux City, May 26, 1965; bishop of Sioux City, Dec. 9, 1970.

Griffin, James A.: b. June 13, 1934, Fairview Park, O.; educ. St. Charles College (Baltimore, Md.), Borromeo College (Wicklife, O.); St. Mary Seminary (Cleveland, O.); Lateran Univ. (Rome); Cleveland State Univ.; ord. priest May 28, 1960; ord. titular bishop of Holar and auxiliary bishop of Cleveland, Aug. 1, 1979.

Grutka, Andrew G.: b. Nov. 17, 1908, Joliet, Ill.; educ. St. Procopius College and Seminary (Lisle, Ill.), Urban Univ. and Gregorian Univ. (Rome); ord. priest Dec. 5, 1933; app. moderator of lay activities in Gary diocese, 1955; ord. first bishop of Gary, Feb. 25, 1957; app. member of Pontifical Marian Academy, Jan. 5, 1970; president, 1971-76, and chairman of board 1976-   , of Catholic Communications Foundation.

Guilfoyle, George H.: b. Nov. 13, 1913, New York, N.Y.; educ. Georgetown Univ. (Washington, D.C.), Fordham Univ. (New York City), St. Joseph's Seminary (Dunwoodie, N.Y.), Columbia Univ. Law School (New York City); ord. priest Mar. 25, 1944; ord. titular bishop of Marazane and auxiliary bishop of New York, Nov. 30, 1964; app. bishop of Camden, installed Mar. 4, 1968.

Guilfoyle, Merlin J.: b. July 15, 1908, San Francisco, Calif.; educ. St. Joseph's College (Mountain View, Calif.), St. Patrick's Seminary (Menlo Park, Calif.), Catholic Univ. (Washington, D.C.); ord. priest June 10, 1933; ord. titular bishop of Bulla and auxiliary bishop of San Francisco, Sept. 21, 1950; app. bishop of Stockton, Nov. 19, 1969, installed Jan. 13, 1970; resigned Sept. 4, 1979.

Gumbleton, Thomas J.: b. Jan. 26, 1930, Detroit, Mich.; educ. St. John Provincial Seminary (Detroit, Mich.), Pontifical Lateran Univ. (Rome); ord. priest June 2, 1956; ord. titular bishop of Ululi and auxiliary bishop of Detroit, May 1, 1968.

H

Hacker, Hilary B.: b. Jan. 10, 1913, New Ulm, Minn.; educ. St. Paul Seminary (St. Paul, Minn.), Gregorian Univ. (Rome); ord. priest June 4, 1938; ord. bishop of Bismarck, N. Dak., Feb. 27, 1957.

Hackett, John F.: b. Dec. 7, 1911, New Haven, Conn.; educ. St. Thomas Seminary (Bloomfield, Conn.), Seminaire Ste. Sulpice (Paris); ord. priest June 29, 1936; ord. titular bishop of Helenopolis in Palaestina and auxiliary bishop of Hartford, Mar. 19, 1953.

Hagarty, Paul Leonard, O.S.B.: b. Mar. 20, 1909, Greene, Ia.; educ. Loras College (Dubuque, Ia.), St. John's Seminary and St. John's Univ. (Collegeville, Minn.); entered Order of St. Benedict, 1931; ord. priest June

6, 1936; ord. titular bishop of Arba and vicar apostolic of the Bahamas, Oct. 19, 1950; first bishop of Nassau, July 5, 1960.

Ham, J. Richard, M.M.: b. July 11, 1921, Chicago, Ill.; educ. Maryknoll Seminary (New York); ord. priest June 12, 1948; missionary to Guatemala, 1958; ord. titular bishop of Puzia di Numidia and auxiliary bishop of Guatemala, Jan. 6, 1968; resigned see 1979; app. vicar for Hispanic ministry in St. Paul and Minneapolis archdiocese, 1980.

Hammes, George A.: b. Sept. 11, 1911, St. Joseph Ridge, Wis.; educ. St. Lawrence Seminary (Mt. Calvary. Wis.), St. Louis Preparatory Seminary (St. Louis, Mo.), Kenrick Seminary (Webster Groves, Mo.), Sulpician Seminary, Catholic Univ. (Washington, D.C.); ord. priest May 22, 1937; ord. bishop of Superior, May 24, 1960.

Hanifen, Richard C.: b. June 15, 1931, Denver, Colo,; educ. Regis College and St. Thomas Seminary (Denver, Colo.), Catholic Univ. (Washington, D.C.), Lateran Univ. (Rome); ord. priest June 6, 1959; ord. titular bishop of Abercorn and auxiliary bishop of Denver, Sept. 20, 1974.

Hannan, Philip M.: b. May 20, 1913, Washington, D.C.; educ. St. Charles College (Catonsville, Md.), Catholic Univ. (Washington, D.C.), North American College (Rome); ord. priest Dec. 8, 1939; ord. titular bishop of Hieropolis and auxiliary bishop of Washington, D.C., Aug. 28, 1956; app. archbishop of New Orleans, installed Oct. 13, 1965.

Harper, Edward, C.SS.R.: b. July 23, 1910, Brooklyn, N.Y.; educ. Redemptorist Houses of Study; ord. priest June 18, 1939; ord. titular bishop of Heraclea Pontica and first prelate of Virgin Islands, Oct. 6, 1960; became first bishop, 1977, when prelacy was made diocese of St. Thomas.

Harrington, Timothy J.: b. Dec. 19, 1918, Holyoke, Mass.; educ. Holy Cross College (Worcester, Mass.), Grand Seminary (Montreal, Que.), Boston College School of Social Work; ord. priest Jan. 19, 1946; ord. titular bishop of Rusuca and auxiliary bishop of Worcester, Mass., July 2, 1968.

Harris, Vincent M.: b. Oct. 14, 1913, Conroe, Tex.; educ. St. Mary's Seminary (La Porte, Tex.), North American College and Gregorian Univ. (Rome), Catholic Univ. (Washington, D.C.); ord. priest Mar. 19, 1938; ord. first bishop of Beaumont, Tex., Sept. 28, 1966; app. titular bishop of Rotaria and coadjutor bishop of Austin, Apr. 27, 1971; bishop of Austin, Nov. 16, 1971.

Harrison, Francis J.: b. Aug. 12, 1912; Syracuse, N.Y.; educ. Notre Dame Univ. (Notre Dame, Ind.), St. Bernard's Seminary (Rochester, N.Y.), ord. priest June 4, 1937; ord. titular bishop of Aquae in Numidia and auxiliary bishop of Syracuse, Apr. 22, 1971; app. bishop of Syracuse, Nov. 9, 1976, installed Feb. 6, 1977.

Hart, Daniel A.: b. Aug. 24, 1927, Lawrence, Mass.; educ. St. John's Seminary (Brighton, Mass.); ord. priest Feb. 2, 1953; ord. titular bishop of Tepelta and auxiliary bishop of Boston, Oct. 18, 1976.

Hart, Joseph: b. Sept. 26, 1931, Kansas City, Missouri; educ. St. John Seminary (Kansas City, Mo.), St. Meinrad Seminary (Indianapolis, Ind.); ord. priest May 1, 1956; ord. titular bishop of Thimida Regia and auxiliary bishop of Cheyenne, Wyo., Aug. 31, 1976; app. bishop of Cheyenne, installed June 12, 1978.

Hastrich, Jerome J.: b. Nov. 13, 1914, Milwaukee, Wis.; educ. Marquette Univ., St. Francis Seminary (Milwaukee, Wis.); ord. priest Feb. 9, 1941; ord. titular bishop of Gurza and auxiliary bishop of Madison, Sept. 3, 1963; app. bishop of Gallup, N.Mex., Sept. 3, 1969.

Hayes, Nevin W., O.Carm: b. Feb. 17, 1922, Chicago, Ill.; entered Carmelite novitiate Aug. 15, 1939; educ. Mt. Carmel College (Niagara Falls, Canada), Whitefriars Hall and Catholic Univ. (Washington, D.C.); ord. priest June 8, 1946; prelate nullius of Sicuani, Peru, 1959; ord. titular bishop of Nova Sinna and prelate of Sicuani, Aug. 5, 1965; resigned November 1970; app. auxiliary bishop of Chicago, Feb. 2, 1971.

Head, Edward D.: b. Aug. 5, 1919, White Plains, N.Y.; educ. Cathedral College, St. Joseph's Seminary, Columbia Univ. (New York City); ord. priest Jan. 27, 1945; director of New York Catholic Charities; ord. titular bishop of Ardsratha and auxiliary bishop of New York, Mar. 19, 1970; app. bishop of Buffalo, Jan. 23, 1973, installed Mar. 19, 1973.

Helmsing, Charles H.: b. Mar. 23, 1908, Shrewsbury, Mo.; educ. St. Louis Preparatory Seminary (St. Louis, Mo.), Kenrick Seminary (Webster Groves, Mo.); ord. priest June 10, 1933; ord. titular bishop of Axomis and auxiliary bishop of St. Louis, Apr. 19, 1949; first bishop of Springfield-Cape Girardeau, Aug. 24, 1956; bishop of Kansas City-St. Joseph, 1962, installed Apr. 3, 1962; resigned June 25, 1977.

Herrmann, Edward J.: b. Nov. 6, 1913, Baltimore, Md.; educ. Mt. St. Mary's Seminary (Emmitsburg, Md.), Catholic Univ. (Washington, D.C.); ord. priest June 12, 1947; ord. titular bishop of Lamzella and auxiliary bishop of Washington, D.C., Apr. 26, 1966; app. bishop of Columbus, June 26, 1973.

Hettinger, Edward Gerhard: b. Oct. 14, 1902, Lancaster, O.; educ. St. Vincent's College (Beatty, Pa.); ord. priest June 2, 1928; ord. titular bishop of Teos and auxiliary bishop of Columbus, Feb. 24, 1942; retired October, 1977.

Hickey, Dennis W.: b. Oct. 28, 1914, Dansville, N.Y.; educ. Colgate Univ. and St. Bernard's Seminary (Rochester, N.Y.); ord.

priest June 7, 1941; ord. titular bishop of Rusuccuru and auxiliary bishop of Rochester, N.Y., Mar. 14, 1968.

Hickey, James A.: b. Oct. 11, 1920, Midland, Mich.; educ. Sacred Heart Seminary (Detroit, Mich.), Catholic Univ. (Washington, D.C.), Lateran Univ. and Angelicum (Rome), Michigan State Univ.; ord. priest June 15, 1946; ord. titular bishop of Taraqua and auxiliary bishop of Saginaw, Apr. 14, 1967; rector of North American College, Rome, 1969-74; app. bishop of Cleveland, June 5, 1974; installed July 16, 1974; app. archbishop of Washington, D.C., installed Aug. 5, 1980.

Hines, Vincent J.: b. Sept. 14, 1912, New Haven, Conn.; educ. St. Thomas Seminary (Bloomfield, Conn.), St. Sulpice Seminary (Paris), Lateran Univ. (Rome); ord. priest May 2, 1937; ord. bishop of Norwich, Conn., Mar. 17, 1960; retired June 17, 1975.

Hoch, Lambert A.: b. Feb. 6, 1903, Elkton, S.D.; educ. Creighton Univ. (Omaha, Nebr.), St. Paul Seminary (St. Paul, Minn.); ord. priest May 30, 1928; ord. bishop of Bismarck, Mar. 25, 1952; app. bishop of Sioux Falls Dec. 5, 1956; retired June 1978.

Hodapp, Robert L., S.J.: b. Oct. 1, 1910. Mankato, Minn.; educ. St. Stanislaus Seminary (Florissant, Mo.), St. Louis Univ. (St. Louis, Mo.); ord. priest June 18, 1941; ord. bishop of Belize, June 26, 1958.

Hodges, Joseph H.: b. Oct. 8, 1911, Harper's Ferry, W.Va.; educ. St. Charles College (Catonsville, Md.), North American College (Rome); ord. priest Dec. 8, 1935; ord. titular bishop of Rusadus and auxiliary bishop of Richmond, Oct. 15, 1952; named coadjutor bishop of Wheeling with right of succession, May 24, 1961; bishop of Wheeling, Nov. 23, 1962; title of see changed to Wheeling-Charleston 1974.

Hoffman, James R.: b. June 12, 1932, Fremont, O.; educ. Our Lady of the Lake Minor Seminary (Wawasee, Ind.), St. Meinrad College (St. Meinrad, Ind.); Mt. St. Mary Seminary (Norwood, O.); Catholic Univ. (Washington, D.C.); ord. priest July 28, 1957; ord. titular bishop of Italica and auxiliary bishop of Toledo, June 23, 1978.

Hogan, James J.: b. Oct. 17, 1911, Philadelphia, Pa.; educ. St. Charles College (Catonsville, Md.), St. Mary's Seminary (Baltimore), Gregorian Univ. (Rome), Catholic Univ. (Washington, D.C.); ord. priest Dec. 8, 1937; ord. titular bishop of Philomelium and auxiliary bishop of Trenton, Feb. 25, 1960; app. bishop of Altoona-Johnstown, installed July 6, 1966.

Hogan, Joseph L.: b. Mar. 11, 1916, Lima, N.Y.; educ. St. Bernard's Seminary (Rochester, N.Y.), Canisius College (Buffalo, N.Y.), Angelicum (Rome); ord. priest June 6, 1942; ord. bishop of Rochester, Nov. 28, 1969; resigned Nov. 28, 1978.

Houck, William Russell: b. June 26, 1926, Mobile Ala.; educ. St. Bernard Junior College (Cullman, Ala.), St. Mary's Seminary College and St. Mary's Seminary (Baltimore, Md.), Catholic Univ. (Washington, D.C.); ord. priest May 19, 1951; ord. titular bishop of Alessano and auxiliary bishop of Jackson, Miss., May 27, 1979, by Pope John Paul II.

Howard, Edward Daniel: b. Nov. 5, 1877, Cresco, Ia.; educ. St. Joseph's College (Dubuque, Ia.), St. Mary's College (St. Mary's, Kans.), St. Paul Seminary (St. Paul, Minn.); ord. priest June 12, 1906; ord. titular bishop of Isauropolis and auxiliary bishop of Davenport, Apr. 8, 1924; app. archbishop of Oregon City, Apr. 30, 1926; title changed to archbishop of Portland, Sept. 26, 1928; resigned Dec. 14, 1966; assigned titular see of Albule.

Howze, (Joseph) Lawson E.: b. Aug. 30, 1923, Daphne, Ala.; convert to Catholicism, 1948; educ. St. Bonaventure Univ. (St. Bonaventure, N.Y.); ord. priest May 7, 1959; ord. titular bishop of Massita and auxiliary bishop of Natchez-Jackson, Jan. 28, 1973; app. first bishop of Biloxi, Miss., Mar. 8, 1977; installed June 6, 1977.

Hubbard, Howard J.: b. Oct. 31, 1938, Troy, N.Y.; educ. St. Joseph's Seminary (Dunwoodie, N.Y.); North American College and Gregorian Univ. (Rome), Catholic Univ. (Washington, D.C.); ord. priest Dec. 18, 1963; ord. bishop of Albany, Mar. 27, 1977.

Hughes, Edward T.: b. Nov. 13, 1920, Landowne, Pa.; educ. St. Charles Seminary, Univ. of Pennsylvania (Philadelphia, Pa.); ord. priest May 31, 1947; ord. titular bishop of Segia and auxiliary bishop of Philadelphia, July 21, 1976.

Hughes, William A.: b. Sept. 23, 1921, Youngstown, O.; educ. St. Charles College (Catonsville, Md.), St. Mary's Seminary (Cleveland, O.) Notre Dame Univ. (Notre Dame, Ind.); ord. priest Apr. 6, 1946; ord. titular bishop of Inis Cathaig and auxiliary bishop of Youngstown, Sept. 12, 1974; app. bishop of Covington, installed May 8, 1979.

Hunthausen, Raymond G.: b. Aug. 21, 1921, Anaconda, Mont.; educ. Carroll College (Helena, Mont.), St. Edward's Seminary (Kenmore, Wash.), St. Louis Univ. (St. Louis, Mo.), Catholic Univ. (Washington, D.C.), Fordham Univ. (New York City), Notre Dame Univ. (Notre Dame, Ind.); ord. priest June 1, 1946; ord. bishop of Helena, Aug. 30, 1962; app. archbishop of Seattle, Feb. 25, 1975.

Hurley, Francis T.: b. Jan. 12, 1927, San Francisco, Calif.; educ. St. Patrick's Seminary (Menlo Park, Calif.), Catholic Univ. (Washington, D.C.); ord. priest June 16, 1951; assigned to NCWC in Washington, D.C., 1957; assistant (1958) and later (1968) associate secretary of NCCB and USCC; ord. titular bishop of Daimlaig and auxiliary bishop of Juneau, Alaska, Mar. 19, 1970; app.

bishop of Juneau, July 20, 1971, installed Sept. 8, 1971; app. archbishop of Anchorage, May 4, 1976, installed July 8, 1976.

Hurley, Mark J.: b. Dec. 13, 1919, San Francisco, Calif.; educ. St. Patrick's Seminary (Menlo Park, Calif.), Univ. of California (Berkeley), Catholic Univ. (Washington, D.C.), Lateran Univ. (Rome), Univ. of Portland (Portland, Ore.); ord. priest Sept. 23, 1944; ord. titular bishop of Thunusuda and auxiliary bishop of San Francisco, Jan. 4, 1968; app. bishop of Santa Rosa, Nov. 19, 1969.

I-J

Imesch, Joseph L.: b. June 21, 1931, Detroit, Mich.; educ. Sacred Heart Seminary (Detroit, Mich.), North American College, Gregorian Univ. (Rome); ord. priest Dec. 16, 1956; ord. titular bishop of Pomaria and auxiliary bishop of Detroit, Apr. 3, 1973; app. bishop of Joliet, June 30, 1979.

Issenmann, Clarence G.: b. May 30, 1907, Hamilton, O.; educ. St. Joseph's College (Rensselaer, Ind.), St. Gregory's Seminary (Cincinnati, O.), St. Mary of the West Seminary (Norwood, O.); ord. priest June 29, 1932; ord. titular bishop of Phytea and auxiliary bishop of Cincinnati, May 25, 1954; bishop of Columbus, 1957-64; app. titular bishop of Filaca, coadjutor bishop of Cleveland and apostolic administrator *"sede plena,"* 1964; bishop of Cleveland, 1966; resigned June 5, 1974, because of ill health.

Johnson, William R.: b. Nov. 19, 1918, Tonopah, Nev.; educ. Los Angeles College and St. John's Seminary (Camarillo, Calif.), National Catholic School of Social Service, Catholic Univ. (Washington, D.C.); ord. priest May 28, 1944; ord. titular bishop of Blera and auxiliary bishop of Los Angeles, Mar. 25, 1971; app. first bishop of Orange, Calif., Mar. 30, 1976, installed June 18, 1976.

Joyce, Robert F.: b. Oct. 7, 1896, Proctor, Vt.; educ. Univ. of Vermont (Burlington, Vt.), Grand Seminary (Montreal, Canada); ord. priest May 26, 1923; ord. titular bishop of Citium and auxiliary bishop of Burlington, Oct. 28, 1954; installed as bishop of Burlington, Feb. 26, 1957; resigned Dec. 14, 1971.

K

Kalisz, Raymond P., S.V.D.: b. 1928, Melvindale, Mich.; educ. St. Mary's Seminary (Techny, Ill.); ord. priest 1954; app. bishop of Wewak, Papua New Guinea, June 4, 1980.

Keeler, William Henry: b. Mar. 4, 1931, San Antonio, Tex.; educ. St. Charles Seminary (Overbrook, Pa.), North American College, Pontifical Gregorian Univ. (Rome); ord. priest July 17, 1955; ord. titular bishop of Ulcinium and auxiliary bishop of Harrisburg, Sept. 21, 1979.

Kellenberg, Walter P.: b. June 3, 1901, New York, N.Y.; educ. Cathedral College (New York, City), St. Joseph Seminary (Dunwoodie, N.Y.); ord. priest June 2, 1928; ord. titular bishop of Joannina and auxiliary bishop of New York, Oct. 5, 1953; app. bishop of Ogdensburg, Jan. 19, 1954; app. first bishop of Rockville Centre Apr. 16, 1957, installed May 27, 1957; retired May 4, 1976.

Kelly, Thomas C., O.P.: b. July 14, 1931, Rochester, N.Y.; educ. Providence College (Providence, R.I.), Immaculate Conception College (Washington, D.C.), Angelicum (Rome); professed in Dominicans, Aug. 26, 1952; secretary, apostolic delegation, Washington, D.C., 1965-71; associate general secretary, 1971-77, and general secretary, 1977- , NCCB/USCC; ord. titular bishop of Tusurus and auxiliary bishop of Washington, D.C., Aug. 15, 1977.

Kenny, Michael H.: b. June 26, 1937, Hollywood, Calif.; educ. St. Joseph College (Mountain View, Calif.), St. Patrick's Seminary (Menlo Park, Calif.), Catholic Univ. (Washington, D.C.); ord. priest Mar. 30, 1963; ord. bishop of Juneau, May 27, 1979.

Kinney, John: b. June 11, 1937, Oelwein, Iowa; educ. Nazareth Hall and St. Paul Seminaries (St. Paul, Minn.); Pontifical Lateran University (Rome); ord. priest Feb. 2, 1963; ord. titular bishop of Caorle and auxiliary bishop of St. Paul and Minneapolis, Jan. 25, 1977.

Kocisko, Stephen: b. June 11, 1915, Minneapolis, Minn.; educ. Nazareth Hall Minor Seminary (St. Paul, Minn.), Pontifical Ruthenian College, Urban Univ. (Rome); ord. priest Mar. 30, 1941; ord. titular bishop of Teveste and auxiliary bishop of apostolic exarchate of Pittsburgh, Oct. 23, 1956; installed as first eparch of the eparchy of Passaic, Sept. 10, 1963; app. eparch of Byzantine-Rite diocese of Pittsburgh, installed Mar. 5, 1968; app. first metropolitan of Munhall, installed June 11, 1969; title of see changed to Pittsburgh, 1977.

Koester, Charles R.: b. Sept. 16, 1915, Jefferson City, Mo.; educ. Conception Academy (Conception, Mo.), St. Louis Preparatory Seminary and Kenrick Seminary (St. Louis, Mo.), North American College (Rome); ord. priest Dec. 20, 1941; ord. titular bishop of Suacia and auxiliary bishop of St. Louis, Feb. 11, 1971.

Krawczak, Arthur H.: b. Feb. 2, 1913, Detroit, Mich.; educ. Sacred Heart Seminary, Sts. Cyril and Methodius Seminary (Orchard Lake, Mich.), Catholic Univ. (Washington, D.C.); ord. priest May 18, 1940; ord. titular bishop of Subbar and auxiliary bishop of Detroit, Apr. 3, 1973.

Krol, John J.: (See Cardinals, Biographies.)

Kucera, Daniel, O.S.B.: b. May 7, 1923, Chicago, Ill.; educ. St. Procopius College (Lisle, Ill.), Catholic Univ. (Washington, D.C.); professed in Order of St. Benedict,

June 16, 1944; ord. priest May 26, 1949; abbot, St. Procopius Abbey, 1964-71; pres. Illinois Benedictine College, 1959-65 and 1971-76; ord. titular bishop of Natchez and auxiliary bishop of Joliet, July 21, 1977; app. bishop of Salina, Mar. 11, 1980.

Kupfer, William F., M.M.: b. Jan. 28, 1909, Brooklyn, N.Y.; educ. Cathedral College (Brooklyn, N.Y.), Maryknoll Seminary (Maryknoll, N.Y.); ord. priest June 11, 1933; missionary in China; app. prefect apostolic of Taichung, Formosa, 1951; ord. first bishop of Taichung, July 25, 1962.

L

Lambert, Francis, S.M.: b. Feb. 7, 1921, Lawrence, Mass.; educ. Marist Seminary (Framingham, Mass.); ord. priest, June 29, 1946; served in Marist missions in Oceania; provincial of Marist Oceania province, 1971; ord. bishop of Port Vila, Vanuatu (New Hebrides), Mar. 20, 1977.

Larkin, W. Thomas: b. Mar. 31, 1923, Mt. Morris, N.Y.; educ. St. Andrew Seminary and St. Bernard Seminary (Rochester, N.Y.); Angelicum Univ. (Rome); ord. priest May 15, 1947; ord. bishop of St. Petersburg, May 27, 1979.

Law, Bernard F.: b. Nov. 4, 1931, Torreon, Mexico; educ. Harvard Univ. (Cambridge, Mass.), St. Joseph Seminary (St. Benedict, La.), Pontifical College Josephinum (Worthington, O.); ord. priest May 21, 1961; editor of *Mississippi Register* (now *Mississippi Today*), 1963-68; director of NCCB Committee on Ecumenical and Interreligious Affairs, 1968-71; vicar general of Natchez-Jackson diocese, 1971-73; ord. bishop of Springfield-Cape Girardeau, Mo., Dec. 5, 1973.

Leech, George Leo: b. May 21, 1890, Ashley, Pa.; educ. St. Charles Borromeo Seminary (Overbrook, Pa.), Catholic Univ. (Washington, D.C.); ord. priest May 29, 1920; ord. titular bishop of Mela and auxiliary bishop of Harrisburg, Oct. 17, 1935; bishop of Harrisburg Dec. 19, 1935; resigned Oct. 19, 1971; app. titular bishop of Allegheny.

Leipzig, Francis P.: b. June 29, 1895, Chilton, Wis.; educ. St. Francis Seminary (Milwaukee, Wis.), Mt. Angel Seminary (St. Benedict, Ore.), St. Patrick's Seminary (Menlo Park, Calif.); ord. priest Apr. 14, 1920; ord. bishop of Baker, Sept. 12, 1950; retired June 30, 1971.

Lemay, Leo, S.M.: b. Sept. 23, 1909, Lawrence, Mass.; educ. Marist College (Washington, D.C.), Gregorian Univ. (Rome); ord. priest Apr. 15, 1933; ord. titular bishop of Agbia and vicar apostolic of North Solomon Islands, Sept. 21, 1960; first bishop of Bougainville, Nov. 15, 1966; resigned July 1, 1974.

Leonard, Vincent M.: b. Dec. 11, 1908, Pittsburgh, Pa.; educ. Duquesne Univ. (Pittsburgh, Pa.), St. Vincent Seminary (Latrobe, Pa.); ord. priest June 16, 1935; ord. titular bishop of Arsacal and auxiliary bishop of Pittsburgh, Apr. 21, 1964; app. bishop of Pittsburgh, installed July 2, 1969.

Lessard, Raymond W.: b. Dec. 21, 1930, Grafton, N.D.; educ. St. Paul Seminary (St. Paul, Minn.), North American College (Rome); ord. priest Dec. 16, 1956; served on staff of the Congregation for Bishops in the Roman Curia, 1964-73; ord. bishop of Savannah, Apr. 27, 1973.

Leven, Stephen A.: b. Apr. 30, 1905, Blackwell, Okla.; educ. St. Gregory's College (Shawnee, Okla.), St. Benedict's College (Atchison, Kans.), St. Mary's Seminary (La Porte, Tex.), American College (Louvain, Belgium); ord. priest June 10, 1928; ord. titular bishop of Bure and auxiliary bishop of San Antonio, Feb. 8, 1956; app. bishop of San Angelo, Tex., installed Nov. 25, 1969; resigned 1979.

Lipscomb, Oscar H.: b. Sept. 21, 1931, Mobile, Ala.; educ. McGill Institute, St. Bernard College (Cullman, Ala.), North American College and Gregorian Univ. (Rome), Catholic Univ. (Washington, D.C.); ord. priest July 15, 1956; ord. first archbishop of Mobile, Nov. 16, 1980.

Lohmuller, Martin J.: b. Aug. 21, 1919, Philadelphia, Pa.; educ. St. Charles Borromeo Seminary (Philadelphia, Pa.), Catholic Univ. (Washington, D.C.); ord. priest June 3, 1944; ord. titular bishop of Ramsbury and auxiliary bishop of Philadelphia, Apr. 2, 1970.

Losten, Basil: b. May 11, 1930, Chesapeake City, Md.; educ. St. Basil's College (Stamford, Conn.), Catholic University (Washington, D.C.); ord. priest June 10, 1957; ord. titular bishop of Arcadiopolis in Asia and auxiliary bishop of Ukrainian archeparchy of Philadelphia, May 25, 1971; app. apostolic administrator of archeparchy, 1976; app. bishop of Ukrainian eparchy of Stamford, 1977.

Lubachivsky, Myroslav J.: b. June 24, 1914, Dolynian, Ukraine; educ. Innsbruck Univ. (Austria), Gregorian Univ. and Biblicum (Rome); began pastoral work in U.S. in 1947; ord. archbishop of Ukrainian rite archeparchy of Philadelphia, Nov. 12, 1979; app. coadjutor archbishop of Lwow of the Ukrainians, Mar. 27, 1980, and apostolic administrator of Philadelphia.

Lucker, Raymond A.: b. Feb. 24, 1927, St. Paul, Minn.; educ. St. Paul Seminary (St. Paul, Minn.); University of Minnesota (Minneapolis), Angelicum (Rome); ord. priest June 7, 1952; director of USCC department of education, 1968-71; ord. titular bishop of Meta and auxiliary bishop of St. Paul and Minneapolis, Sept. 8, 1971; app. bishop of New Ulm, Dec. 23, 1975, installed Feb. 19, 1976.

Lyke, James Patterson, O.F.M.: b. Feb. 18, 1939, Chicago, Ill.; educ. Quincy College (Quincy, Ill.), Antonianum (Rome), Union Graduate School (Cincinnati, O.); professed in Order of Friars Minor, June 21, 1963; ord. priest June 24, 1966; president of National Black Catholic Clergy Caucus; ord. titular bishop of Furnos Maior and auxiliary bishop of Cleveland, Aug. 1, 1979.

Lynch, George E.: b. Mar. 4, 1917, New York, N.Y.; educ. Fordham Univ. (New York), Mt. St. Mary's Seminary (Emmitsburg, Md.), Catholic Univ. (Washington, D.C.); ord. priest May 29, 1943; ord. titular bishop of Satafi and auxiliary bishop of Raleigh Jan. 6, 1970.

Lyons, Thomas W.: b. Sept. 26, 1923, Washington, D.C.; educ. St. Charles College (Catonsville, Md.), St. Mary's Seminary (Baltimore, Md.); ord. priest May 22, 1948; ord. titular bishop of Mortlach and auxiliary bishop of Washington, D.C., Sept. 12, 1974.

M

McAuliffe, Michael F.: b. Nov. 22, 1920, Kansas City, Mo.; educ. St. Louis Preparatory Seminary (St. Louis, Mo.), Catholic Univ. (Washington, D.C.); ord. priest May 31, 1945; ord. bishop of Jefferson City, Aug. 18, 1969.

McCarrick, Theodore E.: b. July 7, 1930, New York, N.Y.; educ. Fordham Univ. (Bronx, N.Y.), St. Joseph's Seminary (Dunwoodie, N.Y.), Catholic Univ. (Washington, D.C.); ord. priest May 31, 1958; dean of students Catholic Univ. of America, 1961-63; pres., Catholic Univ. of Puerto Rico, 1965-69; secretary to Cardinal Cooke, 1970; ord. titular bishop of Rusubisir and auxiliary bishop of New York, June 29, 1977.

McCarthy, Edward A.: b. Apr. 10, 1918, Cincinnati, O.; educ. Mt. St. Mary Seminary (Norwood, O.), Catholic Univ. (Washington, D.C.), Lateran and Angelicum (Rome); ord. priest May 29, 1943; ord. titular bishop of Tamascani and auxiliary bishop of Cincinnati, June 15, 1965; first bishop of Phoenix, Ariz., Dec. 2, 1969; app. coadjutor archbishop of Miami, Fla., July 7, 1976; succeeded as archbishop of Miami, July 26, 1977.

McCarthy, John E., b. June 21, 1930, Houston, Tex.; educ. Univ. of St. Thomas (Houston, Tex.); ord. priest May 26, 1956; assistant director Social Action Dept. USCC, 1967-69; executive director Texas Catholic Conference; ord. titular bishop of Pedena and auxiliary bishop of Galveston-Houston, Mar. 14, 1979.

McCauley, Vincent, C.S.C.: b. Mar. 8, 1906, Council Bluffs, Ia.; educ. Notre Dame Univ. (Notre Dame, Ind.), Holy Cross Seminary (Washington, D.C.); ord. priest June 24, 1943; ord. first bishop of Fort Portal, Uganda, May 18, 1961; resigned to Africanize the diocese Dec. 1, 1972; general secretary of Association of Member Episcopal Conferences in Eastern Africa (AMECEA).

McCormick, J. Carroll: b. Dec. 15, 1907, Philadelphia, Pa.; educ. College Ste. Marie (Montreal), St. Charles Seminary (Overbrook, Pa.), Minor and Major Roman Seminary (Rome); ord. priest July 10, 1932; ord. titular bishop of Ruspae and auxiliary bishop of Philadelphia, Apr. 23, 1947; app. bishop of Altoona-Johnstown, installed Sept. 21, 1960; app. bishop of Scranton, installed May 25, 1966.

McDonald, Andrew J.: b. Oct. 24, 1923, Savannah, Ga.; educ. St. Mary's Seminary (Baltimore, Md.), Catholic Univ. (Washington, D.C.), Lateran Univ. (Rome); ord. priest May 8, 1948; ord. bishop of Little Rock, Sept. 5, 1972.

McDonald, William J.: b. June 17, 1904, Mooncoin, Ireland; educ. St. Kieran's College and Seminary (Kilkenny, Ireland), Catholic Univ. (Washington, D.C.); ord. priest June 10, 1928; rector of Catholic Univ. of America, 1957-67; ord. titular bishop of Aquae Regiae and auxiliary bishop of Washington, May 19, 1964; app. auxiliary bishop of San Francisco, July 26, 1967; retired 1979.

McDonough, Thomas J.: b. Dec. 5, 1911, Philadelphia, Pa.; educ. St. Charles Seminary (Overbrook, Pa.), Catholic Univ. (Washington, D.C.); ord. priest May 26, 1938; ord. titular bishop of Thenae and auxiliary bishop of St. Augustine, Apr. 30, 1947; app. auxiliary bishop of Savannah, Jan. 2, 1957; named bishop of Savannah, installed Apr. 27, 1960; app. archbishop of Louisville, installed May 2, 1967.

McDowell, John B.: b. July 17, 1921, New Castle, Pa.; educ. St. Vincent College, St. Vincent Theological Seminary (Latrobe, Pa.), Catholic Univ. (Washington, D.C.); ord. priest Nov. 4, 1945; superintendent of schools, Pittsburgh diocese, 1955-70; ord. titular bishop of Tamazuca, and auxiliary bishop of Pittsburgh, Sept. 8, 1966.

McEleney, John J., S.J.: b. Nov. 13, 1895, Woburn, Mass.; educ. Boston College (Boston, Mass.), Jesuit Scholasticate (New England Province); entered Society of Jesus, 1918; ord. priest June 18, 1930; app. provincial of New England Province, 1944; ord. titular bishop of Zeugma and vicar apostolic of Jamaica, Apr. 15, 1950; title changed to bishop of Kingston, Feb. 29, 1956; archbishop of Kingston, Sept. 14, 1967; retired Sept. 1, 1970.

McFarland, Norman F.: b. Feb. 21, 1922, Martinez, Calif.; educ. St. Patrick's Seminary (Menlo Park, Calif.), Catholic Univ. (Washington, D.C.); ord. priest June 15, 1946; ord. titular bishop of Bida and auxiliary bishop of San Francisco, Sept. 8, 1970; apostolic adminstrator of Reno, 1974; app. bishop of Reno, Feb. 10, 1976, installed Mar. 31, 1976; title of see changed to Reno-Las Vegas, 1977.

McGann, John R.: b. Dec. 2, 1924, Brooklyn, N.Y.; educ. Cathedral College (Brooklyn, N.Y.), Immaculate Conception Seminary (Huntington, L.I.); ord. priest June 3, 1950; ord. titular bishop of Morosbisdus and auxiliary bishop of Rockville Centre, Jan. 7, 1971; vicar general and episcopal vicar; app. bishop of Rockville Centre May 3, 1976, installed June 24, 1976.

McGarry, Urban, T.O.R.: b. Nov. 11, 1911, Warren, Pa.; ord. priest Oct. 3, 1942, in India; prefect apostolic of Bhagalpur, Aug. 7, 1956; ord. first bishop of Bhagalpur, India, May 10, 1965.

McGucken, Joseph T.: b. Mar. 13, 1902, Los Angeles, Calif.; educ. St. Patrick's Seminary (Menlo Park, Calif.), North American College (Rome); ord. priest Jan. 15, 1928; ord. titular bishop of Sanavus and auxiliary bishop of Los Angeles, Mar. 19, 1941; app. coadjutor bishop of Sacramento with right of succession, Oct. 26, 1955; bishop of Sacramento, Jan. 14, 1957; archbishop of San Francisco, installed Apr. 3, 1962; resigned Feb. 22, 1977.

McGurkin, Edward A., M.M.: b. June 22, 1905, Hartford, Conn.; educ. Maryknoll Seminary (Maryknoll, N.Y.); ord. priest Sept. 14, 1930; ord. first bishop of Maswa, Tanganyika, Oct. 3, 1956; title of see changed to Shinyanga (Tanzania), 1957; resigned Jan. 30, 1975.

McKinney, Joseph C.: b. Sept. 10, 1928, Grand Rapids, Mich.; educ. St. Joseph's Seminary (Grand Rapids, Mich.), Seminaire de Philosophie (Montreal, Canada), Urban Univ. (Rome, Italy); ord. priest Dec. 20, 1953; ord. titular bishop of Lentini and auxiliary bishop of Grand Rapids, Sept. 26, 1968.

McLaughlin, Bernard J.: b. Nov. 19, 1912, Buffalo, N.Y.; educ. Urban Univ. (Rome, Italy); ord. priest Dec. 21, 1935, at Rome; ord. titular bishop of Mottola and auxiliary bishop of Buffalo, Jan. 6, 1969.

McManus, William E.: b. Jan. 27, 1914, Chicago, Ill.; educ. St. Mary of the Lake Seminary (Mundelein, Ill.), Catholic Univ. (Washington, D.C.); ord. priest Apr. 15, 1939; ord. titular bishop of Mesarfelta and auxiliary bishop of Chicago, Aug. 24, 1967; app. bishop of Fort Wayne-South Bend, Aug. 31, 1976, installed Oct. 19, 1976.

McNabb, John C., O.S.A.: b. Dec. 11, 1925, Beloit, Wis.; educ. Villanova Univ. (Villanova, Pa.), Augustinian College and Catholic Univ. (Washington, D.C.), De Paul Univ. (Chicago, Ill.); ord. priest May 24, 1952; ord. titular bishop of Saia Maggiore and prelate of Chulucanas, Peru, June 17, 1967.

McNamara, Lawrence J.: b. Aug. 5, 1928, Chicago, Ill.; educ. St. Paul Seminary (St. Paul, Minn.), Catholic Univ. (Washington, D.C.); ord. priest May 30, 1953; executive director of Campaign for Human Development

1973-77; ord. bishop of Grand Island, Nebr., Mar. 28, 1978.

McNaughton, William J., M.M.: b. Dec. 7, 1926, Lawrence, Mass.; educ. Maryknoll Seminary (Maryknoll, N.Y.); ord. priest June 13, 1953; ord. titular bishop of Thuburbo Minus and vicar apostolic of Inchon, Korea, Aug. 24, 1961; title changed to bishop of Inchon, Mar. 10, 1962.

McNicholas, Joseph A.: b. Jan. 13, 1923, St. Louis, Mo.; educ. Cardinal Glennon College, Kenrick Seminary and St. Louis Univ. (all in St. Louis, Mo.); ord. priest June 7, 1949; ord. titular bishop of Scala and auxiliary bishop of St. Louis, Mar. 25, 1969; app. bishop of Springfield, Ill., July 22, 1975, installed Sept. 3, 1975.

McShea, Joseph M.: b. Feb. 22, 1907, Latimer, Pa.; educ. St. Charles Seminary (Philadelphia, Pa.), Major Pontifical Roman Seminary (Rome); ord. priest Dec. 6, 1931; ord. titular bishop of Mina and auxiliary bishop of Philadelphia, Mar. 19, 1952; app. first bishop of Allentown, installed Apr. 11, 1961.

Madera, Joseph J., M.Sp.S.: b. Nov. 27, 1927, San Francisco, Calif.; educ. Domus Studiorum of the Missionaries of the Holy Spirit (Coyoacan, D.F. Mexico); ord. priest June 15, 1957; ord. coadjutor bishop of Fresno, Mar. 4, 1980; bishop of Fresno, July 1, 1980.

Maginn, Edward J.: b. Jan. 4, 1897, Glasgow, Scotland; educ. Holy Cross College (Worcester, Mass.), St. Joseph's Seminary (Yonkers, N.Y.); ord. priest June 10, 1922; ord. titular bishop of Curium and auxiliary bishop of Albany, Sept. 12, 1957; apostolic administrator of Albany, 1966-69; retired July 8, 1972.

Maguire, John J.: b. Dec. 11, 1904, New York, N.Y.; educ. Cathedral College (New York City), St. Joseph's Seminary (Dunwoodie, N.Y.), North American College (Rome); ord. priest Dec. 22, 1928; ord. titular bishop of Antiphrae and auxiliary bishop of New York, June 29, 1959; app. titular archbishop of Tabalta and coadjutor archbishop of New York, Sept. 15, 1965; retired Jan. 8, 1980.

Maguire, Joseph F.: b. Sept. 4, 1919, Boston, Mass.; educ. Boston College, St. John's Seminary (Boston, Mass.); ord. priest June 29, 1945; ord. titular bishop of Macteris and auxiliary bishop of Boston, Feb. 2, 1972; app. coadjutor bishop of Springfield, Mass., Apr. 13, 1976; succeeded as bishop of Springfield, Mass., Oct. 15, 1977.

Maher, Leo T.: b. July 1, 1915, Mount Union, Ia.; educ. St. Joseph's College (Mountain View, Calif.); St. Patrick's Seminary (Menlo Park, Calif.); ord. priest Dec. 18, 1943; ord. first bishop of Santa Rosa, April 5, 1962; bishop of San Diego, Oct. 4, 1969.

Mahoney, James P.: b. Aug. 16, 1925, Kingston, N.Y.; educ. St. Joseph's Seminary (Dunwoodie, N.Y.); ord. priest May 19, 1951; ord. titular bishop of Ipagro and auxiliary bishop of New York, Sept. 15, 1972.

Mahony, Roger M.: b. Feb. 27, 1936, Hollywood, Calif.; educ. St. John's Seminary (Camarillo, Calif.), National Catholic School of Social Service (Catholic Univ., Washington, D.C.); ord. priest May 1, 1962; ord. titular bishop of Tamascani and auxiliary bishop of Fresno, Mar. 19, 1975; app. bishop of Stockton, installed Apr. 25, 1980.

Malone, James W.: b. Mar. 8, 1920, Youngstown, O.; educ. St. Charles Preparatory Seminary (Catonsville, Md.), St. Mary's Seminary (Cleveland, O.), Catholic Univ. (Washington, D.C.); ord. priest May 26, 1945; ord. titular bishop of Alabanda and auxiliary bishop of Youngstown, Mar. 24, 1960; apostolic administrator, 1966; bishop of Youngstown, installed June 20, 1968.

Maloney, Charles G.: b. Sept. 9, 1912, Louisville, Ky.; educ. St. Joseph's College (Rensselaer, Ind.), North American College (Rome); ord. priest Dec. 8, 1937; ord. titular bishop of Capsa and auxiliary bishop of Louisville, Feb. 2, 1955.

Maloney, David M.: b. Mar. 15, 1912, Littleton, Colo.; educ. St. Thomas Seminary (Denver, Colo.), Gregorian Univ. and Apollinare Univ. (Rome); ord. priest Dec. 8, 1936; ord. titular bishop of Ruspe and auxiliary bishop of Denver, Jan. 4, 1961; app. bishop of Wichita, Kans., Dec. 6, 1967.

Manning, Thomas R., O.F.M.: b. Aug. 29, 1922, Baltimore, Md.; educ. Duns Scotus College (Southfield, Mich.), Holy Name College (Washington, D.C.); ord. priest June 5, 1948; ord. titular bishop of Arsamosata and prelate of Coroico, Bolivia, July 14, 1959.

Manning, Timothy: (See Cardinals, Biographies.)

Marcinkus, Paul C.: b. Jan. 15, 1922, Cicero, Ill.; ord. priest May 3, 1947; served in Vatican secretariat from 1952; ord. titular bishop of Orta, Jan. 6, 1969; secretary (1968-71) and president (1971-   ) of Institute for Works of Religion (Vatican Bank).

Marconi, Dominic A.: b. Mar. 13, 1927, Newark, N.J.; educ. Seton Hall Univ. (S. Orange, N.J.), Immaculate Conception Seminary (Darlington, N.J.), Catholic Univ. (Washington, D.C.); ord. priest May 30, 1953; ord. titular bishop of Bure and auxiliary bishop of Newark, June 25, 1976.

Mardaga, Thomas J.: b. May 14, 1913, Baltimore, Md.; educ. St. Charles College (Catonsville, Md.), St. Mary's Seminary (Baltimore, Md.); ord. priest May 14, 1940; ord. titular bishop of Mutugenna and auxiliary bishop of Baltimore, Jan. 25, 1967; app. bishop of Wilmington, installed Apr. 6, 1968.

Marino, Eugene A., S.S.J.: b. May 29, 1934, Biloxi, Miss.; educ. Epiphany Apostolic College and Mary Immaculate Novitiate (Newburgh, N.Y.), St. Joseph's Seminary (Washington, D.C.), Catholic Univ. (Washington, D.C.), Loyola Univ. (New Orleans, La.), Fordham Univ. (New York City); ord. priest June 9, 1962; ord. titular bishop of Walla Walla and auxiliary bishop of Washington, D.C., Sept. 12, 1974.

Marshall, John A.: b. Apr. 26, 1928, Worcester, Mass.; educ. Holy Cross College (Worcester, Mass.), Sulpician Seminary (Montreal), North American College and Gregorian Univ. (Rome), Assumption College (Worcester); ord. priest Dec. 19, 1953; ord. bishop of Burlington, Jan. 25, 1972.

Matthiesen, Leroy Theodore: b. June 11, 1921, Olfen, Tex.; educ. Josephinum College (Columbus, O.), Catholic Univ. (Washington, D.C.), Register School of Journalism; ord. priest Mar. 10, 1946; ord. bishop of Amarillo, May 30, 1980.

May, John L.: b. Mar. 31, 1922, Evanston, Ill.; educ. St. Mary of the Lake Seminary (Mundelein, Ill.); ord. priest May 3, 1947; general secretary and vice-president of the Catholic Church Extension Society, 1959; ord. titular bishop of Tagarbala and auxiliary bishop of Chicago, Aug. 24, 1967; bishop of Mobile, Ala., Sept. 29, 1969; app. archbishop of St. Louis, installed Mar. 25, 1980.

Medeiros, Humberto S.: (See Cardinals, Biographies.)

Mendez, Alfred, C.S.C.: b. June 3, 1907, Chicago, Ill.; educ. Notre Dame Univ. (Notre Dame, Ind.), Institute of Holy Cross (Washington, D.C.); ord. priest June 24, 1935; ord. first bishop of Arecibo, Puerto Rico, Oct. 28, 1960; resigned Jan. 24, 1974.

Mestice, Anthony F.: b. Dec. 6, 1923, New York, N.Y.; educ. St. Joseph Seminary (Yonkers, N.Y.); ord. priest June 4, 1949; ord. titular bishop of Villa Nova and auxiliary bishop of New York Apr. 27, 1973.

Metzger, Sidney Matthew: b. July 11, 1902, Fredericksburg, Tex.; educ. St. John's Seminary (San Antonio, Tex.), North American College (Rome); ord. priest Apr. 3, 1926; ord. titular bishop of Birtha and auxiliary bishop of Santa Fe, Apr. 10, 1940; app. coadjutor bishop of El Paso, Dec. 26, 1941; bishop of El Paso, Dec. 1, 1942; retired May 29, 1978.

Michaels, James E., S.S.C.: b. May 30, 1926, Chicago, Ill.; educ. Columban Seminary (St. Columban, Neb.), Gregorian Univ. (Rome); ord. priest Dec. 21, 1951; ord. titular bishop of Verbe and auxiliary bishop of Kwang Ju, Korea, Apr. 14, 1966; app. auxiliary bishop of Wheeling, Apr. 3, 1973; title of see changed to Wheeling-Charleston, 1974.

Mihalik, Emil J.: b. Feb. 6, 1920, Pittsburgh, Pa.; educ. St. Procopius Seminary (Lisle, Ill.), Duquesne Univ. (Pittsburgh, Pa.); ord. priest Sept. 21, 1945; ord. first bishop of Byzantine Rite diocese of Parma, O., June 12, 1969.

Minder, John, O.S.F.S.: b. Nov. 1, 1923, Philadelphia, Pa.; ord. priest June 3, 1950; ord. bishop of Keimos, South Africa, Jan. 10, 1968.

Moran, William J.: b. Jan. 15, 1906, San Francisco, Calif.; educ. St. Patrick's Seminary (Menlo Park, Calif.); ord. priest June 20, 1931; Army chaplain, 1933; ord. titular bishop of Centuria and auxiliary to the military vicar, Dec. 13, 1965.

Moreno, Manuel D.: b. Nov. 27, 1930, Placentia, Calif.; educ. Univ. of California (Los Angeles), Our Lady Queen of Angels (San Fernando, Calif.), St. John's Seminary (Camarillo, Calif.); ord. priest Apr. 25, 1961; ord. titular bishop of Tanagra and auxiliary bishop of Los Angeles, Feb. 19, 1977.

Morkovsky, John Louis: b. Aug. 16, 1909, Praha, Tex.; educ. St. John's Seminary (San Antonio, Tex.), North American College, Urban Univ. and Gregorian Univ. (Rome), Catholic Univ. (Washington, D.C.); ord. priest Dec. 5, 1933; ord titular bishop of Hieron and auxiliary bishop of Amarillo, Feb. 22, 1956; app. bishop of Amarillo, Aug. 27, 1958; titular bishop of Tigava and coadjutor bishop of Galveston-Houston with right of succession, June 11, 1963; apostolic administrator; president Texas Conference of Churches, 1970-72; bishop of Galveston-Houston, Apr. 22, 1975.

Morneau, Robert F.: b. Sept. 10, 1938, New London, Wis.; educ. St. Norbert's College (De Pere, Wis.), Sacred Heart Seminary (Oneida, Wis.), Catholic Univ. (Washington, D.C.); ord. priest May 28, 1966; ord. titular bishop of Massa Lubrense and auxiliary bishop of Green Bay, Feb. 22, 1979.

Morrow, Louis La Ravoire, S.D.B.: b. Dec. 24, 1892, Weatherford, Tex.; educ. Salesian School and Palafox (Puebla, Mexico); professed in Salesians of St. John Bosco, Sept. 29, 1912; ord. priest May 21, 1921; ord. bishop of Krishnagar, India, Oct. 29, 1939; resigned Oct. 31, 1969.

Mueller, Joseph M.: b. Dec. 1, 1894, St. Louis, Mo.; educ. Pontifical College Josephinum (Worthington, O.); ord. priest June 14, 1919; ord. titular bishop of Sinda and coadjutor bishop of Sioux City, Oct. 16, 1947; bishop of Sioux City, Sept. 20, 1948; resigned Oct. 15, 1970.

Mugavero, Francis John: b. June 8, 1914, Brooklyn, N.Y.; educ. Cathedral College (Brooklyn, N.Y.), Immaculate Conception Seminary (Huntington, N.Y.), Fordham Univ. (New York City); ord. priest May 18, 1940; ord. bishop of Brooklyn, Sept. 12, 1968.

Mulcahy, John J.: b. June 26, 1922, Dorchester, Mass.; educ. St. John's Seminary (Brighton, Mass.); ord. priest May 1, 1947; rector Pope John XXIII Seminary for Delayed Vocations, 1969-73; ord. titular bishop of Penafiel and auxiliary bishop of Boston, Feb. 11, 1975.

Mulrooney, Charles R.: b. Jan. 13, 1906, Brooklyn, N.Y.; educ. Cathedral College (Brooklyn, N.Y.), St. Mary's Seminary (Baltimore, Md.), Sulpician Seminary (Washington, D.C.); ord. priest June 10, 1930; ord. titular bishop of Valentiniana and auxiliary bishop of Brooklyn, Apr. 22, 1959.

Mulvee, Robert E.: b. Feb. 15, 1930, Boston, Mass.; educ. St. Thomas Seminary (Bloomfield, Conn.), University Seminary (Ottawa, Ont., Canada), American College (Louvain, Belgium), Lateran Univ. (Rome); ord. priest June 30, 1957; ord. titular bishop of Summa and auxiliary bishop of Manchester, N.H., Apr. 14, 1977.

Mundo, Michael P.: b. July 25, 1937, New York, N.Y.; educ. Fordham Univ. (Bronx, N.Y.), St. Jerome's College (Kitchener, Ont., Canada), St. Francis Seminary (Loretto, Pa.); ord. May 19, 1962; missionary in Brazil from 1963; ord. titular bishop of Blanda Julia and auxiliary bishop of Jatai, Brazil, June 2, 1978.

Murphy, Michael J.: b. July 1, 1915, Cleveland, O.; educ. Niagara Univ. (Niagara Falls, N.Y.); North American College (Rome), Catholic Univ. (Washington, D.C.); ord. priest Feb. 28, 1942; ord. titular bishop of Ariendela and auxiliary bishop of Cleveland, June 11, 1976; app. coadjutor bishop of Erie, Nov. 20, 1978.

Murphy, Philip Francis: b. Mar. 25, 1933, Cumberland, Md.; educ. St. Mary Seminary (Baltimore, Md.), North American College (Rome); ord. priest Dec. 20, 1958; ord. titular bishop of Tacarata and auxiliary bishop of Baltimore, Feb. 29, 1976.

Murphy, T. Austin: b. May 11, 1911, Baltimore, Md.; educ. St. Charles College (Catonsville, Md.), St. Mary's Seminary (Baltimore, Md.); ord priest June 10, 1937; ord. titular bishop of Appiaria and auxiliary bishop of Baltimore, July 3, 1962.

Murphy, Thomas J.: b. Oct. 3, 1932, Chicago, Ill.; educ. Quigley Preparatory Seminary (Chicago, Ill.), St. Mary of the Lake Seminary (Mundelein, Ill.); ord. priest Apr. 12, 1958; ord. bishop of Great Falls, Mont. Aug. 21, 1978; title of see changed to Great Falls-Billings, 1980.

Murphy, Thomas W., C.SS.R.: b. Dec. 17, 1917, Omaha, Nebr.; educ. St. Joseph's College (Kirkwood, Mo.); ord. priest June 29, 1943; ord. first bishop of Juazeiro, Brazil, Jan. 2, 1963; resigned Dec. 29, 1973; app. titular bishop of Sululos and auxiliary bishop of Sao Salvador da Bahia, Brazil, Jan. 31, 1974.

N

Nelson, Knute Ansgar, O.S.B.: b. Oct. 1, 1906, Copenhagen, Denmark; educ. Abbey of Maria Laach (Germany), Brown Univ. (Providence, R.I.); professed in the Order of St. Benedict, May 30, 1932; ord. priest May 22, 1937; became an American citizen, Mar. 4,

1941; ord. titular bishop of Bilta and coadjutor bishop of Stockholm, Sweden, Sept. 8, 1947; succeeded as bishop of Stockholm, Oct. 1, 1957; retired; titular bishop of Dura. 1962.

Nevins, John J.: b. Jan. 19, 1932, New Rochelle, N.Y.; educ. Iona College (New Rochelle, N.Y.), Catholic Univ. (Washington, D.C.); ord. priest June 6, 1959; ord. titular bishop of Rusticana and auxiliary bishop of Miami, Mar. 24, 1979.

Newell, Hubert M.: b. Feb. 16, 1904, Denver, Colo.; educ. Regis College and St. Thomas Seminary (Denver, Colo.), Catholic Univ. (Washington, D.C.); ord. priest June 15, 1930; ord. titular bishop of Zapara and coadjutor bishop of Cheyenne, Sept. 24, 1947; bishop of Cheyenne, Nov. 10, 1951; retired Dec. 5, 1977.

Neylon, Martin J., S.J.: b. Feb. 13, 1920, Buffalo, N.Y.; ord. priest June 18, 1950; ord. titular bishop of Libertina and coadjutor vicar apostolic of the Caroline and Marshall Islands, Feb. 2, 1970; vicar apostolic of Caroline and Marshall Is., Sept. 20, 1971; first bishop when vicarate apostolic was raised to diocese, 1979.

Niedergeses, James D.: b. Feb. 2, 1917, Lawrenceburg, Tenn.; educ. St. Bernard College (St. Bernard, Ala.), St. Ambrose College (Davenport, Ia.), Mt. St. Mary Seminary of the West and Athenaeum (Cincinnati, Ohio); ord. priest May 20, 1944; ord. bishop of Nashville May 20, 1975.

Nold, Wendelin J.: b. Jan. 18, 1900, Bonham, Tex.; educ. St. Mary's Seminary (La Porte, Tex.), North American College (Rome); ord. priest Apr. 11, 1925; ord. titular bishop of Sasima and coadjutor bishop of Galveston, Feb. 25, 1948, succeeded as bishop of Galveston, Apr. 1, 1950; title of see changed to Galveston-Houston, 1959; resigned Apr. 22, 1975.

Nolker, Bernard, C.SS.R.: b. Sept. 25, 1912, Baltimore, Md.; educ. St. Mary's College (North East, Pa.), St. Mary's College (Ilchester, Md.), Mt. St. Alphonsus Seminary (Esopus, N.Y.); ord. priest June 18, 1939; ord. first bishop of Paranagua, Brazil, Apr. 25, 1963.

Noser, Adolph A., S.V.D.: b. July 4, 1900, Belleville, Ill.; educ. Quincy College (Quincy, Ill.), St. Mary's Mission House (Techny, Ill.), Angelicum (Rome); received into the Society of the Divine Word, 1921; ord. priest Sept. 27, 1925; ord. titular bishop of Capitolias and vicar apostolic of Accra, Gold Coast, British West Africa, Aug. 22, 1947; title changed to bishop of Accra, Apr. 18, 1950; transferred to titular see of Hierpiniana and vicariate apostolic of Alexishaven, New Guinea, Jan. 8, 1953; first archbishop of Madang, Nov. 15, 1966; retired Dec. 19, 1975.

Novak, Alfred, C.SS.R.: b. June 2, 1930, Dwight, Nebr.; educ. Immaculate Conception Seminary (Oconomowoc, Wis.); ord. priest July 2, 1956; ord. titular bishop of Vardimissa and auxiliary bishop of Sao Paulo, Brazil, May 25, 1979.

O

O'Boyle, Patrick A.: (See Cardinals, Biographies.)

O'Connor, John J.: b. Jan. 15, 1920, Philadelphia, Pa.; educ. St. Charles Borromeo Seminary (Philadelphia, Pa.), Catholic Univ., Georgetown Univ. (Washington, D.C.); ord. priest Dec. 15, 1945; U.S. Navy chief of chaplains, 1975; ord. titular bishop of Cursola and auxiliary to the military vicar, May 27, 1979.

O'Connor, Martin J.: b. May 18, 1900, Scranton, Pa.; educ. St. Thomas College (Scranton, Pa.), St. Mary's Seminary (Baltimore, Md.), North American College, Urban Univ. and Apollinaris (Rome); ord. priest Mar. 15, 1924; ord. titular bishop of Thespia and auxiliary bishop of Scranton, Jan. 27, 1943; rector of North American College 1946-1964; app. titular archbishop of Laodicea in Syria, Sept. 5, 1959; apostolic nuncio to Malta, 1965-69; president emeritus Pontifical Commission for Social Communication.

O'Connor, William A.: b. Dec. 27, 1903, Chicago, Ill.; educ. Quigley Seminary (Chicago, Ill.), St. Mary of the Lake Seminary (Mundelein, Ill.), Urban Univ. (Rome); ord. priest Sept. 24, 1927; ord. bishop of Springfield, Ill., Mar. 7, 1949; retired July 22, 1975.

O'Donnell, Cletus F.: b. Aug. 22, 1917, Waukon, Ia.; educ. St. Mary Seminary (Mundelein, Ill.), Catholic Univ. (Washington, D.C.); ord. priest May 3, 1941; ord. titular bishop of Abritto and auxiliary bishop of Chicago, Dec. 21, 1960; app. bishop of Madison, Feb. 22, 1967, installed Apr. 25, 1967.

O'Keefe, Gerald F.: b. Mar. 30, 1918, St. Paul, Minn.; educ. College of St. Thomas, St. Paul Seminary (St. Paul, Minn.); ord. priest Jan. 29, 1944; ord. titular bishop of Candyba and auxiliary bishop of St. Paul July 2, 1961; bishop of Davenport, Oct. 20, 1966, installed Jan. 4, 1967.

O'Leary, Edward C.: b. Aug. 21, 1920, Bangor, Me.; educ. Holy Cross College (Worcester, Mass.), St. Paul's Seminary (Ottawa, Canada); ord. priest June 15, 1946; ord. titular bishop of Moglena and auxiliary bishop of Portland, Me., Jan. 25, 1971; app. bishop of Portland, installed Dec. 18, 1974.

O'Meara, Edward T.: b. Aug. 3, 1921, St. Louis, Mo.; educ. Cardinal Glennon College and Kenrick Seminary (St. Louis, Mo.), Angelicum (Rome); ord. priest Dec. 21, 1946; app. national director of Society for the Propagation of the Faith, 1967; ord. titular bishop of Thisiduo and auxiliary bishop of St. Louis,

Feb. 13, 1972; app. archbishop of Indianapolis, installed Jan. 10, 1980.

O'Neil, Leo E.: b. Jan. 31, 1928, Holyoke, Mass.; educ. Maryknoll Seminary (Maryknoll, N.Y.), St. Anselm's College (Manchester, N.H.), Grand Seminary (Montreal, Canada); ord. priest June 4, 1955; ord. titular bishop of Bencenna and auxiliary bishop of Springfield, Mass., Aug. 22, 1980.

O'Neill, Arthur J.: b. Dec. 14, 1917, East Dubuque, Ill.; educ. Loras College (Dubuque, Ia.), St. Mary's Seminary (Baltimore, Md.); ord. priest Mar. 27, 1943; ord. bishop of Rockford, Oct. 11, 1968.

O'Rourke, Edward W.: b. Oct. 31, 1917, Downs, Ill.; educ. St. Mary's Seminary (Mundelein, Ill.), Aquinas Institute of Philosophy and Theology (River Forest, Ill.); ord. priest May 28, 1944; exec. dir. National Catholic Rural Life Conference, 1960-71; ord. bishop of Peoria, July 15, 1971.

Ott, Stanley J.: b. June 29, 1927, Gretna, La.; educ. Notre Dame Seminary (New Orleans, La.), North American College and Gregorian Univ. (Rome); ord. priest Dec. 8, 1951; ord. titular bishop of Nicives and auxiliary bishop of New Orleans, June 29, 1976.

Ottenweller, Albert H.: b. Apr. 5, 1916, Stanford, Mont.; educ. St. Joseph's Seminary (Rensselaer, Ind.), Catholic Univ. (Washington, D.C.); ord. priest June 19, 1943; ord. titular bishop of Perdices and auxiliary bishop of Toledo, May 29, 1974; app. bishop of Steubenville, Oct. 11, 1977, installed Nov. 22, 1977.

P

Pardy, James V., M.M.: b. Mar. 9, 1898, Brooklyn, N. Y.; educ. St. Francis College (Brooklyn), Fordham Univ. (New York City), Catholic Univ. (Washington, D.C.); ord. priest. Jan. 26, 1930; ord. titular bishop of Irenopolis and first vicar apostolic of Cheong Ju, Korea, Sept. 16, 1958; title changed to bishop of Cheong Ju, Mar. 10, 1962; retired June 17, 1969.

Paschang, John L.: b. Oct. 5, 1895, Hemingford, Nebr.; educ. Conception College (Conception, Mo.), St. John Seminary (Collegeville, Minn.), Catholic Univ. (Washington, D.C.); ord. priest June 12, 1921; ord. bishop of Grand Island, Oct. 9, 1951; resigned July 25, 1972.

Paul, John J.: b. Aug. 17, 1918, La Crosse, Wis.; educ. Loras College (Dubuque, Iowa), St. Mary's Seminary (Baltimore, Md.), Marquette Univ. (Milwaukee, Wis.), ord. priest Jan. 24, 1943; ord. titular bishop of Lambaesis and auxiliary bishop of La Crosse, Aug. 4, 1977.

Pearce, George H., S.M.: b. Jan. 9, 1921, Brighton, Mass.; educ. Marist College and Seminary (Framingham, Mass.); ord. priest Feb. 2, 1947; ord. titular bishop of Attalea in Pamphylia and vicar apostolic of the Samoa and Tokelau Islands, June 29, 1956; title changed to bishop of Apia, June 21, 1966; app. archbishop of Suva, Fiji Islands, June 22, 1967; resigned Apr. 10, 1976.

Pechillo, Jerome, T.O.R.: b. May 16, 1919, Brooklyn, N.Y.; educ. Catholic Univ. (Washington, D.C.); ord. priest June 10, 1947; ord. titular bishop of Novasparsa and prelate of Coronel Oviedo, Paraguay, Jan. 25, 1966; app. auxiliary bishop of Newark, N.J., Mar. 6, 1976.

Pena, Raymond J.: b. Feb. 19, 1934, Robstown, Tex.; educ. Assumption Seminary (San Antonio, Tex.); ord. priest May 25, 1957; ord. titular bishop of Trisipa and auxiliary bishop of San Antonio, Dec. 13, 1976; app. bishop of El Paso, Apr. 29, 1980.

Pernicone, Joseph M.: b. Nov. 4, 1903, Regalbuto, Sicily; educ. Cathedral College (New York City), St. Joseph's Seminary (Dunwoodie, N.Y.), Catholic Univ. (Washington, D.C.); ord. priest Dec. 18, 1926; ord. titular bishop of Hadrianapolis and auxiliary bishop of New York, May 5, 1954; app. episcopal vicar, 1966. Retired.

Perry, Harold R., S.V.D.: b. Oct. 9, 1916, Lake Charles, La.; educ. St. Augustine Seminary (Bay St. Louis, Miss.), St. Mary's Seminary (Techny, Ill.); ord. priest Jan. 6, 1944; app. provincial of southern province of Society of the Divine Word, 1964; ord. titular bishop of Mons in Mauretania and auxiliary bishop of New Orleans, Jan. 6, 1966.

Pilarczyk, Daniel E.: b. Aug. 12, 1934, Dayton, Ohio; educ. St. Gregory's Seminary (Cincinnati, O.), Urban Univ. (Rome), Xavier Univ. and Univ. of Cincinnati (Cincinnati, O.); ord. priest Dec. 20, 1959; ord. titular bishop of Hodelm and auxiliary bishop of Cincinnati, Dec. 20, 1974.

Pilla, Anthony M.: b. Nov. 12, 1932, Cleveland, O.; educ. St. Gregory College Seminary (Cincinnati, O.), Borromeo College Seminary (Wickliffe, O.), St. Mary Seminary and John Carroll Univ. (Cleveland, O.); ord. priest May 23, 1959; ord. titular bishop of Scardona and auxiliary bishop of Cleveland, Aug. 1, 1979; app. apostolic administrator of Cleveland, 1980.

Pinger, Henry A., O.F.M.: b. Aug. 16, 1897, Lindsay, Nebr.; educ. Our Lady of Angels Seminary (Cleveland, O.), St. Anthony's Seminary (St. Louis, Mo.); professed in the Order of Friars Minor, June 18, 1918; ord. priest June 27, 1924; ord. titular bishop of Capitolias and vicar apostolic of Chowtsun, China, Sept. 21, 1937; title changed to bishop of Chowtsun, Apr. 11, 1946; imprisoned by Reds in 1951, released in 1956; expelled.

Povish, Kenneth J.: b. Apr. 19, 1924, Alpena, Mich.; educ. St. Joseph's Seminary (Grand Rapids, Mich.), Sacred Heart Seminary (Detroit, Mich.), Catholic Univ. (Washington, D.C.); ord. priest June 3, 1950; ord.

bishop of Crookston, Sept. 29, 1970; app. bishop of Lansing, Oct. 8, 1975, installed Dec. 11, 1975.

Power, Cornelius M.: b. Dec. 18, 1913, Seattle, Wash.; educ. St. Patrick's College (Menlo Park, Calif.), St. Edward's Seminary (Kenmore, Wash.), Catholic Univ. (Washington, D.C.); ord. priest June 3, 1939; ord. bishop of Yakima, May 1, 1969, installed May 20, 1969; app. archbishop of Portland, Ore., Jan. 22, 1974, installed Apr. 17, 1974.

Primeau, Ernest J.: b. Sept. 17, 1909, Chicago, Ill.; educ. Loyola Univ. (Chicago, Ill.), St. Mary of the Lake Seminary (Mundelein, Ill.), Lateran Univ. (Rome); ord. priest Apr. 7, 1934; ord. bishop of Manchester, Feb. 25, 1960; resigned Jan. 30, 1974; app. director of Villa Stritch, Rome, 1974.

Prost, Jude, O.F.M.: b. Dec. 6, 1915, Chicago, Ill.; educ. Our Lady of the Angels Seminary (Cleveland, O.), St. Joseph's Seminary (Teutopolis, Ill.); ord. priest June 24, 1942; ord. titular bishop of Fronta and auxiliary bishop of Belem do Para, Brazil, Nov. 1, 1962.

Proulx, Amedee W.: b. Aug. 31, 1932, Sanford, Me.; educ. St. Hyacinthe Seminary (Quebec), St. Paul Univ. Seminary (Ottawa), Catholic Univ. (Washington, D.C.); ord. priest May 31, 1958; ord. titular bishop of Clipia and auxiliary bishop of Portland, Me., Nov. 12, 1975.

Pursley, Leo A.: b. Mar. 12, 1902, Hartford City, Ind.; educ. Mt. St. Mary's Seminary (Cincinnati, O.); ord. priest June 11, 1927; ord. titular bishop of Hadrianapolis in Pisidia and auxiliary bishop of Fort Wayne, Sept. 19, 1950; app. apostolic administrator of Fort Wayne, Mar. 9, 1955; installed as bishop of Fort Wayne, Feb. 26, 1957; title of see changed to Fort Wayne-South Bend, 1960; resigned Aug. 31, 1976.

Q

Quinn, Francis A.: b. Sept. 11, 1921, Los Angeles, Calif.; educ. St. Joseph's College (Mountain View, Calif.), St. Patrick's Seminary (Menlo Park, Calif.), Catholic Univ. (Washington, D.C.); Univ. of California (Berkley); ord. priest June 15, 1946; ord. titular bishop of Numana and auxiliary bishop of San Francisco, June 29, 1978; app. bishop of Sacramento Dec. 18, 1979.

Quinn, John R.: b. Mar. 28, 1929, Riverside, Calif.; educ. St. Francis Seminary (El Cajon, Calif.), North American College (Rome); ord. priest July 19, 1953; ord. titular bishop of Thisiduo and auxiliary bishop of San Diego, Dec. 12, 1967; bishop of Oklahoma City and Tulsa, Nov. 30, 1971; first archbishop of Oklahoma City, Dec. 19, 1972; app. archbishop of San Francisco Feb. 22, 1977, installed Apr. 26, 1977; president NCCB, USCC, 1977-

R

Rausch, James S.: b. Sept. 4, 1928, Albany, Minn.; educ. St. Thomas College (St. Paul, Minn.), Univ. of Minnesota (Minneapolis), Gregorian Univ. (Rome); ord. priest June 2, 1956; associate general secretary of USCC, 1970-72; general secretary of NCCB-USCC, 1972-77; ord. titular bishop of Summa and auxiliary bishop of St. Cloud, Apr. 26, 1973; app. bishop of Phoenix Jan. 25, 1977, installed Mar. 22, 1977.

Raya, Joseph M.: b. July 20, 1917, Zahle, Lebanon; educ. St. Louis College (Paris, France), St. Anne's Seminary (Jerusalem); ord. priest July 20, 1941; came to U.S., 1949, became U.S. citizen; ord. archbishop of Acre, Israel, of the Melkites, Oct. 20, 1968; resigned Aug. 20, 1974; assigned titular metropolitan see of Scytopolis.

Regan, Joseph W., M.M.: b. Apr. 5, 1905, Boston, Mass.; educ. Boston College (Boston, Mass.), St. Bernard's Seminary (Rochester, N.Y.), Maryknoll Seminary (Maryknoll, N.Y.); ord. priest Jan. 27, 1929; missionary in China 15 years; in Philippines since 1952; ord. titular bishop of Isinda and prelate of Tagum, Philippine Islands, Apr. 25, 1962; resigned 1980.

Reh, Francis F.: b. Jan. 9, 1911, New York, N.Y.; educ. St. Joseph's Seminary (Dunwoodie, N.Y.), North American College and Gregorian Univ. (Rome); ord. priest Dec. 8, 1935; ord. bishop of Charleston, S.C., June 29, 1962; named titular bishop of Macriana in Mauretania, 1964; rector of North American College, 1964-68; bishop of Saginaw, installed Feb. 26, 1969; resigned Apr. 28, 1980.

Reicher, Louis J.: b. June 14, 1890, Piqua, O.; educ. St. Mary's Seminary (Cincinnati, O.), St. Mary's Seminary (La Porte, Tex.): ord. priest Dec. 6, 1918; ord. first bishop of Austin, Apr. 14, 1948; resigned Nov. 15, 1971.

Reilly, Daniel P.: b. May 12, 1928, Providence, R.I.; educ. Our Lady of Providence Seminary (Warwick, R.I.), St. Brieuc Major Seminary (Cotes du Nord, France); ord. priest May 30, 1953; ord. bishop of Norwich, Aug. 6, 1975.

Reilly, Thomas F., C.SS.R.: b. Dec. 20, 1908, Boston, Mass.; educ. Mt. St. Alphonsus Seminary (Esopus, N.Y.), Catholic Univ. (Washington, D.C.); ord. priest June 10, 1933; ord. titular bishop of Themisonium and prelate of San Juan de la Maguana, Dominican Republic, Nov. 30, 1956; first bishop of San Juan de la Maguana, Nov. 21, 1969; retired 1977.

Reiss, John C.: b. May 13, 1922, Red Bank, N.J.; educ. Catholic Univ. (Washington, D.C.), Immaculate Conception Seminary (Darlington, N.J.); ord. priest May 31, 1947; ord. titular bishop of Simidicca and auxiliary bishop of Trenton, Dec. 12, 1967; app. bishop of Trenton, Mar. 11, 1980.

Riley, Lawrence J.: b. Sept. 6, 1914; Boston, Mass.; educ. Boston College and St. John's Seminary (Boston, Mass.), North American College and Gregorian Univ. (Rome), Catholic Univ. (Washington, D.C.); ord. priest Sept. 21, 1940; ord. titular bishop of Daimlaig and auxiliary bishop of Boston, Feb. 2, 1972.

Roach, John R.: b. July 31, 1921, Prior Lake, Minn.; educ. St. Paul Seminary (St. Paul, Minn.), Univ. of Minnesota (Minneapolis); ord. priest June 18, 1946; ord. titular bishop of Cenae and auxiliary bishop of St. Paul and Minneapolis, Sept. 8, 1971; app. archbishop of St. Paul and Minneapolis, May 28, 1975; vice-president NCCB/USCC, 1977.

Rodimer, Frank J.: b. Oct. 25, 1927, Rockaway, N.J.; educ. Seton Hall Prep (South Orange, N.J.), St. Charles College (Catonsville, Md.), St. Mary's Seminary (Baltimore, Md.), Immaculate Conception Seminary (Darlington, N.J.), Catholic Univ. (Washington, D.C.); ord. priest May 19, 1951; ord. bishop of Paterson, Feb. 28, 1978.

Rodriguez, Migúel, C.SS.R.: b. Apr. 18, 1931, Mayaguez, P.R.; educ. St. Mary's Minor Seminary (North East, Pa.), Mt. St. Alphonsus Major Seminary (Esopus, N.Y.); ord. priest June 22, 1958; ord. bishop of Arecibo, P.R., Mar. 23, 1974.

Roman, Agustin: b. May 5, 1928, San Antonio de los Banos, Havana, Cuba; educ. San Alberto Magno Seminary (Matanzas, Cuba), Missions Etrangeres (Montreal, Canada), Barry College (Miami, Fla.); ord. priest July 5, 1959, Cuba; vicar for Spanish speaking in Miami archdiocese, 1976; ord. titular bishop of Sertei and auxiliary bishop of Miami, Mar. 24, 1979.

Rosazza, Peter Anthony: b. Feb. 13, 1935, New Haven, Conn.; educ. St. Thomas Seminary (Bloomfield, Conn.), Dartmouth College (Hanover, N.H.), St. Bernard's Seminary (Rochester, N.Y.), St. Sulpice (Issy, France); ord. priest June 29, 1961; ord. titular bishop of Oppido Nuovo and auxiliary bishop of Hartford, June 24, 1978.

Rudin, John J., M.M.: b. Nov. 27, 1916, Pittsfield, Mass.; educ. Maryknoll Seminary (Maryknoll, N.Y.), Gregorian Univ. (Rome); ord. priest June 11, 1944; ord. first bishop of Musoma, Tanzania, Oct. 3, 1957; retired 1979.

Russell, John J.: b. Dec. 1, 1897, Baltimore, Md.; educ. St. Charles College (Catonsville, Md.), St. Mary's Seminary (Baltimore, Md.), North American College (Rome); ord. priest July 8, 1923; ord. bishop of Charleston, Mar. 14, 1950; bishop of Richmond, July 3, 1958; retired Apr. 30, 1973.

Ryan, Gerald: b. Aug. 24, 1923, Brooklyn, N.Y.; educ. Cathedral College (Brooklyn, N.Y.), Immaculate Conception Seminary (Huntington, L.I.), Fordham Univ. Graduate School of Social Work (Bronx, N.Y.); ord. priest June 3, 1950; ord. titular bishop of Munatiana and auxiliary bishop of Rockville Centre, May 9, 1977.

Ryan, James C., O.F.M.: b. Nov. 17, 1912, Chicago, Ill.; educ. St. Joseph's Seraphic Seminary (Westmont, Ill.), Our Lady of the Angels Seminary (Cleveland, O.); ord. priest June 24, 1938; ord. titular bishop of Margo and prelate of Santarem, Brazil, April 9, 1958; first bishop of Santarem, 1979.

Ryan, Joseph T.: b. Nov. 1, 1913, Albany, N.Y.; educ. Manhattan College (New York City); ord. priest June 3, 1939; national secretary of Catholic Near East Welfare Assn. 1960-65; ord. first archbishop of Anchorage, Alaska, Mar. 25, 1966; app. titular bishop of Gabi and coadjutor archbishop of the military ordinariate, Oct. 24, 1975, installed Dec. 13, 1975.

S

Salatka, Charles A.: b. Feb. 26, 1918, Grand Rapids, Mich.; educ. St. Joseph's Seminary (Grand Rapids, Mich.), Catholic Univ. (Washington, D.C.), Lateran Univ. (Rome); ord. priest Feb. 24, 1945; ord. titular bishop of Cariana and auxiliary bishop of Grand Rapids, Mich., Mar. 6, 1962; app. bishop of Marquette, installed Mar. 25, 1968; app. archbishop of Oklahoma City, Sept. 27, 1977; installed Dec. 15, 1977.

Sanchez, Robert: b. Mar. 20, 1934, Socorro, N.M.; educ. Immaculate Heart Seminary (Santa Fe, N.M.), Gregorian Univ. (Rome), Catholic Univ. (Washington, D.C.); ord. priest Dec. 20, 1959; ord. archbishop of Santa Fe, N.M., July 25, 1974.

Scanlan, John J.: b. May 24, 1906, County Cork, Ireland; educ. National Univ. of Ireland (Dublin), All Hallows College (Dublin); ord. priest June 22, 1930; U.S. citizen 1938; ord. titular bishop of Cenae and auxiliary bishop of Honolulu, Sept. 21, 1954; bishop of Honolulu, installed May 1, 1968.

Scarpone, Gerald, O.F.M.: b. Oct. 1, 1928, Watertown, Mass.; ord. priest June 24, 1956; ord. coadjutor bishop of Comayagua, Honduras, Feb. 21, 1979; succeeded as bishop of Comayagua, May 30, 1979.

Schad, James L.: b. July 20, 1917, Philadelphia, Pa.; educ. St. Mary's Seminary (Baltimore, Md.); ord. priest Apr. 10, 1943; ord. titular bishop of Panatoria and auxiliary bishop of Camden, Dec. 8, 1966.

Schexnayder, Maurice: b. Aug. 13, 1895, Wallace (now Vacherie), La.; educ. Chenet Institute (New Orleans, La.), St. Joseph's Seminary (St. Benedict, La.), St. Mary's Seminary (Baltimore, Md.), North American College (Rome); ord. priest Apr. 11, 1925; ord. titular bishop of Tuscamia and auxiliary bishop of Lafayette, La., Feb. 22, 1951; bishop of Lafayette, La., May 24, 1956; retired Nov. 7, 1972.

Schierhoff, Andrew B.: b. Feb. 10, 1922, St. Louis, Mo.; ord. priest Apr. 14, 1948; missionary in Bolivia from 1956; ord. titular bishop of Cerenza and auxiliary of La Paz, Bolivia, Jan. 6, 1969.

Schladweiler, Alphonse: b. July 18, 1902, Milwaukee, Wis.; educ. St. Joseph College (Teutopolis, Ill.), St. Paul's Seminary (St. Paul, Minn.), Univ. of Minnesota (Minneapolis, Minn.); ord. priest June 9, 1929; ord. first bishop of New Ulm, Jan. 29, 1958; retired Feb. 19, 1976.

Schlaefer, Salvator, O.F.M. Cap.: b. June 27, 1920, Campbellsport, Wis.; ord. priest June 5, 1946; missionary in Bluefields, Nicaragua from 1947; ord. titular bishop of Fiumepiscense and vicar apostolic of Bluefields, Nicaragua, Aug. 12, 1970.

Schlarman, Stanley Gerard: b. July 27, 1933, Belleville, Ill.; educ. St. Henry Prep Seminary (Belleville, Ill.), Gregorian Univ. (Rome), St. Louis Univ. (St. Louis, Mo.); ord. priest July 13, 1958, Rome; ord. titular bishop of Capri and auxiliary bishop of Belleville, May 14, 1979.

Schlotterback, Edward F., O.S.F.S.: b. Mar. 2, 1912, Philadelphia, Pa.; educ. Catholic Univ. (Washington, D.C.); ord. priest Dec. 17, 1938; ord. titular bishop of Balanea and vicar apostolic of Keetmanshoop, Namibia, June 11, 1956.

Schmidt, Firmin M., O.F.M.Cap.: b. Oct. 12, 1918, Catherine, Kans.; educ. Catholic Univ. (Washington, D.C.); ord. priest June 2, 1946; app. prefect apostolic of Mendi, Papua New Guinea, Apr. 3, 1959; ord. titular bishop of Conana and first vicar apostolic of Mendi, Dec. 15, 1965; became first bishop of Mendi when vicariate apostolic was raised to a diocese, Nov. 15, 1966.

Schmidt, Mathias, O.S.B.: b. Apr. 21, 1931, Wortonville, Kans.; ord. priest May 30, 1957; missionary in Brazil; ord, titular bishop of Mutugenna and auxiliary bishop of Jatai, Brazil, Sept. 10, 1972; bishop of Rui Barbosa, Brazil, May 14, 1976.

Schmitt, Mark: b. Feb. 14, 1923, Algoma, Wis., educ. Salvatorian Seminary (St. Nazianz, Wis.), St. John's Seminary (Collegeville, Minn.); ord. priest May 22, 1948; ord. titular bishop of Ceanannus Mor and auxiliary bishop of Green Bay, June 24, 1970; app. bishop of Marquette, Mar. 21, 1978, installed May 8, 1978.

Schoenherr, Walter J.: b. Feb. 28, 1920, Detroit, Mich.; educ. Sacred Heart Seminary (Detroit, Mich.), Mt. St. Mary Seminary (Norwood, O.); ord. priest Oct. 27, 1945; ord. titular bishop of Timidana and auxiliary bishop of Detroit, May 1, 1968.

Schuck, James A., O.F.M.: b. Jan. 17, 1913, Treverton, Pa.; educ. St. Joseph's Seminary (Callicoon, N.Y.), St. Bonaventure's University (St. Bonaventure, N.Y.). Holy Name College (Washington, D.C.); ord. priest June 11,

1940; ord. titular bishop of Avissa and prelate of Cristalandia, Brazil, Feb. 24, 1959.

Schulte, Paul Clarence: b. Mar. 18, 1890, Fredericktown, Mo.; educ. St. Francis Solanus College (Quincy, Ill.), Kenrick Seminary (Webster Groves, Mo.); ord. priest June 11, 1915; ord. bishop of Leavenworth, Sept. 21, 1937; archbishop of Indianapolis, July 27, 1946; resigned Jan. 14, 1970; assigned titular see of Elicrora.

Schuster, Eldon B.: b. Mar. 10, 1911, Calio, N. Dak.; educ. Loras College (Dubuque, Ia.), Catholic Univ. (Washington, D.C.), Oxford Univ. (England), St. Louis Univ. (St. Louis, Mo.); ord. priest May 27, 1937; ord. titular bishop of Amblada and auxiliary bishop of Great Falls, Mont., Dec. 21, 1961; app. bishop of Great Falls, Dec. 2, 1967, installed Jan. 23, 1968; resigned Dec. 28, 1977.

Shea, Francis R.: b. Dec. 4, 1913, Knoxville, Tenn.; educ. St. Mary's Seminary (Baltimore, Md.), North American College (Rome), Peabody College (Nashville, Tenn.); ord. priest Mar. 19, 1939; ord. bishop of Evansville, Ind., Feb. 3, 1970.

Sheehan, Daniel E.: b. May 14, 1917, Emerson, Nebr.; educ. Creighton Univ. (Omaha, Nebr.), Kenrick Seminary (Webster Groves, Mo.), Catholic Univ. (Washington, D.C.): ord. priest May 23, 1942; ord. titular bishop of Capsus and auxiliary bishop of Omaha, Mar. 19, 1964; app. archbishop of Omaha, installed Aug. 11, 1969.

Shehan, Lawrence Joseph: (See Cardinals, Biographies.)

Sheldon, Gilbert I.: b. Sept. 20, 1926, Cleveland, O.; educ. John Carroll Univ. and St. Mary Seminary (Cleveland, O.); ord. priest Feb. 28, 1953; ord. titular bishop of Taparura and auxiliary bishop of Cleveland, June 11, 1976.

Shubsda, Thaddeus A.: b. Apr. 2, 1925, Los Angeles, Calif.; educ. St. John's Seminary (Camarillo, Calif.); ord. priest Apr. 26, 1950; ord. titular bishop of Trau and auxiliary bishop of Los Angeles, Feb. 19, 1977.

Skiba, Richard J.: b. Sept. 11, 1935, Racine, Wis.; educ. Old St. Francis Minor Seminary (Milwaukee, Wis.), North American College, Gregorian Univ., Pontifical Biblical Institute, Angelicum (Rome); ord. priest Dec. 20, 1959; ord. titular bishop of Castra and auxiliary bishop of Milwaukee, Dec. 19, 1979.

Skylstad, William: b. Mar. 2, 1934, Omak, Wash.; educ. Pontifical College Josephinum (Worthington, Ohio), Washington State Univ. (Pullman, Wash.), Gonzaga Univ. (Spokane, Wash.); ord. priest May 21, 1960; ord. bishop of Yakima, May 12, 1977.

Smith, Philip F., O.M.I.: b. Oct. 16, 1924, Lowell, Mass.; ord. priest Oct. 29, 1950; ord. titular bishop of Lamfua and vicar apostolic of Jolo, Philippine Islands, Sept. 8, 1972; app. coadjutor archbishop of Cotabato, Philippines, April 11, 1979; archbishop of Cotabato, Mar. 14, 1980.

Snyder, John J.: b. Oct. 25, 1925, New York, N.Y.; educ. Cathedral College (Brooklyn, N.Y.), Immaculate Conception Seminary (Huntington, N.Y.); ord. priest June 9, 1951; ord. titular bishop of Forlimpopli and auxiliary bishop of Brooklyn, Feb. 2, 1973; app. bishop of St. Augustine, installed Dec. 5, 1979.

Soenneker, Henry J.: b. May 27, 1907, Melrose, Minn.; educ. Pontifical Josephinum College (Worthington, O.), Catholic Univ. (Washington, D.C.); ord. priest May 26, 1934; ord. bishop of Owensboro, Apr. 26, 1961.

Sowada, Alphonse A., O.S.C.: b. June 23, 1933, Avon, Minn.; educ. Holy Cross Scholasticate (Fort Wayne, Ind.), Catholic Univ. (Washington, D.C.), ord. priest May 31, 1958; missionary in Indonesia from 1958; ord. bishop of Agats, Indonesia, Nov. 23, 1969.

Speltz, George H.: b. May 29, 1912, Altura, Minn.; educ. St. Mary's College, St. Paul's Seminary (St. Paul, Minn.), Catholic Univ. (Washington, D.C.); ord. priest June 2, 1940; ord. titular bishop of Claneus and auxiliary bishop of Winona, Mar. 25, 1963; app. coadjutor bishop of St. Cloud, Apr. 4, 1966; bishop of St. Cloud, Jan. 31, 1968.

Speyrer, Jude: b. Apr. 14, 1929, Leonville, La.; educ. St. Joseph Seminary (Covington, La.), Notre Dame Seminary (New Orleans, La.), Gregorian Univ. (Rome), Univ. of Fribourg (Switzerland); ord. priest July 25, 1953; ord. first bishop of Lake Charles, La., Apr. 25, 1980.

Stafford, James Francis: b. July 26, 1932, Baltimore, Md.; educ. St. Mary's Seminary (Baltimore, Md.), North American College and Gregorian Univ. (Rome); ord. priest Dec. 15, 1957; ord. titular bishop of Respecta and auxiliary bishop of Baltimore, Feb. 29, 1976.

Steiner, Kenneth Donald: b. Nov. 25, 1936, David City, Nebr.; educ. Mt. Angel Seminary (St. Benedict, Ore.), St. Thomas Seminary (Seattle, Wash.); ord. priest, May 19, 1962; ord. titular bishop of Avensa and auxiliary bishop of Portland, Ore., Mar. 2, 1978.

Stemper, Alfred M., M.S.C.: b. Jan. 2, 1913, Black Hammer, Minn.; ord. priest June 26, 1940; ord. titular bishop of Eleutheropolis and vicar apostolic of Kavieng, New Guinea, Oct. 28, 1957; first bishop of Kavieng, Nov. 15, 1966.

Straling, Phillip F.: b. Apr. 25, 1933, San Bernardino, Calif.; educ. Immaculate Heart Seminary, St. Francis Seminary, Univ. of San Diego and San Diego State University (San Diego, Calif.), North American College (Rome); ord. priest Mar. 19, 1959; ord. first bishop of San Bernardino, Nov. 6, 1978.

Strecker, Ignatius J.: b. Nov. 23, 1917, Spearville, Kans.; educ. St. Benedict's College

(Atchison, Kans.), Kenrick Seminary (Webster Groves, Mo.), Catholic Univ. (Washington, D.C.); ord. priest Dec. 19, 1942; ord. bishop of Springfield-Cape Girardeau, Mo., June 20, 1962; archbishop of Kansas City, Kans., Oct. 28, 1969.

Sullivan, James S.: b. July 23, 1929, Kalamazoo, Mich.; educ. Sacred Heart Seminary (Detroit, Mich.), St. John Provincial Seminary (Plymouth, Mich.); ord. priest June 4, 1955; ord. titular bishop of Siccessi and auxiliary bishop of Lansing, Sept. 21, 1972.

Sullivan, John J.: b. July 5, 1920, Horton, Kans.; educ. Kenrick Seminary (St. Louis, Mo.); ord. priest Sept. 23, 1944; vice-president of Catholic Church Extension Society and national director of Extension Lay Volunteers, 1961-68; ord. bishop of Grand Island, Sept. 19, 1972; app. bishop of Kansas City-St. Joseph, June 27, 1977, installed Aug. 17, 1977.

Sullivan, Joseph V.: b. Aug. 15, 1919, Kansas City, Mo.; educ. Sulpician Seminary (Washington, D.C.), Catholic Univ. (Washington, D.C.); ord. priest June 1, 1946; ord. titular bishop of Tagamuta and auxiliary bishop of Kansas City-St. Joseph, Apr. 3, 1967; app. Bishop of Baton Rouge, Aug. 13, 1974.

Sullivan, Walter F.: b. June 10, 1928, Washington, D.C.; educ. St. Mary's Seminary (Baltimore, Md.), Catholic Univ. (Washington, D.C.); ord. priest May 9, 1953; ord. titular bishop of Selsea and auxiliary bishop of Richmond, Va., Dec. 1, 1970; app. bishop of Richmond, June 4, 1974.

Swanstrom, Edward E.: b. Mar. 20, 1903, New York, N.Y.; educ. Fordham Univ. (New York City), St. John's Seminary (Brooklyn, N.Y.), New York School of Social Work; ord. priest June 2, 1928; director of Catholic Relief Services 1947-76; ord. titular bishop of Arba and auxiliary bishop of New York, Oct. 28, 1960; retired Mar. 20, 1978.

Szoka, Edmund C.: b. Sept. 14, 1927, Grand Rapids, Mich.; educ. Sacred Heart Seminary (Detroit, Mich.), St. John's Provincial Seminary (Plymouth, Mich.), Lateran Univ. (Rome); ord. priest June 5, 1954; ord. first bishop of Gaylord, Mich., July 20, 1971.

T

Tafoya, Arthur N.: b. Mar. 2, 1933, Alameda, N.M.; educ. St. Thomas Seminary (Denver, Colo.), Conception Seminary (Conception, Mo.); ord. priest May 12, 1962; ord. bishop of Pueblo, Sept. 10, 1980.

Tanner, Paul F.: b. Jan. 15, 1905, Peoria, Ill.; educ. Marquette Univ. (Milwaukee, Wis.), Kenrick Seminary (Webster Groves, Mo.), St. Francis Seminary (Milwaukee, Wis.), Catholic Univ. (Washington, D.C.): ord. priest May 30, 1931; assistant director NCWC Youth Department 1940-45; assistant general secretary of NCWC 1945-58; general secretary of NCWC (now USCC) 1958-68; ord. titular bishop of Lamasba, Dec. 21, 1965; bishop of St. Augustine, Mar. 27, 1968; resigned 1979.

Tawil, Joseph: b. Dec. 25, 1913, Damascus, Syria; ord. priest July 20, 1936; ord. titular archbishop of Mira and patriarchal vicar for eparchy of Damascus or the Patriarchate of Antioch for the Melkites, Jan. 1, 1960; apostolic exarch for faithful of the Melkite rite in the U.S., Oct. 31, 1969; app. first eparch when exarchate was raised to eparchy, July 15, 1976; title of see changed to Newton, 1977.

Timlin, James C.: b. Aug. 5, 1927, Scranton, Pa.; educ. St. Charles College (Catonsville, Md.), St. Mary's Seminary (Baltimore, Md.), North American College (Rome); ord. priest July 16, 1951; ord. titular bishop of Gunugo and auxiliary bishop of Scranton, Sept. 21, 1976.

Topel, Bernard J.: b. May 31, 1903, Bozeman, Mont.; educ. Carroll College (Helena, Mont.), Grand Seminary (Montreal), Catholic Univ. (Washington, D.C.), Harvard Univ. (Cambridge, Mass.), Notre Dame Univ. (Notre Dame, Ind.); ord. priest June 7, 1927; ord. titular bishop of Binda and coadjutor bishop of Spokane, Sept. 21, 1955; bishop of Spokane, Sept. 25, 1955; retired Apr. 11, 1978.

Treinen, Sylvester: b. Nov. 19, 1917, Donnelly, Minn.; educ. Crosier Seminary (Onamia, Minn.), St. Paul Seminary (St. Paul, Minn.); ord. priest June 11, 1946; ord. bishop of Boise, July 25, 1962.

Tschoepe, Thomas: b. Dec. 17, 1915, Pilot Point, Tex.; educ. Pontifical College Josephinum (Worthington, O.); ord. priest May 30, 1943; ord. bishop of San Angelo, Tex., Mar. 9, 1966; app. bishop of Dallas, Tex., Aug. 27, 1969.

U-V

Unterkoefler, Ernest L.: b. Aug. 17, 1917, Philadelphia, Pa.; educ. Catholic Univ. (Washington, D.C.); ord. priest May 18, 1944; ord. titular bishop of Latopolis and auxiliary bishop of Richmond, Va., Feb. 22, 1962; app. bishop of Charleston, Dec. 12, 1964, installed Feb. 22, 1965.

Vath, Joseph G.: b. Mar. 12, 1918, New Orleans, La.; educ. Notre Dame Seminary (New Orleans, La.), Catholic Univ. (Washington, D.C.); ord. priest June 7, 1941; ord. titular bishop of Novaliciana and auxiliary bishop of Mobile-Birmingham, May 26, 1966; app. first bishop of Birmingham, Oct. 8, 1969.

Vaughan, Austin B.: b. Sept. 27, 1927, New York, N.Y.; educ. North American College and Gregorian Univ. (Rome), ord. priest Dec. 8, 1951; pres. Catholic Theological Society of America, 1967; rector of St. Joseph's Seminary (Dunwoodie, N.Y.), 1973; ord. titular bishop of Cluain Iraird and auxiliary bishop of New York, June 29, 1977.

Veigle, Adrian J.M., T.O.R.: b. Sept. 15, 1912, Lilly, Pa.; educ. St. Francis College (Loretto, Pa.), Pennsylvania State College; ord. priest May 22, 1937; ord. titular bishop of Gigthi and prelate of Borba, Brazil, June 9, 1966.

Vonesh, Raymond J.: b. Jan. 25, 1916, Chicago, Ill.; educ. St. Mary of the Lake Seminary (Mundelein, Ill.). Gregorian Univ. (Rome); ord. priest May 3, 1941; ord. titular bishop of Vanariona and auxiliary bishop of Joliet, Ill., Apr. 3, 1968.

W

Waldschmidt, Paul E., C.S.C.: b. Jan. 7, 1920, Evansville, Ind.; educ. Notre Dame Univ. (Notre Dame, Ind.), Holy Cross College (Washington, D.C.), Laval Univ. (Quebec), Angelicum (Rome), Louvain (Belgium), Sorbonne (Paris), ord. priest June 24, 1946; president University of Portland, 1962- ; ord. titular bishop of Citium and auxiliary bishop of Portland, Ore., Mar. 2, 1978.

Walsh, James Edward, M.M.: b. Apr. 30, 1891, Cumberland, Md.; educ. Mt. St. Mary's College (Emmitsburg, Md.), Maryknoll Foreign Mission Seminary (Maryknoll, N.Y.); entered Catholic Foreign Mission Society (Maryknoll, N.Y.), 1912; ord. priest Dec. 7, 1915; ord. titular bishop of Sata and vicar apostolic of Kongmoon, China, May 22, 1927; superior general of Maryknoll, July 21, 1936, until Aug. 7, 1946; app. general secretary, Catholic Central Bureau, Shanghai, China, Aug. 24, 1948; placed under house arrest in October, 1958, detained in Shanghai hospital; sentenced to 20 years' imprisonment for "espionage," Mar., 1960; released 1970.

Walsh, Nicholas E.: b. Oct. 20, 1916, Burnsville, Minn.; educ. St. Paul Seminary (St. Paul, Minn.), Catholic Univ. (Washington, D.C.), Pontifical Palafoxianum Seminary (Puebla, Mexico), Register College of Journalism (Denver, Colo.); ord. priest June 6, 1942; first editor of *Idaho Register;* diocesan vicar for Mexican Americans; ord. bishop of Yakima, Oct. 28, 1974; app. titular bishop of Bolsena and auxiliary bishop of Seattle, Aug. 10, 1976.

Ward, John J.: b. Sept. 28, 1920, Los Angeles, Calif.; educ. St. John's Seminary (Camarillo, Calif.), Catholic Univ. (Washington, D.C.); ord. priest May 4, 1946; ord. titular bishop of Bria and auxiliary of Los Angeles, Dec. 12, 1963.

Watson, Alfred M.: b. July 11, 1907, Erie, Pa.; educ. St. Mary's Seminary (Baltimore, Md.), Catholic Univ. (Washington, D.C.); ord. priest May 10, 1934; ord. titular bishop of Nationa and auxiliary bishop of Erie, June 29, 1965; app. bishop of Erie, 1969, installed May 13, 1969.

Watters, Loras J.: b. Oct. 14, 1915, Dubuque, Ia.; educ. Loras College (Dubuque, Ia.), Gregorian Univ. (Rome), Catholic Univ.

(Washington, D.C.); ord. priest June 7, 1941; ord. titular bishop of Fidoloma and auxiliary bishop of Dubuque, Aug. 26, 1965; bishop of Winona, installed Mar. 13, 1969.

Watty Urquidi, Ricardo, M.Sp.S.: b. July 16, 1938, San Diego, Calif.; ord. priest June 8, 1968; ord. titular bishop of Macomedes and auxiliary bishop of Mexico City, July 19, 1980.

Weakland, Rembert G., O.S.B.: b. Apr. 2, 1927, Patton, Pa.; joined Benedictines, 1945; ord. priest June 24, 1951; abbot-primate of Benedictine Confederation, 1967-77; ord. archbishop of Milwaukee, Nov. 8, 1977.

Weigand, William K.: b. 1937, Bend, Ore.; educ. Mt. Angel Seminary (St. Benedict, Ore.), St. Edward's Seminary and St. Thomas Seminary (Kenmore, Wash.); ord. priest 1963; app. bishop of Salt Lake City, Sept. 8, 1980.

Weldon, Christopher J.: b. Sept. 6, 1905, New York, N.Y.; educ. Montreal College (Canada), St. Joseph's Seminary (Dunwoodie, N.Y.), Catholic Univ. (Washington, D.C.); ord. priest Sept. 21, 1939; ord. bishop of Springfield, Mass., Mar. 24, 1950; retired Oct. 15, 1977.

Welsh, Lawrence H.: b. Feb. 1, 1935, Winton, Wyo.; educ. Univ. of Wyoming (Laramie, Wyo.), St. John's Seminary (Collegeville, Minn.), Catholic Univ. (Washington, D.C.); ord. priest May 26, 1962; ord. bishop of Spokane, Dec. 14, 1978.

Welsh, Thomas J.: b. Dec. 20, 1921, Weatherly, Pa.; educ. St. Charles Borromeo Seminary (Philadelphia, Pa.), Catholic Univ. (Washington, D.C.); ord. priest May 30, 1946; ord. titular bishop of Scattery Island and auxiliary bishop of Philadelphia, Apr. 2, 1970; app. first bishop of Arlington, Va., June 4, 1974, installed Aug. 13, 1974.

Whealon, John F.: b. Jan. 15, 1921, Barberton, O.; educ. St. Charles College (Catonsville, Md.), St. Mary's Seminary (Cleveland, O.); ord. priest May 26, 1945; ord. titular bishop of Andrapa and auxiliary bishop of Cleveland, July 6, 1961; app. bishop of Erie, Dec. 9, 1966, installed Mar. 7, 1967; archbishop of Hartford, installed Mar. 19, 1969.

Whelan, Robert L., S.J.: b. Apr. 16, 1912, Wallace, Ida.; educ. St. Michael's College (Spokane, Wash.), Alma College (Alma, Calif.); ord. priest June 17, 1944; ord. titular bishop of Sicilibba and coadjutor bishop of Fairbanks, Alaska, with right of succession, Feb. 22, 1968; bishop of Fairbanks, Nov. 30, 1968.

Wildermuth, Augustine F., S.J.: b. Feb. 20, 1904, St. Louis, Mo.; educ. St. Stanislaus Seminary (Florissant, Mo.), St. Michael's Scholasticate (Spokane, Wash.), Sacred Heart College (Shembaganur, S. India), St. Mary's College (Kurseong, India), Gregorian Univ. (Rome); entered Society of Jesus, 1922;

ord. priest July 25, 1935; ord. bishop of Patna, India, Oct. 28, 1947; retired 1980.

Wirz, George O.: b. Jan. 17, 1929, Monroe, Wis.; educ. St. Francis Seminary and Marquette Univ. (Milwaukee, Wis.); Cath. Univ. (Washington, D.C.); ord. priest May 31, 1952; ord. titular bishop of Municipa and auxilary bishop of Madison, Mar. 9, 1978.

Wurm, John N.: b. Dec. 6, 1927, Overland, Mo.; educ. Kenrick Seminary and St. Louis Univ. (St. Louis, Mo.); ord. priest Apr. 3, 1954; ord. titular bishop of Plestia and auxiliary bishop of St. Louis, Aug. 17, 1976.

Wycislo, Aloysius John: b. June 17, 1908, Chicago, Ill.; educ. St. Mary's Seminary (Mundelein, Ill.), Catholic Univ. (Washington, D.C.); ord. priest Apr. 4, 1934; ord. titular bishop of Stadia and auxiliary bishop of Chicago, Dec. 21, 1960; app. bishop of Green Bay, installed Apr. 16, 1968.

Z

Zayek, Francis: b. Oct. 18, 1920, Manzanillo, Cuba; ord. priest Mar. 17, 1946; ord. titular bishop of Callinicum and auxiliary bishop for Maronites in Brazil, Aug. 5, 1962; named apostolic exarch for Maronites in U.S., with headquarters in Detroit; installed June 11, 1966; first eparch of St. Maron of Detroit, Mar. 25, 1972; see transferred to Brooklyn, June 27, 1977.

Zuroweste, Albert R.: b. Apr. 26, 1901, East St. Louis, Ill.; educ. St. Francis College (Quincy, Ill.), Kenrick Seminary (Webster Groves, Mo.), Catholic Univ. (Washington, D.C.); ord. priest June 8, 1924; ord. bishop of Belleville, Jan. 29, 1948; retired Oct. 29, 1976.

RETIRED U.S. PRELATES

Information, as of Oct. 1, 1980, includes name of the prelate and see held at the time of retirement or resignation; archbishops are indicated by an asterisk. Most of the prelates listed below resigned their sees because of age. See Index: Biographies of American Bishops.

The preferred form of address of retired prelates is *Former Archbishop* or *Bishop of* (last see held).

Richard H. Ackerman, C.S.Sp. (Covington), George W. Ahr (Trenton), Peter W. Bartholome (St. Cloud), Alden J. Bell (Sacramento), Romeo Blanchette (Joliet), John H. Boccella, T.O.R.* (Izmir, Turkey), John Bokenfohr, O.M.I. (Kimberley, S. Africa), James C. Burke, O.P. (Chimbote, Peru, prelate), Charles A. Buswell (Pueblo), L. Abel Caillouet (New Orleans, auxiliary), Cardinal John Carberry* (St. Louis), Mark K. Carroll (Wichita), John J. Cassata (Fort Worth), John E. Cohill, S.V.D. (Goroka, Papua New Guinea), James L. Connolly (Fall River), Thomas Connolly* (Seattle), William E. Cousins* (Milwaukee), Augustine Danglmayr (Ft. Worth, auxiliary), Nicholas

D'Antonio, O.F.M. (Olancha, Honduras).

Edward V. Dargin (New York, auxiliary), James P. Davis* (Santa Fê), Cardinal John F. Dearden* (Detroit), Stephen J. Donahue (New York, auxiliary), Hugh A. Donohoe (Fresno), John A. Donovan (Toledo), Clarence J. Duhart, C.SS.R. (Udon Thani, Thailand), Joseph A. Durick (Nashville), J. Lennox Federal (Salt Lake City), John B. Franz (Peoria), Philip J. Furlong (Military Vicariate, delegate),

James J. Gerrard (Fall River, auxiliary), Francis D. Gleeson, S.J. (Fairbanks), Laurence A. Glenn (Crookston), Ignatius T. Glennie, S.J. (Trincomalee-Batticaloa, Sri Lanka), Lawrence L. Graner* (Dacca, Bangladesh), Lawrence Graziano, O.F.M. (San Miguel, El Salvador), Charles P. Greco (Alexandria), Joseph Green (Reno), John B. Grellinger, (Green Bay, auxiliary), Merlin J. Guilfoyle (Stockton).

J. Richard Ham, M.M. (Guatemala, auxiliary), Charles H. Helmsing (Kansas City-St. Joseph), Edward G. Hettinger (Columbus, auxiliary), Vincent J. Hines (Norwich), Lambert A. Hoch (Sioux Falls), Joseph L. Hogan (Rochester), Edward D. Howard* (Portland, Ore.), Clarence G. Issenmann (Cleveland), Robert F. Joyce (Burlington), Walter P. Kellenberg (Rockville Centre), George L. Leech (Harrisburg), Francis P. Leipzig (Baker), Leo Lemay, S.M. (Bougainville, Solomon Is.), Stephen A. Leven (San Angelo).

William McDonald (San Francisco, auxiliary), John J. McEleney, S.J.* (Kingston, Jamaica), Joseph T. McGucken* (San Francisco), Edward A. McGurkin, M.M. (Shinyanga, Tanzania), Edward J. Maginn (Albany, auxiliary), John J. Maguire* (New York, coadjutor), Alfred Mendez, C.S.C. (Arecibo, P.R.), Sidney M. Metzger (El Paso).

Louis La Ravoire Morrow, S.D.B. (Krishnagar, India), Joseph M. Mueller (Sioux City), Knute Ansgar Nelson, O.S.B. (Stockholm, Sweden), Hubert M. Newell (Cheyenne), Wendelin J. Nold (Galveston-Houston), Adolph A. Noser, S.V.D.* (Madang, Papua New Guinea), Cardinal Patrick O'Boyle* (Washington, D.C.).

Martin J. O'Connor* (Prefect Emeritus, Pontifical Commission for Social Communications), William A. O'Connor (Springfield, Ill.), James V. Pardy, M.M. (Cheong Ju, Korea), John L. Paschang (Grand Island), George H. Pearce, S.M.* (Suva, Fiji Islands), Joseph M. Pernicone (New York, auxiliary), Ernest J. Primeau (Manchester), Leo A. Pursley (Fort Wayne-South Bend), Joseph M. Raya* (Acre), Joseph W. Regan, M.M. (Tagum, P.I., Prelate), Francis F. Reh (Saginaw).

Louis J. Reicher (Austin), Thomas F. Reilly, C.SS.R. (San Juan de la Maguana, Dominican Republic), John J. Rudin, M.M.

(Musoma, Tanzania), John J. Russell (Richmond), Maurice Schexnayder (Lafayette, La.), Alphonse Schladweiler (New Ulm), Paul C. Schulte* (Indianapolis; titular archbishop of Elicora), Eldon B. Schuster (Great Falls).

Cardinal Lawrence J. Shehan* (Baltimore), Edward E. Swanstrom (New York, auxiliary), Paul F. Tanner (St. Augustine), Bernard J. Topel (Spokane), James E. Walsh, M.M. (Kongmoon, China, vicar apostolic), Christopher J. Weldon (Springfield, Mass.), Augustine Wildermuth, S.J. (Patna, India), Albert R. Zuroweste (Belleville).

U.S. BISHOPS OVERSEAS

Cardinal William W. Baum, prefect of the Sacred Congregation for Catholic Education; Archbishop Raymond P. Etteldorf, pro-nuncio to Ethiopia; Bishop Anthony L. Deksnys, pastoral work among Lithuanians in Western Europe; Bishop Paul C. Marcinkus, president of Institute for Works of Religion (Vatican Bank); Bishop Ernest Primeau, former bishop of Manchester, N.H., director of Villa Stritch, Rome.

(See also Missionary Bishops.)

BISHOP-BROTHERS

(See separate entries for biographical data. The asterisk indicates brothers who were bishops at the same time.)

There have been nine pairs of brother-bishops in the history of the U.S. hierarchy.

Living: Francis T. Hurley,* archbishop of Anchorage and Mark J. Hurley* of Santa Rosa.

Deceased: Francis Blanchet* of Oregon City (Portland) and Augustin Blanchet* of Walla Walla; John S. Foley of Detroit and Thomas P. Foley of Chicago; Francis P. Kenrick,* apostolic administrator of Philadelphia, bishop of Philadelphia and Baltimore, and Peter R. Kenrick* of St. Louis; Matthias C. Lenihan of Great Falls and Thomas M. Lenihan of Cheyenne; James O'Connor, vicar apostolic of Nebraska and bishop of Omaha, and Michael O'Connor of Pittsburgh and Erie; Jeremiah F. and John W. Shanahan, both of Harrisburg; Sylvester J. Espelage, O.F.M.,* of Wuchang, China, who died 10 days after the ordination of his brother, Bernard T. Espelage,* O.F.M., of Gallup; Coleman F. Carroll* of Miami and Howard Carroll* of Altoona-Johnstown.

The Catholic Church Extension Society made a donation of $100,000 in August, 1980, to the Archdiocese of Miami to assist in training Puerto Rican students for the priesthood enrolled at St. John Vianney College Seminary, Miami, and St. Vincent de Paul Seminary, Boynton Beach, Fla. Father Robert Lynch, rector of St. John Vianney College Seminary, said that 40 students were in training at the two institutions.

Religious orders and congregations, collectively called **religious institutes,** are special societies in the Church. Their members, called **religious,** commit themselves to observance of the evangelical counsels of poverty, chastity and obedience in a community kind of life in accordance with rules and constitutions approved by church authority.

Religious Institutes

The particular goal of each institute and the means of realizing it in practice are stated in the rule and constitutions proper to the institute. Local bishops, with permission of the Holy See, can give approval for rules and constitutions of **institutes of diocesan rank. Pontifical rank** belongs to institutes approved by the Holy See. General jurisdiction over all religious is exercised by the Congregation for Religious and Secular Institutes. General legislation concerning religious is contained in Canons 487 to 681 of the Code of Canon Law and in subsequent enactments, especially since the Second Vatican Council.

All religious institutes are commonly called religious orders, despite the fact that there are differences between orders and congregations. The best known **orders** include the Benedictines, Trappists, Franciscans, Dominicans, Carmelites and Augustinians, for men; and the Carmelites, Poor Clares, Dominicans of the Second Order and Visitation Nuns, for women. Members of the orders have solemn vows; their communities have papal enclosure and exemption, and are bound to perform the Liturgy of the Hours (Divine Office) in choir as a common practice. Members of the **congregations** have simple vows. The orders are older than the congregations, which did not appear until the 16th century.

Contemplative institutes are oriented to divine worship and service within the confines of their communities, by prayer, penitential practices, other spiritual activities and self-supporting work; engagement in outside active ministry is subordinate to their contemplative pursuits. Examples are the Trappists and Carthusians, the Carmelite and Poor Clare nuns. **Active institutes** are geared primarily for the ministry and many kinds of apostolic work. **Mixed institutes** combine elements of the contemplative and active ways of life. While most institutes of men and women can be classified as active, all of them have some contemplative aspects.

Historical Development

The basis of the life of religious institutes was the invitation Christ extended to men (Mt. 19:16ff.) to follow him with special dedication in a life like his own, which was that of a poor and chaste man under obedience to the Father.

In the earliest years of Christianity, some men and women dedicated themselves to the service of God in a special manner. Among them were holy women, deaconesses and virgins mentioned in the Acts of the Apostles, and confessors and ascetics like St. Clement of Rome, St. Ignatius of Antioch and St. Polycarp.

In the third and fourth centuries, there were traces of a kind of religious profession, and the root idea of the life began to produce significant results in the solitary and community hermitages of Egypt and Syria under the inspiration of men like St. Paul of Thebes, St. Anthony the Abbot and St. Pachomius.

St. Basil, "Father of Monasticism in the East," exerted a deep and still continuing influence on the development of religious life among men and women. His opposite number in the West was St. Benedict, whose rule or counsels, dating from about 530, set the pattern of monastic life for men and women which prevailed for nearly six centuries and which still endures. Before his time, St. Augustine framed guidelines for community life which are still being followed by some men and women religious.

Mendicant orders, whose members were freer than the monks for works of the active ministry, made their appearance early in the 13th century and began to change some of the established aspects of religious life. Religious women, however, continued to live in the monastic manner.

A significant change in religious life developed in the 16th century when several communities of men with simple rather than solemn vows were approved; among them were **clerics regular** like the Jesuits and Barnabites. Some of these communities are considered to be orders, although they differ in some respects from the older orders.

The Sisters of Charity, in 1633, were the first community of women with simple vows to gain church approval. Since that time, the number and variety of female communities have greatly increased. Women religious, no longer restricted to the hidden life of prayer, became engaged in many kinds of work including education, health and social service, and missionary endeavor.

Clerical communities of men — i. e., those whose membership is predominantly composed of priests — are similarly active in many types of work. Their ditinctive fields are education, home and foreign missions, retreats, special assignments and the communications media, as well as the internal life and conduct of their own communities. They also engage in the ordinary pastoral ministry which is the principal work of diocesan or secular priests. They are generally called **regular clergy** because of the rule of life (*regula* in Latin) they follow.

Non-clerical or lay institutes of men are the various brotherhoods whose non-ordained members (called **lay brothers,** or simply **brothers**) are engaged in educational and hospital work, missionary endeavors, and other special fields.

Some of the institutes of men listed below have a special kind of status because their members, while living a common life like that which is characteristic of religious, do not profess the vows of religious. Examples are the Maryknoll Fathers, the Oratorians of St. Philip Neri, the Paulists and Sulpicians. They are called **societies of the common life without vows.**

RENEWAL OF RELIGIOUS LIFE

Following are key excerpts from the *Decree on the Appropriate Renewal of Religious Life* promulgated by the Second Vatican Council.

"A life consecrated by a profession of the counsels (of poverty, chastity and obedience) is of surpassing value. Such a life has a necessary role to play in the circumstances of the present age. That this kind of life and its contemporary role may achieve greater good for the Church, this sacred Synod issues the following decrees. They concern only the general principles which must underlie an appropriate renewal of the life and rules of religious communities. These principles apply also to societies living a community life without the exercise of vows, and to secular institutes, though the special character of both groups is to be maintained. After the Council, the competent authority will be obliged to enact particular laws opportunely spelling out and applying what is legislated here" (No. 1).

"The appropriate renewal of religious life involves two simultaneous processes: (1) a continuous return to the sources of all Christian life and to the original inspiration behind a given community and (2) an adjustment of the community to the changed conditions of the times. . . .

"(a) Since the fundamental norm of the religious life is a following of Christ as proposed by the gospel, such is to be regarded by all communities as their supreme law.

"(b) It serves the best interests of the Church for communities to have their own special character and purpose. Therefore loyal recognition and safekeeping should be accorded to the spirit of founders, as also to all the particular goals and wholesome traditions which constitute the heritage of each community.

"(c) All communities should participate in the life of the Church. According to its individual character, each should make its own and foster in every possible way the enterprises and objectives of the Church in such fields as these: the scriptural, liturgical, doctrinal, pastoral, ecumenical, missionary, and social.

"(d) Communities should promote among their members a suitable awareness of contemporary human conditions and of the needs of the Church. . . .

"(e) Since the religious life is intended above all else to lead those who embrace it to an imitation of Christ and to union with God through the profession of the evangelical counsels, the fact must be honestly faced that even the most desirable changes made on behalf of contemporary needs will fail of their purpose unless a renewal of spirit gives life to them. Indeed such an interior renewal must always be accorded the leading role even in the promotion of external works" (No. 2).

"The manner of living, praying, and working should be suitably adapted to the physical and psychological conditions of today's religious and also, to the extent required by the nature of each community, to the needs of the apostolate, the requirements of a given culture, the social and economic circumstances anywhere, but especially in missionary territories."

Allowance should be made for prudent experimentation in the direction of renewal and adaptation (No. 3).

". . . The hope of renewal must be lodged in a more diligent observance of rule and of constitution rather than in a multiplication of individual laws" (No. 4).

Various Communities

"The members of each community should recall above everything else that by their profession of the evangelical counsels they have given answer to a divine call to live for God alone not only by dying to sin (cf. Rom. 6:11) but also by renouncing the world. They have handed over their entire lives to God's service in an act of special consecration which is deeply rooted in their baptismal consecration and which provides an ampler manifestation of it.

"Inasmuch as their self-dedication has been accepted by the Church, they should realize that they are committed to her service as well.

". . . The members of each community should combine contemplation with apostolic love. By the former they adhere to God in mind and heart; by the latter they strive to associate themselves with the work of redemption and to spread the Kingdom of God" (No. 5).

"Members of those communities which are totally dedicated to contemplation give themselves to God alone in solitude and silence and through constant prayer and ready penance. No matter how urgent may be the needs of the active apostolate, such communities will always have a distinguished part to play in Christ's Mystical Body. . . . Their manner of living should be revised according to the aforementioned principles and standards of appropriate renewal, though their withdrawal from the world and the practices of their contemplative life should be maintained at their holiest" (No. 7).

Communities geared for apostolic action "should skillfully harmonize their observances and practices with the needs of the apostolate to which they are dedicated," with due regard for diversity (No. 8). This norm applies to monastic institutes, which should preserve their special character; to communities which "closely join the apostolic life with choral prayer and monastic observances"; and to "the lay religious life, for both men and women" (Nos. 9 and 10).

[See Secular Institutes for a quotation from the decree on the subject.]

The Vows, Authority

"That chastity which is practiced 'on behalf of the heavenly Kingdom' (Mt. 19:12), and which religious profess, deserves to be esteemed as a surpassing gift of grace. For it liberates the human heart in a unique way (cf. 1 Cor. 7:32-35) and causes it to burn with greater love for God and all mankind. It is therefore an outstanding token of heavenly riches, and also a most suitable way for religious to spend themselves readily in God's service and in works of the apostolate. . . .

"Since the observance of total continence intimately involves the deeper inclinations of human nature, candidates should not undertake the profession of chastity nor be admitted to its profession except after a truly adequate testing period and only if they have the needed degree of psychological and emotional maturity" (No. 12).

"Poverty voluntarily embraced in imitation of Christ provides a witness which is highly esteemed, especially today. Let religious painstakingly cultivate such poverty, and give it new expressions if need be. . . .

". . . Members of a community ought to be poor in both body and spirit, and have their treasures in heaven (cf. Mt. 6:20).

". . . Communities as such should aim at giving a kind of corporate witness to their own poverty. . . .

"To the degree that their rules and constitutions permit, religious communities can rightly possess whatever is necessary for their temporal life and their mission. Still, let them avoid every appearance of luxury, of excessive wealth, and accumulation of possessions" (No. 13).

"Through the profession of obedience, religious offer to God a total dedication of their own wills as a sacrifice of themselves; they thereby unite themselves with greater steadiness and security to the saving will of God. . . . Under the influence of the Holy Spirit, religious submit themselves to their superiors, whom faith presents as God's representatives, and through whom they are guided into the service of all their brothers in Christ. . . . In this way . . . religious assume a firmer commitment to the ministry of the Church and labor to achieve the mature measure of the fullness of Christ (cf. Eph. 4:13).

"Therefore, in a spirit of faith and of love for God's will, let religious show humble obedience to their superiors in accord with the norms of the rule and constitution. . . . Let them bring to the execution of commands and to the discharge of assignments entrusted to them the resources of their minds and wills, and their gifts of nature and grace. Lived in this manner, religious obedience will not diminish the dignity of the human person but will rather lead it to maturity in consequence of that enlarged freedom which belongs to the sons of God.

". . . Each superior should himself be docile to God's will in the exercise of his office. Let him use his authority in a spirit of service for the brethren. . . . Governing his subjects as God's own sons, and with regard for their human personality, a superior will make it easier for them to obey gladly. Therefore he must make a special point of leaving them appropriately free with respect to the sacrament of penance and direction of conscience. Let him give the kind of leadership which will encourage religious to bring an active and responsible obedience to the offices they shoulder and the activities they undertake. Therefore a superior should listen willingly to his subjects and encourage them to make a personal contribution to the welfare of the community and of the Church. Not to be weakened, however, is the superior's authority to decide what must be done and to require the doing of it.

"Let chapters and councils faithfully acquit themselves of the governing role given to them; each should express in its own way the fact that all members of the community have a share in the welfare of the whole community and a responsibility for it" (No. 14).

THEOLOGICAL UNION

The Washington Theological Union, founded by six religious orders in 1968 and with the title, Washington Theological Coalition, until 1977, is a theological and pastoral institute for the training of candidates for the priesthood and other ministries, and for the continuing education of priests.

About 25 religious communities are represented in the current student body of approximately 275, including women religious, lay persons and several non-Catholics. The WTU is the only institute of its kind in the East.

Father Vincent Cushing, O.F.M., is president of the WTU. Father James Coriden is the academic dean. The WTU address is 9001 New Hampshire Ave., Silver Spring, Md.

RELIGIOUS INSTITUTES OF MEN IN THE UNITED STATES

(Sources: *Official Catholic Directory;* Catholic Almanac survey.)

African Missions, Society of, S.M.A.: Founded 1856, at Lyons, France, by Bishop Melchior de Marion Brésillac. Generalate, Rome, Italy; American provincialate, 23 Bliss Ave., Tenafly, N.J. 07670. Missionary work in West Africa, Bahama Islands and inner city parishes.

Assumptionists (Augustinians of the Assumption), AA.: Founded 1845, at Nimes, France, by Rev. Emmanuel d'Alzon; in U.S., 1946. General motherhouse, Rome, Italy; U.S. province, 329 W. 108th St., New York, N.Y. 10025. Educational, parochial, ecumenical, retreat, foreign mission work.

Atonement, Franciscan Friars of the, S.A.: Founded as an Anglican Franciscan community in 1898 at Garrison, N.Y., by Rev. Paul Wattson. Community corporately received into the Catholic Church in 1909. Motherhouse, St. Paul Friary, Graymoor, Garrison N.Y. 10524. Ecumenical, mission, retreat and charitable works.

Augustinian Recollects, O.A.R.: Founded 1588: in U.S., 1944. General motherhouse, Rome, Italy; U.S. provincial residence, 29 Ridgeway Ave., West Orange, N.J. 07052. Missionary, parochial, education work.

Augustinians (Order of St. Augustine), O.S.A.: Established canonically in 1256 by Pope Alexander IV; in U.S., 1796. General motherhouse, Rome, Italy.

St. Thomas of Villanova Province (1796), Villanova, Pa. 19085.

Our Mother of Good Counsel Province (1941), Tolentine Center, 20300 Governors Hwy., Olympia Fields, Ill. 60461.

St. Augustine Province (1969), 2060 N. Vermont Ave., Los Angeles, Calif. 90027.

Good Counsel Vice-Province, St. Augustine Priory, Richland, N.J. 08350.

U.S. Vicariate of Castile, Spain, Province, P.O. Box 578, Vidor, Tex. 77662.

Barnabites (Clerics Regular of St. Paul), C.R.S.P.: Founded 1530, in Milan, Italy, by St. Anthony M. Zaccaria. Generalate, Rome, Italy; American headquarters, 1023 Swann Rd., Youngstown, N.Y. 14174. Parochial, educational, mission work.

Basil the Great, Order of St. (Ukrainian), O.S.B.M.: General motherhouse, Rome, Italy; U.S. province, 31-12 30th St., Long Island City, N.Y. 11106. Parochial work among Byzantine Ukrainian Rite Catholics.

Basilian Fathers (Congregation of the Priests of St. Basil), C.S.B.: Founded 1822, at Annonay, France. General motherhouse, 20 Humewood Dr., Toronto, Ont. M6C 2W2, Canada. Educational, parochial work.

Basilian Salvatorian Fathers: Founded 1684, at Saida, Lebanon, by Eftimios Saifi; in U.S., 1953. General motherhouse, Saida, Lebanon; American headquarters, 30 East St., Methuen, Mass. 01844. Educational, parochial work among Eastern Rite peoples.

Benedictines (Order of St. Benedict), O.S.B.: Founded 529, in Italy, by St. Benedict of Nursia; in U.S., 1846.

• American Cassinese Federation (1855). Rt. Rev. Martin Burne, O.S.B., pres., St. Mary's Abbey, Delbarton, Morristown, N.J. 07960. Abbeys and Priories belonging to the federation:

St. Vincent Archabbey, Latrobe, Pa. 15650; St. John's Abbey, Collegeville, Minn. 56321; St. Benedict's Abbey, Atchison, Kans. 66002; St. Mary's Abbey, Delbarton, Morristown, N.J. 07960; Belmont Abbey, Belmont, N.C. 28012; St. Bernard Abbey, St. Bernard, Ala. 35138; St. Procopius Abbey, Lisle, Ill. 60532; St. Gregory's Abbey, Shawnee, Okla. 74801; St. Leo Abbey, St. Leo, Fla. 33574; Assumption Abbey, Richardton, N. Dak. 58652;

St. Bede Abbey, Peru, Ill. 61354; St. Martin's Abbey, Lacey, Wash. 98503; Holy Cross Abbey, Canon City, Colo. 81212; St. Anselm's Abbey, Manchester, N.H. 03102; St. Andrew's Abbey, 2900 East Blvd., Cleveland, O. 44104; Holy Trinity Monastery, Butler, Pa. 16001; St. Maur Priory, 4545 Northwestern Ave., Indianapolis, Ind. 46208; Newark Abbey, 528 High St., Newark, N.J. 07102; St. Mark's Priory, South Union, Ky. 42283; Benedictine Priory, 6502 Seawright Dr., Savannah, Ga. 31406; St. Benedict's Priory, 304 N. Sheppard St., Richmond, Va. 23221; Woodside Priory, 302 Portola Rd., Portola Valley, Calif. 94025.

• Swiss-American Federation (1870), Rt. Rev. Raphael De Salvo O.S.B., pres., New Subiaco Abbey, New Subiaco, Ark. 72865. Abbeys and priory belonging to the federation:

St. Meinrad Archabbey, St. Meinrad, Ind. 47577; Conception Abbey, Conception, Mo. 64433; Mt. Michael Abbey, Elkhorn, Nebr. 68022; New Subiaco Abbey, Subiaco, Ark. 72865; St. Joseph's Abbey, St. Benedict, La. 70457; Mt. Angel Abbey, St. Benedict, Ore. 97373; Marmion Abbey, Butterfield Rd., Aurora, Ill. 60504;

St. Benedict's Abbey, Benet Lake, Wis. 53102; Glastonbury Abbey, 16 Hull St., Hingham, Mass. 02043; Westminster Abbey, Mission, B.C., Canada; St. Pius X Abbey, Pevely, Mo. 63070; Blue Cloud Abbey, Marvin, S. Dak. 57251; Corpus Christi Abbey, Star Route, Box A-38-A, Sandia, Tex. 78383; Our Lady of Guadalupe Abbey, Pecos N. Mex. 87552; St. Charles Priory, Benet Hill, Oceanside, Calif. 92054.

• English Benedictine Congregation: St. Anselm's Abbey, 4501 S. Dakota Ave. N.E., Washington, D.C. 20017; Abbey of St.

Gregory, Cory's Lane, Portsmouth, R.I. 02871; Priory of St. Mary and St. Louis, 500 S. Mason Rd., St. Louis, Mo. 63141.

• Congregation of St. Ottilien for Foreign Missions, St. Paul's Abbey, Newton, N.J. 07860; Benedictine Mission House, Schuyler, Neb. 68661.

• Congregation of the Annunciation, St. Andrew Priory, Valyermo, Calif. 93563.

• Houses not in Congregations: Mount Saviour Monastery, Pine City, N.Y. 14871; Conventual Priory of St. Gabriel the Archangel, Weston, Vt. 05161.

Benedictines, Olivetan, O.S.B.: General motherhouse, Siena, Italy. U.S. foundation, Our Lady of Mt. Olivet Monastery, 4029 Ave. G, Lake Charles, La. 70601.

Benedictines, Sylvestrine, O.S.B.: Founded 1231, in Italy by Sylvester Gozzolini. General motherhouse, Rome, Italy; U.S. foundations; 17320 Rosemont Rd., Detroit, Mich. 48219; 2711 E. Drahner Rd., Oxford, Mich. 48051; 1697 State Highway 3, Clifton, N.J. 07012.

Bethlehem Missionaries, Society of, S.M.B.: Founded 1921, at Immensee, Switzerland, by Rt. Rev. Canon Peter Bondolfi. General motherhouse, Immensee, Switzerland; U.S. headquarters, 5630 E. 17th Ave., Denver, Colo. 80220. Foreign mission work.

Blessed Sacrament, Congregation of the, S.S.S.: Founded 1856, at Paris, France, by St. Pierre Julien Eymard; in U.S., 1900. General motherhouse, Rome, Italy; U.S. address, 5384 Wilson Mills Rd., Cleveland, O. 44143. Eucharistic apostolate.

Camaldolese Congregation, Cam. O.S.B.: Founded 1012, at Camaldoli, near Arezzo, Italy, by St. Romuald; in U.S. 1958. General motherhouse, Arezzo, Italy; U.S. foundation, Immaculate Heart Hermitage, Big Sur, Calif. 93920.

Camaldolese Hermits of the Congregation of Monte Corona, Er. Cam.: Founded 1520, from Camaldoli, Italy, by Bl. Paul Giustiniani. General motherhouse, Frascati (Rome), Italy; U.S. foundation, Holy Family Hermitage, Bloomingdale, O. 43910.

Camillians (Order of St. Camillus; Clerics Regular, Ministers of the Sick), O.S.Cam.: Founded 1582, at Rome, by St. Camillus de Lellis; in U.S., 1923. General motherhouse, Rome, Italy; North American province, 10100 W. Blue Mound Rd., Wauwatosa, Wis. 53226.

Carmelites (Order of Our Lady of Mt. Carmel), O. Carm.: General motherhouse, Rome, Italy. Educational, charitable work.

Most Pure Heart of Mary Province (1864), 45 E. Dundee Rd., Barrington, Ill. 60010.

St. Elias Province (1931), 69-34 52nd Ave., Maspeth, N.Y. 11378.

Mt. Carmel Hermitage, Pineland, R.D. 1, Box 36, New Florence, Pa. 15944 (immediately subject to Prior General.)

Carmelites, Order of Discalced, O.C.D.: Es-

tablished 1562, a Reform Order of Our Lady of Mt. Carmel; in U.S., 1935. General motherhouse, Rome, Italy. Spiritual direction, retreat, parochial work.

St. Therese of Oklahoma Province (1935), 1125 S. Walker St., P.O. Box 26127, Oklahoma City, Okla. 73126.

Immaculate Heart of Mary Province (1947), P.O. Box 67, Hubertus, Wis. 53033.

Anglo-Irish Province, 510 N. El Molino St., Alhambra, Calif. 91801.

Polish Province of the Holy Spirit, 1628 Ridge Rd., Munster, Ind. 46321.

Carthusians, Order of, O. Cart.: Founded 1084, in France, by St. Bruno; in U.S., 1951. General motherhouse, St. Pierre de Chartreuse, France; U.S. charterhouse, Arlington, Vt. 05250. Cloistered contemplatives; semi-eremitic.

Charity, Servants of, S.C.: Founded 1908, in Italy, by Bl. Luigi Guanella. General motherhouse, Rome, Italy; U.S. headquarters, Don Guanella School, Sproul Rd., Springfield, Pa. 19064.

Christ, Society of, S.Ch.: Founded 1932, General Motherhouse, Poznan, Poland; U.S. address, 3000 Eighteen Mile Rd., Sterling Heights, Mich. 48078.

Cistercians, Order of, S.O. Cist.: Founded 1098, by St. Robert. Headquarters, Rome, Italy.

Our Lady of Spring Bank Abbey, 34639 W. Fairview Rd., Oconomowoc, Wis. 53066.

Our Lady of Gerowval Monastery, Rose Hill, Miss. 39356.

Our Lady of Dallas Monastery, Rt. 2, Box 1, Irving, Tex. 75062.

Cistercian Monastery of Our Lady of Fatima, P.O. Box 295, Moorestown, N.J. 08057. (Staff St. John Neumann Church, Mt. Laurel, N.J.)

Cistercian Monastery of Saint Mary, R.D. 1, New Ringgold, Pa. 17960.

Cistercians of the Strict Observance, Order of (Trappists), O.C.S.O.: Founded 1098, in France, by St. Robert; in U.S., 1848. Generalate, Rome, Italy.

Our Lady of Gethsemani Abbey (1848), Trappist P.O., Ky. 40073.

Our Lady of New Melleray Abbey (1849), Dubuque, Iowa 52001.

St. Joseph's Abbey (1825), Spencer, Mass. 01562.

Holy Spirit Monastery (1944), Conyers, Ga. 30208.

Our Lady of Guadalupe Abbey (1947), Lafayette, Ore. 97127.

Our Lady of the Holy Trinity Abbey (1947), Huntsville, Utah 84317.

Abbey of the Genesee (1951), Piffard, N.Y. 14533.

Our Lady of Mepkin Abbey (1949), Route 3, Box 800, Moncks Corner, S. Car. 29461.

Our Lady of the Holy Cross Abbey (1950), Berryville, Va. 22611.

Our Lady of the Assumption Abbey (1950), Rt. 5, Box 193, Ava, Mo. 65608.

Our Lady of New Clairvaux Abbey (1955), Vina, Calif. 96092.

St. Benedict's Monastery (1956), Snowmass, Colo. 81654.

Claretians (Missionary Sons of the Immaculate Heart of Mary), C.M.F.: Founded 1849, at Vich, Spain, by St. Anthony Mary Claret. General Curia, Rome, Italy. Missionary, parochial, educational, retreat work.

Western Province, 1119 Westchester Pl., Los Angeles, Calif. 90019.

Eastern Province, 400 N. Euclid Ave. Oak Park, Ill. 60302.

Clerics Regular Minor (Adorno Fathers) C.R.M.: Founded 1588, at Naples, Italy, by Ven. Augustine Adorno and St. Francis Caracciolo. General motherhouse, Rome, Italy; U.S. address, 575 Darlington Ave., Ramsey, N.J. 07446.

Columban, Society of St. (St. Columban Foreign Mission Society): Founded 1918. General headquarters, Dublin, Ireland. U.S. headquarters, St. Columbans, Nebr. 68056. Foreign mission work.

Comboni Missionaries of the Sacred Heart (Verona Fathers), M.C.C.J.: Founded 1885, in Italy. General motherhouse, Rome, Italy; North American headquarters, Comboni Mission Center, 8108 Beechmont Ave., Cincinnati, O. 45230. Mission work in Africa and the Americas.

Consolata Society for Foreign Missions, I.M.C.: Founded 1901, at Turin, Italy, by Father Joseph Allamano. General motherhouse, Rome, Italy; U.S. headquarters, P.O. Box C, Lincoln Hwy., Somerset, N.J. 08873.

Crosier Fathers (Canons Regular of the Order of the Holy Cross), O.S.C.: Founded 1210, in Belgium by Bl. Theodore De Celles. Generalate, Amersfoort, Netherlands; U.S. province, 711 Lincoln Ave., St. Paul, Minn. 55105. Mission, retreat, educational work.

Cross, Priests of the Congregation of Holy, C.S.C.: Founded 1837, in France; in U.S., 1841. Generalate, Rome, Italy. Educational and pastoral work; home missions and retreats; foreign missions; social services and apostolate of the press.

Indiana Province (1841), 1304 E. Jefferson Blvd., South Bend, Ind. 46617.

Eastern Province (1952), 835 Clinton Ave., Bridgeport, Conn. 06604.

Southern Province (1968), 1828 S. Carrollton Ave., New Orleans, La. 70118.

Divine Word, Society of the, S.V.D.: Founded 1875, in Holland, by Bl. Arnold Janssen. North American Province founded 1897 with headquarters in Techny, Ill. General motherhouse, Rome, Italy.

Province of the Blessed Virgin (Northern Province), (1964), Techny, Ill. 60082.

Sacred Heart Province (Eastern Province) (1940), 1025 Michigan Ave. N.E., Washington, D.C. 20017.

St. Augustine's Province (Southern Province) (1940), 201 Ruella Ave., Bay St. Louis, Miss. 39520.

St. Therese Province (Western Province) (1964), 2181 W. 25th St., Los Angeles, Calif. 90018.

Dominicans (Order of Friars Preachers), O.P.: Founded early 13th century by St. Dominic de Guzman. General headquarters, Santa Sabina, Rome, Italy. Preaching, teaching, missions, research, parishes.

St. Joseph Province (1806), 141 E. 65th St., New York, N.Y. 10021.

Holy Name of Jesus Province (1912), 5877 Birch Ct., Oakland, Calif. 94618.

St. Albert the Great Province (1939), 1909 S. Ashland Ave., Chicago, Ill. 60608.

St. Martin de Porres Province (1979), 4640 Canal St., New Orleans, La. 70119.

St. Dominic Province (1873), 5353 Notre Dame de Grace Ave., Montreal, Que. H4A 1L2, Canada.

Spanish Province, U.S. foundation (1933), P.O. Box 277, San Diego, Tex. 78384.

Edmund, Society of St., S.S.E.: Founded 1843, in France, by Fr. Jean Baptiste Muard. General motherhouse, Edmundite Generalate, Fairholt, S. Prospect St., Burlington, Vt. 05401. Educational, missionary work.

Eudists (Congregation of Jesus and Mary), C.J.M.: Founded 1643, in France, by St. John Eudes. General motherhouse, Rome, Italy; North American province, 6125 Première Ave., Charlesbourg, Quebec G1H 2V9, Canada. Parochial, educational, pastoral, missionary work.

Francis, Third Order Regular of St., T.O.R.: Founded 1221, in Italy; in U.S., 1910. General motherhouse, Rome, Italy. Educational, parochial, missionary work.

Most Sacred Heart of Jesus Province (1910), 601 Pitcairn Pl., Pittsburgh, Pa. 15232.

Immaculate Conception Province (1925), 2006 Edgewater Parkway, Silver Springs, Md. 20903.

Commissariat of the Spanish Province (1924), 301 Jefferson Ave., Waco, Tex. 76702.

Francis de Sales, Oblates of St., O.S.F.S.: Founded 1871, by Fr. Louis Brisson. General motherhouse, Rome, Italy. Educational, missionary, parochial work.

Wilmington-Philadelphia Province (1906), 2200 Kentmere Parkway, Box 1452, Wilmington, Del. 19899.

Toledo-Detroit Province (1966), Box 4683, Toledo, Ohio 43620.

Franciscans (Order of Friars Minor), O.F.M.: A family of the First Order of St. Francis (of Assisi) founded in 1209 and established as a separate jurisdiction in 1517; in U.S., 1844. General motherhouse, Rome, Italy. Preaching, missionary, educational, parochial, charitable work.

St. John the Baptist Province (1844), 1615 Vine St., Cincinnati, Ohio 45210.

Sacred Heart Province (1858), 3140 Meramec St., St. Louis, Mo. 63118.

Assumption of the Blessed Virgin Mary Province (1887), Pulaski, Wis. 54162.

Most Holy Name of Jesus Province (1901), 135 W. 31st St., New York, N.Y. 10001.

St. Barbara Province (1915), 1500 34th Ave., Oakland, Calif. 94601.

Immaculate Conception Province (1855), 147 Thompson St., New York, N.Y. 10012.

Holy Cross Custody (1912), 1400 Main St., P.O. Box 608, Lemont, Ill. 60439.

Most Holy Savior Custody, 232 S. Home Ave., Pittsburgh, Pa. 15202.

St. John Capistran Custody (1928), 1290 Hornberger Ave., Roebling, N.J. 08554.

St. Stephen Transylvanian Commissariat (1948), 517 S. Belle Vista Ave., Youngstown, Ohio 44509.

Holy Family Croatian Custody, (1927), 4848 S. Ellis Ave., Chicago, Ill. 60615.

St. Casimir Lithuanian Vicariate, Kennebunkport, Me. 04046.

Holy Gospel Province (Mexico), U.S. foundation, 2400 Marr St., El Paso, Tex. 79903.

Saints Francis and James Province (Jalisco, Mexico), U.S. foundation, 504 E. Santa Clara St., Hebbronville, Tex. 78361.

Eastern District, Commissariat of the Holy Land, Mt. St. Sepulchre, 14th and Quincy Sts. N.E., Washington, D.C. 20017.

St. Mary of the Angels Custody, Byzantine Slavonic Rite, P.O. Box 270, Sybertsville, Pa. 18251.

Academy of American Franciscan History, P.O. Box 34440, Washington, D.C. 20034.

Franciscans (Order of Friars Minor Capuchin), O.F.M. Cap.: A family of the First Order of St. Francis (of Assisi) founded in 1209 and established as a separate jurisdiction in 1528. General motherhouse, Rome, Italy. Missionary, parochial work, chaplaincies.

St. Joseph Province (1857), 1740 Mt. Elliott Ave., Detroit, Mich. 48207.

St. Augustine Province (1873), 220 37th St., Pittsburgh, Pa. 15201.

St. Mary Province (1952), 30 Gedney Park Dr., White Plains, N.Y. 10605.

Province of the Stigmata (1918), St. Francis Friary, Newton, N.J. 07860.

Western American Capuchin Province, Our Lady of the Angels, 1721 Hillside Dr., Burlingame, Calif. 94010.

Sts. Adalbert and Stanislaus Province (Warsaw, Poland), Manor Dr., Oak Ridge, N.J. 07438.

Province of Mid-America (1977), St. Conrad Friary, 2 E. 75th St., Kansas City, Mo. 64114.

Texas Capuchin Fraternity (Province of Navarre, Spain), 5605 Bernal Dr., Dallas, Tex. 75212.

Franciscans (Order of Friars Minor Conventual), O.F.M. Conv.: A family of the First Order of St. Francis (of Assisi) founded in 1209 and established as a separate jurisdiction in 1517; first U.S. foundation, 1852. General curia, Rome, Italy. Missionary, educational, parochial work.

Immaculate Conception Province (1872), P.O. Box 830, Union City, N.J. 07087.

St. Anthony of Padua Province (1905), 1300 Dundalk Ave., Baltimore, Md. 21222.

St. Bonaventure Province (1939), 6107 Kenmore Ave., Chicago, Ill.

Our Lady of Consolation Province (1926), Mt. St. Francis, Ind. 47146.

Our Lady of Guadalupe Custody (vice-province), P.O. Drawer F, Hobbs, N. Mex. 88240.

St. Joseph Cupertino Custody (1978), 4532 Torrance Blvd., Torrance, Calif. 90503.

Glenmary Missioners (The Home Missioners of America): Founded 1939, in U.S. General headquarters, Fairfield, Ohio; mailing address, P.O. Box 46404, Cincinnati, Ohio 45246. Home mission work.

Holy Family, Congregation of the Missionaries of the, M.S.F.: Founded 1895, in Holland, by Rev. John P. Berthier. General motherhouse, Rome, Italy; U.S. headquarters, 10415 Midland Blvd., St. Louis, Mo. 63114. Belated vocations for the missions.

Holy Family, Sons of the, S.F.: Founded 1864, at Barcelona, Spain, by Joseph Manyanet; in U.S., 1920. General motherhouse, Barcelona, Spain; U.S. address, 401 Randolph Rd., Silver Spring, Md. 20904.

Holy Ghost, Missionaries of the, M.Sp.S.: Founded 1914, at Mexico City, Mexico, by Felix Rougier. General motherhouse, Mexico City; U.S. headquarters, 4433 Santa Fe Ave., Vernon, Calif. 90058. Missionary work.

Holy Ghost Fathers, C.S.Sp.: Founded 1703, in Paris, by Claude Francois Poullart des Places; in U.S., 1872. General motherhouse, Rome, Italy. Missions, education.

Eastern Province (1872), 6230 Brush Run Rd., Bethel Park, Pa. 15102.

Western Province (1968), 919 Briarcliff, San Antonio, Tex. 78213.

Holy Ghost Fathers of Ireland (1971), U.S. delegate (East), 48-49 37th St., Long Island City, N.Y. 11101.

Jesuits (Society of Jesus), S.J.: Founded 1534, in France, by St. Ignatius of Loyola; received papal approval, 1540; first U.S. province, 1833. Generalate, Rome, Italy. Missionary, educational, literary work.

Maryland Province (1833), 5704 Roland Ave., Baltimore, Md. 21210.

New York Province (1943), 501 E. Fordham Rd., Bronx, N.Y. 10458.

Missouri Province (1823), 4511 W. Pine Blvd., St. Louis, Mo. 63108.

New Orleans Province (1907), 6301 Stratford Pl., P.O. Box 6378, New Orleans, La. 70174.

California Province (1909), College at Prospect Aves., P.O. Box 519, Los Gatos, Calif. 95030.

New England Province (1926), 393 Commonwealth Ave., Boston, Mass. 02115.

Chicago Province, 509 N. Oak Park Ave., Oak Park, Ill. 60302.

Oregon Province (1932), 2222 N.W. Hoyt, Portland, Ore. 97210.

Detroit Province (1955), 7303 W. Seven Mile Rd., Detroit, Mich. 48221.

Wisconsin Province (1955), 2120 W. Clybourn St., Suite 200, Milwaukee, Wis. 53233.

Joseph, Congregation of St., C.S.J.: General motherhouse, Rome, Italy; U.S. vice province, 4076 Case Rd., Avon, Ohio 44011. Parochial, missionary, educational work.

Joseph, Oblates of St., O.S.J.: Founded 1878, in Italy, by Bishop Joseph Marello. General motherhouse, Rome, Italy. Parochial, educational work.

Eastern Province, R.D. No. 2, Route 315, Pittston, Pa. 18640.

Western Province, P.O. Box 82, Tomales, Calif. 94971.

Josephite Fathers, C.J.: General motherhouse, Ghent, Belgium; U.S. foundation, 989 Brookside Ave., Santa Maria, Calif. 93454.

Josephite Fathers (St. Joseph's Society of the Sacred Heart), S.S.J.: Founded 1866, in England, by Cardinal Vaughan; in U.S., 1871. General motherhouse, 1130 N. Calvert St., Baltimore, Md. 21202. Work in Negro missions.

LaSalette, Missionaries of Our Lady of, M.S.: Founded 1852, by Msgr. de Bruillard; in U.S., 1892. Motherhouse, Rome, Italy.

Our Lady of Seven Dolors Province (1933), P.O. Box 6127, Hartford, Conn. 06106.

Immaculate Heart of Mary Province (1945), P.O. Box 538, Attleboro, Mass. 02703.

Mary Queen Province (1958), 4650 S. Broadway, St. Louis, Mo. 63111.

Mary Queen of Peace Vice Province (1967), P.O. Box 95, Georgetown, Ill. 61846.

Legionaries of Christ, L.C.: Founded 1941, in Mexico, by Rev. Marcial Maciel. General motherhouse, Rome, Italy; U.S. novitiate, 393 Derby Ave., Orange, Conn. 06477.

Marian Fathers and Brothers, M.I.C.: Founded 1673; U.S. foundation, 1913. General motherhouse, Rome, Italy. Educational, parochial, mission, publication work.

St. Casimir Province (1930), 6336 S. Kilbourn Ave., Chicago, Ill. 60629.

St. Stanislaus Kostka Province (1948), Eden Hill, Stockbridge, Mass. 01262.

Marianists (Society of Mary; Brothers of Mary), S.M.: Founded 1817, at Bordeaux, France, by Rev William-Joseph Chaminade; in U.S., 1849. General motherhouse, Rome, Italy. Educational work.

Cincinnati Province (1849), 4435 E. Patterson Rd., Dayton, Ohio 45430.

St. Louis Province (1908), 4538 Maryland Ave., St. Louis, Mo. 63156.

Pacific Province (1948), P.O. Box AC, Cupertino, Calif. 95015.

New York Province (1961), 4301 Roland Ave., Baltimore, Md. 21210.

Mariannhill, Congregation of the Missionaries of, C.M.M.: Trappist monastery, begun in 1882 by Abbot Francis Pfanner in Natal, South Africa, became an independent modern congregation in 1909; in U.S., 1920. Generalate, Rome, Italy; U.S.-Canadian headquarters, 23715 Ann Arbor Trail, Dearborn Heights, Mich. 48127. Foreign mission work.

Marist Fathers (Society of Mary), S.M.: Founded 1816, at Lyons, France, by Jean Claude Colin; in U.S., 1863. General motherhouse, Rome, Italy. Educational, foreign mission, pastoral work.

Washington Province (1924), 4408 8th St. N.E., Washington D.C. 20017.

Northeastern Province (1924), 72 Beacon St., Chestnut Hill, Mass. 02167.

San Francisco Western Province (1961), 625 Pine St., San Francisco, Calif. 94108.

Mary Immaculate, Missionary Oblates of, O.M.I.: Founded 1816, in France, by Bl. Charles Joseph Eugene de Mazenod; in U.S., 1849. General motherhouse, Rome, Italy. Parochial, foreign mission, educational work; ministry to marginal.

Southern U.S. Province (1904), 7711 Madonna Rd., San Antonio, Tex. 78216.

Our Lady of Hope, Eastern Province (1883), 350 Jamaicaway, Boston, Mass. 02130.

St. John the Baptist Province (1921), 45 Kenwood Ave., Worcester, Mass. 01605.

Central Province (1924), 104 N. Mississippi River Blvd., St. Paul, Minn. 55104.

Western Province (1953), 290 Lenox Ave., Oakland, Calif. 94610.

Italian Province, U.S. foundation, St. Nicholas Church, 442 Brinkerhoff Ave., Palisades Park, N.J. 07650.

Maryknoll Fathers (Catholic Foreign Mission Society of America), M.M.: Founded 1911, in U.S., by Frs. Thomas F. Price and James A. Walsh. General Center, Maryknoll, N.Y. 10545.

Mekhitarist Order of Vienna, C.M.Vd.: Established 1773. General headquarters, Vienna, Austria. U.S. addresses: Holy Cross Church, 100 Mt. Auburn St., Cambridge, Mass. 02138; Our Lady Queen of Martyrs Church, 1327 Pleasant Ave., Los Angeles, Calif. 90033. Work among Armenians in U.S..

Mercedarians (Order of Our Lady of Mercy), O. de M.: Founded 1218, in Spain, by St. Peter Nolasco. General motherhouse, Rome, Italy; U.S. headquarters, 8692 Lake St., LeRoy, N.Y. 14482.

Mercy, Congregation of Priests of (Fathers of Mercy), C.P.M.: Founded 1808, in France, by Rev. Jean Baptiste Rauzan; in U.S., 1839. General motherhouse, Cold Spring, N.Y. 10516. Mission work.

Mill Hill Missionaries (St. Joseph's Society for Foreign Missions), M.H.M.: Founded 1866, in England, by Cardinal Vaughan; in U.S., 1951. General motherhouse, London, England; American headquarters, Albany, N.Y. 12203.

Missionhurst — CICM (Congregation of the Immaculate Heart of Mary): Founded 1862, at Scheut, Brussels, Belgium, by Very Rev. Theophile Verbist. General motherhouse, Rome, Italy; U.S. province, 4651 N. 25th St., Arlington, Va. 22207. Home and foreign mission work.

Missionaries of St. Charles, Congregation of the, C.S.: Founded 1887, at Piacenza, Italy, by Bishop John Baptist Scalabrini. General motherhouse, Rome, Italy.

St. Charles Borromeo Province (1888), 27 Carmine St., New York, N.Y. 10014.

St. John Baptist Province (1903), 546 N. East Ave., Oak Park, Ill. 60302.

Missionaries of the Holy Apostles, M.Ss.A.: Founded 1962, Washington, D.C., by Eusebe M. Menard. North American headquarters, Box 695, Moorefield, W. Va. 26836.

Montfort Missionaries (Missionaries of the Company of Mary), S.M.M.: Founded 1715, by St. Louis Marie Grignon de Montfort; in U.S., 1948. General motherhouse, Rome, Italy; U.S. headquarters, 101-18 104th St., Ozone Park, N.Y. 11416. Mission work.

Oratorian Fathers (Congregation of the Oratory of St. Philip Neri), C.O.: Founded 1575, at Rome, by St. Philip Neri. A confederation of autonomous houses. U.S. addresses: P.O. Box 11586, Rock Hill, S.C. 29730; P.O. Box 1688, Monterey, Calif. 93940; 4040 Bigelow Blvd., Pittsburgh, Pa. 15213; P.O. Box 211, Yarnell, Ariz. 85362; P.O. Drawer II, Pharr, Tex. 78577.

Pallottines (Society of the Catholic Apostolate), S.A.C.: Founded 1835, at Rome, by St. Vincent Pallotti. General motherhouse, Rome, Italy. Charitable, educational, parochial, mission work.

Immaculate Conception Province (1953), P.O. Box 573, Pennsauken, N.J. 08810.

Mother of God Province (1946), 5424 W. Blue Mound Rd., Milwaukee, Wis. 53208.

Irish Province, U.S. address: 3352 4th St., Wyandotte, Mich. 48192.

Queen of Apostles Province (1909), 448 E. 116th St., New York, N.Y. 10029.

Christ the King Province, 3452 Niagara Falls, Blvd., N. Tonawanda, N.Y. 14120.

Paraclete, Servants of the, s.P.: Founded 1947, Santa Fe, N.M., archdiocese. General motherhouse, Rome, Italy; U.S. motherhouse, Via Coeli, Jemez Springs, N.M. 87025. Devoted to care of priests.

Paris Foreign Missions Society, M.E.P.: Founded 1662, at Paris, France. Headquarters, Paris, France; U.S. establishment, 930 Ashbury St., San Francisco, Calif. 94117. Mission work and training of native clergy.

Passionists (Congregation of the Passion), C.P.: Founded 1720, in Italy, by St. Paul of the Cross. General motherhouse, Rome, Italy.

St. Paul of the Cross Province (1852), 80 David St., South River, N.J. 08882.

Holy Cross Province (Western Province), 5700 N. Harlem Ave., Chicago, Ill. 60631.

Patrick's Missionary Society, St., S.P.S.: Founded 1932, at Wicklow, Ireland, by Msgr. Patrick Whitney; in U.S., 1953. International headquarters, Kiltegan Co., Wicklow, Ireland. U.S. foundations: 70 Edgewater Rd., Cliffside Park, N.J. 07010; 19536 Eric Dr., Saratoga, Calif. 95070; 1347 W. Granville Ave., Chicago, Ill. 60660.

Pauline Fathers (Order of St. Paul the First Hermit), O.S.P.: Founded 1215; established in U.S., 1955. General motherhouse, Czestochowa, Jasna Gora, Poland; U.S. headquarters, P.O. Box 151, Doylestown, Pa. 18901.

Pauline Fathers (Society of St. Paul for the Apostolate of Communications), S.S.P.: Founded 1914, by Very Rev. James Alberione; in U.S., 1932. Motherhouse, Rome, Italy; American province, 6746 Lake Shore Rd., Derby, N.Y. 14047.

Paulists (Missionary Society of St. Paul the Apostle), C.S.P.: Founded 1858, in New York, by Fr. Isaac Thomas Hecker. General offices, 86 Dromore Rd., Scarsdale, N.Y. 10583. Missionary, ecumenical, pastoral work.

Piarists (Order of the Pious Schools), Sch.P.: Founded 1617, at Rome, Italy, by St. Joseph Calasanctius. General motherhouse, Rome, Italy. American province, 1339 Monroe St. N.E., Washington, D.C. 20017; American-Spanish branch (Calasanzian Fathers), 88 Convent Ave., New York, N.Y. 10027. Educational work.

Pontifical Institute for Foreign Missions, P.I.M.E.: Founded 1850, in Italy, at request of Pope Pius IX. General motherhouse, Rome, Italy; U.S. headquarters,17330 Quincy Ave., Detroit, Mich. 48221. Foreign mission work.

Precious Blood, Society of, C.Pp.S.: Founded 1815, in Italy, by St. Gaspar del Bufalo. General motherhouse, Rome, Italy.

Cincinnati Province, 431 E. Second St., Dayton, O. 45402.

Kansas City Province, Ruth Ewing Rd., Liberty, Mo. 64068.

Pacific Province, 5788 Thornton Ave., Newark, Calif. 94506.

Atlantic Vicariate, 381 Robbins Ave., Niles, O. 44446.

Premonstratensians (Order of the Canons

Regular of Premontre; Norbertines), O. Praem.: Founded 1120, at Premontre, France, by St. Norbert. Generalate, Rome, Italy. Educational, parish work.

St. Norbert Abbey, 1016 N. Broadway, De-Pere, Wis. 54115.

Daylesford Abbey, 220 S. Valley Rd., Paoli, Pa. 19301.

St. Michael's Priory, 1042 Star Route, Orange, Calif. 92667.

Providence, Sons of Divine, F.D.P.: Founded 1893, at Tortona, Italy, by Don Aloysius Orione; in U.S., 1933. General motherhouse, Tortona, Italy; U.S. address, 111 Orient Ave., E. Boston, Mass. 02128.

Redemptorists (Congregation of the Most Holy Redeemer), C.SS.R.: Founded 1732, in Italy, by St. Alphonsus Mary Liguori. General motherhouse, Rome, Italy. Mission work.

Baltimore Province (1850), 7509 Shore Rd., Brooklyn, N.Y. 11209.

St. Louis Province (1875), Box 6, Glenview, Ill. 60025.

Oakland Province (1952), 3696 Clay St., San Francisco, Calif. 94118.

New Orleans Vice-Province, 1527 3rd St., New Orleans, La., 70130.

Richmond Vice-Province (1942), P.O. Box 1558, New Smyrna Beach, Fla. 32069.

Resurrectionists (Priests of the Congregation of the Resurrection), C.R.: Founded 1836, in France, under direction of Bogdan Janski. Motherhouse, Rome, Italy;

Chicago Province, 2250 N. Latrobe Ave., Chicago, Ill. 60639.

Ontario Kentucky Province, Resurrection College, Westmont Rd., N., Waterlo, Ont. N2L 3G7, Canada.

Rogationist Fathers, R.C.J.: Founded 1926. General motherhouse, Rome, Italy. U.S. addresses: P.O. Box 248, Mendota, Calif. 93640; P.O. Box 335, Sanger, Calif. 93657.

Rosminians (Institute of Charity), I.C.: Founded 1828, in Italy, by Antonio Rosmini-Serbati. General motherhouse, Rome, Italy; U.S. address, 2327 W. Heading Ave., Peoria, Ill. 61604. Charitable work.

Sacerdotal Fraternity, Congregation of the, C.F.S.: Founded 1901, at Paris, France. General house, 500 Ave. Claremont, Montreal (Westmount), Que. H3Y 2N5 Canada. Care of priests.

Sacred Heart, Missionaries of the, M.S.C.: Founded 1854, by Rev. Jules Chevelier. General motherhouse, Rome, Italy; U.S. province, 305 S. Lake St., P.O. Box 270, Aurora, Ill. 60507.

Sacred Heart of Jesus, Congregation of the (Sacred Heart Priests and Brothers), S.C.J.: Founded 1877, in France. General motherhouse, Rome, Italy; U.S. headquarters, Sacred Heart Monastery, Hales Corners, Wis. 53130. Educational, preaching, mission work.

Sacred Hearts, Fathers of the (Picpus Fathers), SS.CC.: Founded 1805, in France, by Fr. Coudrin. General motherhouse, Rome, Italy. Mission, educational work.

Eastern Province (1946), 3 Adams St. (Box 111), Fairhaven, Mass. 02719.

Western Province (1970), 32481 Sage Rd., Hemet, Calif. 92343.

Hawaiian Province, Box 797, Kaneohe, Oahu, Hawaii 96744.

Sacred Hearts of Jesus and Mary, Missionaries of the, M.SS.CC.: Founded at Naples, Italy, by Ven. Cajetan Errico. General motherhouse, Rome, Italy; U.S. headquarters, 2249 Shore Rd., Linwood, N.J. 08221.

Salesians of St. John Bosco (Society of St. Francis de Sales), S.D.B.: Founded 1859, by St. John (Don) Bosco. General motherhouse, Rome, Italy.

St. Philip the Apostle Province (1902), 148 Main St., New Rochelle, N.Y. 10802.

San Francisco Province (1926), 1100 Franklin St., San Francisco, Calif. 94109.

Salvatorians (Society of the Divine Savior), S.D.S.: Founded 1881, in Rome, by Fr. Francis Jordan; in U.S., 1896. General motherhouse, Rome, Italy; U.S. province, 1735 Hi-Mount Blvd., Milwaukee, Wis. 53208. Educational, parochial, mission work; campus ministries, chaplaincies.

Scalabrinians: See Missionary Fathers of St. Charles, Congregation of the.

Servites (Order of Friar Servants of Mary), O.S.M.: Founded 1233, at Florence, Italy, by Seven Holy Founders. Generalate, Rome, Italy. General apostolic ministry.

Eastern Province (1967) 3401 S. Home Ave., Berwyn, Ill. 60402.

Western Province (1967), 5210 Somerset St., Buena Park, Calif. 90621.

Somascan Fathers, C.R.S.: Founded 1534, at Somasca, Italy, by St. Jerome Emiliani. General motherhouse, Rome, Italy; U.S. addresses: 628 Hanover St., Manchester, N.H. 03104; Pine Haven Boys Center, River Rd., Allenstown, P.O. Suncook, N.H. 03275; Allenbrook Home for Boys, Allen Rd., S. Burlington, Vt. 05401.

Sons of Mary Missionary Society (Sons of Mary, Health of the Sick), F.M.S.I.: Founded 1952, in the Boston archdiocese, by Rev. Edward F. Garesche, S.J. Headquarters, 567 Salem End Rd., Framingham, Mass. 01701. Dedicated to health of the sick; medical, catechetical and social work in home and foreign missions.

Stigmatine Fathers and Brothers (Congregation of the Sacred Stigmata), C.S.S.: Founded 1816, by Bl. Gaspare Bertoni. General motherhouse, Rome, Italy; U.S. headquarters, 36 Fairmont Ave., Newton, Mass. 02158. Parish work.

Sulpicians (Society of Priests of St. Sulpice), S.S.: Founded 1641, at Paris, by Rev. Jean Jacques Olier. General motherhouse, Paris, France; U.S. province, 5408 Roland Ave.,

Baltimore, Md. 21210. Education of seminarians and priests.

Theatines (Congregation of Clerics Regular): C.R.: Founded 1524, at Rome, by St. Cajetan. General motherhouse, Rome, Italy; U.S. headquarters, 1050 S. Birch St., Denver, Colo. 80222.

Trappists: See Cistercians of the Strict Observance.

Trinitarians (Order of the Most Holy Trinity), O.SS.T.: Founded 1198, by St. John of Matha. General motherhouse, Rome, Italy; U.S. headquarters, Park Heights Ave., Box 5719, Baltimore, Md. 21208.

Trinity, Missionary Servants of the Most Holy, S.T.: Founded 1929, by Fr. Thomas Augustine Judge. Generalate, 503 Rock Creek Church Rd. N.W., Washington, D.C. 20010. Home mission work.

Viatorian Fathers (Clerics of St. Viator), C.S.V.: Founded 1831, in France, by Fr. Louis Joseph Querbes. General motherhouse, Rome, Italy: U.S. headquarters, 1212 E. Euclid St., Arlington Hts., Ill. 60004. Educational work.

Vincentians (Congregation of the Mission; Lazarists), C.M.: Founded 1625, in Paris, by St. Vincent de Paul; in U.S., 1817. General motherhouse, Rome, Italy. Educational work.

Eastern Province (1867), 500 E. Chelten Ave., Philadelphia, Pa. 19144.

Midwest Province (1888), 1723 Pennsylvania Ave., St. Louis, Mo. 63104.

New England Province (1975), 1109 Prospect Ave., W. Hartford, Conn. 06105.

American Italian Branch, Our Lady of Pompei Church, 3600 Claremont St., Baltimore, Md. 21224.

American Spanish Branch (Barcelona, Spain), St. Peter's Rectory, 234 Congress St., Brooklyn, N.Y. 11201.

American Spanish Branch (Zaragoza, Spain), Holy Agony Church, 1834 3rd Ave., New York, N.Y. 10029.

Western Province (1975), 649 W. Adams Blvd., Los Angeles, Calif. 90007.

Southern Province (1975), 1302 Kipling St., Houston, Tex. 77006.

Vocationist Fathers (Society of Divine Vocations), S.D.V.: Founded 1920, in Italy; in U.S., 1962. General motherhouse, Naples, Italy; U.S. address, 170 Broad St., Newark, N.J. 07104.

White Fathers of Africa (Society of Missionaries of Africa), W.F.: Founded 1868, at Algiers, by Cardinal C.M.A. Lavigerie. Generalate, Rome, Italy; U.S. headquarters, 777 Belvidere Ave., Plainfield, N.J. 07062. Missionary work in Africa.

Xaverian Missionary Fathers, S.X.: Founded 1895, by Archbishop Conforti, at Parma, Italy. General motherhouse, Rome, Italy; U.S. province, 12 Helene Ct., Wayne, N.J. 07470. Foreign mission work.

INSTITUTES OF BROTHERS

Alexian Brothers, C.F.A.: Founded 14th century in western Germany and Belgium during the Black Plague. Motherhouse, Aachen, Germany; generalate, Signal Mountain, Tenn. 37377. Hospital and general health work.

Carmelite Brothers of the Holy Eucharist, C.F.S.E.: Founded 1975 by Bro. Aloysius Scafidi. Motherhouse, 2264 Marshall Ave., Elm Grove, Wheeling, W. Va. 26003. Educational, clerical, social, nursing work.

Charity, Brothers of, F.C.: Founded 1807, in Belgium, by Canon Peter J. Triest. General motherhouse, Rome, Italy: American District, 1008 N. 70th Ave., Philadelphia, Pa. 19126. Charitable, educational work.

Charity, Missionary Brothers of, M.C.: Founded 1963. U.S. address, 235 Winston St., Los Angeles, Calif. 90013. Work among poor and outcast.

Christian Brothers, Congregation of, C.F.C. (formerly Christian Brothers of Ireland): Founded 1802 at Waterford, Ireland, by Edmund Ignatius Rice. General motherhouse, Rome, Italy. Educational work.

American Province, Eastern U.S. (1916), 21 Pryer Terr., New Rochelle, N.Y. 10804. 354.

American Province, Western U.S. (1966), P.O. Box 85R, Romeoville, Ill. 60441.

Christian Instruction, Brothers of (La Mennais Brothers), F.I.C.: Founded 1817, at Ploermel, France, by Abbe Jean Marie de la Mennais and Abbe Gabriel Deshayes. General motherhouse, Rome, Italy; American province, Notre Dame Institute, Alfred, Me. 04002.

Christian Schools, Brothers of the (Christian Brothers), F.S.C.: Founded 1680, at Reims, France, by St. Jean Baptiste de la Salle. General motherhouse, Rome, Italy; U.S. Conference, 100 De La Salle Dr., P.O. Box 356, Romeoville, Ill. 60441. Educational, charitable work.

Baltimore Province (1845), Box 85, Adamstown, Md. 21710.

Chicago Province (1966), 200 De La Salle Dr., Romeoville, Ill. 60441.

New York Province (1848), 330 Riverside Dr., New York, N.Y. 10025.

Long Island-New England Province (1957), Christian Brothers Center, 635 Ocean Ave., Narragansett, R.I. 02882.

St. Louis Province (1849), 1886 Rue de la Salle, Glencoe, Mo. 63038.

San Francisco Province (1868), P.O. Box A-D, Saint Mary's College, Moraga, Calif. 94575.

New Orleans-Santa Fe Province (1921), De La Salle Christian Brothers, 1522 Breaux Bridge Rd., Lafayette, La. 70501.

Winona Province (1963), 807 Summit Ave., St. Paul, Minn. 55105.

Cross, Congregation of Holy, C.S.C.:

Founded 1837, in France, by Rev. Basil Moreau; U.S. province, 1841. Generalate, Rome, Italy. Educational, social work; missions.

Midwest Province (1841), Box 460, Notre Dame, Ind. 46556.

Southwest Province (1956), St. Edward's University, Austin, Tex. 78704.

Eastern Province (1956), 85 Overlook Circle, New Rochelle, N.Y. 10804.

Francis, Brothers of Poor of St., C.F.P.: Founded 1857. Motherhouse, Aachen, Germany; U.S. province, Mt. Alverno, Fayetteville, Ohio. 45118. Educational work, especially with poor and emotionally disturbed youth.

Francis Xavier, Brothers of St. (Xaverian Brothers), C.F.X.: Founded 1839, in Belgium, by Theodore J. Ryken. Generalate, Rome, Italy. Educational work.

Sacred Heart Province, 10516 Summit Ave., Kensington, Md. 20795.

St. Joseph Province, 704 Brush Hill Rd., Milton, Mass. 02186.

Franciscan Brothers of Brooklyn, O.S.F.: Founded in Ireland; established at Brooklyn, 1858. Generalate, 135 Remsen St., Brooklyn, N.Y. 11201. Educational work.

Franciscan Brothers of Christ the King, O.S.F.: Founded 1961. General motherhouse, 1310 W. Pleasant St., Davenport, Ia. 52804.

Franciscan Brothers of the Good News, O.S.F.: Founded 1970 in Archdiocese of New York. Central friary, Mount Road, Cummington, Mass. 01026. Combine volunteer works of mercy with contemplative life of prayer in hermitages.

Franciscan Brothers of the Holy Cross, F.F.S.C.: Founded 1862, in Germany. Generalate, Hausen, Linz Rhein, West Germany; U.S. region, R.R. 1, Springfield, Ill. 62707. Educational work.

Franciscan Missionary Brothers of the Sacred Heart of Jesus, O.S.F.: Founded 1927, in the St. Louis, Mo., archdiocese. Motherhouse, R.R. 3, Box 39, Eureka, Mo. 63025. Care of aged, infirm, homeless men and boys.

Good Shepherd, Society of Brothers of the, B.G.S.: Founded 1951, by Bro. Mathias Barrett. Motherhouse, P.O. Box 389, Albuquerque, N.M. 87102. Operate shelters and refuges for aged and homeless; homes for handicapped men and boys, alcoholic rehabilitation center.

Guadalupe, Brothers of Our Lady of, H.N.S.G.: Founded 1974 in Gallup, N. Mex., by Bishop Jerome Hastrich. Motherhouse, 500 S. Woodrow Dr., Gallup, N. Mex. 87301. Team ministry apostolate.

Holy Eucharist, Brothers of the, F.S.E.: Founded in U.S., 1957. Generalate, P.O. Box 25, Plaucheville, La. 71362. Teaching, social, clerical, nursing work.

Immaculate Heart of Mary, Brothers of the,

F.I.C.M.: Founded 1948, at Steubenville, Ohio, by Bishop John K. Mussio. Motherhouse, Villa Maria, 609 N. 7th St., Steubenville, Ohio 43952. Educational, charitable work.

John of God, Brothers of the Hospitaller Order of St., O.H.: Founded 1537, in Spain. General motherhouse, Rome, Italy; American province, 2425 S. Western Ave., Los Angeles, Calif. 90018. Nursing work and related fields.

Little Brothers of Jesus: Generalate, London, England; U.S. foundation, 2833 Cochrane, Detroit, Mich. 48216.

Little Brothers of St. Francis, O.S.F.: Founded 1970 in Archdiocese of Boston. General fraternity, 789 Parker St., Mission Hill (Boston), Mass. 02120. Combine contemplative life with evangelical street ministry

Marist Brothers, F.M.S.: Founded 1817, in France, by Bl. Marcellin Champagnat. General motherhouse, Rome, Italy; U.S. address, 1241 Kennedy Blvd., Bayonne, N.J. 07002. Educational, social, catechetical work.

Mercy, Brothers of, F.M.M.: Founded 1856, in Germany. General motherhouse, Montabaur, Germany. American headquarters, 4520 Ransom Rd., Clarence, N.Y. 14031. Hospital work.

Mercy, Brothers of Our Lady of, C.F.M.M.: Founded 1844, in The Netherlands by Abp. J. Zwijsen. Generalate, Tilburg, The Netherlands; U.S. region, 2336 South "C" St., Oxnard, Calif. 93030.

Patrician Brothers (Brothers of St. Patrick), F.S.P.: Founded 1808, in Ireland, by Bishop Daniel Delaney; U.S. novitiate, 7820 Bolsa Ave., Midway City, Calif. 92655. Educational work.

Pius X, Brothers of St.: Founded 1952, at La Crosse, Wis., by Bishop John P. Treacy. Motherhouse, 208 S. 15th St., La Crosse, Wis. 54601. Education.

Presentation Brothers, F.P.M.: Founded 1802, at Waterford, Ireland, by Edmund Ignatius Rice. General motherhouse, Cork, Ireland. U.S. foundation (Canadian Province), 368 S. Ellsworth, Marshall, Mo. 65340.

Rosary, Brothers of the Holy, F.S.R.: Founded 1956, in US. Motherhouse and novitiate, 101 Boynton Lane, Reno, Nev. 89502.

Sacred Heart, Brothers of the, S.C.: Founded 1821, in France, by Rev. Andre Coindre. General motherhouse, Rome, Italy, Educational work.

New Orleans Province (1847), P.O. Box 89, Bay St. Louis, Miss. 39520.

New England Province (1945), Rt. 98, R.R. 1, Pascoag, R.I. 02859.

New York Province (1960), R.D. 1, Box 215, Belvidere, N.J. 07823.

The ninth annual meeting of the Assembly of Religious Brothers, held June 19 to 22 in Detroit, was attended by 70 participants.

ORGANIZATIONS OF MEN RELIGIOUS

Conference of Major Superiors of Men: An association of major superiors of religious institutes of men, founded in 1956 and established officially Mar. 23, 1960, by decree of the Congregation for Religious and Secular Institutes.

Its purposes are to assist religious to fulfill their proper prophetic role in the Church and the world; to provide liaison opportunities among religious and with church officials; to exert Christian influence through its operations, and to serve as a national voice for the corporate views of superiors.

Conference membership consists of 263 major superiors of institutes with a combined total of approximately 30,000 members.

The principal officers are Rev. Alan McCoy, O.F.M., president, and Rev. Donald P. Skwor, S.D.S., executive director.

The national office is located at 1302 18th St. N.W., Suite 601, Washington, D.C. 20036.

National Assembly of Religious Brothers: Founded in 1972 as a grassroots organization open to members of all-brother institutes as well as mixed institutes of priests and brothers. It is a service organization for its members and those affected by their apostolates.

The primary objectives of the NARB are: to publicize the unique vocations of brothers, to encourage the development of the spiritual life of all brothers; to promote increased awareness among brothers of their ministerial power for good; to provide a corporate voice for brothers in shaping the future of religious life; to heighten their concern with and involvement in the needs of the Church and society; and to further communication among brothers and provide liaison with various organizations of the Church.

Membership in the assembly is open to brothers in the U.S. and Canada.

Christian Brother William Mueller is president of the assembly.

The address is 9001 New Hampshire Ave., Silver Spring, Md. 20910.

MEMBERSHIP OF RELIGIOUS INSTITUTES OF MEN

Below are world membership statistics from *Annuario Pontificio* of institutes of men of pontifical right with 500 or more members; the number of priests is in parentheses. Also listed are institutes with less than 500 members with houses in the United States.

Most of the institutes reported decreases in membership between 1978 and 1979.

Jesuits (19,905)	27,249
Franciscans (Friars Minor) (14,579)	21,066
Salesians (11,020)	16,932
Franciscans (Capuchins) (8,778)	12,206
Brothers of Christian Schools	10,446
Benedictines (6,325)	9,856
Dominicans (5,616)	7,252
Marist Brothers	7,056
Redemptorists (4,972)	6,722
Oblates of Mary Immaculate (4,727)	6,072
Society of the Divine Word (3,226)	5,259
Vincentians (3,684)	4,158
Franciscans (Conventuals) (2,730)	4,013
Holy Spirit, Congregation (3,143)	3,910
Augustinians (2,755)	3,583
Discalced Carmelties (2,391)	3,266
Passionists (2,390)	3,129
White Fathers (2,699)	3,098
Trappists (1,505)	3,092
Christian Brothers	2,944
Claretians (1,944)	2,899
Priests of the Sacred Heart (1,928)	2,695
Missionaries of the Sacred Heart of Jesus (1,890)	2,568
Marianists (618)	2,182
Pallottines (1,451)	2,157
Holy Cross, Congregation (961)	2,116
Carmelites (Ancient Observance) (1,602)	2,101
Brothers of the Sacred Heart (41)	2,045

Marists (1,577)	1,936
Combonian Missionaries of the Heart of Jesus (1,260)	1,868
Piarists (1,370)	1,762
Hospitallers of St. John of God (111)	1,755
Brothers of Christian Instruction	1,591
Congregation of the Immaculate Heart of Mary (1,338)	1,574
Picpus Fathers (1,301)	1,573
Brothers of Christian Instruction of St. Gabriel (22)	1,434
Montfort Fathers (1,072)	1,418
Cistercians (Common Observance) (880)	1,393
Society of African Missions (1,253)	1,386
Assumptionists (1,097)	1,304
Servants of Mary (965)	1,287
Premonstratensians (1,025)	1,284
Augustinians (Recollects) (1,018)	1,281
Salvatorians (840)	1,221
Carmelites of BVM (803)	1,213
Pious Society of St. Paul (543)	1,210
Viatorians (461)	1,203
Blessed Sacrament Fathers (833)	1,191
Missionaries of Holy Family (768)	1,055
Consolata Missionaries (854)	1,050
Little Workers of Divine Providence (755)	1,050
Mill Hill Missionaries (896)	1,018
Ministers of Sick (Camillians) (680)	1,017
Brothers of Charity	976
Maryknollers (780)	959
Oblates of St. Francis de Sales (730)	950
Columbans (884)	948
LaSalette Missionaries (659)	890
Franciscans (Third Order Regular) (600)	868
Canons Regular of St. Augustine (728)	853

RELIGIOUS INSTITUTES OF WOMEN IN THE UNITED STATES

(Sources: Catholic Almanac survey; *Official Catholic Directory.*)

Africa, Missionary Sisters of Our Lady of (White Sisters), S.A.: Founded 1869, at Algiers, Algeria, by Cardinal Lavigerie; in US, 1929. General motherhouse, Frascati, Italy; US headquarters, 5335 16th St., N.W., Washington, D.C. 20011. Medical, educational, catechetical and social work in Africa.

Agnes, Sisters of St., C.S.A.: Founded 1858, in US, by Caspar Rehrl. General motherhouse, 475 Gillett St., Fond du Lac, Wis. 54935. Education, health care, social services.

Ann, Sisters of, S.S.A.: Founded 1834, in Italy; in US, 1952. General motherhouse, Rome, Italy; US headquarters, Mount St. Ann, Ebensburg, Pa. 15931.

Anne, Sisters of St., S.S.A.: Founded 1850, at Vaudreuil, Que., Canada; in US, 1866. General motherhouse, Lachine, Que., Canada; US address, 720 Boston Post Rd., Marlboro, Mass. 01752. Retreat work, pastoral ministry, religious education.

Anthony, Missionary Servants of St., M.S.S.A.: Founded 1929, in US, by Rev. Peter Baque. General motherhouse, 100 Peter Baque Rd., San Antonio, Tex. 78209. Social work.

Apostolate, Sisters Auxiliaries of the, A.A.: Founded 1903, in Canada; in US, 1911. General motherhouse, 689 Maple Terr., Monongah, W. Va. 26554. Education, nursing.

Assumption, Little Sisters of the, L.S.A.: Founded 1865, in France; in US, 1891. General motherhouse, Paris, France; US provincial, 1195 Lexington Ave., New York, N.Y. 10028. Social work, nursing, family life education.

Assumption, Religious of the, R.A.: Founded 1839, in France; in US, 1919. General motherhouse, Paris, France; US province, 227 N. Bowman Ave., Merion, Pa. 19066. Educational work.

Assumption of the Blessed Virgin, Sisters of the, S.A.S.V.: Founded 1853, in Canada; in US, 1891. General motherhouse, Nicolet, Que., Canada; American province, North Main St., Petersham, Mass. 01366. Education, mission, pastoral ministry.

Basil the Great, Sisters of St. (Pittsburgh Byzantine Rite), O.S.B.M.: Founded fourth century, by St. Basil the Great. Motherhouse, Mount St. Macrina. West National Pike, Uniontown, Pa. 15401. Education, health care.

Basil the Great, Sisters of the Order of St. (Ukrainian Byzantine Rite), O.S.B.M.: Founded fourth century, in Cappadocia, by St. Basil the Great; in US, 1911. Generalate, Rome, Italy; US motherhouse, 710 Fox Chase Rd., Philadelphia, Pa. 19111. Education.

Benedictine Nuns of the Primitive Observance, O.S.B.; Founded c. 529, in Italy; in US, 1948. US motherhouse, Regina Laudis

Monastery, Bethlehem, Conn. 06751. Cloistered.

Benedictine Sisters, O.S.B.: Founded c. 529, in Italy; in US, 1852. General motherhouse, Eichstatt, Bavaria, Germany. US addresses: St. Vincent's Archabbey, Latrobe, Pa. 15650; St. Emma's Retreat House and Convent, 1001 Harvey St., Greensburg, Pa. 15601; St. Walburga Convent, 6717 S. Boulder Rd., Boulder, Colo. 80302.

Benedictine Sisters (Bedford, N.H.), O.S.B.: Founded 1627, in Lithuania as cloistered community; reformed 1918 as active community; established in US 1857, by Mother M. Raphaela. Regina Pacis, 333 Wallace Rd., Bedford, N.H. 03102.

Benedictine Sisters, Missionary, O.S.B.: Founded 1885. Generalate, Rome, Italy; US motherhouse, 300 N. 18th St., Norfolk, Nebr. 68701.

Benedictine Sisters, Olivetan, O.S.B.: Founded 1887, in US. General motherhouse, Holy Angels Convent, Jonesboro, Ark. 72401. Educational, hospital work.

Benedictine Sisters of Perpetual Adoration of Pontifical Jurisdiction, Congregation of the, O.S.B.: Founded in US, 1874, from Maria Rickenbach, Switzerland. General motherhouse, 8300 Morganford Rd., St. Louis, Mo. 63123.

Benedictine Sisters of Pontifical Jurisdiction, O.S.B.: Founded c. 529, in Italy. No general motherhouse in US. Three federations.

• Federation of St. Scholastica (1922). Pres., Sister Johnette Putnam, O.S.B., St. Scholastica Academy, Box 1118, Covington, La. 70433. Motherhouses belonging to the federation:

Mt. St. Scholastica, Atchison, Kans. 66002; Benedictine Sisters of Elk Co., St. Joseph's Convent, St. Mary's, Pa. 15857; Mt. St. Benedict Motherhouse, 6101 E. Lake Rd., Erie, Pa. 16511; Benedictine Sisters of Chicago, St. Scholastica Priory, 7430 Ridge Blvd., Chicago, Ill. 60645; Benedictine Convent of the Sacred Heart, 1910 Maple Ave., Lisle, Ill. 60532; Our Lady of Sorrows Convent, 5900 W. 147th St., Oak Forest, Ill. 60452; St. Walburga Convent, 851 N. Broad St., Elizabeth, N.J. 07208; Benedictine Sisters, Mt. St. Mary Priory, 4530 Perrysville Ave., Pittsburgh, Pa. 15229;

Red Plains Priory, P.O. Box 60165, Oklahoma City, Okla. 73146; St. Joseph's Convent, 2200 S. Lewis, Tulsa, Okla. 74114; St. Gertrude's Motherhouse, Ridgely P.O., Md. 21660; St. Walburga Convent, Villa Madonna, 2500 Amsterdam Rd., Covington, Ky. 41016; Sacred Heart Convent, Cullman, Ala. 35055; St. Scholastica Priory, Stafford Rd., Covington, La. 70433; Holy Family Convent, Benet Lake, Wis. 53102; St. Benedict's Convent, Bristow, Va. 22013; St. Scholastica Convent, P.O. Box 700, Boerne,

Tex. 78006; St. Lucy's Priory, Glendora, Calif. 91740; Holy Name Priory, St. Leo, Fla. 33574.

• Federation of St. Gertrude the Great (1937). Pres., Sister Julia Hunhoff, O.S.B., Sacred Heart Convent, Yankton, S.D. 57078. Motherhouses belonging to the federation:

Mother of God Priory, Watertown, S. Dak. 57201; Sacred Heart Convent, Yankton, S. Dak. 57078; Mt. St. Benedict Convent, Crookston, Minn. 56716; Sacred Heart Priory, Richardton, N. Dak. 58652; St. Martin's Priory of the Black Hills, R.R. 4, Box 253, Rapid City, S. Dak. 57701; Convent of the Immaculate Conception, Ferdinand, Ind. 47532; Priory of St. Gertrude, Cottonwood, Ida. 83522;

St. Benedict Priory, Fox Bluff Box 5070, Madison, Wis. 53705; Queen of Angels Priory, Mt. Angel, Ore. 97362; St. Scholastica's Convent, Albert Pike and Rogers Ave., Fort Smith, Ark. 72913; Our Lady of Peace Convent, 1511 Wilson, Columbia, Mo. 65201; Queen of Peace Priory, 701 Rolla, Belcourt, N. Dak. 58316. Convent of Our Lady of Grace, Beech Grove, Ind. 46107; Holy Spirit Convent, 9725 Pigeon Pass Rd., Sunnymead, Calif. 92388; St. Benedict's Priory, Winnipeg, Manitoba, Canada.

• Federation of St. Benedict (1947). Pres., Sister Enid Smith, O.S.B., St. Benedict's Convent, St. Joseph, Minn. 56374. Motherhouses belonging to the federation:

St. Benedict's Convent, St. Joseph, Minn. 56374; St. Scholastica Priory, Kenwood Ave., Duluth, Minn. 55811; St. Bede Priory, Priory Rd., Eau Claire, Wis. 54701; St. Mary Priory, Nauvoo, Ill. 62354; Annunciation, Priory, Apple Creek Rd., Bismarck, N. Dak. 58501; St. Paul's Priory, 2675 Larpenteur Ave. E., St. Paul, Minn. 55109; St. Placid Priory, 4600 Martin Way, Olympia, Wash. 98506.

Bethany, Congregation of Oblates of, C.O.B.: Founded 1902 in France; in US, 1959. Motherhouse, Canada; US address: Regina Cleri Home, 4538 Lindell Blvd., St. Louis, Mo. 63108.

Bethany, Sisters of, C.V.D.: Founded 1928, in El Salvador; in US 1949. General motherhouse, Santa Tecla, El Salvador. US address: 850 N. Hobart Blvd., Los Angeles, Calif. 90029.

Bethlemita Sisters, Daughters of the Sacred Heart of Jesus, S.C.I.F.: Founded 1861, in Guatemala. Motherhouse, Bogota, Colombia; US address, St. Joseph Residence, 330 W. Pembroke St., Dallas, Tex. 75208.

Blessed Virgin Mary, Institute of the (Loreto Sisters), I.B.V.M.: Founded 17th century in Belgium; in US, 1954. Motherhouse, Rathfarnham, Dublin, Ireland; US addresses: 6351 N. 27th Ave., Phoenix, Ariz. 85017; 810 Patrick Lane, Prescott, Ariz. 86301; 202 S. Kendrick, Flagstaff, Ariz. 86001.

Blessed Virgin Mary, Institute of the (Loretto Sisters), I.B.V.M.: Founded 1609, in Belgium; in US, 1880. US address, Loretto Convent, Box 508, Wheaton, Ill. 60187. Educational work.

Bon Secours, Sisters of, C.B.S.: Founded 1824, in France; in US, 1881. General motherhouse, Rome, Italy; US motherhouse, Marriottsville Rd., Marriottsville, Md. 21104. Hospital work.

Bridgettine Sisters (Order of the Most Holy Savior), O.SS.S.: Founded 1344, at Vadstena, Sweden, by St. Bridget; in US, 1957. General motherhouse, Rome, Italy; US address, Vikingsborg, Darien, Conn. 06820.

Brigid, Congregation of St., C.S.B.: Founded 1807, in Ireland; in US, 1953. US regional house, 5118 Loma Linda Dr., San Antonio, Tex. 78201.

Carmel, Congregation of Our Lady of Mount, O. Carm.: Founded 1825, in France; in US, 1833. General motherhouse, P.O. Box 476, Lacombe, La. 70445. Education, social services, pastoral ministry, retreat work.

Carmel, Institute of Our Lady of Mount, O. Carm.: Founded 1854, in Italy; in US, 1947. General motherhouse, Rome, Italy; US novitiate, 5 Wheatland St., Peabody, Mass. 01960. Apostolic work.

Carmel Community, C.C.: Founded 1975, Columbus, O. Address, 2065 Barton Pl., Columbus, O. 43209. Contemplative.

Carmelite Missionaries of St. Theresa, C.M.S.T.: Founded 1903, in Mexico. General motherhouse, Mexico City, Mexico; US foundation, 9600 Deertrail Rd., Houston, Tex. 77003.

Carmelite Sisters (Corpus Christi), O. Carm.: Founded 1908, in England; in US, 1920. General motherhouse, Tunapuna, Trinidad, W.I. US addresses: Carmelite Retreat House, 21 Battery St., Newport, R.I. 02840; Mt. Carmel Home, 412 W. 18th St., Kearney, Nebr. 68847; Carmelite Sisters, 765 W. 18th St., Eugene, Ore. 97405. Home and foreign mission work.

Carmelite Sisters for the Aged and Infirm, O. Carm.: Founded 1929, at New York, by Mother M. Angeline Teresa, O. Carm. Motherhouse, Avila-on-Hudson, Germantown, N.Y. 12526. Social work, nursing and educating in the field of gerontology.

Carmelite Sisters of Charity, C.a.Ch.: Founded 1826 at Vich, Spain, by St. Joaquina de Vedruna. General motherhouse, Rome, Italy; US address, 4200 16th St. N.W., Washington, D.C. 20011.

Carmelite Sisters of St. Therese of the Infant Jesus, C.S.T.: Founded 1917, in US. General motherhouse, 1300 Classen Dr., Oklahoma City, Okla. 73103. Educational work.

Carmelite Sisters of the Divine Heart of Jesus, D.C.J.: Founded 1891, in Germany; in US, 1912. General motherhouse, Sittard,

Netherlands. US provincial houses: 1230 Kavanaugh Pl., Milwaukee, Wis. 52313 (Northern Province); 10341 Manchester Rd., St. Louis, Mo. 63122 (Central Province); 8585 La Mesa Blvd., La Mesa, Calif. 92041 (South Western Province). Social services, mission work.

Carmelite Sisters of the Sacred Heart, O.C.D.: Founded 1904, in Mexico. General motherhouse, Guadalajara, Mexico; US provincialate and novitiate, 920 E. Alhambra Rd., Alhambra, Calif. 91801. Social services, retreat and educational work.

Carmelites, Calced (Carmelite Nuns of the Ancient Observance), O. Carm.: Founded 1452, in The Netherlands; in US, 1930, from Naples, Italy, convent. US monasteries: Carmel of the Little Flower, R.D. 3, Box 551, Coopersburg, Pa. 18036; Carmel of Mary, Wahpeton, N.D. 58075; Carmel of the Sacred Heart, 430 Laurel Ave., Hudson, Wis. 54016. Papal enclosure.

Carmelites, Discalced, O.C.D.: Founded 1562, Spain. First foundation in US in 1790, at Charles County, Md.; this monastery was moved to Baltimore. Monasteries in US are listed below, according to states.

Alabama: 716 Dauphin Island Pkwy., Mobile 36606. Arkansas: 7201 W. 32nd St., Little Rock 72204. California: 215 E. Alhambra Rd., Alhambra 91801; 27601 Highway 1, Carmel 93923; 68 Rincon Rd., Kensington 94707; 3361 E. Ocean Blvd., Long Beach 90803; 2150 Stockton Blvd., Sacramento 95817; 5158 Hawley Blvd., San Diego 92116; 721 Parker Ave., San Francisco 94118; 530 Blackstone Dr., San Rafael 94903; 1000 Lincoln St., Santa Clara 95050.

Colorado: 6138 S. Gallup St., Littleton 80120. Georgia: Coffee Bluff, 11 W. Back St., Savannah 31406; Illinois: River Rd. and Central, Des Plaines 60016. Indiana: 2500 Cold Springs Rd., Indianapolis 46222; 63 Allendale Pl., Terre Haute 47802. Iowa: R.R. 1, Eldridge 52748; 2901 S. Cecilia St., Sioux City 51106. Kansas: 3535 Wood Ave., Kansas City, 66102. Kentucky: 1740 Newburg Rd., Louisville 40205. Louisiana: Carmel Ave., Lafayette 70507; 5212 St. Bernard Ave., New Orleans 70122.

Maryland: 1318 Dulaney Valley Rd., Towson, Baltimore 21204. Massachusetts: 61 Mt. Pleasant Ave., Roxbury, Boston 02119; 15 Mt. Carmel Rd., Danvers 01923; Sol-E-Mar Rd., S. Dartmouth 02748. Michigan: 16630 Wyoming Ave., Detroit 48221; 1036 Valley Ave. N.W., Grand Rapids 49504; U.S. 2 Highway, P.O. Box 397, Iron Mountain 49801; 3501 Silver Lake Rd., Traverse City 49684. Minnesota: 8251 De Montreville Trail N., Lake Elmo 55042. Mississippi: 2155 Terry Rd., Jackson 39204.

Missouri: 2201 W. Main St., Jefferson City 65101; 9150 Clayton Rd., Ladue, St. Louis Co. 63124; 424 E. Republic Rd., Springfield

65807. Nevada: 1950 La Fond Dr., Reno 89509. New Hampshire: 275 Pleasant St., Concord, 03301. New Jersey: P.O. Box 785, Flemington 08822; 189 Madison Ave., Morristown 07960. New Mexico: Mt. Carmel Rd., Santa Fe 87501. New York: 745 St. John's Pl., Brooklyn 11216; 1381 University Ave., Bronx, 10452; 75 Carmel Rd., Buffalo 14214; 1931 W. Jefferson Rd., Pittsford 14534; 68 Franklin Ave., Saranac Lake 12983; 428 Duane Ave., Schenectady 12304.

Ohio: 3176 Fairmount Blvd., Cleveland Heights 44118. Oklahoma: 4200 N. Meridian Ave., Oklahoma City 73112. Oregon: 87609 Green Hill Rd., Eugene 97402. Pennsylvania: Thornbrow, Elysburg 17824; 510 E. Gore Rd., Erie 16509; R.D. 6, Box 28, Center Dr., Latrobe 15650; R.D. 1, Box 75-G, Loretto 15940; 66th Ave. and Old York Rd. (Oak Lane), Philadelphia 19126. Rhode Island: Watson Ave. at Nayatt Rd., Barrington 02806.

Texas: P.O. Box 210, Dallas 75211; 1600 Sunset Terr., Ft. Worth 76102; 1100 Parthenon Pl., Roman Forest, New Caney 77357. 1104 Kentucky Ave., San Antonio 78201. Utah: 5714 Holladay Blvd., Salt Lake City 84121. Vermont: Beckley Hill, Barre, 05641. Washington: 2215 N.E. 147th St., Seattle 98155. Wisconsin: W267 N2517 Meadowbrook Rd., Pewaukee 53072.

Casimir, Sisters of St., S.S.C.: Founded 1907, in US by Mother Maria Kaupas. General motherhouse, 2601 W. Marquette Rd., Chicago, Ill. 60629. Education, missions, social services.

Cenacle, Congregation of Our Lady of the Retreat in the, R.C.: Founded 1826, in France; in US, 1892. General motherhouse, Rome, Italy. US provinces: 154-27 Horace Harding Expressway, Flushing, N.Y. 11367; 284 Foster St., Brighton, Mass. 02135; 513 Fullerton Pkwy., Chicago, Ill. 60614.

Charity, Daughters of Divine, F.D.C.: Founded 1868, at Vienna, Austria; in US, 1913. General motherhouse, Rome, Italy. US provinces: 56 Meadowbrook Rd., White Plains, N.Y. 10605; 39 Portage Path, Akron, O. 44303; 1315 N. Woodward Ave., Bloomfield Hills, Mich. 48013. Education, social services.

Charity, Little Missionary Sisters of, P.M.C.: Founded 1915, in Italy; in US, 1949. General motherhouse, Rome, Italy; US headquarters, 201 Washington St., S. Groveland, Mass. 01834.

Charity, Missionaries of, M.C.: Founded 1950, in Calcutta, India, by Mother Teresa. General motherhouse, 54A Acharya Jagadish C. Bose Road, Calcutta 16, India. U.S. address, 335 E. 145th St., Bronx, N.Y. 10451. Service of the poor.

Charity, Religious Sisters of, R.S.C.: Founded 1815, in Ireland; in US, 1953. Motherhouse, Dublin, Ireland; US headquarters,

Marycrest Manor, 10664 St. James Dr., Culver City, Calif. 90230.

Charity, Sisters of (of Seton Hill), S.C.: Founded 1870, at Altoona, Pa., from Cincinnati foundation. Administrative Offices, De Paul Center, Mt. Thor Rd., Greensburg, Pa. 15601. Educational, hospital, social, foreign mission work.

Charity, Sisters of (Grey Nuns of Montreal), S.G.M.: Founded 1738, in Canada by Bl. Marie Marguerite d'Youville; in US, 1855. General administration, Pierrefonds, Quebec H8Y 1T2, Canada; US provincial house, 10 Pelham Rd., Lexington, Mass. 02173.

Charity, Sisters of (of Leavenworth), S.C.L.: Founded 1858, in US. Motherhouse, Leavenworth, Kans. 66048.

Charity, Sisters of (of Nazareth), S.C.N.: Founded 1812, in US. General motherhouse, Nazareth P. O., Nelson Co., Ky. 40048.

Charity, Sisters of (of St. Augustine), C.S.A.: Founded 1851, at Cleveland, O. Motherhouse, 5232 Broadview Rd., Richfield, O. 44286.

Charity, Sisters of Christian, S.C.C.: Founded 1849, in Paderborn, Germany; in US, 1873. General motherhouse, Rome, Italy. US provinces: Mallinckrodt Convent, Mendham, N.J. 07945; Maria Immaculata Convent, 1041 Ridge Rd., Wilmette, Ill. 60091, Education, health services, other apostolic work.

Charity, Vincentian Sisters of, V.S.C.: Founded 1835, in Austria; in US, 1902. General motherhouse, 8200 McKnight Rd., Pittsburgh, Pa. 15237.

Charity, Vincentian Sisters of, V.S.C.: Founded 1928, at Bedford, O. General motherhouse, 1160 Broadway, Bedford, O. 44146.

Charity of Cincinnati, Ohio, Sisters of, S.C.: Founded 1829. General motherhouse, Mt. St. Joseph, Ohio 45051. Educational, hospital, social work.

Charity of Ottawa, Sisters of (Grey Nuns of the Cross), S.C.O.: Founded 1845, at Ottawa, Canada; in US, 1857. General motherhouse, Ottawa, Canada; US provincial house, 975 Varnum Ave., Lowell, Mass. 01854. Educational, hospital work, extended health care.

Charity of Our Lady, Mother of Mercy, Sisters of, S.C.M.M.: Founded 1832, in Holland; in US, 1874. General motherhouse, Rome, Italy; US provincialate, 520 Thompson Ave., East Haven Conn. 06512.

Charity of Our Lady of Mercy, Sisters of, O.L.M.: Founded 1829, in US. Generalate and motherhouse, Charleston, S.C. 29412. Education, campus ministry, social services.

Charity of Quebec, Sisters of (Grey Nuns), S.C.Q.: Founded 1849, at Quebec; in US, 1890. General motherhouse, 2655 rue Le Pelletier, Beauport, Quebec GIC 3X7, Canada. Social work.

Charity of St. Elizabeth, Sisters of (Convent, N.J.), S.C.: Founded 1859, at Newark, N. J.

Generalate, Convent, N. J. 07961. Education, pastoral ministry, social services.

Charity of St. Hyacinthe, Sisters of (Grey Nuns), S.C.S.H.: Founded 1840, at St. Hyacinthe, Canada; in US, 1878. General motherhouse, 665 Avenue Bourdages, SUD, St. Hyacinthe, Quebec J2T 4J8, Canada. Regional house, 98 Campus Ave., Lewiston Me. 04240.

Charity of St. Joan Antida, Sisters of, S.C.S.J.A.: Founded 1799, in France; in US, 1932. General motherhouse, Rome, Italy; US provincial house, 8560 N. 76th Pl., Milwaukee, Wis. 53223.

Charity of St. Louis, Sisters of, S.C.S.L.: Founded 1803, in France; in US, 1910. General motherhouse, Rome, Italy; US provincial house, 29 Casablanca Court, Clifton Park, N.Y. 12065.

Charity of St. Vincent de Paul, Daughters of, D.C.: Founded 1633, in France; in US 1809, at Emmitsburg, Md., by St. Elizabeth Ann Seton. General motherhouse, Paris, France. US provinces: Emmitsburg, Md. 21727; 7800 Natural Bridge Rd., St. Louis, Mo. 63121; 9400 New Harmony Rd., Evansville, Ind. 47712; 96 Menands Rd., Albany, N.Y. 12204; 26000 Altamont Rd., Los Altos Hills, Calif. 94022.

Charity of St. Vincent de Paul, Sisters of, Halifax, S.C.H.: Founded 1856, at Halifax, N. S., from Emmitsburg, Md., foundation. Generalate, Mt. St. Vincent, Halifax, N. S., Canada. U.S. addresses: Boston Province, 50 Aspen Ave., Auburndale, Mass. 02166; New York Province, 410 Grant Ave., Brooklyn, N.Y. 11208. Educational, hospital, social work.

Charity of St. Vincent de Paul, Sisters of, New York, S.C.: Founded 1817, from Emmitsburg, Md. General motherhouse, Mt. St. Vincent on Hudson, New York, N.Y. 10471. Educational, hospital work.

Charity of St. Vincent de Paul, Sisters of, S.V.Z.: Founded 1845, in Croatia; in U.S., 1955. General motherhouse, Zagreb, Yugoslavia; U.S. foundation, 171 Knox Ave., West Seneca, N.Y. 14224.

Charity of the Blessed Virgin Mary, Sisters of, B.V.M.: Founded 1833, in US. General motherhouse, Mt. Carmel, Dubuque, Ia. 52001. Education, pastoral ministry, social services.

Charity of the Immaculate Conception of Ivrea, Sisters of, S.C.I.C.: General motherhouse, Rome, Italy; US address, Immaculate Virgin of Miracles Convent, R.D. 2, Mt. Pleasant, Pa. 15666.

Charity of the Incarnate Word, Congregation of the Sisters of, C.C.V.I.: Founded 1869, at San Antonio, Tex., by Bishop C. M. Dubuis. General motherhouse, 4515 Broadway, San Antonio, Tex. 78209.

Charity of the Incarnate Word, Congregation of the Sisters of (Houston, Tex.), C.C.V.I.: Founded 1866, in US, by Bishop C. M. Dubuis. General motherhouse, 6510 Lawndale Ave., Houston, Tex. 77023. Educational, hospital, social work.

Charity of the Sacred Heart, Daughters of, F.C.S.C.J.: Founded 1823, at La Salle de Vihiers, France; in US, 1905. General motherhouse, La Salle de Vihiers, France; U.S. address, Sacred Heart Province, P.O. Box 642, Littleton, N.H. 03561.

Charles Borromeo, Missionary Sisters of St. (Scalabrini Srs.): Founded 1895, in Italy; in US, 1941. American novitiate, 1414 N. 37th Ave., Melrose Park, Ill. 60601.

Child Jesus, Sisters of the Poor, P.C.J.: Founded 1844, at Aix-la-Chapelle, Germany; in US, 1924. General motherhouse, Simpelveld, Holland; American provincialate, 4567 Olentangy River Rd., Columbus, O. 43214.

Chretienne, Sisters of Ste., S.S.CH.: Founded 1807, in France; in US, 1903. General motherhouse, Metz, France; American provincial house, 297 Arnold St., Wrentham, Mass. 02093. Educational, hospital, mission work.

Christ, Adorers of the Blood of, A.S.C.: Founded 1834, in Italy; in US, 1870. General motherhouse, Rome, Italy. US provinces: Ruma Province, Rt. 1, Box 115, Red Bud, Ill. 62278; 1400 South Sheridan, Wichita, Kans. 67213; Columbia, Pa. 17512. Education, retreats, social services, pastoral ministry.

Christ the King, Sister Servants of, S.S.C.K.: Founded 1936, in US. General motherhouse, Loretto Convent, Mt. Calvary, Wis. 53057. Social services.

Christian Doctrine, Sisters of Our Lady of, R.C.D.: Founded 1910, at New York. Motherhouse, Marydell, Montebello Rd., Suffern, N.Y. 10901.

Christian Education, Religious of, R.C.E.: Founded 1817, in France; in US, 1905. General motherhouse, Paris, France; US provincial residence, 36 Hillcrest Rd., Belmont, Mass. 02178.

Cistercian Nuns of the Strict Observance, Order of, O.C.S.O.: Founded 1125, in France, by St. Stephen Harding; in US, 1949. US addresses: Mt. St. Mary's Abbey, Arnold St. (R.F.D. Box 500), Wrentham, Mass. 02093; Our Lady of the Santa Rita Abbey, Box 97, Sonoita, Ariz. 85637; Our Lady of the Redwoods Abbey, Whitethorn, Calif. 95489; Abbey of Our Lady of the Mississippi, R.R. 3, Dubuque, Ia. 52001.

Clergy, Congregation of Our Lady, Help of the, C.L.H.C.: Founded 1961, in US. Motherhouse, Maryvale Convent, 116 E. First St., Charlotte, N.C. 28202.

Clergy, Servants of Our Lady Queen of the, S.R.C.: Founded 1929, in Canada; in US, 1936. General motherhouse, Lac-au-Saumon, Que., GOJ 1MO, Canada.

Colettines: See Franciscan Poor Clare Nuns.

Columban, Missionary Sisters of St., S.S.C.: Founded 1922, in Ireland; in US, 1930. General motherhouse, Wicklow, Ireland; US region, 1250 W. Loyola Ave., Chicago, Ill. 60626.

Consolata Missionary Sisters, M.C.: Founded 1910, in Italy; in US, 1954. General motherhouse, Turin, Italy; US headquarters, 6801 Belmont Rd., Belmont, Mich. 49306.

Cross, Daughters of the, D.C.: Founded 1640, in France; in US, 1855. General motherhouse, 1000 Fairview St., Shreveport, La. 71104. Educational work.

Cross, Daughters of, of Liege, F.C.: Founded 1883, in Liege, Belgium; in US, 1958. US address, 165 W. Eaton Ave., Tracy, Calif. 95376.

Cross, Sisters of the Holy, C.S.C.: Founded 1841, at Le Mans, France; in US, 1841. General motherhouse, Saint Mary's, Notre Dame, Ind. 46556. Education, health care, social services, pastoral ministry.

Cross and of the Seven Dolors, Sisters of the Holy, C.S.C.: Founded 1847, in Canada; in US, 1881. General motherhouse, St. Laurent, Montreal, Que., Canada; US provincial house, Fairview Rd., Pittsfield, N.H. 03263. Educational work.

Cross and Passion, Sisters of the (Passionist Sisters), C.P.: Founded 1852; in US, 1924. General motherhouse, Bolton, England; US address: Mt. St. Joseph, 670 Tower Hill Rd., Wakefield, R.I. 02880.

Cross and Passion of Our Lord Jesus Christ, Nuns of the (Passionist Nuns), C.P.: Founded 1771, in Italy, by St. Paul of the Cross; in US, 1910. US convents: 2715 Churchview Ave., Pittsburgh, Pa. 15227; 631 Griffin Pond Rd., Clarks Summit, Pa. 18411; 1420 Benita Ave., Owensboro, Ky. 42301; 751 Donaldson Hwy., Erlanger, Ky. 41018; 1032 Clayton Rd., Ellisville, Mo. 63011. Contemplatives.

Crucified, Augustinian Daughters of the: Founded 1840, in Italy. General motherhouse, Rome, Italy; US address, Scalabrini Villa, 860 N. Quidnesset Rd., N. Kingstown, R.I. 02852.

Cyril and Methodius, Sisters of Sts., SS.C.M.: Founded 1909, in US, by Rev. Matthew Jankola. General motherhouse, Danville, Pa. 17821. Education, care of aged.

Disciples of the Divine Master, Sister, P.D.D.M.: Founded 1924; in US, 1948. General motherhouse, Rome, Italy; US headquarters, 60 Sunset Ave., Staten Island, N.Y. 10314.

Divine Compassion, Sisters of, R.D.C.: Founded 1886, in US. General motherhouse, 52 N. Broadway, White Plains, N.Y. 10603. Education, other ministries.

Divine Love, Oblates to, Sisters, R.O.D.A.: Founded 1923, in Italy; in US, 1947. General motherhouse, Rome, Italy; US provincial house, St. Clare's Convent, 1925 Home Ave., Bronx, N.Y. 10461.

Divine Spirit, Congregation of the, C.D.S.: Founded 1956, in US, by Archbishop John M. Gannon. Motherhouse, 409 W. 6th St., Erie, Pa. 16507. Education, social services.

Dominicans

Nuns of the Order of Preachers (Dominican Nuns), O.P.: Founded 1206 by St. Dominic at Prouille, France. Cloistered, contemplative. Two branches in the United States:

• Dominican Nuns having perpetual adoration. First monastery established 1880, in Newark, N.J., from Oullins, France, foundation (1869). Seven autonomous monasteries.

St. Dominic, 13th Ave. and S. 10th St., Newark, N.J. 07103; Corpus Christi, 1230 Lafayette Ave., Bronx, N.Y. 10474; Blessed Sacrament, 29575 Middlebelt Rd., Farmington Hills, Mich. 48018; Holy Name, 3020 Erie Ave., Hyde Park, Cincinnati, O. 45208; Monastery of the Angels, 1977 Carmen Ave., Los Angeles, Calif. 90068; Corpus Christi, 215 Oak Grove Ave., Menlo Park, Calif. 94025; Infant Jesus, 1501 Lotus Lane, Lufkin, Tex. 75901.

• Dominican Nuns devoted to the perpetual Rosary. First monastery established 1891, in Union City, N.J., from Calais, France, foundation (1880). Thirteen autonomous monasteries (some also observe perpetual adoration).

Dominican Nuns of Perpetual Rosary, 14th and West Sts., Union City, N.J. 07087; Presentation Monastery, 217 N. 68th St., Milwaukee, Wis. 53213; Dominican Monastery, 720 Maiden Choice Lane, Catonsville, Md. 21228; Perpetual Rosary, 1500 Haddon Ave., Camden, N.J. 08103; Our Lady of the Rosary, 335 Doat St., Buffalo, N.Y. 14211; St. Dominic, 3000 South Ave., La Crosse, Wis. 54601; Our Lady of the Rosary, 543 Springfield Ave., Summit, N.J. 07901; Mother of God, 1430 Riverdale St., W. Springfield, Mass. 01089; Perpetual Rosary, 802 Court St., Syracuse, N.Y. 13208; Immaculate Heart of Mary, 1834 Lititz Pike, Lancaster, Pa. 17601; Mary the Queen, 1310 W. Church St., Elmira, N.Y. 14905; St. Jude, Marbury, Ala. 36051; Our Lady of Grace, North Guilford, Conn. 06437.

Dominican Rural Missionaries, O.P.: Founded 1932, in France; in US, 1951, at Abbeville, La. General motherhouse, Luzarches, France; US address, 1318 S. Henry St., Abbeville, La. 70510.

Dominican Sisters of Bethany, Congregation, O.P.: Founded 1866, in France. Motherhouse, France; US novitiate, 204 Ridge St., Millis, Mass. 02054.

Dominican Sisters of the Presentation, O.P.: Founded 1684, in France; in US, 1906. General motherhouse, Tours, France; US headquarters, 3012 Elm St., Dighton, Mass. 02715. Hospital work.

Dominican Sisters of the Roman Congregation of St. Dominic, O.P.: Founded 1621, in France; in US, 1904. General motherhouse, Rome, Italy; US province, 2624 Fillmore St., Davenport, Ia. 52804. Educational work.

Eucharistic Missionaries of St. Dominic, O.P.: Founded 1927, in Louisiana. General motherhouse, 1101 Aline St., New Orleans, La. 70115. Parish work, social services .

Maryknoll Sisters of St. Dominic, M.M.: Founded 1912, in New York. Center, Maryknoll, N.Y. 10545.

Religious Missionaries of St. Dominic, O.P.: General motherhouse, Rome, Italy. US foundations: 808 S. Wright St., Alice, Texas 78332; 610 E. Gramman St., Beeville, Tex. 78102; 432 N. Oak St., Santa Paula, Calif. 93060; 459 W. Pleasant Valley Rd., Oxnard, Calif. 93030.

Sisters of St. Dominic, O.P.: Thirty congregations in the US. Educational, hospital work. Names of congregations are given below, followed by the date of foundation, and location of motherhouse.

St. Catharine of Siena, 1822. St. Catharine, Ky. 40061.

St. Mary of the Springs, 1830. Columbus Ohio 43219.

Most Holy Rosary, 1847. Sinsinawa, Wis. 53824.

Most Holy Name of Jesus, 1850. San Rafael, Calif. 94901.

Holy Cross, 1853. Albany Ave., Amityville, N.Y. 11701.

Most Holy Rosary, 1859. Mt. St. Mary on Hudson, Newburgh, N.Y. 12550.

St. Cecilia, 1860. Eighth Ave. N. and Clay St., Nashville, Tenn. 37208.

St. Mary, 1860. 4601 Cleveland Ave., New Orleans, La. 70119.

St. Catherine of Siena, 1862. 5635 Erie St., Racine, Wis. 53402.

Our Lady of the Sacred Heart, 1873. 1237 W. Monroe St., Springfield, Ill. 62704.

Our Lady of the Rosary, 1876. Sparkill, N.Y. 10976.

Queen of the Holy Rosary, 1876. Mission San Jose, Calif. 94538.

Most Holy Rosary, 1892. Adrian, Mich. 49221.

Our Lady of the Sacred Heart, 1877. 2025 E. Fulton St., Grand Rapids, Mich. 49503.

St. Dominic, 1878. Blauvelt, N.Y. 10913.

Immaculate Conception (Dominican Sisters of the Sick Poor), 1879. P.O. Box 231, Ossining, N.Y. 10562. Social work.

St. Catherine de Ricci, 1880. 2850 N. Providence Rd., Media, Pa. 19063.

Sacred Heart of Jesus, 1881. Mt. St. Dominic, Caldwell, N.J. 07006.

Sacred Heart, 1882. 6501 Almeda Rd., Houston, Tex. 77021.

St. Thomas Aquinas, 1888. 423 E. 152nd St., Tacoma, Wash. 98445.

Holy Cross, 1890. P.O. Box 280, Edmonds, Wash. 98020.

St. Catherine of Siena, 1891. 37 Park St., Fall River, Mass. 02721.

St. Rose of Lima (Servants of Relief for Incurable Cancer), 1896. Hawthorne, N.Y. 10532.

Immaculate Conception, 1902. 3600 Broadway, Great Bend, Kans. 67530.

St. Catherine of Siena, 1911. 4600 93rd St., Kenosha, Wis. 53140.

St. Rose of Lima, 1923. 775 Drahner Rd., Oxford, Mich. 48051.

Immaculate Conception, 1929. 9000 W. 81st St., Justice, Ill. 60458.

Immaculate Heart of Mary, 1929. Akron, Ohio 44313.

Immaculate Heart of Mary Province (Dominican Sisters of Spokane). W. 3102 Fort George Wright Dr., Spokane, Wash. 99204.

Dominican Sisters of Oakford (St. Catherine of Siena), 1889. Motherhouse, Oakford, Natal, South Africa. US regional house, 1965. Villa Siena, 1855 Miramonte Ave., Mountain View, Calif. 94040.

(End, Listing of Dominicans)

Dorothy, Institute of the Sisters of St., S.S.D.: Founded 1834, in Italy; in US, 1911. General motherhouse, Rome, Italy; US provincialate, Villa Fatima, Taunton, Mass. 02780.

Eucharist, Religious of the, R.E.: Founded 1857, in Belgium; in US, 1900. General motherhouse, Belgium; US foundation, 2907 Ellicott Terr., N.W., Washington, D.C. 20008.

Eucharistic Missionary Sisters, E.M.S.: Founded 1943, in Mexico. Motherhouse, Our Lady of Loretto Convent, 267 N. Belmont Ave., Los Angeles, Calif. 90026.

Family, Congregation of the Sisters of the Holy, S.S.F.: Founded 1842, in US. General motherhouse, 6901 Chef Menteur Hway., New Orleans, La. 70126. Educational, hospital work.

Family, Little Sisters of the Holy, P.S.S.F.: Founded 1880, in Canada; in US, 1900. General motherhouse, Sherbrooke, Que., Canada. US novitiate, 285 Andover St., Lowell, Mass. 01852.

Family, Sisters of the Holy, S.H.F.: Founded 1872, in US. General motherhouse, P.O. Box 3248, Mission San Jose, Calif. 94538. Educational, social work.

Family of Nazareth, Sisters of the Holy, C.S.F.N.: Founded 1875, in Italy; in US, 1885. General motherhouse, Rome, Italy. US provinces: 353 N. River Rd., Des Plaines, Ill. 60016; Grant and Frankford Aves., Torresdale, Philadelphia, Pa. 19114; 285 Bellevue Rd., Pittsburgh, Pa. 15229; Marian Heights, 1428 Monroe Turnpike, Monroe, Conn. 06468; 1814 Egyptian Way, Box 757, Grand Prairie, Tex. 75050.

Filippini, Religious Teachers, M.P.F.: Founded 1692, in Italy; in US, 1910. General motherhouse, Rome, Italy; US provinces: St. Lucy Filippini Province, Villa Walsh, Morristown, N.J. 07960; Queen of Apostles Province, 474 East Rd., Bristol, Conn. 06010. Educational work.

Francis de Sales, Oblate Sisters of St., O.S.F.S.: Founded 1866, in France; in US, 1951. General motherhouse, Troyes, France; US headquarters, Villa Aviat Convent, Childs, Md. 21916. Educational, social work.

Franciscans

Bernardine Sisters of the Third Order of St. Francis, O.S.F.: Founded 1457, at Cracow, Poland; in US, 1894. Generalate, 647 Spring Mill Rd., Villanova, Pa. 19085. Educational, hospital, social work.

Congregation of the Servants of the Holy Infancy of Jesus, O.S.F.: Founded 1855, in Germany; in US, 1929. General motherhouse, Wuerzburg, Germany; American motherhouse, Villa Maria, P.O. Box 708, Plainfield, N.J. 07061.

Congregation of the Third Order of St. Francis of Mary Immaculate, O.S.F.: Founded 1865, in US, by Fr. Pamphilus da Magliano, O.F.M. General motherhouse, 520 Plainfield Ave., Joliet, Ill. 60435. Educational and pastoral work.

Daughters of St. Francis of Assisi, D.S.F.: Founded 1890, in Austria-Hungary; in US, 1946. Provincial motherhouse, 507 N. Prairie St., Lacon, Ill. 61540. Nursing, CCD work.

Felician Sisters (Congregation of the Sisters of St. Felix), C.S.S.F.: Founded 1855, in Poland; in US, 1874. General motherhouse, Rome, Italy. US provinces: 36800 Schoolcraft Rd., Livonia, Mich. 48150; 600 Doat St., Buffalo, N.Y. 14211; 3800 Peterson Ave., Chicago, Ill. 60659; 260 South Main St., Lodi, N.J. 07644; 1500 Woodcrest Ave., Coraopolis, Pa. 15108; 1315 Enfield St., Enfield, Conn. 06082; 4210 Meadowlark Lane, S.E., Rio Rancho, N. Mex. 87174.

Franciscan Handmaids of the Most Pure Heart of Mary, F.H.M.: Founded 1917, in US. General motherhouse, 15 W. 124th St., New York, N.Y. 10027. Educational, social work.

Franciscan Hospitaller Sisters of the Immaculate Conception, F.H.I.C.: Founded 1876, in Portugal; in US, 1960. General motherhouse, Oporto, Portugal; US novitiate, 300 S. 17th St., San Jose, Calif. 95112.

Franciscan Missionaries of Mary, F.M.M.: Founded 1877, in India; in US, 1904. General motherhouse, Rome, Italy; US provincialate, 225 E. 45th St., New York, N.Y. 10017. Mission work.

Franciscan Missionaries of Our Lady, O.S.F.: Founded 1854, at Calais, France; in US, 1913. General motherhouse, Desvres, France; US motherhouse, 4200 Essen Lane, Baton Rouge, La. 70809. Hospital work.

Franciscan Missionaries of St. Joseph (Mill Hill Sisters), F.M.S.J.: Founded 1883, at Rochdale, Lancashire, England; in US, 1952. General motherhouse, Eccleshall, Stafford, England; US headquarters, Franciscan House, 1006 Madison Ave., Albany, N.Y. 12208.

Franciscan Missionaries of the Divine Motherhood, F.M.D.M.: Founded 1935, in England; US foundation, Convent of the Holy Spirit, East Greenbush, N.Y. 12061.

Franciscan Missionaries of the Infant Jesus: Generalate, Rome, Italy. US novitiate, St. Margaret Convent, Third and Beech Sts., Woodbury, N.J. 08097.

Franciscan Missionary Sisters for Africa, O.S.F.: American foundation, 1953. Generalate, Ireland; US headquarters, 172 Foster St., Brighton, Mass. 02135.

Franciscan Missionary Sisters of Assisi, S.F.M.G.: First foundation in US, 1961. General motherhouse, Assisi, Italy; US address, St. Francis Convent, 1039 Northampton St., Holyoke, Mass. 01040.

Franciscan Missionary Sisters of Our Lady of Sorrows, O.S.F.: Founded 1937, in China, by Bishop R. Palazzi, O.F.M.; in US, 1849. US address, 2385 Laurel Glen Rd., Santa Cruz, Calif. 95060. Educational, social, domestic, retreat and foreign mission work.

Franciscan Missionary Sisters of the Divine Child, F.M.D.C.: Founded 1927, at Buffalo, N.Y., by Bishop William Turner. General motherhouse, 6380 Main St., Williamsville, N.Y. 14221. Educational, social work.

Franciscan Missionary Sisters of the Immaculate Conception, O.S.F.: Founded 1874, in Mexico; in US, 1926. US provincial house, 11306 Laurel Canyon Blvd., San Fernando, Calif. 91340.

Franciscan Missionary Sisters of the Sacred Heart, F.M.S.C.: Founded 1860, in Italy; in US, 1865. Generalate, Rome, Italy; US provincialate, 250 South St., Peekskill, N.Y. 10566. Educational and social welfare apostolates and specialized services.

Franciscan Poor Clare Nuns (Poor Clares, Order of St. Clare, Poor Clares of St. Colette), P.C., O.S.C., P.C.C.: Founded 1212, at Assisi, Italy, by St. Francis of Assisi; in US, 1875. Proto-monastery, Assisi, Italy. Addresses of autonomous motherhouses in US are listed below.

3626 N. 65th Ave., Omaha, Nebr. 68104; 720 Henry Clay Ave., New Orleans, La. 70118; 509 S. Kentucky Ave., Evansville, Ind. 47714; 1310 Dellwood Ave., Memphis Tenn. 38127; 920 Centre St., Jamaica Plain, Mass. 02130; 201 Crosswicks St., Bordentown, N.J. 08505; 1271 Langhorne-Newton Rd., Langhorne, Pa. 19047; 4419 N. Hawthorne St., Spokane, Wash. 99205; 142 Hollywood Ave., Bronx, N.Y. 10465; 421 S. 4th St., Sauk Rapids, Minn. 56379; 8650 Russell Ave. S.,

Minneapolis, Minn. 55431; 3501 Rocky River Dr., Cleveland, O. 44111;

89th and Kean Ave., Hickory Hills, Ill. 60457; 280 State Park Dr., Aptos, Calif. 95003; 2111 S. Main St., Rockford, Ill. 61102; 215 E. Los Olivos St., Santa Barbara, Calif. 93105; P.O. Box 333, Lowell, Mass. 01853; 809 E. 19th St., Roswell, N. Mex. 88201; 28210 Natoma Rd., Los Altos Hills, Calif. 94022; 1916 N. Pleasantburg Dr., Greenville, S.C. 29609; 28 Harpersville Rd., Newport News, Va. 23601; 805 N. Malfalfa Rd., Kokoma, Ind. 46901; 4000 Sherwood Blvd., Delray Beach, Fla. 33445; 200 Marycrest Dr., St. Louis, Mo. 63129.

Franciscan Sisters, Daughters of the Sacred Hearts of Jesus and Mary, O.S.F.: Founded 1860, in Germany; in US, 1872. Generalate, Rome, Italy; US motherhouse, P.O. Box 667, Wheaton, Ill. 60187. Educational, hospital, foreign mission, social work.

Franciscan Sisters of Allegany, N.Y., O.S.F.: Founded 1859, at Allegany, N.Y., by Fr. Pamphilus da Magliano, O.F.M. General motherhouse Allegany, N.Y. 14706. Educational, hospital, foreign mission work.

Franciscan Sisters of Baltimore, O.S.F.: Founded 1868, in England; in US, 1881. General motherhouse, 3725 Ellerslie Ave., Baltimore, Md. 21218. Educational work; social services.

Franciscan Sisters of Chicago, O.S.F.: Founded 1894, in US. General motherhouse, 1220 Main St., Lemont, Ill. 60439. Educational work, social services.

Franciscan Sisters of Christian Charity, O.S.F.: Founded 1869, in US. Holy Family Convent, 2409 S. Alverno Rd., Manitowoc, Wis. 54220. Educational, hospital work.

Franciscan Sisters of Little Falls, Minn., O.S.F.: Founded 1891, in US. General motherhouse, Little Falls, Minn. 56345. Health, education, social services, pastoral ministry, mission work.

Franciscan Sisters of Mary Immaculate of the Third Order of St. Francis of Assisi, F.M.I.: Founded 16th century, in Switzerland; in US, 1932. General motherhouse, Bogota, Colombia; US provincial house, 4301 N.E. 18th Ave., Amarillo, Tex. 79107. Education.

Franciscan Sisters of Our Lady of Perpetual Help, O.S.F.: Founded 1901, in US, from Joliet, Ill., foundation. General motherhouse, 201 Brotherton Lane, St. Louis, Mo. 63135. Educational, hospital work.

Franciscan Sisters of Ringwood, F.S.R.: Founded 1927, at Passaic, N.J. General motherhouse, Mt. St. Francis, Ringwood, N.J. 07456. Educational work.

Franciscan Sisters of St. Elizabeth, F.S.S.E.: Founded 1866, at Naples, Italy; in US, 1919. General motherhouse, Rome; US novitiate, 449 Park Rd., Parsippany, N.J. 07054. Educational work, social services.

Franciscan Sisters of St. Joseph, F.S.S.J.: Founded 1897, in US. General motherhouse, 5286 S. Park Ave., Hamburg, N.Y. 14075. Educational, hospital work.

Franciscan Sisters of the Atonement, Third Order Regular of St. Francis (Graymoor Sisters), S.A.: Founded 1898, in US, as Anglican community; entered Church, 1909. General motherhouse, Graymoor, Garrison P.O., N.Y. 10524. Mission work.

Franciscan Sisters of the Blessed Virgin Mary of the Holy Angels, B.M.V.A.: Founded 1863, at Neuwied, Germany; in US, 1923. General motherhouse, Rhine, Germany; US motherhouse, 1388 Prior Ave. S., St. Paul, Minn. 55116. Educational, hospital, social work.

Franciscan Sisters of the Immaculate Conception, O.S.F.: Founded in Germany; in US, 1928. General motherhouse, Kloster, Bonlanden, Germany; US province, 291 W. North St., Buffalo, N.Y. 14201.

Franciscan Sisters of the Immaculate Conception, O.S.F.: Founded 1901, in US. General motherhouse, 1000 30th St., Rock Island, Ill. 61201. Health care.

Franciscan Sisters of the Immaculate Conception, Missionary, O.S.F.: Founded 1873, in US. General motherhouse, Rome, Italy; US address, 790 Centre St., Newton, Mass. 02158. Educational work.

Franciscan Sisters of the Immaculate Conception and St. Joseph for the Dying, O.S.F.: Founded 1919, in US. General motherhouse, 485 Church St., Monterey, Calif. 93940.

Franciscan Sisters of the Poor, S.F.P.: Founded 1845, at Aachen, Germany, by Bl. Frances Schervier; in US, 1858. Community service center, 23 Middagh St., Brooklyn, N.Y. 11201. Hospital, social work and foreign missions.

Franciscan Sisters of the Sacred Heart, O.S.F.: Founded 1876, in US. General motherhouse, Mokena, Ill. 60448. Education, health care, other service ministries.

Hospital Sisters of the Third Order of St. Francis, O.S.F.: Founded 1844, in Germany; in US, 1875. General motherhouse, Muenster, Germany; US motherhouse, Box 42, Springfield, Ill. 62705. Hospital work.

Institute of the Franciscan Sisters of the Eucharist, F.S.E.: Founded 1973. Motherhouse, 405 Allen Ave., Meriden, Conn. 06450.

Little Franciscan Sisters of Mary, P.F.M.: Founded 1889, in US. General motherhouse, Baie St. Paul, Que., Canada. US province, 55 Moore Ave., Worcester, Mass. 01602. Educational, hospital, social work.

Little Sisters of St. Francis, O.S.F.: Founded 1979, in Boston archdiocese. Address, 785 Parker St., Mission Hill, Mass. 02110. Combine contemplative life with street ministry apostolate.

Missionaries of the Third Order of St. Francis of Our Lady of the Prairies, O.L.P.:

Founded 1960, in US. General motherhouse, Powers Lake, N.D. 58773.

Missionary Sisters of the Immaculate Conception of the Mother of God, S.M.I.C.: Founded 1910, in Brazil; in US, 1922, Generalate, 779 Broadway, Paterson, N.J. 07514; provincialate, P.O. Box 3026, Paterson, N.J. 07509. Mission, educational, health work, social services.

Mothers of the Helpless, M.D.: Founded 1873, in Spain; in US, 1916. General motherhouse, Valencia, Spain; US address, San Jose Day Nursery, 432 W. 20th St., New York, N.Y. 10011.

Philip Neri Missionary Teachers, Sisters of St., R.F.: Founded 1858, in Spain; in US, 1956. Motherhouse, Barcelona, Spain; US address: Sisters of St. Philip Neri, 10634 N.E. 10th Pl., Miami Shores, Fla. 33138.

Poor Clares of Perpetual Adoration, P.C.P.A.: Founded 1854, at Paris, France; in US, 1921, at Cleveland, Ohio. US monasteries: 4200 N. Market Ave., Canton, O. 44714; 2311 Timlin Rd., Portsmouth, O. 45662; 4108 Euclid Ave., Cleveland, O. 44103; 3900 13th St. N.E., Washington, D.C. 20017; 5817 Old Leeds Rd., Birmingham, Ala. 35210. Contemplative, cloistered, perpetual adoration.

School Sisters of St. Francis, O.S.F.: Founded 1874, in US. General motherhouse, 1501 S. Layton Blvd., Milwaukee, Wis. 53215.

School Sisters of St. Francis, O.S.F.: Founded 1843, in Austria; in US, 1913. General motherhouse, Rome, Italy. US provinces: Pittsburgh Province, 934 Forest Ave., Pittsburgh, Pa. 15202; Bethlehem Province, 395 Bridle Path Rd., Bethlehem, Pa. 18017. Education, health care services and related ministries.

School Sisters of the Third Order of St. Francis (Savannah, Mo.), O.S.F.: Founded 1842, in Austria; in US, 1924. Provincial house, La Verna Hts., Savannah, Mo. 64485. Educational, hospital work.

School Sisters of the Third Order of St. Francis (Panhandle, Tex.), O.S.F.: Founded 1845, in Austria; in US, 1942. General motherhouse, Vienna, Austria; US center and novitiate, Sancta Maria Convent, Panhandle, Tex. 79068. Educational, social work.

Sisters of Charity of Our Lady, Mother of the Church, S.C.M.C.: Established 1970, in US. Motherhouse, Baltic, Conn. 06330. Teaching, nursing, care of aged, and dependent children.

Sisters of Our Lady of Mercy (Mercedarians), S.O.L.M.: General motherhouse, Rome, Italy; US addresses: 70 Bay 47th St. Brooklyn, N.Y. 11214; St. Edward School, Pine Hill, N.J. 08021.

Sisters of Mercy of the Holy Cross, S.C.S.C.: Founded 1856, in Switzerland; in US. 1912. General motherhouse, Ingenbohl, Switzerland; US provincial house, Merrill, Wis. 54452.

Sisters of St. Elizabeth, S.S.E.: Founded 1931, at Milwaukee, Wis. General motherhouse, 745 N. Brookfield Rd., Brookfield, Wis. 53005.

Sisters of St. Francis (Clinton, Iowa), O.S.F.: Founded 1868, in US. General motherhouse, Bluff Blvd. and Springdale Dr., Clinton, Ia. 57232. Educational, hospital, social work.

Sisters of St. Francis (Maryville, Mo.), O.S.F.: Founded 1894, in US. Motherhouse, Mt. Alverno Convent, R.R. 3, Box 64, Maryville, Mo. 64468. Hospital work.

Sisters of St. Francis (Millvale, Pa.), O.S.F.: Founded 1865, Pittsburgh, Pa. General motherhouse, 146 Hawthorne Rd., Millvale P.O., Pittsburgh, Pa. 15209. Educational, hospital work.

Sisters of St. Francis of Christ the King, O.S.F.: Founded 1869, in Austria. General motherhouse, Rome, Italy; US provincial house, 1600 Main St., Lemont, Ill. 60439. Educational work, home for aged.

Sisters of St. Francis of Penance and Christian Charity, O.S.F.: Founded 1835, in Holland; in US, 1874. General motherhouse, Rome, Italy. US provinces: 4421 Lower River Rd., Stella Niagara, N.Y. 14144; 2851 W. 52nd Ave., Denver, Colo. 80221; 3910 Bret Harte Dr., P.O. Box 1028, Redwood City, Calif. 94064.

Sisters of St. Francis of Philadelphia, O.S.F.: Founded 1855, at Philadelphia, by Mother Mary Francis Bachmann and St. John N. Neumann. General motherhouse, Convent of Our Lady of the Angels, Glen Riddle, Aston, Pa. 19014. Education, health care, social services.

Sisters of St. Francis of the Congregation of Our Lady of Lourdes, O.S.F.: Founded 1916, in US. General motherhouse, 6832 Convent Blvd., Sylvania, O. 43560. Education, health care, social services, pastoral ministry.

Sisters of St. Francis of the Holy Cross, O.S.F.: Founded 1881, in US, by Rev. Edward Daems, O.S.C. General motherhouse, 3025 Bay Settlement Rd., Green Bay, Wis. 54301. Educational, nursing work, pastoral ministry, foreign missions.

Sisters of St. Francis of the Holy Eucharist, O.S.F.: Founded 1424, in Switzerland; in US, 1893. General motherhouse, Ashland and Prewitt Sts., Nevada, Mo. 64772. Education, health care, social services, foreign missions.

Sisters of St. Francis of the Holy Family, O.S.F.: Founded 1875, in US. Motherhouse, Mt. St. Francis, Dubuque, Ia. 52001. Varied apostolates.

Sisters of St. Francis of the Immaculate Conception, O.S.F.: Founded 1890, in US. General motherhouse, 2408 W. Heading Ave., Peoria, Ill. 61604. Education, care of aging, pastoral ministry.

Sisters of St. Francis of the Immaculate Heart of Mary, O.S.F.: Founded 1241, in

Bavaria; in US, 1913. General motherhouse, Rome, Italy; US motherhouse, Hankinson, N.D. 58041. Education, social services.

Sisters of St. Francis of the Martyr St. George, O.S.F.: Founded 1859, in Germany; in US, 1923. General motherhouse, Thuine, West Germany; US provincial house, Alton, Ill. 62002. Education, social services, foreign mission work.

Sisters of St. Francis of the Mission of the Immaculate Virgin, O.S.F.: Founded 1893, in New York. General motherhouse, Hastings-on-Hudson, N.Y. 10706. Education, parish ministry, social services.

Sisters of St. Francis of the Perpetual Adoration, O.S.F.: Founded 1863, in Germany; in US, 1875. General motherhouse, Olpe, Germany. US provinces: Box 766, Mishawaka, Ind. 46544; P.O. Box 1060, Colorado Springs, Colo. 80901. Educational, hospital work.

Sisters of St. Francis of the Providence of God, O.S.F.: Founded 1922, in US, by Msgr. M. L. Krusas. General motherhouse, Grove and McRoberts Rds., Pittsburgh, Pa. 15234. Education, varied apostolates.

Sisters of St. Joseph of the Third Order of St. Francis, S.S.J.: Founded 1901, in US. General motherhouse, 107 S. Greenlawn Ave., South Bend, Ind. 46617. Education, health care, social services.

Sisters of St. Mary of the Third Order of St. Francis, S.S.M.: Founded 1872, in St. Louis, Mo. General motherhouse, 1100 Bellevue Ave., St. Louis, Mo. 63117. Health care, social services.

Sisters of the Infant Jesus, I.J.: Founded 1662, at Rouen, France; in US, 1950. Motherhouse, Paris, France. Generalate, Rome, Italy. US addresses: 20 Reiner St., Colma, Calif. 94014; St. John the Baptist School, Healdsburg, Calif. 95448; 60 Bellevue Ave., Daly City, Calif. 94014.

Sisters of the Sorrowful Mother (Third Order of St. Francis), S.S.M.: Founded 1883, in Italy; in US, 1889. General motherhouse, Rome, Italy. US provinces: 6618 N. Teutonia Ave., Milwaukee, Wis. 53209; 9 Pocono Rd., Denville, N.J. 07834; Tulsa Provincialate, 17600 E. 51st St. S., Broken Arrow, Okla. 74012. Educational, hospital work.

Sisters of the Third Franciscan Order Minor Conventuals, O.S.F.: Founded 1860, at Syracuse, N.Y. Generalate offices, 100 Michaels Ave., Syracuse, N.Y. 13208. Educational, hospital work.

Sisters of the Third Order of St. Francis, O.S.F.: Founded 1877, in US, by Bishop John L. Spalding. Motherhouse, Edgewood Hills, E. Peoria, Ill. 61611. Hospital work.

Sisters of the Third Order of St. Francis, O.S.F.: Founded 1861, at Buffalo, N.Y., from Philadelphia foundation. General motherhouse, 400 Mill St., Williamsville, N.Y. 14221. Educational, hospital work.

Sisters of the Third Order of St. Francis (Oldenburg, Ind.), O.S.F.: Founded 1851, in US. General motherhouse, Convent of the Immaculate Conception, Oldenburg, Ind. 47036. Education, social services, pastoral ministry, foreign missions.

Sisters of the Third Order of St. Francis of Assisi, O.S.F.: Founded 1849, in US. General motherhouse, 3221 S. Lake Dr., Milwaukee, Wis. 53207. Education, other ministries.

Sisters of the Third Order of St. Francis of Penance and Charity, O.S.F.: Founded 1869, in US, by Rev. Joseph Bihn. Motherhouse, St. Francis Convent, St. Francis Ave., Tiffin, O. 44883. Education, social services.

Sisters of the Third Order of St. Francis of the Perpetual Adoration, F.S.P.A.: Founded 1849, in US. Generalate, 912 Market St., La Crosse, Wis. 54601. Education, health care.

Sisters of the Third Order Regular of St. Francis of the Congregation of Our Lady of Lourdes, O.S.F.: Founded 1877, in US. General motherhouse, Assisi Heights, Rochester, Minn. 55901. Education, health care, social services.

(End, Listing of Franciscans)

Good Shepherd Sisters (Servants of the Immaculate Heart of Mary), S.C.I.M.: Founded 1850, in Canada; in US, 1882. General motherhouse, Quebec, Canada; Provincial House, Bay View, Saco, Maine 04072. Educational, social work.

Good Shepherd, Sisters of Our Lady of Charity of the, R.G.S.: Founded 1641, in France; in US, 1843. Generalate, Rome, Italy. US provinces: 9517 Leebrook Dr., Cincinnati, O. 45231; 82-31 Don Caster Pl., Jamaica, N.Y. 11432; 9407 Stateside Ct., Silver Spring, Md. 20903; 7654 Natural Bridge Rd., St. Louis, Mo. 63121; 389 N. Oxford St., St. Paul, Minn. 55104.

Graymoor Sisters: See Franciscan Sisters of the Atonement.

Grey Nuns of the Sacred Heart, G.N.S.H.: Founded 1921, in US. General motherhouse, Quarry Rd., Yardley, Pa. 19067.

Guadalupe, Sisters of, O.L.G.: Founded 1946, in Mexico City. General motherhouse, Mexico City, Mexico; US address, St. Mary's College, Winona, Minn. 55987.

Guardian Angels, Sisters of the Holy, S.A.C.: Founded 1839, in France. General motherhouse, Madrid, Spain; US foundation, 1245 S. Van Ness, Los Angeles, Calif. 90019.

Handmaids of Mary Immaculate, A.M.I.: Founded 1952 in Helena, Mont. Address: Ave Maria Institute, Washington, N.J. 07882.

Handmaids of the Precious Blood, Congregation of, H.P.B.: Founded 1947, at Jemez Springs, N.M. Motherhouse and novitiate, Cor Jesu Monastery, Jemez Springs, N.M. 87025.

Helpers, Society of, H.H.S.: Founded 1856, in France; in US, 1892. General motherhouse, Paris, France; American province, 303 Barry Ave., Chicago, Ill. 60657.

Hermanas Catequistas Guadalupanas, H.C.G.: Founded 1923, in Mexico; in US, 1950. General motherhouse, Mexico; US foundation, 4110 S. Flores, San Antonio, Tex. 78214.

Holy Child Jesus, Society of the, S.H.C.J.: Founded 1846, in England; in US, 1862. General motherhouse, Rome, Italy. US province: 620 Edmonds Ave., Drexel Hill, Pa. 19026.

Holy Faith, Congregation of the Sisters of the, C.H.F.: Founded 1856, in Ireland; in US, 1953. General motherhouse, Dublin, Ireland; US regional superior, 13817 S. Pioneer Blvd., Norwalk, Calif. 90650.

Holy Ghost, Sisters of the, C.H.G.: Founded 1913, in US, by Most Rev. J. F. Regis Canevin. General motherhouse, 5246 Clarwin Ave., Ross Township, Pittsburgh, Pa. 15229. Educational, nursing work; care of aged.

Holy Ghost and Mary Immaculate, Sister Servants of, S.H.G.: Founded 1893, in US. Motherhouse, 301 Yucca St., San Antonio, Tex. 78203. Education, hospital work.

Holy Heart of Mary, Servants of the, S.S.C.M.: Founded 1860, in France; in US, 1889. General motherhouse, Montreal, Que., Canada; US province, 145 S. 4th St., Kankakee, Ill. 60901. Educational, hospital, social work.

Holy Names of Jesus and Mary, Sisters of the, S.N.J.M.: Founded 1843, in Canada; in US, 1859. General motherhouse, Pierrefonds H9K 1C6, P.Q., Canada. US addresses: Oregon Province, Marylhurst, Ore. 97036; California Province, P.O. Box 907, Los Gatos, Calif. 95030; New York Province, 1061 New Scotland Rd., Albany, N.Y. 12208; Washington Province, W. 2911 Ft. Wright Dr., Spokane, Wash. 99204.

Holy Spirit, Daughters of the, D.H.S.: Founded 1706, in France; in US, 1902. Generalate, Rennes, France; US motherhouse, 72 Church St., Putnam, Conn. 06260. Educational work, district nursing; pastoral ministry.

Holy Spirit, Mission Sisters of the, M.S.Sp.: Founded 1932, at Cleveland, O. Motherhouse, 1030 N. River Rd., Saginaw, Mich. 48603.

Holy Spirit, Missionary Sisters, Servants of the: Founded 1889, in Holland; in US, 1901. Generalate, Rome, Italy; US motherhouse, Convent of the Holy Spirit, Techny, Ill. 60082.

Holy Spirit, Sisters of the, C.S.Sp.: Founded 1890, in Rome, Italy; in US, 1929. General motherhouse, 10102 Granger Rd., Garfield Hts., Ohio 44125. Educational, social, nursing work.

Holy Spirit of Perpetual Adoration, Sister Servants of the: Founded 1896, in Holland; in US, 1915. General motherhouse, Steyl,

Holland; US motherhouse, 2212 Green St., Philadelphia, Pa. 19130.

Home Mission Sisters of America (Glenmary Sisters): Founded 1952, in US. Motherhouse, Morning Star, P.O. Box 39188, Cincinnati, O. 45239.

Home Visitors of Mary, Sisters, H.V.M.: Founded 1949, in Detroit, Mich. Motherhouse, 356 Arden Park, Detroit, Mich. 48202.

Humility of Mary, Congregation of, C.H.M.: Founded 1854, in France; in US, 1864. US address, Convent of Humility of Mary, Ottumwa, Ia. 52501.

Humility of Mary, Sisters of the, H.M.: Founded 1854, in France; in US, 1864. US address, Villa Maria, Pa. 16155.

Immaculate Conception, Little Servant Sisters of the: Founded 1850, in Poland; in US, 1926. General motherhouse, Poland; US provincial house, 184 Amboy Ave., Woodbridge, N.J. 07095. Education, social services, African missions.

Immaculate Conception, Sisters of the, R.C.M.: Founded 1892, in Spain; in U.S., 1962. General motherhouse, Madrid, Spain; U.S. foundation, 867 Oxford, Clovis, Calif. 93612.

Immaculate Conception, Sisters of the, C.I.C.: Founded 1874, in US. General motherhouse, 4920 Kent St., Metairie, La. 70002.

Immaculate Conception of the Blessed Virgin Mary, Sisters of the (Lithuanian): Founded 1918, at Mariampole, Lithuania; in US, 1936. General motherhouse, Lithuania; US headquarters, Immaculate Conception Convent, Putnam, Conn. 06260.

Immaculate Heart of Mary, Daughters of the, I.H.M.: Founded 1952, in US. Diocesan foundation. General motherhouse, Sunset Gardens, Wintersville, Ohio 43952.

Immaculate Heart of Mary, Missionary Sisters, I.C.M.: Founded 1897, in India; in US, 1919. Generalate, Rome, Italy; US address, 1710 N. Glebe Rd., Arlington, Va. 22207. Educational social, foreign mission work.

Immaculate Heart of Mary, Sisters of the: Founded 1848, in Spain; in US, 1878. General motherhouse, Rome, Italy. US province, 4100 Sabino Canyon Rd., Tucson, Ariz. 85715. Educational work.

Immaculate Heart of Mary, Sisters of the (California Institute of the Most Holy and Immaculate Heart of the B.V.M.), I.H.M.: Founded 1848, in Spain; in US, 1871. Generalate, 3431 Waverly Dr., Los Angeles, Calif. 90027.

Immaculate Heart of Mary, Sisters, Servants of the, I.H.M.: Founded 1845, at Monroe, Mich., by Rev. Louis Florent Gillet. Three independent branches: Central Administration, 610 W. Elm St., Monroe, Mich. 48161; Villa Maria, Immaculata, Pa. 19345; Immaculate Heart of Mary Generalate, Marywood, Scranton, Pa. 18509.

Incarnate Word and Blessed Sacrament,

Congregation of, V.I.: Founded 1625, in France; in US, 1853. Incarnate Word Convent, 4600 Bissonnet St., Bellaire, Tex. 77401.

Incarnate Word and Blessed Sacrament, Congregation of the, of the Archdiocese of San Antonio, I.W.B.S.: Motherhouses: 1101 Northeast Water St., Victoria, Tex. 77901; 2930 S. Alameda, Corpus Christi, Tex. 78404.

Incarnate Word and Blessed Sacrament, Sisters of the, S.I.W.: Founded 1625, in France; in US 1853. Motherhouse, 6618 Pearl Rd., Parma Heights, Cleveland, O. 44130.

Infant Jesus, Congregation of the (Nursing Sisters of the Sick Poor), C.I.J.: Founded 1835, in France; in US, 1905. General motherhouse, 310 Prospect Park W., Brooklyn, N.Y. 11215.

Jeanne d'Arc, Sisters of Ste.: Founded 1914, in America, by Rev. Marie Clement Staub, A.A. General motherhouse, 1681 Chemin St. Louis, Quebec, G1S 1G4, Canada; US novitiate, 2121 Commonwealth Ave., Brighton, Mass. 02135. Spiritual and temporal service of priests.

Jesus, Daughters of (Filles de Jesus), F.J.: Founded 1834, in France; in US, 1904. General motherhouse, Kermaria, Locmine, France; American provincial house, 9040 84th Ave., Edmonton, Alberta T6C 1E4, Canada. Educational, hospital, parish and social work.

Jesus, Daughters of, F.I.: Founded 1871, in Spain; in US, 1950. General motherhouse, Rome, Italy; US address, 375 S. 5th St., Apt. 16, Brooklyn, N.Y. 11211.

Jesus, Little Sisters of: Founded 1939, in Sahara; in US, 1952. General motherhouse, Rome, Italy; US headquarters, 700 Irving St. N.W., Washington, D.C. 20017.

Jesus, Society of the Sisters, Faithful Companions of, F.C.J.: Founded 1820, in France; in US, 1896. General motherhouse, Kent, England. US convents: 46 Woodland St., Fitchburg, Mass. 01420; 20 Atkins St., Providence, R.I. 02908; St. Philomena Convent, Portsmouth, R.I. 02871.

Jesus Crucified, Congregation of: Founded 1930, in France; in US, 1955. General motherhouse, Brou, France; US foundations: Regina Mundi Priory, Devon, Pa. 19333; St. Paul's Priory, 61 Narragansett, Newport, R.I. 02840.

Jesus Crucified and the Sorrowful Mother, Poor Sisters of, C.J.C.: Founded 1924, in US, by Rev. Alphonsus Maria, C.P. Motherhouse, 261 Thatcher St., Brockton, Mass. 02402. Education, nursing homes, catechetical centers.

Jesus-Mary, Religious of, R.J.M.: Founded 1818, at Lyons, France; in US, 1877. General motherhouse, Rome, Italy; US province, 8908 Riggs Rd., Hyattsville, Md. 20783. Educational work.

Jesus, Mary and Joseph, Missionaries of, M.J.M.J.: Founded 1942, in Spain; in US, 1956. General motherhouse, Madrid, Spain; US regional house, 12940 Up River Rd., Corpus Christi, Tex. 78410.

John the Baptist, Sisters of St., C.S.J.B.: Founded 1878, in Italy; in US, 1906. General motherhouse, Rome, Italy; US provincialate, Anderson Hill Rd., Purchase, N.Y. 10577. Education, parish and retreat work; social services.

Joseph, Missionary Servants of St., M.S.S.J.: Founded 1874, in Spain; in US, 1957. General motherhouse, Salamanca, Spain; US address, 203 N. Spring St., Falls Church, Va. 22046.

Joseph, Poor Sisters of St.: Founded 1880, in Argentina. General motherhouse, Muniz, Argentina; US addresses, Casa Belen, 305 E. 4th St., Bethlehem, Pa. 78015; St. Gabriel Convent, 4319 Sano St., Alexandria, Va. 22312.

Joseph, Religious Daughters of St., F.S.J.: Founded 1875, in Spain. General motherhouse, Spain; US foundation, 319 N. Humphreys Ave., Los Angeles, Calif. 90022.

Joseph, Religious Hospitallers of St., R.H.S.J.: Founded 1636, in France; in US, 1894. Generalate, 5621 Canterbury Ave., Montreal, Que., Canada. Hospital work.

Joseph, Sisters of St., C.S.J.: Founded 1650, in France; in US, 1836, at St. Louis. US motherhouses:

637 Cambridge St., Brighton, Mass. 02135; 1515 W. Ogden Ave., La Grange Park, Ill., 60525; 480 S. Batavia St., Orange, Calif. 92668; Mt. St. Joseph Convent, Chestnut Hill, Philadelphia, Pa. 19118.

St. Joseph Convent, Brentwood, N.Y. 11717; 23 Agassiz Circle, Buffalo, N.Y. 14214; Avila Hall, Clement Rd., Rutland, Vt. 05701; 3430 Rocky River Dr., Cleveland, O. 44111; Main St. and Division Rd., Tipton, Ind. 46072; Nazareth, Mich. 49074; 1425 Washington St., Watertown, N.Y. 13601; St. Joseph Motherhouse, Baden, Pa. 15005; 819 W. 8th St., Erie, Pa. 16502.

4095 East Ave., Rochester, N.Y. 14610; 13th and Washington Sts., Concordia, Kans. 66901; Holyoke, Mass. 01040; 1412 E. 2nd St., Superior, Wis. 54880; Pogue Run Rd., Wheeling, W. Va. 26003; 3700 E. Lincoln St., Wichita, Kans. 67218.

Joseph, Sisters of St. (Lyons, France), C.S.J.: Founded 1650, in France; in US, 1906. General motherhouse, Lyons, France; US provincialate, 93 Halifax St., Winslow, Me. 04901. Educational, hospital work.

Joseph, Sisters of St., of Peace, C.S.J.: Founded 1884, in England. Generalate, 1302 18th St. N.W., Suite 703, Washington, D.C. 20036. Educational, hospital, social service work.

Joseph of Carondelet, Sisters of St., C.S.J.: Founded 1650, in France; in US, 1836, at St. Louis, Mo. US headquarters, 2307 S. Lindbergh Blvd., St. Louis, Mo. 63131.

Joseph of Chambery, Sisters of St.: Founded 1650, in France; in US, 1885. Generalate, Rome, Italy; US provincial house, 27 Park Rd., West Hartford, Conn. 06119. Educational, hospital, social work.

Joseph of Cluny, Sisters of St., S.J.C.: Founded 1807, in France. Generalate, Paris, France; US provincial house, Cluny Convent, Brenton Rd., Newport, R.I. 02840.

Joseph of Medaille, Sisters of, C.S.J.: Founded 1823, in France; in US, 1855. Became an American congregation Nov. 30, 1977. Central office, 5108 Reading Rd., Cincinnati, Ohio 45237.

Joseph of St. Augustine, Fla., Sisters of St., S.S.J.: General motherhouse, 241 St. George St., St. Augustine, Fla. 32084. Educational, hospital, pastoral, social work.

Joseph of St. Mark, Sisters of St., S.S.J.S.M.: Founded 1845, in France; in US, 1937. General motherhouse, Alsace-Lorraine, France; US motherhouse, 21800 Chardon Rd., Euclid, Cleveland, O. 44117. Nursing homes.

Joseph the Worker, Sisters of St., S.J.W.: General motherhouse, St. Joseph Convent, 143 S. Main St., Walton, Ky. 41094.

Lamb of God, Sisters of the, A.D.: Founded 1945, in France; in US, 1958. General motherhouse, France; US foundation, 1516 Parrish Ave., Owensboro, Ky. 42301.

Living Word, Sisters of the, S.L.W.: Founded 1975, in US. Motherhouse, The Center, 7200 N. Osceola Ave., Chicago, Ill. 60648. Education, hospital, parish ministry work.

Loretto at the Foot of the Cross, Sisters of, S.L.: Founded 1812 in US, by Rev. Charles Nerinckx. General motherhouse, Nerinx, Ky. 40049. Educational work.

Louis, Congregation of Sisters of St., S.S.L.: Founded 1842, in France; in US, 1949. General motherhouse, Monaghan, Ireland; US novitiate, 22300 Mulholland Dr., Woodland Hills, Calif. 91364. Educational, medical, parish, foreign mission work.

Marian Sisters of the Diocese of Lincoln: Founded 1954. Motherhouse, Marycrest, Waverly, Nebr. 68462.

Marian Society of Dominican Catechists, O.P.: Founded 1954 in Louisiana. General motherhouse, Boyce, La. 71409. Community of Alexandria-Shreveport, La., diocese.

Marianites of Holy Cross, Congregation of the Sisters, M.S.C.: Founded 1841, in France; in US, 1843. Motherhouse, Sarthe, France. Congregatonal administration, 10000 Kentsdale Dr., Potomac, Md. 20854. US provinces: 4123 Woodland Dr., New Orleans, La. 70114; Great Rd. and Drakes Corner, Princeton, N.J. 08540.

Marist Sisters, Congregation of Mary, S.M.: Founded 1824, in France. General motherhouse, Rome, Italy; US convents: St. Albert the Great, Dearborn Hts., Mich.

48125; St. Barnabas, E. Detroit, Mich. 48021; Our Lady of Peace, Wheeling, W. Va. 26002.

Maronite Antonine Sisters: Established in US, 1966. US address, 2961 N. Lipkey Rd., R.D. 2, North Jackson, Ohio 44451.

Martha of Prince Edward Island, Sisters of St., C.S.M.: Founded 1916, in Canada; in US, 1961. General motherhouse, 141 Mt. Edward Rd., Charlottetown, P.E.I., Canada.

Marthe, Sisters of Sainte (of St. Hyacinthe), S.M.S.H.: Founded 1883, in Canada; in US, 1929. General motherhouse 800 est, rue St.-Pierre, Hyacinthe, Que., Canada J2T 1N7.

Mary, Company of, O.D.N.: Founded 1607, in France; in US, 1926. General motherhouse, Rome, Italy; US motherhouse, 16791 E. Main St., Tustin, Calif. 92680.

Mary, Daughters of the Heart of, D.H.M.: Founded 1790, in France; in US, 1851. Generalate, Paris, France; US provincialate, 1339 Northampton St., Holyoke, Mass. 01040. Education retreat work.

Mary, Little Company of, Nursing Sisters, L.C.M.: Founded 1877, in England; in US, 1893. General motherhouse, Rome, Italy; US provincial house, 9350 S. California Ave., Evergreen Park, Ill. 60642.

Mary, Missionary Sisters of the Society of (Marist Sisters), S.M.S.M.: Founded 1845, at St. Brieuc, France; in US, 1922. General motherhouse, Rome, Italy; US regional house, 357 Grove St., Waltham, Mass. 02154. Foreign missions.

Mary, Servants of, O.S.M.: Founded 13th century, in Italy; in US, 1893. Generalate, Rome, Italy; US provincial motherhouse, 7400 Military Ave., Omaha, Nebr. 68134.

Mary, Servants of (Servite Sisters), O.S.M.: Founded 13th century, in Italy; in US, 1912. General motherhouse, Our Lady of Sorrows Convent, Ladysmith, Wis. 54848.

Mary, Sisters of St., of Oregon, S.S.M.O.: Founded 1886, in Oregon, by Bishop William H. Gross, C.Ss.R. General motherhouse, 4440 S.W. 148th Ave., Beaverton, Ore. 97007. Educational, nursing work.

Mary, Sisters Servants of, O.S.M.: Founded 1861, in Italy; in US, 1916. Generalate, Rome, Italy; US motherhouse, 13811 S. Western Ave., Blue Island, Ill. 60406. Educational work.

Mary, Sisters Servants of (Trained Nurses), S. de M.: Founded 1851, at Madrid, Spain; in US, 1914. General motherhouse, Rome, Italy; US motherhouse, 800 N. 18th St., Kansas City, Kans. 66102. Home nursing.

Mary and Joseph, Daughters of, D.M.J.: Founded 1817, in Belgium; in US, 1926. Generalate, Rome, Italy; American novitiate, 6037 W. 78th St., Los Angeles, Calif. 90045.

Mary Help of Christians, Daughters of (Salesian Sisters of St. John Bosco), F.M.A.: Founded 1872, in Italy, by St. John Bosco and St. Mary Dominic Mazzarello; in US, 1908. General motherhouse, Rome, Italy; US motherhouse, Haledon, N.J. 07508. Education, youth work.

Mary Immaculate, Daughters of (Marianist Sisters), F.M.I.: Founded 1816, in France, by Very Rev. William-Joseph Chaminade. General motherhouse, Rome, Italy; US foundation, 251 W. Ligustrum Dr., San Antonio, Tex. 78228. Educational work.

Mary Immaculate, Religious of, R.M.I.: Founded 1876, in Spain; in US, 1954. General motherhouse, Rome, Italy: US foundations, 719 Augusta St., San Antonio, Tex. 78215; 251 W. 14th St., New York, N.Y. 10011.

Mary Immaculate, Sisters Servants of, S.M.I: Founded 1892, in Ukraine; in US, 1935. General motherhouse, Rome, Italy; US province, 209 W. Chestnut Hill Ave., Philadelphia, Pa. 19118. Educational, hospital work.

Mary Immaculate of Mariowka, Sister Servants of, S.S.M.I.: Founded 1878 in Poland. General motherhouse, Poland; American provincialate, 1220 Tugwell Dr., Catonsville, Md. 21228.

Mary of Namur, Sisters of St., S.S.M.N.: Founded 1819, at Namur, Belgium; in US, 1863. General motherhouse, Namur, Belgium. US provinces: 3756 Delaware Ave., Kenmore, N.Y. 14217; 3300 Hemphill St., Ft. Worth, Tex. 76110.

Mary of Providence, Daughters of St., D.S.M.P.: Founded 1872, at Como, Italy; in US, 1913. General motherhouse, Rome, Italy; US provincial house, 4200 N. Austin Ave., Chicago, Ill. 60634. Special education for mentally handicapped.

Mary of the Immaculate Conception, Daughters of, D.M.: Founded 1904, in US, by Msgr. Lucian Bojnowski. General motherhouse, 314 Osgood Ave., New Britain, Conn. 06053. Educational, hospital work.

Mary Reparatrix, Society of, S.M.R.: Founded 1857, in France; in US, 1908. Generalate, Rome, Italy. US addresses: 14 E. 29th St., New York, N.Y. 10016; 3350 Ruther Ave., Cincinnati, O. 45220; 13600 Virgil Ave., Detroit, Mich. 48223.

Medical Mission Sisters (Society of Catholic Medical Missionaries, Inc.), S.C.M.M.: Founded 1925, in US, by Mother Anna Dengel. Generalate, Rome, Italy; US headquarters, 8400 Pine Rd., Philadelphia, Pa. 19111. Medical work, health education, especially in mission areas.

Medical Missionaries of Mary, M.M.M.: Founded 1937, in Ireland, by Mother Mary Martin; in US, 1950. General motherhouse, Drogheda, Ireland; US headquarters, 563 Minneford Ave., City Island, Bronx, N.Y. 10464. Medical aid in missions.

Mercedarian Missionaries of Berriz, M.M.B.: Founded 1930, in Spain; in US, 1946. General motherhouse, Berriz, Spain; US headquarters, 918 E. 9th St., Kansas City, Mo. 64106.

Mercy, Daughters of Our Lady of, D.M.: Founded 1837, in Italy, by St. Mary Joseph Rossello; in US, 1919. General motherhouse, Savona, Italy; US motherhouse, Villa Rossello, Catawba Ave., Newfield, N.J. 08344. Educational, hospital work.

Mercy, Missionary Sisters of Our Lady of, M.O.M.: Founded 1938, in Brazil; in US, 1955. General motherhouse, Brazil; US address, 388 Franklin St., Buffalo, N.Y. 14202.

Mercy, Sisters of, R.S.M.: Founded 1831, in Ireland, by Mother Mary Catherine McAuley. US motherhouses:

634 New Scotland Ave., Albany, N.Y. 12208; 273 Willoughby Ave., Brooklyn, N.Y. 11205; S. 5245 Murphy Rd., Orchard Park, N.Y. 14127; 100 Mansfield Ave., Burlington, Vt. 05401; 1125 Prairie Dr., N.E., Cedar Rapids, Ia. 52402; 444 E. Grandview Blvd., Erie, Pa. 16504; 249 Steele Rd., W. Hartford, Conn. 06117.

Windham, N.H. 03087; Merion, Pa. 10966; 3333 Fifth Ave., Pittsburgh, Pa. 15213; 605 Stevens Ave., Portland, Me. 04103; Belmont, N. Car. 28012; 1437 Blossom Rd., Rochester, N.Y. 14610; 535 Sacramento St., Auburn, Calif. 95603.

2300 Adeline Dr., Burlingame, Calif. 94010; US Route 22 at Tirrell Rd., Plainfield, N.J. 07061; 101 Barry Rd., Worcester, Mass. 01609.

Mercy, Sisters of, of the Union in the United States of America, R.S.M.: Founded 1831 in Ireland, by Mother M. Catherine McAuley; union formed in 1929. U.S. provinces:

P.O. Box 10490, Baltimore, Md. 21209; 10024 S. Central Park Ave., Chicago, Ill. 60642; 2301 Grandview Ave., Cincinnati, Ohio 45206; 29000 Eleven Mile Rd., Farmington Hills, Mich. 48024; 541 Broadway, Dobbs Ferry, N.Y. 10522; 1801 S. 72nd St., Omaha, Nebr. 68124; R.D. 3, Cumberland, R.I. 02864; 2039 N. Geyer Rd., St. Louis, Mo. 63131; Dallas, Pa. 18612.

Mercy, Sisters of, Daughters of Christian Charity of St. Vincent de Paul, S.M.D.C.: Founded 1842, in Hungary; US foundation, Rt. 1, Box 353, Hewitt, N.J. 07421.

Mercy of the Blessed Sacrament, Sisters of: Founded 1910 in Mexico. U.S. foundation, 555 E. Mountain View, Barstow, Calif. 92311.

Mill Hill Sisters; See Franciscan Missionaries of St. Joseph.

Minim Sisters of Mary Immaculate, C.F.M.M.: Founded 1886, in Mexico; in U.S. 1926. General motherhouse, Leon, Guanajuato, Mexico; US address, St. Joseph Hospital Convent, Target Range Rd., Nogales, Ariz. 85621.

Misericordia Sisters, S.M.: Founded 1848, in Canada; in US, 1887. General motherhouse. 12435 Ave. Misericorde, Montreal H4J 2G3, Canada. Social work with unwed mothers and their children; hospital work.

Mission Helpers of the Sacred Heart, M.H.S.H.: Founded 1890, in US. General motherhouse, 1001 W. Joppa Rd., Baltimore, Md. 21204. Religious education, evangelization.

Missionary Catechists of the Sacred Hearts of Jesus and Mary (Violetas), M.C.: Founded 1918, in Mexico; in US, 1943. Motherhouse, Tlalpan, Mexico; US address, 209 W. Murray St., Victoria, Tex. 77901.

Missionary Sisters of the Catholic Apostolate (Pallottine Missionary Sisters), S.A.C.: Founded in Rome, 1843; in US, 1912. Generalate, Rome, Italy; US provincialate, Rt. 2, 15270 Old Halls Ferry Rd., Florissant, Mo. 63034.

Mother of God, Missionary Sisters of the, M.S.M.G.: Byzantine, Ukrainian Rite, Stamford. Motherhouse, 711-719 N. Franklin St., Philadelphia, Pa. 19123.

Mother of God, Sisters Poor Servants of the, S.M.G.: Founded 1869, at London, England; in US, 1947. General motherhouse, Maryfield, Roehampton, London. US addresses: Maryfield Nursing Home, Greensboro Rd., High Point, N.C. 27260; St. Mary's Hospital, 916 Virginia Ave., Norton, Va. 24273; Holy Spirit School, 1800 Geary St., Philadelphia, Pa. 19145. Hospital, educational work.

Nazareth, Poor Sisters of: Founded in England; U.S. foundation, 1924. General motherhouse, Hammersmith, London, England; US novitiate, 3333 Manning Ave., Los Angeles, Calif. 90064. Social services, education.

Notre Dame, School Sisters of, S.S.N.D.: Founded 1833, in Germany; in US, 1847. General motherhouse, Rome, Italy. US provinces: 700 W. Highland Rd., Mequon, Wis. 53092; 6401 N. Charles St., Baltimore, Md. 21212; 320 E. Ripa Ave., St. Louis, Mo. 63125; Good Counsel Hill, Mankato, Minn. 56001; 345 Belden Hill Rd., Wilton, Conn. 06897; Rt. 2, Box 4, Irving, Tex. 75062; 9515 S. Loomis St., Chicago, Ill. 60643.

Notre Dame, Sisters of, S.N.D.: Founded 1850, at Coesfeld, Germany; in US, 1874. General motherhouse, Rome, Italy. US provinces: 13000 Auburn Rd., Chardon, O. 44024; 1601 Dixie Highway, Covington, Ky. 41011; 3837 Secor Rd., Toledo, O. 43623; 1776 Hendrix Ave., Thousand Oaks, Calif. 91360.

Notre Dame, Sisters of the Congregation of, C.N.D.: Founded 1653, in Canada; in US, 1860. General motherhouse, Montreal, Que., Canada; U.S. province, 223 West Mountain Rd., Ridgefield, Conn. 06877. Education.

Notre Dame de Namur, Sisters of, S.N.D.: Founded 1803, in France; in US, 1840. General motherhouse, Rome, Italy. US provinces: 328 Dartmouth St., Boston, Mass. 02116; Jeffrey's Neck Rd., Ipswich, Mass. 01938; 1561 N. Benson Rd., Fairfield, Conn. 06431; Landing Rd., Ilchester, Md. 21083; 701 E. Columbia Ave., Cincinnati, O. 45215; 14800 Bohlman Rd., Saratoga, Calif. 95070. Educational work.

Notre Dame de Sion, Congregation of, N.D.S.: Founded 1843, in France; in US, 1892. Generalate, Rome, Italy; US provincial house, 3823 Locust St., Kansas City, Mo. 64109. Creation of better understanding and relations between Christians and Jews.

Notre Dame des Anges, Missionary Sisters of, M.N.D.A.: Founded 1922, in Canada; in US, 1949. General motherhouse, Lennoxville, Canada; US address, St. Mary's Catechetical School, 320 N. Main St., Union City, Conn. 06770.

Notre Dame Sisters: Founded 1853, in Czechoslovakia; in US, 1910. General motherhouse, Javornik, Czechoslovakia; US motherhouse, 3501 State St., Omaha, Nebr. 68112. Educational work.

Our Lady of Mercy, Sisters of: General motherhouse, Wexford, Ireland; US foundation, St. Peter's Convent, 445 W. New York Ave., Deland, Fla. 32720.

Our Lady of Sorrows, Sisters of, O.L.S.: Founded 1839, in Italy; in US, 1947. General motherhouse, Rome, Italy; US headquarters, 10450 Ellerbe Rd., Shreveport, La. 71106.

Our Lady of the Garden, Sisters of, O.L.G.: Founded 1829, in Italy, by St. Anthony Mary Gianelli. Motherhouse, Rome, Italy; U.S. address, St. Brendan School, 445½ Whalley Ave., New Haven, Conn. 06511.

Pallottine Sisters of the Catholic Apostolate, C.S.A.C.: Founded 1843, at Rome, Italy; in US, 1889. General motherhouse, Rome; US motherhouse, St. Patrick's Villa, Harriman Heights, Harriman, N.Y. 10926. Educational work.

Parish Visitors of Mary Immaculate, P.V.M.I.: Founded 1920, in New York. General motherhouse, Box 658, Monroe, N.Y. 10950. Mission work.

Passionist Sisters: See Cross and Passion, Sisters of the.

Paul, Angelic Sisters of St.: Founded 1535, in Milan, Italy; US address, Fatima Shrine, Swan Rd., Youngstown, N.Y. 14174.

Paul, Daughters of St., Missionary Sisters of the Catholic Editions, D.S.P.: Founded 1915, at Alba, Piedmont, Italy; in US, 1932. General motherhouse, Rome, Italy; US provincial house, 50 St. Paul's Ave., Jamaica Plain, Mass. 02130. Apostolate of the communications arts.

Paul of Chartres, Sisters of St., S.P.C.: Founded 1696, in France. General house, Rome, Italy; US address, County Road 492, Marquette, Mich. 49855.

Peter Claver, Missionary Sisters of St., S.S.P.C.: Founded 1894; in US, 1914. General motherhouse, Rome, Italy; US address, 667 Woods Mill Rd. S., Chesterfield, Mo. 63017.

Pious Schools, Sisters of, Sch. P.: Founded 1829 in Spain; in US, 1954. General motherhouse, Rome, Italy; US headquarters, 9925 Mason Ave., Chatsworth, Calif. 91311.

Poor, Little Sisters of the, L.S.P.: Founded 1839, in France; in US, 1868. General motherhouse, St. Pern, France. US provinces: 110-30 221st St., Queens Village, N.Y. 11429; 601 Maiden Choice Lane, Baltimore, Md. 21228; 80 W. Northwest Hwy., Palatine, Ill. 60067. Care of aged.

Poor Clare Missionary Sisters (Misioneras Clarisas), M.C.: Founded Mexico. General motherhouse, Rome, Italy; US novitiate, 1019 N. Newhope, Santa Ana, Calif. 92703.

Poor Clare Nuns: See Franciscan Poor Clare Nuns.

Poor Clares (Sisters of St. Clare), P.C.: General motherhouse, Dublin, Ireland; US foundation, 1120 Cuyamaca Ave., Chula Vista, Calif. 92011.

Poor Handmaids of Jesus Christ (Ancilla Domini Sisters), P.H.J.C.: Founded 1851, in Germany; in US, 1868. General motherhouse, Dernbach, Westerwald, Germany; US motherhouse, Donaldson, Ind. 46513. Educational, hospital work, social services.

Precious Blood, Daughters of Charity of the Most: Founded 1872, at Pagani, Italy; in US, 1908. General motherhouse, Rome, Italy; US convent, 1482 North Ave., Bridgeport, Conn. 06604.

Precious Blood, Missionary Sisters of the, C.P.S.: Founded 1885, at Mariannhill, South Africa; in US, 1925. Generalate, Rome, Italy: US novitiate, New Holland Ave., P.O. Box 97, Shillington, Pa. 19607. Home and foreign mission work.

Precious Blood, Sisters Adorers of the, A.P.B.: Founded 1861, in Canada; in US, 1890. General motherhouses: 2520, rue Girouard, St. Hyacinthe, Que. J2S 7B8, Canada (French); 301 Ramsay Rd., London, Ont. N6G 1N7, Canada (English). Contemplatives.

Precious Blood, Sisters of the, C.Pp.S.: Founded 1834, in Switzerland; in US, 1844. Generalate, 4000 Denlinger Rd., Dayton, Ohio 45426. Education, health care, other ministries.

Precious Blood, Sisters of the Most, C.Pp.S.: Founded 1845, in Steinerberg, Switzerland; in US, 1870. General motherhouse, 204 N. Main St., O'Fallon, Mo. 63366. Education, other ministries.

Presentation, Sisters of St. Mary of the, S.M.P.: Founded 1829, in France; in US, 1903. General motherhouse, Broons, Cotesdu-Nord, France. US address, Maryvale Novitiate, Valley City, N. Dak. 58072. Educational, hospital work.

Presentation of Mary, Sisters of the, P.M.: Founded 1796, in France; in US, 1873. General motherhouse, Castel Gandolfo, Italy. US provincial houses: 495 Mammoth Rd., Manchester, N.H. 03104; 209 Lawrence St., Methuen, Mass. 01844.

Presentation of the B.V.M., Sisters of the, P.B.V.M.: Founded 1775, in Ireland; in US, 1854, in San Francisco. US motherhouses: 2360 Carter Rd., Dubuque, Ia. 52001; R.D. 2,

Box 101, Newburgh, N.Y. 12550; 8931 Callaghan Rd., San Antonio, Tex. 78230; 2340 Turk Blvd., San Francisco, Calif. 94118; Watervliet, N.Y. 12189.

Route 1, Fargo, N. Dak. 58103; 250 S. Davis Dr., P.O. Box 1113, Warner Robbins, Ga. 31093; 1500 N. Main, Aberdeen, S. Dak. 57401; 1300 E. Cedar, Globe, Ariz. 85501; 1555 E. Dana, Mesa, Ariz. 85201; 366 South St., Fitchburg, Mass. 01420; 419 Woodrow Rd., Annadale, Staten Island, N.Y. 10312.

Providence, Daughters of Divine, F.D.P.: Founded 1832, Italy; in US, 1964. General motherhouse, Rome, Italy; US address, 1625 Missouri St., Chalmette, La. 70043.

Providence, Missionary Catechists of Divine, M.C.D.P.: Founded 1930, as a filial society; adjunct branch of Sisters of Divine Providence (San Antonio). Motherhouse, 2318 Castroville Rd., San Antonio, Tex. 78237.

Providence, Oblate Sisters of, O.S.P.: Founded 1829, in US. General motherhouse, 701 Gun Rd., Baltimore, Md. 21227. Educational work.

Providence, Sisters of, S.P.: Founded 1861, in Canada; in US, 1873. General motherhouse, Our Lady of Victory Convent, Brightside, Holyoke, Mass. 01040.

Providence, Sisters of, S.P.: Founded 1843, in Canada; in US, 1854. General motherhouse, Montreal, Canada. US provinces: 1511 Third Ave., Seattle, Wash. 98101; 9 E. 9th Ave., Spokane, Wash. 99202.

Providence, Sisters of (of St. Mary-of-the-Woods), S.P.: Founded 1806, in France; in US, 1840. Generalate, St. Mary-of-the-Woods, Ind. 47876.

Providence, Sisters of Divine, C.D.P.: Founded 1762, in France; in US, 1866. Generalate, Box 197, Helotes, Tex. 78023. Educational, hospital work.

Providence, Sisters of Divine, C.D.P.: Founded 1851, in Germany; in US, 1876. Generalate, Rome, Italy. US provinces: 9000 Babcock Blvd., Allison Park, Pa. 15101; 8351 Florissant Rd., Normandy, Mo. 63121; Box 2, Rte. 80, Kingston, Mass. 02364. Educational, hospital work.

Providence, Sisters of Divine (of Kentucky), C.D.P.: Founded 1762, in France; in US, 1889. General motherhouse, Moselle, France; US province, Melbourne, Ky. 41059. Education, social services, other ministries.

Redeemer, Oblates of the Most Holy, O.SS.R.: Founded 1864, in Spain. General motherhouse, Spain; US foundation, 60-80 Pond St., Jamaica Plain, Mass. 02130.

Redeemer, Order of the Most Holy, O.SS.R.: Founded 1731, by St. Alphonsus Liguori; in US, 1957. US addresses: Mother of Perpetual Help Monastery, Esopus, N.Y. 12429; St. Alphonsus Monastery, Liguori, Mo. 63057.

Redeemer, Sisters of the Divine, S.D.R.:

Founded 1849, in Niederbronn, France; in US, 1912. General motherhouse, Rome, Italy; US motherhouse, 999 Rock Run Road, Elizabeth, Pa. 15037. Educational, hospital work; care of the aged.

Redeemer, Sisters of the Holy, S.H.R.: Founded 1849, in Alsace; in US, 1924. General motherhouse, Wuerzburg, Germany; US provincial house, Huntingdon Valley, Pa. 19006. Personalized medical care in hospitals, homes for aged, private homes; retreat work.

Refuge, Sisters of Our Lady of Charity of the, O.L.C.: Founded 1641, in Caen, France, by St. John Eudes; in U.S., 1855. Autonomous houses were federated in 1944 and in May, 1978, the North American Union of the Sisters of Our Lady of Charity was established. General motherhouse and administrative center, Box 327, Wisconsin Dells, Wis. 53965. Primarily devoted to re-education and rehabilitation of women and girls in residential and non-residental settings.

Reparation of the Congregation of Mary, Sisters of, S.R.C.M.: Founded 1903, in US. Motherhouse, St. Zita's Villa, Monsey, N.Y. 10952.

Resurrection, Sisters of the, C.R.: Founded 1891, in Italy; in US, 1900. General motherhouse, Rome, Italy. US provinces: 7432 Talcott Ave., Chicago, Ill. 60631; Mt. St. Joseph, Castleton-on-Hudson, N.Y. 12033. Education, nursing.

Rita, Sisters of St., O.S.A.: General motherhouse, Wurzburg, Germany. US foundation, St. Monica's Convent, 3920 Green Bay Rd., Racine, Wis. 53404.

Rosary, Congregation of Our Lady of the Holy, R.S.R.: Founded 1874, in Canada; in US, 1899. General motherhouse, C.P. 2020, Rimouski, Que., Canada. US regional house, 20 Thomas St., Portland, Me. 04102. Educational work.

Rosary, Missionary Sisters of Our Lady of the Holy, H.R.S.: Founded 1924, in Ireland; in US, 1954. Motherhouse, Dublin, Ireland. US novitiate, 214 Ashwood Rd., Villanova, Pa. 19085. African missions.

Sacrament, Missionary Sisters of the Most Blessed, M.SS.S.: General motherhouse, Madrid, Spain; US foundation: 1111 Wordin Ave., Bridgeport, Conn. 06605.

Sacrament, Nuns of the Perpetual Adoration of the Blessed, A.P.: Founded 1807, in Rome, Italy; in US, 1925. US monasteries: 145 N. Cotton Ave., El Paso, Tex. 79901; 771 Ashbury St., San Francisco, Calif. 94117.

Sacrament, Oblate Sisters of the Blessed, O.S.B.S.: Founded 1935, in US; motherhouse, St. Sylvester Convent, Marty, S.D. 57361. Care of American Indians.

Sacrament, Religious Mercedarians of the Blessed, R.M.S.S.: Founded 1910, in Mexico; in US, 1926. General motherhouse, Mexico City, Mexico; US convent, 222 W. Cevallos St., San Antonio, Tex. 78204.

Sacrament, Servants of the Blessed, S.S.S.: Founded 1858, in France, by St. Pierre Julien Eymard; in US, 1947. General motherhouse, Rome, Italy; American vice-provincial house, 101 Silver St., Waterville, Me. 04901. Contemplative.

Sacrament, Sisters of the Blessed, for Indians and Colored People, S.B.S.: Founded 1891, in US. General motherhouse, Bensalem, Pa. 19020.

Sacrament, Sisters of the Most Holy, M.H.S.: Founded 1851, in France; in US, 1872. General motherhouse, 409 W. St. Mary Blvd. (P.O. Box 2429), Lafayette, La. 70502.

Sacrament, Sisters Servants of the Blessed, S.S.B.S.: Founded 1904, in Mexico. General motherhouse, Guadalajara, Mexico. US address, Our Lady of Guadalupe School, 536 Rockwood Ave., Calexico, Calif. 92231.

Sacramentine Nuns (Religious of the Order of the Blessed Sacrament and Our Lady), O.S.S.: Founded 1639, in France; in US, 1912. US monasteries: 23 Park Ave., Yonkers, N.Y. 10703; US 31, Conway, Mich. 49722. Perpetual adoration of the Holy Eucharist.

Sacred Heart, Daughters of Our Lady of the: Founded 1882, in France; in US, 1955. General motherhouse, Rome, Italy; US address, 424 E. Browning Rd., Bellmawr, N.J. 08031. Educational work.

Sacred Heart, Missionary Sisters of the (Cabrini Sisters), M.S.C.: Founded 1880, in Italy, by St. Frances Xavier Cabrini; in US, 1889. General motherhouse, Rome, Italy; US provinces: 223 E. 19th St., New York, N.Y. 10003 (Eastern); 467 W. Deming Pl., Chicago, Ill. 60614 (Western). Educational, health, social and catechetical work.

Sacred Heart, Religious of the Apostolate of the, R.A.: General motherhouse, Madrid, Spain; US address, 1120 6th St., Miami Beach, Fla., 33139.

Sacred Heart, Society Devoted to the, S.D.S.H.: Founded 1940, in Hungary; in US, 1956. US motherhouse, 2121 W. Olive Dr., Burbank, Calif. 91506. Educational work.

Sacred Heart, Society of the, R.S.C.J.: Founded 1800, in France; in US, 1818. General motherhouse, Rome, Italy. US provinces: 1177 King St., Greenwich, Conn. 06830; 2047 W. Fargo, Chicago, Ill. 60645; 541 S. Mason Rd., St. Louis, Mo. 63141; 453 Miller Ave., S. San Francisco, Calif. 94080; 842 Commonwealth Ave., Newton, Mass. 02159. Educational work.

Sacred Heart of Jesus, Apostles of, A.S.C.J.: Founded 1894, in Italy; in US, 1902. General motherhouse, Rome, Italy; US motherhouse, 265 Benham St., Hamden, Conn. 06514. Educational, social work.

Sacred Heart of Jesus, Handmaids of the, A.C.J.: Founded 1877, in Spain. General motherhouse, Rome, Italy; US province, 616 Coopertown Rd., Haverford, Pa. 19041. Educational, retreat work.

Sacred Heart of Jesus, Missionary Sisters of the Most (Hiltrup), M.S.C.: Founded 1899, in Germany; in US, 1908. General motherhouse, Rome, Italy; US province, Hyde Park, Reading, Pa. 19605. Education, health care, pastoral ministry.

Sacred Heart of Jesus, Oblate Sisters of the, O.S.H.J.: Founded 1894; in US, 1949. General motherhouse, Rome, Italy; US headquarters, 50 Warner Rd., Hubbard, Ohio 44425. Educational, social work.

Sacred Heart of Jesus, Servants of the Most: Founded 1894, in Poland; in US, 1959. General motherhouse, Cracow, Poland; US address, 231 Arch St., Cresson, Pa. 16630. Education, health care, social services.

Sacred Heart of Jesus, Sisters of the, S.S.C.J.: Founded 1816, in France; in US, 1903. General motherhouse, St. Jacut, Brittany, France; US provincial house, 5922 Blanco Rd., San Antonio, Tex. 78216. Educational, hospital, domestic work.

Sacred Heart of Jesus and of the Poor, Servants of the (Mexican), S.S.H.J.P.: Founded 1885, in Mexico; in US, 1907. General motherhouse, Apartado 92, Puebla, Pue., Mexico; US regional house, 237 Tobin Pl., El Paso, Tex. 79905.

Sacred Heart of Jesus for Reparation, Congregation of the Handmaids of the: Founded 1918, in Italy; in US, 1958. US address, Sunshine Park, R.D. 3, Steubenville, Ohio 43952.

Sacred Heart of Mary, Religious of the, R.S.H.M.: Founded 1848, in France; in US, 1877. Generalate, Rome, Italy. US provinces; 50 Wilson Park Dr., Tarrytown, N.Y. 10591; 8008 Loyola Blvd., Los Angeles, Calif. 90045.

Sacred Hearts, Religious of the Holy Union of the, S.U.S.C.: Founded 1826, in France; in US, 1886. Generalate, Rome, Italy. US provinces: 550 Rock St., Fall River, Mass. 02720; Main St., Groton, Mass. 01450. Varied ministries.

Sacred Hearts and of Perpetual Adoration, Sisters of the, SS.CC.: Founded 1797, in France; in US, 1908. General motherhouse, Rome, Italy; US motherhouse, 491 Hood St., Fall River, Mass. 02720. Varied ministries.

Sacred Hearts of Jesus and Mary, Sisters of the, S.H.J.M.: Established 1953, in US. General motherhouse, Essex, England; US address, 310 San Carlos Ave., El Cerrito, Calif. 94530.

Savior, Company of the, C.S.: Founded 1952, in Spain; in US, 1962. General motherhouse, Madrid, Spain; US foundation, 820 Clinton Ave., Bridgeport, Conn. 06608.

Savior, Sisters of the Divine, S.D.S.: Founded 1888, in Italy; in US, 1895. General motherhouse, Rome, Italy; US motherhouse, 4311 N. 100th St., Milwaukee, Wis. 53222. Educational, hospital work.

Social Service, Sisters of, S.S.S.: Founded 1908, in Hungary; in US, 1926. General motherhouse, 1120 Westchester Pl., Los Angeles, Calif. 90019.

Social Service, Sisters of, S.S.S.: Founded in Hungary, 1923. US address, 440 Linwood Ave., Buffalo, N.Y. 14209. Social work.

Teresa of Jesus, Society of St., S.T.J.: Founded 1876, in Spain; in US, 1910. General motherhouse, Rome, Italy; US provincial house, 154 Fair Ave., San Antonio, Tex. 78223.

Thomas of Villanova, Congregation of Sisters of St., S.S.T.V.: Founded 1661, in France; in US, 1948. General motherhouse, Neuilly-sur-Seine, France; US foundation W. Rocks Rd., Norwalk, Conn. 06851.

Trinity, Missionary Servants of the Most Blessed, M.S.B.T.: Founded 1912, in US, by Very Rev. Thomas A. Judge. General motherhouse, 3501 Solly St., Philadelphia, Pa. 19136. Educational, social work; health services.

Trinity, Sisters of the Most Holy, O.Ss.T.: Founded 1198, in Rome; in US, 1920. General motherhouse, Rome, Italy; US address, Immaculate Conception Province, 21320 Euclid Ave., Euclid, Ohio 44117. Educational work.

Ursula of the Blessed Virgin, Society of the Sisters of St., S.U.: Founded 1606, in France; in US, 1902. General motherhouse, Tours, France; US novitiate, Rhinebeck, N.Y. 12572. Educational work.

Ursuline Nuns (Roman Union), O.S.U.: Founded 1535, in Italy; in US, 1727. Generalate, Rome, Italy. US provinces: 323 E. 198th St., Bronx, N.Y. 10458; Crystal Heights Rd., Crystal City, Mo. 63019; 639 Angela Dr., Santa Rosa, Calif. 95401; 71 Lowder St., Dedham, Mass. 02026,

Ursuline Nuns of the Congregation of Paris, O.S.U.: Founded 1535, in Italy; in US, 1727, in New Orleans. US motherhouses: St. Martin, O. 45170; East and Miami Sts., Paola, Kans. 66071; 3115 Lexington Rd., Louisville, Ky. 40206; 2600 Lander Rd., Cleveland, O. 44124; Maple Mount, Ky. 42356; 2413 Collingwood Blvd., Toledo, O. 43620; 4250 Shields Rd., Canfield, O. 44406; 1339 E. McMillan St., Cincinnati, O. 45206.

Ursuline Nuns of the Congregation of Tildonk, Belgium, R.U.: Founded 1535, in Italy; in US, 1924. Generalate, Tildonk, Belgium; US address, 81-15 Utopia Parkway, Jamaica, N.Y. 11432. Educational, foreign mission work.

Ursuline Sisters (Irish Ursuline Union), O.S.U.: General motherhouse, Blackrock, Cork, Ireland; US address, 1973 Torch Hill Rd., Columbus, Ga. 31903.

Ursuline Sisters of Mount Calvary, O.S.U.: Founded 1535, in Italy; in US, 1910. General motherhouse, Mount Calvary, Germany; US motherhouse, 1026 N. Douglas Ave., Belleville, Ill. 62221. Educational work.

Venerini Sisters, Religious, M.P.V.: Founded 1685, in Italy; in US, 1909. General motherhouse, Rome, Italy; US provincialate; 23 Edward St., Worcester, Mass. 01605.

Verona, Missionary Sisters of (Comboni Sisters), M.S.V.: Founded 1875, in Italy; in US, 1950. US address, 1307 Lakeside Ave., Richmond, Va. 23228. Hospital, social, educational work.

Victory Missionary Sisters, Our Lady of, O.L.V.M.: Founded 1922, in US. Motherhouse, Victory Noll, Box 109, Huntington, Ind. 46750. Educational, social work.

Vincent de Paul, Sisters: See Charity of St. Vincent de Paul, Sisters of.

Visitation Nuns, V.H.M.: Founded 1610, in France; in U.S. (Georgetown, D.C.), 1799. Contemplative, educational work. Two federations in U.S.

First Federation of North America. Major pontifical enclosure. Pres., Mother Mary Gabriella Muth, Monastery of the Visitation, 9001 Old Georgetown Rd., Bethesda, Md. 20014. Addresses of monasteries belonging to the federation: 2300 Springhill Ave., Mobile, Ala. 36607; 9001 Old Georgetown Rd., Bethesda, Md. 20014; 2002 Bancroft Pkwy., Wilmington, Del. 19806; 2209 E. Grace St., Richmond, Va. 23223; 5820 City Ave., Philadelphia, Pa. 19131; 1745 Parkside Blvd., Toledo, O. 43607; 2055 Ridgedale Dr., Snellville, Ga. 30278.

Second Federation of North America. Constitutional enclosure. Pres., Rev. Mother Anne Madeline Ernstmann, Visitation Monastery, 3200 S.W. Dash Point Rd., Federal Way, Wash. 98003. Addresses of monasteries belonging to the federation: 1500 35th St., Washington, D.C. 20007; 3020 N. Ballas Rd., St. Louis, Mo. 63131; 200 E. Second St., Frederick, Md. 21701; Mt. St. Chantal Monastery of the Visitation, Wheeling, W.

Va. 26003; Ridge Blvd. and 89th St., Brooklyn, N.Y. 11209; 1600 Murdock Ave., Parkersburg, W. Va. 26101; 2000 Sixteenth Ave., Rock Island, Ill. 61201; 2475 Dodd Rd., Mendota Heights, St. Paul, Minn. 55120; Visitation Monastery, Georgetown, Ky. 40324; 3200 S.W. Dash Point Rd., Federal Way, Wash. 98003.

Visitation of the Congregation of the Immaculate Heart of Mary, Sisters of the, S.V.M.: Founded 1952, in US. Motherhouse, 900 Alta Vista St., Dubuque, Ia. 52001. Educational work, parish ministry.

Vocationist Sisters (Sisters of the Divine Vocations): Founded 1921, in Italy. General motherhouse, Naples, Italy; US foundation, Perpetual Help Nursery, 172 Broad St., Newark, N.J. 07104.

White Sisters: See Africa, Missionary Sisters of Our Lady of.

Wisdom, Daughters of, D.W.: Founded 1703, in France, by St. Louis Marie Grignon de Montfort; in US, 1904. General motherhouse, Vendee, France; US province, 206 S. Ocean Ave., Islip, N.Y. Education, health care, parish ministry, social services.

Xaverian Missionary Society of Mary, Inc., x.m.m.: Founded 1945, in Italy; in US, 1954. General motherhouse, Parma, Italy; US address, 242 Salisbury St., Worcester, Mass. 01609.

Xavier Mission Sisters (Catholic Mission Sisters of St. Francis Xavier), X.M.S.: Founded 1946, at Warren, Mich., by Cardinal Edward Mooney. General motherhouse, 37179 Moravian Dr., Mount Clemens, Mich. 48043. Educational, hospital, social work in missions.

ORGANIZATIONS OF WOMEN RELIGIOUS

Association of Contemplative Sisters: Founded by nearly 140 representatives of 57 communities in the U.S. and Canada in August, 1969. Its principal purpose is development of the contemplative life-style for effective service to the Church. It has a membership of approximately 700. Sister Lilla Marie Hull, M.M., is president. The central office is located at 920 Centre St., Jamaica Plain, Mass. 02130.

Consortium Perfectae Caritatis: Named Association of Perfect Love after the Latin title of the Second Vatican Council's *Decree on the Appropriate Renewal of Religious Life,* and organized in March, 1971, at a meeting of nearly 150 sisters from 48 communities in the U.S. and Canada. Its purposes are to encourage the development of religious life in line with Vatican II guidelines and related directives, and to share experiences in the renewal of religious life. Sister Mary Elise, S.N.D., is executive director. The association is administered by a group of 14 superiors from 12 states and Canada. The mailing address is

13000 Auburn Rd., Chardon, Ohio 44024. Rev. James A. Viall is coordinator.

Las Hermanas: A national organization of women religious of Hispanic origin formed in 1971 for the purpose of being "actively present to the ever-changing needs" of the Spanish-speaking — through programs of cultural awareness and training for persons in ministry to the Spanish-speaking. The organization, with sister associates and lay affiliates, is directed by a national coordinating team. National coordinators: Sister Margarita Casteneda, Ms. Olga Villa, and Sister Sylvia Sedillo, P.O. Box 4274, Denver, Colo. 80204.

Leadership Conference of Women Religious: An association of major superiors of religious communities of women, with the purpose of promoting the spiritual and apostolic calling and works of sisterhoods in the U.S. Organized in the late 50s and approved by the Congregation for Religious and Secular Institutes June 13, 1962, it has a membership of approximately 600. Its original name, changed in 1971, was the Conference of Major Superiors of Women. With its formerly affiliated Sister Formation Conference, it inaugurated measures for the religious and professional development of sisters and has contributed to the renewal of religious life in this country. Sister Theresa Kane, R.S.M., is president; Sister Lora Ann Quinonez, C.D.P., is executive director. The national secretariat is located at 1302 Eighteenth St. N.W., Washington, D.C. 20036.

National Assembly of Women Religious: Formed in 1970, the assembly is a movement and organization of women and men associates of the Church. Its objectives are the promotion of a ministry of justice particularly, but not exclusively, for women in the Church and in economic systems, and the reconciliation of differences between laywomen and sisters and between men and women in the Church. The membership consists of about 73 diocesan councils and 2,000 individuals. Sister Mary O'Keefe and Sister Merle Nolde are co-directors. Offices are located at 1307 S. Wabash Ave., Chicago, Ill. 60605.

National Black Sisters' Conference: Organized in August, 1968, for the purposes of determining priorities in service to black people, of promoting black vocations and the development of religious life in the unique black life-style, and to influence the formational and recruitment practices of white religious communities. Its members include 150 black sisters belonging to 123 religious communities. Sister Cora Marie Billings, R.S.M., is coordinator. The mailing address of the conference is P.O. Box 28216, Philadelphia, Pa. 19131.

National Coalition of American Nuns: Organized under the leadership of Sister Margaret Traxler, S.S.N.D., in July, 1969, for efforts to secure recognition and development of the role of women in the Church and society, along with advocacy for social activism. Sister Andrea Lee is president. Offices are located at 1307 S. Wabash Ave., Chicago, Ill 60605.

National Sisters' Vocation Conference: Formed in September, 1970, as a national organization dedicated to promoting understanding of the role of women, especially religious, in the Church through work in the vocation apostolate. It coordinates and provides informational and other services to persons and organizations in the vocation apostolate, and assists prospective candidates for religious life. Its membership includes approximately 1,200 women and men. Sister Gertrude Wemhoff, O.S.B., is executive director. The national office is located at 1307 S. Wabash Ave., Chicago, Ill. 60605.

Religious Formation Conference: Originally organized with the title of the Sister Formation Conference in 1952, for the purpose of promoting the spiritual and professional formation of sisters in the U.S. With a current membership of both men and women religious, the conference focuses on initial and on-going formation work in religious communities and secular institutes. Sister Carla Przybilla, O.S.F., is executive director. The national office is located at 1234 Massachusetts Ave. N.W., Washington, D.C. 20005.

Sisters Uniting: Formed in March, 1971, as a council of representatives of national organizations of women religious seeking to promote and express solidarity in defense of Gospel values. Participating bodies included the Association of Contemplative Sisters, Las Hermanas, the Religious Formation Conference, the National Sisters' Vocation Conference, the National Coalition of American Nuns, the Leadership Conference of Women Religious and the National Assembly of Women Religious. Sister Maria Iglesias, S.C., is president. The mailing address is 1234 Massachusetts Ave. N.W., Washington, D.C. 20005.

Other Conferences

International Union of Superiors General (Women): Established in 1965, with approval of its statutes by the Congregation for Religious and Secular Institutes in 1967. Sister Regina Casey of the Missionaries of the Sacred Heart "St. Frances Xavier Cabrini" is president.

Latin American Confederation of Religious: Established in 1959, with approval of its statutes by the Congregation for Religious and Secular Institutes in 1967. Father Carlos Palmes, S.J., is president.

National Conference of Vicars for Religious: Established in 1967 as a national organization of diocesan officials concerned with relations between their respective dioceses and religious communities engaged therein. A service and informational agency for vicars, it also carries on liaison with the Congregation for Religious and Secular Institutes, the National Conference of Catholic Bishops and other organizations concerned with religious. The president is Rev. Angelo Caligiuri, 100 S. Elmwood Ave., Buffalo, N.Y. 14202.

National Conferences: Conferences of religious superiors, generally separate for men and women, have been established in 19 countries in Europe, 14 in North and Central America, 10 in South America, 20 in Africa, and 19 in Asia and Oceania.

Union of Superiors General (Men): Established in 1957, with approval of its statutes by the Congregation for Religious and Secular Institutes in 1967. Father Pedro Arrupe, S. J., is president.

World Conference of Secular Institutes: Established in 1974.

Vocation Council

The National Catholic Vocation Council replaced the National Center for Church Vocations in 1977. The principal purpose of the council is to give the Church in the U.S. visible witness of the mutual collaboration of national vocation organizations in their effort to promote awareness and understanding of dedication to the Church, especially through the ordained ministry and vowed life. The council also services efforts of mutual concern and benefit to membership organizations in the recruitment and development of vocations to the priesthood, diaconate and vowed life.

Member organizations with representatives on the board of directors are: the National Sisters Vocation Conference, the National Conference of Diocesan Vocation Directors, the National Conference of Religious Vocation Directors of Men, Serra International, the Bishops' Committee on Vocations (National Conference of Catholic Bishops), the Leadership Conference of Women Religious and the Conference of Major Superiors of Men.

Brother James Gaffney, C.F.C., is president; Rev. James A.Vedro, O.S.C., is chairman of the administrative committee.

Offices are located at 1307 S. Wabash Ave., Chicago, Ill. 60605

SECULAR INSTITUTES

(Sources: Almanac survey; *Directory of Secular Institutes with Foundations in the U.S.A.*, published by the Publications Office, U.S. Catholic Conference; *Annuario Pontificio*.)

Secular institutes are societies of men and women living in the world who dedicate themselves by vow or promise to observe the evangelical counsels and to carry on apostolic works suitable to their talents and opportunities in the areas of their everyday life.

"Secular institutes are not religious communities but they carry with them in the world a profession of evangelical counsels which is genuine and complete, and recognized as such by the Church. This profession confers a consecration on men and women, laity and clergy, who reside in the world. For this reason they should chiefly strive for total self-dedication to God, one inspired by perfect charity. These institutes should preserve their proper and particular character, a secular one, so that they may everywhere measure up successfully to that apostolate which they were designed to exercise, and which is both in the world and, in a sense, of the world" (*Decree on the Appropriate Renewal of Religious Life,* No. 11; Second Vatican Council).

A secular institute reaches maturity in several stages. It begins as an association of the faithful, technically called a pious union, with the approval of a local bishop. Once it has proved its viability, he can give it the status of an institute of diocesan right, in accordance with norms and permission emanating from the Congregation for Religious and Secular Institutes. On issuance of a separate decree from this congregation, an institute of diocesan right becomes an institute of pontifical right.

Secular institutes, which originated in the latter part of the 18th century, were given full recognition and approval by Pius XII Feb. 2, 1947, in the apostolic constitution *Provida Mater Ecclesia.* On Mar. 25 of the same year a special commission for secular institutes was set up within the Congregation for Religious. Institutes were commended and confirmed by Pius XII in a motu proprio of Mar. 12, 1948, and were the subject of a special instruction issued a week later, Mar. 19, 1948.

The United States Conference of Secular Institutes (CSI) was established in October, 1972, following the organization of the World Conference of Secular Institutes in Rome. Its membership is open to all canonically erected secular institutes with members living in the United States. The conference was organized to offer secular institutes an opportunity to exchange experiences, to do research in order to help the Church carry out its mission, and to search for ways and means to make known the existence of secular institutes in the U.S. Address: 7007 Bradley Blvd., Bethesda, Md. 20034.

Institutes in the U.S.

Caritas Christi: Originated in Marseilles, 1937; for women. Established as a secular institute of pontifical right Mar. 19, 1955. Address: P.O. Box 162, River Forest, Ill. 60305.

Company of St. Paul: Originated in Milan, Italy, 1920; for lay people and priests. Approved as a secular institute of pontifical right June 30, 1950. Address: 52 Davis Ave., White Plains, N.Y. 10605.

Company of St. Ursula, Daughters of St. Angela Merici ("The Angelines"): Founded in Brescia, Italy, 1535; for women. Approved as a secular institute of pontifical right 1958. Addresses: Lina Moser, President, Via Rosmini 128, 38100 Trento, Italy; D. Latz, P.O. Box 265, New Rochelle, N.Y. 10801.

DeSales Secular Institute: Founded in Vienna, Austria, 1940; for women. Pontifical right, 1964. Address: Rev. John Conmy, O.S.F.S., National Assistant, Oblate Novitiate, Childs, Md. 21916.

Diocesan Laborer Priests: Approved as a secular institute of pontifical right, 1952. The specific aim of the institute is the promotion, sustenance and cultivation of apostolic, religious and priestly vocations. Address: 3706 15th St. N.E., Washington, D.C. 20017.

Don Bosco Volunteers: Founded 1917; for women. Established as a secular institute of pontifical right Aug. 5, 1978. For women who love Don Bosco's spirit and choose to follow in his footsteps. Address: Don Bosco College, Newton, N.J. 07860.

Handmaids of Divine Mercy: Founded in

Bari, Italy, 1951; for women. Approved as an institute of pontifical right 1972. Address: Mary I. DiFonzo, 2410 Hughes Ave., Bronx, N.Y. 10458. International membership of 980.

Institute of Secular Missionaries: Founded in Vitoria, Spain, 1939; for women. Approved as a secular institute, 1955. Address: 2710 Ruberg Ave., Cincinnati, O. 45211, Att. E. Dilger.

Institute of the Heart of Jesus: Originated in France Feb. 2, 1791; restored Oct. 29, 1918; for diocesan priests and lay people. Received final approval from the Holy See as a secular institute of pontifical right Feb. 2, 1952. Rev. Jean Grebouval, superior general. Addresses: Central House, 202 Avenue du Maine, Paris 14me, France; U.S. address, Rev. John Lorenz, P.O. Box 4692, Des Moines, Iowa 50306. International membership of approximately 1,400.

Mission of Our Lady of Bethany: Founded in Plessis-Chevet, France, 1948; for women. Approved as an institute of diocesan right 1965. Address: Rev. Alfred Connick, Pope John XXIII Seminary, 558 South Ave., Weston, Mass. 02193.

Missionaries of the Kingship of Christ the King: Under this title are included three distinct and juridically separate institutes founded by Agostino Gemelli, O.F.M. (1878-1959).

(1) Women Missionaries of the Kingship of Christ — Founded in 1919, in Italy; definitively approved as an institute of pontifical rite 1953. Established in 15 countries. U.S. branch established 1950. Age at time of entrance, 21 to 40.

(2) Men Missionaries of the Kingship of Christ — Founded 1928, in Italy, as an institute of diocesan right. U.S. branch established 1962.

(3) Priest Missionaries of the Kingship of Christ — Established in U.S., 1954; approved as institute of pontifical right July 15, 1978. For diocesan priests.

Address: Rev. Stephen Hartdegen, O.F.M., Holy Name College, 14th and Shepherd Sts. N.E., Washington, D.C. 20017.

Oblate Missionaries of Mary Immaculate: Founded, 1952, and approved as a secular institute Feb. 2, 1962; for women. Dedicated to living and bearing witness to the charity of Christ. Addresses: Oblate Missionaries of Mary Immaculate, 91 Brookfield St., Lawrence, Mass. 01843. 7535 Boulevard Parent, Trois Rivieres, P. Q. G9A 5E1, Canada. International membership of approximately 630.

Rural Parish Workers of Christ the King: Originated in Cottleville, Mo., 1942; for women. An approved secular institute of the Archdiocese of St. Louis. Dedicated to the service of neighbor, especially in rural areas. Address: Box 300, Rt. 1, Cadet, Mo. 63630.

Schoenstatt Sisters of Mary: Originated in Schoenstatt, Germany, 1926; for women. Established as a secular institute of diocesan right May 20, 1948; of pontifical right Oct. 18, 1948. Addresses: Schoenstatt Sisters of Mary, W. 284 N. 698 Cherry Lane, Waukesha, Wis. 53186; House Schoenstatt, Star Rt. 1, Box 100, Rockport, Tex. 78382. International membership of more than 2,800.

Secular Institute of Pius X: Originated in Manchester, N.H., 1940; for priests and laymen. Approved as a secular institute, 1959 (first secular institute of diocesan right founded in the U.S. to be approved by the Holy See). Also admits married and unmarried men as associate members. Addresses: Lynchville Park, Goffstown, N.H. 03045. C.P. 1815, Quebec City, P.Q. G1K 7K7, Canada.

Society of Our Lady of the Way: Originated, 1936; for women. Approved as a secular institute of pontifical right Jan. 3, 1953. Addresses: 2701 14th Ave., San Francisco, Calif. 94116; 2339 N. Catalina St., Los Angeles, Calif. 90027; 2117 Penrock Rd., Cleveland Heights, O 44118. International membership, 300.

Teresian Institute: Founded in Spain 1911 by Pedro Poveda. Approved as an institute of pontifical right Jan. 11, 1924. Address: 235 Cypress St., Newton Centre, Mass. 02159.

Voluntas Dei: Originated in Canada, 1958; for secular priests, laymen and couples. Approved as a secular institute May 6, 1965. Addresses: Institute Voluntas Dei, 7385, Blvd. Parent, Trois-Rivieres, Que., Canada G9A 5E1. Rev. Maurice Roy, Immaculate Conception Parish, Drawer A.F., Ajo, Ariz. 85321.

The *Annuario Pontificio* lists the following secular institutes of pontifical right which are not established in the U.S.:

For men: Christ the King; Institute of Our Lady of Life; Institute of Prado; Opus Dei; Priests of the Sacred Heart of Jesus.

For women: Alliance in Jesus through Mary; Apostles of the Sacred Heart; Catechists of the Sacred Heart of Jesus (Ukrainian); Cordimarian Filiation; Daughters of the Nativity of Mary; Daughters of the Queen of the Apostles; Daughters of the Sacred Heart; Evangelical Crusade; Faithful Servants of Jesus; Institute of the Blessed Virgin Mary (della Strada); Institute of Notre Dame du Travail; Institute of Our Lady of Life; Institute of St. Boniface; Little Apostles of Charity; Love and Peace in Christ Jesus; Missionaries of Royal Priesthood; Missionaries of the Sick; Oblates of Christ the King; Oblates of the Sacred Heart of Jesus; Opus Dei; Servants of Jesus the Priest; Servite Secular Institute; Union of the Daughters of God; Workers of Divine Love; Workers of the Cross.

Associations

Association of Mary Immaculate: Founded 1963. Received diocesan approval Jan. 28, 1977. For mature men and women, widows and widowers; separate section for married couples. Training on cassette tape for blind or handicapped. Address: Sr. Mary Matthew, 2923 Lauderdale Dr. E., Jacksonville, Fla. 32211.

Caritas: Originated in New Orleans, 1950; for women. Follow guidelines of secular institutes. Small self-supporting groups who live and work among the poor and oppressed; houses in Louisiana and Guatemala. Address: Box 308, Abita Springs, La. 70420.

Daughters of Our Lady of Fatima: Originated in Lansdowne, Pa., 1949; for women. Received diocesan approval, Jan., 1952. Address: Fatima House, Rolling Hills Rd., Ottsville, Pa. 18942.

Focolare Movement: Inaugurated in Trent, Italy, in 1943, by Chiara Lubich and a small group of companions; for men and women. Approved as an association of the faithful, 1962. It is not a secular institute by statute; however, vows are observed by its totally dedicated core membership of 3,000 who live in small communities called Focolare (Italian word for "hearth") centers. There are 13 resident centers in the U.S. and two in Canada. GEN (New Generation) is the youth organization of the movement. An estimated 70,000 are affiliated with the movement in the U.S. and Canada; 3,000,000, worldwide. Publications include *Living City,* monthly; *GEN II* and *GEN III* for young people and children. Three week-long summer conventions, called "Mariapolis" ("City of Mary"), are held annually. Address for information: P.O. Box 496, New York, N.Y. 10021 (indicate men's or women's branch).

Institute of Apostolic Oblates: Founded in Rome, Italy, 1947; for women. Address: 2125 W. Walnut Ave., Fullerton, Calif. 92633 (provincial house).

Jesus Caritas Priest Fraternities of Charles de Foucauld: An open and loose structure of small groups of priests who meet each month to pray together and share their faith experiences. U.S. address: Rev. Howard W. Calkins (National Responsible), Corpus Christi Church, 529 W. 121st St., New York, N.Y. 10027.

Madonna House Apostolate: Originated in Toronto, Canada, 1930; for priests and lay persons. Diocesan pious union. Address: Madonna House, Combermere, Ontario, Canada K0J IL0 — Catherine Doherty (women), Jim Guinan (men), Rev. J. Callahan (priests). International membership and missions.

Pax Christi: Lay institute of men and women dedicated to witnessing to Christ, with special emphasis on service to the poor in Mississippi. Addresses: St. Francis Center, 708 Ave. I, Greenwood, Miss. 38930; LaVerna House, 2108 Altawoods Blvd., Jackson, Miss. 39204.

SECULAR ORDERS

Secular orders (commonly called third orders) are societies of the faithful living in the world who seek to deepen their Christian life and apostolic commitment in association with and according to the spirit of various religious institutes.

Augustine, Third Order Secular of St.: Founded, 13th century; approved Nov. 7, 1400.

Carmel (The Lay Carmelite Order) (Calced): Founded, 13th century; approved by Pope Nicholas V, Oct. 7, 1452. Address: Aylesford, National Scapular Center, I-55 and Cass Ave. N. Darien, Ill. 60559. Approximately 16,000 members in U.S.

Carmel, Third Order Secular of Our Blessed Lady of Mt., and St. Teresa of Jesus (Discalced): Rule based on the Carmelite reform established by St. Teresa and St. John of the Cross, 16th century; approved Mar. 23, 1594. Office of National Secretariat, U.S.A.; P.O. Box 3079, San Jose, Calif. 95116. Approximately 3,500 members in U.S.

Dominican Laity: Founded in the 13th century. Addresses of provincial coordinators: 487 Michigan Ave. N.E., Washington, D.C. 20017; 1909 S. Ashland Ave., Chicago, Ill. 60608; St. Peter Martyr Priory, 241 S. Detroit St., Los Angeles, Calif. 90036.

Franciscan Order, Secular (SFO): Founded, 1209 by St. Francis of Assisi; approved Aug. 30, 1221. Executive Secretary, Mrs. Mary R. Teoli, 1901 Prior Rd., Wilmington, Del. 19809. Approximately 780,000 throughout the world; 40,000 in U.S.

Mary, Third Order of: Founded, Dec. 8, 1850; rule approved by the Holy See, 1857. Addresses of provincial directors: Marist College, 220 Taylor St. N.E., Washington, D.C. 20017; 7 Harvard St., P.O. Box 66, Charlestown, Mass. 02129; 320 N. 20th Dr. W., Phoenix, Ariz. 85009. Approximately 14,000 in the world, 5,600 in U.S.

Mary, Third Order Secular of Servants of (Servite): Founded, 1233; approved, 1304. Address: Director of Third Order, 1939 Union St., Blue Island, Ill. 60406.

Mercy, Secular Third Order of Our Lady of (Mercedarian): Founded, 1219 by St. Peter Nolasco; approved the same year.

Norbert, Third Order of St.: Founded, 1122 by St. Norbert; approved by Pope Honorius II, 1126. Address: St. Norbert Abbey, De Pere, Wis.

Trinity, Third Order Secular of the Most Holy: Founded 1198; approved, 1219. Address: Trinitarian Provincial Offices, P.O. Box 5719, Baltimore, Md. 21208.

UNITED STATES FOREIGN MISSIONARIES

(Data on U.S. foreign missionary personnel in the following tables were gathered by, and are reproduced with permission of, the United States Catholic Mission Council, 1302 Eighteenth St. N.W., Washington, D.C. 20036.

(For additional information about the Church in mission areas, see News Events and other Almanac entries.)

Field Distribution, 1980

(Under this and following headings, Alaska, Hawaii, etc., are considered abroad because they are outside the 48 contiguous states.)

Africa: 909 (495 men; 414 women). Largest numbers in Tanzania, 159; Kenya, 151; Ghana, 114; Zambia, 71; Nigeria, 63.

Near East: 65 (40 men; 25 women). Largest numbers in Israel, 32; Egypt, 13; Lebanon, 10.

Far East: 1,576 (1,083 men; 493 women). Largest numbers in Philippines, 428; Japan, 343; Taiwan, 174; Korea, 151; India, 139; Hong Kong, 79.

Oceania: 711 (359 men; 352 women). Largest groups in Hawaii, 237; Papua New Guinea, 214; Australia, 62; Mariana Islands, 58; Caroline Islands, 36; Samoa, 32.

Europe: 35 (18 men; 17 women). Largest groups in Finland, 11; Sweden, 10; Denmark, 6.

North America: 294 (112 men; 182 women). Largest group in Alaska, 174.

Caribbean Islands: 548 (298 men; 250 women). Largest groups in Puerto Rico, 251; Jamaica, 128; Haiti, 45.

Central America: 699 (421 men; 278 women). Largest groups in Mexico, 221; Guatemala, 180.

South America: 1,556 (832 men; 724 women). Largest groups in Brazil, 465; Peru, 436; Bolivia, 250; Chile, 181.

TOTAL: 6,393 (3,658 men; 2,735 women).

Men Religious, 1980

Seventy-two mission-sending groups had 3,392 priests and brothers in overseas assignments.

Jesuits: 574 in 37 countries; largest group, 96 in the Philippines.

Maryknoll Fathers: 570 in 25 countries; largest group, 54 in Taiwan.

Franciscans (O.F.M.): 212 in 22 countries; largest group, 69 in Brazil.

Divine Word Missionaries: 173 in 14 countries; largest group, 59 in Papua New Guinea.

Redemptorists: 161 in 8 countries; largest group, 67 in Brazil.

Oblates of Mary Immaculate: 154 in 16 countries; largest group, 39 in Mexico.

Capuchins (O.F.M. Cap): 144 in 10 countries; largest group, 34 in Papua New Guinea.

Marianists: 144 in 13 countries; largest group, 44 in Hawaii.

Benedictines: 87 in 14 countries; largest group, 18 in Guatemala.

Columbans: 80 in 10 countries; largest group, 33 in the Philippines.

Holy Cross Fathers: 71 in 11 countries; largest group, 23 in Bangladesh.

Dominicans: 64 in 8 countries; largest group, 19 in Nigeria.

Brothers of the Christian Schools: 63 in 11 countries; largest group, 28 in the Philippines.

Holy Ghost Fathers: 62 in 6 countries; largest group, 27 in Tanzania.

Holy Cross Brothers: 54 in 6 countries; largest group, 18 in Brazil.

Passionists: 54 in 5 countries; largest group, 26 in the Philippines.

Conventual Franciscans (O.F.M. Conv): 48 in 8 countries; largest group, 16 in Zambia.

La Salette Fathers: 43 in 5 countries; largest group, 14 in Argentina.

Vincentians: 36 in 5 countries; largest group, 21 in Panama.

Marist Fathers: 35 in 8 countries; largest group, 11 in Papua New Guinea.

Augustinians: 31 in 3 countries; largest group, 19 in Peru.

Missionaries of the Sacred Heart: 29 in 3 countries; largest group, 22 in Papua New Guinea.

White Fathers: 26 in 11 countries; largest groups, 5 each in Tanzania, Ghana, and Malawi.

Marist Brothers: 24 in 7 countries; largest group, 10 in the Philippines.

Comboni Missionaries: 22 in 6 countries; largest group, 7 in Uganda.

Franciscan Friars of the Atonement (Graymoor): 22 in 3 countries; largest group, 12 in Japan.

Sacred Heart Brothers: 21 in 4 countries; largest group, 10 in Zambia.

Fathers of the Sacred Hearts: 21 in 4 countries; largest group, 14 in Japan.

Missionhurst-CICM: 20 in 6 countries; largest group, 10 in the Dominican Republic.

Society of African Missions: 20 in 3 countries; largest group, 16 in Liberia.

Forty-two other mission-sending institutes had 19 or less members in overseas assignments.

Diocesan Priests, 1980

One hundred and 88 diocesan priests from 90 dioceses were in overseas assignments in 1980.

The largest groups were from Boston (21 in 4 countries) and St. Louis (14 in 2 countries).

Fifty-four of the diocesan priests in overseas assignments were members of the **Missionary Society of St. James the Apostle,** founded by Cardinal Richard J. Cushing of Boston in 1958. Its director is Reverend George F. Emerson, 24 Clark Street, Boston, Massachusetts 02109.

Fifteen other diocesan priests in overseas assignments are working as Priest Associates with the Maryknoll Fathers, whose headquarters are in Maryknoll, New York 10545.

Sisters, 1980

Two hundred and 11 mission-sending groups had 2,592 sisters in overseas assignments.

Maryknoll Sisters: 411 in 23 countries; largest group, 61 in Hawaii.

Marists: 90 in 13 countries; largest group, 16 in Papua New Guinea.

School Sisters of Notre Dame: 89 in 16 countries; largest group, 15 in Puerto Rico.

Sisters of Notre Dame de Namur: 64 in 8 countries; largest group, 16 in Kenya.

Medical Mission Sisters: 63 in 18 countries; largest group, 17 in Ghana.

Sisters of St. Joseph (Carondelet): 60 in 3 countries; largest group, 29 in Hawaii.

Daughters of Charity: 59 in 11 countries; largest group, 34 in Bolivia.

Franciscan Missionaries of Mary: 55 in 18 countries; largest groups, 8 each in Ghana and Australia.

Ursulines of the Roman Union: 40 in 11 countries; largest group, 8 in Thailand.

Servants of the Immaculate Heart of Mary (Philadelphia): 40 in 2 countries; larger group, 29 in Peru.

Sisters of the Holy Cross: 39 in 4 countries; largest group, 17 in Brazil.

Franciscan Sisters of Allegany: 38 in 3 countries; largest group, 21 in Jamaica.

Benedictines: 36 in 7 countries; largest group, 11 in Colombia.

Sisters of the Third Franciscan Order, Minor Conventuals (Syracuse): 33 in 3 countries; largest group, 21 in Hawaii.

Servants of the Holy Spirit: 31 in 7 countries; largest group, 11 in Ghana.

Society of the Sacred Heart: 30 in 9 countries; largest group, 16 in Japan.

Religious Sisters of Mercy of the Union in the U.S.A.: 30 in 7 countries; largest group, 11 in Honduras.

Little Sisters of the Poor: 27 in 14 countries; largest groups, 4 each in Colombia and India.

Servants of the Immaculate Heart of Mary (Monroe): 27 in 7 countries; largest group, 10 in Puerto Rico.

Sisters of Notre Dame: 26 in 3 countries; largest group, 14 in India.

Adorers of the Blood of Christ: 24 in 5 countries; largest group, 8 in Liberia.

Missionary Sisters of the Immaculate Conception: 22 in 5 countries; largest group, 15 in Canada.

Sisters of the Most Precious Blood (O'Fallon): 22 in 3 countries; largest group, 11 in Finland.

Dominican Sisters (Adrian): 21 in 7 countries; largest group, 7 in Puerto Rico.

Sisters of the Assumption of the B.V.M.: 21 in 3 countries; largest group, 15 in Canada.

Sisters of the Holy Child Jesus: 21 in 5 countries; largest group, 8 in Ghana.

Sisters of St. Joseph (Brentwood): 21 in 3 countries; largest group, 18 in Puerto Rico.

One hundred and 84 other mission-sending institutes had 19 or less members in overseas assignments.

Lay Volunteers, 1980

Two hundred and 21 lay volunteers of 27 sponsoring organizations were in overseas assignments in 1980.

Maryknoll Lay Missioners: 41 in 12 countries; largest group, 7 in Korea.

Jesuit Volunteer Corps: 34 in Alaska.

Lay Mission Helpers: 31 in 13 countries; largest groups, 5 each in Papua New Guinea and Samoa.

Frontier Apostolate: 30 in Canada.

Catholic Medical Mission Board: 16* in 8 countries; largest groups, 4 each in Ghana and Papua New Guinea. (*This figure represents only those whose term of service is for at least one year. In addition, 47 short-term volunteers served in 12 countries during the past year.)

Erie Diocese: 9 in 2 countries; larger group, 8 in Mexico.

Milwaukee Latin American Office: 7 in 6 countries; largest group, 2 in Honduras.

Davenport Diocese: 6 in 3 countries; largest group, 3 in Puerto Rico.

The 19 other sponsoring organizations had 5 members or less in overseas assignments.

U.S. Mission Council

The United States Catholic Mission Council, which took over and expanded functions of the former Mission Secretariat, started operations Sept. 1, 1970, "to provide a forum and organ for the evaluation, coordination and fostering, in the United States, of the worldwide missionary effort of the Church."

Structurally, the council is made up of five seven-member committees representing the National Conference of Catholic Bishops, the Conference of Major Superiors of Men, the Leadership Conference of Women Religious, the National Council of Catholic Laity and mission agencies. Heads of the committees form the executive board which meets at least quarterly to oversee the implementation of policies and programs determined at annual meetings of the whole committee.

Typical activities of the council are educational efforts related to the Church's teaching about its missionary nature, the sponsorship of conferences on theological and pastoral foundations of missionary endeavor, liaison and cooperation with missionary bodies of other Christian churches, the encouragement of mission studies, training programs and refresher courses for departing and returning missionaries, gathering data on missionary activity, and general mission animation.

Rev. Anthony Bellagamba, I.M.C., is executive secretary of the council, with offices at 1302 Eighteenth St. N.W., Washington, D.C. 20036.

U.S. FOREIGN MISSIONARIES, 1960-1980

Year	Diocesan Priests	Religious Priests	Religious Brothers	Religious Sisters	Seminarians	Lay Persons	Total
1960	14	3018	575	2827	170	178	6782
1962	31	3172	720	2764	152	307	7146
1964	80	3438	782	3137	157	532	8126
1966	215	3731	901	3706	201	549	9303
1968	282	3727	869	4150	208	419	9655
1970	373	3117	666	3824	90	303	8373
1972+	246	3182	634	3121	97	376	7656
1973	237	3913*		3012		529	7691
1974	220	3084	639	2916	101	458	7418
1975	197	3023	669	2850	65	344	7148
1976	193	2961	691	2840	68	257	7010
1977	182	2882	630	2781	42	243	6760
1978	166	2830	610	2673	43	279	6601
1979	187	2800	592	2568	50	258	6455
1980	188	2750	592	2592	50	221	6393

+A corrected total for 1972 should read 7937, indicating losses of 436 from 1970 to 1972 and 246 from 1972 to 1973.
*Includes religious brothers and seminarians.

FIELD DISTRIBUTION BY AREAS, 1960-1980

Year	Africa	Far East	Near East	Oceania	Europe	N. Amer.	Carib. Is.	Cent. Amer.	S. Amer.	Total
1960	781	1959	111	986	203	337	991	433	981	6782
1962	901	2110	75	992	93	224	967	537	1247	7146
1964	1025	2332	122	846	69	220	1056	660	1796	8126
1966	1184	2453	142	953	38	211	1079	857	2386	9303
1968	1157	2470	128	1027	33	251	1198	936	2455	9655
1970	1141	2137	39	900	38	233	1067	738	2080	8373
1972	1107	1955	59	826	39	234	819	728	1889	7656
1973	1229	1962	54	811	40	253	796	763	1783	7691
1974	1121	1845	60	883	43	241	757	752	1716	7418
1975	1065	1814	71	808	37	252	698	734	1669	7148
1976	1042	1757	68	795	34	313	671	712	1618	7010
1977	1003	1659	62	784	34	296	629	702	1591	6760
1978	966	1601	57	769	34	339	593	705	1537	6601
1979	923	1562	65	743	37	332	562	686	1545	6455
1980	909	1576	65	711	35	294	548	699	1556	6393

JOHN XXIII CENTER

The John XXIII Center for Eastern Christian Studies was established in 1951 by Father Feodor Wilcock and a group of other Eastern-Rite Jesuits. It operates a wide variety of ecumenical activities related to Eastern Christian studies. One of its projects is the John XXIII Institute, believed to be the only academic institution outside of Rome offering a degree in the theology of the Eastern tradition of Christianity.

Father John C. Geary, S.J., is acting head of the center, located at 2502 Belmont Ave., Bronx, N.Y. 10458.

INFORMATION SERVICE

A new Latin American Church Information Service for 22 episcopal conferences was launched Feb. 13, 1980, in Bogota, Colombia. Its stated purpose was to bring "church information to the media and the public, on what the Church does to implement the teachings of the Gospel . . . to stress the evangelization impact of church thinking and action."

John F. Fink, president of Our Sunday Visitor, Inc., was elected president of the International Federation of Church Press Associations Sept. 23 to 26, 1980, in Rome.

HOME MISSIONS

The expression "home missions" is applied to places in the U.S. where the local church does not have its own resources, human and otherwise, which are needed to begin or, if begun, to survive and grow. These areas share the name "missions" with their counterparts in foreign lands because they too need outside help to provide the personnel and means for making the Church present and active there in carrying out its mission for the salvation of people.

Dioceses in the Southeast, the Southwest, and the Far West are most urgently in need of outside help to carry on the work of the Church. Millions of persons live in counties in which there are no resident priests. Many others live in rural areas beyond the reach and influence of a Catholic center. According to recent statistics compiled by the Glenmary Research Center, there are 545 priestless counties in the United States. Many states generally thought to be well off from a pastoral standpoint include areas in which the Catholic Church and the ministry of priests are virtually unknown.

About 20 per cent of the total U.S. population and less than three per cent of the Catholic population live within the boundaries of the 17 "most missionary" dioceses of the country. A "Survey of the Catholic Weakness" conducted by the National Catholic Rural Life Conference disclosed that the Catholic Church ranked near the bottom of about 40 religious bodies in percentage of rural membership.

Mission Workers

A number of forces are at work to meet the pastoral needs of these missionary areas and to establish permanent churches and operating institutions where they are required. In many dioceses, one or more missions and stations are attended from established parishes and are gradually growing to independent status. Priests, brothers and sisters belonging to scores of religious institutes are engaged full-time in the home missions. Lay persons, some of them in affiliation with special groups and movements, are also involved.

The Society for the Propagation of the Faith, which conducts an annual collection for mission support in all parishes of the U.S., allocates 40 per cent of this sum for disbursement to home missions through the American Board of Catholic Missions.

The Catholic Church Extension Society provides one million dollars or more a year for the building of mission installations and related needs.

Special mission support is the purpose of the Commission for the Catholic Missions among the Colored People and the Indians. Diocesan, parochial and high school mission societies frequently undertake projects in behalf of the home missions.

The **Glenmary Home Missioners,** founded by Father W. Howard Bishop in 1939, is the only home mission society established for the sole purpose of carrying out the pastoral ministry in small towns and the rural districts of the United States. With 74 priests and 29 professed brothers as of Mar. 31, 1980, the Glenmary Missioners had 37 mission bases and 38 satellite missions in the archdioceses of Atlanta and Cincinnati, and in the dioceses of Birmingham, Charlotte, Covington, Dallas, Little Rock, Nashville, Jackson, Tulsa, Owensboro, Savannah, Richmond and Wheeling-Charleston. The Rev. Robert C. Berson is president. National headquarters are located in Fairfield, O. The mailing address is P.O. Box 46404, Cincinnati, O. 45246.

Black Missions

The Commission for Catholic Missions among the Colored People and the Indians reported the following (January, 1980), statistics for 78 dioceses and six religious communities to whom it supplied financial assistance: 955,855 Catholics; 701 churches; 975 priests; 145 predominantly black schools with 34,800 students; 255 integrated schools with 4,200 students. The total number of black Catholics was estimated to be more than 985,000.

Dioceses reporting the largest numbers of black Catholics were: Brooklyn, N.Y., 132,442; Lafayette, La., 80,000; New Orleans, La., 75,500; Washington, D.C., 75,000; New York, N.Y., 50,000; Kansas City-St. Joseph, Mo., 47,000; Philadelphia, Pa., 40,000; Detroit, Mich., 36,800; Galveston-Houston, Tex., 35,000; St. Louis, Mo., 30,400; San Diego, Calif., 28,500; Rockville Centre, N.Y., 20,815; Baltimore, Md., 17,325. The total black Catholic population of these 13 mainly urban dioceses numbered 668,782; they comprised nearly 68 per cent of the total black Catholic population of the 78 dioceses covered in the report.

The report noted that it was impossible to determine "whether, or to what extent, lapsed Catholics are included in a parish or diocesan report."

The commission report, which was limited in scope, did not cover all aspects of the Church's ministry to the black population, which was estimated to number more than 22 million. (See Index: Black Catholics.)

Indian Missions

The Commission for Catholic Missions among the Colored People and the Indians reported the following statistics (May, 1980) for 45 dioceses and one religious community to whom it supplied financial assistance: 218,636 Catholics, 364 churches and chapels, 325 priests, 17 elementary schools, four high schools.

The states with the largest number of missions and Catholic Indians are Arizona, New Mexico, North and South Dakota, Oklahoma and Montana, where almost two-thirds of the reservation Indians now live. Seventy-one churches and chapels and four schools were maintained with 146 priests engaged in serving more than 155,009 Catholic Indians in these areas. Forty-five missions and three schools are located in the states of California, Minnesota, Wisconsin and Wyoming where 41 priests are serving the estimated 31,432 Catholic Indians there. Alaska has 45 mission churches and chapels and 32 priests to minister to approximately 27,000 Indians, Aleuts, Eskimos. In other states, the Commission reported, reservations were small; consequently only several schools and from one to five missions were maintained in most of them.

According to current census tribal reports, it was estimated that 300,000 Indians were living on federal reservations and 307,000 in urban areas. An estimated 25,000 Catholic Indians were not on reservations.

Support Bodies

The Catholic Church Extension Society: This society was established for the purpose of preserving and extending the Church in the U.S. and its dependencies principally through the collection and disbursement of funds for missions. Since the time of its founding in 1905, approximately $75 million have been received and expended for this purpose. Disbursements in fiscal year 1979 amounted to $5 million.

Works of the society are supervised by a board of governors consisting of twelve members: Cardinal John Cody, archbishop of Chicago, chancellor; Rev. Edward J. Slattery, president; five bishops or priests, and five laymen. Society headquarters are located at 35 E. Wacker Drive, Chicago, Ill. 60601.

Commission for Catholic Missions among the Colored People and the Indians: Organized in 1886, this commission provides financial support ($4.020 million allocated in 1978-79 year to 123 dioceses) for religious works among Blacks and Indians in the United States. Funds are raised by an annual collection in all parishes of the country.

Cardinal John J. Krol is head of the board of directors. Msgr. Paul A. Lenz is secretary. Commission headquarters are located at 2021 H St. N.W., Washington, D.C. 20006.

Bureau of Catholic Indian Missions: Established in 1874 as the representative of Catholic Indian missions before the federal government and the public; made permanent organization in 1883 by Third Plenary Council of Baltimore. After a remarkable history of rendering important services to the Indian people, the bureau continues to represent the Catholic Church in the U.S. in her apostolate to the American Indian. Concerns are evange-lization, catechesis, liturgy, family life, education, advocacy. Cardinal John Krol is president of the board; Msgr. Paul A. Lenz is secretary. Address: 2021 H St., Washington, D.C. 20006.

Tekakwitha Conference: Established in 1939, the Conference includes active and former Catholic missionaries among Native American people and Native American people recognized as leaders in their respective churches. The primary focus is evangelization in eight areas of concern: development of Native American ministry, catechesis, liturgy, family life, evangelical liberation, ecumenical cooperation and urban ministry. The annual Conference serves as an opportunity for exchange of ideas, approaches and mutual support. Publications include annual Proceedings and 40th Anniversary Edition of Tekakwitha Conference. President is Rev. Gilbert F. Hemauer, O.F.M. Cap. Address: 1818 Ninth Ave., South No. 5, Great Falls, Mont. 59405.

BLACK CATHOLICS

The National Office for Black Catholics, organized in August, 1970, is a central agency with the general purposes of promoting active and full participation by black Catholics in the Church and of making more effective the apostolate of the Church in the black community.

Walter Hubbard is president of the office's board of directors. Brother Cyprian Lamar Rowe, is executive director. The liaison officer with the National Conference of Catholic Bishops is Auxiliary Bishop Eugene A. Marino, S.S.J., of Washington, D.C.

The NOBC office is located at 1234 Massachusetts Ave. N.W., Washington, D.C. 20005. Its publication is entitled *Impact*.

NOBC Affiliates

The NOBC has affiliates in various cities throughout the country. Three of its member bodies are:

• The National Black Catholic Clergy Caucus, formed at a charter meeting in April, 1968, in Detroit. Its president is Brother Booker Ashe, O.F.M. Cap., House of Peace, 1702 W. Walnut St., Milwaukee, Wis. 53205.

• The National Black Sisters' Conference (see separate entry).

• The National Black Catholic Lay Caucus.

• The National Catholic Conference for Interracial Justice.

Principal support for NOBC operations comes from proceeds of a Black Catholics Concerned collection conducted in parishes annually in October.

Objectives

NOBC operations are in support of the

aspirations and calls of black Catholics for a number of significant objectives. These include:

1. Representation and voice for blacks among those with leadership and decision responsibility in the Church. A strong desire is for the appointment of more black bishops. (Bishop Joseph L. Howze, the first black Ordinary appointed in the U.S. in the 20th century, was installed in the Diocese of Biloxi June 6, 1977. Auxiliary Bishops were: Joseph A. Francis, S.V.D., of Newark; Eugene A. Marino, S.S.J., of Washington; Harold R. Perry, S.V.D., of New Orleans; James P. Lyke, O.F.M., Cleveland.)

2. Vocational recruitment of blacks to the priesthood and religious life, the aim of a campaign inaugurated in 1973. (The number of black priests was approximately 250; black sisters numbered about 700. Father Au-

gustine Tolton (1854-97), ordained in 1886 in Rome, was the first black priest in the U.S. born of African parents.)

3. Recognition of black heritage in the liturgy, community life, theology and education.

Josephite Center

The Josephite Pastoral Center was established in September, 1968, as an educational and pastoral service agency for the Josephites in their mission work, specifically in the black community. St. Joseph's Society of the Sacred Heart, the sponsoring body, has about 185 priests and 20 brothers in 80 mostly southern parishes in 18 dioceses.

Father Joseph A. Benintende, S.S.J., is the executive director of the center, located at St. Joseph Seminary, 1200 Varnum St. N.E., Washington, D.C. 20017.

Black Catholic Population in the U.S.

(Sources: *Statistical Profile of Black Catholics,* published by the Josephite Pastoral Center, Washington, D.C., 1975 figures; *Official Catholic Directory, 1976,* total Catholic population figures. Hawaii and Alaska are not included in totals.)

Region	Black Caths.	Total Black Pop.	Perc. Caths. Black Pop.	Cath. Pop.	Perc. Blacks Cath. Pop.
New England	20,675	386,557	5.3	5,673,372	.4
Middle Atlantic	158,882	3,950,356	4.0	12,941,250	1.2
E. North Central	180,689	3,867,653	4.6	10,420,011	1.7
W. North Central	51,286	697,760	7.3	3,245,895	1.6
S. Atlantic	132,904	6,381,843	2.1	2,715,806	4.8
E. South Central	30,234	2,569,625	1.7	634,349	4.7
W. South Central	237,368	3,005,587	7.9	3,631,334	6.5
Mountain	6,607	178,416	3.7	1,562,453	.4
Pacific	98,209	1,512,018	6.4	5,294,512	1.8
TOTALS	916,854	22,549,815	4.0	46,118,982	2.0

Up to 1926, only 10 black American priests were ordained in the U.S. One hundred and 13 were ordained between 1930 and 1960; 83 of them belonged to religious communities.

MINISTRY TO THE SPANISH-SPEAKING

The number of people of Hispanic origin in the United States is well over the 12 million mark estimated by the U.S. Census Bureau in 1978. In one period alone, between mid-April and late summer, 1980, the Hispanic portion of the population was increased by about 125,000 persons fleeing from Cuba.

The vast majority of persons of Spanish origin in the U.S. have been baptized in the Catholic Church and comprise between 20 and 25 per cent of the Catholic population.

In 1980, there were 12 Hispanic bishops (six heads of dioceses, and six auxiliaries, all named since 1970), approximately 200 Hispanic priests (augmented by others speaking Spanish), 380 Hispanics in U.S. seminaries, more than 450 Hispanic permanent deacons, and a larger number of women religious.

Pastoral ministry to the Spanish-speaking in the United States varies, depending on differences among the people and the avail-

ability of personnel to carry it out.

The pattern in cities with large numbers of Spanish-speaking is built around special churches, centers or other agencies where pastoral and additional forms of service are provided in a manner suited to the needs, language and culture of the people. Services in some places are extensive and include legal advice, job placement, language instruction, recreational and social assistance, specialized counseling, replacement services. In many places, however, even where there are special ministries, the needs are generally greater than the means required to meet them.

Some of the urban dwellers have been absorbed into established parishes and routines of church life and activity. Many Spanish-speaking communities, especially those with transients, remain in need of special ministries.

An itinerant form of ministry best meets

the needs of the thousands of migrant workers who follow the crops.

Special ministries for the Spanish-speaking have been in operation for a long time in dioceses of the Southwest. The total number of dioceses with such ministries is more than 75.

Pastoral care for the Spanish-speaking was the central concern of two national meetings, *encuentros,* held in 1972 and 1977. In line with recommendations made then, particular emphasis has since been focused on meetings and actions for increasing language capability among persons involved in ministry, awareness of Hispanic cultural elements in liturgy and practice, leadership development, and moves for the formation of basic Christian communities (*comunidades de base*). A task force for implementation is chaired by Archbishop Robert F. Sanchez of Santa Fe, N.M.

Agencies and Organizations

Secretariat for the Spanish-Speaking: The national secretariat of the U.S. Catholic Conference, for service in promoting and coordinating pastoral ministry to the Spanish-speaking. Its basic orientation is toward integral evangelization, combining religious ministry with development efforts in programs geared to the culture and needs of Hispanics. Its concerns are urban and migrant Spanish-speaking people; communications and publications in line with secretariat purposes and the service of people; bilingual and bicultural religious and general education; liaison for and representation of Hispanics with church, civic and governmental agencies.

Paul Sedillo, Jr., is director of the national office at 1312 Massachusetts Ave. N.W., Washington, D.C. 20005.

The secretariat has regional offices in California and the Midwest. A Southwest Regional Office for the Spanish-speaking, directed by Ms. Lupe Anguiano, is located at 2114 Commerce St., San Antonio, Tex. 78207.

The secretariat also has working relations with the **Northeast Pastoral Center for Hispanics,** established in 1976 and supported by bishops in 14 states from New England to Virginia. It shares the objectives of the national secretariat in efforts to develop a full array of pastoral programs for the Spanish-speaking.

Mario J. Paredes is executive director of the center, which is located at 1011 First Ave., New York, N.Y. 10022.

In the Southwest, 55 Mexican-American priests organized **PADRES** in February, 1970, to help the Church identify more closely with the pastoral, social, economic and educational needs of the Spanish-speaking. PADRES is an acronym for the Spanish title, "Padres Asociados para Derechos Religiosos, Educativos y Sociales."

Leadership development of Hispanos is one of the principal concerns of PADRES, a national organization with membership open to priests, brothers, deacons, seminarians and others interested in working with the Hispanic community. Father Luis Olivares, C.M.F., is the national president. Brother Trinidad Sanchez, S.J., is the executive director. Offices are located at 3112 W. Ashby St., San Antonio, Tex. 78228.

An analogous organization of Chicano sisters, **Las Hermanas,** was organized in 1971 (see separate entry).

The Mexican American Cultural Center: Founded in 1972 as a pastoral institute with a variety of programs focused on the evangelization of Hispanics in the United States, particularly through lay leadership and liaison between North and South America; named a center of liturgical research by the National Conference of Catholic Bishops.

Fathers Virgil Elizondo and Ricardo Ramirez are president and executive vice president, respectively, of the center, which is located at 3019 French Pl., P.O. Box 28185, San Antonio, Tex. 78228.

Miami Apostolate

(This article was written before the influx of 125,000 or more Cubans into Florida between mid-April and late summer of 1980.)

The Spanish-Speaking Apostolate in metropolitan Miami is one of the most extensive in the country. It serves a population of well over 553,174 people: more than 424,000 Cubans who have established residence there since Fidel Castro rose to power Jan. 1, 1959; a permanent Latin population of more than 50,000; and some 100,000 migrant workers. Directly involved in the apostolate are 71 Spanish-speaking priests and 88 religious brothers and sisters. Spanish-speaking priests are assigned to 39 parishes.

Centro Hispano Catolico (Spanish Catholic Center), founded by Archbishop Coleman F. Carroll in October, 1959, provides many forms of assistance to new arrivals from Latin countries, including: pastoral counseling, orientation to life in the U.S., employment services, medicine-food-clothing distribution, day nursery and kindergarten care, programs for senior citizens, and home visits. Located in the center are Archdiocesan Offices for Immigration Services and the Latin American Affairs Office which fosters cultural relations with Latin American countries.

The staff of the center consists of a chaplain, four Sisters of Social Service, and more than a score of lay persons. Sister Suzanne, S.S.S., is supervisor. of the center. The episcopal vicar for Spanish-speaking peoples in the archdiocese is Bishop Agustin Roman. The center is located at 130 N.E. 2nd St., Miami, Fla. 33132.

LEGAL STATUS OF CATHOLIC EDUCATION

The right of private schools to exist and operate in the United States is recognized in law. It was confirmed by the U.S. Supreme Court in 1925 when the tribunal ruled (Pierce v. Society of Sisters, see Church-State Decisions of the Supreme Court) that an Oregon state law requiring all children to attend public schools was unconstitutional.

Private schools are obliged to comply with the education laws in force in the various states regarding such matters as required basic curricula, periods of attendance, and standards for proper accreditation.

The special curricula and standards of private schools are determined by the schools themselves. Thus, in Catholic schools, the curricula include not only the subject matter required by state educational laws but also other fields of study, principally, education in the Catholic faith.

The Supreme Court has ruled that the First Amendment to the U.S. Constitution, in accordance with the No Establishment of Religion Clause of the First Amendment, prohibits direct federal and state aid from public funds to church-affiliated schools. (See several cases in Church-State Decisions of the Supreme Court.)

Public Aid

This prohibition does not extend to all child-benefit and public-purpose programs of aid to students of non-public elementary and secondary schools.

Statutes authorizing such programs have been ruled constitutional on the grounds that they:

- have a "secular legislative purpose";
- neither inhibit nor advance religion as a "principal or primary effect";
- do not foster "excessive government entanglement with religion."

Aid programs considered constitutional have provided bus transportation, textbook loans, school lunches and health services, and "secular, neutral or non-ideological services, facilities and materials provided in common to all school children," public and non-public.

The first major aid to education program in U.S. history containing provisions benefitting nonpublic school students was enacted by the 89th Congress and signed into law by President Lyndon B. Johnson Apr. 11, 1965. The Elementary and Secondary Education Act was designed to avoid the separation of Church and state impasse which had blocked all earlier aid proposals pertaining to nonpublic, and especially church-affiliated, schools. The objective of the program, under public control, is to serve the public purpose by aiding disadvantaged pupils in nonpublic as well as public schools.

With respect to college and university education in church-affiliated institutions, the Supreme Court has upheld the constitutionality of statutes providing student loans and, under the Federal Higher Education Facilities Act of 1963, construction loans and grants for secular-purpose facilities.

Catholic schools are exempt from real estate taxation in all of the states. Since Jan. 1, 1959, nonprofit parochial and private schools have also been exempt from several federal excise taxes.

Shared and Released Time

In a shared time program of education, students enrolled in Catholic or other church-related schools take some courses (e.g., religion, social studies, fine arts) in their own schools and others (e.g., science, mathematics, industrial arts) in public schools. Such a program has been given serious consideration in recent years by Catholic and other educators. Its constitutionality has not been seriously challenged, but practical problems — relating to teacher and student schedules, transportation, adjustment to new programs, and other factors — are knotty.

Several million children of elementary and high school age of all denominations have the opportunity of receiving religious instruction on released time. Under released time programs they are permitted to leave their public schools during school hours to attend religious instruction classes held off the public school premises. They are released at the request of their parents. Public school authorities merely provide for their dismissal, and take no part in the program.

NCEA

The National Catholic Educational Association, founded in 1904, is a voluntary organization of educational institutions and individuals concerned with Catholic education in the U.S. Its objectives are to promote and encourage the principles and ideals of Christian education and formation by suitable service and other activities.

The NCEA has 14,000 institutional and individual members. Its official publication is *Momentum*. Numerous service publications are issued to members.

Archbishop Joseph Bernardin of Cincinnati, Ohio, is chairman of the association. The Rev. John F. Meyers is president.

Headquarters are located at: Suite 350, One Dupont Circle, Washington, D.C. 20036.

Other Educational Associations

National Association of Boards of Education: Founded in 1971 and made a department of the National Catholic Educational Association in 1973, to develop and promote policy-making boards for the advancement of Catholic education. Has a national membership of 1,307. Publishes *PolicyMaker* four times a year. The executive director is Dr.

Mary-Angela Harper. Office: One Dupont Circle, Suite 350, Washington, D.C. 20036.

National Forum of Catholic Parent Organizations: Founded in 1976 as a commission of the National Catholic Educational Association, to support and promote the role of parents as primary educators of their children. Has a national membership of 625 affiliates. Publishes *Parentcator* 5 five times a year. Office: One Dupont Circle, Suite 350, Washington, D.C. 20036.

CATHOLIC SCHOOLS AND STUDENTS IN THE UNITED STATES

(Source: *The Official Catholic Directory, 1980;* figures as of Jan. 1, 1980. Archdioceses are indicated by an asterisk.)

Section, State Diocese	Univs. Colleges	Students	High Schools	Students	Elem. Schools	Students
NEW ENGLAND	27	56,311	133	67,455	533	146,990
Maine, Portland	1	445	4	1,335	23	5,993
New Hampshire, Manchester	5	4,536	6	2,587	30	8,732
Vermont, Burlington	3	2,429	3	1,308	11	2,745
Massachusetts	9	30,252	76	34,999	237	69,901
*Boston	4	20,966	58	24,510	153	46,999
Fall River	1	2,643	6	3,212	24	6,750
Springfield	1	480	4	3,180	35	10,030
Worcester	3	6,163	8	4,097	25	6,122
Rhode Island, Providence	2	7,943	13	6,689	64	18,228
Connecticut	7	10,706	31	20,537	168	41,391
*Hartford	3	1,868	15	11,246	97	23,782
Bridgeport	2	8,379	11	5,984	50	12,962
Norwich	2	459	5	3,307	21	4,647
MIDDLE ATLANTIC	65	170,534	385	250,076	2,176	698,993
New York	31	96,864	161	109,695	931	323,376
*New York	15	55,001	68	40,106	277	99,862
Albany	3	4,270	13	5,783	63	16,213
Brooklyn	2	19,202	22	25,399	176	93,722
Buffalo	6	13,678	21	9,968	152	34,809
Ogdensburg	1	341	3	1,222	28	5,583
Rochester	—	—	9	7,183	79	20,380
Rockville Centre	2	2,025	16	14,684	90	36,644
Syracuse	2	2,347	9	5,350	66	16,163
New Jersey	7	14,791	97	52,526	470	140,558
*Newark	3	13,352	49	23,092	216	61,468
Camden	—	—	12	7,603	69	21,004
Paterson	3	867	14	6,666	67	17,128
Trenton	1	572	22	15,165	118	40,958
Pennsylvania	27	58,879	127	87,855	775	235,059
*Philadelphia	11	27,729	52	52,840	288	120,511
Allentown	2	1,589	10	5,410	76	14,919
Altoona-Johnstown	2	2,255	3	1,988	41	8,082
Erie	3	5,799	10	4,781	59	15,892
Greensburg	2	1,825	2	1,493	49	9,367
Harrisburg	—	—	10	5,052	56	12,940
Pittsburgh	3	9,031	28	10,716	145	39,399
Scranton	4	10,651	12	5,575	61	13,949
SOUTH ATLANTIC	14	38,831	127	65,891	539	164,324
Delaware, Wilmington	—	—	8	5,126	30	10,989
Maryland, *Baltimore	4	9,148	25	13,354	91	27,426
District of Columbia, *Washington	3	20,841	26	11,780	83	25,632

Section, State Diocese	Univs. Colleges	Students	High Schools	Students	Elem. Schools	Students
Virginia	1	970	14	5,581	56	17,359
Arlington	1	970	4	2,660	28	9,436
Richmond	—	—	10	2,921	28	7,923
West Virginia, Wheeling-Charleston	1	1,197	9	2,384	36	6,401
North Carolina	2	1,327	3	1,187	37	8,726
Charlotte	2	1,327	2	954	18	4,565
Raleigh	—	—	1	233	19	4,161
South Carolina, Charleston	—	—	4	1,541	32	6,361
Georgia	—	—	7	3,898	29	8,947
*Atlanta	—	—	2	1,710	13	4,346
Savannah	—	—	5	2,188	16	4,601
Florida	3	5,348	31	21,040	145	52,483
*Miami	2	4,226	16	11,527	59	24,331
Orlando	—	—	5	2,749	27	8,549
Pensacola-Tallahassee	—	—	1	800	10	2,964
St. Augustine	—	—	2	1,439	16	6,533
St. Petersburg	1	1,122	7	4,525	33	10,106
EAST NORTH CENTRAL	**50**	**111,811**	**322**	**205,968**	**2,169**	**606,166**
Ohio	12	27,717	92	60,506	517	169,205
*Cincinnati	5	19,361	24	18,535	125	43,657
Cleveland	3	5,570	27	20,772	164	62,243
Columbus	1	849	14	5,960	53	15,269
Steubenville	1	677	4	1,400	18	3,497
Toledo	1	508	17	9,011	94	26,352
Youngstown	1	752	6	4,828	63	18,187
Indiana	9	15,891	25	13,620	207	48,084
*Indianapolis	2	1,439	9	5,469	74	16,701
Evansville	—	—	5	2,194	30	5,147
Ft. Wayne-South Bend	5	12,034	5	3,405	44	11,549
Gary	1	1,470	4	2,111	42	11,716
Lafayette	1	948	2	441	17	2,971
Illinois	13	42,429	103	76,326	677	201,437
*Chicago	7	34,058	65	53,600	384	134,089
Belleville	1	958	4	2,537	57	9,023
Joliet	3	5,241	9	6,645	67	19,331
Peoria	—	—	8	4,258	59	12,828
Rockford	—	—	8	4,571	48	11,670
Springfield	2	2,172	9	4,715	62	14,496
Michigan	8	18,179	69	35,931	342	94,934
*Detroit	5	13,984	46	25,301	165	58,408
Gaylord	—	—	5	1,135	20	3,824
Grand Rapids	1	2,163	4	2,920	47	8,632
Kalamazoo	1	540	3	1,098	21	3,965
Lansing	1	1,492	5	3,246	41	10,811
Marquette	—	—	1	116	12	2,659
Saginaw	—	—	5	2,115	36	6,635
Wisconsin	8	7,595	33	19,585	426	92,506
*Milwaukee	4	4,105	15	11,234	180	45,233
Green Bay	2	1,941	9	3,895	99	19,884
La Crosse	1	1,074	7	3,377	77	14,616
Madison	1	475	2	1,079	48	8,967
Superior	—	—	—	—	22	3,806
EAST SOUTH CENTRAL	**9**	**8,122**	**57**	**25,489**	**293**	**67,291**
Kentucky	5	5,383	30	14,058	162	37,140
*Louisville	3	3,196	11	8,247	80	20,951
Covington	1	1,343	14	4,082	54	10,966
Owensboro	1	844	5	1,729	28	5,223
Tennessee	2	1,439	10	5,131	42	10,119
Memphis	1	1,154	5	2,772	16	4,626
Nashville	1	285	5	2,359	26	5,493

Section, State Diocese	Univs. Colleges	Students	High Schools	Students	Elem. Schools	Students
Alabama	2	1,300	5	2,959	52	11,971
*Mobile	1	900	3	1,921	27	7,175
Birmingham	1	400	2	1,038	25	4,796
Mississippi	—	—	12	3,341	37	8,061
Biloxi	—	—	6	1,970	17	3,358
Jackson	—	—	6	1,371	20	4,703
WEST NORTH CENTRAL	35	49,346	171	73,667	913	200,309
Minnesota	9	15,150	27	13,036	225	52,055
*St. Paul and Minneapolis	3	7,824	14	9,168	110	31,886
Crookston	—	—	2	347	12	1,695
Duluth	1	1,159	—	—	15	2,314
New Ulm	—	—	3	807	28	4,291
St. Cloud	3	4,018	3	1,015	37	6,821
Winona	2	2,149	5	1,699	23	5,048
Iowa	8	8,067	30	13,605	159	32,455
*Dubuque	3	3,433	11	5,480	60	15,487
Davenport	4	3,386	8	2,133	38	5,227
Des Moines	—	—	2	2,193	22	4,435
Sioux City	1	1,248	9	3,799	39	7,306
Missouri	7	18,806	48	26,223	282	67,673
*St. Louis	5	13,113	34	19,692	178	46,757
Jefferson City	—	—	2	970	36	6,215
Kansas City-St. Joseph	2	5,693	9	4,865	46	11,978
Springfield-Cape Girardeau	—	—	3	696	22	2,723
North Dakota	2	1,076	7	2,121	34	5,732
Bismarck	1	942	6	1,655	19	3,208
Fargo	1	134	1	466	15	2,524
South Dakota	2	935	5	1,711	27	5,112
Rapid City	—	—	2	468	3	825
Sioux Falls	2	935	3	1,243	24	4,287
Nebraska	1	589	36	10,553	97	18,925
*Omaha	1	589	23	7,705	64	14,184
Grand Island	—	—	7	1,332	9	860
Lincoln	—	—	6	1,516	24	3,881
Kansas	6	4,723	18	6,418	89	18,357
*Kansas City	3	2,615	7	3,475	38	9,200
Dodge City	1	661	—	—	11	1,564
Salina	1	787	7	1,170	12	1,964
Wichita	1	660	4	1,773	28	5,629
WEST SOUTH CENTRAL	12	21,355	125	51,281	507	150,693
Arkansas, Little Rock	—	—	6	2,079	34	5,545
Louisiana	4	7,968	65	29,207	200	79,063
*New Orleans	4	7,968	29	18,076	93	43,406
Alexandria-Shreveport	—	—	7	2,235	25	6,439
Baton Rouge	—	—	9	2,846	25	10,282
Houma-Thibodaux	—	—	3	1,260	15	4,855
Lafayette	—	—	17	4,790	42	14,081
Lake Charles		No separate statistics available.				
Oklahoma	1	337	5	2,145	29	5,064
*Oklahoma City	1	337	2	969	17	2,675
Tulsa	—	—	3	1,176	12	2,389
Texas	7	13,050	49	17,850	244	61,021
*San Antonio	4	6,710	15	4,183	56	15,210
Amarillo	—	—	2	382	12	1,976
Austin	1	2,184	1	251	15	3,096
Beaumont	—	—	2	728	10	2,208
Brownsville	—	—	2	770	8	2,074
Corpus Christi	—	—	4	1,346	25	5,026
Dallas	1	2,391	7	3,311	32	9,362
El Paso	—	—	3	1,202	18	4,178
Fort Worth	—	—	4	1,438	15	3,849

Section, State Diocese	Univs. Colleges	Students	High Schools	Students	Elem. Schools	Students
Texas						
Galveston-Houston	1	1,765	9	4,239	48	13,380
San Angelo	—	—	—	—	5	662
MOUNTAIN	**5**	**6,853**	**37**	**14,859**	**191**	**46,303**
Montana	2	2,507	5	1,326	21	3,281
Great Falls-Billings	1	1,165	3	512	17	2,487
Helena	1	1,342	2	814	4	794
Idaho, Boise	—	—	1	450	12	1,740
Wyoming, Cheyenne	—	—	1	139	7	1,412
Colorado	1	1,083	13	3,907	57	13,846
*Denver	1	1,083	10	3,464	46	12,278
Pueblo	—	—	3	443	11	1,568
New Mexico	2	3,263	4	1,688	30	7,089
*Santa Fe	2	3,263	3	1,601	21	5,408
Gallup	—	—	1	87	9	1,681
Arizona	—	—	8	5,091	45	13,841
Phoenix	—	—	6	3,963	27	8,711
Tucson	—	—	2	1,128	18	5,130
Utah, Salt Lake City	—	—	3	918	8	2,089
Nevada, Reno-Las Vegas	—	—	2	1,340	11	3,005
PACIFIC	**20**	**41,548**	**165**	**91,142**	**779**	**228,246**
Washington	4	8,697	12	7,184	85	20,344
*Seattle	2	4,897	9	5,634	59	15,057
Spokane	2	3,800	2	1,290	19	3,688
Yakima	—	—	1	260	7	1,599
Oregon	2	3,541	11	4,034	55	10,664
*Portland	2	3,541	10	3,941	52	10,054
Baker	—	—	1	93	3	610
California	13	27,074	132	75,513	604	185,842
*Los Angeles	4	6,535	61	35,153	230	75,448
*San Francisco	4	13,326	26	15,226	104	32,049
Fresno	—	—	2	1,400	25	6,325
Monterey	—	—	2	931	14	3,411
Oakland	4	3,090	11	6,447	57	15,401
Orange	—	—	6	4,132	35	13,935
Sacramento	—	—	9	3,981	42	10,953
San Bernardino	—	—	2	1,641	29	8,505
San Diego	1	4,123	5	3,492	43	13,502
Santa Rosa	—	—	6	1,683	13	3,215
Stockton	—	—	2	1,427	12	3,098
Alaska	—	—	2	245	3	512
*Anchorage	—	—	—	—	1	108
Fairbanks	—	—	2	245	1	288
Juneau	—	—	—	—	1	116
Hawaii, Honolulu	1	2,236	8	4,166	32	10,884
EASTERN RITES	**2**	**365**	**5**	**731**	**49**	**7,885**
*Philadelphia	1	357	1	345	17	3,107
St. Nicholas	—	—	1	136	3	815
Stamford	1	8	3	250	10	1,182
*Pittsburgh	—	—	—	—	6	1,020
Parma	—	—	—	—	6	811
Passaic	—	—	—	—	7	950
St. Maron	—	—	—	—	—	—
Newton	—	—	—	—	—	—
TOTALS 1980	**239**	**505,076**	**1,527**	**846,559**	**8,149**	**2,317,200**
Totals 1979	241	483,760	1,542	853,606	8,240	2,379,816
Totals 1970	292	430,863	2,082	1,054,642	9,947	3,665,376

REPORT ON CATHOLIC EDUCATION

The status of Catholic educational institutions and programs in the United States at the beginning of 1980, 1979 and 1970 were reflected in figures (as of Jan. 1) reported by *The Official Catholic Directory, 1980.*

Colleges and Universities: 239 (2 less than in 1979 and 53 less than in 1970).

College and University Students: 505,076 (21,316 more than in 1979 and 74,213 more than in 1970).

High Schools: 1,527 (15 less than in 1979 and 555 less than in 1970).

High School Students: 864,559 (7,047 less than in 1979 and 208,083 less than in 1970).

Public High School Students Receiving Religious Instruction: 996,979 (89,171 less than in 1979 and 371,838 less than in 1970).

Elementary Schools: 8,149 (91 less than in 1979 and 1,798 less than in 1970).

Elementary School Students: 2,317,200 (62,616 less than in 1979 and 1,348,176 less than in 1970).

Public Elementary School Students Receiving Religious Instruction: 3,575,618 (124,261 less than in 1979 and 506,311 less than in 1970).

Teachers, Full-Time: 167,713 (1,436 less than in 1979 and 31,755 less than in 1970).

Lay Teachers: 117,663 (1,368 more than in 1979 and 19,662 more than in 1970).

Sisters: 41,135 (2,578 less than in 1979 and 44,481 less than in 1970).

Priests: 5,444 (356 less than in 1979 and 4,514 less than in 1970).

Brothers: 3,271 (92 more than in 1979 and 2,026 less than in 1970).

Scholastics: 200 (38 more than in 1979 and 396 less than in 1970).

Status of Elementary and Secondary Schools: Father Frank H. Bredeweg, commenting in March, 1980, on a statistical report of the National Catholic Educational Association, said that "Catholic schools are probably at their finest hour." Despite a decline in enrollment and the closing or consolidation of some schools in the 1979-80 academic year, he said the schools were in good shape in terms of academic offerings, class sizes, faculty degrees, experience and certification.

According to the report: "Catholic schools continue to stabilize. Most large-scale reviews of diocesan school systems have been completed and obvious closings or consolidations have been effected. ... Administrative and budget procedures have been improved, with resulting better management. The drastic movement of people from city to suburbs during the 1960s, a significant factor since Catholic schools were built in the cities, has slowed. Finally, and most important of all, Catholic parents and students continue to enthusiastically support Catholic schools."

Minority Enrollment: A 1978 survey reported by the National Catholic Educational Association indicated that Catholic elementary and secondary schools had an average national minority enrollment of 16 per cent. Higher percentages were reported for some urban areas, like: the five boroughs of New York, 38 per cent; Manhattan, 76 per cent; urban District of Columbia, 76 per cent; some inner city areas, 99 per cent.

Early in 1980, the National Catholic Conference for Interracial Justice reported in *Commitment* percentage increases between 1970-71 and 1978-79 for black students, from 4.8 to 7.7 per cent, and Hispanics, from 5 to 7.6 per cent.

Court Decisions: The U.S. Supreme Court, with a 5-to-4 decision Feb. 20, 1980, upheld the constitutionality of a 1974 New York law providing direct cash payment to nonpublic schools for the costs of certain state-mandated testing programs. It was thought the ruling was the first approval ever given by the Court for direct cash payments to nonpublic schools. The majority opinion, written by Justice Byron White, said that reimbursements for costs incurred by the nonpublic schools neither advanced the purposes of religion nor excessively entangled the state in the affairs of religion. "We decline to embrace a formalistic dichotomy that bears so little relationship to common sense or to the realities of school finance," the opinion said in rejecting arguments that direct cash payments would be a new and serious violation of church-state separation. Seven years earlier the Court struck down a reimbursement measure which served secular purposes but had no built-in safeguards against benefitting religion.

The Court decided May 12, 1980, to let stand a Kentucky Supreme Court ruling which limited the power of the state to regulate private schools.

In Louisiana, the First Circuit Court of Appeals ruled in June, 1980, that employees of church-operated schools are not covered by the unemployment security law and that their employers do not have to pay unemployment compensation tax. The ruling, which was in line with an earlier decision of the 19th Judicial Court, was significant because it excluded the state from involvement in the hiring and dismissal policies of Catholic schools.

Tax Credit Not Forthcoming: Perry E. Anthony, director of the U.S. Bishops' Office for Educational Assistance, reported in February, 1980, that there were pending in Congress 34 separate proposals for tuition tax credits for parents of children attending private schools. One of them, proposed by Senator Daniel Moynihan of New York, would have provided up to $750 a year to parents with children in nonpublic schools, by extending the terms of a grant program already available to students at private and religiously oriented colleges and universities. None of the credit bills were enacted into law.

CATHOLIC TEACHER UNIONS

Catholic teacher unions organized in recent years include several in the Archdiocese of New York and locals in Philadelphia, Pittsburgh, Youngstown and Brooklyn. Several of them belong to the National Association of Catholic School Teachers, which has links with groups in Scranton, San Francisco, Los Angeles, Altoona-Johnstown, Kansas City, Mo., Cleveland and Louisville.

The purpose of the association is "to work with diocesan officials in an attempt to draw up acceptable guidelines that can be used by all parties to insure that the teachings of the Church are as applicable to the employer-employee relationship within the institutional Church as the Church has taught for so many years they are in the private and public sectors of industry."

A significant U.S. Supreme Court decision affecting teacher unions in Catholic schools was handed down Mar. 21, 1979. The Court ruled that the National Labor Relations Act of 1935 does not give jurisdiction to the National Labor Relations Board over teachers and their organizations in Catholic schools.

The case originated in representational disputes in the Archdiocese of Chicago and the Diocese of Fort Wayne-South Bend.

Msgr. George G. Higgins, commenting on the decision, pointed out the responsibility of those in charge of Catholic schools to develop agencies of their own analogous to those of the NLRB to deal with union negotiations.

Advocates of unionization argue with justification that teachers have a right to collective bargaining, that they deserve salaries and other contract provisions commensurate with their needs and the quality of their work, and that they need collective protection against authoritative and arbitrary actions by some administrators.

Bishops and school administrators have shown considerable reluctance to deal with unions, especially those which are affiliated with the American Federation of Teachers. Behind the objection is the AFT's record of opposition to public aid for students in nonpublic schools. Also regarded as objectionable is its advocacy of the dissemination of information on birth control and abortion in sex education. Affiliates claim, however, that they are not in sympathy with or bound by these commitments of the federation.

Fears have also been expressed that union demands, financial and otherwise, might drive schools out of existence, change their character, or diminish control over them by the Church.

UNIVERSITIES AND COLLEGES IN THE UNITED STATES

(Sources: Almanac survey; *The Official Catholic Directory.*)

Listed below are institutions of higher learning established under Catholic auspices. Some of them are now independent.

Information includes: name of each institution; indication of male (m), female (w), coeducational (c) student body; name of founding group or group with which the institution is affiliated; year of foundation; number of students, in parentheses.

Albertus Magnus College (w): 700 Prospect St., New Haven, Conn. 06511. Dominican Sisters; 1925 (560).

Albuquerque, University of (c): St. Joseph Pl. N.W., Albuquerque, N.M. 87140. Sisters of St. Francis; 1940 (2,084).

Allentown College of St. Francis de Sales (c): Center Valley, Pa. 18034. Oblates of St. Francis de Sales; 1965 (820).

Alvernia College (c): Reading, Pa. 19607. Bernardine Sisters; 1958 (769).

Alverno College (w): 3401 S. 39th St. Milwaukee, Wis. 53215. School Sisters of St. Francis; 1936; independent (1,327).

Anna Maria College (c): Sunset Lane, Paxton, Mass. 01612. Sisters of St. Anne; 1946 (1,288).

Annhurst College (c): Woodstock, Conn.

06281. Daughters of the Holy Spirit; 1941 (345).

Aquinas College (c): 1607 Robinson Rd. S.E., Grand Rapids, Mich. 49506. Sisters of St. Dominic; 1922 (2,163).

Assumption College (c): 50 Old English Rd., Worcester, Mass. 01609. Assumptionist Fathers; 1904 (2,359).

Avila College (c): 11901 Wornall Rd., Kansas City, Mo. 64145. Sisters of St. Joseph of Carondelet; 1916 (2,000).

Barat College (w): 700 Westleigh Rd., Lake Forest, Ill. 60045. Society of the Sacred Heart; 1919; independent (736).

Barry College (c): 11300 N.E. 2nd Ave., Miami, Fla. 33161. Dominican Sisters; 1940 (2,058).

Bellarmine College (c): 2000 Norris Pl., Louisville, Ky. 40205; Louisville archdiocese, 1950 (1,801).

Belmont Abbey College (c): Belmont, N.C. 28012. Benedictine Fathers; 1876 (777).

Benedictine College (c): Atchison, Kans. 66002. Benedictines, 1971 (1,045).

Biscayne College (c): 16400 N.W. 32nd Ave., Miami, Fla. 33054. Augustinian Fathers; 1962 (2,155).

Boston College (University Status) (c):

Chestnut Hill, Mass. 02167. Jesuit Fathers; 1863 (16,483).

Brescia College (c): 120 W. 7th St., Owensboro, Ky. 42301. Ursuline Sisters; 1925 (832).

Briar Cliff College (c): W. 3303 Rebecca St., Sioux City, Ia. 51104. Sisters of St. Francis of the Holy Family; 1930 (1,258).

Cabrini College (c): Radnor, Pa. 19087. Missionary Srs. of Sacred Heart; 1957 (570, day and evening).

Caldwell College (w): Caldwell, N.J. 07006. Dominican Sisters; 1939 (673).

Calumet College (c): 2400 New York Ave., Whiting, Ind. 46394. Society of the Precious Blood, 1951 (1,470).

Canisius College (c): 2001 Main St., Buffalo, N.Y. 14208. Jesuit Fathers; 1870; independent (4,079).

Cardinal Newman College (c): 7701 Florissant Rd., St. Louis, Mo. 63121. Catholic college with autonomous board of trustees; 1976.

Cardinal Stritch College (c): 6801 N. Yates Rd., Milwaukee, Wis. 53217. Sisters of St. Francis of Assisi; 1932; independent (1,139).

Carlow College (w): 3333 5th Ave., Pittsburgh, Pa. 15213. Sisters of Mercy; 1929 (959).

Carroll College (c): Helena, Mont. 59601. Diocesan Clergy; 1909 (1,342).

Catholic University of America, The (c): Fourth St. and Michigan Ave. N.E., Washington, D.C. 20064. Hierarchy of the United States; 1887. Pontifical University (8,252).

Catholic University of Puerto Rico (c): Ponce, P.R. Hierarchy of Puerto Rico; Pontifical University (9,079).

Chaminade University (c): 3140 Waialae Ave., Honolulu, Hawaii 96816. Marianists; 1955 (2,175).

Chestnut Hill College (w): Philadelphia, Pa. 19118. Sisters of St. Joseph; 1871 (913).

Christian Brothers College (c): 650 E. Parkway S., Memphis, Tenn. 38104. Brothers of the Christian Schools; 1871 (1,154).

Clarke College (w): 1550 Clarke Dr., Dubuque, Iowa 52001. Sisters of Charity, BVM; 1843 (670).

Creighton University (c): 2500 California St., Omaha, Neb. 68178. Jesuit Fathers; 1878 (5,027).

Dallas, University of (c): Irving, Tex. 75061. Private; 1956; independent (2,391).

Dayton, University of (c): 300 College Park Ave., Dayton, Ohio 45409. Marianists; 1850 (8,319).

De Paul University (c): 2323 N. Seminary Ave., Chicago, Ill. 60614. Vincentians; 1898 (12,857).

Detroit, University of (c): McNicholas Rd. at Livernois, Detroit, Mich. 48221. Jesuit Fathers; 1877 (8,300).

Dominican College of Blauvelt (c): Orange-burg, N.Y. 10962. Dominican Sisters; 1952 (1,231).

Dominican College of San Rafael (c): San Rafael, Calif. 94901. Dominican Sisters; 1890; independent (645).

Duquesne University (c): 801 Bluff St., N.W., Pittsburgh, Pa. 15219. Holy Ghost Fathers; 1878 (6,872).

D'Youville College (c): 320 Porter Ave., Buffalo, N.Y. 14201. Grey Nuns of the Sacred Heart; 1908; independent (1,569).

Edgecliff College (c): 2220 Victory Pkwy., Cincinnati, Ohio 45206. Sisters of Mercy; 1935 (752).

Edgewood College (c): 855 Woodrow St., Madison, Wis. 53711. Dominican Sisters; 1927 (475).

Emmanuel College (w): 400 The Fenway, Boston, Mass. 02115. Sisters of Notre Dame de Namur; independent (1,068).

Fairfield University (c): Fairfield, Conn. 06430. Jesuit Fathers; 1942 (4,713).

Felician College (w): S. Main St., Lodi, N.J. 07644. Felician Sisters; 1942 (760).

Fontbonne College (c): 6800 Wydown Blvd., St. Louis, Mo. 63105. Sisters of St. Joseph of Carondelet; 1917 (794).

Fordham University (c): Fordham Rd. and Third Ave., New York, N.Y. 10458. Society of Jesus (Jesuits); 1841; independent (14,964).

Fort Wright College (c): W. 4000 Randolph Rd., Spokane, Wash. 99204. Sisters of the Holy Names of Jesus and Mary; 1939 (405).

Gannon University (c): 109 W. 6th St., Erie, Pa. 16541. Diocese of Erie; 1944 (3,500).

Georgetown University (c): 37th and O Sts. N.W., Washington, D.C. 20057. Jesuit Fathers; 1789 (12,000).

Georgian Court College (w): Lakewood, N.J. 08701. Sisters of Mercy; 1908 (1,258). Coed in evening and graduate divisions.

Gonzaga University (c): Spokane, Wash. 99258. Jesuit Fathers; 1887 (3,340).

Great Falls, College of (c): 1301 20th St. S., Great Falls, Mont. 59405. Sisters of Providence; 1932 (1,165).

Gwynedd-Mercy College (c): Gwynedd Valley, Pa. 19437. Sisters of Mercy; 1948; independent (936).

Holy Cross, College of the (c): Worcester, Mass. 01610. Jesuit Fathers; 1843 (2,570).

Holy Family College (c): Grant and Frankford Aves., Philadelphia, Pa. 19114. Sisters of Holy Family of Nazareth; 1954 (1,142).

Holy Names College (c): 3500 Mountain Blvd., Oakland, Calif. 94619. Sisters of the Holy Names of Jesus and Mary; 1868 (611).

Illinois Benedictine College (c): Lisle, Ill. 60532. Benedictine Fathers; 1887 (1,431).

Immaculata College (w): Immaculata, Pa. 19345. Sisters, Servants of the Immaculate Heart of Mary; 1920 (763).

Incarnate Word College (c): 4301 Broadway, San Antonio, Tex. 78209. Sisters of Charity of the Incarnate Word; 1881 (1,468).

Iona College (c): 715 North Ave., New Rochelle, N.Y. 10801. Congregation of Christian Brothers; 1940; independent (5,400).

John Carroll University (c): North Park and Miramar Blvds., Cleveland, Ohio. 44118. Jesuit Fathers; 1886 (4,000).

Kansas Newman College (formerly Sacred Heart College) (c): 3100 McCormick Ave., Wichita, Kans. 67213. Sisters Adorers of the Blood of Christ; 1933 (652).

King's College (c): Wilkes-Barre, Pa. 18711. Holy Cross Fathers; 1946 (2,115).

Ladycliff College (w): Highland Falls, N.Y. 10928. Franciscan Sisters; 1933; independent (501).

La Roche College (c): 9000 Babcock Blvd., Pittsburgh, Pa. 15237. Sisters of Divine Providence; 1963 (1,260)

La Salle College (c): 20th St. and Olney Ave., Philadelphia, Pa. 19141. Brothers of the Christian Schools; 1863 (6,587)

Le Moyne College (c): Syracuse, N.Y. 13214. Jesuit Fathers; 1946; independent (1,800).

Lewis University (c): Romeoville, Ill. 60441. Christian Brothers; 1930 (2,790).

Loras College (c): 1450 Alta Vista St., Dubuque, Ia. 52001. Archdiocese of Dubuque; 1839 (1,721).

Loyola College (c): 4501 N. Charles St., Baltimore, Md. 21210, Jesuits; 1852; combined with Mt. St. Agnes College, 1971 (5,217).

Loyola Marymount University (c): 7101 W. 80th St., Los Angeles, Calif. 90045. Society of Jesus; Religious of Sacred Heart of Mary, Sisters of St. Joseph of Orange; 1911 (5,879).

Loyola University (c): 6363 St. Charles Ave., New Orleans, La. 70118. Jesuit Fathers; 1904 (4,535).

Loyola University of Chicago (c): 820 N. Michigan Ave., Chicago, Ill. 60611. Jesuit Fathers; 1870 (15,155).

Madonna College (c): 36600 Schoolcraft Rd., Livonia, Mich. 48150. Felician Sisters; 1937 (3,131).

Manhattan College (c): 4513 Manhattan College Pkwy., New York, N.Y. 10471. Brothers of the Christian Schools; 1853; independent (4,600). Cooperative program with College of Mt. St. Vincent.

Marian College (c): Fond du Lac, Wis. 54935. Sisters of St. Agnes; 1936 (500).

Marian College (c): 3200 Cold Spring Rd., Indianapolis, Ind. 46222. Sisters of St. Francis (Oldenburg, Ind.); 1937 (880).

Marist College (c): Poughkeepsie, N.Y. 12601. Marist Brothers of the Schools; 1946; independent (1,899).

Marquette University (c): 615 N. 11th St., Milwaukee, Wis. 53233. Jesuit Fathers; 1881; independent (13,638).

Mary College (c): Bismarck, N.D. 58501. Benedictine Sisters; 1959 (942).

Marycrest College (c): 1607 W. 12th St., Davenport, Iowa 52804. Sisters of the Humility of Mary; 1939 (1,034).

Marygrove College (c): 8425 W. McNicholas Rd., Detroit, Mich. 48221. Sisters, Servants of the Immaculate Heart of Mary; 1910 (958).

Marymount College (w): Tarrytown, N.Y. 10591. Religious of the Sacred Heart of Mary; 1907; independent (1,172).

Marymount College of Kansas (c): Salina, Kans. 67401. Sisters of St. Joseph of Concordia; 1922 (775).

Marymount College of Virginia (w): 2807 N. Glebe Rd., Arlington, Va. 22007. Religious of the Sacred Heart of Mary; 1950 (970).

Marymount Manhattan College (w): 221 E. 71st St., New York, N.Y. 10021. Religious of the Sacred Heart of Mary; 1948; independent (2,252).

Maryville College (c): 13550 Conway Rd., St. Louis, Mo. 63141. Religious of the Sacred Heart; 1872; independent (1,380).

Marywood College (w): Scranton, Pa. 18509. Sisters, Servants of the Immaculate Heart of Mary; 1915 (3,123). Coed in graduate division.

Mater Dei College (c): Riverside Dr., Ogdensburg, N.Y. 13669. Sisters of St. Joseph; 1960 (300).

Mercy College (c): 8200 W. Outer Dr., Detroit, Mich. 48219. Sisters of Mercy; 1941 (2,419).

Mercyhurst College (c): 501 E. 38th St., Erie, Pa. 16501. Sisters of Mercy; 1926 (1,488).

Merrimack College (c): North Andover, Mass. 01845. Augustinians; 1947 (2,188).

Misericordia (College Misericordia) (w): Dallas, Pa. 18612. Religious Sisters of Mercy of the Union; 1924 (947).

Molloy College (w): 1000 Hempstead Ave., Rockville Centre, N.Y. 11570. Dominican Sisters; 1955 (1,500).

Mount Marty College (c): Yankton, S.D. 57078. Benedictine Sisters; 1936 (580).

Mount Mary College (w): 2900 W. Menomonee River Pkwy., Milwaukee, Wis. 53222. School Sisters of Notre Dame; 1913 (1,126).

Mt. Mercy College (c): 1330 Elmhurst Dr. N.E., Cedar Rapids, Ia. 52402. Sisters of Mercy; 1928 (1,042).

Mt. St. Joseph on the Ohio, College of (w): Mt. St. Joseph, Ohio 45051. Sisters of Charity; 1920 (1,480).

Mt. St. Mary College (c): Newburgh, N.Y. 12550. Dominican Sisters; 1959; independent (1,046).

Mt. St. Mary College (c): Emmitsburg, Md. 21727. Diocesan Clergy; 1808; independent (1,260).

Mt. St. Mary's College (w): 12001 Chalon Rd., Los Angeles, Calif. 90049. Sisters of St.

Joseph of Carondelet; 1925 (1,108). Coed in music, nursing and graduate programs.

Mt. St. Vincent, College of (c): Mt. St. Vincent-on-Hudson, New York, N.Y. 10471. Sisters of Charity; 1847; independent (1,200). Cooperative program with Manhattan College.

Mundelein College (w): 6363 N. Sheridan Rd., Chicago, Ill. 60660. Sisters of Charity of the Blessed Virgin Mary; 1929 (1,395).

Nazareth College (c): Nazareth, Mich. 49074. Sisters of St. Joseph; 1924 (540).

Nazareth College (c): East Ave., Rochester, N.Y. 14610. Sisters of St. Joseph of Rochester; 1924; independent (2,772).

New Rochelle, College of (w): 29 Castle Pl., New Rochelle, N.Y. 10801 (main campus). Ursuline Nuns; 1904; independent (4,484). Coed in nursing, graduate, new resources divisions.

Niagara University (c): Niagara Univ., N.Y. 14109. Vincentian Fathers; 1856 (4,905).

Notre Dame, College of (c): Belmont, Calif. 94002. Sisters of Notre Dame de Namur; 1868; independent (1,342).

Notre Dame, University of (c): Notre Dame, Ind. 46556. Congregation of Holy Cross; 1842 (8,731).

Notre Dame College (w): 4545 College Rd., Cleveland, Ohio 44121. Sisters of Notre Dame; 1922 (600).

Notre Dame College (w): Manchester, N.H. 03104. Sisters of the Holy Cross; 1950 (723).

Notre Dame of Maryland, College of (w): 4701 N. Charles St., Baltimore, Md. 21210. School Sisters of Notre Dame; 1873 (752).

Ohio Dominican College (c): Columbus, Ohio 43219. Dominican Srs.; 1911 (849).

Our Lady of Angels College (w): Aston, Pa. 19014. Sisters of St. Francis; 1965 (674).

Our Lady of Holy Cross College (c): 4123 Woodland Dr., New Orleans, La. 70114. Congregation of Sisters Marianites of Holy Cross (766).

Our Lady of the Elms, College of (w): Chicopee, Mass. 01013. Sisters of St. Joseph; 1928 (500).

Our Lady of the Lake University of San Antonio (c): 411 S.W. 24th St., San Antonio, Tex. 78285. Sisters of Divine Providence; 1911 (1,744).

Portland, University of (c): 5000 N. Willamette Blvd., Portland, Ore. 97203. Holy Cross Fathers; 1901; independent (2,708).

Providence College (c): River Ave. and Eaton St., Providence, R.I. 02918. Dominican Friars; 1917 (4,186).

Quincy College (c): 1831 College Ave., Quincy, Ill. 62301. Franciscan Fathers; 1860 (1,646).

Regis College (c): W. 50th Ave. and Lowell Blvd. Denver, Colo. 80221. Jesuit Fathers; 1887 (1,083).

Regis College (w): Weston, Mass. 02193.

Sisters of St. Joseph; 1927; independent (1,270).

Rivier College (w): Nashua, N.H. 03060. Sisters of the Presentation of Mary; 1933; independent (1,703). Coed continuing education and graduate divisions.

Rockhurst College (c): 5225 Troost Ave., Kansas City, Mo. 64110. Jesuit Fathers; 1910 (3,515).

Rosary College (c): 7900 Division St., River Forest, Ill. 60305. Dominican Sisters; 1901 (1,575).

Rosemont College (w): Rosemont, Pa. 19010. Society of the Holy Child Jesus; 1921 (585).

Sacred Heart College (w): Belmont, N.C. 28012. Sisters of Mercy; 1935 (309).

Sacred Heart University (c): Fairfield (P.O. Bridgeport), Conn. 06604. Diocese of Bridgeport; 1963; independent (3,666).

St. Ambrose College (c): Davenport, Ia. 52803. Diocese of Davenport; 1882 (1,955).

St. Anselm's College (c): Manchester N.H. 03102. Benedictine Monks; 1889 (1,932).

St. Basil's College (m): 195 Glenbrook Rd., Stamford, Conn. 06902. Byzantine-Ukrainian Rite Diocese of Stamford; 1939.

Saint Benedict, College of (w): St. Joseph, Minn. 56374. Benedictine Sisters; 1913 (2,023).

St. Bonaventure University (c): St. Bonaventure, N.Y. 14778. Franciscan Friars; 1856; independent (2,781).

St. Catherine, College of (w): 2004 Randolph St., St. Paul, Minn. 55105. Sisters of St. Joseph of Carondelet; 1905 (2,165).

St. Edward's University (c): Austin, Tex. 78704. Holy Cross Brothers; 1885 (2,184).

St. Elizabeth, College of (w): Convent Station, N.J. 07961. Sisters of Charity; 1899; independent (781).

St. Francis, College of (c): 500 N. Wilcox St., Joliet, Ill. 60435. Sisters of St. Francis of Mary Immaculate; 1925; independent (584).

St. Francis College (c): 180 Remsen St., Brooklyn, N.Y. 11201. Franciscan Brothers; 1884; private, independent in the Franciscan tradition (3,100).

St. Francis College (c): 2701 Spring St., Fort Wayne, Ind. 46808. Sisters of St. Francis; 1890 (1,364).

St. Francis College (c): Loretto, Pa. 15940. Franciscan Fathers; 1847 (1,754).

St. John Fisher College (c): 3690 East Ave., Rochester, N.Y. 14618. Basilian Fathers; 1951; independent (1,700).

St. John's University (c): Grand Central and Utopia Pkwys., Jamaica, N.Y. 11439 (Queens Campus); 300 Howard Ave., Grymes Hill, Staten Island, N.Y. 10301 (Staten Island Campus). Vincentian Fathers; 1870 (17,812).

St. John's University (m): Collegeville, Minn. 56321. Benedictine Fathers; 1857 (1,971). Coed in graduate school.

St. Joseph College (w): 1678 Asylum Ave.,

West Hartford, Conn. 06117. Sisters of Mercy; 1932 (1,200). Coed in graduate school.

St. Joseph's College (c): Standish (P.O. N. Windham), Me. 04062. Sisters of Mercy; 1915 (550).

Saint Joseph's College (c): Rensselaer, Ind. 47978. Society of the Precious Blood; 1889 (948).

St. Joseph's University (c): City Ave. at 54th St., Philadelphia, Pa. 19131. Jesuit Fathers; 1851 (5,587).

St. Joseph's College (c): 245 Clinton Ave., Brooklyn, N.Y. 11205 and 155 Roe Blvd., Patchogue, N.Y. 11772. Sisters of St. Joseph; 1916; independent.

St. Joseph the Provider, College of (c): Clement Rd., Rutland, Vt. 05701. Sisters of St. Joseph; 1954; independent (184).

Saint Leo College (c): Saint Leo, Fla. 33574. Order of St. Benedict; 1889; independent (1,002).

St. Louis University (c): 221 N. Grand Blvd., St. Louis, Mo. 63103. Jesuit Fathers; 1818 (10,364).

Saint Martin's College (c): Lacey, Wash. 98503. Benedictine Monks; 1895 (751).

St. Mary, College of (w): 1901 S. 72nd St., Omaha, Neb. 68124. Sisters of Mercy; 1923; independent (589).

St. Mary College (w): Leavenworth, Kans. 66048. Sisters of Charity of Leavenworth; 1923 (798).

St. Mary of the Plains College (c): Dodge City, Kans. 67801. Sisters of St. Joseph of Wichita; 1952 (661).

St. Mary-of-the-Woods College (w): St. Mary-of-the-Woods, Ind. 47876. Sisters of Providence; 1840 (559).

St. Mary's College (w): Notre Dame, Ind. 46556. Sisters of the Holy Cross; 1844 (1,819).

St. Mary's College (c): Orchard Lake, Mich. 48033. Secular Clergy; 1885 (212).

St. Mary's College (c): Moraga, Calif. 94575. Brothers of the Christian Schools; 1863 (1,445).

St. Mary's College (c): Winona, Minn. 55987. Brothers of the Christian Schools; 1913 (1,258).

St. Mary's Dominican College (w): 7214 St. Charles Ave., New Orleans, La. 70118. Dominican Sisters; 1910 (754).

St. Mary's University (c): One Camino Santa Maria, San Antonio, Tex. 78284. Society of Mary (Marianists); 1852 (3,374).

St. Michael's College (c): Winooski, Vt. 05404. Society of St. Edmund; 1904 (1,575).

St. Norbert College (c): De Pere, Wis. 54115. Norbertine Fathers; 1898; independent (1,628).

St. Peter's College (c): 2641 Kennedy Blvd., Jersey City, N.J. 07306. Jesuit Fathers; 1872 (3,973).

St. Rose, College of (c): 432 Western Ave., Albany, N.Y. 12203. Sisters of St. Joseph of

Carondelet; 1920; independent (2,800).

St. Scholastica, College of (c): 1200 Kenwood Ave., Duluth, Minn. 55811. Benedictine Sisters; 1912 (1,159).

Saint Teresa, College of (w): Winona, Minn. 55987. Sisters of St. Francis; 1907 (900).

St. Thomas, College of (c): St. Paul, Minn. 55101. Archdiocese of St. Paul; 1885 (4,784).

St. Thomas, University of (c): 3812 Montrose Blvd., Houston, Tex. 77006. Basilian Fathers; 1947 (1,751).

St. Thomas Aquinas College (c): Sparkill, N.Y. 10976. Dominican Sisters of Sparkill; 1952; independent, corporate board of trustees (1,200).

St. Vincent College (m): Latrobe, Pa. 15650. Benedictine Fathers; 1846 (896).

St. Xavier College (c): 3700 W. 103rd St., Chicago, Ill. 60655. Sisters of Mercy; chartered 1847 (2,153).

Salve Regina — The Newport College (c): Ochre Point Ave., Newport, R.I. 02840. Sisters of Mercy; 1934 (1,600).

San Diego, University of (c): Alcala Park, San Diego, Calif. 92110. San Diego diocese and Religious of the Sacred Heart; 1949; independent (4,000).

San Francisco, University of (c): 2130 Fulton St., San Francisco, Calif. 94117. Jesuit Fathers; 1855 (6,392).

Santa Clara, University of (c): Santa Clara, Calif. 95053. Jesuit Fathers; 1851 (7,295).

Santa Fe, College of (c): Santa Fe, N. Mex. 87501. Brothers of the Christian Schools; 1947 (1,272).

Scranton, University of (c): Scranton, Pa. 18510. Jesuit Fathers; 1888 (4,437).

Seattle University (c): Broadway and East Madison, Seattle, Wash. 98122. Jesuit Fathers; 1891 (3,966).

Seton Hall University (c): South Orange, N.J. 07079. Diocesan Clergy; 1856 (9,991).

Seton Hill College (w): Greensburg, Pa. 15601. Sisters of Charity of Seton Hill; 1883 (790).

Siena College (c): Loudonville, N.Y. 12211. Franciscan Friars; 1937 (2,300).

Siena Heights College (c): Adrian, Mich. 49221. Dominican Sisters; 1919; independent (1,490).

Silver Lake College of Holy Family (c): 2406 S. Alverno Rd., Manitowoc, Wis. 54220. Franciscan Sisters of Christian Charity; 1935 (313).

Spalding College (c): 851 S. 4th St., Louisville, Ky. 40203. Sisters of Charity of Nazareth; 1814 (as Nazareth Academy); independent (928).

Spring Hill College (c): Mobile, Ala. 36608. Jesuit Fathers; 1830 (904).

Steubenville, University of (c): Steubenville, Ohio 43952. Franciscan Fathers; 1946 (977).

Stonehill College (c): North Easton, Mass.

02356. Holy Cross Fathers; 1948; independent (2,643).

Thomas More College (c): 2771 Turkey Foot Rd., Fort Mitchell, Covington, Ky. 41017. Diocese of Covington; 1921 (1,272).

Trinity College (w): Colchester Ave., Burlington, Vt. 05401. Sisters of Mercy; 1925 (670).

Trinity College (w): Michigan Ave. and Franklin St. N.E., Washington, D.C. 20017. Sisters of Notre Dame de Namur; 1897 (808). Coed in graduate school.

Ursuline College (w): 2550 Lander Rd., Cleveland, Ohio 44124. Ursuline Nuns; 1871 (970).

Villa Maria College (w): 2551 W. Lake Rd., Erie, Pa. 16505. Sisters of St. Joseph; 1925 (610).

Villanova University (c): Villanova, Pa. 19085. Augustinian Fathers; 1842 (9,422).

Viterbo College (c): La Crosse, Wis. 54601. Franciscan Sisters; 1890 (1,074).

Walsh College (c): 2020 Easton St. N.W., Canton, Ohio 44720. Brothers of Christian Instruction; 1958 (752).

Wheeling College (c): 316 Washington Ave., Wheeling, W. Va. 26003. Jesuit Fathers; 1954 (703).

Xavier University (c): Victory Pkwy. and Dana Ave., Cincinnati, Ohio 45207. Jesuit Fathers; 1831 (6,382).

Xavier University of Louisiana (c): 7325 Palmetto St., New Orleans, La. 70125. Sisters of Blessed Sacrament; 1925; lay religious administration board (1,934).

Catholic Junior Colleges

Ancilla Domini College (c): Donaldson, Ind. 46513. Ancilla Domini Sisters; 1937 (330).

Aquinas Junior College (c): Harding Rd., Nashville, Tenn. 37205. Dominican Sisters; 1961 (323).

Chatfield College: St. Martin, O. 45118. Ursulines (223).

Donnelly College (c): 1236 Sandusky Ave., Kansas City, Kans. 66102. Archdiocesan College; 1949 (772).

Don Bosco Technical Institute: 1151 San Gabriel Blvd., Rosemead, Calif. 91770. Salenians (296).

Elizabeth Seton College (c): 1061 N. Broadway, Yonkers, N.Y. 10701. Sisters of Charity; 1960; independent (1,259).

Harriman College (c): Harriman Heights Rd., Harriman, N.Y. 10926. Sisters of the Catholic Apostolate; 1956; independent (344).

Hilbert College (c): 5200 S. Park Ave., Hamburg, N.Y. 14075. Franciscan Sisters of St. Joseph; 1957; independent (540).

Holy Cross Junior College (c): Notre Dame, Ind. 46556. Brothers of Holy Cross; 1966 (263).

Lourdes College (c): Sylvania, Ohio 43560. Franciscan Srs.; 1958 (525).

Manor Junior College (w): Fox Chase Manor, Jenkintown, Pa. 19046. Sisters of St. Basil the Great; 1947 (357).

Maria College (c): 700 New Scotland Ave., Albany, N.Y. 12208. Sisters of Mercy; 1963 (512).

Maria Regina College (w): 1024 Court St., Syracuse, N.Y. 13208. Franciscan Sisters; 1963; independent (399).

Marymount Palos Verdes College (c): Rancho Palos Verdes, Calif. 90274. Religious of the Sacred Heart of Mary (360).

Mt. Aloysius Junior College (c): Cresson, Pa. 16630. Sisters of Mercy; 1939 (501).

Mt. St. Clare College (c): Bluff Blvd., and Springdale Dr., Clinton, Ia. 52732. Clinton Franciscans; 1928 (322).

Ottumwa Heights College (c): Grandview Ave., Ottumwa, Ia. 52501. Sisters of the Humility of Mary; 1925.

Presentation College (c): Aberdeen, S.D. 57401. Sisters of the Presentation; 1951 (390).

St. Catharine College (c); St. Catharine, Ky. 40061. Dominican Sisters; 1931 (180).

St. Gertrude, College of (c): Cottonwood, Ida. 83522. Benedictine Sisters.

St. Gregory's College (c): Shawnee, Okla. 74801. Benedictine Fathers; 1876 (282).

St. Mary's College of O'Fallon (c): 200 N. Main St., O'Fallon, Mo. 63366. Sisters of the Most Precious Blood; 1921 (487).

St. Mary's Junior College (c): 2500 S. 6th St., Minneapolis, Minn. 55454. Sisters of St. Joseph of Carondelet. (754).

Springfield College in Illinois (c): 1500 N. Fifth St., Springfield, Ill. 62702. Ursuline Nuns; 1929 (503).

Trocaire College (c): 110 Red Jackett Pkwy., Buffalo, N.Y. 14220. Sisters of Mercy; 1958; independent (845).

Villa Julie College (c): Green Spring Valley Rd., Stevenson, Md. 21153. Sisters of Notre Dame de Namur; 1952; independent (604).

Villa Maria College of Buffalo (c): 240 Pine Ridge Rd., Buffalo, N.Y. 14225. Felician Srs.; 1960 (528).

CAMPUS MINISTRY

"Campus ministry is a pastoral apostolate of service to the members of the entire college community (Catholic and secular) through concern and care for persons, the proclamation of the Gospel, and the celebration of the liturgy," according to a set of guidelines drawn up by an eight-member commission of the National Catholic Educational Association. The general purpose of the ministry is to make the Church present and active in the academic community.

Ideally, according to the guidelines, elements of the ministry — carried on by teams of priests, men and women religious, and lay persons — include liturgical leadership; pastoral counseling; coordination of expressions and energies for religious life on campus; Christian witness on social and moral issues; objective and independent mediation between various groups on campus; participation in religious aspects of the work of the administration, faculty and students.

Status, Agencies

The dimensions and challenge of the campus ministry are evident from estimates that approximately 75 to 80 per cent of 1.8 million Catholics in colleges and universities are on secular or non-Catholic private campuses. Serving them are about 1,500 full-time and 1,000 part-time campus ministry personnel.

The Office of Campus and Young Adult Ministries, under the Department of Education of the U.S. Catholic Conference, has responsibility for continuing support of ministry in this field. Address: 1312 Massachusetts Ave. N.W., Washington, D.C. 20005.

Information and services are furnished by the National Committee of Diocesan Directors of Campus Ministry. This is a committee of members elected from each of the 12 ecclesiastical regions of the U.S., and is an advisory body to the office.

The autonomous Catholic Campus Ministry Association, whose former equivalent was the National Newman Chaplain's Association, is headquartered at 3700 West 103rd St., Chicago, Ill. 60655. Sister Margaret M. Ivers, I.B.V.M., is executive director.

DIOCESAN AND INTERDIOCESAN SEMINARIES

(Sources: Almanac survey; *Official Catholic Directory;* NC News Service.)

Information, according to states, includes names of archdioceses and dioceses, and names and addresses of seminaries. Types of seminaries, when not clear from titles, are indicated in most cases. Interdiocesan seminaries are generally conducted by religious orders for candidates for the priesthood from several dioceses. The list does not include houses of study only for members of religious communities. Archdioceses are indicated by an asterisk.

California: Los Angeles* — St. John's Seminary (major), 5012 E. Seminary Rd., Camarillo. 93010; St. John's College Seminary, 5118 E. Seminary Rd., Camarillo. 93010.

San Diego — St. Francis Seminary (college residence), 1667 Santa Paula Dr., San Diego 92111.

San Francisco* — St. Patrick's Seminary (major), 320 Middlefield Rd., Menlo Park. 94025; St. Patrick's College, P.O. Box 151, Mountain View 94042. Emmanuel (archdiocesan program for priestly formation at high school level), P.O. Box 151, Mountain View 94042.

Colorado: Denver* — St. Thomas Theological Seminary (major), 1300 S. Steele St., Denver 80210.

Connecticut: Hartford* — St. Thomas Seminary (minor), 467 Bloomfield Ave., Bloomfield. 06002.

Norwich — Holy Apostles College (delayed vocation seminary), 33 Prospect Hill Rd., Cromwell 06416.

Stamford Byzantine Rite — Ukrainian Catholic Seminary: St. Basil College (minor), 195 Glenbrook Rd., Stamford 06902; St. Basil's Preparatory School (minor), 39 Clovelly Rd., Stamford 06902.

District of Columbia: Washington* — Theological College, The Catholic University of America, 401 Michigan Ave., N.E. 20064.

Florida: Miami* — St. John Vianney College Seminary, 2900 S.W. 87th Ave., Miami 33165; St. Vincent de Paul Seminary (major), Military Trail, P.O. Box 460, Boynton Beach. 33435.

Hawaii: Honolulu — St. Stephen's Seminary (college level), P.O. Box 699, Kaneohe. 96744.

Illinois: Belleville — St. Henry's Preparatory Seminary, 5901 W. Main St., Belleville 62223.

Chicago* — Quigley Preparatory Seminary (North), 103 East Chestnut St., Chicago 60611; Quigley Preparatory Seminary (South), 7740 South Western Ave., Chicago 60620; Niles College of Loyola University, 7135 N. Harlem Ave., Chicago 60631; St. Mary of the Lake Seminary, Mundelein. 60060.

Springfield — Immaculate Conception Seminary, 1903 E. Lakeshore Dr., Springfield 62708.

Indiana: Indianapolis* — St. Meinrad Seminary, College and School of Theology (interdiocesan), St. Meinrad. 47577.

Iowa: Davenport — St. Ambrose College Seminary, 518 W. Locust St., Davenport 52803.

Dubuque* — Seminary of St. Pius X, Loras College, Dubuque 52001.

Kansas: Kansas City* — Savior of the World Seminary (minor), 12601 Parallel Ave., Kansas City 66109.

Kentucky: Covington — Seminary of St. Pius X (interdiocesan), Erlanger. 41018.

Owensboro — St. Mark's School of Theology Seminary for Belated Vocations, South Union 42283.

Louisiana: Lafayette — Immaculata Seminary (high school), 601 W. St. Mary Blvd., Lafayette 70506.

New Orleans* — Notre Dame Seminary Graduate School of Theology, 2901 S. Carrollton Ave., New Orleans 70118; St. John

Vianney Preparatory School, 3810 Monroe St., New Orleans 70118; St. Joseph Seminary College (interdiocesan), St. Benedict 70457.

Maryland: Baltimore* — St. Mary's Seminary and University, 5400 Roland Ave., Baltimore 21210; Mt. St. Mary's Seminary, Emmitsburg. 21727.

Massachusetts: Boston* — St. John's Seminary, 127 Lake St., Brighton. 02135; St. John's Seminary, College of Liberal Arts, 197 Foster St., Brighton 02135; Pope John XXIII National Seminary, 558 South Ave., Weston. 02193.

Melkite Eparchy of Newton — St. Gregory the Theologian Seminary, 233 Grant Ave., Newton 02159.

Michigan: Detroit* — Sacred Heart Seminary College, Inc., 2701 Chicago Blvd., Detroit 48206; St. Mary's Preparatory, St. Mary's College and Sts. Cyril and Methodius Seminary (independent institution primarily serving Polish-American community), Orchard Lake 48033; St. John's Provincial Seminary (major for dioceses in Detroit province), 44011 Five Mile Rd., Plymouth. 48170.

Grand Rapids — St. Joseph's Minor Seminary, 600 Burton St., S.E., Grand Rapids 49507.

Minnesota: St. Cloud — School of Theology (St. John's Seminary), Collegeville. 56321.

St. Paul and Minneapolis* — St. Paul Seminary, 2260 Summit Ave., St. Paul. 55105; St. John Vianney College Seminary, 2115 Summit Ave., St. Paul. 55105.

Winona — Immaculate Heart of Mary Seminary, St. Mary's College, Winona 55987.

Missouri: Jefferson City — St. Thomas Aquinas Preparatory Seminary, 245 N. Levering Ave. Hannibal. 63401.

Kansas City-St. Joseph — St. John's Diocesan Seminary (high school), 2015 E. 72nd St. Kansas City. 64132.

St. Louis* — St. Louis Roman Catholic Theological Seminary (Kenrick Seminary), 7800 Kenrick Rd., St. Louis 63119; Cardinal Glennon College, 5200 Glennon Dr., St. Louis 63119; St. Louis Preparatory Seminary, 5200 Shrewsbury Ave., St. Louis 63119 (South), 3500 St. Catherine St., Florissant 63033 (North).

Montana: Helena — Diocesan Pre-Seminary Program, Carroll College, Helena 59601.

New Jersey: Newark* — Immaculate Conception Seminary (major), Darlington, Mahwah. 07430; College Seminary of the Immaculate Conception, Seton Hall Divinity School, South Orange. 07079.

New Mexico: Gallup — Cristo Rey College Seminary, 205 E. Wilson, Gallup 87301.

Santa Fe* — Immaculate Heart of Mary Seminary (college house of formation), Mt. Carmel Rd., Santa Fe 87501

New York: Brooklyn — Cathedral Preparatory Seminary of the Immaculate Conception, 555 Washington Ave., Brooklyn 11238; Cathedral Preparatory Seminary of the Immaculate Conception, 56-25 92nd St., Elmhurst. 11373; Cathedral College of the Immaculate Conception, 7200 Douglaston Parkway, Douglaston. 11362.

Buffalo — Christ the King Seminary (interdiocesan), 711 Knox Rd., East Aurora. 14052.

New York* — St. Joseph's Seminary (major), Dunwoodie, Yonkers. 10704: Cathedral Preparatory Seminary, 555 West End Ave., New York 10024.

Ogdensburg — Wadhams Hall, Riverside Dr., Ogdensburg 13669.

Rochester — Becket Hall College Seminary, 80 Fairport Rd., E. Rochester. 14445; St. Bernard's Seminary, 2260 Lake Ave., Rochester 14612.

Rockville Centre — Immaculate Conception Diocesan Seminary, Lloyd Harbor, Huntington, L.I. 11743; St. Pius X Preparatory Seminary, 1220 Front St., Uniondale, L.I. 11553.

St. Maron Diocese, Brooklyn — Our Lady of Lebanon Maronite Seminary, 7164 Alaska Ave. N.W., Washington, D.C. 20012.

Syracuse — Aquinas House, 702 Danforth St., Syracuse 13208.

North Dakota: Fargo — Cardinal Muench Seminary, 100 35th Ave. N.E., Fargo 58102.

Ohio: Cincinnati* — The Atheneum of Ohio: Mt. St. Mary's Seminary of the West, 5440 Moeller Ave., Norwood. 45212; St. Gregory's Seminary College, 6616 Beechmont Ave., Cincinnati. 45230.

Cleveland — St. Mary Seminary, 1227 Ansel Rd., Cleveland 44108; Borromeo College of Ohio, 28700 Euclid Ave. Wickliffe. 44092.

Columbus — Pontifical College Josephinum (interdiocesan), theologate and college, Columbus. 43085.

Toledo — Holy Spirit Seminary High School, 5201 Airport Highway, Toledo 43615.

Oregon: Portland* — Mt. Angel Seminary (college, pre-theology program, graduate school of theology), St. Benedict 97373; St. John Vianney House of Studies, 1538 Southwest Montgomery St., Portland 97201.

Pennsylvania: Erie — St. Mark's Seminary, 429 E. Grandview Blvd., Erie 16504.

Philadelphia* — Theological Seminary of St. Charles Borromeo, Overbrook. 19151.

Philadelphia Byzantine Rite (Ukrainians)* — St. Josaphat's Seminary, 201 Taylor St. N.E., Washington, D.C. 20017.

Pittsburgh Byzantine Rite (Ruthenians)* — Byzantine Catholic Seminary of Sts. Cyril and Methodius, 3605 Perrysville Ave., Pittsburgh. 15214.

Pittsburgh — St. Paul Seminary, 2900 Noblestown Rd. 15205; St. Fidelis Seminary

High School (interdiocesan), Herman. 16039.

Scranton — St. Pius X Seminary (college division), Dalton. 18414.

Rhode Island: Providence — Our Lady of Providence College Seminary, Warwick Neck Ave., Warwick. 02889.

Texas: Corpus Christi — Corpus Christi Minor Seminary, Rt. 1, Box 500. 78415.

Dallas — Holy Trinity Seminary (major), P.O. Box 3068, Irving. 75061.

El Paso — St. Charles Seminary High School, P.O. Box 17548, El Paso 79917.

Galveston-Houston — St. Mary's Seminary (major), 9845 Memorial Dr. Houston. 77024.

San Antonio* — The Assumption-St. John's Seminary (major), 2600 W. Woodlawn Ave., San Antonio 78284.

Washington: Seattle* — St. Edward Hall (high school residence), 204 S. 140th, Seattle 98168.

Spokane — Bishop White Seminary, E. 429 Sharp Ave., Spokane 99202.

West Virginia: Wheeling-Charleston — St. Joseph Preparatory Seminary, Rt. 6, Vienna. 26101; Seminary House of Studies (college residence), 1252 National Rd., Wheeling. 26003.

Wisconsin: Madison — Holy Name Seminary (High School), 3577 High Point Rd., Madison 53711.

Milwaukee* — St. Francis Seminary School of Pastoral Ministry, 3257 S. Lake Dr., Milwaukee 53207; St. Francis de Sales College, De Sales Seminary High School, 3501 S. Lake Dr., Milwaukee 53207.

U.S. SEMINARIES AND STUDENTS, 1962-1980
(Source: *The Official Catholic Directory*.)

Year	Dioc. Seminaries	Total Dioc. Students	Religious Seminaries Scholasticates	Total Rel. Students	Total Seminarians
1962	98	23,662	447	22,657	46,319
1963	107	25,247	454	22,327	47,574
1964	112	26,701	459	22,049	48,750
1965	117	26,762	479	22,230	48,992
1966	126	26,252	481	21,862	48,114
1967	123	24,293	452	21,086	45,379
1968	124	22,232	437	17,604	39,836
1969	122	19,573	407	14,417	33,990
1970	118	17,317	383	11,589	28,906
1971	110	14,987	340	10,723	25,710
1972	106	13,554	326	9,409	22,963
1973	107	12,925	304	8,855	21,780
1974	109	11,765	293	7,583	19,348
1975	104	11,223	269	6,579	17,802
1976	102	11,015	269	6,232	17,247
1977	100	10,344	287	5,599	15,943
1978	98	9,560	278	5,438	14,998
1979	92	8,694	258	5,266	13,960
1980	92	8,552	252	4,674	13,226

SEMINARY STUDY FINDINGS

A task force organized by the Center of Applied Research in the Apostolate reported in August, 1980, these findings from a study conducted during the previous year.

• The number of men in theology programs studying for the diocesan priesthood declined by eight per cent between 1975 and 1979.

• The number of theology students for the priesthood in religious communities declined by 20 per cent between 1976-77 and 1978-79.

• The total 1979 enrollment of students of theology at 54 schools was 4,327.

• It was estimated that the number of young men of age to enter theology schools in the U.S. would decrease by at least 15 per cent during the next 20 years.

• The annual cost per average student rose from $7,772 in 1975-76 to $10,082 in 1978-79.

• It was estimated that contemporary trends would drive up the average per student cost to more than $17,000 a year by the end of the 1982-83 academic year.

NORTH AMERICAN COLLEGE

The North American College was founded by the bishops of the United States in 1859 as a residence and house of formation for U.S. seminarians and graduate students in Rome. The first ordination of an alumnus took place June 14, 1862. Pontifical status was granted the college by Leo XIII Oct. 25, 1884.

Students living at the college study theology and related subjects in the various pontifical universities and institutes in Rome, principally at the Pontifical Gregorian University.

The college is directed by an American rector and staff, and operates under the auspices of a U.S. bishops' committee which was set up in 1924.

PONTIFICAL UNIVERSITIES

(Principal source: *Annuario Pontificio.*)

These universities, listed according to country of location, have been canonically erected and authorized by the Sacred Congregation for Catholic Education to award degrees in stated fields of study.

New laws and norms governing ecclesiastical universities and faculties were promulgated in the apostolic constitution *Sapientia Christiana,* issued Apr. 15, 1979, and scheduled to go into effect in the 1980-81 academic year or the 1981 academic year, according to the scholastic calendar in use in various places.

Argentina: Catholic University of S. Maria of Buenos Aires (June 16, 1960): Juncal 1912, Buenos Aires.

Belgium: Catholic University of Louvain (Dec. 9, 1425; 1834), with autonomous institutions for French- (Louvain) and Flemish- (Leuven) speaking: Place de l'Universite I, 1348 Louvain-La-Neuve (French); Naamsestraat 22B, 3000 Leuven (Flemish).

Brazil: Pontifical Catholic University of Rio de Janeiro (Jan. 20, 1947): Rua Marques de Sao Vicente 209, Rio de Janeiro, Est. de Guanabara.

Pontifical Catholic University of Rio Grande do Sul (Nov. 1, 1950): Praca Dom. Sebastiao 2, Porto Alegre, Estado do Rio Grande do Sul.

Pontifical Catholic University of Sao Paulo (Jan. 25, 1947): Rua Monte Alegre 984, Sao Paulo.

Pontifical University of Campinas (Sept. 8, 1956): Rua Marechal Deodoro 1099, Campinas, Sao Paulo.

Canada: Laval University (Mar. 15, 1876): Case Postale 460, Quebec G1K 7P4.

St. Paul University (formerly University of Ottawa) (Feb. 5, 1889): 223, Rue Main, Ottawa, K1S 1C4, Ontario.

University of Sherbrooke (Nov. 21, 1957): Chemin Ste.-Catherine, Cite Universitaire, Sherbrooke, Que. J1K 2R1.

Chile: Catholic University of Chile (June 21, 1888): Avenida Bernardo O'Higgins 340, Casilla 114D, Santiago de Chile.

Catholic University of Valparaiso (Nov. 1, 1961): Avenida Brasil 2950, Casilla 4059, Valparaiso.

Colombia: Bolivarian Pontifical Catholic University (Aug. 16, 1945): Calle 52, N. 43-53, Medellin.

Pontifical Xaverian University (July 31, 1937): Carrera 7, N. 40-62, Bogota D.E.

Cuba: Catholic University of St. Thomas of Villanueva (May 4, 1957): Avenida Quenta 16,660, Marianao, Havana. Taken over by the Castro government in May, 1961.

Ecuador: Catholic University of Ecuador (July 16, 1954): Doce de Octubre, N. 1076, Apartado 2184, Quito.

El Salvador: José Simeón Cañas University (Sept. 15, 1965): San Salvador.

Ethiopia: University of Asmara (Sept. 8, 1960): Via Menelik II, 45, Post Office Box 1220, Asmara.

France: Catholic Faculties of Lille (Nov. 18, 1875): Boulevard Vauban 60, 59046 Lille.

Catholic Faculties of Lyon (Nov. 22, 1875): 25, Rue du Plat, 69288 Lyon.

Catholic Institute of Paris (Aug. 11, 1875): 21, Rue d'Assas, 75270 Paris.

Catholic Institute of Toulouse (Nov. 15,1877): Rue de la Fonderie 31, 31068 Toulouse.

Catholic University of the West (Sept. 16, 1875): 3, Place Andre Leroy, B.P. 808, 49005 Angers.

Germany: Gesamthochschule Eichstatt (Jan. 25, 1975): Ostenstrasse 26, D-8833 Eichstatt.

Guatemala: Rafael Landivar University (Oct. 18, 1961): 17 Calle 8-64, Z 10 Guatemala.

Ireland: St. Patrick's College (Mar. 29, 1896): Maynooth, Co. Kildare.

Italy: Catholic University of the Sacred Heart (Dec. 25, 1920): Largo Gemelli 1, 20123 Milan.

Japan: *Jochi Daigaku* (Sophia University) (Mar. 29, 1913): Chiyoda-Ku, Kioi-cho 7, Tokyo.

Lebanon: St. Joseph University of Beirut (Mar. 25, 1881): Rue de l'Universite St.-Joseph, Boite Postale 293, Beyrouth.

Netherlands: Roman Catholic University (June 29, 1923): Wilhelminasingel 13, Nijmegen.

Nicaragua: Central American University (1961): Apartado 69, Managua D.N.

Panama: University of S. Maria la Antigua (May 27, 1965): Apartado 2143, Panama 1.

Paraguay: Catholic University of Our Lady of the Assumption (Feb. 2, 1965): Comuneros e Independencia Nacional, Asuncion.

Peru: Catholic University of Peru (Sept. 30, 1942): Apartado 1761, Lima.

Philippine Islands: Pontifical University of Santo Tomas (Nov. 20, 1645): Espana Street, Manila.

Poland: Catholic University of Lublin (July 25, 1920): Aleje Raclawickie 14, Skr. Poczt. 279, 20-950, Lublin.

Portugal: Portuguese Catholic University (Nov. 1, 1967): Palma de Cima, Lisbon 4.

Puerto Rico: Catholic University of Puerto Rico (Aug. 15, 1972): Ponce, Puerto Rico 00731.

Spain: Catholic University of Navarra (Aug. 6, 1960): Ciudad Universitaria, Pamplona.

Pontifical University "Comillas" (Mar. 29, 1904): Canto Blanco, Apartado Postal 3082, Madrid.

Pontifical University of Salamanca (Sept.

25, 1940): Compania 1, Apartado 541, Salamanca.

University of Deusto (Aug. 10, 1963): Avenida de las Universidades, 28, Apartado 1, Bilbao.

Taiwan (China): Fu Jen Catholic University (Nov. 15, 1923, at Peking; reconstituted at Taipeh, Sept. 8, 1961): Hsinchuang, Taipeh Hsien.

United States: Catholic University of America (Mar. 7, 1889): Washington, D.C. 20064.

Georgetown University (Mar. 30, 1833): 37th and O Sts. N.W., Washington, D.C. 20057.

Niagara University (June 21, 1956): Niagara University, N.Y. 14109.

Venezuela: Catholic University "Andres Bello" (Sept. 29, 1963): Esquina Jesuitas, Apartado 422, Caracas.

Ecclesiastical Faculties

(Source: *Annuario Pontificio*)

These faculties in Catholic seminaries and universities, listed according to country of location, have been canonically erected and authorized by the Sacred Congregation for Catholic Education to award degrees in stated fields of study. In addition to those listed here, there are other faculties of theology or philosophy in state universities and for members of certain religious orders only.

Australia: Faculty of Theology, Sydney (Feb. 2, 1954).

Austria: Theological Faculty, Linz (Oct. 15, 1977).

Brazil: Faculty of Philosophy at the Aloysius Institute, Rio de Janeiro (July 15, 1941; Mar. 12, 1977).

Canada: Pontifical Institute of Medieval Studies, Toronto (Oct. 18, 1939).

Dominican Faculty of Theology of Canada, Ottawa (1965; Nov. 15, 1975).

Regis College — Toronto Section of the Jesuit Faculty of Theology in Canada, Toronto (Feb. 17, 1956; Dec. 25, 1977).

Germany: Theological Faculty, Paderborn (June 11, 1966).

Theological Faculty of the Major Episcopal Seminary, Trier (Sept. 8, 1955)

Philosophical Faculty, Munich (1932; Oct. 25, 1971).

Theological-Philosophical Faculty, Frankfurt (1932; June 7, 1971).

Theological Faculty, Fulda (Dec. 22, 1978).

Great Britain: Heythrop College, University of London, London (Nov. 1, 1964). Theology, philosophy.

India: Institute of Philosophy and Theology, Poona (July 27, 1926).

Institute of Theology, Alwaye, Kerala (Feb. 24, 1972).

"Vidyajyoti," Institute of Religious Studies, Faculty of Theology, Delhi (1932; Dec. 9, 1974).

Dharmaran Pontifical Institute of Theology and Philosophy, Bangalore (Jan. 6, 1976).

St. Peter's Pontifical Institute of Theology, Bangalore (Jan. 6, 1976).

"Satya Nilayam," Institute of Philosophy and Culture. Faculty of Philosophy, Shembaganur (Sept. 8, 1932; Dec. 15, 1976).

Italy: Interregional Theological Faculty, Milan (Aug. 8, 1935).

Pontifical Theological Faculty of the Most Sacred Heart of Jesus, Cagliari, of the Pontifical Regional Seminary of Sardinia (July 5, 1927).

Pontifical Ambrosian Institute of Sacred Music, Milan (Mar. 12, 1940).

Theological Faculty of Southern Italy, Naples. Two sections: St. Thomas Aquinas Capodimonte (Oct. 31, 1941) and St. Louis Posillipo (Mar. 16, 1918). Pastoral Ignatian Institute, Messina (July 31, 1972).

Faculty of Philosophy "Aloisianum," Gallarate (1937; Mar. 20, 1974).

Ivory Coast: Catholic Institute of West Africa, Abidjan (Aug. 12, 1975).

Lebanon: University Centre for Religious and Ecclesiastical Sciences, Kaslik (Oct. 20, 1974).

Madagascar: Superior Institute of Theology, at the Regional Seminary of Tananarive, Ambatoroka-Tananarive (Apr. 21, 1960).

Malta: Faculty of Theology, Tal-Virtu (Nov. 22, 1769).

Peru: Pontifical and Civil Faculty of Theology, Lima (July 25, 1571).

Poland: Theological Faculty, Poznan (1969; pontifical designation, June 2, 1974).

Spain: Theological Faculty of Barcelona, of the Major Seminary of Barcelona and the College of St. Francis Borgia of San Cugat del Valles (Mar. 7, 1968).

Theological Faculty, Granada (1940; July 31, 1973).

Theological Faculty of the North, of the Metropolitan Seminary of Burgos and the Diocesan Seminary of Vitoria (Feb. 6, 1967).

Theological Faculty "San Vicente Ferrer," Valencia (Jan. 23, 1974).

Switzerland: Theological Faculty, Chur (Jan. 1, 1974).

Theological Faculty, Luzerne (Dec. 25, 1973).

United States: St. Mary's Seminary and University. School of Theology, Baltimore (May 1, 1822).

St. Mary of the Lake Faculty of Theology, Chicago (Sept. 30, 1929).

The Jesuit School of Theology, Berkeley, Calif. (Feb. 2, 1934, as "Alma College," Los Gatos, Calif.).

Vietnam: Theological Faculty of the Pontifical National Seminary of St. Pius X, Dalat (July 31, 1965). Activities suppressed.

The Pontifical College Josephinum (Theologate and College) at Columbus, Ohio, is a regional pontifical seminary. Established Sept. 1, 1888, it is immediately subject to the Holy See.

Institutes of Higher Studies in Rome
(Source: *Annuario Pontificio.*)

Pontifical Gregorian University (1552). Theology, canon law, philosophy, psychology, science of religion, church history, missiology, social sciences. Associated with the university are:

The **Pontifical Biblical Institute** (May 7, 1909), with faculties of Scripture and ancient Oriental studies.

The **Pontifical Institute of Oriental Studies** (Oct. 15, 1917), with faculties of Oriental ecclesiastical studies and Oriental canon law.

Pontifical Lateran University (1773). Theology, canon law, civil law, philosophy, moral theology, literature.

Pontifical Urban University (1627). Theology, philosophy, missiology.

Pontifical University of St. Thomas Aquinas (Angelicum) (1580), of the Order of Preachers. Theology, canon law, philosophy, social sciences, spirituality.

Pontifical University Salesianum (May 3, 1940; university designation May 24, 1973), of the Salesians of Don Bosco. Canon law, theology, philosophy, pedagogy, and the **Pontifical Institute of Higher Latin Studies** (Feb. 22, 1964).

Pontifical Athenaeum of St. Anselm (1687), of the Benedictines. Theology, philosophy, liturgy, monastic studies.

Pontifical Athenaeum Antonianum (of St. Anthony) (May 17, 1933), of the Order of Friars Minor. Theology, canon law, philosophy, and the affiliated School of Biblical Studies in Jerusalem.

Pontifical Institute of Sacred Music (1911); May 24, 1931).

Pontifical Institute of Christian Archeology (Dec. 11, 1925).

Pontifical Theological Faculty "St. Bonaventure" (Dec. 18, 1587), of the Order of Friars Minor Conventual.

Pontifical Theological Faculty of Sts. Teresa of Jesus and John of the Cross (Teresianum) July 16, 1935), of the Carmelites. Theology, spirituality.

Pontifical Theological Faculty "Marianum" (1398), of the Servants of Mary.

Pontifical Institute of Arabic Studies (1926), of the White Fathers.

The raison d'etre of the Catholic press is to "illuminate current and historical events with the word of God, to defend the human and, Christian values for which modern society feels so deep a need," declared the Pope Mar. 31, 1980, before members of the Society of St. Paul for the Apostolate of Communications.

PONTIFICAL ACADEMY
(Sources: *Annuario Pontificio,* NC News Service.)

The Pontifical Academy of Sciences was constituted in its present form by Pius XI Oct. 28, 1936, in virtue of *In Multis Solaciis,* a document issued on his own initiative.

The academy is the only supranational body of its kind in the world, with a pope-selected, life-long membership of outstanding mathematicians and experimental scientists from many countries. The normal complement of members is 70; the total number, however, includes additional honorary and supernumerary members. Non-Catholics as well as Catholics belong to the academy.

Purposes of the academy are to honor pure science and its practitioners, to promote the freedom of pure science and to foster research.

The academy originated as the Accademia Linceorum (lynxes) in Rome Aug. 17, 1603. Pius IX reorganized this body and gave it a new name — Pontificia Accademia dei Nuovi Lincei — in 1847. It was taken over by the Italian state in 1870 and called the Accademia Nationale dei Lincei, Leo XIII reconstituted it with a new charter in 1887. Pius XI designated the Vatican Gardens as the site of academy headquarters in 1922 and gave it its present title and status in 1936. Four years later he gave the title of Excellency to its members.

Scientists in the U.S. who presently hold membership in the Academy are: Edward Adalbert-Doisy, professor emeritus of biochemistry at St. Louis University (May 29, 1948); Franco Rasetti, professor emeritus of physics at John Hopkins University, Baltimore, Md. (Oct. 28, 1936); George Speri Sperti, director of the Institutum Divi Thomae in the Athanaeum of Ohio (Oct. 28, 1936); William Wilson Morgan, professor emeritus of astronomy at the University of Chicago (Sept. 24, 1964); Albert Szent-Gyorgyi, director of muscle research at the Marine Biological Laboratory, Woods Hole, Mass. (Apr. 10, 1970), Rita Levi-Montalcini, professor of biology at St. Louis University and director of the Cellular Biology Laboratory of the CNR, Rome (June 24, 1974); Severo Ochoa, professor emeritus, of the Roche Institute of Molecular Biology, Nutley, N.J. (June 24, 1974); Marshall Warren Nierenberg, professor of biochemistry at the National Institutes of Health, Bethesda, Md. (June 24, 1974); George Palade, professor of cellular biology at Yale University, New Haven, Conn. (Dec. 2, 1975); Victor Weisskopf, professor of physics at the Massachusetts Institute of Technology, Cambridge, Mass. (Dec. 2, 1975).

Appointed Apr. 17, 1978, were: David Baltimore, professor of biology, Har Gobind

Khorana, professor of biochemistry, and Alexandar Rich, professor of biophysicis — all at the Massachusetts Institute of Technology, Cambridge, Mass.; Roger Walcott Sperry, professor of psychobiology, California Institute of Technology, Pasadena, Calif.

Deceased U.S. members of the Academy were: George D. Birkhoff, Alexis Carrel, Herbert Sidney Langfeld, Robert A. Millikan, Thomas H. Morgan, Theodore von Karman, Victor F. Hess, Peter Debye, Hugh Stott Taylor.

Other members of the Academy are listed below according to country of location; dates of their selection are given in parentheses.

Argentina: Luis F. Leloir (Apr. 22, 1968).

Austria: Hans Tuppy (Apr. 10, 1970).

Belgium: Christian de Duve (Apr. 16, 1970).

Brazil: Carlos Chagas (Aug. 18, 1961); Johanna Dobereiner (Apr. 17, 1978); Crodowaldo Pavan (Apr. 17, 1978).

Canada: Gerhard Herzberg (Sept. 24, 1964); Karel Wiesner (Apr. 17, 1978).

Chile: Hector Croxatto Rezzio (Dec. 2, 1975).

Denmark: Bengt Georg Stromgren (Dec. 2, 1975); Aage Bohr (Apr. 17, 1978).

France: Louis de Broglie (Apr. 5, 1955); Pierre Raphael Lepine (Sept. 24, 1964); Louis Leprince-Ringuet (Aug. 18, 1961); Jerome Lejeune (June 24, 1974); Andre Blanc-LaPierre (Apr. 17, 1978).

Germany: Wolfgang Gentner (Apr. 10, 1970); Rudolf L. Mossbauer (Apr. 10, 1970).

Great Britain: Hermann Alexander Bruck (Apr. 5, 1955); Paul Adrien Dirac (Aug. 18, 1961); Alan Lloyd Hodgkin (Apr. 22, 1968); Alfred R. Ubbelohde (Apr. 22, 1968); Percy C. C. Garnham (Apr. 10, 1970); George Porter (June 24, 1974); Martin Ryle (Dec. 2, 1975).

Greece: George Joachimoglu (Apr. 10, 1970).

Israel: Michael Sela (Dec. 2, 1975).

Italy: Giovanni Battista Bonino (May 23, 1942); Bettolo Giovanni Battista Marini (Apr. 22, 1968); Giuseppe Colombo (Apr. 17, 1978); Giuseppe Moruzzi (Apr. 17, 1978); Giampietro Puppi (Apr. 17, 1978).

Japan: Paul Sanichiro Mizushima (Aug. 18, 1961); Hideki Yukawa (Apr. 8, 1961).

Netherlands: Jan Hendrik Oort (Aug. 18, 1961).

New Zealand: Albert William Liley (Apr. 17, 1978).

Pakistan: Salimuzzaman Siddiqui (Sept. 24, 1964).

Peru: Alberto Hurtado (Aug. 18, 1961).

Portugal: Antonio De Almeida (Apr. 8, 1961).

Spain: Manuel Lora Tomayo (Sept. 24, 1964).

Sweden: Sven Horstadius (Aug. 18, 1961).

Switzerland: John Carew Eccles (Apr. 8, 1961), Thomas Lambo (June 24, 1974).

Vatican City: Daniel J. Kelly O'Connell, S.J. (Sept. 24, 1964).

Venezuela: Marcel Roche (Apr. 10, 1970).

Ex officio members are: Rev. George V. Coyne, S.J., director of Vatican Observatory; Alfons Stickler, S.D.B., prefect of the Vatican Library; Msgr. Martino Giusti, prefect of the Secret Vatican Archives.

President of the Academy is Carlos Chagas (Nov. 9, 1972).

PAPAL ADDRESS

Following are excerpts from an address on faith, science and truth delivered by Pope John Paul Nov. 10, 1979, at a meeting of the Pontifical Academy of Sciences.

Sign of Harmony

"The existence of this Pontifical Academy of Sciences . . . is a visible sign which shows to people, without any form of racial or religious discrimination, the profound harmony which can exist between the truths of science and the truths of faith."

"The title of pontifical attributed to this academy signifies, as you know, the interest and support of the Church, which is manifested under forms quite different, certainly, from those of the ancient patronage system, but which are no less profound and effective. As the distinguished and lamented president of your academy, Msgr. Georges Lemaitre, wrote: 'Would the Church need science? Certainly not; the cross and the Gospel are sufficient for it. But to the Christian nothing human is foreign. How could the Church not be interested in the most noble of strictly human occupations: the search for truth?' "

Search and Respect

"In this academy which is yours and mine, believing and non-believing scientists collaborate, agreeing in the search for scientific truth and in respect for the beliefs of each other. Permit me to quote here again a luminous page of Msgr. Lemaitre: 'Both of them (the believing scientist and the non-believing scientist) strive to decipher the multiple, overlapping palimpsest of nature, where the traces of the various stages of the long evolution of the world have been covered over and mingled. The believer has perhaps the advantage of knowing that the enigma has a solution, that the underlying writing is, after all, the work of an intelligent being; therefore, that the problem posed by nature has been posed to be solved, and that its difficulty is undoubtedly proportionate to the present or future capacity of mankind. That will not perhaps give him any new resources in his investigation, but it will contribute to maintain him in that healthy optimism without which a sustained effort cannot be maintained for a long time.' "

The National Conference of Catholic Charities: Established in 1910 to help advance and promote the charitable programs and activities of Catholic community and social service agencies in the United States. As the central and national organization for this purpose, it services member agencies and institutions by consultation, information and assistance in planning and evaluating social service programs under Catholic auspices.

The principal fields of service in which Catholic Charities agencies are engaged are family counseling, child welfare, services for unmarried mothers, community services, day care centers, neighborhood center programs, and care of the aged. Community organization and social action are also functions of Catholic Charities.

The NCCC conducts research with respect to service to the aging, community self-help programs, the institutional care of children, and other social service projects. It represents the Catholic philosophy of social service to government agencies and personnel, and to professional organizations in the field. Its publications include *Charities USA*, a monthly membership magazine, and *Social Thought,* a quarterly produced jointly with the National School of Social Service of the Catholic University of America.

The NCCC membership includes 549 diocesan agencies and branches, 275 institutions and 3,155 individuals.

Msgr. Lawrence Corcoran is executive director of the conference, with offices at 1346 Connecticut Ave. N.W., Washington, D.C. 20036.

The Society of St. Vincent de Paul, originally called the Conference of Charity: An association of Catholic laity devoted to personal service of the poor through the spiritual and corporal works of mercy. The first conference was formed at Paris in 1833 by Frederic Ozanam and his associates.

The first conference in the U.S. was organized in 1845 at St. Louis. There are now approximately 4,300 units of the society in this country, with a membership of about 34,000.

In the past 50 years, members of the society in this country have distributed among poor persons financial and other forms of assistance valued at approximately $300 million.

U.S. Vincentian councils and conferences participating in "twinning" programs assist their poorer counterparts abroad by sending them correspondence, information and financial aid on a continuing basis.

Under the society's revised regulations, women are being admitted to membership. Increasing emphasis is being given to stores and rehabilitation workshops of the society through which persons with marginal income can purchase refurbished goods at minimal cost. Handicapped persons are employed in renovating goods and store operations.

Joseph Rouast of Paris, France, is president of the Council General, the governing body of the society. There are approximately 750,000 members in the world.

The office of the U.S. Superior Council is located at 4140 Lindell Blvd., St. Louis, Mo. 63108.

Catholic Health Association of the United States, formerly Catholic Hospital Association: Founded in 1915, is a service organization for about 900 Catholic-sponsored health care facilities located throughout the United States.

The association is dedicated to the healing mission of the Church by promoting health of those who are sick or infirm because of age or disability; by respecting human dignity in the experience of sickness and death; and by fostering physical, psychological, emotional, spiritual and social well-being of people.

John Curley is president. Executive offices are located at 1438 S. Grand Boulevard, St. Louis, Mo. 63104.

The Official Catholic Directory, 1980, reported 633 Catholic general hospitals with 166,998 beds treating 34,252,953 patients; 87 special hospitals with 6,748 beds treating 475,869; and 121 nurses' schools with 19,420 students.

National Association of Catholic Chaplains: Founded in 1965. Membership is approximately 3,000.

Rev. Timothy J. Toohey is executive director. Address: 1312 Massachusetts Ave. N.W., Washington, D.C. 20005.

NFPC

The National Federation of Priests' Councils was organized by 233 delegates from 127 priests' organizations at a charter meeting held in Chicago May 20 and 21, 1968.

Its stated purpose is to give priests' councils, official or unofficial, a representative voice in matters of presbyteral, pastoral and ministerial concern to the U.S. and the universal Church.

The NFPC has a membership of 106 senates, councils and associations.

The president is Father Neil McCaulley of Pittsburgh, Pa. Headquarters are located at 1307 S. Wabash Ave., Chicago, Ill. 60605.

Richard W. Daw, director and editor in chief of NC News Service was elected president of the International Federation of Catholic News Agencies during the 12th World Congress of the Catholic Press Sept. 23 to 26, 1980.

FACILITIES FOR RETIRED AND AGED PERSONS

(Sources: Almanac survey, *The Official Catholic Directory*.)

This list covers residence, health care and other facilities for the retired and aged under Catholic auspices. Information includes name, type of facility if not evident from the title, address, and total capacity (in parentheses); unless noted otherwise, facilities are for both men and women. Many facilities for the aged offer intermediate nursing care.

Alabama: Allen Memorial Home (Nursing Home), 735 S. Washington Ave., Mobile 36603 (94).

Good Samaritan Nursing Home, 1107 Voeglin Ave., Selma 36701 (26).

Sacred Heart Residence (Nursing Home), Little Sisters of the Poor, 1655 McGill Ave., Mobile 36604 (125).

Villa Mercy (Nursing Care Facility and Hospice), P.O. Box 1096, Daphne 36526.

Arizona: Sacred Heart Home for the Aged, Little Sisters of the Poor, 1110 N. 16th St., Phoenix 85006 (150).

Villa Maria Geriatric Center (Skilled Nursing Facility and Apartments), 2310 N. Columbus Blvd., Tucson 85712 (87 beds, 50 apartments).

Arkansas: Benedictine Manor (Retirement Home), 2nd and Grand Sts., Hot Springs 71901 (100).

California: Casa Manana Inn, 3700 N. Sutter St., Stockton 95204 (175).

Cathedral Plaza, 1551 Third Ave., San Diego 92101 (221 apartments).

Catholic Women's Center (Residence for Retired Senior Women), 195 E. San Fernando St., San Jose 95112 (48).

Ellis Seniors Residence, 3263 First Ave., Sacramento 95817 (18).

Francis of Assisi Community, 2255 Hayes St., San Francisco (140); for elderly and handicapped.

Little Flower Haven (Residential Care Facility for Retired), 8585 La Mesa Blvd., La Mesa 92041 (93).

Little Sisters of the Poor, 300 Lake St., San Francisco 94118 (140).

Little Sisters of the Poor, Jeanne Jugan Residence, 2100 South Western Ave., San Pedro, Calif. 90732 (120).

Madonna Residence (Retirement Home for Women over 60), 1055 Pine St., San Francisco 94109 (46).

Marian Residence (Retirement Home), 124 S. College Dr., Santa Maria 93454 (58).

Nazareth House, 2121 N. 1st St., Fresno 93703 (80).

Nazareth House, 3333 Manning Ave., Los Angeles 90064 (107).

Nazareth House, 245 Nova Albion Way, Terra Linda, San Rafael 94903 (121).

Nazareth House Retirement Home, 6333 Rancho Mission Rd., San Diego 92108 (122).

Our Lady of Fatima Villa (Skilled Nursing Facility, Women), 20400 Saratoga/Los Gatos Rd., Saratoga 95070 (85).

Our Lady's Home, 3431 Foothill Blvd., Oakland 94601 (154).

St. Francis Home (Elderly and Retired Women), 1718 W. 6th St., Santa Ana 92703 (87).

St. Francis Manor, Inc., 2515 J St., Sacramento 95816.

Villa Scalabrini (Retirement Center), 10631 Vinedale St., Sun Valley 91352 (125).

Villa Siena (Residence), 1855 Miramonte, Mountain View 94040 (48).

Colorado: Little Sisters of the Poor, 3629 W. 29th Ave., Denver 80211 (118).

St. Elizabeth Center (Retirement Home), 2825 W. 32nd Ave., Denver 80211 (147).

Connecticut: Augustana Homes, Simeon Rd., Bethel 06801.

Notre Dame Convalescent Home, 76 West Rocks Rd., Norwalk 06851 (60).

Regina Pacis Villa (Residence), RFD No. 1, Pomfret Center 06259 (16).

St. Joseph Guest Home (Women, Employed and Retired), 311 Greene St., New Haven 06511 (86).

St. Joseph's Home for the Aged, 88 Jackson St., Willimantic 06226 (37).

St. Joseph's Manor, Carmelite Srs. for Aged and Infirm, 6448 Main St., Trumbull 06611 (285).

St. Joseph's Residence, Little Sisters of the Poor, 1365 Enfield St., Enfield, Conn. 06082 (94)

St. Lucian's Home for the Aged, 532 Burritt St., New Britain 06053 (65).

St. Mary's Home (Residence and Health Care Facility), 291 Steele Rd., W. Hartford 06117 (177).

Villa Maria Rest Home for the Aged, West St., Thompson 06277 (30).

Delaware: Jeanne Jugan Residence, Little Sisters of the Poor, 185 Salem Church Rd., Newark 19713.

St. Patrick's House, Inc., 14th and French Sts., Wilmington 19801 (14).

Florida: All Saints Home for the Aged, 2040 Riverside Ave., Jacksonville 32204 (57).

Carroll Manor, 3665 S. Miami Ave., Miami 33133

Casa Calderon, Inc., P.O. Box 2395, Tallahassee 32304. Apartments.

Cor Jesu Retirement Center, 4918 N. Habana Ave., Tampa 33614 (78).

Haven of Our Lady of Peace (Residence and Health Care Facility), 5203 9th Ave., Pensacola 32504 (88).

Maria Manor Health Care Center, 10300 4th St. N., St. Petersburg 33702 (274).

Marian Towers, Inc. (Retirement Apartments), 17505 North Bay Rd., Miami Beach 33160.

Pennsylvania Retirement Residence, 208 Evernia St., W. Palm Beach 33401 (176).

St. Andrew Towers (Retirement Apartments), 2700 N.W. 99th Ave., Coral Springs 33065.

St. Dominic Gardens, 5849 N.W. 7th St., Miami 33126.

St. Elizabeth Gardens, Inc. (Retirement Apartments), 801 N.E. 33rd St., Pompano Beach 33064.

St. Joseph's Residence, 3485 N.W. 30th St., Ft. Lauderdale 33311.

Illinois: Addolorato Villa (Residence), Highway 83, McHenry Rd., Wheeling 60090 (103).

Alvernia Manor (Residence), 1598 Main St., Lemont 60439 (56).

Carlyle Healthcare Center, 501 Clinton St., Carlyle 62231 (128).

Carmelite Retirement Village, Cass Ave. N., at I-55 (Stevenson), Darien 60559 (96 units, 150 residents).

Holy Family Villa (Residence and Health Care,), Lemont 60439 (106).

Huber Memorial Home (Women), 1000 30th St., Rock Island 61201 (17).

Little Sisters of the Poor Center for the Aging, 2325 N. Lakewood Ave., Chicago, Ill. 60614 (120).

Maryhaven, Inc. (Intermediate Care Facility), 1700 E. Lake Ave., Glenview 60025 (147).

Mayslake Village (Retirement Apartments), 1801 35th St., Oak Brook 60521 (481 Apartments).

Meredith Memorial Home, Public Square, Belleville 62220 (88).

Merkle-Knipprath Nursing Home, Rt. 1, Clifton 60927.

Mother Theresa Home, 1270 Main St., Lemont 60439 (58).

Our Lady of Angels Retirement Home, 1201 Wyoming, Joliet 60435 (100).

Our Lady of the Snows Apartment Community (Retirement Apartment Community; Health Care Program), 9500 W. Ill., Rt. 15, Belleville 62223 (200).

Rosary Hill Convalescent Home, 9000 W. 81st St., Justice 60458 (60).

St. Andrew Home, 7000 N. Newark Ave., Chicago 60648 (198).

St. Ann's Health Care Center, 770 State St., Chester 62233 (92).

St. Ann's Home for the Aged, Waukegan and Techny Rds., Techny 60082 (164).

St. Augustine's Home, Little Sisters of the Poor, 2358 Sheffield Ave., Chicago 60614 (110).

St. Benedict Home, 6930 W. Touhy Ave., Niles 60648 (52).

St. Joseph's Home, 3306 S. 6th St. Rd., Springfield 62703 (80).

St. Joseph's Home, 2223 W. Heading Ave., Peoria 61604 (200).

St. Joseph's Home for the Aged, 649 E. Jefferson St., Freeport 61032 (109).

St. Joseph's Home for the Elderly, 80 W. Northwest Hwy., Palatine 60067 (160).

St. Joseph's Home of Chicago, Inc., 2650 N. Ridgeway Ave., Chicago 60647 (173).

St. Patrick's Residence (Sheltered and Intermediate Care; Skilled Nursing Facility), 22 E. Clinton St., Joliet 60431 (202).

Villa Saint Cyril (Residence), 1111 St. John's Ave., Highland Park 60035 (80).

Villa Scalabrini (Residence), Northlake 60164 (155).

Indiana: Providence Home, 520 W. 9th St., Jasper 47546 (64).

Providence Retirement Home, 703 E. Spring St., New Albany 47150 (83).

Regina Pacis Home (Skilled Nursing and Intermediate Care Facility), 3900 Washington Ave., Evansville 47715 (164).

Sacred Heart Home (Residence and Comprehensive Nursing), R.R. 2, Avilla 46710 (130).

St. Anne Home (Residence and Comprehensive Nursing), 1900 Randalia Dr., Ft. Wayne 46805 (140).

St. Anthony's Medical Center, Nursing Home, Main and Franciscan Rd., Crown Point 46307 (211).

St. Augustine Home for the Aged, Little Sisters of the Poor, 2345 W. 86th St., Indianapolis 46260 (186).

St. John's Home for the Aged, Little Sisters of the Poor, 1236 Lincoln Ave., Evansville 47714 (130).

St. Paul Hermitage, 501 N. 17th St., Beech Grove 46107 (105).

Iowa: The Alverno Health Care Facility, 849 13th Ave. N., Clinton 52732 (136).

Bishop Drumm Home for the Aged, 1409 Clark St., Des Moines 50314 (130).

Holy Spirit Retirement Home (Nursing Home), 1701 W. 25th St., Sioux City 51103 (94).

Kahl Home for the Aged and Infirm (Intermediate Care Facility), 1101 W. 9th St., Davenport 52804 (125).

The Marian Home, 2400 6th Ave. North, Fort Dodge 50501 (97) and Marian Village (Apartments), 2320 6th Ave. North, Fort Dodge 50501.

Mary of the Angels Home (Women, Employed and Retired), 605 Bluff St., Dubuque 52001 (85).

Ritter Home for Retired Women, 1837 Sunnyside Ave., Burlington 52601 (6).

St. Anthony Nursing Home, 406 E. Anthony St., Carroll 51401 (78).

St. Francis Continuation Care and Nursing Home, Burlington 52601 (74).

Stonehill Care Center (Residence, Nursing Home), 3485 Windsor, Dubuque 52001 (250).

Kansas: Mt. Joseph (Intermediate Care Facility), 1110 W. 11, R.R. 1, Concordia 66901 (100).

St. John Rest Home (Intermediate Care Facility), 701 Seventh St., Victoria 67671 (60).

St. Joseph Home (Skilled Care Facility), 759 Vermont Ave., Kansas City 66101.

Villa Maria, Inc. (Intermediate Care Facility), 116 S. Central, Mulvane 67110 (66).

Kentucky: Cardome Residence for Women, Georgetown 40324 (30).

Carmel Home (Residence and Nursing Home), Old Hartford Rd., Owensboro 42301 (82).

Carmel Manor (Personal Care Home), Carmel Manor Rd., Ft. Thomas, 41075 (99).

Home for Senior Citizens, P.O. Box R. 1, Philpot 42366 (68).

Madonna Manor Nursing Home, 2344 Amsterdam Rd., Covington 41016 (Cottages for Senior Citizens: 9, with 48 apartments).

St. Charles Nursing Home, 500 Farrell Dr., Covington 41011 (147).

St. Margaret of Cortona Home (Women), 1310 Leestown Pike, Lexington 40508 (24).

Taylor Manor Nursing Home, Versailles 40383 (82).

Louisiana: Bethany M.H.S. Nursing Home (Women), P.O. Box 2308, Lafayette 70501 (40).

Chateau de Notre Dame (Residence and Nursing Home), 2832 Burdette St., New Orleans 70125 (110 residential units, 180 nursing beds).

Christopher Inn Apartments, 2110 Royal St., New Orleans 70116.

Consolata Home (Nursing and Extended Care), 2319 E. Main St., New Iberia 70560.

Lafon Nursing Home of the Holy Family, 6900 Chef Menteur Hwy., New Orleans 70126 (171).

Mary-Joseph Residence for the Elderly, 4201 Woodland Dr., New Orleans 70114 (123).

Mater Dolorosa Adult Group Home, 1215 Dublin St., New Orleans 70118.

Metairie Manor, 4929 York St., Metairie 70001 (200 residential units).

Ollie Steele Burden Manor (Nursing Home), 4200 Essen Lane, Baton Rouge 70809 (60).

Our Lady of Prompt Succor Home (Nursing and Extended Care Facility), 751 E. Prudhomme Lane, Opelousas 70570.

St. Charles Nursing Home, P.O. Box 508, Newellton 71357.

St. Joseph's Home (Nursing Home), 2301 Sterlington Rd., Monroe 71201 (124).

St. Margaret's Home (Nursing Home, Women), 504 Tricou St., New Orleans 70117 (82).

St. Martin Manor, 1501 N. Johnson Rd., New Orleans 70116 (140 residential units).

Wynhoven Apartments (Residence for Senior Citizens), 4600 - 10th St., Marrero 70072 (200).

Maine: Deering Pavilion (Apartments for Senior Citizens), 800 Forest Ave., Portland 04103 (200 units).

Marcotte Nursing Home, 100 Campus Ave., Lewiston 04240 (377).

Mt. St. Joseph (Nursing Home), Highwood St., Waterville 04901 (77).

St. Andre Health Care Facility, Inc. (Nursing Home), 407 Pool Rd., Biddeford 04005 (96).

St. Joseph's Manor, 1133 Washington Ave., Portland 04103.

Seton Village, Inc., 1 Carver St., Waterville 04901 (140 housing units.)

Villa Muir, Home for Women, Bay View, Saco 04072 (15).

Maryland: Cardinal Shehan Center for the Aging, Inc., 2300 Dulaney Valley Rd., Towson 21204. Five services: 400-bed long-term care facility; 200 apartments for elderly; residence for elderly in urban area; outreach programs to elderly in homes; retirement residence for priests.

Carroll Manor (Residence and Nursing Home), 4922 La Salle Rd., Hyattsville 20782 (210).

Little Sisters of the Poor, St. Martin's Home (for the Aged), 601 Maiden Choice Lane, Baltimore 21228 (180).

Sacred Heart Home, 5805 Queens Chapel Rd., Hyattsville 20782 (102).

St. Joseph Nursing Home, 1222 Tugwell Dr., Baltimore 21228 (40).

Villa Rosa (Nursing Home), Lottsford Vista Rd., Mitchellville 20716 (99).

Massachusetts: Beaven-Kelly Home for Men (Rest Home), 1245 Main St., Brightside, Holyoke 01040 (55).

Catholic Memorial Home (Nursing Home), 2446 Highland Ave., Fall River 02720 (289).

Don Orione Nursing Home, 111 Orient Ave., East Boston 02128 (200). Adult day care center (30).

D'Youville Manor (Nursing Home), 981 Varnum St., Lowell 01854 (197). Day care program (20).

Jeanne Jugan Residence, Little Sisters of the Poor (Nursing Home), 186 Highland Ave., Somerville 02143 (120).

Madonna Manor (Nursing Home), Washington St., N. Attleboro 02760 (121).

Marian Manor (Nursing Home), 130 Dorchester St., S. Boston, 02127 (376).

Marian Manor of Taunton Nursing Home, 33 Summer St., Taunton 02780 (83).

Maristhill Nursing Home, 66 Newton St., Waltham 02154 (120).

Mary Immaculate Nursing Home, Bennington St., Lawrence 01841 (250). Adult Day Health Care Center (18).

Mt. St. Vincent Nursing Home, Holy Family Rd., Holyoke 01040 (115).

Our Lady's Haven (Nursing Home), 71 Center St., Fairhaven 02719 (112).

The Protectory, Inc., 189 Maple St., Lawrence 01841. Congregate Housing; Apartments (111 units).

Sacred Heart Nursing Home, 359 Summer St., New Bedford 02740 (215).

St. Francis Home for Aged, 37 Thorne St., Worcester 01604 (83). Adult Day Health Care (30).

St. Joseph Manor Nursing Home, 215 Thatcher St., Brockton 02402 (56).

St. Joseph's Manor (Rest Home, Women), 321 Centre St., Dorchester, Boston 02122 (95).

St. Luke's Home (Rest Home, Women), 85 Spring St., Springfield 01105 (92).

St. Patrick's Manor (Nursing Home), 863 Central St., Framingham 01701 (292).

Michigan: Bishop Noa Home for Senior Citizens, Escanaba 49829 (109).

Burtha M. Fisher Home, Little Sisters of the Poor (Residence and Nursing Home), 17550 Southfield Rd., Detroit 48235 (130).

Casa Maria (Residence), 600 Maple Vista, Imlay City 48444 (48).

Kundig Center (Residence), 3300 Jefferies Freeway, Detroit 48208 (180). Rooms and apartments.

Lourdes Nursing Home (Skilled Facility), 2300 Watkins Lake Rd., Pontiac 48054 (108).

Madonna Villa Senior Residence, 17825 Fifteen Mile Rd., Fraser, 48026 (90).

Marian Hall (Residence), 529 Detroit St., Flint 48502 (116).

Marian-Oakland West, 29250 W. Ten Mile Rd., Farmington Hills 48024.

Marian Place (Residence), 408 W. Front St., Monroe 48161. (42).

Marycrest Manor (Skilled Nursing Facility), 15475 Middlebelt Rd., Livonia 48154 (55).

Marydale Center for Senior Citizens (Board and Apartments), 3147 Tenth Ave., Port Huron 48060 (66).

Maryhaven, 11350 Reeck Rd., Southgate 48195.

St. Ann's Home, (Residence and Nursing Home), 2161 Leonard St. N.W., Grand Rapids 49504 (112).

St. Catherine Cooperative House for Elderly Women, 1641 Webb Ave., Detroit 48206.

St. Elizabeth Briarbank (Residence), 1315 N. Woodward Ave., Bloomfield Hills 48013 (56).

St. Francis Home (Nursing Home), 915 N. River Rd., Saginaw 48603 (100).

St. John Vianney Cooperative House for Men, 4806 Mt. Elliot, Detroit 48207 (30).

St. Joseph's Home for the Aged, 4800 Cadieux Rd., Detroit 48224 (100).

Stapleton Center (Residence), 9341 Agnes St., Detroit 48214 (65).

Villa Elizabeth (Nursing Home), 2100 Leonard St. N.E., Grand Rapids 49505 (136).

Villa Francesca (Residence, Women), 565 W. Long Lake Rd., Bloomfield Hills 48013 (18).

Villa Marie (Board and Apartments), 15131 Newburgh Rd., Livonia 48154.

Minnesota: Assumption Home, Cold Spring 56320 (68).

Bethany Home, Onamia 56359 (80).

Divine Providence Community Home (Intermediate Care), 700 Third Ave. N.W., Sleepy Eye 56085.

Divine Providence Home (Skilled Nursing Home), Ivanhoe 56142 (51).

John Paul Apartments, Cold Spring 56320 (61). For elderly and handicapped.

Little Sisters of the Poor (Skilled Nursing and Intermediate Care), 330 S. Exchange St., St. Paul 55102 (153).

Madonna Towers (Retirement Apartments and Nursing Home), 4001 19th Ave. N.W., Rochester 55901 (200).

Mary Rondorf Retirement Home, 222 N. 5th St., Staples 56479 (84).

Mother of Mercy Nursing Home, Albany 56307 (62).

Regina Nursing Home and Retirement Residence, Hastings 55033. Nursing home (61); retirement home (86).

Sacred Heart Hospice (Nursing Home), 1200 Twelfth St. S.W., Austin 55912 (59).

St. Ann's Residence, 330 E. 3rd St., Duluth 55805 (200).

St. Anne Hospice (Residence and Nursing Care), 1347 W. Broadway, Winona 55987 (118).

St. Benedict Center (Nursing Home), 1810 Minnesota Blvd. S.E., St. Cloud 56301 (220).

St. Elizabeth's Hospital and Nursing Home, 1200-5th Grant Blvd., Wabasha 55981 (53).

St. Francis Home, Breckenridge 56520 (124).

St. Mary's Rehabilitation Center, 2512 S. 7th St., Minneapolis 55454 (240).

St. Mary's Hospital and Nursing Home, Winsted 55395 (95).

St. Mary's Home (Nursing Home), 1925 Norfolk Ave., St. Paul 55116 (140).

St. Mary's Villa (Nursing Home), Pierz 56364 (66).

St. Otto's Home (Nursing Home), Little Falls 56345 (159).

St. Therese Home (Residence and Health Care Facility) (302) and St. Therese Retirement Apartments (220), 8000 Bass Lake Rd., New Hope 55428.

St. William's Nursing Home, Parkers Prairie 56361 (61).

Villa of St. Francis Nursing Home, Morris 56267 (144).

Villa St. Vincent (Skilled Nursing Home and Residence), 516 Walsh St., Crookston 56726. Nursing home (80); residence (95).

Mississippi: Santa Maria Retirement Apartments, 305 E. Beach St., Biloxi, 39530.

Villa Maria Retirement Apartments, 921 Porter Ave., Ocean Springs 39564.

Missouri: The Alverne (Retirement Home), 1014 Locust St., St. Louis 63101 (251).

Cathedral Square Towers, 444 W. 12th St., Kansas City 64105. Apartments for elderly and handicapped.

Chariton Apartments (Retirement Apartments), 4249 Michigan Ave., St. Louis 63111 (122 units; 132 residents).

DePaul Community Health Center — St. Anne's Division (Nursing Home), 12349 DePaul Dr., Bridgeton 63044 (114).

LaVerna Heights Retirement Home (Women), 104 E. Park Ave., Savannah 64485 (40).

LaVerna Village Apartments, 1000-1005 Hall Ave., Savannah 64485 (20).

LaVerna Village Nursing Home, 904 Hall Ave., Savannah 64485 (120).

Little Sisters of the Poor, St. Alexis Home, 5331 Highland Ave., Kansas City 64110 (155).

Little Sisters of the Poor (Home for Aged), 3225 N. Florissant Ave., St. Louis 63107 (210).

Mother of Good Counsel Home (Nursing Home, Women), 6825 Natural Bridge Rd., Normandy, 63121.

Our Lady of Mercy Home (Residence and Nursing Home), 918-24 E. 9th St., Kansas City 64106 (153).

Our Lady of Mercy Country House, Box 451, R.R. No. 4, Liberty 64038 (39).

Our Lady of Perpetual Help Nursing Home, 3419 Gasconade St., St. Louis 63118 (112).

St. Agnes Home for the Aged, 10341 Manchester Rd., Kirkwood 63122 (130).

St. John's Hospital — Mercy Villa Division (Nursing Home), 1845 S. Rogers, Springfield 65804 (150).

St. Joseph Hill Nursing Care Facility (Men), Highway FF, Eureka 63025 (130).

St. Joseph's Home, 723 First Capitol Dr., St. Charles 63301 (101).

St. Joseph's Home for the Aged, 1550 W. Main St., Jefferson City 65101 (75).

Nebraska: Bergen Mercy Care Center (residence), 1870 S. 75th St., Omaha 68124 (193)

Madonna Professional Care Center, 2200 S. 52nd St., Lincoln 68506 (182).

Mt. Carmel Home, Keens' Memorial (Nursing Home), 412 W. 18th St., Kearney 68847 (76).

New Cassel Retirement Center, 900 N. 90th St., Omaha 68114. (75).

St. Joseph's Home (Custodial Foster Home), 320 E. Decatur St., West Point 68788 (51).

St. Joseph's Nursing Home, 401 N. 18th St., Norfolk 68701 (70).

St. Joseph's Villa, David City 68632. (65).

New Hampshire: Mount Carmel Nursing Home, 235 Myrtle St., Manchester 03104 (120).

St. Ann Home, 195 Dover Point Rd., Dover 03820 (53).

St. Francis Home for Aged, Court St., Laconia 03246 (51).

St. Teresa Manor (Nursing Home), 519 Bridge St., Manchester 03104 (49).

St. Vincent de Paul Nursing Home, Providence Ave., Berlin 03570 (80).

New Jersey: Holy Family Residence (Women), 44 Rifle Camp Rd., P.O. Box 536, W. Paterson 07424 (64).

Little Sisters of the Poor, St. Joseph Home, 140 Shepherd Lane, Totowa 07512 (247).

Mater Dei Nursing Home, RD 3, Box 164, Rt. 40, P.O. Newfield 08344 (64).

Morris Hall, Home for the Aged (Residence and Skilled Nursing Home), 2361 Lawrenceville Rd., Lawrenceville 08648 (127).

Mount St. Andrew Villa (Residence), 55 W. Midland Ave., Paramus 07652 (59).

Our Lady's Residence (Nursing Home), Glendale and Clematis Aves., Pleasantville 08232 (104).

St. Ann's Home for the Aged (Residence and Nursing Care, Women), 198 Old Bergen Rd., Jersey City 07305 (106). Adult Medical Day Care.

St. Joseph's Home (women), 240 Longhouse Dr., Hewitt 07421.

St. Joseph's Rest Home for Aged Women, 46 Preakness Ave., Paterson 07502 (30).

St. Joseph's Villa (women), Peapack 07977 (18).

St. Mary's Catholic Home (Skilled Nursing Home), 1730 Kresson Rd., Cherry Hill 08003 (94).

Villa Maria (Residence), 641 Somerset St., N. Plainfield 07061.

New Mexico: Good Shepherd Manor (Residential Care for Aged Persons), Little Brothers of the Good Shepherd, P.O. Box 10248, Albuquerque 87114 (43).

New York: Bernardine Apartments, 417

Churchill Ave., Syracuse 13205.

Consolation Residence, 111 Beach Dr., West Islip 11795 (250).

Ferncliff Nursing Home, P.O. Box 386, River Rd., Rhinebeck 12572 (320).

Frances Schervier Home and Hospital, 2975 Independence Ave., New York 10463 (364).

The Heritage (Residence), 1450 Portland Ave., Rochester 14621.

Holy Family Home, 410 Mill St., Williamsville 14221 (90).

Little Sisters of the Poor, Jeanne Jugan Residence (Skilled Nursing and Health Related), 3200 Baychester Ave., Bronx 10475 (203).

Little Sisters of the Poor, Holy Family Home, 1740-84th St., Brooklyn 11214 (165).

Little Sisters of the Poor, Queen of Peace Residence, 110-30 221st St., Queens Village 11429 (202).

Madonna Home of Mercy Hospital (Nursing Home and Extended Care Facility) (140), and Mercy Hospital Health Related Facility (Residence) (58), Watertown 13601.

Madonna Residence, 1 Prospect Park W., Brooklyn, 11215 (290).

Mary Manning Walsh Home (Nursing Home), 1339 York Ave., New York 10021 (362).

Mercy General Hospital Nursing Home Unit, Tupper Lake 12986 (31).

Mt. Carmel Home (Nursing Home, Women), 539 W. 54th St., New York 10019 (92).

Mt. Loretto Nursing Home, (Skilled Nursing Facility), R.D., 3, Amsterdam 12010 (82).

Nazareth Nursing Home, and Health Related Facility, 291 W. North St., Buffalo 14201 (122).

Our Lady of Hope Residence (Home for the Aged), Little Sisters of the Poor, 1 Jeanne Jugan Lane, Latham 12210 (250).

Ozanam Hall for the Elderly, 42-41 201st St., Bayside 11361 (432).

Providence Rest, 3304 Waterbury Ave., Bronx 10465 (154).

Resurrection Rest Home (Nursing Home and Health Related Facility, Women), Castleton 12033 (50).

Sacred Heart Home (Residence) 4520 Ransom Rd., Clarence 10431. Brothers of Mercy Health Facilities, 10570 Bergtold Rd., Clarence 14031. Brothers of Mercy Housing Co., Inc. (Apartments), 10500 Bergtold Rd., Clarence 14031.

Sacred Heart Nursing Home, 8 Mickle St., Plattsburgh 12901 (89).

St. Ann's Home (Nursing Home and Extended Care Facility), 1500 Portland Ave., Rochester 14621 (354).

St. Anthony's Home for the Aged, 5285 S. Park Ave., Hamburg 14075 (68).

St. Columban's on the Lake (Retirement Home), Silver Creek 14136 (50).

St. Elizabeth Home, 5539 Broadway, Lancaster 14086 (102).

St. Francis Home (Nursing and Health Related Facility), 147 Reist St., Williamsville 14221 (98).

St. Joseph's Guest Home, 350 Cuba Hill Rd., Huntington 11743 (60).

St. Joseph's Home (Nursing Home), 420 Lafayette St., Ogdensburg 13669 (82).

St. Joseph's Nursing Home, 2535 Genesee St., Utica 13501 (120).

St. Joseph's Villa (Residence), 38 Prospect Ave., Catskill 12414 (60).

St. Luke Manor for Chronically Ill, 17 Wiard St., Batavia 14020 (20).

St. Mary's Manor and Bishop McNulty Hall, 515 Sixth St. Niagara Falls 14301 (119).

St. Patrick's Home for the Aged and Infirm, 66 Van Cortland Park S., Bronx 10463 (226).

St. Vincent's Home for the Aged, 319 Washington Ave., Dunkirk 14048 (36).

St. Zita's Home (Women), 143 W. 14th St., New York 10011.

Teresian House, Washington Ave. Extension, Albany 12203 (300).

Uihlein Mercy Center (Nursing Home), Lake Placid 12946 (96).

North Carolina: Maryfield Nursing Home, Greensboro Rd., High Point 27260 (115).

North Dakota: Holy Family Guest Home (Nursing Home), Carrington 58421 (38).

Manor St. Joseph (Residence), Edgeley 58533 (50).

Marillac Manor (Retirement Apartments), 1016 N. 28th St., Bismarck 58501 (42 apartments).

St. Anne's Guest Home, 813 Lewis Blvd., Grand Forks 58201 (100).

St. Olav Guest (Retirement) Home, Powers Lake 58773 (20).

St. Vincent's Nursing Home, 1021 N. 26th St., Bismarck 58501 (94).

Ohio: Alvernia Rest Home (Residence and Nursing Care for Aged), 6765 State Rd., Cleveland 44134 (143).

Archbishop Leibold Home for the Aged, Little Sisters of the Poor, 476 Riddle Rd., Cincinnati 45220 (208).

Assumption Nursing Home, 550 W. Chalmers Ave., Youngstown 44511 (126).

Francesca Residence, 39 N. Portage Path, Akron 44303 (50).

Franciscan Terrace (Residence and Nursing Care), 100 Compton Rd., Cincinnati 45215.

House of Loreto (Nursing Home), 2812 Harvard Ave. N.W., Canton 44709 (98).

Jennings Hall, Inc. (Intermediate Care Facility), 10204 Granger Rd., Garfield Heights 44125 (107).

Kirby Manor (Retirement Apartments),

11500 Detroit Ave., Cleveland 44102 (202 suites).

Little Sisters of the Poor, St. Joseph and Mary Home for Aged, 4291 Richmond Rd., Cleveland 44122 (180).

The Maria-Joseph Living Care Center, 4830 Salem Ave., Dayton 45416 (388).

Mt. St. Joseph (Nursing Home), 21800 Chardon Rd., Cleveland 44117 (100).

Nazareth Towers, 300 E. Rich St., Columbus 43215.

Sacred Heart Home, 4900 Navarre Ave., Oregon 43616 (158).

St. Augustine Manor (Nursing Home), 7818 Detroit Ave., Cleveland 44102 (194).

St. Edward Nursing Home, 3131 Smith Rd., Akron 44313 (143).

St. Francis Home for the Aged, 182 St. Francis Ave., Tiffin 44883 (106).

St. Joseph's Hospice (Nursing Home), 2308 Reno Dr., Louisville 44641 (100).

St. Margaret's Hall (Residence and Nursing Facility), 1960 Madison Rd., Cincinnati 45206 (145).

St. Raphael Home (Nursing Home), 1550 Roxbury Rd., Columbus 43212 (80).

St. Rita's Home (Skilled Nursing Home), 880 Greenlawn Ave., Columbus 43223 (100).

St. Theresa Home for the Aged, 6760 Belkenton Pl., Cincinnati 45236 (120).

Schroder Manor (Residence and Skilled Nursing Care), 1302 Millville Ave., Hamilton 45013 (85).

The Siena Home (Skilled Nursing Home), 235 W. Orchard Spring Dr., Dayton 45415 (99).

Villa Maria Skilled Nursing Home, 401 N. Broadway St., Green Springs 44836 (150).

The Villa Sancta Anna Home for the Aged, 25000 Chagrin Blvd., Beachwood 44122 (68).

Oklahoma: Franciscan Villa, 17110 E. 51st St. S., Broken Arrow 74012. Intermediate nursing care (60); apartments (66).

St. Ann's Nursing Home, 3825 N.W. 19th St., Oklahoma City 73107 (82).

Oregon: Benedictine Nursing Center, S. Main St., Mt. Angel 97362 (105).

Maryville Nursing Home, 14645 S.W. Farmington, Beaverton 97007 (132).

Mt. St. Joseph's Residence and Extended Care Center, 3060 S.E. Stark St., Portland 97214 (317).

St. Catherine's Residence and Nursing Center, 3959 Sheridan Ave., North Bend 97459 (166).

St. Elizabeth's Nursing Home, Baker 97814 (97).

Pennsylvania: Ascension Manor I (Senior Citizen Housing), 911 N. Franklin St., Philadelphia 19123 (140 units).

Ascension Manor II (Senior Citizen Housing), 970 N. 7th St., Philadelphia 19123 (140 units).

Christ the King Manor, 1100 W. Long Ave., Du Bois 15801 (100).

Corpus Christi Residence, 7165 Churchland St., Pittsburgh 15206.

Drueding Infirmary, 413 W. Master St., Philadelphia 19122 (50).

Garvey Manor (Nursing Home), Logan Blvd., Hollidaysburg, 16648 (150).

Holy Family Home, Little Sisters of the Poor, 5300 Chester Ave., Philadelphia 19143 (200).

Holy Family Manor (Skilled Nursing Facility), 1200 Spring St., Bethlehem 18018 (200).

Holy Ghost Guest Home (Women), 4537 Wm. Flynn Hwy., Allison Park 15101 (17).

Immaculate Mary Home, (Skilled and Intermediate Nursing Care), Holme Circle and Welsh Rd., Philadelphia 19136 (300).

John XXIII Home, 2250 Shenango Freeway, Hermitage 16146 (100).

Little Flower Manor Nursing Home, 1201 Springfield Rd., Darby 19023 (122).

Little Flower Manor of Diocese of Scranton, (Long-Term Skilled Nursing and Intermediate Care Facility), 200 S. Meade St., Wilkes-Barre 18702.

Little Sisters of the Poor, 1028 Benton Ave. N.S., Pittsburgh 15212 (140).

Little Sisters of the Poor, Holy Family Residence, 2500 Adams Ave., Scranton 18509 (82).

Maria Joseph Manor, Danville 17821 (94).

Marian Manor (Residence and Nursing Care), 2695 Winchester Dr., Pittsburgh 15220 (172).

Mt. Trexler Skilled Nursing Unit of Sacred Heart Hospital, Limeport 18060 (65).

Redeemer Village, Huntingdon Pike, Meadowbrook 19046 (150 apartments).

Sacred Heart Manor (Nursing Home), 6445 Germantown Ave., Philadelphia 19119 (139).

St. Anne Home (Intermediate and Skilled Nursing Care), R.D. 2, Columbia 17512 (120).

St. Anne Home for the Elderly (Skilled Nursing Facility), 685 Angela Dr., Greensburg 15601 (125).

St. Basil's Home for Women, Uniontown 15401 (18).

St. Ignatius Nursing Home, 4401 Haverford Ave., Philadelphia 19104 (176).

St. John Neumann Nursing Home, 10400 Roosevelt Blvd. Philadelphia 19116 (196).

St. Joseph Home for the Aged, 1182 Holland Rd., Holland 18966 (92).

St. Joseph Home for the Aged (Skilled Nursing Facility), 5324 Penn Ave., Pittsburgh 15224 (150).

St. Joseph's House of Hospitality (Low Income Senior Citizen Residence for Men and Women), 1635 Bedford Ave., Pittsburgh

15219 (65). Under sponsorship of St. Vincent de Paul Society.

St. Joseph Manor (Skilled Nursing Facility), 1616 Huntingdon Pike, Meadowbrook 19046 (250).

St. Joseph's Residence for Men, 1111 S. Cascade St., New Castle 16101.

St. Leonard's Guest Home, 601 N. Montgomery St., Hollidaysburg 16648 (22).

St. Mary's Home of Erie, 607 E. 26th St., Erie 16504. Residential facility (110); geriatric nursing facility (199).

St. Mary's Manor for Sighted and Unsighted, 701 Lansdale Ave., Lansdale 19446 (160).

St. Mary's Villa (Nursing Home), Elmhurst 18416 (121).

Villa de Marillac Nursing Home (Women), 5300 Stanton Ave., Pittsburgh 15206 (50).

Villa St. Teresa (Residence), 1215 Springfield Rd., Darby 19023 (53).

Villa Teresa (Nursing Home), 1051 Avila Rd., Harrisburg 17109 (178).

Vincentian Home for the Chronically Ill., Perrymont Rd., Pittsburgh 15237 (219).

Rhode Island: Jeanne Jugan Residence of the Little Sisters of the Poor, 964 Main St., Pawtucket 02860 (132).

L'Hospice St. Antoine (Home for Aged), 400 Mendon Rd., North Smithfield 02895 (244).

St. Clare Home for the Aged, 309 Spring St., Newport 02840 (44).

Scalabrini Villa (Convalescent, Rest — Nursing Home). 860 N. Quidnessett Rd., North Kingstown 02852 (70).

South Carolina: Carter-May Home, 1660 Ingram Rd., Charleston 29407 (12). Personal care home for elderly ladies.

South Dakota: Brady Memorial Home (Skilled Nursing Facility), 500 S. Ohlman St., Mitchell 57301 (60). Independent living units Maryhouse, Inc. (Skilled Nursing Facility), 717 E. Dakota, Pierre 57501 (82).

Mother Joseph Manor (Skilled Nursing Facility), 1002 North Jay St., Aberdeen 57401 (60). Apartment units (7). Adult day care program.

St. William's Home for the Aged (Intermediate Care, 60), and Angela Hall (Supervised Living, 15), 901 E. Virgil, Box 432, Milbank 57252.

Tekakwitha Nursing Home, Sisseton 57262 (102).

Tennessee: Alexian Brothers Rest Home (Retired Men and Women), Signal Mountain 37377 (150).

Ave Maria Guild Home (Nursing Home), 2805 Charles Bryan Rd., Memphis 38134 (73).

Texas: Home for Aged Women-Men, 920 S. Oregon St., El Paso 79901 (24).

Laurelwood Medical Complex (Home for Aged and Convalescents), 2717 N. Flores St., San Antonio 78212.

Mother of Perpetual Help Home (Intermediate Care Facility), 519 E. Madison Ave., Brownsville 78520 (39).

Mt. Carmel Home (Personal Care Home), 4130 S. Alameda St., Corpus Christi 78411 (92).

The Regis (Retirement Home and Nursing Care), 400 Austin Ave., Waco 76701 (420).

The Retirement Residence, Inc., 2819 Rio Grande, Austin 78705 (100).

St. Ann's Nursing Home, P.O. Box 1179, Panhandle 79068 (52).

St. Anthony's Center (Skilled Nursing, Rehabilitation, Geriatric), 6301 Almeda Rd., Houston 77021 (372).

St. Benedict's Nursing Home, Alamo and Johnson Sts., San Antonio 78204 (197).

St. Dominic Residence Hall, 2401 E. Holcombe Blvd., Houston 77021.

St. Francis Village, Inc. (Retired and Elderly), Crowley. Mailing address — P.O. Box 16310, Ft. Worth 76133 (425).

St. Joseph Residence, 330 W. Pembroke St., Dallas 75208 (49).

San Juan Nursing Home, San Juan 78589 (52).

Utah: St. Joseph Villa (Skilled Nursing Home), 474 Westminster Ave., Salt Lake City 84115 (98).

Vermont: Loretto Home for Aged, 59 Meadow St., Rutland 05701 (54).

Michaud Memorial Manor (Residence), Derby Line 05830 (24).

St. Joseph's Home for Aged, 243 N. Prospect St., Burlington 05401 (53).

Virginia: St. Francis Home, 2511 Wise St., Richmond 23225 (25).

St. Joseph's Home for the Aged, Little Sisters of the Poor, 1503 Michael Rd., Richmond 23229.

Washington: Cathedral Plaza Apartments (Retirement Apartments), W. 1120 Sprague Ave., Spokane 99204 (150).

The Delaney, W. 242 Riverside Ave., Spokane 99201 (84).

The De Paul Retirement Apartments, 4831 35th Ave. S.W., Seattle 98126 (111 units).

Fahy Garden Apartments, W. 1403 Dean Ave., Spokane 99201 (31).

Fahy West Apartments, W. 1523 Dean Ave., Spokane 99201 (55).

The Josephinum (Retirement Home), 1902 2nd Ave., Seattle 98101 (228).

Mt. St. Vincent Nursing Center, 4831 35th Ave., S.W., Seattle 98126 (198).

The O'Malley, E. 707 Mission, Spokane 99202 (100).

St. Joseph Nursing Home, 1006 North H St., Aberdeen 98520 (33).

St. Joseph Care Center (Nursing Home), West 20 — 90th Ave., Spokane 99204 (103). Adult day care center (35).

West Virginia: Knights of St. George Home, Wellsburg 26070 (44).

Welty Home for the Aged (Women), 21 Washington Ave., Wheeling 26003 (44).

Wisconsin: Bethany-St. Joseph Health Care Center, 2507 Shelby Rd., La Crosse 54601 (226).

Divine Savior Nursing Home, 715 W. Pleasant St., Portage 53901 (111).

Franciscan Villa of South Milwaukee, Inc. 3601 S. Chicago Ave., S. Milwaukee 53172 (150).

Hope Nursing Home, 439 Ashford Ave., Lomira 53048 (40).

McCormick Memorial Home for the Aged, 212 Iroquois St., Green Bay 54301 (70).

Marian Catholic Home, 3333 W. Highland Blvd., Milwaukee 53208 (360).

Maryhill Manor Nursing and Retirement Home, 973 Main St., Niagara 54151 (49).

Milwaukee Catholic Home, Inc., 2462 N. Prospect Ave., Milwaukee 53211 (185).

Nazareth House (Skilled Nursing Facility), Stoughton 53589 (100).

Sacred Heart Hospital Nursing Home, Tomahawk 54487 (31).

St. Ann Rest Home (Intermediate Care Facility, Women), 2020 S. Muskego Ave., Milwaukee 53204 (54).

St. Anne's Home for the Elderly (Aged Poor), 3800 N. 92nd St., Milwaukee 53222 (176).

St. Camillus Health Center (Skilled Nursing Home), 10100 W. Bluemound Rd., Wauwatosa 53226 (188).

St. Catherine Infirmary (Nursing Home), 5635 Erie St., Racine 53402 (40).

St. Elizabeth Home, 502 St. Lawrence Ave., Janesville 53545.

St. Elizabeth's Nursing Home (Women), 745 N. Brookfield Rd., Brookfield 53005 (16).

St. Francis Home, 709 S. 10th St., La Crosse 54601 (93).

St. Francis Home (Skilled Nursing Facility), 2325 E. 3rd St., Superior 54880 (52).

St. Francis Home (Skilled Nursing), 365 Gillett St., Fond du Lac 54935 (70).

St. Francis Manor (Retirement Residence), 3553 S. 41st St., Milwaukee 53221 (5).

St. Joan Antida Nursing Home (Women), 6640 W. Beloit Rd., W. Allis 53219 (76).

St. Joseph's Home, 705 Clyman St., Watertown 53094 (28).

St. Joseph's Home, 9244 29th Ave., Kenosha 53140 (89).

St. Joseph's Home, 5301 W. Lincoln Ave., W. Allis 53219 (124).

St. Joseph's Nursing Home, 464 S. St. Joseph Ave., Arcadia 54612 (72).

St. Joseph's Nursing Home, 2415 Cass St., La Crosse 54601 (62).

St. Joseph's Nursing Home, 400 Water Ave., Hillsboro 54634 (75).

St. Joseph Residence, Inc. (Nursing Home), 1925 Division St., New London 54961 (107).

St. Mary's Home for the Aged (Residence and Nursing Care), 2005 Division St., Manitowoc 54220 (172).

St. Mary's Nursing Home (Women), 3516 W. Center St., Milwaukee 53210 (121).

St. Monica's Senior Citizens Home, 3920 N. Green Bay Rd., Racine 53404 (90).

St. Paul Home (Residence and Skilled Nursing Home), 509 W. Wisconsin Ave., Kaukauna 54130 (54).

Villa Clement (Nursing and Convalescent Center), 9047 W. Greenfield Ave., W. Allis 53214 (190).

Villa Loretto Nursing Home, Mount Calvary 53057 (52).

Villa Madonna, 1170 W. Windlake Ave., Milwaukee 53215 (45).

FACILITIES FOR HANDICAPPED CHILDREN AND ADULTS

Sources: Almanac survey; *Directory of Catholic Special Facilities and Programs for Handicapped Children and Adults,* published by the National Catholic Educational Association; *Official Catholic Directory.*

This listing covers facilities and programs with educational and training orientation. Information about other services for the handicapped can generally be obtained from the Catholic Charities Office or its equivalent (c/o Chancery Office) in any diocese. (See Index for listing of addresses of chancery offices in the U.S.)

Abbreviation code: b, boys; c, coeducational; d, day; g, girls; r, residential. Other information includes chronological age for admission. The number in parentheses at the

end of an entry indicates total capacity or enrollment.

Deaf and Hard of Hearing

California: St. Joseph's School for Deaf and Hard of Hearing (d,c; 3-14 yrs.), 1 Santa Maria Way, Orinda 94563.

Illinois: Department of Vision and Hearing, Catholic Charities, 721 N. LaSalle St., Chicago 60610. Special classes (d,c) for hearing-impaired children in Chicago archdiocese, pre-school and elementary level. Marian School for Hearing Impaired (at Most Holy Redeemer School), 9536 S. Millard Ave., Evergreen Park 60642. Itinerant services for children fully mainstreamed in regular Catholic schools. Services for hearing-impaired children under age 3 and their parents.

Holy Trinity Day Classes for the Deaf (c; 3-14 yrs.) 1910 Taylor, Chicago 60612 (35).

Louisiana: Chinchuba Institute (r,d,c; 2-16 yrs.), P.O. Box 187, Marrero. 70072 (123).

Massachusetts: Boston School for the Deaf (r,d,c; 3-17 yrs.), 800 N. Main St., Randolph. 02368 (304).

Missouri: St. Joseph Institute for the Deaf (r,d,c; 3½-15 yrs.), 1483 82nd Blvd., University City, 63132 (150).

New Jersey: Mt. Carmel Guild Pre-School Deaf Program (d,c), 17 Mulberry St., Newark. 07102 (80).

New York: Cleary School for the Deaf (d,c; 2½-14 yrs.), 301 Smithtown Blvd., Lake Ronkonkoma, L.I. 11779 (105).

St. Francis de Sales School for the Deaf (d,c; pre-school through 8th grade), 260 Eastern Parkway, Brooklyn 11225.

St. Joseph's School for the Deaf (d,c; 3-13 yrs.), 1000 Hutchinson River Pkwy, Bronx. 10465 (250).

St. Mary's School for the Deaf (r,d,c; 3-21 yrs.), 2253 Main St., Buffalo. 14214 (260).

Ohio: St. Rita School for the Deaf (r,c; 4 yrs. and older), 1720 Glendale-Milford Rd., Cincinnati. 45215 (150).

Pennsylvania: Abp. Ryan Memorial Institute for Deaf (d,c; parent-infant programs through 8th grade), 3509 Spring Garden St., Philadelphia. 19104 (80).

De Paul Institute (d,c; birth-21 yrs.), Castlegate Ave., Pittsburgh. 15226 (173).

Wisconsin: St. John's School for the Deaf (r,d,c; 3-20 yrs.), 3680 S. Kinnickinnic Ave., Milwaukee. 53207 (160).

Emotionally And/Or Socially Maladjusted

This listing includes facilities for homeless, neglected, emotionally disturbed children and youth.

Arizona: Patterdell, 1820 W. Northern Ave., Phoenix. 85021.

Arkansas: St. Michael School, Monastery of Our Lady of Charity (d,c; 6 yrs. and up), 1125 Malvern Ave., Hot Springs 71901.

California: American Boys Ranch (r; 12-16 yrs.), 14700 Manzanita Park Rd., Beaumont. 92223 (109).

Gracenter, Convent of the Good Shepherd (r, women), 501 Cambridge, San Francisco 94134 (9).

Hanna Boys Center (r; 10-15 yrs.), Box 100, Sonoma. 95476 (80).

Rancho San Antonio (r,b; 12-16 yrs.), 21000 Plummer St., Chatsworth. 91311 (118).

Stanford Lathrop Memorial Home and Group Homes, Sisters of Social Service, 800 N. Street, Sacramento 95814. Conduct six homes for boys and girls.

Colorado: Excelsior Youth Centers (r,g; 12-21 yrs.), 15151 E. Quincy Ave., Denver 80232 (74).

Mt. St. Vincent Home (r,c; 5-13 yrs.), 4159 Lowell Blvd., Denver. 80211 (45).

Connecticut: Highland Heights — St. Francis Home for Children (r,d,c; 8-12 yrs.), 651 Prospect St., New Haven. 06505 (38).

Mt. St. John (r,b; 11-16 yrs.), Kirtland St., Deep River. 06417 (75).

Delaware: Our Lady of Grace Home for Children (r,c; 6-12 yrs.), 487 Chestnut Hill Rd., Newark 19713 (28).

Florida: Boystown of Florida (r; 13-17 yrs.), 11400 SW 137th Ave., Miami 33186 (45).

Georgia: Village of St. Joseph (r,d,c; 6-16 yrs.), 2969 Butner Rd. S.W., Atlanta 30331.

Hawaii: Child Development Center (c; 3-6 yrs; therapeutic day treatment center), 2345 Nuuanu Ave., Honolulu. 96817 (12).

Illinois: Group Home — Virginia Residence (r,g; 14-18 yrs.), 1434 W. Estes Ave., Chicago. 60626 (8).

Group Home, Marcella Residence (g; 14-18 yrs.), 3636 N. Janssen, Chicago. 60657 (8).

Guardian Angel Home (r,d,c; 5-15 yrs.), Plainfield at Theodore St., Joliet 60435.

House of the Good Shepherd, Heart of Mary High School (r,g; 13-18 yrs.), 1126 W. Grace St., Chicago. 60613 (90).

Loyola Univ. of Chicago Child Guidance Center and Day School (c; pre-school to adolescence), 1043 W. Loyola Ave., Chicago 60626 (37).

St. Joseph Carondelet Child Center (r,b; 5-14 yrs.), 739 E. 35th St., Chicago. 60616 (45).

Indiana: Father Gibault School for Boys (r; 10-16 yrs.), 5901 Dixie Bee Rd., Terre Haute. 47802 (108).

Hoosier "Boys" Town (r; 10-15 yrs.), Schererville. 46375 (80).

Kentucky: Boys' Haven (r; 13-18 yrs.), 3201 Bardstown Rd., Louisville. 40205 (51).

Maryhurst School (r,g; 13-17 yrs.), 1015 Dorsey Lane, Louisville 40223.

Our Lady of the Highlands (r,g; teen-age high school age), 938 Highland Ave., Ft. Thomas. 41075 (50).

Louisiana: Hope Haven — Madonna Manor School and Home (r,b; 6-17 yrs.), 1101 Barataria Blvd., Marrero 70072 (158).

Maison Marie Group Home (g; 13-18 yrs.), 3020 Independence St., Metairie 70002 (12).

Maryland: Christ Child Institute for Children (r,d,c; 3-10½ yrs.), Edson Lane, Rockville. 20852 (28r, 15d). Also conducts group home.

Good Shepherd Center (r,d,g; 14-18 yrs.), 4100 Maple Ave., Baltimore. 21227 (90r, 30d).

Massachusetts: Cushing Hall (r,b; 11-14½ yrs.), 279 Tilden Rd., Scituate. 02066 (40). Diagnostic treatment center.

McAuley Nazareth Home (r,c; 10-21 yrs.),

77 Mulberry St., Leicester 01524. Program for autistic.

McAuley Nazareth Home for Boys (r; 6-10 yrs.), 77 Mulberry St., Leicester. 01524 (30).

Madonna Hall (r,g; 13-17 yrs.), Cushing Hill Dr., Marlboro 01752 (55).

Nazareth Child Care Center (r,d,c; 2-12 yrs.), 420 Pond St., Jamaica Plain, Mass. 02130 (112).

Our Lady of Providence Children's Center (r,d,c; 6-12 yrs.), 2112 Riverdale St., W. Springfield. 01089 (50).

St. Vincent Home (r,c), 2425 Highland Ave., Fall River 02720 (85).

Michigan: Barat House, Barat Human Services, League of Catholic Women (r,g; 12-16 yrs.), 5250 John R. St., Detroit. 48202 (24).

Boysville of Michigan, Inc. (r; 13-18 yrs.), 8744 Clinton-Macon Rd., Clinton. 49236 (180).

Don Bosco Hall (r,b; 13-17 years.), 10001 Petoskey Ave., Detroit. 48204 (38).

Jordan House (r,g; 16-21 yrs.), 17487 Alwyne, Detroit 48203 (6). Group home.

St. John's Home (r,c; 9-16 yrs.), 385 E. Leonard N.E., Grand Rapids 49503 (40).

St. Vincent Home for Children (r,c; 5-15 yrs.), 2800 W. Willow St., Lansing 48917 (38).

Villa Maria, Sisters of the Good Shepherd (r,g; 13-17 yrs.), 1315 Walker St. N.W., Grand Rapids. 49504 (40).

Vista Maria School (r,g; 13-17 yrs.), 20651 W. Warren Ave., Dearborn Heights. 48127 (90).

Minnesota: Busch Center (r,c; 8-16 yrs.), 1726 7th Ave. S., St. Cloud 56301 (20). Temporary emergency shelter care facility.

Home of the Good Shepherd, (r,g; 14-17 yrs.), 5100 Hodgson Rd., St. Paul. 55112 (60).

St. Cloud Children's Home (r,c; 12-16 yrs.), 1726 7th Ave. S., St. Cloud. 56301 (72).

St. James Children's Home (r,c), Woodland Hills, Duluth 55803 (120).

Tiffany House Group Home (c), 374 4th Ave. S., St. Cloud 56301 (11).

Missouri: Child Center of Our Lady of Grace (r,d,c; 4-12 yrs.), 7900 Natural Bridge Rd., St. Louis. 63121 (72).

Marillac School (r,d,c; 7-11 yrs.), 310 W. 106th St., Kansas City. 64114 (100 day, 25 boarders).

Marygrove (r,g; 13-17 yrs.), 2705 Mullanphy Lane, Florissant. 63031 (70).

Nebraska: Father Flanagan's Boys' Home (r; 10-18 yrs.), Boys Town, Nebr. 68010 (r, 390; d, 307).

Nevada: St. Yves High School (r,g; 13-17 yrs.), 7000 North Jones Blvd., Las Vegas, 89106 (60).

New Jersey: Catholic Community Services, Mt. Carmel Guild Children's CMHC (d,c; 3-18 yrs.), 17 Mulberry St., Newark 07102 (58).

Christopher House (c), 55 N. Clinton Ave., Trenton 08607. After care day center.

Collier School (d,c; 13-17 yrs.), Wickatunk 07765.

Guidance Clinic (c), 39 N. Clinton Ave., Trenton 08607. After care day center.

Mt. St. Joseph Children's Center (c), Shepherd Lane, Totowa 07512 (17).

Pelletier Day School (c; 13-17 yrs.), 939 Parkside Ave., Trenton 08618 (32).

New York: The Astor Home for Children (r,c; 5-12 yrs.), 36 Mill St., Rhinebeck 12572 (70). The Astor Group Home Program (adolescents), 662 E. 231st St., Bronx 10466 (50). Also has out-patient programs.

Baker Hall (r,d,b; 10-18 yrs.), 150 Martin Rd., Lackawanna. 14218 (90).

Immaculate Heart of Mary Children's Home and School (r,c; 6-12 yrs.), William and Kennedy Sts., Buffalo 14206 (50).

LaSalle School (r,d; 12-18 yrs.), 391 Western Ave., Albany. 12203 (145). Also conducts group homes.

Lincoln Hall (r,b; 12-16 yrs.), Lincolndale. 10540 (250).

Madonna Heights School for Girls (r; 11-17 yrs.), Burrs Lane, Huntington. 11743 (110). Also conducts group homes on Long Island.

Our Lady of Charity School (r,g; 12-18 yrs.), Hamburg. 14075 (50).

Saint Anne Institute (r,d,g; 12-18 yrs.), 25 W. Lawrence St., Albany. 12206 (190).

St. Helena's Residence (r,g; 12-17 yrs.), 120 W. 60th St., New York. 10011 (20).

St. John's of Rockaway Beach (r,b; 10-18 yrs.), 144 Beach 111th St., Rockaway Park. 11694 (112). Also conducts group homes in Rockaway and Richmond Hill.

North Dakota: Home on the Range for Boys (r; 12-18 yrs.), Sentinel Butte. 58654 (36).

Ohio: Children's Village of St. Vincent de Paul (Parmadale) (r,c; 3-21 yrs.), 6753 State Rd., Parma. 44134 (200).

Diocesan Child Guidance Center, Inc. (d,c; preschool), 840 W. State St., Columbus 43222.

Marycrest School for Girls (r,g; 13-18 yrs.), 7800 Brookside Rd., Independence. 44131 (70).

Rosemont School (r,g;d,c; 12-18 yrs.), 2440 Dawnlight Ave., Columbus. 43211 (150).

St. Anthony Home for Boys (r; 14-19 yrs.), 6753 State Rd., Parma. 44134.'

Oregon: Christie School (r,g; 9-16 yrs.), Marylhurst 97036 (26).

St. Mary's Home for Boys (r; 9-17 yrs.), 16535 S.W. Tualatin Valley Highway, Beaverton. 97005 (43).

Villa St. Rose School for Girls (r; 12-18 yrs.), 597 N. Dekum St., Portland. 97217 (51).

Pennsylvania: De LaSalle in Towne (d,b; 13-17 yrs.), 25 S. Van Pelt St., Philadelphia 19103 (100).

De LaSalle Vocational Day Treatment (b;

15-18 yrs.), P.O. Box 344 — Street Rd. and Bristol Pike, Cornwells Hts. 19020 (125).

Gannondale School for Girls (r; 12-17 yrs.), 4635 E. Lake Rd., Erie. 16511 (57).

Good Shepherd Services of Germantown (r,g; 14-18 yrs.), 5301 Chew Ave., Philadelphia 19138 (20). Two group homes.

Harborcreek School for Boys (r; 10-17 yrs.), 5712 Iroquois Ave., Harborcreek. 16421 (135). Also conducts group homes.

Lourdesmont School (r,g; 14-17 yrs.), 537 Venard Rd., Clarks Summit. 18411 (50). Also conducts day school (c).

Pauline Auberle Foundation, The Auberle Home for Boys (r,b; 13-18 yrs.), 1101 Hartman St., McKeesport. 15132 (50).

St. Gabriel Hall (r,d,b; 10-17 yrs.), P.O. Box 390, Phoenixville. 19460 (177). Group homes.

St. Michael's School for Boys (r,b; 12-16 yrs.), Hoban Heights, Tunkhannock 18657 (120).

Toner Institute (r,b; 9-13 yrs.), Castlegate Ave., Pittsburgh. 15226 (52).

Tennessee: DeNeuville Heights School for Girls (r; 12-18 yrs.), 3060 Baskin St., Memphis. 38127 (52).

Texas: Mt. St. Michael Home and School for Girls (r,g; 12-18 yrs.), 4500 W. Davis St., Dallas. 75211 (120).

St. Joseph Youth Center (r,c; 12-17 yrs.), 901 S. Madison St., Dallas. 75208 (48).

Washington: Marian Heights High School (r,g; 13-18 yrs.), 3754 W. Indian Trail Rd., Spokane. 99208 (50).

Morning Star Boys Ranch (Spokane Boys' Ranch, Inc.), (r,b; 11-14 yrs.), Box 781-A Route 3, Spokane. 99203 (56).

Wisconsin: Mary Hill Center (r,g; 13-19 yrs.), 3310 N. Dousman St., Milwaukee 53212 (22).

Our Lady of Charity High School (r,g; 13-18 yrs.), 2640 West Point Rd., Green Bay 54303 (76).

St. Aemilian Child Care Center, Inc. (r&d,b; 6-12 yrs.), 8901 W. Capitol Dr., Milwaukee. 53222 (47).

St. Charles Boys Home (r; 12-18 yrs.), 151 S. 84th St., Milwaukee. 53214 (56).

St. Michael's Home for Children (r,c; 9-18 yrs.), 2902 East Ave. S., La Crosse. 54601 (42).

Wyoming: St. Joseph's Children's Home (r,c; 6-18 yrs.), P.O. Box 1117, Torrington 82240 (60). Also conducts group home.

Developmentally Handicapped

This listing includes facilities for children and youth with learning disabilities and/or mental retardation.

Alabama: Father Walter Memorial Child Care Center (r,c; birth-12 yrs.), 2815 Forbes Dr., Montgomery 36110 (34). Skilled nursing facility.

California: Catholic Charities "Empower" Services to Developmentally Disabled Persons, 433 Jefferson St., Oakland 94607. Services include (in various locations): Tap Center (d; adults); Concord House (r; adults); C.O.R.E. (d; adults outreach program for homebound); Case Management (d; adults, children — social workers); Religious Nurture Program (d; adults, children).

Helpers of the Mentally Retarded, Inc., 2626 Fulton St., San Francisco. 94118. Conducts three homes: Helpers Home for Girls (18 years and older), 2608 Fulton St. and 2626 Fulton St., San Francisco. 94118; Helpers Home for Men (18 years and older), 2750 Fulton St., San Francisco. 94118.

Kennedy Child Study Center (d,c; 5-13 yrs.), 1339 - 20th St., Santa Monica. 90404 (80). Also conducts a developmental nursery (18 mos.-3 yrs.) and a preschool for children from culturally deprived areas (3-5 yrs.).

St. Madeleine Sophie's Training Center (d,c; 18 yrs. and older), 2111 E. Madison Ave., El Cajon. 92021 (80).

St. Vincent School (r,d,c; 8-14 yrs.), P.O. Drawer V, 4300 Calle Real, Santa Barbara. 93102 (135).

Tierra del Sol (d,c; 18 yrs. and older), 9919 Sunland Blvd., Sunland. 91040 (100).

Connecticut: Gengras Center (d,c; 6-21 yrs.), St. Joseph College, 1678 Asylum Ave., W. Hartford 06117 (60).

Special Education Department, Diocese of Bridgeport, 238 Jewett Ave., Bridgeport 06606.

District of Columbia: Lt. Joseph P. Kennedy Jr. Institute (d,c; 5-20 yrs.), 801 Buchanan St. N.E., Washington. 20017 (120). Also conducts group home and sheltered workshop.

St. Gertrude's School of Arts and Crafts (r,d,g; 6-18 yrs.), 4801 Sargent Rd. N.E., Washington. 20017 (48).

Florida: Marian Center Services for Developmentally Handicapped and Mentally Retarded (r,d,c), 15701 Northwest 37th Ave., Opa Locka. 33054. Offers variety of services.

Marian School for Exceptional Children (d,c; 6 mos.-5 yrs.), 326 Pine Terr., W. Palm Beach 33401.

Morning Star School (d,c; 4-12 yrs.), 725 Mickler Rd., Jacksonville. 32211 (70).

Morning Star School (d,c; 3-12 yrs.), 954 Leigh Ave., Orlando. 32804 (45).

Morning Star School (d,c; 4-16 yrs.), 4661 - 80th Ave., N., Pinellas Park. 33565 (50).

Morning Star School (d,c; 6-13 yrs.), 302 E. Linebaugh Ave., Tampa. 33612 (70).

Hawaii: Special Education Center of Oahu (SECO) (d,c; 3-20 yrs.), 708 Palekaua St., Honolulu 96816.

Illinois: Bartlett Learning Center (c;r, 5-12 yrs.; d, 3-12 yrs.), 801 W. Bartlett Rd., Bartlett. 60103 (138).

Good Shepherd Manor (permanent home for men; 18 yrs.), P.O. Box 260, Momence. 60954 (120).

Lt. Joseph P. Kennedy, Jr., School (r,b;d,c; 6-21 yrs.) and Job Training Center (c; 16 yrs. and older), 123rd and Wolf Rd., Palos Park. 60464 (110).

Misericordia Home South (r,c; 1 mo.-6 yrs.), 2916 W. 47th St., Chicago. 60632 (125).

Misericordia Home North (r,c; 4-21 yrs.), 6300 North Ridge, Chicago (60).

Mt. St. Joseph (mentally handicapped women; 20-45 yrs.), Route 3, Box 365, Lake Zurich. 60047 (160).

St. Francis School for Exceptional Children (r,c; 4-12 yrs.), 1209 S. Walnut Ave., Freeport. 61032 (32).

St. Jude School (d,c; 6-16 yrs.), 2nd and Spring Ave., Aviston. 62216 (30).

St. Mary of Providence (r,d,g; 4-21 yrs.), 4200 N. Austin Ave., Chicago. 60634 (190).

St. Rose Center (d,c; 3-15 yrs.), 4911 S. Hoyne Ave., Chicago. 60609 (60).

St. Vincent Residential School (c; 12 yrs. and older), and St. Vincent Community Living Facility (adults), 659 E. Jefferson St., Freeport. 61032.

Special Education Program of the East St. Louis Deanery (d,c; 5-16 yrs.), 8213 Church Lane, East St. Louis. 62203 (48).

Indiana: Marian Day School (d,c; 6-18 yrs.), 625 Bellemeade Ave., Evansville. 47713 (45).

Providence House (r, men; 18 yrs. and up), 520 W. 9th St., Jasper 47546 (66).

St. Bavo Special Class (d,c; 6-15 yrs.), 512 W. 8th St., Mishawaka. 46544 (12).

St. Mary Child Center School (d,c; 3-16 yrs.), 311 N. New Jersey St., Indianapolis. 46204 (32). Developmentally Disabled.

Iowa: Special Services — Office of Education (r,c), P.O. Box 1180, 1229 Mt. Loretto, Dubuque 52001. Conducts several homes which provide training and work experience, organizes and coordinates religion classes for retarded.

Kansas: Holy Family Center (d,c; 6-18 yrs.), 619 S. Maize Rd., Wichita. 67209 (65).

Lakemary Center, Inc. (r,d,c; 3-16 yrs.), 100 Lakemary Dr., Paola. 66071 (72r,35d).

Kentucky: Msgr. Pitt Learning Center (d,c; 5 yrs. and older), 10715 Ward Ave., Louisville 40223 (74).

Ursuline Special Education Learning Center (d,c; 3½-14 yrs.), 3105 Lexington Rd., Louisville. 40206 (50-56).

Louisiana: Department of Special Education, Archdiocese of New Orleans, 1522 Chippewa St., New Orleans. 70130. Conducts day classes, a special day school, and a vocational rehabilitation center for the mentally retarded (300).

Department of Special Education, Diocese of Baton Rouge, P.O. Box 53326, Baton Rouge. 70805. Conducts 10 classes for ele-

mentary and junior high special students and one vocational evaluation and training center for young men and women 16 years and older.

Holy Angels Institute (r,c; teen-age, 14 yrs. and older; nursery, 2 mo. to kindergarten age), 10450 Ellerbe Rd., Shreveport. 71106 (140).

Padua House (r,c; birth-18 yrs.), 200 Beta St., Belle Chase 70037 (44).

Regina Caeli Center (d,c; 6-16 yrs.), 3903 Kingston, Lake Charles. 70605 (45).

St. Francis de Sales Interparochial Special Education School (d,c; 6-16 yrs.), 300 Verret St., Houma 70361 (30).

St. Mary Learning Center, St. Mary's Home (d,c; 6-18 yrs.), 601 W. St. Mary, Lafayette 70506 (50).

St. Mary's Training School (r,c: 3-22 yrs.), P.O. Drawer 7768, Alexandria 71306. (150).

St. Michael Vocational Training Center (d,c; 16-21 yrs.), 1522 Chippewa St., New Orleans 70130.

Maryland: The Benedictine School for Exceptional Children (r,c; 6-16 yrs.), Ridgely. 21660 (100). Also conducts Habilitation Center (r,c; 17 yrs. and older).

St. Elizabeth School for Special Education (d,c; 12 yrs. and older), 801 Argonne Dr., Baltimore. 21218 (145).

St. Francis School for Special Education (d,c; 3-13 yrs.), 2226 Maryland Ave., Baltimore. 21218 (60).

Villa St. Louise, (r), 2520 Pot Spring Rd., Timonium 21093 (30).

Massachusetts: Cardinal Cushing School and Training Center (r,d,c; 6-22 yrs.), Hanover. 02339 (165).

Mercy Centre for Developmental Disabilities (d,c; 3-22 yrs.), 25 West Chester St., Worcester. 01605 (108).

Nazareth Hall on the Cape (d,c; 6-15 yrs.), 261 South St., Hyannis. 02601 (25).

Nazareth Hall for Exceptional Children (d,c; 7-14 yrs.), 887 Highland Ave., Fall River, 02720 (70).

Nazareth Vocational Center (d,c; 18-21 yrs.), 707 Highland Ave., Fall River. 02720 (24).

St. Coletta Day School (d,c; 7-12 yrs., admission age), 85 Washington St., Braintree. 02184 (150).

Michigan: Our Lady of Providence Center (r,d,g; 5-17 yrs., child caring; 18-26, adult foster care), 16115 Beck Rd., Northville. 48167 (100).

St. Louis School (r,b; 8-18 yrs.), 16195 Old U.S. 12, Chelsea. 48118 (90).

Missouri: Department of Special Education, Archdiocese of St. Louis, 4472 Lindell Blvd., St. Louis. 63108. Conducts 27 special day classes (c; 5-16 yrs.) and 2 day classes for pre-school children (c; 2-6 yrs.).

Good Shepherd Manor (residential for developmentally disabled men; 16 yrs. and up),

Little Brothers of the Good Shepherd, 3220 E. 23rd St., Kansas City. 64127 (43).

St. Joseph's Vocational Center (c; 15-21 yrs.), 5341 Emerson Ave., St. Louis. 63120 (135).

St. Mary's Special School (r,c; 5-16 yrs.), 5341 Emerson Ave., St. Louis. 63120 (138).

St. Peter's Special Classes (d,c; 5-21 yrs.), 314 W. High St., Jefferson City. 65101 (38).

Universal Sheltered Workshop (c, adults), 6912 W. Florissant Ave., St. Louis 63136. Sheltered employment.

Nebraska: Villa Marie School (r,d,c; 7-16 yrs.), Rt. 1, Box 109, Waverly. 68462 (25).

Madonna School for Exceptional Children (d,c; 5-21 yrs.), 2537 N. 62nd St., Omaha 68104 (65).

New Jersey: Alhambra Pavilion Child Study Center (c; 5-10 yrs.), 31 Centre St., Newark. 07102 (50).

Archbishop Damiano School (d,c), 532 Delsea Dr., Westville Grove 08093.

Catholic Community Services, Archbishop Boland Rehabilitation and Training Center (d,c; 16-55 yrs.), 450 Market St., Newark 07105.

Child Study Center (d,c; 4-8 yrs.), 272 Main St., Ridgefield Park. 07660 (17).

Department of Special Education, Diocese of Camden, 1845 Haddon Ave., Camden 08108. Services include: Archbishop Damiano School (above), and full time programs at 6 Catholic Schools; adult evening classes (18-65 yrs.); religious education programs.

Department of Special Education, Diocese of Paterson. Murray House (r; adults), 391 Main St., Paterson. 07501. Also conducts two other group homes, an Adult Opportunity Center, a farm and a summer camp.

Felician School for Exceptional Children (r,d,c; 2½-14 yrs.), 260 S. Main St., Lodi 07644.

McAuley School for Exceptional Children (d,c; 5-9 yrs.), Rt. 22 and Terrill Rd., N. Plainfield. 07061 (30).

Marian Center (d,c; 7-14 yrs.), Delsea Dr. and Chestnut St., Vineland. 08360 (30).

Mount Carmel Guild — Department of Special Education and Psychological Services, Archdiocese of Newark, 1180 Raymond Blvd., Newark. 07102. Conducts day classes for the mentally retarded. Also conducts work training programs.

Sr. Georgine Learning Center (d,c; 6-17 yrs.), 544 Chestnut Ave., Trenton. 08611 (30).

New Mexico: Notre Dame on the Rio Grande (r; custodial facility for males, 8 yrs. and older; no maximum age), 1301-15 Mountain Rd., Albuquerque. 87104 (15).

St. Joseph's Manor (r,b; 14-29 yrs.), P.O. Box 610, Bernalillo. 87004. Little Brothers of the Good Shepherd, P.O. Box 610, Bernalillo 87004. Twenty-four-hour child care center for mentally and physically handicapped.

New York: Cantalician Center for Learning (d,c; birth-21 yrs.), 3233 Main St., Buffalo. 14214 (250).

Cantalician Center Workshop (d,c; 18 yrs. and older), 2101 Kenmore Ave., Buffalo. 14207. Also conducts a vocational evaluation and rehabilitation training program.

Cobb Memorial School (r,c; 6-10 yrs.), Altamont. 12009 (50).

Friends of L'Arche of Greater Syracuse, Inc. (r, adults), 1611 Court St., Syracuse 13208. Long-term facility following philosophy of Jean Vanier and L'Arche movement.

Maryhaven Vocational Rehabilitation Center (d,c; 16 yrs. and older), 450 Myrtle Ave., Port Jefferson. 11777 (90).

St. Catherine Center for Children (r,c; birth to 12 yrs. and d,c; 3-12 yrs.), 30 N. Main St., Albany. 12203 (140). Also conducts group home and specialized foster care programs.

St. Joseph School for Exceptional Children (r,d,c; 5-21 yrs.), 10807 Bennett Rd., Dunkirk. 14048 (30).

School of the Holy Childhood (d,c; 7-18 yrs.), 1150 Buffalo Rd., Rochester. 14624 (85). Adult program, 18-50 yrs.

Special Education Department, Diocese of Brooklyn (d,c; 3-18 yrs.), Office of Education, 345 Adams St., Brooklyn, 11201 (235).

Special Education Department, Archdiocese of New York, 1011 First Ave., New York. 10022. Conducts 13 special day classes in 9 parish schools.

North Carolina: Holy Angels Nursery (r,c; birth to 12 yrs.), Belmont. 28012 (66).

Ohio: Good Shepherd Manor (permanent care of men 18 years and older), P.O. Box 387, Wakefield 45687 (104).

Mary Immaculate School for Exceptional Children (d,c; 7-14 yrs.), 3837 Secor Rd., Toledo. 43623 (80). For children with learning disabilities.

Marymount Rehabilitation Services (vocational rehabilitation; 16 yrs. and older), 12215 Granger Rd., Cleveland. 44125.

MRS Industries (c; sheltered workshop), 4765 E. 131st St., Garfield Heights 44105.

Mt. Aloysius (r, men; 21 yrs. and over), Tile Plant Rd., New Lexington. 43764 (100).

Our Lady of Angels Special School (d,c; 7-16 yrs.), 3570 Rocky River Dr., Cleveland. 44111 (30).

Our Lady of the Elms Special School (d,c; 6-15 yrs.), 1230 W. Market St., Akron. 44313 (74).

Rose Mary, The Johanna Graselli Rehabilitation and Education Center (r,c; 3-12 yrs.), 19350 Euclid Ave., Cleveland. 44117 (40).

St. John's Villa (r,c,b, 4-14 yrs; g, 4-18 yrs., continued care, g, 18 yrs. and over), 620 Roswell Rd. N.W., Carrollton. 44615 (221).

St. Joseph Center (d,c; 6-16 yrs.), 2346 W. 14th St., Cleveland. 44113 (70).

Sheltered Workshop and Training Center

(c; 16 yrs. and older), 1890 W. 22nd St., Cleveland. 44113 (35).

Oregon: Emily School for Multi-Handicapped Children (d,c; 2½-5 yrs.), 830 N.E. 47th Ave., Portland. 97213 (12).

Providence Children's Nursing Center (r; nursing care), 830 N. E. 47th Ave., Portland. 97213 (54).

Pennsylvania: Clelian Heights School for Exceptional Children (r,d,c; 6-16 yrs.), R.D. 9, Box 607, Greensburg. 15601 (100). Also conducts re-socialization program (r,d,c; 16-20 yrs.).

Department of Special Education, Diocese of Pittsburgh, 162 Steuben St., Pittsburgh. 15220. Conducts a program consisting of five special day classes.

Don Guanella School (r,d,b; 6-15 yrs.) and C. K. Center (r,c; adults, post-school age), Sproul Rd., Springfield. 19064.

McGuire Memorial (r,d,c; infancy to 7 yrs.), 2119 Mercer Rd., New Brighton. 15066 (99).

Mercy Day School: Center for Special Learning (d,c; 6-18 yrs.), 830 S. Woodward St., Allentown. 18103 (80).

Our Lady of Confidence Day School (c; 5-18 yrs.), 1099 W. Luzerne St., Philadelphia. 19140 (68b, 56g).

St. Anthony School for Exceptional Children (r,d,c; 6-16 yrs.), 13th St. and Hulton Rd., Oakmont. 15139 (150).

St. Joseph Day School (c; 6-18 yrs.), 619 Mahantongo St., Pottsville. 17901 (40).

St. Joseph's Children and Maternity Hospital (r,c; birth-20 yrs.), 2010 Adams Ave., Scranton. 18509 (88).

St. Katherine School (d,c; 4-18 yrs.), William Rd. and Bowman Ave., Philadelphia. 19151 (95 b, 95 g).

St. Mary of Providence Center (r,d,g; 6-14 yrs.), Elverson. 19520 (120).

Tennessee: Madonna Day School for Retarded Children (d,c; 5-16), 4189 Leroy, Memphis. 38108 (50).

St. Bernard School for Exceptional Children, 2021 21st Ave. S., Nashville 37212 (25).

Texas: Notre Dame of Dallas Special School (d,c; 6-12 yrs.), Rt. 2, Box 4, Irving. 75062. (108). Notre Dame Vocational School, at same address, provides work-study program for exceptional young people over 16.

Virginia: St. Coletta School (d,c; 4-21 yrs.), 1305 N. Jackson St., Arlington. 22201 (45).

St. Mary's Infant Home (r,c; 3 days-9 yrs.), 317 Chapel St., Norfolk. 23504 (50).

Wisconsin: St. Coletta School (r,c), Jefferson. 53549 (372). Offers the following programs:

a complete program of special education from kindergarten through elementary and advanced levels (r,d,c);

a work training center in preparation for job placement (r,c; 17-20 yrs.);

a residential care center (r,c; 45-85 yrs.);

a half-way house to give guidance and assist with problems (r,c; 18-24 yrs.);

a sheltered workshop to provide employment for the mentally retarded in a sheltered environment (r,c; 25-45 yrs.).

St. Coletta Day School (c; 8-16 yrs.), 1725 N. 54th St., Milwaukee. 53208 (16).

Orthopedically Handicapped

Alabama: Father Purcell Memorial (r,c; birth to 14 yrs.), 2048 W. Fairview Ave., Montgomery. 36108 (52). Skilled nursing home.

Kentucky: United Cerebral Palsy Center (d,c; birth and up), 71 Orphanage Rd., Fort Mitchell, 41017 (131).

Pennsylvania: St. Edmond's Home for Crippled Children (r,c; 2-10 yrs.)., 320 S. Roberts Rd., Rosemont. 19010 (50).

Visually Handicapped

Illinois: Department of Vision and Hearing, Catholic Charities, 721 N. LaSalle St., Chicago, 60610. Itinerant education services for visually impaired students attending regular Catholic elementary and high schools in Chicago archdiocese.

Maine: The Visual Education Center, Inc. (d,c; 3-20 yrs.), 14 Locust St., Portland. 04111 (18).

Diocesan Human Relations Services, Inc., 41 Birch St., Biddeford 04005; 15 Vaughn St., Caribou 04736. Itinerant services.

New Jersey: St. Joseph's School for the Multiple Handicapped Blind (r,d,c; 3-21 yrs.), 253 Baldwin Ave., Jersey City. 07306 (25).

New York: Catholic Charities Services for Visually Impaired, 272 Merrick Rd., Lynbrook. 11563.

Catholic Guild for the Blind (itinerant teaching program, c; 5-17 yrs.), 345 Adams St., Brooklyn. 11201.

Lavelle School for the Blind (r,d,c; 3-20 yrs.), 221st St. and Paulding Ave., Bronx. 10469 (120).

Pennsylvania: Vision Program, Archdiocese of Philadelphia. St. Lucy Day School (d,c; 5-14 yrs.), 929 S. Farragut St., Philadelphia. 19143 (80). Also provides vision consultant services to parish schools and high schools.

Organizations for Handicapped

(See separate article for a listing of facilities for the handicapped.)

Blind

The **Carroll Center for the Blind** (formerly the Catholic Guild for All the Blind): Located at 770 Centre St., Newton, Mass. 02158, the center conducts diagnostic evaluation and rehabilitation programs for blind people over 16 years of age, and maintains programs in community services for all ages, volunteer and special services, casework and counseling, low-vision training and professional training. It offers a large range of services for blind people who are not in residence, and maintains an office of public education and information. The executive director is Rachel Rosenbaum.

Xavier Society for the Blind: The Society is located at 154 E. 23rd St., New York, 10010. Founded in 1900 by Rev. Joseph Stadelman, S.J., it is a center for publications for the blind and maintains a circulating library of approximately 7,000 volumes in Braille, large type and on tape. Its many publications include *The Catholic Review,* a monthly selection of articles of current interest from the Catholic press presented for the visually handicapped in Braille, on tape, and in large print. The director of Xavier is Rev. Anthony F. La Bau, S.J.

The Deaf

According to the National Catholic Office for the Deaf, there are approximately 95,000 Catholics among the total deaf population of 410,522. (The deaf were defined by the 1974 National Census of the Deaf Population as "those persons who could not hear and understand speech and who had lost — or never had — that ability prior to 19 years of age.) Reported statistics indicated: Students in Catholic schools for the deaf, 1,969; teachers, 570 (147 were religious). Personnel involved in out-of-school pastoral ministry to the deaf included: priests, 97 (35 full-time, 62 part-time); permanent deacons, 6 (part-time); sisters, 72 (27 full-time, 45 part-time); brothers, 3 (1 full-time, 2 part-time); lay people, 69 (4 full-time, 65 part-time).

Organizations involved in work for the deaf include the following.

International Catholic Deaf Association: Established by deaf adults in Toronto, Canada, in 1949, the association has more than 8,000 members in 117 chapters, mostly in the U.S. It is the only international lay association founded and controlled by deaf Catholic adults. It is affiliated with the World Federation of the Deaf. Home office address: 814 Thayer Ave., Silver Spring, Md. 20910. The ICDA publishes *The Deaf Catholic,* a quarterly, and sponsors regional conferences and an annual convention.

National Catholic Office for the Deaf: Formally established in 1976, at Washington, D.C., to provide pastoral service to those who teach deaf children and adults, to the parents of deaf children, to pastors of deaf persons, and to organizations of the deaf. The office develops liturgical and religious education materials; organizes workshops, pastoral weeks, community weeks, leadership programs, cursillos; and serves as a clearinghouse for information concerning ministry to the deaf. It publishes *Listening,* a pastoral service

for the hearing impaired, five times a year. The executive director is Sister Alverna Hollis, O.P. Address: Trinity College, Washington, D.C. 20017.

Mentally Retarded

National Apostolate with Mentally Retarded Persons: Established in 1968, the apostolate has headquarters at Trinity College, P.O. Box 4588, Washington, D.C. 20017. It publishes the quarterly *NAMPR Journal* and a monthly newsletter, and has available a bibliography on the religious education of the retarded. Rev. William Finnegan is president of the apostolate; the executive director is Bro. Joseph Moloney, O.S.F.

Service Agency

Special Education Department, National Catholic Educational Association: Established in 1954 to coordinate under one agency information and service functions for all areas of special education under Catholic auspices. The executive director is Sr. Suzanne Hall, S.N.D. de N. Address: One Dupont Circle N.W., Suite 350, Washington, D.C. 20036.

OTHER SOCIAL SERVICES

Cancer Hospitals or Homes: The following homes or hospitals specialize in the care of cancer patients. They are listed according to state.

Penrose Cancer Hospital, Sisters of Charity of Cincinnati, 2215 N. Cascade Ave., Colorado Springs, Colo. 80907.

Our Lady of Perpetual Help Home, Servants of Relief for Incurable Cancer, 760 Washington St., S.W., Atlanta, Ga. 30315 (54).

Rose Hawthorne Lathrop Home, Servants of Relief for Incurable Cancer, 1600 Bay St., Fall River, Mass. 02724 (35).

Our Lady of Good Counsel Free Cancer Home, Servants of Relief for Incurable Cancer, 2076 St. Anthony Ave., St. Paul, Minn. 55104 (49).

Calvary Hospital, Inc., 1740-70 Eastchester Rd., Bronx, N.Y. 10461 (200). Sponsored by Catholic Charities, Department of Health and Hospitals, Archdiocese of New York.

St. Rose's Free Home for Incurable Cancer, Servants of Relief for Incurable Cancer, 71 Jackson St., New York, N.Y. 10002 (45).

Rosary Hill Home, Servants of Relief for Incurable Cancer, Hawthorne, N.Y. 10532 (82).

Holy Family Home, Servants of Relief for Incurable Cancer, 6707 State Rd., Cleveland, O. 44134 (50).

Sacred Heart Free Home for Incurable Cancer, Servants of Relief for Incurable Cancer, 1315 W. Hunting Park Ave., Philadelphia, Pa. 19140 (59).

Drug Abuse: Rehabilitation centers and outpatient clinics have been established in several dioceses. Facilities include:

Alpha House for Drug Rehabilitation (women) and Dismas House for Drug Rehabilitation (men), 396 Straight St., Paterson, N.J. 07501 (residential rehabilitation programs). Cedar Outpatient Clinic and Cedar Day Care Center, 101-105 Cedar St., Paterson, N.J. 07501 (outpatient services).

St. Joseph's Hospital, L. E. Phillips Center for the Chemically Dependent, 2661 County Trunk I, Chippewa Falls, Wis. 54729 (46).

New Hope Manor (live in therapeutic community for rehabilitation of female drug addicts), Graymoor, Garrison, N.Y. 10524.

St. Luke Center (clinic), 3290 N.W. 7th St., Miami, Fla. 33125.

Alcoholics: Some priests and religious throughout the U.S. are committed in a special way to the personal rehabilitation and pastoral care of alcoholics through participation in Alcoholics Anonymous and other programs. Facilities for the rehabilitation of alcoholics include:

St. Christopher's Inn, Atonement Friars, Graymoor, Garrison, N.Y. 10524 (capacity, 180). Simple detoxification and recovery; 21 days; ages 18-70.

Matt Talbot Inn, 2270 Professor St., Cleveland, Ohio 44113 (capacity 23 men; Halfway House; residential treatment for male alcoholics).

Mt. Carmel Hospital for Alcoholism (20 beds), and Mt. Carmel Rehabilitation Center for Male Alcoholics (50 beds), 396 Straight St., Paterson, N.J. 07501. McNulty House for Male Alcoholics (10 beds), 101 Cedar St., Paterson, N.J. 07501. Straight and Narrow Alcohol Abuse Services (outpatient services), 896 E. 19th St., Paterson, N.J. 07501.

Sacred Heart Rehabilitation Center: 569 Elizabeth St., Detroit, Mich. 48201 (130 beds, early treatment); 400 Stoddard Rd., Memphis, Mich. 48041 (125 beds, advance treatment). Both facilities serve male and female live-in clients. Three Halfway Houses for employed residents who complete full program.

The National Clergy Conference on Alcoholism was established to conduct workshops in various dioceses to instruct priests on ways of dealing with problem drinkers.

Convicts: Priests serve as full- or part-time chaplains in penal and correctional institutions throughout the country. Limited efforts have been made to assist in the rehabilitation of released prisoners in Halfway House establishments.

Dining Rooms; Facilities for Homeless: Representative of places where meals are provided, and in some cases lodging and other services as well, are:

St. Anthony's Dining Room, 121 Golden Gate Ave., San Francisco, Calif. 94102, where nearly 13.5 million free meals have been served since 1950. Founded by Rev. Alfred Boeddeker, O.F.M.

St. Vincent de Paul Dining Room, 675 23rd St., Oakland, Calif. 94604. Administered by Little Brothers of the Good Shepherd. Under sponsorship of St. Vincent de Paul Society.

Ozanam Inn, Little Brothers of the Good Shepherd, 843 Camp St., New Orleans, La. 70130. Under sponsorship of the St. Vincent de Paul Society.

St. Vincent's Dining Room, 505 W. 3rd St., Reno, Nev. 89503.

St. Vincent's Dining Room, 650 S. Main St., Las Vegas, Nev. 89101.

Good Shepherd Refuge, Little Brothers of the Good Shepherd, 601 2nd St. S.W., Albuquerque, N.M. 87102.

Holy Name Centre for Homeless Men, Inc., 18 Bleeker St., New York, N.Y. 10012. A day shelter for alcoholic, homeless men. Provides social services and aid to transients and those in need. Affiliated with New York Catholic Charities.

Mercy Hospice, Sisters of Mercy, 334 S. 13th St., Philadelphia, Pa. 19107. Temporary shelter and relocation assistance for homeless women.

St. Christopher Inn, Graymoor, Garrison, N.Y. 10524. Temporary shelter (21 days for homeless and needy men). A.A. program, referral, counseling.

St. John's Hospice for Men, Little Brothers of the Good Shepherd, 1221 Race St., Philadelphia, Pa. 19107. Founded in 1963. Hot breakfast and dinner served to all in need; accommodations for 35 men for night shelter; clothing distributed daily to needy.

Camillus House, Little Brothers of the Good Shepherd, 726 N.E. First Ave., Miami, Fla. 33132.

Temporary Shelters: Facilities for runaways, the abused and exploited include:

Convent of the Good Shepherd, 2561 Venice Blvd., Los Angeles, Calif. 90019. For battered women with children.

Covenant House, 460 W. 41st St., New York, N.Y. 10036. Non-sectarian. Executive director, Rev. Bruce Ritter, O.F.M. Conv. For homeless and exploited youth aged 21 and under.

Crescent House, 2929 S. Carrollton Ave., New Orleans, La. 70118. Temporary residence for abused women and their children.

Unwed Mothers: Residential and care services for unwed mothers are available in many dioceses.

Committee for Human Values

The U.S. Bishops' Committee for Human Values was established by the National Conference of Catholic Bishops in November, 1974. It is a distinct standing committee for keeping abreast of issues in science, technology and values, as well as relations with nonbelievers.

Retreats, Spiritual Renewal Programs

(Sources: Almanac survey; *1980 Directory of Retreat Houses in the United States and Canada*, compiled by Retreats International; *The Official Catholic Directory*.)

Abbreviation code: m, men; w, women; mc, married couples; y, youth. Houses and centers without code generally offer facilities to all groups. An asterisk after an abbreviation indicates that the facility is primarily for the group designated but that special groups are also accommodated. Houses furnish information concerning the types of programs they offer.

Alabama: Blessed Trinity Shrine Retreat, Holy Trinity 36859.

Visitation Sacred Heart Retreat House, 2300 Spring Hill Ave., Mobile 36607.

Alaska: Holy Spirit Retreat House, Star Route A, Box 2388, Anchorage 99502.

Arizona: Franciscan Renewal Center, Casa de Paz y Bien, 5802 E. Lincoln Dr., Box 220, Scottsdale 85252.

Mount Claret Cursillo Center, 4633 N. 54th St., Phoenix 85018.

Picture Rocks Retreat — A Christian Renewal Center, 7101 W. Picture Rocks Rd., Cortaro 85230. Mailing address, Box 569, Cortaro 85230.

Spiritual Life Institute (individuals only), Nada Contemplative Center, Sedona 86336.

Arkansas: The Abbey Retreat (Coury House), Subiaco 72865.

California: Angela Center (ecumenical), 535 Angela Dr., Santa Rosa 95401.

Camp Mariastella (y*, families, ecumenical), Wrightwood 92397. Office, 1120 Westchester Pl., Los Angeles 90019.

Cenacle Retreat House 5340 Fair Oaks Blvd., Carmichael 95608.

Christ the King Retreat Center, Box 156, Citrus Heights 95610.

Christian Brothers Retreat House (students), 2233 Sulphur Springs Ave., St. Helena 94574.

El Carmelo Christian Renewal Center, 926 E. Highland Ave., Redlands 92373.

El Retiro, Jesuit Retreat House, P.O. Box 128, Los Altos 94022.

Holy Spirit Retreat House, 4316 Lanai Rd., Encino 91436.

Immaculate Heart Retreat House (w, mc), 3431 Waverly Dr., Los Angeles 90027.

La Casa de Maria, 800 El Bosque Rd., Santa Barbara 93108.

Manresa Retreat House (m*), P.O. Box K, Azusa 91702.

Mary and Joseph Retreat House, 5300 Crest Rd., Palos Verdes 90274.

Mater Dolorosa Retreat House (m*), 700 N. Sunnyside Ave., Sierra Madre 91024.

Mission San Miguel, San Miguel 93451.

Mount Mary Immaculate, 3254 Gloria Terr., Lafayette 94549.

Mt. Tabor Monastery, 17001 Tomki Rd., Redwood Valley 95470.

New Camaldoli Immaculate Heart Hermitage (m*, private), Big Sur 93920.

Old Mission San Luis Rey Retreat, P.O. Box 407, San Luis Rey 92068.

Poverello of Assisi Retreat House, 1519 Woodworth St., San Fernando 91340.

Sacred Heart Retreat House (w*), 920 E. Alhambra Rd., Alhambra 91801.

St. Andrew's Priory Retreat House, Valyermo 93563.

St. Anthony's Retreat House, 43816 Siena Dr., Three Rivers 93271.

St. Charles Priory, Benet Hill, Oceanside 92054.

St. Clare's Retreat (w*), 2381 Laurel Glen Rd. Santa Cruz 95065.

St. Francis Retreat, P.O. Box 1070, San Juan Bautista 95045.

St. Joseph's Salesian Youth Center (St. Dominic Savio Retreat House) (y), 8301 Arroyo Dr., Rosemead 91770.

San Damiano Retreat, P.O. Box 767, Danville 94526.

Santa Sabina Center, 1520 Grand Ave., San Rafael 94901.

Serra Retreat (m*), P.O. Box 127, Malibu 90265.

Vallombrosa Center (w*), 250 Oak Grove Ave., Menlo Park 94025.

Villa Maria del Mar, Santa Cruz. Mailing address, 2-1918 E. Cliff Dr., Santa Cruz 95062.

Colorado: Bethlehem Center, RR 1, Box 192, Broomfield 80020.

Convent of St. Walburga (w*), 6717 S. Boulder Rd., Boulder 80303.

El Pomar Renewal Center, 1661 Mesa Ave., Colorado Springs 80906.

Sacred Heart Retreat House, Box 185, Sedalia 80135.

Connecticut: Cenacle Center for Meditation and Spiritual Renewal (w*), Wadsworth St., Box 550, Middletown 06457.

Edmundite Apostolate and Conference Center, Enders Island, Mystic 06355.

Holy Family Retreat (m, mc*), 303 Tunxis Rd., West Hartford 06107.

Immaculata Retreat House, Route 32, Windham Rd., Willimantic 06226.

Mercy Center, 167 Neck Rd., Madison 06443.

Our Lady of Calvary Retreat House, Colton St., Farmington 06032.

Villa Maria Retreat House (w), 159 Sky Meadow Dr., Stamford 06903.

Delaware: St. Francis Renewal Center, 1901 Prior Rd., Wilmington 19809.

District of Columbia: Washington Retreat House (w*), 4000 Harewood Rd. N.E., Washington 20017.

Florida: Cenacle Retreat House, 1400 S. Dixie Highway, Lantana 33462.

Dominican Retreat House (Mary Queen of Apostles), 7275 S.W. 124th St., Kendall 33156.

Franciscan Center, 3010 Perry Ave., Tampa 33603.

Holy Name Priory, P.O. Drawer H, St. Leo 33574.

Our Lady of Florida Retreat House, 1300 US Hwy. No. 1, North Palm Beach 33408.

St. Leo's Abbey (m), St. Leo 33574.

Georgia: Ignatius House, 6700 Riverside Dr. N.W., Atlanta 30328.

Monastery of the Holy Spirit (m), 3780 Hwy. 212 S.W., Conyers 30207.

Idaho: Nazareth, 4450 N. Five Mile Rd., Boise 83702.

Illinois: Aylesford Carmelite Spiritual Center, I-55 at Cass Ave., N, Darien 60559.

Bellarmine Hall (m*), Box 268, Barrington 60010.

Bishop Lane Retreat House, R.R. 2, Box 214 A, Rockford 61102.

Cabrini Contact Center, 9430 Golf Rd., Des Plaines 60016.

Cenacle Retreat House, 513 Fullerton Parkway, Chicago 60614.

Cenacle Retreat and Conference Center, P.O. Box 340, Warrenville 60555.

Childerley Retreat House (university students), 506 McHenry Rd., Wheeling 60090.

Christian Life Center, 1209 W. Ogden Ave., La Grange Park 60525.

Franciscan Apostolic Center, P.O. Box 42, Sangamon Ave., Springfield 67205.

King's House, N. 66th St., Belleville 62223.

King's House of Retreats, Box 165, Henry 61537.

La Salle Manor, Christian Brothers Retreat House (y*), Plano 60545.

Longwood Cenacle, 11600 Longwood Dr., Chicago 60643.

National Shrine of Our Lady of the Snows, 9500 W. Illinois Route 15, Belleville 62223.

Our Lady of Angels Retreat and Renewal Center, 1901 E. 18th St., Chicago 60098.

Resurrection Center, 2710 S. Country Club Rd., Woodstock 60098.

St. Francis Retreat, Mayslake, 1717 31st St., Oak Brook 60521.

St. Joseph Retreat House, 353 N. River Rd., Des Plaines 60016.

St. Mary's Retreat House, P.O. Box 608, 1400 Main St., Lemont 60439.

Techny Towers, International Mission Center, Techny 60082.

Tolentine Center, 20300 Governors Highway, Olympia Fields 60461.

Viatorian Villa, 3015 N. Bayview Lane, McHenry 60050.

Villa Redeemer, Box 6, Glenview 60025.

Indiana: Alverna Center, 8140 Spring Mill Rd., Indianapolis 46260.

Crosier Ministry Center, 2620 E. Wallen Rd., Ft. Wayne 46825.

John XXIII Center, 407 W. McDonald St., Hartford City 47348.

Kordes Enrichment Center, R.R. 3, Box 200, Ferdinand 47532.

Lourdes Retreat House (m*), Box 156, Cedar Lake 46303.

Mount Saint Francis Retreat Center, Mount Saint Francis 47146.

Our Lady of Fatima Retreat House, 5353 E. 56th St., Indianapolis 46226.

Our Lady of Fatima Retreat House, Box O, Notre Dame 46556.

St. Jude Guest House, St. Meinrad 47577.

St. Maur Theological Center, 4545 Northwestern Ave., Indianapolis 46208.

Sarto Retreat House, 4200 N. Kentucky Ave., Evansville 47711.

Seimetz Renewal Center, 1441 Hoffman St., Hammond 46327.

Iowa: American Martyrs Retreat House, 2209 N. Union Rd., Cedar Falls 50613.

Colfax Interfaith Spiritual Center, Box 37, Colfax, 50054.

Kansas: St. Augustine Retreat Center, A 3301 Parallel Parkway, Kansas City 66104.

St. Benedict's Abbey (m, mc*), Atchison 66002.

Villa Christi Retreat House, 3033 W. Second St., Wichita 67203.

Kentucky: Marydale Center, Donaldson Rd., Erlanger 41018.

Our Lady of Gethsemani (m, private), The Guestmaster, Abbey of Gethsemani, Trappist 40073.

Placid House, St. Mark's Priory, South Union 42283.

Saint Thomas Center, 170 Crabbs Lane, Louisville 40206.

Louisiana: Abbey Christian Life Center, St. Joseph's Abbey, St. Benedict 70457.

Ave Maria Retreat House, Route 1, Box 0368 AB, Marrero 70072.

Cenacle Retreat House (w*), 5500 St. Mary St., Metairie 70011.

Manresa House of Retreats (m), P.O. Box 89, Convent 70723.

Maryhill Retreat House (Christian Life Center), 600 Maryhill Rd., Pineville 71360.

Our Lady of the Oaks Retreat House, P.O. Box D, Grand Coteau 70541.

Maine: St. Paul's Center, Oblate Fathers Retreat House (French-English), 136 State St., Augusta 04330.

Maryland: CYO Retreat Center, P.O. Box 4235, 401 Randolph Rd., Silver Spring 20904.

CYO Retreat House (y*), 15523 York Rd., Sparks 21152.

Christian Brothers Retreat House (y*), Rt. 85 South, Adamstown 21710.

Loyola Retreat House-on-Potomac, Faulkner 20632.

Manresa-on-Severn, P.O. Box 9, Annapolis 21404.

Marriottsville Spiritual Center, Marriottsville 21104.

St. Joseph Spiritual Center, 3800 Frederick Ave., Baltimore 21229.

Massachusetts: Calvary Retreat Center, Passionist Community, 59 South St., Shrewsbury 01545.

Campion Renewal Center, 319 Concord Rd., Weston 02193.

Cenacle Retreat House, 200 Lake St., Brighton, Boston 02135.

Christian Formation Center, 475 River Rd., Andover 01810

Eastern Point Retreat House, Gonzaga Hall, Gloucester 01930.

Espousal Center, 554 Lexington St., Waltham 02154.

Esther House of Spiritual Renewal, Sisters of St. Anne, 783 Grove St., Worcester 01605.

Genesis Spiritual Life Center, 53 Mill St., Westfield 01085.

Glastonbury Abbey (Benedictine Monks), 16 Hull St., Hingham 02043.

Guest Retreat House, St. Joseph's Abbey, Spencer 01562.

Holy Cross Fathers Retreat House, 490 Washington St., N. Easton 02356.

Jesuit Center, Sullivan Square, Charlestown, Boston 02129.

La Salette Center for Christian Living, 947 Park St., Attleboro 02703.

Loretto Retreat House, Jeffrey's Neck Rd., Ipswich 01938.

Marian Center (w*), 1365 Northampton St., Holyoke 01040.

Miramar Retreat House, Duxbury, 02332.

Mother of God Retreat House (boys), Old Groveland Rd., Bradford 01830.

Mother of Sorrows Retreat House (m*), 110 Monastery Ave., W. Springfield 01089.

Mt. Carmel Christian Life Center, Oblong Rd., Williamstown 01267.

Sacred Heart Center for Youth Ministry, Salesians of St. John Bosco, P.O. Box 271, Ipswich 01938.

St. Stephen Priory (Dominican), 20 Glen St., Dover, Mass. 02030.

Salvatorian Center, 30 East St., Methuen 01844.

Michigan: Blessed Sacrament Retreat House, Sacramentine Sisters, Conway 49722.

Capuchin Retreat, Box 188, Washington 48094.

Colombiere Retreat/Conference Center, 9075 Big Lake Rd., Clarkston 48016.

Manresa Jesuit Retreat House, 1390 Quarton Rd., Bloomfield Hills 48013.

Mary Reparatrix Retreat Center (w*), 13600 Virgil, Detroit 48223.

Marygrove Center, Garden 49835.

Portiuncula in the Pines, 703 E. Main St., De Witt 48820.

Queen of Angels Retreat, Box 2026, 3400 S. Washington Blvd., Saginaw 48605.

St. Basil's Center, 3990 Giddings Rd., Pontiac 48057.

St. Clare Capuchin Retreat, 1975 N. River Rd., St. Clair 48079.

St. Lazare Retreat House, W. Spring Lake Rd., Spring Lake 49456.

St. Mary's Retreat House (w*), 775 W. Drahner Rd., Oxford 48051.

St. Paul of the Cross Retreat House, 23333 Schoolcraft, Detroit 48223.

Minnesota: The Cenacle, 1221 Wayzata Blvd., Wayzata 55391.

Center for Spiritual Development, 301 S. 10th St., Olivia 56277.

Christian Brothers Retreat Center, Rt. 2, Box 18, Marine-on-St. Croix 55047.

Christian Community Center, Assisi Heights, Box 259, Rochester 55901.

The Dwelling Place, 216 3rd Ave. S., Sauk Rapids 56379.

Epiphany House of Prayer, 266 Summit Ave., St. Paul 55102.

Franciscan Retreats, Conventual Franciscan Friars, Prior Lake 55372.

Jesuit Retreat House (m), 8243 N. Demontreville Trail North, Lake Elmo 55109.

King's House of Retreats, 621 S. First Ave., Buffalo 55313.

Maryhill Retreat House, Society of Daughters of the Heart of Mary, 260 Summit Ave., St. Paul 55102.

Minneapolis Catholic Youth Center (y), 2120 Park Ave. S., Minneapolis 55404.

Welch Center (y), 605 N. Central Ave., Duluth 55807.

Missouri: Cenacle Retreat House (w*), 900 S. Spoede Rd., St. Louis 63131.

Family Life Center (mc*), St. Pius X Abbey, Abbey Rd., Pevely 63070.

Jesuit Retreat House of the Immacolata, RFD 4, Box 450, Liberty 64068. Office, 300 E. 36th St., P.O. Box 1037, Kansas City 64141.

Maria Fonte Solitude (private), P.O. Box 322, High Ridge 63049.

Marian Hall Retreat Center, Conception Seminary College, Conception 64433.

Marianist Apostolic Center, Glencoe 63038.

Our Lady of Assumption Abbey (m, w), Trappists, Rt. 5, Box 193, Ava 65608.

Our Lady of the Ozarks, P.O. Box 424, Carthage 64836.

Pallottine Renewal Center, R.R. 2, 15270 Old Halls Ferry Rd., Florissant 63034.

Passionist Retreat of Our Lady, Retreat House, Passionist Fathers and Brothers, 3036 Bellerive Dr., St. Louis 63121.

Queen of Heaven Solitude (private), Rt. 1, Box 107A, Marionville 65705.

The White House Retreat (m), 7400 Christopher Dr., St. Louis 63129.

Montana: Ursuline Retreat Center, 2300 Central Ave., Great Falls 59401.

Nebraska: Crosier Renewal Center, 223 E. 14th St., P.O. Box 789, Hastings 68901.

Good Counsel, R.R. 1, Box 110, Waverly 68462.

The Mary J. O'Donnell Center (y*), c/o University Chaplains, Creighton Univ., 2500 California St., Omaha 68178.

St. Columbans Foreign Mission Society, St. Columbans 68056.

New Hampshire: The Common - St. Joseph Monastery, Discalced Carmelite Friars, Peterborough 03458.

New Hampshire Monastery, Hundred Acres, New Boston 03070.

Oblate Fathers Retreat House, Rt. 3A, Lowell Rd., Hudson 03051.

St. Francis Friary and Retreat House, 860 Central Rd., Rye Beach 03871.

New Jersey: Bethlehem Center for Prayer and Spiritual Growth (hermitage experience), Pleasant Hill Rd., Box 315, Chester 07930.

Blackwood Center, St. Pius X House, Box 216, Blackwood 08012.

Blessed Trinity Missionary Retreat Cenacle, 1190 Long Hill Rd., Stirling 07980.

Carmel Retreat House, 1071 Ramapo Valley Rd., Mahwah 07430.

Cenacle Retreat House, 411 River Rd., Highland Park 08904.

Franciscan Retreat House, St. Bonaventure Friary, 174 Ramsey St., Paterson 07501.

Good Shepherd Center, 74 Kahdena Rd., Morristown 07960.

Loyola House of Retreats, 161 James St., Morristown 07960.

Marianist Christian Family Living Center (families), Cape and Yale Ave., Cape May Point 08212.

Mt. St. John Academy, Gladstone, N.J. 07934.

Queen of Peace Retreat House, Route 206, Newton 07860.

St. Joseph's Villa (w), Srs. of St. John the Baptist, Peapack 07977.

San Alfonso Retreat House, 755 Ocean Ave., Long Branch 07740.

Villa Pauline Retreat and Guest House (w*), Hilltop Rd., Mendham 07945.

Xavier Center, Convent Station 07961.

New Mexico: Holy Cross Retreat House, P.O. Box 158, Mesilla Park 88047.

Our Lady of Guadalupe Monastery (families - pentecostal), Pecos 87552.

Our Lady Queen of Peace, 5825 Coors Rd. S.W., Albuquerque 87105.

New York: Bergamo East Conference Center, Chaminade Rd., Marcy 13403.

Bethany Retreat House, Route 208, Highland Mills 10930.

Bethlehem Retreat House (m*), Abbey of the Genesee, Piffard 14533.

Bishop Molloy Retreat House (m), 86-45 178th St., Jamaica, L.I. 11432.

Cabrini-on-the Hudson, West Park, N.Y. 12493.

Cardinal Spellman Retreat House, Passionist Fathers, 5801 Palisade Ave., Bronx (Riverdale) 10471.

Cenacle Center for Spiritual Renewal, Cenacle Rd., Lake Ronkonkoma 11779.

The Cenacle: Center for Spiritual Renewal, 693 East Ave., Rochester 14607.

Cenacle Retreat House, State Rd., P.O. Box 467, Bedford Village 10506.

Cenacle Retreat House, Ascension Parish, 302 W. 106th St., New York 10025.

Christ the King Retreat House, 500 Brookford Rd., Syracuse 13224.

Cormaria Retreat House (w*), Sag Harbor, L.I. 11963.

Diocesan Cursillo Center (Spanish), 118 Congress St., Brooklyn 11201.

Dominican Retreat House, 1945 Union St., Schenectady 12309.

Don Bosco Retreat House, Filor's Lane, West Haverstraw 10993.

Graymoor Christian Unity Center, Graymoor, Garrison 10524.

Jesuit Retreat House, North American Martyrs Shrine, Auriesville 12016.

Mary Reparatrix Retreat Center, 14 E. 29th St., New York 10016.

Monastery of the Precious Blood (w), Ft. Hamilton Parkway and 54th St., Brooklyn 11219.

Mount Alvernia Retreat House, Wappingers Falls 12590.

Mount Augustine Retreat House and Apostolic Center, 144 Campus Rd., Staten Island 10301.

Mount Manresa Retreat House, 239 Fingerboard Rd., Staten Island 10305.

Notre Dame Retreat House, Box 342, Foster Rd., Canandaigua 14424.

Queen of Apostles Retreat House, North Haven, Sag Harbor 11963.

Regina Maria Retreat House (w*), 77 Brinkerhoff St., Plattsburgh 12901.

Renewal Center, Diocese of Buffalo, 6969 Strickler Rd., Clarence Center 14032. Poustinia available.

St. Andrew's House, 89 A St. Andrew's Rd., Walden 12586.

St. Columban's Retreat House, P.O. Box 816, Derby 14047.

St. Gabriel Passionist Retreat House, 64 Burns Rd., P.O. Box P, Shelter Island 11965.

St. Ignatius Retreat House, Searington Rd., Manhasset, L.I. 11030.

St. Josaphat's Retreat House, East Beach Rd., Glen Cove 11542.

St. Joseph Center (Spanish Center), 523 W. 142nd St., New York 10031.

Stella Maris Retreat House and Center for

Renewal, 130 E. Genesee St., Skaneateles 13152.

Stella Niagara Center for Renewal, 4421 Lower River Rd., Stella Niagara 14144.

Tagaste Monastery Retreat House (m, y), Suffern 10901.

North Carolina: Maryhurst Retreat House, P.O. Box 1390, Pinehurst 28374.

North Dakota: Queen of Peace Retreat, Redemptorist Fathers, 1310 N. Broadway, Fargo 58102.

Ohio: Bergamo Conference Center, 4435 E. Patterson Rd., Dayton 45430.

Franciscan Renewal Center, 320 West St., Carey 43316.

Friarhurst Retreat House, 8136 Wooster Pike, Cincinnati 45227.

House of Prayer, 6832 Convent Blvd., Sylvania 43560.

Jesuit Renewal Center, P.O. Box 289, Milford 45150.

Jesuit Retreat House, 5629 State Rd., Cleveland 44134.

Loyola of the Lakes, 700 Killinger Rd., Clinton 44216.

Maria Stein Center, 2365 St. Johns Rd., Maria Stein 45860.

Mary Reparatrix Retreat Center (w*), 3350 Ruther Ave., Cincinnati 45220.

Men of Milford Retreat House (m, mc), Box 348, Milford 45150.

MSC Center, Rt. 4, Shelby 44875.

Our Lady of the Pines, 1250 Tiffin St., Fremont 43420.

Sacred Heart, 3128 Logan Ave., Box 6074, Youngstown 44501.

St. Anthony Pilgrim House, 321 Clay St., Carey 43316.

St. Joseph Christian Life Center, 18485 Lake Shore Blvd., Cleveland 44119.

Shrine Center for Renewal, Diocese of Columbus, 5277 E. Broad St., Columbus 43213.

Oklahoma: St. Gregory's Abbey, Shawnee 74801.

Oregon: Loyola Retreat House (Jesuit Center for Spiritual Renewal), 3220 S.E. 43rd St., Portland 97206.

Mt. Angel Abbey Guest-Retreat Center, St. Benedict 97373.

Our Lady of Peace Retreat (w*), 3600 S. W. 170th Ave., Beaverton 97005.

St. Benedict Lodge, 56630 N. Bank Rd., McKenzie Bridge 97401.

Shalom Prayer Center, Mt. Angel 97362.

Trappist Abbey Retreat (m*, private), P.O. Box 97, Lafayette 97127.

Pennsylvania: Byzantine Catholic Seminary (m), 3605 Perrysville Ave., Pittsburgh 15214.

Cenacle Retreat House (w*), 4721 Fifth Ave., Pittsburgh 15213.

Dominican Retreat House (w*), Ashbourne Rd. and Juniper Ave., Elkins Park 19117.

Fatima House, Rolling Hills Rd., Ottsville 18942.

Jesuit Center for Spiritual Growth, Church Rd., Wernersville 19565.

Marian Hall, St. Joseph Convent/Academy, R.D. 2, Columbia 17512.

Marie Wald Retreat House, Convent of the Precious Blood, New Holland Ave., Shillington 19607.

Mercy Center, Box 370, Dallas 18612.

Our Lady of Fatima Center, Griffin Rd., Box 143, Elmhurst 18416.

Retreat Center, Mt. St. Macrina, Box 878, Uniontown 15401.

St. Alphonsus Retreat House (m), Box 218, Tobyhanna 18466 (1,200).

St. Ann's Retreat House, Carrolltown Rd., Ebensburg 15931.

St. Emma Retreat House, 1001 Harvey St., Greensburg 15601.

St. Fidelis Seminary (summer only), Herman 16039.

St. Francis Retreat House, 3918 Chipman Rd., Easton 18042.

St. Francis Retreat House (w), Monocacy Manor, Bethlehem 18017.

St. Gabriel's Retreat House (w), 631 Griffin Pond Rd., Clarks Summit 18411.

St. Joseph's-in-the-Hills (m*), Malvern 19355.

St. Paul of the Cross Retreat House, 148 Monastery Ave., Pittsburgh 15203.

Saint Raphaela Mary Retreat House, 616 Coopertown Rd., Haverford 19041.

St. Vincent Retreat House (m*, summer), Latrobe 15650.

Villa Maria Retreat House, Box 208, Wernersville 19585.

Villa of Our Lady of the Poconos (w), Mt. Pocono 18344.

Rhode Island: Carmel Spiritual Center, 21 Battery St., Newport 02840.

Ephpheta House — A Center for Renewal, 10 Manville Hill Rd; mailing address, P.O. Box 1, Manville 02838.

Our Lady of Peace Retreat House, Ocean Rd., Narragansett 02882.

St. Dominic Savio Youth Center (y*), Broad Rock Rd., Box 67, Peace Dale 02883.

South Carolina: Springbank Christian Center, Dominican Retreat House, Kingstree 29556.

South Dakota: St. Martin's Community Center, R.R. 4, Box 253, Rapid City 57701.

Tennessee: Nazareth, House of the Lord, 1306 Dellwood Ave., Memphis 88127.

Texas: Catholic Renewal Center of North Texas, 4503 Bridge St., Ft. Worth 76103.

Cenacle Retreat House, 420 N. Kirkwood, Houston 77079.

Christian Holiday House and Renewal Center, Oblate Fathers, P.O. Box 635, Dickinson 77539.

Holy Name Retreat House (m*), 430 Bunker Hill Rd., Houston 77024.

Montserrat Jesuit Retreat House, P.O. Box 398, Lake Dallas 75065.

Mt. Tabor Retreat House, 12940 Up River Rd., Corpus Christi 78410.

Our Lady of the Pillar Christian Renewal Center, 2507 N.W. 36th St., San Antonio 78228.

Saint Joseph Retreat House (Casa San Jose), 127 Oblate Dr., San Antonio 78216.

San Juan Retreat House, ("El Rancho Alegre"), Diocese of Brownsville, P.O. Box 998, San Juan 78589.

Utah: Our Lady of the Holy Trinity Retreat House (m), Huntsville 84317.

Our Lady of the Mountains, 1794 Lake St., Ogden 84401.

Virginia: Dominican Retreat (w*), 7103 Old Dominion Dr., McLean 22101.

Franciscan Center for Spiritual Renewal, Rt. 642, Box 825, Winchester 22601.

Holy Family Retreat House, Redemptorist Fathers, Box 3151, Hampton 23363.

Missionhurst Retreat Center, 4651 N. 25th St., Arlington 22207.

Spiritual Renewal Center (Genesis House), Rt. 2, Box 388 B, Richmond 23233.

St. Francis de Sales Retreat, Powhaten 23139.

Washington: Camp Field Retreat Center, P.O. Box 128, Leavenworth 98826.

Immaculate Heart Retreat House, Route 3, Box 653, Spokane 99203.

Redemptorist Palisades Retreat, P.O. Box 3739, Federal Way 98003.

St. Peter the Apostle Diocesan Retreat Center, P.O. Box 86, Cowiche 98923.

Visitation Retreat Center (w), 3200 S.W. Dash Point Rd., Federal Way 98003.

West Virginia: Cenacle Retreat House, 1114 Virginia St. E., Charleston 25301.

St. Joseph Pastoral Center, Rt. 6, Vienna 26105.

Wisconsin: Cardoner Retreat Center, 1501 S. Layton Blvd., Milwaukee 53215.

Holy Name Retreat House (m), Chambers Island; mailing address, 1825 Riverside Drive, P.O. Box 337, Green Bay 54305.

Jesuit Retreat House, 4800 Fahrnwald Rd., Oshkosh 54901.

Marynook — House of the Lord, 500 S. 12th St., Galesville 54630.

Monte Alverno Retreat House, 1000 N. Ballard Rd., Appleton 54911.

Mother of Perpetual Help, 1800 N. Timber Trail Lane, Oconomowoc 53066.

Retreat/Renewal Center, Notre Dame of the Lake, 700 W. Highland Rd., Mequon 53092.

Retreat Programs, St. Benedict's Abbey, Benet Lake 53102.

St. Anthony Retreat Center, Marathon 54448.

St. Benedict Center (ecumenical retreat and conference center), Fox Bluff, P.O. Box 5070, Madison 53705.

St. Francis Friary and Retreat Center, 503 S. Browns Lake Dr., Burlington 53105.

St. Joseph's Retreat Center, Bailey's Harbor 54202.

St. Vincent Pallotti Center, Rt. 3, Box 61, Elkhorn 53121.

Schoenstatt Center, W. 284 N. 698 Cherry Lane, Waukesha 53186.

Siena Center, 5635 Erie St., Racine 53402.

Retreats International Inc.: The first organization for promoting retreats in the U.S. was started in 1904 in California. Its initial efforts and the gradual growth of the movement led to the formation in 1927 of the National Catholic Laymen's Retreat Conference, the forerunner of the men's division of Retreats International. The women's division developed from the National Laywomen's Retreat Movement which was founded in Chicago in 1936. The men's and women's divisions merged July 9, 1977. The services of the organization include the bimonthly *Retreat World* newsletter, the preparation of promotional material for retreat recruiting, the organization of regional retreat groups and sponsorship of a national triennial convention. The officers are: Bishop Albert H. Ottenweller of Steubenville, episcopal advisor; Henry J. Balling, Jr., president; Rev. Thomas W. Gedeon, S.J., executive director. National office: Memorial Library — Room 1112, Notre Dame, Ind. 46556.

Various Programs

There is great variety in retreat and renewal programs, with orientations ranging from the traditional to teen encounters. Features of many of the forms are as follows.

Traditional Retreats: Centered around conferences and the direction of a retreat master; oriented to the personal needs of the retreatants; including such standard practices as participation in Mass, reception of the sacraments, private and group prayer, silence and meditation, discussions.

Team Retreat: Conducted by a team of several leaders or directors (priests, religious, lay persons) with division of subject matter and activities according to their special skills and the nature and needs of the group.

Closed Retreat: Involving withdrawal for a period of time — overnight, several days, a weekend — from everyday occupations and activities.

Open Retreat: Made without total disengagement from everyday involvements, on a part-time basis.

Private Retreat: By one person, on a kind of do-it-yourself basis with the one-to-one assistance of a director.

House of Prayer Experience: see separate entry.

Movement for a Better World: see separate entry.

SPECIAL AGENCIES

Some of the following agencies are engaged in carrying out programs of the United States Catholic Conference. Additional agencies are reported in other Almanac entries.

Religious Education/CCD (Confraternity of Christian Doctrine): Its objective is the religious education of persons from early childhood through adult life.

The modern expansion of Religious Education/CCD dates from publication of the encyclical letter *Acerbo Nimis* by Pope St. Pius X in 1905. His directive, that CCD programs be established in every parish, was incorporated in the Code of Canon Law and was reaffirmed by the Second Vatican Council in the *Decree on the Bishops' Pastoral Office in the Church.*

Religious Education/CCD programs are parish-based. Policies are developed by parish boards or commissions, and responsibility for administering programs rests ideally with a coordinator or director who is a trained professional in religious education.

On the diocesan level, Religious Education is coordinated by a director with a staff operating under the title of an office of religious education or a similar title. The diocesan office coordinates and acts as consultant to the work of local parish and regional programs; it conducts teacher-training courses, issues guidelines for unified programs, provides overall in-service aid and resources for local staffs and programs.

On the national level, Religious Education/CCD (formerly called the National Center for the Confraternity of Christian Doctrine, and since 1969 under the Department of Education, U.S. Catholic Conference) provides field and informational services along with representation for local diocesan programs and staffs. On the international level, it participates in programs which find their roots with the Vatican congregations that deal with religious education or catechesis.

Publications under the direction of Religious Education/CCD include *Living Light,* Catechetical Sunday materials and numerous other publications developed in conjunction with the National Conference of Diocesan Directors of Religious Education.

The Rev. David Beebe is representative for Religious Education/CCD in the Department of Education, U.S. Catholic Conference.

Offices are located at 1312 Massachusetts Ave. N.W. 20005.

National Council of Catholic Men: A federation of Catholic organizations through which Catholic men may be heard nationally on matters of common interest. NCCM is a constituent of the National Council of Catholic Laity.

The president is William H. Sandweg.

Offices are located at 4712 Randolph Dr., Annandale, Va. 22003.

National Council of Catholic Women: A federation of some 10,000 organizations of Catholic women in the U.S.; founded in 1920. NCCW unites Catholic organizations and individual Catholic women of the U.S., develops their leadership potential, assists them to act upon current issues in the Church and society, provides a medium through which Catholic women may speak and act upon matters of common interest, and relates to other national and international organizations in the solution of present-day problems. It is an affiliate of the World Union of Catholic Women's Organizations.

The official publication is *Catholic Women,* issued 6 times a year.

National office: 1312 Massachusetts Ave. N.W., Washington, D.C. 20005.

National Council of Catholic Laity: Formed in 1971 by the National Council of Catholic Men and the National Council of Catholic Women to provide direction and guidance to existing and new lay organizations. It sponsors conferences and is a contact agency for information about specialized groups in the Church. The publication is *NCCL News.*

The principal officers are Thomas Simmons, president; Isabelle Collora and David Bartkus, vice presidents.

The mailing address is **P.O. Box 14525,** Cincinnati, Ohio 45214.

National Catholic Rural Life Conference: Founded in 1923 through the efforts of Bishop Edwin V. O'Hara for the purpose of promoting the general welfare of rural people by a program of extensive services, publications and rural-related activities. Publications include the monthly *Catholic Rural Life.*

The conference has approximately 5,000 members among rural pastors, farmers, teachers, sociologists, economists, agricultural agents and officials. There are 127 officially appointed diocesan rural life directors.

Most Rev. Lawrence J. McNamara, bishop of Grand Island, Neb., is president.

National headquarters are located at 4625 N.W. Beaver Dr., Des Moines, Ia. 50322.

Catholic Relief Services — USCC: The official overseas aid and development agency of American Catholics; it is a separately incorporated organization of the U.S. Catholic Conference.

CRS was founded in 1943 by the bishops of the United States to help civilians in Europe and North Africa caught in the disruption and devastation of World War II.

Initially, CRS collected, purchased and

shipped to war-torn countries huge quantities of food, clothing, medicines and other relief supplies which were distributed to hundreds of thousands of displaced persons, prisoners of war, bombed-out families, widows, orphans and other war victims.

As conditions in Europe improved in the late 1940s and early 1950s, the works conducted by CRS spread to other continents and areas — Asia, Africa and Latin America.

CRS maintains branch offices in 52 countries around the world and, because of its global network of strategically located warehouse facilities, is able to respond instantaneously to meet the needs of those afflicted by disaster or emergencies. Help is given to all those in need regardless of race, creed, color or political affiliation.

In addition to its highly acclaimed disaster relief work, CRS carries on day-to-day development programs in 75 of the poorest countries of the world. These programs, such as "food for work" projects, nutrition-health projects, school-feeding programs, etc., are designed to help people help themselves and to raise the standards of living not only of the individual but of families and entire communities.

CRS operations are funded, for the most part, from the proceeds of an annual collection — Catholic Relief Services Annual Appeal — held during the Lenten season in more than 18,000 Catholic churches in the U.S. Support is also received from individuals and private philanthropic foundations in the U.S., Europe and Australasia. Assistance from the federal government takes four forms: food available under Title II of Public Law 480; defrayment of ocean freight costs on U.S. government-donated foods and all accredited relief supplies generated by CRS itself; grants for refugee relief and resettlement; and grants for community development projects.

Each year, CRS also sponsors a clothing collection during the month of November that yields more than 15 million pounds of used clothing, blankets and material remnants.

In the year ending Dec. 31, 1979, the CRS global program in 75 countries had a total value in excess of $340 million.

Most Rev. Edwin B. Broderick, former bishop of Albany, is the executive director.

CRS headquarters are located at 1011 First Ave., New York, N.Y. 10022.

Family Life, USCC Department of Education: Established in 1931 as a central service agency for assisting, developing and coordinating family life programs throughout the United States. It provides information, program models, services and materials for marriage and family life education. It also provides assistance to dioceses in implementing the Plan of Pastoral Action for Family Ministry.

Rev. Donald Conroy is representative for family life in the Department of Education, USCC. Cecelia M. Bennett is specialist for the family plan project.

Headquarters are located at 1312 Massachusetts Ave. N.W., Washington, D.C. 20005.

SPECIAL APOSTOLATES AND GROUPS

Apostleship of the Sea: An international Catholic organization for the moral, social and spiritual welfare of seafarers and those involved in the maritime industry. It was founded in 1920 in Glasgow, Scotland, and formally approved by the Holy See in 1922. It is promoted and directed by the Pontifical Commission for Migrants and Tourism, Piazza San Calisto 16, Rome, Italy 00153. The U.S. unit is the Apostleship of the Sea in the United States, an affiliate of the NCCB-USCC, established in 1947. It serves 80 port chaplains in 73 U.S. ports on the seacoasts and the Great Lakes. Operations include a hospitality and welcoming program as well as counseling and spiritual services carried on by individual port chaplains through Catholic maritime clubs in Mobile, Ala.; Oakland and San Francisco, Calif.; Seattle, Wash.; New Orleans, La.; Miami, Fla. and interfaith clubs located in Chicago, Ill.; Milwaukee and Green Bay, Wis.; Newark and Port Elizabeth, N.J.; Norfolk, Va.; Houston, Galveston, Corpus Christi and Brownsville, Tex. Recent developments have emphasized the interfaith cooperation on the port level in seamen's ministry. The episcopal promoter of the conference is Most Rev. Rene Gracida, P.O. Drawer 6068, Tallahassee, Fla. 32301. Rev. James E. Dillenburg is national director. Address of the national office is P.O. Box 12824, Pensacola, Fla. 32575. Also affiliated with the Apostleship of the Sea in the United States is the **National Catholic Conference for Seafarers.** The president is Rev. Rivers Patout, St. Theresa Church, 6622 Haskell St., Houston, Tex. 77007.

Auxiliaries of Our Lady of the Cenacle (1878, France): An association of Catholic laywomen, under the direction of the Congregation of Our Lady of the Cenacle, who serve God through their own professions and life styles by means of vows. Members live a fully secular life consecrated according to the spirituality of the Cenacle and pursue individual apostolates. They number approximately 150 throughout the world. U.S. regional director: Sister Agnes Sauer, r.c., 420 N. Kirkwood St., Houston, Tex. 77079.

Catholic Central Union of America (1855): One of the oldest Catholic lay organizations in the U.S., the Union is devoted to the development and vigor of Christian principles in personal, social, cultural, economic and civic life. It was the first society ever given an official mandate for Catholic Action by a committee of the American bishops, in 1936. A bureau in St. Louis is the center for the separate but coordinated direction of the National Catholic Women's Union. The headquarters is also a publishing house (*Social Justice Review, The Catholic Woman's Journal,* other publications), a library of German-Americana and Catholic Americana, a clearinghouse for information, and a center for works of charity. Aid is given to the missions, and maintenance and direction are provided for St. Elizabeth's Settlement and Day Nursery in St. Louis. Union membership is approximately 14,000. Harvey J. Johnson is director of the Central Bureau located at 3835 Westminster Place, St. Louis, Mo. 63108. (See also: National Catholic Women's Union.)

Catholic Medical Mission Board (1928): Founded by Dr. Paluel Flagg and the Rev. Edward Garesche, S.J. Its purposes are to gather and ship medical supplies for the sick poor in mission lands, and to recruit and assign medical and paramedical personnel to overseas mission hospitals and dispensaries. Since its foundation, it has shipped approximately 42 million pounds of supplies. In 1979, more than $8.5 million in medicines were shipped to 1,968 mission distribution centers in 51 countries. Also in 1979, 55 medical volunteers were placed in 12 countries. Rev. Joseph J. Walter, S.J., is the director. Office: 10 W. 17th Street, New York, N.Y. 10011.

Center for Applied Research in the Apostolate (CARA Research Conference Center): A research and development agency in the field of the Church's worldwide religious and social mission. Its purpose is to gather information for the use of decision-makers in evaluating the present status of the Church's mission of service and in planning programs of development toward greater effectiveness of its multiphased ministry in the future. CARA has research and planning programs focused on: church personnel (recruitment, selection training, utilization, effectiveness), overseas areas, diocesan planning, religious life, health care ministry, and other subjects. CARA was incorporated as a non-profit corporation in the District of Columbia Aug. 5, 1964. John V. O'Connor, S.J., is executive director. Offices are located at 3700 Oakview Terrace, N.E., Washington, D.C. 20017.

Christian Family Movement (CFM) (1947): Originating in Chicago and having a membership of married couples and individuals, its purpose is to Christianize family life and create communities conducive to Christian family life. Since 1968, CFM in the U.S. has included couples from all Christian churches. The International Confederation of Christian Family Movements embraces a worldwide membership. National and international headquarters: 2500 New York Ave., P.O. Box 792, Whiting, Ind. 46394. Spanish-speaking, CFM was organized in 1969 under the title **Movimiento Familiar Cristiano (MFC).** Headquarters: 2401 E. Holcombe Blvd., Room 102, Houston, Tex. 77021.

Christian Life Communities: Formerly known as Sodalities of Our Lady, they are groups of men and women, adults and youth, joined with other people involved in living their full Christian vocation and commitment in the world. The governing principles and operating norms of Sodalities, revised in the spirit of documents of the Second Vatican Council, were promulgated and approved by Pope Paul VI in 1971. The Spiritual Exercises of St. Ignatius remain a specific source and characteristic of the spirituality of the movement. Christian Life Communities are located in 42 countries; the U.S. Federation is comprised of approximately 150 communities. Most Rev. Louis Gelineau, bishop of Providence, R.I., is episcopal moderator. National office: 3721 Westminster Blvd., St. Louis, Mo. 63108. The World Federation office is located in Rome.

Cursillo Movement: An instrument of Christian renewal designed to form and stimulate persons to engage in apostolic action individually and in the organized apostolate, in accordance with the mission which individuals have to transform the environments in which they live into Christian environments. The movement originated in Spain, where the first cursillo was held near Palma, Mallorca, in 1949. It was introduced in the U.S. in 1957 and is functioning in more than 120 dioceses. The method of the movement involves a three-day weekend called a cursillo and a follow-up program known as the post-cursillo.

The weekend is an intensive experience in Christian community living centered on Christ and built around 15 talks (10 by laymen, five by priests), active participation in discussions and related activities, the celebration of the liturgy. The follow-up program focuses on small weekly reunions of three to five persons and larger group reunions, called ultreyas, in which participants share experiences and insights derived from their prayer life, study and apostolic action. The movement operates within the framework of diocesan and parish pastoral plans, and functions autonomously in each diocese under the direction of the bishop. Responsibility for growth and effectiveness rests with a diocesan leaders' school, a diocesan secretariat, or both. Most Rev. Joseph Green, former bishop of Reno, is episcopal advisor to the movement. Gerald P. Hughes is coordinator of the National Cursillo Center, P.O. Box 210226, Dallas, Tex. 75211.

Frontier Apostolate (1956): Volunteers for a minimum of two years' service in their professional line (teachers, secretaries, house-parents, etc.) in the Diocese of Prince George, British Columbia, Canada. More than 2,000 have served since the start of the corps by Bishop Fergus O'Grady. There are about 160 men and women from 8 different countries actively engaged in works throughout the diocese. Address: Bishop O'Grady, College Rd., P.O. Box 7000, Prince George, B.C., Canada V2N 3Z2.

Grail, The (1921): An international movement of women concerned about the full development of all peoples, working in education, religious, social and cultural areas. Founded by Rev. Jacques van Ginneken, S.J., in The Netherlands, it was introduced in the U.S. in 1940. Grail participants include women from Australia, Belgium, Brazil, Canada, Egypt, France, Germany, Ghana, India, Indonesia, Italy, Japan, The Netherlands, Nigeria, Philippines, Portugal, Scotland, South Africa, Switzerland, Tanzania, Uganda, United States. U.S. headquarters: Grailville, Loveland, Ohio 45140. International Secretariat: 5, Sayed Sokkar St., Matareya, Cairo, Egypt.

Group Seven (1971): Started by the Glenmary Home Missioners to recruit Catholic men and women (married, single, religious, permanent deacon), 21 years of age and older for periods of two years or more in the U.S. home mission apostolate, particularly in the 17-state area of Appalachia, the South and Southeast. Members support themselves in their own profession or trade. They are given orientation and opportunity for ongoing mission training. Address: P.O. Box 1376, Wise, Va. 24293.

International Liaison (1963): A referral, placement and liaison agency for the volunteer lay ministry; an affiliate of the USCC. It was founded by Rev. George Mader in the Archdiocese of Newark and in 1975 was incorporated as the U.S. Catholic Coordinating Center for Lay Volunteer Ministries. It coordinates efforts of laity seeking placement in U.S. or overseas missions. It issues a Newsletter periodically listing personnel needs in mission areas. Matthew Paratore is the executive director. Office: 1234 Massachusetts Ave. N.W., Washington, D.C. 20005.

Jesuit Volunteer Corps (1956): Established by the Oregon Province of the Jesuits, for service to the poor and oppressed. Regional offices are located in Portland, Ore., Oakland, Calif., Houston, Tex., Cleveland, O., and Philadelphia, Pa. There are 250 volunteers working among Eskimos, on Indian reservations and in inner-city areas. Rev. Lawrence L. Gooley, S.J., is the director of JVC: Northwest. Headquarters: P.O. Box 3928, Portland Ore. 97208.

Lay Mission-Helpers Association (1955): It trains and assigns men and women for work in overseas apostolates for periods of three years. Approximately 560 members of the association have served in overseas assignments since 1955. The Rev. Msgr. Lawrence O'Leary is director of the association. Headquarters: 1531 West Ninth St., Los Angeles, Calif. 90015.

The **Mission Doctors Association** recruits, trains and sends Catholic physicians and their families to mission hospitals and clinics throughout the world for tours of two to three years. Address: 1531 W. Ninth St., Los Angeles, Calif. 90015.

Legion of Mary (1921): Founded in Dublin, its purposes are exclusively spiritual, viz., the sanctification of its members and service to others. It is one of the largest lay organizations in the Church. U.S. address for information: The Legion of Mary, St. Louis Regional Senatus, Box 1313, St. Louis, Mo. 63188. The supreme governing body has offices at De Montfort House, North Brunswick St., Dublin 7, Ireland.

Movement for a Better World (1952): An international movement founded by Rev. Riccardo Lombardi, S.J. The U.S. promoting group, like its counterparts in other countries, conducts various types of renewal programs with a distinctive communitarian thrust for the purpose of motivating Christian witness and action for making a better world in accordance with the plan of God. Father John A. Wilcox is the national coordinator. The mailing address of the national office is P.O. Box H, Far Rockaway, N.Y. 11691. The movement is a non-governmental organization with the United Nations and has a U.N. office at 777 U.N. Plaza, New York, N.Y. 10017.

Opus Dei: An association of Catholic faithful who strive to practice the Christian virtues, in their own states in life and through the exercise of their own professions or occupations in order to carry on an apostolate of witness to Christ. Since the purpose is strictly spiritual, members are free to hold the most diverse views on temporal matters, thus assuring a real pluralism of opinions in all cultural, economic, political and similar areas. Founded in Madrid in 1928 by Msgr. Josemaria Escriva de Balaguer (1902-1975), it received full approval from the Holy See June 16, 1950. Membership: more than 70,000 of 80 nationalities from all continents in separate branches for men and women. In the U.S., members of Opus Dei, along with nonmembers, conduct apostolic works corporately in major cities in the East, Midwest and on the West Coast. Elsewhere, Opus Dei members are engaged in universities, vocational institutes, training schools for farmers, and numerous other educational and charitable initiatives. An information office is located at 330 Riverside Dr., New York, N.Y. 10025. The legal names of the association in the U.S. are: Opus Dei; The Work of God, Inc.

Pax Christi (1948): International Catholic peace movement. Originated in Lourdes, France, as a union of French and German Catholics to symbolize a mutual effort to heal wounds inflicted by World War II, spread to Poland and Italy, and acquired its international title when it merged with the English organization Pax. A general secretariat is located at Antwerp, Belgium. Pax Christi USA, was founded in 1973 to establish peace-making as a priority for the American Catholic Church, to work for disarmament, conscientious objection, a just world order, education for peace, and alternatives to violence. A newsletter is published quarterly; membership, 3,000. Sr. Mary Evelyn Jegen, S.N.D., is national coordinator. Address: 3000 N. Mango Ave., Chicago, Ill. 60634.

Pax Romana — American Graduate and Professional Commission: The U.S. affiliate of Pax Romana, an international Catholic movement for intellectual and cultural affairs (see Catholic International Organizations). The president is Professor Thomas E. Bird, Queens College, CUNY, Flushing, N.Y. 11367. The Pax Romana representative to the United Nations is the Rev. John A. Radano, Seton Hall University, South Orange, N.J. 07079.

Regis College Lay Apostolate (1950): Founded by Sister Mary John Sullivan, C.S.J., it enlists college graduates for a year of teaching service in home and overseas missions. More than 250 lay apostles from Regis College and more than 400 from other colleges have served since the beginning of the program. Headquarters: Regis College, Weston, Mass. 02193

Southwest Volunteer Apostolate: Recruits and places volunteers for work among the Indians and Spanish-speaking of the Diocese of Gallup. Mailing address: P. O. Box 1338, Gallup, N.M. 87301.

Center of Concern (1971): An independent, public-interest group engaged in analysis, education and advocacy relating to issues of global concern. Discussion is carried on within the framework of social justice. A newsletter, *Center Focus,* is published bimonthly. Peter J. Henriot, S.J., is director. Address: 3700 13th St. N.E., Washington, D.C. 20017.

YOUTH ORGANIZATIONS

Boy Scouts in the Catholic Church: The National Catholic Committee on Scouting works in cooperation with the Boy Scouts of America in promoting the basic principles of Catholicism among one million Catholics among the BSA membership of 4 million. *Boy's Life.* Committee Chairman, Henry B. Murphy, 149 N. Warren St., Trenton, N.J. 08608.

Camp Fire, Inc. (1910): 4601 Madison Ave., Kansas City, Mo. 64112. The Youth Activities representative of the USCC acts as advisor in matters pertaining to Catholic participation in the Camp Fire program. To help young people learn and grow in their individual ways through participation in enjoyable activities. Open to youth up to 21 years of age. Membership: approximately 500,000 (no exact statistics available on number of Catholics participating).

Catholic Youth Organization (CYO): Name of official, parish-centered diocesan Catholic youth programs throughout the country. The National CYO Federation is a constituent member of the Youth Activities section, USCC; 1312 Massachusetts Ave. N.W., Washington, D.C. 20005. CYO promotes a program of spiritual, social and physical activities. The original CYO was organized by Bishop Bernard Sheil of Chicago in 1930.

Columbian Squires (1925): P.O. Drawer 1670, New Haven, Conn. 06507. Junior organization of the Knights of Columbus. To train and develop leadership through active participation in a well-organized program of activities. Membership: 12- to 18-year-old Catholic boys. More than 18,500 in 980 circles (local units) active in the U.S., Canada, Puerto Rico, Mexico and the Philippines. *Squires Newsletter,* monthly.

Forest Rangers and Rangerettes, Catholic Order of Foresters: 305 W. Madison St., Chicago, Ill. 60606. To develop physical, mental and moral lives of members. *Catholic Forester.* Membership: youth up to 16 years of age—approximately 26,000 in 786 subordinate courts in U.S. High Chief Ranger, John A. Gorski.

Girl Scouts of the U.S.A.: 830 Third Ave., New York, N.Y. 10022. Girls from most archdioceses and dioceses in the U.S. and its possessions participate in Girl Scouting. The Youth Activities section, USCC, cooperates with Girl Scouts of the U.S.A. *Girl Scout Leader; Daisy.* Membership: more than three million (no exact statistics available on number of Catholic girls participating).

Holy Childhood Association (Pontifical Association of the Holy Childhood) (1843): 1234 Massachusetts Ave. N.W., Washington, D.C. 20005 (national office); 800 Allegheny Ave., Pittsburgh, Pa. 15233 (program distribution center). The official children's mission-aid society of the Church; provides assistance to children in 94 mission countries. Furnishes mission education programs and materials to pupils in Catholic elementary schools and religious education programs. *It's Our World,* four times a year. National Director, Rev. Francis W. Wright, C.S.Sp.

Junior Catholic Daughters of the Americas: 10 W. 71st St., New York, N.Y. 10023. A major department of the Catholic Daughters of the Americas. To promote development of the whole person, service to others, spiritual growth. Membership: Juniors (11 to 18 years old); Juniorettes (6 to 10 years old).

National Christ Child Society Inc. (1887): 5151 Wisconsin Ave. N.W., Washington, D.C. 20016. Founder, Mary V. Merrick. A welfare organization for the care of under-privileged adults and children. Membership: approximately 10,000 adult and junior members in 29 cities in U.S. President, Mrs. Thomas F. Walsh.

St. Dominic Savio Club: Don Bosco, Filor's Lane, West Haverstraw, N.Y. 10993. To promote a program of spiritual, intellectual and recreational activities. *Savio Notes,* monthly. Membership: students in grades three through ten — 12,000 members, 375 unit clubs, 14 foreign country units, home and CCD clubs and more than one million in Lay Savio Movement (past Savios) throughout the world.

Young Christian Students: 7436 W. Harrison, Forest Park, Ill. 60130. A student movement for Christian personal and social change. Membership: 500 in high schools and parishes.

Fraternities and Sororities

Delta Epsilon Sigma (1939): Belmont Abbey College, Belmont, N.C. 28012. National scholastic honor society for students, faculty and alumni of colleges and universities with a Catholic tradition. Membership: 22,000 in 100 chapters. Secretary, Rev. Dr. Neil W. Tobin.

Phi Kappa Theta: 332 Main St., Worcester, Mass. 01608. National collegiate fraternity with a Catholic heritage. Merger (1959) of Phi Kappa Fraternity, founded at Brown Univ. in 1889, and Theta Kappa Phi Fraternity, founded at Lehigh Univ. in 1919. *The Temple Magazine* quarterly, and newsletter, *The Sun.* Membership: 3,000 undergraduate and 36,000 alumni in 65 collegiate and 25 alumni chapters. Executive Director, Kirk Thomas.

Youth Activities, USCC

The Youth Activities section of the Department of Education of the United States Catholic Conference, established in 1940, is a coordinating and service agency for Catholic youth work throughout the country.

The National CYO Federation is the organization within the section which serves diocesan organizations.

USCC Youth Activities maintains liaison with the U.S. Youth Council, the World Assembly of Youth, the World Federation of Catholic Youth and other groups.

Marisa Guerin is the representative for Youth Activities and director of the National Catholic Youth Organization Federation.

Offices are at 1312 Massachusetts Ave. N.W., Washington, D.C. 20005.

ASSOCIATIONS, MOVEMENTS, SOCIETIES IN THE U.S.

(Principal source: Almanac survey.)
See Index for other associations, movements and societies covered elsewhere.

A

Academy of American Franciscan History (1944), Box 34440, Washington, D.C. 20034. Dir., Rev. Alexander Wyse, O.F.M.

Academy of California Church History (1946), P.O. Box 1668, Fresno, Calif. 93717. Pres., Msgr. Denis J. Doherty.

Albertus Magnus Guild (1953). Society of Christian scientists. Pres., Rev. William D. Sullivan, S.J., Boston College, Chestnut Hill, Mass. 02167.

American Benedictine Academy (1947). Scholarly Benedictine society. Pres., Rev. Colman Grabert, O.S.B., St. Meinrad Archabbey, St. Meinrad, Ind. 47577.

American Catholic Correctional Chaplains Association (1952), 275 in 475 institutions. Pres., Rev. Jack T. Heraty; Sec., Rev. Dismas Boeff, O.S.B., 2900 East Blvd., Cleveland, O. 44104.

American Catholic Historical Association (1919), Catholic University of America, Washington, D.C. 20064. *The Catholic Historical Review,* quarterly. Sec., Rev. Robert Trisco.

American Catholic Philosophical Association (1926), Catholic University of America, Washington, D.C. 20064; 1,500. *New Scholas-* *ticism,* quarterly, *Proceedings,* annually. Nat. Sec., George F. McLean, O.M.I.

American Committee on Italian Migration (1952), 373 Fifth Ave., New York, N.Y. 10016; 6,000. *ACIM Newsletter* and *ACIM Nuova Via,* 6 times a year. Sec., Rev. Joseph A. Cogo, C.S.

American Society of Mature Catholics (1962), 1100 W. Wells St., Milwaukee, Wis. 53223; *Mature Catholic,* bimonthly; 6,100 members. Organization for economic advantage.

Ancient Order of Hibernians in America, Inc. (1836); 120,000. *National Hibernian Digest,* bimonthly. Nat. Pres., Thomas D. McNabb; Nat. Sec., John W. Duffy, c/o P.O. Box 700, Riverdale Station, Bronx, N.Y. 10471.

Apostleship of Prayer (1849-France; 1861-U.S.): 114 E. 13th St., New York, N.Y. 10003. *Monthly Leaflet,* 1,200,000. Promotes Daily Offering and Sacred Heart devotion.

Apostolate for Family Consecration (1975), The House of St. Joseph, Box 220, Kenosha, Wis. 53141; 9,906 members. Family reinforcement by transforming neighborhoods into God-centered communities.

Apostolate of Christian Action, P.O. Box 24, Fresno, Calif. 93707. *Divine Love,* quarterly.

Archconfraternity of Christian Mothers (Christian Mothers) (1881), 220 37th St., Pittsburgh, Pa. 15201; over 3,400 branches. Dir., Rev. Bertin Roll, O.F.M. Cap.

Archconfraternity of Our Lady of Perpetual Help and St. Alphonsus (1871), 526 59th St., Brooklyn, N.Y. 11220.

Archconfraternity of the Holy Ghost (1912), Holy Ghost Preparatory School, Bensalem, Pa. 19020 (U.S. headquarters). Nat. Dir., Very Rev. Henry J. Brown, C.S.Sp.

Association for Religious and Value Issues in Counseling (1962), division of American Personnel and Guidance Association. *Counseling and Values,* quarterly. Address, 2 Skyline Pl., Suite 400, 5203 Leesburg Pike, Falls Church, Va. 22041.

Association for Social Economics (formerly the Catholic Economic Association) (1941), De Paul University, 25 E. Jackson Blvd., Chicago, Ill. 60604; 1,200. *Review of Social Economy,* triannually.

Association for the Sociology of Religion (formerly the American Catholic Sociological Society) (1938), Loyola University of Chicago, 6525 N. Sheridan Rd., Chicago, Ill. 60626. *Sociological Analysis,* quarterly. Exec. Sec., Robert McNamara.

Association of Catholic Trade Unionists (1937), 58 Washington Square South, New York, N.Y. 10012. Exec. Sec., John C. Donohue.

Association of Marian Helpers (1946), Stockbridge, Mass. 01262; 750,000, mostly in U.S. *The Marian Helpers Bulletin,* quarterly.

Association of Romanian Catholics of America (1948), 4309 Olcott Ave., E. Chicago, Ind. 46312.

B

Blue Army of Our Lady of Fatima (1946), Washington, N.J. 07882; worldwide membership. *Soul,* bimonthly. Pres., Most Rev. Joao Pereira Venancio, former bishop of Leiria (Fatima), Portugal. U.S. Vice Pres., Most Rev. Jerome Hastrich, bishop of Gallup, N. Mex.

C

Calix Society (1947), 7601 Wayzata Blvd., Minneapolis, Minn. 55426; 2,000 members in U.S. and Canada; *Chalice,* monthly. Association of Catholic alcoholics maintaining their sobriety through affiliation with and participation in Alcoholics Anonymous. Dir., R. D. Dickinson.

Campaign for Surplus Rosaries and the **Mid-America Rosary Museum** (1948), 1821 W. Short 17th St., North Little Rock, Ark. 72114. Collect rosaries and religious articles for free distribution to the poor throughout the world. Lay Internatl. Chairman, P. Marion Chudy, S.F.O.

Canon Law Society of America (1939), 1933 Spielbusch Ave., Toledo, O. 43624. To further research and study in canon law; 1,500. Exec. Coord., Rev. Donald E. Heintschel.

Cardinal Mindszenty Foundation (CMF) (1958), P.O. Box 11321, St. Louis, Mo. 63105. To combat communism with knowledge and facts. Exec. Sec., Eleanor Schlafly.

Catholic Aid Association (1878), 49 W. Ninth St., St. Paul, Minn. 55102; 78,000. *Catholic Aid News,* monthly. Fraternal life insurance society. Pres., F. L. Spanner.

Catholic Alliance for Communications (formerly Catholic Institute of the Press, 1944), 1011 First Ave., New York, N.Y. 10022. To foster Christian principles and action among working members of the communications fields. Pres., Thomas A. Brennan.

Catholic Alumni Clubs International (1957), To advance social, cultural and spiritual well-being of members. Membership limited to single Catholics with professional education; 7,000 in 50 clubs in U.S. and Canada. International Pres., Thomas S. Quinn, 2404 Parkwood, Toledo, O. 43620. Chaplain, Rev. James Auth; International Office, 32 Hewlett Point Ave., East Rockaway, N.Y. 11518.

Catholic Apostolate of Radio, Television and Advertising (1954), 1011 First Ave., New York, N.Y. 10022; 1,700 in New York City. Pres., John Curran.

Catholic Audio-Visual Educators Association (CAVE) (1953), Pres., Rev. Joseph Breslin, Cardinal O'Hara High School, Eagle and Spoul Rds., Springfield, Pa. 19064.

Catholic Bible Society of America, Inc. (1957), P.O. Box 2296, Dallas, Tex. 75221. Place Bibles in hospitals of Diocese of Dallas and elsewhere. Pres. Mrs. James S. Adams.

Catholic Biblical Association of America (1936), Catholic University of America, Washington, D.C. 20064; 947. *The Catholic Biblical Quarterly.* Pres., Rev. Neil J. McEleney, C.S.P.

Catholic Big Brothers, Inc. (of Archdiocese of New York) (1918), 1011 First Ave., New York, N.Y. 10022; Newsletter, quarterly. To provide opportunities for male identification to fatherless boys, 8-15 years of age, through services of qualified adult male volunteers.

Catholic Big Sisters, Inc. (of the Archdiocese of New York), 60 Lafayette St., New York, N.Y. 10013. Voluntary organization providing adjunctive services to Family Court, for girls up to 16 and boys up to 10 years of age. Dir., Hortense Baffa.

Catholic Business Education Association (1945). 2,001. Vice-Pres., Sister Mary Matthew McCloskey, R.S.M., Box 1169, Vicksburg, Miss. 39180.

Catholic Commission on Intellectual and Cultural Affairs (CCICA) (1946), 620 Michigan Ave. N.E., Washington, D.C. 20064; 290. Exec. Dir., Rev. William J. Rooney.

Catholic Committee on Urban Ministry (1967), Notre Dame, Ind. 46556. To support social ministry throughout the country. Dir., Sr. Helen C. Volkomener, S.P.

Catholic Conference on Ethnic and Neigh-

borhood Affairs (1974): 1521 16th St. N.W., Washington, D.C. 20036. Network of Catholic priests, religious and laity working for cultural justice within the church and society. Dir., Bro. Ronald Pasquariello, F.M.S.

Catholic Daughters of the Americas (1903), 10 W. 71st St., New York, N.Y. 10023; 170,000. *Share Magazine.* Nat. Regent, Miss Mary Murray.

Catholic Evidence Guild (1918, in England; 1931, in US), c/o 127 W. 31st St., New York, N.Y. 10001. Lay movement for spread of Catholic truth by means of outdoor speaking.

Catholic Family Life Insurance (1868), 1572 E. Capitol Dr., Milwaukee, Wis. 53211; 47,000. *The Family Friend,* quarterly. Pres., David L. Springob.

Catholic Family Missionary Alliance (1977), Our Lady of the Angels Monastery, 5817 Old Leeds Rd., Birmingham, Ala. 35210. Foundress, Mother M. Angelica, P.C.P.A.

Catholic Golden Age: Scranton Life Bldg., Scranton, Pa. 18503; 600,000. *CGA Newsletter,* bimonthly. Assist Catholics over 50 years of age in their religious and secular needs.

Catholic Guardian Society (1913), 1011 First Ave., New York, N.Y. 10022. Exec. Dir., James P. O'Neill.

Catholic Home Bureau for Dependent Children (1898), 1011 First Ave., New York, N.Y. 10022. Exec. Dir., Sr. Una McCormack.

Catholic Interracial Council of New York, Inc. (1934), 225 E. 52nd St., New York, N.Y. 10022. Sponsors educational programs and publications on Christian principles in intergroup relations; Newsletter, quarterly. Exec. Dir., John J. Garra.

Catholic Interracial Councils: See National Catholic Conference for Interracial Justice.

Catholic Knights of America (1877), 217 E. 8th St., Cincinnati, O. 45202; 15,600. *Catholic Knights of America Journal,* monthly. Fraternal insurance society.

Catholic Knights of St. George (1881), 709 Brighton Rd., Pittsburgh, Pa. 15233; 67,000. *Knight of St. George,* bimonthly. Fraternal insurance society. Pres., Joseph J. Miller.

Catholic Kolping Society of America (1923), 22515 Masonic Blvd., St. Clair Shores, Mich. 48082. *Kolping Banner,* monthly. International society concerned with spiritual, educational and physical development of members.

Catholic Lawyers' Guild. Organization usually on a diocesan basis, under different titles.

Catholic League (1943), 1200 N. Ashland Ave., Chicago, Ill. 60622. Exec. Dir., Most Rev. Alfred Abramowicz.

Catholic Library Association (1921), 461 W. Lancaster Avenue, Haverford, Pa., 19041; 3,640. *Catholic Library World,* monthly (Sept.-April), bimonthly (May-June, July-Aug.); *Catholic Periodical and Literature Index.* Pres., Sr. Franz Lang, O.P., Exec. Dir., Matthew R. Wilt.

Catholic Near East Welfare Association (Near East Missions) (1926), 1011 First Ave., New York, N.Y. 10022. *Near East Missions,* weekly column in 132 diocesan and four national newspapers. Aids missionary activity in 18 countries (under jurisdiction of the Sacred Congregation for the Oriental Church) in Europe, Africa and Asia, including the Holy Land. Nat. Sec., Rev. Msgr. John G. Nolan.

Catholic Negro-American Mission Board (1907), 335 Broadway, Room 1102, New York, N.Y. 10013; 15,000. *Educating in Faith,* bimonthly. Dir., Rev. Benjamin M. Horton, S.S.J.

Catholic One Parent Organization (COPO): To give widows and widowers an opportunity to meet others in the same situation, blending social and spiritual programs. Organized in various dioceses.

Catholic Order of Foresters (1883), 305 W. Madison St., Chicago, Ill. 60606; 168,177 in 28 states. *The Catholic Forester,* bimonthly. Fraternal insurance society. High Chief Ranger, John A. Gorski.

Catholic Pamphlet Society (1938), 2171 Fillmore Ave., Buffalo, N.Y. 14214. Parish pamphlet rack distributors. Dir., Rev. Msgr. Paul T. Cronin.

Catholic Peace Fellowship (1964), 339 Lafayette St., New York, N.Y. 10012; 6,500, *CPF Bulletin.* Peace education and action, development of the pacifist tradition within the Catholic Church; draft counseling. Nat. Sec., Thomas C. Cornell.

Catholic Press Association of the U.S., Inc. (1911), 119 N. Park Ave., Rockville Centre, N.Y. 11570. *The Catholic Journalist* monthly; *Catholic Press Directory,* annually. Pres., Ethel M. Gintoft, Exec. Dir., James A. Doyle.

Catholic Theological Society of America (1946), Office of Secretary, St. Mary of the Lake Seminary, Mundelein, Ill. 60060; 1,200. *Proceedings,* annually. Pres. (1980-81), Rev. Thomas F. O'Meara, O.P.

Catholic Traditionalist Movement (1964), 210 Maple Ave., Westbury, N.Y. 11590.

Catholic Truth Society (1922), 2816 E. Burnside St., Portland, Ore. 97214.

Catholic Union of the Sick in America, Inc. (CUSA) (1947), 63 Wall St., New York, N.Y. 10005 (legal office); 1,200. Admin. Leader, Miss Anna Marie Sopko, 176 W. 8th St., Bayonne, N.J. 07002 (national central office).

Catholic War Veterans (1935), 2 Massachusetts Ave. N.W., Washington, D.C. 20001; 500 posts, *Catholic War Veteran,* bimonthly.

Catholic Worker Movement (1933), 36 E. First St., New York, N.Y. 10003. *The Catholic Worker,* 9 times a year. Lay apostolate founded by Peter Maurin and Dorothy Day; has Houses of Hospitality in 29 U.S. cities and several communal farms in various parts of the country. Promotes pacifism and anarchism in that it is decentralist, and believes in what the popes have termed the principle of subsidiarity, urging decentralization in the school system, community control, and in the economic field credit unions, cooperatives and unions of workers and mutual aid.

Catholic Workman (Katolicky Delnik) (1891), New Prague, Minn. 56071; 18,023. *Catholic Workman,* monthly. Fraternal and insurance society. Pres. Rudy G. Faimon.

Catholic Writers' Guild of America (1919), 65 East 89th St., New York, N.Y. 10028. Exec. Sec., Rev. Bernard J. McMahon.

Catholics United for the Faith (1968), 222 North Ave., New Rochelle, N.Y. 10801; 13,000 in U.S. and Canada; *CUF Newsletter,* monthly. Lay apostolate founded in response to Vatican II's call to the laity. Pres., H. Lyman Stebbins.

Center for Pastoral Liturgy (1975), Catholic University of America, Washington, D.C. 20064. Concerned with promotion of pastoral-liturgical action in the U.S.; sponsors programs, publications, conferences, and workshops oriented toward the service of local churches. Dir., Rev. G. Thomas Ryan.

Central Association of the Miraculous Medal (1915), 475 E. Chelten Ave., Philadelphia, Pa. 19144. *Miraculous Medal,* quarterly. Dir., Rev. Robert P. Cawley.

Chaplains' Aid Association, Inc. (1917), 1011 First Ave., New York, N.Y. 10022. Pres., Most Rev. Philip J. Furlong.

Christopher Movement (1945), 12 E. 48th St., New York, N.Y. 10017. Without formal organization or meetings, the movement stimulates personal initiative and responsible action in line with Christian principles, particularly in the fields of education, government, industrial relations and communications. Christopher radio and TV programs are broadcast by more than 1,500 radio and TV stations; 700,000 copies of *Christopher News Notes* are distributed seven times a year without subscription fee; 110 weekly and 14 daily newspapers carry Christopher columns. Dir., Rev. John Catoir.

Citizens for Educational Freedom (1959): Nonsectarian group concerned with non-public education. National office: Suite 854 Washington Bldg., 15th St. and New York Ave. N.W., Washington, D.C. 20005.

Confraternity of Catholic Clergy (1976), 21-72 43rd St., Astoria, N.Y. 11105; *C.C.C. Newsletter,* bimonthly. To support priests by mutual prayer for personal holiness, loyalty to Pope and adherence to teaching of magisterium. Pres., Rev. Robert I. Bradley, S.J.

Confraternity of the Immaculate Conception of Our Lady of Lourdes (1874), Box 561, Notre Dame, Ind. 46556. Distributors of Lourdes water.

Confraternity of the Most Holy Rosary: See Rosary Altar Society.

Convert Movement Our Apostolate (CMOA) (1945), formerly Convert Makers of America, c/o Our Lady of Grace Rectory, 430 Avenue W, Brooklyn, N.Y. 11223. *Bulletin* quarterly. To train and assist lay persons on a parish level to discuss and present the Faith to interested persons on a one-to-one basis. Dir., Msgr. Erwin A. Juraschek.

Czech Catholic Union of Texas (K.J.T.) (1889), 214 Colorado St., La Grange, Tex. 78945; 16,107. *Nasinec,* weekly, and *K. J. T. News,* monthly. Fraternal and insurance society. Pres., Amos Pavlik.

D

Damien-Dutton Society for Leprosy Aid, Inc. (1944), 616 Bedford Ave., Bellmore, N.Y. 11710; 25,000. *Damien Dutton Call,* quarterly. Provides medicine, rehabilitation and research for conquest of leprosy. Pres., Howard E. Crouch, Dir., Sr. Mary Augustine, S.M.S.M.

Daughters of Isabella (1897), 375 Whitney Ave., New Haven, Conn. 06511; 120,000. International Regent, Mrs. Martine O. Ward.

E

Edith Stein Guild, Inc. (1955), Promotes Judaeo-Christian understanding and assists Jewish converts; 860. ESG *Newsletter.* Address, Church of Our Lady of Victory, 60 William St., New York, N.Y. 10006.

Enthronement of the Sacred Heart in the Home (1907), 3 Adams St., Fairhaven, Mass. 02719; over 2,500,000. Nat. Dir., Rev. Francis Larkin, SS.CC.

Eucharistic Guard for Nocturnal Adoration (1938), 800 North Country Club Rd., Tucson, Ariz. 85716.

Eymard League (1948), 194 E. 76 St., New York, N.Y. 10021; approximately 24,000. *Eymard League Bulletin,* quarterly. Nat. Dir., Rev. Ralph A. Lavigne, S.S.S.

F

Families for Christ (1977), 6026 W. Harwood Ave., Orlando, Fla., 32811; 7,500. Promote social reign of Christ. Pres., Albert Barone.

Family Rosary Crusade (1942), **Crusade for Family Prayer,** and **Families for Prayer** 773 Madison Ave., Albany, N.Y. 12208. Dir., Rev. Patrick Peyton, C.S.C.

Federation of Diocesan Liturgical Commissions (FDLC) (1969), 1307 S. Wabash, Chicago, Ill. 60605. Association of liturgical commission personnel for assisting and coordinating efforts in liturgical renewal. *FDLC Newsletter.* Administrator, Rev. Carl A. Last.

Fellowship of Catholic Scholars (1977), St. John's University, Jamaica, N.Y. 11439; 400 members. Interdisciplinary research and publications of Catholic scholars in accord with the magisterium of the Catholic Church. Pres., Prof. J. Hitchcock; Exec. Sec., Msgr. George A. Kelly.

First Catholic Slovak Ladies' Association,

USA (1892), 24950 Chagrin Blvd., Beachwood, Ohio 44122; 105,000. *Fraternally Yours,* monthly. Fraternal insurance society. Pres., Louise M. Yash.

First Catholic Slovak Union (Jednota) (1890), 3289 E. 55th St., Cleveland, Ohio 44127; 115,097. *Jednota,* weekly. Exec. Sec., Stephen F. Ungvarsky.

First Friday Clubs (1936). Organized on local basis; about 90 clubs in US, others elsewhere. Objectives are to spread devotion to the Sacred Heart, encourage members to receive Holy Communion on First Fridays and to meet at breakfast, luncheon or dinner for discussions of Catholic interest.

Franciscan Apostolate of the Way of the Cross (1949), 174 Ramsey St., Paterson, N.J. 07501. Stations Crucifix available on request. Dir., Rev. Cassian J. Kirk, O.F.M.

Friendship House (1938), 1746 W. Division, Chicago, Ill. 60622. *Community,* quarterly. Work for social justice through nonviolence. Assist prisoners; locate daily employment for day labor workers; promote educational activities related to nonviolence and simple living.

G

Gabriel Richard Institute (1949), 2315 Orleans Ave., Detroit, Mich. 48207. Conducts leadership technique courses in 18 dioceses.

Gelasian Guild (1976), Association of Catholic attorneys working with the USCC; concerned with scholarly study of legal questions affecting Church-state relations. Pres., Rev. Charles Whelan, S.J., 106 W. 56th St., New York, N.Y. 10019.

Guard of Honor of the Immaculate Heart of Mary (1932), 135 West 31st St., New York, N.Y. 10001. An archconfraternity approved by the Holy See whose members cultivate devotion to the Blessed Virgin Mary, particularly through a daily Guard Hour of Prayer.

Guild of Catholic Lawyers (1928), Empire State Bldg., 350 Fifth Ave., Room 316, New York, N.Y. 10001; 600. Pres., Joseph T. Gatti.

Guild of Our Lady of Ransom (1948), c/o St. Timothy's Rectory, 650 Nichols St., Norwood, Mass. 02062. For aid to inmates, former inmates and families of inmates of prisons in the Boston archdiocese. Exec. Dir. and Treas., Rev. Joseph P. McDermott.

Guild of St. Paul (1937), 601 Hill'n Dale, Lexington, Ky. 40503; 13,542; Nat. Spir. Dir., Rev. Msgr. Leonard Nienaber; Pres., Robert Parks.

H

Holy Name Society (in US) (1909), 141 E. 65th St., New York, N.Y. 10021; 5,000,000. Promote reverence for and devotion to the Holy Name of Jesus and develop lay apostolate programs in line with renewal aims of the Second Vatican Council, Nat. Dir., Rev. Brendan Larnen, O.P.

Holy Name Society, National Association (NAHNS) (1970), 516 N. Front St., Minersville, Pa. 17954. Association of diocesan and parochial Holy Name Societies. Exec. Sec., Stephen Andrusisian.

Hungarian Catholic League of America, Inc. (1945), 32 E. 30th St., New York, N.Y. 10016. Member of the National Catholic Resettlement Council. *Catholic Hungarian Sunday,* weekly. Pres., Rev. Msgr. John S. Sabo.

I

Illinois Club for Catholic Women (1920), 720 North Michigan, Chicago, Ill., 60611. *Triune-News,* monthly. Pres., Mrs. James K. Brennan.

Institute on Religious Life (1974), 4200 N. Austin Ave., Chicago, Ill. 60634. *Consecrated Life,* irregularly. To foster more effective understanding and implementation of teachings of the Church on religious life and promote growth in sanctity of all the faithful according to their state in life. Pres., Cardinal John J. Carberry.

International Institute of the Heart of Jesus (1972), 7700 Blue Mound Rd., Milwaukee Wis. 53213 (corporate headquarters); 14 Borgo Angelico, 00193 Rome, Italy (executive offices). Promote awareness and appreciation of the mystery of the Heart of Christ and establish an international forum for the apostolate. Pres., Harry G. John.

Italian Catholic Federation of California, Central Council (1924), 1801 Van Ness Ave., San Francisco, Calif. 94109; 30,000; *Bollettino,* monthly. Sec., Armand De Martini.

J

John Carroll Society, The (1951), 5617 32nd St. N.W., Washington, D.C. 20015. Pres. Ralph H. Brown.

Judean Society, Inc., The (1966), 1075 Space Park Way No. 336, Mt. View, Calif. 94043; over 800. International organization for divorced Catholic women. Self-help, mutual-help counseling groups. Foundress/Internatl., Dir., Frances A. Miller.

K

Knights of Peter Claver (1909), 554 Palmetto St., P.O. Box 204, Mobile, Ala. 36601; 17,000. *The Claverite,* biannually. Fraternal and aid society.

Knights of St. John, Supreme Commandery (1886), 6517 Charles Ave., Parma, O. 44129; Sup. Sec., Brig. Gen. Salvatore La Bianca.

Knights of St. John, Supreme Ladies' Auxiliary (1900), Cheektowaga, N.Y. 14225; 15,000.

Knights of the Immaculata (Militia Immaculatae, M.I.) (1917), National Center, 1600 W. Park Ave., Libertyville, Ill. 60048; canonically established with international headquarters in Rome. A pious association for evangelization and catechesis beginning with members' own inner renewal, under the patronage of the Blessed Virgin Mary.

L

Ladies of Charity of the United States, Association of (1960), 7806 Natural Bridge Rd., P.O. Box 5730, St. Louis, Mo. 63121; 40,000. International Association founded by St. Vincent de Paul in 1617. Pres., Mrs. A. J. Mayer, 5339 N. Santa Monica Blvd., Milwaukee, Wis. 53217.

League of St. Dymphna, National Shrine of St. Dymphna, 3000 Erie St. S., Box 4, Massillon, Ohio 44646. Director, Rev. M. M. Herttna.

Lithuanian Groups: Ateitininkai (1910), 9610 Singleton Dr., Bethesda, Md. 20034; to promote Lithuanian Catholic action; Pres., Juozas Laucka. Lithuanian Catholic Alliance (1889), 73 S. Washington St., Wilkes-Barre, Pa. 18701; 147 branches; *Garsas,* monthly; fraternal insurance organization; Pres., Thomas E. Mack. Lithuanian Roman Catholic Federation of America (1906), 8761 W. Outer Dr., Detroit, Mich. 48219; umbrella organization for Lithuanian parishes and organizations; Pres., Prof Justinas Pikunas. Four organizations with offices at 351 Highland Blvd., Brooklyn, N.Y. 11207 — Knights of Lithuania (1913), educational-fraternal association; Pres., Philip Skabeikis. Lithuanian American Catholic Services (1975); religious, educational, research and service association; Exec. Dir., Rev. Casimir Pugevicius. Lithuanian Catholic Religious Aid, Inc. (1961); to assist persecuted Catholics in Lithuania; Pres., Most Rev. Vincent Brizgys. Lithuanian Roman Catholic Priests' League (1909); religious-professional association; Pres., Rev. Zenonas Smilga.

Little Flower Mission League (1957), P.O. Box 25, Plaucheville, La. 71362. Sponsored by the Brothers of the Holy Eucharist.

Little Flower Society (1923), 11343 S. Michigan Ave., Chicago, Ill. 60628; 40,000, *Little Flower News,* monthly. Nat. Dir., Rev. Quentin Duncan, O. Carm.

Liturgical Conference, The, 810 Rhode Island Ave. N.E., Washington, D.C. 20018. *Liturgy, Living Worship, Homily Service.* Education, research and publication prorams for renewing and enriching Christian liturgical life. Ecumenical. Exec. Dir., Rev. Joseph A. Wysocki.

Loyal Christian Benefit Association (1890), 305 W. 6th St., Erie, Pa. 16512; 56,623. *The Fraternal Leader,* bimonthly. Pres., Mrs. Catherine T. Kelly.

M

Marian Movement of Priests, Nat. Dir., Rev. Albert G. Roux, P.O. Box 8, St. Francis, Me. 04774.

Mariological Society of America (1949), Marian Library, University of Dayton, Day-ton, O. 45469: 275. *Marian Studies,* annually.

Markham Prayer Card Apostolate (Apostolate To Aid the Dying) (1931), Franciscan Sisters of the Poor, 60 Compton Rd., Cincinnati, Ohio 45215. Dir., Rev. Herman H. Kenning.

Maryheart Crusaders, The (1964), 22 Button St., Meriden, Conn. 06450; 1,500. *The Maryheart Crusader,* 4 times a year. To reunite fallen-away Catholics and promote religious education for adults. Pres., Louise D'Angelo.

Men of the Sacred Hearts (1964), Shrine of the Sacred Heart, Harleigh, Pa. 18225. Promote enthronement of Sacred Heart.

Missionary Association of Catholic Women (1916), 1425 N. Prospect Ave., Milwaukee, Wis. 53202. Pres., Mrs. Elizabeth Schneider.

Missionary Cenacle Apostolate (M.C.A.) (1909), 3501 Solly Ave., Philadelphia, Pa. 19136; 1,500. Lay prayer and action community affiliated with Cenacle.

Missionary Vehicle Association, Inc. (MIVA), 514 Allegheny River Blvd., P.O. Box 63, Oakmont, Pa. 15139. To raise funds to provide vehicles of all types to missionaries in need. Nat. Dir., Rev. Leonard J. Tuozzolo, S.S.Sp.

Morality in Media, Inc. (1962), 475 Riverside Dr., New York, N.Y. 10027; 80,000 members. Newsletter, 8 times a year. To stop traffic in pornography constitutionally and effectively, and promote principles of love, truth and taste in the media. A major project is the National Obscenity Law Center which provides legal information for prosecutors and other attorneys. Pres., Rev. Morton A. Hill, S.J.

N

National Alliance of Czech Catholics (1917), 2657-59 S. Lawndale Ave., Chicago, Ill. 60623; 450 parishes. Pres., Mr. Vaclav Hyvnar.

National Association of Church Personnel Administrators (1973), 100 E. 8th St., Cincinnati, O. 45202. Pres., Rev. Joseph Graffis, Exec. Dir., Sr. Sheila McEvoy, S.N.J.M.

National Association of Diocesan Ecumenical Officers, Pres., Rev. Alex J. Brunett, 17500 Farmington Rd., Livonia, Mich. 48152.

National Association of Pastoral Musicians (1976), 225 Sheridan St., N.W., Washington, D.C. 20011; 7,000. *Pastoral Music,* six times a year. For clergy and musicians. Pres. and Exec. Dir., Rev. Virgil C. Funk.

National Association of Priest Pilots (1964), Pres., Rev. John Hemann, 1701 Mulberry St., Waterloo, Iowa 50703.

National Catholic Bandmasters' Association (1953), Box 523, Notre Dame University, Notre Dame, Ind. 46556. *The School Musician Magazine.*

National Catholic Cemetery Conference (1949), 710 N. River Rd., Des Plaines, Ill. 60016. *The Catholic Cemetery,* monthly.

Pres., Rev. Msgr. Joseph F. Rebman.

National Catholic Conference for Interracial Justice (1960), 1200 Varnum St. N.E., Washington, D.C. 20017. *Commitment,* quarterly. Serves 150 Catholic human relations and urban affairs groups; sponsors education and action programs on societal problems. Exec. Dir., Rev. Frederick M. Hinton.

National Catholic Development Conference (1968), 119 N. Park Ave., Rockville Centre, N.Y. 11570. Professional association of organizations and individuals engaged in raising funds for Catholic charitable activities. Pres., Rev. James J. Close; Exec. Dir., George T. Holloway.

National Catholic Disaster Relief Committee, 1346 Connecticut Ave. N.W., Suite 307, Washington, D.C. 20036.

National Catholic Pharmacists Guild of the United States (1962), 400 members; *The Catholic Pharmacist.* Exec. Dir., John P. Winkelmann, 1012 Surrey Hills Dr., St. Louis, Mo. 63117.

National Catholic Society of Foresters (1891), 35 E. Wacker, Chicago, Ill. 60601; 76,693; *National Catholic Forester,* bimonthly. A fraternal insurance society. Pres., Mrs. Dolores M. Johnson.

National Catholic Stewardship Council (1962), 1 Columbia Place, Albany, N.Y. 12207. To promote the total concept of stewardship. Exec. Dir. Rev. James M. Mackey.

National Catholic Women's Union (1916), 3835 Westminster Pl., St. Louis, Mo. 63108; 16,000. *The Catholic Woman's Journal,* 10 times a year.

National Center for Urban Ethnic Affairs (1971): 1521 16th St. N.W., Washington, D.C. 20036. To continue the expression of the Church's concern for problems of urban society. An affiliate of the USCC. Pres., Dr. John A. Kromkowski.

National Church Goods Association, 1114 Greenfield Lane, Mt. Prospect. 60056. Pres., Ted Cotter.

National Clergy Conference on Alcoholism, 3112-7th St. N.E., Washington, D.C. 20017. Exec. Dir., Rev. James J. Powderly.

National Conference of Religious Vocations Directors of Men (NCRVDM), 1307 S. Wabash Ave., Suite 350, Chicago, Ill. 60605. *Call to Growth/Ministry, NCRVDM Newsletter,* quarterlies. Service organization for men and women religious assigned to vocational ministry. Exec. Dir., Rev. James A. Vedro, O.S.C.

National Federation of Catholic Physicians' Guilds (1927), 850 Elm Grove, Suite 11, Elm Grove, Wis. 53122; 6,700 in 88 autonomous guilds in U.S. and Canada, *Linacre Quarterly.* Pres., Eugene Diamond, M.D.

National Federation of Spiritual Directors (1970). Pres., Rev. Robert B. Sidner, St. Meinrad Seminary College, St. Meinrad, Ind. 47577.

National Guild of Catholic Psychiatrists, Inc. (1949). Integration of psychiatry and Roman Catholic theology. *The Bulletin.* Pres. (1976-1981), Sr. Anna Polcino, M.D., 120 Hill St., Whitinsville, Mass. 01588.

National Organization for Continuing Education of Roman Catholic Clergy, Inc. (1973). Membership, 107 dioceses, 62 religious provinces, 27 affiliated institutions. Pres., Rev. Robert M. Schwartz, 212 N. Moore, St. Paul, Minn. 55104; Exec. Dir., Rev. James Dunning, Catholic Theological Union, 5401 S. Cornell, Chicago, Ill. 60615 (national office).

Network (1971), 806 Rhode Island Ave. N.E., Washington, D.C. 20018. A Catholic social justice lobby.

Nocturnal Adoration Society of the United States (1882), 194 E. 76th St., New York, N.Y. 10021; 57,000 in 540 units. Nat. Dir., Rev. Hector C. Lemieux, S.S.S.

O

Order of the Alhambra (1904), 4200 Leeds Ave., Baltimore, Md. 21229. 11,000 in U.S. and Canada. Fraternal society dedicated to assisting retarded children. Supreme Commander, Robert T. Pastel.

P

Paulist League (1924), 415 W. 59th St., New York, N.Y. 10019; 23,700. Dir., Rev. Donald C. Campbell.

Philangeli (Friends of the Angels) (1949 in England; 1956 in U.S.), Viatorian Fathers, 1115 E. Euclid St., Arlington Heights, Ill. 60004; approximately 750,000 in 60 countries. To encourage devotion to the angels.

Pious Union of Prayer (1898), St. Joseph's Home, P.O. Box 288, Jersey City, N.J. 07303; 54,000. *St. Joseph's Messenger and Advocate of the Blind,* quarterly.

Pious Union of the Holy Spirit (1900), 30 Gedney Park Dr., White Plains, N.Y. 10605. Pres., Rev. Jerome McHugh, O.F.M. Cap.

Pontifical Mission for Palestine (1949), c/o Catholic Near East Welfare Association, 1011 First Ave., New York, N.Y. 10022. Field offices in Beirut, Lebanon, Jerusalem and Amman, Jordan. The papal relief agency for 1.5 million Palestinian refugees in Lebanon, Syria, Jordan, and the Gaza Strip. Distributes food, clothing, other essentials; maintains medical clinics, orphanages, libraries, refugee camp schools and chapels, the Pontifical Mission Center for the Blind (Gaza), the Pontifical Mission Libraries (Jerusalem, Bethlehem, Nazareth), the Epheta Institute for Deaf-Mutes (Bethlehem). Pres., Rev. Msgr. John G. Nolan.

Pontifical Missionary Union in the USA (1936), 366 Fifth Ave., New York, N.Y. 10001: *Worldmission,* quarterly. Nat. Dir., Rev. Msgr. William J. McCormack.

Priests' Eucharistic League (1887), 194 E. 76th St., New York, N.Y. 10021; 17,500. *Em-*

manuel, monthly. Nat. Dir., Rev. Paul J. Bernier, S.S.S.

Pro Ecclesia Foundation (1970), 663 Fifth Ave., New York, N.Y. 10022. To answer attacks against Church and promote Church teachings. *Pro Ecclesia,* monthly; *Talks of Pope John Paul II,* semimonthly; *The Common Good,* quarterly. Pres., Timothy A. Mitchell.

Pro Maria Committee (1952), 22 Second Ave., Lowell, Mass. 01854. Promote devotion to Our Lady of Beauraing (See Index).

The Providence Association of the Ukrainian Catholics in America (Ukrainian Catholic Fraternal Benefit Society) (1912), 817 N. Franklin St., Philadelphia, Pa. 19123. *America* (Ukrainian-English).

R

Raskob Foundation for Catholic Activities, Inc. (1945), Kennett Pike and Montchanin Rd., P.O. Box 4019, Wilmington, Del. 19807. Exec. Vice Pres., Gerard S. Garey.

Reparation Society of the Immaculate Heart of Mary, Inc. (1946), 100 E. 20th St., Baltimore, Md. 21218. *Fatima Findings,* monthly. Dir. Rev. John Ryan, S.J.

Rosary Altar Society (Confraternity of the Most Holy Rosary) (1891, in US), 141 E. 65th St., New York, N.Y. 10021; 3,000,000. Prov. Dir., Rev. Frederick M. Jelly, O.P.

Rosary League (1901), Franciscan Sisters of the Atonement, Graymoor, Garrison, N.Y. 10524. 1,600.

S

Sacred Heart League, Walls, Miss. 38680; 600,000. Promote devotion to the Sacred Heart. Its program services include the Sacred Heart Auto League for careful, prayerful driving and the Apostolate of the Printed Word. Dir., Rev. Gregory Bezy, S.C.J.

St. Ansgar's Scandinavian Catholic League (1910), 40 W. 13th St., New York, N.Y. 10011; 1,000. *St. Ansgar's Bulletin,* annually.

St. Anthony's Guild (1924), Paterson, N.J. 07509. *Anthonian,* quarterly. Dir., Rev. Salvator Fink, O.F.M.

St. Jude League (1929), 221 W. Madison St., Chicago, Ill. 60606. *St. Jude Journal,* bimonthly. Dir., Rev. Mark J. Brummel, C.M.F.

St. Margaret of Scotland Guild, Inc. (1938), Graymoor, Garrison, N.Y. 10524; 2,200. Moderator, Bro. Gerard Hand, S.A.

St. Martin de Porres Guild (1935), 141 E. 65th St., New York, N.Y. 10021. Gen. Dir., Rev. Timothy Shea, O.P.

St. Thomas Aquinas Foundation of the Dominican Fathers of the United States (STAF). Mod., Very Rev. Thomas H. McBrien, O.P., Providence College, Providence, R.I. 02918

Serra International (1938), 22 W. Monroe St., Chicago, Ill. 60603; 14,000 members in 440 clubs in more than 31 countries. *Serran,*

bimonthly. Fosters vocations to the priesthood, and religious life, trains Catholic lay leadership. Formally aggregated to the Pontifical Society for Priestly Vocations, 1951. Pres., Gerald J. Murphy.

Slovak Catholic Federation (1911): Founded by Rev. Joseph Murgas to promote and coordinate religious activities among Slovak Catholic fraternal societies, religious communities and Slovak ethnic parishes in their effort to address themselves to the special needs of Slovak Catholics in the U.S. and Canada. *Good Shepherd,* annual. Pres., Rev. Joseph V. Adamec, 1515 Cass Ave., Bay City, Mich. 48706.

Slovak Catholic Sokol (1905), 205 Madison St., Passaic, N.J. 07055; 51,965. *Katolicky Sokol,* weekly; *Priatel Dietok,* monthly.

Society for the Propagation of the Faith (1822), 366 Fifth Ave., New York, N.Y. 10001. *Mission, Worldmission,* quarterlies. Is subject to direction of Sacred Congregation for the Evangelization of Peoples. Nat. Dir., Rev. Msgr. William J. McCormack.

Society of St. Peter the Apostle for Native Clergy (1898), 366 Fifth Ave., New York, N.Y. 10001; 167 branches. Organized as the Pope's own mission aid society for the maintenance of diocesan seminaries and diocesan seminarians in mission countries. Nat. Dir., Rev. Msgr. William J. McCormack.

Spiritual Life Institute of America (1960), R.R. 3, Sedona, Arizona 86336. *Desert Call,* seasonal. An eremetical movement to foster the contemplative spirit in America. Founder, Rev. William McNamara, O.C.D. Second foundation: Primitive Wilderness Hermitage, Kemptville, Nova Scotia, Canada B0W 1Y0.

Stewardship Services, Inc., Suite 913, 1234 Massachusetts Ave. N.W., Washington, D.C. 20005. Non-profit membership organization that provides financial management consulting services for Catholic dioceses, congregations and institutions. Exec. Dir., Thomas J. Jenkins, Jr.

T

Te Deum International (1940), 611 S. 6th St., Springfield, Ill. 62701; 27 chapters. For Catholic adult education on current and international affairs.

Theresians of America (1961), 5326 E. Pershing Ave., Scottsdale, Ariz. 85254; 6,000. Spiritual, intellectual and apostolic organization concerned with the vocation to Christian womanhood in both religious and lay states. Nat. Dir. and founder, Very Rev. Msgr. Elwood C. Voss.

U

United Societies of U.S.A. (1903), 613 Sinclair St., McKeesport, Pa. 15132; 4,318 members. *Prosvita-Enlightenment,* monthly newspaper.

United States Catholic Historical Society

(1884). 300. *Journal,* quarterly; and *Monograph Series,* annually. Exec. Sec., James J. Mahoney, St. Joseph's Seminary, Yonkers, N.Y. 10704.

V

Veneration Society of Sanctity, Inc. (1975), 1322 Cranwood Square S., Columbus, O. 43229.

Vernacular Society (1946), P.O. Box 207, Passaic, N.J. 07055; 500. *Vernacular,* newsletter. Pres., Reinhold Kissner.

W-Y

Western Catholic Union (1877), W.C.U. Bldg., 506-510 Maine St., Quincy, Ill. 62301; 27,351 members. *Western Catholic Union Record,* monthly.

Wisconsin Council of Catholic Women (1915), 810 Farwell Dr., Madison, Wis. 53704. Pres., Mrs. Patrick McCormick.

Word of God Institute (1972), 487 Michigan Ave. N.E., Washington, D.C. 20017. For renewed biblical preaching and evangelization. Dir., Rev. John Burke, O.P.

Young Ladies' Institute (1887), 50 Oak St., San Francisco, Calif. 94102. Grand Sec. Mrs. Sylvia Sharman.

Young Men's Institute (1883), 50 Oak St., San Francisco, Calif. 94102; 4,500. *Institute Journal,* bimonthly. Grand Sec., B. G. Merdinger.

Knights of Columbus

The Knights of Columbus, which originated as a fraternal benefit society of Catholic men, was founded by Father Michael J. McGivney and chartered by the General Assembly of Connecticut Mar. 29, 1882.

In line with their general purpose to be of service to the Church, the Knights are active in many apostolic works and community programs.

Since January, 1947, the Knights have sponsored a program of Catholic advertising in secular publications with national circulation. This has brought some 6 million inquiries and led to more than 600,000 enrollments in courses in the Catholic faith. In recent years the Knights have broadened this program to include other media for spreading Christian and religious ideals. As a result substantial contributions have been made to support the work of the John LaFarge Institute in New York, the Catholic Communications Foundation in New York, and the Center for Applied Research in the Apostolate (CARA) in Washington. In 1975 the Knights also undertook funding of the link-up costs for telecasting papal ceremonies throughout the world via satellite.

K. of C. scholarship funds — two at the Catholic University of America, another for disbursement at other Catholic colleges in the U.S., one at Canadian colleges and others for the Philippines, Mexico and Puerto Rico — have provided college educations for some 1,500 students since 1914.

The order promotes youth activity through sponsorship of the Columbian Squires and through cooperation with other organized youth groups.

Recent programs undertaken by the Knights include: promotion of vocations to the priesthood and religious life; promotion of rosary devotion with free distribution of more than 100,000 rosaries a year; efforts to halt the increased killing of the unborn; assistance to the retarded and other disadvantaged people.

In 1979, local units of the Knights contributed more than $23.9 million to charitable and benevolent causes, and gave more than 8.6 million hours of community service.

K. of C. membership, as of Mar. 1, 1980, was 1,320,667 in 6,711 councils in the U.S., Canada, the Philippines, Cuba, Mexico, Puerto Rico, Panama, Guatemala, Guam and the Virgin Islands. Assets, as of Dec. 31, 1979, amounted to $866,970,743 and total insurance in force, $5,066,826,497.

The Knights' publication, *Columbia,* has the greatest circulation (over 1.2 million) of any Catholic monthly in North America.

Virgil C. Dechant is Supreme Knight.

International headquarters are located at One Columbus Plaza, New Haven, Conn. 06507.

FILM REVIEW ENDS

"Film and Broadcasting Review," the newsletter published twice a month by the Office for Film and Broadcasting of the Department of Communication, U.S. Catholic Conference, published its final issue Sept. 1, 1980.

Established in 1936 as a biweekly film classification list, the publication expanded its coverage and in 1964 became the "Catholic Film Newsletter." The name was changed to "Film and Broadcasting Review" in 1976 to reflect the growing importance of television and other broadcasting activities.

In its 45-year existence, the publication previewed and classified 16,251 feature movies, according to a column written by Father Patrick Sullivan, S.J., retiring editor in chief.

Richard Hirsch, secretary of communication, U.S. Catholic Conference, said the review was dropped as a budget-saving measure discussed by the U.S. bishops at their meeting in May, 1980, when they approved an overall budget model requiring cutbacks in personnel and operations of the U.S. Catholic Conference.

Despite termination of the review, it was announced that publication of media evaluations would continue through coverage provided by NC News Service.

While announcing the end of the review, Hirsch paid tribute to Father Sullivan for rendering "important service to the Church."

CATHOLIC PRESS STATISTICS

The *1980 Catholic Press Directory,* published by the Catholic Press Association, reported a total of 509 periodicals in North America with a circulation of 27,097,851. There were 177 newspapers (five more than the number reported in the 1979 Directory) with a circulation of 5,618,964 (40,377 less). Magazines numbered 332 (an increase of four) and had a circulation of 21,478,887 (an increase of 379,992).

Newspapers

United States: 162; circulation, 5,419,650.

National newspapers, 9; circulation, 693,177.

(Weeklies: *National Catholic Register,* 76,644; *National Catholic Reporter,* 45,135; *Our Sunday Visitor,* 360,498; *Twin Circle,* 66,000; *The Wanderer,* 41,400; *El Visitante Dominical,* 24,000. Monthlies: *Bolletino,* 28,500; *Impact,* 46,000; *Entre Nosotros,* 5,000.)

Diocesan newspapers, 153; circulation, 4,726,473 (includes 7 diocesan editions of *Our Sunday Visitor* with a circulation of 101,946).

Canada: 11; circulation, 173,104.

National newspapers, 2; circulation, 60,786. (*Catholic Register,* weekly, 52,786; *Catholic New Times,* biweekly, 8,000.)

Diocesan newspapers, 9; circulation, 112,228.

West Indies, Others: 4 (diocesan); circulation, 26,300.

Diocesan newspapers in the U.S. with large circulations include: *Chicago Catholic* (168,775); *Long Island Catholic,* Rockville Centre (158,241); *Catholic Herald Citizen,* Milwaukee (135,134); *Pittsburgh Catholic* (113,767); *Clarion Herald,* New Orleans and Houma-Thibodaux (102,057); *The Tablet,* Brooklyn (99,005); *The Evangelist,* Albany (92,000); *The Catholic Standard and Times,* Philadelphia (90,792); *The Catholic Voice,* Oakland (84,631); *The Texas Catholic Herald,* Galveston-Houston (83,973); *Catholic Universe Bulletin,* Cleveland (79,234); *St. Louis Review* (74,163); *The Monitor,* Trenton (70,281); *Denver Catholic Register* (69,672); *The Pilot,* Boston (69,500); *The Michigan Catholic,* Detroit (62,500); *The Tidings,* Los Angeles (60,176).

The oldest Catholic newspaper in the United States is *The Pilot* of Boston, established in 1829 (under a different title).

Magazines

United States and Canada: 332; circulation, 21,478,887.

English-language magazines, 305; circulation, 20,906,471.

Other-language magazines, 27; circulation, 572,416.

America (circulation, 37,092) and *Commonweal* (circulation, 20,000) are the only weekly and biweekly magazines, respectively, of general interest.

The monthly magazine with the largest circulation (1,247,778) is *Columbia,* the official organ of the Knights of Columbus.

General-interest monthly magazines with large circulations include: *Catholic Digest* (540,650); *Liguorian* (487,000); *St. Anthony Messenger* (297,303); *Sign* (124,672); *U.S. Catholic* (58,352).

CATHOLIC NEWSPAPERS AND MAGAZINES IN THE U.S.

(Sources: *Catholic Press Directory, 1980;* Almanac survey; NC News Service.)

Abbreviation code: a, annual; bm, bimonthly; m, monthly; q, quarterly; w, weekly.

Circulation figures for some of these newspapers and magazines are given in the article, Catholic Press Statistics.

Newspapers

Advocate, The, w; 37 Evergreen Pl., E. Orange, N.J. 07018; Newark archdiocese.

Alive, m; 400 East Monroe, Phoenix, Ariz. 85004; Phoenix diocese.

America (Ukrainian-English), daily; 817 N. Franklin St., Philadelphia, Pa. 19123.

Anchor, The w; 410 Highland Ave., Fall River, Mass. 02722; Fall River diocese.

Arizona Catholic Lifetime, biweekly; 64 W. Ochoa St., Tucson, Ariz. 85701.

Arlington Catholic Herald, w; 200 N. Glebe Rd., Suite 614, Arlington, Va. 22203; Arlington diocese.

Bayou Catholic, The, w; P.O. Box 9077, Houma, La. 70360; Houma-Thiboudaux diocese.

Beacon, The, w; Box A, Pequannock, N.J. 07440; Paterson diocese.

Bishop's Bulletin, bm; 1301 E. Austin St., Sioux Falls, S. Dak. 57103.

Bolletino, m; 1801 Van Ness Ave., San Francisco, Calif. 94109; Central Council of Italian Catholic Federation.

Byzantine Catholic World, w; 3643 Perrysville Ave., Pittsburgh, Pa. 15214; Pittsburgh Byzantine archdiocese.

Catholic Accent, w; P.O. Box 850, Greensburg, Pa. 15601; Greensburg diocese.

Catholic Action News, m; P.O. Box 1750,

Fargo, N.D. 58107; Fargo diocese.

Catholic Advance, The, w; 424 N. Broadway, Wichita, Kans. 67202; Wichita diocese.

Catholic Banner, w; P.O. Box 818, Charleston, S.C. 29401; Charleston diocese.

Catholic Bulletin, w; 244 Dayton Ave., St. Paul, Minn. 55102; St. Paul and Minneapolis archdiocese.

Catholic Chronicle, w; P.O. Box 1866, Toledo, O. 43603; Toledo diocese.

Catholic Commentator, The, w; P.O. Box 14746, Baton Rouge, La. 70808; Baton Rouge diocese.

Catholic Communicator, w; 202 Morningside Dr. S.E., Albuquerque, N.M. 87108. Santa Fe archdiocese.

Catholic Crosswinds, semi-monthly; 1001 N. Grand Ave., Pueblo, Colo. 81003; Pueblo diocese.

Catholic Exponent, w; 320 Ohio One Bldg., Youngstown, O. 44503; Youngstown diocese.

Catholic Free Press, w; 47 Elm St., Worcester, Mass. 01609; Worcester diocese.

Catholic Herald, The, w; 5890 Newman Ct., Sacramento, Calif. 95819; Sacramento diocese.

Catholic Herald Citizen, w; P.O. Box 736, Milwaukee, Wis. 53201; Milwaukee archdiocese.

Catholic Herald Citizen — Madison Edition, w; P.O. Box 1176, Madison, Wis. 53701.

Catholic Herald Citizen — Superior Edition, w; 1512 N. 12th St., Superior, Wis. 54880.

Catholic Hungarian's Sunday, w; 1739 Mahoning Ave., Youngstown, O. 44509.

Catholic Key to the News, The, w; P.O. Box 1037, Kansas City, Mo. 64141; Kansas City-St. Joseph diocese.

Catholic Light, biweekly; 300 Wyoming Ave., Scranton, Pa. 18503; Scranton diocese.

Catholic Messenger, w; P.O. Box 939, Davenport, Ia. 52805; Davenport diocese.

Catholic Mirror, w; 200 Jewett Bldg., Des Moines, Ia. 50309.

Catholic Missourian, w; P.O. Box 1107, Jefferson City, Mo. 65101; Jefferson City diocese.

Catholic News, The, w; 80 W. Broad St., Mt. Vernon, N.Y. 10552; New York archdiocese.

Catholic Northwest Progress, w; 907 Terry Ave., Seattle, Wash. 98104; Seattle archdiocese, Yakima diocese.

Catholic Observer, biweekly; 57 Observer St., Springfield, Mass. 01101; Springfield diocese.

Catholic Post, The, w; P.O. Box 1722, Peoria, Ill. 61656; Peoria diocese.

Catholic Register, w; Box 126-C, Logan Blvd., Hollidaysburg, Pa. 16648; Altoona-Johnstown diocese.

Catholic Review, w; 320 Cathedral St., Baltimore, Md. 21203; Baltimore archdiocese.

Catholic Sentinel, w; 2816 E. Burnside St.,

Portland, Ore. 97214; Portland archdiocese, Baker diocese.

Catholic Spirit, The, w; 161 Edgington Lane, Wheeling, W. Va. 26003; Wheeling-Charleston diocese.

Catholic Standard, w; 1711 N. St., N.W., Washington, D.C. 20036; Washington archdiocese.

Catholic Standard and Times, w; 222 N. 17th St., Philadelphia, Pa. 19103; Philadelphia archdiocese; Allentown diocese.

Catholic Star Herald, w; 1845 Haddon Ave., Camden, N.J. 08103; Camden diocese.

Catholic Sun, The, w; 257 E. Onondaga St., Syracuse, N.Y. 13202; Syracuse diocese.

Catholic Telegraph, w; 326 W. 7th St., Cincinnati, O. 45202; Cincinnati archdiocese.

Catholic Times, w; P.O. Box 636, Columbus, O. 43216; Columbus diocese.

Catholic Transcript, w; 785 Asylum Ave., Hartford, Conn. 06105; Hartford archdiocese, Bridgeport and Norwich dioceses.

Catholic Universe Bulletin, w; 1027 Superior Ave. N.E., Cleveland, O. 44114; Cleveland diocese.

Catholic Virginian, w; 14 N. Laurel St., Richmond, Va. 23220; Richmond diocese.

Catholic Voice, The, w; 2918 Lakeshore Ave., Oakland, Calif. 94610; Oakland diocese.

Catholic Voice, The, w; 6060 N.W. Radial, Omaha, Nebr. 68104; Omaha archdiocese.

Catholic Week, w; P.O. Box 349, Mobile, Ala. 36601; Mobile diocese.

Catholic Weekly, The, w; P.O. Box 1405, Saginaw, Mich. 48605; Saginaw diocese.

Catholic Weekly, The, w; 1628 Lambden Rd., Flint, Mich. 48501; Lansing diocese.

Catholic Witness, The, w; P.O. Box 2555, Harrisburg, Pa. 17105; Harrisburg diocese.

Central California Register, biweekly; P.O. Box 1668, 1550 N. Fresno St., Fresno, Calif. 93717; Fresno diocese.

Central Washington Catholic, m; P.O. Box 505, Yakima, Wash. 98907. Yakima diocese.

Challenge, The, semimonthly; P.O. Box 14082, Jefferson Sta., Detroit, Mich. 48214. St. Maron diocese.

Chicago Catholic, The w; 155 E. Superior St., Chicago, Ill. 60611; Chicago archdiocese.

Church Today, biweekly; P.O. Box 7417, Alexandria, La. 71306; Alexandria-Shreveport diocese.

Church World, w; Industry Rd., Brunswick, Me. 04011; Portland diocese.

Clarion Herald, w; 523 Natchez St., New Orleans, La. 70130; New Orleans archdiocese.

Common Sense, w; 1325 Jefferson Ave., Memphis, Tenn. 38104; Memphis diocese.

Community, w; P.O. Box 23370, Jacksonville, Fla.; one-page weekly in Sunday editions of two daily newspapers; Jacksonville diocese.

Compass, The, w; P.O. Box 909, Green

Bay, Wis. 54305; Green Bay diocese.

Concern, m (exc. Aug.); 153 Ash St., Manchester, N.H. 03105; Manchester diocese.

Courier, The, biweekly; P.O. Box 588, Winona, Minn. 55987; Winona diocese.

Courier-Journal, w; 67 Chestnut St., Rochester, N.Y. 14604; Rochester diocese.

Criterion, The, w; P.O. Box 174, Indianapolis, Ind. 46206; Indianapolis archdiocese.

Dakota Catholic Action, 9 times a year; P.O. Box 128, Wilton, N.D. 58579; Bismarck diocese.

Darbininkas (Lithuanian), w; 341 Highland Blvd., Brooklyn, N.Y. 11207; Lithuanian Franciscan Fathers.

Denver Catholic Register, w; P.O. Box 1620, Denver, Colo. 80201; Denver archdiocese.

Dialog, The, w; 1925 Delaware Ave., Wilmington, Del. 19899; Wilmington diocese.

Diocese of Orange Bulletin, m; 440 S. Batavia, Orange, Calif. 92668.

Draugas (Lithuanian), daily; 4545 W. 63rd St., Chicago, Ill. 60629; Lithuanian Catholic Press Society.

Eastern Catholic Life, w; 101 Market St., Passaic, N.J. 07055; Passaic Byzantine eparchy.

Eastern Montana Catholic Register, w; 725 Third Ave. N., Great Falls, Mont. 59403; Great Falls-Billings diocese.

Eastern Oklahoma Catholic, bm; Box 520, Tulsa, Okla. 74101; Tulsa diocese.

El Visitante de Puerto Rico (Spanish), w; Box 1967, San Juan, P.R. 00903; Bishops of Puerto Rico.

El Visitante Dominical (Spanish), w; P.O. Box 96, San Antonio, Tex. 78291; Missionary Society of Oblate Fathers of Texas, Inc.

Entre Nosotros, m; 3112 W. Ashby, San Antonio, Tex. 78228; PADRES.

Evangelist, The, w; 39 Philip St., Albany, N.Y. 12207; Albany diocese.

Florida Catholic, The, w; 321 Hillman Ave., P.O. Box 3551, Orlando, Fla. 32801; Orlando and St. Petersburg dioceses.

Gary Sunday Visitor, w; P.O. Box M-356, Gary, Ind. 46401; Gary diocese.

Georgia Bulletin, w; 756 W. Peachtree St. N.W., Atlanta, Ga. 30308; Atlanta archdiocese.

Globe, The, w; 1821 Jackson St., Sioux City, Ia. 51105; Sioux City diocese.

Good News Visitor of Northwest Florida, w; 855 W. Carolina St., Tallahassee, Fla. 32304; Pensacola-Tallahassee diocese.

Guardian, The, w; P.O. Box 7417, Little Rock, Ark. 72217; Little Rock diocese.

Harmonizer, The, (Edition O.S.V.), w; P.O. Box 390, Fort Wayne, Ind. 46801; Fort Wayne-S. Bend diocese.

Hawaii Catholic Herald, w; 1184 Bishop St., Honolulu, H.I. 96813; Honolulu diocese.

Hlas Naroda (Voice of the Nation) (Czech-English), w; 2657-59 S. Lawndale Ave., Chicago. 60623.

Horizons, semimonthly; 1900 Carlton Rd., Parma, O. 44134; Parma diocese.

Idaho Register, w; P.O. Box 2835, Boise, Idaho 83701; Boise diocese.

Impact! 12 times a year; 1234 Massachusetts Ave. N.W. Suite 1004, Washington, D.C. 20005; National Office for Black Catholics.

Inland Register, w; P.O. Box 48, Spokane, Wash. 99210; Spokane diocese.

Inside Passage, w; 419 6th St., Juneau, Alaska 99801; Juneau diocese.

Intermountain Catholic Register, The, w; P.O. Box 2489, Salt Lake City, Utah 84110; Salt Lake City diocese.

Jednota (Slovak-Eng.), w; Jednota and Rosedale Aves., Middletown, Pa. 17057; First Catholic Slovak Union.

Joliet Catholic Explorer, w; 425 Summit St., Joliet, Ill. 60435; Joliet diocese.

Lafayette Sunday Visitor, w; P.O. Box 1603, Lafayette, Ind. 47902; Lafayette diocese.

Lake Shore Visitor, w; P.O. Box 4047, Erie, Pa. 16512; Erie diocese.

Leaven, The, w; 2220 Central, Kansas City, Kans. 66110; Kansas City archdiocese.

Long Island Catholic, The, w; P.O. Box 700, Hempstead, N.Y. 11551; Rockville Centre diocese.

Message, The, w; P.O. Box 4169, Evansville, Ind. 47711; Evansville diocese.

Messenger, The, w; 224 W. Washington St., Belleville, Ill. 62222; Belleville diocese.

Messenger, The, w; P.O. Box 268, Covington, Ky. 41012; Covington diocese.

Michigan Catholic, The, w; 2701 Chicago Blvd., Detroit, Mich. 48208; Detroit archdiocese.

Mirror, The, biweekly; M.P.O. Box 847, Springfield, Mo. 65801; Springfield-Cape Girardeau diocese.

Mississippi Today, w; P.O. Box 2130, Jackson, Miss. 39205 and P.O. Box 1189, Biloxi, Miss. 39533; Jackson and Biloxi dioceses.

Monitor, The, w; 441 Church St., San Francisco, Calif. 94114; San Francisco archdiocese, Stockton and Santa Rosa dioceses, Calif.; Reno-Las Vegas diocese, Nev.

Monitor, The, w; 139 N. Warren St., Trenton, N.J. 08607; Trenton diocese.

Morning Star, The, w; P.O. Box 3223, Lafayette, La. 70502; Lafayette diocese.

Narod Polski (Polish-Eng.) semi-monthly; 984 Milwaukee Ave., Chicago, Ill. 60622.

Nasa Nada (Eng.-Croatian), m; 4848 S. Ellis Ave., Chicago, Ill. 60615; Croatian Catholic Union.

National Catholic Register, w; 1901 Avenue of the Stars, Suite 1511, Los Angeles, Calif. 90067.

National Catholic Reporter, The, w; P.O.

Box 281, Kansas City, Mo. 64141; published by laymen.

New Star, The, w; 2208 W. Chicago Ave., Chicago, Ill. 60622; St. Nicholas of Chicago Ukrainian diocese.

Newsletter, The, m; 1450 North D St., San Bernardino, Calif. 92405; San Bernardino diocese.

North Carolina Catholic, w; 300 Cardinal Gibbons Dr., Raleigh, N.C. 27606 and 1524 E. Morehead St., Charlotte, N.C. 28207; Raleigh and Charlotte dioceses.

North Country Catholic, w; Box 326, Ogdensburg, N.Y. 13669; Ogdensburg diocese.

Northwestern Kansas Register, w; P.O. Box 958, Salina, Kans. 67401; Salina diocese.

Observer, The, w; P.O. Box 2079, Monterey, Calif. 93940; Monterey diocese.

Observer, The, w; 921 W. State St., Rockford, Ill. 61102; Rockford diocese.

One Voice, w; P.O. Box 10822, Birmingham, Ala. 35202; Birmingham diocese.

Our Northland Diocese, 22 issues annually; P.O. Box 610, Crookston, Minn. 56716; Crookston diocese.

Our Sunday Visitor, w; 200 Noll Plaza, Huntington, Ind. 46750; national edition and official publication for 7 dioceses; Our Sunday Visitor, Inc..

Outlook, m (Sept.-June); 215 W. 4th St., Duluth, Minn. 55806; Duluth diocese.

Pilot, The, w; 49 Franklin St., Boston, Mass. 02110; Boston archdiocese.

Pittsburgh Catholic, The, w; 110 Third Ave., Pittsburgh, Pa. 15222; Pittsburgh diocese.

Polish American Journal, m; 413 Cedar Ave., Scranton, Pa. 18505.

Proclaimer, w; P.O. Box 2824, Kalamazoo, Mich. 49003; Kalamazoo diocese.

Providence Visitor, w; 184 Broad St., Providence, R.I. 02903; Providence diocese.

Record, The, w; 433 S. 5th St., Louisville, Ky. 40202; Louisville archdiocese.

St. Cloud Visitor, w; 810 Germain St., St. Cloud, Minn. 56301; St. Cloud diocese.

St. Joseph's-Blatt (German-Eng.), m; St. Benedict, Ore. 97373; Manfred F. Ellenberger.

St. Louis Review, w; 462 N. Taylor Ave., St. Louis, Mo. 63108; St. Louis archdiocese.

Shlakh — The Way, w; 805 N. Franklin St., Philadelphia, Pa. 19123; Philadelphia archeparchy. Stamford and Chicago eparchies.

Sooner Catholic, The, biweekly; P.O. Box 32180, Oklahoma City, Okla. 73123; Oklahoma City archdiocese.

Southern Cross, The, w; P.O. Box 81869, San Diego, Calif. 92138; San Diego diocese.

Southern Cross, The, w; 601 E. 6th St., Waynesboro, Ga. 30830; Savannah diocese.

Southern Nebraska Register, w; P.O. Box 80329, Lincoln, Nebr. 68501; Lincoln diocese.

Southwest Kansas Register, w; P.O. Box

1317, Dodge City, Kans. 67801; Dodge City diocese.

Steubenville Register, w; 419 S. 4th St., Steubenville, O. 43952; Steubenville diocese.

Tablet, w; 1 Hanson Pl., Brooklyn, N.Y. 11243; Brooklyn diocese.

Tennessee Register, The, w; 2400 21st Ave. S., Nashville, Tenn. 37212; Nashville diocese.

Texas Catholic, w; 3915 Lemmon Ave., Dallas, Tex. 75219; Dallas and Fort Worth dioceses.

Texas Catholic Herald, The, w; 1700 San Jacinto St., Houston, Tex. 77002; Galveston-Houston diocese.

Texas Catholic Herald — Beaumont, w; P.O. Box 3944, Beaumont, Tex. 77704; Beaumont diocese.

Texas Gulf Coast Catholic, w; P.O. Box 2584, Corpus Christi, Tex. 78403; Corpus Christi diocese.

Tidings, The, w; 1530 W. 9th St., Los Angeles, Calif. 90015; Los Angeles archdiocese.

Time and Eternity, w; 514 E. Lawrence St., Springfield, Ill. 62703; Springfield diocese.

Times-Review, The, w; P.O. Box 937, La Crosse, Wis. 54601; La Crosse diocese.

Today's Catholic, w; P.O. Box 12429, San Antonio, Tex. 78212; San Antonio archdiocese.

Twin Circle, w; 1901 Avenue of the Stars, Suite 1511, Los Angeles, Calif. 90067.

Upper Peninsula Catholic, w; P.O. Box 548, Marquette, Mich. 49855; Marquette diocese.

Valley Catholic Witness, P.O. Box 2279, Brownsville, Tex. 98520; one page every other week in three area newspapers; Brownsville diocese.

Vermont Catholic Tribune, biweekly; 351 North Ave., Burlington, Vt. 05401; Burlington diocese.

Voice, The, w; 6201 Biscayne Blvd., Miami, Fla. 33138; Miami archdiocese.

Voice of the Southwest, w; P.O. Box 68, Lumberton, N. Mex. 87547; Gallup diocese.

Wanderer, The, w; 201 Ohio St., St. Paul, Minn. 55107.

WestMont Word, biweekly; P.O. Box 1729, Helena, Mont. 59601; Helena diocese.

West Nebraska Register, w; P.O. Box 608, Grand Island, Nebr. 68801; Grand Island diocese.

West River Catholic, m; 606 Cathedral Dr., Rapid City, S. Dak. 57709; Rapid City diocese.

West Texas Angelus, biweekly; 116 S. Oakes, San Angelo, Tex. 76903; San Angelo diocese.

West Texas Catholic, w; 1800 N. Spring, Amarillo, Tex. 79107; Amarillo diocese.

Western Michigan Catholic, w; 650 Burton S.E., Grand Rapids, Mich. 49507; Grand Rapids diocese.

Western New York Catholic Visitor, w; 100 S. Elmwood Ave., Buffalo, N.Y. 14202; Buffalo diocese.

Witness, The, w; 1229 Mt. Loretta, Dubuque, Ia. 52001; Dubuque archdiocese.

Wyoming Register, w; P.O. Box 1308, Cheyenne, Wyo. 82001.

Magazines, Other Periodicals

ADRIS Newsletter, q; Department of Theology, Fordham University, Bronx, N.Y. 10458. Association for the Development of Religious Information Services.

AIM (Aids in Ministry), q; 1800 W. Winnemac Ave., Chicago, Ill. 60640.

Alaskan Shepherd, 6 times a year; 1312 Peger Rd., Fairbanks, Alaska 99701.

America, w; 106 W. 56th St., New York, N.Y. 10019.

American Benedictine Review, q; 2nd and Division Sts., Atchison, Kans. 66002.

American Midland Naturalist, q; Notre Dame, Ind. 46556.

Americas, The, q; Box 34440, Washington, D.C. 20034: Academy of American Franciscan History.

Amerikanski Slovenec (Slovenian), w; 6117 St. Clair Ave., Cleveland, O. 44103; Slovenian Catholic Union.

Angel Guardian Home Quarterly, The, q; 6301 12th Ave., Brooklyn, N.Y. 11219.

Anthonian, q; Paterson, N.J. 07509; St. Anthony's Guild.

Anthropological Quarterly, q; 620 Michigan Ave. N.E., Washington, D.C. 20064.

Apostolate of Our Lady, m; Carey, O. 43316; Our Lady of Consolation National Shrine.

Apostolate of the Little Flower, bm; P.O. Box 5280, 906 Kentucky Ave., San Antonio, Tex. 78201; Discalced Carmelite Fathers.

Archeparchal Bulletin, q; 815 N. Franklin St., Philadelphia, Pa. 19123.

Atchison Benedictine Community News (ABC News), bm; Mount St. Scholastica Convent, Atchison, Kans. 66002.

Ateitis (Lithuanian), m; 7235 S. Sacramento Ave., Chicago, Ill. 60629; Ateitis Federation.

Ave Maria (Polish), 6 times a year; 600 Doat St., Buffalo, N.Y. 14211; Felician Srs.

Bells of St. Ann, 3 times a year; Belcourt, N.D. 58316; St. Ann's Indian Mission.

Benedictine Orient, bm; 2400 Maple Ave., Lisle, Ill. 60532.

Benedictines, semiannually; Mt. St. Scholastica, Atchison, Kans. 66002.

Bernardine Bulletin, The, semiannually; 647 Spring Mill Rd., Villanova, Pa. 19085; Bernardine Srs..

Best Sellers, m; Univ. of Scranton, Scranton, Pa. 18510.

Better World, q; Belford, N.J. 07718; Mary Productions Guild.

Bible Today, The, bm; Liturgical Press, Collegeville, Minn. 56321.

Brothers' Newsletter, q; Passionist Monastery, P.O. Box 150, West Springfield, Mass. 01089; National Assembly of Religious Brothers.

Call Board, The, 5 times a year; 227 W. 45th St., New York, N.Y. 10036; Catholic Actors' Guild.

Camillian: Journal of the National Association of Catholic Chaplains, q; 1312 Massachusetts Ave. N.W., Washington, D.C. 20005; National Association of Catholic Chaplains.

CHD Newsletter, q; 1312 Massachusetts Ave. N.W. Washington, D.C. 20005; Campaign for Human Development.

Catechist, The, m (exc. Dec., June-Aug.); 2451 E. River Rd., Dayton, O. 45439.

Catholic Aid News, m; 49 W. 9th St., St. Paul, Minn. 55102.

Catholic Apostolate Newsletter, bm; 5424 Blue Mound Rd., Milwaukee, Wis. 53208; Pallottine Fathers.

Catholic Biblical Quarterly, q; Catholic University of America, Washington, D.C. 20064; Catholic Biblical Assn.

Catholic Cemetery, The, m; 710 N. River Rd., Des Plaines, Ill. 60016; National Catholic Cemetery Conference.

Catholic Charismatic, 6 times a year; Paulist Press, 545 Island Rd., Ramsey, N.J. 07446.

Catholic Digest, The, m; P.O. Box 43090, St. Paul, Minn. 55165.

Catholic Forester Magazine, bm; 305 W. Madison St., Chicago, Ill. 60606; Catholic Order of Foresters.

Catholic Golden Age Newsletter, q; Scranton Life Bldg., Scranton, Pa. 18503.

Catholic Historical Review, q; 620 Michigan Ave. N.E., Washington, D.C. 20064; American Catholic Historical Assn.

Catholic Journalist, The, m; 119 N. Park Ave. Rockville Centre, N.Y. 11570; Catholic Press Association.

C.K. of A. Journal, m; 217 E. 8th St., Cincinnati, O. 45202; Catholic Knights of America.

C.L. of C. Index, m; 2770 E. Main St., Columbus, O. 43209.

Catholic Lawyer, q; St. John's University, Jamaica, N.Y. 11439; St. Thomas More Institute for Legal Research.

Catholic League Newsletter, m; 1100 W. Wells St., Milwaukee, Wis. 53233; Catholic League for Religious and Civil Rights.

Catholic Library World, 10 times a year; 461 W. Lancaster Ave., Haverford, Pa. 19041; Catholic Library Association.

Catholic Life Magazine, m (exc. July-Aug.); 35750 Moravian Dr., Fraser, Mich. 48026; PIME Missionaries.

Catholic Mind, The, m (exc. July-Aug.); 106 W. 56th St., New York, N.Y. 10019.

Catholic Near East Magazine, q; 1011 First Ave., New York, N.Y. 10022; Catholic Near East Welfare Assn.

Catholic Periodical and Literature Index, bm; 461 W. Lancaster Ave., Haverford, Pa.

19041; Catholic Library Association.

Catholic Pharmacist, q; 1012 Surrey Hills Dr., St. Louis, Mo. 63117; National Catholic Pharmacists Guild.

Catholic Press Directory, a; 119 N. Park Ave. Rockville Centre, N.Y. 11570; Catholic Press Assn.

Catholic Quote, m; Valparaiso, Nebr. 68065; Rev. Jerome Pokorny.

Catholic Review (Braille), m; 154 E. 23rd St., New York, N.Y. 10010; Xavier Society for the Blind.

Catholic Rural Life, m; 4625 N.W. Beaver Dr., Des Moines, Ia. 50322; National Catholic Rural Life Conference.

Catholic Trends, biweekly; 1312 Massachusetts Ave. N.W. Washington, D.C. 20005; NC News Service.

Catholic University of America Law Review, q; Washington, D.C. 20064.

Catholic War Veteran, bm; 2 Massachusetts Ave. N.W., Washington, D.C. 20001.

Catholic Woman, bm; 1312 Massachusetts Ave. N.W., Washington, D.C. 20005. National Council of Catholic Women.

Catholic Woman's Journal, 10 times a year; 3835 Westminster Pl., St. Louis, Mo. 63108; National Catholic Women's Union.

Catholic Worker, 9 times a year; 36 E. First St., New York, N.Y. 10003; Dorothy Day.

Catholic Workman, m; 112½ E. Main, New Prague, Minn. 56071.

Charities USA, m; 1346 Connecticut Ave. N.W., Washington, D.C. 20036; National Conference of Catholic Charities.

Chicago Studies, 3 times a year; P.O. Box 665, Mundelein, Ill. 60060.

Christian Life Communicator, m; 3721 Westminster Pl., St. Louis, Mo. 63108; National Federation of Christian Life Communities.

Christian Renewal News, 890 Hillcrest Dr., Pomona, Calif. 91768; Apostolate of Christian Renewal.

Christopher News Notes, 7 times a year; 12 E. 48th St., New York, N.Y. 10017; The Christophers, Inc.

City of God, The, 3 times a year; 4545 Northwestern Ave., Indianapolis, Ind. 46208; St. Maur Theological Center.

Classical Bulletin, 6 times a year; 221 N. Grand Blvd., St. Louis, Mo. 63103.

Claverite, The, biannually; 554 Palmetto St., P.O. Box 204, Mobile, Ala. 36601; Knights of Peter Claver.

Columban Mission, m (exc. June, Aug.); St. Columbans, Nebr. 68056; Columban Fathers.

Columbia, m; One Columbus Plaza, New Haven, Conn. 06507; Knights of Columbus.

Columbian, The, w; 188 W. Randolph St., Chicago, Ill. 60601.

Commitment, q; 1200 Varnum St. N.E., Washington, D.C. 20017; National Catholic Conference for Interracial Justice.

Commonweal, biweekly; 232 Madison Ave., New York, N.Y. 10016.

Communio — International Catholic Review, q; Gonzaga University, Spokane, Wash. 99202.

Community, q; 343 S. Dearborn St., Chicago, Ill. 60604; Friendship House.

Consecrated Life, up to 4 times a year; 4200 N. Austin Ave., Chicago, Ill. 60634; Institute on Religious Life. English edition of *Informationes,* official publication of Sacred Congregation for Religious and Secular Institutes.

Consolata, 6 times a year; P.O. Box C, Somerset, N.J. 08873.

Contact, 10 times a year; 123-15 14 Ave., College Point, N.Y. 11356; Sisters of St. Dominic.

Contemplative Review, q; Beckley Hill, Barre, Vt. 05647; Association of Contemplative Sisters.

Continuum, q; St. Xavier College, Chicago, Ill. 60655.

Cord, The, m; St. Bonaventure University, St. Bonaventure, N.Y. 14778.

Counseling and Values, q; 2 Skyline Place, Suite 400, 5203 Leesburg Pike, Falls Church, Va. 22041; Association for Religious and Value Issues in Counseling.

Critic, The (Newsletter), 22 times a year; 225 W. Huron St., Chicago, Ill. 60610; Thomas More Association.

Cross Currents, q; Mercy College, 555 Broadway, Dobbs Ferry, N.Y. 15022.

Crossroads Radio, bm; 1089 Elm St., W. Springfield, Mass. 01089.

Crusader's Almanac, The, biannually; 1400 Quincy St. N.E., Washington, D.C. 20017; Commissariat of the Holy Land.

CRUX of Prayer, m; 75 Champlain St., Albany, N.Y. 12204.

CRUX of the News, w; 75 Champlain St., Albany, N.Y. 12204.

Damien-Dutton Call, q; 616 Bedford Ave., Bellmore, N.Y. 11710.

Daystar, a; 172 Foster St., Brighton, Mass. 02135; Franciscan Missionary Sisters for Africa.

Deaf Blind Weekly, The (Braille), w; 154 E. 23rd St., New York, N.Y. 10010; Xavier Society for the Blind.

Desert Call, q; SLIA-Nada, R.R. 3, Sedona, Ariz. 86336; Spiritual Life Institute of America.

Diakonia, 3 times a year; Fordham Univ., Bronx, N.Y. 10458; John XXIII Center for Eastern Christian Studies.

Dimensions, m; 119 N. Park Ave., Rockville Centre, N.Y. 11570; National Catholic Development Conference.

Divine Love, q; P.O. Box 24, Fresno, Calif. 93707.

Divine Word Messenger, q; Bay St. Louis, Miss. 39520.

Divine Word Missionaries, q; Techny, Ill. 60082.

Ecumenical Trends, m (exc. July-Aug.); Graymoor Ecumenical Institute, Garrison, N.Y. 10524.

Ecumenist, The, 6 times a year; Paulist Press, 1865 Broadway, New York, N.Y. 10023.

Educating in Faith, bm; 335 Broadway, New York, N.Y. 10013; Catholic Negro-American Mission Board.

Emmanuel, m (bm July-Aug.); 194 E. 76th St., New York, N.Y. 10021; Blessed Sacrament Fathers.

Emmaus Letter, q; 1312 Massachusetts Ave. N.W., Washington, D.C. 20005. National CYO Federation.

Encounter, 2 times a year; 200 Lake St., Boston, Mass. 02135; Religious of the Cenacle.

Envoy, q; Office of Public Relations, Catholic University of America, Washington, D.C. 20064.

Eucharist, bm; 194 E. 76th St., New York, N.Y. 10021.

Extension, m; 1307 S. Wabash Ave., Chicago, Ill. 60605; Catholic Church Extension Society.

Family, m; 50 St. Paul's Ave., Boston, Mass. 02130; Daughters of St. Paul.

Family Friend, q; P.O. Box 11563, Milwaukee, Wis. 53211; Catholic Family Life Insurance.

Fatima Findings, m; 100 E. 20th St., Baltimore, Md. 21218; Reparation Society of the Immaculate Heart of Mary.

Fellowship of Catholic Scholars Newsletter, q; St. John's University, Jamaica, N.Y. 11439.

Fiat, The, q; P.O. Box 382, Cohoes, N.Y. 12047; Apostolate of Suffering.

Filipino Catholic Newsmagazine, semimonthly; 114 E. 2nd St., Los Angeles, Calif. 90012; Filipino Catholic Publications, Inc.

Franciscan Herald, m; 1434 W. 51st St., Chicago, Ill. 60609.

F.M.A. Focus, q; 274-280 W. Lincoln Ave., Mt. Vernon, N.Y. 10550; Franciscan Mission Associates.

Franciscan Reporter, q; 3140 Meramec St., St. Louis, Mo. 63138.

Franciscan Studies, a; St. Bonaventure, N.Y. 14778; Franciscan Institute.

Fraternal Leader, bm; 305 W. 6th St., Erie, Pa. 16512; Loyal Christian Benefit Association.

Fund Raising Forum, m; 119 N. Park Ave., Rockville Centre, N.Y. 11570; National Catholic Development Conference.

Glenmary's Challenge, q; P.O. Box 46404, Cincinnati, O. 45246; Glenmary Home Missioners.

God's Word Today, m; P.O. Box 7705, Ann Arbor, Mich. 48107.

Good Shepherd (Slovak and English), q; 205 Madison St., Passaic, N.J. 07055; Slovak Catholic Federation of America.

Grain and Fire, q; P.O. Box 25, Plaucheville, La. 71360; Brothers of the Holy Eucharist.

Harmony, 4 or 5 times a year; 8300 Morganford Rd., St. Louis, Mo. 63123; Benedictine Srs. of Perpetual Adoration.

Holy Name Newsletter, m (exc. July-Aug.); P.O. Box 4033, Rocky Mount, N.C. 27801; National Association of the Holy Name Society.

Homiletic and Pastoral Review, m; 86 Riverside Dr., New York, N.Y. 10024.

Hospital Progress, m; 1438 S. Grand Blvd., St. Louis, Mo. 63104; Catholic Health Association.

Human Development, q; LeJacq Publishing Co., 130 John St., New York, N.Y. 10038.

I.C. Good News, q; P.O. Box 24811, Philadelphia, Pa. 19130; North City Catholic Conference, Inc.

Immaculata, m; 1600 W. Park Ave., Libertyville, Ill. 60048; Franciscan Fathers.

In-Formation, 8 times a year; 1234 Massachusetts Ave., N.W., Washington, D.C. 20005; Religious Formation Conference.

Institute Journal, bm; 50 Oak St., San Francisco, Calif. 94102; Young Men's Institute.

Integrity, m; 6243 S. Fairfield Ave., Chicago, Ill. 60629; Rev. L. Dudley Day, O.S.A.

Interface, q; 1312 Massachusetts Ave. N.W., Washington, D.C. 20005; Bishops' Committee for Ecumenical and Interreligious Affairs.

International Review of Natural Family Planning, q; St. John's University, Collegeville, Minn. 56321; Human Life Center.

It's Our World, 4 times a year; 800 Allegheny Ave., Pittsburgh, Pa. 15233; Holy Childhood Association.

Jesuit, The, q; 39 E. 83rd St., New York, N.Y. 10028.

Jesuit, The (New Orleans Edition), q; 1607 Pere Marquette Bldg., New Orleans, La. 70112.

Jesuit Blackrobe, q; 3601 W. Fond du Lac Ave., Milwaukee, Wis. 53216.

Jesuit Bulletin, 4 times a year; 4511 W. Pine Blvd., St. Louis, Mo. 63108; Jesuit Seminary Aid Association.

Josephite Harvest, The, q; 1130 N. Calvert St., Baltimore, Md. 21202; Josephite Missionaries.

Jurist, The, q; Catholic University of America, Washington, D.C. 20064; School of Canon Law.

Katolicky Sokol (Catholic Falcon) (Slovak-English), w; 205 Madison St., Passaic, N.J. 07055; Slovak Catholic Sokol.

Kinship, q; P.O. Box 39188, Cincinnati, O. 45229; Glenmary Sisters.

KIT — Keeping in Touch, m; 1820 Mt. Elliott Ave., Detroit, Mich. 48207; Capuchin Province of St. Joseph.

Knights of St. John, q; 6517 Charles Ave., Cleveland, O. 44129.

618

Magazines

Kolping Banner, m; 115-14 227th St., Cambria Hghts., N.Y. 11411; Catholic Kolping Society.

Laiskai Lietuviams (Letters to Lithuanians) (Lithuanian), m (exc. Aug.), 2345 W. 56th St., Chicago, Ill. 60636.

Laivas (Lithuanian), m; 4545 W. 63rd St., Chicago, Ill. 60629.

Land of Cotton, q; 400 Government St., Mobile, Ala. 36602; Mobile diocese.

Law Briefs, m; 1312 Massachusetts Ave. N.W., Washington, D.C. 20005; Office of General Counsel, USCC.

Leaves, bm; 23715 Ann Arbor Trail, Dearborn Heights, Mich. 48127; Mariannhill Fathers.

Let's Pray Together, w; 773 Madison Ave., Albany, N.Y. 12208; Families for Prayer.

Letter from St. Paul Newsletter, 8-10 times a year; 955 Lake Dr., St. Paul, Minn. 55120; National Marriage Encounter.

Liguorian, m; 1 Liguori Rd., Liguori, Mo. 63057; Redemptorist Fathers.

Linacre Quarterly, q; 850 Elm Grove Rd., Elm Grove, Wis. 53122; Federation of Catholic Physicians Guilds.

Listening, 5 times a year; Trinity Colege, Washington, D.C. 20017; National Catholic Office for the Deaf.

Little Bronzed Angel, bm; St. Paul's Indian Mission, Marty, S.D. 53761; Benedictine Fathers.

Liturgy, bm; 810 Rhode Island Ave. N.E. Washington, D.C. 20018.

Living Light, The, q; 11 Park Place, New York, N.Y. 10007; Department of Education, USCC.

Love/Life/Death Issues, q; St. John's University, Collegeville, Minn. 56321; Human Life Center.

Marian Helpers Bulletin, q; Stockbridge, Mass. 01262; Association of Marian Helpers and of the Congregation of Marian Fathers.

Marquette Today, q; 1212 W. Wisconsin Ave., Milwaukee, Wis. 53233.

Marriage and Family Living, m; Abbey Press, St. Meinrad, Ind. 47577.

Marriage Encounter, m; 955 Lake Dr., St. Paul, Minn. 55120; National Marriage Encounter.

Mary Magazine and Aylesford News, bm; Cass Ave. N. at I-55, Westmont, Ill. 60559; Carmelite Fathers.

Maryknoll, m; Maryknoll, N.Y. 10545; Catholic Foreign Mission Society.

Master's Work, q; Convent of Holy Spirit, Techny, Ill. 60082; Holy Spirit Missionary Sisters.

Mature Catholic, bm; 1100 W. Wells St., Milwaukee, Wis. 53233; American Society of Mature Catholics.

Media and Values, q; 1962 S. Shenandoah, Los Angeles, Calif. 90034; National Sisters Communication Service.

Medical Mission News, bm; 10 W. 17th St., New York, N.Y. 10011; Catholic Medical Mission Board, Inc.

Medical Mission Sisters News, 4 times a year; 8400 Pine Road, Philadelphia, Pa. 19111.

Men of Malvern, bm; Malvern, Pa. 19355; Laymen's Retreat League of Philadelphia.

Mercy Profile, q; 2303 Grandview Ave., Cincinnati, O. 45206; Sisters of Mercy.

Messenger, The, m; 16010 Detroit Ave., Lakewood, O. 44107.

MHS Review (Franciscanews), q; 232 S. Home Ave., Pittsburgh, Pa. 15202.

Miesiecznik Franciszkanski (Polish), m; Franciscan Printery, Pulaski, Wis. 54162; Franciscan Fathers.

Migration Today, 5 times a year; 209 Flagg Pl., Staten Island, N.Y. 10304; Center for Migration Studies.

Miraculous Medal, The, q; 475 E. Chelten Ave., Philadelphia, Pa. 19144; Central Association of the Miraculous Medal.

Mission, q; 366 Fifth Ave., New York, N.Y. 10001; Society for Propagation of the Faith.

Mission, bm; 1663 Bristol Pike, Bensalem, Pa. 19020; Sisters of the Blessed Sacrament.

Mission Helper, The, q; 1001 W. Joppa Rd., Baltimore, Md. 21204; Mission Helpers of the Sacred Heart.

Missionhurst, 6 times a year; 4651 N. 25th St., Arlington, Va. 22207; Immaculate Heart of Mary Mission Society, Inc.

Mission Intercom, 10 times a year; 1302 18th St. N.W., Washington, D.C. 20036; U.S. Catholic Mission Council.

Missionaries of Africa Report, bm; 1622 21st St. N.W., Washington, D.C. 20009; Society of Missionaries of Africa (White Fathers).

Modern Liturgy, 8 times a year; Resource Publications, 7291 Coronado Dr., San Jose, Calif. 95129.

Modern Schoolman, The, q; 3700 W. Pine Blvd., St. Louis, Mo. 63108; St. Louis University.

Momentum, 4 times a year; Suite 350, One Dupont Circle, Washington, D.C. 20036; National Catholic Educational Asssociation.

Mother Cabrini Messenger, bm; 467 W. Deming Pl., Chicago, Ill. 60614; Mother Cabrini League.

Mount Loretto Review, a; 108 Bedell St., Staten Island, N.Y. 10309.

MSC Spotlite, q; 305 S. Lake St., Aurora, Ill. 60507; Missionaries of the Sacred Heart.

My Daily Visitor, bm; 200 Noll Plaza, Huntington, Ind. 46750; Our Sunday Visitor, Inc.

My Friend, 10 times a year; 50 St. Paul's Ave., Jamaica Plain, Boston, Mass. 02130; for children.

NAWR Trends, m (Sept.-June); 1307 S. Wabash Ave., Chicago, Ill. 60605.

National Catholic Forester, bm; 35 E. Wacker Dr., Chicago, Ill. 60601.

National Communications Office Newsletter, 8-12 times a year; 237 N. Michigan St., South Bend, Ind. 46601; Catholic Charismatic Renewal.

National Jesuit News, m; St. Joseph's College, Philadelphia, Pa. 19131.

Network Quarterly; Newsletter, m; 806 Rhode Island Ave. N.E., Washington, D.C. 20018; Network.

New Catholic World, bm; 1865 Broadway, New York, N.Y. 10023.

New Covenant, m; P.O. Box 8617, Ann Arbor, Mich. 48107; Catholic Charismatic Renewal.

New Scholasticism, q; P.O. Box 495, Notre Dame, Ind. 46556; American Catholic Philosophical Association.

News/Views, 5 times a year; 1307 S. Wabash Ave., Chicago, Ill. 60605; National Sisters Vocation Conference.

News and Views, q; 3900 Westminster Pl.; St. Louis, Mo. 63108; Sacred Heart Program.

Newsletter, The, 3 times a year; 1234 Massachusetts Ave. N.W., Washington, D.C. 20005; International Liaison for Lay Volunteer Service.

Newsletter of the Bureau of Catholic Indian Missions, 10 times a year; 2021 H St. N.W., Washington, D.C. 20006.

North American Voice of Fatima, m; 1023 Swann Rd., Youngstown, N.Y. 14174.

Notre Dame Magazine, 5 times a year; Notre Dame Univ., Notre Dame, Ind. 46556.

Nova et Vetera, m; 300 Broadway, Newark, N.J. 07104.

Nursing Sisters Today, q; 310 Prospect Park W., Brooklyn, N.Y. 11215; Congregation of Infant Jesus.

Oblate World and Voice of Hope, bm; 350 Jamaica Way, Boston, Mass. 02130; Oblates of Mary Immaculate.

On Comm, m; 1511 Third Ave., Seattle, Wash. 98101; Catholic Communications Northwest.

Origins, 48 times a year; 1312 Massachusetts Ave., N.W., Washington, D.C. 20005; NC News Service.

Our Lady of the Snows Newsletter, bm; 15 S. 59th St., Belleville, Ill. 62223; Shrine of Our Lady of the Snows.

Our Lady's Digest, bm; Box 777, Twin Lakes, Wis. 53181; La Salette Fathers.

Our Lady's Missionary, m; 315 Topsfield Rd., Ipswich, Mass. 01938; La Salette Fathers.

Our Sunday Visitor Magazine, w; Noll Plaza, Huntington, Ind. 46750.

Pacer, bm; 500 17th Ave., Seattle, Wash. 98124; Providence Medical Center.

Padres' Trail, 6 times a year; St. Michael's Mission, St. Michael, Ariz. 86511; Franciscan Fathers.

Paraclete, 4 times a year; P.O. Box 2000, Wheaton, Md. 20902; Holy Ghost Fathers.

Parish Ministry, 6 times a year; 299 Elizabeth St., New York, N.Y. 10012; National Conference of Catholic Bishops' Parish Project.

Parish Visitor, q; 25 Elm St., Oneonta, N.Y. 13820; Parish Visitors of Mary Immaculate.

Passionist Orbit, q; 5700 N. Harlem Ave., Chicago, Ill. 60631; Passionist Fathers.

Pastoral Life, m; Route 224, Canfield, Ohio 44406; Society of St. Paul.

Pastoral Music, 6 times a year; 225 Sheridan St., N.W. Washington, D.C. 20011; National Association of Pastoral Musicians.

Paulist Fathers News, 4 times a year; 415 W. 59th St., New York, N.Y. 10019.

People of God Messenger, 10 times a year; 202 Morningside Dr. S.E., Albuquerque, N.M. 87108; Santa Fe archdiocesan office of communications.

Perpetual Help World, q; 294 E. 150th St., Bronx, N.Y. 10451; Redemptorists.

Philosophy Today, q; Carthagena Station, Celina, Ohio 45822.

Pilgrim, q; Jesuit Fathers, Auriesville, N.Y. 12016; Shrine of North American Martyrs.

Pope Speaks, The, q; Our Sunday Visitor, Inc., 200 Noll Plaza, Huntington, Ind. 46750.

Priatel Dietok (Children's Friend) (Slovak), m; 205 Madison St., Passaic, N.J. 07055; Slovak Catholic Sokol.

Priest, The, 11 times a year; 200 Noll Plaza, Huntington, Ind. 46750; Our Sunday Visitor, Inc.

Probe, m (Sept.-June); 1307 S. Wabash Ave., Chicago, Ill. 60605; NAWR.

Professional Placement Newsnotes, bm; 10 W. 17th St., New York, N.Y. 10011; Catholic Medical Mission Board, Inc.

Program Supplement, 18 times a year; Columbus Plaza, New Haven, Conn. 06507; Knights of Columbus.

Provincial Annals, irregularly; St. Bonaventure, N.Y. 14778; Holy Name Province, New York, of Order of Friars Minor.

Quarterly, The, 2021 H St. N.W., Washington, D.C. 20006; Commission for Catholic Missions Among the Colored People and the Indians.

Queen; bm; 40 S. Saxon Ave., Bay Shore, N.Y. 11706; Montfort Fathers.

Reign of the Sacred Heart, m; Hales Corners, Wis. 53130.

Religion Teacher's Journal, m (Sept.-May); W. Mystic, Conn. 06388.

Religious Book Review, q; 125 Mineola Ave., Roslyn Heights, N.Y. 11577.

Religious Life, m; 4200 N. Austin Ave., Chicago, Ill. 60634; Institute on Religious Life.

Religious Media Today, q; 300 Broadway, Newark, N.J. 07104.

Renascence, q; Marquette University, Milwaukee, Wis. 53233.

Respect Life Report, m; 1312 Massachusetts Ave. N.W., Washington, D.C. 20005; Committee for Pro-Life Activities, NCCB.

Response, The, annual; 1234 Massachusetts Ave. N.W., Washington, D.C. 20005; International Liaison.

Review for Religious, bm; Room 428, 3601 Lindell Blvd., St. Louis, Mo. 63108.

Review of Politics, q; Box B, Notre Dame, Ind. 46556.

Review of Social Economy, 3 times a year; 25 E. Jackson Blvd., Chicago, Ill. 60604; Association for Social Economics.

Roses and Gold from Our Lady of the Ozarks, m; 1740 Grand Ave., Carthage, Mo. 64836; Oblate Fathers.

Roze Maryi (Polish), m; Eden Hill, Stockbridge, Mass. 01262; Marian Fathers.

Sacred Music, q; 548 Lafond Ave., St. Paul, Minn. 55103.

St. Anthony Messenger, m; 1615 Republic St., Cincinnati, O. 45210; Franciscan Fathers.

St. Anthony's Newsletter, m; Mt. St. Francis, Ind. 47146.

St. Joseph's Advocate, q; Mill Hill Missionaries, Albany, N.Y. 12203.

St. Joseph's Messenger and Advocate of the Blind, q; St. Joseph Home, P.O. Box 288, Jersey City, N.J. 07303.

Salesian Bulletin, bm; 148 Main St., New Rochelle, N.Y. 10802; Salesian Fathers.

Salesian Missions, q; 148 Main St., New Rochelle, N.Y. 10802; Salesians of St. John Bosco.

Salvatorian Newsletter, The, q; Society of the Divine Savior, Salvatorian Center, New Holstein, Wis. 53062.

Sandal Prints, bm; 1820 Mt. Elliott Ave., Detroit, Mich. 48207; Capuchin Fathers.

Scalabrinians, 4 times a year; 209 Flagg Pl., Staten Island, N.Y. 10304.

School Guide, a; 80 W. Broad St., Mt. Vernon, N.Y. 10552.

School Sister, The, q; Notre Dame of the Lake, Mequon, Wis. 53092; Sisters of Notre Dame.

Science Studies, a; St. Bonaventure University, St. Bonaventure, N.Y. 14778.

SCRC Vision, The, m; 5730 W. Manchester Ave., Los Angeles, Calif. 90045; Southern California Renewal Communities.

Scripture in Church, 4 times a year; P.O. Box 9, Northport, N.Y. 11768.

Second Spring, bm; 121 Golden Gate Ave., San Francisco, Calif. 94102; Adult Benevolent Association.

Serenity, q; 601 Maiden Choice Lane, Baltimore, Md. 21228; Little Sisters of the Poor.

Serran, The, bm; 22 W. Monroe St., Chicago, Ill. 60603; Serra International.

Share, 1312 Massachusetts Ave. N.W., Washington, D.C. 20005; Dept. of Communications, USCC.

Share, q; 16 Acorn Dr., Annapolis, Md. 21401; Catholic Daughters of the Americas.

Shepherd's Call, The, q; 901 Thirteenth St.,

N.W., Albuquerque, N.M. 87103; Brothers of Good Shepherd.

Sign, The, 10 times a year; Monastery Place, Union City, N.J. 07087; Passionist Fathers.

Silent Advocate, bm; St. Rita School for the Deaf, 1720 Glendale-Milford Rd., Cincinnati, O. 45215.

Sister Miriam Teresa League of Prayer Bulletin, q; League Headquarters, Convent Station, N.J. 07961.

Sistersharing, bm; 1962 Shenandoah, Los Angeles, Calif. 90034; National Sisters Communications Service.

SC News, m (Sept.-May); 4400 Churchman Ave., Louisville, Ky. 40215; Sisters of Charity of Nazareth.

Sisters Today, m (exc. July-Aug.); St. John's Abbey, Collegeville, Minn. 56321.

Social Justice Review, bm; 3835 Westminster Pl., St. Louis, Mo. 63108; Catholic Central Union of America.

Social Thought, q; 1346 Connecticut Ave. N.W., Washington, D.C. 20036; National Conference of Catholic Charities.

Sodalis Polonia, 9 times a year; St. Mary's College, Orchard Lake, Mich. 48033; Sts. Cyril and Methodius Seminary.

Sons of Mary Missionary Society, q; 567 Salem End Rd., Framingham, Mass. 01701.

Sophia, m; P.O. Box 43, Newton, Mass. 02165; Newton Melkite eparchy.

Soul, bm; Ave Maria Institute, Washington, N.J. 07882; Blue Army.

Spirit, biannually; Seton Hall University, South Orange, N.J. 08824; poetry magazine.

Spirit and Life, 6 times a year; 8300 Morganford Rd., St. Louis, Mo. 63123; Benedictine Srs. of Perpetual Adoration.

Spirit and the Bride, The, 10 times a year; 4140 Lindell Blvd., St. Louis, Mo. 63108; Catholic Charismatic Renewal Office.

Spiritual Book News, 8 times a year; Notre Dame, Ind. 46556.

Spiritual Life, q; 2131 Lincoln Rd. N.E., Washington, D.C. 20002; Discalced Carmelites.

Spirituality Today (formerly Cross and Crown), q; 1909 S. Ashland Ave., Chicago, Ill. 60608, Dominican Fathers.

Squires Newsletter, m; Columbus Plaza, New Haven, Conn. 06507; Columbian Squires.

Strain Forward, 11 times a year; 50 St. Paul's Avenue, Jamaica Plain, Boston, Mass. 02130; Daughters of St. Paul.

Studies in the Spirituality of Jesuits, 5 times a year; 3700 W. Pine Blvd., St. Louis, Mo. 63108.

Sword, 3 times a year; 29 N. Broadway, Joliet, Ill. 60435.

Theological Studies, q; Georgetown Univ., 37th and O Sts., N.W., Washington, D.C. 20057.

Theology Digest, q; 3634 Lindell Blvd., St. Louis, Mo. 63108.

Theresian, News, The, 6 times a year; 5326 E. Pershing Ave., Scottsdale, Ariz. 85254.

Thomist, The, q; 487 Michigan Ave. N.E., Washington, D.C. 20017; Dominican Fathers.

Thought, q; Fordham University Press, Box L, Bronx, N.Y. 10458; Fordham University.

Today's Catholic Teacher, m (Sept.-May); 2451 E. River Rd., Suite 200, Dayton, O. 45439.

Today's Parish, m (Sept.-May); P.O. Box 180, West Mystic, Conn. 06340.

Topic, semi-annually; 151 Thompson St., New York, N.Y. 10012. Secular Franciscan Order, Province of Immaculate Conception.

Trinity Missions, q; P.O. Box 30, Silver Springs, Md. 20910.

Ultreya Magazine, m; 4500 W. Davis St., Dallas, Tex. 75211. Cursillo Movement.

L'Union (French), 5 times a year; 1 Social St., Woonsocket, R.I. 02895.

UNIREA, The Union (Romanian and English), m; 4309 Olcott Ave., East Chicago, Ind. 46312.

U.S. Catholic, m; 221 W. Madison St., Chicago, Ill. 60606; Claretian Fathers.

Verona Missions, 6 times a year; 8108 Beechmont Ave., Cincinnati, O. 45230.

Venture, 26 times during school year; 200 Noll Plaza, Huntington, Indiana 46750; Our Sunday Visitor, Grades 4-6.

Visions, 26 times during school year; 200 Noll Plaza, Huntington, Ind. 46750; Our Sunday Visitor, Grades 7-8.

Vox Regis Alumni Newsletter, 3 times a year; 711 Knox Rd., East Aurora, N.Y. 14052; Christ the King Seminary.

Waif's Messenger, m; Drawer X, Chicago, Ill. 60690; Mission of Our Lady of Mercy.

Way — of St. Francis, 10 times a year; 109 Golden Gate Ave., San Francisco, Calif. 94102; Franciscan Fathers of California, Inc.

Western Catholic Union Record, m; 906 W.C.U. Bldg., Quincy, Ill. 62301; Western Catholic Union.

Westfriars, m; 2011 38th Ave., Oakland, Calif. 94601; St. Barbara Province, Order of Friars Minor.

Wheeling College Chronicle, 4 times a year; 316 Washington Ave., Wheeling, W. Va. 26003.

Word of God, w; 2187 Victory Blvd., Staten Island, N.Y. 10314; Society of St. Paul.

Working for Boys, q; Box A, Danvers, Mass. 01923; Xaverian Brothers.

Worldmission, q; 366 5th Ave., New York, N.Y. 10001; Society for the Propagation of the Faith.

Worldwide Family Spirit, ten times a year; 23326 Mariano St., Woodland Hills, Calif. 91364, Worldwide Marriage Encounter.

Worship, 6 times a year; St. John's Abbey, Collegeville, Minn. 56321. North American Academy of Liturgy.

Xaverian Missions Newsletter, 9 times a year; 101 Summer St., Holliston, Mass. 01746; Xaverian Missionary Fathers.

Your Edmundite Missions Newsletter, bm; 1428 Broad St., Selma, Ala. 36701; Southern Missions of Society of St. Edmund.

Zeal, q; St. Elizabeth Mission Society of the Sisters of St. Francis, N. Main St., Allegany, N.Y. 14706.

International Periodicals

African Ecclesial Review (AFER), bm; Gaba Publications, P.O. Box 908, Eldoret, Kenya.

Australasian Catholic Record, q; St. Patrick's Seminary, Manly, New South Wales, Australia.

Christ to the World, bm; Via G, Nicoterra 31, 00195, Rome, Italy.

Clergy Review, m; 48 Great Peter St., London, SW1P 2HB, England.

Communio-International Catholic Review, q; Gonzaga Univ., Spokane, Wash. 99258.

Doctrine and Life, m, and **Supplement to Doctrine and Life,** bm; Dominican Publications, St. Saviour's, Dublin 1, Ireland.

Downside Review, q; Newman Bookshop, 87 St. Aldates, Oxford, England.

Dublin Review, q; 14 Howick Place, London, S.W. 1, England.

East Asian Pastoral Review, q; East Asian Pastoral Institute, P.O. Box 1815, Manila, Philippines.

Eastern Churches Review, semi-annual; 9 Alfred St., Oxford, England.

Faith Today, 10 times a year; Dominican Publications, St. Saviour's, Dublin 1, Ireland.

Furrow, m; St. Patrick's College, Maynooth, Ireland.

Heythrop Journal q; Heythrop College, 11 Cavendish Sq., London W1M, OAN, England.

Horizons: Journal of the College Theology Society, biannual; Wilfrid Laurier University Press, Waterloo, Ont., Canada N2L 3C5 (Editorial Office: Villanova University, Villanova, Pa. 19085).

International Philosophical Quarterly, q; Fordham University, Bronx, N.Y. 10458.

Irish Biblical Studies, q; 14 Cadogan Park, Belfast BT9 6HG, N. Ireland.

Irish Theological Quarterly, q; St. Patrick's College, Maynooth, Ireland.

L'Osservatore Romano, w; Vatican City.

Louvain Studies, semi-annual; Naamsestraat 100 B-3000, Louvain, Belgium.

Lumen Vitae, q; International Center for Studies in Religious Education, 184, rue Washington, 1050 Brussels, Belgium.

Maynooth Review, q; St. Patrick's College, Maynooth, Ireland.

Mediaeval Studies, annual; Pontifical Institute of Mediaeval Studies, 59 Queen's Park Crescent East, Toronto, Ont., Canada M5S 2C4.

Month, m; 114 Mount St., London, WIY, 6AH, England.

Music and Liturgy, q; Fowler Wright Books, Ltd., Tenbury Wells, Worcs., England.

New Blackfriars, m; edited by English Dominicans, Blackfriars, Oxford, England.

One in Christ, q; Benedictine Priory, 6A Priory Close — Southgate, London N14 4AT, Eng. (U.S. agency, P. M. Davis, 1937 Lake Ave., Whiting, Ind. 46394.)

Philosophical Studies, annual; St. Patrick's College, Maynooth, Ireland.

Recusant History, biannual; Catholic Record Society, 114 Mount St., London, W1Y 6AH, England.

Religion and Society, q; Christian Institute for the Study of Religion and Society, 17 Miller Rd., P.O. Box 4600, Bangalore 560 046, India.

Scripture in Church, q; Costello Publishing, P.O. Box 9, Northport, L.I., N.Y. 11768.

Social Studies, q; St. Patrick's College, Maynooth, Ireland.

Studies in Religion/Sciences Religieuses (bilingual), q; Wilfrid Laurier University Press, Waterloo, Ont., Canada N2L 3C5.

Sursum Corda—Lift Up Your Hearts, bm; Box 79, Box Hill, Victoria, Australia 3128.

Tablet, The w; 48 Great Peter St., SW1P 2HB, London, England.

Teilhard Review, The, 3 times a year; The Teilhard Centre for the Future of Man, 81 Cromwell Rd., London SW7 5BW, England.

Theology, bm; S.P.C.K. Holy Trinity Church, Marylebone Rd., London, NW1 4DU, England.

Way, The, q; and **Supplements to The Way,** triannual: Campion House College, 112 Thornbury Rd., Middlesex, TW7 4NN, England.

Books

The Official Catholic Directory, annual, P. J. Kenedy and Sons, 866 Third Ave., New York, N.Y. 10022. First edition, 1817.

The Catholic Almanac, annual; Our Sunday Visitor, Inc., 200 Noll Plaza, Huntington, Ind. 46750, publisher; editorial offices, 620 Route 3, Clifton, N.J. 07013. First edition, 1904.

The American Catholic Who's Who, biennial; NC News Service, 1312 Massachusetts Ave., N.W., Washington, D.C. 20005. First volume, 1934-35.

BOOK CLUBS

Catholic Book Club (1928), 106 W. 56th St., New York, N.Y. 10019. Sponsors the Campion Award.

Catholic Digest Book Club (1954), Catholic Digest Magazine, P.O. Box 43090, St. Paul, Minn. 55164.

Herald Book Club (1958), Franciscan Herald Press, 1434 W. 51st St., Chicago, Ill. 60609.

Thomas More Book Club (1939), Thomas More Association, 225 W. Huron St., Chicago, Ill. 60610.

Catholic News Agencies

(Sources: International Catholic Union of the Press, Geneva; Catholic Press Association, U.S.)

Argentina: Agencia Informativa Catolica Argentina (AICA), Rodriguez Pena 846, Casilla de Correo Central 2886, Buenos Aires.

Austria: Katholische Presse-Agentur (Kathpress), Wollzeile 1010 Vienna 1.

Belgium: Centre d'Information de Presse (CIP), 38 avenue des Arts, 1040 Bruxelles (Brussels).

Germany: Katholische Nachrichten Agentur (KN), Adenauer Allee 134, 5300 Bonn 1.

Great Britain: Catholic Information Office of England and Wales (CIOEW), 74, Gallows Hill Lane, Abbots Langley, Herts WD5 OB2.

Hungary: Magyar Kurir, Karolyi w 4-8, Postafiok 41, Budapest V.

India: News Bureau India, 13/16, School Marg, Rajinder Nagar, New Delhi 110060

Italy: Agenzia Stampa Catholica Associata (ASCA), v. uffici del Vicario 30, I-00186 Rome.

Japan: TO-SEI, 10-1 Rokubancho, Chiyodaku, Tokyo 102.

Spain: Prensa Asociada (PA), Alfonso XI, 4—Apartado 14530, Madrid 14.

LOGOS, Mateo Inurria 15, Apartado 466, Madrid — 16.

Switzerland: Katholische Internationale Presse-Agentur (KIPA), Case Postale 1054 CH 1701, Fribourg.

Centre International de Reportages et d'Information Culturelle (CIRIC), 10, av. de la Gare-des-Eaux Vives, CH-1207 Geneva.

United States of America: NC News Service (NC), 1312 Massachusetts Ave. N.W., Washington, D.C. 20005.

Yugoslavia: Aktusinosti Krscanska Sadasnjost (AKSA), Marulicev TRG 14, Zagreb p.p. 02-748.

Zaire: Documentation et Information Africaine (DIA), B.P. 2598, Kinshasa I.

U.S. Press Services

NC News Service (NC), established in 1920, provides a worldwide daily news report by wire throughout the continental U.S. and to Europe, and by mail to Canadian and most overseas subscribers, serving more than 400 Catholic periodicals, foreign news agencies, broadcasters including Vatican Radio, and institutional subscribers. It also provides feature and photo services; "Origins," a documentary and text service; "Catholic Trends," a fortnightly newsletter; "Know Your Faith," a weekly religious education package; *The*

American Catholic Who's Who, a biennial directory. NC is represented in all U.S. dioceses and 40 foreign countries. It has a two-member bureau in Rome. It is a division of the United States Catholic Conference, with offices at 1312 Massachusetts Ave. N.W., Washington, D.C. 20005. The director and editor-in-chief is Richard W. Daw.

Religious News Service (RNS) provides domestic and foreign Catholic and other religious news in daily photos and features; "The Religious News Reporter," a weekly 15-minute radio and/or TV package; "The Week in Religion," a feature. RNS was inaugurated in 1933 by the National Conference of Christians and Jews as an independent news agency. Its offices are located at 43 W. 57th St., New York, N.Y. 10019.

Eastern Rite Information Service (ER), for Eastern Church news; 2208 W. Chicago Ave., Chicago, Ill. 60622.

Spanish-Language Service: A weekly news summary, *Resumen Semanal de Noticias,* issued by NC News Service, is used by a number of diocesan newspapers. Some papers carry features of their own in Spanish.

CATHOLIC WRITERS' MARKET

(Source: Almanac survey.)
Editors call the following suggestions to the attention of writers:

Manuscripts should be typewritten, double-spaced, on one side of the page.

Writers should know the editorial policy, purpose and style of the publication to which they submit manuscripts. Sample copies may easily be obtained, often for the mere cost of postage. Some editors suggest that writers send outlines of proposed material, in order to facilitate editorial decision and direction. "Timely" copy should be submitted considerably in advance of the date of proposed publication; some editors advise a period of three months. Authors are urged to avoid sermonizing. Writers should not expect extensive criticism of their work, although they should profit from advice and direction when these are given. Editors are not required to state their reasons for rejecting manuscripts. Replies regarding the acceptance or rejection of copy are usually made within a few weeks.

All writers should send to editors stamped, self-addressed envelopes for the return of material. Those who write to Canadian editors may use international reply coupons, not U.S. stamps.

Payment is made on acceptance or publication. Rates are sometimes variable because of the reputation of the writer, the quality and length of the manuscript, the amount of editorial work required for its final preparation.

America: 106 W. 56th St., New York, N.Y. 10019. Ed., Rev. Joseph A O'Hare, S.J. Weekly, circulation 37,000; $18 per year.

ARTICLES on important public issues evaluated scientifically and morally; serious and authenticated articles on family life, education, religion, and social and political issues with ethical or religious implications; occasionally, "thought" pieces; 1,000-2,000 words — 3¢ a word. VERSE, short and modern, befitting a Catholic publication but not necessarily religious—$7.50 and up. No fiction.

Annals of St. Anne de Beaupre, The: P.O. Box 1000, St. Anne de Beaupre, Que., Canada G0A 3C0. Ed., Rev. Francois Plourde, C.SS.R. Monthly, circulation 70,000; $4 per year.

FICTION: Stories of general Catholic interest, preferably with slant on devotion to St. Anne; 1,500-1,600 words — 1½-2¢ a word. ARTICLES of solid general interest to Catholics: on aspects of devotion to St. Anne, relative to history of the devotion in North America or elsewhere: on educational or social problems, or situations that should be of concern to all — especially Christians: 1,200-1,700 words — 2¢ a word, Payment on acceptance; report within a month.

Catechist: 2451 E. River Rd., Dayton, O. 45439. Ed., Patricia Fischer. Monthly Sept. through May (exc. Dec.), circulation 51,000; $9 per year.

ARTICLES of interest to teachers of religion in parochial schools and CCD programs: 1,200-1,800 words — rate varies. PHOTOGRAPHS, black and white — rate varies. Payment on publication.

Catholic Digest: P.O. Box 43090, St. Paul, Minn. 55164. Ed., Henry Lexau. Monthly, circulation 560,000; $6.97 per year.

ARTICLES of close-to-home interest for average Catholic — rates vary; most frequent payments are $200 for originals, $100 for reprints; payment on acceptance. FILLERS, short features and jokes — rates vary; payment on publication. Cover pictures — $150. No fiction or verse. No queries necessary.

Columban Mission: St. Columbans, Nebr. 68056. Ed., Rev. Richard Steinhilber. Monthly (exc. June, Aug.); circulation 228,975; $2 per year.

ARTICLES mostly from missions or staff written: occasionally accept feature or factual articles on social and religious aspects of Asian and Latin American life: 2,000 words — $100 and up. PHOTOGRAPHS of Asian and Latin American subjects and photo stories — $10 each.

Columbia: Columbus Plaza, New Haven, Conn. 06507. Ed., Elmer Von Feldt. Monthly, circulation 1,260,000; $3 per year. Official organ of the Knights of Columbus.

ARTICLES dealing with current events, social problems, Catholic apostolic activities: 1,000-3,000 words (must be accompanied by glossy photos) — $100 to $400. FICTION, Christian viewpoint: up to 3,000 words — up to $400. SATIRE: 1,000 words — $100.

CARTOONS, pungènt, wordless humor — $25. COVERS — $750.

Commonweal: 232 Madison Ave., New York, N.Y. 10016. Ed., James O'Gara. Biweekly, circulation 20,000; $20 per year.

ARTICLES, political, religious and literary subjects: 1,000-3,000 words — 2¢ a word. VERSE, serious poetry of high literary merit — about 40¢ a line.

Crusader's Almanac: Franciscan Monastery, 1400 Quincy St. N.E., Washington, D.C. 20017. Ed., Rev. Bartholomew Bengisser, O.F.M. Biannually, circulation 85,000; $1 per year.

ARTICLES about the Holy Land, Bible and Crusades given preference — 1¢ a word.

Emmanuel: 194 E. 76th Street, New York, N.Y. 10021. Editor-in-Chief, Rev. Paul J. Bernier, S.S.S. Monthly, bimonthly July-Aug., circulation 13,000; $10 per year.

ARTICLES, spirituality for those in Church ministry, Eucharistic, pastoral, theological, Scriptural: 2,000-3,000 words — $40-$50.

Eucharist: 194 E. 76th St., New York, N.Y. 10021. Ed., Rev. William J. O'Halloran, S.S.S. Bimonthly, circulation 5,385; $4 per year.

ARTICLES, presenting meaning of Eucharist in Catholic spirituality: average length 1,500 words — 2-3¢ a word. Payment on publication.

Franciscan Herald: 1434 W. 51st St., Chicago, Ill. 60609. Monthly, circulation 8,000; $6 per year.

ARTICLES concerning St. Francis of Assisi and related subjects; application of Gospel principles to living Catholicism today; 2,000 words — $35. BOOK REVIEWS related to Franciscan topics — $10.

Hospital Progress: 1438 S. Grand Blvd., St. Louis, Mo. 63104. Ed., C. S. Boyer. Monthly, circulation 14,000; $20 per year (U.S. and Canada; $22 (foreign).

Official journal of the Catholic Health Association of the United States.

ARTICLES, hospital-oriented; administrative procedures and theories; hospital departmental services: 1,500-3,000 words — $1 per column inch. BOOK REVIEWS, hospital oriented — payment by agreement.

Immaculata: 1600 W. Park Ave., Libertyville, Ill. 60048. Ed., Rev. Bernard M. Geiger, O.F.M. Conv. Monthly, circulation 24,000; $8 per year.

Official publication of Knights of the Immaculata.

FICTION reflecting the interests, problems and lives of Catholics; 1,000-2,500 words — $25 and up. ARTICLES: seasonal, following liturgical calendar of the Church; conversion stories, profiles of saints; analyses of contemporary Catholic events; 900-3,000 words — $25 and up. POETRY, 8-40 lines — payment varies. PHOTOS, DRAWINGS, CAR-TOONS with accompanying article or separately — $5 to $20. BOOK REVIEWS — $10 to $25. Query preferred. Payment on publication.

Institute Journal: 50 Oak St., San Francisco, Calif. 94102. Ed., Thomas P. Brady. Bimonthly, $1 per year.

FICTION — no fixed rate. PHOTOGRAPHS — $15.

Josephite Harvest, The: 1130 N. Calvert St., Baltimore, Md. 21202. Ed., Rev. Earle A. Newman, S.S.J. Quarterly; circulation 40,000; $2 per year.

ARTICLES concerning apostolate of Catholic Church in U.S. to the black community.

Liguorian: One Liguori Dr., Liguori, Mo. 63057. Ed., Norman J. Muckerman, C.SS.R. Monthly, circulation over 500,000; $6 per year.

FICTION concerning current situations; stories with a Christian influence yet without maudlin sentimentality; 1,500-2,000 words — 5¢ a word. ARTICLES on family, Scripture, liturgy; material for older readers and those under 21 needed; 1,500-2,000 words — 5¢ a word. POETRY, 10 lines or less — $10. ILLUSTRATIONS and BOOK REVIEWS on assignment only.

Living Light, The, An Interdisciplinary Review of Christian Education: Editorial offices, Department of Education, 1312 Massachusetts Ave. N.W., Washington D.C. 20005. Quarterly, circulation 4,630; $12 per year.

ARTICLES on religious education, catechetics, Scripture: under 3,000 words — 2¢ per word.

Marian Helpers Bulletin: Eden Hill, Stockbridge, Mass. 01262. Ed., Rev. Walter F. Pelczynski, M.I.C. Quarterly, circulation over 750,000; $1 per year. Overstocked at present.

Marriage and Family Living: St. Meinrad, Ind. 47577. Ed., Ila M. Stabile. Monthly, circulation 60,000; $11 per year.

ARTICLES: (1) aimed at enriching the husband-wife and parent-child relationship by expanding religious and psychological insights or sensitivity: 1,000-2,000 words; (2) informative, aimed at helping couple cope, in practical ways, with problems of modern living: maximum 2,000 words; (3) personal essays relating amusing and/or heartwarming incidents that point up the human side of marriage and family life: maximum 1,500 words — 5¢ a word. PHOTOS: 8x11 b & w glossies, color transparencies — $10 minimum. 4-color cover photo — $150; b & w cover photo — $50; 2-page spread in contents — $35; 1-page in contents — $30. Photos of couples especially desired. Model releases required.

Buys North American serial rights only. Report on submissions in 3 to 4 weeks. Sample copy available for 50¢. Payment on acceptance.

Maryknoll: Maryknoll, N.Y. 10545. Ed., Rev. Darryl L. Hunt, M.M. Monthly, circulation more than 300,000; $1 per year.

ARTICLES must apply in some way to the hopes and aspirations, the culture, the problems and challenges of peoples in Asia, Africa and Latin America: 1,000-1,500 words — average payment, $100. Outline wanted before submission of material. PHOTOS: More interested in photo stories than in individual black and whites and color transparencies. Photo stories — up to $150, black and white; up to $200, color. Individual photos — $15, black and white; $25, color. Transparencies returned after use. Query to be made before sending photos.

Messenger of the Sacred Heart, The: 833 Broadview Ave., Toronto, Ont., Canada, M4K 2P9. Ed., Rev. F. J. Power, S.J. Monthly, circulation 23,000; $5 per year.

FICTION: stories which appeal to men, written with humor—good family reading: maximum, 2,000 words — 2¢ a word. ARTICLES of Catholic interest: 2,500 words — 2¢ a word. Payment upon acceptance.

Miraculous Medal, The: 475 E. Chelten Ave., Philadelphia, Pa. 19144. Ed., Rev. Robert P. Cawley, C.M. Quarterly, circulation 100,000.

FICTION, of general interest. Catholic in principle: 1,500-2,000 words — 2¢ a word and up. VERSE, religious in theme or turn; preferably about Our Lady: maximum 20 lines — 50¢ a line and up. Payment on acceptance. No articles.

Modern Liturgy: 7291 Coronado Dr., San Jose, Calif. 95129. Ed. William Burns. Eight issues a year, circulation, 15,000; $19 per year.

FICTION: parables, fantasy, fables; 1,000 words — 3¢ a word. ARTICLES: how-to, sample services, skills for liturgical artists; 1,200 words — 3¢ a word. POETRY, up to 50 lines — $10. BOOK REVIEWS appropriate for liturgy or religious education — $1 plus book.

Writers' guidelines available, send S.A.S.E.; or, for $3, a recent issue of magazine.

My Daily Visitor: Noll Plaza, Huntington, Ind. 46750. Mng. Ed., Patrick R Moran. Bimonthly, circulation 18,400; $6 per year.

A pocket-sized booklet of reflections for each day of the month.

MATERIAL: Daily reflections based on spiritual meditation, the feast of the day or the liturgical season: maximum 165 words per page (each day's reflection is printed on a separate page) — $100 for series of reflections.

New Catholic World: 1865 Broadway, New York, N.Y. 10023. Mng. Ed., Robert Heyer. Bimonthly, circulation 14,000; $7 per year. Thematic issues.

ARTICLES, related to themes of issue (query editor): about 1,800-2,000 words. Rates of payment supplied.

Our Family: Box 249,Dept. C, Battleford, Sask., Canada SOM OEO. Ed., Rev. Albert Lalonde, O.M.I. Monthly, circulation 13,049; $7 per year.

FICTION, adult only; stories that reflect lives, problems and concerns of audience; anything true to human nature; no sentimentality or blatant moralizing; stories with "woven in" Christian message: 1,000-3,000 words — 3¢ to 5¢ a word. ARTICLES related to family living; religion, education, social, biographical, marriage, courtship, domestic, institutional: 1,000-3,000 words — 3¢ to 5¢ a word. POETRY, in the market for many more poems; should deal with man in search for himself, for God, for others, for love, for meaning in life, for commitment: 8-30 lines — $3-$10. PHOTOS — purchased with manuscript as package (extra payment for photos); also in search of individual photos for editorial use. FILLERS — anecdotes of inspirational value, straight exposition, short humor. Writers' guide and photo specification sheet available on request (free). A sample copy is available for $1. Usually buys first North American serial rights; will consider purchasing second or reprint rights.

Our Sunday Visitor Magazine: Noll Plaza, Huntington, Ind. 46750. Ed., Robert Lockwood. Weekly, circulation 350,000; $9.50 per year.

ARTICLES, no limitation on subjects other than those imposed by good taste and orthodoxy. Picture and text stories, profiles of individuals and organizations; articles that reflect moral, cultural, historical, social, economic and certain political concerns about the U.S. and the world; articles on current problems. Practical, factual and anecdotal material is sought: 750-1,000 words — $75-$100, usual payment. Queries are preferred to unsolicited completed manuscripts. PHOTOGRAPHS, picture stories preferred rather than individual photos. Picture stories (color) — $100 and up.No fiction or poetry.

Parish Family Digest: Noll Plaza, Huntington, Ind. 46750. Ed., Patrick R. Moran. Bimonthly, circulation 140,000.

ARTICLES of timely interest to the young and growing Catholic family as a unit of the Catholic parish — personality profiles, interviews, social concerns, education, humor, inspiration and family and parish-family interrelationships; 1,000 words or less — 5¢ a word. REPRINTS — $25. CARTOONS — $10 each for exclusives. FILLERS — $5 each for exclusives based on personal experience.

Pastoral Music: 225 Sheridan St. N.W., Washington, D.C. 20011. Ed. Connie Szostak. Bimonthly, circulation 8,000; $15 per year.

FICTION and ARTICLES — 4¢ a word.

Priest, The: 200 Noll Plaza, Huntington,

Ind. 46750. Ed., Rev. Vincent J. Giese. Monthly (exc. Aug.), circulation 10,651; $14.50 per year.

ARTICLES of benefit to priests and seminarians in any of the following areas: priestly spirituality, contemporary theology, liturgy, apostolate and ministry, pastoral notes, Scripture. Controversial subject matter acceptable provided it does not go beyond the realm of orthodoxy or respect for authority or demands of fraternal charity: 6-15 double-spaced pages — $25 to $100 (about $5 per manuscript page).

Queen of All Hearts: 40 S. Saxon Ave., Bay Shore, N.Y. 11706. Ed., Rev. James McMillan, S.M.M.; Mng. Ed., Rev. Roger M. Charest S.M.M. Bimonthly; circulation 8,500; $6 per year (U.S.), $7).

FICTION: short stories, preferably with a Marian theme: 1,000-2,000 words. ARTICLES that bring out the importance of devotion to Mary. Payment varies. VERSE with Marian theme — payment, two years' subscription. No artwork or fillers.

Religion Teacher's Journal: Twenty-Third Publications, P.O. Box 180, W. Mystic, Conn. 06388. Ed., Gwen Costello. Eight issues a year, circulation 35,000; $10 per year.

FICTION about teachers relating to children, children and liturgical seasons; maximum length, 7 typewritten, double-spaced pages — $100 maximum. ARTICLES on catechesis, methods, theology, sample programs, how-to ideas, etc.; length and rates same as above. ILLUSTRATIONS, black and white — $15 each; covers/color slides — $25.

Review for Religious: Room 428, 3601 Lindell Blvd., St. Louis, Mo. 63108. Ed., D.F.X. Meenan, S.J. Bimonthly, circulation 19,573; $8 per year.

ARTICLES, of interest to religious: 3,000-6,000 words — $6 per printed page.

St. Anthony Messenger: 1615 Republic St., Cincinnati, O. 45210. Ed., Rev. Jeremy Harrington, O.F.M. Monthly, circulation 300,000; $8 per year.

FICTION: Written out of a totally Christian background, illuminating the truth of human nature for adults. No preachiness, sentimentality. FACT ARTICLES: 3,000-3,500 words. Outstanding personalities (must be based on personal interview). Information and comment on major movements in the Church: application of Christian faith to daily life; real-life solutions in the areas of a) family life, education; b) personal living (labor, leisure, art, psychology, spirituality). Human interest narrative. Humor. Photos and picture stories. Query letters welcome.

St. Joseph's Messenger and Advocate of the Blind: St. Joseph's Home, P.O. Box 288, Jersey City, N.J. 07303. Ed., Sr. Ursula Maphet, C.S.J. Quarterly, circulation 54,000; $2 per year.

FICTION, and ARTICLES, contemporary, mainstream themes, 500-1,500 words — 1¢ to 3¢ a word.

Salesian Missions: 148 Main St., New Rochelle, New York 10802. Ed., Rev. Edward J. Cappelletti, S.D.B. Quarterly, circulation 1,000,000; $1 per year.

ARTICLES: mission interest; pertaining to Salesian Society, life, spirit and educational system of St. John Bosco; adolescent interest and education — 5¢ a word and up. PHOTOGRAPHS — $6. Suggest queries before submitting material. Payment on acceptance. Early report.

Sign: Monastery Pl., Union City, N.J. 07087. Ed., Rev. Patrick McDonough, C.P. Monthly, circulation 150,000; $9.95 per year.

ARTICLES on prayer, sacraments, social concerns, and other topics of Catholic interest: 1,000-3,000 words. Payment varies according to length and quality of article. Photos and drawings welcomed with article submissions. FICTION, religious or providing some insight into the human condition. Payment varies.

Social Justice Review: 3835 Westminster Pl., St. Louis, Mo. 63108. Ed., Harvey J. Johnson, Bimonthly, circulation 1,310; $8 per year.

ARTICLES: research, editorial and review: 2,000-4,000 words — $3.50 per column. No fiction.

Spiritual Life: 2131 Lincoln Rd., N.E., Washington, D.C. 20002. Ed., Rev. Christopher Latimer, O.C.D. Quarterly, circulation 17,000; $6 per year.

ARTICLES, must follow scope of magazine: 3,000-5,000 words — rate varies. Sample copy and instructions for writers sent upon request.

Spirituality Today 1909 S. Ashland Ave., Chicago, Ill. 60608. Ed., Rev. Christopher Kiesling, O.P. Quarterly, circulation 3,500; $5 per year.

ARTICLES concerning any phase of the spiritual life: minimum 3,000-4,000 words — 1¢ a word. No fiction or poetry.

Today's Catholic Teacher: 2451 E. River Rd., Suite 200, Dayton, O. 45439. Ed., Ruth A. Matheny. Monthly Sept. through May (exc. Dec.), circulation 60,000; $8.95 per year.

ARTICLES of professional and personal interest to teachers, administrators, pastors, parish councils and school board members concerning Catholic schools and CCD programs: 600-800 words, 1,500-3,000 words — $15-$75. Premium payment for superior content and writing presentation. Black and white photos helpful. Payment on publication.

Today's Parish: Twenty-Third Publications, P.O. Box 180, W. Mystic, Conn. 06388. Ed., Dr. Robert R. Barr. Eight issues a year, circulation 20,000; $12 per year.

ARTICLES, 1,200-1,500 words — $60 to $100. PHOTOS — $15.

WAY — of St. Francis: 109 Golden Gate Ave. San Francisco, Calif. 94102. Ed., Simon Scanlon, O.F.M. Ten times a year, circulation 8,404; $5 per year.

ARTICLES, in keeping with the purpose of the magazine, to bear effective witness to the ideals and aims of the Order of St. Francis: to view the world through Christian eyes; to point up the relationship between abstract belief and concrete action in the modern world: 1,500-2,200 words — $30 to $50. PHOTOGRAPHS: bought with articles.

Working for Boys: Box A, Danvers, Mass. 01923. Ed., Brother Alphonsus Dwyer, C.F.X. (Mss. to Bro. Alois, C.F.X., Assoc. Ed., St. John's High School, Shrewsbury, Mass, 01545.) Quarterly, circulation 18,000; $1 per year.

FICTION, preferably seasonal: 800-1,000 words — 4¢ a word. ARTICLES, preferably seasonal: All Souls, Christmas, Easter, Summer: 800-1,000 words — 4¢ a word. VERSE, seasonal, 4-16 lines — 25¢-50¢ a line.

Worship: St. John's Abbey, Collegeville, Minn. 56321. Ed., Rev. Aelred Tegels, O.S.B. Bimonthly, circulation 6,784; $10 per year.

ARTICLES related to the engagement of the magazine in ongoing study of both the theoretical and pastoral dimensions of liturgy; examines historical traditions of worship in their doctrinal context, the experience of worship in Christian churches, the findings of contemporary theology, psychology, communications, cultural anthropology, and sociology insofar as they have a bearing on public worship: 5,000-8,000 words — 2¢ a word for commissioned articles. No fiction or poetry.

RADIO, TELEVISION, THEATRE

Radio

Christopher Radio Program: 15-minute interview-discussion series, "Christopher Closeup," weekly, on 288 stations; a one-minute "Christopher Thought for Today," daily, on 1,328 stations. Address: 12 E. 48th St., New York, N.Y. 10017.

Crossroads: Originated in 1954 as the Hour of the Crucified, produced by the Passionist Fathers and Brothers. Weekly, on nearly 700 stations. Director: Rev. Cyril Schweinberg, C.P.; Associate Director: Bro. Damian Carroll, C.P. Address: 1089 Elm St., West Springfield, Mass. 01089.

Guideline: Produced in cooperation with the Office for Film and Broadcasting, NCCB/USCC. Weekly program designed to set forth the teachings of the Catholic Church and to discuss issues the Church faces in the contemporary world; heard on approximately 90 stations (NBC).

On This Rock: Originated in 1941, produced in cooperation with the Office for Film and Broadcasting, NCCB/USCC. A 15-minute weekly program currently employing a youth-oriented music and commentary format; heard on more than 100 stations (ABC).

Sacred Heart Program: Originated in 1939, produced by the Jesuit Fathers. Features five 15-minute programs, one five-minute program and one half-hour program weekly on radio, and one 15-minute TV program weekly. Director, Rev. Denis E. Daly, S.J. Address: 3900 Westminster Place, St. Louis, Mo. 63108.

Television

Directions: Originated in 1960, this weekly half-hour program sustains a news-oriented approach to reporting social, moral and religious issues within a Catholic context. The Office for Film and Broadcasting, NCCB/USCC, cooperates in the production of some 15 segments a year, in addition to interfaith and seasonal specials; carried at variable dates on more than 100 stations (ABC).

For Our Times: Originated in April 1979, this weekly half-hour series produced by CBS in a unique joint cooperative consultation with the Office for Film and Broadcasting, USCC, the National Council of Churches and the New York Board of Rabbis focuses on the ethical and social challenges confronting American society today. Format: documentary and studio discussion (CBS).

Religious Specials: The Office for Film and Broadcasting, NCCB USCC, cooperates in the production of four one-hour Catholic specials a year and occasional seasonal or tri-faith presentations. These programs offer a varied format: film, dramatizations, panel discussions, music and commentary, etc. Catholic portions are telecast on approximately 140 stations (NBC).

Theatre

Catholic University Drama Department: Established in 1937. Offers degree courses in theatre arts, produces five plays a year in The Hartke Theatre. Affiliated with National Players and Olney Theatre. Chairman of the department, William H. Graham. Address: Catholic University of America, Washington, D.C. 20064.

National Players: An operation of University Players, a non-profit organization affiliated with the Drama Department of the Catholic University. It originated in 1949 and is the oldest classical touring company in the U.S.

Olney Theatre Corporation: A non-profit organization affiliated with the Drama Department of Catholic University. It owns and operates Olney Theatre, Olney, Md., an Equity theatre designated the State Summer Theatre of Maryland in 1978.

Catholic Actors' Guild of America, Inc.: Established in 1914 to provide material and spiritual assistance to people in the theatre. Has more than 700 members; publishes *The Call Board* bimonthly. Address: Piccadilly Hotel, 227 W. 45th St., New York, N.Y. 10036.

Communications Services

Centro de Comunicacion, Oblates of Mary Immaculate: National Hispanic communications center. Produces TV and radio programs; publishes religious educational books, audio-visual materials and a weekly Spanish newspaper; organizes annual Chicano Film Festival. Director Adàn Medrano, P.O. Box 96, San Antonio, Tex. 78291.

Christopher TV Series, "Christopher Closeup": Originated in 1951. Half-hour and quarter-hour interviews in color, weekly, on 74 commercial stations, 130 American Forces Network outlets, CBN and PTL syndicate stations and 18 cable systems. Address: 12 E. 48th St., New York, N.Y. 10017.

Father Peyton's Family Theater Productions: Films for TV, for sale and rental. Address: 7201 Sunset Blvd., Hollywood, Calif. 90046.

Franciscan Communications Center: An audio-visual media center dedicated to the production of public service broadcasting material and audio-visual media for religious education. Creators and producers of TeleSPOTS and AudioSPOTS, 10- to 60-second public service messages for radio and TV; TeleKETICS films and media kits, filmstrips, slide programs and phonograph records and tapes, for religious, moral and value education; StorySCAPE, a religious education program for the family. Address: 1229 South Santee St., Los Angeles, Calif. 90015.

Mary Productions "Airtime": Originated in 1950. Offers royalty-free scripts for stage, film, radio and tape production. Audio and video tapes of lives of the saints and historical characters. Address: Mary Productions Guild, 58 Lenison Ave., Belford, N.J. 07718.

Paulist Communications: Contracts with dioceses and parishes to provide public service programs free to radio stations and scripts to priest-broadcasters; contacts stations for dioceses. Address: P.O. Box 1057, Pacific Palisades, Calif. 90272.

Paulist Productions: Producers and distributors of the INSIGHT Film Series (available for TV at no charge), and educational film series. Purchase and rental information available. Address: P.O. Box 1057, Pacific Palisades, Calif. 90272.

Sacred Heart Program — TV: Originated in 1954, produced by the Jesuit Fathers. Director, Rev. Denis E. Daly, S.J. Address: 3900 Westminster Pl., St. Louis, Mo. 63108.

Tele-Vue I Productions: Films for TV, mostly educational, for sale and rental. Also available for rental to Catholic schools. Address: Rev. Paul W. Stauder, Old St. Henry's Church, 525 E. Broadway, E. St. Louis, Ill. 62201.

Catholic Television Network (CTN): Instructional TV operations have been established in the following archdioceses and dioceses. Archdioceses are indicated by an asterisk.

Boston,* Mass.: Rev. James Hawker, Director, 468 Beacon St. 02115.

Brooklyn, N.Y.: Rev. Michael J. Dempsey, Director, 1712 10th Ave., 11215.

Chicago,* Ill.: Mr. Charles E. Hinds, Executive Director, One N. Wacker Dr. 60606.

Los Angeles,* Calif.: Mr. Steven J. Gorski, 1520 W. Ninth St. 90015.

New York,* N.Y.: Sr. M. Irene Fugazy, Director, Seminary Ave., Yonkers, N.Y. 10704.

Rockville Centre, N.Y.: Rev. Thomas Hartman, Director, 1345 Admiral Lane, Uniondale, N.Y. 11553.

San Francisco,* Calif.: Most Rev. Pierre Du Maine, 443 Church St. 94114.

UNDA-USA: A national professional Catholic association for broadcasters and allied communicators organized in 1972. It succeeded the Catholic Broadcasters Association of America which in 1948 had replaced the Catholic Forum of the Air organized in 1938. It is a member of the international Catholic association for radio and television known as UNDA (the Latin word for "wave," symbolic of air waves of communication). Subgroups include Catholic Television Network, the Association of Catholic Radio and Television Syndicators, and the Association of Diocesan Directors. UNDA-USA publishes a newsletter six times a year for members, sponsors an annual general assembly and presents the Gabriel Awards annually for excellence in broadcasting. President, Rev. John Geaney, C.S.P., 320 Cathedral St., Baltimore, Md. 21201. National office: 3015 Fourth St. N.E., Washington, D.C. 20017.

Foundation

The Catholic Communications Foundation (CCF) was established by the Catholic Fraternal Benefit Societies in 1966 to lend support and assistance to development of the broadcasting apostolate of the Church.

The CCF, in addition to making financial grants for religious programs and programming services, has promoted the development of diocesan communications capabilities and has funded scholarship programs at Loyola University, New Orleans.

CCF officers include Bishop Andrew A. Grutka, chairman of the board and treasurer. Address: P.O. Box 80428, San Diego, Calif. 92138.

CHARISMATIC RENEWAL

(Written with the assistance of the National Communications Office Serving the Catholic Charismatic Renewal.)

The movement originated with a handful of Duquesne University students and faculty members in the 1966-67 academic year and spread from there to Notre Dame, Michigan State University, the University of Michigan and to other campuses and cities throughout the country.

According to a Gallup poll reported in the Feb. 22, 1980 issue of *Christianity Today*, 18 per cent of adult Catholics in the United States consider themselves Pentecostal or charismatic Christians. This would include more than 6 million Catholics. The movement is also strong in Canada and is to be found in at least 75 other countries, involving more than 300,000 participants.

Some 11,000 persons attended the national conference at the University of Notre Dame May 30 to June 1, 1980. Teachings from the national conferences and from other special conferences are being shown throughout the country in videotaped seminars called Pastoral Training Weekends. The "Jesus '80" rallies on the eve of Pentecost were more localized in 1980 than in previous years — with 115 rallies in New York and New Jersey alone.

Keys to the Movement

Scriptural keys to the renewal are:
• Christ's promise to send the Holy Spirit upon the Apostles;
• the description, in the Acts of the Apostles, of the effects of the coming of the Holy Spirit upon the Apostles on Pentecost;
• St. Paul's explanation, in the Letter to the Romans, of the charismatic gifts (for the good of the Church and persons) the Holy Spirit would bestow on Christians;
• New Testament evidence concerning the effects of charismatic gifts in and through the early Church.

The personal key to the renewal is baptism of the Holy Spirit. This is not a new sacrament but the personally experienced actualization of grace already sacramentally received.

The experience of baptism of the Holy Spirit is often accompanied by the reception of one or more charismatic gifts.

Among the movement's strongest points of emphasis are prayer, openness to the Holy Spirit, community experience and the sharing of spiritual gifts.

The characteristic form of the renewal is the weekly prayer meeting, a gathering which includes periods of spontaneous prayer, singing, sharing of experience and testimony, fellowship and teaching.

Cardinal Leo J. Suenens has a mandate from Pope John Paul to guide the evolution of the Catholic charismatic renewal so that it may fully enter into the heart of the Church.

Father Tom Forrest, C.Ss.R., is director of the movement's International Communication Office, Boulevard de Smet de Naeyer, 570A, 1020 Bruxelles, Belgium. Kevin M. Ranaghan is director of the National Communications Office, 237 N. Michigan, South Bend, Ind. 46601. Bishop Kenneth Povish of Lansing is chairman of the U.S. Bishops' Ad Hoc Committee for the Charismatic Renewal.

HOUSE OF PRAYER EXPERIENCE

(Source: Sister Ann E. Chester, I.H.M., 529 Stewart Rd., Monroe, Mich. 48202.)

The purpose of the House of Prayer Experience (HOPE) movement is to help active religious and priests and lay persons to acquire a contemporary style of contemplative life for renewal, inner growth and a more joyful personal and communal life in the light of the Gospel.

The starting point of participation in the movement is an extended period, from several weeks to several years, of concentration on intensive prayer with a community — a house of prayer experience. The result sought is the development of a style of prayer and contemplation with a carry-over that integrates and permeates religion and life.

Programs

The communities of houses of prayer consist of a relatively stable core of members with an authentic call to a deeper prayer life and of guests who come and go for shorter or longer periods of participation. The stability of the core group, while not a now-and-forever type of commitment, is such as to guarantee continuity in programs and the resources of experienced personnel in conducting them.

Program elements include the liturgy, meditation, scriptural reading and dialogue, shared prayer in the shared life of community, silence and solitude, search for new forms of prayer and for new adaptations of traditional forms — all against the background of existential conditions. The elements are oriented toward individual and personal needs and to various types of ministry, such as contemplative prayer itself and ministries concerned with a parish, the family, youth, inner-city pastoral work, spiritual development, the charismatic movement.

Houses

Two hundred and four listings were reported in the third *Annual Directory, Houses of Prayer*, released in the spring of 1979 by Clarity Publishing, Inc. (75 Champlain St., Albany, N.Y. 12204). Eighty-two of the houses were sponsored by more than 50 religious congregations of men and women, and

16 by dioceses. The 204 figure represented a 46 per cent increase in listings over those reported in 1978. Fifty-nine of the houses had programs focusing on the spiritual traditions of major religious orders. Houses of prayer or prayer study experience centers were located in 36 of the 50 states. There were also 13 Canadian listings.

Kresge House in Detroit, which provided services to the movement for 10 years, closed its door Aug. 31, 1980.

HUMAN DEVELOPMENT

The Campaign for Human Development was inaugurated by the U.S. Catholic Conference in November, 1969, to combat injustice, oppression, alienation and poverty in this country in three significant ways:

• by making people in this country, especially Catholics, aware of the poverty, oppression and/or injustice afflicting some 35 million persons, through programs of education and public instruction;

• by funding self-help programs begun and carried out by the poor or by the poor and non-poor working together;

• by seeking a re-evaluation of the priorities of individuals, families, the Church and the civic community with respect to the stewardship of God-given goods.

The campaign got under way with a collection taken up in all parishes throughout the country on Nov. 22, 1970. Seventy-five per cent of the money contributed in this and subsequent annual collections was placed in a national fund principally for funding self-help projects and also for educational purposes; 25 per cent remained in the dioceses where it was collected, for similar use on the local levels.

More than $55 million in grants have been allocated by the national office since 1970; grants to 140 projects in 1980 totaled a bit more than $6 million. Diocesan allocations since 1970 have amounted to approximately $20 million.

Aid requests are reviewed by a broadly representative committee of 40 members which passes its recommendations for funding on to the 12-member Bishops' Committee for the Campaign for Human Development. Requests for aid from the national office are about 10 times greater than the some 125 programs funded each year. Local-level requests and funding are handled by diocesan offices for the Campaign for Human Development.

Father Marvin Mottet is executive director of the campaign; his assistant is Timothy Collins. Bishop Joseph H. Hodges of Wheeling-Charleston is chairman of the bishops' committee.

The national office is located at 1312 Massachusetts Ave. N.W., Washington, D.C. 20005.

CATHOLIC RIGHTS LEAGUE

A membership organization founded in 1973, the Catholic League for Religious and Civil Rights seeks to represent the Catholic community in the same way that the Jewish Anti-Defamation League, the American Civil Liberties Union and the National Association for the Advancement of Colored People represent their respective communities.

The League serves as a media watchdog, protesting defamation of Catholic beliefs, values and practices. Its legal department goes to court to defend religious and civil rights. Its research staff serves as a clearinghouse of information on issues of concern to the Catholic community.

Among the League's highest priorities are the right to life of the unborn child and the right of parents to send their children to church-related schools without being denied tax funds for tuition payments.

Supported by contributions from its 30,000 members, the League has no official connection with the Church. League members, as well as opinion leaders and policy makers, receive the League's eight-page *Newsletter* each month.

Father Virgil C. Blum, S.J., presides over operations at the League's national headquarters, 1100 W. Wells St., Milwaukee, Wis. 53233. The League also has local chapters in a dozen U.S. cities.

RIGHT TO LIFE GROUPS

Representative organizations with members of all religious and philosophical convictions who are concerned with the right-to-life of the unborn and related issues include the following: the National Right-to-Life Committee, the National Committee for a Human Life Amendment, the Ad Hoc Committee in Defense of Life, National Nurses for Life, the Committee of Ten Million, the American Association of Pro-Life Obstetricians and Gynecologists, Alternatives to Abortion, Americans against Abortion, Lawyers for Life, the National Youth Pro-Life Coalition, and various groups with Concerned for Life and Right-to-Life titles.

Despite the opinion in some quarters that right-to-life advocates might just as well have fallen over dead after the Supreme Court decisions of 1973, pro-life organizations have shown remarkable vigor.

In the process, however, they have been subject to strong counter-campaigns which have labeled them fanatical, criticized them for sensationalism, scored them as hostile to "rights" of women and privacy and charged them with attempts to subvert the U.S. Constitution.

One of the least credible of the charges is that they are all Catholic inspired and dominated. Such is not the case.

BIRTHRIGHT

Birthright is a nondenominational guidance and referral service organization offering pregnant women alternatives to abortion, in line with the motto, "It is the right of every pregnant woman to give birth and the right of every child to be born."

Started by Mrs. Louise Summerhill of Toronto, Canada, in 1968, it has chapters in Canada, the United States, the United Kingdom, New Zealand, Australia and South Africa. Each of these units, manned by volunteers, operates a crisis center where women can come to discuss their problems privately.

The executive director of Birthright, U.S.A., is Mrs. D. Cocciolone, 62 Hunter St., Woodbury, N.J. 08096.

Birthright, although it has Catholics among its volunteers and draws some support from Catholic sources, insists on its original independent and nondenominational character. Its operations have been adopted by other pro-life groups. Birthright telephone numbers are listed in scores of local directories.

DIOCESAN COMMUNICATIONS OFFICES, DIRECTORS

(Sources: *1980 Directory of Catholic Communications Personnel,* published by the Office of Public Affairs, USCC; *Official Catholic Directory;* NC News Service. Archdioceses are designated by an asterisk.)

Alabama: Birmingham — Rev. Martin Muller (Communications), Box 6147, Birmingham 35209.

Mobile* — Rev. Robert L. Anderson, S.J. (Ed., *The Catholic Week),* 400 Government St., Mobile 36601.

Alaska: Anchorage* — Chancery Office, P.O. Box 2239, Anchorage 99510.

Fairbanks — Rev. Vincent G. Wissman, C.S.P. (Radio-TV), P.O. Box 5001, North Pole 99705. Rev. James Poole, S.J., Box 101, Nome 99762.

Juneau — Miss Carol Crater (Ed., *Inside Passage),* 419 Sixth St., Juneau 99801; Director (Radio-TV), 419 6th St., Juneau 99801.

Arizona: Phoenix — Mr. James Jennings (Communications), Rev. Msgr. Robert J. Donohoe (Community Relations), 400 E. Monroe St., Phoenix 85004.

Tucson — Ms. Susan F. Curtis (Mng. Ed., *Arizona Catholic Lifetime),* 64 W. Ochoa St., Tucson 85701.

Arkansas: Little Rock — Msgr. B. Francis McDevitt (Communications, Radio-TV), 617 Louisiana St., Little Rock 72201.

California: Fresno — Mr. Joseph Jasmin (Information), Box 4273, Fresno 93744.

Los Angeles* — Msgr. Joseph Pollard (Communications), Sr. Mary Carr, O.P. (Director, ETV), 1530 W. 9th St., Los Angeles 90015.

Monterey — Rev. Dennis M. Gilbert (Communications Commission), Old Mission, 941 Chorro, P.O. Box 1483, San Luis Obispo 93406; Rev. Felix Migliazzo (Ed., *The Observer),* Box 2079, Monterey 93940.

Oakland — Mrs. Reggie Finney (Public Relations), Dan Morris (Ed., *The Catholic Voice),* 2900 Lakeshore Ave., Oakland 94610.

Orange — Mr. Thomas A. Fuenter (Communications), 440 S. Batavia St., Orange 92668.

Sacramento — Rev. James T. Murphy (Information), Box 19312, Sacramento 95819.

San Bernardino — Rev. James Fallon (Ed., *Newsletter),* 1450 North D St., San Bernardino 92405.

San Diego — Mr. James Bastis (Communications), Box 80428, San Diego 92138.

San Francisco* — Rev. Harry Schlitt (Executive Director, Communications Center), 50 Oak St., San Francisco 94102; Rev. Miles O'Brien Riley (Director, Information), 441 Church St., San Francisco 94114.

Santa Rosa — Msgr. Walter J. Tappe (Communications), P.O. Box 1297, Santa Rosa 95403.

Stockton — Rev. Lawrence J. McGovern (Information), Box 4237, Stockton 95204.

Colorado: Denver* — Rev. C. B. Woodrich (Information), 200 Josephine St., Denver 80206; Rev. Maurice McInerney (Radio-TV), 4550 Carefree Circle, Colorado Springs 80917.

Pueblo — Ms. Geraldine Carrigan (Communications; Ed., *Catholic Crosswinds),* 1001 N. Grand Ave., Pueblo 81003.

Connecticut: Bridgeport — Rev. Nicholas V. Grieco (Communications), 238 Jewett Ave., Bridgeport 06606; Rev. Alfred J. Sienkiewicz (Radio-TV), 385 Scofieldtown Rd., Stamford 06903.

Hartford* — Rev. Edmund S. Nadolny (Radio-TV), 785 Asylum Ave., Hartford 06105.

Norwich — Jacqueline M. Keller (Communications), 201 Hickory St., Norwich 06360.

Stamford (Ukrainian Diocese) — Rev. Charles Mezzomo, 303 Eddy Glover Blvd., New Britain 06053.

Delaware: Wilmington — Mr. F. Eugene Donnelly (Secretary, Communications), Box 2030, Wilmington 19899.

District of Columbia: Washington* — Rev. Maurice T. Fox (Communications), 1721 Rhode Island Ave. N.W., Washington 20036.

Florida: Miami* — Rev. Donald Connolly (Communications), Marjorie Donohue (Public Information), 6301 Biscayne Blvd., Miami 33138. Rev. Jose P. Nickse (Radio-TV), 6200 N.E. 4th Ct., Miami 33138.

Orlando — Sister Estelle Scully, S.P.

(Communications), Box 3551, Orlando 32802.

Pensacola-Tallahassee — Mr. Gerald Butterfield (Communications), 855 W. Carolina St., Tallahassee 32304.

St. Augustine — Rev. Msgr. R. Joseph James (Diocesan News Service), 1649 Kingsley Ave., Orange Park 32073.

St. Petersburg — Rev. Desmond Daly, P.O. Box 5057, Tampa 33675.

Georgia: Atlanta* — Rev. Msgr. Noel C. Burtenshaw (Ed., *The Georgia Bulletin*), 756 W. Peachtree St. N.W., Atlanta 30308.

Savannah — Rev. Joseph Stranc (Communications), 12 W. Jones Ave., Statesboro 30458.

Hawaii: Honolulu — Msgr. Francis A. Marzen, 1184 Bishop St., Honolulu 96813.

Idaho: Boise — Rev. David L. Riffle (Communications Center), 6003 Overland, Boise 83709.

Illinois: Belleville — Rev. Richard G. Mohr (Communications), 5312 W. Main St. P.O. Box 896, Belleville 62223.

Chicago* — Mr. Peter Foote (Communications), P.O. Box 1979, Chicago 60690. Rev. James Moriarty (Radio-TV), One N. Wacker Dr., Suite 1100, Chicago 60606.

Joliet — Rev. William F. Irwin (Communications), 425 Summit St., Joliet 60435.

Peoria — Mr. Robert England, Sr. Mary Ann Seiler, C.S.J. (Co-Directors, Communications, Evangelization), 607 N.E. Madison, Box 1526, Peoria 61655.

Rockford — Msgr. Thomas G. Doran, Chancellor, 1245 N. Court St., Rockford 61101.

St. Nicholas in Chicago for Ukrainians — Msgr. Jaroslav Swyschuk (Eastern Rite Information Bureau), 2208 W. Chicago Ave., Chicago 60622.

Springfield — Rev. Richard L. Paynic (Information), 514 E. Lawrence, Springfield 62703.

Indiana: Evansville — Rev. Jean F. Vogler (Communications), P.O. Box 4169, Evansville 47711.

Fort Wayne-South Bend — Rev. Vincent J. Giese (Ed., *The Harmonizer*), P.O. Box 390, Ft. Wayne 46801.

Gary — Rev. John F. Morales (Communications), P.O. Box M474, Gary 46401.

Indianapolis* — Mr. Charles J. Schisla (Communications), 136 W. Georgia St., Indianapolis 46225.

Lafayette — Sr. Ann Weller, C.S.J. (Information), 3810 W. Jefferson Rd., Kokomo 46901.

Iowa: Davenport — Rev. Francis C. Henricksen (Communications), Box 939, Davenport 52805.

Des Moines — Sr. Mira Mosle, B.V.M. (Communications), 2910 Grand Ave., Box 1816, Des Moines 50306.

Dubuque* — Rev. Paul L. Weis (Communications), 1229 Mt. Loretta Ave. Dubuque 52001.

Sioux City — Mr. Lewis E. Heifner (Ed., *The Globe*), 1821 Jackson St., Sioux City 51105; Msgr. Frank Brady (Radio-TV), 1212 Morningside Ave., Sioux City 51106.

Kansas: Dodge City — Rev. Daniel V. Heim, Our Lady of Guadalupe Church, 805 Avenue J, Dodge City 67801.

Kansas City* — Rev. William Maher (Ed., *The Leaven*), Box 2329, Kansas City 66110.

Salina — Msgr. Raymond Menard (Information), Box 958, Salina 67401.

Wichita — Rev. Arthur A. Busch, 424 N. Broadway, Wichita 67202.

Kentucky: Covington — Mr. Richard J. Nare (Ed., *The Messenger*), Box 268, Covington 41012; Rev. Paul Arbogast (Communications), 2344 Amsterdam Rd., Covington 41016.

Louisville* — Rev. John H. Morgan, 1305 W. Market St., Louisville 40203.

Owensboro — Msgr. George Hancock (Information), 4003 Frederica St., Owensboro 42301; Rev. Leonard Reisz (Radio-TV), 1001 W. 7th St., Owensboro 42301.

Louisiana: Alexandria-Shreveport — Mr. Al Nassif (Information), Box 7417, Alexandria 71306.

Baton Rouge — Mr. Thomas Barbarie (Ed., *Catholic Commentator*), P.O. Drawer 14746, Baton Rouge 70808.

Houma-Thibodaux — Louis Aguirre (Communications), Rev. Richard Hemenway (Radio-TV), P.O. Box 9077, Houma 70360.

Lafayette — Rev. David Primeaux (Communications), Glenn Norwood (Radio-TV), Box 3223, Lafayette 70502.

Lake Charles — Most Rev. Jude Speyrer, 515 Cathedral St., P.O. Drawer 3387, Lafayette 70502.

New Orleans* — Mr. Thomas M. Finney (Communications, Public Relations), 7887 Walmsley Ave., New Orleans 70125.

Maine: Portland — Mr. Clarence F. McKay (Communications), 510 Ocean Ave., Portland 04103.

Maryland: Baltimore* — Rev. John Geaney, C.S.P. (Communications), 320 Cathedral St., Baltimore 21201.

Massachusetts: Boston* — Mr. George E. Ryan (News Bureau), 49 Franklin St., Boston 02110; Rev. Francis T. McFarland (Radio-TV), 55 Chapel St., Newton 02160.

Fall River — Rev. John F. Moore (Communications), 410 Highland Ave., Fall River 02722; Rev. John F. Hogan, (TV), 494 Slocum Rd., N. Dartmouth 02747.

Springfield — Msgr. David P. Welch (Ed., *Catholic Observer*), Box 1570, Springfield 01101; Rev. Cyril Schweinberg, C.P. (Radio-TV), 1089 Elm St., W. Springfield 01089.

Worcester — Rev. John W. Barrett (Communications), 49 Elm St., Worcester 01609.

Melkite Eparchy of Newton — Rev. James

E. King, 19 Dartmouth St., W. Newton 02165.

Michigan: Detroit* — Rev. Patrick Halfpenny (Communications), 305 Michigan Ave., Detroit 48226.

Gaylord — Sr. Nadine Donnelly, O.P. (Communications), 202 W. Mitchell Ave., Gaylord 49735.

Grand Rapids — Director of Communications, 267 Sheldon Ave. S.E., Grand Rapids 49503.

Kalamazoo — Daniel B. Rebant (Communications), 215 N. Westnedge Ave., Kalamazoo 49005.

Lansing — Rev. Donald L. Eder (Communications), 300 W. Ottawa St., Lansing 48933.

Marquette — Gregory B. Bell (Communications), Box 550, Marquette 49855.

Saginaw — Rev. Donald Eder (Acting Dir. Communications), 5800 Weiss St., Saginaw 48603.

Minnesota: Crookston — Rev. Gerald Noesen (Communications), 812 Stearns, Crookston 56716.

Duluth — Mr. Donald St. Dennis (Information), 215 W. 4th St., Duluth 55806.

New Ulm — Rev. Dennis Labat (Communications), 1400 Chancery Dr., New Ulm 56073.

St. Cloud — Ms. Rosemary Borgert (Information), 810 St. Germain St., Box 1068, St. Cloud 56301.

St. Paul and Minneapolis* — Ms. Joan Bernet (Communications), 226 Summit Ave., St. Paul 55102.

Winona — Ms. Ann DeZell (Communications), Box 588, Winona 55987.

Mississippi: Biloxi — Rev. Michael Tracey (Assoc. Ed., *Mississippi Today*), P.O. Box 367, Biloxi 39533. Rev. William Vollor (Media Communications), Sacred Heart Church, Rt. 1, Box 618, Pass Christian 39571.

Jackson — Mrs. Janna Avalon, Box 2130, Jackson 39205.

Missouri: Jefferson City — Rev. Hugh Behan (Information), Box 1107, Jefferson City 65102; Mr. Mark Saucier (Communications), Box 417, Jefferson City 65101.

Kansas City-St. Joseph — Rev. John C. Weiss (Communications), 1357 N.E. 42nd Terr., Kansas City 64116.

St. Louis* — Msgr. Edward O'Donnell (Information), 462 N. Taylor Ave., St. Louis 63108; Mr. Ronald Coleman (Public Relations), 2249 S. Brentwood Blvd., St. Louis 63144. Rev. Joseph M. O'Brien (Radio-TV), 4140 Lindell Blvd., St. Louis 63108.

Springfield-Cape Girardeau — Sister Emile Morgan, D.C. (Communications), 200 McDaniel Bldg., Springfield 65806.

Montana: Great Falls-Billings — Box 2107, Great Falls 59403.

Helena — Rev. John Robertson, Chancellor, Box 1729, Helena 59601.

Nebraska: Grand Island — Rev. Lawrence McNamara (Communications), P.O. Box 1531, Grand Island 68801.

Lincoln — Rev. James D. Dawson (Information), Box 80328, Lincoln 68501.

Omaha* — Mr. Gregory Pflaum (Communications), 100 N. 62nd St., Omaha 68132.

Nevada: Reno-Las Vegas — Rev. Msgr. Thomas Meger, Chancellor, P.O. Box 1211, Reno 89504.

New Hampshire: Manchester — Mr. Jay Cormier (Communications), 153 Ash St., Manchester 03105.

New Jersey: Camden — Msgr. Charles Giglio (Information), Box 709, Camden 08101.

Newark* — Ann Mary Mullane (Communications), 31 Mulberry St., Newark 07102.

Passaic (Byzantine Rite Eparchy) — Most Rev. Thomas Dolinay, 101 Market St., Passaic 07055.

Paterson — Mr. Gerald M. Costello (Communications Secretariat), 163-65 Newark Pompton Turnpike (Box A), Pequannock 07440; Sister Patricia Kowalski, O.S.M. (Radio-TV), 159 Newark-Pompton Turnpike, Pequannock, N.J. 07440.

Trenton — Sr. Rosemary Jeffries, R.S.M. (Communications), 701 Lawrenceville Rd., Trenton 08648.

New Mexico: Gallup — Rev. Cormac Antram, O.F.M. (Communications, Radio-TV), P.O. Box 39, Tohatchi 87325.

Santa Fe* — Rev. Albert Gallegos (Communications-Media), 202 Morningside Dr. S.E., Albuquerque 87108.

New York: Albany — Rev. Michael Farano (Information), 465 State St., Albany 12206.

Brooklyn — Mr. Frank DeRosa (Information), Box C, Brooklyn 11202.

Buffalo — Rev. Msgr. Robert E. Nesslin (Communications), 100 S. Elmwood Dr., Buffalo 14202.

New York* — Rev. Edwin F. O'Brien (Communications), Revs. Kenneth G. Jadoff and Peter J. Madori (Radio-TV Project Coordinators), Rev. Lester S. Avestruz, O.S.A. (Spanish Media), 1011 First Ave., New York, N.Y. 10022.

Ogdensburg — Rev. David W. Stinebrickner (Information), 622 Washington St., Ogdensburg 13669; Rev. Donald Kramberg (Radio-TV), St. Mary's Rectory, P.O. Box 308, Canton 13617.

Rochester — Rev. Charles J. Latus (Information), 1150 Buffalo Rd., Rochester 14624.

Rockville Centre — Rev. Daniel S. Hamilton (Information), Box 700, Hempstead 11551; Rev. Thomas J. Hartman (Radio-TV), 1345 Admiral Lane, Uniondale 11553.

St. Maron Diocese (Maronite Rite) — Mr. John Hayes (Information), 191 Joralemon St., Brooklyn 11201.

Syracuse — Msgr. Robert F. Lavin (Information), 111 Roberts Ave., Syracuse 13207.

North Carolina: Charlotte — Ms. Mary C. Coyne (Asst. Ed., *North Carolina Catholic*), 1524 E. Moorehead St., Charlotte 28207.

Raleigh — Rev. Joseph G. Vetter (Ed., *North Carolina Catholic*), 300 Cardinal Gibbons Dr., Raleigh 27606.

North Dakota: Bismarck — Rev. John J. Owens, Box 128, Wilton 58579.

Fargo — Sister Mary Ethel Paulus (Ed., *Catholic Action News*), Box 1750, Fargo 58107

Ohio: Cincinnati* — Mr. Daniel J. Kane (Communications), Rev. Theodore Kosse (Radio-TV), 100 E. 8th St., Cincinnati 45202.

Cleveland — Rev. Frank P. Kosem (Delegate, Communications), Mr. J. Jerome Lackamp (Radio-TV), Mr. Patrick DiSalvatore (Public Relations), 1027 Superior Ave., Cleveland 44114.

Columbus — Rev. James P. Hanley (Vicar, Communications), Rev. Michael Reis (Radio-TV), Mr. Richard J. Hatem (Public Relations, Information), 197 E. Gay St., Columbus 43215.

Parma (Byzantine Rite Eparchy) — Rev. Donald Petyo, 1231 Substation Rd., Brunswick 44212.

Steubenville — Rev. Msgr. James C. Marshall, 422 Washington St., Box 969, Steubenville 43952.

Toledo — Mr. Jim Richards (Communications), 2544 Parkwood Ave., Toledo 43610.

Youngstown — Mr. John Lencyk (Communications), 225 Elm St., Youngstown 44503.

Oklahoma: Oklahoma City* — Rev. David F. Monahan (Communications), Box 32180, Oklahoma City 73123.

Tulsa — Rev. Dennis C. Dorney, Chancellor, 820 S. Boulder St., Box 2009, Tulsa 74101.

Oregon: Baker — Rev. Joseph B. Hayes, Sacred Heart Church, 815 High St., Klameth Falls 97601.

Portland* — Rev. Leo Remington (Radio-TV), 2838 E. Burnside St., Portland 97214.

Pennsylvania: Allentown — Rev. Msgr. Vincent E. Lewellis (Information), 202 N. 17th St., Box F, Allentown 18105.

Altoona-Johnstown — Rev. Msgr. Philip Saylor (Information), 126C Logan Blvd., Hollidaysburg 16648.

Erie — Rev. Henry Kriegel (Communications), Box 4047, Erie 16512.

Greensburg — Mrs. Alice Laurich (Communications), Box 850, Greensburg 15601.

Harrisburg — Sr. Arlene Ronollo, S.S.J. (Communications), 4800 Union Deposit Rd., Box 3557, Harrisburg 17105.

Philadelphia* — Msgr. Charles Mynaugh (Acting Dir., Communications), 222 North 17th St., Philadelphia 19103.

Philadelphia* (Ukrainian) — Rev. Ronald Popkivchak, Box 126, Bridgeport 19405.

Pittsburgh* (Byzantine Rite) — Msgr. Edward V. Rosack (Information), 624 Park Rd., Ambridge 15003; Most Rev. John M. Bilock (Radio-TV), 54 Riverview Ave., Pittsburgh 15214.

Pittsburgh — Rev. Ronald P. Lengwin (Communications), Mr. Joseph Williams (Information and Public Relations), 111 Boulevard of the Allies, Pittsburgh 15222.

Scranton — Rev. Joseph P. Gilgallon, 300 Wyoming Ave., Box 708, Scranton 18503.

Rhode Island: Providence — Mr. Brian L. Wallin (Communications), One Cathedral Square, Providence 02903.

South Carolina: Charleston — Rev. Robert J. Millard (Communications), P.O. Box 394, Georgetown 29440.

South Dakota: Rapid City — Mr. Brian T. Olszewski, Box 678, Rapid City 57709.

Sioux Falls — Rev. Thomas J. Ryan, 1301 E. Austin, Sioux Falls 57103.

Tennessee: Memphis — Msgr. Paul W. Clunan (Communications), 203 S. White Station Rd., Memphis 38117.

Nashville — Mr. Joseph A. Sweat (Public Affairs), 2400 21st Ave. S., Nashville 37212.

Texas: Amarillo — Bureau of Information, 1800 N. Spring St., Box 5644, Amarillo 79107; Msgr. Richard F. Vaughan (Radio-TV), 4122 Bonham St., Amarillo 79110.

Austin — Msgr. Lonnie Reyes, N. Congress and 16th, Box 13327, Austin 78711.

Beaumont — Mrs. Edythe Capreol (Communications and Information), P.O. Box 3948, Beaumont 77704.

Brownsville — Sr. Michelle Marie Kuntscher (Communications), Box 2279, Brownsville 78520.

Corpus Christi — Joseph Michael Feist (Public Information), Sr. Janie Barrera (Communications Coordinator), Rev. Robert E. Freeman (Radio-TV), 620 Lipan St., Corpus Christi 78401.

Dallas — Mr. Steve Landregan (Communications-Evangelization), 3434 Highway 67 East, Mesquite 75149.

El Paso — Mr. Andrew Sparke (Parochial Schools TV), 1300 Lamar, El Paso 79903.

Fort Worth — Rev. Eugene Witkowski, 1206 Throckmorton St., Ft. Worth 76102; Mr. Jerry Thomas (Radio-TV), 4801 W. Freeway, Ft. Worth 76107.

Galveston-Houston — Msgr. John L. Fos, 1700 San Jacinto St., Houston 77001; Rev. William L. Young (Radio-TV), P.O. Box 907, Houston 77001.

San Angelo — Mr. Frank Trudo (Communications), Box 1829, San Angelo 76902.

San Antonio* — Rev. Brian Wallace, O.M.I. (Communications), P.O. Box 12429, San Antonio 78212.

Utah: Salt Lake City — Msgr. W. H. McDougall (Information), 331 E. S. Temple St., Salt Lake City 84111; Rev. Thomas J. Meersman (Radio-TV), 1327 E. Second South, Salt Lake City 84102.

Vermont: Burlington — Rev. Joseph T. Sullivan (Communications), 351 North Ave., Burlington 05401.

Virginia: Arlington — Ms. Francis W. McInerney (Communications), 200 N. Glebe Rd., Arlington 22203.

Richmond — Mr. Bob Edwards (Communications), 811 Cathedral Pl., Richmond 23220.

Washington: Seattle* — Rev. Michael G. Ryan, Chancellor, 907 Terry Ave., Seattle 98104.

Spokane — Mr. Maurice Hickey (Communications), Box 1453, Spokane 99210.

Yakima — The Pastoral Office, P.O. Box 505, Yakima 98907.

West Virginia: Wheeling-Charleston — Rev. Victor Seidel, S.T., Box 230, Wheeling 26003.

Wisconsin: Green Bay — Rev. Steven Halbach (Ed., *The Compass*), 1825 Riverside Dr., Green Bay 54301; Mr. Tony Kuick (Radio-TV), Box 66, Green Bay 54305.

La Crosse — Rev. Bernard McGarty (Communications), Box 937, La Crosse 54601.

Madison — Rev. Stephen Umhoefer (Communications), 3577 High Point Rd., Rt. 2, Madison 53711.

Milwaukee* — Sr. Mary Luke Baldwin (Communications), 345 N. 95th, Box 2018, Milwaukee 53201.

Superior — Rev. Robert Urban (Information), 1512 N. 12th St., Superior 54880.

Wyoming: Cheyenne — Rev. Roy Lansing (Information), 412 Randall Ave., Cheyenne 82001.

Catholic Communications Northwest: Regional communications center serving dioceses in Alaska, Idaho, Montana, Oregon and Washington. Executive Director, Dr. Maury Sheridan, 1511 3rd Ave., Seattle, Wash. 98101.

Delaware Valley Catholic Office for Television and Radio: Interdiocesan agency of the Archdiocese of Philadelphia and the dioceses of Camden and Trenton, N.J.; and Wilmington, Del. Address: 222 North 17th St., Philadelphia, Pa. 19103.

Other Communications Offices

International Mission Radio Association: Rev. Jude Bradley, O.S.B., treasurer-administrator, St. Paul's Abbey, Newton, N.J. 07860.

Jesuits in Communication in North America (JESCOM): Rev. Donald R. Campion, S.J., acting director, Suite 402, 1717 Massachusetts Ave., N.W., Washington, D.C. 20005.

Maryknoll Media Relations: Rev. Ronald Saucci, M.M., director, Maryknoll Fathers, Walsh Building, Maryknoll, N.Y. 10545.

National Franciscan Communications Conference: Rev. James J. Gardiner, S.A., president, Graymoor, Garrison, N.Y. 10524.

National Sisters Communications Service: Sister Elizabeth Thoman, C.H.M., executive director, 1962 S. Shenandoah, Los Angeles, Calif. 90034.

National Office

The National Catholic Office for Information (NCOI), successor to the NCWC Bureau of Information, serves as the official spokesman for both the United States Catholic Conference and the National Conference of Catholic Bishops in relating to the news media. The NCOI is part of the NCCB USCC Office for Public Affairs.

The office prepares and distributes news releases; handles inquiries from the press; arranges news media coverage of bishops' meetings; offers public information and public relations counsel on a day-to-day basis to the office of the general secretary of the USCC and the NCCB, and to other agencies and staff members; performs a number of special research and writing functions on behalf of the conferences and their staffs.

The office also provides services and coordination for diocesan information offices.

William Ryan is director of the office, which is located at 1312 Massachusetts Ave. N.W., Washington, D.C. 20005.

CPA AWARDS

Catholic Press Association Awards for material published in 1979 were presented during the CPA convention held May 14-16, 1980, at Nashville, Tenn. First-place awards are listed below.

Newspapers

General excellence, national newspapers: *National Catholic Reporter,* Kansas City, Mo.

General excellence, diocesan newspapers: *Prairie Messenger,* Muenster, Saskatchewan, Canada (1-15,000 circ.); *Green Bay Catholic Compass,* Green Bay, Wis. (15,001-34,000 circ.); *The Record,* Louisville, Ky. (over 34,001 circ.).

Best front page: *The Church World* (tabloid), Portland, Me., *The Tennessee Register* (standard), Nashville, Tenn (1-15,000); *El Visitante Dominical* (tabloid), San Antonio, Tex., *The Catholic News* (standard), New York, N.Y. (15,0001-34,000); *The Catholic Standard and Times* (tabloid), Philadelphia, Pa., *The Record* (standard), Louisville, Ky. (over 34,001).

Best campaign in the public interest: *The Monitor,* St. John's, Newfoundland, Canada, for year-long campaign promoting life (1-15,000); *The Sooner Catholic,* Oklahoma City, Okla., for "The Indians of Oklahoma City: A Poor and Forgotten People" (15,001-34,000); *The Catholic Review,* Baltimore, Md., for "The Energy Crisis" (over 34,001).

Best news report originating with a newspaper: *Catholic Northwest Progress,* Seattle, Wash., for "Bishops Visit Penitentiary, See

Need for Church Action." by Tom Miller.

Best background, in-depth or interpretive reporting: *The Long Island Catholic,* Rockville Centre, N.Y., for "SOS Is Being Sent Out on SSI In-Kind Income Rule," by Nancy Dwyer.

Best editorial: *National Catholic Reporter,* Kansas City, Mo., for "How the Church Actually Works" (unsigned).

Best editorial page or section: *Our Sunday Visitor,* Huntington, Ind.

Best human interest feature story: *National Catholic Reporter,* Kansas City, Mo., for "Raising a Child Alone: 'I Want My Baby To Know Who His Mother Was,' " by Pam Bauer.

Best culture, arts and leisure column: *The Catholic Review,* Baltimore, Md., for theatre columns by Thomas M. Kavanagh.

Best spiritual life column: *The Tablet,* Brooklyn, N.Y., for columns by Father James Tahaney.

Best general commentary column: *Catholic Universe Bulletin,* Cleveland, O., for columns by Russ Faist.

Best syndicated column: *NC News Service,* Washington, D.C., for "Washington Letter," by Jim Lackey.

Best youth coverage: *Courier Journal,* Rochester, N.Y., for Rap-Around section.

Best photo story originating with a newspaper: *Catholic Universe Bulletin,* Cleveland, O., for "Youth Crusade," photos and text by Sigmund J. Mikolajczyk.

Best photograph originating with a newspaper: *The Michigan Catholic,* Detroit, Mich., for photo of man and woman receiving Communion under both species by Dwight Cendrowski.

Best example of circulation promotion: *Chicago Catholic,* Chicago, Ill.

Best special supplement or special issue with editorial emphasis: *St. Cloud Visitor,* St. Cloud, Minn., for "The Pope in Iowa," photos by Vern Bartos, Sister Nancy Bauer, Rosemary Borgert, Dan Musielewicz, Father Ralph Zimmerman.

Best special issue, section or supplement: *The Pilot,* Boston, Mass., 150th anniversary issue.

Best example of effective advertising promotion: *The Monitor,* St. John's, Newfoundland, Canada.

Special Awards for Spanish Material

Best news article in Spanish: *El Visitante Dominical,* San Antonio, Tex., for "Belinda y Sus Dos Hijos," by Irene Sendin.

Best editorial or column: *El Visitante Dominical,* San Antonio, Tex., for "Derechos Humanos en los Estados Unidos," by Juan Jose Gloria.

Best feature article: *The Tablet,* Brooklyn, N.Y., for "El Matrimonio," by Angel Torres.

Magazines

General excellence: *U.S. Catholic* (general interest); *Maryknoll* (mission); *National Jesuit News* (religious order); *Columbia* and *Catholic Lawyer* (professional and special interest); *Pastoral Life* (clergy and religious); *Theological Studies* and *Communio* (scholarly); *God's Word Today* (devotional/inspirational); *Word One,* Claretian Publications (newsletters).

Best cover: *Catholic Charismatic,* June/July (four color, large-size magazine); *Catholic Near East Magazine,* Fall issue (four color, small-size magazine); *The Priest,* July/Aug. (two or three color, large size); *God's Word Today,* October (two or three color, small size); *The Priest,* September (one color, large size); *Way of St. Francis,* January (one color, small size).

Best short story: *Commonweal,* for "Scenes," by Stephen Darst.

Best article originating with the magazine (tie for first place): *Hospital Progress,* for "Abortion: A Changing Morality and Policy?" by Rev. Richard A. McCormick, S.J., and *Columbia,* for "The Secular Sickness," by James Hitchcock.

Best editorial: *Maryknoll,* for "Humanity in Harmony with Earth," by Rev. Darryl L. Hunt, M.M.

Best regular column originating with magazine: *Columbia,* for "Vatican," by Rev. Robert A. Graham, S.J.

Best single photo originating with magazine: *Glenmary's Challenge,* for "Midwife," by Rev. Patrick O'Donnell (large-size magazine); *Maryknoll,* for photo of happy oriental children by Eric Wheater (small-size magazine).

Best photo story originating with magazine: *U.S. Catholic,* for "Brother, Can You Spare Some Time?" photos by Ed Lettau; text by Brian Doyle (large-size magazine); *Maryknoll,* for "In Cities, Life Vies with Death," photos by Eric Wheater and Morgan Vittengl, M.M.; text by Moises Sandoval (small-size magazine).

Best illustration either with art work or photography: *Verona Missions,* for photo of child in a daffodil field by Joanne Moser Gibbons (large-size magazine); *Maryknoll,* for photos by Arthur Tress for "Alone and Abandoned" by Daniel P. Roy (small-size magazine).

Best poetry: *Commonweal,* for "The Weihnachts — Historie," by Anne Porter.

Best treatment on prayer: *U.S. Catholic,* for "Prayer: Just What Do You Think You're Doing?" by Father John Shea.

Best special issue, section or supplement: *Hospital Progress,* for "The Hospice Alternative: Sponsorship, Organizational, Financing, Accreditation, Pastoral, Ethical Issues."

Best single piece of promotion: *St. Anthony Messenger.*

Best interview: *CRUX of Prayer,* for "He

Kept His Vow — Survivor Priest at 74," Patricia A. Crewell's interview of Rev. Walter Ciszek.

Best review or review section: *New Catholic World,* for James Brown's review of "Human Sexuality: A Preliminary Study."

CHRISTOPHER AWARDS

Christopher Awards were presented Feb. 28, 1980, in New York City to writers, directors and producers for their work in books, motion pictures and television.

Award winners were selected on the basis of works which embodied artistic and technical excellence and which had received a significant degree of public acceptance as well as affirming the highest value of the human spirit.

The award is a bronze medallion which bears the Christopher motto: "Better to light one candle than to curse the darkness."

Books for Adults

Blessings, Mary Craig; Morrow.
The Dancing Wu Li Masters, Gary Zukav; Murrow.
A Distant Grief, Kefa Sempangi with Barbara Thompson; Regal.
The Habit of Being: Letters of Flannery O'Connor, selected and edited by Sally Fitzgerald; Farrar, Straus and Giroux.
Lest Innocent Blood Be Shed, Philip Hallie; Harper and Row.
The Medusa and the Snail, Lewis Thomas; Viking.
The Rise of Theodore Roosevelt, Edmund Morris; Coward, McCann and Geoghegan.
The Sinking Ark, Norman Myers; Pergamon Press.
Scott Was Here, Elaine Ipswitch; Delacorte.

Books for Children

Frederick's Alligator, Esther Allen Peterson, illustrated by Susanna Natti; Crown; ages 5-8.
What Happened in Hamelin, Gloria Skurzynski; Four Winds Press; ages 9-12.
All Together Now, Sue Ellen Bridgers; Alfred A. Knopf; ages 12 and up.
The New York Kid's Book, edited by Catharine Edmonds, Joan Gross, Olga Litowinsky, Stephen Mooser, Pamela Morton, Barbara Beasley Murphy, Barbara Seuling, Bebe Willoughby; Doubleday.

Motion Pictures

"The American Game," World Northal. Anthony Jones, Jay Freund and David Wolf.
"The Black Stallion," United Artists. Francis Coppola, Fred Roos, Tom Sternberg, Carroll Ballard, Melissa Mathison, Jeanne Rosenberg and William D. Wittlitt.
"Breaking Away," Twentieth Century-Fox. Peter Yates; Steve Tesich.

"The China Syndrome," Columbia. Bruce Gilbert, Michael Douglas, James Bridges, Mike Gray, T. S. Cook.
"Norma Rae," Twentieth Century-Fox; Tamara Asseyev, Alex Rose, Martin Ritt, Irving Ravetch and Harriet Frank, Jr.
"The Tree of Wooden Clogs," World Northal. Anthony Jones, Jay Freund and David Wolf.

Television

"ABC News Closeup: The Killing Ground," ABC; Pamela Hill, Steve Singer, Tom Priestley, Brit Hume, Michael Connor, Steve Singer.
"... And Your Name Is Jonah," CBS; Charles Fries, Norman Felton, Stanley Rubin, Richard Michaels, Michael Bortman.
"Aunt Mary," CBS; Henry Jaffe, Ellis A. Cohen, Michael Jaffe, Peter Werner, Burt Prelutsky.
"CBS Reports: How Much for the Handicapped?" CBS; Howard Stringer, Marlene Sanders.
"Friendly Fire," ABC; Martin Starger, Philip Barry, David Greene, Fay Kanin.
"The Incredible Journey of Dr. Meg Laurel," CBS; Ron Samuels, Paul Radin, Guy Green, Michael Berk, Douglas Schwartz, Joseph Fineman.
"The Late Great Me: Story of a Teenage Alcoholic," ABC; Daniel Wilson, Linda Marmelstein, Anthony Lover, Jan Hartman.
"The Library of Congress: Portrait of an American Institution," WNET/BBC; Humphrey Burton, Ann Turner, Sir H. Wheldon.
"This Man Stands Alone," NBC; Abby Mann, Harry R. Sherman, Jerrold Freedman.
"The Miracle Worker," NBC; Raymond Katz, Sandy Gallin, Fred Coe, Paul Aaron, William Gibson.
"Orphan Train," CBS; Roger Gimbel, Marian Rees, Tony Converse, Dorothea G. Petrie, William A. Graham, Millard Lampell.
"Paul Robeson," PBS; Don Gregory, Lloyd Richards, Phillip Hayes Dean.
"A Shining Season," CBS; Jim Green, Allen Epstein, Harry Thomason, Stuart Margolin, William Harrison.
"Son-Rise: A Miracle of Love," NBC; Bernard Rothman, Jack Wohl, Richard Rosenbloom, Glenn Jordan, Stephen Kandel, Barry Neil Kaufman, Suzi Lyte Kaufman.
"Walking Through the Fire," CBS; David Susskind, Stan Hough, Robert Day, Sue Grafton.
"Which Mother Is Mine?" ABC; Martin Tahse, Arthur Seidelman, Durrell Royce Crays.

Honors and Awards

Pontifical Orders

The Pontifical Orders of Knighthood are secular orders of merit whose membership depends directly on the pope. Details regarding the various orders are handled by a special agency in the Secretariat of Briefs, an office in the Papal Secretariat of State.

Supreme Order of Christ (Militia of Our Lord Jesus Christ): The highest of the five pontifical orders of knighthood, the Supreme Order of Christ was approved Mar. 14, 1319, by John XXII as a continuation in Portugal of the suppressed Order of Templars. Members were religious with vows and a rule of life until the order lost its religious character toward the end of the 15th century. Since that time it has existed as an order of merit. Paul VI, in 1966, restricted awards of the order to Christian heads of state.

Order of the Golden Spur (Golden Militia): Although the original founder is not certainly known, this order is one of the oldest knighthoods. Indiscriminate bestowal and inheritance diminished its prestige, however, and in 1841 Gregory XVI replaced it with the Order of St. Sylvester and gave it the title of Golden Militia. In 1905 St. Pius X restored the Order of the Golden Spur in its own right, separating it from the Order of St. Sylvester. Paul VI, in 1966, restricted awards of the order to Christian heads of state.

Order of Pius IX: Founded by Pius IX June 17, 1847, the order is awarded for outstanding services for the Church and society, and may be given to non-Catholics as well as Catholics. The title to nobility formerly attached to membership was abolished by Pius XII in 1939. In 1957 Pius XII instituted the Class of the Grand Collar as the highest category of the order; in 1966, Paul VI restricted this award to heads of state "in solemn circumstances." The other three classes are of Knights of the Grand Cross, Knight Commanders with and without emblem, and Knights. The new class was created to avoid difficulties in presenting papal honors to Christian or non-Christian leaders of high merit.

Order of St. Gregory the Great: First established by Gregory XVI in 1831 to honor citizens of the Papal States, the order is conferred on persons who are distinguished for personal character and reputation, and for notable accomplishment. The order has civil and military divisions, and three classes of knights.

Order of St. Sylvester: Instituted Oct. 31, 1841, by Gregory XVI to absorb the Order of the Golden Spur, this order was divided into two by St. Pius X in 1905, one retaining the name of St. Sylvester and the other assuming the title of Golden Militia. Membership consists of three degrees: Knights of the Grand Cross, Knight Commanders with and without emblem, and Knights.

Ecclesiastical Order

Order of the Holy Sepulchre: Critical opinion is divided regarding various details of the history of the order. It is certain, however, that these knights first appeared in the Holy Land and were in existence at the end of the 11th century. Some assign earlier dates or origin, claiming as founders St. James the Apostle, first bishop of Jerusalem, and St. Helena, builder of the Basilica of the Holy Sepulchre. Others hold that Godfrey of Bouillon instituted the order in 1099 and that it took its name from the Holy Sepulchre where its members were knighted.

The order lost a great deal of prestige after the fall of the Latin Kingdom of Jerusalem and the consequent departure of the knights from the Holy Land. It was united with the Knights of St. John in 1489, came under the grand mastership of Alexander VI in 1496 and shortly thereafter was split into three national divisions, German, French and Spanish. Pius IX re-established the Latin patriarchate of Jerusalem in 1847 and gave the patriarch the faculty of conferring the order of knighthood. This right had been held by the Franciscan custos following the appointment of the Friars as guardians of the Holy Land in 1342. Three classes of membership were designated in 1868. Leo XIII later instituted the Cross of Honor (which does not confer knighthood) in three classes — gold, silver and bronze — and also the Dames of the Holy Sepulchre. From 1907 to 1928 the pope was grand master, an office now held by a cardinal. Revised statutes for the order went into effect in 1949, 1962 and 1967. The 1949 constitution enjoined the knights "to revive in modern form the spirit and ideal of the Crusades with the weapons of faith, the apostolate, and Christian charity."

The Order of the Holy Sepulchre now has five classes: 12 Knights of the Collar and four degrees, with separate divisions of each for men and women — Grand Cross, Commanders with Plaque, Commanders and Knights. Three honorary decorations are awarded, vis., Palm of the Order, Cross of Merit (which may be bestowed on non-Catholics), and the Pilgrim's Shell.

Investiture ceremonies combine a profession of faith with the ancient ritual of knighthood dubbing. Candidates do not take monastic vows but pledge an upright Christian life and loyalty to the pope.

The grand master of the order is Cardinal Maximilien de Furstenberg.

There are four lieutenancies of the order in the United States.

Order of Malta

The Sovereign Military Hospitaller Order of St. John of Jerusalem of Rhodes and of Malta traces its origin to a group of men who maintained a Christian hospital in the Holy Land in the 11th century. The group was approved as a religious order — the Hospitallers of St. John — by Paschal II in 1113.

The order, while continuing its service to the poor, principally in hospital work, assumed military duties in the twelfth century and included knights, chaplains and sergeants-at-arms among its members. All the knights were professed monks with the vows of poverty, chastity and obedience. Headquarters were located in the Holy Land until the last decade of the 13th century and on Rhodes after 1308 (whence the title, Knights of Rhodes).

After establishing itself on Rhodes, the order became a sovereign power like the sea republics of Italy and the Hanseatic cities of Germany, flying its own flag, coining its own money, floating its own navy, and maintaining diplomatic relations with many nations.

The order was forced to abandon Rhodes in 1522 after the third siege of the island by the Turks under Sultan Suliman I. Eight years later, the Knights were given the island of Malta, where they remained as a bastion of Christianity until near the end of the 18th century. Headquarters have been located in Rome since 1834.

The title of Grand Master of the Order, in abeyance for some time, was restored by Leo XIII in 1879. A more precise definition of both the religious and the sovereign status of the order was embodied in a new constitution of 1961 and a code issued in 1966.

Religious aspects of the order are subject to regulation by the Holy See. At the same time the sovereignty of the order, which is based on international law, is recognized by the Holy See and by 41 countries with which full diplomatic relations are maintained.

The four main classifications of members are: Knights of Justice, who are religious with the vows of poverty, chastity and obedience; Knights of Obedience, who make a solemn promise to strive for Christian perfection; Knights of Honor and Devotion and of Grace and Devotion, of noble lineage; and Knights of Magistral Grace. There are also chaplains, Dames and Donats of the order.

The order, with five grand priories, three sub-priories and 37 national associations, is devoted to hospital and charitable work of all kinds in some 68 countries.

The Grand Master, who is the sovereign head of the order, has the title of Most Eminent Highness with the rank of Cardinal. He must be of noble lineage and under solemn vows for a minimum period of 10 years.

The present Grand Master is Fra' Angelo de Mojana di Cologna, a lawyer of Milan, who was elected for life May 8, 1962, by the Council of State.

The address of headquarters of the order is Via Condotti, Palazzo Malta, 00187 Roma, Italia.

Papal Medals

Pro Ecclesia et Pontifice: This decoration ("For the Church and the Pontiff") had its origin in 1888 as a token of the golden sacerdotal jubilee of Leo XIII; he bestowed it on those who had assisted in the observance of his jubilee and on persons responsible for the success of the Vatican Exposition. The medal bears the likeness of Leo XIII on one side; on the other, the tiara, the papal keys, and the words *Pro Ecclesia et Pontifice*. Originally, the medal was issued in gold, silver or bronze. St. Pius X ordered that it be of gold only. It is awarded in recognition of service to the Church and the papacy.

Benemerenti: Several medals ("To a well-deserving person") have been conferred by popes for exceptional accomplishment and service. The medals, which are made of gold, silver or bronze, bear the likeness and name of the reigning pope on one side; on the other, a laurel crown and the letter "B."

These two medals may be given by the pope to both men and women. Their bestowal does not convey any title or honor of knighthood.

AMERICAN CATHOLIC AWARDS

Aquinas Medal, by the American Catholic Philosophical Association for outstanding contributions to the field of Catholic philosophy.

Jacques Maritain (1951), Etienne Gilson (1952), Gerald Smith, S.J. (1955), Gerald B. Phelan (1959), Rudolf Allers (1960), James A. McWilliams, S.J. (1961) Charles De Koninck (1964), James Collins (1965).

Martin C. D'Arcy (1967), Dr. Josef Pieper (1968), Leo R. Ward (1969), Bernard Lonergan, S.J. (1970), Henry B. Veatch (1971), Joseph Owens, C.SS.R. (1972), A. Hilary Armstrong (1973), Cornelio Fabro (1974), Anton Pegis (1975), Mortimer J. Adler (1976), Frederick C. Copleston (1977), Fernand Van Steenberghen (1978), John Paul II (1979), W. Norris Clarke, S.J. (1980).

Bellarmine Medal (1955), by Bellarmine College (Louisville, Ky.), to persons in national or international affairs who, in controversial matters, exemplify the characteristics of St. Robert Bellarmine in charity, justice and temperateness.

Jefferson Caffery (1955), Gen. Carlos Romulo (1956), U.S. Rep. John W. McCormack (1957), Frank M. Folsom (1958), Robert D. Murphy (1959), James P. Mitchell

(1960), Frederick H. Boland (1961);

Gen. Alfred M. Gruenther (1962), Henry Cabot Lodge (1963), R. Sargent Shriver (1964), Irene Dunne (1965), Sen. Everett M. Dirksen (1966), Nicholas Katzenbach (1967), Danny Thomas (1968), J. Irwin Miller (1969), Theodore M. Hesburgh, C.S.C. (1970), Sen. John Sherman Cooper (1971), (no award, 1972), Dr. William B. Walsh (1973), Most Rev. Fulton J. Sheen (1974), William F. Buckley, Jr. (1977), Rev. Jesse L. Jackson (1979).

Borromeo Award (1960), by Carroll College (Helena, Mont.), for zeal, courage and devotion in the spirit of St. Charles Borromeo.

William D. Murray (1960), Robert E. Sullivan (1961), Vincent H. Walsh (1962), Leo V. Kelly (1963), Joseph A. Kimmet (1964), Dr. W. E. Long (1965), Frank E. Blair (1968), Gough, Booth, Shanahan and Johnson (1971), Egon E. Mallman, S.J. (1973), Christian Brothers of Ireland (1974), Most Rev. Raymond Hunthausen (1975), Dominican Sisters of Spokane, Wash., of the Province of the Immaculate Heart of Mary (1976), Rev. Emmett Shea (1977), Most Rev. Eldon B. Schuster (1978), Rev. Paul B. Kirchen (1979). Sister Alice Ann Byrne, O.P. (1980).

Brent Award (1976), by the Diocese of Arlington, Va., for distinguished service to fellowman.

Dr. Mildred F. Jefferson (1976), Most Rev. John J. Russell (1977), U.S. Rep. Henry J. Hyde and William B. Ball, Esq. (1978), Mrs. Hazel Hagarty (1979).

Campion Award (1955), by the Catholic Book Club for distinguished service in Catholic letters.

Jacques Maritain (1955), Helen C. White (1956), Paul Horgan (1957), James Brodrick, S.J. (1958), Sister M. Madeleva (1959), Frank J. Sheed and Maisie Ward (1960), John La Farge, S.J. (1961), Harold C. Gardiner, S.J. (1962);

T. S. Eliot (1963), Barbara Ward (1964), Msgr. John T. Ellis (1965), John Courtney Murray, S.J. (1966), Phyllis McGinley (1967), Dr. George N. Shuster (1968), G. B. Harrison (1970), Walter and Jean Kerr (1971), Karl Rahner, S.J. (1974), John J. Delaney (1976).

Cardinal Gibbons Medal (1949) by the Alumni Association of the Catholic University of America for distinguished and meritorious service to the Church, the United States or the Catholic University.

Carlton J. H. Hayes (1949), Gen. Carlos P. Romulo (1950), Fulton Oursler (1951), Most Rev. Fulton J. Sheen (1953), J. Edgar Hoover (1954), Gen. J. Lawton Collins (1955), U.S. Sen. John F. Kennedy and Ignatius Smith, O.P. (1956), Most Rev. Bryan J. McEntegart (1957), Thomas E. Murray (1958);

Gen. Alfred M. Gruenther (1959), Karl F. Herzfeld (1960), Charles G. Fenwick (1961), Luke E. Hart (1962), John W. McCormack

(1963), John A. McCone (1964), R. Sargent Shriver (1965), James J. Norris (1967), Danny Thomas (1968), Theodore Hesburgh, C.S.C. (1969), Dr. Carroll Hochwalt (1970), Danny Thomas (1971), Cardinal Patrick O'Boyle (1972), Helen Hayes (1973), Sen. Mike Mansfield (1974), Judge John J. Sirica (1975), Cardinal Lawrence Shehan (1976), Benjamin T. Rome (1977), Dr. Clarence C. Walton (1978), Cardinal Terence Cooke (1979), Cardinal William Baum (1980).

Cardinal Spellman Award (1947), by the Catholic Theological Society for outstanding achievement in the field of theology.

Revs. Francis J. Connell, C.SS.R., Emmanuel Doronzo, O.M.I., Gerald Yelle, S.S., William R. O'Connor, John C. Murray, S.J. (1947); Eugene Burke, C.S.P. (1948), Bernard J. J. Lonergan, S.J. (1949), John C. Murray, S.J. (1950), Msgr. William R. O'Connor (1951), Emmanuel Doronzo, O.M.I. (1952), Gerald Kelly, S.J. (1953), Francis J. Connell, C.SS.R. (1954), Edmond D. Benard (1955), John C. Ford, S.J. (1956);

Gerard Yelle, S.S. (1957), Msgr. Joseph C. Fenton (1958), Juniper Carol, O.F.M. (1959), Rev. John Quasten (1960), Cyril C. Vollert, S.J. (1961), Walter J. Burghardt, S.J. (1962), Rev. Francis Dvornik (1963), Barnabas Ahern, C.P. (1964), Godfrey Diekmann, O.S.B. (1965), Paul K. Meagher, O.P. (1966), John L. McKenzie, S.J. (1967), Dr. Martin R. P. McGuire (1968), Richard A. McCormick, S.J. (1969), Avery Dulles, S.J. (1970), Raymond E. Brown, S.S. (1971).

For recipients after 1971, see John Courtney Murray Award.

Catholic Action Medal (1934), by St. Bonaventure University (St. Bonaventure, N.Y.).

Alfred E. Smith (1934), Michael Williams (1935), Joseph Scott (1936), Patrick Scanlan (1937), George J. Gillespie (1938), William F. Montavon (1939), John J. Craig (1940), John S. Burke (1941), Dr. George Speri Sperti (1942), Francis P. Matthews (1943);

Jefferson Caffery (1944), John A. Coleman (1945), David Goldstein (1946), Clement Lane (1947), Paul W. Weber (1948), Bruce M. Mohler (1949), Edward M. O'Connor (1950), Richard F. Pattee (1951), James M. O'Neill (1952), John E. Swift (1953);

Frank M. Folsom (1954), Walter L. McGuiness (1955), Carlton J. H. Hayes (1956), Thomas E. Murray (1957), Paul V. Murray (1958), Dr. John L. Madden (1959), Christopher H. Dawson (1960), Stephen Kuttner (1961), Charles De Koninck (1962), Lt. Gen. G. Trudeau (1963), Frank J. Sheed (1964), Danny Thomas (1965), Walter and Jean Kerr (1966), Sir Hugh Stott Taylor (1967), Maurice Lavanoux (1968).

The Catholic University of America Patronal Medal (1974), by the University for outstanding contributions to the Catholic Church and in promoting interest and devotion to Mary, patroness of the University.

Most Rev. Fulton J. Sheen (1974), Sister M. Claudia Honsberger, I.H.M. (1975), Rev. Theodore A. Koehler (1976), Rev. Ross MacKenzie, Presbyterian clergyman (1977), (No award, 1978), Cardinal John J. Carberry, Mother Teresa (1979).

Cecilia Medal (1952), by the Music Department of Boys Town (Nebr.) for outstanding work in liturgical music.

Winifred T. Flanagan (1952), Dom Francis Missia (1953), Omer Westendorf (1954), Dom Ermin Vitry (1955), William A. Reilly (1956), Flor Peeters (1957), Roger Wagner (1958), Most Rev. Gerald T. Bergan (1959), Francis T. Brunner, C.SS.R. (1960), Jean Langlois (1961);

James B. Welch (1962), W. Ripley Dorr (1963), C. Alexander Peloquin (1964), Dr. Louise Cuyler (1965), Dr. Eugene Selhorst (1966), Dr. Paul Manz (1967), Myron J. Roberts (1968), Norman T. Letter (1969), Rev. Elmer Pfeil (1969), Rev. Richard Schuler (1970), Frank Szynski (1979), Evelyn Letter (1980).

Christian Culture Award (1941), by Assumption University (Canada) to outstanding lay exponents of Christian ideals.

Sigrid Undset (1941), Jacques Maritain (1942), Philip Murray (1943), Frank J. Sheed (1944), Arnold M. Walter (1945), Henry Ford II (1946), George S. Sperti (1947), Richard Pattee (1948), Etienne Gilson (1949), Paul Doyon (1950), Christopher Dawson (1951), John C.H. Wu (1952);

Charles Malik (1953), Ivan Mestrovic (1954), F. W. Foerster (1955), Paul Martin (1956), Robert Speaight (1947), Allen Tate (1958), Barbara Ward (1959), John Cogley (1960), Peter Drucker (1961), Benjamin E. Mays (1962), John Quincy Adams (1963);

William Foxwell Albright (1964), Dr. Karl Stern (1965), John Howard Griffin (1966), Edith K. Peterkin (1967), Dr. Mircea Eliade (1968), Dr. James D. Collins (1969), Dorothy Day (1970), Dr. Marshall McLuhan (1971), James M. Cameron (1972), Jean Vanier (1973), Robert J. Kreyche (1974), John T. Noonan, Jr. (1975), Dorothy Donnelly (1976), William Kurelek (1977), Anthony Walsh (1978), Malcolm Muggeridge (1979), Conrad W. Baars, M.D. (1980).

Collegian Award (1949), by "The Collegian," weekly student newspaper of La Salle College (Phila.), for public service in the field of communications.

Ed Sullivan (1949), Morley Cassidy (1950), Bob Considine (1951), Red Smith (1952), George Sokolsky (1953), Edward R. Murrow (1954), David Lawrence (1955), Jim Bishop (1956), Richard W. Slocum (1957), Chet Huntley (1958);

John C. O'Brien (1959), Walter Cronkite (1960), David Brinkley (1961), James Reston (1962), Charles Collingwood (1963), Art Buchwald (1964), Nancy Dickerson (1965), Charles Schulz (1966), Sandy Grady (1967), Harrison E. Salisbury (1968), Ralph W. Howard (1969), (not awarded 1970-77), Lawrence M. O'Rourke (1978).

Damien-Dutton Award (1953), by the Damien-Dutton Society for service toward conquest of leprosy or for the promotion of better understanding of social problems connected with the disease.

Stanley Stein (1953), Joseph Sweeney, M.M. (1954), Sister Marie Suzanne (1955), Dr. Perry Burgess (1956), John Farrow (1957), Dr. H. Windsor Wade (1958), Sister Hilary Ross (1959), Msgr. Louis J. Mendelis (1960), Dr. Kensuke Mitsuda (1961), Pierre d'Orgeval, SS.CC. (1962);

Eunice Weaver (1963), Dr. Robert Cochrane (1964), John F. Kennedy, posthumously (1965), The Peace Corps (1966), Dr. Howard A. Rusk (1967), Dr. Frans Hemerijckx (1968), Dr. Victor G. Heiser (1969), Dr. Dharmendra (1970), Dr. Chapman H. Binford (1971), Dr. Patricia Smith (1972), Dr. Jacinto Convit (1973), Dr. Jose N. Rodriguez (1974), Dr. Oliver Hasselblad (1975), Dr. Yoshio Yoshie (1976), Drs. Paul and Margaret Brand (1977), Dr. Fernando Latapi (1978), Dr. Stanley Browne (1979).

Edith Stein Award (1955), by the Edith Stein Guild for service toward better understanding between Christians and Jews.

Sister Noemi de Sion (1956), Authur B. Klyber, C.SS.R. (1957), Rev. John M. Oesterreicher (1958), John J. O'Connor (1959), Victor J. Donovan, C.P. (1960), Jacques and Raissa Maritain (1961), Gerard E. Sherry (1962), Mother Kathryn Sullivan, R.S.C.J. (1963), Paulist Press (1964), Rev. Edward N. Flannery (1965), Mother Katherine Hargrove, R.S.C.J. (1966), Gregory Baum, O.S.A. (1967), Sr. Rose Albert Thering (1968), Msgr. Vincent O. Genova (1969), Dr. Joseph Lichten (1970), Philip Scharper (1971), Rabbi Marc Tanenbaum (1972), Leon Paul (1973).

Emmanuel D'Alzon Medal (1954), by Assumptionists to persons exemplifying the ideals of their founder.

Jacques Maritain (1954), Michael F. Doyle (1955), Cardinal Richard J. Cushing (1956), Mother Mary St. Elizabeth (1956), Most Rev. John J. Wright (1959), Paolino Gerli (1960), Most Rev. Honoré van Waeyenbergh (1961), J. Peter Grace (1963), Danny Thomas (1967), Miss Mary Dowd, posthumously (1970), Most Rev. Bernard J. Flanagan (1974), Mother Helene-Marie Bories, S.A., and Cardinal Johannes Willebrands (1980).

Father McKenna Award (1950), by the national headquarters of the Holy Name Society, for outstanding service to the society's ideals.

Msgr. John J. Murphy, Msgr. Henry J. Watterson, Msgr. Frederic J. Allchin (1950),

Eustace Struckhoff, O.F.M., Msgr. Joseph A. McCaffrey, Msgr. Francis P. Connelly, Rev. Raymond E. Jones, Msgr. Joseph E. Maguire, Msgr. Edward J. Kelly, Msgr. J. Frederick Kriebs, Rev. Thomas E. O'Connell, Very Rev. Charles L. Elslander, Rev. Joseph J. Heim, Msgr. F. Borgias Lehr (1951);

Rev. Francis J. Hannegan (1954), Rev. Charles A. Hoot, Rev. Louis A. Hinnebusch, O.P., Rev. John O. Purcell, Rev. Paul M. Lackner (1955), Msgr. F. J. Timoney (1958), Rev. Thomas F. McNicholas (1960), James A. Quinn, O.P., and Rev. John C. Griffith (1961), Msgr. Joseph A. Aughney (1962), Msgr. Cornelius P. Higgins (1963), Msgr. Charles P. Mynaugh (1964), Msgr. Charles P. Muth, Rev. Patrick J. Foley (1971), Rev. Msgr. Robert T. Kickham (1973), Rev. John D. Malone, O.P. (1975), Rev. John Bendix (1977), Msgr. Joseph Coughlin (1979).

Franciscan International Award (1958), by the Conventual Franciscans (Prior Lake, Minn.) for outstanding contributions to the American way of life.

Mr. and Mrs. Ignatius A. O'Shaughnessy (1959), Archbishop William O. Brady (1960), Lawrence Welk (1961), Charles Kellstad (1962), Dr. Finn J. Larsen (1963), Dr. Charles W. Mayo (1964), Ara Parseghian (1965), F. K. Weyerhaueser (1966);

Alcoholics Anonymous (1967), James T. Griffin (1968), George S. Harris (1969), Baroness Catherine DeHueck Doherty (1970), Harry Reasoner (1971), Dr. Billy Graham (1972), Dr. and Mrs. John C. Willke (1973), Gov. Patrick J. Lucey (1974), Joe and Jan Rigert (1975), Dr. B. F. Pearson (1976), Francis S. MacNutt, O.P. (1977), Dr. Mildred F. Jefferson (1978), Bruce Ritter, O.F.M. Conv. (1979), John E. McCarthy (1980).

George M. Cohan Award (1970), by the Catholic Actors Guild of America, Inc., for outstanding contribution to Church and the arts.

Gilbert V. Hartke, O.P. (1970), Ruby Keeler (1971), Frances Fuller and Worthington Miner (1972), Patsy Kelly (1973), Earl Wilson (1974), Kate Smith (1975), Hildegarde (1976), Jack O'Brian (1977), Bishop Edwin B. Broderick (1978), Claudette Colbert (1979), Frederick O'Neal (1980).

Good Samaritan Award (1968), by the National Catholic Development Conference to recognize the concern for one's fellowman exemplified by the Good Samaritan.

Bishop Edward E. Swanstrom (1968), Berard Scarborough, O.F.M. (1969), Bishop Joseph B. Whelan, C.S.Sp. (1970), Mother Teresa (1971), Bishop Michael R. Dempsey (1972), Msgr. Ralph W. Beiting (1973), Rev. Daniel Egan, S.A. (1974), Dr. Isabel S. Dumont and Joan Mulder (1975), Msgr. Clement H. Kern (1976), Sister Maria Rosa Leggol, S.S.S.F. (1977), Bruce Ritter, O.F.M.

Conv. (1978), Rev. William Wasson (1979).

Hoey Awards (1942), by the Catholic Interracial Council of New York (225 E. 52nd St., New York, N.Y. 10022) for the promotion of interracial justice. Presented annually to two persons who have worked to promote social and interracial justice.

Frank A. Hall and Edward La Salle (1942), Philip Murray and Ralph H. Metcalfe (1943), Mrs. Edward V. Morrell and John L. Yancey (1944), Paul D. Williams and Richard Barthe (1945), Richard Reid and Charles L. Rawlings (1946), Julian J. Reiss and Clarence T. Hunter (1947), Mrs. Anna McGarry and Ferdinand L. Rousseve (1948), John J. O'Connor and M. C. Clarke (1949), J. Howard McGrath and Lou Montgomery (1950), Mrs. Roger L. Putnam and Francis M. Hammond (1951);

Charles F. Vatterot, Jr., and Joseph J. Yancey (1952), Joseph J. Morrow and John B. King (1953), Mrs. Gladys D. Woods and Collins J. Seitz (1954), Millard F. Everett and Dr. James W. Hose (1955), Frank M. Folsom and Paul G. King (1956), George Meany and James W. Dorsey (1957), James T. Harris and Robert S. Shriver, Jr. (1958), Percy H. Steele, Jr., and John P. Nelson (1959);

William Duffy, Jr., and George A. Moore (1960), Ralph Fenton and Mrs. Osma Spurlock (1961), Benjamin Muse and Dr. Eugene T. Reed (1962), James T. Carey and Percy H. Williams (1963), Arthur J. Holland and Frederick O'Neal (1964), Gerard E. Sherry and James R. Dumpson (1965), Jane M. Hoey and Mrs. Roy Wilkins (1966), Dr. Frank Horne and Lt. Gov. Malcolm Wilson (1967), E. H. Molisani and John Strachan (1968);

Harold E. McGannon and Hulan E. Jack (1969), George P. McManus, Alfred B. Del Bello, Maceo A. Thomas and Cleo Joseph L. Froix, M.D. (1970), Most Rev. Francis J. Mugavero and Most Rev. Harold R. Perry (1971), Joseph F. Crangle and Alen E. Pinado (1972), Meade H. Esposito and Robert B. Boyd (1973), Hon. Harold A. Stevens and Thomas Van Arsdale (1974), Hon. Kenneth E. Sherwood, Joseph Trerotola (1975), William M. Ellinghaus and Hon. Lucille Rose (1976), Hon. Carlos Romero Barcelo and Lena Horne (1977), J. Peter Grace and Hon. Basil A. Paterson (1978), Helen Hayes, Felisa Rincon de Gautier and Cecil E. Ward (1979).

Honor et Veritas Award (1959), by the Catholic War Veterans to outstanding Americans.

Cardinal Francis J. Spellman (1960), Gen. Douglas MacArthur (1961), U. S. Sen. Thomas J. Dodd (1962), Gen. William Westmoreland (1966), Dean Rusk (1967), Col. Martin T. Riley (1968), Theodore M. Hesburgh, C.S.C. (1969), Kenneth D. Wells (1970), Danny Thomas (1971), Thomas V. Cuite (1972), Lawrence Welk (1973), Congressman Melvin Price (1975).

Howard R. Marraro Prize (1973), by the American Catholic Historical Association for a book on Italian history or Italo-American history or relations.

Eric W. Cochrane (1974), Silvano Tomasi (1975), Sarah Rubin Blanshei (1977), Paul F. Grendler (1978), David R. Coffin (1979).

Insignis Medal (1951), by Fordham University for extraordinary distinction in the service of God and humanity.

Dr. Carlos Espinosa Davila, Arthur H. Hayes (1955), Pierre Harmel, Victor Andres Belaunde (1956), M. E. Michelet (1957), Daniel Linehan, S.J., Dr. Victor F. Hess (1958), Dr. George N. Shuster, John H. Tully, Albert Conway (1959), Charles F. Vatterot, Cardinal Agagianian, Charles Norman and Lucy W. Shaffer, David C. Cronin, S.J. (1960);

Cardinal Spellman (1961), Edward P. Gilleran (1962), Joseph A. Martino, William J. Tracy (1963), Brother James M. Kenny, S.J., and Austin Ripley (1966), Vincent T. Lombardi (1967), Melkite Patriarch Maximos V Hakim of Antioch (1968), Joseph and Marian Kaiser (1970), Joseph P. Routh (1973), Edgar Debany and Cardinal Sergio Pignedoli (1975), Eugene J. O'Brien, S.J. (1980).

John Courtney Murray Award (1972), by the Catholic Theological Society for distinguished achievement in theology. Originated in 1947 as the Cardinal Spellman Award.

Rev. Charles E. Curran (1972), Bernard Lonergan, S.J. (1973), George A. Tavard, A.A. (1974), Rev. Carl Peter (1975), Rev. Richard P. McBrien (1976), Frederick E. Crowe (1977), Edward J. Kilmartin, S.J. (1978), Bernard Cooke (1979), David Tracy (1980).

John Gilmary Shea Prize (1944), by the American Catholic Historical Association for scholarly works on the history of the Catholic Church broadly considered.

Carlton J. H. Hayes (1946), John H. Kennedy (1950), George W. Pare (1951), Rev. Philip Hughes (1954), Annabelle M. Melville (1955), Rev. John Tracy Ellis (1956), Rev. Thomas J. McAvoy, C.S.C. (1957), Rev. John M. Daley, S.J. (1958), Rev. Robert A. Graham, S.J. (1959);

Rev. Maynard Geiger, O.F.M. (1960), Rev. John C. Murray, S.J. (1961), Francis Dvornik (1962), Oscar Halecki (1963), Helen C. White (1964), John T. Noonan (1965), Rev. Robert I. Burns, S.J. (1966 and 1967), Rev. Edward S. Surtz, S.J. (1968), Robert Brentano (1969), David M. Kennedy (1970), Jaroslav Pelikan (1971), John T. Noonan (1972), Robert E. Quirk (1973), Bro. Thomas W. Spalding, C.F.X. (1974), Jay P. Dolan (1975), Emmet Larkin (1976), Timothy Tackett (1977), Charles W. Jones (1978), Kenneth M. Setton (1979).

John La Farge Memorial Award for Interracial Justice (1965), by the Catholic Interracial Council of New York. Presented annually to a leading citizen of the community regardless of race, color or creed for promoting social and interracial justice.

Cardinal Francis J. Spellman (1965), U.S. Sen. Jacob K. Javits (1966), Gov. Nelson Rockefeller (1967), George F. Meany (1968), Whitney M. Young, Jr. (1969), Harry Van Arsdale, Jr. (1970), John V. Lindsay (1971), Earl W. Brydges (1972), Louis K. Lefkowitz (1973), Arthur Levitt (1974), Robert F. Wagner (1975), Gustave L. Levy (1976), Cardinal Terence Cooke (1977), E. Howard Molisani (1978), Gov. Hugh L. Carey (1979).

King Award (1971), by the U.S. Catholic Historical Society for significant contribution in the study of the history of the Catholic Church in t he U.S.

Jeremiah F. O'Sullivan (1971), Oskar Halecki (1972), Ross J. S. Hoffman (1973), Joseph G. E. Hopkins (1974), Victor L. Ridder (1975), Elisa A. Carrillo (1976).

Laetare Medal (1883), by the University of Notre Dame for distinguished accomplishment for Church or nation by an American Catholic.

John Gilmary Shea (1883), Patrick J. Keeley (1884), Eliza Allen Starr (1885), Gen. John Newton (1886), Edward Preuss (1887), Patrick V. Hickey (1888), Mrs. A. H. Dorsey (1889), William J. Onahan (1890), Daniel Dougherty (1891), Henry F. Brownson (1892);

Patrick Donahoe (1893), Augustin Daly (1894), Mrs. James Sadlier (1895), Gen. William S. Rosecrans (1896), Dr. Thomas A. Emmet (1897), Timothy E. Howard (1898), Mary G. Caldwell (1899), John Creighton (1900), William B. Cochran (1901, Dr. J. B. Murphy (1902);

Charles J. Bonaparte (1903), Richard C. Kerens (1904), Thomas B. Fitzpatrick (1905), Dr. Francis Quinlan (1906), Katherine E. Conway (1907), James C. Monaghan (1908), Frances Tiernan (Christian Reid) (1909), Maurice F. Egan (1910), Agnes Repplier (1911), Thomas M. Mulry (1912);

Charles G. Hebermann (1913), Edward Douglass White (1914), Mary V. Merrick (1915), Dr. James J. Walsh (1916), Admiral William S. Benson (1917), Joseph Scott (1918), George Duval (1919), Dr. Lawrence F. Flick (1920), Elizabeth Nourse (1921), Charles P. Neil (1922);

Walter G. Smith (1923), Charles D. Maginnis (1924), Dr. Edward F. Zahm (1925), Edward N. Hurley (1926), Margaret Anglin (1927), Jack J. Spalding (1928), Alfred E. Smith (1929), Frederick P. Kenkel (1930), James J. Phelan (1931), Dr. Stephen J. Maher (1932);

John McCormack (1933), Mrs. Nicholas F. Brady (1943), Frank Spearman (1935), Richard Reid (1936), Jeremiah Ford (1937), Dr. Irvin Abell (1938), Josephine Brownson (1939), Gen. Hugh A. Drum (1940), William T. Walsh (1941), Helen C. White (1942);

Thomas F. Woodlock (1943), Anne O'Hare McCormick (1944), G. Howland Shaw (1945), Carlton J. H. Hayes (1946), William G. Bruce (1947), Frank C. Walker (1948), Irene Dunne (Mrs. Francis Griffin) (1949), Gen. Joseph L. Collins (1950), John H. Phelan (1951), Thomas E. Murray (1952);

I. A. O'Shaughnessy (1953), Jefferson Caffery (1954), George Meany (1955), Gen. Alfred M. Gruenther (1956), Clare Boothe Luce (1957), Frank M. Folsom (1958), Robert D. Murphy (1959), George N. Shuster (1960), Pres. John F. Kennedy (1961), Dr. Francis J. Braceland (1962);

Adm. George W. Anderson, Jr. (1963), Phyllis McGinley (1964), Frederick D. Rossini (1965), Mr. and Mrs. Patrick F. Crowley (1966), J. Peter Grace (1967), R. Sargent Shriver (1968), Justice William J. Brennan, Jr. (1969), Dr. William D. Walsh (1970), Walter and Jean Kerr (1971), Dorothy Day (1972), Rev. John A. O'Brien (1973), James A. Farley (1974), Sister Ann Ida Gannon, B.V.M. (1975), Paul Horgan (1976), Mike Mansfield (1977), Msgr. John Tracy Ellis (1978), Helen Hayes (1979), Rep. Thomas P. O'Neill, Jr. (1980).

Marianist Award (1949), by the University of Dayton for outstanding service in America to the Mother of God (until 1966); for outstanding contributions to mankind (from 1967).

Juniper Carol, O.F.M. (1950), Daniel A. Lord, S.J. (1951), Patrick J. Peyton, C.S.C. (1952), Roger Brien, S.G.G. (1953), Emil Neubert, S.M. (1954), Joseph A. Skelly, C.M. (1955), Frank Duff (1956), Eugene F. Kennedy and John McShain (1957), Winifred A. Feely (1958), Abp. John F. Noll (1959), Eamon R. Carroll, O. Carm. (1960), Coley Taylor (1961), Abbe Rene Laurentin (1963), Philip C. Hoelle, S.M. (1964), Cyril O. Vollert, S.J. (1965), Eduardo Frei Montalvo (1967).

Marian Library Medal (1953), by the Marian Library of the University of Dayton for books in English on the Blessed Virgin Mary. Awarded every four years (from 1971), at the time of an International Mariological Congress, to a scholar for Mariological studies.

Most Rev. Fulton J. Sheen (1953), Msgr. John S. Kennedy (1954), Rev. William G. Most (1955), Ruth Cranston (1956), Juniper Carol, O.F.M. (1957), Donald C. Sharkey and Joseph Debergh, O.M.I. (1958);

Edward O'Connor, C.S.C. (1959), John J. Delaney (1960), Sister Mary Pierre, S.M. (1961), Marion A. Habig, O.F.M. (1962), Titus F. Cranny, S.A. (1963), Hilda C. Graef (1964), Edward Schillebeeckx, O.P. (1965),

Cyril Vollert, S.J. (1966), Thomas O'Meara, O.P. (1967), Charles Balic, O. F. M. (1971), Giuseppe M. Besutti (1975), Sergio Alvarez Campos, O.F.M. (1979).

Mater et Magistra Award (1963), by the College of Mt. St. Joseph on the Ohio to women for social action in the pattern and spirit of the encyclical *Mater et Magistra.*

Jane Hoey (1964), Mary Dolan (1965), Mrs. Anne Fremantle (1966), Margaret Mealey (1967), Mrs. Arthur L. Zepf, Sr. (1968), Alice R. May (1969), Mother Teresa (1974).

The O'Neil D'Amour Award (1976), by the National Association of Boards of Education/NCEA, for outstanding contribution of statewide, regional, national or international significance to the Catholic board movement.

Rev. Msgr. Olin J. Murdick (1977), Rev. Gerald A. Gettelfinger (1980).

Peace Award (1950), by the Secular Franciscan Order.

Myron C. Taylor (1950), John Foster Dulles (1951), John W. McCormack (1952), John C. Wu (1953), Ralph Bunche (1954), John R. Gariepy (1956), Most Rev. Richard J. Cushing (1957), Patrick McGeehan, Sr. (1958), Victor Andres Belaunde (1959), J. Edgar Hoover (1960), George K. Hunton (1961);

Mrs. Lester Auberlin (1962), Rev. Martin Luther King (1963), Most Rev. John J. Wright (1964), Pope Paul VI (1965), Cardinal Wyszynski (1966), Bishop Fred Pierce Corson (1967), Robert F. Kennedy, posthumously (1968), Msgr. Robert Fox (1969), Bishop James Walsh, M.M. (1970), Jean Vanier (1972), Mother Teresa of Calcutta (1974), Dom Helder Camara (1975), Archbishop Joseph L. Bernardin (1976), Jose Francisco Garcia Bauer (1977), Manuella Mattioli (1978), Dorothy Day (1979).

Peter Guilday Prize (1972), by the American Catholic Historical Association for articles accepted by the editors of the *Catholic Historical Review* which are the first scholarly publications of their authors.

James P. Gaffey (1972), B. Robert Kreiser (1974), J. Dean O'Donnell, Jr. (1976), Mark A. Gabbert (1977), Virginia W. Leonard (1978).

Poverello Medal (1949), by The College of Steubenville (Ohio), "in recognition of great benefactions to humanity, exemplifying in our age the Christ-like spirit of charity which filled the life of St. Francis of Assisi."

Alcoholics Anonymous Fellowship (1949), Edward F. Hutton (1950), the Court of Last Resort, New York, N.Y. (1951), The Lions International (1952), Variety Clubs International (1953), Llewellyn J. Scott (1954), Dr. Jonas E. Salk and Associates (1955), Mother Anna Dengel (1956), Catherine de Hueck Doherty (1957), D. M. Hamill (1958);

Daniel W. Egan, T.O.R. (1959, posthumously), Mrs. Emma C. Zeis (1960), Donald H. McGannon (1961), Jane Wyatt (1962), Birgit Nilsson (1963), Arthur Joseph Rooney (1964), Joe E. Brown (1965), Project Hope (1966), Lena F. Edwards, M.D. (1967), VISTA (1968), Jack Twyman (1969), The Salvation Army (1970), Most Rev. John K. Mussio (1971). Bro. George J. Hungerman, F.M.S.I., M.D. (1972), The Dismas Committee of the St. Vincent de Paul Society (1973) U.S. Sen Mark O. Hatfield (1974), Sr. Mary Agatha, O.S.F., and Rev Kevin R. Keelan, T.O.R. (1975), Mother Teresa of Calcutta (1976), Dorothy Day (1977), Leon Jaworski (1978), Bishop Bernard J. Topel (1979).

Regina Medal (1959), by the Catholic Library Association for outstanding contributions to children's literature.

Eleanor Farjeon (1959), Anne Carroll Moore (1960), Padraic Colum (1961), Frederick G. Melcher (1962), Ann Nolan Clark (1963), May Hill Arbuthnot (1964), Ruth Sawyer Durand (1965), Leo Politi (1966), Bertha Mahoney Miller (1967), Marguerite de Angeli (1968), Lois Lenski (1969), Ingri and Edgar Parin d'Aulaire (1970), Tasha Tudor (1971) Miendert DeJong (1972); Frances Clarke Sayers (1973), Robert McCloskey (1974), Lynd Ward and May McNeer (1975), Virginia Haviland (1976), Marcia Brown (1977), Scott O'Dell (1978), Morton Schindel (1979), Beverly Cleary (1980).

The Saint De La Salle Medal, by Manhattan College, for significant contribution to the moral, cultural or educational life of the nation.

John F. Brosnan (1951), Cardinal Francis Spellman (1952), Most Rev. Joseph P. Donahue (1953), Most Rev. Edwin V. O'Hara, posthumously (1956), Sr. Mary Emil, I.H.M. (1957), Msgr. Joseph E. Schieder (1958), Very Rev. Bro. Bertrand, O.S.F. (1959), Dr. Roy J. Deferrari (1960).

John Courtney Murray, S.J. (1961), Bro. Clair Stanislaus, F.S.C. (1962), Most Rev. Bryan J. McEntegart (1963), Sr. M. Rose Eileen, C.S.C. (1964), Mother Kathryn Sullivan, R.S.C.J. (1965), Bro. Bernard Peter, F.S.C. (1966), Dr. William Hughes Mulligan (1967), C. Alfred Koob, O. Praem. (1968), Theodore M. Hesburgh, C.S.C. (1970), Most Rev. Edwin B. Broderick (1971), Very Rev. Bro. Charles Henry, F.S.C. (1972), Mary Shea Giordano (1973), Dorothy Day (1974), Henry Viscardi, Jr. (1975), Sister Elinor R. Ford, O.P. (1976), John D. de Butts (1977), Thomas A. Murphy (1978), Gabriel Hauge (1979), Irving S. Shapiro (1980).

St. Francis de Sales Award (1959), by the Catholic Press Association for distinguished contribution to Catholic journalism.

Dale Francis (1959), Frank A. Hall (1960), John C. Murray, S.J. (1961), Albert J. Nevins, M.M. (1962), Floyd Anderson (1963), Rev. Patrick O'Connor (1964), John Cogley (1965), Joseph Breig (1966), John Reedy, C.S.C. (1967), Bishop James P. Shannon (1968), no award (1969), Msgr. Robert G. Peters (1970), Francis A. Fink (1971), Jeremy Harrington, O.F.M. (1972), Robert E. Burns (1973), Gerard E. Sherry (1974), John B. Sheerin, C.S.P. (1975), Lillian R. Block (1976), A.E.P. Wall (1977), Donald Thorman, posthumously (1978), Walter J. Burghardt, S.J. (1979), Thurston Davis, S.J. (1980).

St. Francis Xavier Medal (1954), by Xavier University (Cincinnati) to persons exemplifying the spirit of St. Francis Xavier.

Most Rev. Fulton J. Sheen, Rev. Leo Kampsen, Msgr. Frederick G. Hochwalt (1954), James Keller, M.M. (1955), Gen. Carlos P. Romulo (1956), Stan Musial, Aloysius A. Breen, S.J., Edwin G. Becker (1957), Msgr. (Maj. Gen.) Patrick J. Ryan, Msgr. (Maj. Gen.) Terrence P. Finnegan, Msgr. (Rear Adm.) George A. Rosso (1958);

T. L. Bouscaren, S.J. and Dr. Thomas A. Dooley (1959), Neal Ahern and Celestine J. Steiner, S.J. (1960), Philip J. Scharper (1961), Charles Dismas Clark, S.J. (1962), Pres. John F. Kennedy (posthumously) and J. Paul Spaeth (1963), James B. Donovan (1964), Charles H. Keating, Jr. (1965), Frank Blair (1967), Martin H. Work (1968), Lt. Col. William A. Anders and Archbishop Karl J. Alter (1969), Bishop James E. Walsh, M.M. (1970), Lawrence Welk, Rev. Msgr. Ralph W. Beiting (1971), Paul L. O'Connor, S.J. (1972), James F. Maguire, S.J., and Edward P. VonderHaar (posthumously) (1973), G. Milton Wurzelbacher (1974), D. J. O'Conor (posthumously) (1975), Bishop John K. Mussio (1977), C. Robert Beirne and George H. Brueggeman (1978), Msgr. Robert Sherry and Rev. Emerson Colaw (1979).

St. Vincent de Paul Medal (1948), by St. John's University (Jamaica, N.Y.), for outstanding service to Catholic charities.

Francis D. McGarey (1948), John A. Coleman (1949), Aloysius L. Fitzpatrick (1950), Frank J. Lewis (1951), Howard W. Fitzpatrick (1952), Richard F. Mulroy (1953), Harry J. Kirk (1954), Bernard J. Keating (1955), John M. Nolan (1956), John R. Gariepy (1957);

Charles E. McCarthy (1958), Frederick V. Goess (1959), Maurice J. Costello, M.D. (1960), Thomas F. Hanley (1961), John J. Lynch (1962), William H. Walters (1963), George E. Heneghan (1964), James A. Quigney (1965), Henry J. Shields (1966);

Eugene McGovern (1967), George J. Krygier (1968), James A. Cousins (1969), Edward T. Reilly (1970), T. Raber Taylor (1971), Luke J. Smith (1972), William C. Rohrkemper (1973), Edward V. Murtaugh (1974), Frank V. Buckley (1975), Martin J.

Loftus (1976), John F. Coppinger (1977), Howard E. Halaska (1978), Ronald T. Y. Choo (1979).

Serra Award of the Americas (1947), by the Academy of American Franciscan History for service to Inter-American good will.

Sumner Welles (1947), Pablo Martinez del Rio (1948), Dr. Herbert E. Bolton (1949), Gabriela Mistral (1950), Carlos E. Castaneda (1951), Victor A. Belaunde (1952), Clarence Haring (1953), Alceu Amoroso Lima (1954), France V. Scholes (1956);

Silvio Zavala (1957), John Tate Lanning (1958), John Basadre (1959), Arthur Preston Whitaker (1960), Marcel Bataillon (1961), Javier Malagon y Barcelo (1962), Dr. George P. Hammond (1964), Augustin Millares Carlo (1970), Max Savelle (1976), Miguel Leon-Portilla (1978).

Signum Fidei Medal (1942), by the Alumni Association of La Salle College (Phila.) for noteworthy contributions to the advancement of humanitarian principles in keeping with Christian tradition.

Brother E. Anselm, F.S.C. (1942), Karl H. Rogers (1943), Very Rev. Edward V. Stanford, O.S.A. (1944), Mrs. Edward V. Morrell (1945), Cardinal Dennis Dougherty (1946), Max Jordan (1947), John J. Sullivan (1948), Dr. Louis H. Clerf (1949), Most Rev. Gerald P. O'Hara (1950), Most Rev. Fulton J. Sheen (1951);

John H. Harris (1952), James Keller, M.M. (1953), John M. Haffert (1954), Dr. Francis J. Braceland (1955), Matthew H. McCloskey (1956), Henry Viscardi, Jr. (1957), no award (1958), Dr. Joseph J. Toland, Jr. (1959), Luke E. Hart (1960), Joseph E. McCafferty (1961);

Martin H. Work (1962), R. Sargent Shriver (1963), Mother M. Benedict, M.D. (1964), Sen. Eugene McCarthy (1965), William B. Ball (1966), Frank Folsom (1967), Rev. Leon H. Sullivan (1968), Rev. William J. Finley (1969);

Dr. James W. Turpin (1970), Lisa A. Richette, Esq. (1971), Rev. Melvin Floyd (1972), Elwood E. Kieser, C.S.P. (1973), Msgr. Philip J. Dowling (1974), James C. Giuffre, M.D. (1975), Most Rev. Bernard J. Topel (1976), Mildred Jefferson, M.D. (1977), Judge Genevieve Blatt (1978), Rita Ungaro Schiavone (1979), Rev. Aloysius Schwartz (1980).

Soteriological Award (1967), by the Confraternity of the Passion (Third Order of the Passionists, St. Michael's Monastery, Union City, N.J.) for outstanding exemplification of sharing in the Passion of Christ in contemporary society.

Most Rev. Cuthbert M. O'Gara, C.P. (1967), Mrs. Martin Luther King, Jr. (1968), Veronica's Veil Players (1969), Mother Mary Teresa Benedetti, C.P. (1970), Dr. Billy Graham (1971), Mrs. Flo Kuhn (1972), Rev. Martin J. Tooker, C.P. (1973), Mrs. Mary Sloan (1974), Aileen Leary (1975), Marie

Gallagher (1976), Grete Faber and Georgianna Wendt (1977), Regina Adamecz (1978), Connie Dawson (1979).

Sword of Loyola (1964), by Loyola University of Chicago to person or persons exemplifying Ignatius of Loyola's courage, dedication and service.

J. Edgar Hoover (1964), Col. James McDivitt and Maxime A. Faget (1965), Lt. Dieter Dengler (1966), Brig. Gen. David Sarnoff (1967), Capt. Edward V. Rickenbacker (1968), Dr. Thomas O. Paine and William A. Anders (1969), Most Rev. Fulton J. Sheen (1970), Helen Hayes (1971), James F. Maguire, S.J. (1972), Mr. and Mrs. Foster G. McGaw (1973), John F. Smith, Jr. (1974), Bob Newhart (1975), Arthur Fiedler (1976), Mildred F. Jefferson, M.D. (1977), Rev. Vincent T. O'Keefe, S.J. (1978), George S. Halas (1979).

U.S. Catholic Award (1978), by editors of *U.S. Catholic* magazine for furthering the cause of women in the Church.

Sr. Agnes Cunningham, S.S.C.M. (1978), Sr. Marjorie Tuite, O.P. (1979), Sr. M. Theresa Kane, R.S.M. (1980).

Vercelli Medal (1947), by the Holy Name Society for distinguished service to ideals of the society.

William Bruce, Paul M. Brennan, Joseph Scott, Stephen Barry, Patrick Kennedy (1947), R. W. Hoogstraet (1948), William H. Collins (1949), Ward D. Hopkins (1950), Charles A. Burkholder, James C. Connell, James T. Vocelle, Edwin J. Allen, Fred A. Muth, Austin J. Roche, Michael Lawlor (1951), Michael L. Roche (1953), Maurice J. O'Sullivan, Lucien T. Vivien, Jr. (1954);

John A. Lee, Sr., Daniel M. Hamill, Clarence F. Boggan, Louis J. Euler, Henry J. McGreevy, Ralph F. Nunlist (1955), James J. McDonnell (1957), Joseph J. Wilson (1958), William J. Meehan (1959), Paul Meade (1960), William T. Tavares (1961), David M. Martin (1962), Bert M. Walz (1963), Herbert Michelbrook (1964), Alfred A. McGarraghy (1965), Frank J. Beuerlein (1968), Humbert J. Campana (1970), Richard Asmus (1971), Charles J. Little (1973), William J. Burke, Jr. (1974), Stephen Andrusisian (1975), James P. Bailey (1976), Lanaux Marston (1977), Louis C. Fink (1979).

Other Awards

The following were among other awards presented in 1980.

• The **Good Samaritan Award**, posthumously Sept. 16 to Mother Anna Dengel, foundress of the Medical Mission Sisters, by the National Catholic Development Conference.

• The **Cardinal Wright Award**, Sept. 20 to William May, associate professor of moral theology at The Catholic University of America, by the Fellowship of Catholic Scholars.

DEATHS OCTOBER 1, 1979, TO OCTOBER 1, 1980

Beahan, Msgr. Hugh Michael, 60, July 22, 1980, Grand Rapids, Mich.; communications director for Grand Rapids diocese.

Bengsch, Cardinal Alfred, 58, Dec. 13, 1979, East Berlin, Germany; bishop of Berlin from 1959; cardinal from 1967; president of East German Bishops' Conference.

Bier, Rev. William C., S.J., 68, Mar. 6, 1980, New York, N.Y.; educator; professor of psychology and administrator at Fordham University for 32 years; a founder of the American Catholic Psychological Association.

Biskup, Archbishop George J., 68, Oct. 17, 1979, Indianapolis, Ind.; headed Indianapolis archdiocese from 1970 to March, 1979, when he retired because of ill health.

Blanshard, Paul, 87, Jan. 27, 1980, St. Petersburg, Fla.; author; works directed against Catholic Church; died in a Catholic hospital.

Bottego, Mother Celestine, 84, Aug. 19, 1980, Parma, Italy; a founder with Giacomo Spagnolo of the Missionary Society of Mary (Saverian Missionaries).

Boyer, Rev. Charles, 96, Feb. 23, 1980, Rome, Italy; philosophy professor at Pontifical Gregorian University, Rome, for 47 years; author; ecumenist.

Caggiano, Cardinal Antonio, 90, Oct. 23, 1979, Buenos Aires, Argentina; archbishop of Buenos Aires from 1959 to 1975 when he retired; cardinal from 1946.

Callahan, William M., 69, Mar. 14, 1980, Latrobe, Pa.; journalist and editor in the Catholic press for 40 years.

Cavanaugh, Rev. John J., C.S.C., 80, Dec. 28, 1979, South Bend, Ind.; educator; president of Notre Dame University, 1946-52.

Consedine, William R. (Bud), 69, Apr. 14, 1980, Washington, D.C.; legal officer of the U.S. Catholic Conference and its predecessor, the National Catholic Welfare Conference, from 1958 until his retirement in 1974.

Coughlin, Rev. Charles E., 88, Oct. 27, 1979, Bloomfield Hills, Mich.; retired pastor of the Shrine of the Little Flower Parish, Royal Oaks, Mich.; well known and controversial "radio priest" of the 1930s; forced off the air after the United States entered World War II which he opposed.

DeJaegher, Rev. Raymond J., 74, Feb. 6, 1980, New York, N.Y.; Belgian-born teacher and missionary in China and Vietnam; director of Asian Speakers' Bureau, New York; imprisoned by Japanese early in World War II and later by Chinese communists; special adviser to President Diem in Vietnam; author.

Dengel, Mother Anna, 88, Apr. 17, 1980, Rome, Italy; Austrian-born physician; founded the Medical Mission Sisters (Society of Catholic Medical Missionaries) in 1925, the first religious community of women to practice medicine, surgery and obstetrics.

Donovan, Bernard, 68, Oct. 27, 1979, Saratoga Springs, N.Y.; educator; superintendent of New York City public school system, 1965-69.

Dragonette, Jessica, Mar. 18, 1980, New York, N.Y.; soprano; popular early radio performer.

DuKette, Rev. Norman, 89, Mar. 31, 1980, Flint, Mich.; oldest black priest in the United States; pastor of Christ the King Parish, Flint, Mich., from 1929 to 1970 when he retired.

Durante, Jimmy, 86, Jan. 29, 1980, Santa Monica, Calif.; popular comedian of stage, screen, radio and TV.

Fletcher, Bishop Albert L., 83, Dec. 6, 1979, Little Rock, Ark.; bishop of Little Rock from 1946 to 1972 when he retired.

Gabro, Bishop Jaroslav, 60, Mar. 28, 1980, Chicago, Ill.; Ukrainian-Rite bishop of St. Nicholas of Chicago from its establishment in 1961; strong critic of religious repression in Soviet Union.

Gallagher, Rev. Thomas R., O.P., 65, Dec. 10, 1979, Washington, D.C.; canon lawyer; secretary of apostolic delegation, Washington, D.C., from 1948 to 1979 when he retired.

Gatch, Dr. Don, 50, March, 1980, near Cambodia-Thailand border, in an automobile accident; physician; member of volunteer medical team working with refugees under CRS auspices.

Giordano, Igino, 85, Apr. 18, 1980, Rocca di Papa, near Rome, Italy; noted Italian writer and commentator; first married member of Focolare Movement.

Gorman, Bishop Thomas K., 87, Aug. 16, 1980, Dallas, Tex.; bishop of Dallas from 1954 to 1971 when he retired; active in Catholic press.

Griffin, John Howard, 60, Sept. 9, 1980, Fort Worth, Tex.; author, wrote *Black Like Me,* chronicling his experiences while journeying through the South after blackening his skin; civil rights worker; convert.

Hayes, Archbishop James T.G., S.J., 91, Mar. 28, 1980; Cagayan de Oro, Philippine Islands; American missionary bishop in Philippines from 1933; first archbishop of Cagayan de Oro, from 1951 to 1970 when he retired.

Hebert, F. Edward, 78, Dec. 28, 1979, New Orleans, La.; Democratic congressman from Louisiana for 36 years; former chairman of Armed Services Committee.

Hitchcock, Alfred, 80, Apr. 29, 1980, Beverly Hills, Calif.; London-born film maker; director of 53 works; considered master of suspense; U.S. citizen.

Hume, Ruth Fox, 57, Mar. 1, 1980, Washington, D.C.; author of mysteries and nonfiction works.

Iturbi, Jose, 84, June 28, 1980, Hollywood,

Calif.; Spanish-born pianist, conductor and motion picture performer.

Kolowski, Bro. Stanley Maria, O.F.M. Cap., 62, Mar. 3, 1980, Jersey City, N.J.; Polish-born religious; imprisoned at several concentration camps, including Auschwitz, when he was a seminarian.

Lardone, Archbishop Francesco, 93, Jan. 30, 1980, Italy; Vatican diplomat from 1949-66; U.S. citizen.

McCafferty, Bishop John E., 60, Apr. 29, 1980, Rochester, N.Y.; auxiliary bishop of Rochester from 1968.

McDevitt, Bishop Gerald V., 63, Sept. 29, 1980, Philadelphia, Pa.; auxiliary bishop of Philadelphia from 1962.

Maly, Rev. Eugene, 59, July 30, 1980, Cincinnati, O.; Biblical scholar; author; Catholic press columnist; vice rector and dean of theology at Mt. St. Mary Seminary, Cincinnati.

Marling, Bishop Joseph M., C.Pp.S., 75, Oct. 2, 1979, Kansas City, Mo.; first bishop of Jefferson City from 1956 to 1969 when he retired.

Meany, George, 85, Jan. 10, 1980, Washington, D.C.; long-time labor leader; president of the AFL and first president of merged AFL-CIO from 1952 to late 1979 when he retired.

Murphy, John J., 50, Sept. 23, 1980, Long Island, N.Y.; dean of St. John University Law School.

Niles, John Jacob, 87, Mar. 1, 1980, Lexington, Ky.; folklorist and folk singer; wrote musical accompaniment for poems of Thomas Merton.

O'Brien, Rev. John A., 87, Apr. 18, 1980, South Bend, Ind.; scholar; author of 45 works including the widely read *Faith of Millions;* taught at Notre Dame University; ecumenist; active in convert work; first priest recipient of Notre Dame's Laetare Medal, 1973.

O'Connor, Msgr. Patrick J., 78, Aug. 1, 1980, Atlanta, Ga.; faculty member of Catholic University of America for 20 years; director of National Shrine of the Immaculate Conception, 1950-56.

Ojong, Petrus Kanisius, 59, May 31, 1980, Jakarta, Indonesia; leading figure in Catholic press in Southeast Asia.

Paluch, Chester J., 59, Sept. 14, 1980, Chicago, Ill.; liturgical publisher.

Pignedoli, Cardinal Sergio, 70, June 15, 1980, Reggio Emilia, Italy; Vatican diplomat and curia official; cardinal since 1973; president of Secretariat for Non-Christian Religions at time of his death; considered by observers as a leading contender in the last two papal elections.

Reilly, Rev. Walter A., S.J., 75, Oct. 28, 1979, White Plains, N.Y.; retreat master in New York Jesuit province for nearly 30 years.

Reinert, Rev. Carl M., S.J., 67, Aug. 13, 1980, Omaha, Nebr.; president of Creighton University, 1950-62.

Righi, Archbishop Vittore Ugo, 70, Apr. 28, Rome, Italy; Vatican diplomat.

Robichaud, Archbishop Norbert, 74, Oct. 21, 1979, Canada; archbishop of Moncton, N.B., Canada, from 1942 to 1972 when he retired.

Robles, Gil, 82, Sept. 15, Madrid; parliamentarian; leader of Christian Social Democrats; advocate of democratic rule, exile, during the Franco dictatorship; retired from political life in 1977 to teach law.

Romero y Galdamez, Archbishop Oscar, 62, Mar. 24, 1980, San Salvador, El Salvador; murdered while celebrating Mass. (See March News Events.)

Rongione, Rev. Louis A., O.S.A., 67, June 19, 1980, Philadelphia, Pa.; Villanova University library director; columnist for Philadelphia archdiocesan paper.

Ruocco, Bishop Joseph J., 58, July 26, 1980, Lowell, Mass.; auxiliary bishop of Boston from 1974; first priest of Italian ancestry to become a bishop in Boston archdiocese.

Russo, Rev. Nicholas, 56, Feb. 23, 1980, Queens, N.Y., sociology professor at Cathedral College of the Immaculate Conception, Queens, N.Y.

Sanz Briz, Angel, June 11, 1980, Rome, Italy; Spanish ambassador to the Holy See from 1977.

Sheen, Archbishop Fulton J., 84, Dec. 9, 1979, New York, N.Y. (See December, 1979, News Events.)

Shekleton, Rev. Gerald T., 54, Dec. 5, 1979, Dubuque, Iowa; editor of Dubuque archdiocesan paper for 22 years.

Skehan, Msgr. Patrick W., 70, Sept. 9, 1980, Washington, D.C.; scholar; internationally recognized expert in Semitic and Scripture studies; member of international committee editing Dead Sea Scrolls.

Tracy, Bishop Robert E., 70, Apr. 4, 1980, New Orleans, La.; first bishop of Baton Rouge from 1961 to 1974 when he retired.

Uylenbroeck, Msgr. Marcel, 59, Oct. 2, 1979, Louvain, Belgium; Belgian-born curia official; secretary of Pontifical Council for the Laity from 1969.

Vishnewski, Stanley, 63, Nov. 14, 1979, New York, N.Y.; joined Catholic Worker Movement shortly after its foundation in 1933; associate editor of *The Catholic Worker.*

Vogel, Bishop Cyril J., 74, Oct. 4, 1979, Salina, Kans.; bishop of Salina from 1965.

Yacoub III, Patriarch Ignatius, 67, June 25, 1980, Damascus, Syria; head of the Syrian Orthodox Church from 1957; scholar, writer; devoted to ecumenism; met with both Paul VI and John Paul II at the Vatican.

Zwane, Bishop Aloysius Mandlenkosi, 48, Aug. 9, 1980, South Africa, in an automobile accident; bishop of Manzini, Swaziland, from 1976; outspoken critic of racism and white minority domination in black Africa.